The Encyclopedia of the
United States Congress

Editorial Advisory Board

The
Encyclopedia
of the
United States Congress

Edited by

DONALD C. BACON
ROGER H. DAVIDSON
MORTON KELLER

Volume 1

SIMON & SCHUSTER

A Paramount Communications Company

New York London Toronto Sydney Tokyo Singapore

Simon & Schuster
Academic Reference Division
15 Columbus Circle
New York, New York 10023

Printed in the United States of America

printing number
1 2 3 4 5 6 7 8 9 10

Library of Congress Cataloging-in-Publication Data
The encyclopedia of the United States Congress / edited by
Donald C. Bacon, Roger H. Davidson, Morton Keller.
p. cm.
ISBN 0-13-276361-3 (set : alk. paper)
ISBN 0-13-306655-X (v.1 : alk. paper)
1. United States. Congress—Encyclopedias. I. Bacon,
Donald C. II. Davidson, Roger H. III. Keller, Morton.
JK1067.E63 1995
328.73'003—dc20 94-21203 CIP

*Funding for this publication was received from
the Commission on the Bicentennial of the
United States Constitution. The University of Texas
at Austin and the Lyndon Baines Johnson Library recognize
with gratitude this and other assistance rendered by the
Commission in the development of this project.*

Acknowledgments of sources, copyrights, and
permissions to use previously printed materials
are made throughout the work.

This paper meets the requirements of ANSI/NISO Z39.48-1992
(Permanence of Paper).

About the Editors

DONALD C. BACON is a Washington-based journalist specializing in Congress and the presidency. He has served as staff writer of the *Wall Street Journal* and assistant managing editor for congressional and political coverage of *U.S. News & World Report*. A former Congressional Fellow, he holds major prizes in journalism and has written and contributed to numerous books, including *Rayburn: A Biography* (1987) and *Congress and You* (1969).

ROGER H. DAVIDSON is Professor of Government and Politics at the University of Maryland, College Park. He has taught at several universities and served as a Capitol Hill staff member with the Bolling Committee, with the Stevenson Committee, and as Senior Specialist with the Congressional Research Service, Library of Congress. He is author or coauthor of numerous articles and books dealing with Congress and national policy-making, including the standard textbook, *Congress and Its Members* (4th edition, 1994).

MORTON KELLER is Spector Professor of History at Brandeis University. He has been a visiting professor at Yale, Harvard, and Oxford universities. Dr. Keller's books include *Regulating a New Society: Public Policy and Social Change in America, 1900–1933* (1994); *Regulating a New Economy: Public Policy and Economic Change in America, 1900–1933* (1990); *Parties, Congress, and Public Policy* (1985); and *Affairs of State: Public Life in Late Nineteenth Century America* (1977).

Editorial and Production Staff

Contents

Preface

A perplexing and enduring paradox surrounds the United States Congress. The nation's Founders envisioned a national legislature that would be innovative, forceful, and responsive to the people. For more than two centuries, Congress has largely met that expectation. Its power is unrivaled among legislative assemblies of the world; its structure and procedures are models for burgeoning democracies everywhere; its ethics laws are the strictest of any major democratic legislature, according to a recent Library of Congress survey. Yet, at home, Congress is dogged by ridicule and condemnation and often held to be a failure. Criticism of its actions abounds. Most Americans, seeing Congress as irrelevant to their personal concerns, regard it at best with ambivalence and at worst with contempt.

The Encyclopedia of the United States Congress is constructed with that paradox between reality and perception very much in mind. Designed neither to praise Congress nor to condemn it, the encyclopedia seeks solely to provide in one convenient place the best knowledge and insights available about Congress, its operations, and its history. We have endeavored to make this work comprehensive, balanced, easy to use, and accessible to a wide audience. Our hope is that it will contribute to a better understanding of this unique institution, whose success or failure affects every American.

Not by chance did the authors of the U.S. Constitution devote its first article to the legislative branch. After all, the colonial legislatures, two Continental Congresses, and the Congress of the Confederation had boldly pressed the colonies' grievances against Great Britain, declared the colonies' independence, and managed the new nation's affairs during and after the Revolutionary War. Nearly all the Framers had served in one or more of these assemblies, where a sense of national identity had been planted and nurtured. The powers assigned to Congress in the Constitution are breathtaking in their scope. No one reading the list of responsibilities set down in Article I, section 8 can fail to be impressed by the Framers' vision of a vigorous legislature as the driving force of an energetic government.

Congress has managed to preserve its powers and distinctive character, in part by dividing its work among standing committees and providing itself with adequate professional and clerical staff. Almost alone among the world's legislatures, Congress drafts its own legislation and tries to monitor the vast apparatus of the executive. Its hearings and debates and the scope of its legislative mandate have kept Capitol Hill the principal meeting ground for the diverse interests that shape American public policy. Indeed, the most controversial public issues—territorial expansion, internal development, states' rights, slavery, secession, regulation of private enterprise, trade and tax policies, foreign involvement, social security, civil rights, and the most crucial of all issues—the decision to commit the nation to war—have largely been played out in the chambers and committee rooms of Congress.

Despite Congress's importance, perhaps because of it, Americans have always considered Congress fair game for criticism and derision. The jokes and ridicule began even as its members struggled to attain their first quorum in 1789 and have continued without letup ever since. "Americans are especially fond of running down their congressmen," British scholar James Bryce observed in 1888. From Mark Twain and Will Rogers to Russell Baker and Jay Leno, professional humorists and pundits have never lacked material while Congress has been in session.

This encyclopedia appears at a time when Congress's performance and its members' personal behavior are being scrutinized as never before. Scholars and journalists are asking whether that body might be contributing to the problem rather than the solution concerning the nation's ills. The press speaks almost daily of legislative gridlock, and reports of ethical and moral lapses by senators and House members come with depressing frequency. Voters register their disgust in opinion polls and, more tangibly, in one state after another, in their overwhelming support for term-limitation laws. The proliferation of such statutes, aimed at senior lawmakers who, critics contend, have outstayed their usefulness, are disconcerting testimony to the hardening of public sentiment. A casual reader of today's headlines might well conclude that Congress itself has a shaky future.

But do not be misled; Congress remains strong and vibrant. Arguably, it is doing its job essentially as the Framers envisioned—cautious to a fault, suspicious of panaceas, and, however imperfect, ever vigilant in defending America's interests as it sees them and always capable of surprising its critics with acts of great courage.

How This Encyclopedia Came About

For most Americans, Capitol Hill is a distant place shrouded in mystery and intrigue. Although Congress operates more openly than either of the other branches of the U.S. government, its responsibilities are so diverse and its processes so fraught with labyrinthine complexity that its actions sometimes confuse even the experts. That most nonspecialists profess to be baffled by the lawmaking process is not surprising. What is surprising is that despite Congress's importance as a governing institution, there has not heretofore been a general reference work on Congress—a comprehensive guidebook, if you will—that both specialists and the interested public would find informative, intellectually sound, and easily approachable.

Such a work was first proposed many years ago by the late D. B. Hardeman, an authority on American politics and former aide and biographer of Speaker Sam Rayburn. Hardeman envisioned a comprehensive and reliable resource dedicated to the history and processes of Congress. It would be developed by experts drawn primarily from the fields of history, political science, and journalism. Hardeman theorized that each of these disciplines would bring its own perspectives and insights to the project, thereby producing a work greater than the sum of its parts. It would provide a lasting reservoir of information for those who serve in, study, or simply want to understand the legislative branch.

To further this project, shortly before his death in 1981, Hardeman donated his ten-thousand-volume library on the history of Congress and a portion of his estate to the Lyndon B. Johnson Library in Austin, Texas. The Lyndon B. Johnson Foundation subsequently brought together leading scholars,

journalists, and Capitol Hill staff members to assess the feasibility of Hardeman's plan. The group concluded that a comprehensive reference work on Congress was both desirable and possible. It further concluded that an alphabetically arranged encyclopedia would best serve the interested nonspecialist—the audience Hardeman particularly wanted to reach. Norman J. Ornstein, resident scholar at the American Enterprise Institute, was especially persuasive in urging that this project go forward.

Subsequently, the Senate and House of Representatives endorsed the idea as one of several projects to commemorate Congress's two-hundredth anniversary in 1989. The Commission on the Bicentennial of the United States Constitution followed with vital financial support. The Lyndon B. Johnson Library and Foundation and the University of Texas agreed to serve as the project's joint administrators.

Major Features of This Encyclopedia

This encyclopedia's objective is to be the definitive reference work on the history and character of the United States Congress. Its four volumes contain 1,056 separate entries contributed by 550 leading authorities on Congress, along with several hundred illustrations, tables, and charts. Editors and authors alike have been guided by a strong commitment to make this encyclopedia intelligible to a general audience while satisfying the demanding needs and standards of specialists.

A distinctive feature of this work is its large number of comprehensive essays on major topics. The authorities invited to prepare these articles were asked to bring not only the best current scholarship to their subject but also to illuminate their writing with illustrative examples and their own informed interpretation and analysis. Many of these articles describe and explain major elements of Congress as an institution: its constitutional powers, rules and procedures, committee system (including the history and jurisdiction of every standing committee), budget process, political parties, work load, and staffing. Wherever appropriate, they cover the complex but essential details of congressional structure and procedure relevant to their subject. Legislative terms and concepts of general interest—filibuster, quorum, and referral, for example—are treated in separate entries. Other technical terms and concepts are defined in a separate glossary located in the back of volume 4.

A highlight of this encyclopedia is its series of

eight essays on the historical development of Congress (see under "History of Congress"). Written by leading scholars, they stand as a sequential series of portraits of Congress in its major historical periods. Common themes and topics, such as partisan alignments, political agenda, relations with the executive, internal power patterns, and structural or procedural innovations, connect these essays. Taken together, they comprise a modern history of Congress.

Other major articles identify, discuss, and analyze the important characteristics of members of Congress, such as their careers, electoral concerns, constituencies, ethics, and daily lives as legislators (see "Members of Congress"). There are essays on Congress's African American, Hispanic, Asian, and women members, as well as biographical sketches of 247 former senators and representatives whose impact on the institution and the nation has been especially significant. The editors have omitted biographies of current members, whose careers are still unfolding. The editors also took into account the fact that basic biographical information about the eleven thousand men and women who have served in Congress is readily available elsewhere, notably in the *Biographical Directory of the United States Congress: 1789–1989*.

Still other articles explore the links between Congress and key elements of American political life, such as the president, the federal bureaucracy, the judiciary, interest groups, and the press. There are articles describing the administrations and congressional relations of each president from George Washington to Bill Clinton. Separate entries cover Supreme Court rulings that have had important consequences for Congress as an institution. These and other court cases also are discussed in the context of various topical articles, such as "Contempt of Congress" and "Judicial Review."

A series of articles illuminates every important element of congressional elections: apportionment and districting, candidate emergence, campaigning, and voting patterns. Included with these and related articles are tables, charts, and graphs providing relevant electoral data.

A group of essays deals with the portrayal of Congress in literature, movies, and humor, and explores various aspects of Congress's own culture and mores, including its language and even its cuisine. Additionally, there are several major essays on the Capitol and its surroundings. They range from descriptions of the Capitol's history, architecture, and art treasures to accounts of some of the dramatic,

amusing, and even violent scenes that have taken place within its confines (see, for instance, "Violence," article on "Violence in Congress").

The primary task of Congress is to enact and revise the nation's laws. The encyclopedia underscores this fact in one of its most innovative features: substantial essays on Congress's record in every important area of public policy-making. They include agriculture, art and culture, civil liberties, civil rights, communications, crime and justice, economic policy, education, energy and natural resources, environment and conservation, foreign policy, health and medicine, housing, immigration, Indian policy, labor, public lands, public works, railroads, religion, science and technology, slavery, social welfare and poverty, tariffs and trade, taxation, transportation, treaties, urban policy, and women's issues and rights. Each essay surveys Congress's role in a particular policy area and includes or cross-references a descriptive list of important enactments relevant to the essay topic.

Separate entries discuss landmark laws, such as the Judiciary Act of 1789, Alien and Sedition Acts, Missouri Compromise, Compromise of 1850, Morrill Land-Grant College Act, Sherman Antitrust Act, Civil Rights Act of 1964, and Immigration Act of 1990. Also addressed are the Bill of Rights and every subsequent constitutional amendment. Major treaties and international agreements are covered, as is every major war fought by the United States, emphasizing Congress's role before, during, and after it.

Finally, essays on each of the fifty states describe their historical connection to Congress, including the politics of their admission to the Union and the size, political leanings, and national contributions of their congressional delegations over time.

Acknowledgments

A major reference work is the product of many hands. The three coeditors assume responsibility for important editorial decisions, including the choice of entry topics and authors. But we could not have completed our task without the assistance of many colleagues and friends. We were privileged to have the advice and encouragement of a distinguished editorial board.

Our publisher, Charles E. Smith, president of Simon & Schuster's Academic Reference Division, assembled an able and experienced team. He and editorial director Paul Bernabeo participated in countless meetings, shared their vast knowledge of reference publishing, organized the paperwork and computer file, and gave support and encouragement in ways both large and small. Editorial assistant Debra Alpern capably kept track of information, trafficked manuscripts, and cajoled tardy authors and editors. Copy chief Dorothy Kachouh and her predecessor David Sassian tactfully held authors to rigid standards for syntax and editorial style.

The project received essential financial support from the Commission on the Bicentennial of the United States Constitution, chaired by former Chief Justice Warren E. Burger. The Congressional Research Service of the Library of Congress generously provided office space and facilities, for which we thank especially former director Joseph E. Ross and former Government Division chief Frederick Pauls.

Finally, we salute those special individuals without whom this project would not have been undertaken, much less completed. Michael L. Gillette, working on behalf of the Lyndon B. Johnson Foundation and the Hardeman Bequest, pushed the idea from its inception and helped sustain it through every stage. Richard A. Baker and Raymond W. Smock, respectively the official Senate and House historians, were indispensable participants in this enterprise from beginning to end. We cannot adequately acknowledge their many contributions or adequately express our gratitude to these three individuals. Two members of Congress, Senator Robert C. Byrd and Representative Lindy Boggs, were early advocates of this project and did much to see that it was undertaken. William S. Livingston, vice president and dean of graduate studies at the University of Texas, and Harry J. Middleton, director of the Lyndon B. Johnson Library and Foundation, ensured that the project was efficiently supported.

This work is dedicated to the late D. B. Hardeman, a tribute to his love affair with representative assemblies, his generosity in sharing his knowledge and insights with generations of reporters, scholars, and students, and his foresight in providing through his estate an incentive for the dissemination of knowledge about the United States Congress. We should like to think that this encyclopedia achieves his goal of a definitive reference work about his beloved institution.

Donald C. Bacon
Roger H. Davidson
Morton Keller

Washington, D.C., and
Cambridge, Massachusetts
August 1994

Foreword

The Encyclopedia of the United States Congress required years of planning, correspondence, paperwork, research, editing, and production to complete. The basic resource for this enterprise is the collective knowledge of scholars, journalists, congressional staff members, and other close observers of Congress. Above all, this project owes its existence to the generosity and cooperation of its 550 contributors who made it possible to encompass and convey this field of scholarship. As conceived and inspired by its three principal editors, Donald C. Bacon, Roger H. Davidson, and Morton Keller, this encyclopedia's systematic plan of entries with supporting bibliographies and other scholarly apparatus not only represents the best available research on Congress but also, it is hoped, reproduces that research in a way that will provoke fresh insight and further research.

In addition to the principal editors, who abided the persistent needs of their publisher with patience, wisdom, and good cheer, two members of the editorial advisory board stand out for their willingness to assist and encourage the project in extraordinary ways. Richard A. Baker, Historian of the United States Senate, and Raymond W. Smock, Historian of the United States House of Representatives, provided critical advice and guidance to the publisher throughout years of development.

The publisher also relied in numerous ways on the expertise of scholars employed throughout the U.S. government. Apart from their role as contributors of written material, the staffs of various government offices have assisted in the verification of thousands of particular items of information for the more than one hundred tables in the encyclopedia, for the details of bibliographic entries, and for the location of visual images and the identification of the people and objects in them. This project has relied on assistance from staff members of the Office of the Historian of the United States House of Representatives, the Office of the Historian of the United States Senate, the Office of the Architect of the United States Capitol, several branches of the Library of Congress, the Center for Legislative Archives of the National Archives, the Office of the Curator of the United States Senate, and, above all, from a large number of scholars in the Congressional Research Service.

A few people should be mentioned by name; these are the brightest reflection of the scores of others who endured the questions of the publisher's staff. Ilona Nickels, Congressional Research Service, handled more questions of detail than any other contributor. In addition, she is primarily responsible for the generation of the glossary of technical legislative terms, which appears at the back of volume 4. Sula Dyson Richardson, also of the Congressional Research Service, and Bruce A. Ragsdale, Associate Historian of the Office of the Historian of the United States House of Representatives, were especially helpful in securing accurate and up-to-date information based on current research. Katherine A. Collado, of the National Archives' Center for Legislative Archives, researched and provided information concerning the background and meaning of many of the political cartoons by Pulitzer Prize winners Clifford K. Berryman and Jim Berryman that are reproduced in this work for the first time since their initial publication in the *Washington Evening Star* and other newspapers. John Hamilton, of the Office of the Historian of the United States Senate, assisted in gathering and reproducing numerous visual images from the Senate collection. Dana Strickland and Linnaea A. Dix, of the Curator's Office of the Office of the Architect of the Capitol, helped to secure images related to the Capitol building. The project also owes a large debt of gratitude to Nancy A. Lammers, Director, Book Editorial Design and Production, Congressional Quarterly Books, for her guidance in locating several visual images that are reproduced herein. Sources of visual images are acknowledged in the captions accompanying each illustration, but special thanks are due David J. and Janice L. Frent for permission to reproduce several items of political memorabilia from their personal collection. Finally, the graphs and charts that appear in this work were designed by John W. Hopper and based on information provided by authors and editors.

Structure of This Reference Work

The encyclopedia includes 1,056 signed, original articles ranging in length from approximately 250 to 6,000 words. All articles, with one exception, include a bibliography listing recommendations for further reading. The single exception contains virtually all the information available on its subject.

Some articles, because of the interrelatedness of their subjects, are gathered within *composite entries* made up of two or more *subentries*. For example, certain subjects such as quorum call and parliamentarian divide into two separate articles, one on the subject as it relates to the House of Representatives, followed by one on its aspects in the Senate. Other composite entries, on large subjects such as members of Congress, committees, and the Capitol, include several subentries.

In addition to entries that are articles, the encyclopedia includes more than 150 *blind entries*. Such entries direct readers to articles that are parts of composite entries (such as the blind entry "Spouses of Members," which directs readers to "Members," article on "Spouses of Members"). Others refer to inverted forms of the subject's name, for example, directing readers from "Parties, Political" to "Political Parties." Some also list separate entries; for example, the blind entry "Joint Committee" directs readers to "Committees," article on "Joint Committees," and then names nine particular joint committees each of which is the subject of an entry. In general, blind entries are important alternate names for the same or closely related subjects treated under different headings.

All entries in the body of the work as well as in the index are alphabetized according to the letter-by-letter system. Thus, "Banking, Housing, and Urban Affairs Committee, Senate" is followed by "Bank of the United States," which is followed by "Bankruptcy." Exceptions to this rule include the customary guideline for listing person before place and place before thing. Thus, the article "Washington, George" is followed by "Washington" (an article on the state), which is followed by "Washington, D.C." (a blind entry), which is followed by "Washington's Farewell Address." Names beginning with "Mc" and "St." are alphabetized as if spelled out "Mac" and "Saint." The articles on the Twentieth to the Twenty-seventh Amendments to the Constitution are printed in numerical rather than alphabetical order.

The encyclopedia includes hundreds of *cross-references*, usually given in alphabetical order, that appear at the ends of articles (before bibliographies) or in headnotes. The potential number of cross-references is very large in a work this size. Since many of those that might be included refer to articles that most readers would expect to find in a work devoted to Congress, the editors have sought to avoid clogging the body of the work with cross-references of limited use. Generally, cross-references direct readers to articles of greater specificity rather than to articles of a more general nature. For example, the article "Joint Sessions and Meetings" directs readers to "State of the Union Message" but not to "Sessions of Congress." Furthermore, biographical entries, which might be referenced from hundreds of contexts, are ordinarily not cited in cross-references. Users should refer to the synoptic outline of contents and the comprehensive index at the back of volume 4 for further guidance concerning the organization of the encyclopedia and the interrelationship of its parts.

The front matter of volume 1 includes a complete *Alphabetical List of Entries* as well as a *Directory of Contributors*, giving affiliations and the title of each article written by that contributor. The front matter of each volume includes a table of *Abbreviations and Acronyms* as well as a simple guide to the duration of each Congress from 1789 to 1995: *Years of Each Congress*. This list will assist users in placing particular Congresses in time when an article or table identifies that Congress only by its number. The editors have employed the convention of citing the duration of each Congress as running from the year of its convening to the year of the convening of the subsequent Congress. Thus, although the 84th Congress actually adjourned on 27 July 1956, in references to this Congress its duration is given simply as 1955 to 1957, since the 85th Congress did not convene until 3 January 1957. For a comprehensive account of the precise dates of the convening and adjournment of each session of each Congress, refer to the table accompanying the article "Sessions of Congress."

Another special feature of the encyclopedia is the *glossary of legislative terms* located at the back of volume 4. Included in it are technical terms, especially those related to legislative and budgetary process, that are not the subjects of full articles.

The *Synoptic Outline of Contents*, also at the back of volume 4, reflects the systematic plan of the encyclopedia. This outline will be helpful as a peda-gogical tool and as a guide to the relation between more comprehensive articles and those more nar-rowly defined. For example, although numerous cross-references will direct readers to articles on re-lated House and Senate committees, particular acts of legislation, and Supreme Court cases, the synop-tic outline will be useful for understanding the overall structure of the encyclopedia's plan from the perspective of its broader planning categories. The comprehensive entries on areas of public poli-cy such as labor, currency and finance, and defense, among several others, appear in the synoptic out-line under one heading. The encyclopedia can be used systematically by referring first to an article that surveys the whole history of congressional de-liberations and action concerning a particular area of public policy; interested readers can then follow a trail of cross-references that will guide them to related articles of ever greater specificity. Although the synoptic outline mentions all articles in the en-cyclopedia at least once under a suitable heading, the most convenient entrance into the knowledge collected in this reference work remains the index.

The *comprehensive index* in volume 4 of persons, places, subjects, and glossary terms employs bold-face lettering to indicate pages on which appear ar-ticles devoted entirely to the named subject. Italics indicate that the subject occurs within an illustra-tion or its caption or in a graph or chart. Page numbers referring to the contents of articles and tables, many of which run several pages long, ap-pear in regular type. As in the body of the work, blind entries in the index direct readers to alternate names under which page references will be found. All contributors are listed in the index, with the pages of their articles indicated, following the ex-pression *"as contributor."*

Editorial Style and Standards

In the editing of manuscripts, the publisher's staff employed the guidelines set forth in *The Chicago Manual of Style*, 13th edition, the version current when most of the material was under review and development. In addition, the following sources have provided important although limited guidance concerning proper citation of public laws and other legal documents and for the names, both proper and popular, of acts of legislation and congression-al committees: *The Blue Book: A Uniform System of Citation*, 15th edition; *The Legislative Drafter's Desk Reference*, by Lawrence E. Filson; *Congressional Committees, 1789-1982: A Checklist*, compiled by Walter Stubbs; *Major Acts of Congress and Treaties Approved by the Senate, 1789-1980*, compiled by Christopher Dell and Stephen W. Stathis, published by the Congressional Research Service, U.S. Li-brary of Congress; and *Congressional Directory: One Hundred Third Congress*.

The spelling of proper names presents one of the thorniest problems in editing a large reference work. Several members of Congress are known in the historic literature by variant forms of their names or by popular nicknames. The editors have employed the rosters of each Congress that appear in the *Biographical Directory of the United States Congress: 1774–1989* as the authority on the prop-er forms of names as used by the members themselves. Thus, for example, although California senator John C. Fremont's name frequently appears in other sources with an acute accent over the letter e, this encyclopedia follows the *Biographical Direc-tory* and does not employ the accent. Where a pop-ular name, nickname, or shortened form of a per-sonal name have become current in the literature, alternate forms are given within parentheses on first mention within each article. Thus, James Beauchamp Clark is known in several contexts as Champ Clark.

The publisher has aimed to provide a collection of articles that will be a pleasure to read as well as a source of reliable information. We hope that our effort to forge a coherent and readable whole from the particular strengths of this work's more than one million words will prove useful to a wide vari-ety of readers.

Paul Bernabeo, Editorial Director
September 1994

Directory of Contributors

A

W. ANDREW ACHENBAUM
Institute of Gerontology, The University of Michigan
Older Americans

WILLIAM B. ALLEN
Dean, James Madison College, Michigan State University
Ames, Fisher

WILLIAM C. ALLEN
Architectural Historian, Office of the Architect of the Capitol
Architect of the Capitol
Capitol, The
   History of the Capitol
   Dome and Great Rotunda

MILDRED LEHMANN AMER
Congressional Research Service, The Library of Congress
Attending Physician
Ethics Committee, Senate Select
Extensions of Remarks
Honoraria
Nepotism
Pages
Standards of Official Conduct
   Committee, House

HARRY AMMON
Professor Emeritus, Southern Illinois University at Carbondale
Monroe, James

PERI E. ARNOLD
Department of Government and International Studies, University of Notre Dame
Executive Reorganization

R. DOUGLAS ARNOLD
Woodrow Wilson School of Public and International Affairs, Princeton University
Pork Barrel

RAYMOND O. ARSENAULT
Department of History, University of Southern Florida
Tillman, Benjamin R.

LEROY ASHBY
Department of History, Washington State University
Borah, William E.
Church, Frank

HERBERT B. ASHER
Department of Political Science, The Ohio State University
Freshmen

JACK L. AUGUST, JR.
Department of History, University of Houston
Hayden, Carl

B

STANLEY BACH
Congressional Research Service, The Library of Congress
Amending
Dilatory Motions
Previous Question
Resolutions
Riders
Suspension of the Rules

DONALD C. BACON
Chevy Chase, Maryland
Alcoholic Beverages in Congress

Beaman, Middleton
Boggs, Corinne C. (Lindy)
Bolton, Frances P.
Cannon, Clarence
Court-Packing Fight
Debate, Reporters of
Doughton, Robert L.
Floor Leader
   In the House
Florida
Foote, Henry S.
Gross, Harold R.
Hays, Wayne L.
Historians of the House and Senate
Humor and Satire
   In Congress
Interparliamentary Organizations
Jackson-Vanik Amendment
Longworth, Nicholas
Manhattan Project
National Anthem
Rayburn, Sam
Robinson, Joseph T.
Taber, John
Violence
   Violence against Congress
   Violence in Congress

CHARLES W. BAILEY II
Washington, D.C.
Humphrey, Hubert H.

RICHARD A. BAKER
Historian, United States Senate
Anderson, Clinton P.
Biffle, Les
Chambers
   Senate Chamber
Floor Leader
   In the Senate
McFarland, Ernest W.
Supreme Court

ROSS K. BAKER
Department of Political Science,
Rutgers University
Caucus
    Party Caucus
Clubs
Democratic Party
Mansfield, Mike

DAVID N. BALAAM
Department of Politics and Government,
The University of Puget Sound
Agriculture Committee, House
Agriculture, Nutrition, and Forestry
    Committee, Senate

DANIEL J. BALZ
The Washington Post
Tower, John G.

WILLIAM L. BARNEY
Chapel Hill, North Carolina
Congress of the Confederacy
Secession

ROBERT W. BARRIE
Corporate Federal Relations, General
Electric Company
Hawley-Smoot Tariff Act
Tariffs and Trade

JOHN M. BARRY
Washington, D.C.
Wright, James C., Jr.

RICHARD A. BARTLETT
Tallahassee, Florida
Exploration

EDWIN C. BEARSS
National Park Service, Washington, D.C.
National Cemeteries, Monuments, and
    Battlefields

MICHAEL LES BENEDICT
Department of History, The Ohio
State University
History of Congress
    Sectionalism and Nationalism
        (1840–1872)

A. LEROY BENNETT
Professor Emeritus, University
of Delaware
International Organizations

RICHARD FRANKLIN BENSEL
Department of Government,
Cornell University
Sectionalism

EDWARD D. BERKOWITZ
Department of History, The George
Washington University
Disability Legislation

WINFRED E. A. BERNHARD
Department of History, University of
Massachusetts at Amherst
Dayton, Jonathan
Giles, William B.
Harper, Robert G.
Jay's Treaty
Kentucky and Virginia Resolutions
Macon, Nathaniel
Muhlenberg, Frederick A. C.
Sedgwick, Theodore
Trumbull, Jonathan

ROBERT C. BERRY
Boston College Law School
Sports

RICHARD S. BETH
Congressional Research Service,
The Library of Congress
Calendars
Clerks
Discharge Rules
Points of Order
Private Bill
Public Law

JOHN F. BIBBY
Department of Political Science,
University of Milwaukee
Political Parties

CHARLENE BANGS BICKFORD
First Federal Congress Project, The
George Washington University
First Congress
King, Rufus

MONROE LEE BILLINGTON
Department of History, New Mexico
State University
Cox, Samuel S. (Sunset)
Gore, Thomas P.

SARAH A. BINDER
Department of Political Science,
University of Minnesota
Minority Rights

JEFFREY BIRNBAUM
Wall Street Journal
Tax Reform Act of 1986

G. ROBERT BLAKEY
School of Law, University of
Notre Dame
Racketeer Influenced and Corrupt
    Organizations Act (RICO)

FREDERICK J. BLUE
Department of History, Youngstown
State University
Chase, Salmon P.

BARBARA BLUMBERG
Department of Social Sciences,
Pace University
Celler, Emanuel

MARY ETTA BOESL
President, Policy Research, Inc.,
Washington, D.C.
Children, Youth, and Families
    Committee, House Select
Committees
    Standing Committees
    Select and Special Committees
    Joint Committees
Energy and Natural Resources
    Committee, Senate
Expungement
Ferraro, Geraldine A.
Government Operations Committee,
    House
Green, Edith S.
Griffiths, Martha W.
Hunger Committee, House Select
Jordan, Barbara
Legislative Branch
Library Committee, Joint

Luce, Clare Boothe
Rogers, Edith Nourse
Rules and Administration Committee,
    Senate
Small Business Committee, House
Small Business Committee, Senate
Small Business Legislation
Smith, Margaret Chase
Sullivan, Leonor Kretzer
Taxation Committee, Joint
Urban Mass Transportation Act of 1964
Veterans' Affairs Committee, House
Veterans' Affairs Committee, Senate

PAUL F. BOLLER, JR.
    *Department of History, Texas
        State University*
    Humor and Satire
        About Congress

JON R. BOND
    *Department of Political Science,
        Texas A&M University*
    President and Congress
        Legislative Success

KENNETH R. BOWLING
    *First Federal Congress Project, The
        George Washington University*
    Anti-Federalists
    Articles of Confederation
    Capitals of the United States
    Maclay, William

JOHN BRAEMAN
    *Department of History, University
        of Nebraska*
    Aldrich, Nelson W.
    Allison, William B.
    Beveridge, Albert J.
    Cummins, Albert B.
    Dolliver, Jonathan P.

ALLAN M. BRANDT
    *Department of Social Medicine,
        Harvard Medical School*
    Tobacco

D. CLAYTON BROWN
    *Department of History, Texas
        Christian University*
    Rural Electrification Act of 1936

DANIEL PATRICK BROWN
    *Department of History, Moorpark
        College*
    Wade, Benjamin F.

JEFFREY P. BROWN
    *Associate Dean, College of Arts and
        Sciences, New Mexico State
        University*
    Ohio

THOMAS H. BROWN
    President, Union County College
    Boutwell, George S.

WILLIAM HOLMES BROWN
    *Parliamentarian, United States
        House of Representatives*
    Deschler, Lewis
    House of Representatives
        House Rules and Procedures
    Recommittal

JOHN D. BUENKER
    *Department of Social Sciences,
        University of Wisconsin–Parkside*
    Seventeenth Amendment

TIMOTHY J. BURGER
    Roll Call, Washington, D.C.
    Patronage
    Travel

SUSAN R. BURGESS
    *Department of Political Science,
        University of Wisconsin–Milwaukee*
    War Powers

ROBERT E. BURKE
    *Professor Emeritus, University
        of Washington*
    Wheeler, Burton K.

RICHARD C. BURNWEIT
    *Department of Political Science,
        Westmont College*
    Burton, Phillip
    Morse, Wayne L.
    Reed, David A.
    Snell, Bertrand H.
    Tilson, John Q.

BARBARA C. BURRELL
    *Women's Studies Research Center and
        Wisconsin Survey Research
        Laboratory, University of
        Wisconsin–Madison*
    Family Policies

ROBERT C. BYRD
    Senator, United States Senate
    President Pro Tempore of the Senate

C

BRUCE E. CAIN
    *Institute of Governmental Studies,
        University of California, Berkeley*
    Apportionment and Redistricting

DAN CALDWELL
    *Council on International Studies,
        Pepperdine University*
    Strategic Arms Limitation Talks (SALT)

CHARLES W. CALHOUN
    *Department of History, East
        Carolina University*
    Cleveland, Grover
    Hoar, George F.
    McKinley Tariff Act
    Reed, Thomas B.
    Sherman, John

JOHN F. CALLAHAN
    *Dean of Arts and Humanities,
        Lewis and Clark College*
    McCarthy, Eugene J.

KARL E. CAMPBELL
    Department of History, Pfeiffer College
    Ervin, Samuel J., Jr.

THOMAS M. CAMPBELL
    *Department of History, The Florida
        State University*
    United Nations

LOU CANNON
    The Washington Post
    Reagan, Ronald W.

DAVID T. CANON
Department of Political Science,
University of Wisconsin–Madison
Elections, Congressional
    Becoming a Candidate
    Members
        Demographic Profile

JAMES D. CARROLL
Department of Public Administration,
Florida International University
Congressional Research Service
Library of Congress

FRANK A. CASSELL
Vice-Provost and Dean, Albert A. Robin
Campus, Roosevelt University
Smith, Samuel

DAVID CHALMERS
Department of History, University
of Florida
Muckraking

JOHN WHITECLAY CHAMBERS II
Department of History, Rutgers
University
Conscription

ANTHONY CHAMPAGNE
School of Social Sciences, The
University of Texas at Dallas
Connally, Tom T.
Crockett, David
Garner, John Nance
Houston, Sam
Mahon, George H.
Patman, Wright

RICHARD N. CHAPMAN
Department of History, Francis
Marion University
World War II

ROBERT LEE CHARTRAND
Senior Specialist Emeritus,
Congressional Research Service,
The Library of Congress
Technology in Congress

RONALD S. CHRISTENSON
Department of Political Science,
Gustavus Adolphus College
Treason

WARREN I. CIKINS
Center for Public Policy Education,
The Brookings Institution
Hays, Brooks

GENE CLANTON
Department of History, Washington
State University
Populism

GERARD H. CLARFIELD
Department of History, University
of Missouri–Columbia
Pickering, Timothy

CHARLES E. CLARK
Department of History, University
of New Hampshire
Maine

JAMES W. CLARKE
Department of Political Science,
University of Arizona
Presidential Assassinations
    and Protection

ALAN L. CLEM
Department of Political Science, The
University of South Dakota
Blocs and Coalitions
McGovern, George
Montana
North Dakota
South Dakota

DAVID COHEN
Co-Director, Advocacy Institute
Common Cause

RICHARD E. COHEN
National Journal
Perquisites

WAYNE S. COLE
Professor Emeritus, University
of Maryland
Lend-Lease Act
Nye, Gerald P.
Nye Committee

PAOLO E. COLETTA
Annapolis, Maryland
Bryan, William Jennings
Navy
Service Academies
Smith, Ellison D. (Cotton Ed)
Taft, William Howard
Thurman, Allen G.

KATHERINE A. COLLADO
Center for Legislative Archives,
National Archives
Peace Corps

MELISSA P. COLLIE
Department of Government, The
University of Texas at Austin
Voting in Congress
    Voting Analysis

ELLEN C. COLLIER
Congressional Research Service,
The Library of Congress
Executive Agreement
Genocide Convention
Treaties

TIMOTHY J. CONLAN
Department of Public Affairs,
George Mason University
Finance Committee, Senate

WILLIAM J. COOPER, JR.
Department of History, Louisiana
State University
Davis, Jefferson

DAVID A. CORBIN
Senior Researcher and Writer,
Democratic Policy Committee,
United States Senate
West Virginia

ROBERT E. CORLEW
Dean, Middle Tennessee State University
McKellar, Kenneth D.
Tennessee

GEORGE A. COSTELLO
Congressional Research Service,
The Library of Congress
Bills of Attainder
Ex Post Facto Laws

CECIL V. CRABB, JR.
Department of Political Science,
Louisiana State University
Foreign Policy

BARBARA HINKSON CRAIG
Department of Government,
Wesleyan University
Immigration and Naturalization
Service v. Chadha
Veto
Legislative Veto

JOHN R. CRANFORD
Congressional Quarterly Weekly Review
Savings and Loan Crisis

NICHOLAS CULLATHER
Department of History, University
of Virginia
Philippines
Platt Amendment

NOBLE E. CUNNINGHAM, JR.
Department of History, University
of Missouri–Columbia
Beckley, John
Circular Letters
History of Congress
National Growth and Institutional
Development (1801–1840)

RICHARD N. CURRENT
Professor Emeritus, University of
North Carolina at Greensboro
States' Rights
Webster-Hayne Debate
Whig Party

JAMES T. CURRIE
Department of Political Science,
Industrial College of the Armed Forces
Congress
Customs and Mores of Congress

LEONARD P. CURRY
Department of History, University
of Louisville
Civil War
Homestead Act
Morrill Land-Grant College Act
National Banking Act
Pacific Railroad Acts

D

ROBERT DALLEK
Department of History, University
of California, Los Angeles
Johnson, Lyndon B.

ROGER DANIELS
Department of History, University
of Cincinnati
Chinese Exclusion Policy

MICHAEL DAVIDSON
Counsel, United States Senate
Constitution
Congress in the Constitution

ROGER H. DAVIDSON
Department of Government and Politics,
University of Maryland
American Political Science Association
Aspinall, Wayne N.
Bolling, Richard W.
Clinton, William Jefferson (Bill)
History of Congress
Congress Today and Tomorrow
Legislative Service Organizations
Organization of Congress Committee,
Joint (1993)
Persian Gulf War

LUIS R. DÁVILA-COLÓN
Political Analyst, San Juan, Puerto Rico
Puerto Rico
Statehood

EDWARD DAVIS
Congressional Research Service,
The Library of Congress
Budget Enforcement Act of 1990
Deferral
Deficiency Bills
Gramm-Latta Resolution
Reconciliation
Rescission
Sequestration

CHRISTOPHER J. DEERING
Department of Political Science, The
George Washington University
Armed Services Committee, House
Armed Services Committee, Senate

CHRISTINE DEGREGORIO
Department of Government, School
of Public Affairs, The American
University
Subcommittees

MARTHA DERTHICK
Woodrow Wilson Department of
Government and Foreign Affairs,
University of Virginia
Grant-in-Aid
Social Security Act

ROBERT E. DICLERICO
Department of Political Science,
West Virginia University
Presidential Elections
Twenty-second Amendment

ROBERT JAY DILGER
Director, Institute for Public Affairs,
West Virginia University
Federalism

LAWRENCE C. DODD
Director, Center for the Study of
American Politics, University
of Colorado at Boulder
History of Congress
The Rise of the Modern State
(1933–1964)

GORDON B. DODDS
Department of History, Portland
State University
Oregon

JUSTUS D. DOENECKE
Division of Social Sciences, University
of South Florida
Arthur, Chester A.

KATHLEEN DOLAN
Department of Political Science,
University of Wisconsin–Oshkosh
Backdoor Spending
Entitlement
Fiscal Year
Merchant Marine and Fisheries
Committee, House

ROBERT J. DONOVAN
Falls Church, Virginia
Eisenhower, Dwight D.
MacArthur Firing
Martin, Joseph W., Jr.

ROBERT B. DOVE
Republican Leader's Office,
Washington, D.C.
Adjournment and Recess
In the Senate
Anthony Rule
Motions
In the Senate
Quorum Call
In the Senate
Reconsider, Motion to
In the Senate
Riddick, Floyd M.
Senate
Senate Rules and Procedures
Senator
Unanimous Consent Agreements

JULIE S. DRUCKER
Department of Political Science,
Wellesley College
Caucus
Special Interest Caucus

THOMAS G. DUNCAN
Assistant Parliamentarian, United
States House of Representatives
Pairing
Quorum Call
In the House

A. HUNTER DUPREE
Cambridge, Massachusetts
Science and Technology

PAUL E. DWYER
Congressional Research Service,
The Library of Congress
Contingent Fund
House Administration Committee

E

RALPH LOWELL ECKERT
The Behrend College, Division of
Humanities and Social Sciences, The
Pennsylvania State University, Erie
Crisp, Charles F.

WALTER B. EDGAR
Director, Institute of Southern Studies,
University of South Carolina
South Carolina

GEORGE C. EDWARDS III
Department of Political Science,
Texas A&M University
State of the Union Message

JEROME E. EDWARDS
Department of History, University
of Nevada, Reno
McCarran, Patrick A.

RICHARD C. EHLKE
Congressional Research Service,
The Library of Congress
Bowsher v. Synar
Buckley v. Valeo
Executive Privilege
General Welfare Clause
Gravel v. United States
Morrison v. Olson
Myers v. United States

RICHARD E. ELLIS
Department of History, State University
of New York at Buffalo
Jefferson, Thomas
Jeffersonian Republicans
Louisiana Purchase
McCulloch v. Maryland
Marbury v. Madison
Nullification
Twelfth Amendment

LEON D. EPSTEIN
Department of Political Science,
University of Wisconsin–Madison
La Follette, Robert M.
La Follette, Robert M., Jr.
Wisconsin

ROBERT ERIKSON
Department of Political Science,
University of Houston
Incumbency

C. LAWRENCE EVANS
Department of Government, The College
of William and Mary
Judiciary Committee, Senate

F

WALLACE D. FARNHAM
Professor Emeritus, University of
Illinois at Urbana–Champaign
Railroads

MARTIN L. FAUSOLD
Department of History, State University
of New York, Geneseo
Hoover, Herbert

JOHN D. FEERICK
School of Law, Fordham University
Twenty-fifth Amendment

ESTELLE F. FEINSTEIN
Stamford, Connecticut
Connecticut

LINDA FEINSTEIN
Washington, D.C.
Women in Congress

RICHARD F. FENNO, JR.
Department of Political Science,
University of Rochester
Senate
An Overview

JOHN FERLING
Department of History, West
Georgia College
Washington, George
Washington's Farewell Address

ROBERT H. FERRELL
Department of History, Indiana
University
Coolidge, Calvin
Teapot Dome
World War I

LAWRENCE E. FILSON
Darnestown, Maryland
Drafting
Enacting Clause
Legislative Counsel

EVELYN C. FINK
Department of Political Science,
University of Nebraska–Lincoln
Congress
Congressional Workload

LOUIS FISHER
Congressional Research Service,
The Library of Congress
Constitution
Congressional Interpretation of
the Constitution
Impoundment
Nonstatutory Controls
Removal Power
Salaries
Twenty-seventh Amendment

GILBERT C. FITE
Bella Vista, Arkansas
Russell, Richard B.
Southern Manifesto

MICHAEL W. FLAMM
Department of History,
Columbia University
GI Bill of Rights

WAYNE FLYNT
Department of History, Auburn
University
Alabama

KAREN FOERSTEL
Roll Call, Washington, D.C.
Non-Legislative and Financial
Services, Director of

CHRISTOPHER H. FOREMAN, JR.
The Brookings Institution
Regulation and Deregulation

LINDA L. FOWLER
Department of Political Science,
Syracuse University
Members
Congressional Careers

DANIEL M. FOX
President, Milbank Memorial Fund,
New York City
Health and Medicine
Hospital Survey and Construction Act

MORGAN J. FRANKEL
Office of Senate Legal Counsel,
United States Senate
Constitution
Congress in the Constitution

JOHN B. FRANTZ
Department of History, The
Pennsylvania State University
Pennsylvania

STEPHEN E. FRANTZICH
Department of Political Science,
United States Naval Academy,
Annapolis, Maryland
C-SPAN
Intern and Fellowship Programs

SARA FRITZ
Los Angeles Times, Washington Bureau
Members
Daily Life and Routine in the House
Spouses and Families

ALAN S. FRUMIN
Parliamentarian, United States Senate
Parliamentarian
Senate Parliamentarian

JOSEPH A. FRY
Department of History, University
of Nevada, Las Vegas
Morgan, John T.

ALTON FRYE
Senior Vice President and National
Director, Council on Foreign
Relations
Defense
Defense Production Act of 1950
National Security Act

LAWRENCE H. FUCHS
Department of American Studies,
Brandeis University
Hawaii
Immigration Policy

PATRICK J. FURLONG
Department of History, Indiana
University at South Bend
Indiana
St. Clair Investigation

G

RONALD GARAY
Associate Director, Manship School of
Mass Communication, Louisiana
State University
Broadcasting of Congressional
Proceedings

ROGELIO GARCIA
Congressional Research Service,
The Library of Congress
Confirmation
Government in the Sunshine Act

TED GEST
Senior Editor, U.S. News &
World Report
Abscam
Gun Control

WILLIAM E. GIENAPP
Department of History, Harvard
University
Bell, John
Breckinridge, John C.
Compromise of 1850
Crittenden, John J.
Fugitive Slave Act
Kansas-Nebraska Act
Missouri Compromise
Slavery
Sumner, Charles
Tyler, John
Wilmot Proviso

MICHAEL L. GILLETTE
Director, Center for Legislative Archives,
National Archives
Long, Huey P.

WILLIAM GILLETTE
Department of History, Rutgers
University
Fifteenth Amendment

JOHN B. GILMOUR
Department of Political Science,
Washington University
Bargaining
Blue Ribbon Commissions

ROBERT S. GILMOUR
Department of Political Science, The
University of Connecticut
Governmental Affairs Committee,
Senate

DONNA GIORDANO
Stony Brook, New York
Marcantonio, Vito

BETTY GLAD
Department of Government and
International Studies, University
of South Carolina
Pittman, Key

JAMES K. GLASSMAN
Washington, D.C.
Roll Call

DANNEY GOBLE
Historian, The Carl Albert Center, The
University of Oklahoma at Norman
Monroney, A. S. Mike
Oklahoma

ROBERT U. GOEHLERT
Librarian for Economics, Political
Science, and Criminal Justice,
Indiana University
Congress
Bibliographical Guide

RAIMUND E. GOERLER
University Archivist, The Ohio State
University
Transportation

ROBERT A. GOLDBERG
Department of History, The University
of Utah
Goldwater, Barry

RONALD GOLDFARB
Goldfarb and Graybill,
Washington, D.C.
Contempt of Congress

HAYS GOREY
Time Magazine
Pepper, Claude
Watergate
Watergate Committee

WILLIAM T. GORMLEY, JR.
Graduate Public Policy Program and
Department of Government,
Georgetown University
General Accounting Office

KAY C. GOSS
Associate Director for Preparedness
Training and Exercises, Federal
Emergency Management Agency,
Washington, D.C.
McClellan, John L.
Mills, Wilbur D.

LEWIS L. GOULD
Department of History, The University
of Texas at Austin
McKinley, William
Platt, Orville H.
Roosevelt, Theodore

OTIS L. GRAHAM, JR.
Department of History, University of
California, Santa Barbara
New Deal

GEORGE W. GRAYSON
Department of Government, The College
of William and Mary
Shadow Senators

SHARON STIVER GRESSLE
Congressional Research Service,
The Library of Congress
Postal Service
Post Office and Civil Service
Committee, House

THOMAS N. GUINSBURG
Department of History, University of
Western Ontario
Isolationism

H

VAL J. HALAMANDARIS
President, National Association for
Home Care, Washington, D.C.
Aging Committee, House Select
Aging Committee, Senate Special

ROGER K. HALEY
Librarian, United States Senate
Libraries of the House and Senate

RICHARD L. HALL
Institute of Public Policy Studies,
University of Michigan at Ann Arbor
Commerce, Science, and
Transportation Committee, Senate
Energy and Commerce Committee,
House

ALONZO L. HAMBY
Department of History, Ohio University
Liberalism
Truman, Harry S.

CHARLES V. HAMILTON
Department of Political Science,
Columbia University
Powell, Adam Clayton, Jr.

DAGMAR HAMILTON
Lyndon B. Johnson School of
Public Affairs, The University of
Texas at Austin
Rodino, Peter W., Jr.

VIRGINIA VAN DER VEER HAMILTON
Department of History, The University
of Alabama at Birmingham
Black, Hugo L.
Hill, Lister

SUSAN WEBB HAMMOND
Department of Government, The
American University
Executive Branch

ORVAL HANSEN
Washington, D.C.
Correspondence to Congress

ROBERT L. HARDESTY
President Emeritus, Southwest
Texas State University
Albert, Carl B.
Capitol Hill

CHARLES W. HARRIS
Department of Political Science,
Howard University
District of Columbia
District of Columbia Committee,
   House
Twenty-third Amendment

CYNTHIA HARRISON
Federal Judicial Center, Washington, D.C.
Equal Rights Amendment
Nineteenth Amendment
Women's Issues and Rights

ROBERT J. HAVEL
Longwood, Florida
Iran-contra Committees

ELLIS W. HAWLEY
Department of History, University
of Iowa
Temporary National Economic
   Committee (TNEC)

M. J. HEALE
Department of History, University
of Lancaster
Communism and Anticommunism

JEFFREY HEARN
Takoma Park, Maryland
Ceremonial Activities

C. ROBERT HEATH
Bickerstaff, Heath & Smiley, L.L.P.,
Austin, Texas
Baker v. Carr

HAROLD P. HENDERSON
Division of Social Sciences, Abraham
Baldwin Agricultural College
George, Walter F.
Talmadge, Herman E.
Vinson, Carl

GERALD S. HENIG
Department of History, California
State University
Davis, Henry Winter

PAUL S. HERRNSON
Department of Government and Politics,
University of Maryland
Campaign Committees

ALLEN HERTZKE
The Carl Albert Center, The University
of Oklahoma at Norman
Religion

STEPHEN HESS
The Brookings Institution
Political Dynasties

JOHN R. HIBBING
Department of Political Science,
University of Nebraska
Members
   Tenure and Turnover

DONALD R. HICKEY
Department of History, Wayne
State College
Embargo
Nebraska
War Hawks
War of 1812

DILYS M. HILL
Reader in Politics, University of
Southampton, England
Bush, George H. W.

ROBERT F. HIMMELBERG
Department of History, Fordham
University
National Industrial Recovery Act
Wheeler-Rayburn Public Utility
   Holding Company Act

HARRY HOGAN
Washington, D.C.
Alcohol Policy
Narcotics Abuse and Control
   Committee, House Select
Narcotics and Other Dangerous Drugs

PAUL S. HOLBO
Vice President for Academic Affairs and
Provost, University of Oregon
Spanish American War
Territorial Expansion

JEAN S. HOLDER
Department of History, Gettysburg
College
Adams, John

PAT M. HOLT
Bethesda, Maryland
Foreign Relations Committee, Senate

ARI HOOGENBOOM
Department of History, Brooklyn College,
The City University of New York
Hayes, Rutherford B.
Hepburn Act
Interstate Commerce Act

OLIVE HOOGENBOOM
Brooklyn, New York
Hepburn Act
Interstate Commerce Act

STEPHEN HORN
Representative, United States
House of Representatives
Johnson, Hiram W.
Knowland, William F.

DAVID A. HORROCKS
Supervising Archivist, Gerald R. Ford
Library, Ann Arbor, Michigan
Ford, Gerald R., Jr.

CHARLES T. HOWELL
Chief Counsel, Committee on House
Administration
Contested Elections

FREDERICK E. HOXIE
Director, D'Arcy McNickle Center,
The Newberry Library
Dawes Severalty Act
Indian Policy
Indian Treaties

RANDAL L. HOYER
*Department of History and Social
    Sciences, Madonna University*
Morrill, Justin S.

PAUL HUBBARD
*Department of History, Arizona
    State University*
Arizona
Udall, Morris K.

DAVID C. HUCKABEE
*Congressional Research Service,
    The Library of Congress*
Census

BRIAN D. HUMES
*Department of Political Science,
    University of Nebraska–Lincoln*
Congress
    Congressional Workload

RICHARD HUNT
*Center for Legislative Archives,
    National Archives*
Delaware
New Jersey

R. DOUGLAS HURT
*Director, Ph.D. Program in Agricultural
    History and Rural Studies, Iowa
    State University*
Agriculture

I

HOMER LARRY INGLE
*Department of History, University
    of Tennessee*
Kitchin, Claude

PATRICIA W. INGRAHAM
*Department of Public Administration,
    Maxwell School of Citizenship and
    Public Affairs, Syracuse University*
Hatch Act

GEORGE M. INGRAM
*Senior Staff Consultant, United States
    House of Representatives, Committee
    on Foreign Affairs*
Foreign Aid

J

HARRY V. JAFFA
*Professor Emeritus, Claremont
    McKenna College*
Lincoln-Douglas Debates

RHODRI JEFFREYS-JONES
*Department of History, University of
    Edinburgh, Scotland*
Central Intelligence Agency

ROBERT L. JENKINS
*Department of History, Mississippi
    State University*
Mississippi

RICHARD J. JENSEN
*Department of History, University of
    Illinois, Chicago*
Illinois

JOHN R. JOHANNES
*Department of Political Science,
    Marquette University*
Constituency Service

ROBERT W. JOHANNSEN
*Department of History, University of
    Illinois at Urbana–Champaign*
Douglas, Stephen A.
Polk, James K.

CHARLES W. JOHNSON
*Deputy Parliamentarian, United States
    House of Representatives*
Adjournment and Recess
    In the House
Hinds, Asher C.
Manuals of Procedure
    House Manuals
Precedents
    House Precedents

EVANS C. JOHNSON
*Department of History, Stetson
    University*
Underwood, Oscar W.

LOCH K. JOHNSON
*Department of Political Science,
    University of Georgia*
Intelligence Policy
Investigations

MANFRED JONAS
Department of History, Union College
Fish, Hamilton
Neutrality Debates

CHARLES O. JONES
*Department of Political Science,
    University of Wisconsin–Madison*
Cannon, Joseph G.
Cannon Revolt

CHARLES T. JONES, JR.
*Department of History, University
    of Missouri*
Missouri

ROY STAPLETON JONES, JR.
*Birch, Horton, Bittner, and Cherot
    Washington, D.C.*
Natural Resources Committee, House

DAVID M. JORDAN
*Wisler, Pearlstine, Talone, Craig, Garrity
    & Potash, Blue Bell, Pennsylvania*
Conkling, Roscoe

JANIS JUDSON
*Department of History and Political
    Science, Hood College*
Concurrent Powers
Delegation of Powers
Enforcement
Enumerated Powers
Implied Powers

K

CARL F. KAESTLE
*School of Education, University of
    Wisconsin–Madison*
Education
Elementary and Secondary Education
    Act of 1965
Higher Education Act of 1965
National Defense Education Act of 1958

FREDERICK M. KAISER
  Congressional Research Service,
    The Library of Congress
  Inspectors General
  Intelligence Committee, House
      Permanent Select
  Intelligence Committee, Senate Select
  Subpoena Power

LAWRENCE S. KAPLAN
  Department of History, Kent State
    University
  North Atlantic Treaty

DON E. KASH
  Institute of Public Policy, George
    Mason University
  Office of Technology Assessment (OTA)

KENNETH T. KATO
  Center for Legislative Archives,
    National Archives
  Veterans' Benefits
      An Overview

ROBERT A. KATZMANN
  The Brookings Institution
  Judiciary and Congress
  Legislative Intent
  War Powers Resolution

RICHARD KAZARIAN, JR.
  Providence, Rhode Island
  Seward, William H.

JAMES A. KEHL
  Department of History, University
    of Pittsburgh
  Cameron, Simon
  Penrose, Boies
  Quay, Matthew S.
  Randall, Samuel J.

MORTON KELLER
  Department of History, Brandeis
    University
  Clayton Antitrust Act
  Eleventh Amendment
  Espionage Act
  Federal Reserve Bank Act
  Federal Trade Commission Act
  Grow, Galusha A.

Grundy, Felix
History of Congress
    Progressivism and Normalcy
      (1900–1933)
Interstate Highway System
Literature on Congress
Monroe Doctrine
Norton, Mary T.
Pujo Investigation
Santo Domingo
Securities Acts
Sherman Antitrust Act
X Y Z Affair

MICHAEL P. KELLY
  Stony Brook, New York
  Javits, Jacob K.

SEAN Q KELLY
  Department of Political Science,
    University of Colorado at Boulder
  Elections, Congressional
      Election Results

K. AUSTIN KERR
  Department of History, The Ohio
    State University
  Anti-Saloon League
  Prohibition

THOMAS KESSNER
  Professor of History and Deputy
    Executive Officer, The Graduate
    School and University Center of
    The City University of New York
  LaGuardia, Fiorello H.

RALPH KETCHAM
  Maxwell School of Citizenship and
    Public Affairs, Syracuse University
  Madison, James

ROBERT C. KETCHAM
  Washington, D.C.
  Science, Space, and Technology
      Committee, House

JAMES ROE KETCHUM
  Curator, Commission on Art,
    United States Senate
  Cuisine of Congress

DONALD F. KETTL
  Department of Political Science, The
    Robert M. La Follette Institute of
    Public Affairs, University of
    Wisconsin–Madison
  Government Corporations
  Office of Management and Budget
      (OMB)

EDWARD KEYNES
  Department of Political Science, The
    Pennsylvania State University
  Abortion
  Hyde Amendments

RICHARD B. KIELBOWICZ
  School of Communications,
    University of Washington
  Telegraph

JOHNNY H. KILLIAN
  Congressional Research Service,
    The Library of Congress
  Congress
      Powers of Congress
  Davis et al. v. Bandemer et al.
  Legislative Courts
  Powell v. McCormack
  Wesberry v. Sanders
  Youngstown Sheet and Tube Co. v.
      Sawyer

DAVID C. KING
  John F. Kennedy School of Government,
    Harvard University
  Legislative Reorganization Acts
      Act of 1946
      Act of 1970

JOHN W. KINGDON
  Department of Political Science,
    The University of Michigan
  Agenda
  Congress
      Politics and Influence in Congress

RICHARD S. KIRKENDALL
  Department of American History,
    University of Washington
  Agricultural Adjustment Acts

DICK KIRSCHTEN
National Journal
Atomic Energy Act
Atomic Energy Committee, Joint

FRANK L. KLEMENT
Professor Emeritus, Marquette
University
Vallandigham, Clement L.

MARY-JO KLINE
Silver Spring, Maryland
Morris, Gouverneur

JAMES C. KLOTTER
State Historian and Executive Director,
Kentucky Historical Society, Frankfort
Kentucky

WILLARD CARL KLUNDER
Department of History, The Wichita
State University
Cass, Lewis

ELIZABETH KOED
Department of History, University of
California, Santa Barbara
New Deal

NANCY F. KOEHN
Graduate School of Business
Administration, Harvard University
Economic Policy
Twentieth Century

A. CASH KOENIGER
Department of History and Politics,
Virginia Military Institute
Glass, Carter

DAVID A. KOPLOW
Georgetown University Law Center
Strategic Defense Initiative (SDI)

JESSICA KORN
Department of Political Science,
University of Massachusetts, Amherst
Checks and Balances

JOHN J. KORNACKI
Director, Dirksen Congressional Center,
Pekin, Illinois
Baker, Howard H., Jr.
Michel, Robert H. (Bob)

NICK KOTZ
Washington, D.C.
Automobile Safety

DAVID E. KYVIG
Department of History, The University
of Akron
Eighteenth Amendment
National Prohibition Act
Twenty-first Amendment

L

GARRINE P. LANEY
Congressional Research Service,
The Library of Congress
Territories and Possessions

HAROLD D. LANGLEY
Department of History, The Catholic
University of America
Hayne, Robert Y.

ARLEN J. LARGE
Washington, D.C.
Baker, Robert G. (Bobby)
Long, Russell B.
Muskie, Edmund S.
Panama
Panama Canal Treaty
Stennis, John C.

JOHN L. LARSON
Department of History, Purdue
University
Internal Improvements

ROBERT W. LARSON
Professor Emeritus, University
of Northern Colorado
New Mexico

WILLIAM E. LASS
Department of History, Mankato
State University
Minnesota

ROGER D. LAUNIUS
Chief Historian, National Aeronautics
and Space Administration
Aerospace
National Aeronautics and Space Act
of 1958

LANCE T. LELOUP
Public Policy Research Centers,
University of Missouri, Saint Louis
Balanced Budget Amendment
Budget Process
Budget Reconciliation Act
Congressional Budget and
Impoundment Control Act of 1974

J. STANLEY LEMONS
Department of History, Rhode
Island College
Rhode Island

WILLIAM M. LEOGRANDE
Department of Government, The
American University
Boland Amendments
Cold War

E. RAYMOND LEWIS
Librarian, United States House
of Representatives
Congressional Medal of Honor
Libraries of the House and Senate

GUENTER LEWY
Department of Political Science,
University of Massachusetts
Tonkin Gulf Resolution
Vietnam War

PAUL C. LIGHT
Hubert H. Humphrey School,
University of Minnesota
Members
Daily Life and Routine in the Senate

GLENN M. LINDEN
Department of History, Southern
Methodist University
Fourteenth Amendment

DANIEL LIPINSKI
Chicago, Illinois
Movies on Congress

DONALD J. LISIO
Department of History, Coe College
Bonus March

JOHN EDWIN LITTLE
The Papers of Woodrow Wilson,
Princeton University
New Freedom

THOMAS H. LITTLE
Department of Political Science,
University of Texas, Arlington
Congress
The Study of Congress

BURDETT A. LOOMIS
Department of Political Science,
The University of Kansas
Dirksen, Everett M.
Members
Qualifications

MARK M. LOWENTHAL
Congressional Research Service,
The Library of Congress
Arms Control

RICHARD LOWITT
Department of History, The University
of Oklahoma
Norris, George W.
Twentieth Amendment

STEPHEN E. LUCAS
Department of Communication Arts,
University of Wisconsin–Madison
Debate and Oratory
Eulogies

M

ARTHUR MAASS
Frank G. Thomson Professor Emeritus,
Harvard University
Public Works

LOUIS SANDY MAISEL
Department of Government, Colby
College
Elections, Congressional
Nomination to Candidacy
Mitchell, George J.

VINCENT L. MARANDO
Department of Government and Politics,
University of Maryland
Revenue Sharing

HERBERT F. MARGULIES
Department of History, University of
Hawaii, Manoa
Irreconcilables
League of Nations
Lodge, Henry Cabot

MARK PAUL MARLAIRE
Director, University Outreach, University
of Wisconsin–Parkside
Boardinghouses

THEODORE R. MARMOR
School of Organization and
Management, Yale University
Medicare

FENTON S. MARTIN
Librarian for Political Science Research
Collection, Indiana University
Congress
Bibliographical Guide

KENNETH C. MARTIS
Department of Geology and Geography,
West Virginia University
Districts
Gerrymandering

JACK H. MASKELL
Congressional Research Service,
The Library of Congress
Discipline of Members
Financial Disclosure

NICHOLAS A. MASTERS
Legislative Advisor, Winston and Strawn,
Washington, D.C.
Budget Committee, House
Congressional Operations Committee,
Joint

ROBERT NEIL MATHIS
Department of History, Stephen F. Austin
State University
Brooks, Preston S.

MUFTIAH MCCARTIN
Assistant Parliamentarian, United States
House of Representatives
Jefferson's Manual
Motions
In the House
Recognition

JAMES M. MCCORMICK
Department of Political Science,
Iowa State University
Foreign Affairs Committee, House

RICHARD T. MCCULLEY
Historian, Center for Legislative
Archives, National Archives
Veterans' Benefits
Veterans' Pensions

EILEEN L. MCDONAGH
Department of Political Science,
Northeastern University
Progressive Movement
White Slave-Trade Act

GEORGE MCJIMSEY
Department of History, Iowa State
University
Iowa

G. CALVIN MACKENZIE
Department of American Government,
Colby College
Presidential Appointments
Senatorial Courtesy
Recess Appointments

GARY MCKISSICK
Institute of Public Policy Studies,
University of Michigan at Ann Arbor
Commerce, Science, and
Transportation Committee, Senate

VIRGINIA MCMURTRY
Congressional Research Service,
The Library of Congress
Sunset Laws

GEORGE MEADER
Ann Arbor, Michigan
Former Members of Congress

ELIZABETH R. MEGGINSON
Subcommittee on Coast Guard and
Navigation, United States House
of Representatives
Coast Guard

HANK MEIJER
Grand Rapids, Michigan
Vandenberg, Arthur H.

MARCIA L. MELDRUM
Stony Brook, New York
Health and Medicine
Hospital Survey and Construction Act

R. SHEP MELNICK
*Department of Politics, Brandeis
    University*
Clean Air Act
Comprehensive Environmental
    Response, Compensation, and
    Liability Act of 1980
Endangered Species Act of 1973
Environment and Public Works
    Committee, Senate
National Environmental Policy Act
    of 1969
Occupational Safety and Health Act
    of 1970

MARTIN V. MELOSI
*Department of History, University
    of Houston*
Pearl Harbor Investigation

CAROLYN L. MERCK
*Congressional Research Service,
    The Library of Congress*
Members
    Retirement

MARVIN MEYERS
Professor Emeritus, Brandeis University
Federalist Papers

MICHAEL L. MEZEY
*Department of Political Science,
    DePaul University*
Bicameralism

PATRICIA A. MICHAELIS
Kansas State Historical Society, Topeka
Kansas

MIKE MICHAELSON
C-SPAN, Washington, D.C.
Visitors to Capitol Hill

SIDNEY M. MILKIS
*Department of Politics, Brandeis
    University*
Electoral College
Roosevelt, Franklin D.

CYNTHIA PEASE MILLER
*Assistant Historian, United States
    House of Representatives*
Capitol Historical Society
Mace
Sergeant at Arms

MARK C. MILLER
*Department of Government, Clark
    University*
Judiciary Committee, House

SALLY M. MILLER
*Department of History, University
    of the Pacific*
Berger, Victor L.
Socialism

ALLAN R. MILLETT
*Raymond E. Mason, Jr., Professor of
    Military History, The Ohio State
    University*
Army
Marine Corps

RONALD C. MOE
*Congressional Research Service,
    The Library of Congress*
Communications Satellite Act of 1962
Item Veto

JAMES TICE MOORE
*Department of History, Virginia
    Commonwealth University*
Virginia

WILLIAM HOWARD MOORE
*Department of History, University
    of Wyoming*
Crime and Justice
Kefauver, Estes
Kefauver Crime Committee

WINFRED B. MOORE, JR.
Department of History, The Citadel
Byrnes, James F.

ANNE HODGES MORGAN
Norman, Oklahoma
Kerr, Robert S.

CHESTER M. MORGAN
*Department of History, University
    of Kentucky*
Bilbo, Theodore G.
Eastland, James O.

GARY MUCCIARONI
*Department of Political Science,
    Temple University*
Economic Committee, Joint
Economic Opportunity Act of 1964
Employment Act of 1946
Great Society
Vocational Education Act of 1963

JOHN A. MUNROE
*Professor Emeritus, University of
    Delaware*
Bayard, James A., Sr.

JAMES B. MURPHY
*Department of History, Southern
    Illinois University*
George, James Z.
Lamar, Lucius Q. C.

HYDE H. MURRAY
*Director, Governmental Relations,
    American Farm Bureau Federation*
Language

N

CLAUS-M. NASKE
*Executive Director, University of
    Alaska Press*
Alaska

STEVE NEAL
Chicago Sun-Times
McNary, Charles L.
Sabath, Adolph J.

THOMAS H. NEALE
*Congressional Research Service,
    The Library of Congress*
Special Elections
Twenty-sixth Amendment
Vacancy
Voting and Suffrage

MARK E. NEELY, JR.
*Department of History, Saint Louis
    University*
Lincoln, Abraham

JAMES WARREN NEILSON
*Department of Social Sciences,
    Mayville State University*
Cullom, Shelby M.

CANDICE J. NELSON
*Department of Government, The
    American University*
Campaign Financing
Federal Election Commission
Political Action Committees (PACs)

GARRISON NELSON
*Department of Political Science,
    The University of Vermont*
Bridges, H. Styles
Congressional Quarterly
McCormack, John W.
Massachusetts
New Hampshire
O'Neill, Thomas P. (Tip), Jr.
Vermont

KEITH NICHOLLS
*Department of Political Science and
    Criminal Justice, University of
    South Alabama*
Cabinet and Congress

ILONA B. NICKELS
*Congressional Research Service,
    The Library of Congress*
Call System
Committee of the Whole
Committees
    Markups
    Committee Reports
Congressional Record
House of Representatives
    Daily Sessions of the House
Lawmaking
Managers
Oath of Office
Objectors
One-Minute Speeches
Orders
Presiding Officer

Privilege
Seals
Senate
    Daily Sessions of the Senate
Sponsorship
Unanimous Consent

JOHN NIVEN
*Department of History, The Claremont
    Graduate School*
Calhoun, John C.

PHILIP NORTON
*Department of Politics, University
    of Hull*
Congress
    Comparative Perspectives

MARY ALICE NYE
*Department of Political Science,
    University of North Texas*
Civil Rights
Civil Rights Act of 1964

O

JAMES W. OBERLY
*Department of History, University of
    Wisconsin–Eau Claire*
Public Lands

DAVID M. O'BRIEN
*Woodrow Wilson Department of
    Government and Foreign Affairs,
    University of Virginia*
Commerce Power
Judicial Review

PATRICK G. O'BRIEN
*Director, Center for Great Plains Studies,
    Department of History, Emporia State
    University*
Farm Bloc
McNary-Haugen Farm Relief Bill

MORRIS S. OGUL
*Department of Political Science,
    University of Pittsburgh*
Oversight

WALTER J. OLESZEK
*Congressional Research Service,
    The Library of Congress*
Conference Committees
Kern, John Worth
Leadership
    Senate Leadership
Whips

JAMES A. OLIVER
*Republican Cloakroom, United States
    House of Representatives*
Cloakrooms
Congressional Cemetery

BRUCE I. OPPENHEIMER
*Department of Political Science,
    Vanderbilt University*
Cloture
Divided Government
Filibuster

NORMAN J. ORNSTEIN
*Resident Scholar, American Enterprise
    Institute for Public Policy Research*
Ethics and Corruption in Congress
Interest Groups

SHARI L. OSBORN
Stony Brook, New York
Wagner, Robert F.

DAVID M. OSHINSKY
*Department of History, Rutgers
    University*
Army-McCarthy Hearings
McCarthy, Joseph R.

P

ERIC W. PAFF
*Writer and Editor, Office of the
    Architect of the Capitol*
Capitol, The
    Capitol Grounds

DANIEL J. PALAZZOLO
*Department of Political Science,
    University of Richmond*
Leadership
    House Leadership

DAVID L. PALETZ
*Department of Political Science,
Duke University*
Movies on Congress

GLENN R. PARKER
*Policy Studies Program, The Florida
State University*
Constituency Outreach

JAMES R. PARKER
*Department of History, University of
Wisconsin–La Crosse*
Spooner, John C.

HERBERT S. PARMET
*Department of History, The Graduate
School and University Center of The
City University of New York*
Nixon, Richard M.

JAMES T. PATTERSON
*Department of History, Brown
University*
Taft, Robert A.

SAMUEL C. PATTERSON
*Department of Political Science,
The Ohio State University*
Congress
    Public Perceptions of Congress
Party Committees

FREDERICK H. PAULS
*Congressional Research Service,
The Library of Congress*
Offices, Congressional
Offices, District
Sessions of Congress
Staffing

ROBERT L. PEABODY
*Department of Political Science,
The Johns Hopkins University*
Halleck, Charles A.

WILLIAM D. PEDERSON
*Department of History and Political
Science, Louisiana State University*
Boggs, Hale
Louisiana

THOMAS R. PEGRAM
Department of History, Loyola College
Mann, James R.

ALLAN PESKIN
*Department of History, Cleveland
State University*
Garfield, James A.

RONALD M. PETERS, JR.
*Director and Curator, The Carl Albert
Center, The University of Oklahoma*
Carlisle, John G.
Clark, James Beauchamp (Champ)
Speaker of the House

F. ROSS PETERSON
*Director, Mountain West Center
for Regional Studies, Utah
State University*
Idaho

MARK A. PETERSON
*Graduate School of Public and
International Affairs, University
of Pittsburgh*
Legislative Initiative

PAUL E. PETERSON
*Department of Government, Harvard
University*
Urban Policy

MARK P. PETRACCA
*Department of Politics and Society,
University of California, Irvine*
Term Limitation

JOHN R. PETROCIK
*Department of Humanities and Social
Sciences, California Institute of
Technology*
Alignments and Realignments

JAMES P. PFIFFNER
*Department of Public Affairs, George
Mason University*
Presidential Transitions

MATT PINKUS
The Brookings Institution
Democratic Study Group

DONALD J. PISANI
*Department of History, University
of Oklahoma*
Economic Policy
    Nineteenth Century

MARK A. PLUMMER
*Department of History, Illinois
State University*
Ross, Edmund G.

FORREST C. POGUE
Arlington, Virginia
Marshall Plan

J. R. POLE
*Professor Emeritus and Emeritus
Fellow, St. Catherine's College,
Oxford University*
History of Congress
    The Origins of Congress

JOHN SAMUELS PONTIUS
*Congressional Research Service,
The Library of Congress*
Capitol Police
Franking
Joint Sessions and Meetings

LYNDA W. POWELL
*Department of Political Science,
University of Rochester*
Elections, Congressional
    Congressional Campaigns

KATHRYN PREYER
Professor Emerita, Wellesley College
Judiciary Act of 1789

DOUGLAS PRICE
*Department of Government, Harvard
University*
Wilson, Woodrow

BEN PROCTER
*Department of History, Texas
Christian University*
Mills, Roger Q.
Reagan, John H.

SAMUEL PROCTOR
*Department of History, University
of Florida*
West Florida

Q

JO ANNE MCCORMICK QUATANNENS
Assistant Historian, United States
Senate Historical Office
Harrison, William Henry
Rives, William Cabell

GEORGE H. QUESTER
Department of Government and Politics,
University of Maryland
Antiballistic Missile Systems Treaty
Limited Test Ban Treaty
Nuclear Non-Proliferation Treaty
Nuclear Weapons

R

DOUGLAS RAE
Department of Political Science,
Yale University
Majority and Minority

BRUCE A. RAGSDALE
Associate Historian, United States
House of Representatives
Historical Office
Clerk of the House
Gag Rule
Records of Debate

LYN RAGSDALE
Department of Political Science,
The University of Arizona
President and Congress
An Overview

JACK N. RAKOVE
Department of History, Stanford
University
History of Congress
The Road to Nationhood
(1774–1801)

ANDRÉE E. REEVES
Department of Political Science,
University of Alabama, Huntsville
Education and Labor Committee,
House
Labor and Human Resources
Committee, Senate
Public Works and Transportation
Committee, House

MAVIS MANN REEVES
Professor Emerita, University of
Maryland at College Park
Interstate Compacts

PRISCILLA REGAN
Department of Public Affairs,
George Mason University
Privacy

A. JAMES REICHLEY
Visiting Senior Fellow, Georgetown
University
Republican Party

DAVID M. REIMERS
Department of History, New York
University
McCarran-Walter Immigration and
Nationality Act

HAROLD C. RELYEA
Congressional Research Service,
The Library of Congress
Congress
Congressional Publications
Congressional Directory
Emergency Powers
Federal Register
Freedom of Information Act
Government Printing Office
Investigations, Senate Permanent
Subcommittee on
Printing Committee, Joint

MICHAEL J. REMINGTON
Director, National Commission on
Judicial Discipline and Removal,
Washington, D.C.
Impeachment

ROBERT V. REMINI
Department of History, University
of Illinois
Clay, Henry
Jackson, Andrew

LEONARD L. RICHARDS
Department of History, University of
Massachusetts at Amherst
Adams, John Quincy

HEATHER COX RICHARDSON
Department of History, Massachusetts
Institute of Technology
Conduct of the War Committee, Joint

SULA DYSON RICHARDSON
Congressional Research Service,
The Library of Congress
Voting in Congress
Ratings by Interest Groups

DOUGLAS W. RICHMOND
Department of History, The University
of Texas at Arlington
Corwin, Thomas
Mexican War
Mexico

PATRICK W. RIDDLEBERGER
Professor Emeritus, Southern Illinois
University
Fessenden, William Pitt
Julian, George W.

LEROY N. RIESELBACH
Department of Political Science,
Indiana University
Reorganization of Congress

JAMES R. RIGGS
Emmis Broadcasting, Indianapolis,
Indiana
Korean War

DONALD A. RITCHIE
Associate Historian, United States
Senate Historical Office
Barkley, Alben W.
Forney, John W.
Galleries
Pecora Wall Street Investigation
Press
Press Galleries

PHIL ROBERTS
Department of History, University
of Wyoming
Wyoming

PETER D. ROBINSON
Bailey and Robinson, Washington, D.C.
Authorization

JOHN P. ROCHE
*Professor Emeritus, The Fletcher
School of Law and Diplomacy,
Tufts University*
Constitutional Convention of 1787

WARREN ROGERS
Washington, D.C.
Kennedy, John F.

KENT M. RONHOVDE
*Congressional Research Service,
The Library of Congress*
United States v. Curtiss-Wright Export
Corp.

BERNARD ROSEN
*School of Public Affairs, The
American University*
Accountability

WALTER A. ROSENBAUM
*Department of Political Science,
University of Florida*
Environment and Conservation

DAVID H. ROSENBLOOM
*Department of Public Administration,
The American University*
Civil Service
Civil Service Reform Act of 1978
Pendleton Act

ROGER L. ROSENTRETER
Editor, Michigan History Magazine
Michigan

RODNEY A. ROSS
*Center for Legislative Archives,
National Archives*
Archives
Nevada
Utah

MARC ROTHENBERG
*Office of Research, Joseph Henry Project,
Smithsonian Institution*
Smithsonian Institution

FRANCIS E. ROURKE
*Department of Political Science, The
Johns Hopkins University*
Bureaucracy

WILLIAM D. ROWLEY
*Department of History, University
of Nevada, Reno*
Newlands, Francis G.

PAUL S. RUNDQUIST
*Congressional Research Service,
The Library of Congress*
Calendar Wednesday
Citizenship
Delegates, Nonvoting
Instruction
Journals
Natural Resources Committee, House
Petitions and Memorials
Secrecy of Congress
State Delegations

JERROLD G. RUSK
*Department of Political Science, The
University of Arizona, Tucson*
Elections, Congressional
Theory and Law

ROBERT A. RUTLAND
*Professor Emeritus, University
of Virginia*
Bill of Rights

S

RICHARD C. SACHS
*Congressional Research Service,
The Library of Congress*
Federal Corrupt Practices Act of 1925
Lobbying

ROBERT S. SALISBURY
*Department of History, State University
of New York, Oswego*
Edmunds, George F.
Kelley, William D.
Proctor, Redfield

JAMES V. SATURNO
*Congressional Research Service,
The Library of Congress*
Bills
Continuing Resolution
Executive Communications
Expedited Consideration
Legislative Day

Quorum
Tabling

CHARLES EDWARD SCHAMEL
*Center for Legislative Archives,
National Archives*
Maryland

WENDY SCHILLER
Rochester, New York
Elections, Congressional
Congressional Campaigns

ARTHUR M. SCHLESINGER, JR.
*The Graduate School and University
Center, The City University of
New York*
Kennedy, Robert F.

DAVID A. SCHLUETER
School of Law, St. Mary's University
Military Justice, Uniform Code of

LEONARD SCHLUP
*Akron–Summit County Public
Library, Akron, Ohio*
Gorman, Arthur Pue

JUDY SCHNEIDER
*Congressional Research Service,
The Library of Congress*
Committees
Assignment of Members
Committee Jurisdictions
Grandfathering
Independents
Referral
Seniority

THOMAS E. SCHOTT
Oklahoma City, Oklahoma
Stephens, Alexander H.

MARTIN J. SCHRAM
Washington, D.C.
Carter, James Earl (Jimmy), Jr.

JEAN REITH SCHROEDEL
*Center for Politics and Policy, The
Claremont Graduate School*
Banking, Finance, and Urban Affairs
Committee, House
Banking, Housing, and Urban Affairs
Committee, Senate

PETER SCHUCK
Yale Law School
Immigration Act of 1990

MORTON J. SCHUSSHEIM
Washington, D.C.
Federal Housing Acts
Housing Policy

CARLOS A. SCHWANTES
*Department of History, University
    of Idaho*
Coxey's Army

LARRY SCHWEIKART
*Department of History, University
    of Dayton*
Banking
Banking Act of 1933
Bank of the United States
Currency and Finance
Depository Institutions Deregulation
    and Monetary Control Act of 1980
Emergency Banking Relief Act
Sherman Silver Purchase Act
Silver Issue (Bimetallism)

INGRID WINTHER SCOBIE
*Department of History and Government,
    Texas Woman's University*
Douglas, Helen Gahagan

HAROLD F. SEE
*The University of Alabama
    School of Law*
Bankruptcy
Copyright, Trademarks, and Patents

BRUCE E. SEELY
*Department of Social Sciences,
    Michigan Technological University*
Rural Post Roads Act

TERRY L. SEIP
*Department of History, University of
    Southern California*
California
Electoral Commission of 1877
Electoral Count Act
Force Acts
Johnson, Andrew
Radical Republicans

Reconstruction
Reconstruction Committee, Joint
Stevens, Thaddeus
Thirteenth Amendment

RONALD G. SHAIKO
*Department of Government, School of
    Public Affairs, The American
    University*
Congress Watch
Logrolling

JAMES ROGER SHARP
*Department of History, Syracuse
    University*
Alien and Sedition Acts
Federalists

MACK CLAYTON SHELLEY II
*Department of Political Science,
    Iowa State University*
Conservatism
Conservative Coalition

KENNETH E. SHEWMAKER
*Department of History, Dartmouth
    College*
Webster, Daniel

JOHANNA NICOL SHIELDS
*Department of History, The University
    of Alabama*
Bingham, John A.
Cobb, Howell
Mavericks
Wise, Henry A.

HOLLY H. SHIMIZU
United States Botanic Garden
Botanic Garden

HOWARD E. SHUMAN
Arlington, Virginia
Douglas, Paul H.
Majority and Minority

GEORGE H. SIEHL
*Congressional Research Service,
    The Library of Congress*
National Parks and Forests

JEROLD L. SIMMONS
*Department of History, University
    of Nebraska*
Alien Registration Act
Un-American Activities Committee,
    House

BROOKS D. SIMPSON
*Department of History, Arizona
    State University*
Grant, Ulysses S.

GLENN R. SIMPSON
Roll Call
House Bank

ELBERT B. SMITH
*Professor Emeritus, University of
    Maryland*
Benton, Thomas Hart
Buchanan, James
Fillmore, Millard
Pierce, Franklin
Taylor, Zachary

JENNIFER L. SMITH
*Counsel, Budget Committee, United
    States House of Representatives*
Manuals of Procedure
Senate Manuals

STEVEN S. SMITH
*Department of Political Science,
    University of Minnesota*
Committees
    An Overview
House of Representatives
    An Overview

RAYMOND W. SMOCK
*Historian, United States House
    of Representatives*
Bicentennial of Congress
Black Members
    Nineteenth Century
Chambers
    House Chamber
Chaplains
Doorkeeper of the House
Inspector General of the House
Lame Duck Session
Parliamentarian
    House Parliamentarian

HOMER E. SOCOLOFSKY
*Department of History, Kansas
State University*
Capper, Arthur
Harrison, Benjamin

CHARLES A. SPAIN, JR.
*Staff Attorney, Court of Appeals for the
Third District of Texas, Austin*
Flag of the United States

ROBERT J. SPITZER
*Department of Political Science, State
University of New York, College at
Cortland*
Separation of Powers
Veto
Presidential Veto

HAROLD W. STANLEY
*Department of Political Science,
University of Rochester*
Southern Bloc

STEPHEN W. STATHIS
*Congressional Research Service,
The Library of Congress*
Awards and Prizes
Commemorative Legislation
Federal Holidays
National Floral Emblem

MELVIN STEELY
*Department of History, West
Georgia College*
Georgia

CHARLES STEWART III
*Department of Political Science,
Massachusetts Institute of Technology*
Appropriations Committee, House
Budget and Accounting Act

JAMES BREWER STEWART
*Department of History, Macalester
University*
Giddings, Joshua R.

JOHN G. STEWART
Tennessee Valley Authority
Tennessee Valley Authority

WALTER J. STEWART
Secretary, United States Senate
Secretary of the Senate

ALAN STONE
*Department of Political Science,
University of Houston*
Communications
Communications Act of 1934

RALPH A. STONE
Missoula, Montana
Walsh, Thomas J.

WALTER J. STONE
*Department of Political Science,
University of Colorado at Boulder*
Elections, Congressional
Election Results

RANDALL STRAHAN
*Department of Political Science,
Emory University*
Reed, Daniel A.
Reed's Rules
Ways and Means Committee, House

DAVID H. STRATTON
*Department of History, Washington
State University*
Washington

STEPHEN P. STRICKLAND
President, National Peace Foundation
Sparkman, John J.

PHILIPPA STRUM
*Department of Political Science,
Brooklyn College, The City
University of New York*
Civil Liberties

JOHN V. SULLIVAN
*Assistant Parliamentarian, United States
House of Representatives*
Five-Minute Rule
Reconsider, Motion to
In the House

MARK WAHLGREN SUMMERS
*Department of History, University
of Kentucky*
Colfax, Schuyler

Covode Committee
Crédit Mobilier
History of Congress
    The Age of the Machine (1872–1900)

ROBERT G. SUTTER
*Congressional Research Service,
The Library of Congress*
Formosa Resolution

CAROL M. SWAIN
*Woodrow Wilson School of Public and
International Affairs, Princeton
University*
Black Members
    Twentieth Century
Brooke, Edward W.
Chisholm, Shirley A.
De Priest, Oscar

CLAIRE M. SYLVIA
*Office of Senate Legal Counsel,
United States Senate*
Constitution
    Congress in the Constitution

T

DUANE A. TANANBAUM
*Department of History, Lehman College,
The City University of New York*
Bricker Amendment

DONALD G. TANNENBAUM
*Department of Political Science,
Gettysburg College*
Advice and Consent

WILLIAM R. TANNER
*Department of History, Humboldt
State University*
Internal Security
McCarran Internal Security Act of 1950

ABIGAIL THERNSTROM
*Senior Fellow, Manhattan
Institute and Adjunct Professor,
Boston University*
Twenty-fourth Amendment
Voting Rights Act of 1965

JAMES A. THURBER
Director, Center for Congressional and Presidential Studies The American University
Balanced Budget and Emergency Deficit Control Act
Budget Committee, Senate
Congressional Budget Office
Iron Triangle
Jackson, Henry M.
Magnuson, Warren G.

CHARLES TIEFER
Solicitor and Deputy General Counsel, United States House of Representatives
Germaneness
Investigative Power
Kilbourn v. Thompson
McGrain v. Daugherty
Speech or Debate Clause
Voting in Congress
    Voting Methods
Watkins v. United States
Witnesses, Rights of

SUSAN J. TOLCHIN
Department of Public Administration, The George Washington University
Rankin, Jeannette
Women in Congress

CHRISTOPHER L. TOMLINS
Research Fellow, American Bar Foundation
Fair Labor Standards Act
Labor
Taft-Hartley Labor-Management Relations Act
Wagner-Connery National Labor Relations Act

W. PATRICK TOWELL
Senior Writer, Congressional Quarterly Inc.
Armed Forces

U

CARL UBBELOHDE
Department of History, Case Western Reserve University
Canada
Colorado

JOSEPH K. UNEKIS
Department of Political Science, Kansas State University
Committees
    Committee Hearings

WILLIAM E. UNRAU
Department of History, Wichita State University
Curtis, Charles

ERIC M. USLANER
Department of Government and Politics, University of Maryland
Comity
Elections, Congressional
    Voting
Energy and Natural Resources
Representation
Representative

V

FRANK VAN DER LINDEN
Bethesda, Maryland
Byrd, Harry Flood, Sr.
Smith, Howard W.

MAURILIO E. VIGIL
Department of History and Political Science, New Mexico Highlands University
Chavez, Dennis
Hispanic Members

PAMELA N. VIOLANTE
Museum Specialist and Registrar, Office of the Architect of the Capitol
Congressional Office Buildings

W

ROGER WALKE
Congressional Research Service, The Library of Congress
Indian Affairs Committee, Senate Select

J. SAMUEL WALKER
Historian, U.S. Nuclear Regulatory Commission
Nuclear Power

JOHN F. WALSH
Department of History, Claremont McKenna College
Burr, Aaron
Randolph, John

PAUL Y. WATANABE
Department of Political Science and Co-director of the Institute for Asian American Studies, University of Massachusetts–Boston
Asian American Members

HARRY L. WATSON
Department of History, The University of North Carolina at Chapel Hill
North Carolina

R. KENT WEAVER
The Brookings Institution
Think Tanks

SAMUEL L. WEBB
Department of History, University of Alabama, Birmingham
Bankhead, William B.

JAMES P. WEBER
2d Assistant Parliamentarian, United States Senate
Precedents
    Senate Precedents

TIMOTHY E. WEINER
New York Times, Washington Bureau
Black Budget

MARGARET M. WEIR
The Brookings Institution,
Social Welfare and Poverty

CECIL E. WELLER, JR.
Department of History, San Jacinto
College South
Federal Anti–Price Discrimination Act

JOSEPH WHITE
The Brookings Institution
Appropriations
Appropriations Committee, Senate

CLINTON L. WHITEHURST, JR.
Senior Fellow, Strom Thurmond
Institute of Government and Public
Affairs, Clemson University
Merchant Marine

WILLIAM M. WIECEK
College of Law, Syracuse University
Scott v. Sandford

C. FRED WILLIAMS
Department of History, University of
Arkansas at Little Rock
Arkansas

R. HAL WILLIAMS
Department of History, Southern
Methodist University
Blaine, James G.

DAVID L. WILSON
Department of History, Southern Illinois
University at Carbondale
Harding, Warren G.

MAJOR L. WILSON
Department of History, Memphis
State University
Van Buren, Martin

THEODORE A. WILSON
Department of History, The University
of Kansas
Hull, Cordell
Truman Committee

PHILIP D. WINTERS
Congressional Research Service,
The Library of Congress
Debt Limit

SIDNEY WISE
Professor Emeritus, Franklin and
Marshall College
Scott, Hugh

JULES J. WITCOVER
Baltimore Sun
Vice President of the United States

JOHN F. WITTE
Department of Political Science,
University of Wisconsin–Madison
Sixteenth Amendment
Taxation

BARBARA WOLANIN
Curator, Office of the Architect of
the Capitol
Capitol, The
Art in the Capitol

DONALD R. WOLFENSBERGER
Committee on Rules, United States
House of Representatives
Rule, Special
Rules Committee, House

HERMAN S. WOLK
Historian, Center for Air Force History,
Bolling Air Force Base
Air Force

STEPHEN B. WOOD
Professor Emeritus, University of
Rhode Island
Child Labor

RANDALL B. WOODS
Department of History, University
of Arkansas
Fulbright, J. William
Fulbright Scholars Act

ROBERT WOOSTER
Department of Arts and Humanities,
Texas A&M University–Corpus Christi
Texas

MARGARET JANE WYSZOMIRSKI
Senior Research Fellow, Graduate
Public Policy Program,
Georgetown University
Art and Culture
National Foundation on the Arts and
the Humanities Act of 1965

Y

JAMES HARVEY YOUNG
Decatur, Georgia
Pure Food and Drugs Act

Z

JOSEPH ZIMMERMAN
Department of Political Science, State
University of New York, Albany
New York

Alphabetical List of Entries

Abbreviations and Acronyms Used in This Work

AFL-CIO American Federation of Labor and Congress of Industrial Organizations
amend. amendment
app. appendix
Ala. Alabama
A.M. *ante meridiem,* before noon
Ariz. Arizona
Ark. Arkansas
Art. Article
b. born
c. *circa,* about, approximately
Calif. California
cf. *confer,* compare
chap. chapter (pl., chaps.)
CIA Central Intelligence Agency
Cir. Ct. Circuit Court
cl. clause
Cong. Congress
Colo. Colorado
Cong. Rec. Congressional Record
Conn. Connecticut
CRS Congressional Research Service
d. died
D Democrat, Democratic
D.C. District of Columbia
D.D.C. District Court (federal) of the District of Columbia
Del. Delaware
diss. dissertation
doc. document
DR Democratic-Republican
ed. editor (pl., eds); edition
e.g. *exempli gratia,* for example
enl. enlarged
esp. especially
et al. *et alii,* and others
etc. *et cetera,* and so forth

exp. expanded
F Federalist
f. and following (pl., ff.)
F. Federal Reporter
F.2d Federal Reporter, 2d series
FBI Federal Bureau of Investigation
Fed. Reg. Federal Register
Fla. Florida
F. Supp. Federal Supplement
Ga. Georgia
GAO General Accounting Office
GPO Government Printing Office
GS General Schedule (federal civil service grade level)
H. Con. Res. House Concurrent Resolution
H. Doc. House Document
H. Hrg. House Hearing
H.J. Res. House Joint Resolution
H.R. House of Representatives; when followed by a number, identifies a bill that originated in the House
H. Rept. House Report
H. Res. House Resolution
How. Howard (court reporter)
I Independent (party)
ibid. *ibidem,* in the same place (as the one immediately preceding)
i.e. *id est,* that is
Ill. Illinois
I.L.M. International Legal Materials
Ind. Indiana
J Jeffersonian
Jr. Junior
Kans. Kansas

Ky. Kentucky
La. Louisiana
M.A. Master of Arts
Mass. Massachusetts
Mich. Michigan
Minn. Minnesota
Miss. Mississippi
Mo. Missouri
Mont. Montana
n. note
N.C. North Carolina
n.d. no date
N.Dak. North Dakota
Nebr. Nebraska
Nev. Nevada
N.H. New Hampshire
N.J. New Jersey
N.Mex. New Mexico
no. number (pl., nos.)
n.p. no place
n.s. new series
N.Y. New York
Okla. Oklahoma
Oreg. Oregon
p. page (pl., pp.)
Pa. Pennsylvania
P.L. Public Law
Prog. Progressive
pt. part (pl., pts.)
Pub. Res. Public Resolution
R Republican
Rep. Representative
repr. reprint
rept. report
rev. revised
R.I. Rhode Island
S. Senate; when followed by a number, identifies a bill that originated in the Senate
S.C. South Carolina
S. Con. Res. Senate Concurrent Resolution
S. Ct. Supreme Court Reporter
S.Dak. South Dakota

S. Doc. Senate Document
sec. section (pl., secs.)
Sen. Senator
ser. series
sess. session
S. Hrg. Senate Hearing
S.J. Res. Senate Joint Resolution
S. Prt. Senate Print
S. Rept. Senate Report
S. Res. Senate Resolution
Stat. Statutes at Large
S. Treaty Doc. Senate Treaty Document
supp. supplement
Tenn. Tennessee
Tex. Texas
T.I.A.S. Treaties and Other International Acts Series
U.N. United Nations
U.S. United States, United States Reports
USA United States Army
USAF United States Air Force
U.S.C. United States Code
U.S.C.A. United States Code Annotated
USN United States Navy
U.S.S.R. Union of Soviet Socialist Republics
U.S.T. United States Treaties
v. versus
Va. Virginia
VA Veterans Administration
vol. volume (pl., vols.)
Vt. Vermont
W Whig
Wash. Washington
Wheat. Wheaton (court reporter)
Wis. Wisconsin
W.Va. West Virginia
Wyo. Wyoming

Years of Each Congress

This table provides a simple guide to the dates of each Congress, citing the year in which the following Congress begins as the year in which the previous Congress ends. For the exact opening and closing dates of each session of each Congress from the First Congress to the present, see the table accompanying the entry "Sessions of Congress."

1st	1789–1791	26th	1839–1841	51st	1889–1891	76th	1939–1941
2d	1791–1793	27th	1841–1843	52d	1891–1893	77th	1941–1943
3d	1793–1795	28th	1843–1845	53d	1893–1895	78th	1943–1945
4th	1795–1797	29th	1845–1847	54th	1895–1897	79th	1945–1947
5th	1797–1799	30th	1847–1849	55th	1897–1899	80th	1947–1949
6th	1799–1801	31st	1849–1851	56th	1899–1901	81st	1949–1951
7th	1801–1803	32d	1851–1853	57th	1901–1903	82d	1951–1953
8th	1803–1805	33d	1853–1855	58th	1903–1905	83d	1953–1955
9th	1805–1807	34th	1855–1857	59th	1905–1907	84th	1955–1957
10th	1807–1809	35th	1857–1859	60th	1907–1909	85th	1957–1959
11th	1809–1811	36th	1859–1861	61st	1909–1911	86th	1959–1961
12th	1811–1813	37th	1861–1863	62d	1911–1913	87th	1961–1963
13th	1813–1815	38th	1863–1865	63d	1913–1915	88th	1963–1965
14th	1815–1817	39th	1865–1867	64th	1915–1917	89th	1965–1967
15th	1817–1819	40th	1867–1869	65th	1917–1919	90th	1967–1969
16th	1819–1821	41st	1869–1871	66th	1919–1921	91st	1969–1971
17th	1821–1823	42d	1871–1873	67th	1921–1923	92d	1971–1973
18th	1823–1825	43d	1873–1875	68th	1923–1925	93d	1973–1975
19th	1825–1827	44th	1875–1877	69th	1925–1927	94th	1975–1977
20th	1827–1829	45th	1877–1879	70th	1927–1929	95th	1977–1979
21st	1829–1831	46th	1879–1881	71st	1929–1931	96th	1979–1981
22d	1831–1833	47th	1881–1883	72d	1931–1933	97th	1981–1983
23d	1833–1835	48th	1883–1885	73d	1933–1935	98th	1983–1985
24th	1835–1837	49th	1885–1887	74th	1935–1937	99th	1985–1987
25th	1837–1839	50th	1887–1889	75th	1937–1939	100th	1987–1989
						101st	1989–1991
						102d	1991–1993
						103d	1993–1995

The Encyclopedia of the
United States Congress

A

ABORTION. Since *Roe v. Wade* (410 U.S. 113 [1973]) Congress has attempted to enact legislation limiting the Supreme Court's decision that women have a right to terminate pregnancy by abortion. Although Congress cannot overrule *Roe v. Wade* directly, some members argue that it has legislative power to limit the effects of the Court's decisions. In the 1970s and 1980s these senators and representatives attempted unsuccessfully to limit *Roe* and its progeny by restricting the federal courts' jurisdiction to hear future abortion cases. At the same time Rep. Henry J. Hyde (R-Ill.) was successful in restricting the use of federal funds for both elective and medically necessary abortions. But unless the Supreme Court explicitly overrules *Roe,* the only way to overturn the decision is by amending the Constitution.

According to the Court's congressional critics, the due process clauses of the Fifth and Fourteenth Amendments do not even imply a constitutional right to privacy that includes a woman's decision to end her pregnancy. Since human life begins at conception, the critics continue, Congress has an affirmative duty, under the due process clause of the Fifth Amendment, to protect human life at each stage of biological development. Because the Supreme Court has invented rights that the Framers never contemplated, they conclude, Congress has the authority to curb the justices' continuing usurpation of legislative power. Some members claim that Congress can use its power under the Fourteenth Amendment to define the fetus as a person, deserving due process and equal protection. Using its enforcement power, Congress could prohibit the states from denying these rights to the unborn or, alternatively, the federal courts from interfering with the states' authority to prohibit abortion and protect fetal rights.

In response to these arguments *Roe*'s advocates claim that the due process clauses protect many unenumerated liberties essential to personal freedom, including the right of women to decide when and whether to have children. *Roe* is a natural extension of Supreme Court decisions that establish a private realm of marriage, family life, and reproductive choice into which government cannot intrude without compelling justification. Congress and the states must demonstrate that their interests in safeguarding women's health, potential life, and medical standards are important enough to burden or restrict women's decisional freedom. Since they cannot demonstrate any need to protect women's health until the end of the first trimester, during this time women have a virtually absolute right to choose to have an abortion. Similarly, only after the point of viability can the states and the national government demonstrate a compelling interest in protecting potential life. Even after viability, legislators cannot impose abortion restrictions that endanger a woman's life and health in order to protect a fetus.

Since 1973 *Roe*'s critics have used four methods in their struggle to reverse the decision: constitutional amendments, bills to regulate the jurisdiction of the Supreme Court and the lower federal courts, funding restrictions, and various statutory proposals, including informed consent bills and human life bills—legislation protecting human life in all stages of fetal development. Each of these raises several important questions. Are they legitimate ex-

1

pressions of congressional interest in protecting women's health and potential life? Do they alter the constitutional relationship between the Supreme Court and Congress? Do they impair the Court's authority to enforce the supremacy clause (Article VI) of the Constitution and to provide a uniform interpretation of national law? Only a careful examination of specific proposals can illuminate the answers to these complex questions of constitutional law and national public policy.

In the 1980s the struggle over abortion rights shifted from legislation to the nomination and confirmation of new justices who are more conservative than *Roe*'s judicial advocates. As a result of such decisions as *Webster v. Reproductive Health Services* (492 U.S. 490 [1989]), concerning the use of public facilities and personnel, *Hodgson v. Minnesota* (110 S. Ct. 2926 [1990]), involving notification of parents of minors, and *Rust v. Sullivan* (111 S. Ct. 1759 [1991]), relating to limitations on the use of federal family planning funds for abortion counseling, congressional interest in overturning *Roe* has waned. Furthermore, the Supreme Court's decision in *Planned Parenthood of Southeastern Pennsylvania v. Casey* (112 S. Ct. 2791 [1992]) has expanded the scope of the states' regulatory powers considerably. In response to *Casey*, the struggle has shifted to the federal and state courts as well as the states' legislators.

BIBLIOGRAPHY

Estrich, Susan R., and Kathleen M. Sullivan. "Abortion Politics: Writing for an Audience of One." *University of Pennsylvania Law Review* 138 (1989): 119–155.
Keynes, Edward, with Randall K. Miller. *The Court vs. Congress: Prayer, Busing, and Abortion.* 1989. Pp. 244–312.
Tribe, Laurence H. *Abortion: The Clash of Absolutes.* 1990.

EDWARD KEYNES

ABSCAM. A federal undercover investigation that resulted in convictions of seven members of Congress on corruption charges, "Abscam" began in 1978, when the Federal Bureau of Investigation initiated a property-crime inquiry. Later, the FBI began to check reports that legislators were willing to take bribes in exchange for official favors. Investigators set up a front organization called Abdul Enterprises, Ltd.—whence the name Abscam. Agents or informants made videotapes or audiotapes of suspects accepting cash or agreeing to take bribes to help supposed Arab business executives. One

senator, Harrison A. Williams, Jr. (D-N.J.), was convicted in 1981 of accepting a hidden interest in a titanium mining company for promising to seek federal contracts to purchase the mine's output. Williams, chairman of the Labor and Human Resources Committee, served twenty-one months in prison and was fined $50,000. Six House members were found guilty in 1980 or 1981: John W. Jenrette, Jr. (D-S.C.), Richard Kelly (R-Fla.), Raymond F. Lederer (D-Pa.), Michael O. Myers (D-Pa.), John M. Murphy (D-N.Y.), and Frank Thompson, Jr. (D-N.J.). Myers was expelled from Congress; the others resigned or were defeated for reelection.

In early 1981, the Justice Department issued its guidelines for undercover public-corruption probes, including requirements that the corrupt nature of the activity be "reasonably clear" to the target, that there be "reasonable indications" that the investigation will reveal crimes, and that "entrapment will be scrupulously avoided." In December 1982, a select Senate committee created to review Abscam called for legislation to govern federal undercover probes and to define entrapment more clearly. No bills were enacted, however.

BIBLIOGRAPHY

Greene, Robert W. *The Sting Man: Inside Abscam.* 1981.
U.S. Senate. *Final Report of the Select Committee to Study Law Enforcement Undercover Activities of Components of the Department of Justice to the U.S. Senate.* 97th Cong., 2d sess., 1982. S. Rept. 97-682.

TED GEST

ABSENTEEISM. *See* Voting, *article on* Voting Analysis.

ACCOUNTABILITY. The checks and balances in the U.S. constitutional framework establish the foundation for government accountability. While the judicial branch can hold the legislative and executive branches accountable for acting within the bounds established by the Constitution, the legislative branch has the power to hold the executive branch accountable for making laws work as intended. Competent agency administrators are always mindful of this accountability, because Congress decides what they are authorized to do and how much money they will have to do it.

From the earliest days of the Republic, Congress was engaged in overseeing the executive branch. Yet it was not until 1946, with passage of the Legislative Reorganization Act, that all standing committees were charged with the responsibility for "continuous watchfulness" over the agencies in their jurisdiction. Congress clarified and greatly strengthened the oversight role of committees in 1970 and 1974. The Legislative Reorganization Act of 1970 requires every legislative committee not only to review and study administrative actions on a continuing basis but also to report on its oversight work at the end of each Congress. The Congressional Budget and Impoundment Act of 1974 authorizes committees to require agencies under their jurisdiction to evaluate their programs and report the results to Congress. This law also directed the U.S. General Accounting Office (GAO), an agency in the legislative branch, to recommend to Congress methods for evaluating federally funded programs.

To hold executive branch agencies and officials accountable, Congress, through its committees and subcommittees, focuses primarily on the extent to which the purposes of laws are being fulfilled, the effective and efficient use of resources, and the proper exercise of authority. Such oversight employs both direct and indirect means. Direct means involve investigations, requirements that agencies file reports with the committees that have jurisdiction over them, and hearings. Hearings are held when legislators are considering funding, reauthorizing, or substantively changing existing programs. Allegations of corruption or incompetence in carrying out a law may cause a committee or subcommittee to hold hearings after investigating the charges with its own staff or calling on the GAO to do so. In addition, the casework on constituent problems with specific agencies that is performed by members' staffs provides another direct means for accountability.

The House Committee on Government Operations and the Senate Committee on Governmental Affairs have oversight responsibilities that cut across all executive agencies in the areas of economy and efficiency of operations, budgeting and accounting, reorganization, intergovernmental relationships, and House and Senate oversight procedures. Each of these committees investigates, holds hearings, and proposes legislation. They make extensive use of GAO reports to Congress, which detail the results of audits conducted by the GAO to determine whether federal funds are being used legally, effectively, and efficiently. Audits are initiated by the GAO or performed at the request of a committee or subcommittee. In fiscal years 1991 and 1992 the GAO produced, respectively, 950 and 1,117 such reports.

The facts, analyses, and recommendations developed in GAO reports, committee and subcommittee investigations, and hearings often bring about changes in agency policies and practices. Such agency action is motivated primarily by one or both of the following: (1) agency officials recognize that action is needed and possible; (2) congressional interest in change is strong, and resistance may result in legislation that further limits the discretion of the administrator.

Congress also uses indirect means to hold agency officials accountable. The Inspector General Act of 1978 and later amendments created inspectors general in twenty-six federal agencies. Each inspector general has the responsibility to prevent fraud, abuse, and waste in federal programs by auditing, investigating, recommending corrective action, and reporting to Congress as well as to the agency head. These reports not only stimulate desirable administrative change but also serve as catalysts for additional oversight by committees and subcommittees of Congress.

Another indirect means of accountability was provided by the Civil Service Reform Act (CSRA) of 1978. The law specifically encourages employees to serve as whistle-blowers by exposing mismanagement, violations of laws and regulations, gross waste of funds, abuse of authority, and substantial and specific danger to the public health or safety. To reduce the risk of reprisals against whistle-blowers by agency officials, employees can telephone toll-free numbers in the GAO or the inspector-general offices. Callers do not reveal their identity. They are assigned numbers that they can subsequently use to obtain information on actions taken. Some whistle-blowers, however, prefer to take their criticism directly to Congress or the news media. In either case, if the allegations appear to have merit, they are likely to receive further attention from committee and subcommittee staff members. Depending on their seriousness, the charges may lead to the questioning of agency officials at hearings held by the agencies' authorization or appropriation subcommittees.

Another indirect means Congress uses to hold executive agencies accountable is evident in the authority vested in the U.S. Merit Systems Protection Board, an agency created when the CSRA was enacted. The three members of this bipartisan board, appointed by the president with the approval of the Senate, decide appeals from federal employees who believe their agencies have acted illegally with regard to their employment by such measures as demotion, suspension without pay, or separation. The board also has the authority and responsibility to analyze the activities of one of the federal government's central management agencies, the Office of Personnel Management (OPM), and to report annually to Congress on whether the actions of that office "are in accord with merit principles and free of prohibited personnel practices." Furthermore, the board is required to strike down any OPM policy that violates merit principles or permits prohibited personnel practices.

Through these direct and indirect means, Congress can exercise formidable power in holding executive agencies accountable. Sometimes committees and subcommittees cross the fine line between holding them accountable and subjecting them to micromanagement. While this is discomfiting to administrators and sometimes works contrary to the public interest, the adverse consequences are less serious than those that would follow from failing adequately to oversee the execution of the laws.

The latter still occurs despite the modes of accountability discussed here. That is because legislative goals are sometimes too general, members of Congress and staff have other demands on their time (new legislation, constituent service, and reelection activities), and symbiotic relationships may develop between ranking committee members and staff, agency officials, and representatives of interest groups. Nevertheless, for executive branch officials, the demonstrated capacity of congressional committees and subcommittees effectively to hold them accountable strongly encourages them to act in accordance with the letter and spirit of applicable laws.

[See also Civil Service Reform Act of 1978; Congressional Budget and Impoundment Control Act of 1974; General Accounting Office; Legislative Reorganization Act of 1970; Oversight.]

BIBLIOGRAPHY

Davidson, Roger H., and Walter J. Oleszek. *Congress and Its Members.* 3d ed. 1990.
Keefe, William J., and Morris S. Ogul. *The American Legislative Process.* 6th ed. 1985.
Rosen, Bernard. *Holding Government Bureaucracies Accountable.* 2d ed. 1989.

BERNARD ROSEN

ADAMS, JOHN (1735–1826), leader of the independence movement, Revolutionary War diplomat and first minister to Great Britain, vice president (1789–1797), second president of the United States (1797–1801). A political theorist as well as states-

JOHN ADAMS.   LIBRARY OF CONGRESS

man, John Adams faced both foreign and domestic crises as president and experienced unique problems in his relationship with Congress. Elected by a narrow margin, Adams was opposed by a powerful clique within his own Federalist party. His vice president, Thomas Jefferson, led the Republican opposition, and his cabinet, inherited from George Washington, worked to advance the interests of Adams's Anglophile, intraparty adversary, Alexander Hamilton. Although Hamilton had retired from government in 1795, cabinet members and Federalist leaders in Congress continued to look to the former Treasury secretary for leadership and worked to achieve his congressional program.

Congress divided along lines of Anglophile versus Francophile sentiment when France began undeclared naval warfare against the United States in 1797 in response to the pro-British Jay's Treaty. Congressional Jeffersonian Republicans, believing that Jay's Treaty violated America's 1778 Treaty of Commerce with France, considered French resentment justified but lost public support after French foreign minister Charles-Maurice de Talleyrand-

Périgord, through his negotiators (designated "X," "Y," and "Z" in the dispatches) demanded a bribe from American ministers Elbridge Gerry, John Marshall, and Charles Cotesworth Pinckney. News of the so-called XYZ affair created a national furor and squelched sympathy for France, but worked to Adams's disadvantage in Congress, strengthening the hand of the Anglophile "high" Federalists who supported Hamilton's program in Congress.

The crucial difference between Adams and Hamilton concerned defense. Adams favored a naval buildup, Hamilton a greatly expanded army—which he planned to lead, thereby posing a potential challenge to executive primacy. Adams secured approval from Congress for construction of a navy, but in 1798 the legislature also approved Hamilton's plan for a large provisional force and the augmentation of the regular army. Although Hamilton had been only a junior officer in Revolutionary War service, he succeeded in maneuvering appointment as second-in-command to George Washington, a position that would make him actual commander of the army since Washington had been reluctant to return to service and had indicated that he would take the field only under the most urgent of circumstances. When Adams balked at Hamilton's appointment, Washington threatened to resign; his popularity was such that Adams had to accede.

Because of Hamilton's influence with Washington and the Federalist leadership, Adams spent his presidential years caught in a crossfire between intraparty adversaries and Jeffersonian Republican opponents in Congress. Republicans hoped to use the power of appropriation as a means of giving the House of Representatives a role in foreign policy, claiming that the power to appropriate carried, by implication, the right of decision. Republican representative John Nicholas attempted to secure a reduction of the number of diplomatic ministers, admitting that the measure was intended to reduce the authority of the president. The controversy provoked a constitutional debate on the nature and operation of checks on power within the government. Republicans attempted to push constitutional interpretation to its limits, allowing Congress to use the power of appropriation to restrict executive authority in foreign affairs.

In mid 1798 Congress passed the most controversial legislation of the Adams presidency, the Alien and Sedition Acts. Adams neither sought nor opposed the legislation, which received almost unanimous support from Federalists and provoked an extreme reaction from Republicans. Republican

leaders Jefferson and James Madison framed their replies in the Virginia and Kentucky resolutions, which were precursors of the nullification doctrine (according to which a state could nullify federal law). Controversy over the Alien and Sedition Acts created a climate of domestic unrest that led to fears of insurrection and civil war.

Adams defused the crisis and defeated Hamilton's ambitions by delaying recruitment and formation of the army until a new diplomatic initiative could be undertaken. In February 1799 he appointed William Vans Murray minister plenipotentiary to France, having previously received assurances that Talleyrand now sought rapprochement. When "high" Federalists in the Senate threatened rejection, Adams offered an alternative commission of three, including Murray. As Talleyrand continued to furnish evidence of a new, conciliatory French policy, Adams's diplomacy found popular favor and the Hamiltonian Federalists became isolated from the political mainstream.

Timing deprived Adams of the full benefit of his diplomacy. Long delays in the completion of the negotiation prevented news of the successful completion of the mission and the signing of the Convention of Montfortaine from reaching the United States until electors had been chosen who would give Republicans victory in the presidential election of 1800.

In pursuing a policy of reconciliation with France, Adams brought peace to the country but provoked party schism, thereby diminishing his influence with Congress. In later years he acknowledged that he had had little influence with the legislature. Adams confined his approaches to Congress to the constitutionally authorized processes of speeches, written addresses, and recommendations. There is no evidence that he ever considered initiating a direct effort to influence the legislative process, for his intraparty political opponents controlled Congress. Adams did, however, secure approval of his two major requests: establishment of the navy and a bill for reform of the judiciary.

BIBLIOGRAPHY

The Adams Family Papers. Massachusetts Historical Society, Boston, Massachusetts.
Holder, Jean S. "Sources of Presidential Power: John Adams and the Challenge to Executive Primacy." *Political Science Quarterly* 101 (1986): 601–616.
Kurtz, Stephen G. *The Presidency of John Adams: The Collapse of Federalism, 1795–1800.* 1957.
Smith, Page. *John Adams.* 1962.

JEAN S. HOLDER

ADAMS, JOHN QUINCY (1767–1848), senator and representative from Massachusetts, sixth president of the United States, vigorous opponent of the congressional gag rule and the expansion of slavery.

Adams spent almost all of his long life in politics; his wife, Louisa, characterized him as having an "insatiable passion" for political office and political strife. Yet for many years historians refused to see him as a career politician, some portraying him as a statesman, others as a political misfit.

The trajectory of Adams's career was atypical. He served first in the Senate from 1803 to 1808 and subsequently was secretary of State from 1817 to 1825, president from 1825 to 1829, and finally a member of the House from the Plymouth district of Massachusetts from 1831 until his death in 1848.

Adams took pride in his Massachusetts roots; his distinguished parents, John and Abigail; his knowledge of the classics; his Harvard education; and his acquaintance with nearly all the major cities and leading figures of Europe. He also seemed to relish

JOHN QUINCY ADAMS.

his reputation for being "a man of cold, austere and forbidding manners . . . a gloomy misanthropist . . . an unsocial savage." His dress was casual, his study a mess, his tone often belligerent. Ralph Waldo Emerson, an admirer, thought that his reputation as a "literary gentleman" missed the mark. He was really a "bruiser" who loved a good fight, "an old roué who cannot live on slops, but must have sulphuric acid in his tea."

Upon entering the Senate in 1803, Adams was in many ways like most other New England Federalists. He shared their jealousy of southern power and their hatred for the Constitution's three-fifths rule for counting slaves. Like them, he believed in a strong national government and correspondingly disdained the Jeffersonian attachment to states' rights and strict construction of the Constitution. But he did not share their detestation of the French Revolution, their attachment to Great Britain, their aversion to republics and contempt for ordinary people, or their opposition to western expansion. He first infuriated Federalist Boston by supporting the Louisiana Purchase and criticizing Great Britain's actions on the high seas during the Napoleonic wars. Then, in 1807, Adams advocated stern measures against Britain for attacking the U.S.S. *Chesapeake*, and he not only voted for Jefferson's Embargo Act but in 1808 attended the Jeffersonian Republican caucus to nominate presidential and vice presidential candidates. The Massachusetts legislature publicly rebuked him by electing a replacement six months earlier than usual and ordering both Massachusetts senators to vote for repeal of the embargo, thus forcing him to resign before his term expired. Thereafter, Adams was a despicable "apostate" as far as Federalist Boston was concerned.

Adams joined the Jeffersonian opposition, rose in the ranks of the Jeffersonian Republican party, held a series of diplomatic posts, and became President James Monroe's secretary of State in 1817. By the 1820s, the Federalist party had dropped out of national politics, and the party of Jefferson had become sharply divided along regional and philosophical lines. Therefore, despite the party caucus's selection of William H. Crawford of Georgia as its presidential candidate in 1824, three other men, all claiming the Jeffersonian Republican mantle, ran for the presidency. Adams, one of the three, trounced his rivals in New England but finished second to Andrew Jackson in both the popular and electoral votes. However, since Jackson lacked an electoral majority, the election went to the House of Representatives. There Speaker Henry Clay, who had finished fourth, threw his support to Adams, making him president.

Adams's single-term presidency was marked by bitter partisan squabbling. He appointed Clay secretary of State and thereafter was accused of having bought Clay's support. In his first annual message Adams called for a national system of roads and canals, a national university, a naval academy, exploration of western territories at federal expense, a uniform standard of weights and measures, a more effective patent law to encourage inventors, and an astronomical observatory. He asserted that the federal government had more than enough constitutional authority to carry out his program. Indeed, he argued, failure of the federal government to act in behalf of the public good would be "treachery of the most sacred trust."

His views could not have been less in tune with the philosophy of the strict constructionists of Virginia and New York or with the interests of the southern cotton belt. Adams's message was mocked, and his program of an energetic national government drove thousands of Jeffersonians into the Jackson camp. His vision of an energetic national government, exercising power in behalf of the public good, faded to nothing.

In 1828 Andrew Jackson, the Tennessee slaveholder and hero of the Battle of New Orleans, nearly swept the slave states and ran well in half the free states, defeating Adams by an electoral margin of 178 to 83. After a short retirement, Adams ran for the House of Representatives and in 1831 began serving the first of eight successive terms. At first he won by landslide margins, capturing between 71 and 87 percent of the vote. In 1838 the opposition began to cut into his victory margin, reducing it to 52 percent in 1842; in the next two elections, however, his support widened, reaching 63 percent in his last election, in 1846.

From the beginning, Adams was an anti-Jackson man, and as a rule anti-Jackson candidates had no trouble winning in Massachusetts. Furthermore, he was also a member of the Anti-Masonic party that won majorities in eleven of the twenty-four towns in Adams's Plymouth district.

Adams never spent a day as a backbencher. He was immediately appointed chairman of the Committee on Manufactures and thus began his congressional career in a position of power. His committee was responsible for the tariff revisions of 1832 that provoked John C. Calhoun and his South Carolina followers to nullify the tariff and create a national crisis. Adams also oversaw the passage of legislation in 1846 establishing the Smithsonian Institution. However, his congressional fame rested largely on his savage battles against the gag rule and the expansion of slavery.

The gag rule was enacted by the House in 1836 to stop the American Anti-Slavery Society from placing the slavery issue on the political agenda. The society, thanks largely to the efforts of antislavery women, bombarded Congress with hundreds of thousands of petitions that called for ending slavery and the slave trade in the nation's capital, abolishing the interstate slave trade, adopting legislation barring slavery from western territories, and rejecting the admission of any new slave state. In response, southerners of both parties and northern Democrats rammed through a House resolution automatically tabling and precluding action on antislavery petitions. Adams, with the tacit support of northern Whigs and the enthusiastic backing of northern Anti-Masons, used every parliamentary trick to violate the rule and repeatedly goaded southerners into calling for his censure. Every year he presented a stack of antislavery petitions, which were quickly gagged. In 1842, to his delight, his petitions so angered southern representatives that some accused him of complicity in "high treason" and "perjury" and tried to censure him. In his defense, Adams spoke for days, savagely denouncing slavery as responsible for the South's "backwardness" and depicting his foremost accusers as murderers and common drunks. Two years later, by a vote of 108 to 80, he finally won his nine-year battle to repeal the gag rule.

Adams's concurrent battle against the expansion of slavery took several forms. On one front he lambasted the president, Congress, and the southern states at every opportunity for the horrors growing out of the removal of southeastern Indian tribes to lands west of the Mississippi. Adams left no doubt that the white man was to blame, and especially the southern slavemasters, who hungered for twenty-five million acres of Indian land.

Adams, however, had more hope of keeping slavery out of the West than of preventing further abuse of Indians. Just as the Jacksonians hungered for tribal land, so too did they hunger for the Mexican state of Texas. Adams was vulnerable regarding Texas because as secretary of State and president, he had tried repeatedly to acquire it from Mexico. However, Mexico abolished slavery in 1829, leading Adams to argue that if U.S. slaveholders now took Texas, a vital historical process would be reversed. In a close vote Congress brought Texas into the

Union in 1845 as a slave state with the right to divide into additional states. Adams proclaimed that this vote was "a signal triumph of the slave representation in the Constitution . . . the heaviest calamity that ever befell myself and my country."

A year later, Adams was convinced that President James K. Polk, a Tennessee slaveholder, was engineering a war against Mexico to further slaveholding interests. Although lacking proof, he put his reputation at risk and acted upon his belief. When news arrived in Washington that a Mexican force had attacked Zachary Taylor's dragoons, Adams headed the fourteen House members voting against the president's war bill. Adams told one young colleague that he hoped American officers would resign and the soldiers desert rather than fight such an "unrighteous" war. Throughout the conflict he voted with the dissidents and strongly supported the Wilmot Proviso to bar slavery from all land taken from Mexico.

On 21 February 1848, the House had before it a mundane resolution to tender thanks and decorations to various generals for their gallant actions in the Mexican War. When the Speaker called for ayes and nays, Adams replied with a firm "no." That was his last vote in his long career. A few minutes later, he collapsed at his desk. Two days later he died. By then he had become a legendary figure, hailed in the North as "the conscience of New England" and "Old Man Eloquent," denounced in the South as "the madman from Massachusetts."

BIBLIOGRAPHY

Bemis, Samuel Flagg. *John Quincy Adams and the Foundations of American Foreign Policy.* 1949.
Bemis, Samuel Flagg. *John Quincy Adams and the Union.* 1950.
Lipsky, George A. *John Quincy Adams: His Theory and Ideas.* 1950.
Richards, Leonard L. *Life and Times of Congressman John Quincy Adams.* 1986.

LEONARD L. RICHARDS

ADJOURNMENT AND RECESS. [*This entry includes separate discussions of each house of Congress.*]

In the House

A simple motion to adjourn is highly privileged in the House, and thus, with certain restrictions, is in order whenever the floor can be secured. The motion to adjourn, however, cannot take another member who has the floor from his feet and is not in order in the Committee of the Whole. The motion is nondebatable and does not require a quorum for adoption.

Under clause 4 of Rule XVI, the Speaker has discretion to entertain "at any time" a motion that when the House adjourns *on that day* it stand adjourned to a day and time certain within three calendar days. When the Speaker exercises his discretion, the motion is of equal privilege with the simple motion to adjourn.

Under Article I, section 5 of the Constitution, neither house may adjourn for more than three days (not counting Sundays) without the consent of the other. Adjournment for more than three days (often called a "recess" or a "district work period") is provided by concurrent resolution, which must also be adopted by the Senate; the concurrent resolution is privileged and is nondebatable. In recent years such concurrent resolutions have often contained "recall" provisions authorizing the joint House and Senate leaderships to reconvene the two houses prior to the end of the recess.

Provision for final adjournment (sine die) is made by concurrent resolution, which is also privileged.

Adjourning terminates the legislative day. The House (unlike the Senate) normally adjourns at the conclusion of business each calendar day, thus concluding the legislative day each day.

Under a new clause 12 of Rule I, adopted in the 103d Congress, the Speaker may suspend the business of the House by declaring a short recess at any time as long as no question is pending. Furthermore, under clause 4 of Rule XVI, the Speaker has discretion to entertain "at any time" a motion authorizing the Speaker to declare a recess. As with the motion to adjourn to a day and time certain, this motion is of equal privilege with the simple motion to adjourn when the Speaker exercises his discretion.

In committees, the motion to recess from day to day is highly privileged under clause 1 of Rule XI.

BIBLIOGRAPHY

U.S. House of Representatives. *Constitution, Jefferson's Manual, and Rules of the House of Representatives, 103d Congress.* Compiled by William Holmes Brown. 102d Cong., 2d sess., 1992. H. Doc. 102-405.

CHARLES W. JOHNSON

In the Senate

The Senate can end its daily session either by adjourning or recessing, but the recess is by far the more common. On average, the Senate adjourns three or four times during any legislative month, preferring to recess on all other days.

Generally, if the Senate wants to expedite its proceedings, recessing carries a number of advantages over adjourning. When the Senate reconvenes after a recess, it continues its activities at precisely the point at which it recessed. This provides maximum flexibility for the majority leader.

The procedural requirements for a recess are simple, but the Standing Rules of the Senate stipulate a number of time-consuming activities that must follow an adjournment. These procedures, known as the *morning hour,* were originally designed to consume the first two hours of a session following an adjournment. With one exception, these procedures can only be dispensed with by unanimous consent.

The Morning Hour. During the morning hour, the Senate Rules require that senators approve or correct the journal, conduct morning business, consider resolutions that have been objected to, and consider bills and resolutions on the Senate calendar.

The Constitution requires that the Senate maintain a journal of its proceedings, and the Rules provide that it be read and corrected "if any mistakes be made" as the first item of business following an adjournment. Avoiding this requires either unanimous consent or a nondebatable motion. In practice, the Senate journal is seldom read and a vote on approving it is seldom taken. Unanimous consent is normally granted, allowing the Senate simply to approve the journal.

During the conduct of morning business, several things can happen. Petitions and memorials from private citizens or state legislatures may be presented; the Senate may receive reports from committees (Senate committees report several hundred bills during a congressional session); bills and joint resolutions may be introduced (more than two thousand bills and joint resolutions are introduced by individual senators during each Congress); and concurrent or simple resolutions may be submitted (simple resolutions involve only the Senate; concurrent resolutions involve both houses of Congress).

During the morning hour, the Senate is also required to consider resolutions that have been objected to on a previous day. The Senate must also consider bills and resolutions on the Senate Calendar; these bills and resolutions are laid before the Senate in the order in which they appear, and debate on each question is limited to five minutes.

Reasons for Adjournment. Despite adjournment's cumbersome requirements, on occasion the Senate finds it necessary to adjourn rather than recess. Some procedures can only be accomplished through adjournment. For example, the Rules provide that it is "not in order" to move to consideration of any piece of legislation on the Senate Calendar that has not been on the calendar for one legislative day. The only way to begin a new legislative day is to adjourn. The rules do not require that bills or joint resolutions be referred to a Senate committee. They can be placed directly on the Senate Calendar through a procedure contained in Rule XIV, but this procedure can only be invoked if the Senate adjourns rather than recesses.

BIBLIOGRAPHY

Riddick, Floyd M. *Senate Procedure.* 1981.
Tiefer, Charles. *Congressional Practice and Procedure.* 1989.

ROBERT B. DOVE

ADMINISTRATION COMMITTEE. *See* House Administration Committee.

ADVICE AND CONSENT. The United States Constitution (Article II, section 2) requires that the Senate give its advice and consent to the president on war and treaty-making decisions and on appointments to certain key offices.

In international usage the terms *treaty* and *agreement* are applied interchangeably (Plischke, 1992–1993). In United States practice, however, there are legal and procedural differences between the two terms. A treaty is a formal compact between the United States and one or more nations that must be approved by a two-thirds vote of the Senate. It then becomes part of the supreme law of the United States, equally binding with the Constitution in all places to which the national jurisdiction extends, and taking precedence over state constitutions and laws. The need for Senate consent may be circumvented if the president terms an international accord an executive agreement. The latter needs only presidential consent to bind the government and avoids possible delays involved in gaining Senate approval for a treaty. Still, the treaty route may be elected when implementing legislation or appropriations are required to carry out the terms of the compact.

Most presidential appointments require confirmation by a majority vote in the Senate. However, the Twenty-fifth Amendment, which authorizes the president to fill any vacancy in the office of the vice president, requires for this process the approval of a majority in both houses of Congress. The president may temporarily fill vacancies with recess appointments when the Senate is not in session, but unconfirmed recess appointments expire at the end of the next session of Congress. Since only presidents can nominate, they are thus provided with a powerful tool for pursuing policy objectives through choice of subordinates. They have the power to remove obstructive appointees, except for federal judges, who have life tenure, and members of independent regulatory commissions, who can be dismissed solely for reasons specified by law.

In *Federalist* 76, Alexander Hamilton foresaw the Senate as approving presidential choices almost pro forma, and, actually, Senate approval is the norm. However, almost from the outset, political and policy considerations have entered into the confirmation process. In 1795, the Senate rejected George Washington's nomination of John Rutledge as chief justice of the United States because of the nominee's criticism of Jay's Treaty. Among later presidents, James Madison and Ulysses Grant encountered serious confirmation problems for their nominees. Least successful of all was John Tyler, who had four cabinet and four Supreme Court nominations rejected during his single term.

When a new president is elected, an official document, *U.S. Government Policy and Supporting Positions* (called the "plum book"), lists those positions subject to presidential appointment. Presently, between fifty and seventy thousand individuals are nominated annually. Over 99 percent of nominations are to minor positions (mostly military officers). To prevent strain on Senate time and resources, the process has largely been routinized. When a vacancy occurs, appropriate candidates are identified. Following background checks and other clearances, especially to avoid unnecessary battles over senatorial courtesy, the president selects a nominee, often ratifying a recommendation by White House or executive-branch staff. The nomination is sent to the Senate, where it is referred to a substantive committee (a regular practice since 1868) and investigated by committee staff, after which public hearings are held (until 1929, hearings were closed). The committee then votes on the nomination and sends it to the Senate floor. Following debate and action by the full Senate, successful nominees assume office.

Nominees to major positions (federal judges, members of regulatory bodies, and key executive and diplomatic personnel not covered by merit systems) face the closest scrutiny.

Historically, Supreme Court justices rank first in the proportion of nominations rejected, and, of the twenty-seven rejections or withdrawals since 1789, twenty occurred in the nineteenth century. Although nobody was rejected between 1930 and 1967, since then there has been a resurgence of challenge and rejection (or withdrawal) of presidential nominations to the Court. This is clearly the most controversial office, as befits the long-term impact the justices have on public policy.

Independent regulatory commission members are the next most controversial group because of their power in economic arenas, but they are a distant second in the rate of rejection. Although some nominations of department heads have faced opposition, only three out of several hundred have been rejected in this century, and only eight since 1789.

Nominations may be challenged because of concerns about the nominee's qualifications, ethical judgment, or competence; the standing of the president vis-à-vis what Richard Neustadt (in *Presidential Power*, 1960) has called his "publics"; or personal, political, or policy opposition to a nominee or to the president.

When challenge occurs, even the most powerful president must determine whether a battle over the nomination is worthwhile. In any year, fewer than half a percent of all nominations are withdrawn by the president, while some 3 percent are simply not acted on by the Senate or die in one of its committees. Most others are decided by voice vote, but a few are determined by roll-call vote on the floor of the Senate. Timing is important: more roll-call votes occur in the first year of a president's term, especially when there is a partisan split between the president and the Senate majority. The most controversial nominations are those where ten or more senators are recorded in opposition. Almost all are later approved, but on average the Senate rejects a nomination by roll-call vote once every few years.

Analysis of roll-call votes points to ideology as the major factor prompting support or opposition on Supreme Court appointments. Nominations to executive branch positions have been given little systematic study, but Senate voting on them appears to have been related more to partisanship and personal objection, although there is some evidence of an increased role for ideology since 1981. But while there may be quantifiable givens, these cannot fully explain the success or defeat of a particular nomination. A complete account must include such factors as the strategy of key supporters and opponents. Particularly when they diversify their appeal and address a bipartisan audience, determined opponents united by a leadership armed with a powerful counterstrategy can win over the marginal votes needed to turn challenge into rejection (Tannenbaum, 1987).

Nominations are not a self-contained end game. As G. Calvin Mackenzie observes (in *The Politics of Presidential Appointments*, 1981), beyond the matter of particular appointments, the Senate confirmation process provides legislators with another forum for the ongoing struggle with the executive branch over public policy.

[*See also* Treaties; War Powers.]

BIBLIOGRAPHY

Harris, Joseph P. *The Advice and Consent of the Senate.* 1953

Plischke, Elmer. "Joining International Organizations: The United States Process." *Commonwealth: A Journal of Political Science* 6 (1992–1993): Appendix.

Tannenbaum, Donald G. "Explaining Controversial Nominations: The Fortas Case Revisited." *Presidential Studies Quarterly* 17 (1987): 573–586.

DONALD G. TANNENBAUM

AEROSPACE. Within a short time of the first flight of the Wright brothers in 1903, the U.S. government recognized the importance of fostering aerospace development. Over the years this has taken place in three distinct and significant arenas. The first is the military aerospace endeavor, employing aeronautical and astronautical equipment and proficiency for the defense of the nation. This has been the area of greatest federal spending on the aerospace enterprise and has included the funding of basic research, of the development of new and ever more sophisticated weapons systems, and of operational capabilities. Second, the government has been fundamentally involved in fostering the research and development of air and space technologies, principally through civilian agencies such as the National Advisory Committee for Aeronautics (NACA) and the National Aeronautics and Space Administration (NASA). Finally, the government has been intrinsically involved in the direction and regulation of commercial aerospace activities, both domestic and overseas, to facilitate air commerce and such aerospace operations as satellite communications.

Military Aerospace Activities. As early as 1908 Congress glimpsed something of the potential of

LT. COL. JOHN GLENN. Training in 1961 for his Mercury mission, the first U.S. manned orbital flight. In 1974 Glenn was elected to the U.S. Senate from Ohio.

LIBRARY OF CONGRESS

aviation for the nation's defense. It provided, in the Army Appropriations Act of 1908, for the procurement of one Wright "Flyer" by the Aviation Section of the U.S. Army Signal Corps. The military possibilities of aviation, documented by Lt. Benjamin D. Foulois in a July 1908 staff paper to the Signal Corps School at Fort Leavenworth, suggested that in future conflicts aircraft would be employed to limit "the strategic movement of hostile forces before they have actually gained combat." The possibility of aerial interdiction, coupled with the destruction of an enemy's means of producing war matériel through strategic bombing, ensured that the military would acquire some aircraft for combat missions.

By the beginning of World War I in Europe, therefore, the U.S. government had begun to perceive, albeit reluctantly, the significance of aircraft in the conduct of modern warfare. While as late as 1914, the United States stood fourteenth in total funds allocated by nations to military aviation, far behind even Bulgaria and Greece, Congress began

Major Legislation

Title	Year Enacted	Reference Number	Description
Naval Appropriations Act of 1915	1915	P.L. 63-271	A rider to this appropriations act established the National Advisory Committee for Aeronautics "to supervise and direct the scientific study of the problems of flight, with a view to their practical solution."
Air Mail Act of 1925	1925	P.L. 69-309	The "Kelly Act" authorized the Post Office Department to contract for the delivery of domestic mail by commercial air carriers.
Air Commerce Act of 1926	1926	P.L. 69-254	Instructed Secretary of Commerce to foster air commerce, designate and establish airways, set up air navigation aids, arrange for research and development, license pilots, inspect and certify aircraft, and investigate accidents.
Army Air Corps Act of 1926	1926	P.L. 69-446	Renamed the Air Service as the Army Air Corps and provided for an assistant secretary of War for Air and for a five-year Air Corps expansion program.
Air Mail Act of 1930	1930	P.L. 71-178	The "Watres Act" amended the 1925 Air Mail Act to give the postmaster general broad regulatory control over route locations, route consolidations and extensions, contract bidding conditions, service conditions, equipment and personnel, and compensation.
Air Mail Act of 1934	1934	P.L. 73-308	The "Black-McKellar Act" provided for the commercial contracting of air mail routes throughout the U.S. Also created the Federal Aviation Committee to set broad policy on all phases of aviation and the relation of the government to it.
Civil Aeronautics Act of 1938	1938	P.L. 75-706	Created the Civil Aeronautics Authority and Air Safety Board, both with broad powers to establish and operate airways, and to regulate commercial air operations.
National Defense Act of 1940	1939	P.L. 76-18	Authorized the Army Air Corps to develop and procure 6,000 new airplanes, to increase personnel to 3,203 officers and 45,000 enlisted, and to appropriate $300 million.
Civilian Pilot Training Act of 1939	1939	P.L. 76-153	Established the Civilian Pilot Training Program under the management of the Civil Aeronautics authority to train pilots at various educational institutions in the U.S. as a war preparedness measure.
Federal Airport Act of 1946	1946	P.L. 79-377	Appropriated $500 million for continental U.S. and $20 million for Alaska and Hawaii for the construction of airports on a matching fund basis.
National Security Act of 1947	1947	P.L. 80-253	Abolished the departments of War and the Navy and established in their place the Department of Defense. In so doing, split the Army Air Forces out and made it a separate service, the U.S. Air Force, coequal with the U.S. Army and the U.S. Navy.
Airways Modernization Act	1957	P.L. 85-133	Established the Airways Modernization Board "to provide for the development and modernization of the national system of navigation and traffic control facilities to serve preset and future needs of civil and military aviation."
National Aeronautics and Space Act of 1958	1958	P.L. 85-568	Transformed the National Advisory Committee for Aeronautics into the National Aeronautics and Space Administration.
Defense Reorganization Act of 1958	1958	P.L. 85-599	Provided for a stronger secretary of Defense, vesting control of research and development activities in that office. This provided for more centralized management of aerospace research.

Major Legislation (Continued)

Title	Year Enacted	Reference Number	Description
Federal Aviation Act of 1958	1958	P.L. 85-726	Transformed the Civil Aeronautics Authority into the Federal Aviation Agency and made the Civil Aeronautics Board an independent organization. The new organization had broad powers to manage and regulate commercial aviation in the U.S.
"Crimes in the Sky" Act	1961	P.L. 87-197	Amendment to Federal Aviation Act of 1958 to provide for enforcement of crimes committed in the air, especially for interfering with the performance of duties by flight crews.
Communications Satellite Act of 1962	1962	P.L. 87-624	Created Communication Satellite Corporation, Public/Private Corp., managing satellite communications for U.S.
Department of Transportation Act of 1966	1966	P.L. 89-670	Created the Department of Transportation as a cabinet-level organization. The Federal Aviation Agency was assigned to the new department and given the name Federal Aviation Administration.
National Science and Technology Policy Organization, and Priorities Act of 1976	1976	P.L. 94-282	Created an Office of Science and Technology Policy reporting to the president.
Airline Deregulation Act of 1978	1978	P.L. 95-504	Provided for fare reductions of up to 70 percent without Civil Aeronautics Board (CAB) approval and the immediate entry of air carriers into routes not protected by other carriers. The CAB's regulation of fares, routes, and mergers would be phased out by 1983, and unless Congress acted the CAB would shut down by 1985.
Land Remote Sensing Commercialization Act of 1984	1984	P.L. 98-365	Commercialized the Landsat remote sensing system launched by the U.S. in the 1970s.
Commercial Space Launch Act of 1984	1984	P.L. 98-575	Commercialized launch operations within the U.S. to open it to competition.
Department of Defense Reorganization Act of 1986	1986	P.L. 99-433	The "Goldwater-Nichols Act" provided for greater control of the individual services at the secretary level, and centralized even more aerospace research and development activities.

SOURCES: U.S. Senate, Committee on Commerce, Science, and Transportation, *Space Law and Related Documents: International Space Law Documents, U.S. Space Law Documents* (1990), pp. 443–605; Alex Roland, *Model Research: The National Advisory Committee for Aeronautics, 1915–1958* (1985), 2:393–422; Arnold E. Briddon and Ellmore A. Champie, *Federal Aviation Agency Historical Fact Book: A Chronology, 1926–1963* (1966); Richard I. Wolf, ed., *The United States Air Force: Basic Documents on Roles and Missions* (1987), pp. 325–338.

a buildup of aeronautical capability and created a permanent Aviation Section of the War Department. When the nation entered World War I in April 1917, this process accelerated, with the government making significant investments in the aviation industry and expanding its procurement of military aircraft from 350 on order to an ambitious program to develop and produce 22,000 modern military aircraft by July 1918. Even without achieving this goal—U.S. manufacturers delivered 11,950 planes to the government during the war—the massive military appropriations gave the nascent aviation industry a huge boost. Equally important, the

infrastructure of military aviation was solidified because of the war; indeed, by 1919 the Army Air Service had established sixty-nine airfields in the United States. All these bases became part of a nationwide network of airways and landing fields that permitted rapid movement of units across the country for military purposes.

Interest in military-related aeronautics declined after World War I, and expansion of the aeronautical industry slowed to a trickle. The amount of funding for military aviation declined each year after 1918, reaching a low of $12.6 million in 1924. A major change came with the Army Air Corps Act of 1926, which renamed the Air Service the Army Air Corps, provided for an assistant secretary of War for Air, and mandated a five-year Air Corps expansion program.

As the United States began to rearm in the late 1930s, the nation's leaders came to recognize the importance of the army's air arm. For instance, in 1934 Congress appropriated $23.3 million for the use of the Army Air Corps, only 8.4 percent of all army appropriations. But in 1938, President Franklin D. Roosevelt suggested that the Air Corps was operating with what could politely be called "antiquated weapons" and advocated increasing its strength to thirty thousand airplanes. Congress, however, funded a much more modest three thousand planes. In April 1939, when Congress passed the National Defense Act of 1940, it authorized the Army Air Corps to develop and procure six thousand new airplanes, to increase personnel to 3,203 officers and 45,000 enlisted personnel, and to spend $300 million. As a result, the Army Air Corps received $70.6 million, or 15.7 percent of the army's direct appropriations. These figures continued to climb during the early 1940s.

Although some demobilization took place following World War II, expansion of military aerospace activities continued as a result of the Cold War. The National Security Act of 1947 abolished two cabinet-level organizations, the departments of War and the Navy, and established the Department of Defense in their place. At the same time, the act took the air forces out of army control, making the U.S. Air Force a separate service, coequal with the army and the navy. Since that time, several pieces of legislation have reformed various aspects of the Department of Defense and the aerospace infrastructure but left the basic institutional arrangements intact.

The military air and space component in the Cold War involved a broad range of activities. The development, training, equipping, and employment of aerospace military power extended from aircraft to missiles to satellites to other systems of both a passive and active nature. Much of this activity, such as satellite reconnaissance, was carried out in a highly classified environment. This secrecy was justified as a means of maintaining the integrity of the nation against an aggressive communist menace.

Fostering Aerospace Research and Development. The first important instance of federal action to foster aerospace research and development came as a rider to the Naval Appropriations Act of 1915. In this legislation Congress established the National Advisory Committee for Aeronautics "to supervise and direct the scientific study of the problems of flight, with a view to their practical solution." The NACA became an enormously important government research and development organization for the next half century, materially enhancing the development of aeronautics. All research projects undertaken by the NACA were aimed at expanding fundamental aeronautical knowledge applicable to all flight rather than working on a specific type of aircraft design, because the latter would smack of catering to a particular aeronautical firm. Most NACA research was performed in-house by scientists or engineers on the federal payroll. The results appeared in more than sixteen thousand research reports of one type or another that were distributed widely for the benefit of all.

The NACA's research was conducted in government facilities, and its government scientists and engineers developed a strong technical competence, a commitment to collegial in-house research conducive to engineering innovation, and an apolitical perspective. While it never had more than about eight thousand employees and an annual budget of $100 million, the NACA maintained a small Washington headquarters staff, three major research laboratories, and two small test facilities. The NACA remained a significant entity until it was transformed into the National Aeronautics and Space Administration (NASA) in 1958.

The National Aeronautics and Space Act of 1958 gave NASA a broad mandate to "plan, direct, and conduct aeronautical and space activities"; to involve the nation's scientific community in these activities; and to disseminate information about them. With the avid backing of Congress, NASA became the preeminent public organization conducting aerospace activities during the 1960s. It engaged in a broad-based human spaceflight program that culminated with Project Apollo and the landing of astronauts on the moon on 20 July 1969. Initial NASA estimates of the costs of Project Apollo were about $20 billion by the end of the decade, a figure approaching $150 billion in 1991 dollars. Congress has also supported, albeit with some dissent, the development of the Space Shuttle as the primary human spaceflight program of the nation since Apollo.

Less visible but equally significant was Congress's important role in providing the resources and facilities necessary to execute a wide-ranging program in space science. From *Explorer I* in 1958 to the *Viking* Mars lander to the *Voyager* missions to the outer planets to the Hubble Space Telescope and observatories program, this fostering of aerospace activity has been a persistent theme in the political arena. There have been limits to the political support for these endeavors, however, and space scientists have learned a hard lesson about the pragmatic, and sometimes brutal, politics associated with the execution of "big science." The same can be said regarding space technology applied to everyday problems—communications, navigation, geological study, weather, and a host of other activities. The payoff from these aerospace investments has been enormous; communications, for example, have revolutionized the way in which humanity approaches life since the first *Telstar* was launched in 1962. However, the limits on government support have prompted commercialization of as many of these new technologies as possible.

Regulation of Aerospace Commerce. The third major area of federal involvement in aerospace activities is the regulation of aerospace commerce. The earliest involvement came with legislation to manage an air mail system, but in 1926 the Air Commerce Act assigned responsibility for the fostering of air commerce to the Commerce Department. With this went responsibility to establish airways, to test and license pilots, to inspect and certify aircraft, to establish navigation systems, to investigate accidents, and generally to provide for an orderly development of American aviation. In the process there were fits and starts, regulatory blind alleys, and technological misjudgments, but during the years that followed, the new technology and new industry, as well as the relatively new government regulatory thrust, began to be developed. By the time the Civil Aeronautics Authority was created in 1938, however, the major trends in aeronautical regulation had been established, and much that followed was merely refinement.

Three additional pieces of legislation were important in the regulation of aerospace operations. The Federal Aviation Act of 1958 transformed the Civil Aeronautics Authority into the Federal Aviation Agency (FAA) and gave the FAA broad powers to manage and regulate commercial aviation in the United States. In 1966 the FAA—now renamed the Federal Aviation Administration—was assigned to be a major component of the newly established Department of Transportation. The Airline Deregulation Act of 1978 ended federal enforcement of route structures and prices and allowed competition to reign in service between American cities.

[*See also* Air Force; National Aeronautics and Space Act of 1958; National Security Act.]

BIBLIOGRAPHY

Astronautics and Aeronautics: A Chronology. 21 vols. 1961–1988.
Craven, Wesley Frank, and James L. Cate, eds. *The United States Air Force in World War II.* 7 vols. 1948–1956.
Hechler, Ken. *Toward the Endless Frontier: History of the Committee on Science and Technology, 1959–1979.* 1980.
Maurer, Maurer. *Aviation in the U.S. Army, 1919–1939.* 1987.
Richelson, Jeffrey. *U.S. Military Uses of Space, 1945–1991.* 1991. Microfiche.

ROGER D. LAUNIUS

AFRICAN AMERICAN MEMBERS. *See* Black Members.

AGENDA. The patterns of public policy and the impact of policies on citizens are not simply the results of government officials making choices from the alternatives before them. Whether people get a lot from government, or a little, or who gets what—these matters do not depend merely on the votes cast in the House or Senate. Rather, results are also critically affected by which subjects make their way on to government agendas in the first place and by how the alternatives are generated from which the choices are made.

The word *agenda* has three meanings. First, in its specific parliamentary application, the agenda is the schedule of bills for consideration, either in committee or on the floor. Second, more general scholarly usage takes the government agenda to be that list of subjects or problems to which government officials and those close to them are paying serious attention at a given time. For example, national health insurance is said to be "on the agenda" if politicians, bureaucrats, policy analysts, and interest groups who deal with health policy are paying it serious attention. In this sense, a subject may be on the agenda although choices among the prominent alternatives (e.g., play-or-pay insurance plans, Canadian-style health insurance, or no action) have not been made. Third, in rational-choice modeling, an agenda setter is a presiding officer, parliamentarian, or bill manager who controls the content and ordering of the alternatives from which choices will be made. Where several different winning majorities are theoretically possible, for example, the agenda setter's choice of the order in which various amendments will be proposed determines the outcomes.

The strictly parliamentary meaning of *agenda* focuses attention on various congressional leaders. Chairs, for instance, heavily influence the agendas of their committees. They decide which bills will be taken up and when, how hearings will be structured, and how many of the committee staffers will spend their time. They do so in consultation with their colleagues, of course, but retain a disproportionate control over the committee agenda. Similarly, the majority party leadership in each house determines the agenda for floor consideration. For example, the majority leader of the Senate announces the schedule of bills on the floor for the coming week after an elaborate process of consultation with the minority leader and other actively involved senators. Some potential agenda items are discretionary, in the sense that leaders can affect whether they come up or not, but others are not really within their control. Annual appropriations bills must be brought up, for instance, or governmental agencies would not be able to draw money from the Treasury, and refusing to consider a budget is not a practical option.

Scholars have studied agenda setting in a variety of ways. Some studies track the prominence of items on an agenda by coding and counting the appearance of items in various publicly available documents. These sorts of studies follow the frequency, first and last appearance, and rise and fall of various agenda items in the topics for congressional hearings, mentions of an item in the *Congressional Record*, counts of topics in the *New York Times Index*, and prominence in periodicals more specialized than mass circulation newspapers. A second type of tracking is done by interviewing knowledgeable informants in a given policy area over time and comparing the subjects they are occupied with from one year to another. A third approach, which utilizes case studies, is a detailed analysis of the emergence of a particular issue across time, either within a given country or by comparing two or more countries. A final type of work is theoretical. For instance, some authors specify the types of legislative structures or parliamentary rules that produce a particular majority rule outcome when several different majorities could be possible without those structures.

Studies of agenda setting have emphasized various themes. First, it is apparent that agendas do not change incrementally. Instead, government policy changes in major ways all at once in a tremendous flurry of activity. The New Deal, the Great Society, and the Reagan revolution all illustrate this pattern of eras of substantial change interspersed with periods of rest. Second, several different developments seem to come together at once to produce these major changes. Separate streams of problems, policy proposals, and political events run through government, each with a life of its own. People in and around government recognize and come to concentrate on certain problems rather than others, whether or not such problems are amenable to solution, and they propose and refine policy proposals whether or not they are actually solving problems. And broader political events such as shifts in national mood, changes of administration, or interest-group campaigns move along according to their own dynamics. The greatest agenda changes occur when the streams come together—when a problem is recognized, a solution is available, and the political conditions are right.

Why do some deserving topics fail to capture the attention of people in government or to get on the agenda at all? There are a number of possible explanations. First, one or more of the critical elements may be missing. Governmental officials may not be aware of a problem, for instance, or may not define a factual condition as a problem. Or they may know of a problem, for example, but not yet have worked up a viable solution. Second, severe economic or budgetary constraints may prevent government from spending sufficient money to address a problem, even if potential solutions are available. Third, people with a stake in a solution may lack the necessary resources of time, money, status, or education to organize themselves into interest groups or voting blocs capable of influencing the government's agenda. People who are thus "organized out" of the political process need advocates or patrons, and such advocates do not always materialize. There may be a kind of political-policy underclass, whose interests rarely are heard. Finally, ideas matter. A dominant American ideology seems to emphasize individual advancement and to downplay collective action, and this ideology may result in less government involvement in policy areas such as health, transportation, and housing—and in lower taxes and a smaller public sector—than exists in other industrialized countries.

[*See also* Calendars; Floor Leader.]

BIBLIOGRAPHY

Cobb, Roger, and Charles Elder. *Participation in American Politics: The Dynamics of Agenda-Building.* 1972.

Kingdon, John. *Agendas, Alternatives, and Public Policies.* 1984.

Krehbiel, Keith. "Spatial Models of Legislative Choice." *Legislative Studies Quarterly* 13 (1988): 259–319.

Walker, Jack. "Setting the Agenda in the U.S. Senate." *British Journal of Political Science* 7 (1977): 423–445.

JOHN W. KINGDON

AGING COMMITTEE, HOUSE SELECT.

The House Select Committee on Aging traces its beginnings to the work of Representatives (later Senators) David Pryor (D-Ark.) and John Heinz (R-Pa.). Pryor received national publicity in 1969 when he volunteered as an orderly in Washington, D.C., nursing homes and gave a first-person account of the conditions he found there. He was the first person to offer a resolution to create a house select committee on aging.

Undaunted by opposition from House leaders, Pryor rented a trailer and placed it on the parking lot behind the House Office Building, staffing it with interns paid from the proceeds from Arkansas catfish fries. He created the House "Trailer" Committee on Aging and continued to lobby for the creation of a permanent committee. His ally Heinz was the moving party behind the creation of the House Republican Task Force on Aging. Both Pryor and Heinz began to conduct what they called briefing sessions (instead of hearings), to issue white papers (instead of reports), and to work with the Senate Special Committee on Aging in advancing the interests of older Americans.

In November 1971, President Richard M. Nixon convened the second White House conference on aging. One of its major recommendations was to establish a select committee on aging in the House as a counterpart to the Senate Special Committee on Aging.

In 1974, when the House reformed its committees' structure and jurisdiction, Rep. C. W. Bill Young (D-Fla.), by a vote of 328 to 27, won approval for an amendment creating the House Select Committee on Aging. Heinz won approval for a similar amendment on 8 October 1974. The two measures were consolidated in the final version of the House reorganization plan, H. Res. 988.

Rep. William J. Randall (D-Mo.) was appointed the committee's first chairman, serving during the 94th Congress. The committee came into its own, however, with the ascendancy of Rep. Claude Pepper (D-Fla.) to the chairmanship in the 95th Congress. Pepper, a former senator and, at age seventy-seven, the oldest member of the House, more and more became the personification of "senior power," reflecting older Americans' more prominent role in the political landscape. Under Pepper's leadership, the committee became a coveted and glamorous assignment. In response to the demand, the membership was increased from the original twenty-eight members to sixty-seven, or roughly one out of every seven members serving in the House.

Organized as a "select," or fact-finding, Committee, Aging did not have legislative jurisdiction; however, its in-depth study of issues and numerous substantive reports led to major legislative reforms enacted through other committees. Among these were the abolition of mandatory retirement; the expansion of Medicare and Medicaid; the creation of federal minimum standards for nursing homes; the creation of state-based Adult Protective Service Units to identify and prevent physical, financial, and psychological abuse of the elderly; and granting the U.S. Postal Service, the Food and Drug Administration, and the Federal Trade Commission increased authority to protect seniors from fraud and abuse. The most publicized of these hearings involved abuses in the sale of insurance policies to supplement Medicare.

In 1983, Pepper relinquished the chairmanship to head the Committee on Rules. For the next ten years, the panel continued to hold hearings and focus attention on issues affecting the elderly, especially health care matters and the growing crisis of long-term care.

In 1993, as part of a budget-cutting move, the committee and four other select committees were not refunded. The committee's work was continued by the House Older Americans Caucus, led by Rep. William J. Hughes (D-N.J.), who was joined by eighty-seven cosponsors in support of H. Res. 30, which would re-create and restore the Select Committee on Aging.

[*See also* Aging Committee, Senate Special.]

BIBLIOGRAPHY

Halamandaris, Val J. *Profiles in Caring: Advocates for the Elderly.* 1991.

Pepper, Claude D., and Hays Gorey. *Eyewitness to a Century.* 1987.

VAL J. HALAMANDARIS

AGING COMMITTEE, SENATE SPECIAL.

The Senate Special Committee on Aging grew out of the Subcommittee on Problems of the Aged and Aging of the Committee on Labor and Public Welfare. In 1959, the Senate authorized the subcommittee to make a comprehensive study of the problems of the elderly. After hearings held across the nation, a landmark report was issued the next year by Chairman Pat McNamara (D-Mich.) identifying several major problems confronting the elderly and offering recommendations.

The senior Democrat on the Subcommittee was John F. Kennedy (D-Mass.), who as a presidential candidate integrated the subcommittee's findings into his campaign platform. Wilbur J. Cohen, then dean of the School of Welfare Administration at the University of Michigan (later secretary of the Department of Health, Education, and Welfare) and a close protégé of Senator McNamara, became an adviser to Senator Kennedy in the election campaign. It was Cohen who suggested that Kennedy make health care for the aged one of the key issues in his campaign and who proposed creating a special committee on aging in the Senate to continue the subcommittee's work, to generate public support, and to make an end-run around the Senate Finance Committee, then chaired by conservative senator Harry Flood Byrd, Sr. (D-Va.), who was opposed to the enactment of any federal health insurance program.

The Senate Special Committee on Aging was created on 13 February 1961, with the passage of S. Res. 33, introduced by Senator McNamara. The legislation was enacted over strong objections from the senior committee chairman thanks to President Kennedy's support.

The committee began a series of highly publicized hearings all across America. The hearings achieved greater public awareness of the problems of the elderly and generated grass-roots support for the enactment of Medicare, which was signed into law by President Lyndon B. Johnson on 25 July 1965.

The Senate Aging Committee's greatest achievement has been to raise the visibility of the nation's senior citizens and to sensitize the Congress, the public, and the media to the special problems of the elderly. As a select committee, it does not have legislative authority; however, the committee has worked to bring about the enactment of legislation through other committees. This legislation includes laws barring age discrimination in employment, barring mandatory retirement, creating housing programs for the elderly, providing protection for private pensions, improving access by removing architectural barriers, providing federal minimum standards for nursing homes, creating the National Institute on Aging as part of the National Institutes of Health, and increasing retirement income for the elderly under Social Security, civil service, and veterans' retirement programs.

The committee also played a major role in the enactment of the Social Security amendments in 1972 (P.L. 92-603), which for the first time made the disabled eligible for Social Security and Medicare. The most highly publicized hearings of the committee exposed nursing home abuses and Medicare and Medicaid fraud and resulted in legislation creating the office of inspector general in the Department of Health and Human Services, creating state Medicaid fraud units, and upgrading Medicare and Medicaid fraud from a misdemeanor to a felony.

In September 1976, an effort was made to abolish the Senate Aging Committee as part of the Senate reorganization. This effort failed, although membership in the committee was reduced from a high of twenty-three down to nine members. As part of this downsizing, the committee abolished all subcommittees. In 1978, the Senate voted to make the committee permanent. In subsequent years, the demand for membership on the committee increased, as did the size of the committee, which included twenty-one senators in 1992. In 1993, the committee survived another attempt to abolish it. An amendment offered by Chairman David Pryor (D-Ark.) to extend the committee passed by a vote of 68 to 30 on 24 February 1993. During the 103d Congress, the Senate Aging Committee played an important role in the debate over national health insurance, with the goal of protecting Medicare benefits for senior citizens while extending health coverage to the general population.

[See also Aging Committee, House Select.]

BIBLIOGRAPHY

Halamandaris, Val J. *Profiles in Caring: Advocates for the Elderly.* 1991.
Pepper, Claude D., and Hays Gorey. *Eyewitness to a Century.* 1987.
U.S. Senate. Committee on Labor and Public Welfare. Subcommittee on the Problems of the Aged and Aging. *The Aged and Aging in the United States: A National Problem.* 86th Cong., 2d sess., 1960. S. Rept. 1121.

VAL J. HALAMANDARIS

AGRICULTURAL ADJUSTMENT ACTS

(1933, 1938). The Agricultural Adjustment Acts (AAA) were the main feature of the New Deal's farm program and the foundation of the large role of the federal government in the American agricultural system during and after the 1930s. A great deal of historical experience contributed to the passage of this legislation. Its origins can be traced to old ideas about equal rights and the great importance of farming and farm people, to long-established government and corporate policies, including the protective tariff and production control, to the farm crisis that emerged in the 1920s and worsened in the early 1930s as farmers lost much of their market, and to the battle over the McNary-Haugen plan in the 1920s, which focused on government intervention in that market (chiefly by establishing a government corporation to buy and sell farm products).

AAA also owed much to the rise of two new voices in farm politics: the American Farm Bureau Federation, which led the farm lobby, and agricultural economists who became the acknowledged experts on farm policy. The legislation's sources also lay in Franklin D. Roosevelt's interest in farmers, the promises he had made to them in the 1932 campaign, and his preference for a plan developed by economists as opposed to those favored by farm organizations and members of Congress.

The first Agricultural Adjustment Act (1933; 48 Stat. 31–54) became law only two months after Roosevelt took office in 1933. Sponsored by the administration as represented by the new secretary of Agriculture, Henry A. Wallace, it was supported by the Farm Bureau and passed by the House and the Senate.

The architects of AAA hoped to raise farm prices high enough to give farmers the purchasing power they had enjoyed just before World War I. To accomplish this, the law established an Agricultural Adjustment Administration, housed in the Department of Agriculture, and empowered it to pay farmers to reduce the number of acres devoted to what were termed basic commodities and to work out marketing agreements between producers and processors of farm products. The administration soon emphasized production control, urging farmers to copy a practice of industrial corporations.

Most commercial farmers supported AAA, but the program encountered opposition from people concerned about its harmful impacts on southern sharecroppers and from processors of farm products. The latter persuaded the Supreme Court to overturn the law in 1936.

Forced to offer substitute legislation, the New Dealers moved more boldly in 1938, after the Court had become more friendly to New Deal initiatives. Introduced by Wallace, supported by the Farm Bureau, and passed by a bipartisan bloc led by representatives of farm states and districts, the Agricultural Adjustment Act of 1938 (52 Stat. 31–77) emphasized production control and what Wallace called the "ever normal granary," which stored crops in good years for use when harvests were short.

The program had mixed results. It harmed many sharecroppers, some of whom lost their place on the land as landlords cut back on the acres they devoted to crops, substituted tractors for people, and demoted tenants to wage laborers, but it increased the income of land-owning commercial farmers by paying them for their cooperation and forcing farm prices to rise, and it strengthened the Farm Bureau. The act did not restore purchasing power to pre–World War I levels or achieve its production goals, and it left the government holding huge supplies of grain and other farm products. But those supplies became useful in World War II, and the idea of government aid for farmers, pioneered by AAA, remained sufficiently popular among farmers, their organizations, and their congressional representatives to maintain the role of the federal government as a major part of the agricultural system.

BIBLIOGRAPHY

Hansen, John Mark. *Gaining Access: Congress and the Farm Lobby, 1919–1981.* 1991.

Saloutos, Theodore. *The American Farmer and the New Deal.* 1982.

RICHARD S. KIRKENDALL

AGRICULTURE. Congress, operating under the Articles of Confederation, first addressed agricultural matters with the Land Act of 1785, but this legislation (as well as other land laws) primarily concerned the sale of the public domain for revenue purposes rather than the promotion of farming. In 1820, Congress became more persistently involved with agriculture when the House of Representatives created a Committee on Agriculture at the urging of Rep. Lewis Williams of North Carolina. Five years later, the Senate established a Committee on Agriculture and Forestry. With the founding of these committees, Congress created the procedural structure to consider a wide range of agricultural matters. Nevertheless, it did not provide an appropriation for agriculture until 1839, when it authorized $1,000 for the Patent Office to support the collection of agricultural statistics and the distribution of seeds for experimentation.

Early Congressional Involvement. During the 1850s, Congress became seriously concerned about agricultural affairs. At that time, many agricultural organizations, such as the United States Agricultural Society and the Maryland Agricultural Society, as well as individual farmers and others, urged Congress to create a bureau or department of agriculture within the Department of the Interior. In 1856, Congress also considered legislation to create a land-grant college system for promoting agricultural education. Southern members of Congress, however, blocked both bills; they feared an increase of federal power and the centralization of governmental bureaucracy in the nation's capital at the expense of states' rights. When the southern states seceded from the Union, however, most of the opposition to both bills ended.

On 3 December 1861 in his first annual message to Congress, President Abraham Lincoln urged the creation of a bureau of agriculture. On 7 January 1862, Owen Lovejoy of Illinois, chairman of the House Committee on Agriculture, introduced a bill authorizing such a bureau. The House soon passed the bill in an amended form that authorized a department headed by a commissioner rather than a secretary with cabinet status. Although some senators opposed the creation of a department of agriculture because they believed it would become a burden to the taxpayers, the Senate also approved the establishment of a department under the direction of a commissioner appointed by the president, and Lincoln signed that legislation on 15 May 1862. The new U.S. Department of Agriculture had the responsibility of improving agricultural knowledge and practices. Congress did not, however, authorize it to embark on a host of regulatory activities.

The secession of the South also removed the congressional obstacles to providing a higher education system devoted to agricultural training. On 14 December 1857, Rep. Justin S. Morrill (R-Vt.) had introduced a bill authorizing Congress to provide public lands to the states to support the establishment of colleges emphasizing agriculture and the mechanical arts. Although Congress passed the bill in 1859, President James Buchanan, who owed his election to southern support, vetoed it. In 1862, however, southerners were no longer present in Congress to block this bill, and on 2 July President Lincoln signed the Morrill Land-Grant College Act. This act provided thirty thousand acres of land per representative and senator in states with public lands and certificates for states without public lands to support the founding of an agricultural and mechanical college, one per state. Congress authorized states without public lands to sell their certificates and invest the money to support land-grant colleges, because they could not claim lands in the public land states. This provision avoided potentially troublesome jurisdictional disputes. Alternately, the states without public lands could give the certificates to the colleges, which, in turn, could claim land in the public land states for their support.

After passage of the Morrill act, Congress continued to demonstrate an interest in agricultural education and research. In 1882, Rep. William H. Hatch (D-Mo.) and Sen. James Z. George (D-Miss.) introduced bills to provide financial support for agricultural experimentation at the land-grant colleges. These bills were not successful, but in 1886 Hatch introduced another bill that authorized the creation of federally supported agricultural experiment stations. Congress passed the bill, and President Grover Cleveland signed it on 2 March 1887. This Hatch Act (not to be confused with the Hatch Act of 1939, sponsored by Sen. Carl A. Hatch of New Mexico) enabled Congress to make annual appropriations to support the research conducted at the experiment stations.

Congress further expanded its involvement in agricultural education by passing the Second Morrill Land-Grant College Act in 1890. Whereas the first Morrill act provided only land for the creation of colleges, this act, introduced by Morrill (now a senator), authorized financial support for the land-grant colleges and prohibited racial discrimination in the admissions process at those institutions. President Benjamin Harrison approved the act on 30 August 1890. The states avoided the nondiscrimination requirement by establishing separate institutions for African Americans. Eventually, seventeen states supported institutions of higher education, known as the 1890 colleges, for African American students. Some states assigned funds to public black institutions that already existed, such as Alcorn Agricultural and Mechanical College in Mississippi, Prairie View Agricultural and Mechanical College in Texas, and Lincoln University in Missouri. Maryland gave money to Morgan College, which became the University of Maryland-Eastern Shore. Seven states created new black land-grant schools, such as Delaware State College, West Virginia State College, and Tennessee Agricultural and Industrial State University.

Despite their congressional backing, the land-grant colleges and the agricultural experiment stations had great difficulty influencing farmers. Many refused to believe that anyone could learn to farm by reading books. Moreover, few sons and daughters of farmers enrolled in the land-grant colleges, and those who did seldom returned to the farm. Although the Department of Agriculture began practical demonstration work under the direction of agriculturalist Seaman A. Knapp in 1903, and privately funded county agent work began in some localities as early as 1911, Congress did not support a program for taking new agricultural techniques to farmers until the eve of World War I.

On 6 September 1913, Sen. Hoke Smith (D-Ga.) and Rep. Asbury F. Lever (D-S.C.) introduced a bill that authorized Congress to support cooperative agricultural extension work between the land-grant colleges and the Department of Agriculture. Some members of Congress opposed the bill because it would promote surplus production and low prices. Representative Lever, however, argued that agricultural education through demonstration work would not be limited to increasing agricultural productivity but would also help improve the quality of rural life. Facing little opposition, the bill passed by a voice vote in both houses. President Woodrow Wilson signed the Agricultural Extension Act, commonly known as the Smith-Lever Act, on 8 May 1914. Federal financial support, along with matching state and local aid, would now support home demonstrations to convey practical information on subjects relating to agriculture and home economics.

Although congressional support for educational improvements in agriculture was important, neither the executive nor the legislative branch of the federal government attempted to regulate the agricultural economy; in part, that was because farmers were not united or organized politically. Their interests remained too broad and contradictory to support a single agricultural policy. As a result, Congress addressed general issues such as education, tariff protection, and land disposal or dealt with specific issues such as exempting farmer cooperatives from prosecution under the Clayton Antitrust Act of 1914 and improving storage facilities with the Warehouse Act of 1916.

The Agricultural Depression of the 1920s. In 1920, a precipitous decline in agricultural prices forced Congress to assume a new regulatory role. Many farmers demanded that Congress play a direct role in agriculture by intervening in the economy to maintain favorable agricultural prices. Members of Congress from the agricultural states responded by forming a bipartisan farm bloc. This coalition was organized in May 1921 to push for special legislation beneficial to farmers, agricultur-

al groups, and the rural economy. Senators William S. Kenyon (R-Iowa), Arthur Capper (R-Kan.), and Hoke Smith and Rep. Lester J. Dickinson (R-Iowa) were its most important leaders. In 1921, the farm bloc succeeded in passing important regulatory legislation such as the Packers and Stockyards Act, the Future Trading Act, and the Emergency Agricultural Credits Act. This coalition was then instrumental in the passage of the Capper-Volstead Cooperative Marketing Act in 1922 and the Intermediate Credits Act of 1923. These measures, however, did not have broad economic objectives, and Congress came under increasing pressure to resolve the continuing problems of low prices and overproduction.

At the same time, the American Farm Bureau Federation conducted an aggressive lobbying campaign under the direction of Gray Silver. Silver asked members of Congress to report how they voted on agricultural legislation settled by a voice vote. He also perfected the technique of compiling the results of district-by-district public opinion polls conducted by county farm bureaus. If members of Congress appeared indecisive about supporting agricultural matters of interest to the Farm Bureau, Silver showed them the polls and told state and county offices to overwhelm those members with telegrams and phone calls. Silver's lobbying for the Farm Bureau often proved intimidating, and congressional members from the farm states usually supported bureau causes as a matter of political necessity. These tactics, along with a membership of more than 300,000 and abundant funds, made the Farm Bureau the major agricultural lobbying organization before Congress.

In 1922, George N. Peek, president of the Moline Plow Company, urged Congress to adopt an agricultural policy that would enable farmers to meet domestic demands at fair or parity prices based on the relatively high agricultural prices prevailing from 1909 to 1914. Peek advocated the marketing of surplus commodities on the world market at low prices, with domestic prices rising behind the tariff. Farmers would profit from the domestic price less a charge or equalization fee on each unit sold to pay for the program.

In 1924, Sen. Charles L. McNary (R-Oreg.), chairman of the Senate Committee on Agriculture and Forestry, and Rep. Gilbert N. Haugen (R-Iowa), chairman of the House Committee on Agriculture, introduced Peek's plan. Congress could not agree on the bill and delayed passage until 1927. President Calvin Coolidge, however, vetoed the measure because it would aid some farmers at the expense of others, because it involved federal price fixing behind the protective tariff, and because it authorized an unconditional delegation of taxing power. Although Congress approved the bill again in 1928, it received another veto from Coolidge, which Congress again could not override.

The farm lobby, particularly the Farm Bureau, now began to champion agricultural price-support legislation as something Republicans would have to support in exchange for continuing midwestern and western agrarian support for the Republican party. Farmers demanded economic relief, and agricultural groups began to lobby for beneficial agricultural legislation by providing Congress with reliable information about agricultural problems and by offering solutions that their constituents favored. The severe economic problems in American agriculture during the 1920s convinced Congress that the farm problem would continue; therefore, members increasingly listened to the farm lobby and relied on it to help them devise policy proposals to resolve agricultural difficulties.

When the farm lobby gained access to Congress during the 1920s, it also commanded the power to mobilize public opinion at election time to support or reject representatives and senators based, in part, on the extent of their willingness to aid agriculture. Because neither the Democratic nor Republican party offered solutions to the agricultural problem, the farm lobby filled a power vacuum. Members of Congress now listened to the farm lobby even at the expense of violating party unity because it was politically advantageous to do so. Once the farm lobby gained access to Congress, it maintained influence as long as its information remained reliable and it had the capability to influence the outcome of congressional elections.

After the failure of the McNary-Haugen bill, President Herbert Hoover urged Congress to solve the economic problems of agriculture by providing funds to help farm cooperatives organize and to improve their marketing practices. In 1929, Congress agreed to try Hoover's approach when it passed the Agricultural Marketing Act on 15 June. This legislation created a Federal Farm Board with a $500 million appropriation to help farmers organize cooperatives. Congress also authorized federally supported agricultural stabilization corporations to purchase specific commodities should the agricultural cooperatives fail to solve the surplus problem and to stabilize prices through orderly marketing practices. The Federal Farm Board and the stabilization corporations, however, did not receive sufficient funding to solve the problems of overproduction and low prices.

The Great Depression of the 1930s, together with a severe drought, had a devastating effect on American agriculture. Farm production and prices fell, but operating costs, mortgage payments, and tax levies remained relatively unchanged. Although many people fled the farmlands, others returned to their homes on the farm after they lost urban jobs when the economy collapsed. As a result, the farm population and the number of farms increased but agricultural income remained unchanged. Both farmers and the general public confronted the perplexing problem of want in the midst of plenty, but Congress needed new executive department leadership to solve the problems of agriculture.

The New Deal and World War II. In 1933 during the Hundred Days of the "first" New Deal, the new administration of President Franklin D. Roosevelt proposed the Agricultural Adjustment Act. By so doing, the executive branch, including the Department of Agriculture, took from Congress the major responsibility for proposing agricultural legislation. From then on, the executive branch, often in consultation with the farm lobby, retained its leadership role. Although all legislation, of course, still required congressional approval, Congress was no longer an active force in the development or initiation of agricultural policy, and it has since been content to follow the lead of the executive branch. Because of the increasingly technical nature of agriculture, domestic marketing, and international trade, however, Congress has not so much abdicated its responsibility for agricultural policy as it has recognized the expertise and expense needed to shape such policy. No representative or senator can marshal the financial or technical resources to develop a policy that affects all American agricultural interests. Consequently, Congress after 1933 was content to react to executive leadership while amending proposed legislation to meet the needs of local and national interest groups, particularly in relation to price supports, production adjustments, and farm credits.

When Congress passed the Agricultural Adjustment Act of 1933, it also embarked on a new policy course of federal intervention and regulation in the agricultural economy. By so doing, Congress essentially fulfilled the farm lobby's decade-long fight for equitable treatment of agriculture. The legislation, sponsored by Rep. Hampton P. Fulmer (D-S.C.), enabled farmers to receive federal payments for reducing their planted acreage of surplus crops. Congress intended this legislation to reduce surplus production and increase prices for cotton, wheat, corn, hogs, tobacco, rice, and dairy products. Although the Supreme Court held this legislation unconstitutional in 1936, Congress, responding to direction from the Department of Agriculture, continued to support acreage reductions under the Soil Conservation and Domestic Allotment Act of 1936. This legislation authorized federal payments to farmers who planted soil-conserving grasses and legumes rather than soil-depleting crops, thereby reducing the production of staple crops.

On 16 February 1938, Congress institutionalized this agricultural policy with a new Agricultural Adjustment Act. This act combined the soil conservation provisions of 1936 with a new program that gave the producers of those commodities income parity with workers in other sectors of the economy. Congress also authorized the secretary of Agriculture to limit marketing of specific crops on a prorated basis per producer if excessive surpluses existed, provided that two-thirds of the producers of that commodity authorized that action. Title III of the 1938 legislation created the first major provision for price supports based on congressional authority to regulate commerce. This provision authorized mandatory (nonrecourse) loans for farmers participating in the program. These farmers received loans from the federal government based on a specifically determined market price for their crops. If the market price fell below the loan rate during the year, the farmer could give his crop to the government to cover the debt. If the price rose above the loan rate, he could sell it and pay off the loan. This legislation gave farmers more financial flexibility than ever before. Participants agreed to limit production, and a crop insurance provision enabled them for the first time to protect their incomes against losses due to weather, insects, and disease.

Congress clearly departed from the limited-government philosophy of the past with the Agricultural Adjustment Act of 1938. Thereafter, it continued to be an active participant in government-directed agricultural policy that influenced the daily lives of farm men and women. The 1938 act was the foundation for all succeeding price-support and acreage-adjustment programs. The act and its amendments also provided farmers with the economic support necessary to expand the size of their farms and to purchase new technology. The increased size of farms, however, meant that their number declined, and the new technology often contributed to the surplus production problem. Still, the New Deal years were a watershed for congressional action that changed the course of the federal government's relationship to agriculture.

During the 1930s, the American Farm Bureau Federation, under the leadership of Edward A. O'Neal, effectively supported the policy goals of the Department of Agriculture before Congress. The bureau efficiently and effectively brokered information to Congress, to challengers for congressional seats, and to voters. It served as a barometer of agricultural opinion, suggested policy, offered alternative policy choices, signaled the preferences of constituents, and on a nonpartisan basis supported those members of Congress who followed its advice. As a result, representatives and senators from the farm states endorsed the proposals of the farm lobby during the 1930s, especially those addressing levels of production. Surplus production and consequent low prices remained problems, and the executive branch and Congress continued to rely on the advice of the farm lobby to mitigate them with acreage allotments and price supports. Sen. John H. Bankhead 2d (D-Ala.), chairman of the Finance Committee, supported parity, mortgage adjustment, and other farm-related legislation. Sen. Ellison D. Smith (D-S.C.), chairman of the Committee on Agriculture, protected the interests of cotton farmers, while Sen. Arthur Capper of Kansas supported wheat growers. Representatives Marvin Jones (D-Tex.), chairman of the House Agriculture Committee, and Hampton P. Fulmer of South Carolina championed the needs of cotton and peanut farmers, while Rep. Clifford R. Hope (R-Kans.) became a staunch advocate of the wheat interests. These members were important congressional leaders who supported a variety of agricultural policies during the New Deal years, and they listened closely to the farm lobby for advice.

Congress had provided some federally financed agricultural credit for long-term loans through the federal land bank system with the Farm Loan Act of 1916, and it expanded agricultural credit through the Agricultural Credit Act of 1923. This legislation created twelve federal intermediate credit banks, which Congress authorized to make short-term loans to support agricultural cooperatives. Congress expanded this service with the Farm Credit Act of 1933, which authorized farmer-owned Production Credit Associations to make short- and intermediate-term loans and created a banking system to support the marketing, supply, and service operations of cooperatives. The Farm Credit banks, together with the Farmers Home Administration and the Commodity Credit Corporation, remained the primary federal moneylenders for the agricultural community.

Congress, following the executive branch's leadership, also created the Soil Conservation Service (SCS) on 27 April 1935. Although the agency's forerunner, known as the Soil Erosion Service, had operated in the Department of the Interior, Congress placed the SCS in the Department of Agriculture. The Soil Conservation Act of 1935 gave the SCS responsibility for conserving farmland nationwide. To inform farmers beyond the reach of SCS demonstration projects about the best soil conservation practices, Undersecretary of Agriculture M. L. Wilson urged Congress to pass the Standard State Soil Conservation District Law as an organizational model for the state soil conservation districts. President Roosevelt signed this legislation on 27 February 1937. The statute encouraged state governments and local groups to organize soil conservation districts. The federal government would then help them establish a conservation program and provide trained personnel to instruct the district members about the best soil conservation practices.

Congress also passed the Bankhead-Jones Farm Tenant Act, which the president approved on 22 July 1937. This legislation created the Farm Security Administration (FSA), which replaced the Resettlement Administration, established by executive order on 30 April 1935. The FSA granted loans to farmers who could not qualify for credit at other lending institutions. FSA loans could be used to purchase livestock feed, seed, implements, food, clothing, and land in order to help keep agriculturists on their farms until better economic times returned. The FSA also continued the submarginal land purchase program of the Resettlement Administration as well as the relocation of some destitute farmers on federal lands in areas more suited for agriculture. Southern members of Congress resented the FSA because it provided aid to tenant farmers and sharecroppers, many of whom they believed were no longer needed in agriculture and who usually did not vote or contribute to political campaigns. These members of Congress preferred that federal funds be used to aid the landowners whose financial support and votes they needed at election time.

After World War II began, surplus agricultural production and credit were no longer problems. Even before the United States entered that conflict, Congress guaranteed farmers that they would benefit from high wartime prices when, on 1 July 1941,

Congress increased the price support loan rate to as high as 85 percent of parity for basic commodities with the Steagall amendment to the bill that extended the life of the Commodity Credit Corporation.

As farm prices increased behind the federal loan rate and given high wartime demands, consumers complained about exorbitant food prices, and members of Congress responded to the complaints of their constituents. In January 1942, Congress passed the Emergency Price Control Act, which placed a ceiling on farm prices at not less than 110 percent of parity or below certain prices received on various dates. On 2 October Congress amended this legislation with the Stabilization Act. This measure required the federal government to support twenty commodities at 90 percent of parity for two years after the conclusion of the war in order to protect farmers against a possible rapid postwar price collapse similar to what had occurred in 1920.

The farm lobby—the Farm Bureau, the Grange, the Farmers Union, and other agricultural organizations—pressured Congress for this legislation. Because of these lobbying efforts, wartime price support policy proved highly beneficial to farmers, enabling many of them to enjoy a prosperity that they had never before known. High prices and substantially improved income reaffirmed the belief of many farmers that agriculture provided the economic backbone of the nation and a way of life morally superior to that of those who did not earn a living from the land. After the war, the influence of the farm lobby remained strong in Congress because it accurately reflected the wishes and needs of farmers, whose votes were still crucial in many states.

The Early Postwar Years. After the war ended, Congress debated whether to retain high wartime price supports or return to the prewar system of flexible price supports linked to production or existing supplies. Members of Congress from the Great Plains and the South favored high price supports. However, the Farm Bureau, under new president Allan B. Kline, feared that high price supports would ruin the market for corn farmers and so changed its position to advocate flexible price supports geared to production. This policy shift divided the membership of the Farm Bureau and angered farmers in general. Meanwhile, the Truman administration, represented by Secretary of Agriculture Clinton P. Anderson, advocated slightly reduced price supports on some commodities to lower food prices.

Under the leadership of Rep. Clifford R. Hope (R-Kans.) and Sen. George D. Aiken (R-Vt.), Congress reached a compromise between high and flexible price support proposals in the Agricultural Act of 1948. This legislation maintained high, fixed price supports for one year, after which flexible support prices would go into effect. Basic commodities such as wheat, corn, rice, cotton, tobacco, peanuts, potatoes, hogs, chickens, eggs, and milk would receive price supports at 90 percent of parity through the 1950 crop year. Congress also changed the price support index for determining parity from the base period of 1910–1914 to one dependent on the relationship between farm and nonfarm prices during the previous decade. In 1948, the farm vote endorsed a high price support policy. Many Republicans who had supported the Farm Bureau's policy of lower price supports lost their seats. Democratic members of Congress interpreted the election to mean that the Farm Bureau no longer spoke for the majority of farmers, and the bureau lost influence—that is, it lost access to Congress.

In 1950, the Korean War and Democratic party opposition to flexible price supports caused Congress to postpone the implementation of a reduced agricultural spending program. Instead, Congress passed the Defense Production Act of 1950, which required full parity prices for agricultural products if wartime price controls were implemented; otherwise, mandatory price supports remained at 90 percent of parity for basic commodities. When the Korean War ended, however, Congress feared surplus production and began once again to debate the respective merits of high, fixed, and flexible price supports.

On 11 January 1954, President Dwight D. Eisenhower asked Congress to approve a flexible price support program based on supply. He also urged Congress to expand agricultural exports in order to reduce price-depressing surpluses. After bitter debate, Congress responded in the summer by passing the Agricultural Trade Development and Assistance Act, known as Public Law 480, on 10 July 1954. This legislation authorized the federal government to sell surplus agricultural commodities abroad for foreign currency and to use agricultural surpluses for emergency food aid to friendly and underdeveloped nations. In addition, Congress in August 1954 adopted a flexible price support plan for major crops to help reduce overproduction, but Congress greatly restricted the administration's power to control production and price supports.

Despite the flexible price support program, by the mid 1950s farmers were continuing to produce far more food than was needed domestically by using a package, or systems, approach to farming that inte-grated the use of hybrid seeds, chemical fertilizers, and new technology. High price supports and the federal extension network supported this practice. Congress in 1956 again attempted to resolve the problem of surplus production. In May, it turned to a new agricultural policy with the Agricultural Act of 1956. Informally known as the Soil Bank Program, this two-part plan authorized the government to remove land from production by renting it from farmers. Under the first part, the short-term Acreage Reserve Program enabled participating farmers to receive payments for reducing the amount of land that they planted in basic crops. In contrast to previous legislation, however, they were not allowed to plant the idled acreage with other crops. In the second part, the Conservation Reserve Program, all farmers could divert land to a long-term conservation reserve. Essentially, Congress provided that farmers could be paid for reducing their allotted acreage of certain crops if they used those acres for conservation purposes rather than for other crops. The Soil Bank Program proved more expensive than Congress had anticipated, and it did not reduce production. Moreover, leaders in rural communities complained that idled farmland ruined the local economy. Consequently, Congress abandoned the program in 1959.

During the late 1950s, Democratic members of Congress continued to advocate high price support policies with production controls and direct payments to farmers to maintain adequate agricultural incomes. Republicans in Congress supported reduced federal expenditures for agricultural programs, market expansion, and decreased government interference in agriculture. By 1960, however, technology and science had defeated congressional efforts to reduce surplus production and increase market prices. Furthermore, Congress was becoming increasingly concerned with urban problems and swayed by the consumer movement's opposition to price support programs because price supports increased food prices. Urban members of Congress increasingly criticized high expenditures to aid farmers whose declining numbers substantially decreased their political power. As a result, congressional farm policy no longer remained the sole concern of farmers, particularly after the Supreme Court ruled in 1964 that congressional districts had to be apportioned according to population. That ruling gave increased congressional representation to urban areas and decreased the number of rural representatives.

The 1960s and 1970s. President John F. Kennedy, inaugurated in January 1961, favored mandatory production controls to decrease surplus production and high price supports to maintain adequate farm income. Neither Congress nor the farm lobby supported mandatory controls, but on 22 March 1961, Congress gave Secretary of Agriculture Orville L. Freeman the authority to initiate a payment-in-kind program (expanded in 1983) to address Kennedy's goals while keeping agricultural policy costs from escalating. The payment-in-kind program enabled farmers who raised corn and grain sorghum, and later other grains, to reduce their acreage by 20 percent and to receive the price support rate on 50 percent of their normal yield in the form of negotiable certificates. Congress authorized the Commodity Credit Corporation (CCC) to redeem those notes with grain from its stores, which farmers could then sell, hence the payment-in-kind designation. Under this program, most farmers did not actually receive grain for reducing their production; rather, they allowed the CCC to market it for them. With the Agricultural Act of 1961, Congress also approved a food stamp program and an expanded school lunch program to help increase the consumption of agricultural commodities, reduce surpluses, and maintain adequate price levels.

By 1965, partisanship over agricultural policy began to fade as both Democratic and Republican members of Congress turned their attention to voluntary rather than mandatory acreage reduction for basic commodities while still favoring high price supports. Members continued to support agricultural programs that aided their constituents, but they now listened primarily to specialized commodity groups for information, advice, and political direction. If they determined that their constituents would benefit from a particular agricultural program, they supported it. If, however, a program did not affect their constituents, they usually followed the party leadership.

Congress consolidated and expanded its agricultural programs with the Food and Agriculture Act of 3 November 1965. The act's title indicated that Congress now had agricultural concerns that went beyond farmers to include consumers and that it was using Department of Agriculture programs to aid other constituencies and communities. The law provided voluntary acreage controls for certain basic commodities, with price supports established near world market levels, and economic development programs to fight rural poverty. In contrast to previous short-term legislation that usually covered just one crop year, Congress now extended its agri-

cultural program to encompass a four-year period. This policy ended the annual fighting over a farm bill, and it remained effective through 1970 because, although presidential administrations did change in 1969, the executive branch did not have time to prepare a new farm bill.

In 1970, the Nixon administration's secretary of Agriculture, Clifford M. Hardin, asked Congress to adopt a more market-oriented agricultural policy by expanding exports, reducing government costs, and decreasing planted acreage. Farm groups, however, demanded the maintenance of high price supports, and Congress complied in the Agriculture Act of 1970. The act required farmers to set aside or withdraw a specific number of acres from the production of specified crops and to devote that acreage to conservation. Farmers then could produce any commodity in any amount, except those covered by marketing quotas. Congress also mandated that no farm could receive more than $55,000 per year for participation in price support or acreage diversion programs.

During the 1970s, world crop shortages, a falling dollar, and increased foreign demand for American agricultural commodities helped expand exports and deplete government reserves. Congress responded on 10 August 1973 with the passage of the Agriculture and Consumer Protection Act. This legislation authorized flexible production, and it limited price support payments for grain and cotton farmers to $20,000 annually. It also replaced the concept of price supports with payments (called deficiency payments) based on target prices. The federal government now paid farmers whenever commodity prices dropped below a target price. Congress based target prices on the parity formula of previous programs. Beginning with the 1976 crop year, however, target prices would be linked to an index of production costs based on consideration of tax levies, interest rates, and wages paid plus other operating costs. Although the 1973 act departed from the agricultural policy of the past, the Agricultural Adjustment Act of 1938 still remained in effect and gave the secretary of Agriculture standby authority to return to producer referenda for establishing marketing quotas and to institute the price support systems of the past.

The Reagan Administration and After. By 1980, consumer food prices had increased rapidly, and Congress refused to raise most agricultural price supports even though farmers still suffered from low prices. When President Ronald Reagan assumed office in 1981, Secretary of Agriculture

John R. Block urged Congress to help solve the budget deficit problem by increasing agricultural exports and reducing price support payments. Farm groups, however, wanted a continuation of existing price support programs and protection from embargoes such as President Jimmy Carter had imposed against the Soviet Union in 1980 after its invasion of Afghanistan. Congress responded by reducing agricultural spending in the Agriculture and Food Act of 1981 through limitation of agricultural payments to $50,000 per farm and expansion of commodity donations abroad under Public Law 480. The act also provided some protection against embargoes by requiring the secretary of Agriculture to compensate farmers, in certain circumstances, at the rate of 100 percent of parity for financial losses incurred during times of economic sanction. All farm groups except the Farm Bureau, the largest farm organization, opposed this legislation, a clear indication that members of Congress no longer relied on a unified farm lobby for advice and support.

The worst agricultural depression since the 1930s, together with overproduction, low prices, and high government costs, continued to plague Congress through the 1980s. Members of Congress once again tried to resolve these problems on a bipartisan basis with the Food Security Act of 23 December 1985. This statute attempted to maintain farm income while cutting costs. Congress reduced target prices over five years, bringing price supports closer to market prices and thereby reducing government spending for agriculture. This act also authorized acreage reductions when commodity supplies became excessive, but it failed to help many farmers earn an income sufficient to keep them in agriculture.

In 1990, the old problems of overproduction and low prices remained. That year, Congress once again attempted to address the farm problem with the Food, Agriculture, Conservation, and Trade Act. The act continued the general policies of the past by maintaining loan rates tied to market prices and by preserving price supports through target prices, but it also increased environmental regulations. This legislation, however, still did not enable Congress to balance supply and demand, support an adequate income for farmers, or keep federal expenditures low. Moreover, Congress scaled back price supports beyond what the farm lobby advocated.

Postwar Agricultural Policy: A Summary. The agricultural programs approved by Congress changed relatively little from 1933 to 1992. Con-gressional policy has attempted to support prices through acreage reductions, marketing quotas, and target prices. Before the 1950s, Congress tended to set relatively high price supports that became mandatory on the approval of the various commodity producers. After the early 1950s, Congress linked price support payments to the marketplace, and acreage reductions became voluntary within the various programs. In addition, Congress fell increasingly under the influence of urban constituents, particularly after World War II. With farmers comprising less than 2 percent of the population, the agricultural community no longer exercised great political power, although certain farm and commodity groups remained effective lobbyists for specific programs. Still, the diversity of farmers precluded a unified voice. By the twentieth century, farmers were specialized and therefore came to Congress with different needs. Policies that would benefit grain farmers, for example, would hurt dairy and poultry farmers who needed cheap feeds. As a result, given the complicated and varied nature of agriculture, policy proposals became the domain of the experts in the Department of Agriculture and the farm lobby. By the late twentieth century, senators and representatives from farm states also had to compromise with urban members of Congress to win support for major agricultural legislation. Urban members often approved support payments to farmers in exchange for rural congressional support for food stamps and other social service programs.

Democratic-controlled Congresses and Republican presidents often clashed over agricultural policy after World War II. Republican members of Congress usually favored removing federal involvement in agriculture by allowing the marketplace to dictate demand and prices and thereby to influence production and supply. Democratic members often advocated government intervention to achieve economic and social ends in agricultural and rural communities. Members from both parties relied heavily on the president and the secretary of Agriculture to recommend farm legislation, but they did not automatically approve administration proposals. Often they rejected suggestions for policy changes based on a host of political considerations and the advice of commodity organizations. Moreover, Congress usually treated new agricultural laws as amendments to previous acts.

The basic features of congressional agricultural policy after 1970 were export expansion, measures to increase food consumption domestically, ex-

Landmark Legislation

Title	Year Enacted	Reference Number	Description
Department of Agriculture	1862	12 Stat. 387	Created the U.S. Department of Agriculture, a non–cabinet level department authorized to collect and publish statistical information; collect and distribute new seeds, plants, and animals to farmers; test agricultural technology; and conduct scientific experiments.
Homestead Act	1862	12 Stat. 392	Provided 160 acres, called a quarter section, of public domain to farmers in the trans-Mississippi West. If settlers lived on the land and cultivated the soil, they could gain title to it at no cost after five years; or, after six months of residence, a settler could commute (i.e., purchase) that land for $1.25 per acre.
Morrill Land-Grant College Act	1862	12 Stat. 503	Provided each state with public land or script to support the founding of an agricultural college.
Hatch Act	1887	24 Stat. 440	Created nationwide experiment-station system; authorized annual appropriations to states that agreed to support agricultural research.
Second Morrill Land-Grant College Act	1890	26 Stat. 417	Authorized federal funding for the land-grant colleges and prohibited racial discrimination at those institutions. Eventually, seventeen states used federal funds authorized under this act to support separate institutions of higher education for African American students.
Newlands Reclamation Act	1902	P.L. 57-161	Authorized the construction of federal irrigation projects on the public lands of sixteen western states; established the Reclamation Service, which became the Bureau of Reclamation in 1923.
Smith-Lever Act	1914	P.L. 63-95	Authorized federal aid to help the states disseminate practical information about agriculture and home economics through instruction and demonstrations for farm men and women who did not attend land-grant colleges. State appropriations were to match the federal funds for that work.
Smith-Hughes Act	1917	P.L. 64-347	Created the Federal Board of Vocational Education; provided federal funds to support the teaching of agriculture and home economics in public high schools.
Capper-Volstead Cooperative Marketing Act	1922	P.L. 67-146	Enabled cooperatives to pool resources and eliminate competition for the enhancement of marketing without violating the Clayton Antitrust Act of 1914.
Agricultural Marketing Act	1929	P.L. 71-10	Established the Federal Farm Board to support agricultural cooperatives with federal funds; authorized stabilization corporations to remove surplus commodities from the marketplace through federal purchases.
Agricultural Adjustment Act	1933	P.L. 73-10	Authorized acreage reduction for basic commodities to reduce surplus production, increase prices, and improve agricultural income; created the Agricultural Adjustment Administration, which paid farmers to reduce their planted acreage. The U.S. Supreme Court held this act unconstitutional in 1936.

Landmark Legislation (Continued)

Title	Year Enacted	Reference Number	Description
Tennessee Valley Authority Act	1933	P.L. 73-17	Authorized a massive flood control program for the Tennessee River Valley; made possible the production of hydroelectric power and nitrate fertilizer, as well as reforestation for the agricultural benefit of Appalachia.
Taylor Grazing Act	1934	P.L. 73-482	Prohibited further sales of the public domain but provided for the lease of western range lands for controlled grazing; administered by the Department of the Interior.
Soil Conservation Act	1935	P.L. 46-74	Provided federal financial and technical support for the prevention and control of soil erosion and directed the secretary of Agriculture to establish the Soil Conservation Service.
Soil Conservation and Domestic Allotment Act	1936	P.L. 74-461	Replaced the Agricultural Adjustment Act of 1933 by providing federal aid to farmers who planted soil-conserving instead of soil-depleting crops. The intent remained to increase farm income and decrease production.
Rural Electrification Act	1936	P.L. 74-605	Authorized the Rural Electrification Administration to loan funds to cooperatives for financing the construction of power lines, the wiring of homes, and the purchase or generation of electricity for rural residents.
Agricultural Adjustment Act	1938	P.L. 75-430	Institutionalized the conservation provisions of the Soil Conservation and Domestic Allotment Act of 1936 and established programs for production control, price supports, and benefit payments; new policy features included the provision of marketing quotas under certain circumstances and crop insurance. In the following decades it remained the foundation of agricultural policy.
Emergency Price Control Act	1942	P.L. 77-421	Guaranteed high prices at not less than 110 percent of parity to ensure that farmers benefited from high wartime demands. Amended on 2 October 1942 to extend high price supports for two years after the war to prevent a postwar price collapse.
National School Lunch Act	1946	P.L. 79-396	Provided funds and food to support the school lunch program in public and private schools; intended to help reduce surplus commodities as well as improve the diet of school children.
Farmers Home Administration Act	1946	P.L. 79-731	Abolished the Farm Security Administration and created the Farmers Home Administration to assume its authority for making rehabilitation loans to farmers who could not qualify for credit with other lending institutions.
Agricultural Trade Development and Assistance Act	1954	P.L. 83-480	Provided for the disposal of surplus agricultural commodities abroad as foreign and emergency aid.
Soil Bank Act	1956	P.L. 84-540	Authorized soil bank programs designed to reduce production by removing lands from production so that they could be used for conservation purposes.

Landmark Legislation (Continued)

TITLE	YEAR ENACTED	REFERENCE NUMBER	DESCRIPTION
Food Stamp Act	1964	P.L. 88-525	Authorized the secretary of Agriculture to administer a food stamp program on the request of an appropriate state agency; designed to improve nutrition among low-income households and to utilize food surpluses for the benefit of the agricultural economy.
Food and Agriculture Act	1965	P.L. 89-321	Consolidated and expanded previous agricultural programs and set agricultural policy for four years, thereby eliminating the annual political fighting over farm bills and bringing greater stability to the planning and administrative processes for agricultural programs.
Food Security Act	1985	P.L. 99-198	Established farm policy for five years; continued target prices, specified acreage reductions, authorized erosion controls and wetlands conservation, and gave the secretary of Agriculture broad powers to implement commodity programs.
Food, Agriculture, Conservation and Trade Act	1990	P.L. 101-624	Established a five-year, market-oriented policy; continued the price, income support, and acreage reduction programs of the past with various modifications; contained provisions for the food stamp program, organic food standards, and rural development. Title XXIV created the Climate Change Program in the Department of Agriculture.

panded foreign aid, the establishment of support prices near world levels for basic commodities, direct income payments to farmers participating in production control programs, target prices, deficiency payments, and acreage controls and voluntary production control programs linked to payments and specific loan rates.

None of the government programs after 1933, when Congress first succeeded in approving major agricultural policy, solved the problem of overproduction and low prices. Still, Congress helped contain productivity and stabilize prices, thereby benefiting the farm community, while ensuring adequate production of food and fiber. Congress also achieved compromises acceptable to both private and public interest groups. Congressional agricultural policy was expensive, and it contributed to environmental abuse and increased food prices while driving many small-scale farmers from the land. Yet the recurring problems of surplus production and low prices made Congress unwilling to abandon the price support and acreage reduction programs of the past. Congress's aims remained those of protecting farm income from precipitous de-

cline, maintaining an adequate standard of living, and controlling surplus production. For American agricultural policy, the past continued to serve as prologue.

[*See also* Agricultural Adjustment Acts; Agriculture Committee, House; Agriculture, Nutrition, and Forestry Committee, Senate; Farm Bloc; Hatch Act; Homestead Act; Morrill Land-Grant College Act; Tobacco.]

BIBLIOGRAPHY

Abler, David G. "Vote Trading on Farm Legislation in the U.S. House." *American Journal of Agricultural Economics* 71 (1989): 583–591.

Barton, Weldon V. "Coalition-Building in the United States House of Representatives: Agricultural Legislation in 1973." In *Cases in Public Policy-Making.* Edited by James E. Anderson. 1976.

Benedict, Murray R. *Farm Policies of the United States, 1790–1950: A Study of Their Origins and Development.* 1953.

Blaisdell, Donald C. *Government and Agriculture: The Growth of Federal Farm Aid.* 1940.

Bonnen, James T. "Observations on the Nature of National Agricultural Policy Decision Processes, 1946–76." In

Farmers, Bureaucrats, and Middlemen. Edited by Trudy Huskamp Peterson. 1980.

Bowers, Douglas E., Wayne D. Rasmussen, and Gladys L. Baker. *History of Agricultural Price-Support and Adjustment Programs, 1933–84.* 1984.

Browne, William P. *Private Interests, Public Policy, and American Agriculture.* 1988.

Campbell, Christiana McFayden. *The Farm Bureau and the New Deal: A Study of the Making of National Farm Policy, 1933–40.* 1962.

Christensen, Reo M. *The Brannan Plan: Farm Politics and Policy.* 1959.

Cochrane, Willard W., and Mary E. Ryan. *American Farm Policy, 1948–1973.* 1976.

Fite, Gilbert C. *George N. Peek and the Fight for Farm Parity.* 1954.

Frejohn, John A. "Logrolling in an Institutional Context: A Case Study of Food Stamp Legislation." In *Congressional Policy Change.* Edited by Gerald C. Wright, Jr., Leroy N. Rieselbach, and Lawrence C. Dodd. 1986.

Hadwiger, Don F., and Ross B. Talbot, eds. *Food Policy and Farm Programs.* Proceedings of the Academy of Political Science, vol. 34. 1982.

Hadwiger, Don F., and William P. Browne. *The New Politics of Food.* 1978.

Hansen, John Mark. *Gaining Access: Congress and the Farm Lobby, 1919–1981.* 1991.

Jones, Charles O. "Representation in Congress: The Case of the House Agriculture Committee." *American Political Science Review* 55 (1961): 358–367.

Matusow, Allen J. *Farm Policies and Politics in the Truman Years.* 1967.

Meekhof, Ronald. *Farm Credit Programs for Agriculture.* 1984.

Paarlberg, Don. *American Farm Policy: A Case of Centralized Decision-Making.* 1964.

Pollack, Susan L., and Lori Lynch, eds. *Provisions of the Food, Agriculture, Conservation, and Trade Act of 1990.* 1991.

Schuyler, Michael W. "Politics of Change: The Battle for the Agricultural Adjustment Act of 1938." *Prologue* 15 (1983): 165–178.

Shapsmeier, Edward L., and Frederick H. Schapsmeier. "Farm Policy from FDR to Eisenhower: Southern Democrats and the Politics of Agriculture." *Agricultural History* 53 (1979): 352–371.

Stucker, Barbara C., and Keith J. Collins. *The Food Security Act of 1985: Major Provisions Affecting Commodities.* 1986.

Talbot, Ross B., and Don F. Hadwiger. *The Policy Process in American Agriculture.* 1968.

R. DOUGLAS HURT

AGRICULTURE COMMITTEE, HOUSE.

Established by Congress in 1820, the House Committee on Agriculture shapes the content of farm bills, which are among the most contentious pieces of legislation produced by Congress. These bills authorize the federal government to manage and regulate not only the farm sector of the economy but, increasingly, a broader range of policy issues pertaining to food and natural resources.

The House Agriculture Committee now has jurisdiction and oversight over federal agricultural programs involving adulteration of seeds, insect pests, protection of forest reserve birds and animals, agricultural-industrial chemistry, colleges and experiment and education extension services, economics and research production, marketing and price stabilization of agricultural products, animal industry and diseases, crop insurance and soil conservation, the dairy industry, entomology and plant quarantine, farm credit and security, forestry, human nutrition and home economics, meat and livestock inspection, plant industry, soils and agricultural engineering, and rural electrification.

Until the 1930s a laissez-faire attitude prevailed concerning the role of government in the economy. Federal support for farmers focused mainly on helping them increase production. The late 1920s saw high levels of farm debt and low farm prices and revenues due to a lack of demand for agricultural commodities. Parity—the idea that farm purchasing power (the amount of nonfarm goods and services farmers could buy after selling their produce) should equal urban purchasing power, as it did from 1910 to 1914—became the rallying cry of many farm groups and members of Congress.

The Roosevelt administration's New Deal farm policies attempted to assist farmers and manage the farm economy by expanding the role of the federal government in agriculture in ways rejected by previous administrations and Congresses. The Agricultural Adjustment Act of 1933 (later ruled unconstitutional) restricted production of seven basic crops. Commodity surpluses were distributed through state relief agencies. By executive order the federal Commodity Credit Corporation (CCC) funded nonrecourse loans to cotton and corn farmers. (Farmers could borrow a fixed amount of credit, using their crops as security. If prices fell below the loan value, the CCC kept the crop; if prices rose above it, the farmer paid off the loan and made a profit.) Later, soil conservation programs were used to cut production by reducing the acreage of soil-depleting crops. Marketing quotas also kept down production while farmers were paid to store crops.

These programs were supported in the House Agriculture Committee by the farm bloc, a voting coalition that used the structure and operations of the Agriculture Committee routinely to garner support for measures that benefited the commodity producers enrolled in these programs. Powerful southern Democratic members representing mainly peanut, cotton, and tobacco producers joined with midwestern Republicans representing mainly corn, wheat, and feed grain producers to sustain support for commodity programs and other relief measures. The farm bloc in the House Agriculture Committee allied itself with a variety of actors outside Congress to give producers what they wanted. These actors included farm organizations and the U.S. Department of Agriculture (USDA), which implemented federal farm programs. Until the late 1960s the House Agriculture Committee farm bloc had sufficient political strength to overcome partisan divisions and conflicts among commodity interests within the bloc, demands to cut farm program benefits, and any direct attacks on its own political influence.

After World War II the House Agriculture Committee helped generate measures to dispose of surplus commodities and maintain farm prices. The Agricultural Trade Development and Assistance Act of 1954 (P.L. 480), for instance, shipped food aid abroad both to acquire foreign currencies and to achieve a number of U.S. foreign policy objectives. Yet the Eisenhower administration only grudgingly supported a land diversion program that paid farmers not to produce. Land set-aside programs continued in the 1960s and were utilized again in the 1980s when market conditions worsened, necessitating congressional action.

By the late 1950s the farm population and the number of rural districts in the House had declined to the point where the farm bloc was vulnerable to attacks from congressional liberals, consumer advocates, and the hunger lobby. Their complaints focused on the expensive and exclusive farm programs stemming from the bloc's dominance of the Agriculture Committee. In 1958 Victor L. Anfuso (D-N.Y.) chaired special subcommittee hearings on food stamps. Not until the mid 1970s, however, was the farm bloc forced to logroll with a new coalition of consumer and food stamp interests to obtain their support for commodity programs. In the name of consumers, Peter A. Peyser (R-N.Y.) and Margaret M. Heckler (R-Mass.) led crusades against waste in federal farm subsidies. Later, in 1977, Frederick W. Richmond (D-N.Y.) used his position as chairman of the Subcommittee on Domestic Marketing, Consumer Relations, and Nutrition to champion the food stamp program.

Beginning with the Agricultural and Consumer Protection Act of 1973, farm and food legislation routinely reflected an accommodation of rural and urban interests. This legislation also abandoned the goal of parity but maintained price supports for basic commodities, even under improved market conditions. Many farmers purchased land and new machinery to increase production in response to crop shortages in less developed countries and greater demand in the industrialized countries for wheat and products dependent on feed grains. Deficiency payments were made to farmers on the basis of target prices set in relation to both domestic food prices and the competitiveness of U.S. farm products abroad.

In the late 1970s, surpluses returned and prices fell again as the result of a strong U.S. dollar, increasingly protectionist trade policies in Western Europe, and a U.S. grain embargo imposed on the Soviet Union for its invasion of Afghanistan. Many farm groups staged protests in Washington, D.C., and elsewhere in the nation. In the mid 1980s, farm debt reached record levels and farm foreclosures increased significantly.

Since 1981, faced with budget constraints, administrations have attempted to cut drastically the level of price supports for all commodities, especially for peanuts, tobacco, sugar, and feed grains—all subsidized at prices well above the world market level. The 1981 Agriculture and Food Act and the 1985 Food Security Act preserved price supports for most basic commodities and supported food stamps and other consumer-oriented programs. However, in an effort to make U.S. crops more competitive abroad, the 1985 bill lowered loan rates 25 percent for key commodities, froze target prices, and then gradually reduced them after two years. In short, pressure to cut government spending constrained a weakened farm bloc in the House Agriculture Committee. As a result the farm bloc found it increasingly necessary to ally with urban and western committee members to sustain commodity programs.

Structure and Operations. The House Agriculture Committee has a reputation for being more conservative than the full House. In the past most committee members (many of whom were farmers themselves) came from rural "safe" districts or from districts where farming was big business. Committee membership offered abundant opportunities to satisfy constituents. Since there are fewer strictly rural districts today, however, the committee is not an attractive assignment for as many members of Congress as it once was, and turnover rates have gone up.

Over the years the size of the committee gradually increased from twenty-seven members in the 80th Congress (1947–1949) to thirty-six members in the 88th Congress (1963–1965) to forty-two members in the 94th Congress (1975–1977). After the mid 1970s, southerners on the committee lost seats to midwestern, western, and a few eastern representatives. Along with a nationwide decline in the population of farmers, this shift reflected House leadership efforts to increase representation from liberal districts and from other than southern districts and to broaden the House Agriculture Committee's agenda, all of which gradually diffused the power of the farm bloc.

In the 103d Congress (1993–1995) the committee has forty-five members (twenty-seven Democrats, eighteen Republicans). However, the South regained the lead in seats with the largest share of members (31 percent), followed by the Midwest (27 percent), the West (24 percent), the border states (13 percent), and the East (2 percent, with only one member). Eastern state representation on the committee has decreased from 9 percent in the 89th Congress (1965–1967).

The House Agriculture Committee has been known for the longevity and southern roots of its leadership, both of which contributed to the success of the farm bloc in the committee. Many of the chairs came from southern "safe" districts whose farm constituents were targeted for farm commodity programs. Harold D. Cooley (D-N.C.), for instance, chaired the committee for sixteen years (1949–1953, 1955–1967). Since World War II there have been only six different chairs of the committee. In 1975, however, newly elected and younger Democrats helped overturn the seniority rule that made length of service the basis for selecting the committee chair. William R. Poage (D-Tex.), who chaired the committee from 1967 to 1975, was replaced by a liberal western representative, Thomas S. Foley (D-Wash.). E. "Kika" de la Garza (D-Tex.) has served in the position since 1981.

Since the early 1970s the House Agriculture Committee has followed the initiative of the Senate regarding administration omnibus farm-food bills, which have usually been introduced in the Senate Agriculture Committee every four or five years. However, the House Agriculture Committee normally takes the lead in initiating other farm and food policy measures.

Much of the committee's work is conducted in its six subcommittees (down from a peak of eighteen in the 85th Congress [1957–1959]). They are General Farm Commodities; Livestock; Specialty Crops and Natural Resources; Environment, Credit, and Rural Development; Department Operations and Nutrition; and Foreign Agriculture and Hunger. This division of labor represents a continued shift away from the narrow agenda of commodity producers to a broad range of farm and food policy interests.

Typically, subcommittees investigate those parts of a bill appropriate to their jurisdictions, conduct hearings, and draft legislation in consultation with the USDA (which works closely with producers and other groups). Hearings often educate members about issues being addressed in the bill and provide interest groups with an opportunity to make a case for or against a measure.

In the past, House Agriculture subcommittees have enjoyed a considerable degree of autonomy. Subcommittee working arrangements have usually been informal, with meetings conducted behind closed doors, becoming quite contentious at times. The structure and operation of subcommittees have encouraged members to represent their constituents to the fullest extent, often producing sharp conflicts among different regional, commodity, and partisan interests. After some cajoling by the leadership, members are expected to fall into line and support one another's favorite commodity programs. Coalition building usually rewards members with more comprehensive program support than each would otherwise have received for his or her own commodity; coalitions also help insulate the finished farm bill against attacks in the full committee or on the floor of the House. Very few major farm bills have been defeated on the House floor, although some have had unfriendly amendments added to them.

The full committee is charged with combining the separate pieces of legislation into a comprehensive or omnibus farm bill, but committee members may introduce amendments or specific bills of their own at any time. The expectation traditionally has been that subcommittee bills would be approved by the full committee and would go to the floor in much the same form as they emerged from the subcommittee. This has made it difficult for the committee chair to set legislative priorities and broker the many interests represented in any comprehensive farm bill. Thus, Foley earned the respect and admiration of his peers for fairly addressing the disparate parts of farm bills in full committee and for devising skillful ways of getting the patchwork pieces of the 1981 farm bill through the House and later through the House-Senate conference committee.

Relationships with Other Committees. House-Senate conferences are crucial for putting together a final bill. The House committee deals with its Senate counterpart both formally and informally. The formal House-Senate conferences, however, are the crucial setting for putting together a final bill. The House Agriculture Committee has the reputation of proposing lower expenditures for programs than the Senate committee. These differences in program spending levels are then thrashed out in closed-door conference sessions. Conference leaders have been known to trade votes or make deals with one another to produce a bill.

The House Appropriations Committee is also of great importance to the Agriculture Committee because the chair of the former's Subcommittee on Agriculture usually controls Commodity Credit Corporation spending for farm programs. At one time in the 1980s, Jamie L. Whitten (D-Miss.) chaired both the Appropriations Committee and its Agriculture Subcommittee, making him a central figure in farm legislation. Finally, the House Rules Committee is of strategic importance to the Agriculture Committee, since without a rule, a farm bill is not likely to be reported to the full House.

The House and Senate Agriculture Committees, along with commodity producer groups and their political organizations and the USDA, constitute a relatively influential farm-food policy network in which each player derives benefit from supporting the other. The House Agriculture Committee shares with the USDA much of the responsibility for drafting farm and food bills. The office of the secretary of Agriculture, in consultation with the USDA's Agricultural Stabilization and Conservation Service (which administers commodity programs), has originated most of the major farm bills over the last two decades. USDA officials serve as subcommittee witnesses; they are often loaned to the committee to help prepare it to receive and rule on presidential proposals. Likewise, discussions with the secretary of Agriculture also help the committee gauge the president's views on pending legislation.

Until the early 1970s, commodity groups—backed by the farm bloc—were often quite effective at shaping legislation. But the influence of such farm organizations as the National Farmers Union and American Farm Bureau Federation declined over the next twenty years. This decline reflects many factors, including a decrease in the number of farmers and the restructuring of congressional

districts in favor of urban interests; it also reflects budget constraints that produce major divisions within the farm organization community. Under these constraints the House Agriculture Committee has found it easier to avoid the pressures of general farm organizations.

The House Agriculture Committee also has connections with several other important groups, interests, and institutions that include agribusinesses, the media, the public, academics, and international interests. Most experts claim, however, that these only indirectly influence the legislative process.

Committee Performance. The House Agriculture Committee's current membership, structure, and operating procedures increasingly require it to look beyond commodity producer interests in order to pass legislation that incorporates a wider variety of national food and natural resource policy interests. The committee's relatively large size raises the level of conflict among members but also improves the chances that a farm bill will pass once it has cleared committee. Ironically, having more members on the committee weakened the old farm bloc but at the same time helped it survive, because political realities dictate that the farm bloc compromise with urban and other interests.

However, one can expect the House Agriculture Committee to come under closer scrutiny as budget constraints pressure representatives to cut farm programs significantly. In the past, supporters of the committee have praised it for passing legislation that helped preserve what remains of family farming and the rural sector. Farm programs have benefited a good many farmers, but they have also addressed the needs of consumers and those concerned about broader food policy issues.

However, the committee's detractors argue that the cost of farm-food programs has become exorbitant (averaging $20 billion a year throughout the 1980s), given the declining number of farmers and the fact that bigger and wealthier farmers receive the lion's share of program benefits. Critics charge that commodity programs have stimulated overproduction and merely generated demands for more support measures. Federal programs have raised food prices, which has lessened the competitiveness of U.S. produce abroad, hurt the balance of trade, and generated more demand for trade protectionism. Furthermore, legislation produced by the House Agriculture Committee still smacks of willful, if not malicious, abuses of power and influence. Reform is difficult to achieve, for the committee's structure and operations continue to encourage deal making and coalition building between rural and urban interests.

[*See also* Agriculture, Nutrition, and Forestry Committee, Senate; Farm Bloc; McNary-Haugen Farm Relief Bill.]

BIBLIOGRAPHY

Cochrane, Willard W., and Mary E. Ryan. *American Farm Policy: 1948–1973.* 1976.

Lyons, Michael S., and Marcia Whicker Taylor. "Farm Politics in Transition: The House Agriculture Committee." *Agricultural History* 55 (1981): 128–146.

Peters, John. "The 1977 Farm Bill: Coalitions in Congress." In *The New Politics of Food.* Edited by Don F. Hadwiger and William P. Browne. 1978. Pp. 23–35.

Saloutos, Theodore. *The American Farmer and the New Deal.* 1982.

Talbot, Ross B., and Don F. Hadwiger. *The Policy Process in American Agriculture.* 1968.

DAVID N. BALAAM

AGRICULTURE, NUTRITION, AND FORESTRY COMMITTEE, SENATE.

The first Senate Agriculture Committee was established in 1825 and terminated in 1857. A second committee was established in 1863; in 1884 its name was changed to the Committee on Agriculture and Forestry. In 1977 this committee absorbed the Senate Select Committee on Nutrition and Human Needs and became the Senate Agriculture, Nutrition, and Forestry Committee (commonly known as the Senate Agriculture Committee).

The Senate Agriculture Committee's jurisdiction parallels that of its House counterpart to some extent, especially with regard to oversight of agricultural credit; rural development and electrification development; the Rural Electrification Administration; development of policies concerning food, nutrition, and hunger; food inspection and certification; agricultural education and research; animal welfare; forestry; and soil conservation.

There are three major differences between the responsibilities of the Senate and House Agriculture committees. First, more so than its House counterpart, the Senate Agriculture Committee still categorizes some of the programs and activities under its jurisdiction as traditional farm policy issues. These responsibilities include agricultural commodities, marketing orders, crop insurance, price supports, agricultural product promotion and domestic marketing programs, and production adjustment programs. The House Agriculture Committee combines most of these responsibilities under the heading of "marketing and price stabilization of agricultural products." Second, the Senate Agriculture Committee lists more responsibilities pertaining to international trade and aid than does the House committee. These responsibilities include foreign agricultural trade, foreign market development, oversight of international commodity agreements and export controls on agricultural commodities, foreign assistance programs, and the Food for Peace (food aid) program. Finally, the Senate Agriculture Committee, in contrast to its House counterpart, has recently added to its responsibilities flood control and watershed erosion.

Like its House counterpart, the Senate committee's jurisdiction has broadened over the years as the federal government has firmly involved itself in the management and regulation of farm programs, beginning with New Deal farm support measures in the 1930s. Since then, the Senate committee has joined with the House committee in authorizing a variety of programs involving limits on crop production, loans, food price and farm income support, and the disposal of U.S. commodities abroad through international trade or foreign aid channels.

As in the case of the House Agriculture Committee, these programs have been routinely supported in the Senate Agriculture Committee by a farm bloc whose members formed a voting coalition and logrolled with each other in support of commodity programs and other farm policy measures. Until the 1960s most Senate Agriculture Committee members came from either southern, Democratic party–dominated peanut-, tobacco-, and cotton-producing states or from midwestern wheat- and feed grain–producing states.

In the 1960s the farm bloc gradually lost some of its influence on the Senate committee because of an ongoing decline in the number of farmers and changes in the structure of agriculture that resulted in fewer traditional family farms and fewer but larger mechanized capital-intensive farms (agribusinesses). In the 1970s the Senate Agriculture Committee broadened its agenda to deal more often with urban and suburban liberal consumer concerns such as food stamps, nutrition, and natural resource issues. Now faced with serious budget constraints, the committee generates legislation that usually emerges from coalition building among rural, urban, farm, and national food policy interests.

Structure, Operations, and Culture. In the 89th Congress (1965–1967), southerners and midwesterners together accounted for 70 percent of the seats on the committee. Easterners and westerners each made up 11 percent of the committee, while border states held 6 percent of seats. However, since the 89th Congress there has been a steady decline in the number of southern members, from 47 percent to 28 percent in the 103d Congress (1993–1995). Although not a majority in the committee, in the 103d Congress midwesterners regained their former status of having the largest percentage of seats on the committee—44 percent, up from 41 percent in the 99th Congress (1985–1987). Western representation on the committee remained steady between the 89th and 103d Congresses at approximately 11 percent, while easterners dropped in number from 12 to 6 percent. Altogether, in the 103d Congress the Senate Agriculture Committee has eighteen members, or four more than it did in the 92d Congress (1971–1973), a significant increase of 29 percent.

Despite the decline in southern members and loss of Democratic control over southern states, the farm bloc has remained more entrenched in the Senate Agriculture Committee than in the House Agriculture Committee. The farm bloc wields greater influence in the Senate partly because most senators have more farm and agribusiness constituents than do most representatives and because single-interest commodity groups among these constituents can make or break an election bid. More important, the less populated, more rural-oriented farm states are better represented in the Senate, where each state gets two votes, than in the House, where rural districts have steadily decreased in number. In fact, in their study of committees, Steven S. Smith and Christopher J. Deering (*Committees in Congress*, 1990) found that the Agriculture Committee is the Senate's most constituency-oriented committee.

The overrepresentation of farms in the Senate made it difficult for the various presidential administrations and the consumer movement to influence the Senate farm bloc in any significant way. In the 1970s the Senate Agriculture Committee lagged behind the House Agriculture Committee when it came to congressional efforts to make these committees more responsive to nonfarm interests, which would either broaden the appeal or check the erosion of support for agriculture legislation. Yet because of its smaller size, the Senate Agriculture Committee, after time, found it easier to balance commodity group with urban consumer interests in farm and food bills than did its House counterpart. Under Chairman Herman E. Talmadge

(D-Ga., 1971–1981), the committee was able to produce legislation that rewarded commodity groups and urban special interests for supporting each other. Selection in 1987 of eastern liberal senator Patrick J. Leahy (D-Vt.) to chair the committee signaled committee support for broader consumer, urban, and national food policies.

Because Senate bills are more likely to reflect a favorable balance between rural and urban states than House bills, the Senate Agriculture Committee is usually chosen by each administration to introduce its omnibus farm bill every four or five years. In addition, committee members may amend or introduce legislation of their own at any time.

The committee's small size helps it to function well as a unit. Commodities tend to be represented by individual senators as opposed to specific subcommittees, as is commonly the case in the House Agriculture Committee. Currently, for example, commodity champions include Bob Dole (R-Kans.), wheat and feedgrains; Jesse Helms (R-N.C.), tobacco; and David Pryor (D-Ark.) and Howell Heflin (D-Ala.), cotton.

In the 103d Congress the Senate Agriculture Committee's six subcommittees (one less than in the previous session) are organized mainly along functional lines. They are Agricultural Credit; Agricultural Production and Stabilization of Prices (which oversees commodity programs); Agricultural Research, Conservation, Forestry, and General Liquidation; Domestic and Foreign Marketing and Product Promotion; Nutrition and Investigations; and Rural Development and Rural Electrification.

Because senators serve on more committees (an average of 11) and subcommittees than do representatives, it is usually difficult for them to match the expertise of House subcommittee members in specialized areas. Therefore, senators usually must rely on committee staffers more than do representatives. Consequently, these staffers become more involved and experienced in Senate committee operations than their counterparts in the House. However, a number of senators have developed a reputation for expertise in their work on the Senate Agriculture Committee. These have included George McGovern (D-S.Dak.), Hubert H. Humphrey (D-Minn.), Herman E. Talmadge (D-Ga.), and more recently, Walter D. Huddleston (D-Ky.), Bob Dole, and Thad Cochran (R-Miss.).

Senate subcommittee chairmen are not as powerful as House subcommittee chairmen, nor do they dominate their turf as much as do their House counterparts. Indeed, subcommittee meetings have been known to be unattended by chairmen or important members. Working arrangements are usually informal, and debates can be quite lively, although not as contentious as those in House Agriculture subcommittees. Senate subcommittee members investigate problems, conduct hearings, and often deliberate issues as much on the Senate floor as in subcommittee. As with their House counterparts, the Senate subcommittees' most intense period of work comes every four or five years, when they introduce separate pieces of legislation that are then combined to form a comprehensive, or omnibus, farm bill.

Committee partisanship usually reflects the ratio of Democrats to Republicans in the committee. Since World War II, Republicans have controlled the committee only from 1953 to 1954 and from 1981 to 1986. The 1980 election brought five new Republicans and four new Democrats to the committee, a significant number of new members. Helms replaced Talmadge as committee chairman. Helms was known for his opposition to the food stamp program, and his position as chairman raised questions about his ability to produce a farm bill that balanced rural and urban interests. As was so often the case, however, blatant vote trading easily overrode partisan loyalties; committee members logrolled with one another and produced a legislative package that seemed to satisfy commodity producers as well as consumer and "hunger lobby" interests.

In 1985 the Reagan administration again tried to make the cost of farm programs a partisan issue. But a number of Republican senators who faced reelection in 1986 were torn between supporting farm programs and backing the president's desire to cut them significantly. When it looked as though farm bloc interests would be severely slighted, Senator Dole used his position as majority leader and his position on the Finance Committee (which appropriates funds for farm-food programs) to manage legislation in such a way that Republican senators could easily support farm programs: Dole made deals with Democrats to support their rice, sugar, corn, and soybean programs in exchange for their support of Republican wheat and feed grain programs. Then in conference he joined House Democrats against the administration in supporting a government herd buyout program to help dairy farmers by purchasing their excess cows. The Agriculture Committee chairman Patrick Leahy also engaged in vote trading, when he accepted a number of riders to his farm bill to ensure support for that legislation.

Leahy's vote trading demonstrates the importance of committee leadership skill in ushering farm bills through the Senate and on through House-Senate conferences. The Senate committee is known for recommending higher levels of support for farm programs than its House counterpart. During negotiations with the House committee, program spending is usually reduced to levels below Senate recommendations. In these negotiations, leaders representing both committees are known to make deals with each other to establish funding levels for the various programs that would satisfy both supporters of those programs and the president.

When it comes to appropriation for farm programs, the Senate and House Agriculture committees must also work together. In addition to working with the Senate Finance Committee, the Senate Agriculture Committee must also deal with the House Appropriations Committee. In the 1980s the Senate Agriculture Committee found it as difficult as did the House Agriculture Committee to deal with Rep. Jamie L. Whitten (D-Miss.). He chaired both the House Appropriations Committee and its Subcommittee on Agriculture and thus controlled the Department of Agriculture's funding of farm and food programs. In the late 1980s the leadership of the Senate Agriculture Committee made a concerted effort to legislate CCC funding while bypassing Whitten, but their efforts proved unsuccessful.

Relationships to Other Groups. In conjunction with the legislative responsibilities it shares with its House counterpart, the Senate Agriculture Committee is a member of the farm-food policy coalition that connects Congress to producer groups and the U.S. Department of Agriculture (USDA). Even though commodity producer organizations and their political action committees are less influential than they were through the 1960s, they still make concerted efforts to influence senators. And whereas representatives on the House Agriculture Committee are generally more accessible to their constituents than their Senate counterparts, lobbyists representing a variety of interests have achieved some success working through Senate subcommittees. For instance, as chairman of the Nutrition Subcommittee, George McGovern (D-S.Dak.) was quite receptive to the hunger lobby and to those concerned about such matters as the commercial agriculture industry, nutrition, health, and food additives.

Senators also get political support and a good deal of information about programs from the USDA, especially when omnibus farm bills are under consideration. A good number of senators have developed relationships with a number of executive agencies charged with regulating trade or developing export markets for U.S. agricultural commodities and products. These agencies include not only the USDA but also the Department of Commerce and, in particular, the Office of the Special Trade Representative. Officials from these agencies routinely testify at committee hearings. Key senators have been known to visit or receive foreign dignitaries in conjunction with pending trade agreements or legislation that impacts sales of U.S. agricultural commodities.

Finally, a number of committee members have played a major role in promoting food aid abroad as part of an effort to dispose of surplus commodities and at the same time achieve a variety of political and economic foreign policy objectives. In the 1950s and 1960s, Public Law 480 (the Agricultural Trade and Development Act of 1954) and the Food for Peace aid program accounted for a sizable proportion of commodities shipped abroad.

Committee Performance.   Given that the constituency of a Senate Agriculture Committee member is usually larger than the constituency of a House member (i.e., states are generally bigger than legislative districts), commodity producers and agribusinesses expect the Senate Agriculture Committee to be more responsive to their needs than the House Committee is. This has made it easier for the farm bloc to sustain its influence on the Senate committee than on the House committee.

Yet over the years the environment of the Senate Agriculture Committee has changed to reflect shifts in the structure of farming along with growing urban and consumer concern over a number of national food policy issues. Entering into the twenty-first century, the committee's agenda is likely to encompass a still wider variety of nonfarm interests. As is also the case with the House committee, budget constraints are likely to produce even more public scrutiny of the Senate committee and its legislation, necessitating further coalition building and logrolling on the part of committee members.

[See also Agriculture Committe, House; Farm Bloc; McNary-Haugen Farm Relief Bill.]

BIBLIOGRAPHY

Browne, William P. *Private Interests, Public Policy, and American Agriculture.* 1988.
Hansen, John Mark. *Gaining Access: Congress and the Farm Lobby, 1919–1981.* 1991.
Knutson, Ronald, J. B. Penn, and William Boehm. *Agricultural and Food Policy.* 1983.
Moyer, H. Wayne, and Tim E. Josling. *Agricultural Policy Reform: Politics and Process in the EC and the USA.* 1990.
Paarlberg, Don. *American Farm Policy.* 1964.
Peters, John. "The 1981 Farm Bill." In *Food Policy and Farm Programs.* Edited by Don Hadwiger and Ross B. Talbot. 1982. Pp. 157–170.
Porter, Laurellen. "Congress and Agricultural Policy." In *The New Politics of Food.* Edited by Don F. Hadwiger and William P. Browne. 1978. Pp. 15–22.
Smith, Steven S., and Christopher J. Deering. *Committees in Congress.* 1990.

DAVID N. BALAAM

AIR FORCE. Following the important contribution by the U.S. Army Air Forces to victory in World War II, the Congress and President Harry S. Truman advocated "air parity," that is, an independent air force coequal with the army and navy. The Senate and House Armed Services committees held hearings in late 1946 and 1947 at which leading military and civilian officials testified. On 5 June 1947, the Senate Committee on Armed Services approved the so-called unification bill (S.758) with amendments. The Senate and the House approved the legislation in July by voice vote. On 26 July 1947, President Truman approved the unification legislation known as the National Security Act. The act created the National Military Establishment, headed by a civilian secretary of Defense who exercised control over the executive departments of the Army, Navy, and Air Force, each headed by a civilian secretary.

The National Security Act established the United States Air Force under the Department of the Air Force. However, because of roles and missions clashes during 1947–1949, especially between the air force and the navy, Congress passed amendments to the act in 1949. This legislation began the long process of centralizing authority within the office of the secretary of Defense. Under the 1949 act, the Department of Defense was designated as an executive department; the army, navy, and air force were relegated to military departments; and the service secretaries were removed as statutory members of the National Security Council.

These amendments of 1949 failed to end the roles and missions dispute between the navy and the air force, which centered on the issue of which service would hold responsibility for the strategic atomic mission. Secretary of State James V. Forrestal's "Functions Paper" of April 1948 delineated the functions of the services, giving the air force primary responsibility for conducting strategic air warfare. The severity of the controversy was heightened by the defense budget restraints imposed by the Truman administration—an almost equal three-way split of the defense funding between the services, limiting the funds available to each. During this bitter dispute, Secretary Forrestal resigned and subsequently committed suicide; Secretary of the Navy John L. Sullivan also resigned; and Chief of Naval Operations Adm. Louis E. Denfeld was fired by Truman.

The controversy, known as the "revolt of the admirals," broke out into a rancorous public dispute in hearings before the House Armed Services Committees, then chaired by Rep. Carl Vinson (D-Ga.), in the late summer and autumn of 1949. Two separate hearings were convened, the first focusing on charges that the fledgling air force, and its secretary, Stuart Symington, were guilty of fraud in the procurement of the B-36 bomber, and the second featuring a review of national security strategy and the policy of strategic deterrence.

Chairman Vinson absolved the air force of irregularities in its B-36 procurement. The House Armed Services Committee issued a report in March 1950 that reaffirmed that the air force held primary responsibility for strategic bombing and yet deplored the manner in which the navy's flush-deck aircraft carrier was canceled, which had ignited the navy–air force clash. When the aircraft carrier, the centerpiece of the navy's drive to gain a share of the strategic mission, was canceled by the Truman administration, the navy alleged it had not been given the opportunity properly to present the case for building the carrier. Although the committee's report did not settle the services' struggle over roles and missions, it did recommend ways to ameliorate service rivalry within the structure of the Joint Chiefs of Staff.

In addition to solving issues of roles and missions, the fledgling air force needed to codify its internal structure. The National Security Act gave the new service great latitude in structuring itself, but the air force had not been granted a specific authorized strength. The Army and Air Force Authorization Act of 10 July 1950 stipulated that the air force would be composed of a regular air force of 502,000 officers and airmen, divided into seventy groups and whatever separate squadrons were required. The act also provided for an air national guard of 150,000 personnel and an air force reserve totaling 100,000 personnel.

More than a year later, under the impetus provided by House Military Affairs Committee chairman Vinson, the organization of U.S. Air Force headquarters was codified by the Air Force Organization Act of 1951. The headquarters would be composed of an air staff and not more than five deputy chiefs of staff under the chief of staff of the air force. The act provided for a chief of staff who would command the three combat commands—Strategic Air Command, Tactical Air Command, and the Air Defense Command—and supervised all other air force activities. It also provided for a presidentially appointed judge advocate general to provide comprehensive legal services in support of air force operations.

In 1953, President Dwight D. Eisenhower came to power determined to centralize authority in the office of the secretary of Defense. Eisenhower's Reorganization Plan No. 6 of June 1953, which became law when Congress failed either to amend or disapprove it, abolished a number of boards and staff agencies and replaced them with six new assistant secretaries of Defense. This trend toward centralizing power in the hands of the secretary of Defense culminated in Eisenhower's Department of Defense Reorganization Act of 1958, which stated that the operational chain of command no longer included the service secretaries but rather ran from the president to the secretary of Defense and through the Joint Chiefs of Staff to the unified theater commands and the Strategic Air Command—the latter being a "specified" command, that is, a command having an overall strategic mission not confined to any special geographic theater of operations. Thus the act repealed the legislative authority for the service chiefs of staff to command their respective services. Now, unified and specified commanders would carry out specific military missions with service forces assigned under the operational control of the unified commanders. The 1958 reorganization act survived for almost thirty years without major change.

The Goldwater-Nichols Reorganization Act of 1986 was the most comprehensive revision of the joint military establishment since the 1958 reorganization. The Goldwater-Nichols act gave the air force more responsibility for the military's role in the space program; concentrated more authority in the chairman of the Joint Chiefs of Staff; and directed reviews of the mission, responsibilities, and force structures of the unified and specified commands. This review created the United States Transportation Command in 1987 to supervise joint deployment for land, sea, and air components of the military. The 1986 law also strengthened the authority of the combatant commanders and confirmed the 1958 legislation specifying that the chain of command ran from the president to the secretary of Defense to the combatant commanders.

In the almost half century since Congress established the U.S. Air Force, the evolution of weapons technology and clashes over service roles and missions had led inexorably to the centralization of power and authority in the office of the secretary of Defense. The Goldwater-Nichols Reorganization Act confirmed this drive, gave more power to the chairman of the Joint Chiefs of Staff, and spurred the ongoing trend toward the joint application of doctrine, planning, and strategy supportive of joint operations.

[*See also* Armed Forces; Armed Services Committee, House; Armed Services Committee, Senate; National Security Act.]

BIBLIOGRAPHY

Caraley, Demetrios. *The Politics of Military Unification: A Study of Conflict and the Policy Process.* 1966.
Maurer, Maurer. "The Constitutional Basis of the United States Air Force." *Air University Review* 16 (1965): 63–68.
Wolf, Richard I. *USAF Basic Documents on Roles and Missions.* 1987.
Wolk, Herman S. *Planning and Organizing the Postwar Air Force, 1943–1947.* 1984.

HERMAN S. WOLK

ALABAMA. The creation of Alabama as a territory and as a state owed much to sectionalism. First included as the easternmost portion of the Mississippi Territory created by Congress in 1798, Washington County in what is today Alabama grew more slowly than the Natchez area of Mississippi. The Alabamans resented their feeble voice in the new territorial government and demanded separate status. Their cause appealed to southern lawmakers eager to organize as many slave states as possible. With northern acquiescence, Congress divided the Mississippi Territory in 1817, granting statehood to Mississippi in the western portion and designating the eastern portion as the Territory of Alabama. Alabama became the twenty-second state on 14 December 1819 after meeting all the requirements.

Jacksonian democracy dominated the state's early politics. Alabama's constitution enacted some of America's most liberal voting standards, refusing to restrict suffrage on the basis of property ownership or literacy. At the same time, states' rights appealed to citizens who resented congressional attempts to

BENJAMIN S. TURNER. Alabama's first African American member of Congress (1871–1872).

LIBRARY OF CONGRESS

protect the rights of Indians and the increasingly perceived threat to the institution of slavery.

Sectional issues affected politics more than did party differences. Northern and southern Alabama differed so deeply that the state legislature agreed to select one U.S. senator from northern Alabama and the other from southern Alabama. Class differences also appeared. Felix G. McConnell, elected to Congress from a mountainous district in 1843, first championed the homestead bill to provide free land to farmers. But Sen. Clement C. Clay, representing planter interests, helped kill the legislation.

During the years before the Civil War, Alabama furnished some of America's foremost politicians. Rufus King served as vice president during the Franklin Pierce administration (1853–1857). Rep. William L. Yancey emerged as a chief spokesman for secession. Yancey's 1848 Alabama platform became a major strategy in the states' rights arsenal, and following the death of John C. Calhoun he became the chief southern "fire-eater" as the Civil

War approached. Alabama declared its secession on 11 January 1861; the state was allowed to resume its representation in Congress on 21 July 1868.

The Civil War ended Alabama's national political influence until Rep. Oscar W. Underwood emerged as a presidential contender in 1912. Underwood, who briefly chaired the Committee on Ways and Means, served as Democratic floor leader in both the House (1911–1915) and the Senate (1920–1923). In 1931, John H. Bankhead entered the Senate, the fourth of Alabama's Bankhead family to serve in Congress. He joined his brother, Rep. William B. Bankhead, who later rose to be House majority leader and Speaker. During the 1930s and 1940s Alabama sent to Congress a Democratic delegation notable for its liberalism, except on the overriding issue of racial segregation. The Bankheads, Hugo L. Black, Lister Hill, Kenneth A. Roberts, Robert E. Jones, Jr., Carl A. Elliott, Albert Rains, and John J. Sparkman all supported major social legislation of their times.

As in earlier years, members of Congress from northern Alabama were more liberal than those elected from the southern half. Senator Hill, appointed in 1938 to replace Senator Black when Black moved to the Supreme Court, became chief sponsor of some of America's most advanced education and health legislation. Senator Sparkman served with distinction as chairman of the Senate Foreign Relations Committee (1975–1979).

During the 1960s and 1970s racial conflict launched Gov. George C. Wallace into three third-party presidential efforts. Though he was defeated, Wallace's quixotic crusade deepened racial polarization and hastened the rise of the Republican party in the state. By the 1990s most of the state's congressional seats were hotly contested by both parties, and the delegation was generally split.

BIBLIOGRAPHY

Griffith, Lucille. *Alabama: A Documentary History to 1900.* 1968.
Hamilton, Virginia Van der Veer. *Alabama: A History.* 1977.

WAYNE FLYNT

ALASKA. In March 1867, Secretary of State William H. Seward and Baron Edward de Stoeckel, the Russian minister plenipotentiary, negotiated the sale of Russian territories in America to the United States for $7.2 million. What exactly the United States had purchased remained unclear for many decades. It slowly dawned on Congress that it had bought an arctic and subarctic subcontinent, an enormous territory sweeping across four time zones and encompassing 586,412 square miles, fully one-fifth the size of the contiguous United States.

The U.S. Army arrived in 1867 and for ten years provided the region's only government. From 1877 until 1879 the collector of customs became the sole ruler of Alaska. In 1879, the U.S. Navy took over and administered the colony until 1884.

In 1884 Congress finally recognized the unsatisfactory conditions relative to civil administration, homestead rights, transportation, and mail services in Alaska and passed the Organic Act, which established the foundation on which Alaska's government later rested. In its restrictive aspects, the act prohibited both a legislative branch and a delegate to Congress. It made Alaska a "civil and judicial district," with a presidentially appointed governor, one statutory (rather than constitutional) district judge, four lesser judges, and various other officials. Congress declared that the general laws of the state of Oregon, where applicable and not in conflict with existing statutes, were to be the law of the district of Alaska. Since the management of some territorial affairs would be carried out directly from Washington, D.C., the secretary of the Interior would supervise education in Alaska.

The influx of Klondike-bound gold seekers, beginning in 1897, induced Congress to enact legislation for Alaska. In 1906, Congress finally passed a measure providing for a voteless Alaskan delegate to Congress. James Wickersham, a colorful federal district court judge in Alaska, quit the bench, and Alaskans elected him as their third delegate to Congress in 1908. After much work on his part, Congress finally passed the second Alaska Organic Act in 1912. It gave the territory a legislature, which, however, was more severely limited in its field of action than the legislature of any other territory. It specified that the existing executive and judicial branches that the Organic Act of 1884 (as amended in 1900 and thereafter) had created could not be altered by the territorial legislature.

The drive for admission to the Union began in 1943. A second or "populist" phase of the statehood movement began late in 1953. It involved thousands of ordinary Alaskans and culminated in a constitutional convention in 1955 and 1956 and the adoption of a constitution in the spring of 1956. Employing a strategy first used by Tennessee—the so-called Tennessee Plan—voters sent two shadow senators and a shadow representative to Washington to lobby for Alaska's recognition as a state.

Meanwhile, citizens of Hawaii, which as a noncontiguous U.S. territory with a sizable minority population had much in common with Alaska, had begun their own campaign for statehood. The two drives soon merged as a congressional issue, with statehood proponents arguing on the basis of fairness and "old guard" conservatives fearing that the admission of two new states would upset existing political balances in Congress. Eventually, notably following passage of the Civil Rights Act of 1957, Congress began to reassess its position on statehood. President Dwight D. Eisenhower was persuaded to support the drive, and in August 1958 Congress passed the Alaskan statehood act (72 Stat. 339–352). Hawaii achieved statehood a year later.

Determined to put the new state on solid economic footing, Congress granted the Alaskan government 103,350,000 acres of land, to be selected from the vacant, unappropriated, and unreserved public domain over a twenty-five year period. As the state selected its lands, the native peoples in Alaska grew concerned about threats to their own claims to lands and resources. This conflict accelerated dramatically after the discovery of the Prudhoe Bay oilfield on 16 January 1968. It soon became obvious that a pipeline would be necessary to carry crude oil from the Arctic oilfield to navigable waters, but it could not be built until the claims of the Alaskan natives had been settled. After many months of negotiation, Congress passed the Alaska Claims Settlement Act of 1971 (ANCSA), and President Richard M. Nixon signed the measure into law on 18 December 1971. In exchange for 44 million acres of land and $962.4 million, the native groups relinquished all aboriginal rights. In 1980, Congress completed the division of Alaska among the federal government, the state of Alaska, and native groups with passage of the Alaska National Interest Lands Conservation Act. A complex measure, it set aside an area larger than California for conservation, placing more than 97 million acres into new or expanded national parks and refuges, doubling the total area of national parks and refuges nationwide.

Alaskans elected a Democratic slate to represent them in Congress in 1958. Edward L. (Bob) Bartlett, the territory's last delegate to Congress, became the state's first senior U.S. senator, while former territorial governor Ernest Gruening won the junior seat. Ralph J. Rivers was elected to fill the state's single House seat. Senator Bartlett died in 1968, and Gov. Walter J. Hickel appointed Republican Ted Stevens to take his place. Stevens won election in 1972 and was reelected in 1978, 1988, and 1990. In the mid-1960s, Alaska became a competitive two-party state, and by the 1970s Alaska's three-member congressional delegation was entirely Republican.

BIBLIOGRAPHY

Naske, Claus-M. *A History of Alaska Statehood.* 1986.
Naske, Claus-M., and Herman Slotnick. *Alaska: A History of the 49th State.* 1987.

CLAUS-M. NASKE

ALBERT, CARL B. (1908–), representative from Oklahoma, Democratic whip and majority leader, and Speaker of the House from 1971 to 1977. A political adversary of President Richard M. Nixon, Albert on two occasions was first in line of succession to the presidency.

Carl Bert Albert was born in poverty in rural Bug Tussle, Oklahoma, the oldest of five children. His father was a coal miner and cotton farmer. Albert was a brilliant student and a gifted public speaker. After graduation from the University of Oklahoma, he studied law at Oxford University as a Rhodes scholar. He subsequently practiced law in Oklahoma and Illinois.

During World War II, Albert entered the army as a private and served in the Pacific, rising to the rank of colonel. He returned to Oklahoma in 1946 and was elected to Congress from the 3d District ("Little Dixie"). Albert was five feet, four inches tall and was known as "the Little Giant from Little Dixie."

As a popular centrist Democrat, Albert became a student of House procedures and made a point of getting to know all his Democratic colleagues. He became a protégé of Speaker Sam Rayburn and in 1955 was appointed majority whip. Upon the elevation of John W. McCormack (D-Mass.) to the speakership in 1962, Albert was elected majority leader.

As majority leader he played a crucial role in the passage of the landmark legislation of Lyndon B. Johnson's Great Society—including bills on civil rights, medicare, federal aid to education, environmental and consumer protection, and the "war on poverty." He also chaired the 1968 Democratic convention.

With the retirement of McCormack in 1971, Albert was elected the forty-sixth Speaker, the first born in the twentieth century.

He was a sure-handed, stabilizing influence in the House during six of the twentieth century's most tumultuous years. Those were the years that saw the withdrawal of U.S. troops from Vietnam, the

CARL B. ALBERT. As House majority leader, October 1969.   LIBRARY OF CONGRESS

fall of the Saigon government, rampant inflation and high unemployment, the resignation of Vice President Spiro T. Agnew in a scandal, Watergate, and the threatened impeachment and subsequent resignation of President Nixon. Twice the nation was without a vice president, and Albert, as Speaker, was the proverbial heartbeat away from the presidency.

The years of his speakership were productive for the House. Albert proved a willing and able instrument for overdue institutional reforms. Those reforms strengthened the speakership and expanded the Speaker's role in foreign affairs, rejuvenated the Democratic caucus, modernized the appropriations process, created the Congressional Budget Office, broke the stranglehold of seniority, sped the flow of legislation, and gave more power to junior committee members.

Albert retired from Congress in 1977 and returned to Oklahoma. He will be remembered as a skillful, progressive, and respected Speaker who successfully steered the House through a period of crisis and change.

BIBLIOGRAPHY

Albert, Carl, with Danney Goble. *The Life and Times of Speaker Carl Albert: Little Giant.* 1990.

Howell, Joe. "The Little Giant from Little Dixie." *Tulsa Tribune,* 18 September 1985.

Peters, Ronald M., Jr. *The American Speakership.* 1990. Pp. 156–208.

ROBERT L. HARDESTY

ALCOHOLIC BEVERAGES IN CONGRESS. From the early 1800s, when a purveyor known as the apple woman peddled liquor in the crypt of the Rotunda, into the 1960s, when Sen. Wayne L. Morse campaigned against drinking in the Senate, the sale and consumption of alcoholic beverages in the Capitol has been a recurrent and divisive topic of congressional debate.

Unfettered by rigid rules, senators and representatives of the early congresses could and did drink while they legislated. Rep. John Randolph of Virginia reportedly imbibed while he spoke in Congress, pausing now and then to order more porter from the assistant doorkeeper. By the 1820s the House had its own bar, where congressmen flocked daily, while the Senate had a smaller but equally popular drinking place, aptly named the Hole-in-the-Wall, accessible by private stairway from the Senate chamber.

Congress's drinking habits came under public scrutiny for the first time in 1831, when the burgeoning temperance movement targeted Capitol Hill. Within two years, proponents of the movement had convinced several senators to form the American Congressional Temperance Society, which was joined by more than a hundred senators and representatives, called Cold-Water Congressmen because they advocated cold water as a healthful substitute for alcohol.

Tangible evidence of congressional concern came in 1837 with the passage of a joint resolution prohibiting the "sale or exhibit" of spirituous liquors within the Capitol. As the temperance movement waned, however, so did Congress's commitment to it. Visiting the Capitol refectory in 1838, British writer Frederick Marryat found liquor still being dispensed, albeit by subterfuge. "You go there and ask for a pale sherry, and they hand you gin; brown sherry, and it is brandy; Madeira, whisky; and thus do these potent, grave, and reverent signers evade their own laws beneath the very hall wherein they were passed in solemn conclave," Marryat reported in *A Diary in America* (1839).

GEORGE L. CASSIDAY. His well-known green hat rests on the books at his elbow, October 1930.

A temperance revival gripped Washington in 1842, bringing new pledges of abstinence from many prominent citizens. The moribund Congressional Temperance Society was revived and renamed the Congressional Total Abstinence Society. More than eighty new members signed up, each pledging to shun all forms of alcoholic drink. A new resolution banning from the Capitol "all intoxicating beverages," including beer and wine, was adopted by the two houses. It proved to be as ephemeral as the earlier ban. By 1846, the congressional temperance society had only thirty members. Revived from time to time, it vanished entirely with the death of its last president, Sen. Nelson Dingley, Jr., in 1899.

During the Civil War, liquor was openly dispensed in the Capitol. Vice President Andrew Johnson became incoherent after consuming several brandies at his inauguration on 3 March 1865. Three days later, to humiliate Johnson, his Senate enemies voted to remove all intoxicating liquors from the Senate wing of the Capitol.

New resolutions to remove liquor from the entire Capitol were debated inconclusively in 1866. Sen. James A. McDougall set the debate's tone with his memorable declaration: "I believe in women, wine, whiskey, and war." In 1867, however, Congress's "dry" faction prevailed with an amendment to the joint rules of the House and Senate. It stated that no liquor "shall be offered for sale, exhibited, or kept" in the Capitol, and it was strictly enforced while it lasted. In 1876, after Congress failed to reenact the joint rules, each house again set its own policy, officially continuing to espouse prohibition while unofficially winking at the ban. The House restaurant began serving liquor surreptitiously in teacups.

Washington, D.C., police raided the House and Senate restaurants in 1902 and found them in violation of a liquor-licensing law that Congress had imposed for the District of Columbia. Coming amid rising prohibition agitation, this was a major embarrassment for Congress. The lawmakers responded with a statutory commitment, enacted as an amendment to the Immigration Act of 1903, that "no intoxicating liquor of any character shall be sold within the limits of the Capitol." It did not mention possession and consumption, an exploitable loophole. Thus, prohibition arrived on Capitol Hill years before Congress extended the liquor ban to the District of Columbia in 1917 and before it enacted the Volstead Act of 1919 to enforce the national prohibition mandate of the Eighteenth Amendment.

Congress found it impossible to enforce prohibition, even in Capitol Hill's limited confines. In 1922, Rep. William D. Upshaw charged that members were flagrantly violating their own "dry" laws and was called before the bar of the House to explain his allegation. Upshaw's charge was treated by Congress and the press as a joke. Magazine writer Walter W. Leggett caused a brief stir in 1926 with his article "Wet Washington," which pointed to Capitol Hill as "the wettest place of all."

In the same year, much of the nation chuckled over the attempted arrest of a colorful Washington bootlegger named George L. Cassiday in the House office building. Cassiday, known locally for his green hat, gained immortality in congressional legend when he abandoned his briefcase filled with bottled whiskey and fled the arresting Capitol police officer. As the police scoured the city for the mysterious "Man in the Green Hat," the press kept the story alive, insinuating broadly that he was Congress's own bootlegger and had been deliberately set free. Cassiday was eventually recaptured but never identified his customers.

Following the repeal of Prohibition in 1933, Congress removed all laws prohibiting alcoholic beverages in the District of Columbia, including the 1903 statutory ban on liquor in the Capitol. Each house reclaimed its right to set its own liquor rules, the House delegating the responsibility to the Committee on House Administration and the Senate passing similar authority to its Committee on Rules and Administration. Beer and wine reappeared in the House and Senate restaurants. Both houses retained their ban on the sale of spirituous liquors, policies still in effect in the 1990s. Restrictions on consumption, however, were slowly relaxed to allow the serving of alcoholic beverages at social gatherings in the Capitol, a departure that prompted Senator Morse of Oregon to complain vigorously. The Senate's 1962 rebuff of Morse's resolution to reimpose a total ban marked the last serious assault on Congress's liquor policies, as of 1994.

Given the electorate's traditional interest in the moral behavior of elected officials, remarkably few members of Congress have been accused of excessive drinking. Daniel Webster's fondness for drink emerged briefly as a public issue after moral activist Jane Grey Swisshelm wrote about it in 1850. More recently, Rep. Wilbur D. Mills was forced to resign his Ways and Means Committee chairmanship and retire from Congress after his involvement in alcohol-related incidents in 1974, and retired senator John G. Tower was denied a cabinet position in 1989 after his former Senate colleagues raised doubts about his personal habits, including his sobriety.

Whether alcohol has ever affected the legislative process has been debated but never seriously studied. The most lively discussion of the topic occurred in 1945 when a psychiatrist from Washington's St. Elizabeth's Mental Hospital opined that the stress and strain of their jobs made lawmakers of that period vulnerable to alcohol abuse. "Alcohol is a major factor in Congress and exercises a most damaging effect on legislation," he told a *New York Times* interviewer. The charge, offered without proof and angrily denied by Congress, was later recanted.

In any case, drinking in Congress has shifted dramatically toward moderation in recent years, according to Senator Tower. For various reasons, political and personal, few representatives and senators of the 1980s and 1990s have engaged in the type of after-hours socializing that was once a part of congressional life. "When I arrived in 1961 drinking was a social convention, almost a ritual," Tower stated in his 1991 autobiography.

In Tower's time, senators and representatives would gather informally in small groups at day's end to talk politics and "strike a blow for liberty" (Rep. John Nance Garner's term for having a drink). Such socializing among Congress's male members, usually held in one of the Capitol's out-of-the-way private rooms, was widely practiced at least from the mid

1800s, when Webster hosted colleagues in his "Little Room," into the 1960s, when Speaker Sam Rayburn presided over his famous "Board of Education." Vice President Harry S. Truman was mixing himself a drink in Rayburn's Capitol hideaway on 12 April 1945, when he received word that President Franklin D. Roosevelt was dead. Group socializing was seen as a way for members to bond and was encouraged by Congress's leaders, who used their own sessions for gathering information, mapping strategy, and rallying support.

Most of these groups and their members came and went without history's notice. About others—such as "Johnson Ranch East," hosted in the 1950s by Senate majority leader Lyndon B. Johnson (D-Tex.), "The Clinic," hosted in the 1960s by House minority leader Charles A. Halleck (R-Ind.), and "Twilight Lodge," hosted in the 1970s by Senate minority leader Everett M. Dirksen (R-Ill.)—a few details have been recorded. One exception, unusual for its bipartisan membership, was the "Bureau of Education," hosted in the 1920s by Speaker Nicholas Longworth (R-Ohio) and House minority leader Garner (D-Tex.), who were close friends despite their political differences. As a daily ritual, Garner would appear around 5:00 P.M. at the rear of the chamber and, with a crook of his finger, beckon to Longworth. The urbane Ohioan would promptly adjourn the House and march, arm-in-arm, with the rough-hewn Texan down a little-used corridor of the Capitol to a private room where several of their cronies would be waiting, drinks in hand. Such scenes were rare in the Congress of the 1990s.

BIBLIOGRAPHY

Architect of the Capitol. "History of Legislation concerning Alcoholic Beverages in the U.S. Capitol." 1962.

Brown, George. *Washington: A Not Too Serious History*. 1930.

Johnson, William E. *The Federal Government and the Liquor Traffic*. 1911.

Poore, Ben Perley. *Perley's Reminiscences of Sixty Years in the National Metropolis*. Vols. 1 and 2. 1886.

Sprunger, Keith L. "Cold Water Congressmen: The Congressional Temperance Society before the Civil War." *Historian* (August 1965): 498–515.

Tower, John G. *Consequences*. 1991.

DONALD C. BACON

ALCOHOL POLICY. Prior to national Prohibition, federal action affecting the consumption of alcoholic beverages was essentially limited to the imposition of excise taxes and importation tariffs and to regulation of retail sale in areas under direct fed-

Landmark Enactments

Title	Year Enacted	Reference Number	Description
Tariff Act of 1789	1789	1 Stat. 24	First federal law affecting alcoholic beverages; included liquors among commodities subject to import tariffs.
Revenue Act of 1791	1791	1 Stat. 199–214	First statute to impose an excise tax on the production of distilled spirits; increased a year later, leading to the Whiskey Rebellion.
Eighteenth Amendment to the Constitution	1919[1]	40 Stat. 1050	Prohibited the importation, production, and sale of alcoholic beverages in the United States.
National Prohibition Act (Volstead Act)	1919	41 Stat. 305-323	Established the necessary mechanisms and requirements for enforcing the Eighteenth Amendment.
Twenty-first Amendment to the Constitution	1933[1]	47 Stat. 1625	Repealed the Eighteenth Amendment.
Federal Alcohol Administration Act	1935	P.L. 74-401	Established the post-Prohibition system of regulation of the liquor industry, to the end of maintenance of orderly markets.
Liquor Tax Administration Act	1936	P.L. 74-815	Set forth requirements and procedures for complying with the federal scheme for taxing the importation, production, and sale of alcoholic beverages.
Community Mental Health Centers Act	1963	P.L. 88-164	Established a program of construction (and later, staffing) grants for community centers treating mental illness, defined to include alcoholism, administered by the National Institute of Mental Health in the Public Health Service.
Alcoholic Rehabilitation Act	1968	P.L. 90-574, Title III, Part A	Amended the Community Mental Health Centers Act to establish programs of specialized grants for treatment of alcoholism and narcotic addiction.
Comprehensive Alcohol Abuse and Alcoholism Prevention, Treatment and Rehabilitation Act (Hughes Act)	1970	P.L. 91-616	Created the National Institute on Alcoholism and Alcohol Abuse (NIAAA) within the National Institute on Mental Health and authorized a 3-year program of formula grants to the states and direct project grants to community-based programs for prevention and treatment of alcohol abuse and alcoholism. Also established the National Council on Alcohol Abuse and Alcoholism.

[1]Year ratification was proclaimed

eral control. Although the aim of taxes and tariffs was generally the raising of revenue, alcohol being a major source, records from as early as 1789 show that some legislators also regarded them as tools for reducing consumption. Moreover, tariffs on imported malt liquors and cider were seen by many as a means of encouraging development of domestic breweries, with attendant economic and social benefits.

The American temperance movement, born in the early 1800s, was originally committed to moderation of drinking habits rather than the total abstinence later espoused. For most of the nineteenth century its attention was centered on state law, but the influence of temperance philosophy on national politics grew steadily. Both the Prohibition party and the Anti-Saloon League, outgrowths of the movement, came to take the position that only a federal law could prevent state restrictions from being undermined.

Numerous minor actions marked the progress of temperance ideas in Congress. Beginning with an enactment in 1802, Congress espoused a policy of curbing liquor traffic to the Indian tribes and, later, of total prohibition in the Indian Territory. As early as 1876 a bill was introduced to prohibit, as of 1900, the manufacture and sale of distilled spirits. In the House, a Committee on the Alcoholic Liquor Traffic was established in 1879, remaining in operation until 1927.

In terms of political impact, the Anti-Saloon League became the most important force for na-

Landmark Enactments (Continued)

TITLE	YEAR ENACTED	REFERENCE NUMBER	DESCRIPTION
Comprehensive Alcohol Abuse and Alcoholism Prevention, Treatment, and Rehabilitation Act Amendments	1974	P.L. 93-282	In addition to extending and expanding the NIAAA program, gave statutory backing to a reorganization that placed NIAAA on a co-equal basis with the National Institute on Drug Abuse and the National Institute on Mental Health, in a new agency, the Alcohol, Drug Abuse, and Mental Health Administration (ADAMHA), also in the Public Health Service.
Omnibus Budget Reconciliation Act	1981	P.L. 97-35	Made major changes in the way the federal government provides assistance for a variety of health and social services, including those dealing with treatment and prevention of alcoholism and alcohol abuse—principally by replacing existing categorical grants with block grants to states. Assistance for alcohol abuse, drug abuse, and mental health services was combined in a single block grant, but requirements governing allocation were set forth.
Anti-Drug Abuse Act	1986	P.L. 99-570	Among other things, established the Department of Education's Drug-Free Schools and Communities Program ("drug" defined to include alcohol) and created the Office of Substance Abuse Prevention (in ADAMHA). Also provided biggest increase in funding for alcohol and drug abuse control since 1970.
Anti-Drug Abuse Act	1988	P.L. 100-690	Among other things, created the Office of National Drug Abuse Policy (headed by a "drug czar"). Although the office's mandate was originally considered to be limited to substances subject to the Federal Controlled Substances Act, the 1992 strategy developed by the office included alcohol abuse as a concern of national drug policy.
Alcohol, Drug Abuse, and Mental Health Administration Reorganization Act	1992	P.L. 102-321	Reconstituted ADAMHA as the Substance Abuse and Mental Health Services Administration (SAMHSA), with the former agency's research functions transferred to the National Institutes of Health. Changed block grant concept so that substance abuse and mental health services were to be funded by separate grants and revised formula whereby funds were to be apportioned to the states.

tional restrictions on alcohol. With its help, the strength of the "drys" in Congress, mainly southern and western members, increased measurably after the turn of the century. Their first big victory was the passage in 1913, over the veto of President William Howard Taft, of the Webb-Kenyon Act prohibiting commercial shipment of packaged liquor into dry states.

The real beginning of congressional debate on national prohibition came in 1914 with House consideration of a joint resolution introduced by Richmond P. Hobson (D-Ala.), calling for a constitutional amendment. Although failing then to secure the necessary two-thirds vote, it succeeded two years later in both House and Senate. Also enacted at that time were laws imposing prohibition in Alaska

and Puerto Rico, establishing dry zones around army camps and naval bases, and forbidding liquor consumption by soldiers and sailors. In addition, the sale of liquor was banned in the District of Columbia, mailing of liquor advertisements was proscribed, and an agriculture appropriations act effectively achieved wartime prohibition by forbidding, until demobilization, the use of any foodstuff in the production of alcohol for drinking purposes. Ratification of the Eighteenth Amendment was completed in late 1918, and with enactment of implementing legislation in 1919 (the National Prohibition Act, or Volstead Act), the American temperance movement had—for a period of fourteen years—achieved its goal.

Since repeal of Prohibition in 1933, responsibility

for regulating alcoholic beverage commerce has largely been returned to the states. However, in 1935 Congress passed the Federal Alcohol Administration Act (P.L. 74-401), designed through licensing and other requirements to ensure orderly markets. To collect industry taxes, the Internal Revenue Bureau's Alcohol Tax Unit was established in 1934; and the Liquor Tax Administration Act of 1936 (P.L. 74-815) set forth requirements for compliance. In 1940, regulatory and tax authorities were consolidated and lodged in the tax unit, the forerunner of today's Bureau of Alcohol, Tobacco, and Firearms, which was created in 1972. Thus, the United States embarked upon a regime ostensibly of state control, but in reality a system of federal, state, and local control. The Twenty-first Amendment required the federal government to protect dry states by preventing the transportation or importation of intoxicating liquors for delivery or use therein.

The post-Prohibition era saw growing acceptance of the idea that alcoholics and other drug-dependent persons are ill rather than sinful or merely undisciplined. Thus, such problems were among those studied in research supported by the National Institute of Mental Health, created in 1946. By the 1960s, adherents of this view had sufficient influence in Congress to secure legislation funding nationwide treatment and rehabilitation services for alcoholics, as well as narcotic addicts.

The first major move came with the Community Mental Health Centers Act of 1963 and its definition of "mental illness," which includes both narcotic addiction and alcoholism, thus allowing their treatment in the facilities funded. In 1968 the act was amended to establish the first grant programs specifically for addict and alcoholic treatment (P.L. 90-574), but the most significant step was the 1970 enactment of the Comprehensive Alcohol Abuse and Alcoholism Prevention, Treatment, and Rehabilitation Act (P.L. 91-616). The 1970 legislation signaled full acceptance of the idea that alcoholism is a public health problem, and it is considered by some to mark a triumph of the "disease model" of alcoholism over the psychiatric orientation that had been ascendant since the 1930s. Its passage owed much to the efforts of Sen. Harold E. Hughes (D-Iowa) and Rep. Paul G. Rogers (D-Fla.). An important element in this and subsequent achievements was Senator Hughes's success in getting approval for a Senate Subcommittee on Alcoholism and Narcotics (later, Alcoholism and Drug Abuse; since 1985, Children, Family, Drugs, and Alcoholism).

A salient provision of the Hughes Act established the National Institute on Alcohol Abuse and Alcoholism (NIAAA), later made part of the Alcohol, Drug Abuse, and Mental Health Administration (ADAMHA). Until 1981, the institute was responsible for most federal alcohol abuse treatment and prevention programs as well as related research. In 1981, administration of service grants was turned over to ADAMHA, with NIAAA's mission limited generally to research and training (P.L. 97-85). A 1992 statute assigned services to a new agency called the Substance Abuse and Mental Health Services Administration (SAMHSA), and NIAAA became one of the National Institutes of Health (P.L. 102-321).

Essential federal policy on alcoholic beverages in the post-Prohibition era has evolved over time into a three-sided approach featuring industry regulation, enforcement support for state restrictions, and demand reduction through treatment, prevention, and related research. A summary of prevention efforts should include such recent enactments as those requiring health warning labels on alcohol products and pressuring states to raise the legal drinking age. Also, there is a role in safety-centered regulation and enforcement and the regulation of retail sale and use in areas subject to direct federal jurisdiction.

In addition to those mentioned above, federal alcohol policy is reflected in the legislative mandates, regulations, and actions of such agencies—all subject to congressional oversight—as the Defense Department, Veterans' Administration, Bureau of Indian Affairs, National Park Service, Army Corps of Engineers, Bureau of Land Management, and safety-oriented agencies such as the Consumer Product Safety Commission, National Transportation Safety Board, and Federal Aviation Administration.

[See also Anti-Saloon League; Eighteenth Amendment; National Prohibition Act; Prohibition; Twenty-first Amendment.]

BIBLIOGRAPHY

Blocker, Jack S., Jr. American Temperance Movements: Cycles of Reform. 1989.

Johnson, William E. The Federal Government and the Liquor Traffic. 1911.

Moore, Mark, and Dean R. Gerstein, eds. Alcohol and Public Policy: Beyond the Shadow of Prohibition. 1981.

HARRY HOGAN

ALDRICH, NELSON W. (1841–1915), representative and senator from Rhode Island, the most influential Republican leader of the Senate in the late nineteenth and early twentieth centuries. A wealthy businessman with wide-ranging interests,

THE NELSON GRIP. Political cartoon portraying Nelson W. Aldrich's influence and control over the Senate Republican majority, depicted as a small elephant whose trunk Aldrich firmly holds. Aldrich's power was further cemented by the absence of a vice president following President William McKinley's death and Vice President Theodore Roosevelt's ascension to the presidency, which left vacant the presidency of the Senate. Clifford K. Berryman, 27 July 1903.

U.S. SENATE COLLECTION, CENTER FOR LEGISLATIVE ARCHIVES

Nelson Wilmarth Aldrich was elected to the U.S. House of Representatives in 1878 and was reelected in 1880. He moved up to the Senate after the death of the incumbent in 1881. By the time of reelection in 1886, he had consolidated his position as the dominant influence in the state's Republican machine. Given the Republican stranglehold on the legislature because of a "rotten-borough" apportionment system (heavily weighted in favor of the smaller towns), he retained his seat without significant challenge until his retirement.

Aldrich was not a forceful public speaker. He had thinly veiled contempt for the average voter. His preferred arena was behind the scenes with fellow men of wealth and influence. Energetic and strong-minded, Aldrich made himself a master of Senate rules and parliamentary maneuver. He was a strong believer in the trickle-down theory of prosperity. His twin political passions were the protective tariff and sound money.

Aldrich first made his mark leading the successful resistance by Senate Republicans in 1888 to cuts in the tariff rates advocated by Democratic president Grover Cleveland. He reinforced his standing through his role in the adoption of the McKinley Tariff Act of 1890, in the repeal of the Sherman Silver Purchase Act in 1893, and in the emasculation of the second Cleveland administration's proposed tariff reductions in the Wilson-Gorman tariff of 1894. The election of William McKinley to the presidency in 1896 on a platform of sound money and the protective tariff cemented the ascendancy in the Senate of the so-called Big Four—Aldrich, Orville H. Platt of Connecticut, John C. Spooner of Wisconsin, and William B. Allison of Iowa, with Aldrich the first among equals.

Aldrich was largely responsible for lining up the different interest groups jockeying for favored treatment behind the Dingley Tariff Act of 1897. His most pressing ambition, though, was to place the nation's monetary system firmly on a sound foundation, a goal that he achieved with the adoption of the Gold Standard Act of 1900. Aldrich was no imperialist: he resisted the pressure for war with Spain over Cuba as a threat to political and economic stability until President McKinley's reversal on the issue undercut his position. He was similarly unenthusiastic about acquisition of the Philippines.

The elevation of Theodore Roosevelt to the presidency in 1901 after the assassination of McKinley did not at first endanger Aldrich's power. The new chief executive's first term was marked by wary cooperation with Senate leaders. An implicit—perhaps even explicit—understanding was reached whereby Roosevelt could push for a limited degree of federal government supervision of corporations (e.g., with the establishment of the Bureau of Corporations in 1903) in return for his not disturbing the tariff and monetary status quo. Even this agreement began to break down in 1906 with the angry battle over the Hepburn bill, which would give the Interstate Commerce Commission the power to fix railroad rates.

Roosevelt shied away from an open break with Aldrich over the sensitive tariff issue. The panic of 1907 reopened questions about the nation's monetary system. Aldrich was the chief author of the Aldrich-Vreeland Act of 1908, designed to relieve the money-supply crunch responsible for the panic. After a study tour of Europe in 1908 as chairman of the National Monetary Commission, he came back a strong advocate for replacing the present national banking system, which dated from the Civil War, with what became known as the "Aldrich plan" after its formal publication in early 1911. His goal was a flexible currency, based upon commercial paper, that could adjust to changing business needs; control over the system would be lodged in a so-called national reserve association modeled on the central banks of Europe and having close ties with Wall Street.

The plan faced strong opposition from many bankers outside New York. Its final deathblow was the split within the Republican party over tariff revision in 1909. The Payne bill approved by the House of Representatives made significant reductions in the existing rates, but Aldrich rewrote the measure in the Senate Finance Committee along lines more favorable to eastern manufacturing interests. A revolt ensued by an insurgent group of largely middle-western Republican senators. The climax of the struggle that resulted was the 1912 breakup of the Republican party.

Aldrich appears to have decided as early as 1906 not to run again when his term expired in 1911. He died on 16 April 1915 from heart failure.

BIBLIOGRAPHY

Merrill, Horace S., and Marion G. Merrill. *The Republican Command, 1897–1913*. 1971.
Rothman, David J. *Politics and Power: The United States Senate, 1869–1901*. 1966.
Stephenson, Nathaniel W. *Nelson W. Aldrich: A Leader in American Politics*. 1930.
Sternstein, Jerome L. "Nelson W. Aldrich: The Making of the General Manager of the United States, 1841–1886." Ph.D. diss., Brown University, 1968.

JOHN BRAEMAN

ALIEN AND SEDITION ACTS

ALIEN AND SEDITION ACTS (1798). Following the establishment of the new government in 1789, bitter disputes over domestic and foreign policy divided the political elites of the country into two geographically based, protopolitical parties—the Federalists, mainly concentrated in New England and the Middle Atlantic States, and the Jeffersonian Republicans, centered for the most part in the South. The Alien and Sedition Acts of 1798 were the result of this highly polarized political atmosphere of the 1790s.

In 1798, France refused to accept or to meet with an American delegation sent by the newly elected president, John Adams, to negotiate an end to a quasi-naval war between French and American vessels—a conflict that threatened to blossom into a full-scale war between the two countries. In fact, the French negotiators, code-named "X," "Y," and "Z," declared that formal talks between the two countries could only begin after the United States extended a loan and bribe to France.

The return of two members of the American negotiating team in the spring of 1798, with their news of France's insulting behavior, ignited a fever-pitch political atmosphere. President Adams, claiming that the nation's honor had been insulted by France's haughty action, called for a military buildup and considered a declaration of war. With a wave of political hysteria sweeping the country, both protoparties, the Federalists and the Jeffersonian Republicans, viewed one another as hostile to the Constitution and republican government. To the Federalists, with their exaggerated, crisis-induced fears, the Republicans were no less than agents of Revolutionary France and therefore had to be eliminated as an organized opposition.

It was to this end that a Federalist-dominated Congress passed the Alien and Sedition Acts in June and July 1798. There were in reality three Alien acts, including the Act Concerning Aliens (or Alien Act, 1 Stat. 570–572), the Naturalization Act (1 Stat. 566–569), and the Alien Enemies Act (1 Stat. 577–578). They were aimed at the growing number of immigrants who were coming to the United States—immigrants who the Federalists feared held dangerous ideas and supported the Republicans. The acts established a registration and surveillance system for foreign nationals in the United States and gave the president broad powers to regulate their behavior, including the power of deportation.

The Sedition Act (1 Stat. 596–597) was aimed at stifling the internal Republican opposition. It punished any persons who singly or collectively opposed or impeded the implementation of the laws of the United States or those who were charged with the execution of the laws. The law also prohibited false or malicious writings against the federal government intended to incite hatred and contempt for federal officials. Violators of this law could be fined up to $5,000 and imprisoned for up to five years.

Passage of the Alien and Sedition Acts led to even greater sectional political polarization, with Kentucky and Virginia passing resolutions denouncing the acts and urging their repeal or nullification.

[*See also* XYZ Affair.]

BIBLIOGRAPHY

Sharp, James Roger. *American Politics in the Early Republic: The New Nation in Crisis*. 1993.
Smith, James Morton. *Freedom's Fetters: The Alien and Sedition Laws and American Civil Liberties*. 1966.

JAMES ROGER SHARP

ALIEN REGISTRATION ACT

ALIEN REGISTRATION ACT (1940; 54 Stat. 670–676). A product of pre–World War II fears, the Alien Registration Act, also known as the Smith Act, was one of forty bills considered by the 76th Congress (1939–1941) that contained restrictions on aliens and subversives. Introduced by Rep. Howard W. Smith (D-Va.) on 20 March 1939, the measure sought to criminalize efforts to undermine military recruitment and discipline and to punish those advocating the overthrow of the government. Smith's proposal passed the House in June, but Congress adjourned before the Senate could act. In June 1940, the Senate adopted a substitute version and a conference committee resolved the differences. The final version passed both houses on 22 June 1940 as Title I of the Alien Registration Act. President Franklin D. Roosevelt signed the measure on 29 June.

The most controversial provisions of the act were contained in its sedition section, which made it unlawful to "advocate, abet, advise, or teach" the violent overthrow of "any government in the United States"; to write or distribute printed material toward that end; to organize or join any association with that purpose; or to conspire to do any of the above. Conviction could result in a fine of up to $10,000 and a jail term of up to ten years.

Beginning in 1948, the Justice Department used the Smith Act to secure indictments against leaders of the American Communist party. The Supreme Court upheld the initial convictions and the constitutionality of the act in *Dennis v. United States* (1951), but because the Court later narrowed the law's application in *Yates v. United States* (1957) and *Scales v. United States* (1961), only 29 of the 141 persons indicted under the Smith Act actually served jail terms.

BIBLIOGRAPHY

Belknap, Michael R. *Cold War Political Justice: The Smith Act, the Communist Party, and American Civil Liberties.* 1977.
Chafee, Zechariah, Jr. *Free Speech in the United States.* 1941.

JEROLD L. SIMMONS

ALIGNMENTS AND REALIGNMENTS.

The twin concepts of alignment and realignment have been used to describe two different facets of the electoral status of the political parties. In the more common usage, the two terms refer to the electoral balance between the parties: a party alignment denotes the majority-minority status of the parties and a realignment refers to a change in that status (Key, 1955, 1959; Burnham, 1970). The electoral balance definition expects a Democratic alignment, for example, to produce a Democratic majority among officeholders and Democratic victories in most presidential contests. In the alternative usage, alignment refers primarily to differences in the social and demographic characteristics of party loyalists (Key, 1955, 1959; Petrocik, 1981). The theoretical centerpieces of this second formulation are the notions that (1) parties coordinate the concerns of different constituencies within the society, (2) party alignments reflect policy commitments that are sufficiently shared by some groups to allow them to coalesce within a single party, and (3) a realignment is a shift in each party's social-group profile as a result of changes in the partisanship of the groups.

Historical Alignments. There is general agreement that there have been five different party alignments in American party history. The first party system lasted into the 1820s. Formal party organization was weak, mass participation was limited, and the social divisions of the period were only weakly represented by partylike structures. Quite often, the period is described as a preparty system of deferential politics in which cleavages in local elites, not parties, shaped most of the electoral conflict.

The second party system (from the late 1820s to late 1850s) was a fully developed party system, often viewed as having shaped the particularly American party ethos in which the emphasis is on office seeking over programmatic appeals to voters. It had two well-organized parties, the Whigs and the dominant Democrats, with many "third" parties. It was characterized by extensive and ever-growing mass participation, and there were clear regional, religious, ethnic, economic, and class differences among party supporters. The social heterogeneity of each party's support (linked to office-seeking elites that constructed diverse coalitions) meant that the parties faced many potential internal differences and so were susceptible to the cross-cutting issues that provoke realignments.

The third party system (roughly from 1860 to 1896) was marked by demise of the Whigs and the effective dominance of the Republicans. Further organizational development; sharper regional, religious, and ethnic cleavages; and a political agenda focused on industrial growth and national expansion marked this system.

The fourth party system (often called the "system of '96") was notable for reversing more than seventy years of intensive party control of the electorate. Participation rates declined, party loyalty among voters weakened, regional differences intensified and became more complex, and the Republican party enjoyed more complete supremacy over the Democrats than it had in the previous period.

The fifth, or New Deal, party system emerged with Franklin D. Roosevelt's election as president in 1932. The Democrats replaced the Republicans as the majority party; the central issue dividing the parties became the proper role of the government in regulating and directing social and economic life; and ethnic, religious, and (especially) social class differences distinguished partisans much more sharply than before.

Causes of Realignments. Changes in party alignments, or realignments, have been analyzed in terms of who and what is responsible for them. Concerning the "who," there is an unresolved dispute about whether realignments are mostly dependent on voters changing their party identification or on previously nonparticipating voters becoming active and preferring one party to a disproportionate degree. Both factors seem to have been important. Historically, new voters have probably been more significant, while contemporary shifts may depend more greatly on changes in partisanship. The "what" factor is less controversial. There is general agreement that when the governing party cannot successfully manage social and economic turmoil and when new issues cut across the existing alignment, the parties' electoral foundations are undermined, leading to realignments.

Consequences: Legislative Politics and Policy-Making. Voting patterns in legislatures reflect the electoral alignment because constituency differences are one of the most important sources of party cohesion within an elected legislature. The desire to be reelected encourages legislators to satisfy their usual supporters, as does a general commonality of religious, ethnic, social, and economic interests between a party's legislators and its constituents. Not surprisingly, periodic realignments have had coincident and substantial effects on the programmatic coherence of the parties, as an analysis of roll-call votes illustrates (Brady, 1988).

The pattern is cyclical. The early years of a party alignment are characterized by relatively high levels of party cohesion, particularly on the issues that precipitated the realignment; as time passes, there is a progressive weakening of cohesion. For example, the formation of the second party system in the early 1830s saw voting along party lines surge from just over 60 percent to over 90 percent by the middle of the 1840s. Sectional strains, especially those associated with slavery, eroded party-line voting to less than 40 percent by the late 1850s; then it surged into the 80 to 90 percent range as Democrats faced Republicans in the third party system. The fourth party system realignment galvanized party conflict around another salient set of issues and increased party cohesion in the early 1900s. The decline in party cohesion in Congress through the 1920s was reversed by the New Deal realignment, which saw social welfare and government regulation issues increase party cohesion in Congress from about 55 percent during the 1920s to over 70 percent in the late 1930s and early 1940s.

Future Changes. The gradual decline in party cohesion in Congress after the early 1940s was reversed during the 1980s, which saw levels of party voting well above those of the 1960s and 1970s. The coincidence of this change with (1) the erosion of Democratic partisanship among southern whites, Roman Catholics, and labor-union households since the late 1960s and (2) the decline in Democratic identification after the middle 1980s was seen by some as evidence of a realignment of the New Deal party system and the possible emergence of a sixth party system. Still others, impressed by the slow pace and limits of these changes (Republican success in some areas was matched with Democratic dominance in others), came to doubt the analytic utility of the concepts of alignment and realignment. However, this position was shared by few. Most still found the concept of a party system bounded by realignments to be useful in synthesizing a variety of findings about voters, the social basis of parties, campaign issues, and legislative behavior.

[*See also* Blocs and Coalitions; Political Parties.]

BIBLIOGRAPHY

Burnham, Walter Dean. *Critical Elections and the Mainsprings of American Politics.* 1970.

Brady, David W. *Critical Elections and Congressional Policy Making.* 1988.

Campbell, James E. "Sources of the New Deal Realignment: The Contributions of Conversion and Mobilization to Partisan Change." *Western Political Quarterly* 38 (1985): 357–376.

Key, V. O., Jr. "Secular Realignment and the Party System." *Journal of Politics* 21 (1959): 198–210.

Key, V. O., Jr. "A Theory of Critical Elections." *Journal of Politics* 17 (1955): 3–18.

Petrocik, John R. *Party Coalitions: Realignments and the Decline of the New Deal Party System.* 1981.

Sundquist, James L. *Dynamics of the Party System: Alignment and Realignment of Political Parties in the United States.* Rev. ed. 1983.

JOHN R. PETROCIK

ALLISON, WILLIAM B. (1829–1908), representative and senator from Iowa, one of the inner circle of Republican Senate leaders in the late nineteenth and early twentieth centuries. William Boyd Allison began his political career as a Whig, but aligned with the newly founded Republican party. In 1862 he was elected to the U.S. House of Representatives from Iowa's 3d District for the first of four terms. He served on the influential House Ways and Means Committee and was a loyal party man on Civil War and Reconstruction issues. He strongly backed Mississippi River navigational improvements and government subsidies for railroads; he

WILLIAM B. ALLISON. Steel engraving.
MAGAZINE OF WESTERN HISTORY, COURTESY OF
LIBRARY OF CONGRESS

used his influence to promote the interests of railroads in which he had a personal financial stake.

After a losing bid in 1870, Allison was elected to the Senate in 1872. He was reelected five times. While serving in the Senate, he consolidated his position as an ally of Iowa's most powerful political boss, railroad lawyer Joseph W. Blythe. He sat on the Senate Finance Committee for thirty years; he was chairman of the Appropriations Committee from 1881 until his death, except for two years when the Democrats controlled the Senate; and he was chairman of the Republican Senate caucus from 1897. By the late 1890s, he had become a member of the Senate's ruling quadrumvirate, popularly known as the Big Four, along with Rhode Island's Nelson W. Aldrich, Connecticut's Orville H. Platt, and Wisconsin's John C. Spooner. He was defeated in bids for the Republican presidential nomination in 1888 and 1896.

Allison's skill at walking a political tightrope was most strikingly evident in his handling of the currency issue, given the appeal that inflation had for many Iowa farmers. He played a key role in the adoption of the 1875 law redeeming Civil War greenbacks in gold. As agrarian pressure for bimetallism grew, he was the moving force in watering down a proposal for silver remonetization into a limited silver purchase program as embodied in the Bland-Allison Act of 1878. He voted for the Sherman Silver Purchase Act of 1890 but then worked (unsuccessfully) behind the scenes on the Senate Finance Committee for its repeal in 1893. He supported adoption of the Currency Act of 1900, also known as the Gold Standard Act.

His record was much the same regarding the tariff: he bowed to his constituents' demand for lower rates on industrial products while avoiding antagonizing powerful eastern manufacturing interests. He played leading roles in the Republican Senate's 1888 rewriting of the proposed tariff reductions in the Mills bill adopted by the House Democratic majority, in the adoption of the McKinley Tariff Act of 1890, and in the framing of the Dingley Tariff Act of 1897.

Complaints from Iowans about excessive rates and abuse of power by the railroads constituted Allison's most difficult political problem. Recognizing that a degree of government regulation was required to meet popular demands, he supported adoption of the Interstate Commerce Commission Act of 1887. Later his name was attached to the amendment resolving the conflict between old guard Republicans and President Theodore Roosevelt over the 1906 Hepburn bill authorizing the Interstate Commerce Commission to fix railroad rates.

Allison narrowly defeated factional rival Albert B. Cummins in the June 1908 preferential primary for the Republican Senate nomination, but he died of cancer on 4 August of the same year.

BIBLIOGRAPHY

Merrill, Horace S., and Marion G. Merrill. *The Republican Command, 1897–1913*. 1971.
Sage, Leland L. *William Boyd Allison*. 1956.

JOHN BRAEMAN

AMENDING. [*This entry focuses on the process of amending bills and resolutions in Congress. For discussion of amending the Constitution, see* Constitution, *article on* Congressional Interpretation of the Constitution.] Amending is the process by which members attempt to change the content of legislation as it is considered in committee markup sessions and during House and Senate floor sessions. Introducing a bill begins a process of informal review and formal consideration that can last for the entire length of a two-year Congress. Only under extraordinary circumstances would Congress pass a major bill without first making changes in it. These changes are made during the course of the amending process which, for this reason, is at the heart of the legislative process in Congress.

The legislative process permits a bill to be amended at as many as seven different stages: when it is considered by a subcommittee of the House, by the parent committee of that subcommittee, and by the full House; when it is considered by a subcommittee and committee of the Senate and by the Senate itself; and when the House and Senate try to reach final agreement on the bill's content, either in a conference committee or by a formal exchange of amendments between the two houses. In some cases, one or more of these stages is bypassed; for example, the House and Senate sometimes pass noncontroversial bills without first considering them in formal committee and subcommittee meetings. In other cases, stages are added to the process; for example, some bills are considered by one House or Senate committee only after having been debated and amended by another committee of that house.

Amendments in Committee. Major bills usually are considered first by a subcommittee of the House or Senate. Identical, or "companion," bills frequently are introduced in both houses, so that House and Senate subcommittees can begin to act on the same subject at the same time. After one or more days of public hearings on the bill's merits, the subcommittee decides whether to consider amendments to it at a "markup" session. The text of the bill is marked up (figuratively, at least) as the subcommittee decides to make additions, deletions, or substitutions in its text. Members propose these changes in the form of amendments that specify precisely what alterations in the bill they wish to make. After an amendment has been proposed, members may debate it before voting to accept or reject it. They also may amend the amendment before deciding whether to approve it in its amended form. Ultimately, the subcommittee votes to report the bill, with the amendments it has adopted, to its parent committee, which then may repeat this process.

Much the same process takes place in Senate subcommittees and committees, and the process in both houses generally follows the rules of the full House or Senate for amending legislation on the floor. However, the smaller size of committees and subcommittees usually makes it possible for their markup process to be less formal and structured than the amending process on the floor. There is one other important difference between the amending process in committee and the process as it takes place on the floor. Only the full House and Senate actually may make changes in the text of a bill. Committees and subcommittees only recommend changes in the form of amendments. The full House and Senate then must approve these committee amendments before they actually are incorporated into the bill.

Floor Amendments. When the House or Senate begins to consider the bill on the floor, it acts first on any committee amendments. Members can offer amendments to each committee amendment before voting to accept or reject it, but they usually cannot offer their own amendments to the bill itself until after disposing of all committee amendments. An important exception arises when a committee reports a bill to either house with a single amendment that proposes an entirely different text for the bill. In that case, members generally direct their floor amendments to that committee amendment, often called an "amendment in the nature of a substitute," not to the text of the bill as it was originally introduced. When members eventually agree to the committee substitute, as amended, that completes the amending process because the bill now has been totally amended; the House or Senate then votes on passing the bill as amended by the substitute.

Each amendment must be in writing and read on the floor before members begin to debate it. An amendment to change the text of a measure is known as a "first-degree" amendment. Before the House or Senate votes on that amendment, members may offer amendments to it; an amendment to an amendment is a "second-degree" amendment. Amendments may add (insert) additional language into a bill, strike language from the bill, or replace (strike and insert) language in the bill. For some purposes, it also can be important to distinguish between "perfecting" amendments, which propose to make a limited change in a bill or first-degree amendment, and substitute amendments, which propose to completely replace the text of the bill or first-degree amendment. Once the House or Senate has approved an amendment, it no longer can be amended. Also, members cannot offer amendments that only propose to amend some language that already has been amended. For example, once the House amends a bill by changing a dollar amount from, say, $1 million to $2 million, an amendment is not in order if it proposes only to make another change in the same dollar amount.

Chamber Differences. In these respects, the amending processes on the House and Senate floor are similar. In other respects, however, there are important differences in how the two houses amend legislation. The amending process in the House usually is systematic; members offer amendments to each section or title of a bill in sequence. Senators may offer their amendments to any portion of the bill in any order. Representatives usually may debate each amendment for only five minutes each; senators can debate an amendment at length and even filibuster an amendment they strongly oppose. In the House, each amendment must be germane to the provision or amendment it proposes to change. The Senate requires amendments to be germane only under limited circumstances: for example, senators' amendments to most appropriations and budget measures must be germane as must all amendments that are offered when the Senate has invoked cloture to limit debate. At all other times, senators are free to offer amendments that are totally unrelated to the subject of the bill the Senate is considering.

Representatives and senators do not have the same ability to amend each bill and resolution they consider on the floor. Each house can invoke procedures that limit or even foreclose members' amending opportunities. For example, the House considers many measures under the procedure known as "suspension of the rules," which precludes all amendments except for amendments that are incorporated in the motion to suspend the rules and pass the bill. The House normally considers more important and controversial bills by transforming itself into a Committee of the Whole (formally, a Committee of the Whole House on the State of the Union), which follows procedures that are more convenient for offering and debating amendments. Before the House debates and amends a bill in Committee of the Whole, however, it normally adopts a resolution, known as a "special rule," reported by its Rules Committee to propose special procedures for acting on that particular bill. These procedures may include restrictions on the amendments to the bill that members can offer. A "closed" rule typically prohibits all floor amendments except committee amendments. A "modified open" or "modified closed" rule precludes some but not all amendments; frequently, such a restrictive rule will specifically identify the relatively small number of floor amendments that members can propose. The House must adopt each special rule by majority vote before it takes effect.

In the Senate, members' freedom to offer amendments can be limited by invoking *cloture* to limit further debate on a measure. The effect of cloture, which usually requires support from at least sixty senators, is to permit the Senate to continue considering the measure for no more than thirty more hours, during which senators can only propose germane amendments that were submitted to the Senate in writing before the cloture vote. Alternatively, the Senate sometimes agrees by unanimous consent to limit debate on one or all amendments to a bill. A unanimous consent agreement also may prohibit all amendments to the bill except those identified in the agreement itself. On the other hand, unanimous consent agreements in the Senate and special rules in the House can allow senators or representatives to propose amendments that would not otherwise be in order.

After both houses have passed different versions of the same bill, they again resort to an amending process to resolve the differences between their two versions. The House and Senate must pass a bill in precisely the same form before it can be presented to the president for his approval or disapproval. So after the Senate passes a House bill with one or more amendments, or after the House amends and passes a Senate bill, they must reach agreement on each of these amendments before the legislative process is completed. They may do so through a process by which, for example, the House amends each Senate amendment and the Senate then amends that House amendment. The alternative is for both houses to create a conference committee to report a package settlement of the disagreements that both houses vote to accept or reject without further amendment.

The Importance of Amending. The amending process on the House and Senate floors presents members with the opportunity to shape public policy on subjects that are not within the jurisdictions of the committees on which they serve. Strictly in policy terms, the votes on floor amendments can be considered the most important votes that members cast. During the 95th and 96th Congresses (1977–1981), the House passed 3,013 bills and resolutions and defeated 72; senators rejected only 8 of the 2,634 measures that reached a vote on final passage in that body. Thus, the two houses defeated fewer than 1.5 percent of the measures on which they completed floor action. Each bill must survive the vote on final passage, of course, but these data illustrate that the critical question to be asked of House or Senate floor action on a bill is not whether the bill will pass, but what provisions it will contain when it does pass.

The answer depends on the bill that the standing committee (or committees) brings before the House or Senate for debate, amendment, and passage. This establishes the basic policy approach and framework that chamber will consider. Equally important, however, is how that approach and framework is changed during its floor consideration as a result of the amendments that individual members propose and a majority of their colleagues support. Proposals that members advocate unsuccessfully in subcommittee or committee markup may be presented again as floor amendments in that house, and proposals that are not approved in one house may be revived as floor amendments in the other. The final version of a bill cannot be predicted with confidence until all the stages at which it can be amended have been completed.

Especially in the House of Representatives, the amending process on the floor has become even more important since the House began in 1970 to make organizational and procedural changes. On balance, the effect of many of these reforms has been to reduce the influence of committees and their chairmen. The ability of chairmen to control the agendas and decisions of their committees was reduced at the same time that the House exposed its proceedings to greater public scrutiny and influence. One consequence was to encourage members to offer floor amendments that challenged committee recommendations and for members to support those amendments, especially when they benefited important constituency interests.

As a result, more floor amendments were proposed and adopted, creating greater uncertainty about what would happen to legislation on the floor. Woodrow Wilson's classic dictum that the floor sessions of the House and Senate are merely "Congress on public exhibition," the real work being done in committee rooms, is not nearly as true as it may have been a century ago. In the contemporary Congress, there is no more important aspect of lawmaking than the amending process.

[*See also* Committees, *article on* Markups; Conference Committees; Germaneness.]

BIBLIOGRAPHY

Bach, Stanley. "Parliamentary Strategy and the Amendment Process: Rules and Case Studies of Congressional Action." *Polity* 15 (1983): 573–592.

Smith, Steven S. *Call to Order: Floor Politics in the House and Senate.* 1989.

U.S. House of Representatives. *Deschler's Precedents of the United States House of Representatives,* by Lewis Deschler. 94th Cong., 2d sess., 1977. H. Doc. 94-661. Vol. 9.

U.S. Senate. *Senate Procedure, Precedents, and Practices,* by Floyd M. Riddick. 97th Cong., 1st sess., 1981. S. Doc. 97-2. Pp. 22–113.

STANLEY BACH

AMERICAN POLITICAL SCIENCE ASSOCIATION. Founded in 1903, the American Political Science Association (APSA) is the major professional organization in the United States for people engaged in studying politics and government. Its fifteen thousand members are mainly political scientists who teach and conduct research at colleges and universities.

Congress and other legislative bodies are prime targets of political scientists' research. APSA's presidents, elected annually for their scholarly eminence, have included such students of Congress as Woodrow Wilson, E. E. Schattschneider, Arthur W. Macmahon, David B. Truman, Heinz Eulau, James MacGregor Burns, John C. Wahlke, Richard F. Fenno, Jr., and Charles O. Jones.

In 1941 the association created its Committee on

Congress, chaired by George B. Galloway, to apply managerial expertise to the legislative process. The group's 1945 report faulted Congress's operations and proposed such reforms as professional staffing, committee realignment, consolidated leadership, and delegation of trivial legislation. Many of these proposals found their way into the Legislative Reorganization Act of 1946. APSA's later Committee on Political Parties, chaired by Schattschneider, wrote a notable 1952 report advocating responsible parties headed by strong leaders in Congress and the executive.

Later generations of scholars have avoided reformism, drawing closer to Congress in using it and other legislatures as research subjects. Since 1953 the APSA-sponsored Congressional Fellowship Program has brought scholars, journalists, federal executives, and other professionals from the United States and abroad to Capitol Hill, where they spend ten months working in member or committee offices and attending seminars. The program now selects forty to fifty fellows each year. The more than twelve hundred former Congressional Fellows include some of today's most prominent congressional scholars, reporters, editors, and public officials.

Among APSA's organized sections, the oldest and most active is Legislative Studies. This group sponsors panels, workshops, symposia, and social events at APSA's annual meetings. In addition to distributing an informative newsletter, the section is associated with *Legislative Studies Quarterly*, the leading journal in its field.

[*See also* Intern and Fellowship Programs.]

BIBLIOGRAPHY

American Political Science Association, Committee on Congress. *The Reorganization of Congress*. 1945.
American Political Science Association, Committee on Political Parties. *Toward a More Responsible Two-Party System: A Report of the Committee on Political Parties*, 1950.

ROGER H. DAVIDSON

AMES, FISHER (1758–1808), representative from Massachusetts and leader of the Federalist party's House faction. When John Quincy Adams reviewed *The Works of Fisher Ames*, which appeared posthumously, he acknowledged Ames's role in the struggle between Jeffersonianism and Federalism, a struggle over which would ultimately be considered the "exponent of American principles." But Adams assailed Ames for justifying Britain as

FISHER AMES. Steel engraving, after the original painting by Alonzo Chappel, c. 1860.   LIBRARY OF CONGRESS

"the last hope of the human race" and declaring that Britain "was *right* and we were *wrong*." Adams charged that Ames had founded his political opinions on "scorn and contempt for his own country."

Born in Dedham, Massachusetts, this controversial Federalist was active in public life from 1787 to 1807 and was a member of Congress for the eight years of Washington's presidency. Graduating from Harvard at the age of sixteen, Ames set out on a career that began with intermittent teaching, service in the Revolutionary War, and a subsequent turn to the law. During the turbulent period of 1786 and 1787 Ames identified with the forces of "order" in opposition to the rebellion led by Captain Daniel Shays. He was elected to the first four Congresses, where his oratorical flair and knowledge of political economy stood him in good stead. When James Madison abandoned Washington's party to head the Democratic-Republican party in Congress, Ames emerged as chief spokesman for the Federalists.

Ames crowned his congressional career in his last year of service, 1796. Jay's Treaty had been approved in the Senate, finally settling disputes that still lingered from the Revolutionary War between the United States and Britain. In the House of Representatives Republicans mounted a last-minute effort to scuttle the treaty, seeking to deny appropriations for carrying out American obligations.

Ames, by then ill with the disease that would claim his life twelve years later, sat quietly until the final stage of the debate. When word spread throughout the corridors of Congress that Ames would speak, the Senate and Supreme Court adjourned for the occasion and the galleries filled to capacity.

He did not disappoint. "My God, how great he is," declared Supreme Court Justice James Iredell. When the treaty passed, 51 to 49, the credit went to Ames's speech, the first really great oration delivered on the House floor. Young Daniel Webster memorized the speech and used it as a model for his own oratory; Abraham Lincoln greatly admired it as well and could recite long portions from memory.

With the close of this Congress, Ames closed his official public service. Even John Quincy Adams conceded that Ames was "an ingenious and amiable" patriot of "real wisdom and virtue."

BIBLIOGRAPHY

Ames, Fisher. *Works of Fisher Ames.* Edited and enlarged by W. B. Allen. 1983.
Bernhard, Wilfred E. A. *Fisher Ames: Federalist and Statesman, 1758–1808.* 1965.

WILLIAM B. ALLEN

ANDERSON, CLINTON P. (1895–1975), Democratic representative (1941–1945) and senator (1949–1973) from New Mexico, architect of major conservation, health care, and atomic energy legislation. Born and raised in South Dakota, Anderson attended Dakota Wesleyan University and the University of Michigan, where he pursued interests in law and journalism before family responsibilities ended his studies. In 1917, ill with tuberculosis, he moved to New Mexico, where he regained his health, worked briefly as an investigative reporter, and established a profitable insurance agency.

The genial, sharp-witted, six-foot-two-inch Anderson rose quickly in his state's turbulent political atmosphere and in 1940 was elected as a Democrat to

CLINTON P. ANDERSON.   LIBRARY OF CONGRESS

the U.S. House of Representatives. A protégé of Speaker Sam Rayburn, he received high-profile committee assignments, including an investigation of wartime food shortages. Despite his chronically poor health, Anderson easily won reelection in 1942 and 1944, and in May 1945 President Harry S. Truman appointed him secretary of Agriculture. After earning mixed reviews as an administrator, Anderson returned to legislative work with his election to the U.S. Senate in 1948.

In the Senate Anderson learned to frame issues so that other members found it difficult to vote against him. He quickly absorbed large amounts of information on complex policy issues for which others had little patience. He proved to be a faithful ally as well as a vindictive adversary. A master legislative mechanic with a superior sense of timing, he employed a behind-the-scenes style of quiet persuasion.

During his twenty-four-year Senate career, Anderson chaired, for varying periods, two Senate committees, Interior and Insular Affairs and Aeronautical and Space Sciences, and the Joint Committee on Atomic Energy. As a member of the Finance Committee, he cofounded Medicare. On the Interior and Insular Affairs Committee, he promoted resources conservation and was the principal force behind passage of the Wilderness Act of 1964.

BIBLIOGRAPHY

Anderson, Clinton P., with Milton Viorst. *Outsider in the Senate: Senator Clinton Anderson's Memoirs.* 1970.
Baker, Richard Allan. *Conservation Politics: The Senate Career of Clinton P. Anderson.* 1985.

RICHARD A. BAKER

ANTHONY RULE.

The Anthony Rule is a Senate legislative procedure named for Henry B. Anthony, Republican senator from Rhode Island from 1859 to 1884. It was first used on 5 February 1880 as a way of reducing the congestion on the Senate calendar. The Senate had been spending much of its time arguing over the order in which bills would be considered. The rule forced the consideration of measures in an automatic and orderly way. On 19 March 1884, under a codification of the Senate rules, the Anthony Rule was incorporated into Rule VII of the Standing Rules of the Senate.

Under the Anthony Rule, bills and resolutions appearing on the calendar are taken up automatically in the order in which they appear. Each senator is allowed to speak once, for five minutes only, on any question during the consideration of any calendar measure. The Anthony Rule also expedites removal of calendar items. A single statement of "over" following the initial reading of a bill removes that bill from consideration and allows the Senate to proceed to the next calendar item.

The Anthony Rule has in effect been superseded by the evolution of the job of majority leader, a position that did not exist when the rule was adopted. In current practice, the majority leader decides which items on the calendar will be put before the Senate, and the automatic call of the calendar under the Anthony Rule is routinely avoided by unanimous consent.

BIBLIOGRAPHY

Haynes, George H. *The Senate of the United States: Its History and Practice.* 2 vols. 1938.

ROBERT B. DOVE

ANTIBALLISTIC MISSILE SYSTEMS TREATY

(1972; 23 U.S.T. 3435–3461). The U.S.–U.S.S.R. Antiballistic Missile (ABM) Systems Treaty emerged in 1972 as the product of a decade of negotiations between the United States and the Soviet Union and between the executive branch and Congress. During the Kennedy and Johnson administrations, Secretary of Defense Robert S. McNamara had urged the Soviets to forgo development of antimissile defenses, arguing that such systems could undermine nuclear deterrence and thus be destabilizing. When the Soviets responded that they thought it only appropriate and moral to defend their people against nuclear attack, the Johnson administration launched the Sentinel ABM program.

Congressional opposition to establishing an ABM program, led in the early stages by Sen. John Sherman Cooper (R.-Ky.), stemmed as much from a widespread public distrust of expensive Pentagon proposals in the wake of the Vietnam War as from strategic arguments concerning international stability. The Nixon administration responded that a program of ABM development would help persuade the Soviets to give up their own such defenses.

Thus Soviet agreement in 1972 to a ban on missile defenses in the Strategic Arms Limitation Talks (SALT I) could be viewed as vindicating both Congress and the executive branch, for the ban was put into effect without a full-fledged program of building on the U.S. side. The ABM treaty drew much less criticism during ratification than the accompanying Interim Agreement on Strategic Offensive Arms. The treaty was seen as an important, albeit partial, step toward gaining Soviet acceptance of

SEN. HENRY B. ANTHONY (R-R.I.).
PERLEY'S REMINISCENCES, VOL. 2

arguments concerning the stabilizing influence of "mutual assured destruction."

In 1985 Congress thwarted a Reagan administration attempt to reinterpret the ABM treaty in order to allow development and testing of weaponry proposed in Reagan's Strategic Defense Initiative (SDI, commonly referred to as Star Wars). The administration, yielding to critics, agreed to adhere to the treaty's traditional interpretation. It reopened the issue in 1986, prompting Congress to ban SDI tests that would violate the treaty as traditionally interpreted.

[See also Nuclear Non-Proliferation Treaty; Limited Test Ban Treaty; Strategic Arms Limitation Talks (SALT); Strategic Defense Initiative (SDI).]

BIBLIOGRAPHY

Newhouse, John. *Cold Dawn: The Story of SALT.* 1973.
Yanarella, Ernest J. *The Missile Defense Controversy.* 1977.

GEORGE H. QUESTER

ANTICOMMUNISM. See Communism and Anticommunism.

ANTI-FEDERALISTS. "Anti-Federalist" was the term used between 1787 and 1790 to describe opponents of ratification of the Constitution. In the view of most twentieth-century historians, Anti-Federalists represented a less aristocratic and more democratic alternative to the Federalists. Despite their belief in legislative supremacy, Anti-Federalists worried about a legislature seated in a distant capital, a House of Representatives too small for the size of the population, and a Senate whose powers violated separation of powers. They sought to limit the power of Congress in various areas, including taxation, state militias, federal elections, and jurisdiction over the federal capital; and to deny Congress the power to abridge freedom of religion, press, speech, or assembly. Southern Anti-Federalists in particular advocated a two-thirds or three-fourths vote before Congress could exercise certain of its powers, particularly relating to commerce. Most important, Anti-Federalists sought to attach language that would have limited Congress to expressly delegated powers, thus eliminating the effect of the "necessary and proper" clause of Article I.

Anti-Federalists were not very successful in electing members to the First Congress in 1789. The two members sent by Virginia to the twenty-two-man Senate had no influence. Virginia and South Carolina sent three Anti-Federalists to the fifty-nine-member House; New York and Massachusetts sent two each. Sen. Richard Henry Lee (Va.) and Rep. Elbridge Gerry (Mass.) were the most famous and vocal of these Anti-Federalists. During its first session, these ten House Anti-Federalists, along with six Federalists who frequently voted with them, formed an important but usually ineffective voting block that sought to protect states' rights and limit the powers of the executive and judicial branches.

The most bitter debate between Federalists and Anti-Federalists occurred in August 1789 over the constitutional amendments that became the Bill of Rights. Anti-Federalists lost their effort to amend the Constitution to limit the power of the federal government and its control over the states. After that failure the Anti-Federalists disappeared as a force in Congress and the nation. Most of their leaders, including those who served in Congress, became Jeffersonian Republicans.

[See also Federalists; Jeffersonian Republicans.]

BIBLIOGRAPHY

Bickford, Charlene, and Kenneth R. Bowling. *Birth of the Nation: The First Federal Congress.* 1989.
Main, Jackson T. *The Antifederalists.* 1961.

KENNETH R. BOWLING

ANTI-SALOON LEAGUE. Founded in 1893 as a single-issue nonpartisan organization, the Anti-Saloon League employed professional leaders in its efforts to mobilize a mass constituency, initially focusing on local and state actions. Drawn into congressional lobbying in 1899 by the campaign of the Woman's Christian Temperance Union to outlaw liquor in army canteens, the league fought the entrenched power of committee chairmen and party caucuses who protected the liquor trades. After Congress outlawed the sale of liquor on army posts in 1901, the league attempted to win other restrictive liquor regulations, most notably a ban on the interstate shipment of liquor to dry areas.

The league's power came through mobilization of voters in support of dry candidates of any party. By the early 1910s, this technique had won substantial support in Congress for prohibitory legislation. This support was first demonstrated early in 1913 when Congress overrode William Howard Taft's veto of the interstate shipment bill advocated by the league. The league then announced its campaign for a constitutional amendment for national prohibition. The league used the record of the 1914 House vote on this amendment in subsequent election campaigns to defeat its enemies and elect its supporters. In the 1916 elections the prohibitionists

KNIGHT OF MODERATION. "Ready for the fray—The saloons must go!" Cartoon illustrating the growing conflict between supporters of prohibition, depicted as a chivalrous knight, and liquor interests, portrayed as a drunken mob rushing toward the refuge of the Capitol. Published 10 September 1886.

OFFICE OF THE HISTORIAN OF THE U.S. SENATE

achieved the two-thirds majority of both houses needed to initiate the amendment.

Following the 1919 ratification of the Eighteenth Amendment, the Anti-Saloon League divided on strategy and its power waned. Nevertheless, majorities in Congress favorable to prohibition were sustained, and the league proudly noted the largest majorities ever following the 1928 elections. The depression that began the next year, however, changed public opinion, and league resources evaporated. It never again enjoyed notable influence.

[See also Eighteenth Amendment; National Prohibition Act; Prohibition.]

BIBLIOGRAPHY

Kerr, K. Austin. *Organized for Prohibition: A New History of the Anti-Saloon League.* 1985.

Odegard, Peter. *Pressure Politics: The Story of the Anti-Saloon League.* 1928.

K. AUSTIN KERR

ANTITRUST LEGISLATION. *See* Clayton Antitrust Act; Sherman Antitrust Act.

APPOINTMENTS, RECESS. *See* Recess Appointments.

APPORTIONMENT AND REDISTRICTING.

The boundaries of congressional districts in all but the smallest states are redrawn at the beginning of every decade to equalize their populations. The need for such adjustment stems from the constitutional requirement that congressional districts have equal populations, together with a constantly shifting U.S. population. The alteration of old district lines to achieve new ideal populations is the essence of redistricting, or, as it is sometimes called, reapportionment.

The first step in congressional redistricting is called apportionment. Using a modified proportional representation formula derived by Edward Huntingdon, the Census Bureau calculates each state's share of congressional districts when the decennial census is finished. The second step is to adjust congressional boundaries within each state's border to achieve near equality in district populations. The result of this two-stage process is that district populations are made equal within states but, by strict standards, remain relatively unequal across states. In 1980, Nevada, with its population of 787,000, and Maine, with its population of 1,125,000, were each apportioned two seats, while South Dakota, with 690,000, got only one, producing districts of very unequal size. Congressional districts in Maine had an ideal population of 563,000, in Nevada 393,000, and in South Dakota 690,000.

The authority for congressional apportionment is constitutional. Article I, section 2 states that "Representatives shall be apportioned among the states according to their numbers." In the beginning, Congress expanded its membership to accommodate new states and population increases, but since 1910, House membership has been kept at 435. In 1790, there was one member for each 33,000 people and 106 members total. By 1990, the average ratio was one seat per 570,000 people.

The method of congressional apportionment has changed five times since 1790. The differences between these methods are slight, all of them tending to produce roughly similar and proportionate outcomes. But the small differences associated with the choice of a particular formula mean a lot to states that lose a seat under one method and keep it under another. Some critics, for instance, maintain that the Huntingdon formula, which has been used since 1950, favors small states over large. But for the most part, the Huntingdon method has been widely accepted for its fairness to all states.

Shifting population trends within the United States have caused some enormous variations in the sizes of state delegations over time. New York had ten House seats in 1790, forty in 1830, twenty-one in 1860, forty-five in 1930, and thirty-one in 1990. California, by contrast, grew steadily from eleven seats in 1930 to fifty-two seats in 1990. The original thirteen states had 100 percent of the seats in Congress in 1790, 42 percent in 1870, and 33 percent in 1990. Between 1949 and 1992, nearly sixty seats shifted from the frostbelt to the sunbelt states.

Equal Population Doctrine and Congress. In a number of legislative actions taken prior to the "one person, one vote" judicial decisions of *Baker v. Carr* and *Reynolds v. Sims*, Congress clearly demonstrated its support for the principle of redistricting in favor of districts of equal population. In 1842, Congress legislated that representatives should be "elected by districts of contiguous territory equal in number" with "no district electing more than one representative." Thirty years later, the Reapportionment Act of 1872 also declared that districts should contain "as nearly as possible an equal number of inhabitants." Because Congress had already put itself on a straight and narrow course toward equally populated districts, congressional malapportionment was relatively moderate in 1960. All but 40 of the 435 congressional districts were within 15 percent of the national average.

Prior to 1962, the Supreme Court repeatedly refused to tackle the problem of malapportionment. In *Wood v. Brown* (287 U.S. 1, 8 [1932]), the Supreme Court decided not to overturn a Mississippi law that created unequal congressional districts. In 1946, the Court was given another chance to intervene when a Northwestern University political scientist brought suit against the state of Illinois, arguing that the gross disparities in district populations violated the equal protection clause of the Fourteenth Amendment. As before, the Court refused by a vote of 4 to 3 to take up the case of *Colgrove v. Green* (328 U.S. 549 [1946]), because the issue was, in Justice Felix Frankfurter's words, "of a peculiarly political nature and therefore not meant for judicial interpretation."

The Court's approach changed dramatically with its ruling in *Baker v. Carr* (369 U.S. 186 [1962]).

The plaintiffs had argued that the malapportionment of the Tennessee state assembly violated both the state and federal constitutions. The Supreme Court, by a vote of 6 to 2, decided that it had jurisdiction, despite Frankfurter's objection that this would "catapult the Courts into a mathematical quagmire." In *Wesberry v. Sanders* (376 U.S. 1 [1964]) and *Reynolds v. Sims* (377 U.S. [1964]), the Court applied its "one person, one vote" principle to congressional and state legislative districts, holding in essence that the right to vote is not equal if people vote in unequally sized districts. In particular, according to the logic of malapportionment, a vote in a large district has less value than one in a small district, because a vote's weight varies inversely with an electorate's size. After the initial ruling that malapportionment was justiciable, many of the subsequent cases focused on the issue of how equal new district populations had to be in order to meet the Court's expectations. The congressional standard is that, "as nearly as practicable," one person's vote should be worth as much as another's. The Supreme Court held in *Kirkpatrick v. Priesler* (394 U.S. 526 [1969]) that states should make a good faith effort to achieve exact mathematical equality, and in *White v. Weiser* (412 U.S. 783 [1973]), it struck down the Texas legislature's proposal for a congressional redistricting plan because one with smaller deviations was available. The rejected plan had population deviations from the ideal of less than 5 percent. A decade later, the Court in effect made the equal population requirement even stricter when in *Karcher v. Daggett* (426 U.S. 725 [1983]) it turned down a New Jersey congressional plan with trivial population differences (0.69 percent) in favor of a plan with even smaller deviations.

Vote Dilution and the Evolving Concept of Equity. The first meaning of redistricting equity is described by the principle of "one person, one vote"; namely, that every eligible voter has the right to an equally weighted vote. When districts vary in size, people voting in the larger districts have in a purely mathematical sense less voice in and influence over the outcome of an election than those in smaller districts. In addition, malapportionment gives more representation to some areas of a political jurisdiction than to others.

With the passage of the Voting Rights Act of 1965 and the growing clamor over political gerrymandering, a second sense of redistricting equity emerged—the right to a meaningful or undiluted vote. The logic of a vote-dilution claim is as follows:

even if an individual has a right to an equally weighted vote, the exercise of that right can be frustrated if district lines are drawn in such a manner as to dilute the votes of one group and enhance the electoral prospects of another.

There are two distinct types of vote-dilution claims—partisan and racial. The first points to partisan or political gerrymandering, in which districting arrangements can unfairly favor a particular political party over another (usually the majority over the minority party) or favor incumbents over challengers (the so-called bipartisan or incumbent gerrymander problem). Historically, the Court has been reluctant to involve itself deeply in partisan gerrymandering issues. Indeed, until its ruling in *Davis v. Bandemer* (478 U.S. 109 [1986]), there was no clear indication that it regarded partisan gerrymandering as even a justiciable issue.

In considering the allegation by Indiana's Democrats in *Davis* that the Republican-controlled legislature diluted their voting strength and caused disproportionate gains for Republican candidates, the Supreme Court ruled 6 to 3 that a political gerrymandering claim was justiciable. At the same time, however, the Court cast considerable doubt on whether the potential justiciability of gerrymandering would mean anything of practical significance by overruling the lower court's decision to strike down the Indiana legislature's plan. Some interpret this decision as meaning that a partisan gerrymander claim can only be won by political parties who are able to show that they have suffered exclusion and discrimination comparable to that experienced by racial minorities, and that this threshold virtually rules out any claims by the two major American political parties, the Democrats and Republicans.

At the end of the decade, the Supreme Court further indicated its intention to keep a high threshold for political gerrymandering cases when it affirmed a lower court ruling in *Badham v. Eu* (109 U.S. 829 [1989]). The Court refused to overturn the infamous Burton congressional redistricting plan, holding that Republicans had many avenues of political redress (including the initiative and referendum process) and could not be said to be in a position of political exclusion since they had held a number of statewide offices throughout the 1980s.

Another form of political gerrymandering is the so-called bipartisan or incumbent protection gerrymander. Relative to partisan gerrymandering, the courts have taken a more benign view of explicitly bipartisan plans. In *Burns v. Richardson* (384 U.S. 73 [1966]) and *White v. Weiser* (412 U.S. 783 [1973]), the Court held that drawing lines to minimize contests between sitting incumbents does not in and of itself establish "invidiousness." And in *Gaffney v. Cummings* (412 U.S. 735 [1973]), the Court upheld a purposely political plan that attempted to create proportionate shares of districts for the two political parties based on voting results in the previous three elections. With the growing clamor over the incumbency advantage, however, the Court may find it harder to bless bipartisan gerrymanders in the future.

In addition to the issue of political vote dilution, there is the equally controversial question of racial- and ethnic-group vote dilution. The critical legislation in this regard is the Voting Rights Act (VRA) of 1965 and its subsequent amendments. Although most VRA litigation challenges the use of multi-member districts, sections 2 and 5 also apply to the arrangements of constituency boundaries in single-member district jurisdictions. Areas of the country that are covered by section 5 of the VRA must clear any changes in district boundaries with the Justice Department or the district court of the District of Columbia. The critical issue in clearance is whether any proposed changes in the procedures and rules governing elections in areas with a history of vote discrimination and low voting participation cause retrogression in the voting power of protected minority groups.

Areas that are not covered by section 5 still must meet the standards of section 2, which states: "No voting qualification or prerequisite to voting, or standard, practice, or procedure shall be imposed or applied by any State or political sub-division to deny or abridge the right of any citizen of the United States to vote on account of race or color." Prior to 1982, section 2 was interpreted to mean only the intentional dilution of disadvantaged minority votes (*Bolden v. City of Mobile*, 446 U.S. 55 [1980]). The act was amended in 1982 to cover rules and procedures that had the effect of diluting minority votes regardless of intentions. In *Thornburg v. Gingles* (478 U.S. 30 [1986]), a case involving state legislative districts in North Carolina, the Court singled out three criteria as most important in deciding whether a jurisdiction had complied with the provisions of the VRA: Is a minority group sufficiently large and compact enough to constitute a majority of a district? Is it politically cohesive? Is there evidence of racially polarized voting against minority candidates?

At a minimum, the protection afforded by the VRA prevents the exclusion of groups from the opportunity to elect representatives of their own choice. However, a number of critics maintain that the VRA is being interpreted more expansively by some plaintiffs as a right to proportional representation, a right which the Supreme Court has on several occasions explicitly denied.

More generally, the right to an undiluted vote is problematic in a system that employs single member, simple plurality (SMSP) rules. The logic of such a system is that it exaggerates the share of seats won by the party with the most votes and minimizes that share of seats the other parties get. This is touted by SMSP proponents as an advantage over proportional representation systems because it eases the task of creating a governing majority in the legislature. If the right to an undiluted vote is interpreted to mean anything more than the right to nonexclusion, it puts the courts in the uncomfortable position of enforcing remedies for a right (namely, proportional representation for racial or political groups) that the VRA explicitly denies.

Common Criteria for Redistricting. Broadly speaking, people commonly apply two types of criteria when assessing the quality and fairness of a redistricting: considerations of form and considerations of outcome. The most important considerations of form are equal population, natural communities of interest, and compactness or contiguity. Equal population has already been discussed. It is sometimes referred to as one of the primary criteria, meaning that considerations of population equality must be satisfied absolutely even if they conflict with other considerations of fairness.

By comparison, respect for natural communities of interest is not one of the primary criteria. In the broadest sense, this term encompasses many meanings, including agricultural areas, mountainous counties, desert regions, coastal land, and the like. The political interests associated with these geographical areas may be occupational (e.g., farming), sociological (e.g., areas within one media market), or policy oriented (e.g., the predilection of coastal areas toward environmentalism). The implicit assumption is that district boundaries should respect these natural community boundaries so that important social and economic interests are clearly articulated within the representative body. Opponents of a community-of-interest approach worry that districts so drawn encourage parochialism and factionalism.

A variant of the communities-of-interest criterion is respect for city, county, and local government boundaries. Prior to the "one person, one vote" decisions, several states required that state legislative districts follow county boundary lines exactly. The equal population standard requires that district boundaries stray from local government jurisdictions when necessary to achieve the target population figure. Assuming the satisfaction of the "one person–one vote" principle, a number of states mandate that districting arrangements minimize the splitting of city and county boundary lines to the degree feasible.

The last of the so-called formal criteria is compactness or contiguity. Contiguity means that all parts of the district must be connected at a point or, in other words, that a district cannot consist of unconnected tracts or "islands" surrounded by tracts from another district. However, contiguity can sometimes mean contiguous at a point in the water, as when offshore islands are grouped with an onshore district. Contiguity, rarely violated, is also a primary criterion.

By contrast, compactness is not a primary criterion and is often violated. Compactness can be measured in a variety of technical ways, but the essential notion behind any compactness measure is that districts should have relatively geometrical shapes, without many branches, dips, or jagged edges. At a minimum, compactness is thought to be a virtue because it constrains attempts to gerrymander by means of contorted shapes drawn to favor one party, group, or candidate over another. But some proponents of compactness also believe that it better protects political interests stemming from geographic propinquity. In reality, however, districts are often noncompact, sometimes because it better serves particular political interests, but frequently because compactness conflicts with other redistricting values, such as protecting communities of interest or complying with the VRA.

In sum, the so-called formal criteria—population equality, communities of interest, and compactness or contiguity—focus on the size, shape, and geography of ideal districts, but not on their desired political and ethnic makeup. These latter considerations are covered by outcome criteria, such as fairness between the political parties and fairness to racial and ethnic groups and competitive districts.

At a minimum, fairness between the parties means that the party receiving a majority of the votes should also receive a majority of the seats. With the elimination of gross malapportionment, this so-called majoritarian condition is rarely violated by even the most outrageous partisan gerrymanders. More often, what people mean by partisan fairness is something beyond the violation of the majority principle—namely, that a party's share of seats should match as closely as possible to its share of votes, a condition of at least rough proportionality.

There are a number of problems with this standard. To begin with, SMSP district systems do not yield proportional outcomes in most situations. One of the characteristic features of SMSP systems is that they on average exaggerate the seat share of the majority party and diminish the seat share of minority parties. So even if a redistricting plan is free of any attempt to gerrymander for partisan advantage, it will likely lead to nonproportional seat allocations. Second, the Court and Congress have explicitly acknowledged that there is no right, per se, to proportional representation, so that popular expectations of fairness and legal requirements are at odds with one another. Finally, the best way to achieve proportional outcomes would be to abandon the existing system of single-member districts for some form of proportional or semiproportional rules. While there is evidence of a limited degree of experimentation with such systems (i.e., in certain southern jurisdictions under the threat of voting rights litigation), there has historically been little enthusiasm in the United States for European-style electoral systems.

In response to this dilemma, political scientists have tried to develop alternative ways of measuring fairness in SMSP systems. For instance, some contend that fairness really consists of symmetry between the parties: if party A gets a given share of the seats for a given share of the votes, then party B in a symmetric system would get an identical share of seats given the same share of votes. In other words, a fair system treats the parties in the same way even if it does not yield proportional outcomes. Conceptually, this notion of partisan fairness is much closer to the spirit of SMSP systems than is "proportionality." Unfortunately, it is difficult to implement since it requires knowledge of counterfactual conditions—namely, what seat share a party would have received had it won a different share of the votes.

The idea that redistricting should be fair to all or as many political parties as possible seems intuitively appealing. Unfortunately, it is difficult to implement the concept of partisan fairness in the U.S. electoral system. The same difficulty underlies the concept of racial and ethnic fairness. As with partisan fairness, there are two approaches. At a minimum, racial fairness means that significantly sized minority groups should not be excluded from representation in the political system. A stronger and more widely held version of racial and ethnic fairness is that there should be rough proportionality between population strength and a group's share of elected officials—in short, proportional descriptive representation.

The critical factor for the electoral success of racial and ethnic groups under an SMSP system is numbers large enough and sufficiently concentrated to constitute a viable voting bloc in a given district. At best, the treatment of groups in an SMSP system is arbitrary. Groups that are optimally concentrated (i.e., neither too dispersed nor too packed together) and of sufficient size will tend to be treated more advantageously by the electoral system. Nongeographical groups, whose members are distributed throughout the population randomly (such as women or left-handed people), cannot usually hope to win representation by virtue of constituting a majority of the voters in a particular district. Quasi-geographical groups are loosely clumped by population and can be formed into districts by sensitive drawing of perimeters. Much of the current dispute over racial and ethnic gerrymandering centers on the quasi-geographical category. In essence, how far does the legal obligation of the state legislature or other redistricting body extend under the VRA to draw boundaries that unite geographically disparate minority neighborhoods into minority districts?

In a series of decisions prior to 1982, the courts ruled that electoral rules and institutions, including redistrictings, could not intentionally dilute the voting strength of minority communities. Jurisdictions covered under section 5 of the 1965 VRA had to submit proposed new district boundaries for approval to the Justice Department or the district court of the District of Columbia. In 1982, the language of section 2 of the VRA was amended to cover redistrictings that may not have had the intent to discriminate but had the effect of denying protected minority groups (i.e., blacks, Latinos, and Asians) the equal opportunity to elect a representative of their own choice. The meaning of this was elaborated in the Supreme Court's 1986 decision *Thornburg v. Gingles*. If a protected group can show that it is sufficiently numerous in a given area to constitute a majority of a congressional seat, if it can demonstrate that it tends to act as a politically cohesive force, and if it can demonstrate a pattern of racially polarized voting against it, then districting lines that divide its neighborhoods may be invalidated under this law. Proponents of the VRA proudly point to the significant increase in black and Latino elected officials as a result of VRA litigation. Opponents point out that it has created a special right to proportional representation for some racial and ethnic groups but not others, and they further argue that descriptive representation does not necessarily serve minority communities well.

The third and last of the outcome criteria is competitiveness—the idea that districts should be created to be as competitive as possible, which in effect means maximizing the number of marginal seats where candidates from either party have a chance to win. This is also referred to in political science literature as responsiveness. A responsive system is one in which small changes in the vote result in relatively large changes in seat shares.

Competitiveness is valued as a redistricting goal because it means that changes in voter preferences between elections can be translated into changes in policy. For example, if support for more social spending increases in the period between two elections, then in a responsive system candidates who support those policies should do better in the second election than those who do not. Changes in policy preference should ideally lead to changes in the partisan and ideological composition of the government.

In reality, while the competitiveness of districts is certainly shaped by redistricting, a number of other factors are also important. Disparities in the financial resources or name recognition of candidates, for example, often dampen the responsiveness of elections to shifting public opinion. In principle, however, districts could be drawn to make the underlying distribution of partisanship as even as possible, so that on average districts are more competitive. The chief problem with implementing this criterion is the difficulty of securing agreement from the concerned parties over how to measure and define a competitive seat. Should it be measured by using party-registration data or averages of previous statewide or district races? What are the thresholds that define the difference between competitive and safe districts? An inability to answer these basic questions has reduced competitiveness to a goal toward which much lip service is paid but on behalf of which there is little real effort.

These are the most frequently considered criteria for assessing redistricting plans. Redistricting is so contentious as a political issue because these criteria frequently conflict, forcing those who draw the lines to make difficult choices. Trade-offs between competing values require an implicit or explicit ordering of these values, and, to some degree, the courts have provided guidance in this regard. Equal population, contiguity, the VRA, and the provisions of the Fourteenth Amendment form the primary criteria—none can be violated for the sake of other criteria. Moreover, while it might be possible to do better with respect to one of the primary criteria by violating another, they are treated as forming binding constraints on one another. Thus, districts that satisfy the VRA must be equally populated and contiguous even though in theory many unequally populated and discontiguous districts might better comply with the VRA.

As for the nonprimary criteria, the examples of potential and real conflicts between them are too numerous to enumerate completely. The most common problems arise between fairness of outcome and formal criteria. In some cases, there is simply no logical connection between the two. In some circumstances, they are compatible, and in others, they are not. For instance, compactly drawn districts can produce politically "fair" or "unfair" districts, lessen or increase the number of minority-controlled districts, and discourage or promote political competitiveness. Compactness, for instance, might serve the cause of one criterion or the other in a particular political jurisdiction, but have the opposite effect in another jurisdiction due to different political and demographic circumstances.

The Process of Redistricting. The collection of the decennial census triggers the subsequent redrawing of congressional, state legislative, and local district boundaries. The Census Bureau is directed by law to make its national enumeration as of 1 April in the first year of a decade and to complete it in nine months, reporting the results to the president of the United States by 31 December of the census year. The allocation of congressional seats based on the census data is a purely mechanical exercise based on a "method of equal proportions" that ranks each state's priority of seat assignment by population share.

In recent years the accuracy of the census has been questioned by cities, states, and ethnic and racial groups who believe that they have received less than their fair share of congressional representation and federal spending. In particular, the Census Bureau acknowledges that every decade there is a differential undercount of blacks, Latinos, and, to a somewhat lesser degree, American Indians and Asians. In the 1990 census, for instance, blacks and Latinos were undercounted by approximately 5 percent.

The differential undercount lowers the apportioned share of congressional seats in states with high minority populations and causes malapportionment in inner-city minority districts, as compared to suburban or rural nonminority districts. In anticipation of another undercount in 1990, the Census Bureau designed and tested a postenumeration survey for the purpose of adjusting the enumerated figures to correct for the undercount bias. The Commerce Department sought to end the funding of the postenumeration survey in 1987. In July 1991, Secretary Robert Mosbacher overturned the Census Bureau director's recommendation in favor of adjustment. It seems likely, however, that future censuses will utilize samples and statistical techniques to improve on the data collected by enumeration alone.

Once the apportionment of congressional districts across states is completed, the second phase—the adjustment of boundaries within states—can occur. The Commerce Department secretary is required by law to give to the states by 1 April of the year after the census population counts at the census-tract and census-block level. A critical aspect of this second phase of the reapportionment cycle is the limited timetable in which states must complete their task. In large states especially, this means that a complex process must be completed quickly so that the lines can be in place for the primary elections the following year. For the most part, redistricting remains a state action, although the state's autonomy in these matters has been diminished significantly by three decades of court decisions. States are still free to decide such matters as whether to let legislators draw their own lines or give the task to a commission, whether to use majority or supermajority rules on redistricting bills, and whether to apply additional criteria beyond those mandated by the courts. These choices inevitably affect the nature of redistricting politics that ensues.

A unique feature of the American system is that while most state legislators draw their own district boundaries, members of the U.S. Congress never do. This most sensitive task is in all but three instances delegated to state officeholders. In the typical redistricting procedure in the states, the redrawing of district boundaries is treated like any other piece of legislation. Legislative leaders, including the chairs of committees with jurisdiction over election law and reapportionment, fashion a plan after consultation with some or all incumbent members of Congress, interested state legislators, and sometimes critical interest groups such as the Mexican-American Legal Defense Fund and the National Association for the Advancement of Colored People Legal Defense Fund. They then fashion one or more proposals.

A redistricting plan usually consists of either "metes and bounds" (i.e., detailed, street-by-street descriptions of district boundaries) or a list of census tracts and blocks composing each district. In addition, the legislature will usually produce maps of the new lines and supporting data that give the ethnic and racial breakdowns as well as district populations. Where available, states may also provide party registration figures and data from past elections that give some indication of the likely competitiveness of the district. The redistricting bills are reported out of committee like any other piece of legislation and onto the floor of the two houses of the legislature, where they are debated, sometimes amended, and then sent to the governor's office for approval. The governor can either sign or veto the bill, and in the event of the latter, his or her decision has to be overridden with a supermajority legislative vote. There are some variations in this model of legislative redistricting, but this describes the model process.

The governor's veto is a varying threat. In North Carolina, for instance, there is no gubernatorial veto on any legislative matter, and in New York, it cannot be applied to a redistricting plan. The supermajority vote needed to override the governor's veto is a critical barrier to a majority party's attempt to draw partisan district lines. Except in areas of one-party dominance, such as the South, the majority party will normally lack the votes to override the veto. So if the minority party can gain control of the governor's office, it can force a better deal from the legislature or cause the matter to be resolved by the courts. After *Baker v. Carr,* a number of states sought to escape from the inevitable controversies by referring redistricting to a commission or some other neutral agency. Three states now have pure commission systems: Hawaii, Montana, and Washington give their commissions both the original and final right to decide congressional district boundaries. In Connecticut, redistricting is given to a nine-member commission, but only in the event that an eight-member legislative commission, drawn evenly from both parties, cannot come to agreement. Iowa gives the tasks of changing congressional boundaries to its nonpartisan Legislative Services Bureau, although final approval is reserved to the legislature.

The courts are involved in redistricting in several ways. They sometimes have to take over the process because of a political impasse at the state level. This is most likely to occur when control of a state is split between the two parties. It is commonly assumed that the party that appointed the judges to the bench will get a more favorable plan than the other party. In fact, it often works the other way. In Illinois during the 1981 redistricting, for instance, the task was given over to a three-judge panel that included two Republican appointees; yet, to the dismay of Illinois Republicans, the court chose a plan devised by the Illinois House Democratic leader. When the courts assume the responsibility of drawing district boundaries themselves, it is hard to predict what they will do and whom they will favor.

In a majority of instances, however, the courts are simply asked to review the constitutionality of district lines that are drawn by a state legislature. Several kinds of cases come up frequently. The most common involve claims of racial or ethnic minority vote dilution, usually under the provisions of the VRA. During the 1980 redistrictings, the courts overturned parts of the legislatures' redistricting plans for the states of Georgia, Louisiana, and Mississippi, in order to strengthen the electoral power and representation of black constituents. Latinos also obtained victories in the courts, most notably in Texas.

The courts in the 1980s also overturned several redistricting plans that had excessively large population deviations (e.g., New Jersey). The evolution of these cases, as discussed earlier, has been toward an increasingly strict application of "one person, one vote," especially in cases where deviations from exact equality seem to be coupled with political unfairness.

The least frequent form of constitutional review involves claims of partisan gerrymandering. The definitive statement of the Court on this subject to date is the decision in *Davis v. Bandemer* (1986), a case involving Indiana's state legislative districts. Whether this case signals a more activist posture by the courts in this area is a subject of some controversy.

In the end, however, it may not matter what the courts do. A number of recent studies indicate that there is no evidence of systematic partisan bias in congressional elections. This is not to deny that the parties in control of redistricting seek and gain local advantage through redistricting; it is only to say that the net effect is neutral over the country as a whole. The most common measure of electoral bias used by political scientists is the share of seats a party would receive if it were to get 50 percent of the vote. By this standard, according to one estimate, the Democrats would have received 52.1 percent of the congressional seats with 50 percent of the vote between 1946 and 1964, and 53.9 percent between 1966 and 1988. Correcting for the inflated percentages that result from uncontested seats, the Democrats would be predicted to get 42.8 percent of the congressional seats with 50 percent of the vote before 1966 and 50.6 percent after 1966. Another study concluded that only four of the twenty-six congressional losses the Republicans sustained in 1982 could be attributed to redistricting.

Nonetheless, the quest for a better way to redistrict continues. Reformers frequently argue that it is an unacceptable conflict of interest to allow state legislators to vote on their own district lines. Some point to the success of the Australians, Canadians, and British in removing redistricting from politics, but others point out that this is easier to achieve in parliamentary systems where there is no residency requirement, the civil service and the judiciary are less politicized, and incumbency matters less.

The inability to agree on a better process occurs at a time when expectations about redistricting are rising. Minority groups look for redistricting to remedy decades of underrepresentation. Political parties seek to use redistricting to restore single-party control of the government and to break the logjam of divided government. Good-government advocates envision better redistricting as a means of lessening the incumbency advantage. All of this ensures that redistricting will remain a matter of controversy.

[*See also* Baker v. Carr; Census; Davis et al. v. Bandemer et al.; Districts; Elections, Congressional; Gerrymandering; Representation; Voting Rights Act of 1965; Wesberry v. Sanders.]

BIBLIOGRAPHY

Baker, Gordon E. *The Reapportionment Revolution.* 1967.

Balinski, Michael L., and H. Peyton Young. *Fair Representation: Meeting the Ideal of One Man, One Vote.* 1982.

Browning, Robert X., and Gary King. "Seats, Votes and Gerrymandering: Estimating Representation and Bias in State Legislative Redistricting." *Law and Policy* 9 (1987): 305–322.

Cain, Bruce E. "Assessing the Partisan Effects of Redistricting." *American Political Science Review* 79 (1985): 320–333.

Cain, Bruce E. *The Reapportionment Puzzle.* 1984.

Davidson, Chandler, ed. *Minority Vote Dilution.* 1984.

Dixon, Robert. *Democratic Representation: Reapportionment in Law and Politics.* 1968.

Erikson, R. S. "Malapportionment, Gerrymandering and Party Fortunes." *American Political Science Review* 66 (1972): 1234–1245.

Ferejohn, John A. "On the Decline of Competitive Congressional Elections." *American Political Science Review* 7 (1977): 166–176.

Guinier, Lani. *The Tyranny of the Majority: Fundamental Fairness and Representative Democracy.* 1994.

McCubbins, M. D., and Thomas Schwartz. "Congress, the Courts, and Public Policy: Consequences of the One Man, One Vote Rule." *American Journal of Political Science* 32 (1988): 388–415.

Polsby, Nelson W., ed. *Reapportionment in the 1970s.* 1971.

BRUCE E. CAIN

APPROPRIATIONS. Article I, section 9 of the U.S. Constitution states that "No Money shall be drawn from the Treasury, but in Consequence of Appropriations made by Law." Along with the provisions concerning revenue, this requirement is how Congress maintains, as James Madison wrote in *Federalist* 58, the "power over the purse . . . the most complete and effectual weapon with which any constitution can arm the immediate representatives of the people . . . ." Appropriations involve issues of policy, management, and authority within Congress itself. After two centuries of the American constitutional system, the appropriations power remains a foundation of Congress's role in the Framers' system of checks and balances.

Form of Appropriations. The First Congress adopted the practice of annual appropriations. Each year, each agency would submit estimates of its needs and expected accomplishments. Committees (before 1867, mostly the Senate Finance and House Ways and Means committees, and, from 1867 on, usually the House and Senate Appropriations committees) would hold hearings to consider the estimates and write legislation providing, with conditions, funding (normally known as budget authority) for the coming fiscal year.

The continued process of annual appropriations has allowed Congress to respond to the nation's changing demands. Thus it could raise spending on the space program in the 1960s and on drug enforcement in the 1980s. Congress also can reflect each year's budgetary constraints: for example, the need to balance competing desires for services, the wish to limit taxes, and the need to curtail deficits. Annual review may be used to try to increase the economy and efficiency of agency operations in order to best satisfy demands in the face of con-straints. Not least, annual appropriations are a means of control, forcing agencies each year to ask Congress for life-giving funds.

Yet some programs require longer-term commitments to function effectively. Purchasers of federal debt would hardly accept a return that was subject to an annual vote. Social Security and the payroll tax that funds it would have less political support if benefits were voted on each year. These and other programs are designed so demands will be met regardless of constraints. Such programs are called entitlements because the courts have ruled the laws creating them bestow a property right in the benefit. Instead of being subjected to the annual process, therefore, the largest entitlements have "permanent, indefinite" appropriations established in their organic legislation. For programs with dedicated revenues, such as Social Security, any monies collected for the program trust fund may be withdrawn from the Treasury.

Congress's most important decision about any program's appropriation is whether to make the program an entitlement. If the program is created as an entitlement, it can be altered only through regular authorizations or, since 1980, through the budget reconciliation process. Programs funded through annual appropriations, on the other hand, require positive action each year not only by the separate Appropriations committees but by the entire Congress and the president. They therefore are far more vulnerable to political attack than are entitlements.

There is yet a third group of programs, for which commitments are made outside the annual appropriations process but for which money still must be provided annually. These include appropriated entitlements such as food stamps, funds to cover defaults of guaranteed loans, and programs for which an agency has contract authority, that is, the power to make contracts that will later be funded by a revolving fund or a subsequent appropriation. In the 1980s these programs came to be called mandatory appropriations, and they were exempted from control through the annual appropriations process. A few programs have permanent indefinite budget authority through trust funds, such as the Airport and Highway funds, which are subjected to annual control through obligation limits set in the annual appropriations.

By the early 1990s, when observers spoke of *appropriations* as a separate subject within the budget process, they were referring to the discretionary accounts and obligation limits on the annual bills.

These amounted to only about $532 billion, about 37 percent of all federal spending, in fiscal year 1991. But they represented the vast bulk of the federal bureaucracy's activity, including the great majority of matters of agency discretion and of discrete benefits distributed among districts and states. They therefore remained of great interest to members of Congress and their constituents.

Types of Annual Appropriations. Appropriations are normally made in general appropriations bills. A general appropriation provides funding for some large group of agencies for a given fiscal year. The number of bills and the grouping of agencies within them have varied as new agencies have been created or as political pressures have required. For many years, there have been thirteen annual appropriations bills, each handled by a separate subcommittee in both the House and Senate.

Bills might also be passed for one-time purposes, such as private relief for a widow. Such special appropriations have become less and less common as government has become more routinized and as supplemental appropriations have become more common. A supplemental appropriation may have only one purpose, for instance African famine relief in 1985. More often, supplemental appropriations clean up loose ends across many subcommittees. Contents may be as routine as funding for the federal pay raise, which is usually determined after the fiscal year begins. A supplemental appropriation may also provide relief after a disaster, as after the earthquakes in the San Francisco area in 1989 and the Los Angeles area in 1993. Sometimes a controversial issue is removed from the regular appropriations bill so that that bill can pass and then is settled in a supplemental bill, as with Central America policies in 1984. Or a newly created program may need funding before the next budgetary year, as with the first supplemental appropriation, passed in 1790 (though the word *supplementary* first appeared in a bill title in 1818).

Supplemental appropriations were especially large in the 1970s, amounting to as much as 7.8 percent of total federal spending, because the bad economy meant mandatory accounts needed extra money. In the 1980s a more stable economy reduced supplemental spending. Budget process reforms, moreover, inhibited the old pattern in which general appropriations were held down in a show of restraint and the money later made up amid claims of emergency.

Instead, the 1980s were the heyday of a third way of appropriating, the *continuing resolution* (CR). If Congress does not complete action on a bill (or several bills) by the start of the fiscal year, it and the president agree on a resolution allowing agencies to continue spending at the rate provided in the previous year's appropriations or in some other fairly conservative formula. Because population, prices, and revenues are normally increasing, the CR figure may seem overly frugal, but budget makers reckon that an agency can maintain itself for a period at these levels.

This stopgap method was transformed in a series of steps, beginning with the 1980 defense buildup, into an omnibus appropriations act incorporating the language of all thirteen general appropriations bills. After 1987 criticism by both the president and other members of Congress, who felt the omnibus act gave too much power to the Appropriations committees, as well as the use of "summit agreements" to settle the broadest budget disputes, caused a return to the more usual pattern of only short-term simple CRs.

Appropriations Committees' Work and Influence. At the beginning of each session, agencies prepare their estimates for the House and Senate committees on Appropriations. Since 1921 those estimates have been first reviewed, then altered and submitted by the president's budget office (now the Office of Management and Budget) as the "president's budget." The budget plugs new numbers into an established form (the most recent bill), while suggesting some new conditions and the removal of some old ones.

House and Senate subcommittees then conduct extensive hearings, involving not only representatives of the agencies but also, in a separate round, interested groups and other members of Congress. The House traditionally reports its bill first. This tradition is based on the House's priority on money matters, which the Framers of the Constitution understood as a prerogative of the more popular branch of a legislature, and made part of the text for revenue measures. But the Constitution is silent as to appropriations themselves, so the Senate could, and on very rare occasions does, challenge the House's precedence. Senate subcommittees normally wait for the House version of their bill to clear the House floor before they mark up their amendments to the House measure. In either chamber it is rare for the full committee to make more than a few changes in the subcommittee's bill. In general, House review is both broader and more detailed, but the difference varies by subcommittee and is much less great than it was, say, in 1970.

Both committees have to make their bills fit an

externally imposed total. Once set by the president's budget, that total is now provided by the Congressional Budget Resolution. These 302(a) allocations establish how much new budget authority for discretionary (that is, not mandatory) programs can be appropriated that year. They also set totals for that year's outlays from each program. In any given year outlays differ from budget authority because the money appropriated to buy such items as aircraft carriers is not all spent in one year. The Appropriations committees divide their totals for budget authority and outlays among their subcommittees, and report this division to their respective parent chambers under section 302(b) of the Budget Act. These suballocations are binding, meaning that a point of order prohibits exceeding them on the floor. (Under the 1990 reforms these were temporarily renumbered 602[a] and 602[b]).

The appropriators nearly always use the entire total allowed. Any legislator who wants to add an item must propose an offsetting cut, guaranteeing opposition from supporters of what is cut as well as from the members of the Appropriations Committee. Therefore it is difficult to get money for a program unless Appropriations writes it into the bill, which gives the committees power over other legislators.

Appropriators normally seek the minimum amount required to fund the ongoing activities of existing agencies. Richard Fenno summarized this task as "financ[ing] programs and projects economically." Committee staff look for justifications of concrete resources; they ask about unit costs, change over time, cost per person, administrative overhead, and the like. They ask whether the agency can in fact use the money; in the 1980s, for instance, they continually cut requests for a new air traffic control system, relying on information from General Accounting Office (GAO) auditors that the computer software being developed for the new system was behind schedule, meaning that any funds appropriated for this purpose for the coming fiscal year would go unused.

The committees' second focus is on distributing projects among districts and states. Dams and bridges, veterans' hospitals and visitor facilities in national parks, weapons contracts and blueberry research are among the thousands of items specified in each year's appropriations. This distribution process, frequently scorned as the "pork barrel," is also about the separation of powers. If Congress did not control benefits, the president would and could manipulate Congress by using benefits to punish or reward senators and representatives.

Demand for benefits is intense; the Senate Interior Subcommittee received three thousand requests in 1991. Appropriators see benefits as "glue" to keep members "stuck to the bill." Each subcommittee serves as a broker for requests in its jurisdiction, and it is understood that, as brokers, the appropriators collect a fee—more for their own districts or states—off the top. They have to reject many requests but feel they can do so without backlash from their colleagues so long as they are believed to be fair. Seeking safe margins for bills that must pass, appropriators use their "glue" and argue about programs' minimum needs to build nonpartisan coalitions in committee and substantial majorities in their chambers.

Which programs are most favored in any given year has more to do with events and associated shifts in popular and elite support than with the preferences of committee members. Spending and priorities track the partisan balance in Congress fairly closely. Whether appropriators appear as guardians of the purse, cutting the president's budget, depends far more on the president's request than on their own biases.

If the process does have a bias, it is toward moderation. The committees tend to lean against the wind of any given policy mood, as the political desire to "do something" about a problem is rarely matched by practicality of proposals. The appropriators are more oriented toward maintaining existing organizations, the outputs of which are known, than toward funding new projects with uncertain outputs or cutting existing activities.

Appropriators simplify their extremely complex task by presuming that what had the analytical and political support for approval one year should, barring new information, be continued in the next. In the language of incrementalism, they accept the base and are skeptical of changes, whether increments or decrements.

While the Appropriations committees do not set broad policy, they have immense effects on the detailed ways in which policies are realized. The Appropriations committees have long been considered among the most powerful in Congress because, in the words of one subcommittee chair, "Nothing happens without the money."

Authorizing and Appropriating. The actual and potential effect of appropriations on policy creates one of Congress's central tensions. Most senators and representatives who serve on authorizing committees expect to set basic policy, yet appropriations are what starve or nourish a program. Limitations appropriators set on how money is to be used can have the same effect as conditions written into authorizing legislation.

Appropriators are inherent rivals of authorizers. Yet except in the case of entitlements, Congress rarely allows authorizing committees to fund their own programs. Authorizing committees are expected to pay less attention to competing demands and other constraints and to be less tough on the agencies they create in regard to costs than are the separate Appropriations committees.

Almost any appropriator would acknowledge that boundaries should exist, that the appropriators sometimes exceed their proper role, and that the distinction has something to do with establishing ends (authorization) and providing means (appropriation). But attempts to define and maintain boundaries have caused endless parliamentary strife. These issues are particularly sensitive in the House, where representatives' influence is more closely tied to their committees' influence than in the more individualistic Senate. Rule XXI of the House sets parameters distinguishing appropriations and authorizations, but the rule's terms and interpretations have been in continual flux.

The 1970s saw a proliferation of limitation amendments, when certain factions (usually conservative), thwarted by authorizing committees that refused to consider legislation they proposed, pursued similar goals through limitations on appropriations. In 1977 alone, limitation amendments dealt with abortion, affirmative action, busing, chemical weapons, prayer in schools, the Clinch River Breeder Reactor, and many other issues. A rules change in 1983 did nothing to stop the Appropriations Committee from including limitations in its text, but raised significant barriers to amendments on the House floor.

That appropriations should not be made for programs that are not authorized, that they should not exceed dollar limits set in authorizations, and that they should not include authorizing language are among the limits set by Rule XXI. Events in the 1980s, however, made all these principles hard to keep. When Congress failed to reauthorize the Department of Justice or federal housing programs—because of obstacles that ranged from the controversy over school prayer to authorizing-committee chairmen of opposing parties who could not compromise—it could not simply let those agencies or activities die. Therefore, any adjustments in policy had to be made by tinkering with the appropriations. As more and more appropriations were made through continuing resolutions, factions competed

to attach outright authorizations to those vehicles, which are not subject to Rule XXI limits. At the extreme, a CR in 1984 included an omnibus crime control act.

The relative influence of authorizers and appropriators can be altered by factors as idiosyncratic as personality and as systematic as the budget crisis of the 1980s. The latter reduced everyone's maneuvering room, but hurt authorizers, who like to create new programs, more than appropriators, who work at the margins of existing programs. Personality's role was most evident in the fates of the Foreign Relations and Armed Services committees from 1987 to 1990. Foreign Relations lost influence and Armed Services gained because Foreign Relations had a weak chairman and Armed Services a strong one. The only safe assessment of the tension between authorizing and appropriating is that it will last as long as the committees for appropriations and authorizations remain separate.

Controlling the Executive. Appropriations are central to the power struggle between Congress and the executive. In the nineteenth century the gravest difficulties involved agencies spending money they did not have. In the twentieth century the more common conflict has been a struggle between Congress and the president to control the agencies.

Congress has two basic problems: how to ensure it has enough information for decisions and how to force the administration to comply with its directives. Agencies do not like to reveal embarrassing information. The president wants agencies to support the changes the executive branch has made in their requests. Reliable information on the consequences of spending often does not exist.

Representatives and senators, however, frequently have extensive contacts at the grass-roots level who can provide a variety of information about programs. Interest groups, congressional research agencies (especially the GAO), the press, whistle-blowers, and the rest of Congress all may reveal what an agency wants to conceal. The relationship with agencies, particularly their budget offices, is an iterated game in which Congress can punish agencies next year for deception this year. Agency budget staff therefore feel a need to be honest, and close contact between those civil servants and the subcommittee clerks (staff directors) is at the heart of the appropriations process.

The Office of Management and Budget (OMB) tries to force agencies to support its proposals but cannot forbid agencies from responding to factual questions from Congress. An experienced appropriator knows how to ask the right questions about agencies' needs, but even an inexperienced appropriator might hear an agency's views through a back channel. If an agency is truly recalcitrant about providing information, the House subcommittee will slash its request and then judge from the complaints that the agency makes to the Senate what really hurt and what did not.

The degree of control Congress has wanted to exert over agencies through the appropriations process has varied with political philosophy and partisanship. The Federalists liked broad appropriations, while Jeffersonians (Democratic-Republicans) insisted on minutely specifying the use of funds. Since then, the level of control has oscillated, with a broad trend toward greater generality as the government grew. Nevertheless Congress is continually accused of micromanaging federal operations.

Despite some mutterings in recent administrations, it is understood that the legislature has the right to specify whatever detail it wishes. But both Congress and the executive realize that conditions change, and locking agencies into a workplan by law may lead to poor performance. Over the years they have therefore elaborated an understanding of how the language in the reports that accompany appropriations should be interpreted. Congress may appropriate in large, general categories but then explain how it expects the funds to be divided in extensive reports accompanying the bills. If a report says nothing about the details, the presumption is that the agency will follow its own original justifications. If the agency then wants to vary from its plan, it must usually ask the Appropriations committees for approval of a reprogramming within an account or transfer of funds between accounts.

The process by which justifications, reports, reprogrammings, and transfers are made is informal. Yet when OMB in 1988 told agencies to ignore almost a billion dollars in pork-barrel specifics, the agencies refused. They did so because Appropriations Committee Republicans as well as Democrats warned of retaliation. Forced to choose between OMB and the appropriators, most budget officers feel they must side with the appropriators. As one budget officer said, "OMB never appropriated me one dime."

The appropriations power gives Congress only partial control of the executive because agencies have their own preferences and presidents have many levers, including appointment of officials who respect their preferences. When different parties control the branches and the executive is particularly hostile to Congress, as was the case during the Reagan administration, Congress may have to put more and more instructions into law. The president may fight this but participants agree that a president can threaten veto on only a limited number of items before Congress will override as a matter of pride.

Both the extent and limits of Congress's power were shown in 1987. That year, the Agriculture bill denied funds for the exercise of any authority by an offending assistant secretary of Agriculture, meaning that the appropriators were virtually firing a subcabinet-level appointee. But they had to give the authority to someone, in this case the secretary of Agriculture, who could make decisions on advice from the offending official. Congress can try to block executive action through its appropriations power, but forcing an executive agency to do the right thing is actually very difficult.

[*See also* Appropriations Committee, House; Appropriations Committee, Senate; Authorization; Budget Process.]

BIBLIOGRAPHY

Fenno, Richard F. *The Power of the Purse: Appropriations Politics in Congress.* 1966.
Fisher, Louis. "The Authorization-Appropriation Process in Congress: Formal Rules and Informal Practices." *Catholic University Law Review* 29 (1979): 51–105.
Fisher, Louis. *Presidential Spending Power.* 1975.
Kiewiet, D. Roderick, and Mathew D. McCubbins. *The Logic of Delegation: Congressional Parties and the Appropriations Process.* 1991.
Schick, Allen. *Congress and Money.* 1980.
U.S. Congress. Congressional Budget Office. "Supplemental Appropriations in the 1980s." February 1990.
U.S. Congress. General Accounting Office. Office of General Counsel. *Principles of Federal Appropriations Law.* 2d ed. Vol. 1. 1991.
U.S. House of Representatives. Committee on the Budget. *The Whole and the Parts: Piecemeal and Integrated Approaches to Congressional Budgeting,* by Allen Schick. 1987.
White, Joseph. *Treasured Authority.* Forthcoming.
Wildavsky, Aaron. *The Politics of the Budgetary Process.* 3d ed. 1979.

JOSEPH WHITE

APPROPRIATIONS COMMITTEE, HOUSE.

The House Committee on Appropriations (HAC) has served as the kingpin of the appro-

HOUSE APPROPRIATIONS SUBCOMMITTEE. During a mark-up session with a full audience in the foreground, May 1983.   KEN HEINEN, CONGRESSIONAL QUARTERLY INC.

priations process since its creation in 1865. The democratizing impulse that beset the House in the 1960s and 1970s and the budgetary stalemates of the 1980s undermined some of the traditional authority of the committee. Yet the HAC continues to serve an indispensable function in overseeing appropriations, and membership on the committee is among the most sought-after in the House.

The importance of the Appropriations Committee derives from the importance of the subject matter it considers and its temporal position in the appropriations process. The "power of the purse" is the most fundamental of legislative powers because overseeing the expenditure of funds is typically the most efficient method of shaping the specifics of government programs. Because the HAC is the venue where appropriations are first considered by Congress in any detail, it wields agenda-setting power unmatched by almost any other legislative actor. (For traditional rather than constitutional reasons, the House, and hence its committee, considers appropriations before the Senate does.)

The influence and prestige of the committee can be seen in the resources lavished on it by the House, in the deference of the House to the committee's judgments, and in the demand for membership on the committee. For instance, in the 102d Congress (1991–1993) the HAC had more members and a higher budget than any other legislative committee. Between the 95th and 102d Congresses (1977–1993) no member of the HAC transferred off the HAC to another committee, while sixty members transferred off other legislative committees onto Appropriations, making it the House committee that received the most new members through transfer.

Early History, 1865–1919. The House Ways and Means Committee was the first standing committee created by the House to consider substantive legislation. Until the Civil War, Ways and Means was responsible for reporting legislation in all areas touching on fiscal and monetary policy: taxing, spending, and banking. Before the war, growing federal responsibilities in each of these areas increased the workload of Ways and Means and, in turn, led to calls for the creation of separate appropriations and banking committees. The Civil War put reform on hold, but the comprehensive change in fiscal and monetary politics that attended the war led inevitably to the splitting up of Ways and Means and the creation of the House Appropriations Committee in 1865. (The Banking and Currency Committee was also a product of this reform.) The first chair of the House Appropriations Committee was Rep. Thaddeus Stevens (R-Pa.).

A recurring theme in U.S. appropriations history is the conflict over resources that emerges in the aftermath of war. Fighting a war tends dramatically to increase spending over what it had been in peacetime. During demobilization, members of Congress are faced with the choice of returning spending to prewar levels or of diverting money formerly allocated to the military to domestic uses. In the 1980s this problem was reflected in the coining of the term *peace dividend*—the funds formerly spent to support a war that are freed up for other uses when the conflict ends. Demobilization after the Civil War likewise presented the House with a peace dividend problem, which House leaders wished to solve primarily through returning spending to prewar levels. The HAC, the organ created to implement these designs, rapidly earned a reputation for wielding a sharp budget-cutting knife.

As spending was rapidly reduced in the wake of the war, however, the return of normal politics, economic crises, and events associated with resolving the disputed 1876 presidential election undermined support within the House for the HAC's budget-cutting role. The 1870s and 1880s, therefore, witnessed a steady stream of events that undermined the HAC's authority over appropriations. It lost the authority to report the rivers and harbors appropriations bill in 1877 and the agriculture appropriations bill in 1880. The final blow occurred in 1885, when the authority to report six more appropriations bills—for the army, consular affairs, Indian affairs, military academy, naval affairs, and post office—was taken away and given to the various legislative committees having jurisdiction over these matters. After 1885 the HAC was responsible mostly for appropriations bills that funded the bureaucratic operations of agencies and for bills that spanned the interests of several agencies. On the whole, legislative committees were responsible for reporting both substantive legislation and appropriations for the agencies in their charge.

This decentralized state of affairs remained in effect until 1919. Progressive reformers blamed the decentralization of appropriations authority within the House for the growth in federal appropriations that occurred between 1885 and the turn of the century. (Between 1885 and 1910, federal spending, excluding interest on the debt, grew by 222 percent while prices increased 19 percent, population grew 63 percent, and the gross national product grew 190 percent.) Recent scholarship has questioned not only the degree of actual appropriations decentralization during this period but also whether this spending growth was actually associated with the formal decentralization that occurred between 1877 and 1885. Nonetheless, the formal fragmentation of appropriations authority in the House served as a potent symbol for reform efforts aimed at bringing centralizing, "scientific" methods to the federal government at the turn of the century.

Consequently, the House recentralized formal authority over all appropriations within the Appropriations Committee in 1919. (The second component of the centralization of appropriations, the Budget and Accounting Act of 1921, centralized the executive branch appropriations apparatus.) From then on, the House Appropriations Committee has held sole formal authority over appropriations bills in the House. Yet, as in the 1870s and 1880s, events after 1919 often served to undermine the authority of the HAC to guide appropriations decision making. Compared to what happened in the earlier period, however, much of this undermining was indirect, as in the passage of "entitlement" legislation in which eligibility for program participation is overseen by legislative committees that also permanently authorize expenditures, thus avoiding the annual appropriations process guarded by the HAC.

"Guardian of the Treasury," 1919–1974. The most enduring impressions of the House Appropriations Committee among many policymakers, journalists, and scholars emanate from the committee's activities in the half-century after its authority was consolidated in 1919. With few exceptions, the committee was viewed as standing astride the appropriations process, serving as a faithful "guardian of the Treasury" against independent plans to expand the federal government. Democratic and Republican committees on committees regularly appointed "responsible" senior members to the committee, members whose dedication to prudent financial dealings were well known. The committee was regarded as a tightly integrated social structure whose new members were further socialized into the committee's budget-cutting ways through the naturally conservative appropriations process.

Central to the committee's behavior was its budget-cutting role, combined with the close scrutiny that the committee—and especially its subcommittees—gave to agency requests. Richard Fenno, in his definitive treatment of the "textbook" committee, *Power of the Purse* (1966), expressed the budget-cutting tendency this way:

> The workaday jargon of the Committee is replete with negative verbs, undesirable objects of attention, and effective instruments of action. Agency budgets are said to be filled with "fat," "padding," "grease," "pork," "oleaginous substance," "water," "oil," "cushions," "avoirdupois," "waste tissue," and "soft spots." The action verbs most commonly used are "cut," "carve," "slice," "prune," "whittle," "squeeze," "wring," "trim," "lop off," "chop," "slash," "pare," "shave," "fry," and "whack." (p. 105)

This characterization was hardly hyperbolic. For instance, Fenno studied appropriations decisions for thirty-six executive bureaus between 1947 and 1962. The committee's appropriations recommendations for these bureaus were less than the requested amount in roughly three-quarters of the cases, with cuts usually amounting to between 1 percent and 5 percent of a bureau's request. (Bureau requests tended to be significantly higher than the previous year's appropriation, so that even by cutting the bureau's request, the committee was still able to recommend an increase over the previous year's appropriation 69 percent of the time.) Although changes occurred in the committee's environment and behavior in the years that followed, this is one area that has remained virtually unchanged: from 1962 through 1992 the HAC cut agency requests roughly 70 percent of the time.

Although the HAC gained a reputation for cutting agency requests, it is important to underscore the limited degree of these cuts. The committee rarely hindered agencies from expanding their budgets over time, but merely moderated that growth. Indeed, it is unlikely the HAC would have sustained regular support for its recommendations on the House floor if it had cut spending too sharply. Also, the committee tended to avoid direct policy controversies in its recommendations, often focusing instead on administrative details such as staffing levels, administrative backlogs, and the like.

Adherence to the norm of budget cutting was achieved through a combination of recruitment and socialization. Through careful recruitment, leaders of both parties ensured that new committee members had substantial experience in the House and that their opinions tilted toward the conservative side of mainstream. For instance, Fenno reports that between 1947 and 1964, the median new member of the HAC had already served three terms in the House prior to appointment.

New committee members who were not already inclined to view agency budget requests skeptically were quickly socialized into doing so. This socialization was reinforced by subcommittee practices. Prior to the series of reforms known as the subcommittee bill of rights, subcommittees were appointed by the chair and the ranking minority member of the committee. They tended to avoid appointing subcommittee members who would be advocates on behalf of the agencies they would oversee. Sometimes they would appoint to subcommittees members who might be actively hostile to the interests of the agencies, as when Rep. Alfred E. Santangelo (D-N.Y.) who represented East Harlem, was assigned to the Subcommittee on Agriculture when he was first appointed to the HAC in 1958.

In a practice that continues into the 1990s, virtually all the committee's work was handled in sub-

committees. (In the 103d Congress, 1993–1995, there were thirteen subcommittees for an equal number of appropriations bills.) Indeed, there has generally been a one-to-one correspondence between the annual appropriations bills and HAC subcommittees. The committee enjoyed a system of reciprocity such that the committee would defer to a subcommittee's work when that subcommittee's annual appropriation bill was brought for approval by the full committee. This reciprocity extended within the subcommittees themselves, so that individual members became experts in particular areas of federal spending, and subcommittee members tended to defer to the judgment of these experts when appropriations were under consideration.

The degree of detail that subcommittees could explore while considering appropriations became part of Washington legend. While subcommittees could not go through each bureau's budget with a fine-tooth comb, the close attention to detail in a few bureaus' budgets each year served the purpose of attuning agencies to the committee's economy efforts and assured the full committee—and ultimately the entire House—of the quality of the annual appropriations bills. One classic example of a subcommittee's attention to detail was recounted in Aaron Wildavsky's *Politics of the Budgetary Process* (1964). In this case, the chair of the foreign operations subcommittee, John J. Rooney (D-N.Y.), grilled a State Department official over the assignment of a particular foreign service officer, who had demonstrated a proficiency in the Chinese language, to London.

Many of the broad outlines of the classic, "textbook" view of the House Appropriations Committee remain to the present: almost all business is conducted in subcommittees that wield the upper hand in determining the details of the appropriations bills under their jurisdictions; the full committee and the House floor typically defer to the decisions of the subcommittees; and HAC scrutiny of appropriations bills is the closest scrutiny that most federal agencies receive, year in and year out, of their operations. Nonetheless, the reforms that affected the full Congress in the 1960s and 1970s also had an impact on the HAC, changing it in some ways even as they left it unchanged in others.

The Postreform Committee. Of the various reforms of the House in the 1960s and 1970s, the Congressional Budget and Impoundment Control Act of 1974 (also known as the Budget Act) was probably the most important for the House Appropriations Committee. Among other things, the act established two new committees (a Budget Committee in both the House and the Senate), a new interchamber service organization (the Congressional Budget Office), and an annual budget process structured around a series of budget resolutions. It was—and remains—unclear, however, whether the Budget Act strengthened or weakened the HAC's position within the House.

Arguments that the Budget Act strengthened the position of the HAC start with the origin of the act. Many of its earliest supporters were members of the Appropriations Committee and, in general, were fiscal conservatives. Support for the Budget Act among fiscal conservatives was prompted by the tendency, during the 1960s, for Congress to move more and more spending out of the annual appropriations bills and into entitlement legislation. This had the effect of removing increasing amounts of the budget from the conservative eye of the HAC and giving greater spending-guidance powers to the legislative committees, which were regarded as more friendly to the desires of federal agencies.

The Budget Act prohibited the passage of any additional entitlement legislation, thus stanching the flow of spending responsibility from the Appropriations Committee. In addition, the centralizing tendency of the entire budgetary process was predicted by most to have a conservative influence on spending pressures. Finally, the composition of the House Budget Committee was heavily weighted with members from the two existing fiscal watchdog committees, Appropriations and Ways and Means.

At the same time that the Budget Act promised greater fiscal conservatism in spending matters, the structure of the annual budgetary process reoriented the role of the Appropriations Committee from that of a guardian to that of a "claimant." This argument is associated with Allen Schick's definitive history of the Budget Act's passage, *Congress and Money* (1980). The annual budgetary process was crafted to require all committees that were responsible for spending items, including Appropriations, to justify an aggregate spending level to the House Budget Committee at the beginning of every budgetary cycle. The Budget Committee would, in turn, be responsible for drafting a first budget resolution and shepherding it through the House. Just as agencies had an incentive to overestimate their next year's expenses and oversell the efficacy of their programs to the HAC, the Appropriations Committee now had an incentive to advocate on

their behalf to the Budget Committee. So the games that had been associated with agency-HAC interactions were replicated in HAC–Budget Committee dealings. At least one subcommittee reform of the 1970s also helped to reinforce HAC impulses to advocate for spending programs: after 1974, members were allowed to bid for subcommittee assignments based on committee seniority. Hence, an important mechanism of the "textbook" era vanished: the chairman and ranking minority member no longer controlled subcommittee appointments and, therefore, could no longer keep agency advocates out of the subcommittees.

Whether the HAC has in fact become a claimant rather than a guardian has been difficult to assess empirically. No definitive econometric studies exist comparing the HAC's behavior before and after the Budget Act became effective. There is much evidence that the HAC still treats agency claims skeptically, scrutinizes budgets carefully, and cuts budgets more often than it increases them. In the 1991 consideration of the fiscal year 1992 budget, for instance, the various subcommittees of the House Appropriations Committee spent a total of 255 days in hearings, heard 2,162 witnesses, and produced hearing records amounting to over eighty thousand pages of documents. The appropriations bills that were reported to the House floor by the HAC recommended an aggregate cut of $12 billion from President George Bush's budget.

The chronic deficits that beset the federal government during the 1980s and that continued into the 1990s also affected the position of the Appropriations Committee within the appropriations process. As these deficits persisted, a trend developed in which the regular order of the Budget Act was circumvented in favor of "budget summits" and other centralized negotiating forums involving both congressional leaders and key economic advisers in the executive branch. These negotiations tended to centralize budgetary authority within the federal government generally. Authority was further centralized within the Appropriations Committee itself, as the subcommittee chairs—termed the "College of Cardinals"—became even more important in deciding the allocation of funds among agencies.

Finally, appropriations politics during the 1980s allowed scholars to reassess the traditional view of the House Appropriations Committee as a nonpartisan guardian of the Treasury. The fundamental reason underlying the chronic federal fiscal difficulties in the 1980s was divided government, with one political party (the Republicans) controlling the presidency while the other party (the Democrats) controlled at least one house of Congress. During this period the HAC was less inclined to cut agency budget requests and actually more inclined to augment them. For instance, the net $12 billion cut by the committee in President Bush's fiscal year 1992 appropriations recommendation resulted from cuts of $14 billion in military and foreign aid spending coupled with an increase of $2 billion in domestic spending.

Hence, later revisionist literature focusing on the House Appropriations Committee—work associated with D. Roderick Kiewiet and Mathew D. McCubbins's *Logic of Delegation* (1991)—was aimed at demonstrating how the committee typically served the interests of the majority party caucus, rather than a bipartisan consensus for fiscal prudence. Reforms within the Democratic caucus during the 1970s served to strengthen the degree to which the HAC, working through the Democrats on the panel, served as an agent of the majority party. One reform in particular was aimed at the Appropriations Committee. In addition to subjecting all the chairs of all committees to biennial election, the caucus also began subjecting all the chairs of HAC subcommittees to biennial election in 1974.

The House Appropriations Committee has a long, illustrious history as one of the most critical parts of the policy process. Its chairs—such as Thaddeus Stevens, Samuel J. Randall (D-Pa.), Clarence Cannon (D-Mo.), George H. Mahon (D-Tex.), and Jamie L. Whitten (D-Miss.)—have been among the most influential policymakers of their day. Demand for service on the committee has always exceeded the supply of seats, even during eras, as in the 1870s and 1880s, when the House was whittling away at its authority.

The centrality of the committee lies in the importance of its subject matter. Virtually every member of the House knows that if Congress cannot control how funds are spent, the legislative branch has virtually no chance of controlling the behavior of the executive. Hence the House has always lavished resources on the committee and deferred to its judgment more than to that of other committees. The "democratizing" reforms of the 1960s and 1970s somewhat diminished the stature of the HAC; the prevalence of administrations even more fiscally conservative than the committee during the 1980s diminished its "guardianship" tendencies; and the deficit politics of the 1980s sometimes redirected spending decision making into other venues. Nonetheless, so long as members of Congress insist on having the ability to guide policy independent of the executive branch, the House Appropriations Committee—or some other House committee much like it—will continue to exist and to wield considerable influence.

[*See also* Appropriations Committee, Senate; Banking, Finance, and Urban Affairs Committee, House; Budget Process; Ways and Means Committee, House.]

BIBLIOGRAPHY

Fenno, Richard F., Jr. *The Power of the Purse: Appropriations Politics in Congress.* 1966.
Kiewiet, D. Roderick, and Mathew D. McCubbins. *The Logic of Delegation: Congressional Parties and the Appropriations Process.* 1991.
Schick, Allen. *Congress and Money: Budgeting, Spending, and Taxing.* 1980.
Smith, Steven S., and Christopher J. Deering. *Committees in Congress.* 2d ed. 1990.
Stewart, Charles. *Budget Reform Politics: The Design of the Appropriations Process in the House of Representatives, 1865–1921.* 1989.
Wildavsky, Aaron. *Politics of the Budgetary Process.* 1964.

CHARLES STEWART III

APPROPRIATIONS COMMITTEE, SENATE.

The Senate Appropriations Committee has jurisdiction over the annual appropriations bills that fund the federal bureaucracy. Its annual allocating of more than half a trillion dollars makes the committee one of the most influential in the Senate. Its prestige was both reflected and enhanced by Robert C. Byrd's decision in 1988 that giving up the majority leadership to become Appropriations chairman would not significantly reduce his power.

History. Through the Civil War most appropriations (though not those for rivers and harbors) were reported by the Senate Committee on Finance and the House Committee on Ways and Means. The vast expansion of federal activity during the Civil War convinced Congress that it needed more resources to regain control of the federal purse. The House in 1865 therefore created a new Appropriations Committee, and the Senate followed two years later.

The Appropriations committees quickly joined the revenue committees as the most powerful in their chambers. But in 1885 House Appropriations was stripped of much of its jurisdiction. Representatives argued the appropriators were abusing their authority to change policy, under conditions (a budget surplus) that did not require policy change in the interest of budget control.

Senate Appropriations was temporarily spared,

and this difference foreshadowed later patterns. First, as in the committees' creation, the House tends to seize the initiative in the appropriations process as well as in originating bills. Second, intercommittee jealousy and competition are far more important in the House than the Senate. Senate Appropriations has never had exclusive membership, so appropriators have never seemed a separate group, as their House counterparts do. The Senate's tradition of open debate has meant that appropriations are more easily challenged and there is a greater threat of obstruction in the smaller chamber. Thus the legislative style of Senate appropriators is more accommodating.

Nonetheless, with little controversy the Senate in 1899 followed the House in dispersing much of its Appropriations Committee's authority. Nothing terrible had happened in the wake of the House's doing so, and the majority of senators, who were not on Appropriations, may therefore have seen little reason not to gather a little more power for themselves.

The two decades that followed saw increasing deficits and a campaign to rationalize public administration through such means as the executive budget. The deficits caused by World War I, as with those caused by the Civil War, provided a decisive push for reform. The Budget and Accounting Act of 1921 allowed the president to review and assemble the previously uncoordinated agency estimates in the president's budget. To coordinate its response, the House reconcentrated power in its Appropriations Committee in 1920. The Senate again followed, in 1922.

The process then evolved into a division of labor that lasted until about 1970. House Appropriations held extensive hearings on the agency estimates, usually in search of reasons to reduce them. Senate Appropriations usually held much briefer hearings, often concentrating on the House's changes to the president's request. Participants described the Senate of the 1950s as an "appeals court," and its budget totals regularly exceeded the House's while still falling short of executive-branch estimates. House appropriators viewed their Senate counterparts as dilettantes who did not know the programs; senators claimed that the House committee simply slashed requests, knowing the Senate would undo irresponsible cuts.

The Senate did act as a court of original jurisdiction, however, where agency behavior was particularly important to senators. This was especially the case for agencies that distributed discrete benefits to states. Thus even in the 1960s, when the Senate's ap-

pellate role was conventional wisdom, the Appropriations subcommittees on the departments of the Interior and Agriculture, and on Public Works, were clear exceptions. As Congress's internal workings received more publicity, Appropriations senators and staff also resented the notion that they did less than their House counterparts, and by 1973 virtually all subcommittees would hold hearings on the president's budget request rather than wait for the agencies' appeals. The Congressional Budget and Impoundment Control Act of 1974 then eliminated the rationale for the appellate role. Its procedures, especially as enforced in the 1980s, required that the Senate appropriate the same amount as the House, which made systematic increases impossible.

The 1974 act also created a new set of institutional rivals, the Budget committees. At first, the rivalry between the Senate Appropriations and Budget committees was limited, at least as compared to conflict in the House, because the Senate Budget Committee limited discussion of program details in making its budget resolutions. Senate Appropriations' control of those details was threatened, however, by developments in the 1980s. New procedures created complicated scorekeeping rules under the Budget Committee's control. The Gramm-Rudman-Hollings Act of 1985, largely drafted by Budget Committee staff, threatened devastating sequesters of funds from appropriated programs. In terms of both control of spending results and protection of its procedural independence, Senate Appropriations seemed to be losing power.

With Senator Byrd's accession to the committee's chairmanship, the position of Appropriations changed dramatically. Byrd became the most influential participant in the politics of the budget process, and the 1990 Budget Enforcement Act eliminated Gramm-Rudman's most obnoxious provisions.

Division of Labor. The House and Senate Appropriations committees share a common task that makes them more like each other than either is like the other committees in its respective chamber. If other committees do not act, the status quo continues, so they can afford to exercise power by stalling. But if appropriations are not renewed, the programs that they fund disappear. The act of appropriating is held to be a de facto authorization of a program, but an authorization without appropriations is worthless.

Each year's appropriations bills are much like the previous year's. Numbers may change, a few programs may be added or subtracted, but the bulk of the money goes to agencies that are doing much the same as they did the year before: writing benefit checks, collecting revenues, attempting to control immigration, or whatever.

The committees' organization reflects the fact that although their bills must pass, they are largely routine. The routine involves a great deal of boring work, not much publicity, and an immense array of details, each of which is important to a relatively small group of people. Because their jurisdiction is so broad and detailed, House and Senate Appropriations have long been the largest standing committees in their chambers. In 1991, Senate Appropriations had twenty-nine members. Both committees cope with the detail by dividing labor among highly autonomous subcommittees. In each, the subcommittee staff does the majority of the work and builds networks throughout the bureaucracy, particularly with the agency budget officers.

House and Senate subcommittee leaders in essence function as brokers, balancing colleagues' myriad project requests and trying to assemble a package that will seem "fair" and thus provide what one senator called "glue, so people stick with us." In each Appropriations committee, the subcommittees favor their own members and members of the full committee when doling out funds. Next, they favor the more powerful outsiders, such as party or other committee leaders, and they view a little extra portion of federal monies for their own interests as the brokerage fee.

Each Appropriations committee has norms of budgetary professionalism, and there is the sense that most activity should be nonpartisan. Each subcommittee gathers reams of information, both from hearings and from informal contacts with interest groups and others wishing to support or oppose the president's estimates. The subcommittees mostly ask what aides call "budget questions"— "What did you do with the money last year?" or, "If it's so important, how did you do without it last year?"—rather than policy questions.

While most work is done in subcommittee, the full committees' chairmen and staff have significant power. Small staffs provide computer services and deal with outsiders such as the Congressional Budget Office (CBO) and the Budget committees on issues of scorekeeping or procedure. They also set the committee schedule (when each bill will be considered) and negotiate with chamber leaders as to when each bill will go to the floor. The schedule may be manipulated for advantage in bargaining with the president, as in delaying the defense bill when the drift of opinion is in Congress's favor. Senator Byrd, during his tenure as chairman, also refused to hold full committee markup on a bill when he objected to its contents.

In the 1980s the full committees gained several new, significant roles. Decisions about what would be included in omnibus continuing resolutions were largely made at the committee level. Even more important, the creation of a binding 302(b) process required that the committee set targets for both budget authority and outlays for each subcommittee, before each subcommittee marked up its bill. The process works best if brokered by the chairman and the chair's staff. Chairman John C. Stennis (D-Miss.) in 1987 and 1988 could not manage to do so, but Byrd imposed his allocations with little debate.

The 302(b) pattern is repeated throughout the appropriations process. The chairman provides a mark (a detailed first draft) that uses all the available funds. Anyone who wants to give more to one agency must take from some other agency. So long as the chair reflects the major ideological trends of the time and does not clearly favor some minority, challenge is likely to fail.

Differences from the House. Despite these broad similarities, the Senate Appropriations Committee of the 1980s was distinguishable from the House committee in ways that fit the well-known differences between the chambers.

Senators' responsibilities are spread thin, and this is the way senators like it. Each Appropriations senator serves on four or five subcommittees, as well as in many non-Appropriations assignments. Senators must miss most meetings, and the chairman and ranking member therefore have greater information advantages over their colleagues than the House chairmen and staff have.

Because of the ease and ubiquity of obstruction in the Senate, party matters less and accommodation more there than in the House. A busy subcommittee chairman might even allow the ranking minority member to run many hearings. Chairmen are less likely than in the House to reflexively oppose amendments in subcommittee, in committee, or on the floor. They are more likely to accept proposed legislative language rather than fight it on the floor, allowing a colleague to claim a victory, or to insert report instructions to satisfy a colleague. Often it is understood that the amendment will be dropped in conference, and agencies frequently assume that ignoring report language from the Senate committee is safer than doing so with House language because the Senate appropriators were not themselves committed to the instruction.

Senators influence their subcommittees through

their chairman's efforts to accommodate them, more than by building coalitions or making arguments in subcommittee markup. In the House, representatives serving on subcommittees are more likely to be viewed as experts on the issue at hand than are their Senate counterparts. Staff is therefore more important in the Senate, even though it is smaller than in the House. The norm is two majority aides and one minority aide per subcommittee, though a few subcommittees have more and a few make do with one of each. The majority staffs control schedules, select witnesses for hearings, and draft each stage of a bill; senators cite control of the staff as one advantage of being in the majority. Yet the minority staffs build relationships with both sides, and in some cases are considered the subcommittee experts on large parts of their jurisdiction. Some staff stayed in the majority even as majority control of the Senate changed in 1980 and 1986. In short, even in staffing, personal relationships in the Senate are as important as party affiliation.

The expertise of Senate Appropriations Committee staff and members does not quite match that of the House, so the Senate is at a slight disadvantage in conference. Yet, because the Senate acts last, its bill can better reflect changed substantive or political realities. The conference agreement is therefore often closer to the Senate than to the House version of a bill. And the House has no advantage on those matters about which senators have a particular interest. Rather, it is more likely to win on smaller items, when a representative or the staff knows and cares more than do the Senate appropriators.

The boundary between authorizing and appropriating is weaker in the Senate than in the House. Senators who serve on both an authorizing committee and the appropriating subcommittee for a program are more likely than House authorizers, who cannot simultaneously serve on the appropriating subcommittee, to see the two processes as interchangeable. This is especially true when a senator, as with Ernest F. Hollings (D-S.C.) and J. Bennett Johnston (D-La.) in 1991, chairs both an authorizing committee and an appropriations subcommittee. Thus Hollings chaired the Commerce, Science, and Transportation Committee and the Appropriations Subcommittee on Commerce, Justice, State, and the Judiciary; Johnston chaired the Energy and Natural Resources Committee and the Appropriations Subcommittee on Energy and Water Development. Senate rules make exceptions to the distinction easier. The Senate is also less able to afford the luxury of abiding by some of the rules.

As of 1991 certain House subcommittees had made a point of following the rules against appropriating for agencies for which authorizations had lapsed. If the Senate did not act, there would be less justification for bringing funds out of conference, even when hardly any member of Congress wanted the agency to die.

Place within the Senate. Legislators like to spend money, or at least to decide who will get it, so it is likely that Appropriations will always remain a premier Senate committee. Perhaps the committee's heyday, however, was the late 1950s, when its Democratic membership was virtually identical to that of the informal club that, by wide report, ruled the Senate. Many of its Democratic members chaired other committees, and, at the same time, authorizing chairmen and ranking members sat ex officio in conferences on a number of appropriations bills. Appropriations was at the center of an informal concentration of power among more senior and generally more conservative senators.

By the 1990s the committee was less central, both formally and informally. The prestige authorizing committees had been expanded, and multiple memberships were less common. Appropriations controlled far less of the spending and was constrained by the budget process. The repeated budget battles and growth of entitlement programs also had the effect of moving more and more influence to the Finance Committee.

Yet even when Appropriations' leadership was weak and the committee was losing battles to the Senate Budget Committee, it remained one of the most desired appointments. Half a trillion dollars provides many chits for trading with other senators on other matters. Junior senators could attain influence much more quickly on Appropriations, where they might soon become chair or hold a ranking seat on one of the thirteen subcommittees, than on Finance. Even if Appropriations has to show some deference to authorizing committees on policy matters, an appropriator can act in committee on a much wider range of policies than in any other committee. Armed Services, for example, was one of the prestige committees, yet appropriators wrote a Defense Department bill that virtually duplicated Armed Services' major product while producing twelve other bills as well.

The budget crunch that reduced appropriators' ability to make policy paradoxically increased their apparent power relative to other senators. The scarcity of project resources made them seem more valuable. Appropriators could get their projects in a bill in subcommittee or committee while others needed a floor victory. When Gramm-Rudman-Hollings made the 302(b) process binding, obtaining amendments to add spending on the floor became very difficult, so a seat on the Appropriations Committee became even more useful.

The power that a committee gives its members is not the same as the power it wields as an institution. In the 1980s a seat on Appropriations was quite valuable, but the committee as an institution was weaker than usual. In 1985 (during the Gramm-Rudman-Hollings negotiations), the Senate Budget Committee's chairman and ranking member were both appropriators and favored Budget over Appropriations. The Appropriations Committee had little corporate identity, and even with twenty-nine members it could not exercise much weight in battles over procedure.

In 1990 the Budget Committee chair, Jim Sasser (D-Tenn.), was also an appropriator—and he deferred to Byrd on procedure. Conditions were more favorable, as both a Democratic majority and pent-up demand for domestic spending made senators less willing than in 1985 to threaten the appropriated programs. Byrd's leadership also clearly helped. The Appropriations Committee will always be an attractive assignment, but its place in internal Senate politics will vary with its leadership and external conditions.

[*See also* Appropriations Committee, House; Budget Committee, Senate.]

BIBLIOGRAPHY

Fenno, Richard F., Jr. *The Power of the Purse.* 1966.
Horn, Stephen. *Unused Power.* 1970.
Schick, Allen. *Congress and Money.* 1980.
Sinclair, Barbara. *The Transformation of the U.S. Senate.* 1989.
Smith, Steven S., and Christopher Deering. *Committees in Congress.* 2d ed. 1990.
Stewart, Charles. *Budget Reform Politics.* 1989.
U.S. Senate. *Committee on Appropriations, United States Senate: 100th Anniversary, 1867–1967.* 90th Cong., 1st sess., 1967. S. Doc. 90-21.
White, Joseph. *Treasured Authority.* Forthcoming.
White, Joseph, and Aaron Wildavsky. *The Deficit and the Public Interest.* 1991.

JOSEPH WHITE

ARCHITECT OF THE CAPITOL. The agent of Congress charged with the care and maintenance of the U.S. Capitol, the Senate and House office buildings, the Library of Congress buildings, the Supreme Court, and 274 acres of landscaping, streets, and parking is the Architect of the Capitol. All other congressional facilities, such as the Capitol power plant, the Botanic Garden, and Capitol Police headquarters, also fall under the Architect's jurisdiction. More than twelve million square feet of enclosed space is managed by the Architect's office, which also operates food services for the Senate, oversees the preservation of works of art, and is charged with the planning and construction of such buildings as may be directed by Congress. By law the Architect serves as a member of the Capitol Police Board, the Capitol Guide Board, the House Page Board, the District of Columbia Zoning Commission, the board of directors of the Pennsylvania Avenue Development Corporation, and the Advisory Council on Historic Preservation.

The office of the Architect of the Capitol traces its origins to the Residence Act of 1790, which authorized President George Washington to appoint a board of three commissioners to lay out the federal city and to oversee the design and construction of all government buildings. To the commission Washington named Daniel Carroll of Maryland, a signer of the Constitution and lame-duck member of the first Congress. Second to be named was Thomas Johnson, the chief judge of the Maryland General Court, who had previously served as the first governor of his state. Filling the board's final seat was Dr. David Stuart of Virginia, who through marriage was a member of the president's family and inner circle. The commissioners employed architects and builders, let contracts, negotiated wages, operated a surveyors' department and stone quarry, sold city lots, cleared streets, and performed other such duties associated with the establishment of the permanent seat of government. In 1793 they selected William Thornton's design for the Capitol and soon thereafter began to build it. A series of architects were engaged to oversee the construction of the Capitol, most notably Benjamin Henry Latrobe and Charles Bulfinch, each of whom modified Thornton's original design. As a result, even though the office of Architect of the Capitol did not exist as such, these three men are generally referred to as the first three Architects of the Capitol. Altogether, twelve men served as members of the Board of Commissioners. By 1816, the duties of the board had been consolidated into a single position, that of the commissioner of public buildings, who among other duties was responsible for the care and maintenance of the Capitol. Ten people held the office of commissioner of public buildings.

ARCHITECTS OF THE CAPITOL. *Left to right, top:* William Thornton, Benjamin Henry Latrobe; *bottom:* Charles Bulfinch, Thomas U. Walter.

OFFICE OF THE ARCHITECT OF THE CAPITOL

In 1850 an appropriation to enlarge the Capitol allowed President Millard Fillmore to select an architect to design the addition, oversee its construction, and administer the project. In 1851 Fillmore named Thomas U. Walter of Philadelphia "Architect of the Capitol Extension." During the fourteen years in which Walter served in this role, he also designed the Capitol's great cast-iron dome; the Marine barracks at Brooklyn, New York, and Pensacola, Florida; and additions to the General Post Office, the Treasury Building, and the Patent Office in Washington. Walter's employment on the Capitol extension was separate and distinct from the responsibilities of the commissioner of public buildings.

By 1867 the scope of work directed by the commissioner of public buildings had grown too large for the office as then constituted. The management of all federal buildings, public streets, and parks in the city of Washington, as well as the sale of city lots and other responsibilities, required a larger force with greater resources. Congress abolished the office and transferred to the Army Corps of Engineers all its responsibilities except those related to the Capitol. At the Capitol the commissioner's responsibilities were assumed by the Architect, who thereafter had full responsibility for the care and maintenance of the entire building and grounds. At that time, Edward Clark of Pennsylvania, a protégé of Walter who had succeeded him in 1865, became "Architect of the Capitol," and the word *extension* was soon dropped from the title of the office.

Clark finished the work begun by his predecessor, made improvements to the heating and fireproofing of the older center building of the Capitol, installed the first elevators, and directed the enlargement of the Capitol grounds and related landscaping, including construction of the extensive west terraces. President Theodore Roosevelt appointed Elliott Woods of Indiana, a long-time employee of the Architect's office, to fill the vacancy caused by Clark's death in 1902. Because Woods was not an architect, the name of the office was changed to "Superintendent of the Capitol Building and Grounds." Woods, however, so successfully directed construction of the first Senate and House office buildings that Congress restored the name of the office to Architect of the Capitol in 1921. After Woods died in 1923, President Calvin Coolidge appointed David Lynn of Maryland to the Architect's position. Like Woods, Lynn had been employed in the Architect's office for many years and proved a capable administrator and efficient agent of Congress. He directed the enlargement of the Capitol grounds and the construction of two more congressional office

The Architects of the Capitol

William Thornton	1793
Stephen Hallet	1793–1794
George Hadfield	1794–1798
James Hoban	1798–1802
Benjamin Henry Latrobe	1803–1812
	1815–1817
Charles Bulfinch	1818–1829
Thomas U. Walter	1851–1865
Edward Clark	1865–1902
Elliott Woods	1902–1923
David Lynn	1923–1954
George Stewart	1954–1970
George M. White	1971–

Note: Prior to 1867, the Architects of the Capitol provided design services by contract to the government with the exception of William Thornton, who received the award for his Capitol design. After that year, the architects held a permanent government position.

buildings, a building for the Supreme Court, an annex for the Library of Congress, and underground parking facilities. He retired in 1954 and was succeeded by George Stewart of Delaware, who was appointed by President Dwight D. Eisenhower. Stewart's term in office included construction of the Rayburn House Office Building, completion of the Dirksen Senate Office Building, and the extension of the Capitol's east front. George M. White of Ohio was appointed by President Richard M. Nixon in 1971 and is the first professional architect to hold the position since 1902. His tenure has included construction of the Library of Congress Madison Building and the Hart Senate Office Building, the restorations of the Capitol's west central front and Olmsted Terrace and the Library of Congress's Jefferson and Adams buildings, and the development of a master plan to organize and direct future growth of congressional facilities on Capitol Hill.

BIBLIOGRAPHY

Allen, William C. *The United States Capitol: A Brief Architectural History.* 1990.
Architect of the Capitol. *Records.* 1851–.

WILLIAM C. ALLEN

ARCHIVES. Congress's archives—the records created and received by the House of Representa-

The National Archives was established in 1934 as the depository for the historical records of the executive, legislative, and judicial branches of the federal government. In 1937, the Senate sent the new agency an initial shipment of records. The House followed suit only after enactment of the Legislative Reorganization Act of 1946. This act, among other things, directed the secretary and the clerk to obtain all noncurrent records of the Congress and of each committee and transfer them to the National Archives. These provisions have been incorporated into Senate Rule XI and House Rule XXXVI. In recent decades, both houses of Congress have transferred their records to the National Archives on a regular basis.

The passage of the Federal Records Act of 1950 completed the legal structure governing the preservation and control of congressional records. Whereas the National Archives and Records Administration assumes legal custody of executive agency records transferred to the National Archives, legal

NATIONAL ARCHIVES. Stack area 9E2, which houses records from the House of Representatives. The bound volumes are from the 87th and 88th Congresses.

NATIONAL ARCHIVES

FOURTH FLOOR OF THE CAPITOL BUILDING. File drawers contain records of the early Congresses.

NATIONAL ARCHIVES

tives and the Senate and preserved because of their continuing value—span the entire history of the legislative branch. They are housed with the Center for Legislative Archives in the National Archives Building in Washington, D.C. The center does not hold the collected papers of individual legislators.

Before they were transferred to the National Archives, congressional records suffered over the years through neglect, damage by vermin, and pilferage, as well as from the burning of some House files by the British when they attacked Washington in 1814. The rules of Congress also affected the extant record. Before 1946, Senate Rule XXII instructed standing committees to return to the secretary of the Senate at the end of each Congress only papers "referred" to such committees. The rule said nothing about materials created or received directly by the committee. Nor did it make clear whether records of special and select committees were under the secretary's jurisdiction. The clerk of the House was more fortunate in this regard; in 1880, House rules required all committee records to be delivered to the clerk within three days after the final adjournment of Congress and that appropriate committee permission be obtained for the withdrawal from the custody of the clerk of any records.

control of legislative records remains with the House and the Senate.

Presently each house of Congress has a rule that governs access to its records. Although both Senate and House investigative records and other records potentially detrimental to personal privacy are closed for fifty years, most other unpublished Senate records are available for public inspection twenty years after their creation; most House records are available for research when they are thirty years old. In addition, the House rules require researchers to obtain authorization from the clerk before they can have access to unpublished House records.

From 1938 through 1949, the National Archives administered legislative archives in a separate division. In 1985 the Archives reestablished a division for legislative archives, in 1988 renaming it the Center for Legislative Archives. As part of the 1988 change, the center gained responsibility for the record set of government publications that had been assembled by the superintendent of documents within the Government Printing Office. Two years later, with Public Law 101-509 (5 November 1990), Congress provided momentum for upgrading the status of the Center for Legislative Archives by mandating the creation of the Advisory Committee on the Records of Congress.

[*See also* Clerk of the House; Secretary of the Senate.]

BIBLIOGRAPHY

Advisory Committee on the Records of Congress. *First Report, December 31, 1991.* 1992.
Kepley, David R. "Congressional Records in the National Archives." *Prologue* 19 (Spring 1987): 23–33.

RODNEY A. ROSS

ARIZONA. The forty-eighth state, Arizona was admitted to the Union on 14 February 1912. Annexed to the United States as part of the Mexican Cession of 1848, it was initially included in the New Mexico Territory. In 1862, an Arizona Territory was created by the Confederate States of America, but the Confederacy failed to establish military control. On 20 February 1863, the U.S. Congress created the Arizona Territory as a separate entity from New Mexico, and in January 1864 U.S. officials arrived to establish the first territorial capital at Fort Whipple. An unsuccessful movement for statehood began in the 1890s. In 1906, the voters of the territory rejected an effort by Congress to create one great state (to be called Arizona) by combining the

New Mexico and Arizona territories. By 1910 the movement for Arizona statehood had developed momentum, and President William Howard Taft signed an enabling act allowing the territory to elect a constitutional convention to meet in Phoenix. The resulting document, written at the height of the Progressive era, gained national attention as a model of Progressive thinking; it included provisions for protecting the rights of labor and for the initiative, referendum, and recall.

In 1911, Congress passed a statehood bill, but President Taft vetoed it because he objected to the constitutional provision for the recall of judges. When the people of the Arizona Territory voted to delete that article, Taft approved the statehood bill, but one of the first acts of the sovereign people of the new state of Arizona was to restore the recall of judges to their constitution.

In the early decades of statehood, the Democratic party dominated Arizona's congressional delegation in Washington with such notable orators as Sen. Henry F. Ashurst. The state's first member of the House was Carl Hayden, who in 1927 became a senator and served until his retirement in 1969. He was president pro tempore in the 85th through 90th Congresses (1957–1969). By 1950 the Republican party was challenging the Democrats for control of high office with the election of Howard Pyle, only the third Republican governor since 1912. In 1952, Barry Goldwater was elected senator and led a national resurgence of Republican conservatism that led to his obtaining the party's presidential nomination in 1964. Despite his lopsided loss to Lyndon B. Johnson, Goldwater went on to serve three more senatorial terms and was one of the most influential politicians in Washington.

Other Arizonans gaining national prominence as congressional leaders were Democrat Ernest W. McFarland, Senate majority leader in the 82d Congress (1951–1953) and Republican John J. Rhodes, House minority leader in the 94th through 97th Congresses (1975–1983). Other Arizona members have gone on to high executive posts. Lewis W. Douglas, who served in the House in the 70th through 72d Congresses (1927–1933) was Franklin D. Roosevelt's first director of the budget, and Stewart L. Udall, a House member in the 84th through 86th Congresses (1955–1960), was secretary of the Interior under John F. Kennedy. Arizona had five House seats in the 102d Congress (1991–1993), which were filled by four Republicans and one Democrat. Because of the population growth reflected in the 1990 census, Arizona gained a sixth seat. In the House elections of 1992 one Republican was defeated and two new Democrats were elected, to make a party balance of three each. Among the Democrats is Karan English, Arizona's second woman representative (the first woman to serve in Arizona's delegation was Democrat Isabella S. Greenway, in the 73d and 74th Congresses [1933–1937]).

BIBLIOGRAPHY

Shadegg, Stephen C. *Arizona Politics: The Struggle to End One-Party Rule.* 1986.
Trimble, Marshall. *Arizona: A Cavalcade of History.* 1989.

PAUL HUBBARD

ARKANSAS. The act creating Arkansas Territory in 1819 touched off one of the most acrimonious debates to that date in congressional history. A dispute over the legalization of slavery in the new territory sparked a divisive discussion first in the Committee on Territories and later on the House floor.

The Arkansas territorial bill was a dress rehearsal for the debate leading to the Missouri Compromise. In many respects the "Arkansas Compromise" was the more significant of the two, setting the tone for the status of slavery in the territory of the "Louisiana Purchase" north of the newly created state of Louisiana.

When Arkansas was admitted as a state in 1836, the slavery issue attracted little attention. Of more immediate concern was the region's role in the presidential campaign. Jacksonian Democrats were successful in gaining approval for statehood on 15 June, and the state's voters responded by voting for Democratic presidential nominee Martin Van Buren in November.

The state's minimum of three members in the U.S. Congress was expanded to four following the federal census of 1850, with a second House seat added to the delegation. Additional House seats, for a total of seven, were added after the 1860, 1870, 1880, 1890, and 1900 censuses. Outward migration during and immediately following World War II caused the state to lose one seat in the House after 1950 and two seats after 1960.

Except during Reconstruction, all the states' U.S. senators have been members of the Democratic party. In the House, all have been Democrats except for one Whig, fifteen Republicans, and one Independent. The Arkansas delegation has been one of the most solidly Democratic in the nation.

Three women have served in the House, and one woman, Hattie W. Caraway, served in the Senate. Caraway was that body's first elected female member. No member of a minority group has been chosen to represent the state in Congress.

Members from Arkansas have also had a measure of success outside of the congressional chambers. Sen. Ambrose H. Sevier (1836–1848) was appointed by President James K. Polk as a member of the U.S. delegation to Mexico to negotiate the Treaty of Guadalupe Hidalgo. Sen. Augustus H. Garland (1877–1885) served as U.S. attorney general in President Grover Cleveland's first term. Sen. Joseph T. Robinson (House, 1903–1913; Senate, 1913–1937) was chosen by the Democratic party as its vice presidential nominee in 1928, and later served as Senate majority leader during the first five years of the administration of Franklin D. Roosevelt.

During the 1950s and 1960s, Arkansas had one of the most powerful delegations in Washington. Rep. Wilbur D. Mills (1939–1977), chairman of the House Ways and Means Committee, for two decades wrote most federal tax legislation and was generally regarded as one of the most influential individuals in the nation. Sen. John L. McClellan (1942–1977), chairman of the Appropriations Committee, was a key figure in shaping the nation's domestic fiscal policies, and Sen. J. William Fulbright (House, 1943–1945; Senate, 1945–1974), chairman of the Foreign Relations Committee, played a vital role in developing foreign policy.

BIBLIOGRAPHY

Ashmore, Harry S. *Arkansas: A Bicentennial History.* 1978.
Berry, Fred, and John Novak. *The History of Arkansas.* 1987.

C. FRED WILLIAMS

ARMED FORCES. Congress has implemented its constitutionally mandated authority "to raise and support Armies [and] to provide and maintain a Navy" (Article I, section 8) both through enacting statutes that govern the organization of the armed services and through the routine process it uses to control all federal agencies: by writing the laws that fund their operations.

Through the annual bills that authorize and appropriate defense funds, Congress determines for each service the number of personnel on duty, the number of weapons purchased for its use, the amount of training it can conduct, and myriad other details. Typically, Congress makes only marginal changes in a service's current form, but from time to time it tries to shape more fundamental aspects of the services' character. On the question of who should serve, for instance, Congress has taken the initiative at least three times. In 1862, it authorized the enlistment of blacks in the army; in 1975, it ordered women admitted as cadets and midshipmen to the three service academies; and, in 1991, it repealed the legal ban on assigning women to fly combat aircraft. In 1980, alarmed at a steady decline in the quality and quantity of recruits, Congress enacted a raft of policies to brake the apparent decline of the all-volunteer army, including an 11.7 percent military pay raise.

Control of Services' Missions. Occasionally, Congress has tried to control the services' missions. Sometimes it has restricted deployments by law, as in 1809, when it barred the navy's frigates from operating beyond coastal waters. It was exercising the same power, albeit on a more modest scale, in 1992, when it added to the annual defense authorization bill a provision limiting to 100,000 the number of U.S. military personnel that could be deployed in Europe after 1996.

More typically, however, Congress has exercised a veto over the services' proposed missions by refusing to fund the necessary weapons. Throughout most of the nineteenth century, for instance, it refused to buy enough battleships to allow the navy to plan to challenge any other country's battle fleet instead of merely harassing its commercial shipping.

Congress has also tried to regulate the balance of power between the services' top brass and the nation's political leadership. Partly for fear of diluting civilian control of the services, for example, it rejected nineteenth-century proposals for military reform that would have centralized control of the army or navy in a senior officer or an elite general staff.

But in the twentieth century Congress proved more receptive to such proposals. In 1903, concluding that the army's tangled bureaucracy had hampered operations in the 1898 war with Spain, Congress established a general staff to plan for the army's wartime operations. In 1915, Congress created the post of chief of naval operations to govern "the operations of the fleet," but it stipulated that this officer acted "under the direction of the [civilian] Secretary of the Navy."

Congress took the first big step toward formal unification of the services when it passed the National Security Act of 1947. In addition to making the U.S. Air Force—hitherto part of the army—a separate service alongside the army and navy, the act made all three part of the National Military Establishment headed by a secretary of Defense.

At the time, navy leaders strenuously opposed any organization that would subordinate their service to land-minded army and air force officials, so powerful congressional allies ensured that the new Defense secretary had relatively little authority over the services, each of which would continue to be headed by a civilian secretary with a seat in the president's cabinet. Congress enlarged the scope of the Defense secretary's power in 1949 (when it also dropped the service secretaries from the cabinet) and again in 1958.

The next big step toward service unification came after pro-Pentagon leaders of the House and Senate Armed Services committees were appalled by failures of interservice coordination that stymied a 1980 effort to free U.S. hostages in Iran and complicated the seizure of Grenada in 1983. The resulting Goldwater-Nichols Reorganization Act, passed in 1986, greatly strengthened the authority of the Joint Chiefs of Staff chairman—the nation's highest-ranking officer—partly in hopes of making the services more efficient by eliminating redundancies.

Defense Politics. The issue of whether the United States should have a standing army was one of many that divided the advocates of a stronger federal government from their opponents during the Constitutional Convention of 1787. In the end, the new Constitution divided authority over the new country's military institutions: Congress could raise armies, but it could appropriate funds for no more than two years at a time, and the president would be the army's commander in chief. Even more fundamentally, the country's military power was divided between the national army and the states' militias (today known as the National Guard).

As the country debated ratification of the new political compact, James Madison expressed the prevailing view of the strong-government party in *Federalist* 41: "A standing force . . . is a dangerous, at the same time that it might be a necessary provision." On the other side, Patrick Henry emphasized that the Constitution would empower Congress to raise both taxes and armies. "Where and when did a freedom exist when the sword and the purse were given up from the people?" Henry demanded of the Virginia ratifying convention.

In 1789, once the new political regime was in place, Congress quickly incorporated into it the

War Department, which had already been set up under the Articles of Confederation, and the small standing army that it administered.

Compared to the fears of domestic oppression, which motivated opposition to a standing army, the arguments against a navy were more subtle. Federalists, particularly those from New England and Middle Atlantic states, touted a navy as an essential adjunct to seaborne trade. But Anti-Federalists from the agrarian South and West countered that an effort to build a navy large enough to protect American commerce against the perennially battling British and French navies would be ruinously expensive and probably futile, serving only to draw the United States into a European war.

The small navy organized during the Revolutionary War had been disbanded at its end. By 1794, depredations on U.S. shipping in the Mediterranean by Algiers and other so-called Barbary States forced to a head the issue of whether a new U.S. Navy should be established. The Anti-Federalist argument—that it would be cheaper to buy peace with the North African pirates than to build a navy—was rejected, but narrowly. A preliminary resolution calling for a study of what ships to build passed the House by a vote of 46 to 44. Subsequently, the Navy Act of 1794, which authorized purchase or construction and manning of six frigates, was passed by the House (50 to 39) and Senate and signed into law by President George Washington.

When the country faced the Soviet nuclear threat during the height of the Cold War (from the early 1950s to the late 1980s) the historic skepticism toward military institutions was soft-pedaled. But a concern remained that the wrong kind of force might make the country too easily susceptible to entanglement in an international confrontation—a fear that had fueled the Jeffersonian Republicans' anti-navy stance during John Adams's administration. It was one factor in the widespread bipartisan congressional opposition in 1991 and 1992 to Bush administration proposals that would have made it easier for the army to conduct military operations abroad without taking the politically costly step of mobilizing National Guard units.

Another strand of continuity between past and present congressional attitudes toward the armed forces is Congress's sensitivity to constituents' commercial interests. This responsiveness to constituents has pervaded the process of buying property and equipment for the armed services, either because members have channeled purchases to favored firms or because politically astute executive branch officials have placed contracts with an eye to-

ward ensuring popular, and thus congressional, support. This was already true in Washington's administration, when Secretary of War Henry Knox cannily distributed the contracts to build the navy's first six frigates to shipyards in six cities from New Hampshire to Virginia. And it was still true in 1992, when Congress refused to slash the Pentagon's declining post–Cold War budget further, partly for fear of compounding the severe cutbacks already under way in U.S. defense industries.

Since the 1790s, most legislation dealing with the services has fit into a two-track system: authorization bills to set relatively long-term policies (e.g., the purchase of several warships) and separate appropriations bills to permit funds to be drawn from the Treasury on a year-to-year basis. But it took time for the system of permanent House and Senate Armed Services committees to evolve. Today, the Armed Services committees draft authorization bills, while appropriations bills for the services are drafted by the permanent Appropriations committees.

The modern pattern of annual defense authorization and appropriations bills was set in 1959, when Congress enacted a requirement for a detailed annual bill authorizing major weapons appropriations, to begin in 1961. Over the following two decades, the Armed Services panels expanded the scope of their annual authorization bills step by step until, in 1992, the bill authorizing defense expenditures in fiscal 1993 set an upper limit on the amount that could be appropriated for every program funded in companion bills drafted by the Appropriations committees.

Nevertheless, committee turf wars over defense funding are relatively rare. For one thing, most members of the Armed Services committees and the Defense Appropriations subcommittees have been sympathetic toward the viewpoint of the services' senior uniformed leaders. Also, there has been an informal division of labor: typically, the Armed Services committees have dealt with the really fundamental policy issues in the authorization bills, while the Appropriations panels have concentrated on the details of funding requested for a particular year.

The cutback of the defense establishment begun in 1990 by President George Bush might have exacerbated the rivalry between the two sets of committees. By then, however, particularly influential chairmen were ensconced in the two Armed Services panels—Sen. Sam Nunn (D-Ga.) and Rep. Les Aspin (D-Wis.). By their extraordinary personal stature as defense policy experts and the political skill with which they crafted their committee's annual bills, these two men ensured that the authorization bills would be the vehicle for congressional efforts to restructure the armed services for the post–Cold War world.

When Aspin left Congress to serve as President Bill Clinton's first secretary of Defense, his successor as House Armed Services chair was Ronald V. Dellums (D-Calif.). For more than 20 years, Dellums had been one of the most radical congressional critics of recent U.S. defense policy, but as the chairman of two Armed Services subcommittees, he also had shown finesse as a savvy political broker who eschewed using his role as committee chairman to tilt bills unduly toward his own point of view.

So, under Dellums' lead, House Armed Services essentially backed the Clinton administration's proposal for relatively modest reductions, as drawn up by Aspin during his year at the Pentagon and carried forward by William J. Perry, Aspin's successor as Defense secretary early in 1994.

[See also Air Force; Armed Services Committee, House; Armed Services Committee, Senate; Army; Coast Guard; Defense; Marine Corps; Navy.]

BIBLIOGRAPHY

Cunliffe, Marcus. *Soldiers and Civilians.* 1968.
Hagan, Kenneth J. *This People's Navy.* 1991.
Sprout, Harold, and Margaret Sprout. *The Rise of American Naval Power, 1776–1918.* 1944.
Weigley, Russell F. *The American Way of War.* 1973.
Weigley, Russell F. *History of the United States Army.* Enl. ed. 1984.

W. PATRICK TOWELL

ARMED SERVICES COMMITTEE, HOUSE.

In its current form the House Armed Services Committee dates from the Legislative Reorganization Act of 1946. By other names, however, its roots can be traced to the American Revolution. By one estimate, for example, no fewer than seventeen special subcommittees were created by the Continental Congress to supervise matters as diverse as cannon, muskets, hospitals, clothes, beef, and even saltpeter. These committees were investigative in character and had virtually no authority. The early subcommittees were consolidated into the Board of War and a Marine Committee, and members frequently accompanied Gen. George Washington into the field to observe and to offer advice and counsel.

Without the benefit of standing committees, the First Congress under the new Constitution established a Department of War, which was charged with responsibility for both military and naval affairs. Nine years later, on 30 April 1798, Congress reestablished the U.S. Navy and a separate Department of the Navy.

The first congressional committee on military affairs was a special committee, established in 1782, to investigate the defeat of Gen. Arthur St. Clair during an engagement in the northwest frontier. Separate committees on Expenditures in the War and in the Navy departments—precursors of today's Government Operations Committee—were created in 1816. In 1822, standing committees on Military Affairs and Naval Affairs were established. In 1835, the House also created a separate standing Committee on the Militia. That committee's functions were absorbed by the Military Affairs Committee in 1911. Finally, in 1946, pursuant to the Legislative Reorganization Act, the House Military Affairs Committee and the Naval Affairs Committee were combined as the Armed Services Committee. The combination of these separate committees was paralleled in 1947 by an executive branch reorganization, uniting in the Department of Defense what had been the Department of War and the Department of the Navy.

Jurisdiction. The jurisdiction of the Armed Services Committee is established in House Rule X. That rule makes the committee responsible for the common defense generally, for any activity undertaken by the Department of Defense or by the departments of the Army, Navy, or Air Force, and for the Selective Service system. It oversees all ammunition depots, forts, arsenals, and the reservations and properties of the army, navy, and air force. The pay, promotion, retirement, and other benefits of members of the armed forces fall within the committee's jurisdiction, as do soldiers' and sailors' homes. The committee authorizes research, development, testing, evaluation, and the procurement of all military equipment used by the armed services. Finally, it oversees activities undertaken by other departments and agencies that affect the military uses of space, nuclear energy, research and development in support of the armed services, and strategic and critical materials.

The jurisdiction of the Armed Services Committee has been remarkably stable throughout its history. The committee has acquired authority over the military applications of nuclear energy—inherited when the Joint Committee on Atomic Energy

RONALD V. DELLUMS (D-CALIF.), CHAIRMAN (1993–). *Center,* with committee member Patricia Schroeder (D-Colo.), consulting with staff during a defense authorization bill markup session, July 1993.   R. MICHAEL JENKINS, CONGRESSIONAL QUARTERLY INC.

was eliminated in 1977. It lost jurisdiction when the Select Committee on Intelligence was created, also in 1977. It no longer has authority for the education of military dependents.

Structure and Organization. At the turn of the century, the combined memberships of the Military Affairs and the Naval Affairs committees numbered 37. After these committees' consolidation in 1947, the new Armed Services Committee had 33 members (19 Republicans and 14 Democrats)—including Carl Vinson, L. Mendel Rivers, and F. Edward Hébert (chairs), Lyndon B. Johnson, and Margaret Chase Smith. In 1965 it had grown to only 37 members. By the 102d Congress (1991–1993), however, the committee had grown to 54 members (33 Democrats and 21 Republicans)—an increase of 46 percent. Throughout the entire period, party ratios on the committee have been a rough reflection of those in the whole House.

From the 64th Congress (1915–1917) to the 80th Congress (1947–1949), the Military Affairs and Naval Affairs committees were exclusive ones—

their members could serve on no other House committees. Since that time, both parties have categorized Armed Services as a major committee, which allows each of its members an additional but lesser assignment. Throughout its modern history the Armed Services Committee has employed a set of subcommittees to hold hearings, mount investigations, and draft legislation. With the exception of the 90th (1967–1969) and the 91st (1969–1971) Congresses—when a series of special narrow subcommittees ballooned the total to fifteen or more—the committee has nearly always employed seven subcommittees. And while their subject matter has evolved somewhat, they generally reflect the components of the committee's jurisdiction: investigations, military installations, personnel, procurement, readiness, research and development, sea power, and strategic materials. The committee continues to use subcommittees to craft portions of the annual defense authorization bill and other committee legislation.

The committee's modest size (at least until 1978)

and subcommittee structure have combined with low levels of turnover to make career advancement quite slow for Armed Services' members. For example, on average it takes longer to advance to a coveted subcommittee chair on Armed Services than on any other House committee. From the 86th Congress (1959–1961) to the 91st Congress (1969–1971), Armed Services Democrats averaged eighteen years of committee service before advancing to a subcommittee chair. Only four committee members were able to move up during that time. Since then, advancement has been more rapid but still slow by comparison to other House committees—just over thirteen years on average between the 92d (1971–1973) and the 101st (1987–1989) Congresses. Setting aside the brief, one-Congress tenures of Walter G. Andrews (N.Y., 1947–1949) and Dewey Short (Mo., 1953–1955) during Republican-controlled Congresses, only six people have chaired the committee since World War II: Vinson (Ga.), Rivers (S.C.), Hébert (La.), Melvin Price (Ill.), Les Aspin (Wisc.), and Ronald V. Dellums (Calif.).

Relations between these chairs, committee members, and the party caucus have occasionally been rocky. Prior to the outset of the 94th Congress, Hébert was one of three senior committee chairs to be denied reelection by the caucus. Hébert was replaced by Price, the second-ranking Democrat on the committee. But the aging Price ultimately proved incapable of effective and active committee leadership. This, in turn, led to a contest among several committee Democrats—a race won by the liberal Aspin over six more senior colleagues. During Aspin's tenure, relations between the chairman and the Democratic Caucus remained strained. In fact, Aspin actually lost a routine yes-or-no vote for reelection as chair in 1987 only to engineer a remarkable comeback within weeks after three other committee members had been nominated. Apparently Aspin was chastened, for the remainder of his tenure as chairman was marked by cooperative relations within the committee and with the caucus and party leaders. Aspin, who became secretary of Defense at the outset of the Clinton administration, was succeeded by Dellums, one of the most liberal members of the House.

Motivations and Behavior. The committee attracts conservative, prodefense members from both parties who are interested in protecting the flow of benefits to bases and contractors located in their congressional districts. Asked an open-ended question about their motivations for seeking membership on Armed Services, a majority of members

mentioned constituency concerns. Perhaps unsurprisingly, therefore, committee members and staff traditionally observe that the committee should be regarded as principally concerned with military bases located in congressional districts.

Nonetheless it is neither surprising nor inconsistent that by any measure the party contingents on Armed Services have long been more conservative than their partisan colleagues. According to one popular measure, a 100-point liberalism index published by the Americans for Democratic Action, Armed Services Democrats had a mean score of 41.1 from the 91st to the 100th Congresses while other Democrats averaged 60.6. Although distinctly more conservative, Republican committee members also earned a more conservative average, 10.0, than their Republican House colleagues, 18.8.

The conservatism of the committee makes it a natural ally for and promoter of the uniformed services and the Defense Department. During the post–World War II period this was reinforced by public opinion in strong support of a large active-duty military. Beyond this, however, the committee has supported the development and provision of new, technologically sophisticated weapons—an emphasis that, in turn, channeled defense expenditures to military contractors in a variety of congressional districts. Taken together, this confluence of interests—the committee, the Pentagon, and the contractors—came to be known as the military industrial complex. As public support for the military diminished during the final years of the Vietnam War, the committee remained strongly supportive of the armed forces, of defense-related industries, and of base-dominated communities—blunting calls for budget reductions, elimination of weapons systems, and base closures. Indeed, in the face of overwhelming support for change, including expanding the role of women in the services, reforming procurement practices, reorganizing the Pentagon, and eliminating the ban on gay men and lesbians in the military, the committee became a broker for proposals that were more moderate than many House members preferred and that most in the Pentagon and services opposed outright. Thus, even in an era of change the committee maintained its role at the heart of the military subgovernment by reducing the otherwise negative impacts of a variety of dramatic policy proposals.

Defense Authorizations. Article I, section 8 of the Constitution clearly establishes Congress's responsibilities for national defense: to raise and support the army and the navy; to make rules governing the land and naval forces; to provide for calling forth, organizing, arming, and disciplining the militia; to exercise exclusive legislation over all places purchased for forts, magazines, arsenals, dockyards, and other necessary buildings; and to declare war. By tradition and rule, the last of these responsibilities falls within the jurisdiction of the House and Senate foreign policy committees.

The Armed Services Committee undertakes these other constitutional responsibilities by drafting legislation that provides program authority—statutory authority—for defense activities performed by the executive branch. In 1947, for example, Congress passed the National Security Act that created the Department of Defense, split the U.S. Air Force off from the U.S. Army, transformed the Office of Strategic Services (OSS) into the Central Intelligence Agency (CIA), and created the National Security Council. The committee's authorizing bills may have the additional purpose and effect of setting limits on what may be spent for defense programs. Program authority, in the form of annual Department of Defense authorization bills, covers a vast array of activities—from buying boots, shoes, and uniforms to purchasing multibillion-dollar weapons systems. And at least formally, this means that Congress, subject to presidential veto, may create, alter, or abolish any office, program, or activity undertaken by the Pentagon.

The committee's actual performance of this function has ranged widely—from the close daily supervision of Gen. George Washington in the field to a permissive and detached authorization of military activities immediately after World War II. For example, throughout the postwar period the committee authorized the Defense Department to draft or recruit as many as five million active-duty military personnel annually, a figure never remotely approximated. Likewise, the committee routinely gave open-ended authorizations for the purchase of aircraft, tanks, and other military equipment without specifying their precise characteristics or proportions.

The most important postwar development for the committee has therefore been the expansion of the requirement for annual authorizations. In 1959 Congress passed the so-called Russell Amendment, which required annual program authorization of appropriations for the procurement of aircraft, missiles, and naval vessels. By one estimate, only about 2 percent of defense activity required annual authorization at that time. Because of the Russell Amendment and numerous subsequent legislative requirements, that figure now stands at 100 percent of defense activities. Thus the Armed Services Com-

mittee has ensured at least a cursory role for itself in every activity undertaken in the name of national defense each year.

[See also Armed Services Committee, Senate.]

BIBLIOGRAPHY

Blechman, Barry M. The Politics of National Security: Congress and U.S. Defense Policy. 1990.
Deering, Christopher J. "Decision Making in the Armed Services Committees." In Congress Resurgent: Foreign and Defense Policy on Capitol Hill. Edited by Randall B. Ripley and James M. Lindsay. 1993.
Towell, Pat. "Aspin Moves to Avoid Reruns of His Political Missteps." Congressional Quarterly Weekly Report, 14 April 1990, pp. 1141–1145.
Towell, Pat. "Dellums Walks a Delicate Line from Past to Chairmanship." Congressional Quarterly Weekly Report, 8 May 1993, pp. 1163–1169.

CHRISTOPHER J. DEERING

ARMED SERVICES COMMITTEE, SENATE.
The Senate Armed Services Committee was established by the Legislative Reorganization Act of 1946 and began operation in the 80th Congress (1947–1949). Its roots, like those of its House counterpart, can, however, be traced to Revolutionary times.

Jurisdiction. The Armed Services Committee's jurisdiction is established in Senate Rule XXV. That rule makes the committee generally responsible for the common defense and the departments of Defense, Army, Navy, and Air Force. Maintenance and operation of the Panama Canal Zone and the Selective Service system fall within the committee's jurisdiction, as do naval petroleum reserves (except in Alaska), the national security aspects of nuclear energy, and strategic and critical materials related to defense. The committee is responsible for military research and development and defense-related aeronautical and space activities. Finally, the pay, promotion, retirement, and other benefits of members of the armed forces, including overseas education of military and civilian dependents, also are within the committee's purview. The jurisdiction of the Armed Services Committee has been quite consistent throughout its history. With the elimination of the Joint Committee on Atomic Energy in 1977, the committee acquired authority over the military applications of nuclear energy. It also lost responsibility when the Select Committee on Intelligence was created in 1977.

Structure and Organization. At the turn of the century, the Military Affairs Committee and the Naval Affairs Committee each had 11 members,

SENATE ARMED SERVICES COMMITTEE. Senator Richard B. Russell (D-Ga.), *left*, soon to become chairman of the committee, conferring with Senators John Foster Dulles (R-N.Y.), *center*, and Theodore F. Green (D-R.I.), 1949.   OFFICE OF THE HISTORIAN OF THE U.S. SENATE

with no member serving on both committees. After these committees' 1947 consolidation, the Armed Services Committee had 13 members (7 Republicans and 6 Democrats). By 1967 the committee had grown to 18 members, but it dropped to 15 by 1973. By the 100th Congress (1987–1989), however, the committee had grown to 20 members (11 Democrats and 9 Republicans), an increase of 33 percent. (This number was maintained in the 103d Congress.) Throughout the entire period, party ratios on the committee roughly reflected those in the whole House.

The Armed Services Committee has always used subcommittees to hold hearings and mount investigations. As with most Senate committees, the subcommittees do rather little legislative work. With the exception of the 93d Congress (1973–1975)—when a series of narrow subcommittees (such as Drug Abuse in the Military) increased the total to

twelve—the committee typically has had five or six subcommittees. Until 1980, the subcommittees essentially reflected the appropriations categories: military construction, personnel, research and development, procurement, and so forth. Since 1980, when Republicans briefly gained control of the Senate, the subcommittees have had a more mission-oriented structure. Most subcommittees consider a particular type or set of missions—conventional forces, projection forces, strategic forces, readiness, staffing, and defense industry and technology.

Since World War II, the committee has been chaired by some of the most powerful and illustrious members ever to sit in the Senate. These include Richard B. Russell of Georgia, Leverett Saltonstall of Massachusetts, John C. Stennis of Mississippi, Sam Nunn of Georgia, John G. Tower of Texas, and Barry Goldwater of Arizona. Russell and Stennis had sufficient seniority to gain the chairs of the Armed Services Committee and the Defense Appropriations Subcommittee simultaneously. Lyndon B. Johnson of Texas, Henry M. Jackson of Washington, Margaret Chase Smith of Maine (ranking member from the 90th Congress to the 92d Congress), Gary Hart of Colorado, Dan Quayle of Indiana, and Edward M. Kennedy of Massachusetts have all served on the committee. As of the 102d Congress, Strom Thurmond of South Carolina had served on the committee for thirty-two years—the first four years as a Democrat and the next twenty-eight as a Republican.

Motivations and Behavior. Armed Services is one of four Senate committees—Finance, Appropriations, and Foreign Relations are the others—that falls under the so-called Johnson Rule. When Lyndon Johnson was the Senate majority leader, he guaranteed that each member of his party would be able to obtain a seat on one of the four most desirable Senate committees. Competition among new, and even continuing, members for seats on the committee has generally been quite keen.

The committee attracts conservative, prodefense members from both parties who are interested in promoting a strong national defense while protecting the flow of benefits to bases and contractors located in their states. Asked an open-ended question about why they sought membership on Armed Services, senators mentioned policy and constituency concerns in equal proportions. Committee members and chairs have been disproportionately from the South. For example, during the 102d Congress (1991–1993), eight of the committee's twenty members were from southern or border states. And the committee has been chaired by a southerner for eighteen of the twenty-two postwar congresses.

Party contingents on Armed Services are generally more conservative than their partisan colleagues. According to one popular measure, a 100-point liberalism index published by the Americans for Democratic Action, Armed Services Democrats had a mean score of 52.0 from the 91st to the 100th Congresses while other Democrats averaged 63.2. Although distinctly more conservative, Republican committee members also earned a more conservative average, 13.0, than their Republican Senate colleagues, 26.9.

Defense Authorizations. Article I, section 8 of the Constitution clearly establishes Congress's responsibilities for national defense: to raise and support the army and the navy; to make rules governing the land and naval forces; to provide for calling forth, organizing, arming, and disciplining the military; to exercise exclusive legislation over all property purchased for forts, magazines, arsenals, dockyards, and other buildings; and to declare war. By tradition and rule, the last of these responsibilities falls within the jurisdiction of the House and Senate foreign policy committees.

The Armed Services Committee discharges its other constitutional responsibilities by drafting legislation that provides program authority—statutory authority—for defense activities performed by the executive branch. In 1947, for example, Congress passed the National Security Act, which created the Department of Defense, split the U.S. Air Force off from the U.S. Army, transformed the Office of Strategic Services (OSS) into the Central Intelligence Agency (CIA), and created the National Security Council. The committee's authorizing bills may have the additional purpose and effect of setting limits on defense spending. Annual Defense Department authorization bills cover a host of activities—from buying boots, shoes, and uniforms to purchasing multibillion-dollar weapons systems. At least formally, this means that Congress, subject to presidential veto, may create, alter, or abolish any office, program, or activity undertaken by the Pentagon.

The committee's actual performance of this function has ranged widely—from closely supervising Gen. George Washington in the field every day to a very permissive and detached authorization of military activities immediately after World War II. For example, throughout the postwar period the committee authorized the Defense Department to draft or recruit as many as five million active-duty military personnel annually—a figure never remotely approximated. Likewise, the committee routinely gave open-ended authorizations for the purchase of aircraft, tanks, and other military equipment without specifying their precise characteristics or proportions.

The most important postwar development for the committee has therefore been the expansion of the requirement for annual authorizations. In 1959, Congress passed the so-called Russell Amendment, which required annual program authorization of appropriations for the procurement of aircraft, missiles, and naval vessels. By one estimate, only about 2 percent of defense activity required annual authorization at that time. Because of the Russell Amendment and numerous subsequent legislative requirements, that figure now stands at 100 percent of defense activities. Thus the Armed Services Committee has ensured at least a cursory role for itself in every activity undertaken in the name of national defense each year.

[*See also* Armed Services Committee, House.]

BIBLIOGRAPHY

Blechman, Barry M. *The Politics of National Security: Congress and U.S. Defense Policy.* 1990.

Deering, Christopher J. "Decision Making in the Armed Services Committees." In *Congress Resurgent: Foreign and Defense Policy on Capitol Hill.* Edited by Randall B. Ripley and James M. Lindsay. 1993.

Towell, Pat. "Armed Services Panel: Goldwater in the Cockpit." *Congressional Quarterly Weekly Report,* 16 February 1985, pp. 297–300.

Towell, Pat. "Sam Nunn: The Careful Exercise of Power." *Congressional Quarterly Weekly Report,* 14 June 1986, pp. 1329–1333.

CHRISTOPHER J. DEERING

ARMS CONTROL. Congress's involvement in arms control stems from several constitutional sources: general oversight of all government activities, including foreign and defense affairs, and, more specifically, the Senate's advice and consent role on treaties. Key determinants in Congress's reaction to arms control have been the long-standing tradition of having no permanent foreign obligations, the Senate's regard for its prerogatives, and competing views within Congress and between Congress and the executive of national security needs.

Before World War I. Arms control (or disarmament, as it was first called) is essentially a twentieth-century concept. For the United States, antecedents can be found in nineteenth-century peace movements that emphasized arbitration to settle international disputes, a position with which some members of Congress sympathized, though not as a general principle. In 1897, the Senate first gutted and then rejected Secretary of State Richard Olney's general arbitration treaty with Great Britain. A major reason was Senate concern that its prerogatives in individual foreign policy issues might be lost to arbitrators. Traditional concerns over foreign entanglements and a good dose of Anglophobia contributed to the Senate's action.

The United States attended the first Hague Peace Conference (1899), called by Czar Nicholas II to reduce armaments. The conference reached no agreement on armaments, but it did create the Permanent Court of Arbitration for the voluntary submission of disputes. U.S. peace societies campaigned actively for the idea, which the Senate accepted along with a convention for a moratorium on balloon-borne projectiles. President William McKinley did not submit conventions against expanding bullets and asphyxiating gas, as both agreements faced some U.S. military opposition.

The second Hague Peace Conference (1907) was convened at the call of President Theodore Roosevelt in response to public reaction to the bloody Russo-Japanese War (1904–1905). It achieved little. However, Elihu Root, Roosevelt's secretary of State, negotiated twenty-five arbitration pacts in 1908 and 1909. These were all much weaker than Olney's treaty, exempting "vital interests" and reserving to the Senate the right to approve by two-thirds vote any special treaty referring an issue to arbitration. These the Senate accepted.

Interwar Arms Control. Arms control was not a major factor in the U.S. decision to enter World War I nor in the bitter debate over the Versailles treaty that followed, although it was one of President Woodrow Wilson's Fourteen Points. Disarmament was the centerpiece at the Washington Conference (1921–1922), when Secretary of State Charles Evans Hughes "sank more ships than all the admirals of the world," calling for a limit on capital ships (ships exceeding ten thousand tons displacement, with guns over eight inches in caliber—primarily battleships) and the destruction of much existing tonnage. Perhaps learning from Wilson's mistake at Versailles, Hughes included important congressional leaders on the U.S. delegation: Root (now a senator), Henry Cabot Lodge, and Oscar W. Underwood. The Senate accepted the Five-Power Naval Limitation Treaty and the associated Pacific region political treaties, although there was strong opposition to—and a close vote on—the Four-Power Pacific Treaty, in which the United States, Great Britain, France, and Japan pledged to respect each other's possessions in the Pacific and to consult one another if threatened. Lodge, the leader of opposition to Versailles, found himself in an awkward position in supporting this new pact.

Despite broad opposition to the Versailles treaty, there was strong public interest in joining the League of Nations' autonomous judicial arm, the World Court. Reflecting this, the House passed a favorable resolution in 1925 by a vote of 303 to 28. President Calvin Coolidge submitted the treaty to the Senate in 1925, leading to a repeat of the bitter debate over U.S. membership in the League; opponents saw World Court membership as the first step on the road to entering the dreaded League of Nations. The treaty passed easily (76 to 17) with several reservations, including a U.S. claim that only the United States could authorize the court to render an advisory opinion on matters affecting the United States. The court found this unacceptable. Despite Senator Root's efforts to achieve a compromise, President Herbert Hoover could not overcome strong Senate opposition, nor could President Franklin D. Roosevelt in 1935, when adherence to the treaty fell short by seven votes. A similar fate befell the 1925 Geneva Protocol prohibiting the use of chemical or biological weapons. Although the United States was an active participant in the conference and the Senate Foreign Relations Committee reported the protocol favorably, it was not brought to a vote because of strong opposition.

The Washington Naval Treaty was followed by the London Naval Treaty (1930), slightly increasing Japan's ratio of naval power but placing limits on all classes of warships. This easily passed the Senate (58 to 9), along with a declaration stating that the United States was not bound by any secret understandings. More significant was the 1928 Kellogg-Briand Pact, in which nations forswore war (except in self-defense) as an instrument of policy. Curiously, this pact resulted from U.S. efforts to avoid any guarantee of French security, oddly coupled with a strong popular campaign for a "no war" pledge fostered by staunch isolationist Sen. William E. Borah (R-Idaho). Although many senators saw the inherent weakness of the treaty, it passed overwhelmingly (85 to 1) and without reservations. The Senate Foreign Relations Committee did offer "interpretations" stating that the United States had not given up the right of self-defense or the Monroe Doctrine and was not obliged to act against treaty violators.

These various treaties lulled Congress and the public just as the post–World War I settlement began to unravel. Successive presidents and Congresses saw no need to spend money on even treaty-permitted naval levels (or on the army) so long as the treaties were in force. To a large degree this represented continuing disillusionment with the outcome of World War I and supposedly conspiratorial reasons for U.S. entry into that conflict. Nothing captured this view better than the 1934–1935 hearings chaired by Sen. Gerald P. Nye (R-N.D.), which revealed how the "merchants of death" (arms manufacturers and international bankers) had profited during the war.

The Nuclear Age. The arms-control emphasis after World War II was on nuclear weapons and negotiations with the Soviet Union. After initially emphasizing general disarmament, the United States shifted in the mid 1950s toward partial measures. A key issue was U.S. government organization for arms control, which had been haphazard and not a high priority. Reacting to this, Congress was instrumental in creating the Arms Control and Disarmament Agency (ACDA, 1961) to give focus and long-term expertise to these issues, an effort led by Sen. Hubert H. Humphrey (D-Minn.).

Spurred by the Cuban missile crisis of 1962, the United States, Great Britain, the Soviet Union, and more than a hundred other nations signed the Limited Test Ban Treaty (1963). Although the test ban was widely popular, some senators were concerned about how it would affect future weapons development. President John F. Kennedy garnered support partly by pledging a vigorous underground nuclear test program, and the Senate approved the pact by a vote of 80 to 19.

This pattern of garnering Senate consent by pledging more defense programs was increasingly employed. Such an approach, which Congress abetted, also ran counter to the often unrealistic hope that arms control would result in sizable defense savings. President Richard M. Nixon negotiated the U.S.-U.S.S.R. Antiballistic Missile Systems (ABM) Treaty and the Interim Agreement on Strategic Offensive Arms (also known as Strategic Arms Limitation Talks, or SALT I) in 1972, the latter allowing different levels of U.S. and Soviet missile launchers. This led to Sen. Henry M. Jackson's (D-Wash.) amendment urging that the levels be equal in future agreements. SALT I was also controversial because it was presented as an executive agreement rather than a treaty. The law establishing ACDA allowed the use of executive agreements in such cases, provided they were submitted as joint resolutions for approval by the House and Senate. Nixon's use of an executive agreement for SALT I raised concerns that presidents would prefer having such agreements approved by majority votes rather than risk the Senate's more difficult two-thirds requirement for treaties. Such an approach also created a split between House and Senate, as the House has no constitutional role in treaty approval but has an equal voice in joint resolutions.

Soviet noncompliance with arms control agreements became increasingly controversial following the 1972 agreements, with Congress often having to extract noncompliance information from successive administrations that were reluctant to provide it. Beginning in 1984, Congress required annual presidential reports on Soviet noncompliance,

Landmark Arms Control Treaties

Title	Year Enacted	Reference Number	Description
Washington Naval Treaty (Five-Power Naval Limitation Treaty)	1922	43 Stat. 1655	First treaty to achieve genuine arms reductions. The United States, Great Britain, France, Italy, and Japan agreed to reduce the tonnage of their capital ships (primarily battleships) and to keep these units in strict tonnage ratios to one another.
Kellogg-Briand Pact (Renunciation of War as an Instrument of National Policy)	1928[1]	46 Stat. 2343	Pledge to forswear war by the United States, Great Britain and its major dominions, France, Germany, Japan, et al.; typified idealistic interwar arms control.
Arms Control and Disarmament Act	1961	P.L. 87-297	Under congressional impetus, created Arms Control and Disarmament Agency and established formal goals for U.S. arms control policy.
Limited Test Ban Treaty	1963	14 Stat. 1313	First treaty affecting nuclear weapons, in which the United States, Great Britain, and the Soviet Union agreed to forgo testing in the atmosphere, outer space, and under water; Senate debate also reflected presidential need to pledge continued strong defense programs to ensure passage.
Nuclear Non-Proliferation Treaty	1968[2]	21 UST 483–566	Banned the spread of nuclear weapons, provided for safeguard arrangements, and ensured nondiscriminatory access to peaceful uses of nuclear energy. Signators included the United States, the Soviet Union, and 60 other nations.
Antiballistic Missile Systems (ABM) Treaty; Strategic Arms Limitation Talks (SALT I, Interim Agreement on Strategic Offensive Arms)	1972	23 UST 3435; P.L. 92-448	First U.S.-U.S.S.R. arms control agreements under détente, serving to "cap" nuclear arms race quantitatively by limiting deployments of ABM systems, initially to two sites, and setting upper limits on the number of strategic nuclear missile launchers; also led to Jackson amendment, requiring equal levels in future agreements. ABM treaty was also the subject of a constitutional debate between the Reagan administration and the Senate over treaty interpretation as it related to Strategic Defense Initiative (SDI; Star Wars) testing.
SALT II Treaty	1979[3]	—	Follow-up to SALT I, extending limits to include bombers, and beginning qualitative limits as well; never brought to vote in Senate because of Soviet invasion of Afghanistan, signaling the end of détente.
Intermediate Nuclear Forces (INF) Treaty (Treaty on the Elimination of Intermediate-Range and Shorter-Range Missiles)	1987	S. Treaty Doc. 100-11	First U.S.-U.S.S.R. arms control agreement to eliminate (rather than cap or reduce) an entire class of nuclear weapons systems.
Strategic Arms Reduction Treaty (START)	1991	S. Treaty Doc. 102-20	Perhaps the last of the classic U.S.-U.S.S.R. arms control treaties, negotiated at the end of the Cold War and on the eve of the Soviet collapse, reducing launchers and setting weapons-loading and other qualitative limits. The four nuclear-armed Soviet successor states (Russia, Ukraine, Belarus, and Kazakhstan) undertook to fulfill the same obligations in the Lisbon Protocol (23 May 1992) and the U.S.-Russian-Ukrainian agreement (January 1994).

[1]Year concluded; ratified in 1929.
[2]Year concluded; ratified in 1969.
[3]Year concluded; it was not ratified.

which documents were themselves controversial. Interest in these issues also increased with the creation of the Senate and House intelligence committees in the mid 1970s.

SALT II (1979), which unlike SALT I was a treaty, was a victim of the era's changing politics. The Soviet invasion of Afghanistan doomed Senate approval; though SALT II remained on the calendar, it was never brought to a vote before it expired.

On taking office, President Ronald Reagan subjected the entire U.S. approach to arms control to review, leading to a break in talks. This hiatus helped spawn the nuclear freeze movement, which garnered broad support in Congress, as did various schemes to reduce strategic offensive arsenals, although not enough to force a change in U.S. policy.

Reagan's 1983 Strategic Defense Initiative (SDI; better known as Star Wars) gave rise to a constitutional dispute. SDI proponents in the administration argued that a broad interpretation of the ABM treaty allowed certain types of weapons development and testing that many had previously assumed were banned; SDI opponents and many in the arms control community disagreed. Senators also took strong exception to the underlying argument that presidents could reinterpret treaties after the Senate had voted to accept them under a different interpretation or understanding. Congress repeatedly enacted language effectively barring any such testing.

Reagan and Soviet leader Mikhail Gorbachev in 1987 agreed to the Intermediate Nuclear Forces (INF) Treaty, which passed the Senate easily (93 to 5). However, the Conventional Armed Forces in Europe (CFE) Treaty and Strategic Arms Reduction Treaty (START; both 1991) gave rise to new Senate concerns about post-Soviet instability. CFE passed (90 to 4) with reservations requiring the Bush administration to obtain compliance by Soviet successor states and stating that any significant changes in CFE terms would require Senate approval. START passed (93 to 9), with the proviso that the Soviet Union's four nuclear successor states (Russia, Ukraine, Belarus, and Kazakhstan) were bound by the terms of the treaty.

George Bush and Gorbachev (and, after him, Russian president Boris Yeltsin) exchanged unilateral declarations of lower arms levels. Despite general support of these steps, Congress became concerned that these declarations left it no formal role in approving such measures.

[See also Antiballistic Missile Systems Treaty; Limited Test Ban Treaty; Nuclear Non-Proliferation Treaty; Nuclear Weapons; Strategic Arms Limitation Talks.]

BIBLIOGRAPHY

Clarke, Duncan L. *Politics of Arms Control.* 1979.
Davis, Calvin DeArmond. *The United States and the Second Hague Peace Conference.* 1975.
U.S. House of Representatives. Committee on Foreign Affairs. *Fundamentals of Nuclear Arms Control.* 99th Cong., 2d sess., 1986. See especially "Nuclear Arms Control: A Brief Historical Survey," pp. 1–50.

MARK M. LOWENTHAL

ARMY. Empowered by Article I, section 8 of the Constitution to make laws and allocate money to the land forces of the United States, Congress has exercised its responsibilities with persistent interest in the affairs of the U.S. Army and the various land-force reserve components, now split between the Army Reserve and Army National Guard (the latter the descendant of the state militias). Congress created a Military Affairs Committee and a Naval Affairs Committee in the House of Representatives and in the Senate to deal with the War Department and Navy Department, but it merged these committees in 1947 into two new Armed Services committees, which deal with all four military services, the three service departments (Army, Navy, Air Force), and the Department of Defense. In addition, the Appropriations committees of both houses have always had subcommittees to deal with military budgets, and the chairmen of these subcommittees have often wielded substantial power over land-forces policy. The House and Senate Government Operations committees have occasionally been a third focal point of congressional interest in the Army.

Congress examines the Army's policies and practices on an annual basis through the appropriations and authorization process, and it often dictates policy through the budget bill. It also considers and passes major legislation for the Army, much of which is now incorporated in Title 10 of the U.S. Code. Individual senators and representatives often intercede with the Army on behalf of service constituents and their dependents on individual problems; the Army's congressional liaison office and the Army staff take these concerns very seriously, regardless of their merit.

Land-Force Structure and Recruitment Policy. From its first session Congress focused on the size and structure of the U.S. land forces. It supported a regular army only because it believed such a standing force had two legitimate peacetime missions: patroling the Indian frontier and manning the coastal fortifications built to deter maritime raiders. These two different functional branches of the U.S. Army would presumably provide the professional cadre to train and command a wartime army of citizen-soldiers, whether volunteers or conscripts. In the two Militia Acts of 1792, Congress determined that the War Department would have little influence on the state militias until they were formally called into federal service, which the president could do for up to ninety days per year. The Militia Acts began a struggle over control of the reserve forces that has gone on ever since, with the War Department (after 1947, the Department of the Army) gradually increasing its control over the peacetime organization, recruitment, and training of the militia, now known as the Army National Guard.

Nineteenth-century militia reform left the states in substantial control of their state armies. Congress encouraged the states (with scant success) to improve their militias by offering arms, purchased by special appropriations in 1808. During the Civil War, Congress inched toward conscription by calling for better state management in 1862, but it finally enacted draft legislation the next year, after militia reform and the bounty system had failed to produce an adequate number of recruits. To compensate for militia problems, Congress had allowed the U.S. Army, which it expanded in wartime and reduced in peacetime, to maintain its officers, commissioned and noncommissioned, at wartime regimental strength, a plan first advocated in 1819 by Secretary of War John C. Calhoun. The "expansible army," presumably to be filled by wartime volunteers, would be the first force into action, a policy that worked well in the Mexican War (1846–1848) but that set limits on the size of the wartime army. New units of state and federal volunteers became the norm in the Civil War and the Spanish-American War (1898). In a crisis, Congress sided with the states' rights position on mobilization—that is, that the existing militia be mobilized and manned first and its officers given preferred treatment. The inherent inefficiencies in this system, however, led to the adoption of the Militia Act of 1903 and the Militia Act of 1908 (the so-called Dick Acts), which gave the War Department more control over the peacetime National Guard. The laws, however, did not give clear enough constitutional authorization to use the Guard beyond the continental United States

(a new problem after 1898) for extended periods of time.

Congress then accepted the Army's argument that it required a second land-forces reserve completely under federal control. First authorized in the National Defense Act of 1916, the Army Reserve received even stronger endorsement in the National Defense Act of 1920, which profited from the Army's successful experience with a second wartime draft (the Conscription Act of 1917) and continued wartime problems with ineffective National Guard officers. The War Department and Congress embraced the concept of university-based peacetime officer training with the creation of the Reserve Officer Training Corps (ROTC) through both these acts. It did not, however, reject the Guard, which received additional support for federal training. In return, the National Guard Association, the Guard's lobby, accepted a revision of the law that made it clear that a federally supported Guard recognized no constitutional limits to its federal service since it was now considered the National Guard of the United States.

Congress also took the lead in introducing peacetime conscription, first established in 1940 and reinstituted in 1947 when the Army could not meet its requirements with volunteers. Then Congress, in the Universal Military Training and Service Act of 1951 and the Reserve Forces Act of 1956, attempted to rationalize the relationship between conscripts and volunteers in every portion of the active and reserve Army. The latter act further strengthened regular Army control over its reserve components. Even when conscription ended in the early 1970s, Congress remained concerned that the Army "total force" of regulars and reservists provide ample training and professional opportunities for Army reservists, and it remained the champion of the Army National Guard.

Army Procurement and Construction. From the early nineteenth century on, Congress expected the Army to provide engineering services for national development and to spend its money in ways that would encourage "infant industry." The Army embraced the role as a way to build its popularity in a society not predisposed to value standing armies. By midcentury the Army Corps of Engineers had become the Army's elite and the primary beneficiary of the U.S. Military Academy (founded 1802); the academy itself was a darling of Congress, which assumed the major responsibility for appointing cadets. The Corps of Engineers built coastal fortifications, provided civil engineers to survey and build turnpikes under federal sponsor-ship (the most notable being the east-west National Road), and supplied expertise for the earliest stages of commercial railroad development. In 1824 Congress passed the Rivers and Harbors Act, giving the Corps the task of developing the nation's seaports and inland waterways. This mission shifted from canal building to flood control in the twentieth century, which in turn led to the creation of great inland reservoirs for city water supplies and recreation. No member of Congress would deny the benefits a Corps project might bring to a home district. The Corps also provided the pioneer project managers for construction of the Capitol Building and the Manhattan Project of World War II, as well as the development of the Army's massive base system during the two world wars. Military construction still interests Congress. In fiscal year 1993, for example, Congress approved $28 million for construction in the state of Ohio, $17 million more than the Department of Defense had requested.

Until the twentieth century the Army did not have much impact on American industry, but that changed with the world wars and continued into the Cold War. Except during wartime, the nineteenth-century Army built cannon and firearms in its own armory system; most of its other logistical purchases (clothing, animals, food, forage, fuel, and wagons) came from contractors who also had civilian clients, and these could be readily procured in a rural, agricultural economy. The only consistent industrial recipients of Army dollars were the great firearms companies of New England, but they usually entered the market during wartime expansions. In the twentieth century, the War Department, with congressional support, contributed to the early development of the automotive and aviation industries, especially the latter. The attractiveness of funneling federal aid to commercial aviation through the War Department ensured congressional favor for the Army Air Corps, which received a disproportionate share of the Army budget for planes and bases between the world wars. Congress also approved of growing ties between the Army and industry when it gave the War Department the task of planning for wartime economic regulation and industrial mobilization in the National Defense Act of 1920.

Command of the Army. After the Civil War, Army reformers argued that the United States needed a centralized general staff system to focus the entire Army's effort on wartime mobilization. Fearing that a general staff, viewed as a creation of

autocratic Germany, would lead to militarism and reduce congressional influence, Congress rejected the concept in the 1870s. After the confusions of the war with Spain and the inadvertent creation of an insular empire, Congress approved the General Staff Act of 1903 backed by Secretary of War Elihu Root. With the president's and its own constitutional powers intact, Congress felt safe enough to allow a central planning agency in the War Department.

Congress may have been more comfortable, however, with an Army run by lawyers, engineers, and accountants rather than by warriors, for it continued its informal, horizontal relationships with the department and bureau chiefs who spent the Army's money. It was also wary of ambitious Army chiefs of staff who might use their office for political advancement; three such officers—Leonard Wood, Douglas MacArthur, and Dwight D. Eisenhower—had presidential ambitions. The chief of staff of greatest historical significance, George C. Marshall, set the tone for the office, that of an apolitical professional adviser to the political leadership of both branches of government as well as unchallenged commander of the entire Army. Until the Goldwater-Nichols Defense Reorganization Act of 1986, Congress supported the concept that the Army chief of staff should have no internal rival in determining the Army's business, but the new law gave the chairman of the Joint Chiefs of Staff and the unified and specified commanders in the field unparalleled influence over the Army. Ironically, the reform conformed with the traditional Army view that greater centralization of authority means more efficient and timely defense decision making, especially if it is done by professional officers. Although Congress rejected this assumption in the National Security Act of 1947—which led to greater agency proliferation and civilianization—it came to prefer a chairman of the Joint Chiefs almost coequal with the secretary of Defense, a relationship that also appeals to the Army

Investigations. In April 1792 Congress, with the cooperation of the Washington administration, investigated the conduct of military policy by the War Department, asserting its constitutional authority to review the execution of the laws it had passed and the money it had appropriated. This first use of the investigatory power—on any issue—followed an Indian victory over an Army expedition in the Ohio Territory, the worst such defeat (657 U.S. soldiers died) in the nation's history. The investigation proved inconclusive, though the quartermaster department was shown to have been negligent, forcing the resignation of Quartermaster General Samuel Hodgdon. The expedition's commander, Maj. Gen. Arthur St. Clair, also resigned at Washington's urging at the beginning of the proceedings. Congress concluded that he deserved praise, not censure, but did not order him reinstated. Secretary of War Henry Knox emerged from the inquiry with the taint of ineptness, but his close relationship with Washington ensured that he would remain in office. Although the special House committee of inquiry did not recommend legislation, it showed that it could exercise influence over the War Department outside the normal legislative process.

The St. Clair affair started a tradition of investigatory activism affecting the Army. The most memorable example was the Joint Committee on the Conduct of the War (37th Congress, 1861), which decided that it should review the generalship of the Union army. The joint committee, dominated by "hard war" Republicans, tended to see competence and agreement with its political views as inseparable, and it forced President Abraham Lincoln and Secretary of War Edwin M. Stanton to relieve or reassign generals who fell from congressional favor. The careers of George B. McClellan, Charles P. Stone, William B. Franklin, and Fitzjohn Porter, among others, were blighted by the committee. Lincoln and Stanton managed to hold the committee at bay most of the time, but its enthusiasm for headlines made it a nuisance until war's end. In 1899 Congress (both the 56th and 57th Congresses) established a Senate Committee on the Philippines, which subsequently held hearings on the Army's suppression of the Filipino insurgency. The hearings turned up ample evidence of troop indiscipline and atrocities, although the Senate could not decide whether the criminal behavior had had official approval. Nevertheless, congressional interest ensured that the War Department would investigate suspect officers and enlisted men and discipline the guilty—which won Congress few admirers in the Army.

Responding to complaints by constituents after World War I, Congress conducted an investigation of the administration of the Articles of War in the wartime army. It was aided by the acting judge-advocate, Gen. Samuel Ansell, a liberal legal reformer who shared Congress's concern that the Army gave inordinate weight to command interest in its prosecutions of errant soldiers. Completing its work in 1920, Congress revised the Articles of War to protect soldier-defendants. The next congressional as-

sault on the Army's internal management had far less justification. Acting as chairman of the Senate Government Operations Committee, Sen. Joseph R. McCarthy (R-Wis.) in 1953 established a permanent investigating subcommittee, which he also chaired, to continue his witch-hunts for "communists" and "fellow travelers" in the executive branch, including the Army. His irresponsible actions in the Army-McCarthy hearings led to the first successful resistance to his tactics of fear, and in 1954 his fellow senators and the Eisenhower administration collaborated to both discredit and disempower him through censure. McCarthy's abuse of the investigatory option did not, however, end congressional investigations of the military. Congress has since examined officer education, weapons procurement, recruiting, property management, opportunities for advancement for women and members of racial minorities, and the administration of military justice.

Congress and the land forces of the United States share a common vision: they believe they are an expression of the broadest popular will in regional, class, ethnic, and religious terms, uncontaminated by elitism, false privilege, or excessive wealth. Such hallowed assumptions are truer of the Army than of Congress, but Congress insists that its populism remains intact when it hectors the Army career officer corps for mismanagement and political insensitivity. It champions the Army reserve forces, whose military utility falls short of their numbers and budgets. The ambivalent relationship of Congress and the Army during the Cold War was due in part to the issue of conscription (in the painful wars in Korea and Vietnam, Army infantry represented the majority of casualties) and in part to the reduced influence of the Army in high-dollar defense contracting, a dubious honor now held by the Air Force and Navy. It also in part reflects the professionalization of the Army officer corps and its strong behavioral norms, which predispose it to view politicians and the media with contempt. How the relationship of Congress and the post–Cold War Army will develop is uncertain—except that the Constitution requires that there be such a relationship.

[See also Armed Forces; Armed Services Committee, House; Armed Services Committee, Senate; National Security Act.]

BIBLIOGRAPHY

Hagan, Kenneth J., and William R. Roberts. *Against All Enemies: Interpretations of American Military History from Colonial Times to the Present.* 1986.

Kolodziej, Edward A. *The Uncommon Defense and Congress, 1945–1963.* 1966.

Mahon, John K. *History of the Militia and National Guard.* 1983.

Millett, Allan R. *The American Political System and Civilian Control of the Military: A Historical Perspective.* 1979.

Millett, Allan R., and Peter Maslowski. *For the Common Defense: A Military History of the United States of America.* 1983.

Schlesinger, Arthur M., Jr., and Roger Bruns, eds. *Congress Investigates, 1792–1974.* 1975.

Weigley, Russell F. *History of the United States Army.* 1967.

ALLAN R. MILLETT

ARMY CORPS OF ENGINEERS. *See* Public Works.

ARMY-MCCARTHY HEARINGS.

On 22 April 1954, a huge crowd packed the Capitol Building's Senate Caucus Room for the opening session of the Army-McCarthy hearings. At least forty million people followed the action on radio and television. The news coverage was unprecedented; the hearings overshadowed events of far greater importance, such as the Supreme Court's decision in *Brown v. Board of Education* (1954). As Walter Lippmann, the nation's leading columnist, said, "About affairs which are centered in Washington and govern the nation . . . only McCarthyism is much on people's minds."

The hearings focused upon two distinct questions: Did Sen. Joseph R. McCarthy of Wisconsin and his top aide, Roy M. Cohn, exert improper pressure on the U.S. Army to win preferential treatment for Pvt. G. David Schine, a part-time McCarthy staff member who had been drafted into the army the previous year? And did army officials use Private Schine as a "hostage" in an attempt to derail Senator McCarthy's various investigations of "communist influence" in the armed forces? In reality, the stakes were much higher, and the issues more complex. They ranged from the threat of domestic subversion to the constitutional separation of powers, from the integrity of the armed forces to the political future of Senator McCarthy.

Elected to the Senate from Wisconsin in 1946, McCarthy, a Republican, had gained national attention for his allegations that the Democratic administration of President Harry S. Truman was filled with communists and their supporters. In 1953, fol-

lowing a landslide Republican victory at the polls, McCarthy had been awarded the chair of the Senate Committee on Government Operations and its powerful Subcommittee on Investigations. In short order, Chairman McCarthy held a series of hearings on communist influence in the State Department, the Voice of America, and the Government Printing Office. As the year ended, he turned to the more explosive charge of espionage at Fort Monmouth, New Jersey, headquarters of the Army Signal Corps.

The espionage charge had been proved false several years before, but McCarthy not only continued his investigation; he also broadened it to include allegations that the army's Loyalty Board had promoted and honorably discharged an officer with known communist connections. In response, army officials claimed that McCarthy's keen interest in these subjects was directly related to the status of Roy Cohn's close friend, Private Schine. According to the army's account, Cohn had threatened to "wreck the army" if Schine did not receive special favors, including an exemption from rigorous duty, extra weekend passes, and an assignment close to Washington, D.C.

The controversy alarmed most Republicans. McCarthy had been of tremendous value to them in assaulting a Democratic administration, but now he was attacking a bureaucracy controlled by his own party. In addition, President Dwight D. Eisenhower, a five-star general, deeply resented McCarthy's verbal assaults upon army personnel. It was Eisenhower who urged the army to release a detailed chronology of Cohn's campaign to win special treatment for Private Schine. And it was Eisenhower who convinced Senate Republicans to televise the Army-McCarthy hearings, thereby bringing the senator into the living rooms of millions of Americans who had never seen his behavior at close range.

McCarthy's day-to-day performance—marred by rambling speeches, ugly outbursts, and crude personal attacks—seemed to confirm his critics' portrait of him as a bully and a fraud. The highlight came on 9 June 1954, when the senator charged that a young associate of army counsel Joseph Welch had once been a member of a "pro-communist" organization. Welch's emotional response— "Have you no sense of decency, sir, at long last? Have you left no sense of decency?"—brought thunderous applause.

On 17 June 1954—after 36 days, 72 sessions, 35 witnesses, 42 exhibits, and 2,972 pages of testimo-

SEN. JOSEPH R. McCARTHY (R-WIS.). Lecturing on the Communist menace during the televised Army-McCarthy hearings of 1954, to the manifest incredulity of army counsel Joseph Welch, *far left*.

OFFICE OF THE HISTORIAN OF THE U.S. SENATE

ny—the hearings were recessed sine die. McCarthy's "favorable" rating in the polls had dropped twenty points since the the beginning of the year. On 2 December the Senate voted to censure him for bringing that body "into dishonor and disrepute." Although he remained in office until his death in 1957, McCarthy's political career effectively ended in the spring of 1954.

[*See also* Communism and Anticommunism; McCarthy, Joseph R.]

BIBLIOGRAPHY

Griffith, Robert. *The Politics of Fear: Joseph R. McCarthy and the Senate.* 2d ed. 1970. Repr. 1987.
Oshinsky, David M. *A Conspiracy So Immense: The World of Joe McCarthy.* 1983.
Straight, Michael. *Trial by Television.* 1954.

DAVID M. OSHINSKY

ART AND CULTURE. The Constitution gives Congress one specific direction with regard to arts and culture. Article I, section 8 of the Constitution gives Congress the power to "promote the Progress of Science and useful Arts by securing for limited Times to Authors and Inventors the exclusive Right to their respective Writings and Discoveries." Through the "elastic" clause (Art. 1, sec. 8) the Constitution also left open the prospect that the artistic and cultural well-being of the nation might be addressed by Congress.

During most of the nation's history, Congress exhibited only a sporadic and indirect interest in arts and cultural affairs. Even in the late twentieth century, when it has a more direct and diversified impact on arts and culture, Congress still acts on the belief, stated in the preamble to the National Foundation on the Arts and the Humanities Act of 1965, that "the encouragement and support of national progress . . . in the humanities and the arts . . . [is] primarily a matter for private and local initiative." Congressional action concerning arts and culture can be seen as falling into five policy areas: copyright law, tax law, employment, foreign policy, and direct support.

Copyright Law. The purpose of copyright law is to protect not ideas but the expression of ideas: copyright law seeks to encourage creativity and inventiveness by granting the originators limited rights and privileges for their intellectual property. Congress passed the first copyright law in 1790. Books, maps, and charts were protected for a fourteen-year period, renewable for a second fourteen years. Authors were required to register their works with the U.S. district court where they resided. During the nineteenth century, prints, music, dramatic compositions, photographs, and works of art were added to the list of works protected by copyright. In the first general revision of copyright law (1831), Congress extended the first term of copyright to twenty-eight years and retained the renewal option of fourteen years. In an 1870 revision Congress shifted copyright activities, including deposit and registration of the works, from the district courts to the Library of Congress. In addition, a record of registrations began to be kept. The Copyright Office was established as a separate department of the Library of Congress in 1897.

The 1909 Copyright Act admitted unpublished works to copyright registration for the first time and further extended the renewal term from fourteen to twenty-eight years. Works granted copyright privileges today include not only literary works but also musical works, dramatic works and accompanying music, pantomimes, and choreographic works; pictorial graphic and sculptural works; motion pictures and other audiovisual works; and sound recordings.

As of the Copyright Law Revision of 1976, protection was extended to the life of the author or creator, plus fifty years. In 1990 Congress extended copyright protection beyond economic concerns to the moral rights of the artist. As a consequence, alterations to a creative work were constrained in an effort to protect the integrity of copyrighted works as well as the reputation of the creator. Copyright is secured automatically on creation; no publication, registration, or other action in the Copyright Office is now required to secure copyright, although it is suggested.

The United States has also worked with other countries to establish better international protection for authors' works. As early as 1914 the United States, with the advice and consent of the Senate, recognized the Buenos Aires Copyright Convention of 1910, establishing protection between the United States and certain Latin American nations. In 1955 the United States joined the Universal Copyright Convention (UCC), which establishes copyright protection for artists in all member countries.

In 1988 Congress passed the Omnibus Trade and Competitiveness Act to protect U.S. copyrighted industries—most significantly, motion pictures, recordings, and computer programs—in foreign countries. In addition, the Berne Implementation Act of 1988 enabled the United States to join the Berne Convention for the Protection of Literary and Artistic Works (Paris, 1971), gaining more complete protection for American authors and establishing protection in twenty-five other countries.

Tax Law. Through tax expenditures authorized in the United States tax code, the federal government has contributed significant indirect support for the arts, by allowing tax deductions for charitable donations. In 1993, donations to nonprofit arts, humanities, and cultural organizations were estimated to total $9.6 billion. This indirect federal involvement in the arts began with the ratification of the Sixteenth Amendment in 1913, which allowed the federal government to levy a general income tax. Under this constitutional authority, Congress created the federal income tax structure with the War Revenue Act of 1917. In addition to establishing a personal income tax, this act permitted individuals to deduct charitable contributions to nonprofit organizations, including museums, orchestras, and other cultural, educational, or literary organizations, from their net taxable income. The limitation for deductions was originally set at 5 percent of donors' net income, but was raised to 20 percent in 1952. In 1935 Congress extended this deduction privilege to for-profit corporations.

These tax provisions provided an incentive for private individuals and corporations to donate art and money to nonprofit organizations, with the federal government becoming a sort of co-contributor, in effect donating the amount of money it would otherwise have received in taxes. As tax rates rose after World War II, the charitable deduction provisions became an increasingly important incentive for all private giving, including that to the arts.

Tax-exempt status also allows registered organizations a special third-class postage rate, at 25 percent of the regular cost, and lower rates for bulk mailings. These lower rates are subsidized by an annual congressional appropriation for the U.S. Postal Service.

In the last twenty-five years Congress has enacted many revisions to the tax code that have affected charitable giving. For example, in 1966 Congress passed the Historic Preservation Act, which established a National Register of Historic Places to be kept by the National Park Service. Citizens owning buildings on the register are eligible for the federal rehabilitation tax credit, if they meet certain standards in the rehabilitation of the building. The Tax Reform Act of 1969 stated that any artist giving his or her own work to a nonprofit charitable organization could take a charitable contributions deduction equal only to the cost of the materials, rather than at the market value of the gift. Subsequently, contributions by creators of works of art to libraries, museums, universities, and other cultural institutions declined noticeably.

The 1981 Economic Recovery Tax Act lowered the maximum income tax rate from 70 to 50 percent for high-income individuals, lowered overall tax rates, and included the appreciated value of contributed gifts as part of the alternative minimum tax base. These provisions served to decrease incentives for giving, particularly among upper-income-bracket donors. As a result, the rate of increase in charitable donations fell between 1986 and 1990. At the same time, Congress temporarily extended the charitable deduction to more than 70 million taxpayers who do not itemize deductions, thus providing more incentive for those in lower tax brackets to give. Congress did not renew this charitable deduction privilege for nonitemizers in the Tax Reform Act of 1986.

Thereafter, as both arts organizations and individual artists realized the impact of tax law on the arts, they lobbied Congress for changes. In response Congress passed two tax-related acts addressing the arts. The Technical and Miscellaneous Act of 1988 allows freelance authors, writers, and photographers to deduct creative expenses in the same year they are accrued, instead of waiting until the work is sold, so that artists can create without having to sell their work immediately in order to deduct expenses. Through the Revenue Reconciliation Act of 1990, Congress declared that gifts of appreciated assets from January 1991 through June 1992 were to be considered not at their original price, but at fair market value, providing temporary incentive for donating to charitable organizations.

The continuing concern about the federal deficit, however, means that tax expenditure policy has come under greater scrutiny—including its unintended or peripheral impact on nonprofit organizations.

Employment. Until the 1930s the federal government took a largely laissez-faire approach toward domestic issues. Franklin D. Roosevelt's New Deal marked a change to a more active stance, particularly concerning employment. During the Great Depression, Americans in all professions, including the arts, were unemployed, including twenty thousand people in the theater industry alone. To help stimulate the economy and address domestic needs, Congress authorized and funded a multifaceted relief effort that included national art projects to employ artists.

The first art program, the Public Works of Art Project (PWAP), started in late 1933 and operated under the auspices of the Treasury Department. The Civil Works Administration funded this project, which employed 3,750 painters and sculptors at $350 per artist. These artists produced more than 15,600 works of art for federal and other tax-exempt buildings across the country.

In July 1934 the PWAP project was succeeded by the Section on Fine Arts. Also run by the Treasury Department, the Section on Fine Arts supported the creation of sculptural works and murals for buildings throughout the nation. It relied on local panels to choose artistic themes and recommend artists in the area to receive commissions, thus ensuring that each community had input in the art chosen.

Although the Section on Fine Arts funded many excellent projects, some criticized it for straying from its primary goal of economic relief. Because the Section on Fine Arts emphasized artistic excellence, it sought out first-rate artists, some of whom were already employed, even affluent. Despite this criticism, the program operated until 1943, when World War II had not only prompted new budget priorities but also solved the unemployment problem. During its nine years of activity the Section on Fine Arts awarded 1,124 mural contracts, for which it paid $1,472,199, and 289 contracts for sculpture costing $563,529.

In 1935 Congress passed the Emergency Relief Appropriation Act authorizing the creation of the Works Progress Administration (WPA). Unlike its two predecessors, which were essentially fine arts projects, the WPA took a more inclusive approach, creating five separate projects to employ a wider cultural community. These were the Art Project, the Theater Project, the Writers' Project, the Music Project, and the Historical Survey.

The first of these WPA arts initiatives was the Arts Relief Project, established in July 1935. The Art Project commissioned artists to create murals and paintings for federal buildings, employed approximately 330 people, and operated for four years at a total cost of $735,700. Since the project was funded by the WPA, it emphasized the priority of economic relief rather than artistic competence and achievement. However, in addition to its employment impact, the Art Project also developed the silk-screen process, and established art education centers across the nation where Art Project members taught classes to approximately eight million people.

The Theater Project created the Living Newspaper, a series of staged plays that dramatized controversial current events, among other activities. Actors such as Lee J. Cobb, Canada Lee, Lee Strasberg, and John Houseman began their careers in the project, under directors such as Orson Welles. The Writers' Project conducted folklore studies to preserve the customs, beliefs, and legends of the American people. This project also wrote geographical descriptions and historical accounts of each state, as well as of cities such as New York and Washington, D.C.

The Music Project helped to establish new orchestras, employing 2,533 musicians in 34 symphony orchestras in 1938; 92 million Americans heard these federal musicians in 273 cities in 42 states. The Music Project also undertook music education efforts; more than 13 million people attended WPA music classes in 1939. The Music Project, along with the Art and Writers' projects, was also involved in historical research and preservation efforts.

The original investment of $5 million in these five arts projects produced a body of art work now conservatively valued at around $450 million. Many Americans experienced art for the first time through these outreach programs; in fact, 65 percent of the twenty-five million people who attended Federal Theater productions had never before seen a play. These projects not only fulfilled their purpose of providing jobs for artists, but also lifted public morale by providing cultural experiences and arts education to millions of Americans and by using works of art to improve the community environment.

But the WPA projects came under criticism and were ultimately short-lived. In 1938 Rep. J. Parnell Thomas (R-N.J.) accused the Federal Theater Project of being filled with communists and demanded an official investigation, prompting the House Un-American Activities Committee to investigate the arts projects. Although unable to substantiate Thomas's claims, this investigation set the stage for a second investigation, this one by the House Appropriations Committee, in 1939. That same year, in the Emergency Relief Act, Congress terminated the Federal Theater Project and placed the remaining arts projects under state sponsorship and control. The projects were officially ended along with the WPA in June 1943.

In 1973 Congress again included the arts in employment and training assistance with the Comprehensive Employment and Training Act (CETA). Artists were included both under Title II of the CETA program (for disadvantaged workers) and under Title VI (for those subject to cyclical unemployment). CETA projects were locally initiated and therefore varied from place to place. By 1979, an estimated six hundred projects in approximately two hundred locations were spending as much as $200 million on artist employment through CETA. In addition, many nonprofit arts groups could qualify for CETA employment and training grants to secure clerical support and build their administrative capability. Congress dissolved CETA in September 1983.

Foreign Policy. During the late 1930s the United States began to use the arts as an instrument of foreign policy, prompted by Nazi cultural initiatives in Latin America. Through the Department of State's Division of Cultural Affairs, the United States established a cultural exchange program for university professors, graduate students, and teachers under joint government sponsorship. By 1945 the division was also sending cultural officers to U.S. embassies in Latin America, the Middle East, and Europe.

The post–World War II period saw an unprecedented use of cultural exchanges to reach occupied countries as well as an expansion and the renaming of the division as the Office of International Information and Educational Exchange. In 1946 these efforts in public diplomacy were furthered by passage of the Fulbright Act (P.L. 79-584), which sought to promote international understanding through an academic exchange program administered binationally.

As the Cold War intensified, Congress came to believe that through the arts it could convey the message of democracy to the rest of the world, especially to those countries threatened by the Soviet Union in Eastern Europe and parts of the Near East, such as Turkey. Consequently, Congress passed the United States Information and Educational Exchange Act of 1948, also know as the Smith-Mundt Act (P.L. 80-402) to promote better international understanding of the United States and to counter Soviet propaganda. In compliance with this act, two new offices were created: the Office of Educational Exchange (OEX) and the Office of International Information (OII). In 1953 the United States Information Agency (USIA) replaced both offices.

USIA exibitions often provoked criticism and controversy. When USIA and Department of State exhibits included pieces by modern artists, conservatives labeled the works "depraved" and the artists "communist." Such charges sometimes led to the cancellation of exhibitions, such as the "Sport in Art" exhibit that was scheduled to travel to the 1956 Olympics in Australia.

One of the most significant acts Congress passed concerning the arts and foreign policy was the Mutual Educational and Cultural Exchange Act of 1961 (P.L. 87-256), also known as the Fulbright-Hays Act, named for its sponsors, Sen. J. William Fulbright and Rep. Lawrence Brooks Hays, both from Arkansas. The act effectively recognized the importance of international educational and cultural exchange programs to U.S. foreign relations.

Most of these exchange programs fell under the Division of Cultural Relations. Many types of exchange were undertaken, such as the International Visitors Program, sponsoring visits of foreign leaders to the United States; youth, student, and special programs, involving exchanges of secondary-school and college students and young professionals and political leaders; international athletic programs, involving exchanges of coaches and teams; museum exchanges; and tours of performing arts groups.

In 1978, Congress moved the activities of the Bureau of Educational and Cultural Affairs of the Department of State into the USIA and changed its name to the International Communication Agency (ICA). In 1982, the name was restored to the United States Information Agency.

Direct Support. The most visible form of federal involvement is direct support of the arts. Congress understood the symbolic significance that the city of Washington, D.C., would represent to the new nation about its cultural potential. Therefore Congress funded the design, building, and decoration of the Capitol as its first act of direct support of the arts. The first architect of the Capitol was appointed in 1793 by President George Washington.

Although the construction of the Capitol was completed in 1865, the office of the architect of the Capitol has been continuous since 1851. As an agent of Congress, the architect is responsible for the care and maintenance of the Capitol Building, the grounds, and nearby buildings such as the Library of Congress and the U.S. Supreme Court; in addition, the architect implements reconstruction and landscape improvement projects. Congress also commissioned works by many American painters for the Capitol, including four Revolutionary War scenes by John Trumbull that hang in the Great Rotunda.

Library of Congress. In these early years Congress also appropriated money to help establish some of the nation's foremost cultural institutions. When the American government moved from Philadelphia to the new capital of Washington in 1800, Congress established the Library of Congress, because no library existed for its use. Congressional members took an active role in selecting books for the collection, which soon numbered more than three thousand volumes. The collection was lost in 1814, when the British burned Washington in the War of 1812, whereupon Congress accepted Thomas Jefferson's offer to sell the United States his personal library of seven thousand volumes in order to reestablish the library. Besides continuing to serve as the nation's library, since 1936 the Library of Congress has also sponsored a national poet, first known as the consultant in poetry, and now as the U.S. poet laureate. The poet laureate, whose term runs for one year, advises the Library of Congress on its public literary programs, the acquisition of literary material, and other matters relating to poetry and literature.

Smithsonian Institution. Congress was also involved in the establishment of a number of museums. In 1829 the Englishman James Smithson bequeathed to the United States his fortune of half a million dollars to found, in Washington, "the Smithsonian Institution, an Establishment for the increase and diffusion of knowledge among men." Seventeen years later Congress accepted the gift and established the Smithsonian Institution. In the Smithsonian Act (1846), Congress specified the structure of the institution, the construction of the building, the duties of the secretary, the formation of a library, and the right to amend the provisions of the act. The act also called for the transfer of "all objects of art, natural history, etc., belonging to the United States in Washington" to the institution.

Three other large bequests broadened the scope and depth of the Smithsonian Institution, eventually resulting in a complex of museums and galleries established on or around the Mall in Washington. Charles Lang Freer, a Detroit industrialist who made his money in the railroad and foundry businesses, left his collection of Asian art, totaling about ten thousand objects, to the Smithsonian as well as $500,000 for a building to house the collection. Freer also created an endowment for the study of Far Eastern civilizations. The Freer Gallery of Art opened to the public in 1923.

In 1936, Andrew W. Mellon, a wealthy Pittsburgh banker and secretary of the Treasury under three presidents, gave the Smithsonian his entire collection of Old Master paintings and sculpture, more than $15 million for a building to house the collection, and an endowment for the salaries of executive officers and the acquisition of additional art works. The National Gallery of Art opened in 1941.

Congress accepted a third major private collection from uranium magnate Joseph Hirshhorn in 1966. Hirshhorn's collection consists of nearly five thousand paintings and drawings and more than fifteen hundred pieces of sculpture then valued at about $25 million. He gave $1 million in 1969, and the Hirshhorn Museum opened on the Mall in 1974. Hirshhorn donated the rest of his art when he died in 1981.

The Smithsonian Institution now consists of fifteen museums (thirteen of which are in Washington, D.C.) containing more than 140,000 objects. Its museums host approximately 25 million visitors annually. The Smithsonian's 1992 appropriation from Congress totaled $331 million. Three representatives and three senators sit on the institution's board of regents.

Cultural agencies. In 1910, at the request of President William Howard Taft, Congress established the Commission on the Fine Arts. The commission, consisting of seven members appointed by the president for four-year terms, was created to advise the government about matters concerning the acquisition and commissioning of art for federal properties and to offer opinions on general artistic questions posed by federal officials. This commission assisted Congress by approving the design and location of buildings within the District of Columbia, overseeing the development of the Mall, and advising on projects such as the Lincoln Memorial, the House of Representatives office building (the Cannon House Office Building), the U.S. Supreme Court Building, the Tomb of the Unknown Soldier, and the Jefferson Memorial. However, the commission never effectively broadened its scope beyond the Capitol district.

In 1958 Congress passed legislation calling for the establishment of a National Cultural Center in Washington, D.C. Originally the federal government offered only to donate the land, but following President John F. Kennedy's assassination the center was reconceived as a living memorial, the John F. Kennedy Center for the Performing Arts. Consequently, Congress contributed up to $15.5 million on a matching basis for construction. The Treasury Department was also authorized to lend the center funds for the construction of its parking facilities. The Kennedy Center, which opened in 1971, houses four theaters: the Concert Hall, the Opera House, the Eisenhower Theater, and the Terrace Theater. It is home to the National Symphony Orchestra and the performing arts branch of the Library of Congress.

Historically, most direct congressional arts and culture support has been in the form of one-time projects and commissions; occasional commemorative design activities for monuments, stamps, and coins; and the endorsement of a few national cultural institutions. However, this sporadic tradition changed with the establishment of the National Endowment for the Arts (NEA) and the National Endowment for the Humanities (NEH). In August 1964 Congress passed a bill to establish an advisory National Council on the Arts. At President Lyndon B. Johnson's urging, the following year Congress enacted the National Foundation on the Arts and Humanities Act, which established the NEA and NEH, as two independent agencies. Each agency is headed by a chairperson appointed by the president and confirmed by the Senate. Each chairperson is advised by a twenty-six-member national council of distinguished cultural leaders who are presidentially appointed for staggered six-year terms and subject to senatorial confirmation. The act also established the Federal Council on the Arts and Humanities, composed of directors of government agencies involved in these areas.

The National Endowment for the Arts provides three major types of financial assistance for the arts: fellowships to artists of exceptional talent; matching grants to nonprofit, tax-exempt organizations; and grants to regional arts organizations (nongovernmental) and state arts agencies. These grants and fellowships reflect specific artistic disciplines as well as interdisciplinary fields and are evaluated by rotating panels of experts. These panels, along with the National Council on the Arts, play key roles in informing the endowment of needs and opportunities regarding the arts. The National Endowment for the Humanities undertakes similar activities and performs similar functions with regard to the humanities.

In 1975 Congress passed the Arts and Artifacts Indemnity Act, designating the Federal Council on the Arts and the Humanities as the administrative agency. The act made it easier for U.S. museums to assemble exhibitions of foreign art works such as the Great Bronze Age of China and El Greco of Toledo, by insuring objects up to $400 million total for all exhibitions touring nationwide at any one time.

In 1976 Congress established the Institute of Museum Services (IMS), which was placed within the National Foundation for the Arts and Humanities (NFAH) in 1984. IMS is headed by a director and the fifteen-member National Museum Services Board, all of whom are appointed by the president and approved by the Senate. The institute administers a grant program to aid museums in three areas: general operating support, conservation project support, and the museum assessment program.

In 1985 Congress established a National Medal of Arts to be covered by appropriations to the National Endowment for the Arts. The National Council on the Arts recommends candidates for the medal to the president, who may award no more than twelve medals in any calendar year. American artists, individual patrons, and corporate patrons can receive this prestigious award. Past recipients include painter Georgia O'Keeffe, writer Ralph Ellison, filmmaker Frank Capra, composer Aaron Copland, and architect I. M. Pei.

Congress oversees the arts and humanities endowments through the annual appropriations process as well as through periodic reauthorizations of the NFAH. From the endowments' founding through 1990, the increase and dispersion of arts organizations and growth of support from other public and private sources was exponential. According to figures reported by the NEA, the number of orchestras grew from 58 to 120, professional theaters from 22 to 420, dance companies from 37 to 250, and opera companies from 27 to 120. With more arts available, audiences inevitably grew. According to U.S. census figures, in this twenty-five-year span the number of artists has also tripled.

Even with such success, perennial issues that arise during reauthorization include concerns about the impartiality and representation of advisory panels, the equitable geographic distribution of grants, the risks of funding controversial artists, and the possibility of censorship. In 1989, sharp controversy concerning the purposes and procedures of federal funding for the arts was sparked by two NEA grants that supported exhibitions of the photographs of Robert Mapplethorpe and Andres Serrano. The protracted debate over pornography, offensiveness, censorship, freedom of expression, and public accountability seriously threatened to derail the reauthorization of the agency in 1990. It continued to smolder until controversy erupted again as a campaign issue in the Republican presidential primaries of 1992. One consequence of this lengthy debate was a disruption in the NEA's re-authorization cycle. In 1990, Congress renewed the agency's reauthorization for only three years. Although another two-year extension was proposed in 1993, no formal action had been taken as of June 1994.

Finally, another indication of recent congressional interest in the arts and culture can be seen in the establishment of the Congressional Arts Caucus. Founded in 1981, this legislative service organization cultivates congressional interest in and understanding of the arts by providing information to its members and by fostering communication between its members and special interest constituencies as well as with executive personnel; its members are advocates of arts policy and legislation.

[See also Architect of the Capitol; Capitol, The, articles on Art in the Capitol and Dome and Great Rotunda; Copyright, Trademarks, and Patents; Fulbright Scholars Act; Library of Congress; National Cemeteries, Monuments, and Battlefields; National Foundation on the Arts and Humanities Act of 1965; Smithsonian Institution.]

BIBLIOGRAPHY

Balfe, Judith H. *Paying the Piper: Causes and Consequences of Arts Patronage.* 1993.
Barresi, Anthony L., and Fannie Taylor. *The Arts at a New Frontier.* 1984.
Benedict, Stephen, ed. *Public Money and the Muse: Essays on Government Funding for the Arts.* 1991.
Cummings, Milton C., and Richard S. Katz. *The Patron State: Government and the Arts in Europe, North America, and Japan.* 1987.
Dubin, Steven C. *Bureaucratizing the Muse: Public Funds and the Cultural Worker.* 1987.
Heckscher, August. *The Arts and the National Government: Report to the President.* 1963.
The Independent Commission. *A Report to Congress on the National Endowment for the Arts.* 1990.
Mulcahy, Kevin V., and Margaret Jane Wyszomirski, eds. *America's Commitment to Culture: Public Policy and the Arts.* 1994.
Wyszomirski, Margaret Jane, ed. *Congress and the Arts.* 1988.

MARGARET JANE WYSZOMIRSKI

ARTHUR, CHESTER A. (1829–1886), twenty-first president of the United States. When he assumed the presidency on 22 September 1881, in the wake of the assassination of James A. Garfield, Chester Alan Arthur had never served in either house of Congress. He was, however, a protégé of Sen. Roscoe Conkling (R-N.Y.), leader of the Republican party's "stalwart" faction.

CHESTER A. ARTHUR. Following the assassination of President James A. Garfield, Arthur takes the presidential oath of office in his private residence. From a drawing by J. W. Alexander, *Harper's Weekly*, 1881.

LIBRARY OF CONGRESS

Once president, Arthur acted with dignity and restraint. If leading stalwart cronies were still invited to sumptuous feasts, the man who had made his reputation as the "gentleman boss" usually refrained from granting overt favors to Conkling's faction. He seldom challenged congressional initiative, finding little reason for so doing. When he assumed office, Republican majorities in both houses were quite thin, and after the congressional elections of 1882 the Republicans lost the House.

With Arthur's encouragement, Congress passed the Pendleton (Civil Service) Act of 1883. The law established a five-member commission, instituted competitive examinations for certain jobs, and abolished "assessments," which were compulsory party contributions levied on officeholders. In 1883, Congress heeded Arthur's recommendation to modernize the navy, in a program that included construction of four major ships.

Arthur's major veto centered on a Chinese exclusion bill. The president found the bill's twenty-year ban on Chinese immigration unreasonable and called its registration requirements "undemocratic and hostile to the spirit of our institutions." The veto message also stressed the Chinese contribution to the American economy and warned against insulting a people who might prove to be good trade partners. Heeding the president, Congress revised the bill. In 1882 it also altered a steamboat safety bill that—said Arthur—contained serious technical errors. Congress did override one Arthur veto, a river-and-harbors pork barrel that would have reduced the budget surplus by $19 million.

Arthur's annual presidential messages contained a host of policy suggestions, from erecting a building to house the Library of Congress to establishing a government for Alaska. He reported a large surplus in the treasury, a potential problem in a nation needing more money in circulation. His remedy: the repeal of all internal taxation save excise duties on tobacco and liquor. Arthur wanted a constitutional amendment allowing an item veto whereby the president could block certain parts of a bill while retaining others. In an effort to avoid the kind of political limbo that existed in the two and a half months between Garfield's assassination and his death, Arthur asked Congress to consider the entire matter of presidential succession. And to prevent further confusion of the kind that existed in the immediate aftermath of the Rutherford B. Hayes–Samuel J. Tilden election, he wanted Congress to decide who was to count electoral votes. Accusing the railroads of price collusion and rate discrimination, he endorsed the regulation of interstate commerce.

Congress, absorbed with matters of patronage and pork-barrel projects, felt little compunction in ignoring such suggestions. Moreover, it was a time when presidents were not expected to be legislative leaders, and Arthur—dying of Bright's disease for much of his presidency—was little inclined to break the Gilded Age mold.

BIBLIOGRAPHY

Doenecke, Justus D. *The Presidencies of James A. Garfield and Chester A. Arthur.* 1981.

Reeves, Thomas C. *Gentleman Boss: The Life of Chester Alan Arthur.* 1975.

JUSTUS D. DOENECKE

ARTICLES OF CONFEDERATION. The first constitution of the United States, the Articles of Confederation grew out of the same motion, introduced in the Continental Congress on 7 June

1776 by Richard Henry Lee, that led to the Declaration of Independence. The Articles were then drafted by John Dickinson and a "grand committee." With members of the Congress disagreeing over certain provisions, particularly those relating to western lands and federalism, the document was not sent to the state legislatures for their approval until 15 November 1777. The Articles became effective on 1 March 1781, after the thirteenth state, Maryland, ratified.

The Articles institutionalized state and legislative supremacy, in keeping with the views of the dominant wing of the revolutionary leadership. There was no executive branch, and the only judicial functions related to admiralty jurisdiction and resolution of interstate disputes.

Articles V and IX focused on the powers and operation of the Confederation Congress. It had only those powers "expressly delegated" to it by the states. Most important of these were the sole and exclusive powers of declaring war and peace (unless a state was in danger of imminent invasion) and conducting foreign relations (including those with American Indian nations); requesting money from the states and appropriating its use; borrowing money and issuing bills of credit (paper money); regulating coinage, weights and measures, the post office, and the land and naval forces of the United States; and appointing those civil officers necessary to conduct government business.

The Articles provided that the states choose delegates to the Congress annually. The number (between two and seven) and method of selection were left to each state (most were appointed by state legislatures), and each paid the cost of maintaining its delegation. A member could serve no more than three years in any six and could be recalled at any time. Each state had one vote, but could not cast it if its delegation was evenly divided or had only one member in attendance. A majority vote—seven states—was necessary to take action, but nine votes were required to declare war, form alliances, ratify treaties, coin money, emit bills of credit, request money or appropriate it, determine the size of the army and navy, or appoint a commander in chief. Although it met in secret, Congress was required to publish its journal monthly, excluding only the portions relating to war or foreign affairs that it believed required secrecy.

Amendment of the Articles of Confederation required unanimity, and attempts to strengthen the Articles by further empowering Congress failed. On the basis of its power to propose amendments,

Congress called for a convention to revise the Articles on 21 February 1787. The Federal Convention, which sat from May to September, decided to draft an entirely new constitution. By 13 September 1788, when Congress passed the ordinance calling on the First Federal Congress to meet in March 1789, all but two of the thirteen states had ratified the new instrument of government. The Confederation Congress never again achieved a quorum after 10 October 1788.

[*See also* Constitutional Convention of 1787.]

BIBLIOGRAPHY

Jensen, Merrill, ed. *The Articles of Confederation.* 1940.
Jensen, Merrill, ed. *The Documentary History of the Ratification of the Constitution.* Vol. 1: *Constitutional Documents and Records, 1776–1787.* 1976.

KENNETH R. BOWLING

ASIAN AMERICAN MEMBERS. When twenty-year-old Dalip S. Saund, a Punjabi Sikh, left India in 1920, he commenced a journey that took him from northern India to California's Imperial Valley to Washington, D.C., and the halls of Congress. After studying and working in the United States, Saund decided to make the new land his permanent home. But his desire to become a citizen could not be realized as long as Asian Indians remained ineligible for naturalization. Saund worked to lift the restrictions, principally through the India Association of America, which he organized and led. Finally, in 1946 Asian Indians secured the right to become citizens, and in 1949 Saund was naturalized. Seven years later, he was elected as a Democrat from California to the House of Representatives, the first Asian American elected to Congress. He served three terms.

Sen. Daniel K. Inouye is the best-known Asian American political figure. He has served in Washington since Hawaii gained statehood, first as a representative (1959–1962) and since then as a senator. During World War II, in the midst of virulent anti–Japanese American sentiment and the removal and internment of mainland Americans of Japanese ancestry, Inouye joined the all-Nisei (second-generation Japanese Americans) 442d Infantry Regimental Combat Team of the U.S. Army. Inouye acquired several military commendations and lost his right arm.

Inouye has been chairman of the Select Committee on Intelligence, the Defense Appropriations Subcommittee, the Select Committee on Indian Affairs,

SEN. HIRAM L. FONG (R-HAWAII). In October 1967.
LIBRARY OF CONGRESS

and the Commerce, Science, and Transportation Committee. He first gained national exposure when he delivered the keynote address at the turbulent 1968 Democratic National Convention in Chicago. Inouye's membership on the Senate Watergate Committee thrust him further into the spotlight. Fourteen years later he played a key role as chairman of the Select Committee on Secret Military Assistance to Iran and the Nicaraguan Opposition. From 1979 through 1988, he held the third-ranking leadership position among Senate Democrats as secretary of the Democratic Conference. But he failed in his bid to succeed Robert C. Byrd as majority leader.

Republican Hiram L. Fong, a prominent Chinese American businessman, was elected to the Senate when Hawaii first achieved statehood. Closely paralleling Inouye's career, Fong practiced as an attorney, served in the military during World War II, and was a member of the Territorial Legislature for six-

teen years, including six years as Speaker. In the Senate, Fong held seats on the Post Office and Civil Service, Appropriations, and Judiciary committees. He retired in 1976.

Fong's retirement set off a mad scramble for his seat, and Asian American hopefuls were in the thick of it. Representatives Spark M. Matsunaga and Patsy T. Mink, both Japanese Americans, engaged in a spirited campaign for the Democratic nomination. Matsunaga secured the nomination and then won the general election by a comfortable margin.

Matsunaga, an attorney, had served with distinction along with Inouye in the 442d Regimental Combat Team. He was also a member of Hawaii's Territorial House. Matsunaga was first elected to the U.S. House of Representatives in 1962 and served seven terms before going to the Senate, where he served on the Finance Committee. He died in April 1990 while in his third term.

Rep. Daniel K. Akaka, a native Hawaiian, was appointed to fill Matsunaga's seat. Akaka was a schoolteacher and administrator who held posts in state government before his election in 1976 to the House seat vacated by Mink. He was a member of the House Appropriations and the Select Narcotics Abuse and Control committees. Akaka defeated Rep. Patricia F. Saiki, who is of Japanese ancestry, in the 1990 senatorial contest.

Patsy Mink's initial service in the House of Representatives was from 1965 to 1977; she was defeated in the 1976 Democratic senatorial primary. Mink served in the State Department, as president of Americans for Democratic Action, and as a Honolulu city councillor. Mink, whose vacated House seat had been filled by Akaka in 1976, won a special election in 1990 to serve the remainder of Akaka's term after his appointment to the Senate, and later in the year secured a full term.

The tight Democratic grip on Hawaii's House seats has been broken only once, by Saiki, a former state legislator and leader of the Republican party, who was elected in 1986 and reelected two years later.

Only one United States senator of Asian ancestry has represented a state other than Hawaii. In 1976, seventy-year-old, Canadian-born S. I. Hayakawa defeated California's Democratic incumbent, John Tunney. Hayakawa, a Japanese American, was a well-known semantics scholar and professor at several colleges. Hayakawa presided over San Francisco State College in the late 1960s and early 1970s, earning a national reputation for his staunch opposition to student militants. For the most part, Hayakawa maintained his strong conservative posture as a senator. He retired from the Senate in 1982.

Norman Y. Mineta and Robert T. Matsui were elected to the House from California in 1974 and 1978, respectively. Both had been placed in World War II internment camps, along with some 120,000 other Americans of Japanese ancestry. Mineta was elected mayor of San José in 1971, the first Japanese American to hold that office in a major U.S. city. He has held a House Democratic leadership post as deputy whip, and in the 103d Congress (1993–1995) he became the first Asian American to chair a major House committee, Public Works and Transportation. Matsui has chaired the Subcommittee on Human Resources of the House Ways and Means Committee, and was elected treasurer of the Democratic National Committee in 1991.

In 1992 Jay C. Kim, a civil engineer, became the first Asian American of Korean ancestry elected to Congress. Kim, a Republican, was formerly mayor of Diamond Bar, California.

Asian American members of Congress, both Democrats and Republicans, have generally been liberal to moderate in their positions, especially on social issues and civil rights. Hayakawa was the most consistently conservative. There has not been a broad coherent Asian American legislative agenda. But Asian American members of Congress understandably took the lead in establishing the Commission on Wartime Relocation and Internment of Civilians in 1980, and successfully guided passage of the

Asian American Members of Congress

SENATORS	CONGRESS
Hiram L. Fong (R-Hawaii)	86th–94th
Daniel K. Inouye (D-Hawaii)	88th–
S. I. Hayakawa (R-Calif.)	95th–97th
Spark M. Matsunaga (D-Hawaii)	95th–101st
Daniel K. Akaka (D-Hawaii)	101st–

REPRESENTATIVES	CONGRESS
Dalip S. Saund (D-Calif.)	85th–87th
Daniel K. Inouye (D-Hawaii)	86th–87th
Spark M. Matsunaga (D-Hawaii)	88th–94th
Patsy Mink (D-Hawaii)	89th–94th, 101st
Daniel K. Akaka (D-Hawaii)	95th–101st
Patricia F. Saiki (R-Hawaii)	100th–101st
Norman Y. Mineta (D-Calif.)	94th–
Robert T. Matsui (D-Calif.)	95th–
Jay C. Kim (R-Calif.)	103d–

Civil Liberties Act of 1988, which offered redress for surviving Japanese Americans interned during World War II and a formal apology from the government.

BIBLIOGRAPHY

Kim, Hyung-Chan, ed. *Dictionary of Asian American History.* 1986.
Takaki, Ronald T. *Strangers from a Different Shore: A History of Asian Americans.* 1989.

PAUL Y. WATANABE

ASPINALL, WAYNE N. (1896–1983), Democratic representative from Colorado, chairman of the Committee on Interior and Insular Affairs, and champion of western water projects; called "the ruler of the land" by the *Wall Street Journal.*

Born in Ohio, Wayne Norviel Aspinall moved with his family to a peach orchard near Palisade, in western Colorado's Grand Valley. He graduated from the University of Denver and its law school, taught high school in Palisade, drove a school bus, managed a peach orchard, and practiced law. He served in World Wars I and II and for sixteen years in the Colorado legislature.

In 1948 Aspinall defeated a Republican incumbent in the first of eleven congressional election victories. His huge, thinly settled 4th Congressional District covered the state's entire western slope of the Continental Divide. To obtain population parity, northeastern plains counties were added to the district in the mid 1960s; 1970s redistricting removed nineteen of his loyal southwestern counties.

On the Interior and Insular Affairs Committee, Aspinall managed the 1956 Colorado River Storage Act and the Alaska and Hawaii statehood bills. As chairman from 1959 to 1973, he guided acrimonious debates on the Wilderness Act of 1964, the Redwoods Act of 1968, the Central Arizona Project, and legislation creating the Public Land Law Review Commission. In an era of domineering committee leaders, Aspinall prevailed through schoolmasterly preciseness, parliamentary skill, and detailed knowledge of water law and other matters dear to the West: reclamation, national parks, wilderness, and other uses of public lands. A colleague (quoted in Richard F. Fenno, Jr.'s *Congressmen in Committees,* 1973) said of him:

He knows more about that jurisdiction than any other person in the country, bar none. He's in at 8 A.M., works all day, no social life. He dominates those subcommittee chairmen; they have no autonomy at all. . . . And everything's by the numbers, according to good parliamentary procedure. . . . He lets everybody talk; he's fair. . . . It's time consuming, time consuming as hell; but it's run perfectly.

Witnesses before his committee had to "have their ducks in order." If they didn't, he said "piffle" to their interests. Of some one thousand measures he managed on the House floor, he lost not a single one.

Environmentalists found Aspinall a crusty foe. "We have seen dream after dream dashed on the stony continents of Wayne Aspinall," the Sierra Club's head lamented. Environmentalism surged in Colorado in 1972, dooming Aspinall's renomination.

BIBLIOGRAPHY

Edmonds, Carol. *Wayne Aspinall: Mr. Chairman.* 1980.

ROGER H. DAVIDSON

ASSASSINATIONS OF PRESIDENTS.

See Presidential Assassinations and Protection.

ATOMIC ENERGY ACT (1946; 60 Stat.

755–775). On 31 December 1946, with a stroke of his pen, President Harry S. Truman transferred control of the world's most powerful weapon from the military authorities that had overseen its development to a panel of five civilians. His order implementing the Atomic Energy Act of 1946, which had become law on 1 August 1946, marked the culmination of a historic debate over custody of the awesome secrets of the atom bomb.

Even before the destruction of Hiroshima, Japan, on 6 August 1945, Army lawyers had drafted legislation calling for a significant military presence (four out of nine members) on a commission to oversee the post–World War II development of atomic energy. In the House, the Military Affairs Committee moved swiftly, reporting out a bill on 5 November 1945 that was in keeping with the War Department's desires.

The Senate's Military Affairs Committee, however, was denied jurisdiction over the matter. On 23 October 1945, Brien McMahon (D-Conn.) and Arthur H. Vandenberg (R-Mich.) persuaded the Senate to create a select panel to deal with the subject. McMahon, a freshman, was appointed chairman of the Special Committee on Atomic Energy.

In the ensuing months, scientists, including many who had participated in the military's top-secret Manhattan Project, actively led a public education

THE IDEAL CHOICE. Sen. Kenneth D. McKellar (D-Tenn.) presents the "ideal" candidate to head the Atomic Energy Commission to Senators Kenneth S. Wherry (R-Nebr.) and H. Styles Bridges (R-N.H.). The cartoon reflects the difficulty of finding a commission head who would be acceptable to the Senate, the advice and consent of which was needed for appointment. McKellar had previously opposed one of President Harry S. Truman's nominees, David Lilienthal, and so offers the straw man as the perfect choice who has never said nor done anything to tarnish his reputation. Clifford K. Berryman, *Washington Evening Star*, 18 February 1947.

U.S. SENATE COLLECTION, CENTER FOR LEGISLATIVE ARCHIVES

and lobbying campaign for free exchange of atomic information and the establishment of international controls over nuclear weaponry. They helped assemble an effective coalition that included such newly formed groups as the Federation of Atomic Scientists, the National Committee on Atomic Information, and the National Committee for Civilian Control of Atomic Energy.

McMahon introduced a bill on 20 December 1945 that would win the backing of the Truman administration and the lobby of citizens and scientists. Passed by the Senate the following June, it was approved—in drastically amended form—by the House on 20 July 1946. In conference, the Senate prevailed on the key issue of civilian control, but the final measure included a strong advisory role for the military. The final version of the McMahon bill was approved by both chambers on 26 July 1946.

The law created two uniquely powerful institutions: the Atomic Energy Commission (AEC) and the congressional Joint Committee on Atomic Energy (JCAE). The AEC, headed by five civilian commissioners appointed by the president, was charged with developing atomic energy for peaceful purposes. Subject to oversight by the JCAE, it ran the government's atomic research laboratories and facilities for the production of fissionable materials.

Major amendments to the Atomic Energy Act in 1954 led to greater private participation in, and government assistance to, the production of electrical power at nuclear facilities. After serving for two decades as both the promoter and the regulator of the nation's atomic power industry, the AEC was dissolved in 1974, and its functions were divided between the Energy Resource and Development Administration and the Nuclear Regulatory Commission. Congress abolished the JCAE in 1977.

[See also Atomic Energy Committee, Joint.]

BIBLIOGRAPHY

Green, Harold P., and Alan Rosenthal. *Government of the Atom: The Integration of Powers.* 1963.
Hewlett, Richard G., and Oscar E. Anderson, Jr. *The New World, 1939–1946: A History of the United States Atomic Energy Commission.* Vol. 1. 1962.

DICK KIRSCHTEN

ATOMIC ENERGY COMMITTEE, JOINT.

On 5 August 1977, without so much as a roll-call vote in either chamber, the House and the Senate quietly abolished the once-mighty Joint Committee on Atomic Energy. In its heyday, the panel had been described by scholars Harold P. Green and Alan Rosenthal as "probably the most powerful congressional committee in the history of the nation."

Created by the Atomic Energy Act of 1946, the Joint Atomic Energy Committee enjoyed unique powers. Granted exclusive jurisdiction over "all bills, resolutions and other matters" relating to civilian and military aspects of nuclear power, it was the only joint congressional committee in modern times authorized to report legislation.

Perhaps even more extraordinary was the panel's exclusive access to the information upon which its secretive deliberations were based. As overseer of the Atomic Energy Commission (AEC), which also was created by the 1946 act, the joint committee was entitled by statute to be kept abreast of all commission activities.

The committee's power to control information within the legislative branch and to require it from the executive branch was unprecedented. Not surprisingly, over the course of its three-decade history, it attracted prominent and influential members.

The original appointees to the eighteen-member panel included Sen. Brien McMahon (D-Conn.), who was the chairman and primary author of the Atomic Energy Act, and fellow Democratic senators Tom T. Connally of Texas and Richard B. Russell of Georgia. Senate Republicans on the committee included Bourke B. Hickenlooper of Iowa and Michigan's Arthur H. Vandenberg. House Democrats Chet Holifield of California and Charles Melvin Price of Illinois, also appointed at the outset, became committee fixtures.

Texas Democrat and future president Lyndon B. Johnson joined the panel as a House member in 1947 and later rejoined it as a senator. Other major names from the joint committee's roster include Senators Clinton P. Anderson (D-N.Mex.), Wayne N. Aspinall (D-Colo.), Howard H. Baker, Jr. (R-Tenn.), Clifford P. Case (R-N.J.), Everett M. Dirksen (R-Ill.), Albert A. Gore, Sr. (D-Tenn.), Henry M. Jackson (D-Wash.), John O. Pastore (D-R.I.), and Stuart Symington (D-Mo).

The Joint Atomic Energy Committee's dominance over the AEC was challenged during the Eisenhower administration. In 1953, Lewis L. Strauss, a Wall Street financier and naval reservist who had risen to the rank of admiral during World War II, became the commission's chairman. Strauss won a measure of increased autonomy for the AEC through the 84th Congress (1955–1957) but then ran into a wall of congressional opposition.

Leading the charge against Strauss was Anderson of New Mexico. Richard A. Baker described their relationship in this way:

> Relations between the Admiral and the Senator had been strained since 1953 when Strauss had opposed plans to have the Tennessee Valley Authority sell power to AEC installations in the area and refused to support J. Robert Oppenheimer against Sen. Joseph R. McCarthy's charges of disloyalty. . . . At the heart of Anderson's bitter and unyielding attitude toward Strauss lay his determination that Congress must take an active part in the work of executive branch agencies. Accordingly, he reacted angrily at Strauss's efforts to withhold information from the Joint Committee on Atomic Energy.

In late 1958, Strauss threw in the towel, declining Eisenhower's offer of reappointment for another term. The joint committee, in what many considered to be an exception to the separation of powers

COMMITTEE HEARINGS. Rep. Chet Holifield (D-Calif.), *left,* and Sen. Bourke B. Hickenlooper (R-Iowa), during hearings on radioactive fallout, May 1957.   LIBRARY OF CONGRESS

principle, thus reigned as a legislative body with quasi-executive powers. The AEC was subordinated to the role of an operating board under the policy guidance of Congress.

Amendments to the Atomic Energy Act in 1954 shifted emphasis from weapons development (the hydrogen bomb was successfully tested in 1951) to civilian uses of atomic energy. Over the next two decades, as electricity from commercial reactors came on-line, the policies of the Joint Atomic Energy Committee and the AEC attracted criticism. Groups concerned about the safety of nuclear power plants contended that the AEC's dual role as promoter and regulator of atomic energy constituted an inherent conflict of interest.

By 11 October 1974, when President Gerald R. Ford signed a law abolishing the AEC and creating the Nuclear Regulatory Commission (NRC) and the Energy Research and Development Administration, the glory days of the Joint Atomic Energy Committee were over. Earlier that year, the House Select Committee on Committees, led by reform-minded Rep. Richard W. Bolling (D-Mo.), recommended

stripping the joint panel of its jurisdiction over civilian nuclear power.

The overseers of the atomic energy establishment also were under attack for failing to erect safeguards against nuclear weapons proliferation. Lax supervision of exports of U.S. nuclear technology drew scathing criticism from NRC commissioner Victor Gilinsky in a November 1976 speech. For twenty years, Gilinsky said, the ultimate destination of nuclear exports had gone largely unchecked by "a myopic Atomic Energy Commission and its own congressional committee."

In that climate, other congressional committees succeeded in chipping away at various aspects of the Joint Atomic Energy Committee's jurisdiction. An August 1976 report by the Atomic Industrial Forum, a trade group, provided an advance epitaph for the committee: "Its voice in nuclear affairs, which at one time was dominant, has now been joined by other voices in the halls of Congress which demand to make independent assessments on matters that once were the sole province of the committee."

When the 95th Congress convened in January 1977, reorganization plans in both the House and Senate rang the death knell of a Joint Committee on Atomic Energy that had outlived its usefulness.

[*See also* Atomic Energy Act; Nuclear Power; Nuclear Weapons.]

BIBLIOGRAPHY

Baker, Richard A. *Conservation Politics: The Senate Career of Clinton P. Anderson.* 1985.
Green, Harold P., and Alan Rosenthal. *Government of the Atom: The Integration of Powers.* 1963.
Kirschten, J. Dicken. "Is Doomsday at Hand for the Joint Atomic Committee?" *National Journal,* 20 November 1976, p. 1658.
Nieburg, H. L. "The Eisenhower AEC and Congress." *Midwest Journal of Political Science* 6 (1962): 115.

DICK KIRSCHTEN

ATTENDING PHYSICIAN. Congress established the Office of Attending Physician in 1928 after a succession of medical emergencies in which several members of Congress collapsed and three died in their offices. In each case, medical care was delayed for up to several hours awaiting the arrival of a physician.

The office is housed in the Capitol and comprises the attending physician, who traditionally has been an active duty U.S. naval officer, other navy medical personnel, and civilian nurses. Since 1928, five navy doctors have served as attending physician.

Originally an emergency facility for members of Congress, the Office of Attending Physician has undertaken additional medical duties over the years. It has a highly trained medical response team that serves some 80,000 of the more than 1.5 million tourists who visit the Capitol each year as well as members of Congress, congressional staff, and the Capitol Police. It also provides minor first aid to members, staff, and tourists; participates with the Military District of Washington, D.C., the chief of the Capitol Police, and other officials in planning medical care for mass casualties; provides medical support for joint sessions of Congress and other special events; and oversees aspects of environmental and occupational health requirements in the Capitol complex.

From 1928 to 1992, senators and representatives received free, routine medical care, including prescription drugs, from the Office of Attending Physician. Since 1992, members wishing to use the office for routine medical care have been charged an annual fee. The change followed a spate of press and public criticism of congressional perquisites. Members, as well as staff and tourists, continue to receive emergency care at no charge.

Individuals who have served as attending physician include Rear Admirals George Calver (1928–1966), Rufus Pearson (1966–1973), Freeman Carey (1973–1986), William Narva (1986–1990), and Robert Krasner (1990–).

BIBLIOGRAPHY

U.S. Congress. *Congressional Record.* 102d Cong., 2d sess., 2 April 1992. "The Attending Physician," pp. S4707–S4708.

MILDRED LEHMANN AMER

AUTHORIZATION. Authorization legislation has two functions: to provide legal authority for federal programs and activities and to authorize subsequent appropriations to fund them. Authorizations are within the jurisdiction of all House and Senate legislative committees, except the committees on appropriations. The bifurcated process of setting policy through authorizations and then separately appropriating annual funding, in place since 1836, is not constitutionally required but was instituted under the rules of the House and Senate to facilitate both policy-making and annual appropriations. Congressional committee structure and procedure draw clear distinctions between authorizing and appropriating and the committees with those respective responsibilities.

The form, content, and scheduling of authorization bills vary from case to case. Language authorizing appropriations typically provides that "there are authorized to be appropriated" to the designated agency or department a specified amount of dollars for the particular fiscal year or years. The purpose of the authorization, whether for general operations or for designated programs, also is stated in the legislation. While a dollar limit for the authorization usually is set, occasionally a bill will authorize appropriation of "such sums as may be necessary."

An authorization may be for one fiscal year, or two or more, but may also allow spending from an appropriation after the specified fiscal year by authorizing that the money "remain available until expended." Authorizations for the Department of Defense are on a one-year cycle, others are for two, and some for three or more. An example of a multiyear authorization is P.L. 103-43 of 10 June 1993, to amend the Public Health Service Act to revise and extend the programs of the National Institutes of Health. The bill authorized the enactment of appropriations for three years, fiscal years 1993 through 1996. Permanent authorizations do exist in law, but because periodic congressional review is a main purpose of authorization legislation, an annual or biennial authorization is much more typical.

In developing authorization bills through investigation, hearings, and markup, committees examine how well government agencies are performing in their assigned programs and how well those programs are working. Authorizations may redirect or restrict government activities and create new ones. Some authorization measures relate only to programmatic rather than funding issues, but it is a rare authorization that does not have a budgetary effect in some manner.

In the Congressional Budget Act of 1974, Congress attempted to regularize the scheduling of authorization bills by requiring that they be reported by 15 May preceding the fiscal year for which funds are to be authorized. The act envisioned early reporting and consideration of authorizations in order to provide timely funding. Compliance was spotty, impractical, and often waived; the requirement was removed in 1985. Because appropriation bills can be considered as early as 15 May, however, early consideration is encouraged. The 1974 budget act does require authorizing committees to file views and estimates of spending programs within their jurisdictions with the Budget Committee by 25 February of each year. The views of the authorizing committees are taken into account as the Budget Committee fashions a budget resolution specifying overall funding amounts for each broad budget function.

Levels of authorization for appropriations are not technically regulated by the budget process because authorization sets an upper level within which appropriations are made, consistent with congressional budget resolutions and other constraints. Authorization bills may contain direct spending that is immune to control by the appropriations process. The congressional budget process strictly controls direct spending in authorizations, such as entitlements and direct contract authority (so-called backdoor spending), as to amount, timing, and overall budgetary effect.

It is the authorizing committees, not the appropriators, that are instructed by budget resolutions to produce spending cuts and receipts through reconciliation bills. Much of the work of authorizing committees is done through reconciliation when this process occurs. The goal of reconciliation is to have authorizing committees raise revenues or designate other types of receipts, such as user fees for government services, or to cut spending. In the balancing act encouraged by reconciliation, new authorizations and program changes may be offset by additional spending cuts. Entire entitlement programs may be rewritten in reconciliation to provide spending cuts that will free money for increased spending for priorities. Even simple authorizations creep into reconciliation, where they are protected from ordinary legislative scrutiny because votes on reconciliation measures do not permit members to vote on programs separately.

When considered separately, authorizations are considered under normal House and Senate procedures on the floor; less controversial authorizations may be processed by unanimous consent, and many authorizations come up under suspension of the rules in the House. Authorization bills do not have the privileged procedural status (to be brought up at any time without a rule from the Rules Committee) that appropriation bills and certain other measures have under the rules. Authorization legislation may start in the House or Senate unless it also contains revenue provisions or direct appropriations, which are constitutionally required to originate in the House.

The separate authorization and appropriations processes envision that authorizations will actually be enacted into law before the relevant appropriation is considered by the House and Senate. It often does not work that way. Some authorizations are passed by the House or Senate before appropriations are considered, but few are enacted before movement on appropriations. Typically, authorizations are enacted simultaneously with, and even later than, appropriation bills. Late authorizations still serve a fundamental purpose, however: they dictate in specific detail the policies and programs for which an appropriation is to be spent. And some appropriations provide that they are available to carry out authorizing legislation enacted later.

The record of successful completion of authorizations has waned since the 1970s and many programs are funded without authorizing legislation. One reason programs go unauthorized is the increased complication and overlap in committee jurisdiction since that time. Authorizations for the Department of Energy, for example, are within the jurisdiction of a number of House committees and several in the Senate. No discrete Energy Department authorization has been enacted in the last ten years. Another reason for inaction on authorizations is the congressional budget process itself: program and funding decisions often are made through the budget process rather than through the authorizing committees. Finally, the appropriations process has remained viable and has become a forum for program and policy decisions, sometimes, but not always, with the encouragement of authorizing committees.

In 1837, the House adopted a rule, now clause 2(a) of Rule XXI, prohibiting general appropriation bills from containing appropriations not previously authorized by law. The rule also prohibits amendments that include unauthorized appropriations. The Senate has no such general prohibition. The House rule is often, and strictly, enforced. When appropriations are not authorized, it is customary for the House to waive the rule against unauthorized appropriations. The lack of authorization is no legal bar to appropriating. However, a variety of statutes prohibit, for particular agencies and programs, the obligation and expenditure of appropriations unless previously authorized by law. The statutes were enacted to protect the integrity of authorizations for specific agencies and activities. Such a statute applies, for example, to the Department of State (section 2580 [a] [1] of Title 22, U.S.C.). For an unauthorized appropriation to be spent in such circumstances, the appropriation bill must specifically override the provision of law.

The House of Representatives has a host of decisions on what does or does not constitute an authorization in law for an appropriation. Voluminous precedents are catalogued in Hinds', Cannon's, and Deschler's precedents of the House, as well as in the House Rules and Manual. Generally, the failure to authorize annually does not necessarily subject an appropriation to a point of order; the statute creating or empowering a department or program may be sufficient authorization. The authorization requirement does have consequences for the Senate because House conferees on an appropriation bill cannot agree in conference to Senate provisions that are unauthorized. These must be reported back for a separate vote in the House in connection with the conference report.

With respect to authorization legislation contained in appropriation bills, Rule XXI of the House Rules also prohibits legislation in appropriations. While an authorization for future appropriations rarely appears in an appropriation bill, authorization language in the more general sense—autho-

rizing, restricting, or changing government activities—does appear in appropriation bills with some frequency. While such provisions are sometimes included at the behest of authorizing committees that have been unable to process authorizing legislation, House authorizing committees frequently complain about the appropriations process overstepping its bounds. At the beginning of the 103d Congress, the House amended Rule XXVIII to allow the chairman of the appropriate authorizing committee the right to floor time to urge the rejection of Senate legislative amendments to appropriation bills.

There was renewed interest in the 103d Congress in the separate authorization and appropriation processes, in light of the examination by the Joint Committee on the Organization of Congress of the organization, structure, and efficiency of Congress. Testimony before the joint committee, by members of Congress as well as others, suggested that the authorizing committees should also assume responsibility for appropriating. The joint committee did not adopt that recommendation, but did recommend consideration of two-year budgeting, with authorizations or appropriations considered every other year. This is more likely to take place with authorizations than appropriations. The lively debate may produce improvements and greater coordination and efficiency in the bifurcated congressional funding system but is unlikely to result in more fundamental change.

[See also Appropriations; Budget Process.]

BIBLIOGRAPHY

U.S. Congress. General Accounting Office. *Principles of Federal Appropriation Law.* 2d ed. 1991.
U.S. House of Representatives. *Constitution, Jefferson's Manual, and Rules of the House of Representatives, 103d Congress.* Compiled by William Holmes Brown. 102d Cong., 2d sess., 1992. H. Doc. 102–405.
U.S. Senate. *Riddick's Senate Procedure, Precedents, and Practices,* by Floyd M. Riddick and Alan S. Frumin. 101st Cong., 2d sess., 1992. S. Doc. 101–28.

PETER D. ROBINSON

AUTOMOBILE SAFETY. On 9 September 1966, President Lyndon B. Johnson signed into law the National Traffic and Motor Vehicle Safety Act (P.L. 89-563) and a companion piece of legislation, the Highway Safety Act (P.L. 89-564). These laws, marking America's first legislative effort to stem the growing death rate on the nation's highways, had been a long time in coming.

Since the dawn of the age of the automobile, the auto industry had been unfettered by government regulation. Americans—citizens and politicians alike—believed that what was good for Detroit was indeed good for the nation. In the late 1950s, however, as traffic fatalities increased, many concluded the industry needed regulation.

Although many scholars, activists, and politicians can be credited for bringing about the landmark safety laws of 1966, the efforts of two men stand out: Daniel Patrick Moynihan and Ralph Nader. In 1959, Moynihan, then chairman of the New York State Traffic Policy Committee, wrote a seminal article, "Epidemic on the Highway." In it, he challenged auto industry assertions that drivers—not their machines—were to blame for most auto accidents. Moynihan called for laws to force the industry to build safer cars. In 1965, Ralph Nader, who would become the automobile industry's nemesis and the hero of the consumer movement, wrote *Unsafe at Any Speed*. The book exposed design hazards of one of General Motors' models, the Corvair, and generally criticized U.S. automakers for placing sales, style, and horsepower before safety. General Motors launched an undercover investigation into Nader's private life. In February 1966, Capitol Hill police caught two detectives hired by General Motors trailing Nader.

While the works of Moynihan and Nader popularized the safety movement, legislators such as Democratic senators Abraham A. Ribicoff (Conn.), Warren G. Magnuson (Wash.), and Gaylord Nelson (Wis.) pushed Congress for safety standards. The automakers resisted, claiming that restyling cars to fit proposed standards would prove too costly. The fight for legislation gained unusually broad media attention. For many, the auto safety issue pitted activist heroes against industry villains; it made for good news.

Under the media glare and over Detroit's opposition, Congress passed the safety laws with widespread political support, including that of President Johnson. The laws set mandatory minimum safety standards for new autos, required state safety programs and allocated federal funds for them, and established an agency, the National Highway Traffic Safety Administration, commissioned to find ways to reduce highway accidents.

The 1966 laws intensified a long-lasting tug-of-war between industry and safety advocates. In the ensuing years, each side was able to claim small victories. For instance, the Ford Motor Company won a battle with consumer groups in April 1971 when it convinced the Nixon administration to rescind inflatable air bag standards. The top two Ford executives, Henry Ford II and Lee Iacocca, met with the president and persuaded him that installing air bags would financially hamstring the auto industry and thus hurt the national economy.

In 1974, Congress—bending to the auto lobby and public complaints—rescinded the requirement of ignition interlock systems, gadgets that prevented cars from starting unless seat belts were fastened. In the early 1980s consumer groups won a legislative battle, and eventually a Supreme Court fight, over the air bag. Although air bag standards were postponed, by the early 1990s most new cars were equipped with these protective devices.

Safety advocates also forced automakers to design cars with safer brakes and tires, full-harness seat belts, stronger bumpers, and other lifesaving features.

BIBLIOGRAPHY

Crandall, Robert W., Howard K. Gruenspecht, Theodore E. Keeler, and Lester B. Lave. *Regulating the Automobile*. 1986.

Graham, John D. *Auto Safety: Assessing America's Performance*. 1989.

Claybrook, Joan. *Retreat from Safety*. 1984.

NICK KOTZ

AWARDS AND PRIZES. Military as well as civilian awards are periodically authorized by Congress. Recipients of these prizes have been as diverse as the nation itself. Initially, both the Continental Congress and the U.S. Congress approved individually struck medals as tributes for military exploits. Following the outbreak of the Civil War, the contributions of private citizens also began to attract congressional attention. Standardized medals for particular types of actions, contributions, initiatives, and service were first authorized late in the nineteenth century.

The first awards—individually struck gold medals—were for unique contributions to the fight for American independence. Less distinguished but still notable accomplishments occasionally prompted the awarding of silver and bronze medals and ceremonial swords. Only gold medals, however, have been continuously awarded to the present day. They have been bestowed upon prominent as well as relatively unknown individuals in the arts, athletics, aviation, diplomacy, exploration, politics, medicine, science, and entertainment. Although

Congress has approved legislation that stipulates specific requirements for numerous other awards and decorations, there are no permanent statutory authority provisions that relate to the creation of congressional gold medals. When such an award has been deemed appropriate, Congress, by special action, has provided for the creation of a personalized medal to be given in its name to show the approbation of a grateful nation in each instance.

Military Awards. Throughout its history, Congress has approved a variety of different military awards. Brevet promotions (honorary rank) were authorized for gallant action or meritorious conduct from 1812 to 1870. Certificates of Merit for extraordinary service were given under the direction of Congress from 1854 until the Civil War. Congress next approved the Medal of Honor (Navy, 1861; Army, 1862), which would become the keystone of the military medal system that Congress would enact into law. Current military decorations authorized by Congress are:

Distinguished Service Cross for extraordinary heroism not justifying the award of the Medal of Honor.

Distinguished Service Medal for exceptionally meritorious service to the United States.

Silver Star for gallantry in action not warranting a Medal of Honor or Distinguished Service Cross.

Distinguished Flying Cross for heroism and extraordinary achievement while participating in an aerial flight.

Soldier's Medal, Navy and Marine Corps Medal, Coast Guard Medal, and Airman's Medal for heroism involving voluntary risk of life under conditions other than those of conflict with an enemy.

Legion of Merit (first U.S. decoration created specifically for award to citizens of other nations) for exceptionally meritorious conduct in the performance of outstanding service to the United States since 8 September 1939.

Good Conduct Medal (Air Force) for exemplary behavior, efficiency, and fidelity during a three-year period of service.

Prisoner of War Medal for prisoners of war held captive after 5 April 1917, during World War I, World War II, the Korean War, and the Vietnam War.

Congress also approved decorations to honor the officers and men who participated in the

Indian Wars, 1865–1898 (Indian War Medals).

Spanish American War, 1898 (Cárdenas Medal of Honor, Manila Bay [Dewey] Medal, Specifically Meritorious Service Medal, West Indies Naval Campaign [Sampson] Medal).

Philippine Insurrection, 1899–1913 (Philippine Service Medal).

Mexican War, 1911–1917 (Mexican Border Service Medal).

World War I (Army of Occupation of Germany Medal).

World War II (World War II Victory Medal, Merchant Marine Distinguished Service Medal, Atlantic War Zone Bar, Mediterranean–Middle East War Bar, Pacific Zone Bar, Combat Bar, Merchant Marine Victory Medal, Mariner's Medal).

Berlin Airlift (Medal of Humane Action).

Korean War (Service Bar).

During the twentieth century, Congress authorized a national trophy and medals for military personnel (1901, 1918). Congress awarded the Medal of Honor to the Unknown Soldiers of World War I from Great Britain, France, Italy, and the United States; to the American Unknown Soldiers of World War II, the Korean War, and the Vietnam conflict; and to the city of Verdun, France, for its assistance during World War I. In commemoration of the fiftieth anniversary of World War II, Congress authorized a Congressional Medal for the Attack on Pearl Harbor.

On several occasions from the 1930s to the 1960s, Congress approved private bills authorizing certain members of Congress, as well as other U.S. government personnel, to accept and wear the decorations tendered to them by foreign nations. In August 1958, Congress authorized more than four hundred retired federal personnel to accept such awards.

Presidential and Other Awards. Seventeen awards currently presented by either the president or a member of the cabinet are authorized by Congress.

Young American Medal for Bravery and Young American Medal for Service (1950) recognizes young Americans, eighteen years and younger, who exhibit exceptional courage in a lifesaving effort.

Presidential Cash Awards to Federal Employees (1954) rewards federal employees whose job performance and ideas have benefited the government and are substantially above normal job requirements.

Enrico Fermi Award (1954) recognizes meritorious contribution to the development, use, or control of atomic energy.

National Medal of Science (1959) recognizes individuals who have made outstanding contributions in physical, biological, mathematical, and engineering sciences.

Congressional Space Medal (1969) honors astronauts whose contributions have been exceptionally meritorious.

President's Award for Outstanding Public Safety Service (1974) recognizes public safety officers for extraordinary valor in the line of duty or for outstanding contribution to public safety.

Presidential Rank Awards for the Senior Executive Service (1978) recognize career members of the Senior Executive Service for outstanding contributions. Recipients are awarded the rank of either meritorious or distinguished executive.

National Technology Medal (1980) recognizes outstanding contributions to the promotion of technology or technological manpower for the improvement of the economic, environmental, or social well-being of the United States.

President's Foreign Affairs Medal (1980) recognizes distinguished, meritorious service to the nation, including extraordinary valor in the face of danger to life or health by members of the Foreign Service.

Presidential Awards for the Senior Foreign Service (1980) recognizes members of the Senior Foreign Service for having performed especially meritorious or distinguished service in the conduct of U.S. foreign policy.

Presidential Award for Cost Savings Disclosures (1981) recognizes federal employees whose disclosure of waste, fraud, or mismanagement results in substantial savings to the federal government.

Presidential Rank Award for the Senior Cryptologic Executive Service (1982) recognizes outstanding service by civilian personnel in the National Security Agency and the Defense Intelligence Agency.

National Medal of Arts (1984) recognizes individuals or groups for outstanding contributions to the excellence, growth, support, and availability of the arts in the United States.

Presidential Award of Excellence in Science and Mathematics Teaching (1984) recognizes annually two teachers from each state, the District of Columbia, and Puerto Rico who specialize in science and mathematics for grades seven through twelve.

Presidential Award for Outstanding Private Sector Involvement in Job Training Programs (1986) recognizes individuals and organizations who have demonstrated outstanding achievement in planning and administering job training partnership programs or contributed to the success of job training partnership programs.

Malcolm Baldrige National Quality Award (1987) recognizes companies and organizations that have substantially benefited the economic or social well-being of the United States through improvements in the quality of their goods and services resulting from the effective practices of quality management.

Presidential Awards for Teaching Excellence in Foreign Languages (1988) recognizes annually one elementary school teacher and one secondary school teacher from each state, the District of Columbia, Puerto Rico, the Trust Territories of the Pacific Islands, the Northern Mariana Islands, and other commonwealths, territories, and possessions of the United States, and from the United States Department of Defense Dependents' School who have demonstrated outstanding teaching ability in foreign languages.

Civilian awards approved by Congress include Gold and Silver Lifesaving Medals for rescue attempts in U.S. waters (1874), a Selective Service Medal (1945) awarded for faithful and loyal service during World War II, medals for meritorious service by the District of Columbia police and fire departments, and a heroism medal for courageous young Americans. Medals of various types have also been bestowed in recognition of the contributions of those involved in exploration expeditions such as Adm. Robert E. Peary (Polar expedition of 1908–1909) and Adm. Richard E. Byrd (Antarctic expeditions of 1928–1930, 1933–1935, 1939–1941, 1946–1947).

In 1979, Congress created the Congressional Award Program to promote initiative, achievement, and excellence among youths who dedicated specific amounts of time to public service, personal development, physical fitness, and expeditions. Any youth from fourteen through twenty-three years of age who satisfies the standards of achievement designated for these activities can earn gold, silver, or bronze medals. Medal recipients are also eligible for scholarships. The program is operated by the Congressional Award Board, which established a private, nonprofit corporation, the Congressional Award Foundation, to carry out daily operations. The foundation serves as the national office for local and statewide councils. Prior to December

1987, the program was financed totally from private sector sources.

A Civic Achievement Award Program in Honor of the Speaker of the House of Representatives was approved in 1987 to recognize achievement in civic literacy by students, classes, and schools throughout the nation in grades 5 through 8. The Civic Award Program, administered under the direction of the librarian of Congress, is conducted by the Close Up Foundation in cooperation with the National Association of Elementary School Principals. Annual awards, in the form of certificates signed by the Speaker of the House, are given annually to individuals, classes, and schools.

[*See also* Congressional Medal of Honor.]

BIBLIOGRAPHY

Kerrigan, Evans E. *American War Medals and Decorations*. 1971.

McDowell, Charles P. *Military and Naval Decorations of the United States*. 1984.

Stathis, Stephen W. "Congressional Gold Medals." *Numismatist* 104 (July 1991): 1064–1070, 1109–1112.

STEPHEN W. STATHIS

B

BACKDOOR SPENDING. Budget authority provided in substantive legislation outside the regular appropriations process is known as "backdoor" spending. Since this type of spending is "locked in" by the legislative committees, it cannot be reduced by cutting appropriations. As the term suggests, backdoor spending evolved as legislative committees sought to gain a more direct voice in spending decisions. They achieved this by sidestepping normal appropriations procedures and funding government actions in the same legislation that authorizes them.

There are several types of backdoor spending. The three most common are entitlement authority, contract authority, and borrowing authority. Entitlements are provisions of law that require the federal government to make payments to eligible individuals. Some entitlements, such as social security and medicare, have permanent appropriations that provide funds annually without any specific action by Congress. Others, such as veterans' benefits, require annual appropriations, but the Appropriations committees have very little control over the amount of money spent. Instead, they must approve enough money to pay benefits to all eligible people. The only way Congress can modify entitlement spending levels is to change the laws that established the entitlements.

Borrowing authority allows an agency of the federal government to borrow money, while contract authority allows agencies to enter into contract obligations. Since both of these represent commitments the federal government must honor, the money to pay for borrowing or contract authority must be appropriated at some point. Since 1974, however, Congress has required that amounts of new contract or borrowing authority be provided for by Congress in appropriations bills and that new borrowing or contract authority must fall within these levels.

[*See also* Entitlement.]

BIBLIOGRAPHY

Cranford, John. *Budgeting for America.* 2d ed. 1989.
Schick, Allen. *Congress and Money: Budgeting, Spending, and Taxing.* 1980.

KATHLEEN DOLAN

BAKER, HOWARD H., JR. (1925–), Republican senator from Tennessee, Senate minority leader (1977–1981), Senate majority leader (1981–1985), White House chief of staff (1987–1988). Howard Baker was born in Huntsville, Tennessee, in 1925. His father and then his stepmother were Republican members of the U.S. House of Representatives. Like John F. Kennedy, he served on a PT boat in the South Pacific during World War II. He practiced law in Tennessee after the war and later married Joy Dirksen, daughter of Sen. Everett M. Dirksen (R-Ill.), in 1951. As Everett Dirksen rose to positions of leadership in the Senate, his young son-in-law was nearby, observing and learning.

With the landslide election of Ronald Reagan in 1980, Howard Henry Baker, Jr., became the first Republican majority leader of the U.S. Senate since William F. Knowland (1953–1954). Although he had been a presidential rival of Reagan and was skeptical of Reagan's economic plan, once calling it a "riverboat gamble," Baker quickly moved to accommodate the new president by leading a rather unwieldy group of Republican senators into a unit of solid support. It would not be the first time that he would accommodate this president at some sacrifice to his own political interests.

Baker first ran for the Senate in 1964, but lost by a narrow margin. In 1966, however, he became the first popularly elected Republican senator from Tennessee. A strong supporter of civil rights legislation, he sought the minority leadership position in 1969 after Dirksen's death, but was unsuccessful. He tried again in 1970, but again lost. In 1973, however, Baker became a celebrity as vice chairman of the Senate Watergate Committee, and his easy style, telegenic presence, and penetrating, yet judicious questions, revealed to the nation a legislator of stature and charisma. It was Baker who inquired: "What did the president know and when did he know it?"

After Watergate, Baker returned to the Environment and Public Works Committee. In 1976, he narrowly defeated Robert P. Griffin of Michigan to

HOWARD H. BAKER, JR. During the Senate Watergate hearings, 1973.
OFFICE OF THE HISTORIAN OF THE U.S. SENATE

become minority leader. Despite political fallout, Baker played a key role in garnering Republican support for passage of the Panama Canal Treaty for Jimmy Carter. After a lackluster presidential bid in 1980, Baker returned to the new Republican-controlled Senate as majority leader.

Baker, as Senate leader, was known as a consensus builder. Folksy, hard-working, articulate, and a master of the art of gentle persuasion, he worked cooperatively with Democratic leader Robert C. Byrd as well as with conservatives of his own party to fashion the Reagan economic package of 1981. Although they distrusted each other, both Speaker Thomas P. (Tip) O'Neill and President Reagan trusted Baker, and that put him at the pivot of decision making during Reagan's first term. This closeness and respect from both the president and the opposition led to a different job for Baker in Reagan's second term.

In 1984 Baker decided not to seek reelection. In 1987, as he was considering another run for president, the Reagan administration became embroiled in the Iran-contra affair. With public confidence eroding and relations with Congress souring, Reagan summoned Baker to assist him in the White House. Putting his own presidential ambitions aside, he agreed to serve the president as chief of staff. With the administration back on course and Reagan's popularity restored, Baker retired to private law practice in 1988.

BIBLIOGRAPHY

Annis, James. "Howard H. Baker Jr.: A Public Biography." Ph.D. diss., Ball State University, 1985.
Davidson, Roger H. "Senate Leaders: Janitors for an Untidy Chamber?" In *Congress Reconsidered.* Edited by Lawrence C. Dodd and Bruce I. Oppenheimer. 3d ed. 1985.

JOHN J. KORNACKI

BAKER, ROBERT G. (BOBBY) (1928–),
Senate staff aide whose behavior led to an internal ethics crackdown in the 1960s. Robert Gene Baker went to work for the Senate in 1943 as a fourteen-year-old page. He stayed for twenty years, longer than most senators. On becoming Democratic floor leader in 1955, Lyndon B. Johnson picked Baker as secretary to the majority, a job that soon assumed new dimensions of internal power.

Baker became skilled at giving Johnson advance counts of how senators would vote on important roll calls, effectively displacing party whip Mike

ROBERT G. (BOBBY) BAKER. *Left,* with lawyer Edward Bennett Williams.   LIBRARY OF CONGRESS

Mansfield. Senate observers noted that Mansfield was sometimes frustrated in trying to direct floor business during the majority leader's absence, as Baker circulated quietly in the back of the chamber urging delay in Johnson's name. Baker also helped Johnson maintain leadership control through the distribution of committee assignments and funds from campaign contributors.

Baker's world collapsed in September 1963, when a vending-machine company sued him for using political influence to further his own outside business interests. In months of hearings the Senate Rules Committee probed his involvement in vending machines, insurance, banking, and the Carousel Motel, a Maryland beach resort. The committee in July 1964 judged him "guilty of many gross improprieties." In 1967 he was convicted in federal court of tax evasion, theft, and conspiracy, and eventually served eighteen months in prison. The Senate tried

to repair its image by establishing in 1964 the six-member Select Committee on Standards and Conduct, chaired by Mississippi's conspicuously upright John C. Stennis.

BIBLIOGRAPHY

Baker, Bobby. *Wheeling and Dealing: Confessions of a Capitol Hill Operator.* 1978.

ARLEN J. LARGE

BAKER V. CARR (369 U.S. 186 [1962]). Involving a challenge to the apportionment of the Tennessee legislature, *Baker v. Carr* is generally recognized as the keystone of the one person–one vote doctrine and the basis for the ensuing reapportionment revolution. The Tennessee legislature had last been redistricted in 1901, even though significant shifts in population had occurred in the succeeding six decades. As a result, the largest legislative district had about nineteen times the population of the smallest. The vote of the residents of the smaller districts was therefore much more powerful than the vote of residents of the larger districts. This same pattern of malapportionment existed throughout the United States, as state legislators were reluctant to redraw legislative and congressional districts that were highly advantageous to the areas they represented. Consequently, rural areas tended to have more members of the U.S. Congress and the state legislatures than their population justified, while urban, and particularly suburban, areas typically had fewer.

The Supreme Court did not hold that the Tennessee legislature was malapportioned or even that the use of legislative districts with grossly disparate populations violated the Constitution. Those principles were established later in other cases. *Baker v. Carr,* however, was the essential first step, since it established that federal courts were appropriate forums in which to decide redistricting issues, or, in other words, that cases concerning redistricting were justiciable.

The justiciability issue was critical because an earlier Supreme Court case, *Colegrove v. Green* (328 U.S. 549 [1946]), had determined that a challenge to Illinois's congressional districts should be dismissed on the ground that redistricting presented a political question that is appropriately reserved to the legislative branch of government. Justice Felix Frankfurter, who was still on the Court in 1962 and who vigorously dissented in *Baker v. Carr,* stated in *Colegrove* that the redistricting issue was a "political thicket" that the courts should not enter. Although *Colegrove* was decided by a sharply divided court, and no opinion was joined by more than three justices, federal courts routinely dismissed subsequent redistricting cases on the basis of Frankfurter's reasoning.

Baker v. Carr rejected the *Colegrove* analysis and opened the doors of the federal courts to reapportionment cases. Once the Supreme Court had decided that such cases could be heard, the legal principles controlling reapportionment cases developed rapidly. In *Gray v. Sanders* (1963), the Court announced the principle of "one person–one vote." In 1964, the Supreme Court decided that the one person–one vote doctrine applied to the U.S. Congress *(Wesberry v. Sanders)* and to both houses of state legislatures *(Reynolds v. Sims)*. By 1967, all but nine states had either redrawn congressional district lines or elected at-large members to the U.S. House of Representatives. Gross population disparities between districts had become a thing of the past. Because *Baker v. Carr* had such a direct relationship to the basic issues of representative government, Chief Justice Earl Warren contended that it was the most important case decided during his tenure on the Supreme Court.

[*See also* Wesberry v. Sanders.]

BIBLIOGRAPHY

Graham, Gene. *One Man, One Vote: Baker v. Carr and the American Levelers.*1972.

McKay, Robert B. *Reapportionment: The Law and Politics of Equal Representation.*1965.

Schwab, Larry M. *The Impact of Congressional Reapportionment and Redistricting.*1988.

C. ROBERT HEATH

BALANCED BUDGET AMENDMENT.

The goal of a balanced budget amendment to the U.S. Constitution is to prevent deficit spending on the part of the federal government by requiring the nation's tax revenues and spending to be in balance. Issues related to balanced budgets extend as far back in U.S. history as 1690 (in the colony of Massachusetts). In 1798, Thomas Jefferson made the first proposal to amend the Constitution to require a balanced budget. Congress considered such an amendment on four separate occasions from 1970 through 1992.

Led by Republicans and other conservatives, efforts to enact and ratify a balanced budget amendment gathered momentum in the 1970s as federal deficits increased. With Democratic majorities in Congress generally opposed to the idea, proponents such as the National Taxpayers' Union attempted to employ the never-used alternative method for proposing a constitutional amendment, whereby if two-thirds of the states—now thirty-four out of fifty—so petition, Congress must call a constitutional convention.

By 1982, thirty-one states had endorsed the call for a convention, and President Ronald Reagan endorsed the balanced budget amendment. Members of Congress were spurred to action, and a balanced budget amendment was brought to the House and Senate floors. The proposed amendment would also have limited total revenues to a proportion of national income and provided that the balanced budget requirement could be waived in cases of war or by a vote of three-fifths of senators and representatives. The amendment was adopted in the Republican-controlled Senate by a vote of 69 to 31, more than the two-thirds majority required to pass a constitutional amendment, but fell forty-six votes short in the House by a vote of 236 to 187.

Momentum for the balanced budget amendment declined following the 1982 defeat. During the 1980s, two states withdrew their call for a constitutional convention to draft a balanced budget amendment. Congress turned to statutory efforts to balance the budget, including the Gramm-Rudman-Hollings Act of 1985, which mandated deficit reduction. In 1986, the Senate fell one vote short of adopting a balanced budget amendment in a 66 to 34 vote. In 1990, the House fell seven votes short, defeating a balanced budget amendment 279 to 150. As deficits continued to grow, reaching record levels in the early 1990s, proponents renewed their efforts.

The balanced budget amendment remains a controversial approach for dealing with budget deficits. Proponents argue that only by changing the Constitution itself can a profligate Congress be forced to balance the budget. The current system, they argue, has a built-in bias towards government growth and borrowing. Supporters note that forty-nine of the fifty states have balanced budget requirements and successfully balance their spending and revenue. In addition, public opinion polls over the past two decades have consistently shown that the overwhelming majority of Americans support the idea of a balanced budget amendment.

Most economists oppose such an amendment, suggesting that deficit spending is not always bad for the economy and that a fiscal straitjacket would unnecessarily constrain economic policy. Opponents also argue that a balanced budget is a policy issue, not a constitutional one, and that current political preferences should not be imposed on future generations. Despite balanced budget requirements, they note, states engage in deficit spending through their capital budgets by keeping these separate from their operating budgets. Finally, critics argue that a balanced budget amendment is unenforceable. Because, they argue, revenues and spending totals are highly sensitive to the economy, it is impossible to guarantee a balanced budget. They warn that a balanced budget requirement would involve the courts not only in determining who is responsible for violations but in actually writing budgets.

BIBLIOGRAPHY

White, Joseph, and Aaron Wildavsky. *The Deficit and the Public Interest.* 1989.

Savage, James D. *Balanced Budgets and American Politics.* 1988.

LANCE T. LELOUP

BALANCED BUDGET AND EMERGENCY DEFICIT CONTROL ACT (1985; 99 Stat. 1038).

In 1985, after a decade of persistently high deficits and increasing budgetary deadlock, Congress passed the Balanced Budget and Emergency Deficit Control Act, which is commonly referred to as the Gramm-Rudman-Hollings (GRH) Act. The act is named after its authors, Senators Phil Gramm (R-Tex.), Warren B. Rudman (R-N.H.), and Ernest F. Hollings (D-S.C.). The primary objective of GRH was to balance the federal budget by the early 1990s.

The central enforcement mechanism of the GRH Act in its original form was a series of automatic spending cuts that were to occur if the federal budget failed to meet or to fall within $10 billion of the deficit targets for fiscal years 1986–1990. The process by which these automatic spending cuts were to be made is referred to as sequestration. Sequestration was intended to ensure that the deficit targets were adhered to even if Congress and the president failed to reduce the deficit sufficiently through legislative action. It required federal spending to be cut automatically if Congress and the president did not enact laws to reduce the deficit to the maximum amount allowed for a given year. Under GRH, sequestration involved issuing a presidential order that would permanently cut budgetary resources to achieve the amount of outlay savings required to reduce the deficit. Trust funds, such as Social Security and other special funds, were exempt from sequestration. Once sequestration was triggered by a determination made by the executive, spending reductions were to be made automatically. This automatic cutting process was regarded by many as a strong incentive for Congress and the president to reach agreement on legislation and on a budget that would avoid a sequester. If the proposed federal budget failed to meet the annual deficit target established under GRH, the act would force the president to make across-the-board spending cuts evenly divided between domestic and defense programs until those targets were reached. Congress made major revisions in the GRH Act in 1987 and 1990. The Budget Enforcement Act (BEA) of 1990 changed the sequestration process substantially and established more flexibility in the annual deficit targets.

The GRH sequestration process was tied solely to the enforcement of fixed deficit targets until its revision by the BEA in 1990. If a sequester occurred, a formula set forth in the GRH Act required that 50 percent of the budget-outlay reductions be made in defense programs and 50 percent in social programs. Since defense made up less than 25 percent of the budget during the late 1980s and early 1990s, there was a strong incentive for members of Congress who did not want cuts in defense to avoid a sequester. Under sequestration, budget cuts were to be made uniformly across the range of accounts covered by the process. About two-thirds of federal budget outlays, however, were exempt from sequestration, and certain entitlement programs, such as Medicare, which could not be cut more than 2 percent, had special sequestration rules. The burden of sequestration was therefore unevenly distributed among defense and certain social-spending programs.

The GRH Act in its original form established a fixed deficit target for each fiscal year covered by the process (see table 1). The targets were not adjusted to account for changes in economic conditions, such as growth or inflation rates, or demographic trends that changed the number of persons receiving federal payments under entitlement programs. The five-year enforcement procedures under GRH and the Congressional Budget Act of 1974 could be suspended for two reasons: if war were declared, or if Congress were to enact a special joint resolution triggered by the issuance of a low-growth report by the Congressional Budget Office.

Originally, GRH provided for the automatic issuance of a sequestration order by the president on receiving a report by the comptroller general identifying a deficit that exceeded the limit set by the law. In *Bowsher v. Synar* (1986), the Supreme Court invalidated this feature of GRH on the grounds that the constitutional separation-of-powers doctrine was violated because the comptroller general is a legislative branch official. The Supreme Court's decision would have prevented GRH's implementation, but Congress significantly revised the original act with the Balanced Budget and Emergency Deficit Control Reaffirmation Act of 1987, commonly called Gramm-Rudman-Hollings II (GRH II), by placing the function that triggers sequestration in the hands of the director of the Office of Management and Budget, an executive branch official. GRH II also revised the original deficit-reduction targets and extended the deadline for balancing the budget to 1993 (see table 1).

The GRH acts promised long-term lower deficits and a balanced budget, but these goals were elusive and overly optimistic. After the enactment of GRH in 1985 and its revision in 1987, the deficit never met the limits required by law. Sequestration was supposed to threaten the interests of all participants in the congressional budget process enough to make them want to avoid it. This threat, however, did not always have the intended effect. Congress avoided sequestration by substituting overly optimistic economic and technical assumptions for actual policy changes. Also, enforcement of the deficit targets was not effective after the final budget "snapshot." Before the BEA was passed in 1990, Congress evaluated the budget only once a year to ascertain whether or not it was meeting the GRH deficit-reduction targets. The result was a snapshot of the budget situation. After the snapshot was taken, indicating that the deficit target had been met, Congress could adopt legislation that would raise the deficit in the current and following years.

[*See also* Bowsher v. Synar; Budget Enforcement Act of 1990; Congressional Budget and Impoundment Control Act of 1974; Reconciliation; Sequestration.]

BIBLIOGRAPHY

Havens, Harry. "Gramm-Rudman-Hollings: Origins and Implementation." *Public Budgeting and Finance* 6 (1986): 4–24.

Penner, Rudolph G., and Alan J. Abramson. *Broken Purse Strings: Congressional Budgeting 1974–1988.* 1988.

Thelwell, Raphael. "Gramm-Rudman-Hollings Four Years Later: A Dangerous Illusion." *Public Administration Review* 50 (1990): 190–197.

Thurber, James A. "New Rules for an Old Game: Zero-Sum Budgeting in the Postreform Congress." In *The Postreform Congress.* Edited by Roger H. Davidson. 1992. Pp. 257–278.

JAMES A. THURBER

BANK. *See* House Bank.

BANKHEAD, WILLIAM B. (1874–1940), Democratic representative from Alabama, served as chairman of the House Committee on Rules (1934–1935), as House majority leader (1935–1936), and as Speaker of the House of Representatives (1936–1940). William Brockman Bankhead was the scion of a political family described by its opponents as the "Royal Bankheads." His father, John H. Bankhead, had been a member of the House and a senator, and his brother, John H. Bankhead II, served in the Senate from 1931 until his death in 1946. His daughter Tallulah was one of the most acclaimed actresses of the twentieth century.

Both William and his father represented a U.S. House district that included counties from both the North Alabama hill country, an area inhabited primarily by small farmers and coal miners, and the lowland Black Belt, which was dominated by large plantation owners. Hill country farmers often had a radical agrarian or populist political stance that distinguished them from the wealthy and conservative Black Belt planters. The Bankheads reached

TABLE 1. *Federal Deficit Reduction Targets, 1986–1993 (in billions of dollars)*

FISCAL YEAR	1985 GRH TARGETS	1987 GRH TARGETS	ACTUAL DEFICITS
1986	172	—	221
1987	144	—	150
1988	108	144	155
1989	72	136	152
1990	36	100	195
1991	0	64	269
1992	—	28	399
1993	—	0	255

SOURCE: J. Thurber and S. Durst. "The 1900 Budget Enforcement Act: The Decline of Congressional Accountability." In *Congress Reconsidered.* 5th ed. Edited by L. Dodd and B. Oppenheimer. 1993.

WILLIAM B. BANKHEAD.   LIBRARY OF CONGRESS

out to both groups. Father and son supported many progressive measures, but they were careful not to offend wealthy plantation owners. William also balanced his strong support for the coal and iron industry in his district by backing the growing demands of union labor. This struggle to balance the interests of disparate forces led the Bankheads to prefer conciliation over rigid policy positions.

William was born on 12 April 1874 in Lamar County, in northwestern Alabama. After earning a bachelor's degree from the University of Alabama in 1893, he took a law degree from Georgetown University in 1895. For a brief period, Bankhead lived in New York City, where he practiced law and tried his hand on the Broadway stage. In 1900 he returned to Alabama, was elected to the state legislature, and was subsequently elected prosecuting attorney for an area that included several counties. In 1916 he was elected to the U.S. House of Representatives from Alabama's Tenth District. He was reelected eleven times.

The amiable Bankhead was always well liked in Congress, but did not exercise much influence until Franklin D. Roosevelt was elected President and Democrats won majorities in both houses of

Congress in 1932. Bankhead was quickly elevated to chairman of the House Rules Committee in 1934, named majority leader in 1935, and elected Speaker a year later. He cautioned Roosevelt not to take radical positions, but he loyally supported nearly all the New Deal measures, including the controversial Court-packing plan of 1937. In 1940, Bankhead was considered to be a serious candidate for the Democratic vice presidential nomination, and he blamed President Roosevelt when the nomination went to Henry A. Wallace instead. Only a few weeks after the Democratic convention, Bankhead, who had been ill through much of his tenure as Speaker, died at the Naval Hospital in Washington.

Bankhead entered politics under the guidance and patronage of a powerful father, but he demonstrated his own natural aptitude for the political game. He was a fine debater with an excellent command of the language, but he did not engage in rhetorical demagoguery. He was, according to one Alabama newspaper, "the patient workmanlike statesman." Bankhead rarely introduced major legislation, but he consistently championed southern cotton farmers, from big cotton planters to small tenant farmers, and others who operated on the margins of the agricultural economy. His greatest achievement was the passage of the New Deal legislative program, which he skillfully, if sometimes reluctantly, guided through the House of Representatives.

BIBLIOGRAPHY

Burns, James McGregor. *Roosevelt: The Lion and the Fox.* 1956.

Heacock, Walter J. "William B. Bankhead and the New Deal." *The Journal of Southern History* 21 (1955).

Tindall, George Brown. *The Emergence of the New South, 1913–1945.* 1967.

SAMUEL L. WEBB

BANKING. Banks were a feature of the Republic from its earliest days. The first American bank, the Bank of North America, received its charter from the Continental Congress on 31 December 1781. Although the bank received a Pennsylvania charter in 1782, its creation raised concerns about the relationship between government and business. Periodically, that relationship generated criticism, as it did when Alexander Hamilton submitted a plan for a new national bank, the Bank of the United States (BUS), in 1790. Chartered in 1791, the first BUS avoided some friction by selling four-fifths of the capital stock to the public.

By 1801 there were some thirty commercial banks in the United States, virtually all of them under state charters. Large numbers of so-called private banks (i.e., uncharted banks) also conducted business, although exactly how many of these existed is undetermined. Nevertheless a stiff competition developed in money. Any bank could issue its own money ("notes" or "paper") backed by gold and silver ("specie") as long as the bank would redeem, or pay on demand, the specie for the paper. That simple fact—competitive money based on commodity backing—dominated all debates about banking for more than one hundred years. Political parties differed on how to control competition and how to ensure rapid "convertibility" into gold or silver. Other debates, such as those between Jacksonians and Whigs in the 1830s, were over the degree to which the state should support banking, and, especially, whether or not the federal government should involve itself in banking.

One of the most difficult issues concerned the government's need to keep its money somewhere, either in a private bank or in some sort of publicly owned institution. Visionaries such as Hamilton wanted to put the government's money to use through the creation of a government-owned bank that, in turn, would generate a market for government securities. That, consequently, would stabilize the credit of the young republic and ensure that its bonds would sell. Others, such as the Jeffersonian Democrats (also known as the Democratic Republicans, or simply Republicans), abhorred such use of government power. To the extent that the government had to conduct its financial business, it should do so with private banking firms, they believed.

In 1811, the recharter bill for the first BUS failed by a single vote in each house, despite the support of President James Madison and his secretary of the Treasury, Albert Gallatin. But five years later the financial dislocations following the War of 1812 persuaded Congress to charter a second BUS. The second BUS received much of the blame for the panic of 1819 and for many years was seen as the culprit for the inflation of the 1830s.

Far more than had the first, the second Bank of the United States became a political issue. Although far from the common conception of a modern "central" bank with modern monetary tools, the BUS could, when it chose, force some banks to maintain high reserves by threatening to present them with huge amounts of their own notes and demand redemption in gold, silver, or BUS notes. Both the first and second BUS were allowed to have branch offices in many states—a true interstate branch-banking network that state laws denied to state-chartered institutions.

A political power play by BUS president Nicholas Biddle doomed the bank. He attempted to gain a recharter for the bank in 1832, four years before the old charter expired. President Andrew Jackson vetoed the charter bill and set off the famous "Bank War," which he won. Congress could not override his veto, and Jackson subsequently withdrew the

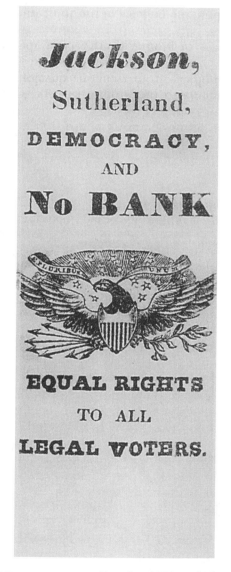

SILK CAMPAIGN RIBBON. For the 1832 presidential and congressional elections, bearing a campaign slogan opposing the rechartering of the Second Bank of the United States.   COLLECTION OF DAVID J. AND JANICE L. FRENT

government's deposits from the BUS, leaving it an empty shell. Recent scholarship suggests that Jackson opposed the BUS not because he found the notion of a national bank distasteful but rather because he would not tolerate a political opponent such as Biddle having such a large base of patronage and power.

With the demise of the second BUS, the "money vacuum" in the United States was filled by the state-chartered banks. Several state legislatures found the constant petitions for charters and recharters so time-consuming that they passed free banking laws that essentially resembled modern general incorporation laws, wherein anyone with the capital to post a bond could open a bank. The primary control over banking was not legislative, but remained instead the requirement that banks convert their notes into specie on demand.

The Civil War revised national banking politics. Secretary of the Treasury Salmon P. Chase, looking for a way to increase bond sales to finance the war, hit on the Hamiltonian concept of national banking, except that Chase decided to charter not one but many banks, as many as could put up the required bond backing. Receiving their charters from the federal government rather than the states, these national banks had merely to purchase and hold U.S. securities as collateral for their note issues. Congress on 25 February 1863 passed the National Bank Act, which established the bond requirement for the banks and set reserve requirements of "greenbacks" and specie to national bank notes and deposits. "Greenbacks" were the specially created non-interest-bearing Treasury notes authorized under the Legal Tender Act of 25 February 1862. They had special designation as "lawful money, and a legal tender in payment of all debts, public and private," the first time in American history that the government had required individuals to accept any particular form of money in payment for goods or services. The acceptance of greenbacks came from the promise by the government to redeem them at par value, in gold, at some future point. People had faith in the government's promise, on which it indeed made good.

At the same time, the National Bank Act created a competition between the state and federal governments to charter banks. National charter requirements, especially the reserve and capital requirements, were stiff, and states found that they could attract banks by offering lower capital and reserve requirements. As a result, whereas in 1870 national bank numbers exceeded those of nonna-

tional banks by a factor of five, by 1890 nonnational banks had surpassed national banks by almost thirteen hundred.

In the next decades, financial unrest grew, fed by the falling prices brought about by expectations of a return to the gold standard (accomplished in 1879), and, after 1879, by a worldwide deflation that lasted until 1900. Prices for farm goods fell, but farmers still had to repay their original loan and mortgage commitments. Faced with falling prices and overall deflation, farmers and miners joined forces to lobby Congress for inflationary policies, either through coinage and monetization of the vast new silver supplies (at old silver prices, which would expand the money supply) or through new government issues of unbacked paper money (i.e., greenbacks without the promise to return to gold redemption).

Congress in fact had gone in the other direction in 1873 by abandoning the coinage of silver dollars and attempting to disengage from bimetallism and move to a strict gold standard, in which only gold would constitute money and only gold would back paper note issues. A hue and cry went up, and the act was dubbed the "Crime of '73." Agitation over silver led in 1878 to passage of the Bland-Allison Act, in which the government again made silver into "money" by authorizing the Treasury to purchase between $2 million and $4 million worth of the metal each month to coin silver dollars. Those amounts did not significantly decrease the excess silver, nor did they substantially inflate the currency. By then, seventeen times more silver was mined than gold, but the silver fans (and later, the Populists) wanted the government to buy it and coin it at a ratio of 16 to 1, in effect giving an extra silver dollar per sixteen transactions to everyone with access to that metal.

Further bimetallist pressure led Congress in 1890 to pass the Sherman Silver Purchase Act, which required the Treasury to buy 4.5 million ounces of silver at market prices and issue legal tender Treasury notes redeemable in gold. The government bought a specific quantity, not a dollar amount, and was partly responsible for touching off a gold drain. After all, foreign countries also had silver to convert to gold, and the price offered at the U.S. Treasury was attractive. Although Congress repealed the Sherman Act after President Grover Cleveland called the legislators into special session in 1894, the outflow of gold already had brought on the panic of 1893, which J. P. Morgan almost singlehandedly ended by lending the U.S. government 3.5 million ounces of gold.

It was recognized that the nation could not rely on such a private rescue in the next panic. Calls for reform of the banking system, especially for making the currency more "elastic" (that is, more expandable during crisis periods), led to a number of high-level commissions and plans for reform. In 1906 investment banker Jacob Henry Schiff prodded the New York Chamber of Commerce into naming a five-man committee to prepare a plan to reform the banking and currency systems.

Then the panic of 1907 sent new tremors through the banking system. Morgan again served as the rampart, lending $25 million to support the sagging system. And in 1908 Congress passed the Aldrich-Vreeland Emergency Currency Act, which authorized the secretary of the Treasury to issue emergency currency in future panics. Two components of the new reforms needed had come into focus: the system had to be elastic—it had to be able to expand or contract the money supply as necessary—and there had to be a "lender of last resort"— some individual or institution that could lend to the banks until public fears subsided. To that end, the Aldrich-Vreeland Act also created the National Monetary Commission (NMC) to make recommendations for dealing with future crises. After the committee named by the NMC went to Europe, Senate Finance Committee chairman Nelson W. Aldrich and others returned convinced of the need for a national bank.

Legislators, meanwhile, sought to address another issue related to banking, namely the lack of banking facilities in some parts of the country. To that end Congress in 1910 passed an act establishing the Postal Savings System, which authorized selected post offices to receive deposits and pay 2 percent interest on accounts. The system grew slowly, and had deposits of $3.8 billion by 1929. It remained in place until Congress abolished it in 1967. Again, the need for reform was clear, as the Postal Savings Banks would not have been popular if branch banking had been a viable alternative.

Aldrich's committee continued to work throughout 1910 on a national bank plan, but he did not get far. In November 1910, four of the most influential men in banking, plus a Harvard professor, met in secrecy at Jekyll Island, Georgia, where they designed the scope, functions, management, and organization of a new banking structure. It put most of the control of that system in the hands of the federal government. While Congress ruminated over that plan, in 1912 Louisiana represen-

tative Arsène P. Pujo, a member of the House Committee on Banking and Currency, conducted an investigation into the so-called Money Trust, a largely New York–based concentration of financial power among the nation's largest banks. The committee's report, issued in February 1913, contributed to the passage of the Federal Reserve Bank Act by revealing a great concentration of financial assets among the largest banks in the nation, including extensive interlocking directorates.

Rep. Carter Glass of Virginia, chairman of the House Committee on Banking and Currency, introduced a bill to create the Federal Reserve System. Both houses quickly passed the bill and President Woodrow Wilson signed it on 23 December 1913. The act addressed three major areas of concern: providing elasticity in the money supply, establishing a lender of last resort, and reducing the power of the Money Trust. Twelve Federal Reserve Banks would be created around the nation, with the majority in the South and West (Missouri received two; California, Texas, Georgia, and Minnesota, one each). Each Federal Reserve Bank was a corporation that the member banks supported with an investment of 6 percent of their paid-up capital. A Federal Reserve board of governors, including five members chosen by the president, with the comptroller of the currency and the secretary of the Treasury serving as ex officio members, oversaw the operation. The Reserve banks could expand or contract the money supply by lowering or raising the discount rate to their member banks. Funds could be rapidly transferred among the district banks, thereby (or so advocates hoped) containing any runs that might develop. But no deposit insurance existed, and any thoughts that the power of New York might quickly diminish faded as the New York Federal Reserve Bank emerged as the dominant institution in the system.

Certain pressures on the Federal Reserve System's membership developed, however, and by 1910, out of twenty-five thousand banks in the United States, more than eighteen thousand were nonnational banks. Part of the attraction for a bank to obtain a state charter, particularly in some western and southern states, came from the branch-banking laws of the states. National banks, for all intents, could not establish branches, but several states permitted setting up branches, particularly California, where A. P. Giannini built up his huge group of branch bank systems under the Bank of America aegis. By the mid 1920s, the government realized that for national banks to compete with the state banks they had to be able to set up branches. Accordingly, on 25 February 1927 the McFadden Act, a bill introduced into the House by Banking and Currency Committee chairman Louis T. McFadden of Pennsylvania, became law. The act permitted national banks to have branches if state laws permitted them to do so, and any state bank that joined the national system could retain all branches in existence when the act went into effect. Several restrictions still applied to the setting up of branches by national banks, but McFadden made the national system more competitive with the state banks. Some historians suggest that the McFadden Act was drafted specifically out of a compromise with Giannini to bring his huge Bank of Italy, with its three hundred branches, into the system. Giannini indeed joined, changing the name of the bank to the Bank of America.

But the McFadden Act did not permit interstate branch banking, which meant that the American banking system still had a serious weakness. That weakness showed up in the failures of rural banks during the farm depression of the 1920s. From 1919 to 1929, the number of banks fell by forty-two hundred, with the most failures coming in states that had enacted deposit insurance laws.

As bank failures spread, larger institutions found themselves in danger with the acceleration of the downturn after the failure of the New York–based Bank of the United States in 1930. Recent scholarship points to the international gold standard as the ultimate culprit in the country's banking woes. The United States held steadfastly to the gold standard, even as gold flowed out of American vaults. In a system in which gold served as the final backing for paper money, the result was predictable.

When Franklin D. Roosevelt assumed the presidency in 1933, he immediately ordered a national bank holiday on 6 March to give the banks a respite and to allow federal investigators to determine which banks could remain open. Of the more than 17,700 banks in operation before the holiday, 11,800 reopened after, with many others reorganized. Roosevelt's actions were confirmed by the Emergency Banking Relief Act, approved 9 March 1933. Some deposits started to return to the banks, and more followed after Congress enacted the Glass-Steagall Act (also called the Banking Act of 1933), which established the Federal Deposit Insurance Corporation (FDIC), an agency that insured deposits through a fund paid for by member banks. Historians once credited the holiday and the deposit insurance as the factors that restored stability to the banking system. It now seems much more likely, however, that a provision of the Emergency Banking Relief Act permitting the president to leave the gold standard ended the banking instability of the 1930s. At the time, however, the creation of the FDIC appeared beneficial, and few looked at the problems associated with deposit insurance at the state level in the 1920s. Glass-Steagall also required banks to separate themselves from their securities affiliates (those companies that dealt in stocks and bonds), thus reducing the competitive range of banks' activities.

Another law with unexpected side effects, the National Housing Act of 1934, created the Federal Savings and Loan Insurance Corporation (FSLIC), an agency that insured the deposits of savings and loans (S&Ls). FSLIC was not a part of FDIC, nor did it have even as much independence from Congress as the FDIC had. A related statute, the Home Owners' Loan Act of 1933, allowed federal chartering of S&Ls to place them in competition with commercial banks, although for the most part the government restricted their lending to mortgage loans.

From 1945 until the mid 1960s, the banking industry generally ran along the guidelines formulated during the New Deal. Comptrollers of the currency differed as to their chartering policy—but commercial banks, S&Ls, and investment houses carved out their own segments of the market and did not compete with each other directly. Internationally, from 1944 to 1971 the United States worked within the Bretton Woods Agreement, wherein the nations of the world agreed to peg their currency values to the dollar. Domestically, few changes in the legal structure of banking occurred from 1945 to 1975, with only the Bank Holding Company Act of 1956 having a major impact on the way commercial banks conducted business. The law, passed after Transamerica Corporation won a victory over federal prosecution for monopoly, forced holding companies to choose between banks and other businesses. It limited multibank holding companies, preventing them from engaging in unrelated activities and from acquiring banks in more than one state (although it allowed existing arrangements to stand). In 1970 Congress brought one-bank holding companies, excluded from the 1956 act, under the provisions of the law.

Several states had started to modify their antibranching laws in the Great Depression, and the march toward nationwide branching picked up momentum in the 1970s, when several states modified their laws to permit some intrastate expansion. By 1990, only four states still prohibited branching.

Other laws such as those designed to permit the S&Ls to compete with banks resulted in rising interest rates paid by the S&Ls for deposits in the inflationary 1970s. As long as the interest rates on deposits remained below what the S&Ls took in on mortgage interest, they were healthy. But after inflation drove deposit interest rates up, the S&Ls suffered from an interest rate "mismatch" and soon faced disaster. Congress had restricted their lending primarily to mortgages, but the S&Ls needed something that paid better. In 1982, the Garn–St Germain Act sought to address that problem by expanding the S&Ls' power to pursue investments such as those commercial banks made. The law also allowed the S&Ls to offer adjustable-rate mortgages.

By the time Garn–St Germain went into effect, the S&Ls already had been pushed to the brink, and for most of them the only hope was to invest in extremely high-return securities. Unfortunately, "high-return" meant high-risk securities, especially high-yield "junk" bonds—that is, securities that did not carry an investment grade rating by the large investment houses. At that point, the legacy of the New Deal played its part: because the S&Ls carried deposit insurance—which by then had been shown to play a major role in the bank failures of the 1920s and 1930s—they had an added incentive to engage in high-risk behavior, since their depositors could not lose money. Only the owners and stockholders, who were certain to lose without an influx of cash, stood to lose with these investments. The drop in oil prices and the corollary plummet in real estate prices destroyed much of the S&Ls' assets, so that only a very few survived. And in 1989, due in part to the perverse incentives for S&L owners to engage in risky behavior under the protection offered by deposit insurance, the FSLIC went bankrupt. Congress created a new financing entity, the Resolution Funding Corporation (later called the Resolution Trust Corporation), to cover the FSLIC's obligations.

The most recent legislative change for commercial banks came in March 1980 with the Depository Institutions Deregulation and Monetary Control Act (DIDMCA). Title II of that legislation provided for limited deregulation of the financial industry, permitting nonbank institutions to issue demand deposits (checks) and allowing some banks to pay interest on their demand obligations, which S&Ls had done for some time. It also eliminated Federal Reserve interest rate ceilings for time deposits, providing for a "level playing field" for all competitors in the financial industry. Despite the act's title, however, DIDMCA in many ways expanded federal control over banks by subjecting members and nonmembers alike to the control of the Federal Reserve's board of governors over a key banking variable, reserve requirements.

DIDMCA did not address interstate banking, legislation concerning which remains a work in progress. States and regions are still wrestling with tailoring state laws to make interstate banking a reality without national regulation, and have succeeded. More difficult, they have found, has been changing the federal laws dating back to Glass-Steagall—laws most bankers find outdated and poorly conceived. In the mid-1990s, the state bankers' associations and the American Bankers Association were lobbying to allow banks to compete in previously prohibited areas and were meeting with slow but steady success.

[See also Banking, Finance, and Urban Affairs Committee, House; Banking, Housing, and Urban Affairs Committee, Senate; Bank of the United States; Currency and Finance; Savings and Loan Crisis; Silver Issue. For discussion of related legislation, see Banking Act of 1933; Depository Institutions Deregulation and Monetary Control Act of 1980; Emergency Banking Relief Act; Federal Reserve Bank Act; National Banking Act; Securities Acts.]

BIBLIOGRAPHY

Friedman, Milton, and Anna J. Schwartz. *A Monetary History of the United States, 1867–1960.* 1963.

Hammond, Bray. *Banks and Politics in America from the Revolution to the Civil War.* 1957.

Klebaner, Benjamin. *American Commercial Banking: A History.* 1990.

Perkins, Edwin J. "The Divorce of Commercial and Investment Banking: A History." *Banking Law Journal* 88 (1971): 483–529.

Schweikart, Larry, ed. *Encyclopedia of American Business History and Biography: Banking and Finance to 1913.* 1990.

Schweikart, Larry, ed. *Encyclopedia of American Business History and Biography: Banking and Finance, 1913–1989.* 1990.

White, Eugene N. *The Regulation and Reform of the American Banking System, 1900–1929.* 1983.

LARRY SCHWEIKART

BANKING ACT OF 1933 (48 Stat. 162–195). Following the banking collapse of the early 1930s and the advent of the New Deal administration of

President Franklin D. Roosevelt, Democrats Carter Glass of Virginia (who had just won reelection to the Senate) and Rep. Henry B. Steagall of Alabama drew up legislation called the Banking Act of 1933 (which soon became known as the Glass-Steagall Act). The act was based on Glass's conviction that commercial banking should be separated from lending for investment purposes. The Glass-Steagall Act also prohibited partners or officers of securities firms from serving as directors of Federal Reserve member banks. Finally, it created the Federal Deposit Insurance Corporation (FDIC) and enabled banks to qualify for deposit insurance if they showed solvency. All member banks of the Federal Reserve System, as well as many nonmembers, soon were insured.

The stock market crash and the collapse of the securities market led many to blame the relationship between the banks and their securities affiliates. Congress at first rejected calls to separate the activities of the two. Glass responded by putting the banks "on trial" in front of the Senate Banking and Currency Committee, which he chaired, eventually convincing Congress to force the banks to dissolve their securities affiliates. Subsequent research by Eugene N. White has shown that banks with securities affiliates were less likely to fail than those without securities affiliates.

The act left some investment activities to banks, including the underwriting of debt instruments of federal government and municipal bonds. Criticism of deposit insurance (as abused by savings and loan institutions) and of the act's limits on banking activities has grown in recent years. But the act remains in place as of 1994, although some minor inroads have been made toward reducing its scope.

[See also Emergency Banking Relief Act.]

BIBLIOGRAPHY

Edwards, Franklin R. "Banks and Securities Activities: Legal and Economic Perspectives." In *The Deregulation of the Banking and Securities Industries*. Edited by Lawrence G. Goldberg and J. White. 1979.

Huertas, Thomas F. "The Economic Brief against Glass-Steagall." *Journal of Bank Research* 15 (1984): 148–159.

Peach, Nelson W. *The Securities Affiliates of National Banks*. 1941.

White, Eugene N. "Before the Glass-Steagall Act: An Analysis of the Investment Banking Activities of National Banks." *Explorations in Economic History* 23 (January 1986): 33–55.

LARRY SCHWEIKART

BANKING, FINANCE, AND URBAN AFFAIRS COMMITTEE, HOUSE. For the first one hundred years of the United States' existence, the Ways and Means Committee had jurisdiction over banking legislation in the House of Representatives. Throughout the nineteenth century the House regularly increased the number of committees to handle the increase in the legislative work load. The 1865 creation of the Banking and Currency Committee was part of this move toward rationalizing the work load. The bulk of the committee's work load during the late nineteenth and early twentieth centuries involved the regulation and supervision of financial institutions. The committee, under the leadership of Chairman Carter Glass (D-Va.), played a leading role in developing the country's central banking system through the enactment of the Federal Reserve Act of 1913, the Glass-Steagall Act of 1933, and the Bank Act of 1935. After World War II housing and urban policy issues became increasingly important and the committee changed its name in 1975 to the Committee on Banking, Currency, and Housing. Two years later the committee was renamed the Banking, Finance, and Urban Affairs Committee.

Structure and Jurisdiction. In the 103d Congress, the Banking Committee is the fifth largest standing committee in the House. Most of its business is handled through subcommittees, which hold hearings and do the initial markup of legislation. All proposed legislation is referred to the following six subcommittees: Housing and Community Development; Financial Institutions Supervision, Regulation, and Deposit Insurance; International Development, Finance, Trade, and Monetary Policy; General Oversight, Investigations, and the Resolution of Failed Financial Institutions; Economic Growth and Credit Formation; and Consumer Credit and Insurance.

In general, the size of a subcommittee's membership indicates its importance. The three largest, each with thirty members, are the Financial Institutions Supervision, Regulation, and Deposit Insurance Subcommittee; the Housing and Community Development Subcommittee; and the Consumer Credit and Insurance Subcommittee.

The Financial Institutions Supervision, Regulation, and Deposit Insurance Subcommittee, which has jurisdiction over all policies governing the operations of financial institutions and their regulatory agencies, has been a top priority of Chairman Henry B. Gonzalez (D-Tex.), as it was for his predecessor, Fernand J. St Germain (D-R.I.). Membership on the Housing and Community Development Subcommittee was deemed somewhat less important during the 1980s, when the subcommittee was unable to get increases in housing funds passed over staunch White House opposition; after 1992, however, when the Los Angeles riots and the election of a Democratic president increased the political importance of housing and urban affairs, membership on this subcommittee again became very desirable. In 1993, when the Banking Committee reorganized its internal structure, the jurisdiction of the Consumer Credit and Insurance Subcommittee was increased to include matters involving the insurance industry.

The next largest subcommittee is International Development, Finance, Trade, and Monetary Policy, with twenty-five members. Because of its involvement with international credit and the funding of trade through the Export-Import Bank, this subcommittee works closely with the Foreign Affairs Committee. The Subcommittee on Economic Growth and Credit, with fifteen members, deals with economic stabilization policies and financial aid to various sectors of the economy. The 1975 federal loan guarantees that enabled New York City to resolve its fiscal crisis and the 1978 loan guarantees that kept the Chrysler Corporation from going bankrupt were under its purview. It also oversees the production of goods and services essential to military performance as required by the 1950 Defense Production Act.

The six-member Subcommittee on General Oversight, Investigations, and the Resolution of Failed Financial Institutions has a mandate to provide continuous oversight of all administrative agencies under the Banking Committee's jurisdiction. Due to the large number of agencies under the committee's jurisdiction, most receive only cursory ongoing oversight. This subcommittee is also responsible for overseeing the disposition of failed financial institutions.

Committee Staff. According to the rules of the House, all staff members work for the committee chairman. In hiring decisions at the full committee level, Gonzalez tried to "team on each issue a member of the professional staff with someone coming out of a more political background." He chose to give the Republican leadership and subcommittee chairs discretion in making some hiring decisions. In 1992 there were twenty-five majority staff working directly under the chairman at the full committee level, nine Republican staff working under the committee's ranking minority member, and seventy-two staff assigned to the subcommittees. The partisan split between Democratic and Republican sub-

committee staff strongly favored the majority party, which had 80 percent of the staff members. Senior policy staff have responsibility for writing most bills, but they are careful to write bills that are consistent with the sponsoring members' legislative philosophy and electoral needs.

Membership. Richard Fenno in his 1973 book, *Congressmen in Committees*, categorized congressional committees into three ideal types based on three types of personal political goals of committee members: achieving reelection, gaining influence within the House, or creating good public policy. He classified the Banking Committee as a policy-oriented committee, but there are indications that the reforms of the 1970s, which opened up hearings and meetings to outsiders, have increased reelection-oriented behavior within the committee. Members have become increasingly susceptible to pressure from their constituents and from powerful organized interests, and staffers describe most of the current members as motivated by both policy and electoral goals.

When representatives were asked to rank their committee preferences, the Banking Committee fell into the middle range. During the 1950s and 1960s most members chose the committee because they wanted to influence housing policy. This changed in the 1970s when financial-sector lobbying groups began to urge newly elected representatives with proindustry views to seek service on the committee. Conflicts between different sectors of the financial community are reflected in campaign funding: some legislators get a large portion of their campaign contributions from banking groups, while others receive more from competing industries, such as savings and loans or the insurance industry.

In 1994 the partisan makeup within the Banking Committee was almost identical to the 60 percent to 40 percent split within the House as a whole. On the Democratic side there were thirty party members and one independent who normally votes with them; there were twenty Republicans. Most of the legislative matters before the committee cut across traditional party lines. While one might classify Republicans as being more concerned with the profitability of the financial sector and Democrats as being more concerned with the credit needs of the community, these generalizations are of only limited utility in predicting the outcome of a vote. For example, on controversial votes, Democratic members who represent financial center districts may vote with the proindustry Republican coalition.

In one sense Gonzalez has used a participatory leadership style, seeking input from a large group of committee members and giving the subcommittee chairmen a great deal of latitude in crafting and marking up legislation. However, unlike his predecessor, Gonzalez has not been a deal maker; when formulating legislation, he has made few accommodations to his opponents. In contrast, St Germain initially consulted very few members but was more willing to bargain at later stages. Because he would not allow a bill to go to the floor unless he knew he had the votes to pass it, St Germain lost only one floor vote during his entire chairmanship. Gonzalez's unwillingness to compromise has caused the Banking Committee to have one of the lowest floor passage rates of any committee. In 1990 some Democratic members of the committee supported a more junior member's bid to be elected chairman; although Gonzalez defeated the challenge, it was a clear indication of dissatisfaction.

Policy Environment. In the post–World War II period, the Banking Committee was extremely ac-

tive, attempting to carry out Congress's 1949 pledge to provide "a decent home" for every citizen. Under the leadership of Brent Spence (D-Ky.) and then Wright Patman (D-Tex.), the committee directed the development of the Federal Home Loan Bank System to provide funds to the savings and loan industry, public housing programs to provide affordable housing for the urban poor, urban renewal programs to revitalize inner cities, and mortgage guarantee programs administered by the Federal Housing Administration. By the early 1970s Patman's liberal-activist orientation was completely out of step with the proindustry orientation of most of his fellow committee members, and he lost his chairmanship in 1974.

During the latter half of the 1970s, when Henry S. Reuss (D-Wis.) was chairman, one staffer described the Banking Committee's policy environment as "sleepy." The liberal Reuss was never able to muster majorities to continue the activist poli-

BANKING COMMITTEE CHAIRMAN HENRY B. GONZALEZ (D-TEX.). *Left*, consulting with Rep. Barney Frank (D-Mass.) prior to a markup session, June 1992.   R. MICHAEL JENKINS, CONGRESSIONAL QUARTERLY INC.

cies of his immediate predecessors. Instead, committee members were primarily concerned with the practical needs of various industry groups. The operating environment changed radically during the 1980s due to the public perception that the savings and loan crisis had been caused by the deregulation of the early 1980s and that the Banking Committee had allowed the industry to make billions off bad loans, which the public, through deposit insurance guarantees, was forced to make good. Heightened press scrutiny and a desire among committee members to avoid blame for any further scandals have made it much more difficult in the 1990s for the committee to resolve many issues.

One of the major problems is the need to overhaul the financial regulatory structure to eliminate overlapping state and federal jurisdictions and place all financial institutions in a similar competitive position. Without reforms, the U.S. banking industry will continue to be at a disadvantage in competing with foreign institutions. The 1980 Depository Institutions Deregulation and Monetary Control Act and the 1982 Garn–St Germain Act eliminated some of these problems, but given the situation in the early 1990s, legislators are wary of passing any laws that might appear to be proindustry. More recent laws, such as the 1987 Competitive Equality Banking Act and the 1989 Financial Institutions Reform, Recovery, and Enforcement Act, have included provisions that make it more difficult for healthy firms to acquire failing institutions. One staffer described committee members' motivations in passing these provisions as simply a "desire to avoid blame for the next crisis."

[See also Banking, Housing, and Urban Affairs Committee, Senate.]

BIBLIOGRAPHY

Fenno, Richard F. Congressmen in Committees. 1973.
Salamon, Lester M. The Money Committees. 1975.
Schroedel, Jean Reith. "Campaign Contributions and Legislative Outcomes." Western Political Quarterly 39 (September 1986): 371–389.

JEAN REITH SCHROEDEL

BANKING, HOUSING, AND URBAN AFFAIRS COMMITTEE, SENATE.

Initially the Senate assigned all banking legislation to the Finance Committee. Since banking legislation was only a secondary concern of the Finance Committee, the panel was not significantly involved in crafting the most important nineteenth-century

banking legislation, the 1863 National Bank Act, which created the Office of the Comptroller of the Currency to regulate nationally chartered banks. Following major financial liquidity crises in 1907, the Finance Committee under the chairmanship of Nelson W. Aldrich (R-R.I.) played an important role in creating support for the development of a central banking system. Although Aldrich had retired by the time the Federal Reserve Act was passed in 1913, he had helped prepare the country for its enactment.

When population growth and industrialization in the late nineteenth century led to increased demands on Congress, Senate leaders chose to transfer some responsibilities from existing committees to newly created ones. In 1913 the Senate created a separate Banking and Currency Committee with jurisdiction over banking and currency. The Depression-era banking reforms were a product of extensive collaboration between President Franklin D. Roosevelt and the leadership of both congressional banking committees. After World War II, when housing issues came to dominate the committee's agenda, it was renamed the Banking, Housing, and Urban Affairs Committee.

Structure and Jurisdiction. Even though the Banking, Housing, and Urban Affairs Committee in 1993 had nineteen members, most important decisions are made at the full committee level. Subcommittees hold hearings and make recommendations, but all markup is done by the full committee. Unlike its House counterparts, the Senate committee as a whole oversees the regulation of financial institutions rather than delegating this responsibility to a subcommittee.

In 1993 the committee had the following four subcommittees: Housing and Urban Affairs, Securities, International Finance and Monetary Policy, and Economic Stabilization and Rural Development. The largest and traditionally most influential of the subcommittees is Housing and Urban Affairs, which in 1993 had eleven members. Its jurisdiction includes all matters relating to housing and mortgage credit and community development. Even though the White House opposed increases in federal funding to housing and cities throughout the 1980s, this subcommittee was able to maintain its preeminent status because its chairman, Alan Cranston (D-Calif.), took an activist, confrontational stance toward the Reagan and Bush administrations.

The Securities Subcommittee, with eleven members in 1994, has responsibility for overseeing the stock markets and the agricultural commodities markets. Because the responsibility for securities legislation is parceled out among different House committees, the Securities Subcommittee is often embroiled in jurisdictional conflicts. The international Finance and Monetary Policy Subcommittee, with eleven members in 1994, has responsibility for all legislation dealing with international financial entities (e.g., the International Monetary Fund and the Defense Production Act of 1950.) Since the mid 1970s, this subcommittee has not been very active. The Economic Stabilization and Rural Development Subcommittee, considered the least desirable of the subcommittees, was created in 1993 with nine members as a replacement for the Consumer and Regulatory Affairs Subcommittee.

Committee Staff. According to Senate rules, committee chairmen are responsible for making all decisions about the allocation of committee staff. Traditionally, Banking Committee chairmen have chosen to delegate many of these decisions to those working most directly with the staff. Like his predecessors, Sen. Donald W. Riegle, Jr. (D-Mich.), the chairman since 1989, chose to give subcommittee chairmen and the ranking minority member the responsibility for hiring their own staff. Riegle differed from his predecessors, however, in his more partisan strategy of allocating only about a third of the total staff to minority members. As might be expected given the subcommittees' relative weakness, only about a third of the fifty staffers in 1993 were assigned full-time to the subcommittees.

Traditionally, Banking Committee staff positions were among the most sought-after in Congress. More than half the staffers had law degrees or advanced degrees in economics. Many had experience working in private-sector financial institutions or for governmental regulatory agencies before joining the Banking Committee staff. Even though major policy positions are determined by committee members, the staff plays a large role in formulating these positions and writing legislation. On important issues senior staffers provide members with summaries of the policy options and make recommendations. The staff handles the actual writing of the bills and ends up making decisions about many of the details.

Membership. According to John Bibby's and Roger Davidson's *On Capitol Hill* (1967), many senators sought appointment to the Banking Committee during the years immediately following World War II. Committee membership then offered a chance to participate in major policy de-

DONALD W. RIEGLE, JR. (D-MICH.). Chairman (1989–), during a hearing of the Senate Committee on Banking, Housing, and Urban Affairs.
OFFICE OF THE HISTORIAN OF THE U.S. SENATE

bates about price controls, economic reconversion, and full employment and housing policies. But as policy decisions became more routine in the mid 1950s, the attractiveness of Banking Committee service declined, and it became one of the least sought-after of committee assignments. In 1963 Sen. Joseph S. Clark (D-Pa.) went so far as to describe the committee as an "Orphan Annie" bereft of supporters. The 1965 reduction in the size of committee membership was indicative of its declining popularity. Subsequent studies indicated that the Banking Committee had regained some of its attractiveness to both policy- and constituency-oriented senators by the late 1970s.

The impact of the Keating Five scandal on the membership of the committee cannot be overstated. In 1990 the Senate Ethics Committee held two months of televised hearings into the activities of five senators, who had received a total of $1.5 million in campaign contributions from wealthy investor Charles Keating, Jr., and were accused of trying to improperly influence federal regulators on his behalf. The involvement of Chairman Riegle and Senator Alan Cranston, the second-ranking Democrat, in efforts to prop up the bankrupt Lincoln Savings and Loan, which eventually cost the taxpayers $2 billion, raised serious questions about campaign contributors' influence on committee decisions. Cranston chose to not seek reelection after being reprimanded by the full Senate. Even though Riegle was found not to have broken any Senate rules, the Ethics Committee concluded that his "conduct gave the appearance of being improper." Many committee members felt that they had been personally tainted by the scandal.

During the 102d and 103d Congresses there was little cooperation among the Democrats and Republicans on the committee. While a large portion of the partisanship resulted from a need to assign blame for the savings and loan bailout, it was also partly due to a change in leadership. During the chairmanships of Senators Jake Garn (R-Utah) and William Proxmire (D-Wis.) collegiality predominated and committee cleavages ran along regional and rural-urban lines rather than partisan ones. Democratic and Republican staff worked together on writing the major financial-sector legislation. For example, Garn asked both Democratic and Republican staffers to work on the 1982 Depository Institutions Act and Proxmire did the same on the 1988 financial modernization bill. But when Riegle became chairman he instructed Democratic members' staff to stop cooperating with Republicans' staffers. Republican staffers were allowed to make recommendations only after bills were written. Interparty battles became so bad that Republican and Democratic staffers engaged in shouting matches, and enormous conflicts sometimes flared over relatively minor issues.

The greatest conflicts between Democratic and Republican senators occurred during appointment and oversight hearings. The 1991 hearings over whether to reappoint Robert Clark to head up the Office of the Comptroller of the Currency were especially acrimonious. Republicans believed that Riegle led the attack on Clark to deflect attention from his own problems, while Democrats argued that Clark and other Bush administrative appointees were lax in their regulation of financial institutions.

Policy Environment. The Banking Committee is one of the most contentious in Congress. Its tendency toward partisanship was exacerbated by the deep problems of the financial sector during the 1980s. As long as deposit insurance programs were funded by the industry, there was very little public awareness of financial institutions' problems. When taxpayer money became involved the press began to pay a lot of attention to the issue. For example, Sen. Howard M. Metzenbaum (D-Ohio) generated a great deal of favorable press coverage for his attacks on the Reagan administration's handling of the sale of bankrupt thrifts in 1988. Republicans, however, charged that Metzenbaum actually made the situation worse by discouraging healthy institutions from acquiring failing ones.

By the end of the 102d Congress (1991–1993) scandals had made it very difficult for the committee to focus on the real policy issues. There was hope, however, that the influx of six new members in the 103rd Congress (1993–1995) would have a positive effect on the committee. The issues remained substantially the same. In the short run the committee had to deal with immediate issues such as raising at least $130 billion to refund the deposit insurance system and trying to find solutions to the host of urban ills that caused the Los Angeles riots in 1992. In the long term, the committee was faced with the need to reach agreement on policies for overhauling the entire financial regulatory structure. Among these was the need to eliminate overlapping federal and state jurisdictions and restrictions that hamper the ability of American firms to compete in an increasingly global financial market.

[*See also* Banking, Finance, and Urban Affairs Committee, House.]

BIBLIOGRAPHY

Bibby, John. "Committee Characteristics and Legislative Oversight of Administration." In *The Legislative Process in the U.S. Senate.* Edited by Lawrence K. Pettit and Edward Keynes. 1968.
Bibby, John, and Roger Davidson. *On Capitol Hill.* 1967.
Salamon, Lester M. *The Money Committees.* 1975.
Schroedel, Jean R. *Congress, the President, and Policymaking: A Historical Approach.* 1994.

JEAN REITH SCHROEDEL

BANK OF THE UNITED STATES. On 13 December 1790 Alexander Hamilton, the secretary of the Treasury, proposed that Congress charter a national bank patterned after the Bank of England. Calling it a "political machine of the greatest importance to the state," Hamilton saw a national bank as indispensable to his broader plan for restoring the public credit of the new nation.

The bank, he suggested, would act as the agent of the Treasury in the marketplace and would provide credit at a low cost to the government. To bolster sales of government bonds, bank stock could be purchased with government securities. Government funds would be deposited in the bank, and the bank could issue up to $10 million in notes, or paper currency, that would be redeemable on demand in gold or silver coin (specie). The government would hold one-fifth of the capital stock of $10 million, with four-fifths going into private hands (and much of that, eventually, went into foreign ownership).

Opposition quickly developed, led by James Madison and Thomas Jefferson. Hamilton's opponents argued that a national bank would put too much power in the hands of the government. Nevertheless, the Federalists gained passage of the bill, which gave the institution a twenty-year charter.

The first Bank of the United States (BUS), according to most historians, displayed conservative management under Thomas Willing, the first president, and throughout its twenty-year life it remained conservative. Yet by no stretch of the imagination did the bank wield control over the nation's money supply or use any of the modern tools associated with "central banking." Rather, through its uniform notes it provided one source of currency of relatively stable value in a competitive note market.

In 1811, when the BUS's twenty-year charter came up for renewal, the Republicans in the legislature defeated the recharter bill by a single vote in each house despite lukewarm support from Republican president James Madison and enthusiastic backing by Secretary of the Treasury Albert Gallatin.

FIRST BANK OF THE UNITED STATES. On Third Street, Philadelphia. Engraving by W. Birch and Son, 1799.

As a consequence of the War of 1812, the nation's debt had soared from $45 million to $127 million. The number of state-chartered banks had expanded to 246 by 1816. By 1814, pressure on the banks to redeem their notes in specie forced them to suspend convertibility (i.e., paying gold and silver for their notes). New calls went up for a national bank.

On 10 April 1816 Madison signed a new charter giving life to the second Bank of the United States. Like the first, the second BUS had a twenty-year charter, and the government again owned one-fifth of the capital stock. The government appointed five of the twenty-five directors. But unlike the first, the second BUS had a larger capital stock base—$35 million—and the bank had to pay the government a $1.5 million bonus for its charter. Specifically designated the government's depository, the second BUS had a huge advantage over private competitors in that it always had a large deposit base, on which it did not have to pay interest! (It did have to make transfers of government funds free of charge.)

Eventually the bank had twenty-five branch offices around the nation. When the size of the bank's capital and deposit base was combined with its ability to shift funds to any point around the nation, BUS did indeed have incomparable financial powers. The bank, however, was no more a "central bank" than its predecessor. The bank influenced the nation's financial policies, but it could not control them.

The limits of the second BUS's power appeared in 1819, when a financial panic struck. Langdon Cheves, a South Carolinian, replaced William Jones as president and called in loans in a credit contraction one historian described as "ruthless." BUS notes and deposits fell by more than 50 percent within a year, sending state banks, which had based their own expansionary note issues on the national bank's expansion, into suspension. The actions of the BUS left a sour taste in the mouths of many farmers and debtors, including Andrew Jackson, who later came to oppose the bank vehemently.

Nicholas Biddle, the Philadelphian who replaced Cheves in 1823, ran a more aggressive BUS that generated profits. He also, however, refused to honor notes worth more than five dollars at any

SECOND BANK OF THE UNITED STATES. Philadelphia, 1834.

branch other than the one that had issued them, thus negating one of the goals of a national system—namely, creating a uniform national currency. Some also perceived that Biddle was restraining the note issues of the state-chartered banks by that move, although several years later, when Jackson attempted to kill the BUS, state bankers sent in hundreds of petitions showing their support for the institution.

Biddle pushed for an early recharter of the BUS in 1832—an election year. Congress passed the recharter bill, but on 10 July 1832 Jackson vetoed it on the grounds that the BUS was a monopoly (i.e., it received special government privileges) and that it catered to foreign stockholders. Recent scholarship suggests that Jackson actually had a vision of a national bank that was scarcely different from the one he sought to destroy. When the Democrats had power in the states, they used it not to enforce competition, but to gain monopoly powers for their own banks, often under the guise of centralized "state banks." That constituted an attempt by the Jacksonians to control the nation's currency at the federal level, despite their "hard money" reputation.

A running battle between Biddle and Jackson ensued, with the BUS president attempting to change Jackson's mind through his own "ruthless" credit contraction, but Biddle only alienated some of his supporters. Jackson appointed his attorney general, Roger B. Taney, secretary of the Treasury in October 1833. Although his nomination was later rejected by the Senate, Taney meanwhile removed the government's cash, parceling it out to some twenty state banks, most of them run by Jacksonian supporters. Only a husk of a bank remained alive as the BUS until 1836, when its charter expired. At that time it gained a charter from the state of Pennsylvania, but failed in the midst of the subsequent panic of 1837.

[*See also biographies of Clay and Jackson.*]

BIBLIOGRAPHY

Hammond, Bray. *Banks and Politics in America: From the Revolution to the Civil War.* 1957.
McFaul, John. *The Politics of Jacksonian Finance.* 1972.
Schweikart, Larry. "Jacksonian Ideology, Currency Control, and 'Central' Banking: A Reappraisal." *Historian* 51 (1988): 78–102.

LARRY SCHWEIKART

BANKRUPTCY. Article I, section 8, clause 4 of the Constitution empowers Congress to enact a uniform bankruptcy law. The First Congress formed a House committee to draft such a statute, but none was passed until 1800. The 1800 act, which provided for involuntary bankruptcy, was repealed in 1803 due to its ineffectiveness, abuse of its provisions, and the awkwardness of dealing with the nascent federal court system.

The difficult economic times and bank failures of the 1830s prompted the Bankruptcy Act of 1841, which provided for involuntary bankruptcy for merchants and added voluntary bankruptcy for the citizenry in general. The end of the national economic crisis, dissatisfaction among creditors, and complaints by debtors that the national act did not offer the exemptions available under state bankruptcy acts led to repeal of the 1841 act only a year after it had become effective.

The economic crisis of the late 1850s and the destabilizing effects of the Civil War and its aftermath led to the Bankruptcy Act of 1867. This statute permitted involuntary bankruptcy on the petition of a creditor who was owed at least $250 or voluntary bankruptcy by a debtor who owed at least $300. Although amended, the act did not resolve the ongoing tension between debtors and creditors and was repealed in 1878.

The next bankruptcy act was that of 1898. It addressed earlier debtor dissatisfaction by permitting state exemptions to remain intact and addressed the problem of federal court administration by permitting dual jurisdiction with state courts. Numerous amendments followed, the most important of which was the Chandler Act of 1938, a thoroughgoing revision and reorganization of the law as it had evolved to that time.

The Bankruptcy Reform Act of 1978 was the culmination of a congressional review of the bankruptcy laws that began in the 1960s. It broadened and more clearly defined federal bankruptcy court jurisdiction and procedures for administration of estates and enhanced the powers of bankruptcy judges. Chapter 7, which governs liquidation, brought treatment of secured creditors into line with modern financing methods and the Uniform Commercial Code. Chapter 11 consolidated the reorganization treatment of businesses under a single procedure, eliminating the preliminary litigation concerning which reorganization rules to apply. The amendments of 1984 made bankruptcy courts adjuncts of U.S. district courts, which derive their power from Article III of the U.S. Constitution, in order to address the unconstitutionality of bestowing certain Article III powers on them.

Late-twentieth-century legislative issues in bankruptcy include the application of bankruptcy to in-

Landmark Bankruptcy Legislation

TITLE	YEAR ENACTED	REFERENCE NUMBER	DESCRIPTION
Bankruptcy Act of 1800	1800	2 Stat. 19–36	First national bankruptcy act; provided for involuntary bankruptcy.
Bankruptcy Act of 1841	1841	5 Stat. 442	Short-lived act that provided for both involuntary (merchants) and voluntary (individuals) bankruptcy.
Bankruptcy Act of 1867	1867	15 Stat. 227	Provided both voluntary and involuntary bankruptcy when debts were sufficiently large.
Bankruptcy Act of 1898	1898	30 Stat. 544	Retained state exemptions and allowed state as well as federal courts to administer.
The Chandler Bill of 1938	1938	52 Stat. 840	Revised and reorganized the 1898 act; added provisions on corporate reorganization and administrative protection for debtors.
Bankruptcy Reform Act of 1978	1978	92 Stat. 2549	Broadened and expanded the powers of the federal bankruptcy courts.
Bankruptcy Amendments and Federal Judgeship Act of 1984	1984	98 Stat. 333	Responded to unconstitutionality of conferring Article III judicial powers on Article I administrative bankruptcy judges.

tellectual property, such as patents, copyrights, and trademarks. Also of fundamental importance is the appropriateness and manner of the use of bankruptcy as a device for handling mass torts, such as those involving the Dalkon Shield or the asbestos cases, or for avoiding the effects of collective bargaining agreements, pension obligations, or environmental claims. It is likely that future Congresses will continue to legislate changes in U.S. bankruptcy law.

BIBLIOGRAPHY

Frimet, Rhett. "The Birth of Bankruptcy in the United States." *Commercial Law Journal* 96 (1991): 160.
Norton, William L., Jr., ed. *Norton Bankruptcy Law and Practice.* 2d ed. 1992.
Warren, Charles. *Bankruptcy in United States History.* 1935.

HAROLD F. SEE

BARGAINING. When individuals seek to achieve goals that require the cooperation of others but cannot compel cooperation by either violence or authority, they must bargain. Because Congress is a largely nonhierarchical organization, bargaining is a pervasive phenomenon. Typically this means that members of Congress must exchange favors, benefits, or other resources they control to induce cooperation from others. Members of Congress bargain to influence votes in committee and on the floor, to get committees to consider bills they favor, to persuade the leadership to schedule a floor vote, and to keep other members from offering obnoxious amendments. They bargain with interest groups to overcome objections to legislation. The House and Senate must bargain with one another to resolve differences between House and Senate versions of bills. To head off vetoes, Congress bargains with the president as bills work their way through the legislative process. This list, which could be extended indefinitely, suggests the importance of bargaining in the work of Congress.

To understand congressional bargaining, one must first comprehend the resources possessed by senators, representatives, and the president. The basic power that all members of Congress have is to say no—that is, to vote on the floor against legislation favored by others or to block it in committee. Committee and subcommittee chairmen have a more powerful "no" than most members by virtue of their influence over the agendas of committees and subcommittees. Members of the majority party leadership also have extraordinary bargaining power because of their control over the floor schedule. The rules of the Senate grant individuals exceptional power to block legislation by filibustering or objecting to unanimous consent requests. Insistent senators thus have the ability to "blackmail" the rest of the Senate by threatening to block popular legislation unless some provision they find objectionable is removed or modified, or a benefit for their state is included. Unless the demand is truly outrageous the Senate may have no practical choice but to submit to such "holdups." The veto provides the president with an extremely powerful tool with which to influence legislation; provided he has the support of a third of either chamber of Congress, he can single-handedly stop any bill. Thus Congress must normally consult carefully with the executive branch as a bill moves toward enactment, and serious objections must be accommodated.

To get a bill through the House or the Senate, one must persuade a majority of members to vote for it. How can they be induced to do so? Many votes will be won on the basis of ideological agreement or common interest. Where these factors fail to produce enough votes, however, other kinds of persuasion are required. Representatives trying to gather votes for their bill may trade their votes, promising to support other legislation in the future in exchange for a vote for their bill today. An interesting vote trade was the so-called corn-for-porn swap of 1991, in which supporters of farmers and of the National Endowment for the Arts (which was being hamstrung by censorship efforts) agreed to help each other's legislation. It is impossible to determine how much explicit vote-trading occurs, but it is undoubtedly a powerful element in congressional bargaining. Implicit vote-trading is also important. Some legislators reportedly will vote for any legislation favored by other members provided that it is not terribly expensive or offensive to their own constituents, expecting that favors will be returned someday.

In high-stakes issues where legislators are unwilling to trust that a favor will be returned, a useful tactic is "logrolling." Representatives bundle two or more legislative proposals that appeal to largely different constituencies and produce an enthusiastic majority coalition. This accounts for the marriage of farm price supports to food stamps at a time when agricultural assistance was threatened by dwindling rural representation. To obtain the votes of urban liberals who might otherwise have voted against farm subsidies, food stamps were added to the bill, creating an unbeatable combination.

What distribution of benefits will legislative bargaining produce? William Riker conjectured that rational legislators ought to form "minimum winning coalitions"—coalitions that distribute benefits to just over half of all districts and that are funded by all districts. While attractive on a theoretical level, this notion has found little empirical support. Far more often researchers have found patterns of universalism, whereby benefits are distrib-

uted very widely. Why do legislators not employ more cutthroat tactics? This question has not been answered definitively, but it is likely that the shifting, unstable nature of congressional coalitions leaves legislators unsure of the future, uncertain whether they might be in the minority on the next bill. Because one never knows whose assistance will be needed to pass a bill next week or next year, legislators are understandably reluctant to make enemies. Consequently, benefits are more commonly distributed according to norms of universalism.

The idea of a *reversion point* helps in understanding many kinds of bargaining, including much that occurs in Congress. A reversion point is the policy that will obtain should no agreement be reached and no legislation passed. The more odious a negotiator finds the reversion point, the greater his or her incentive to reach an agreement. If one side is disproportionately harmed by the reversion, it will naturally have less bargaining power and be forced to accept a bad bargain. In policy disputes where neither side finds the reversion point particularly objectionable, the incentive to compromise is scant, and it is likely that no agreement will be reached. Such was the situation surrounding the budget deficit in the 1980s. The enactment of the Gramm-Rudman-Hollings law to balance the budget was an innovative effort to shift the reversion point in budget politics to a policy universally regarded as disastrous—massive, across-the-board spending reductions—and thereby to inspire compromise. It did not work, mostly because in the process of enactment the reversion point was shifted from a policy that was unimaginable to one that was merely unpleasant.

[*See also* Blocs and Coalitions; Logrolling.]

BIBLIOGRAPHY

Ferejohn, John. "Logrolling in an Institutional Context: A Case Study of Food Stamp Legislation." In *Congress and Policy Change.* Edited by Gerald Wright, Leroy Rieselbach, and Lawrence Dodd. 1986.
Riker, William. *The Theory of Political Coalitions.* 1962.

JOHN B. GILMOUR

BARKLEY, ALBEN W. (1877–1956), senator from Kentucky, Democratic floor leader (1937–1949), vice president of the United States (1949–1953). Barkley was known for his intense loyalty to the Franklin D. Roosevelt administration, yet ironically he gained his greatest power and respect by resigning as majority leader in protest over one of Roosevelt's vetoes.

Born in a log house in western Kentucky, Barkley helped plow tobacco fields as a youth and worked his way through college and law school. As a young lawyer in Paducah, he entered politics in 1905 by campaigning on horseback to become prosecuting attorney and county judge. By 1912 he had won election to the House of Representatives, and in 1926 he took a Senate seat. Barkley's legendary talents as a stump-speaker led to his selection to deliver the 1932 Democratic keynote address. His speaking ability and conciliatory nature helped Barkley to become one of the top assistants of Senate Democratic leader Joseph T. Robinson during the early New Deal years.

In 1937, Robinson died unexpectedly during the congressional fight over Roosevelt's Court-packing plan, and Barkley announced his candidacy to succeed Robinson as majority leader. Mississippi senator Pat Harrison, chairman of the Finance Committee, was his chief opponent. Considering Harrison too conservative for the post, President Roosevelt intervened in the race with a public letter addressed personally to "dear Alben" as the acting leader, which implied his support for Barkley. White House aides worked backstage to pressure Democratic senators into voting for Barkley. When Barkley won by a single vote, it was widely perceived that he owed his position to the president. As a result, he became more an administration spokesman than a leader of the Senate.

Despite holding a majority of seventy-six of the ninety-six senators in 1937, the Democrats had split badly over Roosevelt's Court plan. The party's conservative and liberal wings began to diverge further over New Deal social and economic policies. As many of the president's programs were defeated, Barkley's unwavering support for the administration frequently left him voting in the minority, further undermining his standing as a leader. The press dubbed him "Bumbling Barkley," which he admitted stuck "like tar did to Br'er Rabbit."

As World War II approached, international issues restored Democratic unity in the Senate, while at the same time the war distracted the president from domestic issues. Barkley led successful fights for lend-lease legislation and restoration of the draft, but frequently complained of being neglected by the White House and of having his advice ignored. In 1944 he argued strongly against a presidential veto of a revenue bill, but Roosevelt went ahead and vetoed a bill he called tax relief "not for

ALBEN W. BARKLEY.   LIBRARY OF CONGRESS

the needy but the greedy." In an angry and dramatic Senate speech, Barkley urged the Senate to override the veto, if it had "any self-respect left," and then announced that he would resign as majority leader. The next day the Democratic caucus unanimously reelected him as leader. "By his one-vote margin in the 1937 contest when he was first elected leader, the impression was given, and it has been the impression ever since, that he spoke to us for the President," said Sen. Elbert D. Thomas (D-Utah). "Now that he has been unanimously elected, he speaks for us to the President."

Barkley's reelection elevated his status in the Senate but cost him the Democratic vice presidential nomination in 1944. A loyal party member, he continued to support President Roosevelt and his successor, Harry S. Truman. As minority leader during the Republican 80th Congress he worked especially hard to forge bipartisanship in foreign policy. Carrying his theory of Senate leadership to the extreme, he argued that "no matter what party is in power—no matter who is President—the majority leader of the Senate is expected to be the legislative spokesman of the administration."

In 1948, Barkley's long years of service were rewarded with his nomination and election as vice president. He was a popular vice president and was last holder of that office to preside routinely over Senate debates. He made a bid for the presidential nomination in 1952 that was blocked when organized labor pronounced him too old to make the race. Barkley returned to Kentucky and two years later ran once again for the Senate, beating the incumbent, John Sherman Cooper. He enjoyed taking a seat in the back row with the other freshman senators. "I'm glad to sit on the back row," he told an audience at Washington and Lee University in 1956. "For I would rather be a servant in the House of the Lord than to sit in the seats of the mighty." With those words he collapsed and died on the platform.

BIBLIOGRAPHY

Barkley, Alben W. *That Reminds Me.* 1954.
Davis, Polly Ann. *Alben Barkley: Senate Majority Leader and Vice President.* 1979.
Drury, Allen. *A Senate Journal, 1943–1945.* 1963.

DONALD A. RITCHIE

BAYARD, JAMES A., SR. (1767–1815), representative and senator from Delaware and a congressional Federalist leader. James Asheton Bayard, Sr., was reared in Philadelphia by his uncle, a merchant, after the early death of his parents. Graduating from Princeton in 1784, he began the practice of law in 1787 in Wilmington, Delaware, near his ancestral property in Cecil County, Maryland. His marriage in 1795 to Ann Bassett was critical to his career as it connected him to Richard Bassett and Joshua Clayton, leaders of the Federalist party in Delaware.

In winning election to the House of Representatives in 1796, 1798, and 1800, Bayard relied on Federalist strength in rural downstate Delaware, where the high standing of the Bassett family among the dominant Methodists gave him a special advantage. His oratorical talent, especially in extemporaneous debate, won him early attention, as, for instance, in his prominence among the House managers of the impeachment case against William Blount. His most notable role was in 1801, when he led moderate Federalists in casting blank ballots in the contested presidential election and thus permitting the choice of Thomas Jefferson over Aaron Burr. Bayard preferred Burr and had supported him through thirty-five ballots, but he was not will-

ing to persist in face of the danger to the Constitution and the Union that a drawn election might occasion. From Jefferson's friends he had received assurances, apparently not authorized by Jefferson, that the navy and the public credit would be preserved and that Federalist officials in minor positions who had performed their duties well would be retained.

After serving as unofficial House minority leader in the Seventh Congress, Bayard lost his seat in 1802 by fifteen votes. In 1804 he won a fourth term by a much larger margin but gave it up to accept election to the Senate. There he sought to defend U.S. commerce and the national bank and pleaded for evenhanded treatment of Great Britain and France. Resenting attacks on U.S. ships and seamen, he still hoped to prevent or postpone war. Once the War of 1812 began, however, he loyally supported all defense measures and subsequently was chosen by President James Madison to be part of a commission sent abroad in 1813 to negotiate peace. After completion of a peace treaty at Ghent in late 1814, Madison appointed Bayard minister to

JAMES A. BAYARD, SR. Engraving after a painting.
LIBRARY OF CONGRESS

Russia, but he rejected this post as he had previously rejected appointment as minister to France by President John Adams in 1801. Ill when he returned to the United States, Bayard died six days later, at the age of forty-eight.

Bayard lived well, enjoying cards, wine, and good food. He frequently arrived in Washington late in the session and left early, discouraged by the weakness of his party in the Senate. In Delaware his support of a strong Union, his castigation of a government that left the coast inadequately defended, and his agency in securing peace helped strengthen his party for the next decade.

BIBLIOGRAPHY

Borden, Morton. *The Federalism of James A. Bayard.* 1955.

Craven, Wesley Frank. "James A. Bayard." In *Princetonians, 1784–1790.* Edited by Wesley Frank Craven and Ruth L. Woodward. 1991. Pp. 4–9.

Munroe, John A. *Federalist Delaware, 1775–1815.* 2d ed. 1987.

JOHN A. MUNROE

BEAMAN, MIDDLETON (1877–1951), early advocate of a systematic approach to the drafting of laws, first House legislative counsel. A House staff member from 1919 to 1949, Beaman was long regarded as the dean of American legislative draftsmen. He earlier had served as law librarian of the Library of Congress and research director of the Legislative Drafting Research Fund at Columbia University, where his campaign for precisely written laws won him in 1916 an invitation to serve as a volunteer adviser to Congress. The idea of scientific development of statute law was novel only to Congress; such reform had been adopted years earlier by the Progressive legislatures of several states, most notably Wisconsin.

Beaman's initial assignment was to help the House Committee on Merchant Marine and Fisheries draft a proposal to create the United States Shipping Board. So useful were his suggestions for eliminating inconsistencies and improving the arrangement, expression, and additional details of the bill that other committees soon sought his services. Among legislators clamoring for his advice were former skeptics who originally had doubted that legal scholars had much to teach professional legislators about the writing of laws. In 1919, Congress formalized Beaman's role by creating, largely around him, the Legislative Drafting Service (later renamed the Office of the Legislative Counsel). The office was divided into two branches, with Beaman heading the House branch and a second draftsman, Thomas I. Parkinson, heading the Senate branch.

Meticulous, unassuming, and apolitical, Beaman epitomized the indispensable staff member. His crucial role in helping elected officials, regardless of political party, draft laws in precise legal language was rarely publicized. Even so, his imprint is on hundreds of statutes, including all revenue legislation enacted between 1917 and 1948 and two landmark measures in which he took special pride: the Securities Act of 1933 and the Social Security Act of 1935.

BIBLIOGRAPHY

Landis, James M. "The Legislative History of the Securities Act of 1933." *George Washington Law Review* (October 1959): 36–38.

Lee, Frederic P. "Office of the Legislative Counsel." *Columbia Law Review* (April 1929): 380–402.

McCarthy, Charles. *The Wisconsin Idea.* 1912. Pp. 194–216.

U.S. Congress. Joint Committee on the Organization of Congress. *Hearings on H. Con. Res. 18.* 79th Cong., 1st sess., 1945. See statement of Middleton Beaman, pp. 413–430.

DONALD C. BACON

BECKLEY, JOHN (1757–1807), first clerk of the House of Representatives and first librarian of Congress. John Beckley was elected clerk of the House of Representatives at the opening session of the First Congress on 1 April 1789. Clerk of the Virginia House of Delegates for the previous ten years, Beckley brought to his new post a long record of local and state government service.

Regarding Beckley's performance in Congress, Rep. John Page declared that "there never was a more correct and diligent clerk . . . who so happily united Accuracy with Dispatch" and noted "the Facility with which he could turn to any Paper which had ever been committed to his care." Present-day scholars and archivists are less satisfied with Beckley's system. An early practitioner of records management, Beckley decided what papers were worth keeping and what could be destroyed; in the process, he disposed of many original manuscript drafts that archivists and historians would prize today.

Beckley is even more notable for his involvement in the partisan politics of the young republic. An early champion of the Jeffersonian Republican party, Beckley was active in Pennsylvania politics. He directed the 1796 Republican presidential campaign for Thomas Jefferson in Pennsylvania, employing techniques that often were ahead of their time. Republicans carried fourteen of the fifteen electoral districts of Pennsylvania for Jefferson in 1796. However, John Adams won the presidency, and the Federalists elected a majority to Congress. One of their first acts was to replace Beckley as clerk of the House.

Four years later, when Jefferson was elected president and Jeffersonian Republicans gained control of Congress, they promptly restored Beckley to the House clerkship. In 1802, Jefferson appointed Beckley to the newly created post of librarian of Congress, an office that he held simultaneously with his clerkship until his death in 1807.

BIBLIOGRAPHY

Berkeley, Edmund, and Dorothy Berkeley. *John Beckley: Zealous Partisan in a Nation Divided.* 1973.

Cunningham, Noble E., Jr. "John Beckley: An Early American Party Manager." *William and Mary Quarterly* 3d ser., 13 (1956): 40–52.

DePauw, Linda Grant, ed. *Documentary History of the First Federal Congress of the United States of America.* Vol. 3 of *House of Representatives Journal,* pp. vii, x–xv, 7, 75–76n., 606. 1977.

NOBLE E. CUNNINGHAM, JR.

BELL, JOHN (1797–1869), representative and senator from Tennessee, candidate for president. Born into a pioneer Tennessee family, Bell received a good education and quickly became a prominent Nashville attorney. He was elected to the House of Representatives in 1827 and served for fourteen consecutive years, including one term as Speaker (1834–1835). Initially a supporter of Andrew Jackson, he broke with the president over the issue of the Bank of the United States and over the selection of Martin Van Buren as Jackson's successor. Bell became the leader of the Whig party in Tennessee, and in 1841 William Henry Harrison appointed him Secretary of war, but Bell soon resigned. He was elected U.S. senator in 1847 and held this post until 1859.

Throughout his congressional career the cautious, unimpassioned Bell was a leading southern moderate. Though a large slaveholder, he was never an ardent defender of the institution of slavery and distrusted both pro- and antislavery agitators in

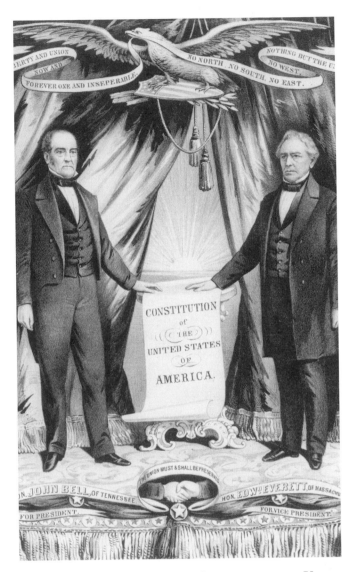

CAMPAIGN BANNER FOR THE CONSTITUTIONAL UNION PARTY, 1860. Presidential candidate John Bell, *left,* and vice presidential candidate Edward Everett. Lithograph on wove paper, published by Currier and Ives, 1860.
LIBRARY OF CONGRESS

both sections of the country. He voted against the gag rule in the House, upheld the power of Congress over slavery in the territories, and supported the Compromise of 1850. In 1854, he was one of the few southern members of Congress to oppose the Kansas-Nebraska Act, which he correctly predicted would reinvigorate the slavery controversy. Four years later he defied the instructions of the Tennessee legislature and voted against the proslavery Lecompton constitution for Kansas. His national outlook weakened him at home, and he was defeated for reelection.

After running unsuccessfully for president in 1860 on the Constitutional Union ticket, he retired from public life. He supported the Confederacy during the war and died in 1869. Like other advocates of conciliation, he was ultimately overwhelmed in the end by the growing sectional conflict.

BIBLIOGRAPHY

Caldwell, Joshua W. "John Bell of Tennessee." *American Historical Review* 4 (1899): 651–664.
Parks, Joseph Howard. *John Bell of Tennessee.* 1950.

WILLIAM E. GIENAPP

BENTON, THOMAS HART (1782–1858), Democratic senator (1821–1851) and representative (1853–1855) from Missouri. Benton was born near Hillsboro, North Carolina, and briefly attended the University of North Carolina. In 1801 his widowed mother moved her large family to a farm near Nashville, Tennessee, where Benton educated himself, taught school, and became a successful attorney. Elected to the Tennessee senate in 1809, Benton authored an extensive judicial reform program and sponsored laws to protect settlers on public land.

During the War of 1812 he recruited troops for Andrew Jackson's army and, as a colonel in charge of a regiment of volunteers, commanded a raft on Jackson's downriver expedition to Natchez. But Jackson's participation as second in a duel involving Benton's younger brother, Jesse, led to a gunfight in which Thomas participated and in which Jackson was badly wounded by Jesse.

To escape Jackson's powerful political enmity, Benton moved to frontier St. Louis, where he flourished as a lawyer and an editor. In 1820 he was elected one of Missouri's first U.S. senators. Along the way he fought two duels with political rival Charles Lucas—the second one fatal for his opponent. In 1820 he married Elizabeth MacDowell of Virginia. As a husband and father, Benton became known as a "house lamb" in contrast to his public reputation as a "street lion."

Benton and Jackson reconciled in 1824, and after 1828 Benton was Jackson's most devoted senatorial partisan against the Bank of the United States and in favor of Jackson's monetary and tariff policies. His support of hard money earned him the sobriquet "Old Bullion." He argued for the expansion of American settlement to the Pacific and later helped promote the western expeditions of his explorer

THOMAS HART BENTON.   LIBRARY OF CONGRESS

son-in-law, John C. Fremont. For thirty years Benton forcefully supported the principle of selling public land at low prices to actual settlers, and gradually lowering prices for land that remained unsold.

As a magnetic senator from the key border state of Missouri, Benton took an active, conspicuous part in the developing sectional controversy over slavery in the territories. He took the position that the nullification crisis of 1833 was a sham caused by then-senator John C. Calhoun's political ambitions. In 1844, Calhoun, now secretary of State, signed a treaty with Texas annexing it to the United States without settling the border dispute with Mexico and announced that Texas must be annexed to prevent a Texas-British agreement to abolish slavery in Texas. Benton led the opposition that prevented Senate ratification of the treaty, arguing that the threat of abolition was nonsense and that premature annexation—before the boundary and slavery questions were settled—would precipitate both war with Mexico and civil war in the United States.

After Congress annexed Texas by joint resolution and President James K. Polk initiated the Mexican War, however, Benton helped arrange the peaceful surrender of New Mexico and the nearly bloodless U.S. takeover of California. He also led the movement to achieve a compromise with Britain over the northern border of the Oregon Territory, fixing it at the forty-ninth parallel. Polk's efforts to make Benton the commanding general of the U.S. armies in Mexico were blocked by Congress, and the two men became irrevocably estranged when Benton's son-in-law Fremont was court-martialed for disobedience in California.

During the angry 1846 debates over the Wilmot Proviso, which would have prohibited slavery in the new territories acquired from Mexico, Benton, though he denounced the proviso, refused to support the southern demand for equal rights for slavery. He argued that where it already existed slavery was in no danger but that geography, climate, and the objections of territorial populations would make its expansion impossible. Ultimately, his conflicts with Calhoun and his refusal to obey Missouri's legislature on this issue led to his defeat for reelection in 1850. During the debates of 1850 he denounced the "omnibus" compromise bill of Henry Clay as a southern ploy to give most of New Mexico to Texas. When the bill was defeated by amendments that broke it into separate measures, however, he accepted most of the resulting bills that actually passed. In 1852 he was elected to the House, where he denounced the Kansas-Nebraska Act, which repealed the Missouri Compromise, as an unnecessary betrayal of a sacred trust.

Defeated for reelection in 1854, Benton turned to the history of the political system in which he had played so conspicuous a role. He published his widely read *Thirty Years' View* in two volumes in 1854 and 1856, and in 1857 offered the public a book-length refutation of the Supreme Court's Dred Scott decision. In 1856 he made twenty-one speeches against the presidential candidacy of his son-in-law Fremont because he feared that the election of a northern Republican president would cause secession and civil war. In 1858, though dying of cancer, he completed his sixteen-volume *Abridgment of the Debates in Congress.*

BIBLIOGRAPHY

Benton, Thomas Hart. *Historical and Legal Examination of the Dred Scott Case.* 1858.

Benton, Thomas Hart. *Thirty Years' View.* 2 vols. 1854, 1856.

Chambers, William N. *Old Bullion Benton: Senator from the New West.* 1856.

Fremont, Jessie Benton. *Souvenirs of My Time.* 1887.

Smith, Elbert B. *Magnificent Missourian: The Life of Thomas Hart Benton.* 1959.

ELBERT B. SMITH

BERGER, VICTOR L. (1860–1929), representative from Wisconsin and the first of only two members of the U.S. Congress to belong officially to a socialist party. Born in Transylvania (then part of the Austro-Hungarian Empire), Victor L. Berger immigrated to the United States in 1878. He became a Milwaukee newspaper editor and publisher and a founder of the Socialist Party of America. He built a strong base in the local German-dominated labor movement and was elected from the 5th Congressional District of Wisconsin in 1910 as the first socialist to serve in Congress.

Berger introduced legislation to create a system of public pensions and to establish social ownership and operation of major industries. Among other measures, he sponsored a resolution for a constitutional convention to further democratize the political system. Berger sat on the Committee on the District of Columbia, where he supported home rule and labor and consumer legislation. In foreign affairs, he espoused international solidarity and opposed immigration restrictions and the stationing of troops on the Mexican border. He sought to promote social-democratic ideas and reforms whose purpose was to modify capitalism toward collectivism.

Beginning in 1912, Berger lost three successive election campaigns to fusionist Democratic and Republican tickets. During World War I, he was convicted of conspiracy under the Espionage Act for his open opposition to and criticism of the war but was thereafter elected to the 66th Congress (1919–1920). The House excluded him and did so again after he won a special election to fill his seat. His conviction was overturned by the Supreme Court, and Berger was elected by his district, and seated, in 1922, 1924, and 1926. He continued to publicize his social-democratic concepts while always differentiating them from Bolshevism. He was defeated for reelection in 1928.

VICTOR L. BERGER. At the Socialist National Convention headquarters, Cleveland, Ohio, 6 July 1924.

BIBLIOGRAPHY

Berger, Victor L. *The Voice and Pen of Victor L. Berger.* 1929.
Miller, Sally M. *Victor Berger and the Promise of Constructive Socialism, 1910–1920.* 1973.

SALLY M. MILLER

BEVERIDGE, ALBERT J. (1862–1927), senator from Indiana, one of the insurgent Republicans during the presidency of William Howard Taft, and a distinguished historian. Albert Jeremiah Beveridge practiced law in Indianapolis, Indiana, until 1899, when a skillful lobbying effort brought him victory in the Republican legislative caucus and

thus election to the U.S. Senate as one of its youngest members ever. He was reelected in 1905.

Beveridge first made his mark as an advocate of U.S. imperialism. The depression of the 1890s had convinced him that continued prosperity required United States access to new markets and investment opportunities abroad. He was in the forefront of the clamor for war with Spain in 1898, championed U.S. acquisition of the Philippines, and even favored retention of Cuba. He could be a political maverick, as when he broke with Senate leaders to support free trade with Puerto Rico in 1900.

After Theodore Roosevelt ascended to the White House in 1901, Beveridge tied his political future to the president's coattails. During Roosevelt's first term, however, the president—and Beveridge—usually cooperated with the party's congressional leaders. The first signs of a more independent stance came in 1906, when Beveridge sponsored, and led the fight for, the Meat Inspection Act of 1906 and a national child-labor bill to prohibit the interstate shipment of child-made goods. He further aroused old guard suspicions by calling for tariff revision and for the establishment of an independent tariff commission to depoliticize tariff making.

The turning point in Beveridge's political career came when he joined the insurgent Republican revolt in 1909 against the Payne-Aldrich tariff bill. He remained on the insurgent side in the controversy between Gifford Pinchot and Richard A. Ballinger regarding conservation policy, the battle over new railroad-rate regulation that resulted in the Mann-Elkins Act of 1910, and the fight concerning the postal-savings-bank measure.

The unpopularity of the Taft administration, combined with factionalism in the Indiana Republican party, resulted in the Democrats' winning control of the state legislature in the 1910 elections. Beveridge consequently lost his Senate seat. He not only supported Roosevelt for the 1912 Republican presidential nomination, but followed him into the Progressive party. One of the more powerful orators of his generation, he was the keynote speaker at the new party's national convention in 1912, its candidate for governor of Indiana that year, and its Senate nominee in 1914.

Beveridge was preeminently an American nationalist. The primary aim of his brand of progressivism was to promote national efficiency and cohesion. By 1916, the reform agenda of the Progressive party had moved beyond what he was willing to support, and he returned to the Republican party. Committed to retaining a free hand for the United

ALBERT J. BEVERIDGE.

States in foreign affairs, he was an irreconcilable opponent of U.S. membership in the League of Nations.

Turning to writing history after his Senate service, Beveridge published the first two volumes of his majestic biography of Chief Justice John Marshall in 1916 and the last two volumes in 1919. The work remains the standard life of Marshall. In 1922 Beveridge again sought congressional office, winning the Indiana Republican senatorial primary; however, he lost in the general election. Before his death on 27 April 1927, Beveridge substantially completed the first two volumes of a planned four-volume biography of Abraham Lincoln.

BIBLIOGRAPHY

Bowers, Claude G. *Beveridge and the Progressive Era.* 1932.
Braeman, John. *Albert J. Beveridge: American Nationalist.* 1971.

JOHN BRAEMAN

BIBLIOGRAPHY. *For a review of sources on the study of Congress, see* Congress, *article on* Bibliographical Guide.

BICAMERALISM. The United States Congress, like most of the world's legislatures, is a bicameral institution, that is, composed of two chambers. The U.S. Congress consists of a House of Representatives, whose members represent small districts and serve two-year terms, and a Senate, whose members are elected by statewide constituencies and serve six-year terms. Seats in the House are apportioned among the states on the basis of population, but each state, regardless of population, is represented by two senators. Unlike the chambers of bicameral legislatures in most other countries, the House and the Senate are essentially equal in power. Neither can enact laws on its own; the consent of both chambers is required for all legislation. There are, though, some differences in their powers; revenue legislation must originate in the House, and the Senate alone ratifies treaties and approves appointments of federal officials and judges.

That Congress would have a bicameral structure was barely a subject of debate at the Constitutional Convention, although the precise details of the arrangement were discussed extensively. Bicameralism was a foregone conclusion because it served three important goals, each subscribed to by most Convention delegates.

The first goal was to recognize the federal structure that was to be created by the new Constitution. By providing each state with equal representation in the Senate, the concept of the new nation as a union of federating states was emphasized. Further, the interests of the smaller states would have greater protection than they would receive in the House, where representation was to be based on population. Finally, the selection of senators by state legislatures suggested that the Senate represented the state governments themselves, with the people represented in the House.

A second goal of bicameralism was to protect against what many of the Founders believed to be the dangers of a legislature elected by the people. Such a body, James Madison wrote, draws "all powers into its impetuous vortex," is disposed "to sacrifice the aggregate interest to the local views of their constituents," and tends to disregard "the rules of justice and the rights of the minor party." Therefore, the power of the House needed to be checked, and bicameralism, along with a presidency electorally independent of Congress, were to be the primary checks. It was inevitable, said Madison, that the legislature would dominate in a republican form of government, but "the remedy for this inconvenience is to divide the legislature into different branches." Thus, Edmund Randolph promised, the unelected Senate would provide a cure for the "evils" that arose from "the turbulence and follies of democracy."

A third goal of bicameralism was to increase the likelihood of better government. Not only would the Senate protect against the democratic excesses of the House, but as Madison said, the Senate would act with "more coolness, with more system, and with more wisdom than the popular branch." It would be wiser because its members would not be elected by the public at large, but rather by state legislators who presumably would pick men of stature. Its small size would make it less chaotic than the larger House—more like a king's privy

council than a legislature, some believed—thereby facilitating sober deliberation. Its members would serve six-year rather than two-year terms and would therefore be more able than members of the House to resist the pressures of public opinion. And senators would likely be men of substance, people who, in Gouverneur Morris's words, would "have great personal property" and exhibit "aristocratic pride." Better government decisions would result because, as George Washington suggested, the Senate would function in a manner analogous to the saucer into which one poured one's coffee; the saucer cools the hot coffee as the Senate would cool the hot passions of the House.

Of the two chambers, the role of the Senate has changed most dramatically over the years. Contrary to the hopes of the Founders, the Senate in its early days was clearly inferior to the House, primarily because it lacked democratic legitimacy. The principle of appointment of senators by state legislatures began to erode as early as the 1830s, however, and by 1913, when popular election of the Senate was constitutionally mandated, more than half of the states had already adopted procedures that provided the functional equivalent. Also, the end of the United States' geographic isolation in the beginning of the twentieth century brought a greatly enhanced role to the Senate because of its special powers over foreign policy. And, as the responsibilities of the federal government increased, the Senate's role in the appointment process became more significant as well. Finally, modern mass media increased the public importance of the Senate. Because there are fewer senators than representatives, members of the Senate were more visible than their House counterparts and could more readily be turned into national figures by the media.

Although the Senate has come to be as democratic as the House, important distinctions between the two chambers persist, distinctions attributable primarily to the smaller size of the Senate, the longer terms that its members serve, and the larger constituencies that they usually represent. Because of its size, the Senate has procedures that enhance the power of its individual members. Unlimited debate is only one example of Senate procedures that allow a minority of senators to bring the legislative process to a halt. The House, in contrast, has a more complex and rigid set of procedures that curbs the autonomy of its individual members. Because of its large size, the House also depends heavily on its committee system and is more likely to be characterized by strong party leadership. Senators, in contrast, demonstrate an extreme reluctance to be led, either by their committees or their party leaders.

Popular election has made the Senate as electorally volatile as the House and, as a result, senators have become more attentive to constituency and electoral pressures than in the past. Nonetheless, there is reason to believe that long electoral cycles and large constituencies enhance the capacity of senators to think and act on the basis of long-term policy considerations and with a national perspective.

But there is no evidence that the Senate in particular provides the braking action on unwise or controversial legislation that the Founders had anticipated. Rather, it is bicameralism itself—with its requirement that both chambers approve of legislation—that slows down, inhibits, moderates, and often prevents government action. More positively, it can be argued that the dual consideration required by bicameralism enhances the deliberative nature of the Congress by providing more opportunities for the gathering of information and the detection of errors. In that case, bicameralism would produce, as the Founders hoped, better—albeit slower—government decision making.

[*See also* Checks and Balances; House of Representatives; Legislative Branch; Representative; Senate; Senator.]

BIBLIOGRAPHY

Baker, Ross K. *House and Senate*. 1989.

Carmines, Edward G., and Lawrence C. Dodd. "Bicameralism in Congress: The Changing Partnership." In *Congress Reconsidered*. 3d ed. Edited by Lawrence C. Dodd and Bruce I. Oppenheimer. 1985.

Fenno, Richard F., Jr. *The United States Senate: A Bicameral Perspective*. 1982.

Longley, Lawrence D., and Walter J. Oleszek. *Bicameral Politics: Conference Committees in Congress*. 1989.

Page, Benjamin I. "Cooling the Legislative Tea." In *American Politics and Public Policy*. Edited by Walter Dean Burnham and Martha Wagner Weinberg. 1978.

MICHAEL L. MEZEY

BICENTENNIAL OF CONGRESS. A series of commemorative events and projects, conceived and planned under the guidance of separate Senate and House commissions, marked the two-hundredth anniversary of the convening of the First Federal Congress on 4 March 1789.

The Senate established a Commission on the Bi-

centennial of the U.S. Senate in 1983 with Sen. Robert C. Byrd as chairman, and the House established a Commission on the Bicentenary of the U.S. House of Representatives in 1985 with Rep. Corinne C. (Lindy) Boggs as chairman. The purpose of these commissions was to oversee publications, exhibits, and ceremonies designed to illuminate the two-hundred-year history of Congress.

Congress authorized a number of publications as part of the observance. These include *The Biographical Directory of the United States Congress, 1774–1989: Bicentennial Edition*, which contains sketches of the more than eleven thousand individuals who have served in the House and Senate, including the Continental Congresses; Sen. Robert C. Byrd's *The Senate, 1789–1989: Addresses on the History of the United States Senate*; Sen. Bob Dole's *Historical Almanac of the U.S. Senate*, a guide to the research collections of former members of the House and Senate; *Black Americans in Congress, 1870–1989*; *Women in Congress, 1917–1989*; *The Origins of the House of Representatives: A Documentary Record*; and *The U.S. Capitol: A Brief Architectural History*. The Library of Congress mounted three major exhibits while the Smithsonian Institution's National Portrait Gallery featured one on the First Federal Congress.

On 16 July 1987, as part of the commemoration of the bicentennial of the Constitution, more than two hundred members of the House and Senate journeyed to Philadelphia on a special train to take part in ceremonies at Independence National Historical Park commemorating the "Great Compromise" in the Federal Convention of 1787 that resulted in the creation of the House and Senate. The senators and representatives convened in the same room in Independence Hall in which the Federal Convention had met, where they held a joint ceremony. The senators and representatives then proceeded to their respective chambers in Congress Hall.

On 2 March 1989 the House and Senate held a joint meeting in the House chamber, during which the leaders of both bodies spoke on the two-hundred-year history of Congress. The session included the reading of a poem prepared for the occasion by Howard Nemerov, poet laureate of the United States, and an address by the historian David McCullough. The ceremony included unveiling designs for commemorative postage stamps and three commemorative coins. By law, the surcharges from the coin sales went to the U.S. Capitol Preservation Commission to preserve the art and architecture of the Capitol for future generations.

Other features of the observance included a ninety-minute documentary underwritten by Ameritech, *The Congress: The History and Promise of Representative Government,* prepared by filmmaker Ken Burns, which premiered at the National Theater in Washington, D.C., and appeared on the Public Broadcasting System, and this multivolume *Encyclopedia of the United States Congress,* underwritten in part by the Commission on the Bicentennial of the U.S. Constitution.

The congressional activities in support of the bicentennial were in marked contrast to those one hundred years earlier. While the nation celebrated the centennial of the Constitution from 1886 to 1890 with parades and speeches, most of the activities took place in Philadelphia and New York. Congress failed to pass a bill to provide financial support and federal commissioners to cooperate with the Constitutional Centennial Commission under the leadership of former Rep. John A. Kasson of Iowa. On 4 March 1889, the centennial anniversary of Congress, the focus of the day's events was the inauguration of President Benjamin Harrison. On 11 December that year, Congress met in joint session to commemorate the centennial of George Washington's inauguration; it featured an oration by Chief Justice Melville W. Fuller.

BIBLIOGRAPHY

Baker, Richard Allen. "Documenting the History of the United States Senate." *Government Publications Review* 10 (1983): 415–426.

Kammen, Michael. *A Machine That Would Go of Itself: The Constitution in American Culture.* 1986.

U.S. House of Representatives. *Final Report of the Commission on the Bicentenary of the United States House of Representatives.* 101st Cong., 2d sess., 1990. H. Rept. 101-815.

U.S. Senate. *Final Report, Study Group on the Commemoration of the United States Senate Bicentenary.* 98th Cong., 1st sess., 1983. S. Rept. 98-13.

RAYMOND W. SMOCK

BIFFLE, LES (1889–1966), secretary of the U.S. Senate and key legislative strategist in the Truman administration. Raised in Piggott, Arkansas, the son of a local official, Leslie Biffle attended business school and in 1909 moved to Washington as secretary to Democratic representative Robert B. Macon. With Macon's retirement in 1913, Biffle secured a Senate patronage post, courtesy of his state's newly elected senator, Joseph T. Robinson. In 1925, Robinson, who had become Senate Demo-

cratic leader, named Biffle assistant party secretary. When the Democrats took control of the Senate in 1933, Robinson advanced Biffle to the role of majority secretary.

The dapper five-foot-eight-inch secretary proved to be an astute legislative vote counter and political operative. At once gregarious and poker-faced, Biffle won and kept confidences among senators of both parties. A master of the Senate's obscure folkways, the courtly Biffle regularly assisted new Democratic senators, including Harry S. Truman, who entered the Senate in 1935. The two men, close in age, political views, and modest demeanor, developed an intimate friendship.

In February 1945, the Senate unanimously elected Biffle as its secretary; two months later his considerable influence soared when Truman became president. The president relied on Biffle for his accurate and frank political counsel. During the 1948 presidential campaign, disguised in overalls and straw hat, Biffle toured several midwestern states to test sentiment behind formal polls predicting Truman's defeat. He correctly advised Truman that he had a "fighting chance." Biffle's forty-four-year congressional career ended in 1953 with the conclusion of Truman's presidency and the return of the Senate to Republican control.

BIBLIOGRAPHY

Barcella, Ernest. "They Call Him Mr. Baffle." *Collier's,* 29 January 1949.

Bell, Jack. "When Biffle's Phone Rings He Knows Who It Is." *Washington Star,* 4 March 1951.

Wood, Lewis. "Sage of Capitol Hill." *New York Times,* 26 August 1945.

RICHARD A. BAKER

BILBO, THEODORE G. (1877–1947), Democratic senator from Mississippi, ardent New Dealer, and archangel of white supremacy. Bilbo "was, is and evermore shall be," said his only biographer Wigfall Green, "God or Satan. He dwelled—dwells—in heaven or hell, but never in limbo." Born in the last year of Reconstruction, Bilbo died barely eleven months before his party—the Democratic party of the solid South—first adopted a civil rights plank in its national platform. Class conflict, within the context of white supremacy, dominated the single-party polity of the age of Jim Crow in the South, and Bilbo mastered the contours of that political landscape as perhaps no one else did. His first Senate term (1935–1941) encompassed the high tide of New Deal reform while his second (1941–1947) coincided with the first stirrings of a national repudiation of southern racial sensibilities. In ardent defense of the former and contemptuous assault on the latter, Bilbo's political passion was, as always, unrestrained.

Bilbo came to the Senate with a remarkably successful record in state politics and an unsavory reputation for sexual and financial scandal. A peerless practitioner of earthy stump oratory and a tireless champion of progressive reform, he brushed aside the ubiquitous attacks upon his character, casting himself as a martyr to the cause of Mississippi's "runt pigs," the poor white tenants, sharecroppers, and one-mule farmers whose votes first made him state senator (1908–1912), then lieutenant governor (1912–1916), and twice governor (1916–1920, 1928–1932) before electing him to the U.S. Senate in 1934.

In Washington, Bilbo displayed a relentless loyalty to Franklin D. Roosevelt's New Deal. His unflinching support for relief spending, social security, public housing, labor legislation, corporate regulation, redistributive taxes, public power, executive reorganization, and judiciary reform would have been the envy of any urban liberal. As a member of the Committee on Agriculture and Forestry, he was particularly vigilant in protecting the interests of his rural constituents. He was an early supporter of tenant resettlement, but the only significant legislation he sponsored that passed was a 1938 act creating regional agricultural research laboratories.

During World War II Bilbo found the atmosphere of national unity less conducive to his combative style than the class politics on which he had always thrived. While generally supporting the administration's war policies, he grew increasingly uneasy with the incipient civil rights sentiment that was taking root, especially within the Democratic party.

During the 1940s, the predictable stridence of Bilbo's rhetoric made him an irresistible target for growing national outrage against racial intolerance. He fought anti–poll tax and antilynching measures, helped talk the Wartime Committee on Fair Employment Practice to death with a marathon filibuster in 1946, and resurrected a bill he had introduced in 1939 to divert relief funds to a scheme of "voluntary repatriation" of American blacks to West Africa. The publication in 1947 of his volatile *Take Your Choice: Separation or Mongrelization* earned him the inglorious crown of undisputed potentate of white supremacy.

Facing reelection in 1946, Bilbo for the first time made race the central issue in a victorious campaign that sparked two separate investigations of his conduct. The Senate Special Committee to Investigate Senatorial Campaign Expenditures, in a strictly partisan vote, exonerated him of charges that his racist invective had intimidated black voters. The Senate Special Committee Investigating the National Defense Program, however, uncovered evidence of his questionable dealings with war contractors that provoked an effort to deny Bilbo his seat. His imminent death from cancer led to a compromise that allowed him to retain his Senate salary but refused him the oath of office for a third term. He died on 21 August 1947, an enduring symbol, not of the economic liberalism he championed for so long, but of the racial bigotry that consumed him in the end.

BIBLIOGRAPHY

Green, A. Wigfall. *The Man Bilbo*. 1963.
Morgan, Chester M. *Redneck Liberal: Theodore G. Bilbo and the New Deal*. 1985.

CHESTER M. MORGAN

BILL OF RIGHTS. The first ten amendments to the U.S. Constitution were fowarded to the states by the First Congress in 1789 and ratified two years later by the necessary number of states to become "the supreme law of the land." The events preceding their ratification form an essential part of the history of human rights in the British colonies that in 1776 became the United States.

Background. Although there is mention in the Magna Carta of 1215 of curbs on the use of arbitrary power, the common law of England was long the chief protector of an Englishman's right to hold property and live peaceably. Common law as it evolved assumed the right of an accused person to have a jury trial, to have counsel, and to be protected against excessive fines and bails. But in most cases, the way a prisoner was treated and the punishment meted out by the court was often a matter of local circumstances and the quality of the legal counsel.

The history of English law is essentially the story of a society's gradual transition from a feudal condition to modernity. This means that for many centuries little change took place. But by 1640, a clash between Charles I and Parliament resulted in civil war; the central issues of the conflict were an Englishman's right to his liberty of person, his right to own and keep property, and his right to express himself on public matters. The Petition of Right (1628) had forced Charles to acknowledge that no freeman could lose his life, liberty, or property without the due process of law; illegal and arbitrary demands for money were to end; and the obnoxious practice of quartering sailors and soldiers in private households was forbidden.

Charles clashed with Parliament and with the New Army led by Oliver Cromwell, and the king forfeited his life. Out of the tumult of civil war that followed, the Glorious Revolution of 1688 created an atmosphere that allowed an ordinary Englishman more personal freedom than the citizen of any other country enjoyed. Within two decades the encrusted arbitrary machinery of government had been overhauled to eliminate the Star Chamber (with its secrecy, arbitrary arrests, and torture), and defendants in criminal trials were granted the right to remain silent or at least not give self-incriminating testimony.

Other important concessions were wrung from Charles II and James II. The Toleration Act helped end strife between Protestants and Catholics, and in the 1689 Bill of Rights Parliament laid down certain principles for the future governance of England: the royal authority was limited and citizens were guaranteed the right to bail, freedom from cruel or unusual punishments, and the right to petition against grievances. These were specific guarantees, proclaimed by Parliament to be the supreme law of England, and their enactment showed the huge gulf between medieval law and the concern for a citizen's rights that had emerged from the battle between headstrong monarchs and the elected representatives serving in Parliament. A series of common law decisions emerged at the same time to make the bailing of prisoners held in custody (habeas corpus) a routine rather than an unusual circumstance to ensure that trials were held in the vicinity of the alleged crime, and to protect people from being tried twice for the same offense (double jeopardy).

British colonists in North America accepted the protection of the new laws; in some cases they themselves had dealt with similar matters earlier on. In colony after colony, laws were enacted by the colonial assemblies to provide a broad spectrum of personal liberties. Some curbs on the rights of Catholics remained on the statute books, but when the Stamp Act crisis erupted in 1765, most of the British colonies in North America had laws conferring on colonial subjects the same rights they would have possessed as native-born Englishmen.

When Parliament began searching for new sources of tax revenues after the expensive French and Indian War, a clash with American lawmakers brought an unexpected wave of dissension that rocked the established order. An informal body, the Stamp Act Congress of 1765, met to form a protest addressed to George III and "both Houses of Parliament." Resolutions were passed to warn Parliament that Americans believed their most fundamental liberties were involved, and among the jeopardized rights they catalogued were trial by jury, the right of petition, and the "full and free enjoyment of their rights and liberties."

The aftermath of the Boston Tea Party brought on a crisis that was resolved only by the outbreak of fighting in April 1775. Before those first shots of the American Revolution were fired, colonial leaders had reacted to British oppression by calling for a Continental Congress to give voice to their protests against the usurpations of Parliament.

One firebrand who served in the Continental Congress, Samuel Adams, pushed his colleagues for a propaganda weapon that would focus on human rights. "Should America hold up her own Importance to the Body of the Nation and at the same Time agree in one general Bill of Rights," Adams suggested, "the Dispute might be settled on the Principles of Equity and Harmony restored between Britain and the Colonies." In October 1774 Congress had issued a "Declaration of Rights" that listed royal or parliamentary errors and enumerated the rights claimed by British Americans. Ten in number, these rights included the right "to life, liberty, and property"; the safeguards provided by the common law for accused persons; the right "peaceably to assemble"; and the right to petition for redress of grievances. With an echo from the Glorious Revolution in England, the delegates also insisted that "the keeping [of] a standing army in these colonies, in times of peace . . . is against the law."

Leaders from all of the thirteen colonies met in Philadelphia again in 1775. While the Continental Congress debated the next move, all the colonies used their legislatures to keep a semblance of government in place. In Virginia, a convention had replaced the old House of Burgesses, and its elected members met in May 1776 at Williamsburg. With what now seems to be blinding speed, the convention called for a complete break with Great Britain and the establishment of an independent nation. It appointed a committee to draft a constitution and

declaration of rights for the "free state of Virginia."
George Mason, a Virginia planter and patriot, drafted a plan that was soon enacted and broadcast to
other states, with a prefatory declaration of rights
and a constitution calling for a republic with executive, legislative, and judicial branches.

Formally proclaimed on 12 June 1776, the Virginia Declaration of Rights set the tone and format
for all subsequent bills of rights. Mason's list of sixteen rights, which was reported by a committee
and passed by the makeshift legislature, began with
the statement "that all men are by nature free and
independent" and cannot be deprived of their lives
or liberties or the means of "pursuing and obtaining happiness and safety." The declaration went on
to call for free elections of representatives, to repeat the safeguards for accused persons embedded
in the common law, and to call for trial by jury, a
free press, a ban on standing armies in peacetime,
and "the free exercise of religion." James Madison,
a fledgling delegate, helped broaden the scope of
the article on religious freedom and thus established his credentials as a libertarian.

Copies of the Virginia Bill of Rights were printed
in newspapers from Georgia to Massachusetts, and
as the last tie with Great Britain was legally severed
in July 1776, most of the new "free and independent" states passed laws similar to those Mason
and his committee had written. By 1781 nearly all
the former colonies either had explicit laws creating bills of rights or prefaces to their constitutions
embodying those principles regarded as basic
human liberties.

The Constitution and the First Congress. This
lawmaking process was completed by 1781, and the
war ended in 1783, but the United States of America was a new nation moving in uncharted waters.
Farm prices fell, taxes went unpaid, and commerce
languished when England imposed punishing duties on American commodities. Searching for a solution to the new nation's dilemma, the Virginia
legislature issued a call for all states to meet in
Philadelphia in May 1787 to consider ways of revising the Articles of Confederation, which had provided a loose-knit interim government for thirteen
"sovereign" states. Virginia sent a strong delegation, headed by George Washington and guided by
Madison, who had devised a plan for a republican
form of government that he thought could cure the
ills afflicting the country. Madison's plan, which
dealt with the specific shortcomings of the
makeshift confederation, did not mention a bill of
rights.

The debates at the Constitutional Convention
lasted until mid September, when a final draft was
in preparation. Some delegates had mentioned the
rights of accused persons, and in piecemeal form
the ban on bills of attainder and ex post facto laws
were added, along with a prohibition on religious
tests for officeholders. The writ of habeas corpus
was not to be suspended except when "the public
safety may require it."

On 12 September George Mason, perhaps with
lingering memories of May 1776, called for the addition of a bill of rights, observing that "it would
give great quiet to the people." Impatient delegates
quickly squelched Mason's motion, which lost by a
unanimous vote. Over the next few days, Mason
and several other delegates tried to insert provisions for a free press and civil jury trials, but their
overall strategy failed. When the delegates signed
the engrossed Constitution on 17 September 1787,
Mason and two others abstained despite last-
minute efforts to persuade them that a bill of rights
was unnecessary.

The ensuing contest for the Constitution's ratification proved closer than its supporters had reckoned. Mason wrote his *Objections to this Constitution* before he left Philadelphia, and its opening
phrase became the tocsin of the opposition. "There
is no Declaration of Rights," Mason began, and his
phrase became the battle cry of Anti-Federalists
who wanted either to alter the Constitution or to
reject it outright. Early in 1788, Federalists supporting ratification realized their tactical error and
began talking about the enactment of a bill of
rights once the Constitution had been ratified.
Madison not only joined Alexander Hamilton and
John Jay in writing *The Federalist* to counteract dissension but was forced to concede that a bill of
rights might be needed to calm apprehension. At
the Virginia ratifying convention, Madison made
his compromise explicit, and the Constitution was
narrowly ratified by Virginia and the other key
state, New York.

When the contest was settled, Madison heard
from his friend Thomas Jefferson, then in Paris,
who assured him that a bill of rights was needed. "I
hope . . . a bill of rights will be formed to guard
the people against the federal government, as they
are already guarded against their state governments in most instances," Jefferson observed.

Madison got the point and acknowledged the
promised bill of rights when he campaigned for a
seat in the First Congress. Opposed by James Monroe, Madison promised voters in his district that he

would work for "such amendments as will . . . guard essential rights, and will render certain vexatious abuses of power impossible." To erase all doubt, Madison said that he would seek amendments protecting "the rights of Conscience in the fullest latitude, the freedom of the press, trials by jury, security against general warrants &c."

Voters reacted by electing him by a comfortable margin, and Madison went to the First Congress prepared to fulfill his campaign promise. But he soon learned that most other members gave a bill of rights a low priority. Since debates in the House of Representatives were printed in newspapers, Madison soon learned of the impatience in his district and elsewhere because there had been no mention of amendments encompassing a bill of rights. On 25 May 1789 Madison announced on the House floor that he would soon be offering the promised amendments. Despite some grumbling, he kept his word, and on 8 June he presented amendments covering all the personal liberties brought forward during the ratification struggle.

Madison's proposed list added to the usual provisions—for a free press and freedom of speech and of religion—the right to petition, key provisions relating to justice for accused criminals, and two amendments to increase congressional representation and prohibit members of Congress from raising their salaries. He confronted critics who said a bill of rights was not needed by insisting that such rights would have "a salutary effect against the abuse of power. If they are incorporated into the constitution, independent tribunals of justice will consider themselves in a peculiar manner the guardians of those rights."

Madison had an easier time convincing the general public that a bill of rights was needed than he did his fellow members of Congress. His original idea was to place the amendments into the Constitution as part of the original plan, but this proposal was soon dropped. A committee was appointed 21 July to draft the amendments; the committee reported a week later, and the debate over each proposed amendment began. A list of seventeen amendments survived. The fourteenth, which Madison said he valued above all others, provided that "no State shall infringe the right of trial by Jury in criminal cases, nor the rights of conscience, nor the freedom of speech, or of the press."

On 24 August 1789 the House of Representatives sent the seventeen amendments to the Senate. Extensive debate and and even more extensive nitpicking led to the dropping of Madison's favorite fourteenth proposal, which made states responsible for personal rights, and the melding together of the several articles into one amendment dealing with personal liberties with the prefatory clause "Congress shall make no law," which clarified the federal government's role in preserving a citizen's personal liberty. A joint conference worked out a compromise that left twelve amendments, and by 28 September both houses had passed this trimmed-down version, keeping the first two to deal with congressional matters, and the proposed amendments were sent to the state legislatures for ratification.

More than two years were required to complete the business of ratifying the Bill of Rights. Former opponents of the Constitution (such as George Mason) were won over by the proposals, but a segment of the Anti-Federalist opposition dismissed the amendments as "good for nothing." Sen. William Grayson of Virginia held that view, writing in a letter to Patrick Henry, "I believe as many others do, that they will do more harm than benefit." Henry was all-powerful in the Virginia legislature, and his faction managed to argue over the amendments until all but one of the necessary states had ratified.

North Carolina and Rhode Island, both of which had so far remained outside the Union because of their delayed ratifications, finally accepted the Constitution together with the amendments. Meanwhile, however, Vermont had been admitted as a state, which meant that eleven states were required to adopt the amendments before they became law. The first two amendments were dropped in the ratifying process, so that what had been the third amendment now became the first in the renumbering that took place in Secretary of State Jefferson's office. Jefferson decided that the ten amendments became effective on the date of the Virginia ratification, 15 December 1791. (Three states that had never acted on the proposals made a ceremonial gesture of ratification in 1941, and the "lost" amendment dealing with congressional salaries was revived and finally ratified in 1992.)

In a sense the whole ratification process had been ceremonial, for in 1791 the Bill of Rights was more symbol than reality. Before the decade was over, Congress had passed the Sedition Act proscribing freedom of speech and shackling newspapers during the Quasi-War with France of 1798–1800. Vigorous prosecutions of dissident editors led to jail sentences. Jefferson and Madison responded with the Kentucky and Virginia resolutions, hoping that state legislatures would call the obnoxious law un-

Congress of the United States,

begun and held at the City of New-York, on

Wednesday the Fourth of March, one thousand seven hundred and eighty nine.

THE Convention of a number of the States, having at the time of their adopting the Constitution, expressed a desire, in order to prevent misconstruction or abuse of its powers, that further declaratory and restrictive clauses should be added: And as extending the ground of public confidence in the Government, will best ensure the beneficent ends of its institution

RESOLVED by the Senate and House of Representatives of the United States of America, in Congress assembled, two thirds of both Houses concurring, that the following Articles be proposed to the Legislatures of the several States, as amendments to the Constitution of the United States, all, or any of which Articles, when ratified by three fourths of the said Legislatures, to be valid to all intents and purposes, as part of the said Constitution: viz.

ARTICLES in addition to, and amendment of the Constitution of the United States of America, proposed by Congress, and ratified by the Legislatures of the several States, pursuant to the fifth Article of the original Constitution.

Article the first. After the first enumeration required by the first Article of the Constitution, there shall be one Representative for every thirty thousand, until the number shall amount to one hundred, after which, the proportion shall be so regulated by Congress, that there shall be not less than one hundred Representatives, nor less than one Representative for every forty thousand persons, until the number of Representatives shall amount to two hundred, after which the proportion shall be so regulated by Congress, that there shall not be less than two hundred Representatives, nor more than one Representative for every fifty thousand persons.

Article the second. No law, varying the compensation for the services of the Senators and Representatives, shall take effect, until an election of Representatives shall have intervened.

Article the third. Congress shall make no law respecting an establishment of religion, or prohibiting the free exercise thereof; or abridging the freedom of speech, or of the press; or the right of the people peaceably to assemble, and to petition the Government for a redress of grievances.

Article the fourth. A well regulated militia, being necessary to the security of a free State, the right of the people to keep and bear arms shall not be infringed.

Article the fifth. No Soldier shall, in time of peace be quartered in any house, without the consent of the owner, nor in time of war, but in a manner to be prescribed by law.

Article the sixth. The right of the people to be secure in their persons, houses, papers, and effects, against unreasonable searches and seizures, shall not be violated, and no warrants shall issue, but upon probable cause, supported by oath or affirmation, and particularly describing the place to be searched, and the persons or things to be seized.

Article the seventh. No person shall be held to answer for a capital, or otherwise infamous crime, unless on a presentment or indictment of a Grand Jury, except in cases arising in the land or naval forces, or in the Militia, when in actual service in time of war or public danger; nor shall any person be subject for the same offence to be twice put in jeopardy of life or limb; nor shall be compelled in any criminal case to be a witness against himself, nor be deprived of life, liberty, or property, without due process of law; nor shall private property be taken for public use, without just compensation.

Article the eighth. In all criminal prosecutions, the accused shall enjoy the right to a speedy and public trial, by an impartial jury of the State and district wherein the crime shall have been committed, which district shall have been previously ascertained by law, and to be informed of the nature and cause of the accusation; to be confronted with the witnesses against him; to have compulsory process for obtaining witnesses in his favor, and to have the assistance of counsel for his defence.

Article the ninth. In suits at common law, where the value in controversy shall exceed twenty dollars, the right of trial by jury shall be preserved, and no fact tried by a jury, shall be otherwise re-examined in any Court of the United States, than according to the rules of the common law.

Article the tenth. Excessive bail shall not be required, nor excessive fines imposed, nor cruel and unusual punishments inflicted.

Article the eleventh. The enumeration in the Constitution, of certain rights, shall not be construed to deny or disparage others retained by the people.

Article the twelfth. The powers not delegated to the United States by the Constitution, nor prohibited by it to the States, are reserved to the States respectively, or to the people.

Frederick Augustus Muhlenberg, Speaker of the House of Representatives

John Adams, Vice-President of the United States, and President of the Senate.

ATTEST,

John Beckley, Clerk of the House of Representatives.

Sam. A. Otis Secretary of the Senate

BILL OF RIGHTS. Facsimile of the first page as sent to the states in 1789.

constitutional through "interposition." They knew that the Federalist judges would deny their claim that the law was clearly in violation of the First Amendment. But they found few state lawmakers eager to tackle these thorny constitutional problems. The laws expired, untested in the courts.

Slavery, the Civil War, and Reconstruction. Through the nineteenth century, citizens' rights remained tied to local circumstances. The Supreme Court held in *Barron v. Baltimore* (1833) that the Bill of Rights was binding only on the federal government, not the states—a ruling that made the Bill of Rights a dormant relic. The slavery crisis worsened, but Congress by its "gag rule" ignored antislavery petitions between 1836 and 1844; state and local officials banned abolitionist newspapers; Mormons were persecuted by mobs and denounced by state officers; and Indian tribes were pushed around by federal troops, with no public mention that the Bill of Rights was being violated. During the Civil War President Abraham Lincoln suspended the writ of habeas corpus and citizens suspected of disloyalty were thrown into Northern prisons, often without a formal charge or hearing. Preoccupied with winning the war, Congress overlooked these arbitrary acts.

After the Confederate surrender at Appomattox the nation attempted to address the problems faced by the new citizens created when the former slaves were freed. Three constitutional amendments ending slavery and trying to guarantee the civil and political rights of the freed slaves were passed by Congress and ratified between 1865 and 1870. Although their intent now seems clear, at the time the efforts to make former (male) slaves free men with all the rights of citizenship, including suffrage, led to much constitutional confusion. Southern states adopted various strategies to deny blacks full status as citizens, and in the North there was deep reluctance to accept blacks as social equals.

Change came slowly. In 1873 the Supreme Court in the *Slaughterhouse Cases* narrowly defined the meaning of the Fourteenth Amendment's guarantee of the "privileges and immunities of citizens." Instead of declaring the protection of the substantive and procedural rights that form the heart of the Bill of Rights as due to all citizens, the Court refused to erase important distinctions between state and national citizenship, in effect allowing states to enact laws that left southern blacks as second-class citizens. A hammer blow to full rights for blacks came in the Court's decision in *Plessy v. Ferguson* (1896), in which the Court gave its seal of approval to the growing number of laws that mandated "separate but equal" public facilities for blacks and whites. The effect was firmly to implant a Jim Crow society throughout the South—a society in which blacks were denied access to public restaurants, hotels, theaters, railroad passenger cars, and even seats on trolleys.

Congress chose to ignore the situation, even after the Supreme Court reinforced the *Slaughterhouse* decision with more restrictive rulings between 1900 and 1908 (although in 1907 Justice John Marshall Harlan had taken a minority position and suggested that free speech and freedom of the press were rights now protected by the due process clause of the Fourteenth Amendment).

Violations of Civil Liberties. More setbacks came in the wave of hysteria that followed America's entry into World War I in April 1917. Congress passed the Espionage Act in 1917, which gave the imprimatur of statutory approval to a powerful crackdown on those who criticized or dissented from the war effort. And in *Schenck v. United States* (1919), the Supreme Court for the first time handed down a ruling on the claim that an act of Congress per se was a violation of the First Amendment guarantee of freedom of expression. Charles Schenck, a secretary of the Socialist party, had helped distribute leaflets urging young men to resist the draft for military service. His counsel pleaded that the Espionage Act violated a citizen's right to speak freely, even in wartime. The act was upheld, but a warning signal was hoisted by Justice Oliver Wendell Holmes, who said that the test was whether such expressions presented "a clear and present danger that they will bring about the substantive evils that Congress has a right to prevent."

An even tougher law, the Sedition Act of 1918, held that "disloyal, profane, scurrilous, or abusive language about the form of government, the Constitution, soldiers and sailors, flag or uniform of the armed forces" could be punished. More arrests were made, and the statute was upheld by the Supreme Court.

A legal breakthrough came in 1925 when the Court declared in *Gitlow v. New York* "that freedom of speech and of the press—which are protected by the First Amendment from abridgment by Congress—are among the fundamental personal rights and 'liberties' protected by the due process clause of the Fourteenth Amendment from impairment by the States." Then in 1931 the Court began opening an umbrella of protection for all First Amendment rights, and a generation later the work was virtually completed. In a series of decisions that were not always popular, the Court decided that the First Amendment protected schoolchildren from having to salute the flag or to pray in the classroom. The "wall of separation" that Thomas Jefferson yearned to erect between church and state was fitted firmly in place to prevent public expenditures for parochial schools. New tests of "symbolic speech" permitted protest groups to burn the American flag without fear of arrest. And to thwart censorship the Supreme Court liberally interpreted the rights of free speech in art and literature as well as in political discussion.

The Court persistently used the due process and equal protection clauses of the Fourteenth Amendment to resurrect the First through the Ninth Amendments. Not only Congress but state governments and their officers likewise were forbidden to interfere with citizens' personal rights. By 1969 the whole catalog of personal liberties, including guaranteed rights for accused persons, made the Bill of Rights a shield against unconstitutional acts by both federal and state officials. Only in the murky areas of obscenity and pornography did doubts remain as to where Congress might wander without abridging a citizen's personal liberty; the Supreme Court was still trying to define those limits as the twentieth century entered its final decade.

One of the major fields of contention had finally closed with the end of the Cold War between the Western democracies and the former Soviet Union. Fears of the Bolsheviks translated into legislative efforts to stifle activities of the Communist party in the post–World War I era, as many states passed syndicalism laws covering a broad range of activities that were considered subversive. Congress remained aloof until 1940, when the Alien Registration Act (Smith Act) was passed to provide the federal government with a legal weapon to trap communists who plotted or advocated the overthrow of the government by force. The McCarran Internal Security Act of 1950 went further, and came close to outlawing the Communist party. But a generation after the red scares and the brief flurry of McCarthyism (when Congress had been used as a forum to cast aspersions on left-wing bureaucrats and scholars) there were few memories of the hysteria of the 1950s. Indeed, by 1992 the Soviet Union had disbanded and Congress was approving laws that provided aid for the republics that had once constituted that "Evil Empire."

Civil Rights. As the spotlight shifted away from personal rights, the scope of the Bill of Rights broadened with public concern over racially motivated segregation. President Harry S. Truman ordered the integration of the armed forces in 1947, despite outspoken protests by congressional critics from the South. State laws that prevented voting by blacks were challenged, as were the segregated school systems in southern public schools and colleges. First to go were the state laws separating white and black college students, and in 1954 the Supreme Court threw away the 1896 *Plessy* concept, ruling in *Brown v. Board of Education* that segregated public-supported schools were unconstitutional. Enforcement of the decision proved a long and arduous process, but the nation's commitment to "equal protection" was beyond doubt.

Except for passing the Civil Rights Act of 1960, which attempted to protect the rights of black citizens to vote in both state and federal elections, Congress was a reluctant participant in the desegregation process until after the assassination of President John F. Kennedy in 1963. National attention increasingly focused on the remnants of the old schemes of segregated facilities and racial discrimination still permitted by state codes. The resulting Civil Rights Act of 1964 created commissions to handle grievances, barred discrimination in public facilities, and made voting registration accessible to all citizens. Civil rights law was strengthened with another Civil Rights Act in 1968, which struck at segregated housing practices and acknowledged the civil rights of Native Americans. Congress passed legislation in 1980 to tighten enforcement procedures and accelerate the process of creating a color-blind social order.

Modern congressional responses to equal rights have taken the form of legislation directed toward a redress of old grievances suffered by minorities. Meanwhile, the Supreme Court has carried forward its traditional role of redefining and expanding the Bill of Rights. Thus the First Amendment has been broadly interpreted to strike down the use of public land or funds to erect a Christmas nativity scene (*City of Birmingham v. ACLU*, 1986) but to permit newspapers to attack elected officials with extreme charges so long as there is no "malice aforethought" (*New York Times v. Sullivan*, 1971). The flag-burning cases (*Texas v. Johnson*, 1989) provoked much public outrage and even a call for a constitutional amendment to punish such acts, but the furor dissipated with the passage of time.

In 1991 Americans celebrated the bicentennial of the Bill of Rights with public displays and ceremonies in every state of the Union. A visit to view the original manuscript deposited in the National Archives had become a kind of pilgrimage for thousands of citizens. Over two hundred years the public perception of government's role in preserving a citizen's rights had become manifest in the calendar of the Supreme Court rather than in the Congress. Madison, Jefferson, and others present when the Bill of Rights was created had predicted that the courts—not the legislature—would be the ultimate guardians of the people's liberties. More than two hundred years later, their judgment was confirmed in every Supreme Court term.

The role of Congress in protecting a citizen's right of privacy or the right to fair treatment in the marketplace remained controversial in the 1990s. The vexing matters of a woman's right to have an abortion or an African American's claim of job discrimination were thorny issues debated in Congress and the nation. In a country of more than 250 million people, where freedom is at the heart of most human problems, the Bill of Rights was a part of every lawmaker's consciousness. Legislators, judges, and juries were aware, as Justice William J. Brennan, Jr., once remarked, that the Bill of Rights exists because it is in the interest of the whole nation "that justice shall be done." The Bill of Rights had become the nation's conscience as well as "the supreme law of the land."

[See also Bills of Attainder; Civil Liberties; Civil Rights; Constitution.]

BIBLIOGRAPHY

Abraham, Henry. *Freedom and the Court. Civil Right and Liberties in the United States.* 5th ed. 1988.
Brant, Irving. *The Bill of Rights: Its Origin and Meaning.* 1965.
Cox, Archibald. *The Court and the Constitution.* 1987.
Hickok, Eugene W., Jr., ed. *The Bill of Rights: Original Meaning and Current Understanding.* 1991.
Levy, Leonard. *Constitutional Opinions: Aspects of the Bill of Rights.* 1986.
Levy, Leonard. *Original Intent and the Framers' Constitution.* 1988.
Rutland, Robert A. *The Birth of the Bill of Rights, 1776–1791.* 1991.
Schwartz, Bernard, ed. *The Bill of Rights: A Documentary History.* 2 vols. 1971.
Smolla, Rodney A. *Free Speech in an Open Society.* 1992.

ROBERT A. RUTLAND

BILLS. One of the four forms of legislation considered in the House and the Senate, bills are designated by chamber of origin (with "H.R." or "S.") and number. When a bill is passed by both chambers in identical form, it is enrolled and presented to the president for his signature. By statute, all bills begin with the following enacting clause: "Be it enacted by the Senate and House of Representatives of the United States of America in Congress assembled."

Current rules allow bills to be introduced by any member of Congress on any subject, and they are then generally referred to the appropriate committee or committees of jurisdiction for consideration. In the Senate, it has been a long-standing practice to allow multiple sponsorship of legislation. Limited cosponsorship was introduced in the House only in 1967, however, and just since 1979 has Rule XXII allowed for an unlimited number of House members to cosponsor legislation.

The early rules of both chambers carried over provisions inherited from English practice and the Continental Congress that restricted members' freedom to introduce bills. It was the expectation that committees would draft legislation, and motions for leave for individual members to introduce bills were not common and often were debated extensively. During the nineteenth century, the practice of requiring motions for leave fell into disuse, but as late as 1876 the House refused to receive a bill introduced without leave. A vestigial restriction remains in Senate Rule XIV, which refers to measures introduced "on leave," although modern practice makes no such requirement.

[*For comprehensive discussion of how a bill becomes a law, see* Lawmaking. *See also* Deficiency Bills; Private Bill.]

BIBLIOGRAPHY

Cooper, Joseph, and Cheryl D. Young. "Bill Introduction in the Nineteenth Century: A Study of Institutional Change." *Legislative Studies Quarterly* 14 (February 1989): 67.
U.S. House of Representatives. *Constitution, Jefferson's Manual, and Rules of the House of Representatives, 103d Congress.* Compiled by William Holmes Brown. 102d Cong., 2d sess., 1992. H. Doc. 102–405. Rule XXII.
U.S. House of Representatives. *Hinds' Precedents of the House of Representatives of the United States*, by Asher C. Hinds. 59th Cong., 2d sess., 1907. Vol. 4, chap. 91.
U.S. Senate. *Senate Procedure, Precedents, and Practices*, by Floyd M. Riddick. 97th Cong., 1st sess., 1981. S. Doc. 97–2.

JAMES V. SATURNO

BILLS OF ATTAINDER. Legislative enactments that prescribe punishment for named or easily identifiable individuals without a judicial trial are bills of attainder, which are prohibited by the Constitution. Article I, section 9, clause 3 imposes the prohibition on Congress; Article I, section 10, clause 1 applies it to the states. A bill of attainder is an abuse of power by which the legislature exceeds its proper role of prescribing general rules of conduct and takes on the additional functions of prosecutor, judge, and jury. Congress assumes these very roles by targeting individuals in impeachments, but there remedies are limited to removal and disqualification from office.

The constitutional prohibition on bills of attainder covers the original English bill of attainder, which imposed death and confiscation of property (note that Article III prohibits Congress from prescribing "corruption of blood" as punishment for treason), as well as the English bill of pains and penalties, which inflicted noncapital penalties. More is covered, however; the clause is a general prohibition of legislative imposition of punishment of any kind, whether in the criminal sense or not. Statutes invalidated under the clause include a law prohibiting the payment of salary to federal employees identified by name (*United States v. Lovett*, 1946) and a law limiting federal court practice to attorneys who would swear that they had not aided the Confederate cause during the Civil War (*Ex parte Garland*, 1867). On the other hand, a statute providing for government custody of President Richard M. Nixon's papers was upheld (*Nixon v. Administrator of General Services*, 1977). Although the law applied to only one individual, he constituted "a legitimate class of one," and, furthermore, the law was not punitive.

BIBLIOGRAPHY

Chafee, Zechariah, Jr. *Three Human Rights in the Constitution of 1787*. 1956.
Tribe, Laurence H. *American Constitutional Law*. 2d ed. 1988. Pp. 641–663.

GEORGE A. COSTELLO

BINGHAM, JOHN A. (1815–1900), Republican representative from Ohio, prosecutor at the trial of the conspirators in the assassination of Abraham Lincoln, coauthor of the Fourteenth Amendment. Bingham approached politics with the zeal of an evangelical minister. Initially a Whig, he became famous for his oratory, which he placed in service of the Republican cause after entering the House in 1855. Bingham served four terms, lashing the slave states with dramatic invective, but he lost his reelection bid in 1862. His party provided him with appointive positions during the Civil War, including one as judge advocate for the army. Again elected to the House in 1865 where he served four more terms, Bingham was made a special judge advocate in the trial of Lincoln's assassins, a role he performed with characteristic fervor.

Despite his rhetoric, Bingham, who served as chairman of the Judiciary Committee from 1869 to 1873, was a constitutional conservative. He balanced his desire to protect individual rights with respect for the states, and he believed amendments to be a more prudent means of extending national power than loose construction. These principles became apparent during his service on the Joint Committee on Reconstruction in the 39th and 40th Congresses (1865–1869). Bingham drafted the key first section of the Fourteenth Amendment to protect personal liberties, apparently not anticipating later interpretations that extended substantive property rights to corporations. He supported the right of the freedmen to vote, but he wanted the

JOHN A. BINGHAM.   LIBRARY OF CONGRESS

southern states to reassume their former status quickly, and he opposed extended disfranchisement of former Confederates. As a prosecutor in the 1868 impeachment trial of Andrew Johnson, Bingham again relied on dramatic invective that disguised his conservative tendencies. Following his defeat in the 1872 election, he was rewarded by his party with an appointment as U.S. ambassador to Japan.

BIBLIOGRAPHY

Beauregard, Erving E. "John A. Bingham and the Fourteenth Amendment." *The Historian* 58 (1987): 67–76.
Benedict, Michael Les. *A Compromise of Principle: Congressional Republicans and Reconstruction, 1863–1869.* 1974.

JOHANNA NICOL SHIELDS

BLACK, HUGO L. (1886–1971), Democratic senator from Alabama, onetime member of the Ku Klux Klan, vigorous supporter of the New Deal, and Franklin D. Roosevelt's first Supreme Court nominee. Black, a former county solicitor, police court judge, and highly successful attorney for unions and workers, defeated four prominent politicians in 1926 to win the Democratic senatorial nomination, a virtual assurance of election in Alabama at that time. The son of a small-town merchant, Black had earned his law degree at the two-year school of the University of Alabama, which in 1905 had only two faculty members and did not require that entering students hold bachelor's degrees.

Black's supporters in 1926 included prohibitionists, small farmers, newly enfranchised women, Methodists, Baptists, union members, veterans, and some 80,000 Alabamans who belonged to the Ku Klux Klan. In the decade following World War I, the Klan flourished in Alabama, largely due to its outspoken opposition to Catholic immigrants who, pouring into industrialized Birmingham, appeared willing to work even more cheaply than the native labor force.

Through rampant anti-Catholicism, illegal violence, and elaborate rituals, the Klan appealed to Alabama's largely uneducated and powerless majority of lower-class whites. It became a tightly controlled political machine that represented the prejudices of its members as well as their frustration over having been excluded from economic gains and political power. In a pragmatic act serving his own ambition, Black had joined the Klan in 1921.

As a freshman Democrat during the Hoover administration, Black could only complain that the nation's economic catastrophe resulted from a concentration of wealth in the hands of a few, while the majority lacked purchasing power. Prosperity, he argued, would not trickle down from Herbert Hoover's Reconstruction Finance Corporation but would rise upward from a well-paid, regularly employed work force.

Although the Klan had faded from political power in Alabama by 1932, Black, through adroit political maneuvering, won a second term. Amid the innovative atmosphere of the New Deal, he proposed a law to mandate a thirty-hour workweek. President Franklin D. Roosevelt persuaded Black to sponsor a less radical plan that eventually emerged as the Fair Labor Standards Act of 1938. By instigating and insisting on nationwide standards of minimum wages and maximum work hours, Black made his most substantive contribution as a senator. A fervent New Dealer, he also supported social security, the abolition of child labor, government health insurance, the Tennessee Valley Authority, subsidized housing, a permanent work program for unemployed youth, and Roosevelt's controversial Court-packing plan to enlarge the Supreme Court. As a zealous investigator he focused national attention on the flaws of subsidy programs for airlines and merchant shippers and the behind-the-scenes maneuvering of airline lobbyists.

In 1937, facing a tough reelection fight against anti–New Deal business, industrial, and timber interests that vigorously opposed the pending wage and hour law, Black was removed from the political arena through his nomination by Roosevelt to the U.S. Supreme Court.

Unaware of Black's former Klan affiliation, Roosevelt wanted to place on the Court an ardent New Dealer and a person whom the Senate, because of its courtesy tradition, would be certain to confirm. Black won confirmation 63 to 16 and quickly took his judicial oaths.

By unearthing proof of Black's onetime Klan membership, the anti–New Deal press created a controversy that subsided only after Justice Black, in a short nationwide radio address, announced that he had resigned from the Klan before entering the Senate and declared firmly that he refused to discuss the subject further. In October 1937 he took his seat on the Court. During three decades of service the onetime Klansman established a distinguished record as a civil libertarian.

BIBLIOGRAPHY

Hamilton, Virginia Van der Veer. *Hugo Black: The Alabama Years.* 1972.

Virginia Van der Veer Hamilton

BLACK BUDGET. *Black budget* is the term for the billions of dollars kept in thousands of covert accounts by the Department of Defense. *Black* is a term of art in espionage signifying complete secrecy. Under the cover of national security laws, the funds pay for all U.S. intelligence activities and for scores, perhaps hundreds, of secret weapons programs. The costs of the highly classified military and intelligence projects, an estimated $30 billion or more a year, are concealed in the Defense budget by falsified line items, censored financial figures, and other forms of accounting legerdemain.

Congressional defenders of the black budget maintain it is necessary for national security. Critics say it violates Article I, section 9, clause 7 of the Constitution, which states that "a regular Statement and Account of the Receipts and Expenditures of all public Money shall be published from time to time." The black budget is not published in any form understandable to taxpayers, nor is it easily examined by members of Congress.

The black budget began with the Manhattan Project for developing the atomic bomb. From 1942 to 1945, $2.19 billion flowed secretly from the Treasury to the atomic bomb program. In 1944, House Speaker Sam Rayburn of Texas became the first and only legislator to be told by the War Department precisely how the funds were hidden: in two line items labeled "Engineer Service: Army" and "Expediting Production." A handful of other House members and senators were informed subsequently of the secret funding and participated in its cover-up.

The practice flourished during the Cold War. The black budget's formal origins lie in the Central Intelligence Agency Act of 1949, which stated that the CIA could spend money "without regard to the provisions of law and regulations relating to the expenditure of Government funds." Along with the CIA, the National Security Agency, established in 1952 to conduct global electronic espionage, and the National Reconnaissance Office, established in 1960 to operate spy satellites, were created and funded through secret appropriations buried in Department of Defense accounts. Throughout the 1950s and 1960s, only a few senior members of Congress were aware of the covert accounts, and

those members chose not to examine the matter. Years went by in which the Armed Services subcommittees on intelligence never met. No oversight existed.

Congress began to address the subject of secret appropriations in the 1970s. The first public discussion of the issue on the Senate floor came in April 1971. Brandishing a Pentagon budget, Sen. J. William Fulbright (D-Ark.) told his colleagues that billions of dollars for intelligence were contained in the appropriation. "No one can tell where in this bill those funds are," Fulbright said. "When they read a line item and find that there is so much for aircraft, or for a carrier, those may or may not be the real amounts."

In the next five years, Watergate-era revelations of illegal CIA activities both at home and abroad led to the first congressional investigations of secret spending. A committee led by Idaho Democratic senator Frank Church found in April 1976 that the black budget "violates Article I, Section 9, Clause 7 of the Constitution," and said that the publication of "the aggregate figure for national intelligence would begin to satisfy the Constitutional requirement and would not damage the national security." However, no publication of the black budget ensued.

The 1980s saw a counterreformation and an explosion of secret spending. Weapons systems, many created to fight nuclear war, increasingly were funded through secret accounts, a practice that became common in the Reagan administration. Secret spending on weaponry grew dramatically, as some of the most expensive weapons systems in history—the $2-billion-a-copy B-2 nuclear bomber, for example—were developed under the black budget. Meanwhile, intelligence spending by the CIA and the Pentagon also increased rapidly. By one estimate, the black budget grew from about $9 billion in 1980 to about $36 billion in 1987—making the black budget larger than the military budget of any nation in the world, save the Soviet Union.

The Iran-contra affair and its public exposure of excessive executive-branch secrecy, along with the diminished threat of nuclear war, the dissolution of the Soviet Union, and above all the end of the Cold War, brought calls for increased openness from members of Congress. But after fifty years, secrecy still surrounds the costs of immense military and intelligence programs. As the twentieth century draws to a close, the White House has done nothing and Congress has done little to dismantle the mechanisms of the national security era. The black budget and the costs of the lingering Cold War-era programs it sustains remain secret.

BIBLIOGRAPHY

Burrows, William E. *Deep Block: Space Espionage and National Security.* 1986.

Groves, Leslie R. *Now It Can Be Told: The Story of the Manhattan Project.* 1962.

Richelson, Jeffrey T. *The U.S. Intelligence Community.* 1985.

Weiner, Tim. *Blank Check: The Pentagon's Black Budget.* 1990.

TIM WEINER

BLACK MEMBERS. [*This entry includes two separate discussions of African American members of Congress, one focusing on the nineteenth century and the other on the twentieth century.*]

Nineteenth Century

The enforcement of the Reconstruction Act of 1867 and the ratification of the Fifteenth Amendment made it possible for black Americans to seek election to the U.S. Congress for the first time. While more than two thousand blacks were elected to various state and local posts during Reconstruction, only fourteen were elected to the House and two to the Senate during Reconstruction, and only six others served in the House during the nineteenth century, bringing the total number of black members of Congress to twenty-two. As a group, the black members of the nineteenth century fought to protect the voting rights of freedmen, supported public education in the South, sought land grants for freedmen, spoke out against the vigilante violence against blacks, including lynching, and in general championed civil rights at a time of great racial strife in the United States.

FIRST BLACK MEMBERS OF CONGRESS. *Left to right,* Sen. Hiram R. Revels (R-Miss.), Representatives Benjamin S. Turner (R-Ala.), Robert C. De Large (R-S.C.), Josiah T. Walls (R-Fla.), Jefferson F. Long (R-Ga.), Joseph H. Rainey (R-S.C.), and Robert B. Elliott (R-S.C.). Currier and Ives, 1872.

LIBRARY OF CONGRESS

COMMEMORATION OF EMANCIPATION. Center depicts Rep. Robert B. Elliott (R-S.C.) delivering a speech to the House of Representatives, 6 January 1874. *Frank Leslie's Illustrated Newspaper*, 1874.   LIBRARY OF CONGRESS

All the black members who served in Congress during the nineteenth century were Republicans, the party of Abraham Lincoln, which had supported civil rights for the newly freed slaves. The first black to serve in the Senate was Hiram R. Revels (1827–1901) of Mississippi, an African Methodist Episcopal minister and former chaplain of a black regiment during the Civil War, who was elected by the Mississippi state legislature to fill the unexpired term of Jefferson Davis, the former president of the Confederacy. Revels entered the Senate on 25 February 1870, after attempts to disqualify him from office failed. The first black to serve in the House of Representatives was Joseph H. Rainey (1832–1887) of South Carolina, who was born a slave. He was a

barber by trade and during the Civil War had worked on a Confederate blockade runner and on the fortifications of Charleston before escaping to Bermuda, where he remained until 1866. Rainey was elected to the South Carolina state legislature in 1870, but when a special election was held for a seat in Congress he won the election and was sworn in on 12 December 1870. In May 1874 he became the first African American to preside over the House when Speaker James G. Blaine turned the gavel over to him. The first African American to preside over the Senate was Mississippi senator Blanche K. Bruce (1841–1898) on 14 February 1879, during debate on a Chinese exclusion bill.

With the end of Reconstruction and the withdrawal of the protection of federal troops it became increasingly difficult for black officeholders to keep their offices. White supremacy groups such as the Ku Klux Klan launched campaigns of voter intimidation throughout the South. Beginning in the 1890s, Democrats and "lily white" Republicans combined forces to redraft state constitutions and election laws that made it all but impossible for blacks to hold elective office. The last of the black members of Congress elected in the nineteenth century was Rep. George H. White, an educator, lawyer, and banker from North Carolina. In his last speech on the floor of the House, on 29 January 1901, he predicted blacks would one day return to Congress. That did happen, but not until Oscar De Priest of Illinois took his seat in the House of Representatives on 15 April 1929.

Following service in Congress, some of the nineteenth-century black members went on to other political offices or professional careers. Still others returned to trades they had practiced before being elected to Congress. About half had attended college. Senator Bruce turned down an opportunity to be U.S. minister to Brazil because that country still had slaves. Instead he became registrar of the Treasury (until 1885) and later recorder of deeds in the District of Columbia. In the last year of his life he again assumed the position of registrar of the Treasury. Richard H. Cain of South Carolina, the first black clergyman to serve in the House (1873–1875 and 1877–1879), was elected bishop of the African Methodist Episcopal Church and helped establish a college in Waco, Texas. John R. Lynch of Mississippi held several appointed federal posts after serving three terms in the House; he practiced law and received a commission as a paymaster during the Spanish-American War, eventually becoming paymaster of the regular army and retiring in 1911 with the rank of major. In 1913 he published *Facts of Reconstruction*. His autobiography, *Reminiscences of an Active Life*, was not published until 1970. Joseph H. Rainey was the Republican candidate to be clerk of the House, but the Democrats gained control of the House in the 46th Congress, ending his chances. He opened a banking firm in Washington, D.C., which failed. Charles E. Nash, Louisiana's only black representative during Reconstruction, was a bricklayer and a veteran of the Civil War who had lost part of his right leg in battle. He returned to bricklaying following his service in the 49th Congress. Senator Revels went on to become the first president of Alcorn University. Robert Smalls of South Carolina, a well-known Civil War hero who

Nineteenth-Century African American Members of Congress

SENATORS	CONGRESS
Hiram R. Revels (R-Miss.)	41st
Blanche K. Bruce (R-Miss.)	44th–46th

REPRESENTATIVES	CONGRESS
Jefferson F. Long (R-Ga.)	41st
Joseph H. Rainey (R-S.C.)	41st–45th
Robert C. DeLarge (R-S.C.)	42d
Robert B. Elliot (R-S.C.)	42d–43d
Benjamin S. Turner (R-Ala.)	42d
Josiah T. Walls (R-Fla.)	42d–44th
Richard H. Cain (R-S.C.)	43d and 45th
John R. Lynch (R-Miss.)	43d
Alonzo J. Ransier (R-S.C.)	43d
James T. Rapier (R-Ala.)	43d
Jeremiah Haralson (R-Ala.)	44th
John A. Hyman (R-N.C.)	44th
Charles E. Nash (R-La.)	44th
Robert Smalls (R-S.C.)	44th–45th, 47th–49th
James E. O'Hara (R-N.C.)	48th–49th
Henry P. Cheatham (R-N.C.)	51st–52d
John M. Langston (R-Va.)	51st
Thomas E. Miller (R-S.C.)	51st
George W. Murray (R-S.C.)	53d–54th
George H. White (R-N.C.)	55th–56th

served four terms in the House of Representatives, was appointed by President Benjamin Harrison to the position of collector of the port of Beaufort, South Carolina, a position he held against political opposition until 1913. Rep. George H. White later developed a town for blacks in Cape May County, New Jersey, called Whitesboro.

While the black members of Congress in the nineteenth century experienced great difficulties in gaining office and holding it, they nonetheless represented an important breakthrough on the path to racial justice in the United States. They were political pioneers at the state and federal level. They arrived in a segregated capital and encountered much hostility from white members. The fact that most served only one or two terms meant they were never in Congress long enough to develop the political power that comes with seniority, a system of advancement within Congress that was beginning to take hold even in the 1870s. Several never received a chance fully to participate in Congress because they spent much of their terms fighting for their seats in contested elections. Josiah T. Walls (1842–1905), for example, the first African American elected to the House from Florida, was unseated twice, serving only half his second term. Nonetheless Walls championed public education and internal improvements for Florida.

The legacy of these twenty-two members, however, remains a vital part of American political history. Those African Americans who have followed in their footsteps in the twentieth century are keenly aware of the debt they owe to this first generation of black political leadership.

[*See also* Reconstruction.]

BIBLIOGRAPHY

Foner, Eric. *Freedom's Lawmakers: A Directory of Black Officeholders during Reconstruction.* 1993.

Litwack, Leon, and August Meier. *Black Leaders of the Nineteenth Century.* 1988

McFarlin, Annjennette Sophie. *Black Congressional Reconstruction Orators and Their Orations, 1869–1879.* 1976.

Ragsdale, Bruce A., and Joel D. Treese. *Black Americans in Congress, 1870–1989.* 1990.

RAYMOND W. SMOCK

Twentieth Century

Of the more than eleven thousand men and women who have served in the U.S. Congress, less than one hundred have been African American. African Americans entered Congress in two distinct waves, one in the nineteenth century and the other in the twentieth. Twenty-two blacks served during the first wave: twenty in the House and two in the Senate. The second wave started in 1928 and continues today. The 103d Congress, elected in 1992, has the largest African American contingent ever, with thirty-eight House members, a delegate, and the nation's first black Democratic senator.

The reentry of African Americans into Congress in 1929 after a twenty-eight-year hiatus was not easy. The first black Congress member of the second wave was Oscar De Priest (R-Ill.), elected in 1928 from a majority-black Chicago district after the death of the white incumbent. After serving in the 71st, 72d, and 73d Congresses (1929–1935), De Priest was defeated in 1934 by Arthur W. Mitchell, the first black Democrat elected to Congress.

Mitchell's election was followed two years later by the 1936 Democratic landslide and the electoral realignment in which African Americans left the Republican party and became part of President Franklin D. Roosevelt's New Deal coalition. The mass departure of African Americans from the party of Abraham Lincoln was based, in part, on the public policies of President Herbert Hoover, which were seen as clearly favoring whites over blacks.

The early black members of Congress attempted to provide representation to a national black constituency. Mitchell sponsored legislation covering civil service reform, the abolition of lynching, desegregated interstate travel, and the creation of a "Negro exposition." He resigned in 1942 and William L. Dawson, another black Democrat, succeeded him. Two years later, Adam Clayton Powell, Jr., was elected from Harlem, in New York City, and for the first time since 1891 there was more than one black representative in the House. While De Priest, Mitchell, and Dawson worked within the system to accomplish their goals, Powell was an outsider who became a fearless spokesman for black America.

Trailing half a century behind white women, the first black woman entered Congress in 1969 when Shirley A. Chisholm was elected from a majority-black Brooklyn, New York, district. She immediately rocked the institution with her outspoken style. Chisholm criticized the seniority system. After she protested her assignment to the Agriculture Committee, Chisholm was given a seat on the Rules Committee. She resigned from Congress in 1983.

Black female representatives have included Yvonne Brathwaite Burke (Calif.), Barbara Jordan (Tex.), and, more recently, Cardiss Collins (Ill.), Maxine Waters (Calif.), Eva Clayton (N.C.), Cynthia McKinney (Ga.), Corrine Brown (Fla.), Carrie Meek (Fla.), and Eddie Bernice Johnson (Tex.). Furthermore, in November 1992, Carol Moseley Braun (Ill.) became the first African American woman elected to the Senate. Unlike many of the white women elected in past decades, all but one of the black women have been elected on their own, rather than after the death of a spouse.

Twentieth-century African American representatives cannot readily be distinguished from other members of Congress by their backgrounds alone. Like white politicians, they tend to be of higher socioeconomic standing than their constituents. They are well educated, and many have held political office previously, most often in state legislatures and on city councils. Others have been clergy, morticians, teachers, professors, and business executives. Just as with white representatives, law is their predominant profession, followed by education, busi-

MEMBERS OF THE BLACK CAUCUS, 92D CONGRESS. *Left to right,* Representatives George W. Collins (D-Ill.), Ronald V. Dellums (D-Calif.), William L. Clay (D-Mo.), Charles C. Diggs, Jr. (D-Mich.), and Shirley A. Chisholm (D-N.Y.).

LIBRARY OF CONGRESS

ness or banking, social work, and religion. A large number worked for state or local government before being elected to Congress, and many have served in the armed forces. The predominant religion among them is Baptist.

Twentieth-century African American representatives have had a collective impact since 1971, when nine black Democratic House members formed the Congressional Black Caucus, an organization that has successfully used its power to negotiate for greater inclusion of blacks in the institutional structure. The caucus has grown into a formidable institution. It has its own foundation, research group, and political action committee.

Prior to 1974, black representatives sat mostly on nonprestigious committees such as Education and Labor, Government Operations, and Public Works and Transportation. By 1990, however, they were well represented on all major committees, including Rules, Ways and Means, and Appropriations, and high seniority had led to five chairmanships.

In recent years, much has been accomplished through individual initiative. William H. Gray III (D-Pa.) was able to penetrate the House power structure in an unprecedented manner. He quickly moved from co-chairman of the Democratic Leadership Council to Budget Committee chairman, Democratic Caucus chairman, and finally majority whip. He has since resigned his seat in Congress, but other African Americans are still in key positions.

The turnover rate for twentieth-century African American representatives has been extremely low, as it has been for white incumbents. Since the 1950s, the overall reelection rate for House members has rarely dipped below 90 percent. For 1988 and 1990, it was 98.4 and 96.9 percent, respectively. By April 1993, only a handful of incumbent blacks had ever been defeated (most in primaries). They were Oscar De Priest (1934), Adam Clayton Powell, Jr. (1970), Robert N. C. Nix (1978), Bennett Stewart (1981), Katie Hall (1984), Alton R. Waldon, Jr. (1986), Charles A. Hayes (1992), and Gus Savage

Twentieth-Century African American Members of Congress

SENATORS	CONGRESS
Edward W. Brooke (R-Mass.)	90th–95th
Carol Moseley Braun (D-Ill.)	103d–

REPRESENTATIVES	CONGRESS
Oscar De Priest (R-Ill.)	71st–73d
Arthur W. Mitchell (D-Ill.)	74th–77th
William L. Dawson (D-Ill.)	78th–91st
Adam Clayton Powell, Jr.[1] (D-N.Y.)	79th–90th, 91st
Charles C. Diggs, Jr. (D-Mich.)	84th–96th
Robert N. C. Nix (D-Pa.)	85th–95th
Augustus F. (Gus) Hawkins (D-Calif.)	88th–101st
John Conyers, Jr. (D-Mich.)	89th–
Shirley A. Chisholm (D-N.Y.)	91st–97th
William L. Clay (D-Mo.)	91st–
George W. Collins (D-Ill.)	91st–92d
Louis Stokes (D-Ohio)	91st–
Ronald V. Dellums (D-Calif.)	92d–
Ralph H. Metcalfe (D-Ill.)	92d–95th
Parren J. Mitchell (D-Md.)	92d–99th
Charles B. Rangel (D-N.Y.)	92d–
Yvonne Brathwaite Burke (D-Calif.)	93d–95th
Cardiss Collins (D-Ill.)	93d–
Barbara Jordan (D-Tex.)	93d–95th
Andrew Young (D-Ga.)	93d–95th
Harold E. Ford (D-Tenn.)	94th–
George W. Crockett, Jr. (D-Mich.)	96th–101st
Julian C. Dixon (D-Calif.)	96th–
William H. Gray III (D-Pa.)	96th–102d
Mickey Leland (D-Tex.)	96th–101st
Bennet Stewart (D-Ill.)	96th
Mervyn M. Dymally (D-Calif.)	97th–102d
Katie Hall (D-Ind.)	97th–98th
Gus Savage (D-Ill.)	97th–102d
Harold Washington (D-Ill.)	97th–98th

REPRESENTATIVES	CONGRESS
Charles A. Hayes (D-Ill.)	98th–102d
Major R. Owens (D-N.Y.)	98th–
Edolphus Towns (D-N.Y.)	98th–
Alan Wheat (D-Mo.)	98th–
Alton R. Waldon, Jr. (D-N.Y.)	99th
Mike Espy (D-Miss.)	100th–102d
Floyd H. Flake (D-N.Y.)	100th–
John Lewis (D-Ga.)	100th–
Kweisi Mfume (D-Md.)	100th–
Donald M. Payne (D-N.J.)	101st–
Craig Washington (D-Tex.)	101st–
Lucien E. Blackwell (D-Pa.)	102d–
Barbara-Rose Collins (D-Mich.)	102d–
Gary Franks (R-Conn.)	102d–
William J. Jefferson (D-La.)	102d–
Maxine Waters (D-Calif.)	102d–
Sanford Bishop (D-Ga.)	103d–
Corrine Brown (D-Fla.)	103d–
Eva Clayton (D-N.C.)	103d–
James E. Clyburn (D-S.C.)	103d–
Cleo Fields (D-La.)	103d–
Alcee L. Hastings (D-Fla.)	103d–
Earl F. Hilliard (D-Ala.)	103d–
Eddie Bernice Johnson (D-Tex.)	103d–
Cynthia McKinney (D-Ga.)	103d–
Carrie Meek (D-Fla.)	103d–
Mel Reynolds (D-Ill.)	103d–
Bobby L. Rush (D-Ill.)	103d–
Robert C. Scott (D-Va.)	103d–
Walter R. Tucker (D-Calif.)	103d–
Melvin Watt (D-N.C.)	103d–
Albert R. Wynn (D-Md.)	103d–

[1]The 90th Congress refused to seat him.
SOURCE: Congressional Black Caucus.

(1992). Sen. Edward W. Brooke (R-Mass.) was defeated in a general election after serving for twelve years.

After leaving Congress, African Americans have served in a variety of jobs. Jordan and Chisholm have lectured widely at universities and in other public forums. Gray became chairman of the United Negro College Fund, a nonprofit organization. Mike Espy (Miss.) became secretary of Agriculture in the Clinton administration.

Despite much progress, the future growth of black membership in Congress is uncertain. Many of the gains from the 1990s can be attributed to a combination of forces, including urban migration, which concentrated large numbers of blacks in cities like Chicago, Philadelphia, Detroit, and New York; the passage, implementation, and extensions of the Voting Rights Act of 1965; and court decisions that have mandated the creation of majority-minority districts wherever possible. In the 1992 elections, thirteen of the sixteen newly elected blacks came from districts created to have black majorities. The other three replaced retiring or defeated black incumbents.

REP. CHARLES B. RANGEL (D-N.Y.). *Left*, with Jesse Jackson, June 1993.

R. MICHAEL JENKINS, CONGRESSIONAL QUARTERLY INC.

It is the concentration and dispersion of the African Americans in the population that places a ceiling on the potential gains from drawing black districts to elect black politicians. Not only do the newly created districts have on average lower black voting-age populations than those of the past, but it has become increasingly difficult to sustain population levels in existing black districts. Thus, paradoxically, though African American representation seems to be on the rise, it may soon stagnate or even decline.

[*See also* Caucus, *article on* Special Interest Caucus; Civil Rights; Civil Rights Act of 1964; *and biographies of figures mentioned herein.*]

BIBLIOGRAPHY

Barnett, Marguerite R. "The Congressional Black Caucus." *Proceedings of the Academy of Political Science* 32 (1975): 34–50.
Barone, Michael, et al. *The Almanac of American Politics.* 1978 and subsequent editions.
Christopher, Maurine. *Black Americans in Congress.* 1976.
Ragsdale, Bruce, and Joel D. Treese. *Black Americans in Congress, 1870–1989.* 1990.
Swain, Carol M. *Black Faces, Black Interests: The Representation of African Americans in Congress.* 1993.
Weiss, Nancy J. *Farewell to the Party of Lincoln.* 1983.
Wilson, James Q. "Two Negro Politicians: An Interpretation." *Midwest Journal of Political Science* 5 (1960): 349–369.

CAROL M. SWAIN

BLAINE, JAMES G. (1830–1893), representative and senator from Maine, Speaker of the House, leader of the Republican party's "Half-Breed" faction, secretary of State, and unsuccessful presidential candidate in 1884. A political leader of great influence and popularity, James Gillespie Blaine was the most prominent figure in U.S. politics from the 1870s to the 1890s. Blaine began as a Whig but then became an early member of the Republican party. He grew to prominence within it and remained loyal to its organization and principles for the rest of his life, proud of the party's record on such issues as slavery, preserving the Union, currency, and the tariff. As Speaker of the House during much of Reconstruction, he helped shape legislation dealing with the postwar economy, the South, and the freed slaves. Blaine was a deft debater who participated in several of the most dramatic moments in the history of the House.

Blaine was born in West Brownsville, Pennsylvania, to a family that, once prominent and well-to-do, had fallen on hard times. Blaine was educated at home, in local schools, and for a year in a private academy in Ohio. At the age of thirteen he entered Washington (now Washington and Jefferson) College in Washington, Pennsylvania. Because he could not afford law school, Blaine taught for several years at a military institute near Lexington, Kentucky, and at a school for the blind in Philadelphia. Kentucky introduced him to slavery, which he detested. When he decided to embark on a career in journalism, he moved in 1854 with his wife, Harriet Stanwood Blaine, to her home town of Augusta, Maine, and became part owner and editor of the *Kennebec Journal*, a leading Whig newspaper.

Blaine was a fervent Whig but soon grew impatient with his party's response to the issue of slavery in the territories. Working to join antislavery elements in a new political organization, he became one of the first editors in New England to back the Republican party, was a delegate to the party's first national convention in 1856, and as a journalist watched the Lincoln-Douglas debates, an experience that gave him a lifelong admiration for Abraham Lincoln. Blaine was wary of many abolitionists because he thought their views harmed the antislavery cause, but he wanted slavery kept out of the territories, opposed the Kansas-Nebraska Act, and favored the Whig-Republican doctrines of national authority. He also favored internal improvements, homesteading on public lands, and a protective tariff.

Running as a Republican in 1858, Blaine won a seat in the lower house of the Maine legislature. He

JAMES G. BLAINE.   LIBRARY OF CONGRESS

That fall Blaine won a seat in the 38th Congress (1863–1865) from Maine's 3d District, a seat he occupied for the next seven terms. When he arrived in the House he was told, "Don't speak when you want to speak, but only when you can't help it." Impulsive and self-confident, Blaine spoke when he chose. He spoke for the use of greenback currency as a war measure, the recruitment of black troops, and the commutation clause of the Conscription Act. He proposed a constitutional amendment for a tax on exports to help pay off war debts. In a challenge to Thaddeus Stevens, the fearsome Pennsylvanian, he called for the federal assumption of state war debts and wound up heading a House committee to study the matter.

Blaine was reelected easily in 1864 and was named to the Military Affairs Committee, which he preferred to the Post Office and Militia committees of his first term. He voted that year for a constitutional amendment abolishing slavery—a vote that took courage—and spent much of his time on measures to enfranchise blacks, which he saw as the key to reconstruction. States withholding the franchise or other rights "on account of race or color," he proposed, should not count those people toward representation, a principle adopted in the second section of the Fourteenth Amendment. Lincoln's assassination upset Blaine's hopes, and he shortly lost faith in Andrew Johnson when he failed to protect citizens in the South who had been loyal to the Union. In anger he voted to impeach Johnson but later regretted having done so.

Blaine's influence grew after the war. As a third-termer he was placed on the Rules Committee, a rare tribute for one so new to Congress, and he was untouched by the Crédit Mobilier and "salary grab" scandals of the Grant era. In the debates over reconstruction he sometimes sided with the Radicals, especially over the franchise, but more often he took moderate stands. In 1867 he tangled again with Stevens, sponsoring the Blaine Amendment, which set the terms for reconstruction by providing that a state could be readmitted once it accepted the Fourteenth Amendment and black suffrage. In a less fortunate incident, Blaine lost his temper in an 1866 squabble with Roscoe Conkling of New York, describing Conkling's "grandiloquent swell, his majestic, supereminent, overpowering, turkey-gobbler strut." The insult, among the most scathing ever spoken in the House, made a lifelong enemy of Conkling, who helped defeat Blaine in the 1884 presidential race.

Blaine became Speaker of the House in 1869 and served until 1875, longer than all but two of his

was reelected three times and served in 1861 and 1862 as speaker of the state house of representatives. Blaine was a thorough, innovative, and conscientious legislator. He headed a committee to investigate conditions in the state prison; he studied prisons in fifteen states and borrowed their best features to improve the prison system in Maine. At the outbreak of the Civil War he worked with the governor to raise and equip troops and rally public opinion for the Union cause. Angered by a Democratic attack on Lincoln and the war, he spoke out early in 1862 in the statehouse for the confiscation of Confederate property, the freeing of rebels' slaves, and the enlistment of freedmen in the Union army.

predecessors. As Speaker he lacked Thomas B. Reed's daring and Sam Rayburn's power, but he is ranked among the best who have ever held the office. He was known for his fairness, firmness, mastery of procedure, and attentiveness to the interests of the House. Contemporaries compared him to Henry Clay, though unlike Clay he rarely left the chair to join in debate. Blaine loved being Speaker and worked behind the scenes to shape legislation he wanted. Because he opposed a provision permitting presidents to suspend the writ of habeas corpus to suppress disorders, he helped sidetrack the federal elections bill of 1875. He promoted measures aimed at a sound currency and moderate tariff. Anticipating Reed by fifteen years, he helped push the adoption of a rule to cut down on dilatory debate.

When the Republicans lost the House in 1874, Blaine led them on the floor, in the minority for the first time since the Civil War. In a dramatic speech in January 1876 he opposed amnesty for former Confederate president Jefferson Davis, whom he accused of committing "gigantic murders and crimes" at the Confederate prison in Andersonville, Georgia. The speech was popular among Republicans, but angered Democrats, who soon accused Blaine of having used his influence as Speaker to aid an Arkansas railroad in which he had once invested. Blaine was innocent of that charge but not of some dubious business dealings, as shown in the so-called Mulligan letters, a set of letters to an old business associate. Citing his right to privacy, Blaine refused to make the letters public, then read them one by one to a packed House on 5 June 1876. Many people rallied to him, but the issue of tainted dealings trailed Blaine for the rest of his life.

Troubles in the House made it easier for Blaine to accept appointment to the Senate that July; in the fall he was elected to a full term. He had wanted to move to the Senate but when he got there found it dull, a contrast to the rapid give and take of the House. He served on Appropriations and other influential committees and worked for favorite causes such as specie resumption, expanded trade, a larger merchant marine, and the exclusion of "cheap" Chinese labor. He was still worried about voting rights for blacks and refused to support Rutherford B. Hayes's policy of conciliating the South. Instead, Blaine led a forward-looking faction of "Half-Breed" Republicans who wanted to move the party toward the newer issues of economic nationalism, the tariff, and a developing urban industrial society.

In March 1881 Blaine resigned from the Senate to become James A. Garfield's secretary of State, ending a nineteen-year career in Congress. Energetic and farsighted, he set in motion some important policies, including a peace congress with Latin American nations, that were cut short by Garfield's assassination. In 1884 Blaine narrowly lost his own race for the White House after a campaign so dirty it ended any presidential ambitions he had. Blaine was the party favorite and could have had the Republican nomination in 1888 but declined to run. Instead, he was pleased when Benjamin Harrison named him secretary of State in 1889; the initiatives he embarked on included the Pan-American Congress, which laid the groundwork for the Organization of American States. When Harrison questioned Blaine's pledge not to run for president, Blaine became so upset that in June 1892 he resigned suddenly, stunning the country. He had been in ill health for many years and died in Washington on 27 January 1893, a few days short of his sixty-third birthday.

For more than two decades Blaine exerted a remarkable influence on American policy and public opinion. Thaddeus Stevens called him "magnetic" because he attracted countless followers, becoming a commanding party leader and the most popular figure of his time. Blaine was a person of great energy, but he was also a hypochondriac. Three of his children died suddenly in the 1890s and he never recovered from the shock. More farsighted than most, Blaine had a rare capacity for change and vision, which served him well in Congress and the State Department. He wrote a perceptive history of Congress from 1861 to 1881 and took pride in having served there, believing, as he once said, that "there is no test of a man's ability in any department of public life more severe than service in the House of Representatives."

BIBLIOGRAPHY

Blaine, James G. *Twenty Years of Congress*. 2 vols. 1884, 1886.

Morgan, H. Wayne. *From Hayes to McKinley: National Party Politics, 1877–1896*. 1969.

Muzzey, David Saville. *James G. Blaine: A Political Idol of Other Days*. 1934.

R. HAL WILLIAMS

BLOCS AND COALITIONS. Composed of members of legislative assemblies who work and vote together in pursuit of particular legislative goals, blocs and coalitions have arisen despite attempts by political party leaders to maintain strict party discipline. Examples from congressional experience include the War Hawks in the era of the War of 1812, the silver bloc of the late nineteenth century, the farm bloc of the early twentieth century, and the conservative coalition that has existed since the New Deal, composed of Republicans and southern Democrats.

Such groups coalesce around policy issues on which neither political party has established a position that satisfies the constituents of group members. Congressional coalitions do not form with the intention of dominating the entire legislative agenda. Rather, they are interested in the resolution of particular and immediate policy questions. The payoff for congressional coalitions is the achievement of policy goals, and failure to win a floor vote does not necessarily or invariably result in coalition instability or decline. Generally, congressional coalitions do not follow "minimum winning coalition" strategies described in the political science literature, again largely because their interests are policy-specific.

Coalitions are inherently important when they affect national political decisions. In the United States they take on enhanced significance when they appear to be, or to have been, precursors of a new national party or a realignment of the old parties. Although contemporary observers tend to think of coalitions, blocs, and factions as derivatives of more formal, permanent political parties, in many cases these groupings were actually predecessors to parties in the evolution of modern representative assemblies. The study of coalitions is a central concern of political science. As Barbara Hinckley wrote in *Coalitions and Politics* (1981), "Politics in general may be justifiably defined as the process of coalition formation."

The World Context. Coalitions and blocs in Congress take on connotations different from those found in other national legislatures. In multiparty parliamentary democracies such as Italy and France, party coalitions are formed in the national legislature in order to establish a responsible government; in this sense, a coalition is a combination of entire parties. The Craxi coalition that governed Italy during much of the 1980s consisted of Christian Democrats, Socialists, Social Democrats, Republicans, and Liberals; outside the coalition were Communists, the Italian Social Movement, Radicals, and several lesser parties. Coalitions of entire parties are almost inevitable in multiparty systems,

sometimes necessary in a system such as the British where there are two dominant and one or two smaller parties, and absent in two-party systems where one party is bound to have a majority of seats. In Congress the odd number of seats in the House of Representatives militates against the possibility of no party having a majority; in the Senate a tie between Democrats and Republicans would be broken in favor of the party of the vice president, as happened in the organization of the Senate in the 83d Congress (1953–1954), with Vice President Richard M. Nixon exercising the tie-breaking vote.

A bloc may be distinguished from a parliamentary coalition in that members of a given party might join different blocs, whereas entire parties establish parliamentary coalitions. In the essentially two-party U.S. Congress, however, the terms *coalition* and *bloc* are interchangeable.

Another related term, *faction*, usually refers to members of one political party who feel loyalty to a particular leader or have an interest in a particular issue that other party members do not share. These congressional intraparty factions are especially important when changes in party leadership positions are being contemplated, ordinarily at the beginning of a new Congress. Prior to the Civil War, factions fought for control within their party caucus and then hoped that all caucus members would vote together for the caucus choice in electing the chamber's leading officers. The southern Democrats in the days of the one-party "solid South" were an example of a faction operating inside one party.

Past Coalitions. The size and behavior of congressional coalitions are important in congressional decision making. Congressional parties are by no means perfectly cohesive in roll-call voting. If they were, the larger party would always win. Where the larger party fails to win, blocs assume critical importance. "Majorities are built in Congress, not elected to it," John Manley has written in "The Conservative Coalition in Congress" (1973).

Throughout American history, blocs have played central roles in some of the most important congressional debates and decisions. The War Hawks, led by Henry Clay of Kentucky and John C. Calhoun of South Carolina, were the effective leaders of the House who led a reluctant President James Madison into the War of 1812 against Great Britain. Factionalism in the House carried over into the presidential nomination process in 1816, when the congressional caucus picked James Monroe of Virginia to succeed Madison by a vote of 65 to 54 over William H. Crawford of Georgia. The end of the reign of "King Caucus" came in the wake of the 1824 election, when presidential support was split among John Quincy Adams, Andrew Jackson, Clay, and Crawford. The eventual House decision for Adams over the popular-vote leader Jackson so offended the nation that a new political party emerged in 1828 to carry the Tennessean into the White House and to democratize the presidential selection process.

From the era of Jackson to the Civil War, the related questions of slavery, national supremacy, and national expansion dominated the congressional agenda. With northern and southern factions continually contending against each other in both the Democratic and Whig parties, critical decisions on the speakership of the House and on national expansion were often determined by the relative size of interparty blocs. The two largest parties were seldom able, let alone inclined, to establish a party position and to enforce party loyalty on critical roll-call votes. Free-Soilers, abolitionists, secessionists, native Americanists (native whites who felt threatened by immigrants), Know-Nothings, and other groups confounded efforts to reduce congressional politics to a neat and permanent two-party pattern.

Even after the Republicans emerged as the antislavery party in the 1850s, and the Civil War was fought, cross-party coalitions continued to play significant roles. Administration efforts to reconcile the Confederate states were vehemently opposed by Radical Republicans in Congress, whose efforts to protect the former slaves provoked bitterness and violence in the South.

The Republican party split into Stalwart and Half-Breed factions in the generation following the war. Stalwarts during the Grant and Hayes administrations (1869–1881) resisted reconciliation with the South, which was more and more firmly tied to the Democratic party, and also opposed civil service reforms. Prominent Stalwarts included Roscoe Conkling of New York, John A. Logan of Illinois, Zachariah Chandler of Michigan, and Simon Cameron of Pennsylvania. Half-Breed leaders included James G. Blaine of Maine, James A. Garfield and John Sherman of Ohio, and George F. Hoar of Massachusetts. The Half-Breed faction, insurgent and reformist, supported President Garfield in his patronage disputes with Senators Conkling and Orville H. Platt. The Blaine-Logan ticket of 1884 was an attempt to unify the two wings of the Republican party. The Stalwarts tried to control the entire Senate by means of their majority status

in the Republican caucus; to thwart them, Half-Breeds often cooperated with the Democrats.

Agrarian movements appeared in the last quarter of the nineteenth century, first as a series of third-party movements. The culmination of this effort came in 1896 when Populists and Democrats fused their presidential candidacies in the person of Nebraska's William Jennings Bryan, who fought for free and unlimited coinage of silver and opposed continuation of the gold standard that had been national policy for several decades. Though unsuccessful as the Democratic presidential nominee in 1896, 1900, and 1908, Bryan did establish the electoral base on which Woodrow Wilson and Franklin D. Roosevelt later won.

The bases of division within the Republican party around the turn of the century were the tariff question and efforts to enhance federal involvement in the economy. Nelson W. Aldrich of Rhode Island, author of the high protective tariff, was the center of the eastern Republican bloc. When Theodore Roosevelt became president after the assassination of William McKinley in 1901, he became the leader of progressive Republicans. Aligned with Aldrich were Senators William B. Allison of Iowa, Platt of Connecticut, and John C. Spooner of Wisconsin, and Rep. Joseph G. Cannon of Illinois, the Speaker of the House. Cannon used his immense powers to stifle and obstruct progressive legislation favored by liberal Republicans and many Democrats. On the progressive side of the Republican party were Senators Robert M. La Follette of Wisconsin, Albert B. Cummins of Iowa, William E. Borah of Idaho, and Albert J. Beveridge of Indiana. Within a few years they were to be joined in the Senate by George W. Norris of Nebraska (whose House career peaked in his leadership of the successful effort to oust Cannon from the speakership) and Hiram W. Johnson of California. Some of these progressives, notably Borah and Johnson, later joined Sen. Henry Cabot Lodge (R-Mass.) in blocking U.S. entry into the League of Nations in 1919.

Republican progressives divided into two segments, an eastern-oriented faction that followed Theodore Roosevelt's "upper middle-class liberalism," which was supported by such midwesterners as William Allen White, editor of the Emporia, Kansas, *Gazette*, and a western faction known for its "Granger-Populist radicalism," including La Follette, Cummins, and Coe I. Crawford of South Dakota. In the first third of the twentieth century, the Democratic party was also fragmented between an eastern, urban, industrial, antiprohibitionist ("wet"), immigrant wing associated with leaders such as Alfred E. Smith of New York, and a rural, western and southern, prohibitionist ("dry"), nativist, Protestant wing associated with Bryan.

The farm bloc emerged in the 1920s out of the radical agrarian segments of the two major parties. The bloc's perennial legislative interest was the McNary-Haugen bill, which called for farm price supports based on pre–World War I "parity" to maintain farmers' incomes. It was backed by the American Farm Bureau Federation. McNary-Haugen was one of the central congressional controversies of the decade. Heartland Republicans were unable, despite persistent efforts, to overcome the opposition of their eastern colleagues and President Calvin Coolidge. In one Congress, the McNary-Haugen bill was favorably reported by one committee but got no further; then in 1926 it passed the Senate but failed in the House; and, finally, it passed both chambers only to be vetoed by Coolidge on 25 February 1927. The depth of party divisions is evident in the fact that 113 Republicans and 97 Democrats voted for McNary-Haugen in the House, as did 24 Republicans and 22 Democrats in the Senate.

Although it lost on McNary-Haugen, the farm bloc was strong enough in 1924 to thwart the tax proposals of the Coolidge administration and Treasury Secretary Andrew Mellon and to finally secure federal government operation of the nitrate plant at Muscle Shoals, Alabama, despite Coolidge's obstruction. This was an important step toward adoption of the Tennessee Valley Authority, the product of cooperation between such diverse politicians as Norris of Nebraska and Oscar Underwood of Alabama. Progressive Republicans were the backbone of the farm bloc. They were in a strong strategic position immediately after World I, when the party division in Congress was close, but as the Republican margin grew larger, especially after the 1924 election, progressives lost much of their leverage.

In the last two years of President Herbert Hoover's administration (1931–1932), Republican progressives regularly voted against the president and with the Democratic side in both chambers. The farm bloc declined after the New Deal. By the advent of the Eisenhower administration in 1953, it had disappeared, in large part because the corn-belt–based, feed-crop–oriented Farm Bureau and the wheat-belt–based, food-crop–oriented Farmers Union took sharply opposing positions on the issues of production controls and high, rigid price supports.

Modern Coalitions. The modern bloc arrangement in Congress, one that had by the early 1990s persisted for more than fifty years, emerged in the late 1930s largely in response to conflicts associated with President Roosevelt's New Deal. What brought the conservative coalition together, as noted by Clinton Rossiter in *Conservatism in America: The Thankless Persuasion* (1962) and confirmed by James Patterson (1967) was growing opposition to most of the New Deal's domestic programs, particularly to the growing influence of organized labor, a swelling federal bureaucracy, expanded welfare programs, and increasing budget deficits. The conservative coalition was later to be defined by Congressional Quarterly as a bloc of Republicans and southern Democrats. At every stage, however, there have been several mavericks in both these groups, such as liberals Jacob K. Javits of New York and Clifford P. Case of New Jersey among Republicans, and Claude Pepper of Florida and J. William Fulbright of Arkansas among southern Democrats. Opposed to the conservative coalition has been a liberal-labor bloc consisting largely of northern Democrats, with occasional exceptions such as conservatives Frank J. Lausche of Ohio and Edward Zorinsky of Nebraska.

One conservative nucleus at the outset of the New Deal in 1933 was composed of five "irreconcilibles," Democratic senators Carter Glass and Harry Flood Byrd, Sr., of Virginia, Millard E. Tydings of Maryland, Thomas P. Gore of Oklahoma, and Josiah W. Bailey of North Carolina. These warm friends opposed Roosevelt's program from the start. But in the honeymoon period Roosevelt was generally able to count on sufficient support from the large Democratic majorities as well as progressive Republicans to carry critical votes in both chambers. After the 1934 congressional elections, the potential for a conservative coalition seemed most unpromising, and no congressional session in American history had ever augured so well for its chief executive (Patterson, 1967, p. 33). But the tide began to turn in 1935, when the percentage of conservatively inclined Democrats more than doubled in both chambers. In the Senate this conservative shifting was reflected in seven roll calls where several Democrats defected from Roosevelt (the votes concerned the World Court, the Works Progress Administration, public utilities regulation, the Wagner Act, social security, a wealth tax, and the Guffey coal bill). Patterson identifies four Senate blocs in these votes: (1) proadministration Democrats, numbering about half the Senate;

(2) antiadministration Democrats, including the five irreconcilables, several other southerners, and Royal S. Copeland of New York, Peter G. Gerry of Rhode Island, and Edward R. Burke of Nebraska; (3) perhaps a dozen old guard Republicans; and (4) a group of holdover Republican progressives who generally supported Roosevelt, including Borah, Norris, Johnson, the younger La Follette, Arthur Capper of Kansas, and Charles L. McNary of Oregon.

In 1937 several controversial welfare and relief programs were making it difficult for Democratic leaders in Congress—including Senate majority leader Joseph T. Robinson of Arkansas, Pat Harrison of Mississippi, James F. Byrnes of South Carolina, and Vice President and former House Speaker John Nance Garner of Texas—to hold their party together. The most important issue in forming the conservative coalition was Roosevelt's plan to pack the Supreme Court with additional, pro–New Deal justices. This united Senate Republicans for the first time in three decades, under the leadership of Borah, McNary, and Arthur H. Vandenberg of Michigan. These Republicans welcomed the cooperation of many congressional Democrats who opposed Roosevelt's plan not so much on ideological grounds as from a concern for maintaining the position of Congress vis-à-vis the president. The sudden death of Senator Robinson in July 1937, in the midst of the Court-packing debate, resulted in a divisive leadership election in which the president's preference, Alben W. Barkley of Kentucky, carried the day against Harrison.

Republican gains in the 1938 congressional elections did much to cement the new coalition, which reached its zenith in 1939. Civil rights struggles in the 1930s and 1940s saw growing use of the filibuster by Senate conservatives and tended to solidify the coalition. In the 1960s, however, with aggressively liberal Democratic presidents and large Democratic majorities in both House and Senate, the filibuster rule was weakened and conservative control of the House Rules Committee was ended by expanding its size with new liberal appointments.

It may be said by way of summary that two cross-party coalitions–one "establishment" and one "insurgent"—have existed since the Civil War and have been more consistent than either the Republican or the Democratic party in terms of ideological and economic policy orientation. But the coalitions have themselves been amorphous and transient, shifting over the years because the leaders and reg-

ulars who formed them left Congress and because public recognition of salient political issues changed. Still, some congressional leaders did remain for several decades as prominent members of various coalitions and blocs. This lent a sense of permanence and continuity to congressional debates and blocs, and in some degree bound the politics of the 1890s to the politics of the 1920s, the 1930s, and later decades. This point is underscored by the long congressional service of such twentieth-century leaders as Republicans Curtis, Borah, Norris, Capper, Vandenberg, and Dole as well as Reed Smoot (Utah), Hiram W. Johnson (Calif.), Everett M. Dirksen (Ill.), Barry Goldwater (Ariz.), and Strom Thurmond (S.C.) and Democrats Robinson, Barkley, Glass, Byrd, Fulbright, Ted Kennedy, Ellison Smith (S.C.), Kenneth D. McKellar (Tenn.), Carl Hayden (Ariz.), Walter F. George (Ga.), Robert F. Wagner (N.Y.), Richard B. Russell (Ga.), Lister Hill (Ala.), Mike Mansfield (Mont.), and Hubert H. Humphrey (Minn.).

Recent decades have seen the emergence of small but cohesive coalitions based on ideology, region, particular policy areas, ethnicity, and gender. Examples include the Democratic Study Group, the Industrial Belt Caucus, the Sunbelt Council, the "boll weevils" (conservative Democrats), the "gypsy moths" (moderate and liberal Republicans from the Northeast and Midwest), the Alcohol Fuels Caucus, the Coal Caucus, the Metropolitan Area Caucus, the Suburban Caucus, the Copper Caucus, the Textile Caucus, the Western State Coalition, the Children's Caucus, the Members of Congress for Peace through Law, the Pro-Life Caucus, the Solar Coalition, the Women's Caucus, and the Black Caucus.

Scholars and journalists have utilized several quantitative approaches to identify and measure legislative voting blocs. A. Lawrence Lowell, Stuart Rice, Bruce Russett, and Aage R. Clausen have been among the most inventive and widely cited. In these efforts to quantify congressional blocs, two methodological decisions are fundamental: which roll calls are to be investigated (all in a given session, a random selection, or a purposive selection based on policy domains such as agriculture, economic regulation, or foreign affairs), and what level of agreement among or between members (50 percent, 60 percent, etc.) is considered sufficiently high to merit inclusion of a member in a bloc.

[*For discussion of particular blocs, coalitions, and interest groups in Congress, see* Asian American Members; Black Members; Conservative Coalition; Farm Bloc; Hispanic Members; Southern Bloc; War

Hawks; Women in Congress. *See also* Caucus, *article on* Special Interest Caucus; Legislative Service Organizations; Political Parties.]

BIBLIOGRAPHY

Barone, Michael. *Our Country: The Shaping of America from Roosevelt to Reagan.* 1990.

Burner, David. *The Politics of Provincialism: The Democratic Party in Transition, 1918–1932.* 1986.

Crunden, Robert M. *Ministers of Reform: The Progressive Achievement in American Civilization, 1889–1920.* 1982.

Hinckley, Barbara. *Coalitions and Politics.* 1981.

Manley, John. "The Conservative Coalition in Congress." *American Behavioral Scientist* 7 (1973): 224.

Nye, Russel B. *Midwestern Progressive Politics: A Historical Study of Its Origins and Development, 1870–1958.* 1959.

Patterson, James T. *Congressional Conservatism and the New Deal: The Growth of the Conservative Coalition in Congress, 1933–1939.* 1967.

Rossiter, Clinton. *Conservatism in America: The Thankless Persuasion.* 2d rev. ed. 1962.

Saloutos, Theodore, and John Hicks. *Twentieth-Century Populism: Agricultural Discontent in the Middle West, 1900–1939.* 1951.

ALAN L. CLEM

BLUE RIBBON COMMISSIONS.

Blue ribbon commissions are temporary advisory bodies, usually established to find broadly acceptable solutions to contentious problems. Because commissions lack the power to implement the recommendations they make, they are influential only to the extent that Congress or the president heeds their advice.

There is great variety in commissions, which can be uniquely crafted to meet the needs of the moment. They are created by presidential decree, by statute, or informally by the mutual consent of Congress and the president. They normally consist of prominent individuals representing a wide range of opinion whose findings will command respect—experts, prominent private citizens, and politicians. Although commissions were used sporadically throughout the nineteenth century, they did not come into common usage until the presidency of Theodore Roosevelt.

Among the best known and most effective was the National Commission on Social Security Reform, established by presidential order in 1981 to deal with a crisis in the funding of social security and medicare. Its report was issued in 1983. Representing a wide range of opinion from both parties, the commissioners joined in nearly unanimous support of the recommendations, which President Ronald Reagan and House Speaker Thomas P. (Tip) O'Neill, Jr., also embraced. Soon after, Congress adopted the commission's proposals with few changes. In this notable case, a commission transformed what had been the most partisan, contentious issue in American politics into a most tractable one. Summit negotiations between members of Congress and senior White House advisers helped to produce bipartisan agreements on budget deficit reduction in both 1987 and 1990.

Sharply divided reports do little or nothing to resolve problems. The National Economic Commission (1988–1989), modeled on the Social Security Commission, was intended to produce bipartisan recommendations on how to reduce the budget deficit. Its members divided along partisan lines and issued a majority report accompanied by a sharp dissent from the minority. The result was a continuation of previous conflict. The Pepper Commission (named for Rep. Claude Pepper [D-Fla.], an advocate for the elderly) was designed to produce a consensus on reform of the American health care system. Its members could not reach a consensus and issued a divided report, which did nothing to promote either consensus or action in Congress.

Countless politicians, pressed to make decisions that could prove unpopular however they are made, have taken the easy way out by appointing a commission. This time-honored practice encourages a cynical view that politicians create commissions mostly to fob off unwanted responsibilities. But commissions can help elected officials make difficult decisions by providing an ostensibly disinterested, expert justification. Moreover, research indicates that most commission recommendations are accepted and implemented. At the very least, appointing a commission can shift responsibility from government officials for a year or so while its members deliberate.

At their most effective, commissions allow Congress to realize purposes its members could not endorse directly. A 1967 law established a quadrennial Commission on Executive, Legislative, and Judicial Salaries, and instructed it to issue a recommendation for salary levels for the three branches of government. Because the proposal would take effect automatically unless Congress voted to oppose it, the use of the commission helped insulate members of Congress from the political hazards of voting for their own pay increase.

As the use of commissions increased in the

1980s, so did criticism of them, principally on the ground that elected officials were abdicating their responsibilities, but also on the ground that decisions were being made behind closed doors. There is some basis for these arguments, but it is the elected officials who must decide whether or not to adopt commission recommendations. Thus it is they who accept ultimate responsibility.

BIBLIOGRAPHY

Flitner, David. *The Politics of Presidential Commissions: A Public Policy Perspective.* 1986.

Light, Paul. *Artful Work: The Politics of Social Security Reform.* 1985.

Wolanin, Thomas R. *Presidential Advisory Commissions.* 1975.

JOHN B. GILMOUR

BOARDINGHOUSES. During the relatively brief legislative sessions of pre–Civil War Washington, the great majority of members of Congress resided in boardinghouses, or messes. Located near the Capitol, housing from three to thirty representatives and senators who shared bedrooms and board, the boardinghouses were an important ingredient in the life of the new city.

In his seminal study *The Washington Community: 1800–1828*, James Sterling Young found these messes to have been very significant in organizing congressional voting behavior. Young demonstrated that agreement on critical votes among boardinghouse members was substantially higher than among representatives of the same political party, region, or state. On arrival in Washington, members of Congress formed a fraternity of like-minded individuals based on the boardinghouse, and the mess effectively became a caucus in which political issues were discussed and consensus on roll-call votes determined. The relative weakness of the political parties and their leadership in addition to the social isolation of the mess reinforced the strength of the "boardinghouse caucus," making it the strongest determinant of how a member would vote. Young used the terms "fraternity," "mess," "boardinghouse," and even "party" interchangeably, revealing his belief in the importance of the boardinghouses.

A later study by Allan G. Bogue and Mark Paul Marlaire analyzed voting agreements to test the

CARROLL ROW. First Street between East Capitol and A Streets, S.E., site in the 1840s of Mrs. Sprigg's Boardinghouse, which catered to members of Congress.   LIBRARY OF CONGRESS

consensus-building strength of the boardinghouses. Bogue and Marlaire found that on most congressional roll calls the strongest determinant of voting behavior was not boardinghouse membership but state party agreement; often state delegation agreement was also higher than that of the mess. Throughout the period, a party member from one state was more likely to agree with another member of the same party and state than with another member of Congress, regardless of mess residence or other variables. Boardinghouse voting agreements seem to have resulted from the much higher rates of agreement among members of state delegations and state parties rather than being determining factors in themselves.

When selecting a mess, members of Congress clearly felt more comfortable in joining others from their home states and/or those who shared their political views. But considerations concerning price, quality, and location of the accommodations as well as other practical matters were most often mentioned in contemporary letters and diaries. Rather than feeling isolated in their boardinghouses and spending all their free time with their messmates, members of Congress described a very active Washington social life, with frequent guests in the mess and convivial visits to an abundance of local taverns. Far from resembling fraternities or caucuses, boardinghouses were only one site of the legislators' lively political and social lives.

By the time of the Civil War, increasing numbers of members of Congress were living in private residences or hotels and strongly identified with their political parties and those parties' leadership, resulting in a decline of boardinghouses as influences on roll-call voting. Descriptions of members' actual living conditions and their effect on political behavior have added greatly to present-day understanding of congressional history, but in the early national period the strength of loyalty to party and to state were the most critical factors in determining legislative voting.

BIBLIOGRAPHY

Bogue, Allan G., and Mark Paul Marlaire. "Of Mess and Men: The Boardinghouse and Congressional Voting, 1821–1842." *American Journal of Political Science* 19 (1975): 207–230.

Goldman, Perry M., and James S. Young. *The United States Congressional Directories, 1789–1840.* 1973.

Young, James Sterling. *The Washington Community: 1800–1828.* 1966.

MARK PAUL MARLAIRE

BOGGS, CORINNE C. (LINDY) (1916–), Democratic representative from Louisiana. Congress lost one of its most popular and politically astute members when Lindy Boggs retired in 1991, after representing Louisiana's 2d Congressional District, which includes the French Quarter of New Orleans, for eighteen years. She and her husband, Hale Boggs, the House majority leader at the time of his death in 1972 and whom she succeeded in Congress, formed one of the longest-running and most effective husband-and-wife teams in U.S. political history. Their combined tenures in the House began in 1941 and spanned half a century.

Born in Pointe Coupee Parish, Louisiana, Lindy Claiborne graduated from Newcomb College of Tulane Unversity and taught high-school history. She entered politics through a New Orleans reformist movement that ousted remnants of the Huey Long machine and in 1941 sent her twenty-six-year-old husband to the U.S. House of Representatives. In Washington, she remained closely associated with her husband's career, serving as his campaign manager, adviser, and all-around assistant, while at

CORINNE C. (LINDY) BOGGS.   LIBRARY OF CONGRESS

the same time establishing herself as one of the capital's most popular figures.

From day one as a lawmaker, Lindy Boggs had the political know-how and entrée to power of a senior House member. A master of quiet persuasion, she pursued the interests of her port-city constituency through her seat on the Appropriations Subcommittee on Energy and Water Development. Only rarely did she lead on national issues, but when she did she usually won, as in achieving pay equality for women in the civil service and in barring banks from discriminating against women borrowers.

Her district shifted to a black majority in the 1980s, but Boggs continued to win reelection handily. Analysts attributed her appeal across racial lines to her record of support for civil rights, social programs, and other minority concerns and to her emphasis on service to her constituents. But most important, they noted, the voters simply liked her.

BIBLIOGRAPHY

Barone, Michael, and Grant Ujifusa. *The Almanac of American Politics 1990.* 1989. Pp. 497–500.
U.S. House of Representatives. *Women in Congress, 1917–1990.* Prepared by the Office of the Historian. 101st Cong., 2d sess., 1991. H. Doc. 101-238. Pp. 17–18.
Will, George. "50 Years in Washington." *Washington Post,* 6 December 1990.

DONALD C. BACON

BOGGS, HALE (1914–1972), Democratic representative from Louisiana, majority whip (1962–1971), majority leader (1971–1972). Thomas Hale Boggs was five years old when his family moved from Mississippi to Gretna, Louisiana, just west of New Orleans. He graduated from Tulane University law school in 1937, entered law practice in New Orleans in the same year, and soon married Corinne "Lindy" Claiborne, a cousin of his young law partners, deLesseps S. ("Chep") Morrison and Jacob Morrison.

The Morrisons and the Boggses formed a political group to oppose the corrupt and moribund Huey P. Long machine. Running in the 2d Congressional District, Boggs defeated Rep. Paul H. Maloney in 1940 to become the youngest member of the House. He lost the seat in 1942, but, after service in the navy, reclaimed it in 1946. A crowd pleaser with old-fashioned oratorical skills, Boggs kept the congressional seat until his death.

Hale Boggs's climb in the House leadership was tied to his friendship with Speaker Sam Rayburn.

HALE BOGGS. In May 1970.   LIBRARY OF CONGRESS

The witty, partisan, and urbane Boggs was assigned to the Ways and Means Committee in 1949, and that put him in a position to influence major social and economic legislation and, through the Democratic Committee on Committees, on which all Ways and Means Democrats then served, to affect the committee assignments of other Democrats. In 1955, Rayburn brought him into the party leadership as deputy whip. Boggs held moderate-to-liberal views on most issues. He was the principal author of legislation to finance the federal interstate highway system, to provide tax allowances for working mothers, and to preserve dependency allowances on dependents enrolled in college. He pressed for liberal trade policies as chairman of the Ways and Means Subcommittee on Foreign Trade Policy and the Joint Economic Committee's Subcommittee on Foreign Economic Policy, and he was a major force behind the Trade Expansion Act of 1962.

A friend of John F. Kennedy and Lyndon B. Johnson, Boggs was a central figure in the dramatic behind-the-scenes negotiations that produced the Kennedy-Johnson ticket in 1960. When Kennedy was killed in 1963, President Johnson appointed Boggs to the Warren Commission, which investigated the assassination. Boggs helped to steer much of Johnson's Great Society legislation through Congress.

Boggs's regional and national loyalties were often in conflict with his drive to ascend the House leadership ladder. Boggs staunchly supported the Vietnam policies of both Johnson and Richard M. Nixon but remained a partisan critic of the latter's domestic programs. Boggs's shift to support civil rights in 1965 had caused such severe criticism in his district that he only narrowly won the 1968 campaign against Republican challenger David C. Treen. In 1971, despite opposition from both conservatives and liberals as well as growing concern over his frequent mood swings, Boggs ran for House majority leader. On the second ballot, he defeated Morris K. Udall of Arizona by a margin of almost two to one.

In a speech on 5 April 1971, Boggs issued a stunning call for the resignation of J. Edgar Hoover, director of the Federal Bureau of Investigation and an American law-and-order icon. Claiming to have evidence of an FBI-led surveillance program aimed at opponents of the Nixon administration (including members of Congress and college students), Boggs charged that "the way Mr. Hoover is running the FBI today it is no longer a free country." In a speech on 22 April, Boggs laid out his evidence of tapped telephones and other spying activities that he said the FBI had directed at himself and others. Critics found the evidence inconclusive, and the issue soon faded. Boggs's suspicions, though not his specific charges of massive illegal FBI activity, were generally confirmed the following year with the unfolding of the Watergate scandal.

Boggs was in Alaska on 16 October 1972 to campaign for Rep. Nicholas J. Begich (D-Alaska); the plane carrying the two congressmen was lost after leaving Anchorage. No trace was found. Boggs was declared presumed dead in December 1972. His widow, Lindy Boggs, was elected to replace him in the House. She held the seat until her retirement in 1990.

BIBLIOGRAPHY

Ferrell, Thomas F., and Judith A. Haydel. "Lindy and Hale Boggs: Louisiana's National Democrats." In *Louisiana's Political Leaders: Ratings and Case Studies.* Edited by Vincent J. Marsala and William D. Pederson. 1993.

Kirn, Dorothy N. *Hale Boggs: A Southern Spokesman for the Democratic Party.* 1980.

Peabody, Robert L. *Leadership in Congress.* 1976.

WILLIAM D. PEDERSON

BOLAND AMENDMENTS.

Named for Rep. Edward P. Boland (D-Mass.), chairman of the House Permanent Select Committee on Intelligence (1977–1984), the Boland amendments were three distinct measures adopted between 1982 and 1985 that limited the president's authority to covertly aid the Contra rebels fighting the leftist Sandinista government in Nicaragua. The debates over Contra aid were among the most bitter and divisive foreign policy debates of the Reagan era.

President Reagan initiated covert support for the Contras in late 1981. In the summer of 1982, the House Intelligence Committee added the first Boland amendment (Boland I) to the Classified Annex to the Intelligence Authorization Act for Fiscal Year 1983. It prohibited U.S. aid to paramilitary groups "for the purpose of overthrowing the Government of Nicaragua or provoking a military exchange between Nicaragua and Honduras."

The full House publicly reaffirmed Boland I in December 1982, adding it to the 1983 defense appropriation on a vote of 411 to 0. The administration did not oppose Boland I, because it was substituted for a proposal with more restrictive language. Reagan interpreted Boland I as allowing continued U.S. aid to the Contras as long as the purpose of U.S. policy was not among those proscribed—even though the Contras themselves admittedly sought to overthrow the Sandinistas.

The escalation of the Nicaraguan war in 1983 convinced many members of Congress that the administration was violating Boland I. Consequently, Representative Boland and the House Democratic leadership developed a new measure (Boland II) to prohibit all U.S. assistance to the Contras. The first appearance of Boland II was House Resolution 2760, which passed the House 228 to 195 in July 1983, but was not taken up by the Republican-controlled Senate. In October, the House added Boland II to the intelligence authorization and defense appropriations bills for fiscal 1984, but the Senate refused to accept it in conference. As a compromise, U.S. assistance to the Contras was capped at $24 million for fiscal 1984, half of what Reagan had requested.

In May 1984, the House reaffirmed its support

for Boland II, voting 241 to 177 to delete $21 million in additional Contra aid that the Senate had added to an emergency supplemental appropriation. The House also added Boland II to the intelligence bill for fiscal 1985. After revelations that the CIA had mined Nicaragua's harbors without adequately informing the congressional Intelligence committees, the Senate acceded to the House position in October, and Boland II became law. It read:

No funds available to the Central Intelligence Agency, the Department of Defense, or any other agency or entity of the United States involved in intelligence activities may be obligated or expended for the purpose or which would have the effect of supporting, directly or indirectly, military or paramilitary operations in Nicaragua by any nation, group organization, movement, or individual.

After President Reagan's 1984 reelection, Congress was more receptive to his determined advocacy of Contra aid. In June 1985, the House rejected a proposal to extend Boland II without regard to fiscal year and approved a Republican-backed proposal to provide the Contras with $27 million in "nonlethal aid," which included both nonmilitary and military assistance excluding arms and ammunition.

The intelligence authorization for fiscal 1986 included modified Boland language that subsequently came to be known as Boland III. The modification, introduced by administration supporters, created an exception to the ban on military aid, allowing "intelligence sharing" with the Contras. The exception produced considerable uncertainty about what sorts of aid the CIA could legally provide. Although Republicans later criticized Boland III for its ambiguity, they were glad to be rid of the unambiguous prohibition of Boland II. Boland III was finally repealed in 1986 when Congress approved President Reagan's $100 million aid package for the Contras without any significant restrictions.

The Iran-contra investigation in 1987 revealed that senior administration officials, led by Oliver North, an aide to the National Security Council, had continued aiding the Contras, despite the Boland II and Boland III prohibitions, and had actively concealed their actions from Congress. Although Reagan denied knowledge of North's activities, anger over the revelation contributed to Congress's decision in early 1988 to end all further military assistance to the Contras.

BIBLIOGRAPHY

Arnson, Cynthia J. *Crossroads: Congress, the Reagan Administration, and Central America.* 1993.
LeoGrande, William M. "The Contras and Congress." In *Reagan versus the Sandinistas.* Edited by Thomas W. Walker. 1987.
U.S. Congress. House of Representatives Select Committee to Investigate Covert Arms Transactions with Iran; Senate Select Committee on Secret Military Assistance to Iran and the Nicaraguan Opposition. *Report of the Congressional Committees Investigating the Iran-Contra Affair.* 100th Cong., 1st sess., 1987. H. Rept. 100-433, S. Rept. 100-216.

WILLIAM M. LEOGRANDE

BOLLING, RICHARD W. (1916–1991), Democratic representative from Missouri (1949–1983), chairman of the Committee on Rules (1979–1983), and a skilled legislative strategist and reformer. Though born in New York City, Richard Walker Bolling had Alabama roots. He was educated at the University of the South and at Vanderbilt University, became a teacher and school administrator, and then served with distinction in World War II. Three years after moving to Kansas City, Missouri, he won election to Congress as an anti-machine Democrat. He won reelection easily until his retirement in 1983.

Immersing himself in the House's work, Bolling gained mastery of its procedures and practices. Soon he became a protégé of Speaker Sam Rayburn and a regular in his inner circle, the "Board of Education." In 1955 Bolling moved to the Rules Committee, where for the next twenty-eight years he was the most respected strategist and reformer of his generation.

A liberal in the Roosevelt-Truman mold, Bolling pushed civil rights and forged close ties with organized labor. He was Rayburn's link with the growing circle of liberals chafing at the conservative barons who controlled key committees.

On the Rules Committee, Bolling was described as Rayburn's hatchet man. He schemed to pry labor and civil rights bills from the conservative panel and its chairman, Howard W. Smith of Virginia. In 1961, he and others persuaded Rayburn to enlarge the Rules Committee in order to loosen the conservatives' grip and ease passage of President John F. Kennedy's program.

After Rayburn died late that year, Bolling made a surprise bid for the majority leader's job against party whip Carl B. Albert of Oklahoma. Although the two had similar voting records, Bolling was touted as the liberal candidate by labor and civil rights lobbyists and the press. But while Bolling hesitated to ask colleagues for support, Albert was on the telephone securing votes. It was a triumph of inside strategy over outside strategy; Bolling withdrew and in the caucus moved that Albert's election be unanimous.

Bolling was excluded from leadership circles during the nine-year reign of Rayburn's successor, John W. McCormack of Massachusetts, who shunned liberal reformers in favor of senior cronies who retained their grip, albeit a weakening one, on key committees. Helped by his friend Wes Barthelmas, Bolling wrote two books, *House Out of Order* (1965) and *Power in the House* (1968), advocating reforms to strengthen party leaders and curb committee chairs' power.

McCormack's successors relied on Bolling's knowledge and skills. Many of his proposals were adopted in the 1970s, strengthening party leaders and caucuses at the expense of committee leaders. Bolling played a key role in drafting the landmark Congressional Budget and Impoundment Control Act of 1974.

Less successful was Bolling's proposed reform of the committee system. At the behest of Speaker Albert and Minority Leader Gerald R. Ford, Bolling chaired a bipartisan select committee that in 1973 and 1974 examined all aspects of committee operations and designed a wide-ranging plan to realign jurisdictions, eliminate obsolete panels, and bolster oversight of the executive. The plan was defeated by members who feared losing their turf, though a watered-down version was adopted in 1975.

The next year Bolling tried again for the majority leader's job against wily Phillip Burton of California, a chief antagonist of the committee reform plan. On the second ballot Bolling was bumped from the race when he fell two votes behind the compromise candidate, James C. Wright, Jr., of Texas, who finally won.

Bolling's last two terms were spent at the helm of the Rules Committee, where he had sat for twenty-four years under less able people. Now he made the panel an arm of the leadership, devising special new rules to strengthen the majority party's hand in scheduling and managing floor debates.

Bolling was a proud, articulate man of striking appearance. "I like Dick," a colleague once said, "but if I told him they had just found a bomb in the basement of the Capitol, he would say, 'Yes, I knew it was there all the time and I told them to do something about it years ago.'" His seeming aloofness, even arrogance, flowed from an innate reticence, impatience with small talk, and total absorption with the House's business. He failed to follow his mentor Rayburn's path to leadership, yet as much as anyone he reshaped the House that Rayburn left.

BIBLIOGRAPHY

Bolling, Richard. *House Out of Order.* 1965.
Bolling, Richard. *Power in the House: A History of the Leadership of the House of Representatives.* 1968.
Davidson, Roger H., and Walter J. Oleszek. *Congress against Itself.* 1977.
Polsby, Nelson W. "Two Strategies of Influence: Choosing a Majority Leader, 1962." In *New Perspectives on the House of Representatives.* Edited by Robert L. Peabody and Nelson W. Polsby. 1963. Pp. 237–270.

ROGER H. DAVIDSON

BOLTON, FRANCES P. (1885–1977), representative from Ohio, ranking Republican on the Committee on Foreign Affairs, and first woman congressional delegate to the United Nations General Assembly. Born Frances Payne Bingham, she was the daughter of wealthy and well-connected Cleveland parents. Her marriage in 1907 to Chester C. Bolton, a rich, politically ambitious lawyer whose father had been a law partner of Republican boss Marcus A. Hanna, awakened her to the challenge of public service to which, along with philanthropy, she devoted the rest of her long life.

Chester C. Bolton was elected to the U.S. House in 1928. Following his death in 1939, Frances Bolton won a special election to serve out his term. The first woman elected to Congress from Ohio, she remained in the House until redistricting in 1968 led to her defeat, at age eighty-three. Her political opponents contemptuously labeled her "Congress's richest member," which she probably was.

She ran in 1940 as an anti–Franklin D. Roosevelt isolationist, but at the outbreak of World War II she joined the war effort, concentrating in an area that had long attracted her interest—public health and nursing. During World War I she had pressured the army into establishing a school of nursing. As a congresswoman in 1943, she sponsored the Bolton Act, which created a U.S. Cadet Nurse Corps and provided training for some 124,000 nurses. She also championed a law to provide regular officers' commissions for members of the Army Nurse Corps. In 1944, she made a widely publicized in-

FRANCES P. BOLTON.

spection tour of U.S. military hospitals in Europe, becoming the first woman lawmaker to visit a war zone.

The one-time isolationist became an avowed internationalist after the war, traveling extensively as a member of the Foreign Affairs Committee, speaking out against the spread of communism, and gaining status as an authority on Africa. She and her son, Oliver P. Bolton (R-Ohio), made history in 1952 when his election to the House made them the only mother and son ever to have served in Congress concurrently.

BIBLIOGRAPHY

Cheshire, Maxine. "Congresswoman Travels a Long Way Forward." *Washington Post and Times Herald,* 12 May 1957, pp. F-1, F-3, F-6.

Loth, David. *A Long Way Forward: The Biography of Congresswoman Frances P. Bolton.* 1957.

U.S. House of Representatives. *Women in Congress, 1917–1990.* Prepared by the Office of the Historian. 101st Cong., 2d sess., 1991. H. Doc. 101-238. Pp. 21–22.

DONALD C. BACON

BONUS MARCH. Following World War I, two new veterans' organizations, the American Legion and the Veterans of Foreign Wars, steadily intensified their congressional lobbying for increased veterans' benefits. In 1924 Congress avoided a third presidential veto by delaying payment of a World War I "bonus" until 1945, when compound interest from a trust fund could pay an average bonus of $1,000. By 1929 renewed lobbying had generated more than forty pending veterans' bills. In response, President Herbert Hoover convinced Congress to create the Veterans Administration and to increase benefits for all veterans. But veterans severely criticized Hoover when he opposed their demand for immediate payment of the bonus, which would have amounted to $4 billion—equivalent to the entire federal budget.

In 1932 more than twenty thousand veterans responded with a spontaneous march on the capital. Throughout June and July the bonus marchers lobbied Congress. Hoover secretly protected the marchers' civil liberties and provided food, tents, equipment, and an army field hospital while steadfastly resisting demands to evict them. The House passed a bill for immediate payment, but on 16 July the Senate overwhelmingly rejected it. Under pressure of a threatened lawsuit from a wrecking contractor, Hoover agreed to the eviction on 28 July of a small contingent of veterans from several condemned buildings. These veterans attacked the police, and in the process, two veterans were killed. The frightened police demanded that federal troops be summoned.

Hoover directed that the troops be limited to the small riot area and that they only assist the police. However, when army chief of staff Gen. Douglas MacArthur took command, he deliberately disobeyed Hoover's repeated orders to stop operations and instead attacked the veterans' camps, driving the bonus marchers and their wives and children out of the capital.

The bonus march delivered an irreparable blow to Hoover's reputation. MacArthur falsely justified his disobedience by insisting that his troops faced armed communist insurrectionists, and Hoover unwisely believed him. But when neither MacArthur nor any federal agency could prove a communist plot, Hoover bore the blame for the cruel rout.

President Franklin D. Roosevelt twice vetoed immediate bonus payment, but in 1936 Congress overrode him.

BONUS MARCHERS. On the lawn of the Capitol, 1932.   OFFICE OF THE HISTORIAN OF THE U.S. SENATE

BIBLIOGRAPHY

Lisio, Donald J. *The President and Protest: Hoover, Conspiracy, and the Bonus Riot.* 1974.
Lisio, Donald J. "A Blunder Becomes Catastrophe: Hoover, the Legion, and the Bonus Army." *Wisconsin Magazine of History* 51 (1967): 37–50.

DONALD J. LISIO

BORAH, WILLIAM E. (1865–1940), senator from Idaho, progressive Republican maverick, famed orator, and vigorous opponent of U.S. commitments abroad. Elected in 1907 as the leader of the reform wing of Idaho's Republican party, Borah served in the U.S. Senate until he died of a brain hemorrhage in 1940. By then, *Time* magazine had already decided that he was "the most famed Senator of the century." His eloquence, his celebrated independence, his influence as chairman of the Senate Foreign Relations Committee from 1924 to 1933, and his stands on the major issues unquestionably made him one of the nation's dominant political figures.

As a prominent progressive, he fought for many reforms, including the graduated income tax, the direct election of senators, laws to protect workers, and Prohibition. He had "an instinctive sympathy for the underdog," as he said, although his sympathies sometimes did not cross racial lines. He was a strong defender of small-town agrarian life. A resolute foe of concentrated power, Borah wanted to destroy corporate monopolies, which he viewed as bastions of the rich. He backed direct primary elections and women's suffrage to make government more responsive to the people. Although he urged government to protect the public interest, he resisted federal bureaucratization. Regulatory agencies, he believed, would ultimately fall victim to the very groups they were supposed to regulate. During the Great Depression, he supported New Deal relief programs for the unemployed and pensions for the elderly, but he bitterly fought measures, such as the National Industrial Recovery Act (1933), that consolidated economic and political power or upset the constitutional balance between the branches of government.

Borah vigilantly guarded civil liberties. He voted against the World War I Espionage Act and campaigned after the war for amnesty for political prisoners. "Instead of persecuting men with ideas to express," he said, "we should hire halls for them."

Republicans often questioned his loyalty to the party, particularly during the 1920s when he was a leading critic of the Harding and Coolidge administrations. Calvin Coolidge scoffed that no one could have seen Borah riding on horseback, because the senator could never go in the same direction as the horse. Presidential ambitions unquestionably influenced Borah. In 1936, he finally declared his candidacy but failed to capture the Republican nomination.

An individualist and a loner, he nevertheless shrewdly cultivated the press and had a remarkable knack for publicity. Supporters labeled him "the Lion of Idaho." Because he viewed politics as a moral undertaking and tended to lecture and sermonize, detractors called him "Saint Borah."

For all his concerns about political principles, however, Borah frequently substituted rhetoric for action. He thus often disappointed reformers who looked to him as their champion. As Nebraska senator George W. Norris said, Borah shoots "until he sees the whites of their eyes."

Borah was one of the distinguished orators in U.S. history. Well-prepared and knowledgeable, he dazzled audiences with facts and logic, not theatrics or demagogic appeals. "Borah's up!" brought a stampede of reporters and spectators to the Senate.

In foreign policy, Borah was a dedicated nationalist who fiercely battled foreign entanglements. He regretted voting for the U.S. declaration of war in 1917, because that conflict had encouraged such entanglements. After the war, he joined with a small group of like-minded senators, known as the "irreconcilables," and played a pivotal role in blocking America's entry into the League of Nations. In his opinion, the League threatened U.S. independence and would be the instrument by which powerful European countries controlled their empires. Borah worried also that the United States itself was turning imperialistic. By sending marines into Central America again and again, he said, the United States was bullying other nations in order to protect the investments of wealthy bankers.

Borah astutely recognized that nationalism and revolution were transforming the world. The United States, he firmly believed, should allow countries to work out their own destinies. For fifteen years, he pushed for the United States to recognize Soviet Russia, a policy that the Franklin D. Roosevelt administration adopted in 1933.

As war spread around the world during the 1930s, Borah's aversion to U.S. foreign entanglements fueled his struggle to keep America neutral. He was apprehensive about German and Japanese

WILLIAM E. BORAH.   LIBRARY OF CONGRESS

expansion but suspected that the British and the French were also pursuing imperial goals. By the late 1930s, however, his influence was fading and events were leaving him behind.

Borah's death in 1940 spared him from having to witness America's entry into World War II and the events that followed. The war accelerated trends that he had long opposed—trends that made the United States more urban, bureaucratic, corporate, and interventionist.

BIBLIOGRAPHY

Ashby, LeRoy. *The Spearless Leader: Senator Borah and the Progressive Movement in the 1920s.* 1972.
Johnson, Claudius O. *Borah of Idaho.* 1936.
Maddox, Robert James. *William E. Borah and American Foreign Policy.* 1969.
McKenna, Marian C. *Borah.* 1961.

LeRoy Ashby

BOTANIC GARDEN. The U.S. Botanic Garden was chartered by Congress in 1820 to collect, cultivate, and grow the various flora of this and other countries for exhibition and display to the public and for use by interested students, scientists, and garden clubs. Situated near the Capitol, the garden is the oldest continually operating botanic garden in North America. The first greenhouse for the garden was constructed in 1842 to accommodate a botanical collection brought to Washington from the South Seas by the U.S. Exploring Expedition of 1838 to 1842. The greenhouse was located behind the first federal Patent Office building on 8th and F Streets, N.W. In 1850, the garden was relocated to a conservatory on the eastern end of the Mall, at the base of Capitol Hill.

Eventually, the conservatory became inadequate for carrying out the objectives of the garden, and Congress authorized the preparation of plans for the construction of a new building. In 1931, the cornerstone of the present U.S. Botanic Garden Conservatory was laid. The main location, at Maryland Avenue and First Street, S.W. includes the conservatory and surrounding terrace; Frederic Auguste Bartholdi Park, which features the majestic Bartholdi Fountain and an outdoor display area; and an administration building. Plants are grown and produced at a separate location in Anacostia, Washington, D.C.

The U.S. Botanic Garden highlights the importance of plants to the well-being of humankind and to the fragile ecosystems that support all life.

The conservatory houses collections of plants from subtropical, tropical and arid regions. There are also special exhibits that showcase orchids and carnivorous, medicinal, and endangered plants. The garden's outdoor and indoor displays further our appreciation of the aesthetic, cultural, economic, therapeutic, and environmental value of plants worldwide.

Since 1856, the Botanic Garden has been under the jurisdiction of the Joint Committee on the Library of Congress. The architect of the Capitol, who has been serving as acting director since July 1934, is responsible for the operation and maintenance of the Botanic Garden and for any construction and improvements made to it.

Seasonal flower shows throughout the year provide color, beauty, and an educational experience. Classes covering subjects as diverse as plant conservation, plant ecology, ethnobotany, medicinal plants, paleobotany, and folklore are offered from September through June, and tours are available by appointment.

BIBLIOGRAPHY

Haskell, Daniel C. *The United States Exploring Expedition, 1838–1842.* 1942.
Rathbun, Richard. *The Columbian Institute for the Promotion of Arts and Sciences.* Bulletin 101 of the Smithsonian Institution. 1917.

Holly H. Shimizu

BOUTWELL, GEORGE S. (1818–1905), representative and senator from Massachusetts, leader of the impeachment of President Andrew Johnson, and coauthor of the Fourteenth and Fifteenth Amendments to the U.S. Constitution. An early and consistent spokesman for mass participation in politics and for universal education, Boutwell began his political career as a Democrat. He was elected as such six times to the Massachusetts House of Representatives (1840–1850) and then as the youngest governor in the state's history (1851–1853).

His antagonism toward slavery, however, led him to help form the Massachusetts Republican party. An early and consistent supporter of Abraham Lincoln and the Civil War, he advocated the use of black troops in the Union army. Boutwell became the first commissioner of Internal Revenue in 1862. Within a year, he returned to the political arena as a Republican member of the U.S. House of Representatives. Boutwell's views on slavery, emancipation, black suffrage, and the punishment of the Con-

GEORGE S. BOUTWELL.   LIBRARY OF CONGRESS

federate states were much more militant than Lincoln's, and he became a leader of the so-called Radical Republicans. Unlike some Radicals, however, he opposed black colonization overseas and strongly advocated black suffrage. Always loquacious, occasionally tactless, he rarely hid his feelings. Within a few weeks of entering the 38th Congress (1863–1865), Boutwell urged confiscation of Confederate-owned land.

Boutwell believed that congressional, not executive, control of southern economic power was central to reconstruction. When Andrew Johnson assumed the presidency in 1865 and openly supported the former Confederate states' return to the Union without black suffrage, Boutwell became more strident. His membership on the House Judiciary Committee and on the Joint Committee on Reconstruction made him quite influential. On 11 December 1865, he proposed extending the franchise to blacks. Boutwell's fear that Johnson was attempting to undo Civil War victories and thwart

black civil rights led him, in October 1866, to suggest impeachment. He drafted the twenty-eight charges of impeachment and became an influential manager of the impeachment process. Although the "Massachusetts Impeacher," as Boutwell was called, was unsuccessful, he never waivered in his belief in black suffrage. His commitment paid off when on 11 January 1869 the Judiciary Committee proposed what became the Fifteenth Amendment.

After four years as President Ulysses S. Grant's secretary of the Treasury (1869–1873), Boutwell returned to Congress for a four-year term as a senator from Massachusetts. He continued to fight for black civil rights, now turning his attention to educational opportunity for both blacks and whites. Long a congressional supporter of the Freedman's Bureau, he strongly supported passage of the Civil Rights Act of 1875. Boutwell sought to secure from the Senate Judiciary Committee a bill prohibiting school segregation, and he unsuccessfully proposed a tax-supported integrated public school system. His 1877 reelection attempt failed, and he returned to private life as an international lawyer. To the end of his long life he remained an advocate of human rights. In the words of his memorial tablet, he was a "Consistent, Brave, and Devoted Friend of Human Liberty."

BIBLIOGRAPHY

Brown, Thomas H. *George Sewall Boutwell: Human Rights Advocate.* 1989.
Boutwell, George, S. *Reminiscences of Sixty Years in Public Affairs.* 2 vols. 1902.

THOMAS H. BROWN

BOWSHER V. SYNAR (478 U.S. 714 [1986]). The Balanced Budget and Emergency Deficit Control Act of 1985, popularly known as the Gramm-Rudman-Hollings Act, established budget deficit targets for the years 1986 to 1991. Failure to achieve those targets in a given year would trigger a process whereby across-the-board cuts in programs would be made. Both the Congressional Budget Office (CBO) and the Office of Management and Budget (OMB) would report to the comptroller general on the cuts necessary to achieve the deficit amount specified. The comptroller would evaluate the reports of CBO and OMB and report to the president the cuts required.

In *Bowsher v. Synar*, the Supreme Court struck down this statutory scheme as unconstitutionally involving Congress in the supervision of officials charged with executing the laws. The comptroller general is the head of the General Accounting Office, an entity independent of the executive branch. While the comptroller is appointed by the president with the advice and consent of the Senate for a fixed term, the comptroller is removable by impeachment or by joint resolution of Congress for certain statutorily prescribed causes. Applying the reasoning of *Immigration and Naturalization Service v. Chadha* (1983), which struck down the legislative veto, the Court held that to permit an officer subject to congressional removal for causes short of impeachment to execute the laws would be in effect to permit a congressional veto.

The lower court in *Bowsher* had raised doubts not only about the congressional removal provisions governing the comptroller general but also about confining the president to for-cause removal of members of independent regulatory commissions. The Supreme Court, however, distinguished between direct congressional involvement in the removal of the comptroller general and the statutes establishing independent agencies, which either specify the causes for which the president may remove an officer or are silent on removal. Later cases—particularly *Morrison v. Olson* (1988), which upheld the special prosecutor law—seemed to confirm the continued legitimacy from a separation-of-powers standpoint of the independent agency structure.

[*See also* Balanced Budget and Emergency Deficit Control Act.]

BIBLIOGRAPHY

Gifford, David J. "The Separation of Powers Doctrine and the Regulatory Agencies after *Bowsher v. Synar.*" *George Washington Law Review* 55 (1987): 441–481.

Currie, David P. "The Distribution of Powers after *Bowsher.*" *Supreme Court Review* 19 (1986): 19–40.

RICHARD C. EHLKE

BRECKINRIDGE, JOHN C. (1821–1875), Democratic representative and senator from Kentucky, vice president, presidential candidate, soldier. Breckinridge was a member of a distinguished Kentucky family. After attending several colleges he studied law, set up practice, saw brief service in the Mexican War, and went to the state legislature. A staunch Democrat, he won a seat in the U.S. House of Representatives in 1851 in a heavily Whig district and was reelected two years later. Quickly emerging as an important leader in the House, he played a leading role in the repeal of the Missouri Compromise, helping to draft the Kansas-Nebraska bill and to secure its passage in the House. He was a member of the Ways and Means Committee and increasingly served as its main spokesman on the floor. Despite his national stature, his enemies in Kentucky gerrymandered his district, forcing him to retire at the end of his second term.

In 1856, at the age of thirty-five, he was elected vice president. His impartial and dignified service as presiding officer of the Senate earned widespread praise. During these years his southern sympathies grew progressively stronger: he worked privately for approval of the proslavery Lecompton constitution for Kansas, and, in his one important vote, he broke a tie against a homestead bill in 1859. After the national Democratic party split, the southern wing nominated him for president in 1860. Although he steadfastly denied that he favored disunion, he was backed by southern radicals and led all other presidential candidates in the South. During the secession crisis, he supported the compromise efforts of John J. Crittenden and others; when it became his duty to preside over the official counting of the electoral votes, he thwarted southern efforts to disrupt the proceedings. Nevertheless, he upheld the right of secession and strenuously opposed any coercion of a state.

JOHN C. BRECKINRIDGE.

Breckinridge had earlier been elected to the Senate, and he assumed his seat in the special session in July 1861. He gained notoriety as a vigorous opponent of the Civil War, which he denounced as illegal. When Kentucky abandoned its neutrality in September, Breckinridge fled the state to avoid arrest by the Union military for disloyalty. The state legislature requested that he resign his Senate seat, which he did in October. The following month he was indicted for treason, and, despite his resignation, the Senate on 2 December 1861 formally proclaimed him a traitor and expelled him.

In the meantime, Breckinridge had accepted a Confederate military commission. He served without particular distinction until February 1865, when he became the Confederate secretary of war. After the Confederacy's surrender, he fled to Europe and Canada; returning to Kentucky in 1869, he withdrew from public affairs and died in 1875.

Breckinridge's congressional career revealed a growing divergence between his professed ideals and his actions. Torn by conflicting emotions, he insisted throughout the 1850s that he was a defender of the Union at the same time that he adopted increasingly radical proslavery positions. In the final crisis, he almost impulsively endorsed disunion without carefully considering this decision. His erratic, unsteady course negated his considerable talents and prevented him from achieving the promise of his early congressional career.

BIBLIOGRAPHY

Davis, William C. *Breckinridge: Statesman, Soldier, Symbol.* 1974.
Heck, Frank H. "John C. Breckinridge and the Crisis of 1860–1861." *Journal of Southern History* 21 (1955): 316–346.

WILLIAM E. GIENAPP

BRICKER AMENDMENT. Sen. John W. Bricker, a conservative Republican from Ohio, first introduced his constitutional amendment in 1951. Bricker and the leaders of the American Bar Association feared that the United Nations Charter, the Genocide Convention, and the UN's draft covenant on human rights would allow the federal government to encroach further on the reserved powers of the states in economic and social matters. They thus proposed amending the Constitution to limit the use and effects of treaties and executive agreements within the United States.

In June 1953 the Senate Judiciary Committee recommended approval of an amendment that reit-

SEN. JOHN W. BRICKER (R-OHIO). Holding copy of the Bricker Amendment.   LIBRARY OF CONGRESS

erated the Constitution's supremacy over treaties, required implementing legislation "which would be valid in the absence of [a] treaty" before a treaty would have force within the United States and gave Congress the power to regulate all executive agreements. If approved, the Bricker amendment would have weakened the authority of the president and the federal government to enter into and carry out international agreements.

The Bricker amendment had sixty-four cosponsors in the Senate, including almost all the Republicans, isolationists, and conservative Democrats. But President Dwight D. Eisenhower opposed the amendment, fearing that it would limit his authority and flexibility in foreign affairs. The administration's supporters joined with liberal Democrats to defeat the Bricker amendment in the Senate in 1954.

Although the Bricker amendment was never adopted, the debate over the measure made senators more aware of the domestic effects of international agreements. It also delayed U.S. ratification of the Genocide Convention until 1986.

BIBLIOGRAPHY

Reichard, Gary. "Eisenhower and the Bricker Amendment." *Prologue* 6 (1974): 88–99.

Tananbaum, Duane. *The Bricker Amendment Controversy: A Test of Eisenhower's Political Leadership.* 1988.

Tananbaum, Duane. "The Bricker Amendment Controversy: Its Origins and Eisenhower's Role." *Diplomatic History* 9 (1985): 73–93.

DUANE TANANBAUM

BRIDGES, H. STYLES (1898–1961), governor, Senate Republican leader from New Hampshire, Appropriations Committee chairman. Henry Styles Bridges was born in West Pembroke, Maine, and graduated from the University of Maine in 1918. Involvement in rural outreach led him to relocate to New Hampshire in 1921. After serving in a number of nonelective posts, he narrowly won the state's governorship in 1934, becoming New Hampshire's youngest chief executive.

When Bridges came to the U.S. Senate in 1937, he was one of only seventeen Republicans—the party's twentieth-century nadir. Bridges early defined himself as a fervent anticommunist and staunch domestic conservative. Although his fiscal conservatism placed him at odds philosophically with the Republican party's moderate and liberal eastern wing, it enabled him to a play a major role in the Senate Republican establishment. His geographical links to the Senate's eastern liberals and his philosophical links to conservative midwestern Republicans gave him access to both wings of the Senate Republican party as it came to grips with postwar political power.

Bridges held important assignments on the Appropriations and Armed Services committees. He was the senior Republican on the Senate Appropriations Committee, chairing it in both the 80th (1947–1949) and 83d (1953–1955) Congresses and serving as ranking minority member in six other Congresses from 1949 until his death in 1961. He also served as minority leader in 1952 and 1953 after the death of Sen. Kenneth S. Wherry of Nebraska. Bridges much preferred committee work to floor leadership and willingly relinquished the party leadership post to Sen. Robert A. Taft of Ohio, whose presidential ambitions had been thwarted a year earlier by Dwight D. Eisenhower.

Although less publicly visible than his contemporaries, Bridges played a powerful behind-the-scenes

H. STYLES BRIDGES. In March 1961.

LIBRARY OF CONGRESS

role that was crucial as Senate Republicans sought to balance their regional and philosophical rivalries in the 1940s and 1950s.

BIBLIOGRAPHY

Cotton, Norris. *In the Senate: Amidst the Conflict and the Turmoil.* 1978.

Horn, Steven C. *Unused Power: The Work of the Senate Committee on Appropriations.* 1970.

Reichard, Gary W. *The Reaffirmation of Republicanism: Eisenhower and the Eighty-third Congress.* 1975.

GARRISON NELSON

BROADCASTING OF CONGRESSIONAL PROCEEDINGS. The relationship between Congress and radio and television is rooted in the earliest days of American broadcasting. In 1922—only two years after the first U.S. radio station became operational—Rep. Vincent M. Brennan (R-

Mich.) introduced the first bill to authorize a radio service to broadcast congressional proceedings. The measure failed, but the idea persisted. By the late 1940s, television's displacement of radio as America's preeminent electronic mass medium had begun to change attitudes toward the broadcasting of congressional proceedings. Even House and Senate members who firmly opposed televising chamber deliberations welcomed television coverage of committee hearings.

Televised Committee Proceedings. Television cameras first were admitted to congressional hearing rooms in 1948, to cover Senate Armed Services Committee hearings. Soon they were covering House Un-American Activities Committee hearings on the spread of communism. The small number of households with television sets during the period, however, meant that few Americans were able to watch the hearings. Television sets had become more numerous by the early 1950s, when the hearings of the Senate Special Committee to Investigate Organized Crime in Interstate Commerce were broadcast. The so-called Kefauver Crime Committee, named for its chairman, Estes Kefauver (D-Tenn.), conducted hearings in fourteen U.S. cities as it investigated the spread of organized crime in the United States. Kefauver Crime Committee testimony was televised locally in a number of these cities, but when the committee moved to New York City and Washington, D.C., its televised hearings caused a sensation when millions of people interrupted jobs and household chores alike to watch them.

Televised hearings led by Sen. Joseph R. McCarthy to investigate alleged communist infiltration of the U.S. armed forces generated even greater public attention than the Kefauver committee hearings. Senator McCarthy used his position as chairman of the Senate Committee on Government Operations' permanent investigations subcommittee to conduct thirty-six days of hearings lasting from 22 April to 17 June 1954. The ABC and Dumont television networks provided live coverage of all 187 hours of what came to be known as the Army-McCarthy hearings. The NBC television network carried only the first two days of the hearings live before it joined CBS in providing viewers with only filmed highlights of each day's proceedings. An opening-day estimated television audience of some thirty million people leveled off to an average of nine to ten million per day as the Army-McCarthy hearings wore on.

Viewer reaction to what they saw of the Army-McCarthy hearings centered on the demeanor of

Senator McCarthy. Whereas some saw the senator as a courageous American, many of McCarthy's colleagues regarded his hearing tactics as intimidating and voted to censure him shortly after the Army-McCarthy hearings ended.

Nearly twenty years passed before televised congressional hearings again so thoroughly seized public attention. By the summer of 1973, when the Senate Select Committee on Presidential Campaign Activities—known as the Ervin committee after its chairman, Samuel J. Ervin, Jr. (D-N.C.)—opened its hearings on the Watergate affair to television cameras, practically every U.S. household had one or more television sets. An estimated 85 percent of these households tuned in to watch at least some portion of the Ervin committee hearings. Evidence of presidential misdeeds uncovered by the Ervin committee was eventually transferred to the House Judiciary Committee. During several days of high drama in July 1974, television viewers watched the committee initiate impeachment proceedings against President Richard M. Nixon. Nixon's resignation saved the nation from the trauma of an impeachment trial, but, had a trial occurred, television would have been there: both houses of Congress had already established ground rules to allow full coverage.

More recent hearings have also attracted extended television coverage. When the House Select Committee to Investigate Covert Arms Transactions with Iran and the Senate Select Committee on Secret Military Assistance to Iran and the Nicaraguan Opposition conducted joint hearings in 1987 on the Iran-contra affair, television cameras were there. And more drama than was anticipated accompanied televised coverage of the Senate Judiciary Committee's confirmation hearings for U.S. Supreme Court nominee Clarence Thomas in 1991. The routine hearings that supposedly had concluded in September were reconvened in October, when the Judiciary Committee was forced to consider charges of sexual harrassment leveled against Thomas.

Televised Chamber Proceedings. In 1973 the Joint Committee on Congressional Operations returned House and Senate attention to the possibility of televising chamber proceedings. The committee's purpose was twofold: to explore ways in which Congress could better communicate its role to the American public, and to explore ways that Congress might compete with the extensive media attention given the president.

The joint committee's eventual recommendation that Congress test the televising of chamber proceedings won only a lukewarm reception in the Senate. The House showed more enthusiasm, forming a special broadcasting subcommittee to explore implementation of the joint committee's recommendation. One of the most controversial issues with which the subcommittee had to grapple pertained to the ultimate authority over a House television system. The subcommittee preferred a system controlled by the television networks, whereas Speaker Carl B. Albert (D-Okla.) insisted that ultimate control should reside with the Speaker.

Efforts to resolve the dispute over the system's control delayed further action on televising House proceedings until the 95th Congress, when the new Speaker, Thomas P. (Tip) O'Neill, Jr. (D-Mass.), surprised colleagues by announcing that a ninety-day test to judge the feasibility of a House television system would commence in March 1977. Remote-control cameras would provide various House offices with daily closed-circuit coverage of chamber activity. House members surveyed at the conclusion of the ninety-day experiment appeared pleased with chamber television. Few noted any of the feared adverse effects on House conduct or procedures.

The successful ninety-day test was followed by the introduction of legislation to make House television permanent. In October 1977, the House voted 342 to 44 to approve the measure in principle. Implementation of a House television system, however, had to await a final decision regarding who would control the television cameras. Advocates of network control claimed that House leaders could easily censor whatever they did not want the public to see, but advocates of a House-controlled system argued that network news managers could do the same.

The House Rules Committee considered the matter thoroughly and recommended that the House maintain control over its own television system. The recommendation was approved by a vote of 235 to 150 in June 1978, and on 19 March 1979, the House inaugurated live television coverage of its chamber proceedings. Rep. Albert A. Gore, Jr. (D-Tenn.), briefly noted the significance of the occasion before the House returned to routine business. The Public Broadcasting Service (PBS) and the Cable-Satellite Public Affairs Network (C-SPAN) were the only networks to carry the proceedings in their entirety.

The Senate's interest in televising its proceedings was slow to take hold, but by April 1981 the Senate Rules Committee had begun hearings on a measure, introduced by Sen. Howard H. Baker (R.-Tenn.), providing for continuous televised coverage of Senate chamber proceedings. Arguments on the issue were similar to ones voiced earlier in the House. Those who favored televising Senate chamber proceedings felt that it could help restore public esteem for the body. Opponents argued that it would encourage grandstanding and that the intricacies of Senate debate would confuse television viewers. The Baker bill won the approval of the Senate Rules Committee but encountered strong opposition on the Senate floor. A powerful block of senators, led by Russell B. Long (D-La.), successfully stymied any chance for televising Senate proceedings in the foreseeable future.

Sen. Robert C. Byrd (D-W.Va.) assumed retired senator Baker's advocacy role in 1985, introducing legislation calling once more for implementation of a Senate chamber television system. Senators' recognition of the success of House television had improved chances for Senate television, and Senator Long's pending retirement significantly diminished the strength of Senate television opponents.

A Rules Committee recommendation that the Senate commence testing of a closed-circuit television system was approved by the full Senate by a vote of 67 to 21 on 27 February 1986. Live television coverage of Senate chamber proceedings began on a temporary basis in June 1986, continuing through July while senators judged its effectiveness. They were satisfied enough to vote on 29 July 1986 to make television a permanent Senate fixture. Television cameras attached to gallery railings (as in the House) covered chamber activity as the Senate inaugurated its television system on 2 June. C-SPAN arranged a satellite feed (separate from its House feed) to carry Senate proceedings to interested cable-television systems nationwide. Several senators, including then–majority leader Bob Dole (R-Kan.) delivered brief remarks commemorating the occasion.

Rules for Broadcast of Committee Proceedings. Senate rules regulating television and radio coverage of committee hearings began evolving in the 1950s, when such coverage was first instituted. The Kefauver Crime Committee hearings that generated so much interest in 1952 also raised questions concerning the proper conduct of hearings in general. Some critics argued that televised interrogation abused the due process and privacy rights of witnesses. Others claimed that the bulky cameras and bright lights that were required for TV broadcasts in television's early days disrupted hearing-room decorum. Efforts by several senators to create formal codes for conducting televised hearings proved unsuccessful. Rather than to create blanket rules, the Senate instead decided to allow each committee to adopt its own procedures. Current Senate rules specify that television and radio may be allowed to cover committee and subcommittee hearings that are open to the public in accordance with whatever rules a committee or subcommittee has set for that coverage.

Some committees empower their chairmen with authority to determine the proper conduct of hearings covered by television and radio; others require that the chairman share that authority with the committee's ranking minority member; and still others require that decisions pertaining to television and radio coverage of hearings be made by majority vote of the committee. Where specific rules exist, they generally require that the chairman order that television and radio coverage be interrupted at the request of any committee witness who objects to having his or her testimony broadcasted. Other rules require that television cameras, microphones, and lighting be unobtrusive and that television and radio personnel in the hearing room conduct themselves in an orderly fashion and forbid commercial sponsorship of committee hearings.

In the early 1950s, House members shared their Senate colleagues' concern and interest in developing a code to regulate televised hearings. That concern became moot, though, when House Speaker Sam Rayburn (D-Tex.) ruled in 1952 to prohibit television and radio coverage of House committee hearings. Speaker Joseph W. Martin, Jr., had allowed the broadcast of selected hearings during his tenure, but Speaker Rayburn took a narrower view. He held in 1952 and reaffirmed in 1955 that committees were bound by the same House rules that, as he interpreted their silence on the issue, barred broadcasts of House proceedings. House Rule XI specifically extended the rules of the House to committees, and Rayburn announced on 24 January 1955 that until the rules were changed, he could not permit broadcast or photographic coverage of committee hearings, whether they were held in Washington or elsewhere. Some observers felt that the prohibition was due to the Speaker's general distrust of the media coupled with his particular reservations over the conduct of the televised Kefauver committee hearings. Whatever the reasons, the Rayburn ban remained virtually undisturbed until the 1970 Legislative Reorganization Act once again opened House committee room doors to television and radio.

Current rules for television and radio coverage of House committee hearings resemble Senate rules

"BAD NEWS FOR WASHINGTON ACTORS." Political cartoon depicting Speaker Sam Rayburn's opposition to the televising of House debates. Cy Hungerford, 1 March 1952.
REPRINTED WITH PERMISSION FROM THE *PITTSBURGH POST-GAZETTE*

in that their intentions are to protect witnesses' rights and to preserve the decorum of committee proceedings. But the House provides a more precise and extensive list of blanket rules applying to all House committees than does the Senate. For instance, the House requires that committee hearings be open to television and radio coverage for the benefit of the public, that they be covered in an impartial fashion, and that coverage not be used for partisan or campaign-related purposes. A majority vote of committee members is required to allow television and radio coverage of the committee's hearings, and each House committee may determine its own procedural rules for such coverage as long as these rules contain provisions prohibiting commercial sponsorship of the coverage, forbidding television and radio coverage of witnesses upon their request, guaranteeing fair access to accredited news organizations that request television and radio coverage of committee hearings, prohibiting the removal of television and radio apparatus while hearings are in progress, forbidding excessive lighting, and requiring that television and radio personnel conduct themselves with dignity.

Rules for Broadcast of Proceedings of Full Chamber. Rules for television and radio coverage of House chamber proceedings are likewise more precise than are rules for such coverage in the Senate chamber. The Speaker of the House has clear authority to oversee operation of the House television and radio system. The Speaker controls the manner in which chamber proceedings are covered and approves the distribution of House-oriented television and radio signals to authorized media representatives. House rules stipulate that coverage, as it originates, be unedited, that it not be used for political purposes, and that it not be used in commercial advertisements.

One House rule stipulated that television cameras be allowed to focus only on members as they addressed their colleagues from lecterns in or near the well of the House. Speaker Tip O'Neill modified this particular rule in 1984 in response to his political opponents' use of so-called special order speeches. (Special orders are reserved for members wishing to speak on topics of their choice at the conclusion of daily legislative business.) Several conservative Republican representatives took advantage of the special orders privilege in 1984 to criticize the Speaker and his political agenda. Speaker O'Neill decided to embarrass his antagonists by ordering television cameras to pan the nearly empty House chamber. Although criticized for what Republicans cited as a breach of authority, O'Neill nonetheless refused to reverse the new rule allowing panning of the chamber.

Rules for television and radio coverage of Senate chamber proceedings are enforced by a less centralized authority than in the House. The Senate Rules and Administration Committee has the ultimate authority over the use of television and radio in the Senate chamber. Operation of the television and radio systems themselves are under the authority of the Senate sergeant at arms. Like the House, the Senate requires that the television and radio signals originating from the Senate chamber be unedited and that they not be used for political campaign purposes. Television cameras must focus on senators whenever they speak (and wherever they are speaking from) and are prohibited from panning the chamber, except during roll-call votes.

Congressional Television's Impact. The amount and kind of television coverage given House and Senate activity can affect public policy. Television can influence the legislative conduct of individual members of Congress and, ultimately, their chances for reelection.

Some members of Congress have been known to seek committee assignments based on the amount of television exposure a particular committee is expected to receive and to participate actively in committee hearings only when television cameras are present. Regardless of whether a member of Congress seeks television exposure or prefers to work far from the camera's eye, any senator or representative may be thrust into the television limelight and achieve celebrity by virtue of his or her participation in newsworthy committee hearings. This is especially true of committee chairs.

No less affected by their television appearances are noncongressional House and Senate hearing participants. Attorney Anita Hill, for instance, became known to millions when she testified before the Senate Judiciary Committee's confirmation hearings for Supreme Court nominee Clarence Thomas. It was Hill's charges of sexual harrassment against the nominee that called into doubt his qualifications to serve on the Court. Another attorney—Joseph N. Welch—had achieved similar fame many years before. Welch had been appointed special counsel to represent the U.S. Army during the 1954 Army-McCarthy hearings. He not only defended the army successfully, but his mild-mannered and gentlemanly rebuff of Sen. Joseph McCarthy won him the respect of practically everyone who witnessed his performance. Welch continued to practice law after concluding his special counsel duties, but he also was in demand for television appearances to discuss legal matters.

The presence of television cameras in the House chamber has not appreciably changed legislative proceedings, although the House leadership has lost some control over younger House members who have used television to build public recognition and to increase their influence on colleagues and constituents alike. Television has been blamed for increasing partisan rhetoric in the House chamber, particularly during special order speeches (as noted above) and "one-minute" speeches delivered prior to the beginning of daily legislative business.

Senate chamber proceedings have not experienced any major departure from tradition as a result of television. Senate special order speeches increased when television first entered the chamber, but their number has since returned to a pretelevision level. Some observers contend that television actually has led to a more disciplined Senate, with senators making better, shorter, and more substantive remarks.

TELEVISED PROCEEDINGS. A congressman watching floor proceedings from his office.   LIBRARY OF CONGRESS

Self-policing has held grandstanding in both the Senate and House chambers to a minimum, and members of Congress have become more sensitive to what they say, and how they say it, because of their constituents' ability to view them on television. More important, a speaker's opponents may videotape his or her floor remarks for use in political campaigns. Although incumbent members of Congress are prohibited from such use of videotapes, nonincumbents are not.

Indirect effects of congressional television have included the improved appearance of senators and representatives: men, especially, are now taking more care to outfit themselves with telegenic suits and accessories, and some have reportedly resorted to makeup and hairpieces to improve their looks. Members have also become more proficient in the use of visual aids during debate. Outside the congressional chambers, members of Congress have found office television monitors an excellent means of keeping up with chamber debate and of becoming better informed about legislative matters.

The self-censorship that television network news organizations thought would happen unless they controlled House and Senate chamber television has not materialized. Nonetheless, networks give scant airtime to the televised proceedings, in part because of union rules that prohibit the networks from carrying more than a few minutes of programming originated by nonunion personnel. As a result of the limited time provided by the networks, members of Congress have become experts at producing comments that can easily fit into thirty-second sound bites.

There is no indication that public esteem for either the House or the Senate has improved as a result of television, but there is plenty of evidence that the public has benefited from televised House and Senate proceedings. Congressional television has increased awareness of particular issues, allowed the public to hear a wide spectrum of views on these issues, and instructed viewers in the fundamentals of the legislative process.

[*See also* Congress, *article on* Public Perceptions of Congress; C-SPAN; Press; Technology in Congress.]

BIBLIOGRAPHY

Bates, Stephen, ed. *The Media and the Congress.* 1987.
Clark, Timothy B. "The House on Cable." *The Journal of the Institute for Socioeconomic Studies* 9 (Summer 1984): 12–22.
Crain, W. Mark, and Brian Goff. *Televised Legislatures: Political Information Technology and Public Choice.* 1988.
Garay, Ronald. *Congressional Television: A Legislative History.* 1984.
Hess, Stephen. *Live from Capitol Hill! Studies of Congress and the Media.* 1991.

RONALD GARAY

BROOKE, EDWARD W. (1919–), Republican from Massachusetts, first African American to be popularly elected to the U.S. Senate. Edward W. Brooke III, a Washington, D.C., native, graduated from Howard University in 1941, joined the army, and served in World War II. He earned two law degrees from Boston University, in 1948 and 1950. From 1950 to 1961, Brooke practiced law in Massachusetts. After one year as the chairman of Boston's Finance Commission, he served as the Massachusetts attorney general from 1962 until 1966, when he was elected to the Senate.

Though Brooke was a Republican, he often took liberal positions in the Senate. A strong advocate of civil rights, he supported integrated schooling and criticized the Nixon administration's lack of support for the civil rights movement. Brooke lobbied for improvements in many social services, including mass transit and public housing. He also supported expanding the minimum wage structure. Brooke frequently opposed the Nixon administration in areas besides civil rights. He did not support the U.S. invasion of Cambodia or American involvement in Vietnam. He opposed many of Nixon's conservative Supreme Court nominees and was the first senator to publicly request Nixon's resignation after the exposure of the Watergate scandal.

Brooke's committee assignments included the Banking, Housing, and Urban Affairs Committee;

EDWARD W. BROOKE. In July 1968.

the Committee on Appropriations; the Committee on Aging; and the Select Committee on Equal Educational Opportunity. Throughout his career, he remained an active civil rights spokesman.

Running for a third term in 1978, Brooke was defeated by Paul E. Tsongas.

BIBLIOGRAPHY

Christopher, Maurine. *Black Americans in Congress.* 1976.
Ragsdale, Bruce, and Joel D. Treese. *Black Americans in Congress, 1870–1989.* 1990.

CAROL M. SWAIN

BROOKS, PRESTON S. (1819–1857), Democratic representative from South Carolina and self-styled defender of southern honor. A native of Edgefield District, South Carolina, Preston Smith

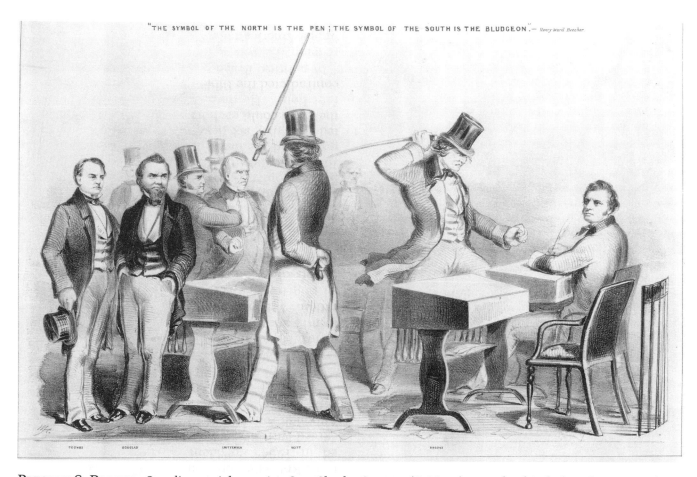

"THE SYMBOL OF THE NORTH IS THE PEN ; THE SYMBOL OF THE SOUTH IS THE BLUDGEON." — *Henry Ward Beecher.*

PRESTON S. BROOKS. Standing at right, caning Sen. Charles Sumner (R-Mass.), seated at his desk in the Senate chamber. Lithograph by Winslow Homer.

LIBRARY OF CONGRESS

Brooks campaigned as a states' rights Democrat in 1852 and won a seat in the U.S. House of Representatives. He was reelected in 1854. Brooks took moderate positions on such divisive sectional issues as chartering a transcontinental railroad and organizing the Kansas Territory.

Brooks is best known for one impulsive act—the brutal caning of antislavery senator Charles Sumner of Massachusetts in the Senate chamber on 22 May 1856. Brooks, who had previously fought two duels over questions of honor, alleged that Sumner, in a two-day speech attacking southern-inspired violence in Kansas, had slandered the reputations of his native state and his absent kinsman, Sen. Andrew P. Butler. A district court in Baltimore fined Brooks for assault; a special Senate committee called for prompt action by the House; and a select committee in the House investigated the episode and recommended that Brooks be expelled for a serious breach of congressional privilege. Even though the full House failed to endorse expulsion,

Brooks resigned and then promptly won a special election. Skilled propagandists used the Sumner-Brooks affair to heighten sectional tensions both inside and outside Congress. Brooks lamented the notoriety and the estrangement from many of his northern friends. On 27 July 1857, he suddenly died from an acute inflammation of the throat.

BIBLIOGRAPHY

Donald, David. *Charles Sumner and the Coming of the Civil War.* 1967.
Mathis, Robert Neil. "Preston Smith Brooks: The Man and His Image." *South Carolina Historical Magazine* 79 (1978): 296–310.

ROBERT NEIL MATHIS

BRYAN, WILLIAM JENNINGS (1860–1925),

lawyer, Democratic representative from Nebraska, three-time presidential candidate, secretary of

State, world peace advocate, religious fundamentalist. Bred in the moral values of his religious parents and the *McGuffey Reader*, Bryan represented the agrarian America of the last frontier. Finding his law practice in Illinois unrewarding, he moved to Lincoln, Nebraska, in 1887. There he called for tariff, banking, and currency reform and railroad regulation. Supported by Populists as well as Democrats, and by both urbanites and agrarians eager to defeat entrenched Republicans, he won a congressional seat in 1890.

During his two terms in Congress from 1891 to 1895, Bryan met every representative and as many senators as possible. He and other pro-silver Westerners backed Charles F. Crisp of Georgia in his bid to become House Speaker; in return, Speaker Crisp appointed Bryan to the Ways and Means Committee.

In the belief that the wisdom of average Americans could provide solutions for all their political and economic ills, Bryan sought laws that would operate equally for all, give special privilege to none, and make the government more responsive to the people. He won national acclaim by demanding a tariff for revenue only, the regulation of corporations and destruction of trusts, the direct election of senators, an income tax amendment to the Constitution, and, most notably, free silver at a ratio of 16 to 1 with gold. The rationale for inflating the currency in this way was to increase farm prices and so enable mortgaged farmers to pay off their indebtedness.

After leaving Congress, Bryan sought to solidify sentiment against conservative Grover Cleveland and for himself as the leader of the Democratic party. His "Cross of Gold" speech at the Democratic national convention in 1896 undoubtedly helped him win the presidential nomination. He was defeated because conservatives opposed him, labor could not see how increased farm prices would help their cause, and Republicans had much more money to spend and used various "dirty tricks" to defeat him.

Bryan supported President William McKinley's demand for a free Cuba in 1898 but opposed the acquisition of an American empire. Renominated in 1900, he was defeated again. He then bided his time. Not only were conservative Democrats defeated in 1904; President Theodore Roosevelt now agreed with Bryan on many of his reform demands. Although renominated in 1908, Bryan was defeated for a third time. As a reward for helping Woodrow Wilson win nomination and election in 1912, Bryan became Wilson's secretary of State.

Bryan helped Wilson win his New Freedom reforms. He also helped obtain the Sixteenth, Seventeenth, and Eighteenth Amendments to the Constitution. Yet his monument while secretary was writing treaties with thirty nations calling for attempts at reconciliation before going to war. But his fear that Wilson's handling of the attack on the *Lusitania* would drag the nation into the Great War led him to resign on 8 June 1915.

Throughout his life, but most prominently after 1921, Bryan concentrated on moral issues such as prohibition and conservative religion. At the trial of John T. Scopes for violating the Tennessee law that prohibited the teaching of evolution, Bryan admitted that the "six days" during which God created the earth could each have been longer than twenty-four hours. He thus agreed with evolutionists and contradicted the Bible.

In politics, Bryan was a progressive reformer. In religion, he was a fundamentalist who sought to imbue American life with Christian ethics.

WILLIAM JENNINGS BRYAN.   LIBRARY OF CONGRESS

BIBLIOGRAPHY

Ashley, LeRoy. *William Jennings Bryan: Champion of Democracy.* 1987.

Coletta, Paolo E. *William Jennings Bryan.* 3 vols. 1964–1969.

Clements, Kendrick. *William Jennings Bryan: Missionary Isolationist.* 1982.

PAOLO E. COLETTA

BUCHANAN, JAMES (1791–1868), Democratic representative and senator from Pennsylvania, fifteenth president of the United States (1857–1861). Born near Mercersburg, Pennsylvania, Buchanan graduated from Dickinson College in 1809 and became a successful attorney. In 1819 his fiancée died, and he vowed to remain a bachelor. This decision was politically significant because later, in Washington, he shared bachelor quarters with southern legislators who became his closest personal friends.

Buchanan served in the Pennsylvania legislature (1814–1816) and in the U.S. House of Representatives (1821–1831); he was minister to Russia (1832–1833) and a U.S. senator (1834–1845). As a laissez-faire Jacksonian, he opposed homestead laws, federal support of river and harbor improvements, land grants for schools, and tariffs, even though he represented a manufacturing state.

Buchanan expressed regret that slavery existed but offered no moral objections to the practice. He supported the annexation of Texas, and as James K. Polk's secretary of State (1845–1849), he opposed the treaty ending the Mexican War because it did not allow the United States to annex an even greater portion of Mexican territory. In the boundary dispute between the United States and Britain over the northern border of the Oregon Territory, Buchanan argued for the 54° 40′ line and against the compromise that set the border at the 49th parallel. In 1850 Buchanan supported the compromise and opposed the Wilmot Proviso. As minister to England (1853–1857), he coauthored the Ostend Manifesto recommending the conquest of Cuba from Spain to protect American slavery.

Elected president in 1856, Buchanan failed to realize that the greatest danger to the Union in 1860 would be the election of a Republican president. As chief executive, he offered the South concessions that had the effect of greatly strengthening the Republican party in the North. He appointed a cabinet composed largely of southerners and in patronage appointments ignored the northwestern

JAMES BUCHANAN. LIBRARY OF CONGRESS

Democrats led by Sen. Stephen A. Douglas of Illinois. He influenced and publicly approved the Supreme Court's Dred Scott decision, which held that neither the federal government nor any state government could bar slavery from any territory. Believing that slavery had reached its natural geographical limit, Buchanan thought that the Scott verdict would bring peace. Most northerners, however, saw it as legitimizing a southern grab for power and territory.

Throughout his administration, Buchanan and the Democrats controlled both houses of Congress, and Buchanan did not hesitate to use his power over appointments, printing contracts, and other government favors to gain northern Democratic support for his prosouthern policies. The Senate was more compliant than the House, but before secession Buchanan had his way on most important issues. In 1858, Buchanan asked Congress to admit Kansas as a slave state, even though the proslavery Lecompton constitution represented the will of only a fraction of the Kansas people because its opponents had refused to vote. The Senate agreed by a vote of 33 to 25, but the House, despite Buchanan's pressures, returned the constitution to Kansas with a promise of extra land if it should be again ratified. This time, however, the Kansans rejected the constitution by a majority of 6 to 1. Angry southerners felt that Kansas had been stolen from them, while northerners were equally enraged by Buchanan's efforts on behalf of the slave-holding South.

As the sectional crisis deepened, Buchanan continued his stubborn allegiance to the South. Because most of the northeastern delegates were his appointees, he exercised great influence over the Democratic presidential nominating convention at Charleston in 1860 and played a major role in preventing the nomination of Stephen A. Douglas, which split the Democratic party into two factions supporting separate candidates. He openly supported John J. Breckinridge, the southern candidate, and thereby helped ensure the election of Abraham Lincoln. Buchanan's annual message of 1860 endorsed the arguments of the southern radicals and recommended a national convention to enact a constitutional amendment for the federal protection of slavery in all territories. Secession, said Buchanan, was unconstitutional, but the federal government had no power to suppress it by force. He did, however, flatly refuse to negotiate with the South with regard to Fort Sumter and at one point tried unsuccessfully to reinforce the fort by ship.

Meanwhile, Buchanan sent an army to Utah to crush the rebellious Mormons. Only the skillful negotiations of Thomas L. Kane, lawyer and abolitionist, prevented an all-out war. Buchanan advocated equally aggressive foreign policies, but they were usually rejected by the Congress. He confronted the British successfully in Central America and Puget Sound and perhaps inadvertently fostered the illegal African slave trade by sending a fleet to protect ships flying the American flag from search by British warships trying to suppress the trade. Acting as commander in chief, Buchanan, by military order, released the American adventurer William Walker after Walker had been arrested by the U.S. Navy while trying to invade Nicaragua. At various times he asked Congress for authority to invade Mexico or to purchase parts of that country, and he also made a request of Congress for $30 million to buy Cuba.

In retirement, Buchanan was subjected to vicious charges of treason, but he loyally supported the Union cause in the Civil War. In his memoirs he ably defended himself against charges of wrongdoing, but he still argued that Republican "fanatics" had caused the war. He died on 1 June 1868.

BIBLIOGRAPHY

Buchanan, James. *Mr. Buchanan's Administration on the Eve of the Rebellion.* 1866.
Klein, Philip S. *President James Buchanan.* 1962.
Moore, John B. *The Works of James Buchanan.* 2 vols. Repr. 1960.
Smith, Elbert B. *The Presidency of James Buchanan.* 1975.

ELBERT B. SMITH

BUCKLEY V. VALEO (424 U.S. 1 [1976]). The Supreme Court in *Buckley v. Valeo* rendered a landmark decision on the constitutionality of the most comprehensive election reform legislation ever enacted by Congress. In its opinion, the Court examined constitutional questions surrounding federal election funding and separation-of-powers challenges to the composition of the Federal Election Commission (FEC), the agency established to administer the law. Its holdings have since launched a remarkable series of cases on congressional power to influence execution of the law.

The Federal Election Campaign Act of 1971 had restricted amounts that could be contributed to political campaigns, limited spending by candidates for various federal offices and by political parties, required reporting and public disclosure of contributions and expenditures, and established a system of public financing of campaigns. It also created the FEC, composed of congressional and presidential appointees, to administer the law. The Court struck down the expenditure limits as representing substantial restraints on political speech and thus violating the First Amendment, noting that "a restriction on the amount of money a person or group can spend on political communication . . . necessarily reduces the quantity or expression by restricting the number of issues discussed, the depth of their exploration, and the size of the audience reached." Limits on contributions, on the other hand, were viewed as only marginally restrictive of the contributor's ability to communicate because the "transformation of contributions into political debate involves speech by someone other than the contributor." The Court also upheld the recordkeeping and disclosure requirements (even as applied to minor parties) and public financing of campaigns.

The FEC appointees were named by the Speaker of the House, the president pro tempore of the Senate, and the president; all appointees were subject to the approval of both the Senate and House. The Court found that this arrangement violated Article II of the Constitution, which provides that "Officers of the United States" must be appointed by the president with Senate confirmation, or, in the case of so-called "inferior officers," by the president alone, department heads, or the courts. An officer subject to Article II appointment is any appointee "exercising significant authority pursuant to the laws of the United States." The commission's rule-making and enforcement powers had to be performed by "Officers of the United States," the Court found, and could not be vested in an entity composed of congressional appointees or appointees subject to confirmation by both Senate and House. On the other hand, the commission's investigative and informational powers—which Congress could have delegated to its own committees—could be exercised by the commission as constituted.

The Court thus interpreted the appointments clause as restricting the power of Congress to establish entities that perform significant functions under public law with officers not appointed in accordance with Article II. While Congress may establish offices, prescribe qualifications of officers, and limit removal of officers in certain circumstances, it may not participate directly in appointing officers who perform significant executive functions.

BIBLIOGRAPHY

U.S. Senate. *The Constitution of the United States of America: Analysis and Interpretation.* 99th Cong., 1st sess., 1985. S. Doc. 99-16. Supplement. 101st Cong., 2d sess., 1990. S. Doc. 101-36. Pp. 540, 1070, S3.
Polsby, Daniel D. *"Buckley v. Valeo:* The Special Nature of Political Speech." *Supreme Court Review* 1 (1976): 1–43.

RICHARD C. EHLKE

BUDGET ACT OF 1974. *See* Congressional Budget and Impoundment Control Act of 1974.

BUDGET AND ACCOUNTING ACT (1921; 42 Stat. 20–27). The basic parameters of the annual appropriations process were established by the Budget and Accounting Act of 1921. Although the Congressional Budget and Impoundment Control Act of 1974 altered how Congress and the president develop an annual budget, the fundamentals of the Budget and Accounting Act have remained unchanged. The act established the president's budget, the General Accounting Office (GAO), and the Bureau of the Budget, now called the Office of Management and Budget (OMB). Coupled with congressional reforms that strengthened the House and Senate Appropriations committees, the act was the crowning achievement of Progressive politicians who endeavored to reform the budget process at the turn of the century.

Prior to the Budget and Accounting Act, appropriations authority within the executive branch was diffuse. The president did not prepare an overall budget; executive agencies dealt directly with Congress for funding. Annual agency requests were submitted formally through the Treasury secretary, who was required by law to forward them unchanged to Congress. The lack of centralized appropriations authority within the executive branch was compounded by a similar decentralization within Congress: the House (in 1865) and the Senate (in 1899) had granted several legislative committees the right to report appropriations bills.

Agitation for budget reform began during the Taft administration (1909–1913). The argument to centralize appropriations authority in both the executive branch and Congress was initially carried by President William Howard Taft's Treasury secretary, Franklin MacVeagh. Taft eventually managed to persuade Congress to authorize the President's Commission on Economy and Efficiency (the so-called Taft Commission) to study government efficiency generally. The commission issued reports arguing in favor of strong presidential leadership in appropriations and for a single congressional budget committee. One of its last acts was to help President Taft prepare a model "executive" budget for submission to Congress. But because of Republican defeats in the 1912 election, this budget was merely printed by the Senate and then ignored.

After the Taft Commission went out of existence in 1913, former members actively agitated for budget reform. Congress, too, regularly considered reform proposals during the 1910s, although, for a variety of reasons, none passed. Management difficulties associated with fighting World War I heightened interest in reform, and many Republicans credited their campaigning on the issue in the 1918 election for helping them recapture control of Congress.

Hence, the House Budget Study Committee was appointed for the 66th Congress (1919–1921) to consider executive and legislative appropriations reform. Chaired by James W. Good (R-Iowa), the committee recommended the Accounting Act, which would establish an annual presidential budget, an executive Budget Bureau, and a legislative Accounting Department. The Accounting Act passed Congress in 1920 but was vetoed by President Woodrow Wilson because of the bill's provisions for removing the comptroller general, the head of the Accounting Department. Congress failed to override the veto. Republican Warren G. Harding was elected president in 1920, along with a Republican Congress. The Accounting Act was renamed the Budget and Accounting Act and was quickly passed in 1921 and signed by Harding.

The Budget and Accounting Act has remained virtually unchanged since then. One change concerns the Budget Bureau, which was transferred from the Treasury to the newly created Executive Office of the President in 1939. Its name was later changed to the Office of Management and Budget, and its role was expanded in 1970.

[*See also* General Accounting Office; Office of Management and Budget.]

BIBLIOGRAPHY

Fisher, Louis. *Presidential Spending Power.* 1975.
Stewart, Charles. *Budget Reform Politics: Reforming the Appropriations Process in the House of Representatives, 1865–1921.* 1989.

CHARLES STEWART III

BUDGET COMMITTEE, HOUSE. The first article of the U.S. Constitution firmly fixes major control over the nation's purse in the House of Representatives by requiring that revenue bills originate there. By custom, appropriations also originate in the House. The Senate, however, must act on all House decisions before they can become law.

Despite such clear constitutional delegation of monetary responsibility, the executive has asserted its own authority over the years, particularly in time of war. Congress itself has also assigned the executive responsibility through statute, such as the Budget and Accounting Act of 1921. Presidential assertiveness peaked during the Vietnam War and the presidency of Richard M. Nixon. Nixon not only circumvented the regular appropriations process by spending money that had not been directly appropriated (backdoor spending) but, more important, refused—through the procedure known as impoundment—to spend money that had been

constitutionally appropriated. Out of the ensuing impoundment crisis came the Congressional Budget and Impoundment Control Act of 1974.

Congress previously had no means independent of the executive to analyze the president's budget or develop a fiscal policy of its own. The 1974 act changed this by establishing permanent standing budget committees in the House and Senate and a Congressional Budget Office to give Congress the capacity to perform its own independent, nonpartisan budget analysis. The establishment of a new budget process gave the House of Representatives in particular a greater decision-making capacity and new responsibilities.

Although the House Budget Committee shares much in common with its Senate counterpart, there are important differences. The House committee, with forty-three members (twenty-six Democrats and seventeen Republicans), has nearly twice the membership of its Senate counterpart (twenty-one members). The ratios are determined at the beginning of every Congress based on each party's strength.

Both the House and Senate Budget committees were superimposed on the existing committee structure. Unlike its Senate counterpart, however, the House Budget Committee has no legislative jurisdiction of its own, except for a provision (the "Gephardt Rule") that allows an increase in the debt limit as a part of the House Budget Committee's reported resolution. Other than that, it cannot report to the floor any changes in existing legislation, including the Budget Act itself. The Senate panel, however, has legislative jurisdiction over the Budget Act, and any amendments to that act.

The House Budget Committee, also unlike the Senate panel, has a rotating membership. That is, none of its members (other than a member of the House leadership) may serve for more than six out of every ten years. The chairmanship is not permanent as it is in the Senate; in each new Congress the House Budget chairman must be reelected. The House also requires that the total membership of its Budget Committee include five members from the Ways and Means Committee (three from the majority party and two from the minority), another five members (three majority and two minority) from the Appropriations Committee, and one (a majority member) from the Rules Committee. The Senate committee has no similar provision.

The House and Senate Budget committees also differ in matters of procedure. The House panel pays more attention to budget detail; that is, line items. For example, it might write a line item mandating the top salary level for public employees, or it might propose to limit the amount spent for an aircraft carrier in a fiscal year. The Senate panel, in contrast, deals more frequently in broadly based actions. For example, it might make a 2 percent across-the-board cut in nondefense discretionary spending while leaving the specifics of how that would be achieved to the Senate Appropriations Committee.

Most votes of the House Budget Committee are cast along party lines: minority members do not vote for their own committee's budget resolution, either in committee or on the House floor. The divisiveness is occasionally acrimonious, as in the early days of the Clinton presidency. The Senate committee's divisions were seldom along strictly party lines until 1993, the first year of the Clinton presidency.

Since 1975 both Budget committees have had the responsibility each year of drafting a concurrent resolution on the budget that relates the disparate parts of the budget to the whole. The resolution, to be passed by 15 April each year, sets targets in five areas: (1) total budget authority (new legal obligations that will affect the immediate or future year's outlay of government spending); (2) total budget outlays (actual spending in that particular year); (3) total budget revenues; (4) total budget surplus (or deficit); and (5) total public debt. The 1975 resolution marked the first time that members of Congress were required to vote on budget totals.

The concurrent resolution also sets budget authority and outlay targets for the various functional categories in the budget. There are twenty-one categories in all, covering such areas as defense, veterans' affairs, education, income security, health, and interest on the debt.

Congress originally planned to have two budget resolutions each year. The second (to be passed by 15 September) was designed to modify the five aggregates as changing economic circumstances might require. It was to be followed by a concurrent reconciliation resolution (25 September) that would force committees to respect spending ceilings if they had been exceeded or had not been met.

The House Budget Committee was the first to decide that a second resolution was not needed, arguing that it was unnecessary because the reconciliation process had evolved into the primary means of controlling spending in entitlement and mandatory programs. The Senate later agreed with the House and dropped the second concurrent resolution.

Reconciliation is a two-stage process. First, the budget resolution contains instructions to the authorizing committees about how much they should decrease (or increase) budget authority, outlays, and revenues under their jurisdictions. Then these changes are put in a reconciliation bill drafted by the authorizing committees with spending and revenue jurisdiction. Both House and Senate chambers must approve the reconciliation bill. The bill is then sent to the president for his signature. The Appropriations committees are generally not subject to reconciliation instructions. Instead, they are governed by the binding spending limits on discretionary spending set forth in the budget resolution for the next fiscal year.

It sometimes is very difficult for the House and Senate Budget committees to agree on a concurrent resolution. Since the Budget and Impoundment Control Act was passed in 1974, the House generally has favored less defense and more domestic spending than the Senate. Despite these and other policy differences, the budget and impoundment control provisions have strengthened congressional control of the purse, which was the original intent of the act. The act set procedures and timetables to establish a comprehensive congressional program for the nation's taxing and spending policies. Previously, only the president had the means or procedures for this. The impoundment control procedures succeeded in preventing the president from unilaterally abrogating legislative decisions on appropriations. By joining budget and impoundment control into a single act, Congress sought to ensure that the power of the purse assigned to it by the Constitution was exercised more fully. These changes led to the rising power and visibility of the House Budget Committee as a leadership mechanism.

Two later reforms have pushed the budget agenda in the direction of deficit reduction. The first, known as Gramm-Rudman-Hollings II, or GRH II (the initial act was declared unconstitutional), set rigid, inflexible budget targets for five consecutive years, requiring that fixed deficit targets be met each year. If the required deficit reductions were not met, an automatic across-the-board sequestration of funds would go into effect to meet the legal deficit-reduction requirements. Within three years it became clear to congressional leaders that this was not a workable solution to eliminate deficit spending.

The second reform, crafted through long negotiations between House and Senate leaders and the executive branch, was the Budget Enforcement Act of 1990. It placed yearly caps on all discretionary spending, required that any reduction in revenues must be accompanied by an equal reduction in entitlement spending, nullified the GRH II legislation, and provided pay-as-you-go provisions for any new spending. Pay-as-you-go prevents any spending increase unless revenues are raised at the same time by an equal amount or spending is cut somewhere else by an equal amount.

[See also Budget Committee, Senate.]

BIBLIOGRAPHY

Davis, Edward. *"Pay-as-You-Go" Enforcement Procedures in 1991.* Congressional Research Service, Library of Congress. 1992. Revised regularly.
Hager, George. "Budget Drama, Act II: Scenarios for Chaos." *Congressional Quarterly Weekly Report,* 25 January 1992, pp. 156–159.
Schick, Allen, ed. *Making Economic Policy in Congress.* 1983.
Schick, Allen, Robert Keith, and Edward Davis. *Manual on the Federal Budget Process.* Congressional Research Service, Library of Congress. 24 December 1991.
U.S. Congress. General Accounting Office. *GAO's Budget Enforcement Act Compliance Report Regarding Activities under Gramm-Rudman-Hollings Act Occurring in 1991.* GAO Doc. AFMD-92-43. 1992.
U.S. House of Representatives. Committee on the Budget. *Management Reform: A Top Priority for the Federal Executive Branch.* 102d Cong., 1st sess., 1991.
U.S. Senate. Committee on Government Operations. *Congressional Budget and Impoundment Control Act of 1974: Legislative History.* 93d Cong., 2d sess., 1974.

NICHOLAS A. MASTERS

BUDGET COMMITTEE, SENATE. The Congressional Budget and Impoundment Control Act of 1974 (P.L. 93-344; 88 Stat. 297–339) established the Senate Budget Committee with sixteen members to be chosen by the party caucuses and to serve indefinitely. Because the act establishes no tenure limitations on committee members, the committee is quite different from the House Budget Committee, which has service limitations. The Senate committee also does not provide for direct representation of other committees or the party leadership, as is the case in the House. The Senate Budget Committee was originally established with ten Democrats and six Republicans but has varied in its size over time. In the 103d Congress, it had grown to twenty-one members, twelve Democrats and nine Republicans. The committee does not have subcommittees with legislative jurisdiction. Nearly all legislation it considers is a self-initiated part of the congressional budget process, so few bills are referred to the committee in comparison with all other Senate committees.

In the early years under the leadership of Chairman Edmund S. Muskie (D-Maine) and ranking minority member Henry L. Bellmon (R-Okla.), the committee had a strong bipartisan consensus on basic goals and often on policy directives. It has generally not suffered the ideological split nor extreme partisan friction that the House Budget Committee has experienced; however, partisan battles over the budget increased during the presidency of Bill Clinton. Although most senators regard the committee as an attractive and even powerful assignment, it does not have the power of the Appropriations or Finance committees.

The principal budgetary functions of the Senate Budget Committee are similar to the functions of the House Budget Committee. The primary responsibilities are to report budget resolutions; draft reconciliation instructions and compile a reconciliation bill; allocate new budget authority, outlays, and new entitlement and credit authority for committees; monitor and advise Congress on the status of the budget; report resolutions waiving certain budget procedures; and oversee the Congressional Budget Office.

The 1974 Budget Act created a congressional budget process centered on a "concurrent resolution on the budget," prepared in the Senate by the committee. The concurrent budget resolution is scheduled for adoption before the legislature considers spending or revenue bills, thus centralizing budget decision making and often calling for other Senate committees to stay within the spending limits set by the Budget Committee's resolution. The central purpose of the budget process established by the act is to coordinate the various revenue and spending decisions that are made in the separate tax, appropriations, and legislative measures. Thus, the Senate Budget Committee plays a central role in the congressional budget process. Since 1976, when the congressional budget process was initiated, the Budget Committee's procedures have adapted to changing circumstances (such as the Gramm-Rudman-Hollings acts of 1985 and 1987 and the Budget Enforcement Act of 1990), but the role of the committee has remained relatively stable and has increased in importance as the national deficit and debt have come to dominate the budget process.

To ensure that the budget resolution serves as a guideline for subsequent action on budget-related measures, the Budget Committee and Congress are supposed to adopt it before turning to the consideration of revenue, spending, or debt-limit measures for the next fiscal year. However, Congress has often failed to adopt the budget resolution by the 15 April deadline specified in the Congressional Budget Act of 1974.

Under the 1974 act, the Senate Budget Committee is required to issue a "views and estimates" report on the budget matters in its jurisdiction, within six weeks of receiving the president's budget. The committee holds hearings and receives the views and estimates and receives reports from other committees and the Congressional Budget Office, in order to draft the annual budget resolution. In its initial hearings each year, the Senate Budget Committee also receives testimony from the director of the Office of Management and Budget, the secretary of the Treasury, the head of the President's Council of Economic Advisers, and the director of the Congressional Budget Office. The views and estimates reports from Senate committees provide information on the preferences and legislative plans of the committees in regard to budgetary matters within their jurisdiction. The Budget Committee uses the reports, along with Congressional Budget Office analyses, to prepare the budget resolution for the next fiscal year. It uses baseline estimates to project the cost of continuing programs, assuming no policy or statutory changes. The budget resolution contains revenue and spending levels for five fiscal years, but only the figures for the first year are binding. It is a concurrent resolution, which means it has no statutory effect; the president does not sign a concurrent resolution. In marking up the budget resolution, the committee often is divided along party lines, although it has been more consistently bipartisan and consensual than the House Budget Committee. The Senate Budget Committee has always been much more aggressive than its House counterpart in attempting to cut spending and in confronting the authorizing, tax, and appropriations committees on the floor in order to enforce spending cuts.

The committee's concurrent budget resolution does not mention specific programs or accounts; the aggregates, functional allocations, and reconciliation instructions typically are based on assumptions about particular programs. Although the extent to which committee members consider particular programs when they act on the budget resolution varies from year to year, they have been more careful than their House counterparts in attempting to stay out of the jurisdiction of the other Senate committees. Specific program decisions are supposed to be the domain of the Senate Appropriations Committee and other committees of jurisdiction, but major issues often are discussed in markup and the Budget Committee reports. Although no programmatic assumptions in this process are binding on the committees of jurisdiction, they often influence the final outcome. The concurrent budget resolution aggregates include total revenue, total new budget authority, total outlays, the surplus or deficit, the debt limit, and total new direct loan obligations. Reconciliation instructions from the Budget committees direct designated House and Senate committees to report legislation that brings spending, revenue, or debit-limit levels under existing law into conformity with current budget policies.

The role of the Senate Budget Committee has been greatly affected in recent years by the reliance on budget summit negotiations between the executive and Congress. A summit agreement in 1987 (Gramm-Rudman-Hollings II) established overall budget policy for fiscal years 1988 and 1989, a 1989 summit agreement set overall policy for fiscal year 1990, and a summit agreement in 1990 established the Budget Enforcement Act, a framework for fiscal years 1991 to 1995.

[See also Balanced Budget and Emergency Deficit Control Act; Budget Committee, House; Congressional Budget and Impoundment Control Act of 1974; Congressional Budget Office; Office of Management and Budget.]

BIBLIOGRAPHY

Rubin, Irene S. The Politics of Public Budgeting: Getting and Spending, Borrowing and Balancing. 2d ed. 1993.

Thurber, James A. "New Rules for an Old Game: Zero-Sum Budgeting in the Postreform Congress." In The Postreform Congress. Edited by Roger H. Davidson. 1992.

Thurber, James A., and Samantha L. Durst. "The 1990 Budget Enforcement Act: Zero-Sum Budgeting and the Decline of Governmental Accountability." In Congress Reconsidered. Edited by Lawrence C. Dodd and Bruce I. Oppenheimer. 1993.

White, Joseph, and Aaron Wildavsky. The Deficit and the Public Interest: The Search for Responsible Budgeting in the 1980s. 1989.

Wildavsky, Aaron. The New Politics of the Budgetary Process. 2d ed. 1992.

JAMES A. THURBER

BUDGET ENFORCEMENT ACT OF 1990

(104 Stat. 1388). Set forth in Title XIII of the Omnibus Budget Reconciliation Act (OBRA) of 1990, the Budget Enforcement Act of 1990 (BEA) established temporary procedures (covering fiscal years 1991–1995) to enforce a five-year agreement for reducing the federal deficit reached between President George Bush and congressional leaders in September 1990. OBRA of 1990 made about half of the total savings called for in the deficit reduction agreement by changing spending and tax laws directly. The BEA was enacted to ensure that future budgetary legislation affecting fiscal years 1991–1995 would be consistent with the deficit reduction agreement and that the remaining savings called for in the agreement would be realized.

The BEA made major changes in the sequestration process under the Gramm-Rudman-Hollings Act of 1985 and in enforcement procedures under the Congressional Budget Act of 1974. It amended Gramm-Rudman in two respects: by (1) revising and extending the annual deficit targets and making them adjustable for changes unrelated to new policy and (2) establishing limits on discretionary spending and a pay-as-you-go requirement for mandatory spending and tax legislation. It amended the Congressional Budget Act principally to make the congressional budget process conform to the discretionary spending limits and pay-as-you-go requirement.

In August of 1993, the discretionary spending limits and pay-as-you-go requirement were extended through fiscal year 1998 as part of the Omnibus Budget Reconciliation Act of 1993 (P.L. 103-66; 107 Stat. 312–685). OBRA of 1993 embodied President Bill Clinton's five-year deficit reduction plan.

[See also Balanced Budget and Emergency Deficit Control Act; Congressional Budget and Impoundment Control Act of 1974.]

BIBLIOGRAPHY

Doyle, Richard, and Jerry McCaffery. "The Budget Enforcement Act after One Year." *Public Budgeting and Finance* 12 (Spring 1992): 3–15.

Joyce, Philip G., and Robert D. Reischauer. "Deficit Budgeting: The Federal Budget Process and Budget Reform." *Harvard Journal on Legislation* 29 (Summer 1992): 429–453.

EDWARD DAVIS

BUDGET PROCESS.

The power of the purse granted to Congress in Article I of the Constitution has long been an essential element of Congress's role as a policymaker. In recent years, the budget process has become the central feature of the internal operations of Congress. It affects the relative power of committees, the resources of majority party leaders, the rules and floor procedures, and Congress's ability to negotiate with the president.

Three important factors help explain the evolution of the congressional budget process and judgments about its performance. First, congressional budget reforms were in part spurred by basic changes in the nature of the budget itself. From the 1960s on, as outlays became dominated by entitlements and mandatory spending, discretionary spending shrank as a share of total outlays. The budget became increasingly sensitive to macroeconomic changes. Taxing and spending decisions were no longer strictly annual choices but increasingly encompassed multiyear commitments. The traditional authorization-appropriations process, which considered the budget in parts rather than as a whole, proved inadequate to the task of managing relatively inflexible budget figures. In short, the experimentation in congressional budgeting since the late 1960s reflects legislative attempts to adapt to a rapidly changing budgetary, economic, and political environment.

Second, the development of the congressional budget process reflects the constitutional separation of powers and institutional combat between the executive and legislative branches. Interbranch conflict was exacerbated in the late twentieth century by the prevalence of divided government. For example, the 1974 Budget Act was adopted not only to increase Congress's ability to control the budget but to check President Richard M. Nixon's power and ability to thwart congressional priorities. In the 1980s, the sharp divisions between President Ronald Reagan and congressional Democrats were reflected in the recurrence of chronic budget deficits. The major changes in the budget process after 1982 in large part occurred in response to growing deficits, procedural attempts to resolve prolonged institutional conflict, and divergent policy preferences.

Third, apparent inconsistencies in Congress's budgeting performance reflect the tension between two basic roles of members of Congress: that of responsible national policymakers versus that of local district representatives concerned about reelection and oriented toward providing tangible benefits for constituents. Wishes that are rational and desirable for each individual member may make it difficult for Congress to demonstrate collective responsibility. This tension makes the necessary tasks of increasing taxes and cutting spending to reduce deficits much more difficult than spending for (albeit worthy) programs in education, health, defense, and other policy areas. As a result, even when Congress imposes strict rules and requirements on itself to control spending, members use gimmicks, tricks, and "blue smoke and mirrors" to avoid fiscal discipline. While many other forces have shaped the congressional budget process, structural changes in the budget, legislative-executive conflict, and divergent legislative roles help explain the unusual path that the budgeting process has taken.

Congressional Budgeting before 1974. The congressional budget process has evolved through a number of stages over two hundred years. The House Ways and Means Committee initiated both taxing and spending bills until the Civil War. In 1865, the House created the Appropriations Committee to consider expenditures, and the Senate followed suit two years later, leaving the Ways and Means Committee and the Senate Finance Committee with jurisdiction over taxes. The process became more fragmented over the ensuing decades as standing committees gained control over various money bills. The Budget and Accounting Act of 1921 created the executive budget, strengthening the president's role, but Congress continued to use the decentralized authorization-appropriations process. The president's power in budgeting increased dramatically during the New Deal and World War II as part of a larger and more activist executive branch.

Following World War II, Congress attempted to improve its budget process. The 1946 Legislative Reorganization Act included provisions that provided for a legislative budget; a Joint Committee on the Budget was established to review the president's requests and report a legislative budget to both houses. But jurisdictional struggles, partisanship, and tension between the White House and Congress doomed efforts to make the congressional budget process more comprehensive. Although a number of solutions were attempted, efforts to create a legislative budget had ceased by 1950.

The authorization-appropriations process functioned adequately through much of the 1960s, when the economy was robust, and growing revenues made it possible gradually to increase the size and scope of programs. By the late 1960s, however, both the process and congressional control over the budget were deteriorating. Congress at-

"TRYING TO PIN THE TAIL ON THE DONKEY." Cartoon depicting president-elect Franklin D. Roosevelt, whose 1932 presidential campaign emphasized economy in government, advising the House not to go about balancing the budget in a haphazard way. The cartoon reveals how strong was the belief in economy in government even at the depth of the Great Depression, and how little expectation there was of the New Deal spending to come. Clifford K. Berryman, 5 January 1933.

LIBRARY OF CONGRESS

tempted to enact legislation to cap expenditures in five out of the six years from 1967 to 1972. With a frustrated Congress seemingly unable to stem the tide of rising expenditures, President Nixon attacked Congress's lack of discipline and impounded (refused to spend) funds appropriated by Congress. The expansion of federal programs and the escalating conflict between Congress and the president created the environment for major budget reform.

Budget and Impoundment Control Act of 1974. The Joint Study Committee on Budget Control issued a report in 1973 stressing the importance of developing procedures that would allow Congress to take an overview of the budget, coordinate spending and revenues, and integrate separate spending bills. During the committee's year-long deliberations, various political and committee interests were represented. As a result, instead of instituting an entirely new process, the Budget Impoundment and Control Act created an additional set of procedures that was layered on top of the old system.

Budget committees. The act created new committees in both the House and Senate. The Senate Budget Committee (SBC) was established as a regular standing committee with sixteen members, subject to the same principles of committee assignments, seniority, and rules that applied to other Senate committees. Membership on the House Budget Committee (HBC), however, was defined and limited. Of the HBC's twenty-five members, five came from the Ways and Means Committee and five from the Appropriations Committee; House Republican and Democratic leadership supplied one member each. (Both the HBC and SBC have subsequently been enlarged.) Service on the HBC was limited to four years out of any ten (subsequently six years out of ten). These provisions were designed to keep the new panel broad in perspective and representative of the House, but they also left the HBC in a secondary position in relation to the existing money committees.

Congressional Budget Office. To help provide analytical support and better budget data, Title II of the act created the Congressional Budget Office (CBO). This nonpartisan agency was given responsibility for monitoring the economy and its effect on the budget, improving budgetary information, and providing cost estimates of legislation.

Budget resolutions. The congressional budget was to be specified in a series of resolutions to be reported by the budget committees. Concurrent resolutions were the chosen vehicle, since they were binding only on Congress, did not require the president's signature, and did not in themselves provide the authority to spend funds. The Budget Act required enactment of a first resolution, which established targets, by 15 May and a second resolution, which set binding totals, by 15 September. Each resolution would specify: (1) total budget authority (BA) and outlays, (2) budget authority and outlays for fifteen functional subtotals (e.g., function 050, national defense, or function 350, agriculture), (3) total revenues, (4) resulting surplus or deficit, and (5) resulting public debt.

Timetable. To help ensure that the new process would work, the law included a strict timetable. The original timetable, which has been revised on a number of occasions since, is summarized in table 1.

Using the president's budget, CBO analysis, the views and estimates of other committees, and testimony from economists and budget experts, each of the Budget committees was to draw up the first resolution and report it to its chamber by 15 April. By 15 May a single budget resolution was to be passed

TABLE 1. *Congressional Budget Timetable, 1975*

ACTION TO BE COMPLETED	ON OR BEFORE
President submits annual budget message to Congress	15 days after Congress meets
Congressional committees make recommendations to Budget committees	15 March
Congressional Budget Office reports to Budget committees	1 April
Budget committees report first budget resolution	15 April
Congress passes first budget resolution	15 May
Legislative committees complete reporting of authorizing legislation	15 May
Congress passes all spending bills	Seven days after Labor Day
Congress passes second budget resolution	15 September
Congress passes budget reconciliation bill	25 September
Fiscal year begins	1 October

by both the House and Senate and all authorizing bills were to be reported by committees. After passage of the first resolution, the Budget committees translated the functional totals into committee allocations, informing the spending committees how much budget authority and outlays they could provide under the resolution. The Appropriations committees further subdivided the totals for their subcommittees. By September, all spending bills were to be passed. The Budget committees, reviewing these bills in light of current economic conditions, were to draft and report a second concurrent resolution by 15 September. It was to contain binding totals and subtotals, and once it was enacted, any legislation violating the totals would be ruled out of order. If the spending bills and the second resolution did not agree, a reconciliation bill ordering adjustments in the individual spending bills was to be passed by 25 September. Because the new fiscal year (FY) began on 1 October, a three-month transition quarter, from 1 July to 30 September 1976, was created to facilitate the change.

Impoundment. The Budget and Impoundment Control Act moved to prevent the president from thwarting Congress's wishes by refusing to spend appropriated moneys. Congress did recognize the need for some executive discretion, however, and created two new processes: deferral and rescission. The president requests a *deferral* to delay temporarily the spending of money appropriated by Congress. Deferrals are automatically effective unless either house passes a disapproval resolution. The president requests a *rescission* to eliminate spending authority permanently. To take effect, rescissions must be approved by an affirmative vote of both the House and Senate within forty-five days of the request.

Passage of the legislation. Despite the many significant changes encompassed in the Budget Impoundment and Control Act and the many compromises it reflected, there was strong bipartisan support for the legislation in both houses. The House passed it 401 to 6 and the Senate 75 to 0. President Richard Nixon, in part the target of the legislation, signed the bill in July 1974, only weeks before he would resign the presidency. The consensus on final passage belied members' widely differing goals and expectations, however. Liberal Democrats saw it as opening an opportunity to debate national spending priorities for the first time—for example, to make explicit comparisons between amounts going to defense versus money spent on domestic programs. Conservative Republicans saw the legislation as providing a method for restraining spending and reducing deficits, since for the first time members would be accountable should they vote for an unbalanced budget. Because of these conflicting interpretations, the consensus over the new procedures, which had been designed to improve the policy performance of Congress and to check the president's power, crumbled as soon as real budget choices were faced.

Implementing the Congressional Budget Process, 1975 to 1980. During its first five years of operation, the new budget process inspired sharp partisan disputes in the House of Representatives, often to the point where many members feared the process would collapse. In the Senate, bipartisan support for the budget process was much greater and the new

system seemed stronger and more secure.

In the first-year trial run in 1975, House Republicans objected to proposed changes in President Gerald R. Ford's budget and refused to cooperate. House Budget Committee chairman Brock Adams (D-Wash.) worked with the Democratic leaders in the House to fashion a slim majority. The first resolution in 1975 passed by a narrow margin of 200 to 196, with Democrats supporting it 197 to 68 and Republicans opposing it 3 to 128. This partisan voting pattern on budget resolutions would remain remarkably consistent over the next five years, as shown in table 2. Because Republicans and the more conservative Democrats opposed the budget resolutions, the Democratic leaders had to appeal to their party's liberal wing to gain a majority. As a result, budget resolution figures in the House tended to be higher on social spending and lower on defense than in the Senate.

As table 2 also shows, the process was more bipartisan and more secure on the Senate side. Some observers suggested that the six-year terms in the Senate insulated senators from the intense reelection pressure faced by House members, making it easier for senators to vote for budget resolutions. Furthermore, since the SBC was a regular Senate standing committee, its members had more incentive to restrain partisanship as a means of protecting the prestige and influence of the committee. Also, the Senate Budget Committee, in the eyes of many analysts, benefited from enlightened leadership. SBC chairman Edmund S. Muskie (D-Maine) and ranking minority member Henry L. Bellmon (R-Okla.) worked closely together to present a united front on the Senate floor to promote and strengthen the process.

The congressional budget process made some important changes in the way Congress handled taxing and spending decisions. In 1976, for the first time in years, all thirteen regular appropriations

TABLE 2. *Votes on First Budget Resolutions, 1975–1980*

	DATE	TOTAL VOTE YES/NO	REPUBLICANS YES/NO	DEMOCRATS YES/NO		DATE	TOTAL VOTE YES/NO	REPUBLICANS YES/NO	DEMOCRATS YES/NO
HOUSE					SENATE				
	1975	200–196	3–128	197–68		1975	69–22	19–18	50–4
	1976	221–155	13–111	208–44		1976	62–22	17–16	45–6
	1977	213–179	7–121	206–58		1977	56–31	15–17	41–14
	1978	201–197	3–136	198–61		1978	64–27	16–19	48–8
	1979	220–184	9–134	211–50		1979	64–20	20–15	44–5
	1980	225–193	22–131	203–62		1980	68–28	19–22	49–6

bills were enacted before the start of the fiscal year. Congress showed that it could use the process to modify the president's budget, as it did with Ford's budgets in 1975 and 1976. Congress also demonstrated that it could accommodate the plans of a new president when it enacted a third budget resolution in 1977 at the request of President Jimmy Carter. The CBO's reports and analyses raised the level of budget-related information available to Congress. Yet after five years most participants and observers were disappointed with the performance of the congressional budget process.

Despite the changes that had followed in the wake of the Budget Impoundment and Control Act—the two Budget committees, the new voting coalitions, and the exacerbated partisanship in the House—there was no great shift in budget policy after 1975. The new budget process had survived, and Congress for the first time was approving budget totals and functional subtotals, but the process appeared to have little overall effect on fiscal policy or national priorities. Scholars who have studied the congressional budget process of the late 1970s agree that the second budget resolutions were little more than the sum of the actions of the spending committees. Rather than creating top-down influence on subsequent budget choices, the Budget committees—referred to by one observer as "adding machine committees"—largely accommodated the desires of the authorizing and appropriations committees. There was little evidence of priorities being restructured or spending being restrained, and the deficits continued to mount. The tension between the congressional roles of delivering benefits to constituents and of imposing overall budgetary discipline was reflected in many of the debates and deals struck during the late 1970s. In most cases, spending prevailed over restraint.

The reconciliation process, one of the most potent creations of the Budget, Act, was simply ignored in the 1970s. In 1979, efforts to use reconciliation were rejected by a coalition of committees. After the 1980 election, however, congressional leaders reported a reconciliation bill that reduced spending by some $8 billion. Significantly, it had both Democratic and Republican support and established an important precedent for the use of reconciliation in 1981.

Reagan, Deficits, and Budget Process, 1981 to 1985. The 1980 elections resulted in a shakeup in both the legislative and executive branches. Republicans regained control of the presidency after a four-year hiatus and took control of the Senate for

the first time since 1955. The size of the Democratic majority in the House was reduced from 117 to 51. This meant that House Republicans had to attract only twenty-six Democratic defectors to create a majority. With Republicans replacing Democrats as Senate chairmen, Pete V. Domenici (R-N.Mex.) became chairman of the Senate Budget Committee. James R. Jones (D-Okla.), who was narrowly elected chairman of the House Budget Committee, had a more conservative perspective than his predecessor, Robert N. Giaimo (D-Conn.).

In his 1980 campaign, Ronald Reagan had promised three general changes in budgetary priorities: a rapid increase in defense spending, a significant reduction in taxes, and large cuts in domestic spending and entitlements. Led by Office of Management and Budget director David Stockman, the administration moved quickly, presenting revised budget proposals to Congress within weeks of taking office. An extremely important change in the congressional budget process assisted Reagan in accomplishing his "revolution" in U.S. government: the decision to move reconciliation from the end to the beginning of the budget process. A reconciliation bill instructed committees and subcommittees to make cuts in the programs under their jurisdiction, reconciling individual authorizations and appropriations with totals in the budget resolution. This was achieved using the so-called elastic clause of the 1974 Budget Act, which allowed Congress to change "such other matters relating to the budget as may be appropriate to carry out the purposes of this Act." In 1980, Congress had established that reductions in authorizations would count toward reconciliation totals. This meant that reconciliation instructions could mandate a wide range of cuts in appropriations, entitlements, borrowing and contract authority, and authorizations.

With solid support in the Senate, the Reagan administration still needed to win the backing of conservative, southern House Democrats commonly referred to as boll weevils. The initial confrontation took place over the first concurrent resolution on the budget for fiscal year 1982. HBC chair Jones reported a resolution that, while giving the president much of what he wanted, did not satisfy the administration. Representatives Phil Gramm (D-Tex.) and Delbert L. Latta (R-Ohio) drafted a substitute reflecting the president's wishes. In May, the substitute, dubbed Gramm-Latta I, was adopted 253 to 176. Republicans supported the substitute budget resolution 190 to 0, while 63 of the 229 Democrats voting defected to the president. The Senate adopt-

BUDGET BALANCING. A sweating and worn "old man Congress," Clifford Berryman's recurring personification of Congress, delivers to the door of the Senate a budget balancing bill approved by the House. The cartoon reflects the importance of budget making in the agenda of the House and the difficulty of balancing the budget during the Depression. Clifford K. Berryman, *Washington Evening Star*, 3 April 1932.   LIBRARY OF CONGRESS

ed the resolution 78 to 20, with a majority of both parties supporting the president.

Despite the defeat, House Democrats believed that they could derail the administration's plans when the crucial reconciliation bill was considered in June. Once again, the Democratic version included most of the president's requests, cutting $39 billion from the budget for fiscal year 1982. The Rules Committee reported a rule for the bill that allowed the cuts to be voted on in six parts, greatly increasing the chances that many of the cuts would be rejected. However, on 25 June the Republican-

boll weevil alliance narrowly defeated the rule 217 to 210, substituting instead a single yes-or-no vote on the entire package of cuts. This victory virtually assured the coalition the margin it needed to defeat the Democratic leadership on the reconciliation bill itself. The Republican substitute, the Budget and Reconciliation Act (known as Gramm-Latta II), was hurriedly drafted overnight and passed the next day by a six-vote margin. The third and final key vote occurred a month later, when the House and Senate, by large margins, approved the Economic Recovery Tax Act (ERTA), which slashed income taxes by 25 percent across the board.

The events of 1981 had lasting effects on budgeting for several reasons. First, when combined with the recession that began late in the year, the tax cuts and defense increases (which were not compensated for by domestic cuts) resulted in historically large, chronic budget deficits. These deficits would become the driving force for additional reforms and changes in the congressional budget process. Second, reconciliation at the beginning of the process became an integral part of congressional budgeting even though it was extremely unpopular with many members. Third, the process in 1981 demonstrated that the second budget resolution played no meaningful role in overall budget control, and it was effectively dropped after 1982. Because the budget process itself remained unpopular, many of the changes were adopted informally, an approach that avoided the necessity of opening up the 1974 act to revision on the House and Senate floors.

The 1982 elections resulted in Democratic gains in the House and effectively ended the ability of Republicans and conservative Democrats to create a majority coalition. Table 3 examines voting alignments in the House and Senate on the first budget resolution votes between 1981 and 1985. Only in 1981 and 1982, when they were able to build a ma-

TABLE 3. *Votes on Budget Resolutions, 1981–1985*

	DATE	TOTAL VOTE YES/NO	REPUBLICANS YES/NO	DEMOCRATS YES/NO		DATE	TOTAL VOTE YES/NO	REPUBLICANS YES/NO	DEMOCRATS YES/NO
HOUSE					SENATE				
	1981	253–176	190–000	63–176		1981	78–20	50–2	28–18
	1982	219–206	156–32	63–174		1982	49–43	46–2	3–41
	1983	229–196	4–160	225–36		1983	50–49	21–32	29–17
	1984	250–168	21–139	229–29		1984	41–34	40–3	1–31
	1985	258–170	24–155	234–15		1985	50–49[1]	48–4	1–45

[1]Vice President George Bush cast the tie-breaking vote.

jority coalition, did Republicans vote for a budget resolution. After 1982, the House reverted to voting patterns similar to those of the 1970s. On the Senate side, bipartisanship in voting disappeared after 1981. With the exception of 1983, Senate Democrats and Republicans divided sharply over the budget, matching the partisanship of the House.

Deficits continued to rise in the early 1980s, hitting a record $208 billion in fiscal year 1983, with the deficit representing 6.3 percent of gross domestic product (GDP). Although several deficit reduction measures, which raised taxes and cut spending, were passed, the deficits remained at more than 5 percent of GDP through 1987. As had been true before 1975, some appropriations bills were not enacted by the start of the fiscal year; continuing resolutions were frequently needed when spending bills were not ready by 1 October. On several occasions when agreement could not be reached, the federal government had to shut down nonessential operations. Increasingly, both authorizations and appropriations were lumped together in "megabills." This must-pass legislation became the target for nongermane amendments of every description. A growing number of appropriations were enacted without authorizing legislation, a violation of House and Senate rules. Supplemental appropriations to restore cuts or avoid discipline were more frequent. Procedural controls and enforcement mechanisms weakened, while waivers to the Budget Act increased in frequency. These changes in the budget process, given the context of the large budget deficits, created the impetus to revise the Budget Act in 1985.

Balanced Budget and Emergency Deficit Control Act, 1985. In December 1985, Congress made the most dramatic changes in its budgetary process in a decade when it enacted the Balanced Budget and Emergency Deficit Control Act, better known as Gramm-Rudman-Hollings after its Senate cosponsors Phil Gramm (who had switched to the Republican party and gone to the Senate), Warren B. Rudman (R-N.H.), and Ernest F. Hollings (D-S.C.). The main thrust of the legislation was to create a mechanism for making across-the-board cuts in outlays should deficit targets not be met. Although the legislation was originally greeted with skepticism and derision, members frustrated with the inability to break the deadlock over deficits proved willing to sign on to almost anything that promised deficit reduction. The cosponsors forced congressional action by linking the deficit plan to the statutory debt-limitation legislation that had to

pass for the government to operate and pay its bills. For several months, House and Senate negotiators tried to hammer out a compromise version of the mandatory deficit reduction plan. Finally, when Republicans agreed that half the automatic cuts would come from defense, a final agreement was reached. Expressing some misgivings, President Reagan signed the bill.

Gramm-Rudman-Hollings established maximum allowable federal deficits over a five-year period: $172 billion for fiscal year 1986, $144 billion for fiscal year 1987, $108 billion for fiscal year 1988, $72 billion for fiscal year 1989, and $36 billion for fiscal year 1990. The budget was to be balanced in fiscal year 1991 and beyond. The act mandated that the president submit a budget with deficits that met the targets. It required that the Office of Management and Budget and the Congressional Budget Office issue estimates each August of the deficits for the coming year. If the deficits exceeded the targets, the General Accounting Office (GAO) would list the amounts that needed to be cut to reach the deficit targets. The president would then have to issue a sequestering order making mandatory cuts. Congress would have until 15 October to either raise taxes or cut spending to meet the target and avoid sequestration. Under the Gramm-Rudman-Hollings rules, the sequester would impose half of all cuts on defense and half on domestic spending. However, the law exempted many categories of spending, including Social Security, interest on the federal debt, Medicaid, food stamps, veterans' benefits, existing contracts, and several other welfare and child nutrition programs. Provisions of the mandatory plan could be waived only during war or a recession.

Gramm-Rudman-Hollings also revised the congressional budget process, accommodating the new deficit plan, advancing the timetable, and attempting to strengthen enforcement procedures. Table 4 shows the revised timetable that was implemented in 1986. It advanced the date by which the president had to submit his budget to Congress, although this requirement was dropped two years later. It moved up the date for CBO reports, the views and estimates of standing committees, and the budget resolution, and it formally dropped the second budget resolution. Perhaps the most important changes were the 15 June deadline for reconciliation and the 30 June deadline for appropriations bills.

In addition, Gramm-Rudman-Hollings attempted to strengthen enforcement procedures. First, totals and subtotals in the budget were made binding

TABLE 4. *Revised Budget Process under Gramm-Rudman-Hollings*

ACTION TO BE COMPLETED	ON OR BEFORE
President submits budget	Monday after 3 January
CBO reports to Congress	15 February
Committees submit views and estimates to Budget committees	25 February
Senate Budget Committee reports budget resolution	1 April
Congress passes budget resolution	15 April
House Appropriations Committee reports appropriations bills	10 June
Congress passes reconciliation bill	15 June
House passes all appropriations bills	30 June
Initial economic, revenue, outlay, and deficit projections made by OMB and CBO	15 August
OMB and CBO report tentative contents of sequester order to GAO	20 August
GAO issues deficit and sequester report to the president	25 August
President issues sequester order	1 September
Fiscal year begins and sequester order takes effect	1 October
OMB and CBO issue revised projections based on subsequent congressional action	5 October
GAO issues revised sequester report to president	10 October
Final sequester order becomes effective	15 October
GAO issues compliance report on sequester order	15 November

rather than mere targets. Second, committees were given ten days to publish their internal allocation of outlays, budget authority, and entitlements among their subcommittees. Third, no legislation providing new spending authority could come to the House or Senate floor unless a budget resolution had been passed. Fourth, any resolution that exceeded the Gramm-Rudman-Hollings deficit targets would be ruled out of order. Fifth, any committee or subcommittee that exceeded its allocations was subject to a point of order on the floor. Finally, all waivers of these provisions in the Senate and most in the House needed a three-fifths majority to be granted.

The act appeared to expand the scope of the budget process and strengthen the power of the Budget committees and party leaders at the expense of the other spending committees. As in the past, howev-

er, members and committees would prove creative in avoiding the discipline imposed by the budget rules. Under the compromise that allowed the passage of Gramm-Rudman-Hollings, a limited sequester for fiscal year 1986—which was already in progress—was ordered in early 1986. When all exempt programs were removed from the calculations, only around 25 percent of outlays were subject to sequestration. Through a complex formulation, the cuts amounted to 4.9 percent in defense accounts and 4.3 percent in domestic accounts. Gramm-Rudman-Hollings affected congressional budgeting in other ways. In particular, the new rules meant that amendments to taxing or spending legislation had to be revenue neutral; that is, any tax reduction or spending increase had to be offset or would be ruled out of order. This in particular affected the procedures surrounding Senate consideration of the Tax Reform Act of 1986.

The revised timetable proved impossible for Congress to meet as it struggled to reach the $144 billion deficit target for the fiscal year 1987 budget. In July 1986, the Supreme Court in *Bowsher v. Synar* struck down the mechanism that triggered automatic cuts. The Court ruled that because the GAO is an agent of Congress, it could not instruct the president to order sequestration without violating the constitutional doctrine of separation of powers. Nonetheless, both Republicans and Democrats in Congress agreed that it was essential to meet the deficit target. When Congress returned in August, CBO and OMB revealed that the deficit projections had suddenly gotten worse. The difficult cuts that had already been agreed to were now nearly $20 billion short of reaching the deficit target of $144 billion. Members agreed, however, that sequestration must be avoided at all costs.

To meet the target, the House and Senate used a variety of budgetary tricks and gimmicks to avoid across-the-board cuts. First, because Gramm-Rudman-Hollings allowed a $10 billion cushion, budgetmakers simply shot for $154 billion rather than $144 billion. Second, they used devices such as unrealistic economic assumptions, the proposed sale of government assets, and the elimination of an unspecified amount of government waste to reach the target. Even so, the process remained deadlocked through October, when an omnibus spending bill of $576 billion was enacted.

The experience of 1986 revealed some fundamental flaws in the Gramm-Rudman-Hollings process. Despite the new timetable, members would not know how big the deficit would be until August, which eliminated any incentives to make hard choices earlier in the year. Congress was chasing a moving target; most of the deficit increases between February and August stemmed from changes in the economy or technical errors in estimating revenues and outlays, not from the actions of Congress. As a result, Congress resorted to any expedient to get a short-term fix rather than the long-term solution to deficits that Gramm-Rudman-Hollings had promised. If it had not done so, the sequester would have had disastrous consequences on the outlays that were not exempt from cuts.

Balanced Budget and Emergency Deficit Control Reaffirmation Act, 1987. Through 1986, Congress was unable to agree on how to fix the constitutional flaw in Gramm-Rudman-Hollings. In 1987, however, it enacted the Balanced Budget and Emergency Deficit Control Reaffirmation Act, dubbed Gramm-Rudman II, which gave the OMB rather than the GAO the power to order across-the-board cuts. It had become clear to members of both parties that the original deficit targets were unrealistic. Therefore, the date for balancing the budget was extended from 1991 to 1993, the targets were revised, and the ambitious timetable was relaxed. The new targets were as follows: $144 billion for fiscal year 1988, $136 billion for fiscal year 1989, $100 billion for fiscal year 1990, $64 billion for fiscal year 1991, $28 billion for fiscal year 1992, and a balanced budget thereafter. While mandatory cuts continued to be divided equally between defense and domestic programs, Gramm-Rudman II gave the president more flexibility in determining where cuts in defense could be made. In an attempt to reduce budget gimmickry, the revised law restricted what could be counted as savings and limited Congress's ability to use unrealistic economic assumptions in order to show deficit reduction. Gramm-Rudman II also disallowed items that increased outlays in future years, made it harder to waive the budget rules, and called for an experiment with biennial budgeting in certain agencies.

Abandonment of the original deficit targets only two years after they were adopted sent a negative signal to the financial markets about Congress's commitment to deficit reduction. On 19 October 1987, U.S. securities markets plunged, losing 23 percent of their value in a single day, the largest one-day drop in history. The crash had a chilling effect on Congress and the Reagan administration, and they agreed to meet in a summit to work out budget differences. In December 1987, an agreement covering fiscal years 1988 and 1989 was reached that was designed to meet the deficit targets through the beginning of the next administration.

Reacting to the eight years of partisan interbranch warfare over the budget, President George Bush promised a more constructive engagement with the Congress. In April 1989—the earliest that the two branches had reached such an accord—Bush and congressional leaders announced that they had come to tentative agreement on the budget for fiscal year 1990. Unfortunately, the agreement for the most part merely papered over lingering differences concerning taxes, social programs, and defense. By autumn, the agreement had unraveled as Congress and the president battled over the administration's proposal for a reduction in the capital gains tax. But the major budget crisis in the Bush administration would not occur until 1990, when once again the deficit targets were scrapped and yet another approach to congressional budgeting was adopted.

Budget Summit Agreement and Budget Enforcement Act, 1990. The path toward a balanced budget took a tortuous turn in 1990. In February, Bush submitted a budget for fiscal year 1991 that projected a deficit of $64 billion, which met the Gramm-Rudman II target. But six months later, an economic downturn, technical errors in forecasting revenues, and larger-than-anticipated outlays for a bailout of the savings and loan industry combined to leave the projected deficit near $250 billion. A sequester of nearly $200 million—which would gut more than 50 percent of domestic and defense discretionary spending—was unthinkable. Once again, the deficit targets would have to be scrapped and a new solution found.

On 30 September 1990, after five months of work, a summit composed of top congressional and White House leaders reached agreement on a five-year, $500 billion deficit reduction package and revised budget process. The plan both raised taxes and cut spending, with approximately one-third of the projected net savings from tax increases, one-third from defense cuts, and one-third from domestic spending cuts. Both sides compromised: Bush agreed to new taxes despite his "no new taxes" pledge during the 1988 presidential campaign, and congressional Democrats accepted large cuts in domestic programs such as Medicare. Both President Bush and Democratic leaders in Congress endorsed the plan, but restive members voted the measure down. Within weeks, however, a revised version encompassing most of the basic framework was adopted. The Omnibus Budget Reconciliation Act

(OBRA) of 1990 not only was the largest deficit reduction package ever but also included a major revision of the congressional budget process in the Budget Enforcement Act (BEA).

The budget agreement embodied a number of important policy and procedural changes. Two of the most crucial were the suspension for three years of Gramm-Rudman-Hollings and the creation of separate appropriations caps for discretionary spending. Under Gramm-Rudman-Hollings, Congress had been held responsible for budget changes that were not of its own making. The new process eliminated fixed deficit targets and shifted the emphasis from deficit reduction to spending control, focusing on maintaining budgetary discipline in those areas where Congress actually has the power to determine how much taxes are raised and how much money is spent.

The Budget Enforcement Act divided discretionary appropriations into three categories with separate outlay and budget authority limits for fiscal years 1991 to 1993. For 1994 and 1995, the three discretionary caps were to be merged and a single discretionary appropriation cap imposed. The shares of domestic, defense, and international spending were fixed for three years; but in years four and five, trade-offs among the three components would be possible. The caps would be enforced by a new set of rules. Under Gramm-Rudman-Hollings, budget resolutions covered a single year, allowing spending increases and tax cuts to be shifted ahead. Under the Budget Enforcement Act, the resolutions cover five years and limits must be maintained for that period.

If any of the caps is exceeded, excess spending is eliminated by a minisequester within the offending category. For example, if international program spending should exceed allowable budget authority, an across-the-board cut would be assessed on all programs within the category. Before 1 July, the sequester takes place fifteen days after the cap is broken. After 1 July, a "look back" sequester is assessed in the next fiscal year. Under OBRA, the assumptions and targets were to be reassessed in early 1993. If the process was maintained as originally written in 1990, the Gramm-Rudman-Hollings process was to be reactivated to enforce the totals in 1994 and 1995.

The other major change in budget enforcement concerned the treatment of entitlements and revenues in the budget. Under the old system, a sequester of discretionary programs could be triggered by revenue shortfalls or increases in entitlement spending due to greater utilization or higher inflation. Under the Budget Enforcement Act, both revenues and entitlements were put on a pay-as-you-go basis. Any action to increase entitlement eligibility or reduce revenues had to be offset by spending cuts or tax increases elsewhere in the budget. These provisions affected the total of all legislation in a given year, not individual measures.

Increases in entitlement spending were to be compensated for by a sequester across certain entitlement categories. Reconciliation procedures were extended to revenues for the first time to enforce the pay-as-you-go rules. The Budget committees were given power to issue reconciliation instructions to the House Ways and Means or Senate Finance committees to mandate an offset for a revenue loss. Social Security was exempted from the pay-as-you-go requirement, and what the act called a "firewall" was created to protect the Social Security trust fund from legislation that would expand benefits or reduce payroll taxes.

Unlike appropriations caps, which focused on spending control, these entitlement provisions focused on deficit neutrality. Any discretionary or entitlement spending determined by both the president and Congress to be necessitated by an emergency was exempted from the requirement. In general, OBRA represented a dramatic change from past efforts to eliminate deficits because it retreated from fixed deficit targets. The deficit could increase because of economic changes, reestimation, or emergencies without triggering spending reductions. The revised process was more flexible and realistic than earlier efforts in its assertion of discipline over the aspects of budgeting that Congress actually controls: discretionary spending, entitlement expansion, and tax reductions.

Even with the critical changes in both policy and process that OBRA rendered, the deficit problem would not simply disappear. Despite the spending cuts and tax increases, the deficit increased in the early 1990s because of a recession, the savings and loan bailout, and spiraling Medicare and Medicaid costs. After Bill Clinton became president, projections showed that the deficits would remain in the range of $300 to $560 billion through the year 2000 without further policy changes. As a result, Clinton proposed a controversial five-year, $500 billion deficit reduction package in 1993. This suggests that Congress will continue to innovate and improvise with its budget procedures in an effort to find the means to assert fiscal discipline.

When the authorization-appropriations process

was judged to be inadequate, Congress embarked on a quest to develop a budget process that could serve both the needs of individual members to serve their constituencies and the duty of Congress as a whole to set responsible national policy. The growth of entitlements and other inflexible mandatory spending and the decline of discretionary spending helped change the very nature of budgeting. In 1974, legislators developed a system intended to provide greater overall coordination and control and to allow Congress to compete more effectively with the president. Some wanted the budget process to restrain spending, but others wanted it to reallocate or rationalize greater spending. With the onset of chronic deficits and the recurring deadlock between congressional Democrats and the White House, the process was oriented almost exclusively to spending restraint and deficit reduction. Yet this did not reduce the members' interest in pursuing various policy goals and protecting pet programs and projects.

Scholars and observers have come to different conclusions about the performance of the congressional budget process. Some argue that it has been an unmitigated disaster that has failed to deal constructively with budget deficits. They criticize devices such as Gramm-Rudman-Hollings for making mindless cuts and restricting the options of both Congress and the president. Some see the instability and improvisational nature of the congressional budget process as a sign of weakness.

Yet many of the criticisms are based on unrealistic expectations of the process. In some ways, Congress has made extraordinary changes. It has emerged with stronger leadership and more centralized policy-making mechanisms. It is better equipped to compete with the president when priorities collide or to cooperate when priorities coincide. Reconciliation has proved to be a potent weapon in shaping the budget. Despite the repeated failure to reduce deficits, in 1982, 1987, 1990, and other years Congress made many hard, responsible choices that prevented the deficits from being significantly larger than they might have grown to be.

Congress's budgeting-performance problems are more a reflection of underlying conflicts in national government than of an inherent institutional inability to manage the budget effectively. The congressional budget process has been so unstable in part because of the divergent policy preferences of legislative and executive branches and the partisanship that has often dominated their relationship. Rules, procedures, and processes play an important role in shaping the context of congressional behavior and in influencing policy outcomes, but they cannot on their own resolve fundamental political and ideological conflicts.

[See also Appropriations; Backdoor Spending; Budget Committee, House; Budget Committee, Senate; Congressional Budget Office; Entitlement; General Accounting Office; Office of Management and Budget. For discussion of particular budget-related legislation, see Balanced Budget and Emergency Deficit Control Act; Budget and Accounting Act; Budget Enforcement Act of 1990; Budget Reconciliation Act. See also Balanced Budget Amendment.]

BIBLIOGRAPHY

Gilmour, John B. Reconcilable Differences? Congress, the Budget Process, and the Deficit. 1990.
Haas, Lawrence J. Running on Empty: Bush, Congress, and the Politics of a Bankrupt Government. 1990.
Ippolito, Dennis. Congressional Spending. 1981.
Kettl, Donald E. Deficit Politics: Public Budgeting in Its Institutional and Historical Context. 1992.
LeLoup, Lance T. The Fiscal Congress: Legislative Control of the Budget. 1980.
Makin, John H., Norman J. Ornstein, and David Zlowe, eds. Balancing Act: Debt, Deficit, and Taxes. 1990.
Mills, Gregory B., and John Palmer. Federal Budget Policy in the 1980s. 1984.
Penner, Rudolph G., and Alan J. Abramson. Broken Purse Strings: Congressional Budgeting, 1974–88. 1988.
Savage, James D. Balanced Budgets and American Politics. 1988.
Schick, Allen. The Capacity to Budget. 1990.
Schick, Allen. Congress and Money. 1980.
White, Joseph, and Aaron Wildavsky. The Deficit and the Public Interest: The Search for Responsible Budgeting in the 1980s. 1989.

LANCE T. LELOUP

BUDGET RECONCILIATION ACT (1981; 95 Stat. 357). The Omnibus Budget Reconciliation Act of 1981 (OBRA) (P.L. 97-35) was the centerpiece of President Ronald Reagan's far-reaching budget and economic plan during his first year in office. Called "the most sweeping legislation in modern American history," the act contained instructions to dozens of House and Senate committees to implement reductions and substantive changes in programs to reduce spending by more than $35 billion in the first year and more than $100 billion over three years. Thousands of federal programs, from food stamps to Amtrak, were affected. More important, perhaps, than the sheer amount of deauthorization that OBRA required was how seriously the act eroded congressional committees' power by replacing the committees' discretion to shape legislation with a reconciliation process dominated by floor majorities.

Nicknamed Gramm-Latta II after its House cosponsors Phil Gramm (D-Tex.) and Delbert L. Latta (R-Ohio), OBRA occasioned an intensely bitter partisan fight. With the Republican-controlled Senate solidly behind him, Reagan worked hard with his congressional supporters to secure the necessary defections from conservative southern Democrats to create a working majority in the House. Democrats, led by Speaker Thomas P. (Tip) O'Neill, Jr., attempted to thwart the president by dividing OBRA into six separate bills. This move failed, and Democrats were forced to vote on a single substitute that represented the administration's program. The bill was hastily prepared through the early morning hours of 25 June 1981 by Representative Gramm and Office of Management and Budget director David Stockman. The final version, although laden with typographical errors, was adopted by the House 214 to 208. It represented the most significant element of Reagan's 1981 economic blitz and introduced a revolutionary change in the congressional budget process.

BIBLIOGRAPHY

LeLoup, Lance T. "After the Blitz: Reagan and the U.S. Congressional Budget Process." *Legislative Studies Quarterly* 7 (August 1982): 321–339.
White, Joseph, and Aaron Wildavsky. *The Deficit and the Public Interest.* 1989.

LANCE T. LELOUP

BUREAUCRACY. One of the clearest of all clauses in the U.S. Constitution is the provision in Article II, section 1 that states with stark simplicity that "executive power shall be vested in a President of the United States." In awarding the president such preeminent authority over an executive branch that would in time become a vast and complex bureaucratic establishment with authority extending throughout the land, the Framers of the Constitution rejected a variety of proposals that would have required the chief executive to share that power with other government officials. They feared that dispersion of executive authority would weaken both the presidential office and the ability of the public to hold all government offi-

cials accountable for their decisions.

But even as the Framers were giving the president this exclusive title to executive authority, they also granted Congress the right to establish and empower all the agencies that might thereafter lie within the domain of the executive branch, along with the ability to determine how much financial support they would receive to carry out the tasks they might be assigned.

Here indeed was a prime example not of the separation of powers for which the Constitution is so famous, but of what Richard Neustadt was later to describe in *Presidential Power* (1992) as "separate institutions sharing power." Under the terms of the written Constitution, executive officials high and low would have to defer to the president as the head of their sphere of government, but Congress rather than the chief executive would ultimately determine both the scope of their power and the extent of their resources.

Over the years, both the president and Congress have sought an advantageous answer to the question inherent in the design of the Constitution: Whose executive branch is this, anyway? For its part, Congress has used the authority granted it to define the duties of each agency in the executive branch and to spell out in what is sometimes seen as excruciating detail how the agency should carry out its responsibilities. The legislature has done so both by statute and through a variety of informal ways for communicating its preferences and priorities to the bureaucracy.

Historical Development

Very early in American history, attempts were made to stake out the claim that Congress rather than the president had lawful authority to issue commands to at least some agencies in the executive branch. During the presidency of Andrew Jackson, for example, Whig party leaders argued that the national legislature had legal authority over the affairs of the Treasury Department, since Treasury, unlike the Department of State, did not perform functions that were inherently executive in character but derived its role in government from its responsibility for handling congressional appropriations.

These Whigs argued that the right to provide such appropriations was a central feature of the authority granted Congress under the Constitution, as well as a fiscal responsibility that historically had been at the heart of all legislative power. Consequently, it would be entirely proper for the secretary of the Treasury to take his instructions on the disposition of government funds from Congress rather than the president.

Congressional Domination of the Bureaucracy. The president's legislative opponents could draw some support for their position from the decisions Congress made at the beginning of the Republic when it established executive departments. At that time, as Lloyd Short put it (*The Development of National Administrative Organization in the United States*, 1923), the

> secretaries of War and Foreign Affairs were made solely responsible and subordinate to the President, and only a general indication was made as to the scope of their duties. On the contrary, the Secretary of the Treasury, although he was also responsible to the President, was more minutely controlled and directed in the discharge of the specific duties assigned to him by Congress. (p. 100)

This attempt to wrest control over the Treasury Department from the president did not succeed. Jackson simply removed the Treasury secretary who had complied with the legislature and replaced him with an official who would submit to his control. Disputes over the proper extent of Congress's role in such matters as the appointment and removal of executive officials continued to surface, however. President Andrew Johnson's defiance of congressional restrictions on his appointment power brought him to the brink of impeachment in the years immediately following the Civil War.

But while Johnson was able to dodge the legislative bullet in his impeachment trial, the bureaucracy was not. As Richard M. Pious has noted (*The American Presidency*, 1979):

> By the time the House voted its impeachment, control of the departments already rested in the hands of congressional leaders. They instituted a system of congressional supremacy, involving a close connection between department secretaries and committee chairs, which remained in effect for the remainder of the century. . . . Woodrow Wilson made his academic reputation as a political scientist with a description of how congressional committees controlled departments, and urged adoption of cabinet government to bring order out of the chaos the rival committees had created. (p. 74)

Thus, in the nineteenth and early twentieth centuries, the chief impact of congressional involvement in the affairs of the bureaucracy was to decentralize power within the executive branch, with each of its major segments coming under the strong influence of a different set of legislative mas-

ters. In this way, the executive power that the Constitution had so carefully centered in the presidency was eventually spread among many hands. Agency executives found that their success in Washington depended less on staying on good terms with the White House than on their ability to get along well with Congress. While the Framers had sought to create unity within the executive through their provisions on presidential power, they had sown the seeds of disunity through the equally important clauses they included on legislative power.

Congress thus became a dominant presence in the lives of executive agencies very early on in U.S. history through its ability to define agency missions and to measure out agency appropriations. As it developed an elaborate committee structure, Congress also acquired the capacity to keep itself better informed on how well its instructions were being carried out, a process that eventually came to be known as congressional oversight of the bureaucracy.

Throughout U.S. history, Congress exercised enormous influence over what is now called "state-building," an area of research in which Stephen Skowronek has pioneered (1982). Over the years Congress has approved the establishment of a variety of bureaucratic organizations designed to give the American state the muscle needed to handle an expanding set of responsibilities.

The legislature has been criticized for the slowness with which it acted, but the most remarkable aspect of congressional involvement in state-building is the extent to which it served to keep the character of American bureaucracy in tune with the democratic character of the country. The establishment of organizations such as the Agriculture, Commerce, and Labor departments occurred not as a result of needs originated or defined in highly placed government circles, as might ordinarily be expected in Europe, but in response to pressures from within American society itself.

The Department of Labor, for example, was born in 1913, before the national government itself had assumed any significant responsibilities in this field (Francis E. Rourke, "The Department of Labor and the Trade Unions," *Western Political Quarterly* 7 [1954]: 656–672). Like the departments of Agriculture and Commerce (and later Veterans' Affairs and Housing and Urban Development), Labor was a department created to assure a significant sector of the population that it too had a voice in the affairs of government. Thus, "creating a bureaucracy that looks like America" is one of the major legislative contributions to state-building in the United States.

Congress versus the President. Inevitably, the performance of each of these roles brought Congress into conflict with the White House, as neither was able to resist the invitation the Constitution had issued to vie for control over the bureaucracy. But it is important to note that, while the efforts of the rival branches of government to manage the affairs of executive bureaucracies did produce conflict, such efforts also led to a great deal of constructive constitutional innovation. This occurred as these separate institutions searched for political compromises to reconcile their conflicting legal authority over the operation of the national government's executive machinery.

As a result, the struggle for control over bureaucracy has been a powerful force for change in the way in which both the presidency and Congress now function. Because it is a written document, the Constitution has sometimes had the appearance of a fundamental law that is highly resistant—if not totally impervious—to change. In the case of the congressional relationship with the bureaucracy, however, the record suggests that the Constitution can also be viewed as a set of governing arrangements that have largely been invented as the country's history unfolded. In this area of governmental operations, the Constitution has revealed its great flexibility and capacity for adaptation.

Executive Privilege. For example, U.S. presidents have always insisted that they alone have the ultimate right to determine whether information in the hands of executive officials should be released beyond the executive branch when, in their view, such disclosure might adversely affect vital national interests or the effective operation of the executive branch. The validity of this claim of executive privilege to withhold information from Congress was challenged at the very beginning of the Republic when President George Washington sought to withhold information about an unsuccessful military expedition against the Indians and about the negotiations preceding a peace treaty with Great Britain. Here Washington eventually compromised, supplying Congress information it requested on the military expedition but denying access to executive records on treaty negotiations.

Presidential assertion of executive privilege continued to plague the relationship between legislative committees and the chief executive. Not until the presidency of Richard M. Nixon was the legal issue finally resolved when in 1974 the Supreme Court held, in *United States v. Nixon*, that presidents did indeed enjoy such a privilege, although in this dispute Nixon's own claims of prerogative were disallowed.

The Court's decision in the *Nixon* case did not, however, alter the long-standing preference of Congress and the White House for negotiating a political solution to the legal conflicts that arose whenever the legislature sought access to information that an executive-branch organization refused to disclose. These legal disputes have customarily been settled by political bargains. Usually, the information requested by Congress is eventually released, with executive officials perhaps deleting particularly sensitive material. Too, access to the material is frequently confined to those legislators with an unmistakable "need to know."

Shaping Structural Change in the Bureaucracy. Such constitutional innovation has also been necessary when changes in the organizational structure of the bureaucracy are contemplated. For a very long time, decisions regarding structural change were shaped almost entirely by congressional statutes. This led to a great deal of organizational rigidity within the executive branch. Presidents who wanted to shift programs from one agency to another or otherwise to alter patterns of authority within their executive household usually had to persuade Congress to pass laws permitting such changes. These statutes were difficult to enact, since the agencies affected could easily rally the groups they served or their supporters in Congress to block such reorganizations. Legislative opponents of reorganization feared that it could shrink their influence over agency policies from which they or their constituents benefited.

So from the 1930s to the 1990s, the two branches of government made frequent use of a mutually satisfactory arrangement. By statutory enactment, modern presidents have generally been given the right to reorganize the executive branch at their own initiative, but their reorganization plans go into effect only if, within a specified period of time, the legislature has not chosen to pass a resolution vetoing the change. It was here that the legislative veto first came into prominent use as a means of breaking deadlocks between Congress and the president.

This legislative veto system puts the burden on the opposition to defeat the president's plans rather than requiring the White House to overcome the roadblocks in congressional procedures that ordinarily impede new legislation. Indeed, the obstacles posed by congressional procedures increase the likelihood that the president's reorganization plans will go into effect, since the legislative veto system

BUREAU OF THE CENSUS. Operators recording census data, late 1930s. LIBRARY OF CONGRESS

converts them into impediments that opponents of reorganization (rather than its supporters) must surmount. As Peri E. Arnold has shown in *Making the Managerial Presidency: Comprehensive Reorganization Planning, 1905–1980* (1986), a great deal of executive reorganization has been accomplished as a result of this arrangement, under which, in contrast to the ordinary constitutional process, Congress exercises the power of veto.

The Role of Partisanship. It can therefore fairly be said that cooperation has characterized the various efforts by Congress and the White House to control the development and operation of American bureaucracy as often as has conflict. The compromises that have emerged are generally the product of a willingness of members of both political parties in Congress to modify what are often deemed to be its institutional prerogatives in order to produce some desired result. Conflict, on the other hand, is often rooted in the jockeying for partisan or ideological

advantage that is an inevitable feature of legislative life. Congressional Democrats and Republicans alike have usually been inclined to allow the White House much more leeway in running the bureaucracy when a member of their party is president.

Thus, in the 1960s, congressional Democrats who had been highly critical of administrative secrecy within the executive branch while Republican Dwight D. Eisenhower held the presidency became strangely quiet about this issue when Democrat John F. Kennedy moved into the White House. Through most of the 1970s and 1980s, Republicans in Congress were highly supportive of grants of extensive discretion to executive agencies as their party began to win presidential elections with great regularity, reversing their strong opposition to this practice during the long period of Democratic ascendancy.

The divided government that emerged in the 1950s and generated growing conflict in the 1980s tended to heighten competition between Congress and the president for control over the bureaucracy. The Democrats, who held a majority in both houses of Congress during much of this period, were highly supportive of measures designed either to narrow the power of bureaucrats or to enhance the ability of the courts and groups outside government to challenge the decisions of executive agencies. These steps were triggered by Democratic fears that Republican presidents had saturated the bureaucracy with political appointees who were shifting agency policies in directions Congress never intended to go.

On the other hand, Republicans in the White House or at the head of executive agencies in this era of divided government were no less outspoken in their criticism of what they regarded as the efforts of Democratic legislators to micromanage administrative decisions. Their heaviest fire was directed at legislative efforts to intervene in foreign policy decisions that they viewed as entirely within the president's constitutional authority.

Congressional Acquiescence. Political combat has not been the only factor shaping the relationship between Congress and bureaucracy in modern times. As *United States v. Nixon* suggests, Supreme Court rulings have also had a major impact. In 1935, the Court handed down a decision in *Humphrey's Executor v. the United States* that effectively carved out a sphere of autonomy for the various independent regulatory agencies that had been created by Congress to prevent the abuse of economic power in broad sectors of the American society, beginning with the establishment of the Interstate Commerce Commission in 1887. In this case, the Court decided that these agencies administered functions that were not truly executive responsibilities but were, in the justices' view, quasi-legislative or quasi-judicial in character.

As a result of this ruling, independent regulatory commissions were entitled to greater immunity from presidential control and subjected to a larger degree of congressional supervision than other organizations within the bureaucracy. In *Humphrey's Executor,* the Court upheld a congressional statute that set limits on the president's right to remove the chief officials of a regulatory agency, although the Court had previously ruled that, as chief executive, the president enjoyed an unlimited power to fire heads of executive organizations.

The *Humphrey's Executor* decision, however, can be regarded as part of a losing effort that was mounted in the 1930s to hold back the tide of grow-

ing presidential ascendancy within the executive branch. This effort was visible also in a 1939 Brookings Institution study that reflected the views of conservatives in Congress. It argued that "the departments and agencies constituted an administrative branch set up by acts of Congress and were therefore under the Congress rather than the President" (Don K. Price, *America's Unwritten Constitution,* 1983, p. 125). However, Congress eventually took its cue from the President's Committee on Administrative Management (which reported to Franklin D. Roosevelt in 1937) rather than from the Brookings Institution study, and in 1939 it approved a set of reorganization proposals that greatly strengthened presidential authority over the bureaucracy.

Thus, neither Supreme Court decisions nor isolated pockets of congressional resistance could prevent the onset of change in the New Deal era. As the number and power of federal agencies swelled, it became apparent in Congress and elsewhere that an increasingly complicated executive structure needed some kind of centralized, hierarchical direction and control and that such management could only come from the White House. In the end, therefore, presidential ascendancy within the executive branch came about with congressional acquiescence as the need for greater efficiency, effectiveness, and economy in the executive branch's operation became a matter of urgent necessity for legislative as well as executive officials.

Bicameralism. Another way in which the Constitution has affected the congressional relationship with the bureaucracy is the division of legislative power between the House and the Senate. This bicameral arrangement has had some negative consequences for bureaucracy, since it subjects executive agencies to a kind of double jeopardy. Agencies' policies and activities must pass muster with both houses of the legislature—both powerful and often very different. This situation is without parallel in other highly industrialized societies. But the bicameral system has also had one positive aspect for bureaucracy: it has enabled executive agencies to win reversals in one chamber of unfavorable decisions in the other.

Congressional Committees as Channels of Interaction

The relationship between Congress and the bureaucracy is primarily an encounter between individual executive agencies and the small number of legislative committees with which these organizations are obliged to interact. It is to such committees that both the House and the Senate ordinarily delegate the cutting edge of their legislative power, and it is only with them that agencies are required to have an ongoing connection.

The interests of executive agencies and the congressional committees with which they deal can be seen as either conflicting or converging. The conventional image of the relationship is one of confrontation. Framed by the traditional view of the Congress as the overseer of the bureaucracy, this view sees legislative committees as subjecting the executive agencies under their jurisdiction to vigorous and unrelenting scrutiny to determine how well or poorly they are carrying out their assigned duties.

Many studies of the legislative-bureaucratic relationship have drawn a quite different picture, however. Consensus rather than conflict is perceived to prevail as each party discovers that the other can generously serve its interests in many ways. The easiest and safest conclusion to draw from these contrasting images of the tie between Congress and the bureaucracy is that, as with many other relationships in human affairs, it can generate conflict while also providing comfort for the parties involved.

Adversarial Relations with Congress. The image of the relationship as adversarial is prominent in studies of Congress that focus on its ability to cut agency appropriations, strip executive organizations of major programs, or threaten agencies with reprisals unless they make major changes in their policies. This image of conflict is also prominent in studies of the Senate's use of its confirmation power. While Senate committees often appear willing to give routine approval to a president's nominees, the confirmation power can be used as a potent instrument of congressional control over bureaucracy. It enables the legislature to send strong signals to a newly appointed agency executive of its dissatisfaction with an organization's past performance.

Symbiosis with Congress. There is strong support in both the political arena and academic analysis, however, for the view that the interests of Congress and the bureaucracy more often converge than conflict. Public interest groups have led the way in criticizing what they perceive as the indulgent attitude of congressional committees toward the programs and activities of executive organizations. Witness the heavy fire directed at congres-sional intelligence committees with jurisdiction over the activities of the Central Intelligence Agency when it was revealed in the post-Vietnam years that they had often failed to detect or censure questionable CIA activities.

Academic studies of congressional behavior lend strong support to the view that the interests of Congress and the bureaucracy dovetail more often than they conflict. For example, Morris Fiorina's analysis of the bureaucratic-legislative relationship describes the connection between the two institutions as a cozy partnership from which each party derives substantial benefits (*Congress: Keystone of the Washington Establishment*, 2d ed., 1989).

According to Fiorina, this partnership provides members of Congress with the opportunity to gain political favor in their own districts by helping voters obtain information or benefits they need from executive agencies. It also allows legislators to intervene in their constituents' behalf with agencies that are imposing regulations that voters find objectionable. Such favors enable members to build coalitions of support within their own constituencies that transcend party lines and so to convert their districts into safe seats.

The bureaucracy benefits from this partnership as well, since members of Congress inevitably develop a vested interest in maintaining the health of executive organizations whose activities provide them with so many opportunities to serve their constituencies. In the modern U.S. administrative state, the hand of bureaucracy is everywhere, and, as Fiorina notes, "The more decisions the bureaucracy has an opportunity to make, the more opportunities there are for the congressman to build up credits" (p. 46).

Fiorina was by no means the first observer to note the presence of such symbiosis in the relationship between Congress and the bureaucracy. A number of earlier studies of policy-making in the United States highlighted how executive agencies and legislative committees could enter into alliances in the pursuit of common interests. Arthur Maass's *Muddy Waters* (1951), a study of the relationship between the U.S. Army Corps of Engineers and the House and Senate Public Works committees, was a pioneer investigation of how an executive agency and the committees that were expected to patrol its activities could instead organize into a mutual benefit society.

The Iron Triangle. In *The Political Process: Executive Bureau–Legislative Committee Relations* (1965), J. Leiper Freeman generalized this relationship into a model of policy-making designed to apply throughout the entire political system. He argued that executive agencies responsible for running particular government programs commonly forged close ties with both the legislative committee responsible for enacting the statutes on which their authority rested and the clientele groups served by their programs and policies. This "iron triangle" or "subgovernment" model of U.S. policy-making ultimately became (with some fine-tuning over the years) the dominant paradigm for explaining the way government policy is shaped in modern American democracy.

Each segment of the triangle, or subgovernment, is expected to serve its own interests by supporting the goals of both other participants in the policy-making system. The most salient characteristic of such an alliance is the fact that it is a closed system of decision making. Members of Congress not on the committee included in the triangle and segments of the population not part of the agency's clientele are excluded from effective participation in policy decisions in the many policy-making areas in which subgovernments have long held the reins of power.

The Evolution of Legislative-Bureaucratic Relationships. There are thus two competing views of the relationship between Congress and the bureaucracy: one that sees their interests as diverging and another that sees them as converging. But it must be remembered that what is perceived may depend on the vantage point. White House officials who have difficulty imposing their policy preferences on an executive agency may come to view it as being in cahoots with the legislative committees with which it deals even as officials at that same agency may see those committees as trying to impose detailed and misguided controls over their organization's programs.

It should also be noted that the relationships between executive agencies and legislative committees are far from static. Developments in the environment in which they operate exert constant pressure for change in these relationships as in other aspects of the political system. For a number of reasons, for example, it has become increasingly difficult for both the committees and the agencies to prevent "outsiders" from invading the enclaves of public policy over which they maintained such close and exclusive control in the heyday of the iron triangle system.

For one thing, a proliferation of subcommittees is now characteristic of congressional organization as a result of various efforts the legislature has made to reform its operation since World War II. By reducing the number of committees, these reforms spawned an increasing number of subcommittees and provided additional points of entry through which legislators not part of traditional iron triangles could gain a voice in areas of policy-making over which subgovernment cartels once held exclusive power. By the early 1970s, as Steven S. Smith and Christopher J. Deering point out (*Committees in Congress*, 1990), "Few members considered deference to committee recommendations a viable norm" (p. 180). Moreover, by the 1980s a new vehicle for the expression of dissenting opinion had emerged in Congress: the special interest caucus. Made up of legislators who seek to promote the interests of a single group or region of the country, more than a hundred of these congressional caucuses seek to enact legislation or to tilt government agencies toward actions or decisions favorable to their constituencies.

The domination of policy formulation by iron triangles has also been weakened by another development. Today, executive agency jurisdictions increasingly overlap, with the external effects of one agency's decisions reverberating in other policy settings. Environmental groups, for example, have shown growing interest in the activities of a great many executive agencies other than those specifically concerned with environmental affairs. When these groups suspect that a government construction project will have an adverse impact on the environment, the responsible agency may suddenly discover that a new set of environmentally conscious legislators has become very interested in its activities and that these legislators are not at all reluctant to launch strong attacks on the agency. As a result, a once-harmonious relationship between an executive agency and its congressional network begins to show increasing signs of friction.

Activist groups in other policy areas, such as civil rights and consumer issues, have also opened opportunities for greater participation in systems of policy-making previously closed to outsiders. The net effect of these various aspects of "movement politics" has thus been to make the relations between legislative committees and executive agencies much less predictable. When the National Endowment for the Arts was charged in the late 1980s and early 1990s with having provided financial support for "pornography," its activities, which had formerly been of interest only to the appropriate specialized committees, suddenly caught the attention of every member of Congress.

One major effect of these changes is that agency executives in the 1990s often discover that it is not enough to be working diligently toward the achievement of their organizations' programmatic goals, such as transportation or public works. To avoid criticism and possible retaliation from Congress, they must now be able to show that their agencies work out of buildings that provide easy access for the handicapped, avoid projects that will have an adverse impact on the environment, and otherwise comport themselves in ways that meet the expectations of the activist movements across the political spectrum that have become so conspicuous a feature of contemporary American political life.

It is, however, much too early to say that the iron triangle is a spent force. Symbiosis still characterizes the relationship between agencies and committees. Agencies cannot survive or prosper without the support they receive from the legislative committees concerned with their affairs. Nor can members of Congress ignore the fact that these agencies commonly provide services that are highly prized by their many constituents or can impose restrictions that will anger voters in their districts.

It thus becomes difficult for Congress or its committees to penalize a bureaucratic organization without imposing burdens on the voters on whom the legislators depend for reelection. Aware of this fact, agencies have become quite adept at making it more difficult for legislators to impose sanctions on them. For instance, agencies may respond, or threaten to respond, to cuts in appropriations by eliminating or cutting back on services that are especially cherished or badly needed by constituents in a great many congressional districts. Thus, Congress and the bureaucracy are bound together not only by the favors they exchange but also by the reprisals they can visit on one another.

The Growth of Congressional Staff

Also of great importance to legislative-bureaucratic relationships has been the proliferation of expertise throughout the political system on a growing number of subjects for which executive agencies are now charged with responsibility. Congress is one of the chief beneficiaries of this diffusion of expertise. Highly skilled professional staff organizations now serve all members, and legislative committees and many congressional offices have acquired their own stables of experts. These developments have greatly enhanced the ability of Congress to second-guess the decisions and policies of executive agencies. To be sure, the system of committee government already described has for a long time generated a great deal of legislative expertise, and participation in the work of such committees has allowed many members to acquire specialized knowledge.

Hugh Heclo has suggested that the term *issue network* describes the setting in which government policies are now forged better than does the traditional notion of the iron triangle. But, according to Heclo, participation in such a network is only open to those who are qualified by virtue of their expertise to discuss the policy issues salient to the network. To hold its own in this new setting, Congress has had to upgrade its own professional capacities. This development has led Lawrence C. Dodd to describe the modern Congress as a technocracy in which power has come increasingly to be centered in the hands of "technical experts" (Richard A. Harris and Sidney M. Milkis, eds., *Remaking American Politics*, 1989, pp. 89–111).

The growth in the size and skill of its professional staff has had a number of effects on Congress's relationship with the bureaucracy. It has saved legislators from having to deal with executive officials who are better informed than they on the finer points of policy issues. Closing the expertise gap has created a more level playing field in the policy debate that often characterizes the relationship between Congress and the executive branch.

The presence of a professional staff has also given Congress a much greater capacity for continuity in its involvement in the affairs of executive agencies. Staff members have both the time and knowledge to track decision making within the executive branch much more closely than can the members of Congress for whom they work, since the legislators must focus so much of their attention on getting reelected.

Mathew D. McCubbins and Thomas Schwartz have made the persuasive argument that Congress can pursue two strategies in overseeing the work of executive agencies ("Congressional Oversight Overlooked: Police Patrols Versus Fire Alarms," *American Journal of Political Science* 2 [1984]: 165–179). The first is a continuous process of legislative surveillance that they describe as a "police patrol" system. Under this arrangement, Congress undertakes to keep itself continuously informed on how well executive agencies are performing the various tasks that the legislature has given them. The other strategy open to the legislature is a system of "fire alarm" oversight. Congress leaves it to others, including the courts and various groups affected by an agency's decisions, to patrol each organization's activities on an ongoing basis. The legislature intervenes only when these other oversight mechanisms prove inadequate.

McCubbins and Schwartz conclude that, in view of various factors that limit their time and attention, legislators cannot police every executive agency and that fire-alarm oversight is therefore a rational option for them. But it can also be argued that the growth of legislative staff allows Congress to follow both strategies simultaneously. Members can confine themselves to dealing with the infrequent crises that trigger "fire alarms," while the legislative staff patrols the activities of executive agencies in an ongoing way.

Its ability to draw on the resources of a professional staff provides Congress with another asset as well: the legislature can look ahead and anticipate policy issues that may not yet have appeared on the congressional agenda. The Office of Technology Assessment (OTA) now plays this role for Congress. Fire-alarm oversight allows the legislature to become involved in policy problems only after they have assumed major proportions; OTA's expertise permits Congress to anticipate some fires beforehand. Of course, given the number of immediate issues that crowd the everyday congressional agenda, problems that are on the horizon always face an uphill struggle for legislative attention.

Finally, it should be noted that the steady expansion in the size and functions of legislative staff is one of the chief ways in which Congress has responded to the emergence of the national bureaucracy as a major force in the American political system. The United States was the last of the major industrial powers to accept the necessity of such a bureaucratic establishment. One "exceptional" feature of its political institutions—in which Americans long took great pride—was the fact that bureaucracy played a very small role in the national government. But a national bureaucracy came to Washington with a vengeance in the middle of the twentieth century. Its arrival forced both the executive and Congress to bureaucratize themselves in order to cope with the presence and the power of what soon came to be called a fourth branch of government. Beginning in the 1930s, a complex staff structure employing highly skilled professionals began to evolve in and around the White House, and Congress has since followed suit by spawning its own wide-ranging legislative staff system.

It used to be said in the Progressive era that the cure for the ills of democracy was more democracy. In the 1990s the United States confronts the irony that the cure for the ills of bureaucracy seems to be more bureaucracy in both the presidency and Congress.

[*See also* Executive Privilege; Executive Reorganization; Iron Triangle; Oversight.]

BIBLIOGRAPHY

Aberbach, Joel D. *Keeping a Watchful Eye: The Politics of Congressional Oversight.* 1990.

Davidson, Roger H., and Walter J. Oleszek. *Congress and Its Members.* 1981.

Dodd, Lawrence C., and Richard L. Schott. *Congress and the Administrative State.* 1979.

Fisher, Louis. *The Politics of Shared Power: Congress and the Executive.* 1987.

Foreman, Christopher H., Jr. *Signals from the Hill: Congressional Oversight and the Challenge of Social Regulation.* 1988.

Harris, Joseph P. *Congressional Control of Administration.* 1964.

Maass, Arthur. *Congress and the Common Good.* 1983.

Malbin, Michael J. *Unelected Representatives: Congressional Staff and the Future of Representative Government.* 1980.

Ogul, Morris. *Congress Oversees the Bureaucracy: Studies in Legislative Supervision.* 1976.

Rourke, Francis E. *Bureaucracy, Politics, and Public Policy.* 1984.

Skowronek, Stephen. *Building a New American State: The Expansion of National Administrative Capacities, 1877–1920.* 1982.

FRANCIS E. ROURKE

BURR, AARON (1756–1836), vice president under Thomas Jefferson, U.S. senator, New York assemblyman, Revolutionary War officer, and lawyer. Burr personified the political and imperialist intriguer that many of the founding generation believed to be a threat to the new American republic. His schemes of western conquest and personal ambition earned him the antipathy of Alexander Hamilton and Thomas Jefferson as well as a charge of treason against the United States.

Burr came from an eminent family. His father, Aaron Burr, was president of the College of New Jersey (Princeton); his maternal grandfather was the great divine Jonathan Edwards. After graduating from Princeton, Burr became an officer in the Continental Army. His war experience revealed a pattern repeated later: he was well liked and com-

AARON BURR. As vice president, 1802.

petent, but his self-assurance and ambition won him distrust.

Burr became a successful New York lawyer and a heavy land speculator. Able to stitch rival state factions together to oppose Hamilton's financial program, he was elected to the U.S. Senate in 1790, a seat he held until 1797. In the Senate Burr became a clear opponent of the Federalists, helping to lead the opposition to Jay's Treaty with Great Britain. Defeated for reelection in 1796 because of claims of financial impropriety regarding the Holland Land Company, Burr entered the New York assembly and remained there until 1799.

Burr became a key member of the New York City Republican party. Clever politicking and forceful self-advocacy placed him on the Jeffersonian Republican party's national ticket as vice president in 1800. The presidential election of 1800 went to the floor of Congress because Jefferson, whom the Republicans had chosen as their presidential candidate, and Burr had an equal number of electoral votes. The Federalists, perhaps assisted by Burr himself, saw an opportunity to elect Burr as president. But after thirty-six ballots Jefferson was elected. As vice president Burr antagonized both Republicans and Federalists; the Republicans replaced him with George Clinton on the 1804 ticket. On 2

March 1804, Burr gave a moving farewell speech to the Senate, apologizing for his indiscretions as vice president.

After an unsuccessful attempt to win the New York State governorship, Burr entered into an extended and bitter public quarrel with Hamilton that led to their famous duel of 11 July 1804 in which Burr shot and killed his opponent. Burr fled south, traveling to east Florida with his old friend Gen. James Wilkinson. He and Wilkinson made vague plans of annexing Mexico, possibly with British aid, if there were a war with Spain. In late 1804 Burr returned to Congress for his last session as vice president, presiding over the impeachment trial of Supreme Court Justice Samuel Chase.

Burr's western expansionist dreams accelerated after he left the vice presidency. With Jonathan Dayton of New Jersey and Thomas Truxtun, he planned the annexation of western lands. In the summer of 1806, Burr gathered a small band of mercenaries and adventurers in Kentucky. President Jefferson proclaimed that the group was illegally plotting war against Spain. Burr finally surrendered to the federal government on 10 January 1807. Justice John Marshall subsequently found Burr not guilty of the charge of treason on the ground that treason depended on an overt act of "levying war," thus tightening the constitutional definition of that offense.

Burr fled the United States after his trial, returning in 1812 and renewing his New York law practice.

BIBLIOGRAPHY

Abernathy, Thomas P. *The Burr Conspiracy.* 1954.
Schnachner, Nathan. *Aaron Burr.* 1937.
Vidal, Gore. *Burr.* 1973.

JOHN F. WALSH

BURTON, PHILLIP (1926–1983), liberal Democratic representative from California (1964–1983) who as Democratic caucus chairman played a key role in democratizing the institutional rules of the House during the early 1970s. Elected to the California Assembly from an urban San Francisco district in 1956, Burton earned a reputation as an expert on social welfare and reapportionment. A champion of the underrepresented working class and the poor, Burton was elected to the U.S. House of Representatives in 1964; as a member of the Education and Labor Committee and a consummate wheeler-dealer, he achieved the passage of legislation establishing benefits for coalminers who suffered from occupation-related black lung disease, and he won increases in the minimum wage.

Burton served as chairman of the liberal Democratic Study Group from 1971 to 1973. In that role and as chairman (1975–1977) of the Democratic caucus, which had been revitalized by the assertive seventy-five-member Democratic freshman class of the 94th Congress, Burton promoted institutional reforms in committee assignment and committee chair selection that restricted the seniority system and enhanced the power of junior Democrats. An opponent of the committee reorganization reform plan proffered by Rep. Richard W. Bolling (D-Mo.), Burton subsequently faced Bolling, Majority Whip John J. McFall of California, and James C. Wright, Jr., of Texas in a bitter contest for the majority leader position vacated by newly elected Speaker Thomas P. (Tip) O'Neill, Jr., in 1976. Burton's loss to the more conservative Wright by one vote stemmed more from his abrasive, tempestuous personal style and obvious ambition for power than from his ideological position.

A brilliant legislative strategist, Burton, as a senior member of the Committee on Interior and Insular Affairs, managed the largest expansion of the national park and wilderness system through Congress in 1978. In the early 1980s, Burton outraged Republicans by engineering a California redistricting plan that protected Democratic incumbents and helped ensure Democratic control of the House through the decade.

BIBLIOGRAPHY

Jacobs, John. "The Power Game." *San Francisco Examiner,* 10 July 1989, *Image Magazine,* pp. 15–27.

Leary, Mary Ellen. "I Aim to Open Up the System: Phillip Burton of the Caucus." *The Nation,* 18 January 1975, pp. 37–40.

RICHARD C. BURNWEIT

BUSH, GEORGE H. W. (1924–), Republican representative from Texas, vice president, 41st president of the United States. George Bush moved to Texas in 1948 following war service in the Pacific and graduation from Yale with a B.A. in economics. Bush built a successful business in oil exploration. By the early 1960s, he was active in Republican party politics, becoming party chairman in Harris County in 1962. Bush made an unsuccessful bid for the U.S. Senate in 1964, mounting a conservative campaign against the liberal Democratic incumbent, Ralph W. Yarborough.

GEORGE BUSH. As president, January 1990.
BUSH PRESIDENTIAL MATERIALS PROJECT

In 1966, Bush ran successfully for the House of Representatives for the 7th District in the affluent suburbs of Houston against conservative Democrat Frank Briscoe. In 1968, he was returned unopposed. Bush became a member of the House Ways and Means Committee (the first freshman representative to become a member of the committee in many years). Bush's record in the House was conservative: Americans for Democratic Action rated him in 1967 at 7 out of a scale of 100, while the Chamber of Commerce of the United States rated him at 90 and Americans for Constitutional Action at 83. In view of his later diplomatic and foreign affairs experience, it is interesting to note that Bush took little part in foreign policy issues while in Congress. He did, however, support a number of liberal measures, including a code of official conduct, the abolition of the military draft, the enfranchisement of eighteen-year-olds, and, most notably, voted in April 1968 in support of an open housing civil rights bill that was not popular in his own district. In September 1968 he also pressed, as part of a small group of House Republicans and Democrats, for legislation on campaign spending reform.

In 1970, Bush failed in a bid for a Senate seat against conservative Democrat Lloyd Bentsen, in the process losing his House seat. In December 1970, President Richard M. Nixon appointed him first as permanent representative of the United States to the United Nations and then, early in 1973, as chairman of the Republican National Committee. In 1974, President Gerald R. Ford, Jr., appointed Bush to be chief of the U.S. Liaison Office in the People's Republic of China and in December 1975 selected him as head of the Central Intelligence Agency.

Ronald Reagan defeated Bush for the Republican presidential nomination in 1980; Bush then accepted Reagan's offer of the vice presidential nomination. Bush's vice presidency was marked by his high-profile loyalty to President Reagan and the extensive foreign visits he made on behalf of the administration.

The Bush Presidency. Bush won the 1988 presidential election over Michael Dukakis with 53.4 percent of the popular vote and carried forty states. But the Republicans lost seats in both houses of Congress; the Democrats controlled the Senate by a margin of ten seats and the House by eighty-five. There were only 175 Republicans in the House, the smallest number for the president's party at the beginning of a presidential term since the Civil War. Candidate Bush emphasized continuity with the Reagan administration but with a "kinder, gentler" approach. The campaign had been negative and largely issueless but Bush, well-known and generally liked in Congress for his service in the House and presiding role in the Senate, stressed in his Inaugural Address that this was "the age of the offered hand" to Congress. Consistent with this promise, Bush initially used his considerable skills as a Washington insider to establish a cooperative relationship with Capitol Hill. Bipartisan agreements were reached over Bush's first budget and help for the ailing savings and loan industry. Bush enjoyed good relations with Dan Rostenkowski, chairman of the House Ways and Means Committee; Speaker Thomas S. Foley, who succeeded James C. Wright, Jr., when the latter resigned in June 1989; and Senate minority leader and former rival for the presidential nomination, Bob Dole.

Conflict with Congress. But Bush's "let's deal" approach increasingly foundered on the constraints of a Democratic-controlled Congress and, it was argued, by White House chief of staff John Sununu's abrasive style in handling congressional relations.

Bush's difficulties were highlighted early on, when his nominee for secretary of Defense, Sen. John G. Tower of Texas, was rejected by the Senate; it was the first time a president's initial nominee for the cabinet had been defeated.

Presidential success is measured in *Congressional Quarterly's* assessments as how often the president won his way on roll-call votes on which he took a clear position. Support reached a new low in 1992, when Bush won only 43 percent of roll-call votes—the worst score since *Congressional Quarterly* began keeping records in 1953. By comparison, Presidents Eisenhower (in his first term), Kennedy, Johnson, Nixon (in his first term), Carter, and Reagan (in his first term) all had average success scores, over a four-year term of office, of over 70 percent. Most of Bush's lost votes were over social and economic issues; on foreign policy matters, he had a winning record. The White House blamed the low support ratings on the intransigence of a Democratic-led Congress. Commentators pointed to the problems of "gridlock" with the government divided between a Republican White House and a Democratic Congress in a period of high deficits and low economic growth.

Achievements and constraints. Despite these difficulties, President Bush recorded a number of important achievements. Though Democrats criticized Bush for failing to take a stand against China's human rights abuses following the Tiananmen Square massacre, Congress generally supported his foreign policy, as in the 1991 Persian Gulf War against Iraq's Saddam Hussein (after vigorous debate on the constitutional authority to declare war); the 1989 invasion of Panama and the successful indictment of that nation's former president, General Manuel Noriega, on drug charges; and assistance to the former Soviet republics.

Domestically, Bush's legislative successes included bills pertaining to the savings and loans rescue operation, clean air, child care, transportation, housing, and help for Americans with disabilities (though there were disputes over the funding and implementation of these laws, particularly over environmental regulations). Bush had to make major concessions to Congress in 1990 over the budget that came at the cost of relations with the right wing of the Republican party. The budget agreement did not include the capital gains tax cut that Bush had long sought; it did, however, increase taxes on gasoline and home heating oil and, most damagingly, increase the tax rate on high income taxpayers, which Bush had vigorously opposed. House minority whip Newt Gingrich of Georgia attacked Bush for reneging on the "no new taxes" pledge of his presidential campaign, and while the Republican leadership still supported Bush, there was growing unease on the right over the administration's commitment to conservative positions on taxes, abortion, and school choice.

President Bush's relations with Congress were highlighted by his use of the veto as a major policy tool. Bush exercised the veto on forty-six occasions during his presidency, applying them to such controversial political issues as taxes, abortion, civil rights, family leave, "motor voter" registration, and most-favored-nation trade status for China. This strategy had certain advantages for Bush. The threat of a veto forced compromises, and the use of it, overruled on only one occasion (over cable television reregulation), limited a Democratic Congress's ability to pass legislation the administration opposed.

Relations with Congress were also influenced by Bush's popularity. Following the Persian Gulf War, his approval rating reached a peak of 89 percent; but as Bush's poll ratings fell sharply with the onset of recession in the second half of 1991, Congress had less incentive to work with him.

In assessing Bush's domestic record, his style is a major consideration. Though Bush's communication skills were sometimes seen as ineffective, the central issue was the vigor with which domestic issues were pursued. Here Bush's leadership was seen as weak; while urging support for plans he said were necessary to deal with issues of education, health, drugs, and homelessness, he did not supply the sustained pressure needed to turn them into law. Bush was also criticized for a vacillating response to the Los Angeles riots of April 1992 that followed the acquittal of four police officers accused of severely beating black suspect Rodney King. Bush called for emergency aid and longer-term tax incentives (in the form of enterprise zones) for the inner cities. The size of the congressional aid as proposed by the Democrats in Congress, however, aroused strong Republican opposition. In June 1992 a compromise halved the supplemental appropriations bill for aid to Los Angeles and Chicago (which had suffered severe flood damage) and the enterprise zone initiative failed in November 1992, when Bush vetoed the tax bill that contained it on the grounds that it raised taxes.

Although domestically Bush followed a minimalist agenda characterized by risk aversion, deregulation, and laissez-faire, he left office on an activist note as foreign relations again came to the fore. In

August 1992, the administration authorized negotiation of the North American Free Trade Agreement with Mexico. In December 1992, he decided in favor of the use of American troops as part of the UN-mandated multinational force to protect humanitarian relief programs in Somalia. Finally, on 3 January 1993, Bush and Russian president Boris Yeltsin signed the Further Reduction and Limitation of Strategic Offensive Arms Treaty (the Start II treaty).

BIBLIOGRAPHY

Fleisher, Richard, and Jon R. Bond. "Assessing Presidential Support in the House II: Lessons from George Bush." *American Journal of Political Science* 36 (1992): 525–541.

Hill, Dilys M., and Phil Williams, eds. *The Bush Presidency: Achievements and Constraints.* 1994.

Sinclair, Barbara. "Governing Unheroically (and Sometimes Unappetizingly): Bush and the 101st Congress." In *The Bush Presidency: First Appraisals.* Edited by Bert A. Rockman and Colin Campbell. 1991. Pp. 155–184.

DILYS M. HILL

BYRD, HARRY FLOOD, SR. (1887–1966), Democratic senator from Virginia, chairman of the Committee on Finance, leader of Senate conservatives. A direct descendant of William Byrd of Westover, Virginia, Byrd inherited an aristocratic "FFV" (first family of Virginia) name but no family fortune. He left school at fifteen and took charge of his father's debt-burdened newspaper, building it into a successful daily, the *Winchester Evening Star.* Later he acquired apple orchards, which became a profitable family enterprise.

Byrd and his brothers were called Tom, Dick, and Harry. Tom managed the apple business; Dick became Adm. Richard Evelyn Byrd, the aviator who flew over the North and South poles; Harry served in the state senate (1915–1925) and became governor at age thirty-eight.

His record of progressive reform made the governor a candidate for the Democratic presidential nomination in 1932. Byrd was Virginia's "favorite son" candidate and had some support outside his home state as an attractive young executive (age forty-five) who had streamlined his state's government and had achieved enactment of a tough anti-lynching law. In 1933, President Franklin D. Roosevelt named Sen. Claude A. Swanson of Virginia his secretary of the Navy, opening the way for Byrd's appointment to the vacated seat.

HARRY FLOOD BYRD, SR. In January 1961.

For thirty-two years, Senator Byrd battled for the principles of an earlier Virginia country gentleman, Thomas Jefferson, advocating a frugal federal government, fiscal integrity, and states' rights. Roosevelt had campaigned on a platform calling for a 25 percent cut in the federal budget, but he soon switched to bigger spending and greater government power through policies that Byrd opposed as state socialism. In later years, as a lone figure demanding a balanced budget, Byrd would say: "I campaigned for the New Deal platform in 1932—and I'm still standing on it." Byrd became an influential member of "the club," the ruling circle of conservative Senate Democrats. During his last decade on Capitol Hill (1955–1965), Byrd wielded great power as the Finance Committee chairman, dealing with all tax measures and with Social Security.

In character Byrd personified the Virginia gentleman: courteous, kind, genial, soft-spoken, a man of impeccable integrity. The apple-cheeked patrician reigned over the "Byrd machine," credited with ruling the Old Dominion for decades through a coalition of courthouse politicians and businessmen who valued honest, low-budget state government. Critics branded Byrd an absentee landlord and boss who gave the state a pinchpenny government. He referred to his organization as "just a loose association of friends who believe in sound government."

Byrd was criticized for stubbornly opposing court-ordered school desegregation through his state's "massive resistance," which included various measures by the Virginia General Assembly including repeal of the compulsory school attendance laws, tuition grants for some students to attend private schools, and authorization for the governor to close any school under court order to integrate and to cut off all state funds from any school that tried to reopen in obedience to court orders. Public schools at Norfolk, Charlottesville, and Front Royal were closed in the autumn of 1958. Resistance, however, proved a losing battle, for the courts nullified the "massive resistance" statutes. Nevertheless, the senator was able to retain his power in the Senate. At election times Byrd maintained a "golden silence," refusing to endorse the Democrats' presidential nominees, and that sent a clear signal to his constituents that they should feel free to vote as they pleased. Consequently, the Republicans were able to carry Virginia in several presidential elections.

President John F. Kennedy courted his favor by dropping in, by helicopter, at Byrd's Rosemont estate, where the senator was hosting a luncheon one spring Sunday in 1961. President Lyndon B. Johnson, who had become the Senate majority leader as a protégé of the southern grandees, figuratively worshiped at Byrd's feet.

However, Kennedy failed to soften Byrd's opposition to his New Frontier programs. Byrd proceeded to sink several of the young president's key proposals, including a boost in unemployment benefits and a plan for medicare. President Johnson fared somewhat better. In 1964, Johnson convinced Byrd to allow a vote by the Finance Committee on a tax reduction and planned deficit measure originally sought by Kennedy and later embraced by the new Johnson administration. Byrd disliked the legislation but agreed to step aside. The committee approved the bill, as did the Senate two weeks later.

Byrd was something of a naturalist. He often hiked over the Blue Ridge trails and up Old Rag and Hawks Bill mountains in Virginia, and in Washington he took daily hikes through Rock Creek Park. As governor, he developed the Shenandoah National Park, and the Park Service was one of the few federal agencies he liked.

He retired from the Senate on 10 November 1965 and died of a brain tumor on 20 October 1966. His son, Harry, Jr., succeeded him in the Senate.

BIBLIOGRAPHY

Krock, Arthur. "In the Nation: The Last Heir of Monticello." *New York Times,* 7 July 1966.
Wilkinson, J. Harvie. *Harry Byrd and the Changing Face of Virginia Politics, 1945–1966.* 1968.

FRANK VAN DER LINDEN

BYRNES, JAMES F. (1882–1972), Democratic representative and senator from South Carolina, justice of the Supreme Court, director of war mobilization, secretary of State, governor of South Carolina, and one of the most influential advocates of the New Deal. James Francis Byrnes was a third-generation Irish American. Born in Charleston, South Carolina, six weeks after the death of his father, a municipal clerk, he quit school at age thirteen and took a job as a stenographer to ease the financial burdens on his mother, a dressmaker. In 1900, he moved to Aiken, where he read law and was admitted to the bar. A quick mind and an infectious charm helped him to win election as district attorney in 1908.

His success as a prosecutor coupled with his pledge to support progressive reforms for the white farmers of his rural district won Byrnes a seat in the U.S. House of Representatives in 1910. He fulfilled his pledge and stayed in the House, without a major electoral threat, for the next fourteen years. A staunch Democrat, Byrnes supported nearly all the domestic and foreign policy initiatives of President Woodrow Wilson. As a member of the Roads Committee, he played a prominent role in the adoption of the Federal Highways Act of 1916. He received further national attention as one of the most vocal critics of the Republican administrations of the early 1920s.

Following an unsuccessful bid in 1924, Byrnes was elected to the Senate in 1930 on a platform that called for aggressive federal action to combat the Great Depression. From 1933 through 1936, he voted for virtually all of President Franklin D. Roosevelt's New Deal legislation. Moreover, he played a major role in steering much of it through the Senate while earning a widespread reputation as a compromiser and as the Senate's most effective legislative whip. Occupying a key position on the Appropriations Committee, Byrnes helped in the adoption of the Emergency Relief Appropriations Act of 1935, which led to the creation of the Works Progress Administration. He won a landslide re-election in 1936 as the "honest broker" of federal benefits to South Carolina.

By Roosevelt's second term, Byrnes began to fear that the New Deal was being transformed from an emergency program to combat the Depression into a permanent approach toward American government. He also feared that northern Democrats were beginning to cater to African Americans and organized labor at the expense of white southern interests. Byrnes responded by participating in a coalition of southern Democrats and Republicans that fought minimum-wage legislation, blocked an anti-lynching law, attempted to cut relief funds to northern cities, and opposed the further expansion of federal authority.

Byrnes continued, however, to endorse Roosevelt's foreign policy. From 1939 to 1941, he supported every administration effort to lead the nation into a more active role against Germany and Japan. His greatest contributions as floor whip came when he spearheaded the Senate's repeal of the U.S. arms embargo in 1939 and its adoption of the Lend-Lease Act of 1941. Roosevelt rewarded Byrnes by appointing him to the Supreme Court in June 1941. He resigned from the Court in October 1942 to head the wartime Office of Economic Stabilization. President Harry S. Truman named him secretary of State in 1945.

BIBLIOGRAPHY

Alsop, Joseph, and Robert Kintner. "Sly and Able: Jimmy Byrnes Knows How to Make the Senate Work." *Saturday Evening Post,* 20 July 1940.
Byrnes, James F. *All in One Lifetime.* 1958.
Moore, Winfred B., Jr. "The 'Unrewarding Stone': James F. Byrnes and the Burden of Race, 1908–1944." In *The South Is Another Land.* Edited by Bruce Clayton and John Salmond. 1987.

WINFRED B. MOORE, JR.

C

C-SPAN. The Cable-Satellite Public Affairs Network (C-SPAN) is a nonprofit corporation created by the cable-television industry to disseminate gavel-to-gavel coverage of congressional proceedings, as well as other public-affairs programming, to cable subscribers. The service was made possible by decisions of the House in 1979 and the Senate in 1986 to televise their legislative sessions and make the signals available for public broadcast.

With a television "feed" available, Brian Lamb, the founder of C-SPAN, convinced the cable industry to create a nonprofit corporation to cover public affairs, funded by subscriber fees. C-SPAN is overseen by a board of directors composed of cable operators. It receives no government funds, nor does it accept commercial advertising. Each subscriber with C-SPAN access contributed approximately three cents per month to provide the network with an operating budget of $16 million in 1991. While real-time sessions of the House and Senate still preempt all other programming, C-SPAN also provides coverage of selected committee hearings, proceedings of foreign legislatures, press conferences, speeches, "state of the state" reports by governors, national party conventions of both major and minor parties, and presidential inauguration ceremonies.

C-SPAN is "long form" television—it covers events in their entirety without editing or editorial commentary and presents them without the high production values and technological wizardry that characterize commercial public-affairs programming. The network seeks out public-affairs events that the major networks do not cover or cover only partially. It also takes the lead in encouraging polit-ical institutions to open their sessions to the public, arguing that televised proceedings are a vital extension of the public gallery that democracy requires. C-SPAN has also established an educational division to encourage academic use of its programming, which is recorded for research and educational use by the Purdue University Public Affairs Video Archives.

With approximately fifty-five million subscribers in 1992, C-SPAN is available to more than half of the households in the United States. It is estimated that forty-three million adults are at least occasional viewers. The actual audience at any one time is much smaller, numbering in the hundreds of thousands for most programming. While it attracts a smaller audience than major commercial networks, C-SPAN's viewers are politically active. The people who view C-SPAN are much more likely to vote, to make campaign contributions, and to contact elected officials. Citizens and elected officials alike report that C-SPAN has made it more likely that individuals will monitor the political process and make their views known.

[*See also* Broadcasting of Congressional Proceedings.]

BIBLIOGRAPHY

Frantzich, Stephen. *Using C-SPAN in the Classroom: A Faculty Guide to Integrating Public Affairs Programming.* 1989.

Garay, Ronald. *Congressional Television: A Legislative History.* 1984.

Lamb, Brian. *America's Town Hall.* 1988.

STEPHEN E. FRANTZICH

SENATE ON C-SPAN. The first day of televised Senate sessions, 2 June 1986. Pictured are Senators Bob Dole (R-Kans.) and Robert C. Byrd (D-W.Va.). *(See previous page.)*   NAN M. GIBSON, C-SPAN

CABINET AND CONGRESS. Interactions between Congress and the cabinet occur in three general areas. The most basic, ongoing relationship results from congressional responsibility to organize, reorganize, and fund the executive bureaucracy. A second area involves recruitment issues, including the Senate's advice-and-consent role in the appointment process and the historical controversy over senatorial limitation of the president's power to fire departmental secretaries. A third area encompasses broad issues of executive-branch accountability as well as specific provisions for congressional oversight of departmental operations and congressional power to impeach departmental secretaries.

Organization and Funding. Since the cabinet is nowhere mentioned in the Constitution, it has no formal constitutional standing. The Constitution does refer to the "executive departments" and their "principal officers," over which Congress wields considerable power. In this context, the cabinet is a general term for the collectivity of departmental heads, and the president's use of this group of officers as an advisory body is only indirectly and minimally relevant to the Congress. Much more important is the congressional responsibility to organize the executive branch of government and regularly to provide guidance and funding for its operation.

Administrative departments were traditionally used in colonial governments and under the Articles of Confederation. The Constitution refers to "executive departments" and gives Congress the power "to make all laws which shall be necessary and proper" for executing governmental functions.

It is clear that the Framers intended that the First Congress should establish the necessary departments. Indeed, during the summer of 1789, Congress did establish the departments of State, Treasury, and War.

Over the course of American history, the expanding size and increasing complexity of society and government have resulted in the need for an expanded cabinet, and Congress has fulfilled its responsibility to meet that need. The first expansion occurred in 1798, when the Department of the Navy was created. The creation of the Department of Veterans' Affairs in 1988 brought the total number of cabinet departments to fourteen.

In addition, Congress has from time to time found it necessary to reorganize existing cabinet departments. In 1913, the Department of Commerce and Labor was split into separate departments. In 1947, the theretofore separate departments of War and Navy were combined to become the Department of Defense, and in 1979 the Department of Health, Education, and Welfare was split into the Department of Health and Human Services and the Department of Education. Only once has Congress removed a department from the cabinet: in 1970, the Post Office was downgraded from a cabinet department to a government corporation.

Once established, the executive departments maintain their dependence on Congress for legislative authorization of policies and programs and for the appropriation of funds for day-to-day operations. The president certainly plays an important role in recommending legislation and drafting a budget, but is finally responsible for policy formulation Congress and funding the departments. It is in this area that the relationship between Congress and the cabinet becomes very complicated and somewhat unpredictable. Given the sharing of powers by the separate branches, cabinet officers are often strongly pulled in different directions, not only by the president and Congress but also by their own subordinates and constituents. Because Congress controls the purse, departmental heads tend to appeal directly to Congress for resources and support. But tradition has limited their opportunities for formal interaction with Congress. With very few exceptions (occurring early in the administration of George Washington), cabinet members have neither participated in congressional debate nor even answered questions on the House or Senate floor. As a result, much of the interaction between Congress and cabinet members has taken place at the committee and subcommittee levels, and the frequency and manner of interaction have become dependent on the moods, interests, and predispositions of the cabinet officers and their congressional counterparts.

Recruitment Issues. The recruitment of cabinet officers involves the Constitution's provision that the president "shall nominate, and, by and with the Advice and Consent of the Senate, shall appoint" all of the officers of the executive branch. The Senate has generally considered cabinet appointments to be a presidential prerogative; only in the most extreme circumstances has the Senate rejected a president's choice. In one of the more peculiar of these extreme circumstances, the Senate in 1843 three times rejected John Tyler's repeated nomination of Caleb Cushing as secretary of the Treasury. A more recent example is the Senate's 1988 rejection of John Tower, George Bush's nominee to head the Defense Department. From the time of Washington's first cabinet nominations in September 1789 until today, the Senate has rejected only nine nominees. But the power of the Senate in this area should not be underestimated; senatorial opposition has undoubtedly preempted certain nominees and caused the withdrawal of others. An excellent recent example is President Bill Clinton's withdrawal of Zoe Baird as his nominee for attorney general.

Another area of interaction involves the Senate's potential ability to limit the president's power to fire cabinet members. Much controversy raged over this issue during congressional debate over the establishment of the first executive departments. In their effort to maintain an independent executive, opponents of a senatorial role fought hard and won. Rep. James Madison went so far as to insist that the legislation be worded to avoid conveying the impression that Congress controlled the issue.

In 1867, however, Congress attempted to usurp the president's removal powers through the passage of the Tenure of Office Act. That act required that the Senate give its consent before presidential removals of cabinet officials could become effective. The Senate's first attempt to exercise such power came when President Andrew Johnson removed Secretary of War Edwin M. Stanton without senatorial advice or consent. The House impeached Johnson for violating the removal provisions of the act, and, though the attempt to remove Johnson from office failed in the Senate by one vote and Secretary Stanton's dismissal stood, the law re-

REJECTED NOMINEES. *At left,* Charles Warren, President Calvin Coolidge's nominee for attorney general. *Above,* Adm. Lewis Strauss, President Dwight D. Eisenhower's choice for secretary of Commerce. *Facing page,* John G. Tower, President George Bush's nominee for secretary of Defense.   LIBRARY OF CONGRESS AND OFFICE OF THE HISTORIAN OF THE U.S. SENATE

mained on the books until it was repealed in 1887. The issue was not finally settled, however, until all attempts at senatorial interference in the president's powers of removal were declared unconstitutional by the Supreme Court's decision in *Myers v. United States* (1926).

The Accountability Function. Congress's primary constitutional power for holding cabinet officers accountable is the impeachment power. While the availability of this power may have significant impact on the behavior of departmental secretaries, its actual use has been quite rare. In fact, up to 1992, only three impeachment proceedings had ever been instituted against cabinet members. Ulysses S. Grant's secretary of war, William Belknap, was impeached in the House of Representatives in 1876 but was subsequently acquitted by the Senate. Impeachment proceedings were undertaken against Attorney General Harry Daugherty in 1922 and against Secretary of Treasury Andrew Mellon in 1932, but in both cases the proceedings were rendered moot by the secretaries' resignations.

Under statutory interpretations of the Constitution, Congress has also assumed broad powers to oversee the functioning of the executive branch.

Congress exercises these powers regularly through reporting and audit requirements, often formalized through the General Accounting Office, and occasionally through committee and subcommittee hearings and investigations of administrative activities. This latter category of oversight activity may subject cabinet officers to an unwelcome and uncomfortable burden, such as when the secretary of State is grilled on foreign policy or the attorney general is forced to defend the Department of Justice's treatment of religious fanatics. These powers are applied to the executive branch generally, and their availability and use have significant and ongoing impact on the operation of cabinet departments.

[*See also* Bureaucracy; Executive Branch; Presidential Appointments.]

BIBLIOGRAPHY

Cohen, Jeffrey. *The Politics of the U.S. Cabinet.* 1988.
Fenno, Richard F., Jr. *The President's Cabinet.* 1959.
Horn, Stephen. *The Cabinet and Congress.* 1960.
Lammers, Nancy, ed. *Powers of Congress.* 1982.
Ripley, Randall B., and Grace A. Franklin. *Congress, the Bureaucracy, and Public Policy.* 1980.

KEITH NICHOLLS

CALENDARS. A chamber's calendar is essentially a list of the matters available for floor consideration; procedurally, to say a measure is "on the calendar" is to say that it is available for consideration. (Most measures reach this status by being reported from committee.) Such lists are printed daily for each chamber when in session. Committees also publish calendars, but usually in only two editions per Congress. The Senate Calendar lists only pending matters, but the House Calendar and those of most committees are cumulative and contain indexes and legislative histories of measures that have been on the calendar, making the final editions for each Congress valuable historical records.

House Calendar System

The House has five formal calendars: the House Calendar, the Union Calendar (also known as the Calendar of the Committee of the Whole House on the State of the Union), the Private Calendar (Calendar of the Committee of the Whole House), the Consent Calendar, and the Discharge Calendar (Calendar of Motions to Discharge Committees). Every measure reported is routinely placed on one of the first three.

This system reflects the House's establishment of separate procedures for considering different kinds of measures; each calendar carries measures governed by a distinct procedure. The heart of these distinctions is House Rule XXIII, clause 3, which provides that all matters "involving a . . . charge upon the people . . . be first considered in a Committee of the Whole." In the House, procedure in the Committee of the Whole is that which most fully secures the opportunity for amendment. Accordingly, this provision helps ensure the ability of the House to exercise the powers of the purse that the Constitution assigns it, as the institution of government whose members' short terms and (comparatively) small electorates tie it most closely to the people. Such a provision has been part of the rules since 1794.

Under this rule, not only tax measures but all measures appropriating funds or authorizing appropriations, as well as congressional budget resolutions, are to be considered in the Committee of the Whole and are accordingly, when reported, placed on its calendar, the Union Calendar. Private bills go to the Private Calendar. Measures falling into neither category may be considered "in the House, under the one-hour rule," and therefore go to the House Calendar.

Under House Rule XIII, clause 4, any member may have any bill on the House or Union Calendar placed on the Consent Calendar. On first and third Mondays, measures on this calendar are called up in order of their placement thereon. Any measure to which one member objects is postponed until the next call; if three members then object, the measure is stricken from this calendar. Each party appoints official objectors to monitor the Consent Calendar and to object to measures they find inappropriate thereunder. If no sufficient objection occurs at either stage, the measure is considered "in the House as in Committee of the Whole," a procedure permitting debate only under the five-minute rule. A measure pending on the Consent Calendar, or defeated when considered from that calendar, may still also be considered from its original calendar.

The Discharge Calendar, in order on second and fourth Mondays, contains only measures on which discharge petitions have received the requisite 218 signatures.

The original premise of the House calendar system was that measures on each calendar be in order at a specified time and be considered in order of their placement on that calendar. Because this system early showed itself too inflexible in handling major legislation, the House also developed the concept of privilege, which in this sense means a measure's right to consideration in preference over the otherwise prescribed order of business. Although the calendar on which a measure is placed indicates the procedure under which it may be considered, it can receive actual consideration only through obtaining privilege.

The rules distribute privilege among measures both by making certain calendars privileged on specified days and by making certain measures privileged over others on the same calendar. The Private, Consent, and Discharge calendars are privileged on specified days, and measures on these calendars come up in the order of their placement thereon. Among Union Calendar measures, general appropriations bills and measures under the Budget Act are privileged, as imperative legislation. Among those on the House Calendar, privilege extends to special rules, disciplinary resolutions, committee funding resolutions, and certain other housekeeping measures (House Rule XI, clause 4[a]). The committee reorganization of 1974–1975 abolished the privilege of several other categories of measure.

Certain other House procedures, which are also in order only on designated days, are sometimes called "calendars" as well. The "suspension calendar" is really just a list issued by the majority whip that announces which measures the leadership intends to call up by motions to suspend the rules, in order on Mondays and Tuesdays. The "District calendar" refers to measures that the Committee on the District of Columbia calls up pursuant to its privilege to do so on second and fourth Mondays. To be eligible for consideration on Calendar Wednesday, a measure must already be on the House or Union Calendar and cannot be otherwise privileged.

Measures belonging to no privileged category may obtain privilege in several ways. They may be called up on suspension, on the Consent Calendar, or on Calendar Wednesday. More significantly, a special rule, itself privileged, may grant privilege to the measure; this possibility underlies the key role of special rules in managing the House floor agenda.

Development of House Calendars. The House brought together the essentials of today's calendar system in its rules recodifications of 1880 and 1890, associated with Thomas B. Reed (R-Maine, Speaker 1889–1891 and 1895–1899). These rules, conceived

with the objective of permitting the House "to go at once to any measure upon its calendars," consolidated control of the floor agenda by the Speaker, acting for the majority party.

At first, special orders granting privilege to otherwise nonprivileged measures were adopted by suspension of the rules (then in order only on first and third Mondays); only later did the Rules Committee begin reporting such resolutions as privileged. After 1890, a "Morning Hour" permitted committees in rotation to call up nonprivileged House Calendar measures. Although this provision persists today, it was soon vitiated by the continual intervention of more privileged business.

The House refined this system until the Speaker's virtually absolute control of access to the floor led to the 1910 "revolt" against Speaker Joseph G. Cannon (R-Ill.; Speaker 1903–1911). Reforms of 1909 instituted the Consent Calendar and Calendar Wednesday; the revolt itself resulted in the first discharge rule. The Consent Calendar was designed to permit members to secure consideration for bills of individual interest; Calendar Wednesday, which was modeled on the Morning Hour call of committees but given high privilege, was designed to allow committees to bring their measures to the floor. For securing consideration of otherwise nonprivileged measures, the use of both Calendar Wednesday and the Consent Calendar remained common through the 1920s, but declined thereafter, when Speaker Sam Rayburn (D-Tex.; Speaker 1940–1946, 1949–1952, 1955–1961) recentralized control of the floor. More recently, such measures have instead been increasingly considered under suspension of the rules, and in the 1970s the days on which that procedure is in order were increased.

The Printed House Calendar. Since 1911, rules have required the daily printing of the House Calendar. It lists measures pending on each of the five formal calendars and provides legislative histories of the measures that have been on them, including short title, committee referral, calendar reported to, and subsequent actions, with dates. It also lists bills in conference and bills through conference, identifying conferees from both chambers. Lists indicate unfinished business and correlate measure numbers with private or public law numbers. Tables display dates of reporting and further action on key appropriations and other measures. Discharge petitions filed are listed, oddly, only in the index, under "Discharge."

The index to the House Calendar appears only on Mondays. Since 1988, the list of "Measures through

Conference" and certain inactive legislative histories have also appeared only on Mondays. Since 1983 the calendar has also listed measures sequentially referred, and since 1979 a calendar in the everyday sense has displayed the days on which House sessions have occurred. The House Calendar no longer lists pending special orders (including special order speeches), committees called on Calendar Wednesdays, or titles of measures enacted into law or vetoed, as it formerly did.

Senate Calendar System

The Senate has not found it necessary to develop as elaborate a system of calendars as has the House, but it too arrived at the foundations of its present system in the late nineteenth century. A measure generally reaches the Senate floor, by motion or unanimous consent request that the Senate proceed to consider it, from a single Calendar of General Orders. Nominations and treaties submitted by the president for the advice and consent of the Senate are carried on separate calendars of executive business, however.

Ever since 1789, Senate rules have required one day's notice of introducing a bill and two readings before referral, on separate legislative days. Normally, measures are introduced, immediately read twice, and referred, all by unanimous consent. Under rules originating in 1877, however, if objection is raised after the second reading, the bill goes directly to the Calendar of General Orders.

Corresponding procedures apply to simple and concurrent resolutions, which the Senate normally either refers when submitted or considers immediately by unanimous consent. Under the procedures from 1877, though, any objection puts off consideration for one legislative day; the measure is then listed in the calendar as having been laid "Over, Under the Rule." It may then be laid before the Senate at a specified point in the Morning Hour that, under rules rooted in the recodifications of 1877 and 1884, is to begin each legislative day.

In the Morning Hour, after disposition of several categories of "morning business," the Calendar of General Orders is to be called, and measures not objected to are taken up under rules limiting each senator to five minutes' debate. This call may be interrupted, however, on any day except Monday by a nondebatable motion to consider some other measure. These Morning Hour procedures were still in active use at least into the 1950s and remain in the rules, but today the Morning Hour occurs only rarely and is used chiefly to make possible a nonde-batable motion to consider some measure. This possibility is important because, outside the Morning Hour, a motion to proceed to consider a measure is normally debatable, and so can be filibustered.

The Senate reaches its executive business by a nondebatable motion to go into executive session. Executive or legislative matters to which no objection will be made may also be disposed of by routinized unanimous consent procedures.

Printed Senate Calendars. The bulk of the printed Senate Calendar consists of the Calendar of General Orders, which gives measure numbers, sponsors, titles, committees of referral, senators reporting, and dates reported; a separate list correlates measure numbers with calendar numbers. Besides "Resolutions and Motions Over, Under the Rule" and "Bills and Joint Resolutions Read the First Time," the document also lists "Subjects on the Table," which are placed under this heading by unanimous consent and can come up by motion but not by calendar call. Also set forth are texts of unanimous consent agreements currently in effect that govern consideration of specific measures; "Bills in Conference," paralleling the list in the House Calendar; and "Motions for Reconsideration" entered but not yet acted on. Finally, there are lists of Senate and Senate committee members, a table of action on appropriation bills, and, nowadays, a literal calendar showing days on which the Senate has been in session. The document is not indexed, and few collected sets appear to exist.

The Senate's Executive Calendar, published separately, contains only lists of treaties and nominations reported and pending. It does not appear to be widely distributed.

Printed Committee Calendars. Most committees have published calendars since the 80th Congress (1947–1949), and a few published before then. These generally set forth committee membership, subcommittees, jurisdiction, and (sometimes) rules. The heart of a committee calendar is a list of measures referred, showing sponsors, official titles, and dates of action; these are often indexed by topic and by sponsor, and are sometimes supplemented with information about subcommittee referral or subsequent action.

Committee calendars also generally include lists of hearings held or printed and of reports and other committee documents published, sometimes cross-indexed to measures; lists of memorials, petitions, and executive communications received; and, in the Senate, lists of nominations received and action thereon. Some calendars list such additional matters as committee legislation enacted and measures over which the committee asserts jurisdiction. They may also summarize committee activities, legislation reported, or historical background, or they may set forth statistical summaries or excerpts from pertinent laws and executive orders.

[*See also* Calendar Wednesday; Committee of the Whole; Discharge Rules; Five-Minute Rule; House of Representatives, *article on* Daily Sessions of the House; Legislative Day; Private Bill; Privilege; Senate, *article on* Daily Sessions of the Senate.]

BIBLIOGRAPHY

Haynes, George H. *The Senate of the United States.* 1938. Pp. 339–379.
Oleszek, Walter J. *Congressional Procedures and the Policy Process.* 3d ed. 1989. Chaps. 5–8.
Riddick, Floyd M. *The United States Congress: Organization and Procedure.* 1949.
U.S. House of Representatives. *Cannon's Precedents of the House of Representatives of the United States,* by Clarence Cannon. 8 vols. 74th Cong., 1st sess., 1935. Vol. 6, chap. 210; vol. 7, chaps. 211–215; vol. 8, chaps. 237–241.
U.S. House of Representatives. *Deschler's Precedents of the United States House of Representatives,* by Lewis Deschler. 94th Cong., 2d sess., 1977. H. Doc. 94-661. Vol. 7, chap. 22, "Calendars."
U.S. House of Representatives. *Hinds' Precedents of the House of Representatives of the United States,* by Asher C. Hinds. 5 vols. 59th Cong., 2d sess, 1907. Vol. 4, chaps. 87–89, 107–110; vol. 5, chap. 111.
U.S. Senate. *Riddick's Senate Procedure, Precedents, and Practices,* by Floyd M. Riddick and Alan S. Frumin. 101st Cong., 2d sess., 1992. S. Doc. 101-28. Pp. 253–267.

RICHARD S. BETH

CALENDAR WEDNESDAY.

The Calendar Wednesday procedure in the House of Representatives was adopted in 1909. Republican and Democratic progressives charged that the Speaker, then also the chairman of the Rules Committee, effectively blocked House floor action on bills reported from legislative committees. The Calendar Wednesday procedure was offered by Rep. John J. Fitzgerald (D-N.Y.) as a compromise aimed at opening up House procedures while preserving the Speaker's role in major legislation.

Under the current form of the rule (Rule XXIV, cl. 7), any bill on the House Calendar or the Union Calendar (lists of major public bills awaiting chamber action) may be called up for consideration on Wednesdays on a motion by the committee chairman or by a member of the committee authorized to do so. Committees are called alphabetically, and a committee not answering the call is passed over. After the House adjourns its Calendar Wednesday business, the call of committees begins the next time Calendar Wednesday occurs where it left off. Privileged measures, including general appropriations bills and rules from the Rules Committee, may not be called up through Calendar Wednesday.

Under the Calendar Wednesday procedures, bills on the Union Calendar must be considered in Committee of the Whole under the five-minute rule, with no more than two hours of general debate time. Matters on the House Calendar are considered under the one-hour rule. Calendar Wednesday can be set aside only by a two-thirds vote of the House or by unanimous consent. The Rules Committee is prohibited from reporting a rule that would directly or indirectly prevent action under Calendar Wednesday. Except in rare circumstances, Calendar Wednesday has not been proven to be a generally effective procedure for bringing bills to the floor.

BIBLIOGRAPHY

Baker, John D. "The Character of the Congressional Revolution of 1910." *Journal of American History* 60 (December 1973): 679–691.
U.S. House of Representatives. *Constitution, Jefferson's Manual, and the Rules of the House of Representatives of the United States, 103d Congress.* Compiled by William Holmes Brown. 102d Cong., 2d sess., 1992. H. Doc. 102-405, Sec. 897.

PAUL S. RUNDQUIST

CALHOUN, JOHN C.

(1782–1850), representative and senator from South Carolina, secretary of War, secretary of State, vice president of the United States. John Caldwell Calhoun was born in the back country of South Carolina eight months before the preliminary treaty of Paris ended the Revolutionary War. The third son of a wealthy planter, he received his primary education at home and at at a frontier school in Georgia. Calhoun completed his education at Yale College, from which he graduated in 1803. He went on to study law at Tapping Reeve's celebrated school in Litchfield, Connecticut.

Calhoun practiced law briefly but was more interested in pursuing a career as a politician and a planter. He was able to realize these objectives

JOHN C. CALHOUN.

disregarded their country's weakness and pushed President James Madison into declaring war on Britain in 1812. When the war went badly for the United States and the northeastern states threatened secession, Calhoun felt painfully his responsibility for his part in promoting the rash venture. Nevertheless, he regarded the War of 1812 as a final determination of American nationhood. After the Treaty of Ghent ended the war in 1815, Calhoun pushed through Congress such nationalist measures as the chartering of the second Bank of the United States and the protective tariff of 1816. But President Madison vetoed Calhoun's "bonus bill" for a federally financed system of internal improvements.

As President James Monroe's secretary of War, Calhoun reorganized the department, made reforms in Indian affairs, and managed to maintain the efficiency of the regular army, although an economy-minded Congress forced him to reduce its size. Calhoun sought the presidency during Monroe's second term, but he was unable to muster enough support to compete against Andrew Jackson, John Quincy Adams, Henry Clay, and William H. Crawford, the leading contenders. Elected vice president, he served in that office for over seven years under Presidents Adams and Jackson.

During his vice presidency, Calhoun began formulating his political theories designed to protect minority interests, as he saw them, against the rule of a class-driven majority. It was in this context that he became an eloquent defender of a plantation-based, slaveholding socioeconomic order against an emerging industrial state based on free labor.

This issue came to the fore in the debate over the tariff of 1828, which protected northern industries at the expense of southern consumers. Stigmatized as the Tariff of Abominations by southern politicians and journalists generally and South Carolina cotton planters in particular, the tariff called forth Calhoun's first important essay on political theory. Entitled the "South Carolina Exposition and Protest," Calhoun's essay was embodied in a series of resolutions passed by the South Carolina legislature.

Based loosely on Thomas Jefferson's and James Madison's ideas on states' rights, Calhoun's "Exposition" went further, claiming that each state possessed original sovereignty and therefore could and should nullify a federal law that it deemed harmful. Three years later, in his famous Fort Hill Address, Calhoun publicly reiterated these arguments in general terms, though he substituted the word "in-

when he married his cousin Floride Bonneau, a Tidewater heiress, on 8 January 1811. He served two sessions in the South Carolina legislature, to which he had been elected in 1810 and where he came to the attention of leading planters and lawyers for his marked ability in debate and in carefully reasoned discourse. This group, together with Calhoun's numerous and politically important relatives, made sure that he was elected to the 12th Congress, which convened in 1811.

His obvious intellectual and political talents won him an important place in the House of Representatives. A fervent nationalist, Calhoun was a member of the small group of Congressmen who were labeled War Hawks because of their insistence on challenging Great Britain to redress wrongs that they believed their youthful nation had suffered and still was suffering from that imperial power. Although the United States was woefully unprepared for military conflict with Britain, the War Hawks

terposition" for nullification. Both documents demanded noncompliance with the tariff. They effectively ruled out his candidacy to succeed Jackson, a candidacy that Secretary of State Martin Van Buren had already imperiled. President Jackson had taken violent exception to the proposed nullification of a federal law, and for a time civil war was threatened in South Carolina. Calhoun steered a middle course between the extremist nullifiers and the unionists in his native state, and he joined with Clay in forging the Compromise Tariff of 1833.

By now Calhoun had resigned the vice presidency; the South Carolina legislature promptly elected him to the U.S. Senate, in which he would serve for nearly twenty years. As a senator, he was a vigorous defender of southern institutions, including slavery. His powers of logic, his intellectual prowess, and his wealth of knowledge were all mobilized to defend his region, his state, and the South's culture against the antislavery activists who were gaining ground in the rapidly industrializing North.

During the early 1830s, the abolitionist movement, at first a tiny minority of northern reformers, began to utilize various techniques of mass persuasion to publicize the moral evil of slavery. Among these were the establishment of abolitionist newspapers, the holding of large public meetings, and the presentation of abolitionist petitions to Congress.

Ex-president John Quincy Adams, then serving as a representative from Massachusetts, was no abolitionist, but he firmly believed in the constitutional right of petition. Until gagged by a Congressional rule he regularly presented such petitions, even though many of them arraigned southern planters in the most invidious terms. With Calhoun's vehement support the Senate adopted a similar rule to stifle such petitioning. But the gag rules simply exacerbated the debate over slavery. Calhoun assumed the leadership of the more extreme bloc of southern members of Congress in threatening secession as a last resort if the antislavery movement prevailed.

Never a strict party man, Calhoun in 1836 supported William Henry Harrison, the unsuccessful Whig candidate for the presidency, against the Democrat Van Buren. But he endorsed Van Buren's Independent Treasury scheme as a less centralized form of fiscal management than was likely to be proposed by the nationalist-minded Whigs. And when Van Buren and Harrison staged a rematch of their presidential contest in 1840, Calhoun supported the Democratic incumbent. In the wake of Van

Buren's defeat, Calhoun sought the 1844 Democratic nomination but was blocked by the party's Van Buren wing.

At the same time, Calhoun strongly supported the policy of John Tyler (who became president when Harrison died shortly after his March 1841 inauguration) that sought the annexation of Texas as a state. Not an expansionist in principle, Calhoun saw Texas as a mighty addition to the power of the slave states and as a buffer that would protect New Orleans and the Gulf states from a possible European threat. In 1843, when Secretary of State Abel P. Upshur was killed in an explosion aboard the USS *Princeton*, President Tyler selected Calhoun as Upshur's successor. As secretary of State, he pursued a diplomatic policy that culminated in a treaty of annexation with Texas. Both houses of Congress approved the treaty by joint resolution. It became law in March 1845. Reelected to the Senate, Calhoun continued to play an important role in foreign affairs, setting the stage for compromise with Great Britain on the Oregon territorial boundary at the 49th parallel.

Calhoun and his South Carolina colleagues opposed President James K. Polk's declaration of war against Mexico. His reasons were not those of a pacifist, though he did oppose a war of aggression. He was deeply concerned about the future of the Union. If, as he suspected, a defeated Mexico were to make a huge cession of western land, that would create a dangerous situation regarding the question of slavery in the new territories. His other major concern was that extremist expansionists would gain control of the Polk administration and insist that all or much of Mexico be absorbed into the Union. Should this occur, Calhoun feared that Mexico's large population, indifferent to republican institutions, Roman Catholic in religion, and of mixed racial stock, would endanger the largely Protestant, ethnically Anglo-Saxon culture of the United States.

In August 1846, one of his original reservations about the war and its possible consequences was confirmed. Rep. David Wilmot of Pennsylvania succeeded in adding to an appropriation bill a rider, or proviso, that would have banned slavery in all the territory that might be gained from Mexico. The so-called Wilmot Proviso passed the House but failed in the Senate. Thereafter, opponents of slavery sought every opportunity to secure test votes on the proviso. Calhoun led the antiproviso forces, charging that there was a conspiracy on the part of both major parties to restrict and eventually destroy slavery. The abolitionists, he claimed, might be a minority in the northern states, but in many they held the balance of power between the Whigs and Democrats and were thus in a position to extort concessions. The peace treaty of Guadalupe Hidalgo, which ended the Mexican War with a huge cession of western lands to the United States, did indeed reopen the slavery controversy on a national basis.

Calhoun had no use for the popular sovereignty idea promoted by Lewis Cass, the Democratic candidate for president in 1848. Cass's solution to the slavery issue was to let the inhabitants of a territory decide whether it would enter the Union as a free or slave state. To Calhoun, this formula would permit transient, irresponsible populations to prescribe the organic law of a state. There could be, he contended, no protection for slavery under these circumstances.

But Calhoun's worst fears regarding the eventual fate of the South and its institutions came with the organization of the Free-Soil party, which nominated Martin Van Buren for president in 1848. Though it gained no electoral votes and polled only about 10 percent of the popular vote, the Free-Soil presence underlined the fact that opposition to extending slavery into the territories was a compelling political topic in the North. The South, as Calhoun saw it, was being forced into a minority position, in which its way of life would eventually be destroyed.

Though in failing health, Calhoun delivered a series of important speeches on the floor of the Senate in 1849. In what came to be known as the Southern Address, he charged that the slave states could expect united action on the part of northern fanatics and spoilsmen bent on freeing black slaves and elevating them to equality with whites. The entire region, he prophesied, would become "the permanent abode of disorder, anarchy, poverty, misery and wretchedness."

The Southern Address, with its overblown rhetoric, was meant to warn the North not to trifle with slavery in the new territories or wherever federal power extended, as in the District of Columbia or in the regulation of the interstate slave trade. It was also designed to encourage the slave states to stand united against what he termed northern aggression. Otherwise, Calhoun claimed, they would be exposed in piecemeal fashion to eventual northern domination. Only through concerted action, threatening the integrity of the Union, could the slave states protect their economy and their racial system.

Soon after these pronouncements, the new president, Zachary Taylor, insisted that since California had adopted its own constitution banning slavery, it must be admitted as a free state. Over Calhoun's vigorous opposition Oregon had already joined the Union as a free state. Now Calhoun would draw the line. During the debate over the California enabling act, he and his lieutenants made preparations for calling a convention of the southern states at Nashville, Tennessee. It was their avowed purpose to have the convention adopt a secession resolution if California entered the Union as a free state. Whig leaders in Congress recognized the gravity of this threat. Headed by Sen. Henry Clay, they drew up a series of compromise bills that were being debated when Calhoun on 4 March 1850 made his last appearance on the Senate floor for a formal speech.

Still hopeful that the South, with its institution of slavery and its agrarian economy, could coexist in an industrializing nation, Calhoun sought to convince the free states that secession was no bluff. So weak that he had to have Sen. James M. Mason of Virginia deliver his speech, Calhoun reiterated a strict definition of the powers of Congress over the territories. He accused northern politicians of distorting the Constitution for their own ends.

He denounced President Taylor's demand that California be admitted as a free state as "the Executive Proviso." The North, he said, was solidly opposed to slavery, and he argued that its call for "free soil" in the territories was a pretext for an eventual attack on slavery in the states. The South, admittedly the weaker section, was prepared to separate from the Union unless concrete steps (probably nonrepealable constitutional amendments) were taken. Calhoun's speech was direct enough to call forth a plea for compromise from Sen. Daniel Webster in his famous Seventh of March Address. Calhoun died three weeks later, on 31 March 1850.

As an antebellum statesman, Calhoun ranks with those other great political figures Webster and Clay. As a political theorist he must be considered one of the foremost champions of minority rights. An elitist, he was in his speeches and remarks in Senate debates vigorously opposed to the concept of natural rights. His two essays on political theory, *Disquisition on Government* and *Discourse on the Constitution* (1851), form a notable contribution to the understanding, if not the solution, of the tension between liberty and power in a social setting.

In his nearly seventeen years in the U.S. Senate, Calhoun came to represent the foremost defender of the South as a distinct region and of its social and economic institutions, which included slavery. He shared with Clay, Webster, and Jackson the role of leadership in the nation's political affairs. As a debater in the Senate he had few equals. He lacked a colorful oratorical style, but he more that made up for this deficiency with his logical discourse and his mastery of his subject. Calhoun could not compete with the fiery eloquence of Henry Clay or the dramatic presentation of Webster, but his thoughtful speeches commanded attention and respect even from those who disagreed with his contentions.

For his defense of the plantation South and slavery, he relied on the property protection afforded by the Fifth Amendment of the federal Constitution. His thinking on this topic had significant impact on Chief Justice Roger B. Taney's decision in the Dred Scott case. His insistence on state sovereignty and his belief in the doctrine of secession of a state or states from the Union for what he termed just cause was a contributing factor in the explosive growth of sectional sentiment among southern leaders that eventually provoked the political and constitutional crisis of 1860 and 1861.

BIBLIOGRAPHY

Bartlett, Irving H. *John C. Calhoun: A Biography.* 1993.
Capers, Gerald M. *John C. Calhoun, Opportunist: A Reappraisal.* 1960.
Coit, Margaret L. *John C. Calhoun: An American Portrait.* 1950. Repr. 1990.
Current, Richard N. *John C. Calhoun.* 1963.
Niven, John. *John C. Calhoun and the Price of the Union.* 1988.
Wilson, Clyde, et al., eds. *The Papers of John C. Calhoun.* 1959.
Wiltse, Charles M. *John C. Calhoun.* 3 vols. 1949–1951.

JOHN NIVEN

CALIFORNIA. Originally part of the northern reaches of Spain's New World empire, California remained a province of Mexico when that country won its independence from Spain in 1821. American presence in the area began with the fur trappers and traders in the 1820s and 1830s and increased with the first organized parties of settlers who came overland in the early 1840s. The U.S. push to acquire California and other portions of Mexican territory accompanied the American dispute with Mexico over the southern boundary of Texas, which had been admitted to the Union in December 1845. Mexico rebuffed U.S. offers to buy California and New Mexico, and after the Mexican-American War broke out following a military clash in the disputed Texas territory, American settlers in Sonoma touched off hostilities in California with the Bear Flag Revolt against Mexican authority in June 1846. With the help of U.S. naval and military forces, California was safely in American hands by early 1847. As part of the Treaty of Guadalupe Hidalgo, which formally ended the war in February 1848, Mexico ceded California to the United States.

The discovery of gold in early 1848 dramatically increased California's population, from approximately 15,000 to 100,000 by late 1849. In the interim, Congress had failed to pass legislation organizing California as a formal territory because of a sharp dispute between North and South over whether to allow slavery in the territory acquired from Mexico. Faced with rampant lawlessness in the goldfields, Californians took matters into their own hands and, with the approval of the military governor, convened a constitutional convention in October 1849, adopted a constitution prohibiting slavery, and one month later elected a state government that promptly petitioned Congress for admission to the Union. When the 31st Congress convened in December 1849, President Zachary Taylor recommended the admission of California as a free state, but southern members of Congress, led by Sen. John C. Calhoun of South Carolina, resolutely opposed California's admission because of its exclusion of slavery. The stage was thus set for a rancorous congressional controversy over California's admission and a host of other sectional issues, including the status of slavery in other portions of the Mexican Cession. In January 1850 Sen. Henry Clay of Kentucky offered eight compromise proposals to resolve the disputes, including the admission of California as a free state. The ensuing sectional debate occupied Congress until the forces for compromise, then led by Illinois senator Stephen A. Douglas, packaged Clay's proposals into five separate bills and shepherded each to passage in August and September 1850. The bill admitting California as the thirty-first state was passed on 9 September 1850.

As the state stabilized during the 1850s, Democrats tended to dominate state politics, but the new Republican party had gained a strong foothold by the time of the Civil War. Party competitiveness remained high through the remainder of the nineteenth century with the strong influence of the Southern Pacific Railroad lobby at all levels of state government and in the congressional delegations. The railroad lobby was not curbed until a thoroughgoing progressive reform movement elected Republican Hiram W. Johnson governor in 1910. Johnson and a bipartisan progressive bloc in the state legislature passed a broad range of political reforms, including the direct primary; woman suffrage; the initiative, referendum, and recall; and allowance of cross-filing and nonpartisan elections at the state and local levels of government. While Californians preferred moderate Republican leadership at the state level until the late 1950s, the Democrats have generally had a majority in the congressional delegations since the 1930s.

Buttressed by dramatic population growth since the beginning of World War II, California replaced New York as the most populous state by the early 1960s. Since the reapportionment following the 1970 census it has had the largest House delegation, presently fifty-two, far eclipsing the next two delegations, New York and Texas, with thirty-one and thirty representatives, respectively. But the sheer numbers have not translated into proportional power in Congress for the state, largely because of a high turnover rate due to the mercurial state politics and a frequently acute split between conservative Republicans and liberal Democrats in the state's delegations. California has contributed a few prominent congressional leaders, such as Sen. William F. Knowland, who served as Republican majority and minority leader during the 1950s, but comparatively speaking, the state's representatives and senators have rarely been able to accumulate the seniority necessary to achieve the key leadership positions and to chair the most prominent standing committees in each chamber. Still, with fifty-four electoral votes, the state is a force to be reckoned with in presidential politics.

BIBLIOGRAPHY

Delmatier, Royce D., Clarence F. McIntosh, and Earl G. Waters, eds. *The Rumble of California Politics, 1848–1970.* 1970.
Hamilton, Holman. *Prologue to Conflict: The Crisis and Compromise of 1850.* 1964.
Rolle, Andrew F. *California: A History.* 4th ed. 1987.

TERRY L. SEIP

CALL SYSTEM. A system of electronic bells and corresponding lights throughout the Capitol and in all the House and Senate office buildings is used to summon members to the floor when their presence is required. During a day of session, members must balance the need for their presence on

SENATE CLOCK. With call lights.

OFFICE OF THE CURATOR, U.S. SENATE

the floor with competing demands from their committees, visiting constituents, and office staff. Televised floor proceedings, personal beepers, and portable telephones are used by many members to keep track of when they must go to the floor. Official notification, however, comes via a call system that is referred to by many names: bells and lights, legislative buzzers and signal lights, electric bell signals.

The call system sounds throughout the Capitol and the House and Senate office buildings. Simultaneously, a corresponding set of lights—usually in the shape of stars—is illuminated. The lights are either installed as part of a clock face or are mounted directly on the wall. While not every room in the Capitol complex contains them, most member offices and committee hearing rooms clearly display such lights.

Although frequently called "bells," the sound is more like that of an electronic buzzer. It is loud, intrusive, and is meant to interrupt the meetings, conversations, and phone calls that create the constant din of noise heard throughout the halls of Congress.

Prior to the introduction of electricity to the Capitol, pages and other employees were sent throughout the building to let members know they were needed on the floor. A direct-current bell system was first installed in the Capitol about 1891. In 1957, the then-new Dirksen Senate Office Building was the first to receive electronic clocks and buzzers. The call system throughout the Capitol complex has been modernized and upgraded several times since.

The call system uses different types of rings with different meanings. Each house of Congress employs a code unique to that chamber. Since the House and Senate officially share only one room in the Capitol, there is no chance that members will confuse the two separate codes; in the shared room the signal lights for the House are on the east side of the room, those for the Senate are on the west side.

The signals used in the Senate and their meanings are as follows:

One long continuous ring indicates the Senate is convening.

One ring indicates a yea and nay vote.

Two rings indicate a quorum call.

Three rings indicate a call for the absentees.

Four rings indicate the adjournment or recess of that day's session.

Five rings indicate that seven and one-half minutes remain on a yea and nay vote.

Six rings indicate that morning business has concluded (if all lights are cut off), or that the Senate is in a short recess (if the lights remain on).

The signals used in the House are as follows:

One long continuous ring indicates the House is convening.

One ring indicates a teller vote.

One long continuous ring followed by three brief rings indicates a notice quorum call (terminated when 100 members appear on the floor.)

One long continuous ring indicates the termination of a notice quorum call.

Two rings indicate an electronic recorded vote.

Two rings followed by a pause followed by two rings indicate a manual roll-call vote.

Two rings followed by a pause followed by five rings indicate the first vote of a series of clustered votes postponed from earlier consideration.

Three rings indicate a recorded quorum call.

Three rings followed by a pause followed by three rings indicate a manual recorded quorum call.

Three rings followed by a pause followed by five rings indicate a quorum call in Committee of the Whole, to be immediately followed by a five-minute recorded vote.

Four rings indicate adjournment of the House.

Five rings indicate a five-minute electronic recorded vote.

Six rings indicate a recess of the House.

Twelve rings indicate a civil defense warning.

BIBLIOGRAPHY

Bassett, Isaac. Papers. Office of the Curator of Arts and Antiquities, U.S. Senate, Washington, D.C. Unpublished memoirs of the nineteenth-century Senate.

Brown, Glenn. *History of the United States Capitol.* 1900. Repr. 1970.

U.S. House of Representatives. Committee on Public Buildings and Grounds. *Electric Lights and Call-Bells for House Wing, Rotunda and Tholus of the Capitol.* 50th Cong., 2d sess., 1889. H. Rept. 3699.

ILONA B. NICKELS

CAMERON, SIMON (1799–1889), senator from Pennsylvania (1845–1849, 1857–1861, 1867–1877). In the first stage of his career, Cameron was a printer and editor. Advocacy of the protective tariff became his editorial trademark, and he began to exercise considerable influence on state and national politics. By 1830 he had shifted to more lucrative economic pursuits—such as banking, railroads, ironworks, and canal construction—from which he amassed a fortune. As a protariff Jacksonian Democrat who had the support of many Whigs and nativists, he was appointed to the Senate when James Buchanan moved to the State Department.

Cameron failed to win retention to a full Senate term of his own in 1849, and he left the Democratic party in 1854 to become one of the founders of the Republican party in Pennsylvania. He again unsuccessfully attempted to reenter the Senate in 1855, but he did achieve that goal two years later. He resigned in 1861 to accept the secretaryship of the War Department, an appointment that President Abraham Lincoln reluctantly bestowed after his managers struck a deal with Cameron at the 1860 Republican convention.

Lincoln's hesitation proved justified. Cameron mismanaged the department and had to be replaced in 1862. He was sent to Russia as minister, a post he resented. He arrived in the fall of 1862 and immediately requested a furlough, which was denied; he nonetheless returned home to contend for a Senate seat in 1863. Rebuffed for a third time, he became a strong supporter of Lincoln's reelection. This struck a responsive chord with the public; he seized a firm hold on both the state legislature and his party's or-

SIMON CAMERON. *PERLEY'S REMINISCENCES*, VOL. 2

BIBLIOGRAPHY

Bradley, Erwin S. *The Triumph of Militant Republicanism.* 1964.

Crist, Robert G., ed. *Pennsylvania Kingmakers.* 1985.

JAMES A. KEHL

ganization, was elected to the Senate in 1867, and was reelected without opposition in 1873.

When Rutherford B. Hayes became president in 1877, Cameron requested that his son J. Donald be retained as secretary of War. The president refused, and Cameron resigned to demonstrate his power. His control of the Pennsylvania legislature was so complete that it promptly named his son as his successor.

As this incident indicates, Cameron was a dogged man intent on punishing his enemies, but he was equally eager to reward his friends. He viewed his Senate seat as a vehicle to achieve both goals through the power of federal patronage. This attitude led to a Senate career that was neither statesmanlike nor brilliant. He was among those who worked with President Ulysses S. Grant to depose Charles Sumner (R-Mass.) from the chairmanship of the Senate Foreign Relations Committee. Cameron then assumed the chairmanship himself. His most notable feat in that capacity was to bring to ratification the Washington treaty of 1871, which introduced the concept of arbitration to all American-British disputes, a milestone in the development of the general harmony that has pervaded relations between the two countries for generations.

CAMPAIGN COMMITTEES. The four congressional campaign committees—the Democratic Congressional Campaign Committee (DCCC), the Democratic Senatorial Campaign Committee (DSCC), the National Republican Congressional Committee (NRCC), and the National Republican Senatorial Committee (NRSC)—were founded to assist in the reelection of members of the House of Representatives and the Senate. Though they continue to pursue this mission, their focus has broadened to include the recruitment and election of challengers and of candidates for open seats. They have also increased the kinds and quantity of the assistance they provide to candidates.

History. The two House campaign committees were established during the period of instability that followed the Civil War. The NRCC was formed in 1866 by Radical Republicans who were feuding with President Andrew Johnson and wanted to distance themselves from him and the Republican National Committee. The Democrats formed their House campaign committee as a countermeasure in 1868. Senate leaders created the two senatorial campaign committees in 1916 after the Seventeenth Amendment had transformed the upper chamber into a popularly elected body.

Throughout most of their history, the campaign committees (and party organizations in general) played fairly modest roles in congressional elections. They gave small contributions to candidates running for reelection and arranged for prominent speakers to attend campaign events. Congressional candidates were largely on their own when running for election, and the congressional campaign committees were for the most part peripheral to the electoral process.

The committees developed dramatically from the mid 1970s through the 1980s. They used direct mail and telemarketing fund-raising techniques to increase the number of individuals from whom they received contributions and to enlarge their revenues. They hired large professional staffs, became more involved in candidate recruitment, increased the amounts of money they contributed to and spent on behalf of congressional candidates, and began to provide candidates with valuable campaign services. The Republican campaign committees began this process first and made the most progress. In the early 1990s they continued to have substantial advantages over their Democratic counterparts.

Organization. Each campaign committee has a two-tiered organization. The first tier consists of members of Congress who are selected by their party colleagues in the House or Senate. The second tier consists of professional staff who possess political, administrative, or technical skills. Each committee has five or six divisions that are responsible for administration, fund-raising, research, public relations, and campaign assistance to candidates. The communications divisions of the two House campaign committees have media centers that candidates can use to record television and radio commercials. Each committee has a political division responsible for identifying competitive districts, recruiting candidates, and providing selected candidates with strategic advice, money, fund-raising assistance, and campaign services.

Committee staffs have a great deal of autonomy in daily operations and are extremely influential in formulating committee campaign strategies. In the case of the NRCC, for example, Republican House members have allowed their staff to take the lead in setting committee priorities and have adopted a hands-off attitude similar to that of a board of directors. In 1992, the DCCC, DSCC, NRCC, and NRSC employed staffs of 64, 35, 89, and 135 full-time employees, respectively.

Campaign Assistance and Decision Making. Campaign committee election activities take four basic forms: candidate recruitment, campaign contributions and expenditures, campaign services, and generic party-focused campaigning. Campaign committee recruitment is usually limited to competitive districts. Committee members and staff, in conjunction with state and local party leaders, encourage prospective candidates to run for Congress by promising them party contributions and campaign services in the general election. Party organizations may also help clear the field of primary opposition, thereby helping the party and the favored candidate avoid the damage that can result from a primary fight.

Other campaign committee activities also tend to focus on competitive contests, reflecting the committees' overriding goal of maximizing the number of seats their parties hold in Congress. National political and economic conditions are additional factors influencing the distribution of committee resources. When the president is popular and the economy is strong, the campaign committees of the president's party invest more resources in competitive challenger and open-seat races. Conversely, the out-party committees use more of their resources to protect incumbents. When national conditions do not favor the president's party, the patterns are reversed: the in-party committees take a defensive, incumbent-protecting posture, and the out-party committees go on the offensive, using more of their resources to help nonincumbent candidates.

To try to predict which elections will be close, the committees use several kinds of information: returns from previous elections, information about the demographics of election districts, and polls. Congressional roll-call votes and constituent service activities give insights into which incumbents might be vulnerable. Research that assesses the electoral experience and levels of name recognition of challenger and open-seat candidates helps the committees to identify those who have the potential to wage competitive campaigns.

The unpredictable nature of electoral politics means that campaign committee decision making and targeting are necessarily imperfect. District, statewide, or national political conditions that threaten incumbents can also distort committee decision making and resource distribution, with some safe incumbents demanding, and receiving, substantial committee assistance while some competitive nonincumbents get little or no help.

Party activity in congressional elections is limited by the Federal Election Campaign Act of 1971 and its amendments. The House campaign committees and national and state party committees are each allowed to contribute a maximum of $5,000 to House candidates during the general election. The senatorial campaign committees and their affiliated national committees are allowed to give a combined total of $17,500 to Senate general election candidates; state party organizations can give an additional $5,000. Party committees can also contribute money in congressional primaries and runoff elections, but campaign committees rarely give contributions in contested nomination races.

Party committees are also allowed to make coordinated expenditures on behalf of candidates. These expenditures are made in cooperation with the candidates' campaign committees, giving both the party and the candidate a measure of control over spending. Originally set at $10,000 each for a state and national committee, the limits for coordinated expenditures on behalf of House candidates are adjusted for inflation and reached $27,620 in 1992. The limits for coordinated expenditures in Senate elections vary by the size of a state's voting-age population and are also indexed to inflation. In 1992 they ranged from $55,240 in the smallest states to $1,277,322 in California, the nation's most populous state. The campaign committees give most competitive House or Senate candidates the maximum contribution; most also benefit from a large coordinated expenditure. The House and Senate campaign committees distribute more money to congressional candidates than any other party organization.

The committees also provide candidates with assistance in aspects of campaigning that require technical expertise or in-depth research. The committees help candidates plan campaign strategies, conduct issue research, and produce television and radio advertisements. They hold training colleges for candidates and campaign managers. They also introduce competitive candidates to political consultants and political action committee (PAC) managers to help channel the flow of money and election services in their direction.

The campaign committees also help finance generic party-focused television and radio advertisements as well as voter registration and get-out-the-vote drives. These activities—like most campaign committee contributions, campaign services, and voter mobilization efforts—are primarily targeted toward competitive elections. The Republican committees gave their candidates more money and campaign services than the Democrats during the 1976 through 1992 elections, but the Democrats began to close the gap in the late 1980s. Party assistance typically has a bigger impact on campaigns waged by nonincumbents because these candidates generally possess less experience, little of the clout that incumbents have with PACs and wealthy individual contributors, and none of the other advantages of incumbency.

Relationship with Congress. Like most other extragovernmental party organizations in the United States, the campaign committees devote little effort to advancing ideological or policy-oriented goals. They do, however, serve as arenas where members of Congress can discuss the partisan implications of policy issues. They provide individual members of Congress with political advice and occasionally help party leaders in Congress coordinate their public messages. The committees do not provide or withhold campaign assistance to encourage legislators to support the policy positions of their party's congressional leadership. In fact, campaign committee staffs occasionally advise members to break ranks with their party leadership in order to solidify support among their local constituents. The support that the campaign committees provide for party leaders' and members' congressional activities pales in comparison to their involvement in election-related ventures.

[*See also* Campaign Financing; Elections, Congressional, *especially the article on* Congressional Campaigns; Party Committees; Political Action Committees; Political Parties.]

BIBLIOGRAPHY

Frantzich, Stephen E. *Political Parties in the Technological Age.* 1989.
Herrnson, Paul. *Party Campaigning in the 1980s.* 1988.
Jacobson, Gary. "Party Organization and Campaign Resources: Republicans and Democrats in 1982." *Political Science Quarterly* 100 (1985–1986): 603–625.
Jacobson, Gary, and Samuel Kernell. *Strategy and Choice in Congressional Elections.* 1981.
Kayden, Xandra, and Eddie Mahe, Jr. *The Party Goes On.* 1985.
Price, David E. *Bringing Back the Parties.* 1984.

PAUL S. HERRNSON

CAMPAIGN FINANCING. Prior to 1972 the only restrictions on congressional campaign finance were the Tillman Act (1907) and the Taft-Hartley Labor-Management Relations Act (1947), which prohibited candidates from accepting contributions from corporate and union treasury funds, respectively. While the Federal Corrupt Practices Act of 1925 required disclosure of campaign receipts and expenditures, it was so poorly written and enforced that there was in practice no disclosure. Consequently, while academic and journalistic accounts provide some insights into the financing of presidential campaigns prior to 1972, little is known about the financing of congressional elections. With no effective disclosure of campaign receipts and expenditures, sources of congressional campaign funds were unknown prior to 1972. It was not until January of 1972, when the Federal Election Campaign Act of 1971 was passed, that meaningful disclosure of campaign finance contributions occurred.

In 1972 Congress passed the first of three campaign finance reform bills that would determine the way congressional elections are financed. The Federal Election Campaign Act of 1971 required a po-

TWO CAMPAIGN HUSTLERS
FROM 'WAY BACK

BOOZE

$ BOODLE

CAMPAIGN CONTRIBUTIONS. Political cartoon satirizing the influence of alcohol and bribery in political campaigns. George F. Coffin, c. 1880–1900.

LIBRARY OF CONGRESS

litical committee or candidate to disclose receipts and expenditures in excess of $100 and required all political committees with receipts in excess of $1,000 to file a statement of organization. The act also required candidates to file regular reports of contributions and expenditures and to provide the names, addresses, and occupations of their contributors.

In 1974 the Federal Election Campaign Act (F.E.C.A.) was amended to limit both contributions and spending in congressional elections. Contributions by individuals were limited to $1,000 per candidate per election, with a total aggregate annual contribution limit of $25,000. Political and party committees were limited to $5,000 per election, but, unlike individuals, there was no aggregate limit placed on contributions. Senators and their families could contribute no more than $35,000 to their own campaigns; for House members and their families the limit was $25,000. Finally, independent expenditures on behalf of a candidate were limited to $1,000.

Spending by House candidates was limited to $70,000 in primary elections and another $70,000

in the general election. Senate candidates could spend up to $100,000 or eight cents per eligible voter, whichever was greater, in primary elections and $150,000 or twelve cents per eligible voter, whichever was greater, in general elections. Spending by the national political parties was limited to $10,000 for House candidates and $20,000 or two cents per eligible voter, whichever was greater, for Senate candidates. Spending limits were indexed to the Consumer Price Index.

The Federal Election Campaign Act of 1974 also established a Federal Election Commission to administer the act. The commission was to consist of six members, two appointed by the president, two by the Speaker of the House, and two by the president pro tempore of the Senate.

The constitutionality of the 1974 amendments was challenged in federal court soon after they were passed. The resulting Supreme Court case, *Buckley v. Valeo* (424 U.S. 1 [1976]), upheld the constitutionality of the contribution limits, but struck down the constitutionality of the spending limits; struck down limits on spending by House and Senate candidates; held that there could be no limits on independent expenditures; and ordered that all six members of the Federal Election Commission be appointed by the president.

In response to the Supreme Court's decision the F.E.C.A. was again amended in 1976. These amendments required that the Federal Election Commission consist of six members, three Democrats and three Republicans, appointed by the president and confirmed by the Senate. The amendments also limited contributions by individuals to political action committees (PACs) to $5,000 per year and to a political party to $20,000 per year. The individual contribution limits of $1,000 per candidate per election and the aggregate individual contribution limit of $25,000 per year remained in effect. The F.E.C.A. amendments of 1976 limited contributions from multicandidate committees to no more than $15,000 to a national party committee and limited the amount the senatorial campaign committees could give to Senate candidates to $17,500 per year. Finally, the 1976 amendments established that, for contribution purposes, all PACs created by a corporation, membership organization, or union would be considered one PAC.

The final changes to F.E.C.A. occurred in 1979, when Congress amended the act to promote "party building" activities. This allowed individuals to contribute unlimited amounts of money to the Democratic and Republican parties for activities such as registration and get-out-the-vote drives. This so-called soft money has been used primarily in presidential campaigns but also plays a role in congressional campaigns.

Campaign Finance Laws. The contribution limits enacted in 1974 continue to apply to congressional campaigns. Individuals may contribute $1,000 to a candidate per election (i.e., $1,000 in the primary election and $1,000 in the general election), up to $20,000 to a national party committee, and $5,000 to any other political committee (e.g., a PAC), but the total contributions an individual may give to candidates for federal office may not exceed $25,000 in any one calendar year. Political action committees may give up to $5,000 per candidate per election (i.e., $5,000 in the primary election and $5,000 in the general election), up to $15,000 to a national political party committee per year, and up to $5,000 to any other political committee per year, but there is no aggregate limit on the amount of money PACs may give to candidates.

Political parties give money to congressional candidates in two ways: through direct contributions to the candidates and through indirect, or coordinated, expenditures. Coordinated expenditures are funds spent by the national and state party committees to help a candidate, but the expenditures are made by the party committee. For example, a party committee could commission a poll or media ad for a candidate, and the costs would be paid by the committee, not by the candidate's campaign.

The national party committees (the Democratic National Committee and the Republican National Committee), the Senate campaign committees (the Democratic Senatorial Campaign Committee and the National Republican Senatorial Committee), and the House campaign committees (the Democratic Congressional Campaign Committee and the National Republican Congressional Committee) may each contribute $10,000 to House candidates. In addition, the state party committees may contribute $10,000 to House candidates. The national party committees and the Senate campaign committees may together contribute $17,500 to Senate candidates, and the House campaign committees and the state party committees may each contribute $10,000 to Senate candidates.

The coordinated expenditure limits are the limits set in 1974 and then indexed for inflation. The coordinated expenditure limit for House races is $10,000, plus a cost-of-living increase. For the 1994 election cycle the coordinated expenditure limit for House candidates was $29,300, except for states with only one congressional candidate, where the limit was $58,600. For Senate elections the coordinated expenditure limit is two cents times the state voting-age population and then adjusted for inflation or $20,000 plus a cost-of-living adjustment, whichever is higher. In 1994 the coordinated expenditure for the least populous states was $58,600, the same as the coordinated expenditure limit for House candidates who ran statewide, while the coordinated expenditure limit for California, the most populous state, was $1,325,415. The state party committees have the same coordinated expenditure limits as the national party committees. The state party committees may make their own coordinated expenditures or give that authority to the national party committees, thus doubling the amount of money the national party committees control for House and Senate elections.

While there are limits on what individuals, political parties, and PACs may contribute to congressional candidates, there are no limits on what a

TABLE 1. *Limits on Contributions to Congressional Campaigns*

	RECIPIENT			
CONTRIBUTOR	CANDIDATE (EACH ELECTION)[1]	NATIONAL PARTY COMMITTEES (CALENDAR YEAR)	ANY OTHER COMMITTEE (CALENDAR YEAR)	TOTAL LIMIT (CALENDAR YEAR)
Individuals	$1,000	$20,000	$5,000	$25,000
PACs	5,000	15,000	5,000	None
Party committees	5,000	None	5,000	None
All other groups	1,000	20,000	5,000	None

[1]Includes contributions to a candidate's campaign committee
SOURCE: David B. Magleby and Candice J. Nelson, *The Money Chase: Congressional Campaign Financing.* 1990.

candidate may spend on his or her own race, nor are there limits on individual or PAC independent expenditures. Independent expenditures are those made by an individual or PAC to support or oppose someone's candidacy, but there can be no consultation or communication between the candidate and his or her campaign and the individual or group making independent expenditures. While individuals rarely make individual expenditures of any size, some PACs have used independent expenditures to influence congressional elections. For example, in 1992 the National Rifle Association spent more than $100,000 on independent expenditures in an ultimately successful effort to unseat Rep. Beryl Anthony (D-Ark.). Altogether PACs spent $6 million dollars on independent expenditures in congressional elections in 1992.

Sources of Funds. Congressional candidates receive campaign contributions from three sources: individual contributors, political action committees, and the party committees. The relative importance of these three groups depends in large part upon a candidate's status (incumbent, challenger, or open seat), party affiliation, and the office for which the candidate is running (House or Senate). Senate candidates, regardless of status, receive more than half of their campaign contributions from individuals. The same is true for House Republicans, but for House Democrats PACs are an important and, in some cases, major source of campaign funds.

Incumbents are more likely to receive contributions from PACs than are challengers and candidates for open seats. Party contributions, while less important for most candidates than contributions from PACs and individuals, are more important, or at least a larger percentage of total contributions, for Republicans than for Democrats.

Although Senate incumbents receive approximately two-thirds of their campaign contributions from individuals and between one-quarter and one-third of their contributions from PACs, House incumbents are much more dependent on PAC contributions. House Republican incumbents receive approximately 40 percent of their campaign contributions from PACs, while House Democratic incumbents receive over 50 percent of their campaign contributions from PACs.

For challengers and open-seat candidates, the campaign finance picture is quite different. Of challengers for a House seat, Democrats receive approximately one-third of their campaign funds from PACs, while Republicans receive only about

10 percent. Figures for Senate challengers are similar to those for House Republican challengers; in the Senate the difference between PAC receipts of Republican and Democratic challengers is much less than in the House. Open-seat candidates in both parties and in both the House and Senate generally receive more money from PACs than do challengers, but still considerably less than incumbents.

Expenditures of Funds. While the Federal Election Campaign Act requires extensive disclosure of campaign contributions, its requirements for disclosure of campaign expenditures are much less strict. While campaign expenditures exceeding $200 must be reported to the Federal Election Commission, F.E.C.A. requires only that the name, address, date, amount, and purpose of the expenditure be disclosed. Because describing the purpose of the expenditure is left up to the candidate, there is no uniformity in the reporting of expenditures.

Following the 1989 to 1990 election cycle, two *Los Angeles Times* reporters and their colleagues analyzed the expenditure reports of candidates who ran for Congress in 1990. In *The Handbook of Campaign Spending: Money in the 1990 Congressional Races* (1992), Sara Fritz and Dwight Morris grouped congressional expenditures into eight major categories, several with subcategories (see table 3).

Fritz and Morris's efforts to categorize and compare campaign expenditures by congressional candidates illustrate the difficulty in tracing expenditures in House and Senate elections. Their research led to two very interesting findings. First, contrary to popular opinion, electronic media, particularly television, is not the primary expenditure for most congressional candidates. Senate candidates spent 35 percent of their resources on radio and television, House candidates 23 percent. The difference in the relative amounts spent on broadcast media is not surprising because in many House districts television and, to a lesser extent, radio are not efficient advertising mechanisms. However, the fact that only one-third of Senate spending was for radio and television was a surprise, since the common assumption had been that nearly two-thirds of all Senate campaign expenditures were for television advertising.

The second interesting finding was how little total spending was directed at traditional campaign activities such as voter contact. Fritz and Morris estimated that in House races over half of all campaign expenditures were unrelated to contacting voters. For Senate campaigns a larger percentage of expenditures was directed to voter contact, due

TABLE 2. *Individual and PAC Contributions to Congressional Candidates, by Candidate Status, 1986–1992 (percent)*

	HOUSE			
	DEMOCRATS		REPUBLICANS	
	INDIVIDUALS	PACs	INDIVIDUALS	PACs
INCUMBENTS				
1992	42%	51%	52%	40%
1990	38	53	51	41
1988	39	52	52	40
1986	43	49	54	38
CHALLENGERS				
1992	51	22	59	9
1990	49	24	55	10
1988	48	26	58	10
1986	51	26	56	10
OPEN SEATS				
1992	50	25	54	17
1990	44	28	53	20
1988	38	23	55	19
1986	48	23	55	19

	SENATE			
	DEMOCRATS		REPUBLICANS	
	INDIVIDUALS	PACs	INDIVIDUALS	PACs
INCUMBENTS				
1992	54%	39%	67%	27%
1990	68	26	69	23
1988	64	30	67	28
1986	67	28	68	26
CHALLENGERS				
1992	66	10	65	9
1990	62	13	57	16
1988	72	17	69	12
1986	57	20	75	8
OPEN SEATS				
1992	70	17	51	13
1990	48	14	46	35
1988	50	16	61	29
1986	63	19	64	21

SOURCE: "1992 Congressional Election Spending Jumps 52% to $678 Million," Federal Election Commission Press Release, 4 March 1993.

in large part to the greater percentage of Senate expenditures on electronic media and direct mail.

Campaign Finance Reform. While the Federal Election Campaign Act was a reform of campaign finance laws when it was initially passed in 1972, and amended in 1974, 1976, and 1979, the act was little more than a decade old when the first efforts to reform congressional campaign finance laws began anew. In 1985 Senators David Boren and Barry Goldwater introduced an amendment to

TABLE 3. *Where the Campaign Dollars Go: Percentage of Funds Spent by Candidates in the 1990 Elections*[1]

| | HOUSE | | SENATE | |
EXPENSE	INCUMBENTS	CHALLENGERS	INCUMBENTS	CHALLENGERS
Advertising and media	22%	31%	33%	43%
Office	28	28	24	26
Fund-raising	18	9	31	19
Campaigning and voter contact	17	26	6	9
Polling	3	3	3	2
Constituent gifts and entertainment	2	—	—	—
Donations	7	—	2	—
Other	4	3	1	1

[1]A dash indicates an expenditure of less than 1 percent

Note: Figures include percentages of all expenditures by candidates in the 1990 elections. For House candidates this covers a two-year cycle (1989–1990); for Senate candidates there is a six-year cycle (1985–1990). Percentage column totals may not equal 100 because of rounding.

SOURCE: Computed from data reported in Sara Fritz and Dwight Morris, *Gold-Plated Politics: Running for Congress in the 1990s*, 1992. The database was compiled from Federal Election Commission reports by the *Los Angeles Times*'s Washington bureau staff.

limit the amount of money candidates for Congress could accept from PACs: $100,000 for House candidates and between $175,000 and $750,000 for Senate candidates (depending on the size of the state); and to reduce individual PAC contributions to $3,000 per candidate per election. The Boren-Goldwater amendment passed the Senate in December 1985, but because it was a nongermane amendment to a nuclear waste bill, and because there was no enforcement mechanism included in the bill, the amendment was merely symbolic of renewed interest in campaign finance reform in the U.S. Congress.

The attention that the Boren-Goldwater amendment received, however, began a debate on campaign finance reform that continued throughout the 1980s and into the 1990s. In 1987, prior to the start of the 100th Congress, Senators David Boren, Robert Byrd (the majority leader), George Mitchell, and Alan Cranston (the majority whip) were all at work on campaign finance legislation. Soon after the start of the Congress, Senator Byrd called together the other three senators, as well as Sen. Wendell Ford, the chairman of the Senate Rules Committee, to try to create a campaign finance bill that was acceptable to all of them.

Senate Bill 2 (S. 2, the Senatorial Election Campaign Act of 1987), the legislation drafted by the Senate leadership, established a state-by-state general election spending limit based on the voting-age population of the state and limited spending in primary elections to two-thirds of the general election limit. A candidate who raised 20 percent of the state general election spending in amounts of $250 or less received a grant of public funds equal to the 80 percent of the general election spending limit. While individual PAC contribution limits were not changed, candidates could accept no more than 30 percent of the state primary spending limit from all PACs during the six-year election cycle. S. 2 also limited the amount the party committees could receive from PACs, placed restrictions on bundling (the practice of an organization collecting individual checks and then giving them to a candidate in a bundle, thereby enabling the organization to get credit for raising the funds), required disclosure of soft money, and provided additional public funds to candidates who had independent expenditures made against them.

Senate Republicans offered their own campaign finance reform bill. Senators Mitch McConnell and Bob Packwood introduced legislation to prohibit direct contributions from PACs to candidates, require disclosure of soft money, and require full disclosure by party committees of all receipts, expenditures, and soft money.

During the summer and fall of 1987 and into the winter of 1988, Republicans filibustered Democratic efforts to debate campaign finance reform. There were a record eight cloture votes on S. 2, but the Democratic leadership was unable to cut off the filibuster.

During the 101st (1989–1991) and 102d (1991–1993) Congresses campaign finance continued to be debated. In 1990 campaign finance bills passed both the House and Senate, but conferees never met to work out differences in the legislation. In 1992 legislation passed both the House and Senate, only to be vetoed by President George Bush in May 1992. The 1992 bill established spending limits in both House and Senate elections, further restrictions on PAC contributions, and public funding (in different forms) for House and Senate candidates.

The 1992 legislation established a spending limit of $600,000 for House elections and a limit of between $636,500 and $8.9 million for Senate elections. The lower amount would have applied to the least populous states; the limit of $8.9 million applied to California. Spending limits in each state for Senate elections were based on the voting-age population of the state. The limits on PAC contributions also differed for House and Senate candidates. House candidates could accept no more than $5,000 from any one PAC and no more than $200,000 from all PACs. Senate candidates could accept no more than $2,500 from any one PAC and no more than 20 percent of their general election spending limit from PACs. A House candidate who qualified for public funding by winning the primary and raising $60,000 in contributions of $250 or less, and who had an opponent in the general election, would receive $200 in federal matching funds for each $200 in individual contributions received, up to a limit of $200,000. Senate candidates, like their House counterparts, also had to win a primary and have a general election opponent. In addition, Senate candidates had to raise $250,000 or 10 percent of the general election spending limit, whichever was less, in amounts of $250 or less, and half of those $250 contributions had to come from within the state.

When the 103d Congress convened in January 1993, campaign finance reform was once again on the legislative agenda, but the probability of reform was considerably higher. Unlike in prior years, reform advocates in 1993 had the support of the president, Bill Clinton, who had pledged support for campaign finance reform legislation during his campaign and who had mentioned campaign finance reform as a priority of his administration during his State of the Union address. During the 100th, 101st, and 102d Congresses there was little

likelihood that campaign finance legislation passed by Congress would be signed by Presidents Ronald Reagan and George Bush. Thus some members of Congress viewed a vote for campaign finance reform as a win-win vote; they could support reform, and thus be perceived as on the progressive side of the issue in the minds of both their constituents and special interest groups such a Common Cause, and yet not fear that they would actually have to run under the proposed changes in the law. In contrast, in 1993, reformers could be fairly confident that President Clinton would sign a campaign finance bill, and thus the provisions of that bill needed careful thought.

During the winter and spring of 1993 the Senate Rules Committee held hearings on Senate Bill 3 (S. 3, the Congressional Campaign Spending Limit and Election Reform Act), the same campaign finance reform bill that had been vetoed by President Bush a year earlier. In May 1993 President Clinton announced his proposals for campaign finance reform: spending limits in House and Senate campaigns, communications vouchers for candidates who accepted spending limits, further limits on the amount of money House and Senate candidates could accept from political action committees, and the elimination of soft money in presidential and congressional elections.

In June of 1993, following three weeks of intensive debate on the Senate floor, campaign finance reform legislation once again passed the Senate. The Senate legislation established spending limits in the general election of between $1.2 and $5.5 million, depending on a state's population, and limited spending in primary elections to 67 percent of the general election spending limit or $2.75 million, whichever was less. The bill also prohibited candidates from accepting PAC contributions, prohibited candidates for federal office from raising soft money, and severely curtailed the use of soft money by national party committees. What distinguished the bill that passed the Senate in 1993 from previous bills considered or passed by the Senate was that it did not include the public funding provisions included in earlier Senate legislation. While 1993 differed from 1987 and 1988 in that the president supported campaign finance reform, in 1993, just as in 1987 and 1988, the Democrats in the Senate still needed some bipartisan support for campaign finance reform legislation to avoid a Republican filibuster. To gain enough support to avoid a filibuster, Democrats in the Senate dropped federally funded communications vouchers for candidates who agreed to spending limits, thus passing a bill with spending limits but no public funding.

In November 1993 the House of Representatives passed its campaign finance bill. The House bill, H.R. 3, also called the Congressional Campaign Spending Limit and Reform Act of 1993, established spending limits of $600,000 for House candidates but indexed the spending limits to inflation. House candidates who accepted spending limits would receive up to $200,000 in federal communications vouchers, which could be used for paid media, postage, and other forms of voter contact, such as brochures, bumper stickers, and campaign buttons. The legislation also limited the aggregate amount of money House candidates could accept from PACs. All House candidates, whether or not they accepted spending limits, could accept no more than $200,000 from PACs. H.R. 3, like its Senate counterpart, also sharply restricted soft money. What H.R. 3 did not do, however, was provide a funding mechanism to pay for the federal communications vouchers. That mechanism was to be included in future legislation.

Well into 1994, campaign finance reform remained elusive. Representatives and senators continued to differ on the role of PACs in congressional elections: senators wanted to ban PACs; representatives, to continue to allow PAC contributions of $5,000 per election. A second contentious issue was public funding. Members of the House and Senate differed over whether campaign finance legislation should include partial public funding and, if so, where the revenues to support public funding would come from.

The debate over campaign finance reform presents a conflict between self-interest and philosophical interest for Democrats and Republicans, and House and Senate members, and the conflict was particularly brought to the fore with the election of a Democratic, reform-minded president. The three most controversial issues in the debate over congressional campaign finance reform continue to be spending limits, public funding, and political action committees. Because of differences in costs of campaigns, sources of funds, and House and Senate rules and procedures, partisan and institutional differences within Congress make agreement on campaign finance reform extremely difficult.

For example, the debate over spending limits is viewed differently by House and Senate members and by Republicans and Democrats. Because Senate races are more expensive than House races, on average, Senators spend more time raising money;

thus limits on spending, and thus on the time spent raising money, are more important to senators than to representatives. At the same time, however, Republicans, in the minority in both the House and Senate, fear that any spending limits will preclude them from ever becoming the majority party in either the House or the Senate, because nonincumbent candidates often need to spend more than incumbents to overcome the inherent advantages of incumbency.

Similar conflicts exist over the issue of public funding. For nonincumbent candidates, particularly for the House, public funding would provide seed money to build a campaign organization, achieve initial name recognition, and attract campaign contributions from PACs, individuals, and the party committees. The group of candidates who would most benefit from public funding are those who are most underfunded in the current system, namely, Republican nonincumbents seeking election to the House. However, because Republicans philosophically oppose government funding of congressional elections, Republicans oppose what likely is in the best interests of their candidates.

Political action committees are also targets for campaign finance reform. They are viewed by some advocates of reform as the epitome of special interest influence over congressional behavior, and proposals to further restrict PAC contributions to members of Congress, or to ban PACs entirely, are touted as a means to remove this influence. However, enthusiasm for further restricting or banning PACs varies from chamber to chamber and from one political party to the other. Senators receive less than one-third of their campaign contributions from PACs, so restrictions on PACs would not significantly change their sources of campaign funds. Further, because business-related PACs, despite their general philosophical alignment with Republicans, tend to give almost one-half of their contributions to influential majority-party Democrats, Republican senators do not receive as many contributions from groups whose interests they support and thus have been the most vocal in the call for banning PAC contributions.

House members, however, are much more dependent on PAC contributions than are their Senate colleagues. Because House members receive over 40 percent of their campaign contributions from PACs, and House Democratic incumbents receive over half of all their campaign contributions from PACs, House members, particularly House Democrats, are much less enthusiastic than their Senate colleagues about banning or further restricting PAC contributions.

While spending limits, public funding, and restrictions on PACs are the most contentious issues in the debate over campaign finance reform, other issues also raise controversy. For example, while there is general agreement that soft money needs to be curtailed, the political parties want to ensure that the programs supported by soft money continue. Similarly, proposals to restrict bundling by individuals and PACs abound, but the parties want to create legislation that exempts organizations whose bundling helps their candidates. For instance, EMILY's List, a PAC that supports Democratic women candidates who favor abortion rights, raised $6.2 million dollars in 1992, and candidates who were the recipients of those dollars want to pass reform legislation that enables the bundling practices of EMILY's List to continue.

The debate over congressional campaign finance reform that began in earnest in 1987 continued into the 1990s. The issues first addressed in the original Senate bill (S. 2) continued to be the issues that plagued members of Congress in the 1990s, and the positions of the two parties and two chambers changed little. The difference between the late 1980s and early 1990s was the presence of a pro-reform president, a difference that influenced the debate over campaign finance reform.

Congressional campaign finance is an issue that increasingly pits the haves against the have-nots. As members of Congress have become increasingly adept at raising money under the provisions of the Federal Election Campaign Act, the disparity between the amount of money raised and spent by incumbents and challengers increases. After the flurry of open seats created in 1992 by redistricting and retirements, the 1990s will likely be another decade of high reelection rates for incumbents, helped in large part by their spending advantage over their generally underfunded challengers.

[See also Buckley v. Valeo; Campaign Committees; Elections, Congressional; Federal Election Commission.]

BIBLIOGRAPHY

Fritz, Sara, and Dwight Morris. The Handbook of Campaign Spending: Money in the 1990 Congressional Races. 1992.
Herrnson, Paul S. Party Campaigning in the 1980s. 1988.
Jackson, Brooks. Honest Graft: Big Money and the American Political Process. 1988.
Johannes, John R., and Margaret Latus Nugent. Money, Elections, and Democracy: Reforming Congressional Campaign Finance. 1990.
Magleby, David B., and Candice J. Nelson. The Money Chase: Congressional Campaign Finance Reform. 1990.
Mutch, Robert E. Campaigns, Congress, and the Courts: The Making of Federal Campaign Finance Law. 1988.
Sorauf, Frank J. Inside Campaign Finance: Myths and Realities. 1992.
Sorauf, Frank J. Money in American Elections. 1988.
Stern, Philip M. The Best Congress Money Can Buy. 1988.

CANDICE J. NELSON

CANADA. Congressional interest in what became the Dominion of Canada began in 1775, when the Continental Congress dispatched agents northward with appeals to residents of the British territory to join the rebellion. Later that year forces of the rebellious colonies invaded but failed to conquer Quebec. Hopes for incorporating Canada into the federal union, by peaceful or other means, continued to color congressional attitudes, and were reflected in another invasion during the War of 1812 and in the continuing annexationist vision of a "manifest destiny" that would push the border northward. All the while Americans on both sides of the border confronted an ever-shifting array of specific issues: boundaries, fisheries, trade, and use of lake and river waterways. Until the 1920s, Great Britain handled Canada's external affairs. In the 1923 Halibut Fishing Treaty, Canada for the first time negotiated directly and independently with the United States.

Boundary disputes, often bound up with annexation rhetoric, have consumed much congressional time and energy. Sometimes the issues seemed dangerously volatile, as in the Maine–New Brunswick "Aroostook war" of 1839. This conflict arose when the Maine legislature granted lands within disputed border areas, lands on which New Brunswick lumberjacks began logging operations. Maine and Massachusetts called out their militias and Congress authorized a force of fifty thousand men and voted $10 million for a possible emergency. Gen. Winfield Scott arranged a truce, and the lands were divided by treaty in 1842.

Despite the occasional strains, however, historically, with very brief exceptions, nationals from both countries have moved freely across the border without passports. Thus there has been much mingling of Canadians and U.S. citizens, especially in the border states and provinces. When Congress established immigration quotas in the 1920s, Canada was exempted from the restrictions.

In 1854, the Senate approved a treaty reciprocally reducing tariffs. But a decade later, rising U.S. protectionism and anger about lapses in Canadian neutrality during the Civil War pressured Congress to request that the president give the required one-year notice of intent to abrogate the treaty. Reciprocity proved difficult to revive. In 1911, Congress approved a trade agreement, only to have it fail in Canada when it become entangled in a parliamentary election.

As older antagonisms faded, however, cooperative ventures multiplied. The International Joint Commission, which has successfully mediated U.S.–Canadian boundary and boundary-water disputes, dates from 1909. But the commission alone could not broker the sixty-year effort to authorize a jointly beneficial inland waterway that would open up the interiors of both countries to ocean-going ships. Not until 1954 was this joint undertaking, the Saint Lawrence and Great Lakes Waterway, agreed to.

The Permanent Board on Joint Defense was initiated by President Franklin D. Roosevelt (without reference to Congress) and Prime Minister W. L. Mackenzie King in 1940. By 1958 the North American Air Defense Command (NORAD) was in place.

Limited reciprocal reductions in tariffs, begun in the 1930s, led by 1965 to a free-trade agreement covering automobiles and automobile parts. In 1989, Congress approved a trade accord that will virtually eliminate all trade barriers by 1999. An even broader trade compact, the North American Free Trade Agreement (NAFTA), that would eventually eliminate customs duties and most other restrictions on the sale of goods and services between the United States, Canada, and Mexico, was approved in 1993.

Rising concern over the environment, particularly air and water pollution, has complicated relations between the two neighbors in recent years. At the same time, customary methods of settling disputes have weakened, partly because Congress has demanded a greater voice in foreign policy and partly because of shifts in federal-provincial relationships in Canada. In response to this change, Canada in 1981 hired a U.S. law firm to assist it in lobbying Congress to act on legislation to reduce acid rain, much of which has been blamed on emissions from midwestern U.S. utility and industrial plants. Acid rain, which forms when wind-borne sulfur dioxide and nitrogen oxide mix with rain or snow, can harm lakes, fish, and vegetation far from the polluting source. While Canadians fumed, Congress took its time deliberating the acid-rain issue

before finally enacting strict emissions-control measures as part of the Clean Air Act of 1990.

BIBLIOGRAPHY

Curtis, Kenneth M., and John E. Carroll. *Canadian-American Relations: The Promise and the Challenge.* 1983.

CARL UBBELOHDE

CANDIDACY. *See* Elections, Congressional.

CANNON, CLARENCE (1879–1964), House parliamentarian, Democratic representative from Elsberry, Missouri, and Appropriations Committee chairman. A onetime professor of history and Latin, Clarence Andrew Cannon was hired as a clerk by Speaker James Beauchamp (Champ) Clark in 1911. He became journal clerk of the House in 1914 and clerk at the Speaker's Table (parliamentarian) in 1917. As the House's chief parliamentary authority, he compiled several procedural manuals, including *Cannon's Precedents of the House of Representatives of the United States*, first published in 1936 and still in use in the 1990s. He served as parliamentarian until 1922, when he was elected to the House as the representative of Missouri's 9th Congressional District.

Assigned to the Appropriations Committee, Cannon became chairman in 1941 and, except for 1947–1949 and 1953–1955, when the Republicans controlled Congress, served in that role until his death. His knowledge of House rules, his ability to unify his committee, and his resourceful and combative nature made him one of the most effective chairmen of his era. Strongly committed to government economy, he routinely sought to cut spending programs—except for farm subsidies, which he invariably defended. He was easily aroused, and he rarely lost a legislative fight, either in the House or in confrontation with the Senate. An autocrat who exercised total dominance over his committee and its members, Cannon epitomized a leadership style that had begun to fade by the early 1960s and would virtually vanish with the passage of committee-reform legislation in the 1970s.

Proponents of new and enlarged spending programs frequently tried to circumvent Cannon and his committee. One device, known as "backdoor spending," flourished in the 1950s and early 1960s. It allowed committees to bypass the appropriations process by providing for the financing of a program in the original authorization bill. Agencies were au-

CLARENCE CANNON.   LIBRARY OF CONGRESS

thorized simply to borrow funds from the Treasury to carry out a particular program. Cannon relentlessly opposed this and any other practice that undermined his committee. In 1961, he waited until Congress was within hours of year-end adjournment to introduce a supplemental appropriations bill that included a provision permanently outlawing backdoor spending. The House passed the measure and adjourned, leaving angry senators no choice but to approve the bill without change or risk closing down essential government services. Backdoor spending fell from a high of $19 billion in 1961 to less than $500 million in 1962.

In 1962 final action on appropriations bills was held up for months as Cannon and Senate Appropriations Committee chairman Carl Hayden, Democrat of Arizona, engaged in an acrimonious dispute that exposed long-festering resentment between the houses over their respective roles in the appropriations process. Cannon, challenging the Senate's traditional practice of hosting and chairing all House-Senate conferences on appropriations, demanded that half the meetings be held in the House wing of the Capitol. Hayden said he would agree, provided the House renounce its claimed right to originate all appropriations measures. Cannon rejected that idea but accepted Hayden's offer to hold future conferences near the center of the Capitol. Cannon added, however, a new demand—that the conference chairmanship rotate between the two houses. Hayden refused. Only pressure of adjournment and the intercession of House and Senate leaders brought the two chairmen to a negotiated settlement. Cannon was the clear winner: future conferences would take place midway between the House and Senate; House conferees would have opportunities to chair some of the meetings; and the House would retain its right to initiate all spending bills.

BIBLIOGRAPHY

Berman, Daniel M. *In Congress Assembled.* 1964. Pp. 337–352.
Fenno, Richard F., Jr. *Congressmen in Committees.* 1973. Pp. 123–127.
MacNeil, Neil. *Forge of Democracy.* 1963. Pp. 393–400.

DONALD C. BACON

CANNON, JOSEPH G. (1836–1926), Republican representative from Illinois, chairman of the House Committee on Appropriations (1895–1903), and Speaker of the House of Representatives (1903–1911). Joseph Gurney Cannon was one of the most powerful and colorful representatives to serve in the House of Representatives. Born in North Carolina of Quaker parents, his family moved to Indiana in 1840. He studied law at the Cincinnati Law School and began practice in Terre Haute, Indiana. In 1858, he moved to Tuscola, Illinois, just south of Champaign-Urbana, where he was immediately involved in Republican Party politics. He met Abraham Lincoln in 1860 at the Republican State Convention in Decatur.

Cannon's political career began in 1861 with his service as Illinois state's attorney, a position he held until 1868. The 1870 Census resulted in an increase in the number of representatives for Illinois from nine to fourteen. In 1872, Cannon was elected to the House for the first time, beginning an extraordinary career that continued, with two interruptions, for fifty years.

During his initial period of House service (1873–1891), Cannon served at different times on the Committee on Expenditures in the Post Office Department, the Committee on Appropriations,

JOSEPH G. CANNON. LIBRARY OF CONGRESS

and the Committee on Rules. In the 51st Congress, Cannon was a candidate for Speaker but was defeated by Thomas B. Reed (R-Maine). Accepting his loss, Cannon nevertheless kept the speakership as his ultimate goal. He worked closely with Reed in the 51st Congress and observed the invocation of the famed Reed Rules to thwart the dilatory tactics of the Democrats. The 1890 midterm elections resulted in a net loss of eighty-five Republican House seats, which nearly halved the party's numbers. Cannon was among those defeated.

In 1892, Cannon was once again elected to the House, serving in the minority. When the Republicans recaptured the House in 1894, nearly doubling their number of seats, Cannon became chairman of the House Committee on Appropriations and served on the Committee on Rules. Once again Reed was Speaker. In 1896, William McKinley (R-Ohio), who had served in the House with Reed and Cannon, was elected president.

When Reed retired in 1898, House Republicans disregarded Cannon's ambition and selected David B. Henderson of Iowa as Speaker. After compiling a rather lackluster record, Henderson unexpectedly retired in 1902. Cannon, finally given his chance, was elected Speaker in the 58th Congress and served through the 61st Congress.

Cannon's speakership earned him the nickname "Czar." His long experience in parliamentary maneuvering and service on major committees helped him to utilize to the fullest the awesome authority of his post. During this time, the Speaker chaired the House Committee on Rules and was therefore in a position to determine the scheduling of major legislation for floor debate along with the conditions under which debate would take place. He also had the power to appoint committees, including their chairmen, and to recognize members for purposes of debate. In her classic late-nineteenth-century study of the speakership, Mary Parker Follett observed that "he serves not as the creature of his party, he is its leader." "Czar" Cannon accepted this characterization and sought to impose strong party discipline during his entire tenure.

Cannon was not the author of major legislation. He seemingly preferred to serve in leadership positions and to build majorities for and against the legislative proposals of others. Important legislation was enacted during Cannon's tenure as Speaker, including major military support bills, immigration restrictions, employers' liability regulation, regulation of interstate commerce, food and drug controls, meat inspection, and currency regulation. But the issue of most interest to Cannon was the protective tariff, which was a matter of continuing concern to presidents and Congresses during this period and was of particular concern to the Republican party. For his part, Cannon was determined to use his position as party leader to get his way on this important issue.

Cannon competed with President Theodore Roosevelt, a rising number of insurgent Republicans, and the Democrats in seeking to control the House. In preserving his authority, Cannon relied heavily on his powers to reward his friends and punish his enemies. In 1909, the Payne-Aldrich Tariff became a defining issue of Cannon's power. Insurgents resisted both the proposal and Cannon's arbitrary use of power in building majority support for it. The Speaker, however, got his way.

In March 1910, insurgent Republicans fought back by joining the Democrats to support a change in the House Rules to alter the makeup of the House Committee on Rules, including the removal

"THE HOUSE IN SESSION (ACCORDING TO THE MINORITY POINT OF VIEW)!" The House depicted as an unruly place where the majority, portrayed as clones of despotic Speaker Joseph G. Cannon, has no ear for the minority. Clifford K. Berryman, *Washington Evening Star*, 16 April 1908.

U.S. SENATE COLLECTION, CENTER FOR LEGISLATIVE ARCHIVES

of the Speaker as its chairman. In 1910, the Democrats won a majority in the House and James R. Mann (R-Ill.) was elected minority leader. Cannon was defeated for reelection in 1912, when Woodrow Wilson won the White House and the Democrats gained control of the House by a more than two-to-one majority.

In 1914, Cannon returned to the House for the third and last time. He was then seventy-eight years old. He was reelected to three more Congresses before finally retiring in 1923 at eighty-seven. He died 12 November 1926. In the foreword to L. White Busbey's biography, Cannon modestly wrote, "I am one of the great army of mediocrity which constitutes the majority. . . . All my experiences have been as an average man." Few who knew him would agree with that statement.

BIBLIOGRAPHY

Bolles, Blair. *Tyrant from Illinois: Uncle Joe Cannon's Experiment with Personal Power.* 1951.
Brown, George Rothwell. *The Leadership of Congress.* 1922.
Busbey, L. White. *Uncle Joe Cannon: The Story of a Pioneer American.* 1927.
Peters, Ronald W., Jr. *The American Speakership: The Office in Historical Perspective.* 1990.

CHARLES O. JONES

CANNON REVOLT. The so-called Cannon Revolt was a controversy of 1910 in the House of Representatives through which the power of the Speaker of the House—and, consequently, of party leadership in Congress—was redefined. It is named for Joseph G. Cannon (R-Ill.), who served as Speaker from 1903 to 1911 (the 58th through 61st Congresses).

The status and power of the Speaker of the House were then quite substantial, having been enhanced by Thomas B. Reed (R-Maine), Speaker from 1889 to 1891 and 1895 to 1899. In addition to the standard parliamentary authority of applying the rules of debate and recognizing members on the floor, the Speaker chaired the Committee on Rules and appointed committees and their chairs.

Cannon served as Speaker during a period in which the majority Republicans were seriously divided between the progressive and "stalwart" wings of the party. He was a stalwart, and he used all of his power to thwart the progressives, or "insurgents." In particular, he frustrated the policy goals of the progressives through his appointing power and his scheduling power as chairman of the Rules Committee.

The Committee on Rules had just five members—"three very distinguished Republicans and two ornamental Democrats," as one Democrat sarcastically described the group (*Congressional Record*, 61st Cong., 2d sess., 17 March 1910, p. 3294). Cannon appointed his stalwart friends to the committee (John Dalzell, R-Pa.; Charles H. Grosvenor, R-Ohio; James S. Sherman, R-N.Y.; and Walter I. Smith, R-Iowa, served at various times), and together they controlled the flow of important legislation to the floor, as well as the manner in which it would be debated there.

Speaker Cannon used his power to appoint committees to further his policy interests. He followed the seniority principle in appointing chairmen when it suited his purposes; otherwise he violated it. On several occasions he chose as chairman a member who had not previously served on the committee. For example, Cannon appointed Jesse Overstreet (R-Ind.) as chairman of the Committee on Post Offices and Post Roads in 1903 and James

WHO'LL BELL THE CAT?

CANNON REVOLT. Cartoon depicting insurgent Republicans as mice preparing to bell a smug cat, Speaker Joseph G. Cannon. Shortly before the publication of the cartoon, Cannon had publicly taunted his opponents and defied them to attack his power. The following spring, House Democrats and insurgent Republicans succeeded in stripping Cannon of much of his power. Clifford K. Berryman, *Washington Evening Star*, 3 December 1909.

U.S. SENATE COLLECTION, CENTER FOR LEGISLATIVE ARCHIVES

A. Tawney (R-Minn.) as chairman of the Committee on Appropriations in 1905. Cannon also punished insurgents by changing their committee assignments (even while they were serving as chairmen) and placing more junior members ahead of them (sometimes to prevent their serving as chairmen). In the 61st Congress, he appointed the committees on Rules and Ways and Means on the second day of the first (and special) session but delayed most other appointments for nearly five months, until the Payne-Aldrich tariff (favored by stalwarts) had cleared the House-Senate conference on the last day of the session.

"Cannonism," the arbitrary exercise of power to thwart the progressive program, became an issue in the 1908 elections. The insurgents won a sufficient number of seats to hold the balance of power in the 61st Congress. Twelve of them refused to vote for Cannon as Speaker at the start of the special session in 1909—not enough to defeat him but a

sufficient number to provide a warning. A coalition of Progressive Republicans and Democrats voted against adopting the rules of the previous Congress, but a subsequent motion to enlarge the Committee on Rules, remove the Speaker as chairman, and take away his power to appoint committees (except for Ways and Means) was defeated by a coalition of regular Republicans and twenty-three Democrats. One of these Democrats, John J. Fitzgerald (N.Y.), then introduced other, milder reforms (notably a consent calendar and motion of recommittal for use by the minority), which were passed.

The stage was set for a confrontation between Speaker Cannon and the insurgents when Congress met in its second session, beginning 9 December 1909. It was only a question of time and opportunity. On 16 March 1910, Cannon was overruled by the House on a procedural point. Emboldened by this action, one of the insurgents, George W. Norris (R-Nebr.), introduced a resolution on 17 March to enlarge the Committee on Rules, to require its members to be selected by groups of state delegations, and to remove the Speaker as chairman. Norris argued that the resolution was privileged under the constitutional guarantee that "each House may determine the rules of its proceedings."

A classic debate ensued, one that defined differing interpretations of the role of political parties in Congress. It continued for twenty-six hours. The Cannon forces argued for a party-responsibility position: to wit, that a majority within the party had selected its leaders, that those leaders in turn were authorized to act for the party, and that those who rejected party leadership should be punished. This was what Speaker Cannon himself believed; as he said, "Results cannot be had except by a majority, and in the House of Representatives a majority, being responsible, should have full power and should exercise that power" (*Congressional Record*, 61st Cong., 2d sess., 19 March 1910, p. 3436).

The insurgents argued that party leaders must always be attentive to changes and that their power was not absolute. John M. Nelson (R-Wis.) explained, "We are no less Republicans because we would be free Members of Congress. We do not need to be kept on leading strings" (*Congressional Record*, 61st Cong., 2d sess., 17 March 1910, p. 3304).

On 19 March 1910, Cannon ruled that "the [Norris] resolution is not in order." Norris appealed the decision and Cannon was overruled, with 34 insurgents joining 148 Democrats in voting against the Speaker. An amended version of Norris's resolution then passed the House, with 43 Republicans voting with 150 Democrats in support of the changes. Speaker Cannon then invited a resolution to declare the speakership vacant and to call for an election. Such a resolution was introduced but defeated.

In 1910, the Democrats won a majority in the House of Representatives. When the new Congress met, another significant change was made to limit the Speaker's authority: his power to appoint committees was taken away. The Democrats gave this power to their members on the Committee on Ways and Means (the selections to be approved by the caucus). The Republicans created a special committee for this purpose.

The Cannon revolt produced lasting changes in the power exercised by party leaders in the House of Representatives. Following these reforms, committee chairmen came to possess significant power—power that was itself the subject of reform during the 1970s. The debate of 17–19 March 1910 remains one of the most important in congressional history in defining the functions of congressional party leaders.

BIBLIOGRAPHY

Atkinson, Charles R. *The Committee on Rules and the Overthrow of Cannon.* 1911.

Brown, George R. *The Leadership of Congress.* 1922.

Hechler, Kenneth W. *Insurgency: Personalities and Politics of the Taft Era.* 1964.

Jones, Charles O. "Joseph G. Cannon and Howard W. Smith: An Essay on the Limits of Leadership in the House of Representatives." *Journal of Politics* 30 (1968): 617–646.

CHARLES O. JONES

CAPITALS OF THE UNITED STATES.

Since 1774, when it first convened at Philadelphia, Congress has met in nine locations. While they are now collectively referred to as capitals, prior to 1789 the word *capital* was used almost exclusively to refer to a seat of state government. Referring to Washington, D.C., as the capital did not gain wide acceptance until well into the nineteenth century. Until then, "meeting place of Congress," "residence of Congress," and "seat of federal government" were used, with the last being the preferred term after 1788.

The Continental and Confederation Congresses met in Philadelphia from 1774 to 1783, with excursions to Baltimore (20 December 1776 to 4 March 1777), Lancaster (27 September), and York (30 September to 27 June 1778) under the threat of British troops; and to Princeton (30 June to 4 November 1783) to assert federal power and influence when Pennsylvania refused to meet federal demands during a Continental Army meeting at Philadelphia. Congress informed the states that it would determine its permanent postwar residence in October 1783. By then a dozen sites had been proposed. On 7 October 1783, Elbridge Gerry of Massachusetts moved that Congress establish the federal town either on the Delaware River near Trenton, New Jersey, or on the Potomac River near Georgetown, Maryland. When the Trenton site won, southern congressmen complained bitterly, pointing out that the durability of the Union was at stake. As a compromise Gerry proposed a second federal town near Georgetown, with Congress alternating between them every six months. Congress accepted the compromise and agreed to alternate between Annapolis and Trenton until the two federal towns were built. While the decision subjected Congress to ridicule, especially from the middle states, it was considered true to republican principles because it acted to prevent the centralization of power, particularly by the executive wing of the government. Furthermore, it served to hold the Union together at a critical time.

Congress sat at Annapolis from 26 November 1783 until 3 June 1784 and at Trenton from 1 November to 24 December 1784. Just before leaving Trenton, it resolved to have only one federal town with an area between four and nine square miles and appointed a commission to oversee construction at a site near Trenton. This ordinance was never implemented because of successful southern efforts in 1785, privately backed by George Washington, to block the $100,000 appropriation. In spite of a bitter ten-week fight that threatened implementation of the new Constitution, Congress decided on 13 September 1788 to convene the First Federal Congress at New York, which began meeting in March 1789. Congress had begun meeting at New York on 11 January 1785 and continued to meet there until 12 August 1790, the end of its second session as a federal Congress.

During the first session of the First Federal Congress, in September 1789, members fought over a location for the seat of government. Southerners favored a Potomac site and threatened a dissolution of the Union unless the North agreed. They lost out to the Susquehanna River, a location backed by a coalition of New England and middle states, but

CAPITOL BUILDINGS OF THE UNITED STATES. From *Harper's Weekly*, 1900.

ELMER HOLMES BOBST LIBRARY, FALES LIBRARY, NEW YORK UNIVERSITY

last-minute efforts by James Madison blocked a final decision.

In the spring of 1790 Congress concentrated on Alexander Hamilton's plan for establishing public credit. Southern opposition to the proposal that the federal government assume the Revolutionary War debts of the states and northern opposition to a Potomac capital were compromised in an arrangement crafted by Hamilton, Thomas Jefferson, and Madison. Hamilton agreed to prevent New Englanders and New Yorkers from interfering with a bargain previously worked out between the South and Pennsylvania under which Congress would reside at Philadelphia for ten years and then move to the Potomac River site. Once such a bill was signed by the president, Madison agreed to produce the necessary votes for the assumption of state debts.

President George Washington signed the Act for Establishing the Temporary and Permanent Seat of Government of the United States on 16 July 1790. It provided that the permanent capital be located on the Potomac River somewhere between its eastern branch, just below Georgetown, and Conococheague Creek at Williamsport, Maryland. President Washington was given complete control over the development of the capital. Congress appropriated no funds and created a presidential commission, the first in U.S. history, to oversee the city's development. Washington chose the specific site himself. It surrounded Georgetown, an important Potomac River port. When the First Federal Congress convened at Philadelphia for its third session on 6 December 1790 he asked it to pass a supplemental act that would allow for the inclusion of Alexandria, Virginia, his hometown south of the limit set by the original act. Although shocked, congressmen dared not attack him publicly. Instead they used the bill as leverage to secure his signature on the controversial bill creating the first Bank of the United States.

The site Washington chose for the district was at the exact north-south center of the United States at the time. While he owned twelve hundred acres within its boundaries, Washington's primary motive was not to make money. He believed the site to be the best location for the survival both of the sectionally divided Union and of his name in the nation's history. At the same time, the site choice represented the capstone of a lifetime devoted to the political and economic promotion of the Potomac and Ohio rivers, and Washington did not hide the fact that the choice could raise the value of the approximately forty thousand acres of land he owned along these rivers, particularly his Mount Vernon plantation.

In September 1791 the presidential commission named the federal city Washington and the district around it, amounting to one hundred square miles, the Territory of Columbia. Washington minutely managed the city's development during the remainder of his presidency, wanting to deny Congress any excuse not to move there in 1800.

Congress convened at Washington on 17 November 1800 and, except for a ceremonial occasion on the bicentennial of the signing of the Constitution, has met there ever since. Opponents of the location attempted to move Congress to Baltimore or Trenton in 1804 and to Philadelphia in 1808. Heavier pressure for a removal in the wake of the British attack on the city in 1814 dwindled away as President Madison opposed it. The question did not arise again in Congress for half a century. But as the nation expanded westward there was talk of relocating to a site in the Ohio River valley, particularly Cincinnati. The late 1860s saw a flood of petitions in favor of a Mississippi River site, most of them specifying St. Louis. This campaign almost succeeded in 1870. But it was dealt a deathblow by President Ulysses S. Grant's declaration that, because of the importance of the 1790 decision, he would veto any such bill unless it received a two-thirds majority in Congress. The 1870 discussion settled the question: Washington would be, as the bill establishing it stated, "the Permanent Seat of the Government of the United States."

[See also Capitol, The; District of Columbia.]

BIBLIOGRAPHY

Bowling, Kenneth R. "A Place to Which Tribute Is Brought." *Prologue* 8 (1976): 129–139.

Bowling, Kenneth R. *The Creation of Washington, D.C.: The Idea and Location of the American Capital.* 1991.

Bowling, Kenneth R. "Neither in a Wigwam nor the Wilderness." *Prologue* 20 (1988): 163–179.

Fortenbaugh, Robert. *The Nine Capitals of the United States.* 1948.

KENNETH R. BOWLING

CAPITOL, THE. [*This entry includes four articles:*

    History of the Capitol
    Art in the Capitol
    Capitol Grounds
    Dome and Great Rotunda
See also Architect of the Capitol; Chambers.]

History of the Capitol

As the seat of the legislative branch of the federal government, the U.S. Capitol is one of the most widely recognized buildings in the world. It is part office building and part museum, part forum and part stage, as well as a forceful symbol of the country, its people, and its government.

Most basically, the Capitol is a building covering an area of 175,170 square feet, 751 feet long and 350 feet wide. It contains more than 540 rooms, 650 windows, and approximately 850 doorways. Many architects have played roles in designing the Capitol, which was constructed in ten major stages beginning in 1793. In the course of its fascinating and occasionally bewildering history, the Capitol has been built, burned, rebuilt, extended, restored, domed, and redomed.

The authority to construct a capitol for the federal government in the City of Washington was provided by the Residence Act of 1790. Passed after a hard-fought battle, the act was part of a compromise: southerners in Congress agreed to federal assumption of state Revolutionary War debts in exchange for a capital located on the Potomac. The act directed President George Washington to appoint three commissioners to acquire land and "to erect thereon within 10 years good and suitable buildings." The commissioners in turn hired Pierre Charles L'Enfant, a talented French engineer who had served in Washington's army during the Revolution. L'Enfant was given the task of laying out the future capital and selecting the sites for the president's house and the Capitol; he was also expected to design these two key structures. His design for the city is often cited as one of the world's most beautiful, with broad diagonal avenues superimposed on a street grid dotted with numerous parks and public gardens. A prominent elevated site, known locally as Jenkins' Hill, was selected for the Capitol because, in L'Enfant's words, it was "a pedestal waiting for a monument." To accentuate the site's prominence L'Enfant plotted major avenues converging on it and began the principal public garden, the Mall, at its foot. On his map L'Enfant labeled the site "Congress House." Secretary of State Thomas Jefferson carefully crossed that out and wrote the word "Capitol," from the Latin *capitulum*, literally a temple on a hill but more generally associated with the great national temple of ancient Rome dedicated to Jupiter Optimum Maximus. The change in name was indicative of the Washington administration's political and architectural aspirations for the capital city.

The Early Capitol. Despite his brilliant city plan, L'Enfant found himself at odds with the three commissioners in charge of establishing the federal capital. He felt responsible only to the president and refused to follow any but Washington's orders. In the inevitable series of conflicts that resulted from L'Enfant's insubordination, perhaps his most brazen act was committed in November 1791, when he ordered the destruction of Daniel Carroll's house, then under construction, because it lay in the path of a future avenue. He had also refused to produce the plans for the Capitol and the president's house, claiming he carried them in his head. L'Enfant's dismissal in 1792 left the commissioners

THE HOUSE AND SENATE WINGS. Completed before the construction of the central portion.   LIBRARY OF CONGRESS

THE CAPITOL. The first known photograph, attributed to John Plumbe, Jr., c. 1846.

without a design for the Capitol, but, on Jefferson's advice, they decided to advertise for one. Newspapers described the commissioners' intention to award $500 and a city lot to the architect who "shall produce to them the most approved PLAN." This competition drew at least sixteen entries, all of which were deemed unsuitable, if not architecturally absurd.

Still without a plan in the fall of 1792, the commissioners permitted an amateur architect from the British West Indies named William Thornton to submit a design. Although trained in Scotland as a physician, which profession he rarely practiced, Thornton had displayed a talent for architectural composition and drafting. His 1789 design for Library Hall in Philadelphia had won the first architectural competition staged in America. Upon seeing Thornton's design for the Capitol, Washing-

ton recommended it to the commissioners for its "grandeur, simplicity and convenience." Thornton took the prize on 5 April 1793.

The winning design for the Capitol consisted of a domed center section inspired by the Pantheon, a second-century Roman temple much admired by Secretary of State Jefferson. Flanking this section were identical wings, one for the House of Representatives and one for the Senate. The elevation was designed with Corinthian pilasters standing on rusticated piers and supporting a full entablature with a balustrade above to mask a low pitched roof. A seven-bay portico standing on a one-story arcade was placed in front of the dome. Part of the composition, notably the wings, was in the conservative style of the Palladian-Georgian architectural style current in England in the 1720s and 1730s. The domed center building, however, with its direct

EXTENSIONS AND NEW DOME OF THE CAPITOL. The building in various stages of construction, 1856 and 1857. *This page, top,* view of west front, showing temporary workshops; *bottom,* view from Pennsylvania Avenue. *Facing page, top,* beginnings of the construction of the cast-iron dome; *bottom,* the east front, with the dome's iron columns in place.

LIBRARY OF CONGRESS AND OFFICE OF THE ARCHITECT OF THE CAPITOL

Roman precedent, was an early and important development in the emerging Neoclassical style.

Workers began digging the Capitol's foundation on 1 August 1793. The cornerstone was laid by President Washington on 18 September 1793, in a Masonic ceremony highlighted by orations and salutes and concluding with "every abundance of other recreation." Work on the foundations proceeded at an unusually slow pace, however, because of the scarcity of workers and materials. The sale of city lots, which was intended to fund construction of the Capitol and president's house, fell far short of expectation. With funds low and only part of the foundation complete, the commissioners decided in 1796 to concentrate all construction work on the north wing of the Capitol. When the government moved to its permanent home in Washington in November 1800, the House of Representatives, the Senate, the Supreme Court, the Library of Congress, and the district courts, along with their sundry clerks, took up quarters in the north wing, which had been hurriedly and badly finished. During this first phase of construction three architects had been hired to build the Capitol from Thornton's plan. Stephen Hallet and George Hadfield were dismissed because of the changes they wanted to impose on the accepted design. James Hoban, better known as the architect of the president's house, brought the north wing to completion.

In the middle of President Jefferson's first term, Congress passed a $50,000 appropriation to continue construction of the Capitol. The former board of commissioners was replaced by a single superintendent, and Benjamin Henry Latrobe was appointed surveyor of public buildings, with the principal responsibility of constructing the Capitol's south wing. After studying Thornton's plan, Latrobe concluded that a totally new interior design was needed. The original plan for the south wing contained but one room, the Hall of the House of Representatives. Latrobe's alternative provided for committee rooms and offices on the ground floor with the Hall of the House above. Jefferson recognized the advantages of Latrobe's plan and approved the change. Construction began in 1804, and in October 1807 the House of Representatives took up quarters in its splendid hall, complete with carved Corinthian columns, a ceiling with one hundred skylights, rich drapery, central heating, and impressive sculptural decoration.

While work on the south wing was under way, Latrobe was asked to make repairs to the north wing, which had already reached an advanced state of decay because of inferior materials and workmanship. Typically, Latrobe studied the problem and developed a completely new interior arrangement that could be built using masonry vaults. He had built the south wing by using vaults, the most permanent and fireproof construction method then known, and intended the repairs in the north wing to be as solid. Again Jefferson approved Latrobe's proposed alterations, but he directed that construction be limited to the eastern half of the wing. The Senate chamber would be raised to the main level and a room designed specifically for the Supreme Court would be built below. Thus the Senate, which had been located on the ground level, would be raised to the same level as the House of Representatives. The rebuilding of the north wing was begun in 1808, but tragedy soon struck. John Lenthall, the clerk of the works, prematurely removed the wooden centering on which the vaulted ceiling of the Supreme Court chamber was built. The vaults collapsed, and Lenthall was killed instantly. Although Latrobe's reputation suffered greatly because of Lenthall's death, he carried on the work with resolve. He rebuilt the fallen vault in a remarkable way, imposing little weight on the existing walls. In a similar fashion he rebuilt the vestibule leading to the Court chamber using sandstone columns to carry the weight of the vaulted ceiling. The capitals of these columns incorporated a thoroughly American design element: ears of corn.

When the Senate occupied its rebuilt chamber in 1811, little more reconstruction work could be done because funding was being diverted to prepare America's defense for a second war with Great Britain. Latrobe left Washington in 1813; returning two years later, he described the Capitol as a "most magnificent ruin." It had been nearly destroyed by British troops under the command of Sir George Cockburn, who set fire to the public buildings in Washington on 24 August 1814. Only a sudden rainstorm had prevented the Capitol's total destruction.

The Capitol had been under construction for twenty-two years when Latrobe was rehired to restore the north and south wings. In Congress there was a serious but ultimately unsuccessful movement to relocate the capital. This effort failed when Congress authorized President James Madison to borrow $500,000 to repair Washington's public buildings.

The restoration of the Capitol began with the demolition of the ruined colonnades in the House chamber; the vaults of the Supreme Court and Senate chamber were also removed. The blackened exterior sandstone walls were patched and scrubbed. Little work was required on the ground floor of the south wing because of the solidity of its construction. The domed vestibule to the Hall of the House and the Senate lobby, famous for its corncob capitals, also escaped injury. Changes to the floor plan were made to enlarge the Senate chamber, while the Hall of the House was redesigned into a half-domed semicircle much like the amphitheaters of ancient Greece and Rome. A beautiful marble from the upper Potomac was used for the columns that Latrobe designed for these two principal chambers. The Corinthian columns in the House chamber were modeled after the Choragic Monument of Lysicrates in Athens, while the Ionic order of the Erechtheion, also in Athens, was used in the Senate chamber.

Although Latrobe is today considered one of the giants of American architectural history, in his own day he was unpopular with those accustomed to speedy, economical construction. Latrobe's temper grew short with officials placed over him who could not appreciate the splendor and solidity of his restored Capitol. After he physically attacked the commissioner of public buildings, a lame veteran of the Revolutionary War, in the presence of President James Monroe, Latrobe's employment with the government came to an abrupt close.

Charles Bulfinch, a well-respected architect from Boston, was chosen to replace Latrobe at the Capitol. He arrived in Washington in January 1818 and continued the work of his predecessor in restoring the north and south wings. On 24 August 1818, the fourth anniversary of the British invasion, workers set the cornerstone for the long-delayed center building that would at last connect the two wings. Designs for this part of the Capitol had been handed down by Thornton and Latrobe, but Bulfinch created his own within the limits imposed by the existing work. For the west portico facing the Mall, Bulfinch recalled his design for the Massachusetts State House of 1795–1797. A basement story for committee rooms and offices was cleverly hidden by an earthen terrace that also created courtyards along the western elevation. These courtyards were convenient spots in which privies and other necessary evils could be kept out of public view. Bulfinch also built the long-awaited dome, the Capitol's most symbolically important feature. On orders from President Monroe and his cabinet, who wished the building to be as prominent as possible, Bulfinch was obliged to raise the outer wooden dome higher than his own taste or classical proportion would

have allowed. The last part of the Capitol, the east portico, was finished in 1826. In the next three years Bulfinch completed the remaining details, landscaped the grounds, and brought the Capitol to a finish after thirty-six years of construction.

For the next twenty years the Capitol remained virtually unchanged. Running water, piped from a nearby spring, was brought to the building in 1832. Gas lighting replaced whale-oil lamps in the 1840s. An iron mast one hundred feet tall was erected above the wooden dome in 1847 to hold a 30,000-candlepower gaslight, the light from which could be seen, it was claimed, from Baltimore, nearly forty miles away. After a few months, however, the lantern was removed as a precaution against fire. Desks and chairs were crowded into the House and Senate chambers as lands acquired by the Louisiana Purchase and from the Mexican War were organized into territories that were soon admitted to the Union as states. The nation was rapidly outgrowing its Capitol, and by 1850 it became necessary to enlarge the building.

Extension and New Dome. In the spring of 1850, the Senate Committee on Public Buildings and Grounds reviewed a scheme prepared by Washington architect Robert Mills for an enlargement of the Capitol. Unsatisfied, the committee later announced in newspapers a competition that would award $500 for the best design. It reserved the right to divide the prize any way it saw fit (the money was eventually split five ways). When the competition was announced, Congress passed a $100,000 appropriation to enlarge the Capitol and directed President Millard Fillmore to select the manner in which the addition would be made and to name the architect who would design it. The two houses of Congress held differing opinions on the question of enlargement: the Senate wanted two wings added to the Capitol, while the House wanted one large addition placed on the building's east front. Unable to agree, Congress left the question to the president to decide. While the Senate-sponsored competition failed to produce a viable design, it drew into the field several prominent architects from whom the president would eventually choose. On 11 June 1851 Fillmore appointed Thomas U. Walter of Philadelphia as architect of the Capitol extension, having been impressed by Walter's design for two wings placed at right angles to the Capitol and connected to it by narrow corridors. Walter's plan changed the existing structure as little as possible while almost tripling the size of the Capitol.

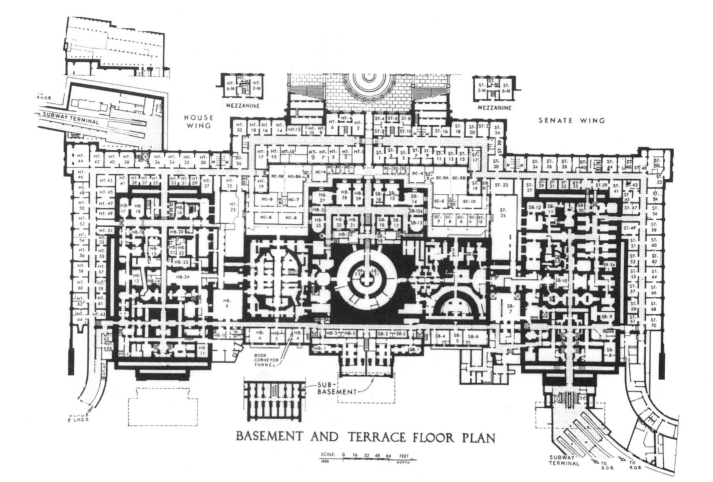

BASEMENT AND TERRACE FLOOR PLAN

SCALE: 0 16 32 48 64 FEET
1993   NORTH

HOUSE SIDE

BASEMENT

HB–1. House Sergeant at Arms.
HB–1A. Clerk of the House.
HB–4. Library of Congress station.
HB–5, 6. General Counsel of the House.
HB–9, 10. House Restaurant. Coffee shop.
HB–13, 13B. Minority Clerk.
HB–15. Architect of the Capitol. House engineers.
HB–16, 17, 18. Committee on Appropriations.
HB–19. Architect of the Capitol. Custodial service.
HB–21, 22, 23, 24. House Restaurant. Kitchen.
HB–25. House Chaplain.
HB–26, 27, 28, 29, 31, 32, 32A, 33. Architect of the Capitol.

TERRACE

HT–1. Committee on House Administration
HT–2, 2M, 4, 4M, 6, 6M. Committee on Standards of Official Conduct.
HT–3, 5, 7. Architect of the Capitol. Curator.
HT–8, 10. Doorkeeper of the House. Pages.
HT–9, 13, 15, 17. Clerk of the House. Legislative Operations.

HT–12, 14, 16, 18. Architect of Capitol. Flag office.
HT–20, 23, 25, 26, 49, 62. Architect of the Capitol. Mechanical rooms.
HT–30, 32, 34, 36. Architect of the Capitol. Sheetmetal shop.
HT–33. Architect of the Capitol. Carpenter's key shop.
HT–35, 37, 39. Architect of the Capitol. Elevator shop.
HT–38, 40, 41. Architect of the Capitol. Electrical shop.
HT–42, 44. Architect of the Capitol.
HT–43. Architect of the Capitol. Paint shop.
HT–45, 47. Architect of the Capitol. Laborers' shop.
HT–46. Architect of the Capitol. Plumbers' shop.
HT–50, 52. Doorkeeper of the House. Document Room.
HT–53, 55, 57. House television control.
HT–54. Non-Legislative and Financial Services.
HT–58, 59, 60, 61. Clerk of the House. Official Reporters of Debates.
HT–65, 66, 67. Committee on Appropriations.

COURTYARD

HC–1, 2, 3. Director of Non-Legislative and Financial Services.
HC–5. Foyer.

HC–5A, 5B. Conference / Hearing room.
HC–5C. Kitchen.

SENATE SIDE

BASEMENT

SB–7. Senate restaurant. Kitchen.
SB–8. Senate Sergeant at Arms. Recording studio.
SB–9. Senate Sergeant at Arms.
SB–10. Senate Restaurant. Carry-Out.
SB–11, 12. Architect of the Capitol. Senate engineers.
SB–13, 13A, 14, 15, 16, 17, 18, 19, 21. Architect of the Capitol.
SB–20. Secretary of the Senate.
SB–22. Architect of the Capitol. Masonry shop.
SB–23. Senate Sergeant at Arms. Custodial service.
SB–36. Secretary of the Senate. Newspaper room.

TERRACE

ST–1, 3, 5, 7, 9, 11, 17, 18, 48. Capitol Police.
ST–13. Senate Sergeant at Arms. Special Services.
ST–15. Capitol Guide Service.
ST–16. Architect of the Capitol. Insulation shop.

ST–19, 23, 24, 25, 27, 28, 30, 49, 52, 59, 61, 68. Architect of the Capitol. Mechanical rooms.
ST–20, 60, 62. Senate Sergeant at Arms. Custodial service.
ST–21. Hallway.
ST–34, 36, 38. Senate Sergeant at Arms. Senate television control.
ST–41. 44. Secretary of the Senate. Printing Services.
ST–43, 45, 70. Senate Sergeant at Arms.
ST–47. Senate Sergeant at Arms. Human Resources.
ST–50. Democratic Policy Committee.
ST–51, 52, 64, 66. Architect of the Capitol, Paint shop.
ST–54. Secretary of the Senate. Captioning services.
ST–56, 58. Secretary of the Senate. Daily Digest.
ST–57. Republican Policy Committee.
ST–71, 73. Senate Sergeant at Arms. Recording studio (old Senate subway tunnel).

COURTYARD

SC–5. Foyer.
SC–5A, 5B. Conference / Hearing room.
SC–5C. Kitchen.

SOURCE. This page and following four pages: U.S. Congress. Joint Committee on Printing. Congressional Directory, 1993–1994.

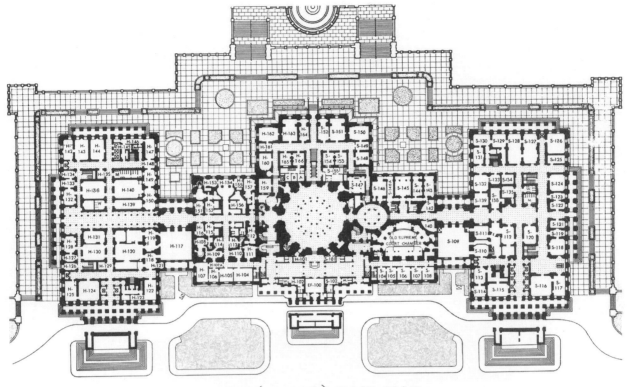

FIRST (GROUND) FLOOR PLAN

SCALE: 0 16 32 48 64 FEET
1993   NORTH

HOUSE SIDE

Hall of Columns.
Hall of Capitols.
Great Experiment Hall.
Cox Corridor.
H–101. House Post Office.
H–102, 104, 105. Clerk of the
House.
H–106, 107, 107A, 108, 109, 115,
116. Majority Whip.
H–110, 113, 114, 156. Chief
Deputy Whips.
H–111, 112. General Counsel of
the House.
H–117. House Restaurant [Ernest
Petinaud Room].
H–118, 119, 121. House
Restaurant.
H–120. House Restaurant [Charles
E. Bennett Room].
H–122, 123. Private dining room
(Speaker).
H–123A. House Restaurant.
Catering Office.
H–124, 125. Sergeant at Arms.
H–126. Parliamentarian.
H–127, 128. Speaker of the House.

H–129. Wright Patman
Congressional Federal Credit
Union.
H–130, 131. Members' private
dining rooms.
H–132, 133, 134. Majority Leader.
H–135, 144. Subcommittee on
Defense (Appropriations).
H–136. Committee on Ways and
Means.
H–139. Committee on Foreign
Affairs.
H–140. Committee on
Appropriations [George Mahon
Room].
H–142, 143. Subcommittee on
HUD—Independent Agencies
(Appropriations).
H–145, 146, 147, 148, 149, 150.
Majority Leader.
H–151. Clerk of House.
H–152. Committee on Rules.
H–153, 154, 155. Doorkeeper of
the House.
H–157. Committee on Ways and
Means.

H–159, 160, 161, 162, 165, 166,
166A, 166B, 166C. Attending
Physician.
H–163, 164. Subcommittee on
Treasury, Postal Service, and
General Government
(Appropriations).

SENATE SIDE

BRUMIDI CORRIDORS.

S–101. Railroad Ticket Office.
S–102. Capitol Guide Service.
S–109, 110, 111, 112, 113, 114,
115. Senate Restaurant.
S–113A. Senate Restaurant.
Catering Office.
S–116, 117. Committee on Foreign
Relations.
S–118, 119, 121. Democratic
Policy Committee.
S–120. Reception Room
(Restaurant) [Hugh Scott Room].
S–122, 123. Republican Legislative
Scheduling Office.
S–125, 126, 127, 128, 129, 130,
131. Committee on
Appropriations.

S–132, 133. Parliamentarian.
S–134. Executive Clerk.
S–138. Reception Room
(Restaurant) [Arthur H.
Vandenberg Room].
S–139. Engrossing and Enrolling
Clerks.
S–141. Old Supreme Court
Chamber.
S–145. Senate Wives' Reception
Room.
S–146. Committee on
Appropriations.
S–146A. Subcommittee on
Commerce, Justice, State, and the
Judiciary (Appropriations).
S–147. Architect of the Capitol.
S–148, 149, 150. Democratic Whip.
S–153, 154. Attending Physician.
First Aid.
S–155. Attending Physician.

CRYPT

The Special Services Office is
located at the northwest wall of
the Crypt.
EF–100. Reception Room (center,
East Front).

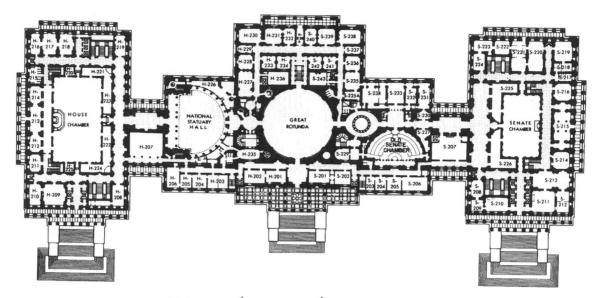

SECOND (PRINCIPAL) FLOOR PLAN

scale: 0   16   32   48   64 feet
1993   NORTH

HOUSE SIDE

National Statuary Hall.
Hall of the House of Representatives.

H–201, 202, 203, 204, 205, 206. Speaker.
H–207. House Reception Room [Sam Rayburn Room].
H–208. Committee on Ways and Means.
H–209, 210. Speaker's Rooms.
H–211. Parliamentarian.
H–212, 213, 214. Representatives' retiring rooms.
H–216, 217, 218. Committee on Appropriations.
H–219. Republican Whip.
H–220. House Republican Leader's floor office.
H–221, 223. Republican cloakroom.
H–222, 224. Democratic cloakroom.
H–225. Speaker's floor office.
H–226. Democratic Steering and Policy Committee.
H–227, 228, 229, 230, 231, 232, 232A, 233, 236. Republican Leader.
H–234. Prayer Room.
H–235. Congressional Women's Reading Room [Lindy Claiborne Boggs Room].

SENATE SIDE

Senate Chamber.

S–205. Committee on Appropriations.
S–206. President Pro Tempore.
S–207. Senators' Conference Room [Mike Mansfield Room].
S–208, 209. Secretary of the Senate.
S–210. Secretary of the Senate [John F. Kennedy Room].
S–211. Secretary of the Senate [Lyndon B. Johnson Room].
S–212. Vice President.
S–213. Senate Reception Room.
S–214. Ceremonial Office of the Vice President.
S–215. Senators' retiring room [Marble Room].
S–216. President's Room.
S–218, 219. Secretary of the Senate. Official Reporters of Debates.
S–220. Secretary of the Senate. Bill Clerk and Journal Clerk.
S–221, 222, 223, 224. Majority Leader [Robert C. Byrd Rooms].
S–225. Democratic cloakroom.
S–226. Republican cloakroom.
S–228. Old Senate Chamber.
S–229, 243. Assistant Republican Leader.
S–230, 231, 232, 233, 234, 235, 235A, 236. Republican Leader [Howard H. Baker, Jr., Rooms].
S–238. [Strom Thurmond Room].

Rotunda

The exterior of each wing was designed to follow closely the architectural vocabulary of the existing building. As in the old Capitol, Corinthian pilasters standing on rusticated piers support a full entablature and balustrade. Porticos were placed on the side elevations as well as the east and west fronts. Evidence of the period's taste for Greek architecture appears in the carving of the exterior marble and throughout the interior decoration. Segmental-ly arched windows on the first floor are somewhat Italianate, while Gothic Revival makes a showing, although a minor one, in the interior. Walter designed these huge wings to be compatible with the existing Capitol while introducing subtle references to the architectural styles of his own day.

Several types of marble were considered for the facing of the extensions. After extensive scientific testing, marble from Lee, Massachusetts, was se-

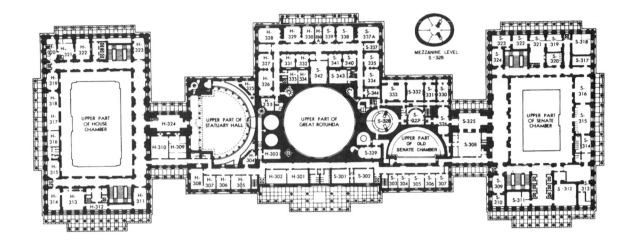

THIRD (GALLERY) FLOOR PLAN

scale 0   16   32   48   64 feet
1993   NORTH

HOUSE SIDE

H–301, 302. Subcommittee on Legislative—D.C. (Appropriations).
H–303, 308. Committee on Appropriations.
H–304. Periodical Press Gallery.
H–305. Committee on Rules.
H–306. Members' Families Lounge.
H–307. Subcommittee on Foreign Operations (Appropriations).
H–309, 310. Subcommittee on Commerce, Justice, State, and the Judiciary (Appropriations).
H–311, 312, 313, 314. Committee on Rules.
H–315, 316, 317, 318, 319. Press Gallery.
H–320, 321, 322, 322A. Radio and Television Correspondents' Gallery.
H–323. Committee on Appropriations.
H–324, 324M. Democratic Steering and Policy Committee [Thomas P. O'Neill, Jr., Room].
H–325. Democratic Steering and Policy Committee.
H–326, 327, 327A, 328, 329, 330, 330A, 331, 332, 333, 334, 335. Committee on House Administration.

SENATE SIDE

S–308. Radio and Television Studio.
S–309, 310. Democratic Secretary.
S–311. Senate Wives' Lounge.
S–312, 312A. Assistant Secretary of the Senate.
S–313, 314, 315, 316. Press Gallery.
S–317. Press Photographers' Gallery.
S–318. Democratic Policy Committee.
S–319, 321, 322, 323, 324. Sergeant at Arms.
S–320. Periodical Press Gallery.
S–325. Radio and Television Correspondents' Gallery.
S–326, 327. Hallway.
S–331, 332, 333. Secretary of the Senate. Senate Library.
S–337, 337A. Secretary for the Minority.

lected. Another quarry near Baltimore supplied the one hundred monolithic shafts for the exterior Corinthian columns. There was never a thought of using Virginia sandstone to match the veneer of the old Capitol. It had proved a weak material that weathered poorly.

In June 1851 construction began on the extension of the Capitol. The cornerstone was laid by President Fillmore on 4 July 1851 in a ceremony highlighted by a rousing oration by Secretary of State Daniel Webster.

When Franklin Pierce succeeded Fillmore as president in 1853, control of the work was transferred to the War Department, and Montgomery C. Meigs, a captain in the Army Corps of Engineers,

was placed in charge. He immediately ordered changes to Walter's design, particularly the location of the new House and Senate chambers. Walter had planned these two-story rooms to occupy positions in the western half of each wing, with access to natural light and ventilation. Meigs altered this scheme by bringing the chambers into the center and surrounding them with corridors and committee rooms. Thus positioned, the chambers would be lighted by skylights and ventilated by steam-powered fans. While access to these rooms was greatly improved, Meigs's windowless chambers would prove highly controversial until air-conditioning was installed in the 1920s.

At the beginning of their association, Meigs, the

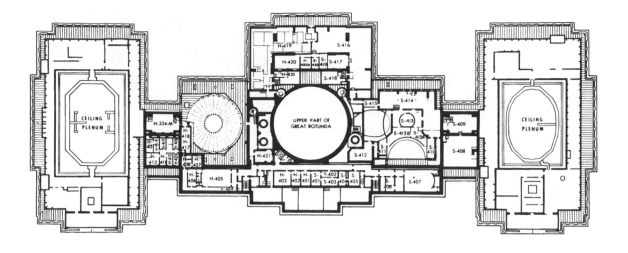

FOURTH (ATTIC) FLOOR PLAN

scale: 0   16   32   48   64 feet
1993   NORTH

HOUSE SIDE

H–324. (mezzanine). Democratic Steering and Policy Committee.
H–405. Permanent Select Committee on Intelligence.
H–419A, 419B. Clerk of the House.
H–419C. Committee on House Administration.
H–419D. Subcommittee on the Legislative Process (Rules).
H–420. Architect of the Capitol. Curator.
H–420A, 421. Architect of the Capitol.

SENATE SIDE

S–406. Secretary of the Senate. Senate Security.
S–408, 409. Radio and Television Correspondents' Gallery.
S–410. Secretary of the Senate. Conservation and Preservation.
S–411, 413A, 413B, 420. Secretary of the Senate. Curator of Art.
S–412, 417. Architect of the Capitol. Mechanical room.
S–413, 414, 415, 416, 148. Secretary of the Senate. Senate Library.
S–414A. Secretary of the Senate. Director of Preservation.
S–419. Capitol Historical Society.

engineer, and Walter, the architect, seemed to work together harmoniously. Relieved of administrative burdens, Walter was able to channel his energies into solving the thousands of design problems associated with colossal construction projects. Meigs thrived on the fame of being in charge of such an important work at a relatively young age. As the project progressed, however, Meigs began to feel that too much credit was being given to the architect and that he himself deserved most, if not all, of it. By 1858 Meigs and Walter were engaged in a bitter fight for control of the work that would drag on for two years. Still, despite their animosity, construction proceeded at a reasonable rate. With work remaining to be done in the wings, the House of Representatives first met in its new chamber on 16 December 1857, and the Senate occupied its new chamber on 4 January 1859.

The interior design of the Capitol extensions was largely directed by Meigs, who with the support of Secretary of War Jefferson Davis aimed to produce the most elaborate finish possible. He commanded an international army of sculptors and painters, who designed elaborate and expensive decorations that were sometimes criticized as un-American. According to one Italian-born artist, Meigs thought the Capitol "required a superior style of decoration in real fresco, like the palace of Augustine and Nero, the Baths of Titus and Liva in Rome and the admired relics of the paintings at Herculaneum and Pompei [sic]." Frescoed walls and ceilings, encaustic tile floors, marble columns and ceilings, stained-glass skylights, and bronze railings and door decorations were part of Meigs's extensive interior decorations, which still contrast sharply with the plain finish of the earlier building.

On Christmas Eve 1851, a spark from one of the stoves in the Library of Congress started a fire that destroyed the room and much of its contents. Lost were thirty-five thousand books; thousands of maps and manuscripts; paintings by Gilbert Stuart, John Cranch, and John Trumbull; and sculptures by

Luigi Persico, Giuseppe Ceracchi, and Pierre-Jean David d'Angers. Thomas U. Walter was asked to investigate the cause of the fire and to design a new room that would be both elegant and fireproof, and so he designed and supervised installation of the first room in America built entirely of cast iron. Alcoves for bookshelves, balconies, railings, and the ceiling were made of iron cast in New York and brought to Washington by train. Particularly notable were the massive ceiling consoles, each weighing a ton. They were profusely ornamented with foliage, scrolls, and shells and marked a high point in the Rococo Revival style in American architecture.

In the 1870s and early 1880s a debate was waged over additional accommodations for the Library of Congress. The debate centered on whether to house the library in its own building or to enlarge the Capitol to house the rapidly expanding collections. Passage of the Copyright Act of 1870 required that two copies of every work protected by the law be deposited in the congressional library. Eventually, it was decided that the library should be removed and that its former space in the Capitol would be rebuilt into committee rooms, offices, and corridors. In 1901 Walter's cast-iron interior was removed and sold for scrap. The loss of this important evidence of mid-nineteenth-century taste and technology was unfortunate. Walter's greatest creation in cast iron, however, was to become the Capitol's most familiar feature: the dome.

On 16 December 1854, Walter completed a drawing of the Capitol as it would appear when the extensions were finished. Instead of Bulfinch's wooden dome, Walter's drawing showed a new dome with a high, two-story drum, an attic, and a cupola crowned by a statue standing on a tall lantern. Such a dome would complement a vastly enlarged building, unifying the composition into a more harmonious whole. The use of cast iron would also make the new dome fireproof, a mounting concern after the Library of Congress fire of 1851. On the strength of this lone drawing, Congress passed a $100,000 appropriation on 3 March 1855 to begin construction of a new cast-iron dome. Clearly, the success of Walter's iron library was an important factor in the decision to replace the wooden dome with one of cast iron.

Construction of both the extensions and the new dome slowly transformed the old Capitol into its present, well-known form. Work slowed during the two-year battle between Meigs and Walter, but the pace quickened when Meigs was replaced in No-

vember 1859 by William B. Franklin, a captain in the Corps of Topographic Engineers.

The outbreak of the Civil War caused work on the extensions to stop for one year (May 1861 to May 1862). Walter was given a leave of absence and moved with his family to the relative safety of Philadelphia. Work continued on the dome, however, with Walter making frequent visits to Washington and corresponding regularly with the contractor, Janes, Fowler, Kirtland and Company of New York, which had been awarded the project in February 1860.

By the spring of 1862, the war effort was at a point at which the Capitol extension project could be restarted. Continuing the stalled construction was considered an important boost to morale, worthy, according to Walter, of "half a dozen victories." But it was obvious that the work could no longer be directed by the War Department. The Department of the Interior oversaw the completion of the Capitol extension and new dome.

On 2 December 1863 the War Department returned to the Capitol, this time to celebrate the installation of the fifth and final section of the Statue of Freedom on top of the new dome. As a flag was raised over the head of the statue, a thirty-five-gun salute was answered by salutes from the twelve forts that encircled the city. Walter ordered his men not to make any speeches or even wave their hats, because the celebration was exclusively in the hands of the War Department.

Walter resigned his position at the Capitol on 26 May 1865 in a dispute over contracts and authority. With the dome almost finished and the design of the extension complete, he thought it time to retire to Philadelphia. After fourteen years in Washington, Walter was exhausted and in poor health. He was succeeded by his longtime assistant and former pupil Edward Clark, who finished the remaining details of the dome and extensions.

Modernizations and Improvements. After the office of commissioner of public buildings was abolished in 1867, Clark became responsible for the care and maintenance of the entire Capitol and its grounds. His constant concerns were making the old building fireproof and improving the heating and ventilation equipment. Under Clark's supervision the first elevators and electric lighting were installed, and improvements in sanitation were also made. But Clark's principal achievement was the improvement of the grounds. In 1873, the Capitol grounds were enlarged by closing A Streets North and South and annexing them and the adjacent

THE CAPITOL. As seen from the Jefferson Building of the Library of Congress.

squares. The old iron fence and the sandstone piers and gatehouses, which had been designed by Bulfinch in the 1820s, were removed and the grounds made ready for landscaping. Acting on Clark's recommendation, Congress called on the first great American landscape architect, Frederick Law Olmsted, to design the enlarged grounds. Shortly after his appointment in 1874 Olmsted produced a general plan for landscape improvements that called for broad, open lawns, tree-shaded walks, low stone walls, and a picturesque summerhouse (sometimes called the Grotto). The Olmsted design surrounded the Capitol with an open park that would welcome visitors and invite them to linger.

The most ambitious and controversial aspect of Olmsted's plan was to build a great marble terrace along the north, south, and west elevations of the Capitol. The terrace would replace Bulfinch's stepped earthen berms, which Olmsted regarded as too insignificant and weak to uphold the Capitol visually. The marble terrace would correct the illusion that the Capitol was about to slip off the edge of Jenkins' Hill. Work began on the terrace in 1884 and was completed eight years later. While the terrace also added one hundred rooms to the Capitol, its foremost purpose was to provide a suitable pedestal.

After the completion of the Olmsted terrace, the construction history of the Capitol becomes relatively quiet. Expansion of congressional facilities on Capitol Hill took the form of office buildings connected to the Capitol by underground tunnels. During the first half of the twentieth century the Capitol's appearance was only slightly altered when the old Library of Congress space was remade into committee rooms and offices and when the roofs of the original north and south wings were fireproofed and rebuilt with a lower pitch.

The only significant twentieth-century alteration to the Capitol was begun in 1958, when the east portico, finished by Bulfinch in 1826, was dismantled in preparation for the east front extension. An addition to this elevation of the Capitol had first been proposed by Walter in 1864 to correct the illusion that the iron dome was inadequately supported. Extending the portico beyond the base of the dome would overcome the impression of instability. An addition would also protect the crumbling sandstone walls and help to buttress the old vaulting. Further, the Capitol would gain another ninety rooms. Speaker Sam Rayburn and Senate majority leader Lyndon B. Johnson guided the enabling legislation through Congress while loud protests were sounded by preservation groups who wished the Capitol to remain unchanged. The exterior of the east front extension, which is an exact reproduction of the sandstone original in Georgia marble, was completed in time for President John F. Kennedy's inauguration on 20 January 1961. The extension project was directed by J. George Stewart, who was appointed Architect of the Capitol in 1954.

Since the 1970s, work on the Capitol has emphasized a high standard of maintenance and technology as well as a renewed appreciation of the building's unique history. These concerns have been fostered by George M. White, who was appointed Architect of the Capitol in 1971. In 1973 electronic voting was introduced into the Hall of the House to expedite the previously time-consuming procedure of roll-call voting. Nationwide television coverage of House debates began in 1979, and coverage of the Senate followed in 1986. Electronic security systems, improved climate control, and new computer and communications capabilities are among the modern technologies that allow the Capitol to function efficiently and safely.

Restoration and Adaptation A series of restorations was begun in anticipation of the nation's bicentennial in 1976. The old Senate and Supreme Court chambers, which had suffered ill-advised alterations, were returned to their mid-nineteenth-century appearances. The old Hall of the House, which had been sensitively converted into National Statuary Hall in 1864, was partially restored with reproductions of original lighting fixtures and drapery. The most ambitious restoration project in the history of the Capitol was begun in 1983 and completed in 1987. It involved the restoration of the sandstone walls of the west central front, the only elevation of the old Capitol that had not been covered over by marble additions. To return the deteriorated walls to pristine condition, about 40 percent of the original sandstone was replaced with Indiana limestone. The stone replacement was preceded by a careful analysis of each stone's structural stability. Many layers of paint, which had concealed some defects, were removed. Over one thousand holes, some as long as thirty-eight feet, were drilled through the walls; stainless steel rods set in concrete grout were installed to reinforce the structure. After a consolidant was applied to strengthen the stone, the west front was repainted. Because this project was completed under budget, the remaining funds appropriated for the restoration of the west front were applied to the restoration of the Olmsted terraces, a project begun in 1991.

In 1993 the Capitol marked its two hundredth an-

niversary. The growth of the Capitol has aptly reflected the growth of the nation, and it will continue to be adapted to meet the needs of the Congress. No matter how these needs and the building that serves them evolve, the Capitol will remain a place where, in Alexander Hamilton's words, "the people govern."

BIBLIOGRAPHY

Allen, William C. *The Dome of the United States Capitol: An Architectural History.* 1992.

Brown, Glenn. *History of the United States Capitol.* 2 vols. 1900, 1902.

Fairman, Charles E. *Art and Artists of the Capitol of the United States of America.* 1927.

Frary, I. T. *They Built the Capitol.* 1940.

U.S. House of Representatives. *Documentary History of the Construction and Development of the Capitol Building and Grounds.* 58th Cong., 2d sess., 1904. H. Rept. 646.

WILLIAM C. ALLEN

Art in the Capitol

The aesthetic appearance, historical significance, and symbolic meaning of the U.S. Capitol are enhanced by the works of art in numerous media that grace its halls and chambers. From the beginning, sculptural decoration was envisioned for the new center of government. The early Architects of the Capitol, Benjamin Henry Latrobe and Charles Bulfinch, personally directed the artists embellishing the building. Later Architects of the Capitol have made recommendations to Congress on commissioning, moving, caring for, and transferring the works of art. Since 1806 the Joint Committee on the Library has had jurisdiction over acquisition and placement of works of art. In recent years some of the committee's responsibilities have been assumed by three other bodies. The Senate Commission on Art and the House Fine Arts Board were created in 1968 and 1988, respectively; the United States Capitol Preservation Commission, for which the Architect of the Capitol acts as a consultant, was also created in 1988.

Until the latter part of the nineteenth century many sculptures in the Capitol were created by artists born and trained in Europe. Italian sculptors were first brought to the Capitol in 1806 to carve capitals, reliefs, and statues. Unfortunately, most of the earliest carvings were destroyed in the 1814 fire. Among the most beautiful works created after

ART IN THE CAPITOL. *Above, Statue of Freedom,* designed by Thomas Crawford in 1856, located on top of the dome of the Capitol. The final section of the bronze statue was placed on 2 December 1863. *Above, right,* bronze staircase railing, sculpted by Edmond Baudin, located on the first floor of the House wing. *At right, The Car of History,* carved by Carlo Franzoni in 1819 from Benjamin Latrobe's design.

OFFICE OF THE ARCHITECT OF THE CAPITOL

APOTHEOSIS OF WASHINGTON.   Fresco located in the canopy of the dome of the Capitol. By Constantino Brumidi, 1865.

the fire is the *Car of History,* the clock for the Hall of the House of Representatives (now National Statuary Hall), which Carlo Franzoni carved from Latrobe's design in 1819. Across the hall is Enrico Causici's *Liberty and the Eagle,* still in its original plaster because Congress never commissioned the marble version. In the Old Supreme Court Chamber, the 1817 relief by Franzoni showing Justice with her scales, also in plaster, is the focal point of the room. The central east front pediment, *Genius of America,* was sculpted by Luigi Persico, who also created the figures of War and Peace on either side

THE ROGERS DOORS. Bronze doors at the eastern entrance of the Rotunda, portraying events in the life of Christopher Columbus, designed and sculpted by Randolph Rogers in Rome in 1858. Installed between Statuary Hall and the House extension in November 1863, the doors were moved to the Rotunda entrance in 1871.   OFFICE OF THE ARCHITECT OF THE CAPITOL

of the central door. Over the door is *Fame and Peace Crowning George Washington*, carved by Antonio Capellano in 1827. The deteriorated originals were reproduced in marble in 1958 during the extension of the east front.

As the central Rotunda was being completed, plans were being made for eight mural-sized oil paintings to be set into frames built into the wall. In 1817 John Trumbull received the commission for four of the paintings. His Revolutionary-era subjects range from *Declaration of Independence* to *George Washington Resigning his Commission*. They contain the earliest of over two dozen representations of George Washington in the Capitol. The other frames were filled by the work of four artists: John Vanderlyn's *Landing of Columbus*, William H. Powell's *Discovery of the Mississippi*, Robert W. Weir's *Embarkation of the Pilgrims*, and John G. Chapman's *Baptism of Pocahontas*.

Other significant early paintings are the portraits of the Marquis de Lafayette, given by the artist, Ary Scheffer, in 1824, and of George Washington, commissioned by Congress from John Vanderlyn in 1832. These paintings were hung in the new House Chamber and remain there today. In 1832 the Senate purchased one of its finest paintings, Rembrandt Peale's porthole portrait of George Washington, which now hangs in the restored Old Senate Chamber. Many other paintings and busts displayed in the Capitol were destroyed in the 1851 Library of Congress fire.

The construction of the extensions and new dome (1851–1866) greatly widened the opportunity to commission new art for the Capitol. Both Architect Thomas U. Walter and Supervising Engineer Montgomery C. Meigs took a keen interest in the decoration. Meigs was interested in every detail; he determined that fresco would be the most permanent and monumental medium for wall paintings, he sought out talented sculptors—he even caught the snakes used as models for the bronze handles for the chamber doors. Meigs allowed the mature Italian artist Constantino Brumidi to begin painting in the Capitol in 1855. Brumidi had been trained in Rome in the art of true fresco, which must be painted in small sections on fresh plaster. He was able to create the illusion of three-dimensional forms on flat surfaces, following the style and technique of the Italian Renaissance and Baroque masters. After successfully completing the fresco decoration of the House Agriculture Committee Room, one of the most beautiful rooms in the Capitol, Brumidi was hired as the master painter. His mas-

terpiece, *The Apotheosis of George Washington*, is the canopy in the eye of the dome above the Rotunda. The revered first president rises in glory, surrounded by maidens representing the first thirteen states. Below him are scenes that combine classical gods and goddesses with American historical figures and technological advances, such as the transatlantic cable and the McCormick reaper. Brumidi also created a design for the frieze encircling the base of the dome, but almost twenty years passed before he was allowed to begin painting. He died in 1880 with the frieze less than half completed; his designs were carried out by a compatriot, Filippo Costaggini. A gap remained that was not filled until the last three scenes were added in 1953 by Allyn Cox.

Brumidi left his mark throughout the Senate wing, decorating important rooms such as the President's Room. He designed the intricate wall and ceiling decoration and painted the frescoed lunettes for the area now called the Brumidi Corridors. He also suggested the design for the four graceful bronze railings, sculpted by Edmond Baudin, for the Members' Staircases. Brumidi's classical motifs and style were criticized by some, but he worked for a quarter century, contributing to the beauty and richness of the Capitol. In an ongoing campaign begun in the 1980s his frescoes are being cleaned and conserved, a process that has revealed the original beauty of his colors and forms.

The extensions provided space for large historical and landscape paintings. Emanuel Leutze's thirty-foot-wide mural, *Westward the Course of Empire Takes Its Way*, was painted in the House stairway in 1862. In 1940 the opposite stairway received an equally large oil painting, *The Scene of the Signing of the Constitution of the United States*, by Howard Chandler Christy. Two large landscape paintings by Albert Bierstadt were purchased for the Hall of the House: *The Discovery of the Hudson River* now hangs in the Members' Dining Room, and *Entrance into Monterey* hangs in the members' stairwell.

The enlarged Capitol also provided new places for sculpture, starting at the top of the dome with the Statue of Freedom by Thomas Crawford, placed in 1863. Crawford also received the commission for the Senate pediment, *Progress of Civilization;* the statues depicting Justice and History over the Senate doors; and two sets of bronze doors, which were completed by William Rinehart after Crawford's death. Randolph Rogers created the central bronze doors, which depict scenes of the life of Christopher Columbus and were modeled after Lorenzo Ghiber-

LEGACY OF CONSTANTINO BRUMIDI. *Above, left*, portrait of Benjamin Franklin, located on the ceiling of the President's Room, Senate wing, in a Brumidi mural. *At left*, Senate Reception Room, walls and ceiling decorated by Brumidi. On the left wall of the room is a portrait of Sen. Robert M. La Follette, Sr. (R-Wis.), added to the room in 1959 along with portraits of Senators John C. Calhoun (R-S.C.), Henry Clay (W-Ky.), Daniel Webster (W-Mass.), and Robert A. Taft (R-Ohio). *Above*, Brumidi, photographed by Mathew Brady.

OFFICE OF THE HISTORIAN OF THE U.S. SENATE

THE LANDING OF COLUMBUS ON SAN SALVADOR. Painting by John Vanderlyn, installed in the Rotunda in 1847.

ti's *Gates of Paradise.* The House pediment, *The Apotheosis of Democracy* by Paul Wayland Bartlett, was not completed until 1916.

A major impetus for adding sculpture to the Capitol was the creation of National Statuary Hall in the Old Hall of the House in 1864. Each state is allowed to contribute two bronze or marble statues of prominent citizens. (By the early 1990s, five states had yet to commission their second statues.) The collection is a wealth of American history, showing citizens from many professions and periods, from Revolutionary hero Nathanael Greene, of Rhode Island, the first statue placed (1870), to Philo T. Farnsworth of Utah, pioneer of television (1990). The collection also richly documents the history of American sculpture because many major artists are represented and the collection has always been indoors and well cared for. The style of the statues varies from the delicate details of the 1883 marble of Robert Fulton of Pennsylvania by Howard Roberts to the abstract power of the 1983 statue of Father Damien of Hawaii by Marisol Escobar. On the Senate side is the open-ended collection of marble busts of vice presidents, which was begun in 1885. The busts of the earliest vice

presidents ring the Senate Chamber. A comparable group on the House side is the collection of oil portraits of Speakers of the House, which have been systematically added since 1910.

Other sculpture has been added to commemorate historically important figures, such as the marble statue of Abraham Lincoln by Vinnie Ream Hoxie and the bronze bust of Martin Luther King, Jr., by John Wilson. Adelaide Johnson's unique *Suffrage Monument,* a four-ton block of marble carved with portraits of Elizabeth Cady Stanton, Susan B. Anthony, and Lucretia Mott, was dedicated in the Rotunda and installed in the Crypt in 1921.

To the west of the Capitol grounds stand the marble *Peace Monument* by Franklin Simmons (1877) and the bronze *Garfield Monument* by John Quincy Adams Ward (1887), both restored in the 1990s. The only other statue on the grounds is the 1959 portrait of Robert A. Taft, which is part of the Taft Memorial.

Among the most recent additions to the art of the Capitol are the oil-on-canvas murals in the first-floor House corridors begun by Allyn Cox in 1973. The Hall of Capitols was completed in 1974 and the Great Experiment Hall in 1982. The theme of west-

Statues in the Capitol by State

STATE	STATUE	SCULPTOR
Alabama	Jabez Lamar Monroe Curry	Dante Sodini
	General Joseph Wheeler	Berthold Nebet
Alaska	Edward L. Bartlett	Felix W. de Weldon
	Ernest Gruening	George Anthonisen
Arizona	John Campbell Greenway	Gutzon Borglum
	Eusebio F. Kino	Suzanne Silvercruys
Arkansas	Uriah M. Rose	Frederic W. Ruckstull
	James P. Clarke	Pompeo Coppini
California	Thomas Starr King	Haig Patigian
	Junipero Serra	Ettore Cadorin
Colorado	Dr. Florence Rena Sabin	Joy Buba
Connecticut	Roger Sherman	Chauncey B. Ives
	Jonathan Trumbull	Chauncey B. Ives
Delaware	Caesar A. Rodney	Bryant Baker
	John Middleton Clayton	Bryant Baker
Florida	Dr. John Gorrie	Charles Adrian Pillars
	Gen. Edmund Kirby Smith	Charles Adrian Pillars
Georgia	Dr. Crawford W. Long	H. Massey Rhind
	Alexander H. Stephens	Gutzon Borglum
Hawaii	King Kamehameha I	Thomas R. Gould
	Father Damien	Marisol Escobar
Idaho	George L. Shoup	Frederick Ernst Triebel
	William E. Borah	Bryant Baker
Illinois	General James Shields	Leonard Wells Volk
	Frances E. Willard	Helen Farnsworth Mears
Indiana	Oliver H. P. T. Morton	Charles H. Niehaus
	General Lew Wallace	Andrew O'Connor
Iowa	James Harlan	Nellie V. Walker
	Samuel Jordan Kirkwood	Vinnie Ream
Kansas	John J. Ingalls	Charles H. Niehaus
	George Washington Glick	Charles H. Niehaus
Kentucky	Henry Clay	Charles H. Niehaus
	Dr. Ephraim McDowell	Charles H. Niehaus
Louisiana	Huey P. Long	Charles Keck
	Edward D. White	Arthur C. Morgan
Maine	William King	Franklin Simmons
	Hannibal Hamlin	Charles E. Tefft
Maryland	Charles Carroll of Carrollton	Richard E. Brooks
	John Hanson	Richard E. Brooks
Massachusetts	Samuel Adams	Anne Whitney
	John Winthrop	Richard S. Greenough
Michigan	Lewis Cass	Daniel Chester French
	Zachariah Chandler	Charles H. Niehaus
Minnesota	Henry Mower Rice	Frederick Ernst Triebel
	Maria L. Sanford	Evelyn Raymond
Mississippi	Jefferson Davis	Augustus Lukeman
	James Z. George	Augustus Lukeman
Missouri	Francis P. Blair, Jr.	Alexander Doyle
	Thomas Hart Benton	Alexander Doyle

Statues in the Capitol by State (Continued)

STATE	STATUE	SCULPTOR
Montana	Charles Marion Russell	John B. Weaver
	Jeannette Rankin	Terry Mimnaugh
Nebraska	William Jennings Bryan	Rudulph Evans
	J. Sterling Morton	Rudulph Evans
Nevada	Patrick A. McCarran	Yolande Jacobson
New Hampshire	John Stark	Carl Conrads
	Daniel Webster	Carl Conrads
New Jersey	Richard Stockton	Henry K. Brown and H. K. Bush-Brown
	Philip Kearny	Henry Kirke Brown
New Mexico	Dennis Chavez	Felix W. de Weldon
New York	Robert Livingston	Erastus Dow Palmer
	George Clinton	Henry Kirke Brown
North Carolina	Zebulon Baird Vance	Gutzon Borglum
	Charles Brantley Aycock	Charles Keck
North Dakota	John Burke	Avard Fairbanks
Ohio	James A. Garfield	Charles H. Niehaus
	William Allen	Charles H. Niehaus
Oklahoma	Sequoyah (Sequoya)	Vinnie Ream and G. Julian Zolnay
	Will Rogers	Jo Davidson
Oregon	Reverend Jason Lee	Gifford MacG. Proctor
	John McLoughlin	Gifford MacG. Proctor
Pennsylvania	John Peter Gabriel Muhlenberg	Blanche Nevin
	Robert Fulton	Howard Roberts
Rhode Island	Nathanael Greene	Henry Kirke Brown
	Roger Williams	Franklin Simmons
South Carolina	John C. Calhoun	Frederic W. Ruckstull
	Wade Hampton	Frederic W. Ruckstull
South Dakota	William H. H. Beadle	H. Daniel Webster
	Joseph Ward	Bruno Beghe
Tennessee	Andrew Jackson	Belle K. Scholz and Leopold F. Scholz
	John Sevier	Belle K. Scholz and Leopold F. Scholz
Texas	Stephen F. Austin	Elisabet Ney
	Samuel Houston	Elisabet Ney
Utah	Brigham Young	Mahonri Young
	Philo T. Farnsworth	James R. Avati
Vermont	Ethan Allen	Larkin G. Mead
	Jacob Collamer	Preston Powers
Virginia	Robert E. Lee	Edward V. Valentine
	George Washington	Jean-Antoine Houdon
Washington	Marcus Whitman	Avard Fairbanks
	Mother Joseph	Felix W. de Weldon
West Virginia	John E. Kenna	Alexander Doyle
	Francis H. Pierpont	Franklin Simmons
Wisconsin	Père Jacques Marquette	Gaetano Trentanove
	Robert M. La Follett, Sr.	Jo Davidson
Wyoming	Esther Hobart Morris	Avard Fairbanks

ward expansion will be carried out in the third corridor. In recent years, historical treasures such as nineteenth-century architectural drawings and photographs and gilded mirror and picture frames have been considered part of the art collection and have been restored as needed.

BIBLIOGRAPHY

U.S. Congress. Architect of the Capitol. *Art in the United States Capitol.* 94th Cong., 2d sess., 1978. H. Doc. 94-660.

U.S. Congress. Joint Committee on the Library. *Art and Artists of the Capitol of the United States of America,* by Charles E. Fairman. 69th Cong., 1st sess., 1927. S. Doc. 95.

Frary, I. T. *They Built the Capitol.* 1940.

Murdock, Myrtle Cheney. *Constantino Brumidi: Michelangelo of the United States Capitol.* 1950.

BARBARA A. WOLANIN

Capitol Grounds

The U.S. Capitol grounds provide a parklike setting for the nation's Capitol, offering a picturesque counterpoint to the building's formal architecture. The grounds comprise a total area of 274 acres; the square immediately surrounding the Capitol covers an area of 58.8 acres, bounded by Independence Avenue on the south, Constitution Avenue on the north, First Street NE/SE on the east, and First Street NW/SW on the west. More than one hundred varieties of trees and bushes are planted around the grounds, and thousands of flowers are used in seasonal displays.

The immediate grounds, as well as the marble terraces on three sides of the Capitol, were designed by Frederick Law Olmsted (1822–1903), who planned the expansion and landscaping of the area that was carried out from 1874 to 1892. Olmsted, most famous as the designer of New York City's Central Park, is considered the greatest American landscape architect of his day; he was a pioneer in the development of public parks in this country. To ensure the prominence of the Capitol on the grounds, he refrained from grouping trees or other landscape features in ways that would distract the viewer from the building.

The paved Capitol plaza lies east of the Capitol

WEST FRONT OF THE CAPITOL. Painting by August Kollner, 1839.   OFFICE OF THE ARCHITECT OF THE CAPITOL

AERIAL VIEW OF WASHINGTON, D.C. Looking southwest, showing the Capitol with construction on the dome interrupted because of the Civil War. *Harper's Weekly*, 27 July 1861.   LIBRARY OF CONGRESS

and is entered via extensions of Delaware Avenue, New Jersey Avenue, and East Capitol Street. At the East Capitol Street entrance to the plaza are two large, rectangular stone fountains. Red granite lamp piers and smaller bronze light fixtures line the paved plaza. Seats are placed at intervals along the sidewalks. Three pavilions with benches were originally shelters for streetcar passengers.

In the northwestern corner of the grounds, a small brick structure that Olmsted named the Summer House contains shaded benches, an ornamental fountain, and public drinking fountains; it also offers a view of a grotto with a splashing waterfall. Two stone towers in the western portion of the grounds contain air shafts for the Capitol ventilation system.

The land on which the Capitol stands was part of the territory occupied by subtribes of the Algonquian Indians. At the time of its acquisition by the federal government, the land was owned by Daniel Carroll of Duddington.

The Residence Act of 1790 provided that the federal government should be established in a permanent location by the year 1800. In March 1791 the commissioners of the City of Washington, who had been appointed by President George Washington, selected the French engineer Pierre-Charles L'Enfant to plan the new federal city. L'Enfant decided to locate the Capitol at the elevated east end of the Mall on what was called Jenkins' Hill; he described the site as "a pedestal waiting for a monument."

At this time, the site of the Capitol was a relative wilderness partly overgrown with scrub oak. A muddy creek with swampy borders flowed at the base of the hill, and a swamp stood nearby. For some years the land around the Capitol was regarded as a common, crossed by roads in several directions.

In 1825 the grounds were divided into rectangular grassy areas bordered by trees, flower beds, and gravel walks. The trees grew quickly but soon depleted the soil, and a lack of proper pruning and thinning left most of the area's vegetation ill-grown,

AERIAL VIEW OF THE CAPITOL. Looking east, November 1992.   OFFICE OF THE ARCHITECT OF THE CAPITOL

feeble, or dead. Virtually all of it had been removed by the early 1870s.

The mid-nineteenth-century extension of the Capitol required also that the Capitol grounds be enlarged, and in 1872 and 1873, Congress appropriated money to purchase additional land. In 1874 Olmsted was commissioned to plan and oversee the development of the grounds around the Capitol. In addition, he addressed an architectural problem that had existed for some years: from the west, the earthen terraces at the building's base made it seem inadequately supported. The solution, Olmsted believed, was to construct marble terraces on the north, west, and south sides of the building. This proposal was reviewed, discussed, and approved by the Joint Committee on Public Buildings and Grounds, which had oversight of the project, and was later adopted by Congress.

Work began on the east side of the grounds in 1874 and progressed to the west, north, and south sides in 1875. After the old, depleted soil was removed, new soil enriched with fertilizers was brought in. By 1876 gas and water service had been completed for the entire grounds, and electrical lamp-lighting apparatuses had been installed. Also by then, stables and workshops had been removed from the grounds, and the nearby streetcar system had been relocated farther from the Capitol. The granite and bronze lamp piers and ornamental bronze lamps for the east plaza area were completed. The pedestrian walks and approaches were laid in 1877, and the roads throughout the grounds were paved in 1878.

The east side of the grounds was virtually completed by 1879, and work then largely shifted to the west side. In the years 1880 to 1882, the perimeter walls, the approaches and entrances, the House air tower, and the Summer House were completed. The terraces were begun in 1884. Olmsted retired from superintendency of the terrace project in 1885 but continued to direct the work on the grounds until 1889, adapting the landscape to the new construction. The Senate air tower was installed in 1888–1890. In 1892, the terraces were completed and occupied, and the streetcar track that had extended into the grounds from B Street South (now Independence Avenue) was removed.

In the last years of the nineteenth century, trees, lawns, and plantings were tended, pruned, and thinned. A hurricane in September 1896 damaged or destroyed many trees, requiring extensive removals in the following year. Also in 1897, electric lighting replaced gas lighting on the grounds.

Between 1910 and 1935, areas totaling 61.4 acres north of Constitution Avenue were added. Additions in subsequent years brought the total area to 274 acres. Since 1983, security has been improved with, among other measures, the installation of barriers at vehicular entrances. The area still functions in many ways as a public park, however, and visitors are welcome to use the walks to tour the grounds. Demonstrations and ceremonies are often held on the grounds. During the summer, many high-school bands perform in front of the Capitol, and a series of evening concerts by the National Symphony Orchestra and the bands of the armed forces is offered on the west lawn.

BIBLIOGRAPHY

U.S. Congress. Architect of the Capitol. *Report of the Architect of the Capitol Extension*. 1874–1875.
U.S. Congress. Architect of the Capitol. *Report of the Architect of the Capitol*. 1876–.

ERIC W. PAFF

Dome and Great Rotunda

The Capitol's most distinguishing feature is the dome, a cast-iron structure that was begun in 1856 and completed ten years later. It was designed by Thomas U. Walter, who modeled it after some of Europe's most famous domes, notably Saint Paul's in London, Saint Isaac's in Saint Petersburg, and the Panthéon in Paris. It is composed of a two-story drum surrounded by a one-story circular colonnade of thirty-six Corinthian columns. Seventy-two brackets embedded in more than five million pounds of brickwork hold the columns in place. Above the drum are an attic with decorated consoles and a ribbed cupola supporting a lantern with twelve columns. Capping the dome is the Statue of Freedom, an allegorical bronze figure by Thomas

Crawford. Standing 19 feet 6 inches tall, the statue was cast in five sections that together weigh 14,985 pounds. The fifth and final section of the statue was hoisted into place on 2 December 1863.

The dome measures 135 feet 5 inches in diameter at its base, and it rises 287 feet 6 inches above the ground level of the east plaza. Most of the ironwork for the dome was cast near New York City by the firm of Janes, Fowler, Kirtland and Company, brought to Washington by train, and installed by the foundry's workers, all for seven cents per pound. Finished at a total cost of $1,047,291, the dome includes 8,909,200 pounds of ironwork.

SECTIONAL DRAWING OF THE DOME OF THE CAPITOL. 1859, by Thomas U. Walter, Architect of the Capitol (1851–1865).   OFFICE OF THE ARCHITECT OF THE CAPITOL

The iron dome replaced an earlier dome constructed of wood covered in copper, which had been designed and built by Charles Bulfinch. Finished in 1824, it was among the last parts of the original Capitol to be completed. By the 1850s, however, it was considered too small for the Capitol, which was then being enlarged. The wooden dome was also a fire hazard and expensive to maintain. The present dome was designed to correct the defects of the original.

The interior of the dome, the Great Rotunda, is the physical and symbolic heart of the Capitol. It is a circular room 96 feet in diameter and 185 feet tall. The lower 48-foot section of the Rotunda wall is made of Virginia sandstone and is original to the first dome and rotunda. Resting on that is the cast-iron addition begun in the 1850s. Eight monumental paintings placed around the Rotunda depict events of the Revolutionary War and scenes from the discovery, exploration, and settlement of America. The Revolutionary War scenes by John Trumbull, commissioned in 1817, are among the oldest works of art in the Capitol. Above the paintings are sculpted panels with portrait busts of early explorers and scenes from colonial history. Part of the design for the second, much grander dome included a frieze 300 feet in circumference that was originally intended to be filled with sculpture. It was eventually painted in imitation of sculptural relief. Over the eye of the inner dome is a colossal (4,664 square feet) allegorical painting titled *The Apotheosis of Washington*. This fresco and the frieze were painted by the Italian-born artist Constantino Brumidi, who spent twenty-five years decorating the Capitol in the third quarter of the nineteenth century.

Forty sandstone columns sustaining a series of groin vaults support the Rotunda's expansive stone floor. An opening was originally provided in the center of the floor to light the Crypt below, but it was closed in 1828 to protect the Rotunda's artwork from dampness. Below the center of the Crypt is a tomb intended for the remains of the first president, but, because his heirs would not permit his reinterment there, the space is now used to store the catafalque made in 1865 for Lincoln's lying in state. The Crypt was provided for the sole purpose of supporting the Rotunda's floor; however, soon after it was finished, it became home to a motley assortment of peddlers and hawkers. Apples, nuts, cakes, and liquor were sold from stands, while coachmen and servants loitered about. This condition was soon condemned as an "intolerable nui-

sance," and the Crypt was cleared of commercial activity.

Since 1882 use of the Rotunda has been guided by *Hinds' Precedents of the House of Representatives*. Special events, such as the unveiling of statues or receptions for visiting heads of state, are usually authorized by concurrent congressional resolutions. The first recorded event to take place in the Rotunda was a reception for the Marquis de Lafayette in 1824. In its early history the Rotunda was used for such diverse activities as an "Exhibition of American Manufacturers" (1825), an Independence Day oration delivered by Francis Scott Key (1831), and a bazaar to raise money for a statue of slain President James A. Garfield (1882). For a few weeks at the beginning of the Civil War in 1861, the 8th Massachusetts Regiment was bivouacked in the Rotunda.

The nation pays final tribute to its leaders when they lie in state in the Rotunda. Prominent people have been so honored on twenty-six occasions (see table 1).

TABLE 1. *Final Tributes in the Rotunda*

Henry Clay	1852
Abraham Lincoln	1865
Thaddeus Stevens	1868
Charles Sumner	1874
Henry Wilson	1875
James A. Garfield	1881
John A. Logan	1886
William McKinley	1901
Pierre Charles L'Enfant	1909
George Dewey	1917
Unknown Soldier of World War I	1921
Warren G. Harding	1923
William Howard Taft	1930
John Joseph Pershing	1948
Robert A. Taft	1953
Unknown Soldiers of World War II and the Korean War	1958
John F. Kennedy	1963
Douglas MacArthur	1964
Herbert C. Hoover	1964
Dwight D. Eisenhower	1969
Everett M. Dirksen	1969
J. Edgar Hoover	1972
Lyndon B. Johnson	1973
Hubert H. Humphrey	1978
Unknown Soldier of the Vietnam Era	1984
Claude Pepper	1989

EULOGIES TO PRESIDENT JOHN F. KENNEDY. Services in the Great Rotunda, 24 November 1963.

LIBRARY OF CONGRESS

BIBLIOGRAPHY

Allen, William C. *The Dome of the United States Capitol: An Architectural History.* 1992.
Brown, Glenn. *History of the United States Capitol.* 2 vols. 1900, 1902.

WILLIAM C. ALLEN

CAPITOL HILL. A Washington, D.C., neighborhood with loosely defined boundaries, Capitol Hill today is a mix of government buildings, parks, and restored Federal-style brick row houses set on wide avenues and narrow, tree-lined streets. In 1791, Maj. Pierre L'Enfant, commissioned to prepare a plan for laying out the new national capital, selected this area as the site for the congressional building. He described the site—a plateau eighty-eight feet above the level of the Potomac River—as "a pedestal waiting for a superstructure." Today, even though the Supreme Court Building is also promi-

nently located there, "the Hill" has come to be synonymous with the legislative branch. When people say they are "going up to the Hill," they usually mean they have business with Congress.

In 1608, when Captain John Smith led a small exploratory party up the "Patawomeke" River, the area now designated Capitol Hill was a lush, wooded plateau inhabited by the Powhatan Indians, a subtribe of the Algonquians. Their council house was located at the foot of the hill.

By the mid 1600s, English settlers began infiltrating the area. The original patent, taken out in 1664 by George Thompson, referred to the place as New Troy. By the time the federal government purchased Duddington Manor, the site of the future Capitol, from Daniel Carroll, the area was known as Jenkins Hill—even though there is no evidence of a Jenkins ever owning the land.

L'Enfant's grand plan for the national capital placed the Capitol Building—that is, the meeting-

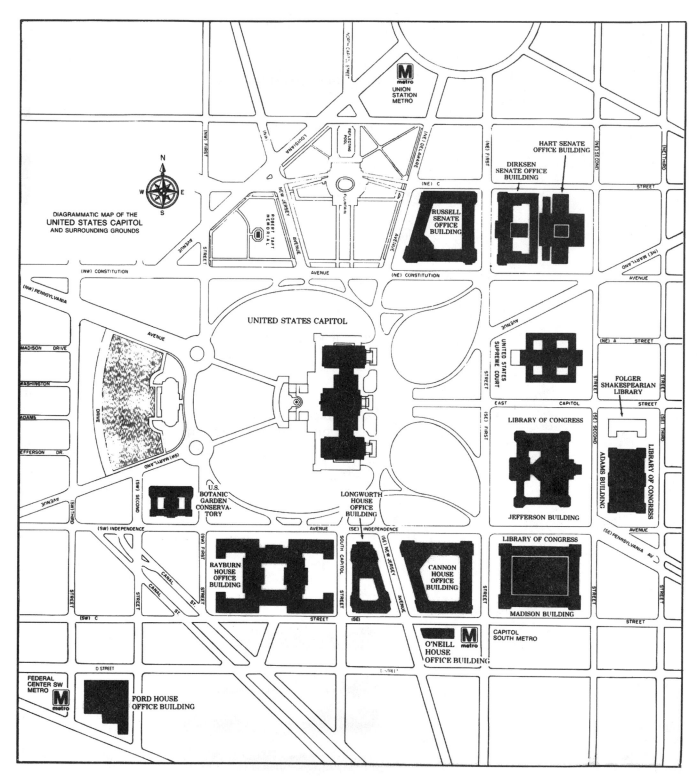

MAP OF CAPITOL HILL. In the 1990s.

CONGRESSIONAL QUARTERLY INC.

CAPITOL HILL. Aerial view, looking west, mid 1970s.

place of Congress—in the geographical hub of the city. Thus, the four sectors of Washington—northwest, northeast, southwest, and southeast—are designated by their relationship to the Capitol; all four sectors converge there.

By the time the first wing of the Capitol was completed in 1800, Capitol Hill was teeming with private homes, businesses, boardinghouses, and taverns. Very few of those structures survive today. Most of the graceful row houses, churches, and commercial buildings on Capitol Hill were built during and after the administration of Abraham Lincoln.

Over the years, the federal government's physical presence on Capitol Hill has expanded considerably, most notably with the Library of Congress (1889), the Supreme Court Building (1935), and the various Senate and House office buildings.

During the first half of the twentieth century, the Capitol Hill neighborhood went into serious decline. Not until after World War II did people begin restoring the rundown old buildings and rejuvenating the area. Today, Capitol Hill boasts some of the most beautiful streets and most elegant old homes in Washington.

The Capitol Hill neighborhood is relatively compact, generally considered to be bounded by Massachusetts Avenue on the north, the foot of the Capitol on the west, E Street on the south, and Lincoln Park and 11th Street on the east. The most important buildings are the Capitol, the Supreme Court, the Library of Congress (now in three separate structures), the Folger Shakespeare Library, the Botanic Gardens, and Union Station. The Capitol complex includes the Russell, Dirksen, and Hart Senate office buildings and the Cannon, Longworth, and Rayburn House office buildings.

[*For discussion of other institutions and buildings on Capitol Hill, see* Botanic Garden; Capitol, The; Congressional Office Buildings; Library of Congress; Supreme Court; Visitors to Capitol Hill. *See also* Congressional Cemetery.]

BIBLIOGRAPHY

Herron, Paul. *The Story of Capitol Hill.* 1963.
Reps, John W. *Washington on View: The Nation's Capital since 1790.* 1991.
Spencer, Duncan. "The Hill's Architecture." *Roll Call* (4 April 1991): 23–24.
U.S. Congress. "Capitol Buildings and Grounds." *Congressional Directory: 1991–1992.* Pp. 642–643.

ROBERT L. HARDESTY

CAPITOL HISTORICAL SOCIETY. A private, nonprofit educational organization, the United States Capitol Historical Society was founded in 1962 by Fred Schwengel, Republican representative from Iowa (1955–1965, 1967–1973), to encourage interest in the Capitol building and the U.S. Congress. The society was chartered by Congress (92 Stat. 1643) in 1978. Schwengel served as its president until his retirement in 1992 and as chairman of the board of trustees until his death in 1993.

The society has undertaken a wide range of activities that aim to serve the professional scholar, the amateur historian, and the general public. Chief among these are a variety of research projects and publications, including a guidebook of the Capitol published in seven languages, films on the history of the District of Columbia and the Capitol, a visitors' booth in the Capitol, an oral history program with former members of Congress, and a research fellowship program on the art and architecture of the Capitol. The society also conducts a series of symposia that include professional scholarly conferences, a secondary school program, and publication of scholarly presentations and conference proceedings.

The Capitol Historical Society has sponsored projects to preserve and enhance the Capitol, including a program begun in 1970 to decorate the walls and ceilings of the House wing. The society also acquires artwork, historical documents, and furnishings to donate to the Capitol collection.

BIBLIOGRAPHY

Office of the Architect of the Capitol. Records, 1793–. Washington, D.C.
U.S. Capitol Historical Society. *The U.S. Capitol Historical Society, 1962–1992: A Brief History.* 1992.

CYNTHIA PEASE MILLER

CAPITOL POLICE. The central and enduring function of the U.S. Capitol Police is to provide an environment of security that enables Congress to perform its legislative functions free from threats of violence, while at the same time preserving the constitutional rights of all citizens to peacefully assemble and petition their elected representatives for redress of grievances.

In 1801, there was only one night watchman for the entire Capitol grounds. In 1993, the U.S. Capitol Police force numbered 1,352 sworn and civilian members with a $64 million budget, indicative of the increase in population and crime in the Capitol complex area. The force patrols a 40-block, 200-acre area that includes the Capitol and grounds and some twenty buildings that constitute the Capitol Hill complex. The nearby Supreme Court and Library of Congress have their own police forces. The Capitol Police also assist numerous visitors to Capitol Hill, of which there were more than 2.4 million in 1992. The force also provided crowd control and security for 45 official visits by ranking U.S. officials and foreign dignitaries, 73 outdoor concert events, and 248 scheduled demonstrations on the Capitol grounds during 1992.

Despite tightened security throughout the government in recent years, Congress remains probably the most accessible legislature in the world, with the Capitol itself serving as a universally recognized symbol of freedom to the world.

In accordance with a national tradition that the Capitol and its attendant buildings belong to the people, Congress continues to insist on virtually unlimited access for any citizen or visitor. No other national government permits unescorted access to its legislative body. The problem is that security and accessibility are essentially opposing concepts, and the greater accommodation of one must be at the expense of the other. It is the challenge of ensuring freedom of access to the Capitol, while providing adequate security for members of Congress, their staffs, and the visiting public, that makes the tasks of the Capitol Police unique and unlike those faced by other domestic law enforcement bodies of similar size.

In response to shootings and other episodes of violence, the threat of international terrorism, and the growth in congressional staff, Congress has gradually increased the size of the police force and has provided funding for a variety of security enhancements. An electronic surveillance and an intrusion detection system have been installed. All incoming mail to congressional offices is x-rayed. Packages delivered to the Capitol complex are first examined for explosives and weapons. Visitors and congressional staff must pass through metal detectors both at designated entrances to Capitol buildings and at the entrances to the House and Senate galleries. Guards and barriers limit vehicular access to the grounds surrounding the Capitol.

This security improvement program includes the training of the Capitol Police Technical Security Division to examine suspicious packages, to handle bombs, and to provide electronic countersurveillance. Specially trained dogs assist some of the police units.

Since members typically desire to maintain close and easy contact with the public, Congress has been slow to impose security restrictions injurious to that value. In 1954, following a shooting incident in the House chamber in which five representatives were wounded, Congress considered a proposal to place bulletproof glass in the House and Senate galleries, but rejected that idea because it would both literally and symbolically isolate members from the public.

CAPITOL POLICE. In the mid 1850s.   OFFICE OF THE ARCHITECT OF THE CAPITOL

The House and Senate sergeants at arms are officially responsible for security for the House and Senate, respectively. They submit the budgets of the Capitol Police and the Capitol Police Board to the legislative branch subcommittees of the House and Senate Appropriations committees. The Capitol Police Board determines police policy and therefore has the greatest effect on the daily operations and policies of the police. The board, comprising the Architect of the Capitol and the House and Senate sergeants at arms, is involved with such matters as prescribing hiring standards and detailing police officers for duty. The board's chairmanship rotates yearly between the two sergeants at arms. The U.S. Capitol Police chief oversees the daily operations of the force.

The Senate Committee on Rules and Administration and the House Committee on House Administration have exercised primary legislative and oversight jurisdiction over the Capitol Police, while the House Committee on Public Works and Transportation and the Senate Committee on Environment and Public Works have jurisdiction over legislation relating to the Capitol buildings and security.

Prior to the mid 1960s, patronage appointees constituted a large percentage of the Capitol Police and the turnover rate for the entire force was 80 percent per year, primarily because many on the force at the time were college students. Because of concern over the professional quality of the force and its capability to meet certain emergency situations, the U.S. Capitol Police frequently relied on the Metropolitan Police of the District of Columbia for assistance.

Since that time, a policy has been developed to establish a professional, merit-based force. New appointees must meet standard physical and mental requirements, and promotions are competitive, based upon a written examination, a supervisor's performance appraisal, and an oral board evaluation. As a result, the annual turnover rate decreased to less than 5 percent in 1993.

Critics of the current congressional security apparatus note that there are almost three police officers for every member of Congress. Over the years, they have argued that the Capitol Police force is too large and too costly to be an effective law enforcement unit, and that similar size police forces elsewhere serve much larger populations and geographic jurisdictions. Opponents also point to the availability of several nearby police security agencies that can be called upon as necessary, including the Metropolitan Police for the District of Columbia, the Secret Service, the Federal Bureau of Investigation, the U.S. Park Police, and others. The protective function of the Capitol Police, they argue, could be performed less expensively by contracting out to a private security company, thereby enabling the Capitol Police to concentrate on criminal activities.

Supporters of the present policy note that the Capitol Police force has become increasingly professional, is well trained, and is paid comparably to other federal law enforcement services in the Washington, D.C., metropolitan area. They note the constitutional significance of providing Congress with a law enforcement entity under its control and not under the control of the executive branch as both a symbolic and practical application of the separation of powers doctrine.

BIBLIOGRAPHY

Byrd, Robert C. *The Senate, 1789–1989. Addresses on the History of the United States Senate.* Vol. 2. 1991. Pp. 327–345.
Kaiser, Fred. "The U.S. Capitol Police and Supreme Court Police: Expanding their Protective Mandates and Jurisdictions." *Police Studies* 11 (Summer 1988): 81–91.
Nichols, Dan. *U.S. Capitol Police. The United States Capitol Police: A Tradition of Service and Protection.* 1993.
Pontius, John. "Protecting the Congress: The Role of the U.S. Capitol Police." *Congressional Research Service Review,* January 1986, pp. 22–24.
U.S. House of Representatives. Committee on House Administration. *A Statutory History of the U.S. Capitol Police.* 99th Cong., 1st sess., 1985. Committee Print.

JOHN SAMUELS PONTIUS

CAPPER, ARTHUR (1865–1951), five-term Republican senator from Kansas, first native-born Kansan to become governor of Kansas, and leading farm-paper publisher who was known in Congress as the "Farmer's Friend." After graduating from Garnett High School in 1884, Capper was a printer and then a reporter and editor for the Topeka *Daily Capital.* He became owner of a weekly newspaper and other publications, including the financially burdened *Capital,* which became profitable under his tutelage. He developed a farm-paper syndicate covering Kansas and neighboring states. Although never previously a seeker of elective office, he was the party's candidate for governor in 1912. He lost by just twenty-nine votes in a statewide and national Democratic landslide, his only loss in sixteen primary and general statewide races. Elected governor in 1914 and reelected two years later, he then won his seat in the U.S. Senate in 1918.

In the Senate, Capper served continuously on the Agriculture and Forestry and District of Columbia committees. He was second chairman of the farm bloc, a bipartisan caucus seeking to improve conditions for farmers. His name was attached to a number of pieces of legislation in his first two terms: the Capper-Volstead Cooperative Marketing Act providing antitrust exemptions for cooperative marketing and producers' associations, the Capper-Tincher Act regulating grain futures, the Capper-Lenroot-Anderson Act (Agricultural Credits Act) affording intermediate credit for farmers, the Capper-Ketchum Act granting federal funds for 4-H clubs, and the Capper-Crampton Act authorizing a system of roads between Washington, D.C., and Mount Vernon.

Although a man of wealth, Capper lived modestly. His primary asset in the Senate was his familiarity with the concerns of his constituents. He was active in committees but rarely spoke in front of the full Senate.

BIBLIOGRAPHY

Capper, Arthur. *The Agricultural Bloc.* 1922. Repr. 1972.
Socolofsky, Homer E. *Arthur Capper: Publisher, Politician, Philanthropist.* 1962.

HOMER E. SOCOLOFSKY

CAREERS. *See* Members.

CARLISLE, JOHN G. (1835–1910), Democratic representative (1877–1890) and Senator (1890–1893) from Kentucky, Speaker of the House (1883–1888), and secretary of the Treasury (1893–1897). John G. Carlisle was born in Campbell (now Kenton) County, Kentucky, and was largely self-educated, up through reading for the law in Covington,

JOHN G. CARLISLE.   LIBRARY OF CONGRESS

Kentucky, where he was admitted to the bar in 1858. A year later he was elected to the state legislature, beginning a political career that lasted until 1897. He served in the state's lower house from 1859 to 1865, in the state senate from 1866 to 1871, and as Kentucky's lieutenant governor from 1871 to 1875.

Carlisle joined the U.S. House of Representatives in 1877, and his rise to prominence there was rapid. He became a leader in the tariff-reform faction of the Democratic party. In the election of 1878, the Democrats swept into power and elected Samuel J. Randall of Pennsylvania as their Speaker. Randall's Philadelphia constituency supported high tariffs. Rural constituents like Carlisle's bore the brunt of the higher consumer costs that protective tariffs produced. The tariff reformers were a majority within the Democratic caucus but were consis-

tently outvoted by a coalition of Republicans and high-tariff Democrats.

Carlisle was elected Speaker in 1883 and the tariff reformers finally had control of the House. Carlisle struck an alliance with President Grover Cleveland in the cause of tariff reform. Against the opposition of the Randall faction and the Republicans of the 49th Congress, Carlisle led the tariff-reform group in proposing rate reductions. Working with Rep. William R. Morrison of Illinois, chairman of the Committee on Ways and Means, Carlisle sought a moderate tariff bill that could win the support of both Democrats and Republicans. The Pennsylvania delegation, led by Randall, held the balance of power, and the Morrison tariff bill was twice defeated. It was not until the 50th Congress, in 1888, that Carlisle and President Cleveland were able to push through a tariff-reform bill drafted by the new chairman of the Ways and Means Committee, Roger Q. Mills of Texas. The House victory proved hollow, however, when the Mills bill was gutted in the Senate. Carlisle, an effective and respected Democratic Speaker, serving during a Democratic administration, ultimately failed to see his main policy enacted into law.

Nonetheless, the alliance between Carlisle and Cleveland paid dividends for the Kentuckian. He served as minority leader in the House during the first two years of the Benjamin Harrison administration and was then sent by Kentucky to the Senate, where he fought against the protectionist McKinley tariff bill. The enactment of the McKinley tariff proved a pyrrhic victory for the Republicans, enabling Cleveland to reclaim the White House in the 1892 election. Cleveland still regarded Carlisle as his right-hand man on fiscal issues and named him secretary of the Treasury.

Carlisle was caught in the middle of the conflict between eastern capital and western economies in the early 1890s. He was instinctively conservative and inclined to husband the nation's gold supply, a position favored in the eastern financial markets. Yet his constituency and that of the Democratic party were centered in the South and West, which were bastions of free silver. Finally, Cleveland and Carlisle allied themselves with the East by issuing government bonds to cover its liabilities, a move that alienated them from their congressional supporters. William Jennings Bryan arose as the voice of populist discontent, and the Democratic party was rent asunder. The country returned the presidency to the Republicans for the next sixteen years.

The end of the second Cleveland administration marked the end of Carlisle's political career. He became an attorney in New York City, where he enjoyed moderate success.

BIBLIOGRAPHY

Barnes, James A. *John G. Carlisle: Financial Statesman.* 1931. Repr. 1967.
Kennon, Donald R., ed. *The Speakers of the U.S. House of Representatives, 1789–1984.* 1986. Pp. 178–182.
Peters, Ronald M., Jr. *The American Speakership: The Office in Historical Perspective.* 1990. Pp. 59–97.

RONALD M. PETERS, JR.

CARTER, JAMES EARL (JIMMY), JR.

(1924–), governor of Georgia, thirty-ninth president of the United States, noted for forging historic peace among adversaries in the Middle East but faltering in his dealings with a Congress controlled by his own Democratic party. Jimmy Carter—the name he used even in his official signature—was the quintessential Washington outsider, even in the Oval Office. It was a status he carefully cultivated after he began his long-shot campaign for the presidency in 1976 as a former governor of Georgia. Born in tiny, rural Plains, Georgia, on 1 October 1924, Carter achieved political gains by emphasizing his politically nontraditional roots: peanut farmer, warehouse businessman, U.S. Naval Academy graduate, nuclear engineer.

Although unknown nationally, Carter recognized early that his image as an outsider could help him win the presidency. The fact that political analysts and even many of his close associates gave him no chance to win the 1976 nomination made Carter more tenacious—a trait that would eventually bring him his greatest successes and failures. Carter defeated his better-known Democratic opponents, and narrowly defeated the never-elected Republican incumbent President Gerald R. Ford. Crucial to understanding Carter's triumph as a political outsider is the fact that it came in the wake of the nation's most infamous political scandal—the so-called Watergate affair, which forced Republican president Richard M. Nixon to resign in midterm.

The tenacity that led Carter to defy political experts by running for president also led him to defy diplomatic experts by waging an unorthodox mission to bring peace to the Middle East's historic enemies, Israel and Egypt. In 1978, Carter invited to his Camp David retreat Israel's prime minister Menachem Begin and Egypt's president Anwar Sadat, and doggedly prodded until an accord was reached. A year later, his unprecedented, unscripted shuttle between Cairo and Jerusalem risked a very public failure, but succeeded in forging the Israeli-Egyptian peace treaty.

Carter made human rights the centerpiece of U.S. international policy, applying it to both communist and anticommunist dictatorships. He also signed two major treaties that were the culmination of negotiations begun by President Ford—yet were vigorously opposed by Republican conservatives. The United States and Soviet Union concluded a Strategic Arms Limitation Talks treaty known as SALT II, which sharply reduced strategic nuclear weapons, but after the Soviet military invaded Afghanistan, the treaty was never ratified. In his memoir, *Keeping Faith,* Carter called the failure to ratify the SALT II treaty "the most profound disappointment of my Presidency."

Carter also signed two Panama Canal treaties under which the United States would relinquish control of the canal to Panama on the last day of 1999. Conservative Senate Republicans opposed ratification, but the Senate's top Republican, Minority Leader Howard H. Baker, Jr., of Tennessee, backed Carter's effort. After a prolonged political fight and several technical compromises, the Senate ratified the treaties.

Domestically, Carter's program initiatives were hampered by his failure to build close ties with con-

PRESIDENT JAMES EARL (JIMMY) CARTER, JR. *Left, front,* addressing Congress. Standing behind are Vice President Walter F. Mondale, *center,* and Speaker Thomas P. (Tip) O'Neill, Jr. (D-Mass), *right.*

LIBRARY OF CONGRESS

gressional leaders, whom he had not known before coming to Washington. Congressional Democratic leaders complained that top Carter advisers did not consult them and often did not return their phone calls. They privately and publicly criticized Carter's advisers, including congressional liaison chief Frank Moore, a Georgian who came to Washington with Carter. Things got so bad that House Speaker Thomas P. (Tip) O'Neill, the wily Massachusetts Democrat, dubbed Carter's chief White House adviser, Hamilton Jordan, "Hannibal Jerkin'."

Carter got his relations with Congress off to the worst political start, for what he considered the best populist motives. After one month in office, he fulfilled his campaign promise to cut the worst examples of waste and pork-barrel projects by proposing to eliminate funds for constructing nineteen dams and other water projects affecting seventeen states. Senators and representatives were furious at this attack on the pet projects they had bragged about to voters back home; Carter responded by targeting thirteen more projects for review. Although Carter's actions may have been valid on the environmental and budgetary merits, his zealotry on water projects stirred up so much political ill will on Capitol Hill that his presidency never recovered.

When Carter engineered his own comprehensive energy reform plan, members of Congress balked, saying that they were not fully consulted. As a result, Carter never got the full reform package he sought. He succeeded in creating departments of Energy and Education, and in deregulating energy, finance, transportation, and communications programs. He enacted the first comprehensive reform of the civil service system in a century and installed inspectors general to probe mismanagement in each agency.

The Carter years were tough for consumers, largely due to circumstances beyond Carter's control. An Arab oil embargo led to gasoline shortages and fueled a disastrous cycle of high inflation and high interest rates.

In November 1979, Iranian radicals invaded the U.S. embassy in Tehran, captured fifty-two American employees, and held most as hostages throughout Carter's first year as president. Carter focused the world spotlight on their plight, but his presidency seemed to be held hostage to their fate. A U.S. commando attempt to rescue the hostages failed due to military miscalculations and mishaps.

Carter was challenged for the 1980 Democratic presidential nomination by Sen. Edward M.

Kennedy of Massachusetts, who was supported by discontented liberals. Carter emerged victorious but weakened, and in November he was defeated decisively by California's former governor Ronald Reagan, a conservative Republican who won the votes of many disillusioned blue-collar Democrats.

Carter's public stature has grown significantly in his years out of office. He founded the Carter Center of Emory University, a policy institute that focuses on resolving world crises. In a notable endeavor as an elder statesman, Carter traveled privately to North Korea in 1994 to negotiate with communist leader Kim Il Sung. Private citizen Jimmy Carter has won widespread public appreciation as a former president who works tirelessly for noble causes.

BIBLIOGRAPHY

Carter, Jimmy. *Keeping Faith: Memoirs of a President.* 1982.
Jones, Charles O. *The Trusteeship Presidency: Jimmy Carter and the United States Congress.* 1988.
Schram, Martin. *Running for President, 1976: The Carter Campaign.* 1977.

MARTIN SCHRAM

CASEWORK. *See* Constituency Service.

CASS, LEWIS (1782–1866), senator from Michigan, the "father of popular sovereignty," Democratic presidential candidate. A New Hampshire native, Cass was elected to the Senate of the 29th Congress by the Michigan legislature in 1845 after a varied career as an Ohio legislator, army general during the War of 1812, governor of the Michigan Territory, secretary of War, and minister to France.

Senator Cass was an unabashed promoter of territorial expansion and sectional compromise. Appointed to the Foreign Relations Committee, he championed the "all of Oregon" claim in the dispute with Britain and advocated an aggressive military policy during the Mexican War. His letter to Alfred Nicholson (24 December 1847) tacitly rejected the antislavery Wilmot Proviso in favor of "popular sovereignty"—allowing territorial residents to decide the slavery question. In 1848 Cass was nominated for president by the Democrats, but the Whig Zachary Taylor won the election.

Returning to the Senate in 1849, Cass accepted only one standing committee assignment: the Library. He joined Henry Clay on the Committee of

LEWIS CASS.   LIBRARY OF CONGRESS

BIBLIOGRAPHY

Dunbar, Willis Frederick. *Lewis Cass.* 1970.
Woodford, Frank B. *Lewis Cass: The Last Jeffersonian.* 1950.

                                    WILLARD CARL KLUNDER

CAUCUS. [*This entry includes two separate articles:* Party Caucus *and* Special Interest Caucus. *For related discussions, see* Political Parties *and* Interest Groups.]

Party Caucus

The term *caucus* is used both in a legislative and extralegislative sense. Most generally, it is simply a meeting of party members, open to all who consider themselves affiliated with the party, for the purpose of nominating candidates for election. The more common current use of the term is in a legislative context where *caucus* simply means the organization of all members of a particular party within a legislative body.

In either case, the word seems to be a genuinely American term and not a borrowing from British parliamentary practice. William Safire considers it an American Indian word, but Noah Brooks and others have judged it to be a corruption of the word *caulkers,* a term for shipyard workers who caulked the seams of wooden ships. As early as 1725, caulkers organized in Boston for the purpose of nominating candidates for local office.

In recent and contemporary legislative practice in the United States, party caucuses have performed four functions: (1) nominating and electing party officers and candidates; (2) reviewing the assignment of party members to legislative committees and ratifying committee chairmen; (3) serving as forums for discussion of matters of party policy and, on occasion, of binding party members to the policy decisions arrived at; and (4) imposing party discipline on party members who have been adjudged guilty of violating some fundamental condition of party membership and defining a member's standing in the party.

The Party Caucus in the Early Congress (1796–1824). The caucus of the anti-Federalist Republican party (later the Democratic party) was a major force in the early years of the Republic. These followers of Thomas Jefferson met for the first time on 2 April 1796 for the purpose of formulating a strategy to defeat Jay's Treaty. Because the Federalist-dominated Senate had already ratified the

Thirteen, which drafted the Compromise of 1850 legislation, and was easily reelected to a second term. Cass supported the Kansas-Nebraska bill introduced by Stephen A. Douglas in 1854 because it embraced popular sovereignty. The subsequent founding of the Republican party served notice that his moderate position on slavery was losing support. He denounced the violence of "Bleeding Kansas" but focused his criticism on free staters. After the Republicans swept Michigan in 1856 Zachariah Chandler replaced him in the Senate. James Buchanan then appointed Cass secretary of State.

An obese teetotaler and an uninspired orator, Cass was not a colorful politician. He espoused a narrowly legalistic interpretation of the Constitution and viewed slavery as a political issue, not a moral one. He personified the vigorous Americanism prevalent in the Old Northwest.

treaty, Republicans in the House hoped to block the appropriation to implement it.

The next important meeting of the party caucus was in 1796, to nominate Thomas Jefferson as the party's candidate for president. The Federalist members of Congress also used the caucus as the presidential nominating vehicle but abandoned it after their defeat in 1800.

The first genuine caucus debate over presidential nominations took place in 1808, when both James Madison and James Monroe sought the nomination. By the time of the 1816 gathering, increasing protests were heard against "King Caucus" as the presidential nominating vehicle.

The opposition burst into the open on 14 February 1824, when only sixty-six of the 216 Republican members of Congress attended the caucus. Andrew Jackson denounced the caucus and had himself nominated by the Tennessee legislature. He, William H. Crawford, John Quincy Adams, and House Speaker Henry Clay competed for the presidency in 1824, all within the confines of a single party now beginning to refer to themselves as "Democrats."

The caucus as a presidential nominating device did not survive the 1824 election, but for legislative purposes it remained a powerful force used by Speaker Clay to establish party positions on bills before they reached the floor. Clay was able to assist Adams in the House, but the Senate was now coming into its own and was filled with friends of Andrew Jackson bent on frustrating Adams. The party caucus in the Senate was led by Vice President John C. Calhoun, a Jackson partisan and adversary of Clay.

The election of Jackson signaled a period of transition for the parties. The Federalists had disappeared by 1820, and by 1832 the old Jeffersonian Republicans had degenerated into warring factions. By 1833 and 1834, however, disgruntled ex-Jacksonians and followers of Clay established themselves as the National Republican, or Whig, party.

The brief twenty-five-year life of the Whig party was haunted by the slavery question. Having a much stronger antislavery wing than the Democrats and desiring to be a truly national party, the Whigs were perennially threatened by any broaching of the slavery question within its caucus in Congress.

Party Regularity and Caucus Discipline in the Late Nineteenth Century. The Republicans, as the successors to the Whigs, confronted problems of party discipline during the impeachment and trial of Andrew Johnson in 1866. The four senators who

voted to acquit Johnson were excluded from the Senate Republican caucus in 1868. The liberal Republican faction in the 1870s likewise posed problems of party regularity. The caucus denied Carl Schurz of Missouri the chairmanship of a committee and later expelled Schurz and seven other liberal Republicans from the caucus. Denial of committee assignments or chairmanships to members found to be at odds with their caucus over matters of policy or for supporting opposing party candidates made its first appearance at this time. The Senate Democratic caucus accommodated the rejected Republicans by allocating them seats out of the Democratic quota.

The Republicans in both the House and Senate in the 1880s and 1890s were also forced to confront the problem of members elected with some combination of Republican and third-party support. In 1893, for example, the Senate Republicans were presented with the defection of long-time Republican senator William M. Stewart of Nevada to the Populists. The Democrats who gained control of the Senate in the elections of 1892 permitted Stewart to retain his chairmanship of the Committee on Mines, but Stewart's erstwhile Republican colleagues were unwilling to see him retain his seat on the Appropriations Committee, and he was removed.

Throughout the later nineteenth and early twentieth centuries, Democrats on the whole were more willing to submit to party discipline than were Republicans. More often in the minority during this period (1895–1910), the Democrats in both houses used the caucus to build cohesion in their outnumbered ranks. Without a Democratic president between 1897 and 1913, the party caucus was a natural rallying place.

In the Senate, where members enjoy greater personal influence and latitude than in the House, caucus discipline has always been more problematic. Nonetheless, when Arthur Pue Gorman was elected caucus chairman in 1889, he attempted to exert the kind of leadership of Senate Democrats that Republican caucus chairman William B. Allison of Iowa was applying on the Republican side. Gorman's efforts culminated in 1903 with the adoption of a policy in the caucus that a two-thirds vote on policy matters would be binding on all Democratic senators. Within three years, this rule was challenged when, in February 1906, the Democratic caucus adopted the policy that all Democratic senators must vote against the treaty with Santo Domingo. Sen. Thomas M. Patterson of Colorado not only withdrew from the caucus but denounced the caucus rule on the floor of the Senate as unconstitutional. In 1915, after a similar two-thirds vote on a ship-purchase bill (culminating in the Shipping Act), Sen. Gilbert M. Hitchcock of Nebraska defied the caucus and denounced the binding rule. Senate Republicans have generally not attempted to bind members to caucus policy decisions but seem to have been even more exacting than the Democrats in admitting members to the caucus whose credentials as Republicans were the least bit unorthodox, as was seen in the case of the members elected with third-party support in the period from 1870 to 1900.

The Golden Age of the Caucus in the House (1909–1920). Caucuses of both parties in the House played a major role in the 1910 revolt against Speaker Joseph G. Cannon, when Democrats threw their support behind the efforts of progressive Republicans to oust Cannon from the speakership. But when the 61st Congress convened in January 1909, twenty House Democrats defied the caucus and supported Cannon, who rewarded them with seats on the Rules and Ways and Means committees. This was done without the approval of Democratic floor leader James Beauchamp (Champ) Clark and in violation of a caucus rule adopted in 1909 that stipulated that "no Democrat should accept a committee assignment unless it has the approval of the minority leader." While an effort was made to strip the errant Democrats of their rewards by a caucus meeting in March 1909, the only punishment meted out was a resolution condemning their acceptance of Cannon's largess; significantly, no action was taken to deny them their choice committee assignments.

In 1909, the House Democratic caucus also adopted the 2 to 3 rule that Senate Democrats had passed in 1903. In the House, however, the rule was applied more stringently and with greater effect.

Under caucus chairmen Albert S. Burleson of Texas and A. Mitchell Palmer of Pennsylvania (chairman for the 63d Congress, 1913–1915), the organization reached its zenith of influence. So powerful did the caucus become that bills were first introduced in the caucus and marked up there. Only after caucus approval by a 2 to 3 vote were they introduced on the floor. Committee action became a hollow formality.

Even more remarkable were two additional caucus practices in the 62d and 63d Congresses. One was that no report would issue from a standing committee without express caucus approval. Another was that the Committee on Rules would not

issue a rule without instructions from the caucus, except on bills reported out by the Ways and Means or Appropriations committees.

Upon assuming the presidency in 1913, Democrat Woodrow Wilson gave to the caucus the task of revising the thorny and controversial tariff law. Since the two-thirds rule applied on caucus policy decisions, Wilson could secure approval for the changes he desired with the certainty that they would pass the Democrat-dominated House.

The powerful and commanding role of the caucus, however, did not survive the loss of Democratic control of the House after World War I. Its disciplinary role curtailed by its loss of the ability to designate committee chairmen, the caucus reverted to its earlier role as an organization that approved ranking minority members and then dissolved for the rest of the life of the Congress.

The Eclipse and Revival of the House Caucus (1933–1965). When the Democrats regained control of the House after the 1930 elections, and then had their numbers augmented in the election of 1932 with the coming to power of Franklin D. Roosevelt, the role of the caucus became crucial. When the House organized itself in 1933 there were 310 Democrats. To cope with the unwieldy group, the caucus modified its whip system by designating fifteen regional assistant whips. This provided congressional Democrats with a rare degree of cohesion and enabled the first New Deal legislation to sail through the House.

The period of the late 1920s and the dramatic period of the New Deal caused a shift of emphasis in the activities of the various congressional party caucuses. Until the election of 1928 it had tended to be the dominant Republicans who were more occupied with enforcing party regularity and dealing with bolters or members elected with minor-party endorsement. The desertion of the national ticket in 1928 by a number of southern Democratic members—the "Hoovercrats"—forced Democratic caucuses into the somewhat unfamiliar role of enforcing party regularity. In 1943, the Democratic caucus in the House denied a seat on the Judiciary Committee to Rep. Vito Marcantonio of New York because he had been elected with the support of the American Labor party, which was adjudged to be a communist front organization. In 1963, the House Democratic caucus stripped Representatives John Bell Williams of Mississippi and Albert W. Watson of South Carolina of their committee seniority for their open support of Republican presidential candidate Barry Goldwater. This was the first time that loss of seniority was used as a punishment by a congressional party caucus, but it was repeated in 1969 when Louisiana's John R. Rarick lost his Agriculture Committee seniority for supporting the Republican presidential candidate in the 1968 election. In a more unusual case, the House Democratic caucus in 1983 ratified a decision from the party's Steering and Policy Committee to strip Rep. Phil Gramm of Texas of his seat on the Budget Committee, while allowing him to retain his seat on the Energy and Commerce Committee. Gramm had been accused of leaking Democratic Budget Committee strategy to Republicans in the White House in 1981.

The Caucus as a Reform Vehicle (1965–1975). Beginning in 1965 with a decision to hold monthly meetings of the Democratic caucus rather than on an ad hoc basis, the party panel served as the major

instrument of change against entrenched committee and subcommittee chairmen.

In 1971, both party caucuses in the House adopted new rules allowing them to use criteria other than seniority in ratifying committee chairmen. Seniority had been the sole basis since the 1910 revolt against Speaker Cannon. Both caucuses also established for themselves the right to accept or reject the slates of committee chairs and ranking members sent to them by their respective parties' assignment panels, but it was not until 1975 that a caucus challenge was actually mounted to sitting chairmen who had been recommended to the body. The House Democratic caucus rejected the names of three incumbent chairmen. This power was extended by the caucus to chairmen of Appropriations subcommittees the same year. The 1973 "Subcommittee Bill of Rights" of the Democratic caucus

SENATE DEMOCRATIC CAUCUS MEMBERS. *Foreground, facing front, left to right,* Hubert H. Humphrey (Minn.), Majority Leader and vice president–elect Lyndon B. Johnson (Tex.), Mike Mansfield (Mont.), and George A. Smathers (Fla.), 3 January 1961.   LIBRARY OF CONGRESS

greatly strengthened the subcommittees vis-à-vis the full committees.

The caucus was less successful in this period as a vehicle for developing party policies on the Vietnam War. The Democrats struggled with the issue in the House, and it was not until the spring of 1973 that the Democratic caucus first endorsed an antiwar resolution. On issues on which there are intraparty divisions, caucuses with their diverse memberships find policy consensus difficult.

However, in the aftermath of the 1980 Reagan victory and the capture of the Senate by the Republicans, the House was the only national-level institution still in Democratic hands, and the caucus, under Rep. Gillis W. Long of Louisiana, used the organization as a forum to air grievances among the various party factions in the House. In a modest effort at unifying the party behind a policy, the House Democratic caucus in 1982 endorsed a broad statement of party principle entitled "Rebuilding the Road to Opportunity," which called for the adoption of an industrial policy to promote U.S. economic competitiveness.

Because of its numerical predominance in the House since 1955, the Democratic caucus has been able to shape House practice much more consistently than the Republican conference. Republicans, in recent years, have tended to use their conference (they dropped the use of the term *caucus* in 1911) as a place to air their differences with the Democrats and to promote media coverage of Republican positions on legislation.

The role of the Senate party conferences (the Democrats now use that term as well in the Senate) has also been more media-oriented and informational than policy-making. There has been no effort to revive a binding rule, which, even in those days of greater party unity, was never effective.

The increasingly individualistic nature of U.S. politics makes it unlikely that congressional party caucuses will ever again be the focus of important policy deliberations. As forums for debate, the caucuses, which are closed to the press and public, can be quite useful. They will also continue in their role of ratifying leadership nominations that emanate from party steering committees and committees on committees. They may even be used in novel ways, as in the House Democrats' decision in 1983 to invite all of the party's presidential hopefuls to address the membership and answer questions. Another enduring function of party caucuses will be to determine qualifications for caucus membership and party perquisites.

Historically, House caucuses have been much more effective in enforcing party unity and discipline than those in the Senate. This bicameral difference is a reflection of the larger role accorded to leadership in the more populous House and the greater power of individual members in the more compact Senate.

BIBLIOGRAPHY

Baker, Richard A., and Roger H. Davidson, eds. *First among Equals.* 1991.
Galloway, George B. *History of the House of Representatives.* 1961.
Haines, Wilder H. "The Congressional Caucus of Today." *American Political Science Review* 9 (November 1915): 696–706.
Jones, Charles O. *The Minority Party in Congress.* 1970.
Rothman, David J. *Politics and Power: The United States Senate, 1869–1901.* 1966.
Sinclair, Barbara. *Majority Leadership in the U.S. House.* 1983.

ROSS K. BAKER

Special Interest Caucus

Congressional caucuses and legislative service organizations are informal voluntary groups of members who seek to have some impact on the policy process. While caucuses are a relatively recent phenomenon, viewed initially with some misgivings, membership in such groups is now an accepted and legitimated form of member behavior. From the 1970s on, however, there was considerable change in the status, activity, and number of these groups. Before the 1970s, there were only a few recognizable caucuses in Congress, and most of these were concentrated in the House of Representatives. With the exception of the Democratic Study Group and one or two others, these informal groups were short-lived and not influential. This changed dramatically with the formal establishment of the Congressional Black Caucus in 1971. In response to a series of galvanizing incidents, including President Richard M. Nixon's refusal to meet with them as a group, black members began to coordinate their activities. After fourteen months of negotiation, Nixon agreed to a meeting, and in response to their success black members of the House officially formed the Congressional Black Caucus. Unlike most congressional interest groups of the time, the Congressional Black Caucus had a chair and formal membership. More important, it had policy agenda that it actively and vocally promoted. The

Congressional Black Caucus targeted issues and policies that were of unique and specific interest to their caucus, as opposed to their party.

Over the next few years the number of caucuses and their degree of institutionalization increased. By the early 1980s, caucuses had become a part of the congressional establishment. In 1980, there were almost 70 groups; by 1987, the number had grown to 120; and in 1993, the Congressional Research Service listed 127 caucuses operating in the 103d Congress. While the growth was bicameral, the majority of these groups formed in the House.

The proliferation was relatively sudden, so until 1981 there were no formal rules or procedures governing the funding or activities of these groups. This changed, however, when the House acted on the recommendation of the House Administration Committee to regulate the funding of caucuses. The 1981 ruling required all caucuses to register with the House Administration Committee in order to secure office space and congressional funding. A few caucuses decided to create shadow foundations to accept outside funding and grants prohibited by the ruling. Though there are interactions between caucuses and their foundations, legal restrictions prohibit mingling of funds, offices, and staff.

With the growing heterogeneity in Congress, political parties have been hard pressed to respond to the growing and divergent demands of members. Over the years, caucuses have formed in response to the special needs of certain members. Arthur G. Stevens and his coauthors (1974) suggest that frustration of key junior members of the Democratic party in the House of Representatives led to caucus formation. Thus, with the growing decentralization in Congress, members of both parties formed smaller, more cohesive subparty units in an attempt to improve their policy success on the floor.

Caucuses give members specific benefits that they may have more difficulty attaining from their party. The particular benefits depend on the type of caucus the member joins. According to Susan Webb Hammond's typology (1989), caucuses may be categorized as party, personal-interest, or constituency oriented. Party caucuses are oriented toward specific intraparty concerns, which are usually ideologically based. Such groups include the Democratic Study Group, the Wednesday Group (a Republican caucus) and the Conservative Democratic Forum. Personal-interest caucuses are issue based and usually form around a specific concern that members (regardless of party or ideology) hold in common. Examples have included the Arts Caucus and the Senate Caucus on the Family. Finally, constituency-based caucuses are formed to represent the interests and concerns of a specific constituency group. These caucuses vary by the size of their constituencies, and they have ranged from large, nationally based groups (Congressional Black Caucus) to state or district groups (Wine Caucus). Not surprisingly, constituency-based groups comprise the majority of caucuses in Congress.

Caucus activity corresponds to the type of group and the interests it represents. These informal groups are increasingly significant in the policy process because they perform many of the same functions as political parties and legislative committees, but with greater efficiency. Among the most important are information gathering and management, agenda setting, and coalition building.

Information gathering is one of the caucuses' most vital functions. Congressional office and committee staffs are constrained by a variety of duties and responsibilities that limit the amount of time they can devote to a given issue, but caucuses, because of their narrower focus, can devote more time and energy to intensive study. This has helped some caucuses, such as the Democratic Study Group, to become centralized sources of information for the entire party concerning issues before Congress. Other caucuses provide more specific information reflecting their more particular concerns. In addition, caucuses use their information-gathering skills to build bridges with nonmembers. By providing research to those who are not members and making information available to personal and committee staffs, caucuses allow working relationships to form that may eventually help them achieve their policy goals.

Another important caucus activity is agenda setting. Because all caucus members are also party members, these groups are able to promote issues and ideas to the larger congressional audience through their membership. Finally, caucuses help to build coalitions through intraparty, bipartisan, or even bicameral negotiation. Regardless of the type of coalition building that occurs, caucuses may play an important broker's role between parties or chambers, helping to create consensus on an issue by coordinating the diverse efforts that result from overlapping committee jurisdictions. More often, they may provide support for the position of their party.

Caucus members may receive benefits from these organizations that are as tangible as the benefits they receive from their party. A sense of belonging

TABLE 1. *Caucuses and Legislative Service Organizations, 103d Congress*

HOUSE

PARTISAN

CAUCUS	NO. OF MEMBERS
Conservative Democratic Forum (also known as the Boll Weevils)	50
Conservative Opportunity Society [Republican]	50
Democratic Budget Study Group	35
Democratic Freshman Class [103d Congress]	66
Democratic Freshman Class of 1990 [102d Congress]	25
Democratic Freshman Class of the 101st Congress	18
Democratic Freshman Task Force on Reform	NA[1]
Democratic Study Group [LSO][2]	255
House Republican Study Committee [LSO]	130
House Wednesday Group [LSO]	38
Mainstream Forum [Democratic]	50
Ninety-two Group [Republican]	35
Republican Class of the 101st Congress	14
Republican Class of the 100th Congress	18
Republican Class of '85 [99th Congress]	NA
Republican Freshman Members, 103d Congress	48
Republican Freshman Task Force on Reform	47
Republican Sophomore Class of the 103d Congress	18

BIPARTISAN

CAUCUS	NO. OF MEMBERS
Albanian Issues Caucus	NA
Army Caucus	80
Chesapeake Bay Congressional Caucus	22
Congressional Automotive Caucus [LSO]	52
Congressional Aviation Forum	75
Congressional Bearing Caucus	40
Congressional Biomedical Research Caucus	67

BIPARTISAN (Continued)

CAUCUS	NO. OF MEMBERS
Congressional Boating Caucus	72
Congressional Caucus on Unfounded Mandates	93
Congressional Children's Working Group	113
Congressional Coalition on Population and Development	44
Congressional [House] Footwear Caucus	80
Congressional Friends of the Caribbean Basin	80
Congressional [House] Grace Caucus	170
Congressional Human Rights Caucus [LSO]	200
Congressional Hunger Caucus [LSO]	NA
Congressional Narcotics Abuse and Control Caucus [LSO]	NA
Congressional Property Rights Caucus	NA
Congressional Social Security Caucus	50
Congressional Space Caucus [LSO]	NA
Congressional [House] Steel Caucus [LSO][3]	100
Congressional Task Force on Tobacco and Health	50
Congressional Task Force to End the Arab Boycott	55
Congressional [House] Textile Caucus [LSO]	NA
Congressional [House] Travel and Tourism Caucus [LSO]	160
Congressional [House] Truck Caucus	NA
Congressional U.S.–Former Soviet Union Energy Caucus	36
Congressional Urban Caucus	75
Constitutional Forum	NA
Delta Caucus	24
Depot/Plant Caucus[4]	NA
Fair Trade Caucus	NA

[3]The Congressional Steel Caucus no longer has LSO status.
[4]The Depot/Plant Caucus was originally organized as the Depot Caucus in 1986, subsequently became inactive, then was reactivated in 1992 under its current name.

[1]NA = not available at this time
[2]Legislative Service Organization

TABLE 1. *Caucuses and Legislative Service Organizations, 103d Congress (Continued)*

HOUSE

BIPARTISAN *(Continued)*

CAUCUS	NO. OF MEMBERS
Fairness Network[5]	37
Forestry 2000 Task Force	100
House Beef Caucus	NA
House Character Counts Group	NA
House Corn Caucus	60
House Empowerment Caucus	30
House Mining Caucus	40
House Working Group on Mental Illness and Health Issues	13
Insurance Caucus	NA
Law Enforcement Caucus	NA
Long Island Sound Caucus	13
Medical Technology Caucus	NA
New England Congressional Energy Caucus	23
Northeast Agricultural Caucus	56
Northeast Gas Congressional Caucus	NA
Northeast-Midwest Congressional [House] Coalition [LSO][6]	100
Notch Coalition	12
Older Americans Caucus [LSO]	NA
Progressive Caucus	NA
Pro-Life Caucus	NA
[House] Rural Health Care Coalition[7]	148

SENATE

PARTISAN

CAUCUS	NO. OF MEMBERS
Senate Republican Task Force on Health Care	NA
Senate Steering Committee [Republican]	NA

SENATE *(Continued)*

PARTISAN CAUCUS *(Continued)*

CAUCUS	NO. OF MEMBERS
Senate Wednesday Group [Republican][8]	

BIPARTISAN

CAUCUS	NO. OF MEMBERS
Caucus on Deficit Reduction and Economic Growth	40
Concerned Senators for the Arts	68
Northeast-Midwest Senate Coalition	36
Senate Anti-Terrorism Caucus	14
Senate Beef Caucus	44
Senate Character Counts Group	NA
Senate Children's Caucus	30
Senate Coal Caucus	30
Senate Cuba Freedom Caucus	NA
Senate Delta Caucus	14
Senate Drug Enforcement Caucus	NA
Senate Empowerment Caucus	NA
Senate Footwear Caucus	32
Senate Grace Caucus	30
Senate National Guard Caucus	NA
Senate Rail Caucus	NA
Senate Rural Health Caucus	60
Senate Steel Caucus	NA
Senate Sweetener Caucus	23
Senate Textile Steering Committee (also known as the Senate Textile Caucus)	10
Senate Tourism Caucus	60
Senate Western State Coalition	30

BICAMERAL

CAUCUS	NO. OF MEMBERS
Ad Hoc Congressional Committee for Irish Affairs	90
Arms Control and Foreign Policy Caucus [LSO][9]	140

[5]The Fairness Network is a group of House members whose districts are affected by proposals to close or realign military bases. It seeks to ensure that the bases slated for closing have a fair hearing.
[6]The Northeast-Midwest Congressional Coalition changed its name from the Northeast-Midwest Economic Advancement Coalition in 1978. The coalition has a standing subunit called the House Great Lakes Task Force (HGLTF), which serves a number of functions previously conducted by the Conference of Great Lakes Congressmen.
[7]The Rural Health Care Coalition has a number of subunits that focus on issues of particular concern to the group, including grants programs, health education, hospitals and clinics, long-term care, and rural development.

[8]"The Senate Wednesday Group provides liberal-to-moderate Republican senators a forum for informal discussion on subjects of common interest. The Senate Wednesday Group does not take a position on legislation, nor does it act as a lobbying group. Because of the group's informal nature, no listing of membership is available." (*Congressional Yellow Book*, Spring 1993, pp. vi–13).
[9]The Arms Control and Foreign Policy Caucus changed its name from Members of Congress for Peace through Law in 1983.

TABLE 1. *Caucuses and Legislative Service Organizations, 103d Congress (Continued)*

BICAMERAL *(Continued)*			
CAUCUS	NO. OF MEMBERS	CAUCUS	NO. OF MEMBERS
California Delegation Bipartisan Task Force on Defense Reinvestment and Economic Development	54	Congressional Friends of Animals	25
California Democratic Congressional Delegation [LSO]	35	Congressional Friends of Human Rights Monitors	155
Congressional Alcohol Fuels Caucus	90	Congressional Hispanic Caucus [LSO]	18[15]
Congressional Arts Caucus [LSO]	280	Congressional Leaders United for a Balanced Budget (CLUBB)	100
Congressional Asian Pacific American Caucus	10	Congressional Minor League Baseball Caucus	61
Congressional Biotechnology Caucus	84	Congressional Olympic Caucus	35
Congressional Black Caucus [LSO][10]	40[11]	Congressional Populist Caucus [LSO]	30
Congressional Border Caucus [LSO]	27	Congressional Rural Caucus [LSO]	100
Congressional Caucus for Women's Issues [LSO][12]	145	Congressional Soybean Caucus	100
Congressional Caucus on Advanced Materials	37[13]	Congressional Sportsman's Caucus	168
Congressional Caucus on India and Indian-Americans	20	Congressional Sunbelt Caucus [LSO]	150
Congressional Caucus on Syrian Jewry	75	Congressional Task Force on International HIV/AIDS	60
Congressional Clearinghouse on Recycling and Solid Waste Solutions	30	Environmental and Energy Study Conference [LSO][16]	390[17]
Congressional Coalition for Soviet Jewry	NA	Federal Government Service Task Force [LSO]	56
Congressional Coalition on Adoption	90	Friends of Ireland	160
Congressional Competitiveness Caucus	214	Military Reform Caucus	NA
Congressional Copper Caucus[14]	35	National Security Caucus[18]	183
Congressional Defense Caucus	50	New York State Congressional Delegation [LSO]	36
Congressional Ferroalloy Caucus	36	Pennsylvania Congressional Delegation[19] [LSO]	23
Congressional Fire Services Caucus	363	Tennessee Valley Congressional Caucus	38
		Vietnam Era Veterans in Congress	64

[10]The Congressional Black Caucus changed its name from Democratic Select Committee (founded in 1969) when it formally reorganized in 1971.

[11]The Black Caucus has a number of "associate" members of the House and Senate not included in this count.

[12]The Congressional Caucus for Women's Issues changed its name from Congresswomen's Caucus in 1981.

[13]1992 membership; the number of members of the Caucus on Advanced Materials could not be confirmed for 1994.

[14]The Congressional Copper Caucus is the result of a merger (in 1985) of the former Senate Copper and House Copper caucuses.

[15]In addition, the Hispanic Caucus has a number of "honorary" members of the House and Senate.

[16]The Environmental and Energy Study Conference changed its name from the Environmental Study Conference in 1981.

[17]1992 membership

[18]The National Security Caucus changed its name from the Coalition for Peace through Strength in 1988.

[19]The Pennsylvania Congressional Delegation includes the Pennsylvania Congressional Delegation Steering Committee (which has appeared as a separate House group in earlier versions of this compilation).

SOURCE: Sula P. Richardson, *Caucuses and Legislative Service Organizations of the 103d Congress, Second Session: An Informational Directory.* Congressional Research Service, Library of Congress. CRS Rept. 94-707 GOV. 1994.

and a reduction in the alienation that a member may feel in as large an institution as the U.S. Congress are among the more personal benefits of caucus membership. But Hammond suggests that membership in a caucus may also result in specific legislative benefits that allow members to pursue their goals of power, policy, and reelection with greater efficiency and success. That is, membership in some caucuses allows members to claim greater responsiveness to constituent concerns, while membership in other caucuses may also allow junior members to develop leadership skills that they would otherwise be unable to develop so early in their congressional careers. As members become increasingly ambitious, this benefit should not be underestimated.

These activities lead to concern that caucuses contribute to fragmentation in Congress (especially the House) by providing yet another source of input to decision making. As caucuses become more institutionalized, they may supplant some of the traditional legislative functions of party and the existing institutional machinery. Indeed, in recent years, some caucuses have even held informal hearings, traditionally the responsibility of congressional committees. Yet some have suggested that while caucuses do increase structural fragmentation, they may simultaneously reduce other types of fragmentation because they help to supplement the activity of established congressional institutions. Because these groups unite around narrower interests, they usually exhibit a higher degree of unity than the party as a whole. These blocs of unity may in turn be used by the party leadership to build winning coalitions on the floor. Proliferation of these blocs may initially lead to greater confusion and diffusion within each party and in Congress as a whole. If these blocs are consistent and recognizable over time, however, then both parties may use them to organize and unite key factions of their membership. Evidence of this type of activity in the pre–floor negotiation stage has begun to emerge. Caucus staffs often interact with congressional committees, providing information and support for specific pieces of legislation. This kind of interaction may eventually lead to more centralized control of issues by the party leadership and a recentralization of power in Congress.

While caucuses were initially viewed with concern and suspicion by more senior members and party leadership, today they are an accepted and vital part of the congressional environment. The election of Thomas S. Foley (D-Wash.) as Speaker of the House in June 1989 marked the first time that a former chair of the Democratic Study Group reached the House's highest leadership position. It may also have marked a turning point in the development and institutionalization of this congressional phenomenon.

[See also Legislative Service Organizations.]

BIBLIOGRAPHY

Hammond, Susan Webb. "Congressional Caucuses in the Policy Process." In *Congress Reconsidered*. Edited by Lawrence C. Dodd and Bruce Oppenheimer. 4th ed. 1989.
Loomis, Burdett. "Congressional Caucuses and the Politics of Representation." In *Congress Reconsidered*. Edited by Lawrence C. Dodd and Bruce Oppenheimer. 2d ed. 1981.
Stevens, Arthur G., Arthur H. Miller, and Thomas E. Mann. "Mobilization of Liberal Strength in the House, 1955–1970: The Democratic Study Group." *American Political Science Review* 68 (1974): 667–681.

JULIE S. DRUCKER

CELLER, EMANUEL (1888–1981), Democratic representative from New York (1923–1973), chairman of the House Judiciary Committee (1949–1953, 1955–1973), and architect of civil rights and other liberal legislation. In 1922, running in Brooklyn's 10th Congressional District, which had never gone Democratic, Celler squeaked to victory, denouncing prohibition and nativism to his Jewish, Italian, Greek, and Irish neighbors. As his district (repeatedly redrawn and renumbered) became increasingly multiethnic, multiracial, and Democratic, Celler, ever sensitive to his minority constituents, was reelected time and again by huge margins.

Appointed chairman of the Judiciary Committee in 1949, the grandfatherly, genial "Manny" introduced and battled through Congress each of the civil rights acts from 1957 through 1968. He sponsored four constitutional amendments, the Twenty-third through the Twenty-sixth. Chairing the Judiciary Monopoly Subcommittee, he investigated mergers and monopolistic practices in baseball, banking, newsprint, and many other industries. The most important legislation resulting from the investigative hearings was a Celler-cosponsored 1950 amendment to the Clayton Antitrust Act of 1914 that prohibited corporations from acquiring the assets of competitors. Committed to loosening immigration restrictions, Celler authored measures

EMANUEL CELLER. On 12 March 1963.

in the 1940s permitting Indians and Filipinos to immigrate and become naturalized U.S. citizens and allowing over 300,000 displaced persons to enter the country. He was a House sponsor of the Immigration and Nationality Act of 1965, which ended discriminatory immigration quotas based on national origins.

The seniority system, which placed Celler in powerful chairmanships, along with Celler's dedication to the New Deal, Fair Deal, and Great Society help account for his achievements. Also contributing to his political successes were his skills in drafting legislation, stacking subcommittees, conducting investigative hearings, and floor managing bills.

In 1972, Elizabeth Holtzman defeated Celler in the Democratic primary. His age, overconfidence, lessened contact with constituents, and unpopular pro–Vietnam War and anti–Equal Rights Amendment stands contributed to his loss.

BIBLIOGRAPHY

Celler, Emanuel. *You Never Leave Brooklyn: The Autobiography of Emanuel Celler.* 1953.
Rubin, Lawrence. "Oral History Memoir of Congressman Emanuel Celler." 24 June 1970 and 1 August 1972.

William E. Wiener Oral History Library of the American Jewish Committee, New York, N.Y.

BARBARA BLUMBERG

CENSUS. The United States Census is the foundation of the American statistical system, providing much of the demographic information on which Congress depends in making domestic policy. Although the census is required by the Constitution, the data that it collects are also important to state and local governments and private enterprise.

The census is not just an information-gathering activity. As with most activities of government, it is also political. The form, contents, and length of the questionnaires are intensely debated and negotiated within the executive and legislative branches. Most questions are designed to provide information used in federal programs, but the fundamental purpose of the census—the apportionment of representatives among the states and the resulting redistricting within states—remains a primary focus for Congress.

Apportioning Representatives and Taxes. The apportionment concept is central to understanding the census as it relates to Congress. Two sections of the Constitution pertain to using the census to apportion representatives and taxes. Article 1, section 2 (subsequently modified by the Fourteenth Amendment) provided that

> Representatives and direct Taxes shall be apportioned among the several States which may be included within this Union, according to their respective Numbers, which shall be determined by adding to the whole Number of free Persons, including those bound to Service for a Term of Years, and excluding Indians not taxed, three fifths of all other Persons.

The Fourteenth Amendment removed the references to free persons and the rule providing that three-fifths of all other persons would be counted for apportionment. What remained was the concept that both representation in the House and taxation would be apportioned among the states according to their populations. As Margo Anderson (1988) points out, the concept was an example of constitutional checks and balances. More representation in the House was to carry a price—more taxes allocated to the state. This carrot-and-stick was intended to prevent states from inflating their populations for the census, but the importance of the stick faded along with attempts to impose "direct taxes." A national property tax, for example, failed as a revenue source in the late 1790s, was not very successful in the 1810s, and failed again during the Civil War. Thus, with exception of a successful Civil War income tax, throughout the nineteenth century most revenue for the federal government was obtained from duties and other fees. The Sixteenth Amendment (1913) removed the constitutional requirement that all taxes be apportioned among the states based on the census.

Determining the Form, Contents, and Method. How the census is to be conducted is left to Congress. Article I, section 2 of the Constitution provides that "the actual Enumeration shall be made within three Years after the first Meeting of the Congress of the United States, and within every subsequent Term of ten Years, in such Manner as they shall by Law direct."

The phrase "in such Manner as they shall by Law direct" has given Congress wide latitude to specify census form and contents. The first censuses asked relatively few questions, but in the late nineteenth century the scope and complexity of the questionnaires increased to include information from a wide variety of sources, including schools, farms, and industries. During the twentieth century, the questions relating to education, agriculture, and manufacturing were separated from the decennial census and put into separate surveys and censuses.

Changing Counting Methods. The first census takers were federal marshals. The marshals and their assistants conducted the census until 1880, but the census has always required mobilization of a large temporary labor force. In 1990, for example, the Census Bureau hired approximately 300,000 temporary staff members.

The census is not strictly a head count. In fact, arguably, the census is basically (with some exceptions) a count of housing units, and the people are among the characteristics of the housing units. Census forms are sent to housing units, and one person in each unit is asked to fill out the form for all the others living there. Although every U.S. household receives a census questionnaire containing a core of basic questions, slightly fewer than a fifth of the households get a much longer questionnaire, from which much of the detailed information in the census is derived.

How the census is taken has changed in two centuries, and the methods changed significantly after 1960. The 1960 census was the last one for which enumerators visited every U.S. household. In 1970, 60 percent of the nation's households were asked to

APPORTIONMENT. Political cartoon that refers to the determination of representation in the House on the basis of population. Uncle Sam prepares to measure a figure representing the House with results of the fourteenth census. Clifford K. Berryman, *Washington Post*, 11 May 1904.

U.S. SENATE COLLECTION, CENTER FOR LEGISLATIVE ARCHIVES

complete their census forms themselves and mail them back for processing. These households were contacted by enumerators only if they failed to return their forms or if the forms contained errors. Enumerators visited the remaining 40 percent of households. The 1980 census expanded the mail-based census to cover approximately 90 percent of the nation's households, and 1990 mail coverage extended to nearly all households.

Continuing Controversy: Census Error. The Census Bureau has always had to control costs while attempting to count everyone in the country. The costs of enumerating a household have risen substantially, from $6.85 in 1970 to $12.10 in 1980, and to $17 in 1990 (figures in constant 1980 dollars). As costs have risen, increasing attention has been paid to the issue of miscounts. Postcensus research has shown that certain minority groups are more difficult to count than whites; while overall population coverage of the census has generally improved (from 94.4 percent in 1940 to an estimated 98 percent in 1990), the differential undercount between blacks and whites (the difference between the white under- or overcount and the black undercount) has improved little if at all (it was 5.2 percent in 1940 and again in 1980, with fluctuations during the intervening decades). The tendency for large segments of the minority population to settle in specific regions of the country and in certain large cities has politicized the undercount issue. Some cities and states see themselves as victims of census miscounts. Because representation in legislative bodies (at the federal, state, and local level) is allocated by population, and federal funds are distributed in part on the basis of population, those areas that believe they have been undercounted have sought redress in Congress and the courts.

At issue are the methods used to take the census and whether the census should be adjusted using statistical methods. As the U.S. population becomes more heterogeneous, traditional census-taking techniques may not work as well as in the past. The mailed census form was developed in part to reduce costs and speed up enumeration. The development of the technique coincided with the increase of women in the work force and a consequently smaller pool of potential part-time census workers, on whom the Census Bureau had relied during much of the twentieth century. Because the mail-based census requires an accurate address list and a cooperative population, changing living patterns and attitudes toward government could negatively affect the census.

As the twentieth century waned, nontraditional living patterns threatened the mail-based census. The 1990 census takers found a homeless population living either on the streets or in shelters. Portions of the large immigrant population (both legal and illegal) were perceived to be living in crowded conditions that might discourage compliance with the census, from fear that illegal immigrants would be found out or that landlords would find lease requirements being violated. People dependent on public assistance were believed to be similarly less likely to cooperate with the census, if they were violating rules that would affect their eligibility for continued assistance. As the 1990 census was analyzed, these concerns suggested that the mail-based census might not be a good technique for enumerating hard-to-count populations.

Early planning for the year 2000 census had to take into account the competing needs of producing better information about the U.S. population and finding a way to be fair to all the different groups in U.S. society. Should the census be a head count, or should the Census Bureau use statistical techniques (based on postcensus surveys) to adjust the counts to even out differential coverage? Given the apparent problems of getting people to respond to a mailed census questionnaire, either because people were less willing to provide personal information to the government or because the questionnaires were lost in a sea of direct mail, should the entire process be rethought? Should the census questionnaire count only that information necessary for reapportionment and redistricting and leave the rest of the questions for a sample survey? Should the entire census be a large-sample survey? These questions and others faced Congress and the Census Bureau as they planned for the 2000 census.

[*See also* Apportionment and Redistricting.]

BIBLIOGRAPHY

Anderson, Margo J. *The American Census: A Social History.* 1988.
Halacy, Daniel Stephen. *Census: 190 Years of Counting America.* 1980.
U.S. Senate. Committee on Governmental Affairs. *The Decennial Census: An Analysis and Review.* 96th Cong., 2d sess., 1980. Committee Print.

DAVID C. HUCKABEE

CENTER FOR LEGISLATIVE ARCHIVES. *See* Archives.

CENTRAL INTELLIGENCE AGENCY.

The National Security Act of 1947 established the Central Intelligence Agency (CIA) and supplied it with its legislative charter. By this step, the United States acquired the world's first democratically sanctioned secret intelligence agency. President Harry S. Truman secured a direct line of responsibility to himself through the newly established National Security Council, which, over the years, developed a succession of secret subcommittees to guide the CIA. Yet there was little opposition in Congress to the agency's establishment and not much debate, for the clause setting up the CIA was just part of a wide-ranging bill that prepared the way for the reform of the defense establishment as a whole. Thus Congress had many contentious issues to discuss, and the creation of a new intelligence agency seemed of relatively minor importance.

The absence of a full debate left the purpose of the CIA clouded in ambiguity, a circumstance that in later years would lead to heated controversy. In some ways, the motives were clear: the United States did not want another Pearl Harbor; there was a need to combat the clandestine methods of the Soviet Union; and a measure of centralization in intelligence gathering was desirable. As a protection against abuses, the CIA was forbidden from engaging in domestic operations. But Truman had in mind a narrower field of action than that constructed by later agency expansionists. Truman wanted an agency that would keep him informed about foreign affairs and assist with foreign economic policy, notably the implementation of the Marshall Plan. By the 1950s, however, the CIA was organizing coups d'état and paramilitary operations of the type that culminated in the disastrous Bay of Pigs invasion of 1961. Truman eventually claimed that the agency had gone beyond its original intent.

The CIA Act of 1949 made provision for an unvouchered intelligence budget. Neither this law nor that of 1947 allowed for congressional scrutiny. Senior members of the Appropriations and Armed Services committees in the House and Senate would agree to broad expenditure guidelines; they would not ask for details regarding CIA expenditures; and they would channel the money via the financially intricate byways of the defense program in a way that not only obscured the nature of the CIA's activities but also made it difficult to ascertain its overall budget. Congress accepted this arrangement in the 1950s because clandestine operations self-evidently require the utmost discretion if they are to be effective, because the CIA seemed a trustworthy organization, and because it seemed so desirable to close ranks behind the agency at the height of the Cold War. Sen. Joseph R. McCarthy's clumsy attempts to red-bait the palpably patriotic agency in 1953 discouraged subsequent initiatives by other legislators to institute a responsible form of congressional oversight.

Improving relations between the Soviet Union and the United States and growing friction between the White House and Congress eventually brought a renewed determination to investigate and supervise the CIA's activities. By the mid 1970s, the agency was being held to account on a variety of fronts. It had, for instance, illegally spied on Americans at home; it had conspired to assassinate foreign heads of state; it had contributed to the overthrow of democratically elected governments in Guatemala, Guyana, and Chile. The House established an investigative committee chaired by Rep. Otis G. Pike, and the Senate an inquiry under Sen. Frank Church. CIA director William E. Colby decided to cooperate with the Church committee. The

ensuing congressional investigations disproved the widely publicized allegations that the CIA was a "rogue elephant" rampaging "out of control": rather, the agency had almost invariably acted on the instructions of the White House.

Nevertheless, in 1976 both houses of Congress decided to set up permanent oversight committees. The principle of oversight acquired bipartisan respectability in the 1980s, when Barry Goldwater, hitherto a supporter of the Republicans' aim to "revive" the CIA, took a critical line as chairman of the Senate Intelligence Committee. It became politically hazardous to ignore the intelligence committees. At the time of the Iran-contra affair, the Reagan administration met with a hostile response when it attempted to bypass congressional scrutiny by giving the National Security Council some duties previously performed by the CIA. Hearings in 1991 to confirm the selection of Robert M. Gates as CIA director significantly focused on the nominee's willingness to keep congressional committees appropriately informed.

The congressional relationship with the CIA has some disturbing facets. The agency is a tempting target for ambitious legislators who wish to make a name for themselves in a sensational manner. Investigative committees can be overaggressive in the short run and then neglectful of follow-through duties once the immediate furor has died down. Oversight committees can, as they did in the 1950s, degenerate into rubber-stamp bodies. But, beyond providing democratic sanction for the CIA's activities and a safeguard against presidential abuses, the Congress-CIA relationship has benefited both sides by enabling the CIA to receive counsel from experienced members of oversight committees and by ensuring that Congress is kept informed of intelligence activities through discreet channels.

[See also Intelligence Committee, House Permanent Select; Intelligence Committee, Senate Select; National Security Act.]

BIBLIOGRAPHY

Jeffreys-Jones, Rhodri. The CIA and American Democracy. 1989.
Smist, Frank John, Jr. Congress Oversees the United States Intelligence Community, 1947–1989. 1990.

RHODRI JEFFREYS-JONES

CEREMONIAL ACTIVITIES. Among the earliest questions to be considered by Congress when it first convened in April 1789 was that of the

CEREMONY IN THE HOUSE OF REPRESENTATIVES. Commemoration of the hundredth anniversary of the Marquis de Lafayette's death, 28 May 1934.   LIBRARY OF CONGRESS

proper form of address for the president. Such possibilities as "His Majesty," "His Highness," and "His Elective Highness" were under consideration in the Senate, which addressed its reply to George Washington's first Inaugural Address to "His Highness the President of the United States and Protector of their Liberties." The House of Representatives chose a simpler form: "to George Washington, President of the United States."

At the time of the founding, forms of political life were taken very seriously. In the late eighteenth century, monarchical tradition provided the only available precedent for state ceremonial activity. For some the adaptation of royal pomp and circumstance to the cause of the new nation was both a natural and desirable development; for others it was a cause for concern. This division—between the proponents of republican simplicity, on the one hand, and those who gave evidence of monarchical tendencies, on the other—contributed to the growth of factionalism and influenced the develop-

ment of ceremonial traditions in the early years of the Republic.

Some congressional ceremonial events fulfilled no particular legislative function. The laying of the cornerstone for the future Capitol on 18 September 1793 was primarily a Masonic ritual. At the ceremony for the extensions of the Capitol, which began in 1851, the Grand Master of the Masons of the District of Columbia officiated, and President Millard Fillmore wore the same Masonic apron that Washington had worn in 1793. The ceremony took place on the Fourth of July, however—a date with more patriotic than Masonic significance. Masonic rituals remained a part of the proceedings over one hundred years later, when President Dwight D. Eisenhower laid the cornerstone for the extension of the east front of the Capitol on the Fourth of July in 1959, but by this point the symbolic center of the ceremony had shifted. The meaning of this ceremony became less tied to the actual construction of the building and the attendant mysteries of Freemasonry, as the Capitol itself became an important symbol of the nation as a whole.

Other moments in the life of the Capitol have also been recognized ceremonially. Throughout the years, gifts of art and historic relics have been received in formal ceremonies. Upon the completion of the new Senate wing in 1859, the body took up residence in its new chamber by means of a simple, yet formal, procession from the old to the new, attended by an overflow crowd of the general public. Many gathered at the Capitol on 2 December 1863 to see the final section of Thomas Crawford's *Statue of Freedom* raised to the top of the dome. When the statue was in place, a thirty-five-gun salute, one shot for each state, was sent forth by a field battery on the Capitol grounds, and a dozen forts across the District answered in succession with thirty-five-gun salutes of their own. Coming as it did in the middle of the Civil War, when President Abraham

Lincoln had seen to it that construction continued on the Capitol as "a sign we intend the Union shall go on," this ceremonial assertion of union could not have been more clear.

Perhaps the most significant recurring congressional ceremonies are those that reach beyond the capital city and capture the attention of the entire nation: inaugurations, state of the union and other presidential addresses, appearances before Congress by American citizens and visiting foreign dignitaries, and state funerals. In the case of inaugurations, many of the festivities, such as the parades to and from the Capitol or the inaugural balls, are not properly a part of the congressional ceremony, which consists of the constitutionally appointed duty of administering the oath of office to the president-elect and the vice president-elect. During the early administrations, the ceremony commonly took place in either the Senate or House chamber; George Washington, though, took the oath before

FUNERAL SERVICES. For Sen. Joseph T. Robinson (D-Ark.) in the Senate chamber, July 1937.

CHARLES DE GAULLE. President of the French Fifth Republic addressing a joint session of Congress, 25 April 1960.   LIBRARY OF CONGRESS

the general public in 1789. A dispute between the House and Senate led to a public inaugural in 1817 as well, but it was not until the arrival of Andrew Jackson in 1829 that the inauguration was firmly established as more than a private congressional procedure. The movement of the ceremony out of the Capitol and into public view, like the election of Jackson, was a sign of the growth of democracy in U.S. politics. The vice president's swearing-in and inaugural address, however, continued to take place inside the Capitol until 1937.

Like the inaugural address, the president's annual message to Congress (known as the State of the Union Address since 1945) fulfills a constitutional requirement. The proceedings are based upon the precedent of the royal address at the opening of parliament. The Jeffersonians, however, believed the balance of power should rest with the legislative branch, and through the course of the nineteenth century the president's annual message devolved into a dry bureaucratic report delivered to

Congress in writing. It was not until the election of Woodrow Wilson, an advocate of a strong presidency, that the annual message came to be delivered in person once again. With this tradition renewed, Wilson and some of his successors, particularly Warren G. Harding, Harry S. Truman, and Ronald Reagan, have made further use of the "bully pulpit" that a joint session of Congress affords to deliver speeches in addition to the annual message. And since the passage of the Twentieth Amendment in 1934, the final State of the Union message by a defeated president has sometimes been used to deliver a farewell address, a notable example being Eisenhower's 1961 speech, which warned of the growing influence of the military-industrial complex in American life.

The ceremonial drama of an appearance before Congress has not been the province of presidents alone; numerous American citizens and foreign visitors also have been the centerpiece of such ceremonies, but until the twentieth century such events were rare. The first person to speak before a joint meeting of Congress, other than members and presidents, was the Marquis de Lafayette in 1824. Lafayette and exiled Hungarian revolutionary leader Louis Kossuth, who visited the House and the Senate in 1852, were welcomed as compatriots who carried American ideals into the world even as the United States itself remained resolutely isolationist. Visits by representatives of China, Japan, and the Hawaiian Islands between 1868 and 1874 were a sign of the expansion of America's interest beyond the continental United States. The vast majority of foreign visitors to Congress have been received during World War I, World War II, and since 1945, as the country has assumed a world leadership role.

Appearances by Americans before Congress have been no more common than those by foreign visitors. In the late nineteenth century, the House would, on occasion, recess in order to allow the introduction of visitors such as Chief Justice Morrison R. Waite in 1874, or various Civil War generals in the 1860s and 1880s. During the course of the last century, returning military leaders (from Adm. George Dewey in 1899 after the victory at Manila Bay to Gen. Norman Schwarzkopf in 1991 after the Persian Gulf War) have been received by Congress. It was at such an appearance in 1951 that Gen. Douglas MacArthur brought a military career of almost a half century to a close with the words "Old soldiers never die, they just fade away." Astronauts, too, have been so honored after a number of historic journeys into space.

Since its early days, Congress has also had the duty of conducting funeral services. Individual memorial exercises were commonly held on Saturdays for members who died while Congress was in session, while those who died during a recess would be remembered early in the following session. In 1929 it was decided that a general service would be held at the close of a Congress. Henry Clay became the first person to lie in state in the Rotunda upon his death in 1852. Since that time the honor has been accorded to a number of prominent Americans. Many of these have been presidents, whose deaths Congress has regularly observed since the death of Washington in 1799. When Congress was first presented with the circumstance of a president who died in office, namely William Henry Harrison in 1841, the chambers of both houses were draped in black and mourning badges were worn. For the funeral of Zachary Taylor in 1850 Congress assembled at the Capitol and moved in joint procession to the services at the White House.

On occasion a joint session has been held at which a memorial address has been delivered on the life, character, and public services of the deceased, most commonly when the death has occurred while Congress has been in recess. Historian and statesman George Bancroft spoke on Abraham Lincoln in 1866; former Speaker, senator, and secretary of State James G. Blaine delivered an address on James A. Garfield in 1882; and in 1902 Secretary of State John Hay spoke at the joint session for William McKinley. Theodore Roosevelt, Warren G. Harding, Woodrow Wilson, Calvin Coolidge, and Vice President James S. Sherman have also been remembered in such ceremonies.

Other ceremonial activities include the various commemorations undertaken by Congress to celebrate great people and events of America's past. The most honored individuals have been Washington and Lincoln, the preeminent symbols of union in the United States. In the midst of the Civil War a joint session was held at which Washington's farewell address was read. Washington was remembered again in the 1880s with joint sessions celebrating the completion of the Washington Monument and the centennial of his first inauguration and in 1932 for the 150th anniversary of his birth. A 1959 joint session in honor of Lincoln's sesquicentennial, at which the poet Carl Sandburg delivered a stirring address, was followed by centennial celebrations of Lincoln's first and second inaugurals in 1961 and 1965. Most recently, joint sessions

have been held for the centennials of the births of Franklin D. Roosevelt, Harry S. Truman, and Dwight D. Eisenhower.

Congress has also regularly celebrated events associated with its own past. In 1893 Congress adjourned to attend as a body the 100th anniversary celebration of the laying of the cornerstone of the Capitol. In 1900 the centennial of the establishment of Washington, D.C., as the seat of government was commemorated with a joint session, as were the 150th and 200th anniversaries of the first Congress in 1939 and 1989. As part of the commemoration of the bicentennial of the Constitution, a delegation of more than two hundred members of Congress traveled together to Philadelphia in 1987 to celebrate the anniversary of the Great Compromise of 16 July 1787.

Ceremonial activity is as much an instrument of power as any other practice associated with Congress. Its component parts—processions, oaths, oratory, and other symbolic practices—are the building blocks common to all ritual, and ritual is one means by which messages are given legitimacy. In the midst of all the pageantry, pomp, and circumstance certain values and beliefs are being promoted—some explicitly, others implicitly. Ceremony, like legislative activity, is the stuff of politics.

BIBLIOGRAPHY

Aikman, Lonnelle. *We the People: The Story of the United States Capitol.* 14th ed. 1991.
Fersh, Seymour. *The View from the White House: A Study of the Presidential State of the Union Messages.* 1961.
Hazelton, George C., Jr. *The National Capitol: Its Architecture, Art, and History.* 1914.
Kerr, Mary Lee, ed. *Foreign Visitors to Congress: Speeches and History.* 2 vols. 1989.
Mossman, B. C., and M. W. Stark. *The Last Salute: Civil and Military Funerals, 1921–1969.* 1971.

JEFFREY HEARN

CHAMBERS. [*This entry includes separate discussions of the House and Senate chambers, focusing on their physical features. See also* Capitals of the United States; Capitol, The. *For broad discussion of the legislative function of the houses of Congress, see* House of Representatives; Senate.]

House Chamber

The chamber of the House of Representatives is the single most important room on the House side of the Capitol because it is where legislation is in-

THE OLD HOUSE CHAMBER IN THE CAPITOL. Now called Statuary Hall. Lithograph.   LIBRARY OF CONGRESS

troduced, debated, and voted upon. It is also the location of joint sessions of Congress, where events such as the president's annual State of the Union address and ceremonial sessions take place, and where outstanding Americans and citizens of other nations, as well as foreign heads of state, address Congress and the nation.

The first House chamber was in Federal Hall at the corner of Broad and Wall streets in New York City, where the First Federal Congress met from 4 March 1789 to 12 August 1790. Originally built to house City Hall, it was redesigned for Congress by Pierre Charles L'Enfant. Precise details of the architectural features of the interior are not known. The House chamber was the central feature of the interior; it was two stories (thirty-six feet) high, approximately seventy feet long, and fifty feet wide in a "somewhat octagonal" shape. Along the eight walls were four fireplaces alternating with four octagonal windows, and there were six large windows sixteen feet from the floor, several Ionic columns, and two visitors' galleries on the south wall, one above the other. There was also space on the floor

of the chamber "confined by a bar" to which the public was admitted. After Congress moved to Philadelphia, the building that housed the First Congress served as a customs house before being torn down and sold for scrap in 1812.

For ten years, beginning 4 January 1790, Congress resided in Philadelphia. The House chamber was on the first floor of the newly built Philadelphia County Court House, renamed Congress Hall. House members sat at adjoining individual wooden desks in a sweeping semicircle facing a raised Speaker's dais. A small elevated visitors' gallery occupied the west side of the room. In 1793, as a result of the first reapportionment, the House increased in size from 69 to 105 members, and the House chamber was extended twenty-six feet to make room for the new representatives. When Congress moved to Washington, D.C., the chamber was remodeled and restored for use as a court house. In the 1890s restoration of the building began, but it was not until 1913 that the room was restored to resemble approximately its appearance when it had served as the House chamber. Congress Hall is now preserved as part of Independence National Historical Park, where it has been under the jurisdiction of the National Park Service since 1951 as the oldest building still standing that once housed Congress.

In November 1800, when Congress moved to Washington, D.C., the new Capitol building was in the early stages of construction; only the north, or Senate wing, was nearly complete. The House, the Senate, the Supreme Court, the District Courts, and the Library of Congress all met in this wing until 1801, when the House moved into a temporary brick structure known as "the Oven" because of its shape and poor ventilation; it was connected to the north wing by an enclosed wooden walkway 145 feet long. The House occupied the Oven until 1804, when it was torn down to make room for the south wing. During this construction the House again met in the north (Senate) wing. The new House chamber that emerged in the south wing, designed by Benjamin Henry Latrobe, was considered the most beautiful room in the nation with its marble floor, carved stone columns, numerous skylights, elegant draperies, and central heating. The House occupied this chamber from 1806 to 1814, when on 24 August British soldiers burned the Capitol and other buildings in the city. During the four-year restoration of the Capitol from 1815 to 1819, the House chamber was located first in a building at Eighth and E streets, N.W., known as Blodgett's Hotel, which quickly proved inadequate. In 1815, fearing Congress might not stay in the District of Columbia, a number of citizens formed the Capitol Hotel Company to erect a temporary Capitol at the corner of First and A streets, N.E., on the site of the current Supreme Court building. The House met at this site until 1819 when the House chamber in the Capitol was reoccupied.

The rebuilt House chamber, embellished with a wooden ceiling painted in classical coffers and fea-

INTERIOR OF THE HOUSE CHAMBER. Occupied by the House of Representatives since 1857. Wood engraving by Theodore R. Davis, *Harper's Weekly*, 14 March 1868.

turing sculpture that included *Statue of Liberty* by Enrico Causici, an eagle by Giuseppe Valaperta, and the magnificent *Car of History* by Carlo Franzoni, served as the House Chamber from 1819 until 1857. This "Splendid Hall," despite its considerable architectural beauty, had a serious flaw. The acoustics were so bad because of the semicircular ceiling that members often had difficulty hearing the debates.

The extensions added to the Capitol in the 1850s provided the House with a new chamber, which it occupied for the first time on 16 December 1857. The old hall was abandoned and used temporarily for storage and during the Civil War became a gathering place for vendors who sold to members of Congress and visitors a range of products such as food, tobacco, and refreshments. In 1864 Congress passed an act that set aside the old House Chamber as Statuary Hall, with each state allowed to submit two statues of prominent individuals to the collection. In the 1970s Statuary Hall was partially restored to its former grandeur and serves today as a site for important ceremonies, including the luncheon in honor of the president following an inauguration.

The current chamber has undergone several renovations, which have altered its appearance. In 1913 the individual desks of members were replaced with benches. A major renovation, from 1949 to 1951, gave the chamber the appearance it has today. Originally the chamber was more ornate. The Speaker's dais and the working desks that surround it, now of wood, were of marble. The now paneled walls were richly covered and hung with several large oil paintings, including two by Albert Bierstadt and a fresco by Constantino Brumidi. An elaborate gilded clock with caryatids of a pioneer and an Indian by William Henry Rinehart was placed on the gallery ledge opposite the Speaker's rostrum. The clock and the paintings have been relocated, and today only two portraits hang in the chamber, those of George Washington by John Vanderlyn and of the Marquis de Lafayette by Ary Scheffer.

The remodeling of the chamber also included removal of the original stained glass ceiling that depicted the seals of the states. It was replaced by a frosted glass skylight with an eagle, surrounded by fifty stars and the seals of the states and territories. Above the gallery doors were added twenty-three bas-reliefs of outstanding lawgivers through the ages, beginning with Moses and ending with two Americans, George Mason and Thomas Jefferson.

Centered in the series, above the Speaker's rostrum, is a quotation from the speech Daniel Webster gave at the laying of the cornerstone of the Bunker Hill Monument: "Let us develop the resources of our land, call forth its powers, build up its institutions, promote all its great interests and see whether we also in our day and generation may not perform something worthy to be remembered." Above the American flag behind the Speaker's table is the motto "In God We Trust." The most recent changes to the House chamber came in 1972 with the installation of the electronic voting system, and in 1977 television cameras were added to provide gavel-to-gavel coverage of the floor proceedings.

BIBLIOGRAPHY

Brown, Glenn. *History of the United States Capitol.* 1903. Repr. 1970.
Torres, Louis. "Federal Hall Revisited." *Journal of the Society of Architectural Historians* 29 (December 1970): 327–328.
U.S. Department of the Interior, National Park Service. *Congress Hall: Capitol of the United States, 1790–1800.* Handbook 147. 1990.
U.S. House of Representatives. *Art in the United States Capitol.* 94th Cong., 2d sess., 1978. H. Doc. 94-660.
U.S. House of Representatives. *The United States Capitol: A Brief Architectural History.* 101st Cong., 1st sess., 1990. H. Doc. 101-144.

RAYMOND W. SMOCK

Senate Chamber

In its first two centuries, the Senate met in eight chambers—one each in New York and Philadelphia, and six in Washington. These rooms reflected, as well as shaped, the Senate's self-image, offering a magnificent theatrical setting in the first half of the nineteenth century and a drafty, acoustically annoying place in the hundred years that followed. Not until the second half of the twentieth century did the Senate have a chamber that truly suited its needs.

The Senate of the First Congress took up temporary quarters on the second floor of New York City's handsomely restored Federal Hall on 4 March 1789. The richly carpeted forty-by-thirty-foot room was distinguished by a high arched ceiling, tall windows curtained in crimson damask, fireplace mantels in handsomely polished marble, and a canopied presiding officer's chair. Noticeably absent from the chamber was a spectators' gallery, reflecting the Senate's intention to conduct its proceedings in private.

THE SENATE CHAMBER IN THE CAPITOL. As restored after the War of 1812. The Senate occupied this room until 1859. Mezzotint and etching by Thomas Doney, 1846.   NATIONAL PORTRAIT GALLERY, SMITHSONIAN INSTITUTION

After two years, Congress moved to Philadelphia for a ten-year stay, awaiting construction of permanent quarters in the newly designated federal city on the banks of the Potomac. On 6 December 1790, the Senate convened on the upper floor of Philadelphia's new county courthouse, renamed Congress Hall. In addition to the double row of members' desks and chairs upholstered in red leather, the room's furnishings included a large carpet, brightly designed with an eagle clutching an olive branch and thirteen arrows, and full-length portraits of Louis XVI and Marie Antoinette. In 1794 the Senate decided to open its proceedings to the public; a gallery was added a year later.

On 21 November 1800, the Senate took up residence in basement quarters of the unfinished Capi-

tol in Washington. This chamber, although smaller than that of Philadelphia, seemed appropriate to the Senate's needs. Soon, however, dry-rotted timbers, spoiled plaster, a leaky roof, and demands for more space resulted in a plan to restore the room and divide it into two chambers, with the Supreme Court occupying the ground-floor portion and the Senate located on the floor above. The Senate, after a brief stay in an adjacent room, met in the new second-floor room from 1810 until August 1814, when the British set fire to the Capitol. For the next four and a half years the Senate convened first in a downtown Washington location and then in the temporary "Brick Capitol" a block away.

In 1819, the Senate returned to a grandly restored chamber. This large semicircular room, with its low-vaulted domed ceiling, provided an ideal setting, both acoustically and dramatically, for the Senate during the troubled four decades that led to civil war. By the mid 1830s, the chamber's striking features included six skylights, a large twenty-four-light brass chandelier, crimson carpeting and wall hangings, a Rembrandt Peale portrait of George Washington, white statuary mantels, a graceful semicircular gallery, and a carved gilt eagle with shield affixed to the canopy over the presiding officer's desk.

Between 1845 and 1850 five new states entered the Union, and more were expected in the years immediately ahead. In the early 1850s construction began on larger Senate and House chambers to accommodate Congress's growing membership, and on 4 January 1859 the Senate moved to its current meeting place.

The new chamber measured 113 by 82 feet, with spacious gallery seating for six hundred along all four walls. The 35-foot-high ceiling featured stained glass panels decorated with symbols of national progress and plenty. Natural light illuminated the room by day and gas by night, until electricity was added in the late 1880s.

Mahogany desks for the sixty-four senators of 1859 were arranged in three semicircular rows, with members of the new Republican Party sitting to the presiding officer's left, while Democrats sat to the right. Many of these desks dated to 1819, when a New York cabinetmaker fashioned them to form a perfect semicircle, with those in the center wide and square, and those toward the aisle narrow and angled. Each desk held an inkwell and a container of blotting sand, an indication of how before the twentieth century the chamber served as the senators' principal office space.

THE MODERN SENATE CHAMBER. Used by the Senate since 1859.

OFFICE OF THE HISTORIAN OF THE U.S. SENATE

Until 1877, desks were arranged in equal numbers on both sides of the center aisle. Since then, desks have been moved back and forth across that aisle to permit all members of a party to sit together. By the late 1930s it had become customary for the majority and minority floor leaders to occupy the center-aisle, front-row desks on their parties' respective sides. Individual members have tended to select their seats according to length of service, moving toward the center and front with increasing seniority.

For decades after the 1859 move, senators complained about the chamber, citing stagnant air, suffocating heat, intolerable dryness, and impossible acoustics. In the late 1930s, Capitol engineers discovered that the braces supporting the chamber's ninety-ton iron ceiling had become corroded, placing it in danger of collapsing. A full-scale renovation was delayed until 1949 by the intervening war. Reconstruction of the ceiling, walls, and galleries was completed by the end of 1950, dramatically altering the chamber's appearance and significantly improving its acoustics and ventilation. For several months during this period, the Senate met in its pre-1859 quarters.

The chamber of 1951 appeared much as it does today, with the exception of a voice amplification system installed in the 1960s and minor decorative changes to accommodate the introduction of television cameras in 1986.

Seats are provided at the long marble desk in front of the presiding officer for key legislative staff, including the journal clerk, parliamentarian, legislative clerk, and assistant secretary. Adjacent to the presiding officer are places for key officials, including the secretary of the Senate, the sergeant at arms, and individual party secretaries. Two mahogany desks placed in front of the clerks' desk offer seating for the staffs of the party secretaries and the Democratic Policy Committee and Republican Scheduling Office, which provided information to senators as votes are conducted.

The current chamber contains several reminders of the Senate's earlier days, including lacquer snuffboxes and spittoons. Along the upper walls, in tribute to past Senate presidents, are the busts of twenty vice presidents from John Adams to Thomas A. Hendricks.

BIBLIOGRAPHY

Byrd, Robert C. *The Senate, 1789–1989: Addresses on the History of the United States Senate.* Vol. 2. 1991. Chap. 18.

Goodwin, Stephen. "Safeguarding the Senate's Golden Age." *Historic Preservation,* November-December 1983, 19–23.

U.S. Senate. *History of United States Senate Roof and Chamber Improvements and Related Historical Data.* 82d Cong., 1st sess., 1951. S. Doc. 82-20.

RICHARD A. BAKER

CHAPLAINS. The Constitution provides that the House and Senate shall determine the officers of each body, and since 1789 Congress has included a chaplain among its officers. It has been the custom since the First Congress to open each legislative session with a prayer. The Supreme Court implicitly upheld the practice in 1983, citing the use of a chaplain in the Continental Congress in 1774 and the long tradition in the Congress under the Constitution, arguing that the custom is "deeply embedded in the history and tradition of this country."

The first chaplain appointed to the Continental Congress in 1774 was the Episcopalian rector of Christ Church in Philadelphia, Jacob Duché, who served until 1776. The first chaplain of the House of Representatives was William Lynn of Philadelphia (Dutch Reformed–Presbyterian) and the first in the Senate was Samuel Provoost, rector of New York's Trinity Church (Episcopal) and the first Episcopal bishop of New York. While each chamber had its

REV. SAMUEL PROVOOST. Episcopal Bishop of New York, elected as the first Senate chaplain on 25 April 1789, five days before George Washington took his presidential oath of office.   LIBRARY OF CONGRESS

Chaplains of the House of Representatives

NAME	DENOMINATION	DATE SERVICE BEGAN[1]
William Lynn	Presbyterian	4 March 1789
Samuel Blair	Presbyterian	4 January 1790
Ashbel Green	Presbyterian	5 November 1792
Thomas Lyell	Methodist	17 November 1800
W. Parkinson	Baptist	7 December 1801
James Laurie	Presbyterian	5 November 1804
P. Elliott	Presbyterian	1 December 1806
O. B. Brown	Baptist	26 October 1807
Jesse Lee	Methodist	22 May 1809
N. Sneathen	Methodist	4 November 1811
Jesse Lee	Methodist	2 November 1812
O. B. Brown	Baptist	19 September 1814
S. H. Cone	Baptist	4 December 1815
Burgess Allison	Baptist	2 December 1816
J. N. Campbell	Presbyterian	18 November 1820
Jared Sparks	Unitarian	3 December 1821
J. Breckenridge	Presbyterian	2 December 1822
H. B. Bascom	Methodist	1 December 1823
Reuben Post	Presbyterian	6 December 1824
Ralph Gurley	Presbyterian	6 December 1830
Reuben Post	Presbyterian	5 December 1831
William Hammett	Methodist	3 December 1832
Thomas H. Stockton	Methodist	2 December 1833
Edward Dunlap Smith	Presbyterian	1 December 1834
Thomas H. Stockton	Methodist	7 December 1835
Oliver C. Comstock	Baptist	5 December 1836
Septimus Tustan	Presbyterian	4 September 1837
Levi R. Reese	Methodist	4 December 1837
Joshua Bates	Congregationalist	2 December 1839
T. W. Braxton	Baptist	7 December 1840
J. W. French	Episcopalian	31 May 1841
John N. Maffit	Methodist	6 December 1841
J. S. Tiffany	Episcopalian	5 December 1842
J. S. Tinsley	Baptist	4 December 1843
William M. Daily	Methodist	4 December 1844
William H. Milburn	Methodist	1 December 1845

[1]The date of the beginning of the congressional session in which each chaplain first served, not necessarily the date of the appointment.

own chaplain, they rotated duties weekly between the House and Senate, a custom that was continued until the 1850s. From 1855 to 1861 the House did not appoint or elect regular chaplains and relied instead on various members of the clergy in the District of Columbia. The Senate did likewise from 1857 to 1859.

Chaplains have been Protestant or Anglican, except for Charles C. Pise, a Roman Catholic who served as Senate chaplain for one year beginning in December 1832. Guest chaplains representing many religions, including Islam, Judaism, and Native American faiths, are regularly invited to offer the opening prayer. The chaplains are elected by the entire membership of their respective bodies. The House elects all its officers every two years at the be-

Chaplains of the House of Representatives (Continued)

NAME	DENOMINATION	DATE SERVICE BEGAN[1]
W. S. S. Sprole	Presbyterian	7 December 1846
Ralph Gurley	Presbyterian	6 December 1847
L. F. Morgan	Methodist	1 December 1851
James Gallagher	Presbyterian	6 December 1852
William H. Milburn	Methodist	5 December 1853
Thomas H. Stockton	Methodist	4 July 1861[2]
W. H. Channing	Unitarian	7 December 1863
Charles B. Boynton	Congregationalist	4 December 1865
J. G. Butler	Presbyterian	4 March 1869
S. L. Townsend	Episcopalian	6 December 1875
John Poise	Methodist	15 October 1877
W. P. Harrison	Methodist	3 December 1877
Frederick D. Power	Christian	5 December 1881
John S. Lindsay	Episcopalian	3 December 1883
William H. Milburn	Methodist	7 December 1885
Samuel W. Haddaway	Methodist	7 August 1893
Edward B. Bagby	Christian	4 December 1893
Henry N. Couden	Universalist	2 December 1895
James Shera Montgomery	Methodist	11 April 1921
Bernard Braskamp	Presbyterian	3 January 1950
Edward G. Latch	Methodist	10 January 1967
James D. Ford	Lutheran	15 January 1979

DENOMINATIONAL TOTAL

Methodist	21
Presbyterian	17
Baptist	8
Episcopalian	4
Christian	2
Congregationalist	2
Unitarian	2
Lutheran	1
Universalist	1
Total	58[3]

[2] From 1855 until 1861 the House of Representatives did not elect chaplains but invited the clergy of the District of Columbia to alternate in opening the daily sessions with a prayer and in preaching on Sundays.
[3] Only fifty individuals have served as chaplain of the House; several held the post on more than one occasion.
SOURCE: Adapted by the author from U.S. House of Representatives, *History of the United States House of Representatives*, by George B. Galloway. 87th Cong., 1st sess, 1962. H. Doc. 87-246.

ginning of each new Congress. The Senate, being a continuing body, holds elections for officers more infrequently. Since the 1950s the chaplains have had office space to meet the needs of their increased responsibilities, which have expanded to include full-time pastoral services to members of Congress and staff. Chaplains are selected and serve as individuals, not as representatives of a particular denomination or religion. During an 1854 inquiry into the value of having an official chaplain, the House Judiciary Committee concluded, "If there be a God who hears prayer—as we believe there is—we submit, that there never was a deliberative body that so eminently needed the fervent prayers of righteous men as the Congress of the United States."

Chaplains of the Senate

NAME	DENOMINATION	APPOINTMENT DATE
Samuel Provoost (First Bishop of New York)	Episcopalian	25 April 1789
William White (First Bishop of Pennsylvania)	Episcopalian	9 December 1790
Thomas John Claggett (First Bishop of Maryland)	Episcopalian	27 November 1800
Edward Gantt	Episcopalian	9 December 1801
A. T. McCormick	Episcopalian	7 November 1804
Edward Gantt	Episcopalian	4 December 1805
John J. Sayrs	Episcopalian	3 December 1806
A. T. McCormick[1]	Episcopalian	10 November 1807
Robert Elliott	Presbyterian	10 November 1808
James Jones Wilmer	Episcopalian	24 May 1809
O. B. Brown	Baptist	5 December 1809
Walter D. Addison	Episcopalian	12 December 1810
John Brackenridge	Presbyterian	13 November 1811
Jesse Lee	Methodist	27 September 1814
John Glendie[2]	Presbyterian	8 December 1815
S. E. Dwight	Congregationalist	16 December 1816
William Hawley	Episcopalian	9 December 1817
John Clark	Presbyterian	19 November 1818
Reuben Post	Presbyterian	9 December 1819
William Ryland	Methodist	17 November 1820
C. P. McIlvaine	Episcopalian	9 December 1822
William Staughton	Baptist	10 December 1823
C. P. McIlvaine	Episcopalian	14 December 1824
William Staughton	Baptist	12 December 1825
William Ryland	Methodist	8 December 1826
Henry Van Dyke Johns	Episcopalian	14 December 1829
J. P. Durbin	Methodist	19 December 1831
Charles C. Pise	Roman Catholic	11 December 1832
Frederick W. Hatch	Episcopalian	10 December 1833
Edward Y. Higbee	Episcopalian	23 December 1835
John Reinhard Goodman	Episcopalian	28 December 1836
Henry Slicer	Methodist	11 September 1837
George G. Cookman	Methodist	31 December 1839
Septimus Tustan	Presbyterian	12 June 1841
Henry Slicer	Methodist	16 December 1846
C. M. Butler[3]	Episcopalian	9 January 1850
Henry Slicer	Methodist	7 December 1853

[1]On 29 October 1807 Edward Gantt was elected but declined to serve.
[2]On 6 December 1816 John Glendie was elected but declined to serve.
[3]Vice President Millard Fillmore voted for C. M. Butler, breaking a tie vote (30 for Henry Slicer, 30 for C. M. Butler).

Chaplains of the Senate (Continued)

NAME	DENOMINATION	APPOINTMENT DATE
Henry C. Dean	Methodist	4 December 1855
Stephen P. Hill	Baptist	8 December 1856
P. D. Gurley	Presbyterian	15 December 1859[4]
Byron Sunderland	Presbyterian	10 July 1861
Thomas Bowman	Methodist	11 May 1864
Edgar H. Gray	Baptist	9 March 1865
John P. Newman	Methodist	8 March 1869
Byron Sunderland	Presbyterian	8 December 1873
Joseph J. Bullock	Presbyterian	24 March 1879
E. DeWitt Huntley	Methodist	18 December 1883
John G. Butler	Lutheran	15 March 1886
W. H. Milburn[5]	Methodist	6 April 1893
F. J. Prettyman	Methodist	23 November 1903
Edward Everett Hale[6]	Unitarian	14 December 1903
U. G. B. Pierce	Unitarian	18 June 1909
F. J. Prettyman	Methodist	13 March 1913
Joseph J. Muir[7]	Baptist	21 January 1921
ZeBarney Thorne Phillips[8]	Episcopalian	5 December 1927
Frederick Brown Harris	Methodist	10 October 1942
Peter Marshall[9]	Presbyterian	4 January 1947
Frederick Brown Harris	Methodist	3 February 1949
Edward L. R. Elson	Presbyterian	9 January 1969
Richard Halverson	Presbyterian	2 February 1981

DENOMINATION TOTAL

Episcopalian	19
Methodist	17
Presbyterian	13
Baptist	6
Unitarian	2
Congregationalist	1
Lutheran	1
Roman Catholic	1
Total:	60[10]

[4]During the 35th Congress (1857–1859) the Senate did not elect a chaplain but invited the clergy of the District of Columbia to alternate in opening the daily sessions with a prayer.
[5]Resigned because of ill health on 2 December 1902, his resignation to take effect when the Senate elected a new chaplain. He was officially listed as Senate chaplain until the election of F. J. Prettyman, although apparently Prettyman began serving as chaplain prior to his election.
[6]Died in office on 10 June 1909.
[7]Died in office on 16 November 1927.
[8]Died in office on 10 May 1942.
[9]Died in office on 25 January 1949.
[10]Only fifty individuals have served as chaplain; several held the post on more than one occasion.
SOURCE: Senate Historical Office

REV. HENRY N. COUDEN. Chaplain of the House of Representatives, offering a prayer for the recovery of President Woodrow Wilson, c. 1920.

LIBRARY OF CONGRESS

BIBLIOGRAPHY

Byrd, Robert C. *The Senate, 1789–1989: Addresses on the History of the United States Senate.* Vol. 2. 1991.

Byrd, Robert C. *The Senate, 1789–1989: Historical Statistics, 1789–1992.* Vol. 4. 1993.

Galloway, George B. *History of the United States House of Representatives.* 1962.

U.S. House of Representatives. Committee on the Judiciary. *Chaplains in Congress and in the Army and Navy.* Report prepared by James Meacham. 33d Cong., 1st sess., 1854. H. Rept. 124.

Whittier, Charles H. *Chaplains in Congress.* Congressional Research Service, Library of Congress. CRS Rept. 90-65 GOV. 1990.

RAYMOND W. SMOCK

CHASE, SALMON P. (1808–1873), antislavery advocate, third-party leader, senator, governor of Ohio, Republican party founder, secretary of the Treasury during the Civil War, and chief justice of the United States. One of the founders of the Free-Soil party in 1848, Salmon P. Chase was elected to the U.S. Senate in 1849 by a Free-Soil–Democratic coalition in the Ohio legislature. He served one eventful term in the Senate, combining with the small band of Free-Soilers in opposing passage of the Compromise of 1850 put forward by Henry Clay. Chase strenuously argued against the harsh fugitive slave bill that was part of the compromise proposal. He and his antislavery colleagues were able to manage only a delaying action, however, and after nine months of often dramatic debate the bills became law. Ostracized by Democrats and Whigs from North and South because of his insistence that the federal government divorce itself from all support of slavery, Chase was denied significant committee assignment.

SALMON P. CHASE.   LIBRARY OF CONGRESS

Johnson, Dick. "The Role of Salmon P. Chase in the Formation of the Republican Party." *The Old Northwest* 3 (1977): 23–38.

FREDERICK J. BLUE

CHAVEZ, DENNIS (1888–1962), representative and senator from New Mexico, chairman of the Senate Public Works Committee, and the first Hispanic senator born in the United States. Dionisio (Dennis) Chavez, born in Los Chaves, New Mexico, in 1888, attended grammar school in Albuquerque, then took a job delivering groceries. In 1916, Chavez translated speeches into Spanish for U.S. senator Andrieus A. Jones and was rewarded with a job on the U.S. Senate staff. Chavez resumed his education and graduated from Georgetown University Law School in 1920. He returned to New Mexico and practiced law.

In 1930 Chavez was elected to New Mexico's single seat in the U.S. House of Representatives. His four-year tenure in the House was highlighted by

The next several years in Congress were characterized by major-party efforts to avoid discussion of sectional issues. But in early 1854, with the introduction of Stephen A. Douglas's Kansas-Nebraska bill repealing the Missouri Compromise of 1820, debate exploded. Unable to block passage of the bill, Chase joined with Joshua R. Giddings of Ohio, Charles Sumner of Massachusetts, and others in condemning the measure as a surrender to slave interests and calling for a new, more effective, antislavery party.

In 1855, Chase won election as governor of Ohio on the ticket of the new Republican party, which he had helped form. Denied his most cherished goal, nomination and election to the presidency, he was elected again to the Senate in 1860. Instead of serving, he accepted Abraham Lincoln's appointment as Treasury secretary. A constant advocate of emancipation and racial equality, he completed his career as chief justice of the U.S. Supreme Court.

BIBLIOGRAPHY

Blue, Frederick J. *Salmon P. Chase: A Life in Politics.* 1987.

DENNIS CHAVEZ.   LIBRARY OF CONGRESS

his sponsorship of the Pueblo Lands bill recognizing Indian land claims and legislation creating the Farm Credit Administration.

In 1934, Chavez challenged incumbent U.S. senator Bronson Cutting. Chavez narrowly lost, but he contested the outcome, charging voting fraud. Amid the controversy, Cutting was killed in an airplane crash. Governor Clyde Tingley appointed Chavez to the vacant seat, and Chavez was reelected to the Senate five times.

Chavez's Senate career was notable for his contributions in civil rights and public works projects. In 1944 he introduced the first Fair Employment Practices bill. Although the bill was killed by a conservative majority in Congress, Chavez's pioneering effort foreshadowed the passage of the 1964 Civil Rights Act. Chavez also worked to make New Mexico a center for national defense and atomic research, playing a role in the creation of the Los Alamos Scientific Laboratory, Sandia Laboratory, and the White Sands Proving Grounds.

Under Chavez's chairmanship (1949–1962), the Committee on Public Works initiated the Interstate Highway System and oversaw a vast expansion of other federal projects from post offices to power-producing dams throughout the country. Chavez's combined House and Senate service totaled thirty-one years, longer than that of any Hispanic predecessor.

BIBLIOGRAPHY

Vigil, Maurilio E. *Los Patrones: Profiles of Hispanic Political Leaders in New Mexico History.* 1980.
Vigil, Maurilio E., and Roy Lujan. "Parallels in the Careers of Two Hispanic U.S. Senators." *The Journal of Ethnic Studies* 13–14 (1986): 1–20.

MAURILIO E. VIGIL

CHECKS AND BALANCES. The mixing of legislative, executive, and judicial powers in the U.S. Constitution is known as the system of checks and balances. The mixing is particularly noteworthy because the Constitution is based on the doctrine of separation of powers, which requires clear demarcation of the powers and responsibilities of the institutions entrusted with different government functions. The separation of powers is an institutional device fashioned partly to prevent the tyranny thought to result from concentrating legislative, executive, and judicial powers in a single person or in one part of the government. From their study of history, however, the Framers of the Constitution understood that the complete separation of functions had failed to prevent the accumulation of different types of powers in one institution. To help ensure that the powers would remain separated, the Framers qualified the separation-of-powers doctrine by mixing executive, legislative, and judicial powers, thereby giving each branch a set of tools with which to prevent encroachment on its powers by either of the other branches.

The Constitution mixes powers in a variety of ways to create checks and balances. Congress has the power to act as a court in impeaching executive or judicial officers. The consent of the Senate is required in the executive activity of appointing ambassadors, ministers, and judges and in the making of treaties. The president has a share of legislative power through the authority to exercise a qualified veto over legislation and can convene and in certain circumstances adjourn Congress. The judiciary exercises its check on executive and legislative power through its power to review the constitutionality of congressional statutes and executive actions.

Industrialization, immigration, and urbanization at the turn of the twentieth century brought new political problems that prompted critical reassessments of the capacity of the constitutional structure to provide for effective government. The most influential of the critics, Woodrow Wilson, based his analysis on the novel assumption that the doctrine of separation of powers is synonymous with checks and balances. Wilson characterized the constitutional structure as a machinelike system devoted solely to preventing the excessive exercise of government power. Noting that Congress in the late nineteenth and early twentieth centuries dominated both of the other branches and was not held in check and balanced by them, Wilson concluded that the constitutional system had broken down.

Although contemporary critics of American government face novel political circumstances, their criticisms rest on Wilson's interpretation of checks and balances. Contemporary characterizations of the U.S. political system as one that can do no more than produce gridlock and deadlock in policy-making are based on the Wilsonian assumption that checks and balances represent the whole of the constitutional structure. To use checks and balances as a synonym for the tripartite system, however, is to misunderstand the possibilities and varied capacities built into the Constitution. The separation of executive, legislative, and judicial functions was meant both to ensure that the exercise of government power by any one of the three branches would be checked and balanced by the other two as well as to make government better able to fulfill the particular objectives associated with each function. It was meant to prevent Congress, for example, from aggrandizing its power into executive and judicial responsibilities. At the same time, it was intended to improve Congress members' capacity to carry out their representative functions by freeing them from direct responsibility for administration. In other words, the separation of power was meant to make government less threatening to individual liberty and more efficient at governing. Thus, checks and balances represent one important aspect—though not the essence—of the constitutional framework within which American political institutions operate.

[See also Separation of Powers.]

BIBLIOGRAPHY

Epstein, David. The Political Theory of The Federalist. 1984.
Sundquist, James. Constitutional Reform and Effective Government. 1992.

JESSICA KORN

CHICANO MEMBERS. See Hispanic Members.

CHILD LABOR. During the early years of the Republic, the employment of children in productive enterprise was widely regarded as essential and socially beneficial. By the end of the nineteenth century, however, public attitudes had begun to shift significantly, reflecting profound changes occurring in the organization of production and the use of youthful operatives in largely unregulated industrial employment. As public attention focused on the exploitation of children, the emerging child labor reform movement began to seek protective legislation within the states. By 1907, the advanced industrial states had enacted remedial legislation, typically barring children under fourteen from labor and regulating the hours and conditions under which those between fourteen and sixteen were employed.

The Progressive Era. The perception increasingly took root in public consciousness, however, that industrial problems were national in character, amenable only to national solutions. In response, Congress began to utilize its commerce and taxing powers to achieve social welfare purposes. When the Supreme Court sustained these pioneering forms of legislation, it appeared to have sanctioned a substantial national police power.

Led by Sen. Albert J. Beveridge (R-Ind.), who in January 1907 first proposed national child labor legislation, and responding to the growing public commitment to the quest for social justice, many members of Congress who had once rejected federal control of child labor began to endorse federal regulation. In 1914, leading Progressives introduced a regulatory bill sponsored by a coalition of reform organizations spearheaded by the National Child Labor Committee.

Two years later, after extensive hearings, this measure, now known as the Keating-Owen bill, was decisively enacted by bipartisan majorities in each chamber, 337 to 46 in the House and 52 to 12 in the Senate. The only opposition came from representatives from the southern textile-manufacturing states. The Keating-Owen Child Labor Act prohibited the shipment in interstate commerce of products from manufacturing establishments where children under fourteen were employed, where those between fourteen and sixteen worked more than eight hours or at night, or where children under sixteen were engaged in hazardous employment. To many, this remedial legislation represented the climax of the Progressive movement.

Although constitutional challenge was expected, the sponsoring organizations and congressional leaders believed that the numerous Supreme Court decisions legitimating national police power enactments afforded ample constitutional justification. Nevertheless, the Court in Hammer v. Dagenhart (1918), a test case initiated by southern textile manufacturers, overturned the Keating-Owen law by the narrow margin of 5 to 4. Justice William R. Day's majority opinion condemned the legislation as an overly broad assertion of congressional power to regulate interstate commerce, and one that interfered in purely local matters that properly came under state control.

Undeterred by the overturning of the Keating-Owen law, Progressive spokesmen in Congress, again supported by reform organizations concerned with children and spurred by "the national sentiment of humanity," sought other means of ending the exploitation of children. Within months they settled on the taxing power as a viable instrument with which to extend federal protection, again relying on seemingly conclusive police-power precedents. A rider was attached to the Revenue Act of 1918 providing for a 10 percent tax on the

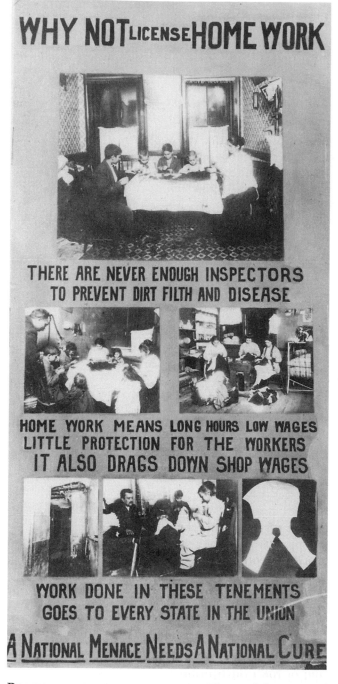

WHY NOT LICENSE HOME WORK

THERE ARE NEVER ENOUGH INSPECTORS
TO PREVENT DIRT FILTH AND DISEASE

HOME WORK MEANS LONG HOURS LOW WAGES
LITTLE PROTECTION FOR THE WORKERS
IT ALSO DRAGS DOWN SHOP WAGES

WORK DONE IN THESE TENEMENTS
GOES TO EVERY STATE IN THE UNION

A NATIONAL MENACE NEEDS A NATIONAL CURE

POSTER OPPOSING HOME WORK. The mobilization of public opinion helped to pass the child labor acts.

LIBRARY OF CONGRESS

net profits of corporations for each violation of the now familiar national child labor standards. This legislation, too, was decisively approved by large, bipartisan majorities in each house.

The child labor tax remained in effect for three years, while the Supreme Court under Chief Justice Edward D. White avoided a conclusion on its validity. Once William Howard Taft assumed the Court's leadership, however, a second test case was brought forward, again generated by southern textile interests. Once more the justices, in *Bailey v. Drexel Furniture Company* (1922), nullified federal child labor legislation. Speaking for an eight-judge majority, Taft held that Congress had exceeded its authority to tax, imposing an impermissible penalty on manufacturers, and again, as in *Hammer,* had interfered with labor conditions within the jurisdiction of the states.

Thwarted by the Supreme Court's narrow construction of congressional commerce and taxing powers, the reform forces that had led the drive for the two national child labor statutes decided to confront the constitutional question directly. Working together, congressional Progressives and child labor spokesmen formulated the Twentieth Amendment, employing broad language that would empower Congress "to limit, regulate, and prohibit the labor of persons under eighteen years of age." This resolution was adopted by Congress in June 1924 and transmitted to the states for ratification.

But the progressive temper of the country had waned significantly, with the result that the amendment languished. In a nation desperately seeking to recover "normalcy," the sponsoring organizations were unable to generate the requisite popular support. Only six states had ratified the amendment by the end of 1931, while nineteen had rejected it.

The New Deal. The transformation of American political culture brought about by the Great Depression revived interest in providing federal protection for child laborers. This objective, however, was decidedly a secondary consideration to President Franklin D. Roosevelt and the congressional leaders who framed the numerous New Deal emergency measures to spur recovery of the nation's economy. Child labor provisions were included as part of a series of national employment standards in the National Industrial Recovery Act (NIRA) in 1933. But these standards were vitiated when the Supreme Court struck down the NIRA in *Schechter Poultry Corporation v. United States* (1935), condemning it for reasons not directly related to its child labor provisions.

Two years later, the Supreme Court, responding to the decisive change in the nation's political attitudes embodied in the New Deal, embraced "a new Constitution of powers." Encouraged by this revolution in constitutional interpretation, Congress in 1938 enacted the Fair Labor Standards Act, which imposed wage and hour regulations on the production of goods intended for interstate commerce and prohibited their shipment when manufactured in violation of these standards. Among these comprehensive standards were child labor provisions. Persons under sixteen years of age were excluded from employment, while those aged sixteen to eighteen were barred from "particularly hazardous" activities.

The Supreme Court finally legitimated national child labor legislation in 1941. Writing for a unanimous bench in *United States v. Darby Lumber Company*, Justice Harlan F. Stone not only sustained child labor regulations that were significantly more far reaching than those incorporated in the Keating-Owen law but also declared *Hammer v. Dagenhart* to have been wrongly decided. Congress's conception of national policy, as embodied in the 1916 legislation, had then been, as it now was pronounced, the law of the land.

Interest in the Twentieth Amendment also quickened after the realignment of the electorate in the early 1930s. By 1937, twenty-eight states had ratified. But the length of time the amendment had been pending was called into question by opponents, and it became superfluous after the Fair Labor Standards Act was sustained.

[*See also* Fair Labor Standards Act; National Industrial Recovery Act.]

BIBLIOGRAPHY

Karis, Thomas G. "Congressional Behavior at Constitutional Frontiers: From 1906, the Beveridge Child Labor Bill, to 1938, the Fair Labor Standards Act." Ph.D. diss., Columbia University, 1951.
Wood, Stephen B. *Constitutional Politics in the Progressive Era.* 1968.

STEPHEN B. WOOD

CHILDREN, YOUTH, AND FAMILIES COMMITTEE, HOUSE SELECT. Proposed in a resolution cosponsored by a bipartisan group of 229 representatives, the House Select Committee on Children, Youth, and Families was approved without controversy by voice vote on 29 September 1982. As a select committee, this committee was temporary and had to be reconstituted in each new Congress. The Select Committee on Children, Youth, and Families was reestablished in each succeeding Congress from the 98th (1983–1985) through the 102d (1991–1993); it was disbanded in the 103d Congress in 1993.

The functions of the committee remained un-

changed during its existence. Although the committee lacked legislative authority and therefore reported no measures to the House, it had the following responsibilities: (1) to conduct a continuing comprehensive study and review of the problems of children, youth, and families, including but not limited to income maintenance, health (including medical and child development research), nutrition, education, welfare, employment, and recreation; (2) to study the use of all practical means and methods of encouraging the development of public and private programs and policies that would assist American children and youth in taking a full part in national life and becoming productive citizens; and (3) to develop policies that would encourage the coordination of both governmental and private programs designed to address the problems of childhood and adolescence.

During the decade in which the committee existed, public interest in family issues intensified. As family issues became more salient, additional numbers of representatives sought appointment to the panel. Twenty-five representatives served on the committee in the 98th and 99th Congresses (1983–1987); the committee had thirty members in the 100th and 101st Congresses (1987–1991). The committee did not attract a full contingent of thirty-six members until the 102d Congress (1991–1993), years when issues affecting children, youth, and families were of widespread public interest.

During the 102d Congress, the select committee addressed a variety of timely issues. Topics included: the state of families in the United States; health care reform for women, children, and teens; creation of a friendly workplace for fathers; police stress and family well-being; prevention of underage drinking; teens and AIDS; the rising cost of college tuition and its impact on families; community-based mental health services for children; cost-effective 1990 programs for children; innovative strategies for healthy infants and children; the effects of noise on the hearing of children and youth; and exploration of public-private partnerships to prevent child abuse.

In the 103d Congress (1993–1995), many members sought to end all four existing House select committees as a cost-saving measure. With a majority in favor of disbanding the select committees, Speaker Thomas S. Foley (D-Wash.) did not need to bring the issue to a vote; the select committees, including the House Select Committee on Children, Youth, and Families, quietly died when their authorization expired on 31 March 1993.

BIBLIOGRAPHY

U.S. Congress. *Congressional Record.* 97th Cong., 2d sess., 29 September 1982. See "Providing for the Establishment of a Select Committee on Children, Youth, and Families," pp. H7953–H7963.

Taylor, Paul. "Schroeder Pitches Families' Plight." *Washington Post,* 12 March 1991.

Alston, Chuck, and Richard Sammon. "Foley Foresees Quiet Death for Select Committees." *Congressional Quarterly Weekly Report,* 20 March 1993, p. 647.

MARY ETTA BOESL

CHINESE EXCLUSION POLICY. The Chinese Exclusion Act of 1882, although directly affecting only a small group, was in fact the hinge on which U.S. immigration policy turned. Prior to its passage, no significant number of free immigrants had been barred from the country; once it had set a precedent, further limitations on the immigration of ethnic groups became standard procedure for more than eight decades.

Chinese began to emigrate to the American West Coast just before the 1849 gold rush. Between then and 1882, perhaps 300,000 came, but because many remigrated, there were only about 125,000 in the country in 1882. They were highly concentrated in the Far West, particularly in California. Predominantly male laborers, their toil was vital to the development of western mining, transportation, and agriculture.

Although racist hostility was directed at Chinese from their first arrival, the major anti-Chinese movement began in the 1870s. Sparked by the Irish-born agitator Dennis Kearney—whose slogan was "The Chinese Must GO!"—it quickly captured the support of all western political parties. Its arguments were both economic and cultural; the "Chinaman," almost all laboring men and their allies insisted, "worked cheap and smelled bad." By 1876 enough political pressure existed to cause a congressional investigation.

In 1879 President Rutherford B. Hayes vetoed the Fifteen Passenger bill (which limited Chinese immigrants to fifteen per ship), while assuring Congress that diplomacy would secure a better result. An 1880 treaty gave the United States the unilateral right to "regulate, limit or suspend" the immigration of Chinese laborers, canceling the right of Chinese to enter the country, which had been established by the Burlingame treaty of 1868. Congress then suspended the immigration of Chinese laborers for twenty years, but President Chester A. Arthur vetoed the bill, arguing that a "shorter experiment" was more prudent. Congress quickly complied and passed a bill that Arthur signed on 6 May 1882.

Although called the Chinese Exclusion Act, the law only suspended the immigration of Chinese laborers for ten years while exempting teachers, students, merchants, and tourists. It also specifically

"THE CHINESE QUESTION." Published at the beginning of an upsurge of anti-Chinese hostility in the United States, the cartoon depicts Liberty protecting a Chinese man from an armed mob, declaring, "Hands off gentlemen! America means fair play for all men." The wall behind is plastered with anti-Chinese posters. In the background is a ruined "colored orphanage" and a noose hanging from a tree, evoking comparison between hostility toward Chinese and racist violence against African Americans. On the ground in front of the armed group is a poster reading: "Crimes and Drunkenness. Riots by 'Pure White' strikers." Thomas Nast, *Harper's Weekly,* 18 February 1871. LIBRARY OF CONGRESS

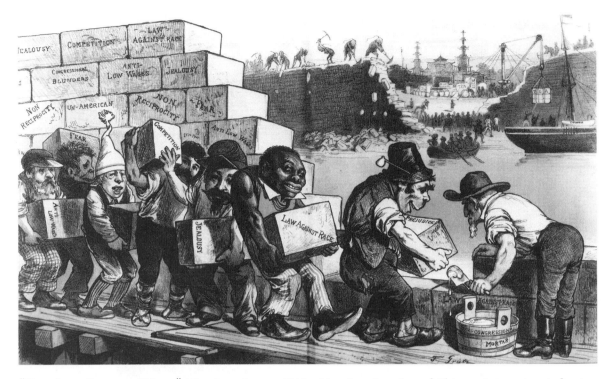

"THE ANTI-CHINESE WALL." The American wall blocking immigration of Chinese is constructed using "congressional mortar." At the same time, the Chinese wall blocking trade with the West is being demolished. The caption reads: "The American Wall Goes Up as the Chinese Original Goes Down." Lithograph from *Puck*.   LIBRARY OF CONGRESS

denied all Chinese persons the right to become naturalized citizens. Once this first exception to free and unrestricted immigration had been made, others followed. Between 1882 and 1924 a series of restrictive acts shoved the once wide-open "golden door" of immigration nearly closed. During that period, Chinese exclusion was tightened steadily; the law was renewed for a second ten-year period in 1892 and made "permanent" in 1902. The Immigration Act of 1924 barred all Asians as "aliens ineligible to citizenship."

In 1943, in what can now be seen as another turning point in U.S. immigration policy, Congress repealed the fifteen separate statutes that had implemented Chinese exclusion, gave the Chinese an immigration quota, and permitted Chinese naturalization. Both the debates in Congress and President Franklin D. Roosevelt's messages about the changes stressed the need to show the nation's Chinese allies the "affection and regard" of Americans. Three years later, similar changes were made regarding Filipinos and natives of India, and in 1952 the McCarran-Walter Act removed all special bars to Asian immigration and naturalization.

[*See also* McCarran-Walter Immigration and Nationality Act.]

BIBLIOGRAPHY

Daniels, Roger. *Asian America: Chinese and Japanese in the United States Since 1850.* 1988.
Riggs, Fred. *Pressures on Congress: A Study of the Repeal of Chinese Exclusion.* 1950.
Sandmeyer, Elmer C. *The Anti-Chinese Movement in California.* Rev. ed. 1991.

ROGER DANIELS

CHISHOLM, SHIRLEY A. (1924–), Democratic representative from New York, the first black woman elected to the House and the first black woman to be a presidential candidate. Born in Brooklyn, New York, to West Indian parents, Shirley Chisholm attended public schools, graduated with an advanced degree from Columbia University in 1952, and began her political career as a member of the New York State assembly (1964–1968). In 1968, she was elected to the House from New York's 12th Congressional District.

SHIRLEY CHISHOLM. Announcing her candidacy for the Democratic presidential nomination, 25 January 1972.

LIBRARY OF CONGRESS

BIBLIOGRAPHY

Christopher, Maurine. *Black Americans in Congress.* 1976.
Ragsdale, Bruce, and Joel D. Treese. *Black Americans in Congress, 1870–1989.* 1990.

CAROL M. SWAIN

CHURCH, FRANK (1924–1984), senator from Idaho, chairman of the Committee on Foreign Relations, and opponent of U.S. interventionism. In 1956, eight years after he had almost died of cancer, Frank Forrester Church III was elected to the U.S. Senate as a Democrat. He was thirty-two and had never before held political office. No Democrat in largely Republican Idaho had served more than one Senate term; Church was reelected three times.

A brilliant speaker and a moralist, he nevertheless excelled at consensus politics and compromise. He championed civil liberties, social welfare programs for the disabled and the elderly, environmen-

Chisholm began her twelve-year congressional career by opposing the House seniority system. She fought to be reassigned from the Committee on Agriculture to committees that would have a direct relationship to the needs of her inner-city district. She was soon moved to the Committee on Veterans' Affairs and later served on both the Rules and the Education and Labor committees. Chisholm was a staunch supporter of civil rights and equal opportunity programs. She opposed the draft in 1969 and was an early advocate of federally funded day-care facilities for working mothers. In 1971, she cosponsored the Adequate Income Act, which guaranteed all families a certain income level.

As a presidential candidate in 1972, she won delegates in several states and received 152 first-round votes at the Democratic national convention.

Throughout her congressional career, Chisholm emphasized educational and employment opportunities for minorities. She also lobbied for an extension of the minimum wage laws to include domestic workers and urged Congress to establish nondiscriminatory housing standards for low-income families and minorities.

Frustrated with the increasingly conservative and sluggish political atmosphere in Washington, Chisholm retired from the House in 1980.

FRANK CHURCH. During an interview, 27 January 1975.

LIBRARY OF CONGRESS

tal protection laws, and civil rights. He delivered the keynote address at the 1960 Democratic National Convention. An opponent by 1965 of the Vietnam War, he cosponsored major amendments (1970–1973) to end America's military involvement in Southeast Asia.

Church's growing opposition to U.S. interventionism, the "imperial presidency," and an expansive concept of national security that encouraged secrecy, surveillance, deception, and covert actions made him a national figure in the 1970s. He chaired several of the most significant Senate committees in modern U.S. history—one leading to the National Emergency Powers Act (1976), another probing the influence of multinational corporations on foreign policy (1973–1976), and another investigating the abuse of power by intelligence-gathering agencies such as the Central Intelligence Agency and Federal Bureau of Investigation (1975).

In 1976 he unsuccessfully sought the Democratic presidential nomination. He directed the Panama Canal treaties (1978) through the Senate and chaired the Foreign Relations Committee (1979–1980). In 1980 he lost his Senate seat by less than 1 percent of the vote. He died in 1984 of cancer.

BIBLIOGRAPHY

Ashby, LeRoy, and Rod Gramer. *Fighting the Odds: The Life of Senator Frank Church.* 1994.
Church, F. Forrester. *Father and Son: A Personal Biography of Senator Frank Church of Idaho.* 1985.

LeRoy Ashby

CIRCULAR LETTERS.

Beginning with the First Congress, some members sent printed circular letters to their constituents reporting on legislative proceedings and national affairs. In various forms, the practice has continued ever since, with many members mailing newsletters to voters in their home districts. In the early Congresses, when the Senate was not popularly elected, circular letters were sent mostly by members of the House of Representatives. And for decades they were sent primarily by members from southern and western states.

Circular letters varied widely in content. Some were largely copied from official reports or provided mere listings of laws enacted. Others offered insightful commentary on congressional proceedings and national affairs. Most letters were written with the next election in view. All were mailed under the congressional franking privilege, but for many

years they were privately printed at members' expense. Most surviving early circular letters were addressed to individuals, but some went to postmasters. "Circular Letter" was printed on many of them, and sometimes a gentle admonishment was added—such as this note from a Mississippi representative on his 1815 circular: "Let this pass from hand to hand."

Until the 1820s the only records of congressional debates contemporaneously published were in newspapers, whose reporters prepared the transcripts. Circular letters thus provide historians with valuable firsthand accounts of congressional proceedings during the early years of the Republic.

BIBLIOGRAPHY

Cunningham, Noble E., Jr., ed. *Circular Letters of Congressmen to Their Constituents, 1789–1829.* 3 vols. 1978.
Cunningham, Noble E., Jr. *The Jeffersonian Republicans in Power: Party Operations, 1801–1809.* 1963.

Noble E. Cunningham, Jr.

CITIZENSHIP.

In a nation of immigrants, the political status of those born in foreign territories takes on great importance. The British colonies in North America increasingly found themselves at odds with the views of the British Parliament on political involvement by the foreign-born, and by the time of the Constitutional Convention (1787) the need for a national policy with regard to citizenship acquired by birth or by legislative policy was clear. Despite this, national citizenship status was not formally recognized until the Fourteenth Amendment, and it was not until World War II that the final remnants of racism directed against certain foreign-born residents were removed from the naturalization laws.

With the Declaration of Independence, the traditional British citizenship doctrine of perpetual allegiance was clearly overturned. The establishment of the new state governments and the adoption of the Articles of Confederation brought new challenges. Article VI of the Articles declared that "the free inhabitants of each of these States . . . shall be entitled to all privileges and immunities of free citizens in the several States." This confusing language, conceivably entitling an alien resident in one state to the same rights as a citizen of another state, led to considerable squabbling, as did the lack of a definition of national citizenship. Each of the states remained free to grant citizenship status to anyone it wished, and there was great disparity between states on the matter of residence requirements, religious affiliation, naturalization fees, and other subjects. In the Constitutional Convention, there was ready agreement on the portion of the New Jersey Plan that called for uniform naturalization requirements among the states, leading to the constitutional proviso granting Congress the power to establish "a uniform rule for naturalization."

The Framers also recognized the right of naturalized citizens to participate in national political life. The Constitution stipulated that senators had to have been citizens for seven years at the time of their selection, and representatives for five years. Only the president (and by implication, the vice president) were required to be "natural born citizens." The citizenship qualification for members of Congress has occasioned some contentious congressional debate over the years, most notably the Senate's decision (in its first sessions opened to the public) that Anti-Federalist leader Albert Gallatin had not been a citizen for the required seven years and was not entitled to a Senate seat.

The Federalist era saw three separate naturalization laws, each increasingly restrictive. In 1790, at the request of President George Washington in his annual message, the Congress adopted the first U.S. naturalization law. "Free white" aliens who had resided in the United States for two years, and for one year in the state where the application would be made, were declared eligible for naturalization. Any common-law court of record in any state could receive naturalization petitions and, when satisfied with the applicant's good character, could administer the oath of allegiance. If a naturalized citizen had minor children who resided in the United States, they became citizens as well, and children born abroad of American citizens were declared to be natural-born citizens. In 1795, these rather liberal provisions were restricted by a five-year residence requirement, the filing of a preliminary declaration of intent, and a requirement that courts additionally be "satisfied of applicant's attachment to the principles of the Constitution." In 1798, coincident with the passage of the Alien and Sedition Acts, Congress amended the naturalization law to require a fourteen-year residence, with a five-year period between the preliminary declaration and taking the oath of allegiance.

The Jefferson administration quickly moved to overturn the 1798 act. In 1802 a revised act was passed requiring a five-year residence and alien registration with a federal or state court clerk to estab-lish a residence record. As before, state or federal courts could issue naturalization certificates to free white persons who satisfied the court as to their character and attachment to the Constitution. The basic provisions of the act remain in law today, with the exception that now only federal courts may conduct naturalization proceedings.

Not until after the Civil War did blacks become eligible for citizenship. The post–Civil War amendments to the Constitution established a national citizenship standard for the first time, and specified that freed blacks born in the United States were citizens. Congress, in 1872, approved the Revised Statutes—the first attempt at creating a United States Code—and in the recodification deleted the phrase "free white person" from the U.S. naturalization law. This action stood until American Indians and Asians sought naturalization, when Congress amended the law to make naturalization available only to "free white persons and persons of African nativity or descent." Not until 1943 did Congress pass a bill, sponsored by Rep. Warren G. Magnuson (D-Wash.), eliminating racial barriers to naturalized citizenship for residents of Chinese descent. Similar bans against residence by immigrants from India and the Philippines were ended in 1946. Remaining racial barriers to naturalization were removed by the McCarran-Walter Act of 1952, although that act retained the ethnically biased "national origins" quotas for immigration that dated from 1924. More recent immigration legislation, including the Immigration Reform and Control Act of 1986 and the Immigration Reform Act of 1990, have set overall annual numerical limits for admission of immigrants to the United States while ending discriminatory, restrictive annual quotas for individual countries.

The legal status of American Indians was in doubt for many years. Citizenship was not conferred on them by the Fourteenth Amendment because American Indians still residing with their tribes were not technically "subject to the jurisdiction of the United States." Under the Dawes Severalty Act of 1887, Indians who severed their ties to their tribes and elected to take a portion of tribal lands as a personal allotment could become citizens when they showed their self-sufficiency. Most American Indians acquired citizenship through this act, and the remainder did so under the Citizenship Act of 1924.

If one could acquire citizenship, naturally one could also lose it—voluntarily or involuntarily. Nativist and anticommunist sentiment led to stricter scrutiny of political ideology during the naturalization process, especially after its federalization in the Naturalization Act of 1907, and later in the Nationality Act of 1940, when still greater attention was paid to denaturalization for criminal activities, departure from the United States, and participation in suspect political activities ostensibly threatening national security.

Until 1924, an American-born woman lost her citizenship and acquired that of her spouse if she married an alien (in the nineteenth century this was an accepted standard of international law). The racial barrier exacerbated such hardships: an American woman of Asian descent who married a foreigner lost her citizenship, and even if the marriage was later terminated, she could not be naturalized. In 1924, Congress passed the Women's Independent Citizenship Act ending a woman's automatic loss of citizenship upon marriage to a foreigner and permitting married women to seek naturalization in their own right.

With the repeal in the 1940s and 1950s of the remaining racial barriers to naturalized citizenship, legislative attention focused primarily on immigration to the United States rather than on the acquisition of citizenship. The McCarran-Walter Act of 1952, which removed the final racial restriction, nevertheless continued the geographic and ethnic bias of earlier acts which had set an overall annual limit for immigrants from the Eastern Hemisphere and had established annual country-by-country limits. These limits severely restricted the migration of Southern and Eastern Europeans, Africans, and Asians, while giving preference to immigrants from northern and western Europe. The McCarran-Walter Act included additional restrictions banning persons with political views deemed dangerous to the United States.

The quota system was overhauled for the first time by the 1965 Immigration Act. An overall numerical quota for persons born in the Western Hemisphere was set for the first time. In return for this concession by immigration reformers, the ethnic bias in the Eastern Hemisphere quota was ended. In 1990, the Simpson-Mazzoli Immigration Reform Act finally passed Congress after nearly six years of preliminary work. That earlier action included passage of amnesty legislation designed to regularize the status of foreigners who had long resided in the United States illegally. The Simpson-Mazzoli Act substantially increased the number of annual quota slots and gave the Immigration and Naturalization Service expanded discretion to per-

mit "non-quota" immigrants into the country. The act also simplified the court proceedings for naturalization in an effort to end lengthy administrative backlogs.

The 1965 and 1990 reforms encouraged greater ethnic and geographic diversity among those seeking permanent admission to the United States. Coupled with the end of racial barriers to naturalized citizenship, these acts sought to produce a more ethnically diverse citizenry that would take part in the political affairs of the country more quickly than had earlier immigrants to the United States. If the 1990 act and other related measures prove successful, the U.S. Congress in the future should more closely mirror the diversity of the American populace.

[See also Dawes Severalty Act; Fourteenth Amendment; Immigration Policy; McCarran-Walter Immigration and Nationality Act.]

BIBLIOGRAPHY

Curran, Thomas J. *Xenophobia and Immigration, 1820–1930.* 1975.
Franklin, Frank G. *The Legislative History of Naturalization in the United States.* 1906. Repr. 1969.
Kettner, James H. *The Development of American Citizenship, 1608–1870.* 1978.
Mann, Arthur. *The One and the Many: Reflections on the American Identity.* 1979.

PAUL S. RUNDQUIST

CIVIL LIBERTIES. Congress's mixed record in the area of civil liberties is scarcely surprising, given the complex tensions between the majority and the individual that are inherent in a democratic political system.

Civil Rights and Majority Rule. Democracy is usually defined as rule by the majority with protection of individual and minority rights. The role of a legislature in a democracy is to represent the majority that elected it. Representation implies action. Civil liberties are those areas of life in which the majority is not perceived as having a legitimate interest and in which government therefore is not permitted to take action or into which it is permitted to intrude only under limited circumstances.

Among the liberties basic to the free exchange of ideas that is necessary if citizens are to be informed are the liberties to speak and hear, publish and read, and organize and assemble with others. Other civil liberties minimize the government's power to abridge life, liberty, and property, which it can do only after providing the individual with due process of law. This means, for example, that the government cannot deny bail to accused persons unless there is a likelihood that they will not appear for trial, punish even the most heinous lawbreakers with cruel or unusual punishment, or convict anyone of a criminal act in the absence of safeguards such as a fair trial, a jury of one's peers, the power to call witnesses and to cross-examine witnesses for the prosecution, and the right to be tried only once for a criminal act.

As it is the primary function of Congress to act on behalf of the very majority from which the individual may need protection, congressional action and civil liberties often clash. Such clashes are all the likelier during periods of national crisis, particularly wartime, when patriotism can degenerate into a popular belief that disagreement with government policy constitutes disloyalty or subversion. And, indeed, Congress has proved least responsive to civil liberties concerns at such times.

From the Bill of Rights to the Civil War. The First Congress established the legal basis for many of the civil liberties recognized by the U.S. government. In 1791 it sent to the states for ratification the Bill of Rights, the First through Tenth Amendments to the Constitution, keeping a promise that had been made by supporters of the Constitution while it was being ratified. As the amendments limited the powers of the national government, Congress in effect agreed to minimize its own freedom of action in areas such as speech, press, rights of the accused, and additional areas not enumerated but reserved to the people and the states in the Ninth and Tenth Amendments.

The Second Congress was less friendly to civil liberties. Slavery was recognized as legitimate by the Constitution; acting under it, Congress passed the Fugitive Slave Act of 1793. The act provided that an owner or agent's oral testimony or affidavit, given to any federal or state magistrate, was adequate proof of a runaway slave's ownership. As future chief justice Salmon P. Chase unsuccessfully argued, the act violated the Fourth Amendment's prohibition of unreasonable searches and seizures, the Fifth Amendment's due process clause, and every person's right to a jury trial and habeas corpus protections.

The Fifth Congress passed the next anti–civil libertarian statute in 1798, when the country was engaged in the so-called quasi-war with France and many considered an actual war imminent. The ruling Federalist party regarded the occasionally alarmist Jeffersonian Republican newspapers as

aiding the enemy. It therefore enacted four measures, known jointly as the Alien and Sedition Acts. One act increased the period of residence before immigrants could become citizens from five years to fourteen. A second and third gave the president the power to deport aliens in times of peace and war, depriving aliens of any right to defend themselves in court. The fourth, the Sedition Act, provided fines and jail sentences for those found guilty of writing, publishing, or saying anything "false, scandalous, and malicious" against Congress or the president if their intent was to defame those officers or excite "the hatred of the good people of the United States" against them. In effect, the act made criticism of the government a crime. Tragically, only one of the seventeen prosecutions under the Sedition Act, including ten of journalists for Jeffersonian newspapers, resulted in an acquittal.

No further congressional action antithetical to civil liberties was taken until 1850, during the crisis of the pre–Civil War period and the increasingly tense debate over slavery. The Compromise of 1850, an unsuccessful attempt by the 31st Congress to reconcile differences between the North and the South, included the new Fugitive Slave Act. It permitted locally appointed commissioners to order the arrest and return of fugitive slaves upon an owner or agent's oral or written affidavit, denying the slave access to a judge and other constitutional guarantees such as habeas corpus, trial by jury, cross-examination, and the right to testify on his or her own behalf.

From the Civil War to World War I. On 5 May 1863, Union military forces in Ohio arrested Clement L. Vallandigham, a former member of Congress, charging him with treason. The speech he had made denouncing the war was interpreted by military officials as contradicting the local commander's order prohibiting expressions of sympathy for the enemy. On 8 May the 37th Congress passed a statute permitting the president to suspend the writ of habeas corpus at will. (The writ is an order to produce someone being held prisoner, articulate any charges, and proceed with the normal hearing process.) Ohio was no longer under martial law and the civil courts were operating there, but a military commission tried and sentenced Vallandigham. A number of other such military tribunals tried civilians under this congressional authority during the Civil War, all of them violating the accused's rights to a jury of his peers, cross-examination, and the subpoenaing of witnesses.

In 1866, after the Civil War ended, the Supreme

Court declared in *Ex parte Milligan* that the 1864 conviction of a civilian in an area not under martial law violated the right to habeas corpus. A year later, the 39th Congress restored the right to appeal denials of habeas corpus in federal courts, including the Supreme Court. A Southern newspaper editor, jailed by a military commander for publishing "incendiary and libelous" articles about the post–Civil War Reconstruction governments established in the South by Congress, relied on the 1867 statute and appealed to the Supreme Court. His appeal implicitly challenged the substitution of the Reconstruction governments for popularly elected state governments. While it was pending, the 40th Congress repealed the statute, thereby taking the appeal (*Ex parte McCardle* [1869]) out of the Court's jurisdiction and safeguarding the Reconstruction acts.

The so-called Reconstruction amendments—the Thirteenth, Fourteenth, and Fifteenth Amendments to the Constitution—were passed by the 38th and 39th Congresses. Their impact on the course of civil liberties in the United States has been a major one. The Thirteenth Amendment outlawed slavery; the Fifteenth was an attempt to protect the right of former slaves to vote. But the most important of these amendments is the Fourteenth, which declares that no state may "deprive any person of life, liberty, or property, without due process of law; nor deny to any person within its jurisdiction the equal protection of the laws." Beginning in 1925, this clause would gradually be interpreted by the Supreme Court to mean that the limitations on governmental power included in the Bill of Rights extended to the states as well as to the federal government, and that the "liberty" mentioned in the Fourteenth Amendment referred to the liberties detailed in the first eight amendments. As a result, limitations by local, state, and federal governmental actions in fields such as speech, religion, search and seizure, and privacy can be opposed in federal courts.

Congress next turned its attention to civil liberties when the United States entered World War I. The 65th Congress enacted the Selective Service Act of 1917, which established criminal penalties for people obstructing the draft or refusing to be conscripted, without reference to whether they did so on grounds of religion or conscience. The same Congress passed the vaguely worded Espionage Act of 1917, which punished not only treason but attempts to cause "disobedience" in the armed forces or to impede recruitment. It enacted the Trading with the Enemy Act of 1917, permitting the postmaster general to ban from the mails virtually any foreign-language publications he chose. Finally, Congress passed the Sedition Act of 1918, in part to curb the radical laborers organized as the Industrial Workers of the World. Among the activities that were branded as "crimes" by the Sedition Act were "uttering, printing, writing, or publishing any disloyal, profane, scurrilous, or abusive language." Strictly interpreted, the act would have made it impossible for Americans to criticize their government at all. The Alien Act of 1918 legitimated deportation of alien anarchists or those who openly espoused the use of force to overthrow the government, whether or not they had engaged in subversive activities.

World War II and Its Aftermath. One result of the fear that swept the United States in the decades after the Russian Revolution of 1917 was the 76th Congress's Alien Registration Act of 1940, also known as the Smith Act. It criminalized speech that attempted to create disloyalty among members of the military, speech or distribution of printed matter that advocated violent overthrow of the government, and membership in any organization that advocated overthrow. The act thus limited the rights of speech and association. The 76th Congress's McCarran Internal Security Act of 1950, also known as the Subversive Activities Control Act or the McCarran Act, required organizations that advocated communist causes to register with the Subversive Activities Control Board and disclose their officers, finances, and membership. As membership in such organizations implied advocacy of violent overthrow of the government, individuals who registered under the McCarran Act made themselves liable to prosecution under the Smith Act and thereby were deprived of their Fifth Amendment right against self-incrimination. President Harry S. Truman vetoed the bill, saying that it endangered freedom of speech and put the government "in the thought control business"; Congress nonetheless overrode his veto.

The Supreme Court initially upheld the registration requirement in *Communist Party v. Subversive Activities Control Board* (1961) but subsequently overturned it as a violation of the Fifth Amendment right against self-incrimination in *Albertson v. Subversive Activities Control Board* (1965). Members of communist front and communist action groups were ineligible for passports (this provision was struck down by the Supreme Court in *Aptheker v. Secretary of State* [1964]), or for employment in national defense jobs (overturned by the Supreme Court in *United States v. Robel* [1967]). Title II of the McCarran Act, also called the Emergency

Landmark Civil Liberties Enactments

TITLE	DATE ENACTED	REFERENCE NUMBER	DESCRIPTION
Bill of Rights (First through Tenth Amendments to U.S. Constitution)	1791	1 Stat. 97–98	Codified the basic rights of the people.
Fugitive Slave Act	1793	1 Stat. 302–305	Abridged constitutional rights; first federal law to do so. Permitted runaway slaves to be arrested in free as well as slave-holding states, and enabled owners or their agents to reclaim slaves upon no more than an oral or written affidavit before any magistrate. Provided a penalty of $500 for harboring runaway slaves or obstructing their capture, with the fine to go to the claimant.
Naturalization Act[1]	1798	1 Stat. 566–569	Raised probationary residence period before an immigrant could gain citizenship from five to fourteen years.
Act Concerning Aliens[1]	1798	1 Stat. 570–572	Gave the president authority, without any judicial proceedings, to deport any alien whom he judged dangerous to the peace and safety of the U.S.
Act Respecting Alien Enemies	1798	1 Stat. 577–578	Gave the president authority in time of war or threatened invasion to seize or deport all resident male aliens of fourteen years or over who were citizens of the enemy nation.
Act for the Punishment[1] of Certain Crimes	1798	1 Stat. 596–597	First federal law restricting freedom of speech and press. Established terms of imprisonment and fines for any person who conspired to defeat the operation of any U.S. law by criticizing it through speeches or articles, or who attempted to defame federal officials by criticizing them in "scandalous and malicious" writings.
Fugitive Slave Act	1850	9 Stat. 462–465	Continued abridgment of rights; led to passage of state acts limiting its effect.
Habeas Corpus Act	1863	13 Stat. 755–758	Denied habeas corpus by permitting arrest and trial of civilians by the military in areas not under martial law and where civilian courts were functioning.
Thirteenth Amendment to the Constitution	1865[2]	13 Stat. 774–775	Outlawed all forms of involuntary servitude, including slavery.
Fourteenth Amendment to the Constitution	1866[2]	14 Stat. 358–359	Prohibited states from depriving persons of due process or equal protection of the laws, giving Congress power to enact remedial legislation, and became basis for later applications of the Bill of Rights as limitations on state governments.
An Act to Amend "An Act to Establish the Judicial Courts of the United States"	1867	14 Stat. 385–387	Restored right of appeal to all federal courts in habeas corpus cases.
Amendment to "An Act to Amend the Judiciary Act"	1868	15 Stat. 44	Reinstated right to appeal denial of habeas corpus to Supreme Court.
Fifteenth Amendment to the Constitution	1868[2]	15 Stat. 346	Declared the right of former slaves to vote.
Selective Service Act	1917	40 Stat. 76–83	Imposed military draft with no provision for conscientious objection.
Espionage Act	1917	40 Stat. 217–231	Penalized attempts to cause "disobedience" in the armed forces or to impede recruitment.
Trading with the Enemy Act	1917	40 Stat. 411–426	Permitted postmaster general to ban foreign-language publications from the mail.

[1]Alien and Sedition Acts
[2]Date ratified

Landmark Civil Liberties Enactments (Continued)

TITLE	DATE ENACTED	REFERENCE NUMBER	DESCRIPTION
Sedition Act	1918	40 Stat. 553–554	Made criticism of government difficult by criminalizing "disloyal" language.
Alien Act	1918	P.L. 65-221	Permitted deportation of aliens on the basis of their beliefs.
Alien Registration Act (Smith Act)	1940	54 Stat. 670–676	Criminalized advocacy of violent overthrow of the government.
To Provide a Penalty for Violation of Restrictions or Order with Respect to . . . Military Areas	1942	P.L. 77-503	Established criminal penalties for civilians refusing to leave areas designated as military zones by the president or authorized military commander. Designed and used to move Japanese Americans from the West Coast and inter them in camps.
McCarran Internal Security Act (Subversive Activities Control Act)	1950	64 Stat. 987–1031	Required communist organizations and their members to register with the government and disclose names and addresses; prohibited members from using U.S. passports or working in defense jobs; required attorney general to keep register of such organizations. Title II, entitled Emergency Detention Act, permitted government to keep lists of suspected communists; permitted president to declare national emergency during which they would be interned.
McCarran-Walter Immigration and Nationality Act	1952	66 Stat. 163–282	Excluded aliens from the U. S. for ideological reasons.
Communist Control Act	1954	68 Stat. 775–780	Specifically outlawed the Communist party.
Postal Service and Federal Employees Salary Act	1962	P.L. 87-793	Permitted postmaster general to seize any mail from foreign countries that he believed to be communist propaganda or obscene material and to notify addressee, who had sixty days to request that the mail be forwarded.
Legal Services Corporation Act of 1974 (became Title X of Economic Opportunity Act of 1964)	1974	P.L. 93–355	Created legal services for the indigent in the Office of Economic Opportunity; later created independent Legal Services Corporation to provide the services.
Amendment of 1974 (to Freedom of Information Act of 1966)	1974	P.L. 93-502	Established procedures for getting information from the government; authorized courts to examine information the government withheld under the law's exemptions.
Omnibus Crime Control and Safe Streets Act	1968	P.L. 90-351	Permitted law enforcement officials to ignore Miranda warning in some circumstances.
Limitation on Detention	1971	P.L. 92-128	Repealed Emergency Detention Act of 1950.
Foreign Intelligence Surveillance Act	1978	P.L. 95-511	Created special courts to hear search warrant requests in cases of suspected spying.
Privacy Protection Act	1980	P.L. 96-440	Required the government to get a subpoena before searching a newsroom for information about crimes committed by third parties.
Bail Reform Act	1984	P.L. 98-473	Made "dangerousness" grounds for denying pre-trial bail.
Foreign Relations Authorization Act	1988	P.L. 100-204	Prohibited exclusion of aliens from the U. S. on the basis of their beliefs.
Anti-Terrorism Act	1988	P.L. 100-204	Prohibited Palestine Liberation Organization from setting up an office in the U.S. and limited its ability to distribute information.
Civil Liberties Act of 1988	1988	P.L. 100-383	Ordered restitution to be made to Japanese Americans interned under 1942 executive order.
Flag Protection Act	1989	P.L. 101-131	Criminalized "desecration" of the American flag.

Detention Act of 1950, declared that Americans participating in the world communist movement thereby repudiated their allegiance to the United States, and it authorized the president to declare a state of "Internal Security Emergency," during which people who had participated in the movement could be interned by order of the attorney general in special places of detention that the Bureau of Prisons was ordered to keep in readiness. The Detention Review Board, created to review a detention order on the petition of any detainee, had total control over its own procedures and criteria for evaluating cases. This part of the act, with its abridgment of the right to jury trial, witnesses, cross-examination, and other due process rights, was repealed by the 92d Congress in 1971, partly in reaction to disclosures that the Federal Bureau of Investigation had created a Security Index of more than twenty thousand people to be detained in an emergency and partly in response to pleas from Japanese Americans and their congressional representatives.

Japanese American internment. Japanese Americans had particular reason to be fearful. After the Japanese attack on Pearl Harbor in 1941, the U.S. Army claimed that Japanese American citizens were likely to aid a Japanese attempt to invade the West Coast. The 77th Congress acted in 1942 to legitimize President Franklin D. Roosevelt's Executive Order 9066, which empowered the secretary of War to designate military zones from which any persons he chose could be excluded. The law also provided criminal penalties for refusing to obey exclusion orders. Under the law, 120,000 Japanese American citizens were summarily forced from their homes on the West Coast and placed in ten primitive, hastily erected internment camps. In *Hirabayashi v. United States* (1943) and *Korematsu v. United States* (1944) the Supreme Court denied the internees judicial recourse even though they were being deprived of their liberty and property without any indication of wrongdoing. In 1988, the 100th Congress ordered that restitution of $20,000 be made to each person interned and still living. As of 1993, however, Congress had not appropriated funds adequate to carry out the law.

Anticommunist hysteria. Fear of Japanese Americans had abated by the 1950s, but fear of communists had not. In 1952, the 82d Congress enacted the McCarran-Walter Immigration and Nationality Act, barring aliens who advocated anarchism or communism from entering the United States and strengthening the government's power to deport similarly suspect resident aliens without trial or al-

legation of specific crimes. In the Communist Control Act of 1954, the 83d Congress outlawed the Communist party, declaring it "an instrumentality of a conspiracy to overthrow the Government of the United States." Finally, in 1962, the 87th Congress authorized the postmaster general to seize mail he believed to be communist propaganda (or obscene material) and required any addressee who wanted the material to file a request in writing (P.L. 305). The Supreme Court struck down this act as an abridgment of free speech in *Lamont v. Postmaster General* (1965).

The congressional authority to undertake investigations was used during the 1930s, the late 1940s, and the 1950s to publicize the names of people who were considered by various congressional committees to be "subversive" but who were never accused of specific crimes or tried in a courtroom. The House Un-American Activities Committee (HUAC), initially established as a special committee by the 71st Congress in 1930 and transformed into a standing committee by the 79th Congress in 1945, relied on secret "information" about purported membership in communist organizations to summon individuals to testify before it and accuse them of belonging to subversive groups, without giving them their constitutional rights of trial, cross-examination, or confrontation of their accusers. HUAC was particularly active during the early 1950s, when the Korean War (1950–1953) seemed to validate the threat of the relentless spread of communism. Under the leadership of Sen. Joseph R. McCarthy (R-Wis.), similar activities were undertaken by the Senate Permanent Subcommittee on Investigations of the Committee on Government Operations. Growing antipathy for McCarthy's misuse of publicity to violate civil liberties finally led to his being censured by a special session of the Senate on 12 November 1954.

Recent Congressional Actions. Citizens' rights in the criminal justice system have been the repeated targets of congressional action. A federal wagering tax statute passed by the 82d Congress in 1951, for example, required professional gamblers to register with the Internal Revenue Service and pay an occupation tax. If the gamblers complied with the registration requirement, they thereby exposed themselves to criminal charges for gambling, in violation of their Fifth Amendment right against self-incrimination. The statute was overturned by the Supreme Court in *Marchetti v. United States* (1968). Title VIII of the Omnibus Crime Control and Safe Streets Act of 1968, enacted by the 90th Congress, was an attempt to repeal the Supreme Court's decision in *Miranda v. Arizona* (1966) requiring law enforcement officials to inform suspects of their constitutional rights. In passing the Bail Reform Act of 1984, the 98th Congress ignored the Eighth Amendment's protection of accused persons from imprisonment unless they are likely to flee before trial. It authorized judges to refuse bail if they believed an accused could "pose a danger to any other person or the community," making a vague concept of "dangerousness" sufficient reason for imprisonment. In a move protective of civil liberties and aimed at limiting warrantless wiretapping, however, the 95th Congress passed the 1978 Foreign Intelligence Surveillance Act, creating special courts to hear warrant requests if the government believed a citizen to be spying for a foreign power.

On occasion, Congress has used its appropriations power rather than its legislative power to affect civil liberties. In 1976, for example, the 94th Congress became the first to attach to an appropriations bill (P.L. 94-206) an amendment banning the use of Medicaid funds for abortions, which the Supreme Court had declared a constitutionally protected right in *Roe v. Wade* (1973). This limitation on reproductive freedom was reenacted by subsequent Congresses.

Although the Legal Services Corporation was created by Congress to provide attorneys for the indigent (Economic Opportunity Act of 1964, 89th Congress; Legal Services Corporation Act of 1974, 93d Congress), access of the poor to legal services has been substantially impeded by the sharply reduced funding provided to the corporation beginning with the 98th Congress's Appropriations Act of 1984, which also placed various limitations on the kinds of cases for which funds could be utilized.

Since the mid 1960s, the record of Congress in the civil liberties field has been as mixed as ever. The Freedom of Information Act passed by the 89th Congress in 1966 made large bodies of data available to citizens by establishing procedures by which they could get information from the government. The act, however, included exceptions such as one permitting the executive branch to keep secret any information it believed might endanger national security. Following an unsuccessful courtroom challenge to the law by several members of Congress in *Environmental Protection Agency v. Mink* (1973), the 93d Congress (1974) altered the law to authorize courts to examine material the government wished to withhold in order to ascertain whether the security claims were valid. In

Zurcher v. The Stanford Daily (1978), the Supreme Court held that judges who believed journalists might have evidence relevant to a criminal investigation could issue warrants for searches of their newsrooms, even if the journalists themselves were not suspected of crime. The 96th Congress, however, undid that decision with the Privacy Protection Act of 1980, which prohibits such searches from taking place until after a subpoena has been issued. As subpoenas can be challenged in court before a search takes place, this makes government invasion of newsrooms less likely. Similarly, in Title IX of the Foreign Relations Authorization Act of 1988, the 100th Congress negated some of the harm of the 1952 McCarran-Walter Immigration and Nationality Act by forbidding the executive branch from excluding any alien from the United States because of beliefs or associations that would be protected under the Constitution were the alien a U.S. citizen. Congress, however, limited the duration of the act (from 31 December 1987 through 1 March 1989) and incorporated the Anti-Terrorism Act of 1987 into it. The latter, which declared the Palestine Liberation Organization (PLO) to be a terrorist organization, made it illegal for Americans to receive anything other than information from the PLO and prohibited the PLO from establishing an office in the United States, thereby making the exchange of ideas between the PLO and U.S. citizens extremely difficult. The airing of ideas was also at issue in *Texas v. Johnson* (1989), in which the Supreme Court struck down a conviction for flag-burning as an abridgment of "symbolic speech." The 101st Congress then enacted the Flag Protection Act of 1989, making "desecration" of the flag punishable by up to one year in jail. This act was overturned by the Supreme Court in *United States v. Eichman* (1990).

While Congress has occasionally moved to protect civil liberties, it has more often sought to limit them. Individual members of Congress have been concerned with civil liberties; most, however, have not. Civil liberties issues have on occasion brought Congress into conflict with the Supreme Court, with the Court usually more wary of the majority's abridgment of individual liberties. In the final analysis, however, the best method for safeguarding civil liberties is to ensure that they are understood by the people of the United States, whom it is Congress's function to represent.

[*See also* Alien and Sedition Acts; Alien Registration Act; Bill of Rights; Espionage Act; Ex Post Facto Laws; Fourteenth Amendment; Fugitive

Slave Act; Internal Security; McCarran Internal Security Act of 1950; Slavery; Un-American Activities Committee, House.]

BIBLIOGRAPHY

Irons, Peter. *Justice at War.* 1983.
Kutler, Stanley I. *The American Inquisition: Justice and Injustice in the Cold War.* 1982.
Smith, James M. *Freedom's Fetters: The Alien and Sedition Acts and American Civil Liberties.* 1956.
Murphy, Walter F. *Congress and the Court.* 1962.
Nye, Russel B. *Fettered Freedoms: Civil Liberties and the Slavery Controversy.* 1963.
Preston, William, Jr. *Aliens and Dissenters: Federal Suppression of Radicals, 1903–1933.* 1966.
Taylor, Telford. *Grand Inquest: The Story of Congressional Investigations.* 1955.

PHILIPPA STRUM

CIVIL RIGHTS. Congressional civil rights policy-making in the twentieth century has had many different facets. Legislative action has included antilynching, school desegregation, voting rights, equal employment, and fair housing. Since the 1970s, congressional attention to such traditional civil rights concerns has waned, and the focus has shifted to minority vote dilution and protection for groups other than racial minorities. On some occasions, presidential leadership has been crucial to congressional passage of civil rights bills; at other times, chief executives have sought to reduce the scope of existing civil rights protections.

For more than half of the twentieth century, Congress failed to pass any civil rights legislation. The failure of most civil rig hts bills prior to 1964 reflected the success of a united minority in thwarting the goals of the majority. Conservative southern Democrats, in conjunction with Republicans, manipulated congressional procedures through the Rules Committee in the House and the filibuster in the Senate to defeat civil rights proposals. When the passage of civil rights protections became inevitable, as with the Civil Rights Acts of 1957 and 1960, southern Democrats successfully weakened the original proposals. The passage of momentous civil rights bills in 1964, 1965, and 1968 was the result not only of strong executive leadership but also of electoral developments that enabled the pro–civil rights majority to overcome the coalition of southern Democrats and Republicans.

On many civil rights issues, Republicans in Congress represented the swing votes. After President Richard M. Nixon's election in 1968, northern Democrats relied on congressional procedures and Republican defections to halt conservative attempts to weaken voting rights legislation. The passage of fair housing laws in 1968 hinged on compromises offered by the Republican leadership. In the area of employment, Republican support of southern Democrats deprived the Equal Employment Opportunity Commission of enforcement power. Regarding school desegregation, there has been a complete reversal in the position of northern Democrats and Republicans who initially supported such policies.

Any discussion of civil rights policy-making is also a discussion of southern politics. The eleven states with the greatest loyalty to the Democratic party from 1876 to 1944 were the eleven states of the Confederacy: Alabama, Arkansas, Florida, Georgia, Louisiana, Mississippi, North Carolina, South Carolina, Tennessee, Texas, and Virginia. Representatives from a group of border states that had slaves in 1860 and required statewide public school segregation in May 1954—Delaware, Kentucky, Maryland, Missouri, Oklahoma, and West Virginia—generally voted with their southern colleagues.

A conservative coalition of southern Democrats and Republicans appeared in congressional roll-call votes from the late 1930s on. But for the most part, up to the mid 1940s the alliance rested on similar views regarding labor policy and other economic issues rather than on civil rights.

Early Civil Rights Policies. The Thirteenth, Fourteenth, and Fifteenth Amendments to the U.S. Constitution provided the foundation for congressional protection of civil rights. Passed in the aftermath of the Civil War, the amendments respectively prohibited slavery; defined citizenship, equal protection, and due process; and protected the right of African Americans to vote. They also authorized Congress to pass appropriate legislation for the enforcement of each article. Pursuant to these amendments Congress passed the Civil Rights Acts of 1866, 1870, 1871, and 1875. These laws protected the right of newly freed slaves to make and enforce contracts and to inherit, lease, or sell property; guaranteed their voting rights; provided for civil action in discrimination cases; and prohibited discrimination in places of public accommodation. In a period of pervasive racism, these laws had little impact. The Supreme Court interpreted them narrowly; in the *Civil Rights Cases* (1883), it ruled that the Act of 1875 prohibited only state actions and therefore did not prohibit private or individual acts of discrimination.

Twentieth-century civil rights policy-making by Congress began with efforts to pass a federal anti-lynching law. The Tuskegee Institute estimated that 4,643 persons were lynched in the United States between 1882 and 1934; African American victims numbered 3,352, or 72 percent. Legislation introduced from 1900 through 1902 called on Congress to investigate lynching and make the crime a federal offense. These early efforts failed to obtain broad support, and antilynching legislation receded from the congressional agenda.

The first antilynching bill to draw serious attention in Congress was introduced in 1921 by Rep. Leonidas C. Dyer (R-Mo.). Reported favorably by the House Judiciary Committee, the bill was passed by the House of Representatives on 26 January 1922 by a vote of 213 to 119, but southern Democrats blocked its passage in the Senate with a filibuster. Neither house took action on various antilynching measures introduced in the years immediately following 1921. The next major antilynching bill, introduced in 1935 and known as the Costigan-Wagner Act, fell victim like its 1921 predecessor to filibuster by the southern Democrats. President Franklin D. Roosevelt, though publicly favoring antilynching laws, did not urge Congress to pass such a measure. He did, however, create a Committee on Fair Employment Practices in 1941 by executive order.

The 75th Congress (1937–1939) marked the beginning of a significant and persisting civil rights presence on the congressional agenda. The House passed several antilynching bills between 1937 and 1940, and from 1942 to 1949 supported measures prohibiting poll taxes as a requirement for voting. None of these bills passed the Senate, however. Greater support for these civil rights measures came from Republicans than from northeastern Democrats prior to the 79th Congress (1945–1947); but immediately thereafter, as the electoral impact of the great migration of African Americans from the South to the northern cities began to be felt, northern Democrats demonstrated higher levels of civil rights support than did Republicans.

Post–World War II Era. Progress on civil rights in the years immediately following World War II stemmed from executive-branch action and judicial decisions rather than from Congress. President Harry S. Truman sent Congress a comprehensive civil rights program in 1948, but none of his proposals came to a floor vote in either chamber. Through executive order, President Truman ended segregation in the armed forces and prohibited discrimination in federal employment and any work carried out under government contract.

Proposals to ban poll taxes were introduced regularly in Congress beginning in the 1940s. While the House passed five anti–poll tax bills from 1942 to 1947, the Senate either failed to act on the bills or saw the measures die due to southern-led filibusters. Debate over the elimination of poll taxes centered on whether poll taxes were a voting qualification that states could properly set and whether a statutory ban on them was sufficient or a constitutional amendment was required. In 1964 the issue finally was laid to rest when thirty-eight states ratified the Twenty-fourth Amendment to the Constitution, prohibiting poll taxes.

Southerners continued to defeat civil rights bills during most of the 1950s. Sen. Richard B. Russell (D-Ga.) led a 1950 filibuster to prevent the creation of a permanent Fair Employment Practices Commission and Sen. James O. Eastland (D-Miss.), as chairman of the Judiciary Committee, thwarted President Dwight D. Eisenhower's attempt in 1956 to establish a U.S. Commission on Civil Rights. Rep. Howard W. Smith (D-Va.), chair of the House Rules Committee, stalled progress on the Civil Rights Act of 1957 by conducting lengthy hearings before granting a rule on the bill. House procedures necessitate a privileged resolution or rule that allows important legislation to be considered before other less significant bills. Smith's power as chairman of the Rules Committee gave him the opportunity to delay or even kill legislation by refusing to grant such a rule.

Pressure on Congress for action on civil rights mounted in the years following the Supreme Court's school desegregation decision (*Brown v. Board of Education*) in 1954. Rosa Parks's refusal to move to the back of the bus in 1955 started a year-long bus boycott in Montgomery, Alabama. The enrollment of African American students at Central High School in Little Rock, Arkansas, touched off mob violence that required the U.S. National Guard to restore order in 1956.

Ultimately, the Civil Rights Act of 1957 passed the House 286 to 126. It established the U.S. Commission on Civil Rights and provided for limited protection of African Americans' right to vote. Southerners who voted for the bill represented border state districts with relatively small black populations. Opposition to the bill, aside from the anti–civil rights southerners, came primarily from northern Republican members who represented predominantly white rural areas. They saw no political advantage in voting for civil rights because they had few minority constituents and many had no desire to alienate their conservative southern colleagues. While southerners overwhelmingly opposed the 1957 Civil Rights Act, they also knew they could not prevent its passage. Therefore they focused on a strategy to modify and thus weaken the bill.

Like their House colleagues, southern senators took a moderate stance toward the 1957 Civil Rights Act, avoiding an organized filibuster. Pro–civil rights senator Paul H. Douglas (D-Ill.) and Senate minority leader William F. Knowland (R-Calif.) bypassed the Senate Judiciary Committee and brought the bill before the full Senate. After an eight-day debate, the Senate passed the bill in August. Following House-Senate negotiations to resolve differences regarding jury trials, President Eisenhower signed the bill on 9 September 1957. Senate majority leader Lyndon B. Johnson (D-Tex.) played a crucial role in the passage of the Senate version of the bill. He discouraged a potential filibuster by threatening to require the Senate to meet continuously if one was attempted. At the same time he worked out a compromise in the Senate's version of the jury-trial provision that was acceptable to most southerners.

Two factors important to the passage of the 1957 law—the first civil rights measure enacted since 1875—were the lack of a sustained filibuster by southern senators and increased Republican support for the bill. Southern senators avoided a filibuster because of their fear that it might result in a strengthening of cloture procedures for ending a filibuster. The Republican election strategy in 1956 was to contrast civil rights progress under Eisenhower's leadership with the obstructionism of southern Democrats in Congress. This helped attract African American voters to the Republican party. In the presidential race, the number of African Americans voting Republican was higher than it had been since the New Deal, although Republicans in Congress failed to improve their party strength.

The weakness of the Civil Rights Act of 1957 soon became apparent. Civil rights advocates in and out of Congress criticized the legislation from the beginning, and condemned the Justice Department for not aggressively enforcing the law. The Commission on Civil Rights, in its 1959 special report, noted the inadequacy of existing voting rights protections. Civil rights bills dealing with school desegregation, housing, and antibombing proposals were introduced in Congress in 1959; some originated

with the president, others reflected the position of party leaders such as Johnson, and still others resulted from bipartisan efforts. This legislative activity laid the foundation for the passage of another civil rights bill in 1960.

Patterns of support and opposition to the Civil Rights Act of 1960 followed the trend established in 1957. Representatives from border states such as Kentucky and Missouri voted for the bill, while, as before, rural nonsouthern legislators from Iowa, Idaho, and Indiana opposed it. Most southerners opposed the act; Republicans and northern Democrats split into liberal and moderate factions. Moderates, House and Senate leaders such as Johnson, Dirksen, Rayburn, and Halleck, supported the administration bill. Liberals sought to strengthen it, but their efforts failed. Southerners succeeded in weakening the measure, aided in their efforts by northern Republicans. The key provision of the act, eliminated as a result of southern efforts, called for the use of federal voting registrars to remedy voting rights violations. Instead, judicial remedies were established. Other provisions of the 1960 act required that voting and registration records for federal elections be preserved, extended the Civil Rights Commission, and set criminal penalties for transporting or possessing explosives. Originally, antibombing proposals were limited to assaults on churches and schools; as passed, the bill made any type of criminal act involving explosives a federal offense.

Pressure on the federal government for additional civil rights protections increased in the years after 1960. Lunch counter sit-ins in North Carolina and school boycotts in New Orleans in 1960, the arrest in 1961 in Jackson, Mississippi, of "freedom riders" who sought to desegregate interstate buses, Martin Luther King, Jr.'s "I Have A Dream" speech in 1963, and protests and church bombings in Alabama all heightened the sense of urgency. President John F. Kennedy took various actions, such as petitioning the Interstate Commerce Commission to ban segregation in bus terminals and sponsoring a bill to outlaw poll taxes and to make a sixth-grade education sufficient in states with literacy tests. The literacy bill died because of a Senate filibuster. Pro–civil rights forces in Congress blamed its failure on the conservative coalition, the indifference of civil rights groups, and lack of attention from the executive branch.

Civil Rights Act of 1964. Passage of the Civil Rights Act of 1964 marked the beginning of a new era of significant progress by pro–civil rights forces

THE MARCH ON WASHINGTON, D.C. The culmination of a nationwide civil rights movement, the march of 28 August 1963 drew over 250,000 demonstrators to the capital to press for congressional passage of the Civil Rights Act.

LIBRARY OF CONGRESS

in and out of Congress. The 1964 act was the product of a combination of factors, among them the efforts of pro–civil rights members of Congress including Senators Hubert H. Humphrey (D-Minn.) and Thomas H. Kuchel (R-Calif.) and the membership of the Democratic Study Group, and of organizations such as the Leadership Conference on Civil Rights, the AFL-CIO, and Catholic and Jewish groups. The assassination of President Kennedy also had an impact on passage, with President Johnson invoking the slain president's name and urging congressional support. The most important legislative factor in the passage of the 1964 act was the defeat of the conservative coalition in the Senate after a seventy-four-day filibuster. On 19 June 1964 the Senate passed the Civil Rights Act by a vote of 73 to 27. Twenty southern senators opposed the bill. The House passed the Senate version on 2 July 1964 by a margin of 289 to 126, with 12 southerners in favor and 88 opposed. President Johnson signed the bill just hours later on nationwide television.

The Civil Rights Act of 1964 prohibited discrimination in places of public accommodation and in programs receiving federal funds. It also barred discrimination in employment and established the Equal Employment Opportunity Commission. Regarding voting rights, the act barred unequal application of voting registration requirements, prohibited the rejection of voter applications because of administrative or technical errors, and allowed literacy requirements to be met by a sixth-grade education.

The 1964 election gave the Democratic party an overwhelming majority in the House and strengthened President Johnson's position. It also further diminished the strength of the conservative coalition: eleven northern Republicans and three southern Democrats who had voted against the Civil Rights Act of 1964 lost their bids for reelection. These setbacks for the coalition opened the door for future civil rights legislation.

Voting Rights Act of 1965 and Amendments. The battle over the Civil Rights Act of 1964 lasted

CIVIL RIGHTS ACT OF 1968. President Lyndon B. Johnson signing the bill into law, 11 April 1968.

over a year; passage of the Voting Rights Act of 1965 took less than three months. Television coverage of the violence in Selma, Alabama, against civil rights activists pushed many in Congress to action. Thirty-four southern Democrats voted for the voting rights bill, a threefold increase over the eleven southerners who had voted for the Civil Rights Act of 1964.

The Voting Rights Act of 1965 suspended the use of literacy tests for five years and authorized the dispatch of federal voting registrars and poll watchers to states where discrimination in voting was most prevalent. The act made interference with an individual's right to vote a federal crime. It also required the prior approval of the Justice Department for any changes in existing election procedures.

The act applied in those states or political subdivisions where literacy tests were in use or where less than 50 percent of the eligible voting age population was registered as of November 1964. Implementation of the law thus focused on the South. In a compromise necessary for its passage, the Voting

Rights Act of 1965 was to expire in 1970. Extensions of the act in 1970, 1975, and 1982 showed a continuing congressional commitment to voting rights, although new concerns have arisen, most notably the issue of minority vote dilution.

In sharp contrast to President Johnson's leadership in civil rights, President Nixon sought to lessen the impact of voting rights legislation on the South. Civil rights advocates in Congress, especially House Judiciary chairman Emanuel Celler (D-N.Y.) and Senator Philip A. Hart (D-Mich.), attempted to extend the Voting Rights Act in 1970. Nixon preferred to diminish the impact of the law by making coverage nationwide and eliminating preclearance. House minority leader Gerald R. Ford, Jr. (R-Mich.), spoke in favor of the Nixon proposals. After a protracted battle, the House accepted the Nixon version of the Voting Rights Act on 11 December 1969. Many civil rights supporters thought that the vote represented a serious defeat for civil rights.

A number of Senate Republicans, most of whom had supported the original voting rights bill, opposed Nixon's changes. Pro–civil rights senators engineered a compromise that maintained the law's original content for five more years, although it now applied to jurisdictions where less than 50 percent of the voting age population was registered as of November 1968. Opposition to the bill collapsed, southerners abandoned a proposed filibuster, and the Voting Rights Act Amendments of 1970 passed the Senate 64 to 12. The fate of the extension then rested in the House. Unless it accepted the Senate version of the bill, effectively nullifying the Nixon proposals, passage might be jeopardized. Fifty-nine House Republicans voted with 165 Democrats to pass the Senate version without further amendments. The remaining 117 Republicans and 66 Democrats voted against the bill. Only 34 southern Democrats voted for the bill. President Nixon reluctantly signed the Voting Rights Act Amendments of 1970 into law on 22 June 1970.

President Gerald R. Ford chose not to oppose the Voting Rights Act Amendments of 1975. Congress, lobbied by the Mexican American Legal Defense Fund, expanded the Voting Rights Act to cover linguistic minorities by making bilingual voting materials available where 5 percent of the population was of a single-language minority. Republicans sought to weaken the voting rights bill in 1975 and offered numerous amendments in the House. Fifty-six southern House Democrats voted for the seven-year extension of voting protections, compared with 34 in 1970.

The pro–voting rights stance of so many southern Democrats reflected the election of southern representatives with more moderate positions on race. Turnover among the ranks of southern Democrats in 1972 and 1974 delivered new members to Congress who were more supportive of civil rights. The change in attitude was a consequence of the increasingly important role of African American voters in the South and of a moderating trend in the racial views of the region's white voters.

The 1982 extension of the Voting Rights Act brought new issues to the fore. Once again a Republican, Ronald Reagan, was in the White House, and Republican gains in the Senate had given the party a majority. These circumstances caused concern among voting rights proponents.

The two most important problems concerned bailout procedures and the Supreme Court's ruling in *Mobile v. Bolden* (1980). Rep. Henry J. Hyde (R-Ill.) called for an amendment to the Voting Rights Act so that preclearance coverage was not automatic. Instead, the House added a bailout provision whereby a jurisdiction able to prove a ten-year clean voting rights record in federal court could bail out from under preclearance coverage. The House passed the measure by a vote of 385 to 24. Seventy-one southern Democrats voted for the extension, more than twice as many as had voted for the original bill.

Although pro–civil rights senators had enough support to pass the bill, controversy surrounded the House's amendments to section 2. In response to *Mobile v. Bolden*, which required proof of intent to discriminate, the House specified that the courts accept evidence of discriminatory results. Sen. Orrin G. Hatch (R-Utah) fought to alter the House version of section 2. His efforts and those of Sen. Bob Dole (R-Kans.) led to a compromise, which added a requirement that the courts look at the totality of the circumstances in discrimination cases. The compromise also extended the Voting Rights Act for twenty-five years rather than permanently.

The Senate passed the Voting Rights Act Amendments of 1982 by a vote of 85 to 8. Fourteen southern Senators voted for the bill while only five had supported the original act. In *Thornburg v. Gingles* (1986) the Supreme Court interpreted the extension as requiring states, where possible, to create districts in which members of a racial minority constitute a majority of voters, thus reducing minority vote dilution.

Fair Housing Act of 1968 and Amendments. Prior to the 1970 extension of the Voting Rights Act, Congress confronted one of the most contentious issues in civil rights policy-making—fair housing legislation. Southern senators for many years successfully filibustered against housing acts. President Johnson's proposed civil rights bill of 1966, which passed the House, included fair housing provisions and authorized the attorney general to initiate desegregation suits in schools and public accommodations. But the fair housing sections of the bill brought about its defeat in the Senate. Illinois senator Everett M. Dirksen's lack of support for cloture in 1966, a departure from his pro-cloture votes in 1964 and 1965, was the key element in the bill's demise. His failure to support cloture reflected his conservative ideology and long-standing opposition to fair housing proposals.

President Johnson resubmitted his 1966 civil rights proposals in 1967, this time with its components divided into separate bills. The only provision passed by both chambers that year was a five-year extension of the U.S. Commission on Civil Rights. The House also passed and sent to the Senate a bill

Landmark Civil Rights Legislation

Title	Year Enacted	Reference Number	Description
Civil Rights Act of 1866	1866	14 Stat. 27, Ch. 31	Guaranteed the rights of all citizens to make and enforce contracts and to purchase, sell, or lease property.
Civil Rights Act of 1870	1870	16 Stat. 140, Ch. 114	Prohibited discrimination in voter registration on the basis of race, color, or previous condition of servitude. Established penalties for interfering with a person's right to vote.
Civil Rights Act of 1871	1871	16 Stat. 433, Ch. 99	Prohibited discrimination in voting in congressional elections. Allowed for the appointment of election supervisors by circuit judges.
Civil Rights Act of 1875	1875	18 Stat. 148, Ch. 114	Barred discrimination in places of public accommodation, public conveyances on land and water, and other places of public amusement.
Civil Rights Act of 1957	1957	P.L. 85-315	Established a U.S. Commission on Civil Rights. Empowered the attorney general to seek court injunctions to enforce voting rights.
Civil Rights Act of 1960	1960	P.L. 86-449	Authorized federal judges to aid in the voting registration of African Americans.
Civil Rights Act of 1964	1964	P.L. 88-352	Barred discrimination in places of public accommodation, banned unequal application of voting registration requirements, made sixth-grade education sufficient for a presumption of literacy, required that literacy tests be administered in writing.
Voting Rights Act of 1965	1965	P.L. 89-110	Prohibited the use of literacy tests for five years, provided federal voting registrars and federal poll watchers to prevent discrimination in voting, required preclearance by the Justice Department before election changes are instituted.
Civil Rights Act of 1968	1968	P.L. 90-284	Outlawed discrimination in the sale or rental of housing.
Voting Rights Act Amendments of 1970	1970	P.L. 91-285	Extended for five years the provisions of the Voting Rights Act of 1965. Made the act applicable to areas where less than 50 percent of the eligible voting age population was registered as of November 1968.
Voting Rights Act Amendments of 1975	1975	P.L. 94-73	Extended for seven years the provisions of the Voting Rights Act of 1965. Established coverage under the act to language minorities and required bilingual voting materials.
Voting Rights Act Amendments of 1982	1982	P.L. 97-205	Extended for twenty-five years the provisions of the Voting Rights Act of 1965. Established bailout procedures where jurisdictions proving a clean voting rights record could terminate preclearance coverage. Allowed the courts to accept evidence of discriminatory results, rather than intent, as proof of discrimination.
Civil Rights Restoration Act of 1987	1987	P.L. 100-259	Established that antidiscrimination laws are applicable to an entire organization if any part of the organization is receiving federal funds.
Civil Rights Act of 1991	1991	P.L. 102-166	Allowed plaintiffs to receive monetary damages in cases of intentional discrimination or harassment based on sex, religion, or handicap.

protecting civil rights workers and an individual's right to serve on a jury, to participate in government or government-aided programs, to work, to attend school, or to enjoy public accommodations. The Senate took action on this measure early in 1968. Sen. Samuel J. Ervin, Jr. (D-N.C.), led the opposition to the bill. His substitute bill, approved in subcommittee, substantially weakened the administration's measure, and the full Judiciary Committee rejected the Ervin proposal.

Senators Walter F. Mondale (D-Minn.) and Edward W. Brooke (R-Mass.) added a fair housing amendment to the Senate version of the bill. The Mondale-Brooke amendment prohibited discrimination in the sale or rental of 90 percent of the nation's housing. The southern filibuster of the bill survived initial cloture votes. In a surprising move, Minority Leader Dirksen joined civil rights supporters to work out a compromise on the fair housing provisions of the bill. Dirksen indicated that his change of position had resulted in part from the summer riots of 1967 in places such as Chicago, Cleveland, and New York City. Republicans who supported fair housing, including Dirksen's son-in-law Howard H. Baker (R-Tenn.), urged Dirksen to support the bill in order to improve Republican fortunes in the upcoming 1968 elections. The housing compromise covered approximately 80 percent of housing in the United States. On 11 March 1968, H.R. 2516 passed the Senate 71 to 20.

House approval was doubtful because many who supported the original open housing legislation in 1966 had fallen victim to electoral defeat later that year. In 1968, controversy in the House centered on whether to send the bill to conference committee or to accept the Senate version. Civil rights supporters feared that the opposition would rally and defeat the act if it were sent to conference committee. They wanted quick action by the House, but the House Rules Committee, chaired by William M. Colmer (D-Miss.), postponed granting a rule on the bill until 9 April 1968. The delay was designed to give the opposition time to rally its forces and demand that the bill go to conference committee. But on 4 April, five days before the scheduled Rules Committee meeting, Martin Luther King, Jr., was assassinated. Riots across the nation followed the news of King's death. In light of King's death and the violent aftermath, the Rules Committee reversed itself and together with the House rejected attempts to send the bill to conference. Instead the House voted on 10 April 1968 to accept the Senate version of the fair housing bill.

Lobbying both for and against passage of the 1968 fair housing law was vigorous in the final stages of the legislative process. Clarence M. Mitchell, Jr., chief lobbyist for the Leadership Conference on Civil Rights, did much to organize and mobilize support for its passage. Lobbying by the National Association of Real Estate Boards (NAREB) to prevent House passage of the Senate version of the bill resulted in a flood of letters, telegrams, and telephone calls to members of Congress.

The Fair Housing Act of 1968 was amended in 1974 to include provisions prohibiting discrimination on the basis of gender. In 1980 Rep. Don Edwards (D-Calif.), a longtime advocate of stronger fair housing laws, played a key role in proposing a bill that extended fair housing enforcement to include those involved in selling, brokering, and appraising real estate. The measure, heavily amended in committee by southern Democrats and Republicans, survived a motion to recommit, which would have killed the bill, by only thirteen votes. But Senators Orrin Hatch and Strom Thurmond (D-S.C.) led a filibuster that brought about the withdrawal of the bill from Senate consideration and thus its defeat. Lobbying by the real estate industry appears to have been responsible for the final defeat of the 1980 fair housing bill.

The Fair Housing Amendments Act of 1988 marked a significant step forward in the government's effort to enforce fair housing legislation. The new statute gave the Department of Housing and Urban Development access to administrative law judges and procedures with the capacity to award damages to victims of discrimination and levy fines for discrimination that ranged from $10,000 to $50,000. Support by Vice President George Bush helped pass the legislation. Hamilton Fish, Jr. (R-N.Y.), played an important role in negotiations between civil rights groups and real estate interests that contributed to the bill's success.

School Desegregation. In contrast to the incremental progress of fair housing legislation, congressional action to desegregate schools completely reversed its original direction. In *Brown v. Board of Education* (1954), the Supreme Court ruled that the separate-but-equal doctrine violated the equal protection clause of the Fourteenth Amendment, but it left the manner of enforcement undefined. At first, the federal government's school desegregation efforts focused on the South, where state laws mandated segregated schools. Congress eventually threatened to withhold federal Elementary and Secondary Education Act funds to force desegregation in the region.

When the focus of school desegregation shifted to the North, support in Congress rapidly declined. The federal courts continued to support busing to desegregate schools, but pro–civil rights members of Congress from that region began to respond to the anti-busing sentiment of their constituents. Particularly crucial in Congress's change of position was the court-ordered desegregation plan for Detroit, Michigan, handed down by a federal district court in June 1972. Many Michigan representatives, longtime civil rights advocates, voted in favor of a constitutional amendment to ban school busing. Opposition to school busing from northern representatives, coupled with traditional opposition from the South, led to frequent appropriations bill amendments prohibiting the use of Justice Department funds to force school busing.

Equal Employment Opportunity Commission. Civil rights forces continued to make progress in the area of equal employment. Congress created the Equal Employment Opportunity Commission (EEOC) in the Civil Rights Act of 1964, but from its inception, the EEOC lacked adequate enforcement powers. Under the original bill, the commission could use only conciliation to solve employment discrimination cases. In ensuing years, Congress struggled with the issue of granting broader enforcement powers to the EEOC.

Conservative coalition forces actively sought to defeat proposals to strengthen the EEOC. In 1970 Rules Committee chairman William M. Colmer used his position to block passage of the Equal Employment Opportunities Enforcement Act. Civil rights forces in the Senate, unable to end a southern filibuster, were forced to compromise on enforcement powers for the commission. The resulting bill, passed in 1972, brought about some improvement but left many problems unsolved. While the EEOC could take its cases directly to court rather than relying on the Justice Department, the commission continued to lack adequate enforcement powers. The only other legislative action concerning the EEOC during the 1970s involved a 1978 reorganization that transferred to the commission enforcement responsibilities previously parceled out among the Office of Personnel Management, the Department of Labor, and other agencies. The Justice Department, however, retained its power to bring discrimination suits against state and local governments.

The 1980s and Beyond. With the exception of the 1982 extension of the Voting Rights Act, congressional attention to civil rights diminished during the 1980s. Changes in the South, specifically the increasing turnout of African American voters and the lessening resistance of whites to civil rights laws, were responsible for declining national attention to the issue. There are different opinions regarding the extent to which these developments have affected the voting patterns of southern members of Congress, but clearly, both new and long-term members from that region have had to adapt to the new realities of black voting power and de-

clining white resistance. The voting record of South Carolina senator Strom Thurmond, at one time the leading spokesman of southern resistance to desegregation, is a case in point.

In the late 1980s, civil rights returned to the congressional agenda. The civil rights movement of the 1960s and most civil rights laws thereafter focused primarily on racial discrimination; age or gender discrimination was considered a separate issue. The Civil Rights Restoration Act of 1988 was the Democrat-led Congress's response to a 1984 Supreme Court decision narrowing the applicability of various antidiscrimination laws. The law stipulated that any organization receiving federal funds must abide by all antidiscriminatory laws and that this proviso covered the entire organization, not just the portion receiving federal funds. However, legislation passed in 1988, 1990, and 1991 included provisions aimed at discrimination based on age, gender, and physical handicap or other disability. The Americans with Disabilities Act, passed in 1990, prohibited discrimination against the disabled in areas including employment, public accommodations, and public services and transportation. The Civil Rights Act of 1991, a response to Supreme Court decisions concerning the right of plaintiffs to seek damages in discrimination cases, provided for limited monetary damages in cases of intentional harassment or discrimination based on sex, religion, or disability. Racial minorities, covered under earlier laws, could already win unlimited damages in discrimination cases. The 1991 act also prohibited racial discrimination by all participants in government contracts. President Bush had vetoed an earlier 1990 version of the act because of his concern over quotas.

Civil rights in American politics originally focused on the rights of African Americans, especially in the area of voting. Voting continues as the center of controversy in the 1990s, although the nature of the conflict has changed dramatically. Voting rights once meant primarily the access of minorities to the ballot; today the courts face questions such as whether the equal protection rights of white voters are diminished when extreme measures are taken to create majority African American and majority Hispanic districts. Nevertheless the Voting Rights Act of 1965 stands as the most successful legislative instrument designed to protect the rights of minorities to register and participate in the political process.

As the end of the century approaches, civil rights is much more broadly conceived than it was a hundred years ago, when legislators began to attempt to pass antilynching laws. The U.S. civil rights laws in the mid 1990s prohibit discrimination based on age, race, gender, and disability. The greatest need for ongoing efforts in antidiscrimination policy concern the workplace—where evidence of continued discrimination such as sexual harassment abounds. There is much progress to be made in the area of fair housing as well, and calls are mounting for protection of groups defined by their sexual orientation and those infected with the virus that causes AIDS (Acquired Immunodeficiency Syndrome).

[*For discussion of related public policy issues, see* Slavery; Voting and Suffrage; Women's Rights and Issues. *See also* Civil Rights Act of 1964; Equal Rights Amendment; Fifteenth Amendment; Fourteenth Amendment; Fugitive Slave Act; Thirteenth Amendment; Voting Rights Act of 1965.]

BIBLIOGRAPHY

Black, Merle. "Racial Composition of Congressional Districts and Support for Federal Voting Rights in the American South." *Social Science Quarterly* 59 (1978): 435–450.

Carmines, Edward G., and James A. Stimson. *Issue Evolution: Race and the Transformation of American Politics.* 1989.

Graham, Hugh Davis. *The Civil Rights Era: Origins and Development of National Policy, 1960–1972.* 1992.

Nye, Mary Alice, and Charles S. Bullock III. "Civil Rights Support: A Comparison of Southern and Border State Representatives." *Legislative Studies Quarterly* 17 (1992): 81–94.

Orfield, Gary. *Congressional Power: Congress and Social Change.* 1975.

MARY ALICE NYE

CIVIL RIGHTS ACT OF 1964 (78 Stat. 241–268).

Passage of the Civil Rights Act of 1964 signaled a turning point in congressional protection of minority rights. Statutes enacted in 1957 and 1960 were marked by compromises dictated by anti–civil rights southerners and failed to advance minority rights. In sharp contrast, the 1964 law included substantive protections aimed at eliminating discrimination.

As with many landmark pieces of legislation, the origins of the 1964 act cannot be traced to just one source. The measure contained provisions that had been the focus of numerous earlier legislative battles. As early as 1948, President Harry S. Truman advocated an end to discrimination in employment and established the Fair Employment Practice Commission. A variety of bills aimed at protecting minority rights were introduced during the 1950s. In 1963 President John F. Kennedy sent Congress a civil rights bill that became the basis for the Civil Rights Act of 1964.

The passage of the 1964 law resulted from the efforts of a host of civil rights groups as well as President Lyndon B. Johnson and pro–civil rights members of Congress. The leading civil rights organizations included the National Association for the Advancement of Colored People (NAACP), the National Urban League, the Congress of Racial Equality, the Southern Christian Leadership Conference, and the Student Nonviolent Coordinating Committee. Other groups fighting for civil rights progress were the American Federation of Labor–Congress of Industrial Organizations (AFL-CIO), the National Council of Churches, Americans for Democratic Action, and the American Civil Liberties Union. These groups, whose primary role was to keep civil rights supporters in the House of Representatives united behind the bill and focused on its substantive aspects, were crucial to the measure's passage. Congressional civil rights supporters included members of the Democratic Study Group

"DON'T PUSH TOO HARD—LET HIM WORK." In 1963 and 1964 civil rights groups stepped up their pressure on Congress to enact civil rights legislation. Gib Crockett, *Washington Star,* 21 June 1963.   LIBRARY OF CONGRESS

PASSING THE BILL. Senate majority leader Mike Mansfield (D-Mont.), *left*, and Senate minority leader Everett M. Dirksen (R-Ill.) worked closely to pass the Civil Rights Act of 1964.   OFFICE OF THE HISTORIAN OF THE U.S. SENATE

(DSG) and individuals such as Senate majority leader Mike Mansfield (D-Mont.) and Senate majority whip Hubert H. Humphrey (D-Minn.). Senate leaders of both parties helped defeat southern efforts to kill the bill through a filibuster. President Johnson urged passage of the bill in recognition of President Kennedy's efforts for civil rights. The Senate on 19 June 1964 voted to pass the Civil Rights Act, 73 to 27. The House passed the Senate's version on 2 July 1964 by a vote of 289 to 126. President Johnson signed the bill just hours later on nationwide television.

The bill dealt with several major aspects of discrimination. Title I focused on voting rights. It contained provisions barring the unequal application of voter registration requirements, stipulating that literacy tests be uniformly administered in writing, accepting a sixth-grade education as a presumption

of literacy, and forbidding the rejection of voter applications for administrative or technical errors. Title VIII required the Census Bureau to collect registration and voting statistics as recommended by the U.S. Commission on Civil Rights. The limited voting provisions of Title I proved insufficient and were strengthened by the Voting Rights Act of 1965.

Title II of the 1964 Civil Rights Act banned discrimination in places of public accommodation based on race, color, religion, or national origin. The law covered private businesses providing services to the public, including but not limited to restaurants, cafeterias, lunchrooms, lunch counters, hotels, motels, and theaters. In addition, the law permitted anyone denied access to such places to sue in court for preventive relief. Subsequent titles of the bill (III and IV) also outlawed segregation in state or locally owned public facilities, including public schools.

The 1964 act, in Title VII, established equal employment as the law of the land, prohibiting discrimination on the basis of race, color, religion, sex, or national origin. The law covered hiring procedures as well as other employment practices. It established the Equal Employment Opportunity Commission (EEOC), a five-member bipartisan commission appointed by the president and subject to confirmation by the Senate. The EEOC's responsibilities consisted of investigating written charges of employment discrimination and providing assistance to public and private organizations to assist in their compliance with the law.

Title V prohibited discrimination in any program receiving federal funds. Its provisions allowed the federal government to terminate federal funds for programs that violated the antidiscrimination guidelines.

The results of the 1964 act varied. The Equal Employment Opportunity Commission, for instance, has been hampered by a lack of enforcement powers. Conservative southern Democrats and Republicans in Congress have forced compromises in legislation that attempted to increase the EEOC's power. The Supreme Court upheld Congress's power to prohibit discrimination in places of public accommodation, and private business gradually complied with the law. The federal government used Title V to deny federal funds to southern schools refusing to desegregate. The virtual end to discrimination in places of public accommodation is the most readily available evidence of the success of the 1964 act, while the government's power to withhold or cut off federal funds continues today as an important tool in the fight for equality. In historical perspective, the Civil Rights Act of 1964 is likely to remain a landmark in Congress's response to the issue of minority rights, the most sensitive and contentious area of U.S. public policy.

[See also Voting Rights Act of 1965.]

BIBLIOGRAPHY

Bullock, Charles S., III, and Charles M. Lamb. *Implementation of Civil Rights Policy.* 1984.
Orfield, Gary. *Congressional Power: Congress and Social Change.* 1975.

MARY ALICE NYE

CIVIL SERVICE. In the United States, *civil service* is not a precise legal category or term of political art. It generally refers to civilian employees, though not politically appointed officers, in the executive branch of government. The civil service includes employees of legislative agencies, such as the U.S. General Accounting Office, and some judicial employees, but not judicial clerks or legislative staff. Further, the term typically connotes white-collar employment, though police and firefighters are within its purview, whereas public school teachers and public university professors generally are not. In some contexts, civil service refers to employees who, under a merit system, enjoy legal job security that distinguishes them from temporary, conditional, and politically appointed public employees.

Congressional Involvement. The federal government has historically faced difficulty in fully integrating the civil service into the separation of powers and the dominant political culture. The constitutional scheme places the president at the head of the executive branch but makes the civil service highly dependent on Congress. Article I, section 8 of the Constitution authorizes Congress "to make all Laws which shall be necessary and proper for carrying into Execution" its legislative

"THE CIVIL SERVICE AS IT IS." Prior to passage of the Pendleton Act in 1883, federal employees were hired on the basis of partisan patronage rather than on the basis of merit. This cartoon depicts a congressman "presenting a few of his constituents" for appointment to federal office. Wood engraving, *Harper's Weekly,* 3 February 1872.

LIBRARY OF CONGRESS

powers and "all other Powers vested by [the] Constitution in the Government of the United States, or in any Department or Officer thereof." Because the civil service is the main vehicle for translating legislation into action, Congress displays considerable interest in civil service matters large and small. The main areas of congressional involvement in the civil service are as follows.

Legal direction. Federal departments, other administrative units, and offices must be established pursuant to legislation. They are partly agents of Congress. Ministerial duties can be vested in executive branch personnel, including the president, who are required to follow the law. Congress can also vest discretion in agencies regarding the enforcement of policies embodied in legislation. High-level civil servants and street-level bureaucrats (e.g., law enforcement agents, inspectors, social workers) often exercise substantial discretion in the course of doing their jobs. Additionally, Congress can use resolutions to convey direction to administrative agencies.

Empowerment. The legal authority of civil servants and executive officers depends overwhelmingly upon statutes. Whatever independent executive power may exist under Article II of the Constitution does not have a great impact on the day-to-day functioning of civil servants, especially those in domestic agencies. For example, the Administrative Procedure Act (APA) of 1946 authorizes and regulates agency rule making and adjudication. As amended by the Freedom of Information Act of 1966 and the Privacy Act of 1974, the APA regulates the withholding and release of information held by the government. Many statutes specify the legal authority and processes available to agencies in minute detail.

Accountability. Congress seeks to hold civil servants accountable for their actions. The Legislative Reorganization Act of 1946 charged standing committees with exercising "continuous watchfulness" over the agencies under their jurisdiction. Hearings and investigations are routine. Members of Congress often engage in casework for constituents who contact them regarding some difficulty they are having with federal agencies. Perhaps casework is primarily constituency service aimed at obtaining reelection, but it also serves to inform legislators about the performance of civil servants. Casework on civil service issues (e.g., obtaining jobs, retirement and health benefits) is so voluminous that the U.S. Office of Personnel Management has a liaison office in the Rayburn House Office Building. Many additional statutes and processes bear on civil service accountability, including conflict of interest, tort claims, and whistle-blowing legislation. The U.S. General Accounting Office conducts a variety of studies and investigations of the civil service on issues that include work force diversity and labor relations.

Funding. Article I, section 9 provides that "No Money shall be drawn from the Treasury, but in Consequence of Appropriations made by Law." Consequently, Congress has major responsibility for funding the civil service. Civil servants' pay and benefits depend on statutes. In practice, this means that a great deal of lobbying by civil service unions is directed toward Congress, as is opposition to higher compensation by groups representing taxpayers. Since federal employees and taxpayers are located in all states and legislative districts, the politics of civil service is usually salient to legislators.

Staffing. The civil service cannot properly execute the law if it is severely understaffed; nor will it be efficient if it is seriously overstaffed. Congress can place staffing ceilings in legislation to indicate how large or small it wants agencies to be. Although sometimes circumvented, such ceilings cannot be exceeded legally. Agencies may generally operate below them in the interests of economy and efficiency.

Personnel policy. Federal civil service law is highly detailed. Congress has been involved in the following personnel areas, among others: equal employment, political activity, collective bargaining, veterans' preference, recruitment, examination, selection, assignment, performance evaluation, discipline, adverse actions, grievances, dismissals, promotions, transfers, retirement, reductions in force, training, travel, position classification, holidays, leaves, hours, and compensation. The House standing Committee on Post Office and Civil Service and the Senate standing Committee on Governmental Affairs are key actors in these personnel matters. Legislators from districts with many federal employees, such as those in the Virginia and Maryland suburbs of Washington, D.C., often serve on the House committee.

Delegations of legislative authority. In practice, Congress has delegated a good deal of legislative authority for civil service issues to the president and executive-branch agencies. However, Congress retains interest in the use of such authority and remains so deeply entrenched in civil service matters that it is often accused of micromanagement. For instance, members of Congress sometimes pressure agencies to retain or relocate employees who live in their districts.

Congress's authority and interest in the civil service inevitably pit it against the presidency, which frequently claims independent authority for faithful execution of the laws under Article II of the Constitution. Presidents are apt to claim responsibility for good management, meaning efficiency, economy, and effective hierarchical control. Congress does not by any means eschew the values of good management but has often been more concerned with the political values of responsiveness, representativeness, and accountability within government agencies. The tensions inherent in these different approaches are complicated by judicial rulings requiring civil service procedures and civil servants' actions to embrace constitutional rights and values, such as due process and equal protection. Because the civil service is at the center of contemporary government and is subordinate to the three constitutional branches, it remains an area where ostensibly separated powers tend to collide.

Current Organization of the Federal Civil Service. The federal civil service is now organized according to the Civil Service Reform Act of 1978 (92 Stat. 1111–1227). The act was a response to the vast changes in the civil service that began during the New Deal. In 1931, there were 610,000 federal civil servants; in 1978, there were about 2.8 million. Expansion and the development of newer concerns, such as equal opportunity and collective bargaining, made it increasingly difficult for the central personnel agency, the U.S. Civil Service Commission (CSC), to fulfill its mission. Established as an independent commission in 1883, the CSC was no longer able to perform most personnel functions on a centralized basis. More authority for personnel was delegated to the departments and agencies, with the commission engaging in audits, investigations, and other policing functions. Increasingly, this policing role, appropriate earlier as a check on patronage practices, was viewed as a barrier to modern management and flexibility. The 1978 legislation was engineered by President Jimmy Carter, who believed that the federal bureaucracy was bloated, inefficient, and badly in need of reform.

The Civil Service Reform Act included the following changes:

1. The Civil Service Commission was abolished. Its legal successor is the Merit Systems Protection Board (MSPB). The board is headed by a chairperson and two members, appointed to seven-year terms by the president with the advice and consent of the Senate. No more than two of these appointees may be of the same political party. The MSPB is responsible for assuring that merit principles, personnel laws, and regulations are upheld. It hears employee appeals of adverse actions, such as dismissals and demotions, and has specific authority to protect whistle-blowers against reprisals for exposing waste, fraud, abuse, or gross mismanagement. The MSPB also has responsibility for evaluating the performance of the Office of Personnel Management and conducting special studies of aspects of federal personnel administration.

2. The position of special counsel was established. Initially attached to the MSPB, the special counsel is appointed to a five-year term by the president with the advice and consent of the Senate. The special counsel is now an independent entity responsible for investigating allegations of violations of personnel laws, rules, and regulations. The Special Counsel can bring cases before the MSPB for adjudication. It reports suspected criminal violations to the attorney general.

3. The Office of Personnel Management (OPM) was created to take over most of the Civil Service Commission's managerial functions. It is headed by a director, appointed to a four-year term by the president with the advice and consent of the Senate. OPM is considered the president's arm for personnel management and is more directly responsible to him than was the commission. It has authority for various aspects of the retirement system, training, position classification, examinations, and developing and overseeing merit-pay procedures for upper-level federal managers.

4. A section on labor-management relations (Title VII) placed labor relations affecting most of the civil service on a comprehensive statutory basis for the first time. Title VII establishes a bipartisan Federal Labor Relations Authority (FLRA), consisting of a chairperson and two members appointed by the president, with the advice and consent of the Senate, for five-year overlapping terms. The FLRA has general responsibility for oversight of the federal labor relations program, including employee representational matters, determination of bargaining units, grievances, unfair labor practices, and definition of the scope of bargaining. Title VII provides for a relatively narrow scope of bargaining that excludes pay and many personnel matters such as hiring, promotion, and position classification. A Feder-

al Service Impasses Panel works under the FLRA's general direction to assist employee organizations and management in resolving disputes. Title VII does not cover the Postal Service and several smaller agencies, including the General Accounting Office, the Federal Bureau of Investigation (FBI), the Central Intelligence Agency (CIA), and the Tennessee Valley Authority (TVA).

5. A Senior Executive Service (SES) was created from most super-grade civil service positions. Containing about eight thousand positions, it is comprised predominantly of top-level career civil servants, though by law 10 percent of its ranks may be filled with political appointees. The SES is a kind of higher civil service long thought desirable for the federal government. It reflects the beliefs that (a) there is a body of professionalism called public management that can be transferred from agency to agency; (b) it is politically desirable for top federal managers to move among bureaus and agencies in order to develop a more comprehensive view of the public interest; and (c) political executives need greater flexibility in assigning and directing top career civil servants. In the SES, rank (designated Executive Service [ES] 1–6) is essentially vested in the person, not the position. Consequently, reassignments, transfers, and changes in job content are not treated as promotions or demotions subject to complicated personnel rules or adverse action procedures. Involuntary transfers between agencies are prohibited. Members of the SES are eligible for bonuses and cash awards based on performance. They retain fallback rights to positions at the GS (General Schedule) 15 level.

6. An equal employment opportunity recruitment program was established within OPM. The reform act established the policy that the federal work force should reflect the nation's diversity and be drawn from all segments of society; there should be no "underrepresentation" of minority group members in any category of federal employment. In conjunction with the act, adjudicatory authority for equal employment opportunity complaints was transferred to the Equal Employment Opportunity Commission in 1979.

7. OPM was given authority to suspend many personnel regulations in order to permit the development and implementation of personnel research and demonstration projects involving up to five thousand employees and lasting up to five years.

8. Federal personnel management was to make

greater use of performance appraisal systems and merit pay. The latter was for those in management positions in GS 13 through 15 (subsequently labeled GM positions). Both performance appraisal and merit pay have been difficult to implement and have undergone almost continual revision.

Current Issues. The size of the civil service, which stands at approximately three million employees, and its costs are constant issues. Efforts to control taxes and budget deficits often focus on reducing the size of the civil service and making it operate more efficiently. At the core of current efforts to change the civil service is a desire to use marketlike thinking and processes to reduce costs while enhancing responsiveness to the public. One leading strategy has been to privatize civil service functions—that is, to contract them out to private firms. Reducing government functions, either by deregulation or some other means, is a comple-

Growth of Federal Employment

Year	Number of Employees
1791	4,479
1821	6,914
1831	11,491
1841	18,038
1851	26,274
1861	36,672
1871	51,020
1881	100,020
1891	157,442
1901	239,476
1911	395,905
1921	561,143
1931	609,746
1941	1,437,682
1951	2,482,666
1961	2,435,808
1971	2,862,926
1981	2,865,000
1985	3,020,531
1988	3,112,823
1994	2,991,373[1]

[1]Figure supplied by Office of Personnel Management.
SOURCES: Richard Stillman, *The American Bureaucracy* (1987); U.S. Bureau of the Census and Social Science Research Council, *Statistical History of the United States from Colonial Times to the Present* (1965); U.S. Civil Service Commission, *Annual Report*, 78, 88; U.S. Bureau of the Census.

mentary approach. There is also a new focus on customer service, or meeting the needs of the individuals, groups, firms, and other agencies with whom civil servants deal. Although it is uncertain how successful changes along these lines will be, it is certain that Congress will continue to play a very strong role in determining the structure and operation of the civil service.

[See also Bureaucracy; Civil Service Reform Act of 1978; Governmental Affairs Committee, Senate; Pendleton Act; Post Office and Civil Service Committee, House.]

BIBLIOGRAPHY

Ingraham, Patricia, and David H. Rosenbloom, eds. *The Promise and Paradox of Civil Service Reform*. 1992.
Mosher, Frederick. *Democracy and the Public Service*. 2d ed. 1982.
Shafritz, Jay, Norma Riccucci, David H. Rosenbloom, and Albert Hyde. *Personnel Management in Government*. 4th ed. 1992.
Skowronek, Stephen. *Building a New American State*. 1982.

DAVID H. ROSENBLOOM

CIVIL SERVICE REFORM ACT OF 1978

(92 Stat. 1111–1227). Viewed by President Jimmy Carter as the centerpiece of his efforts to make the government more efficient and responsive, the Civil Service Reform Act of 1978 was the first major reorganization of federal personnel administration since the enactment of the Civil Service Act of 1883. Political support for the reform was very broad, encompassing career and political executives in government, labor unions, and civil rights and good-government groups.

The act included the following changes:

1. The Civil Service Commission was succeeded by the Merit Systems Protection Board (MSPB). The bipartisan board is headed by a chairperson and two other members, who are appointed to seven-year terms by the president, with the advice and consent of the Senate. The MSPB is responsible for assuring that merit principles, laws, and regulations are not violated. It hears employee appeals of adverse actions and has specific authority to protect against reprisals whistle-blowers who expose waste, fraud, abuse, or gross mismanagement. It conducts special studies of aspects of federal personnel administration.

2. A special counsel was created. Initially attached to the MSPB, the special counsel is appointed to a five-year term by the president, with the advice and consent of the Senate. The special counsel is now an independent entity responsible for investigating allegations of violations of personnel laws, rules, and regulations.
3. The Office of Personnel Management (OPM) was created to assume most of the Civil Service Commission's managerial functions. It is headed by a director appointed to a four-year term by the president, with the advice and consent of the Senate. OPM is considered the president's arm for personnel management and is more directly responsible to him than was the commission. Its responsibilities include operating the retirement system, training, position classification, designing and administering merit examinations, and developing and overseeing merit-pay procedures for upper-level federal managers.
4. A section on labor-management relations (Title VII) placed labor relations affecting most of the civil service on a comprehensive statutory basis for the first time. Title VII established the bipartisan Federal Labor Relations Authority (FLRA), consisting of a chairperson and two members appointed by the president, with the advice and consent of the Senate, for five-year overlapping terms. The FLRA has responsibility for oversight of the federal labor relations program, including employee representational matters, determination of bargaining units, grievances, unfair labor practices, and definition of the scope of bargaining. Bargaining, however, does not extend to pay or to many personnel matters such as hiring, promotion, and position classification. Title VII does not cover the U.S. Postal Service or several smaller agencies.
5. The Senior Executive Service (SES) was created out of positions in grades GS (General Schedule) 16 through 18 (previously called super-grades). The SES comprises predominantly top-level career civil servants, though by law 10 percent of its positions may be filled with political appointees. The SES reflects the beliefs that (a) there is a body of professional skill called public management that can be transferred from agency setting to agency setting; (b) top federal managers should move among bureaus and agencies in order to develop a more comprehensive view of the public interest; and (c) political executives need greater flexibility in assigning and directing top career civil servants. Personnel

procedures within the SES are far more flexible than within most of the federal service.

6. A minority recruitment program was established within OPM. The Reform Act included a policy that the federal work force should reflect the nation's diversity and be drawn from all segments of society. Although not part of the act, adjudicatory authority for equal employment opportunity complaints within the civil service was transferred from the defunct Civil Service Commission to the Equal Employment Opportunity Commission in 1979.

7. OPM was given authority to suspend many personnel regulations to permit the development and implementation of personnel research and demonstration projects. These can involve up to five thousand employees and last up to five years.

8. There was to be greater use of performance appraisal systems and merit pay, the latter for those in management positions in GS 13 through 15 (subsequently labeled GM positions). Both performance appraisal and merit pay have been difficult to implement, and they have undergone almost continual revision.

[*See also* Pendleton Act.]

BIBLIOGRAPHY

Ingraham, Patricia, and Carolyn Ban, eds. *Legislating Bureaucratic Change.* 1984.
Ingraham, Patricia, and David H. Rosenbloom, eds. *The Promise and Paradox of Civil Service Reform.* 1992.

DAVID H. ROSENBLOOM

CIVIL WAR. The 37th (1861–1863) and 38th (1863–1865) Congresses were among the most remarkable in American history, because of their makeup and because of what they accomplished. Neither was a national Congress—the Confederate states (except for a few members from Virginia, Tennessee, and Louisiana) were not represented. In 1861 and 1862, when focusing on the nullity of secession, the House had been anxious to welcome as members Southern Unionists whose arrival was made possible by federal military advances. But when their thoughts turned to reconstructing the nation, the members of the House Republican majority perceived the presence of such representatives as disturbing precedents that threatened to limit their options.

Political Alignments. The political complexion of the Civil War Congresses is difficult to deter-

AERIAL VIEW OF THE U.S. CAPITOL. During the Civil War, work on the extensions of the Capitol, including the cast-iron dome, was suspended from May 1861 to May 1862. C. H. Andrews, *Illustrated London News*, 25 May 1861.

LIBRARY OF CONGRESS

mine, in part because of continual changes in membership (especially in the 37th Congress) and, more importantly, because of confusion about the political affiliation of the members; the more commonly published figures are erroneous or misleading. If there had been no secession, there would not have been Republican majorities in either house of the 37th Congress. Indeed, the elections of 1860 and 1861 had reduced the number of Republicans in the lower house from 114 to 106; 50 Democrats and 28 Unionists completed the postsecession House membership. The Senate consisted of 28 Republicans, 13 Democrats, and 7 Unionists. In addition, one Senate seat from Oregon was filled consecutively by Republican Edward D. Baker, Democrat Benjamin Stark, and Unionist Benjamin F. Harding.

By the time of the elections (1862–1863) for the 38th Congress, the distribution of seats had been modified to reflect the 1860 census count. The number of congressional seats for the states that had not passed secession ordinances increased from 173 to 184. This meant that congressional district lines had to be redrawn in a dozen states, three-quarters of which had Republican majorities in their legislatures.

But in their zeal to increase their congressional representation, the Republican state legislators created too many closely divided districts, and so when the political tide ran even moderately against them, as was the case in 1862 and 1863, the results were nearly disastrous. Of the 106 Republican members of the House in the 37th Congress, only 31 were reelected to the 38th Congress, compared to 28 of 49 Democrats and 10 of 28 Unionists. Although many of the vacancies were filled by men of the same political affiliation (when incumbents withdrew or were not renominated), the Republicans suffered severely. In state after state, the Republican proportion of the delegation declined. Overall, the Republican House membership in the 38th Congress dropped to 92 of 184 seats. The big gainers were, of course, the Democrats, whose numbers grew from 50 to 76. Fortunately for the Republicans, 13 Unionists attended the Republican caucus and voted with the members of that party to organize the House. In the Senate, the Republicans fared better. There they controlled 33 seats, compared to 30 in the previous Congress, while the Democrats held steady at 13 and the Unionists declined from 6 to 5.

When the members of Congress gathered in Washington in July 1861, the Republicans elected Galusha A. Grow of Pennsylvania as Speaker of the House. Grow was chosen largely because of his ardent championship of homestead legislation; Republican support for that proposal was credited with producing that party's narrow (and essential) 1860 victories in Indiana and Illinois. In organizing the House committees, Grow, after some rebuffs, offered the most influential position—the chairmanship of Ways and Means—to fellow Pennsylvanian Thaddeus Stevens. This was a crucial decision, for Stevens may well have been the most dominant member of the House since Henry Clay had served as Speaker.

Grow was an accommodationist who tried to satisfy and placate his party colleagues. When he went down to defeat in the 1862 and 1863 anti-Republican tide, he was succeeded by Schuyler Colfax, who was cast in the same mold.

Meanwhile, Stevens quickly seized control of the business of the House and retained it through the 37th and 38th Congresses. He was able to push forward measures he favored while condemning others to a lingering death in committee, and he was expert at using parliamentary devices to limit amendment and debate. He was not, however, always able to control his colleagues' votes, and on some major issues found himself in the minority.

Ideological Alignments. Ideological divisions in Congress during the Civil War were considerably more complex than has sometimes been assumed. For one thing, Democratic senators and representatives were, on the whole, quite supportive of the Union war effort. Measures dealing with military appropriations and raising troops were usually passed without notable opposition, so long as no effort was made to enlist black troops. Similarly, a simple bipolar view that divides Republican members into Radicals and Moderates grossly oversimplifies a range of much more subtle gradations, ranging from the ultraconservative, rigid, and narrow constitutionalism of Sen. Edgar Cowan of Pennsylvania to the advanced radicalism of Senators Benjamin F. Wade of Ohio, Charles Sumner of Massachusetts, and David Wilmot of Pennsylvania, who favored emancipation of the slaves and confiscation of property on the extraconstitutional ground of the congressional "war power."

Indeed, it is possible to speak of such subdivisions as ultraconservatives, conservatives, moderates, advanced moderates, radicals, and advanced radicals. The votes indicating where congressional Republicans stood along the radical-conservative spectrum were on issues including emancipation,

THE NEW YORK FIRE ZOUAVES. A volunteer Union regiment in the Civil War, shown quartered in the House chamber. Wood engraving, *Harper's Weekly*, 1861.

the enlistment of black troops, the confiscation of personal property, the suspension of constitutional guarantees of personal liberty, the granting of political rights to blacks, the use of military tribunals for trying civilians, the reconstruction of the Union, and (early on) the question of overtures to the Confederate states.

There were, of course, some differences among Democrats and Unionists as well, but they tended to cluster more tightly and to overlap the moderate and conservative end of the Republican spectrum. Several of the Democrats were decidedly pro-Southern, and some left Congress to cast their lot with the Confederacy. Probably the most pro-Southern members remaining in the 37th Congress were Rep. Henry May of Maryland and Senators James A. Bayard of Delaware and Jesse D. Bright of Indiana. Bright was expelled from the Senate for

having addressed Jefferson Davis as president of the Confederate States of America in a letter. At the other end of the Democratic scale, Senators John B. Henderson of Missouri, Andrew Johnson of Tennessee, and James A. McDougall of California, together with Representatives George H. Browne of Rhode Island, Edward Haight of New York, and John W. Noell of Missouri, occupied positions similar to those of the advanced moderate Republicans. A substantial portion of the Unionists had similar views.

Legislation. There were three sessions of the 37th Congress—the special session that convened on 4 July 1861 and the two regular sessions, which began in December 1862 and December 1863—and two regular sessions of the 38th Congress. The earlier Congress was in session more than six weeks longer than the second.

The scope of action in the special session of the 37th Congress was limited by a resolution, introduced by Democratic representative William S. Holman of Indiana, that permitted consideration only of measures dealing with military matters and related financial legislation and "general legislation of a judicial character." But no such restraints bound the House during the other four Civil War sessions. The number of acts and resolutions passed in the 37th and 38th Congresses were to 521 and 515, respectively; only three times before had a single Congress's enactments exceeded five hundred. The increase, not surprisingly, was in the area of public acts and resolutions, which slightly exceeded four hundred in each Congress; no earlier Congress had enacted even half as many.

The legislative output of these Congresses—especially the 37th—was of exceptional importance. The desperate financial straits brought about by the war caused Congress to authorize the issuance of non-interest-bearing Treasury notes of modest denominations, which circulated as currency. As state-chartered banks declined to accept these notes at par, Congress (reluctantly at first) authorized additional issues and made them a legal tender for all debts, public and private. In 1863 Congress established a national banking system that not only created a national currency with uniform backing and, hence, national acceptability, but also established a major market for the interest-bearing federal securities that backed the currency. Supplemental legislation in these areas continued in succeeding Congresses. The net result was a complete change in the nation's banking and currency structures.

Wartime financial exigency also led Congress to restructure the nation's tax system by passing an extensive internal revenue measure that taxed, in the words of one representative, "everything except coffins." It levied the nation's first income tax and a broad array of excise taxes and led to the establishment of the Bureau of Internal Revenue. The Morrill Tariff of 1861 (passed late in the 36th Congress) was followed by additional legislation on import duties (frequently tied to increases in internal taxation) in both Civil War Congresses. This legislation shifted the national tariff policy sharply away from the tendency toward a revenue-oriented policy that had prevailed since 1833 and reintroduced a protective policy that (with a couple of exceptions) would continue for the next two-thirds of a century.

Also directly related to the war were the Conscription Acts of 1863 and 1864, by which the federal government for the first time established a national draft. The same might be said of the various acts of both Congresses that aimed at confiscating the property owned by persons supporting the rebellion, despite provisions of the Constitution that inhibit such seizures.

Opportunity as well as necessity sparked innovative legislation. The war itself, and the sectionalism that produced it, made possible extensive legislation dealing with slavery and blacks. Congressional action in this area addressed such matters as slave enlistment in the army and the resulting emancipation of black soldiers and their families, schemes for freeing slaves with compensation to their masters, colonization efforts, the removal of some civil disabilities for free blacks, and—early in 1865—passage of the Thirteenth Amendment, which formally abolished slavery throughout the Union, and creation of the Freedmen's Bureau.

The absence of members of Congress from the Deep South also made possible (or, at least, easier) the enactment of various measures on which there had been sectional division. The passage of the Homestead Act in 1862 marked both the end of a series of laws pertaining to the purchase of public land and the beginning of decades of legislation based on the assumption of access of settlers to public lands without purchase. The Morrill Land-Grant College Act (1862), too, embodied policies that had little support in the Deep South. And the Pacific Railway Acts of 1862 and 1864 represented the ultimate (for this era) embodiment of the use of federal resources to construct internal improvements—something that many southerners had long opposed—and made possible the railroad's construction on a nonsouthern route.

Also notable during these war years, and at least in part resulting from differences among Republicans over war aims and methods of achieving those aims, were the efforts of the legislature to exert more influence over the executive branch. The investigative activities of various committees—most notably the Joint Committee on the Conduct of the War—frequently appeared to be directly related to increasing legislative (and, especially, Radical Republican) influence in areas of executive responsibility. Also, in 1862 and 1863, a scheme was mounted in Congress to oust Secretary of State William H. Seward from the cabinet, and some congressional leaders certainly supported the attempt within the Republican party to deny renomination to President Abraham Lincoln in 1864.

The efforts by Republican members, in particular those on the Committee on the Conduct of the War, to play an active role in the prosecution of the war were largely unsuccessful; their views, though, were doubtless influential (though not determinative) in the choice of senior military commanders. Meanwhile, Lincoln, though his messages to Congress espoused various measures, rarely attempted to influence congressional legislation. He gave rather late (and successful) support to the National Banking Act. His endorsement of compensated, state-mandated emancipation coupled with voluntary colonization of the freed slaves produced only minimal action. But the executive prevailed in the conflict between the president and Congress over Reconstruction policy, thanks to Lincoln's pocket veto of the Wade-Davis bill.

The members of the 37th and 38th Congresses were both bitterly condemned and extravagantly praised by their contemporaries. Members' motives during these Congresses doubtless ranged from meanly spiteful to grandly visionary. In any event, the legislation they passed was of exceptional importance and had great influence on the postwar development of the nation.

[*See also* Conduct of the War Committee, Joint; Congress of the Confederacy; Radical Republicans; Secession; Thirteenth Amendment.]

BIBLIOGRAPHY

Bogue, Allan G. *The Congressman's Civil War.* 1989.
Bogue, Allan G. *The Earnest Men: Republicans of the Civil War Senate.* 1981.
Curry, Leonard P. *Blueprint for Modern America: Nonmilitary Legislation of the First Civil War Congress.* 1968.
McPherson, Edward. *The Political History of the United States during the Great Rebellion.* 1865.

LEONARD P. CURRY

CLARK, JAMES BEAUCHAMP (CHAMP)

(1850–1921), Democratic representative from Missouri, floor leader (1907–1911), Speaker of the House (1911–1918). Raised and educated in Kentucky and Ohio, Champ Clark moved to Bowling Green, Missouri, in 1876. He became city attorney in 1880, county attorney in 1884, and a member of the state house of representatives in 1888. Before leaving the state legislature in 1891, he authored the state's antitrust and secret ballot laws. Clark was defeated for the Democratic nomination to Congress in 1890. In 1892 he won his party's nomination and was elected to Congress, only to lose the seat to a Republican in 1894. He regained the office in 1896, serving continuously thereafter until he was defeated in 1920.

JAMES BEAUCHAMP (CHAMP) CLARK. As Speaker of the House, at the Speaker's table.   LIBRARY OF CONGRESS

In Congress he served on the Foreign Affairs and Ways and Means committees and became the protégé of Democratic floor leader John Sharp Williams of Mississippi. In the 60th Congress (1907–1909), he succeeded Williams as Democratic leader and led the Democrats in their fight against dictatorial Republican Speaker Joseph G. Cannon of Illinois. Working with a group of Republican insurgents led by George W. Norris of Nebraska, Clark's Democrats revolted against the Speaker's power over the House Committee on Rules. In March 1910, the House voted to remove the Speaker from the committee and to limit its power. Public disaffection with the Republican-controlled House led to a Democratic landslide in the elections of that year, propelling Clark into the speakership.

Clark sought to change the Speaker's role in House affairs. Turning over most of the party leadership responsibilities to his floor leaders, Oscar W. Underwood of Alabama and Claude Kitchin of North Carolina, Clark chose to play the dual role of impartial presiding officer of the House and active participant in legislative debate when the House met in the Committee of the Whole to consider legislation. In the latter capacity, he spoke to issues more frequently than any other twentieth-century Speaker. This activism was related to his presidential ambitions. In part as a result of his role in the overthrow of Cannon, Clark became the leading Democratic candidate for the presidency in 1912, running well ahead of Woodrow Wilson and William Jennings Bryan on the first ballot and retaining a lead through the fourteenth ballot. Bryan and Clark had become political adversaries, and when Bryan threw his support to Wilson, Clark's presidential ambitions were defeated for good.

Clark later claimed, with some justification, that the revolt against Cannon had been the first wedge dividing the Republican party between its stalwart (conservative) and insurgent (progressive) wings, leading to the breaking up of the party by Theodore Roosevelt's Bull Moose faction in 1912. Ironically, division within the Democratic party between the Bryanites and the party's mainstream was to deny Clark the ultimate object of his ambition. But, by March 1913, the Democrats controlled the federal government and the door was open to progressive enactments under Woodrow Wilson. Whatever Clark's disappointment in being denied the White House, he had the satisfaction of seeing realized many of the progressive legislative goals for which he had labored. As Speaker, he continued to play a vital role in pressing for the progressive cause. During his tenure, Congress enacted the Underwood-Simmons tariff, the Federal Trade Commission Act, the Clayton Antitrust Act, and the Federal Reserve Bank Act. Congress also passed on to the states constitutional amendments providing for direct taxation of income, direct election of U.S. senators, and woman suffrage, all progressive policies.

He remained as Speaker through the 65th Congress (1917–1919) and served as Democratic leader in the 66th Congress (1919–1921). The reforms that the progressive Democrats implemented in House procedure—especially the enhanced roles for the party caucus and the Rules Committee—represented significant change from what had existed under the Republican leadership. Of the two, the strengthening of the Rules Committee and of the committee system in general proved more enduring than the strengthening of the party caucus. Southern Democrats took advantage of the seniority system to control the committees, and the brief period of party governance gave way to a prolonged era of conservative control of the House.

BIBLIOGRAPHY

Clark, Champ. *My Quarter Century of American Politics.* 2 vols. 1920.

Kenon, Donald R., ed. *The Speakers of the U.S. House of Representatives, 1798–1984.* 1986. Pp. 212–219.

Peters, Ronald M., Jr. *The American Speakership: The Office in Historical Perspective.* 1990. Pp. 77–97.

RONALD M. PETERS, JR.

CLAY, HENRY (1777–1852), representative and senator from Kentucky, Speaker of the House, secretary of State, Whig leader, and three-time unsuccessful presidential candidate. Henry Clay was born in Hanover County, Virginia, on 12 April 1777, the seventh of nine children. In his youth, Clay several times heard Patrick Henry speak, which made a lasting impression on him. He read law with Chancellor George Wythe in Richmond, Virginia. Wythe later secured Clay a position in the office of the attorney general, where he completed his legal training. The young lawyer migrated to Kentucky and settled in Lexington, where he opened a law office and won immediate success pleading both civil and criminal cases. Clay married Lucretia Hart, the daughter of one of the state's largest landowners, who also had extensive manufacturing and commercial interests, and thus Clay allied himself to the Blue Grass gentry. Initially a Jeffersonian Republican, Clay quickly developed political and economic ideas more in tune with the mercantile and banking establishment. This constituency decided to send him to the state legislature, where his outstanding speaking talents and powers of persuasion

HENRY CLAY.   LIBRARY OF CONGRESS

could better serve their needs and interests. He was duly elected to the state's lower house in 1803 and immediately assumed an active and influential role in the conduct of legislative business. Clay was rewarded with election to the U.S. Senate on 19 November 1806 to fill the unexpired term of John Adair, even though he had not reached the constitutionally mandated minimum age of thirty. Apparently no one noticed this infraction, and his election was never challenged. Clay gained immediate distinction as a senator. John Quincy Adams noted his oratorical and political skills and pronounced him a "republican of the first fire." Anxious to involve the federal government in public works to assist his western constituents, Clay chaired committees that reported favorably on building the Ohio River Canal and a canal to connect Chesapeake Bay with Delaware Bay.

Clay returned to the Kentucky state legislature in 1807 and was elected Speaker. In 1810 he was again elected to the U.S. Senate, to complete the term of Buckner Thruston. Although he thoroughly enjoyed the Washington scene, he felt the Senate too tame for his tastes, preferring the tumult and excitement of the House. He won a seat there in 1810 and was chosen Speaker of the House on the first ballot on the first day of the new congressional session in 1811.

A group known as the War Hawks demanded war with Great Britain to avenge the United States' many grievances. They believed that Clay, who counted himself among their number, could provide the leadership to force the government into declaring war. He did not disappoint them. But he did more. For the first time he established the role of the Speaker as the political leader of the House. Over time, he infused so much authority into the office as to make the Speaker the second most powerful person in the government after the president. He did so by retaining his right to debate and vote in the House; by presuming the right to refer all bills to standing committees (whose members he chose); by strictly enforcing House rules; and by blocking filibusters by having his floor leaders move the previous question which, when approved, cut off debate. Most particularly, he possessed the intelligence, eloquence, charm, and political skill to find compromises by which to create majorities for the bills he wished to see passed. He served as Speaker of the 12th through 16th and 18th Congresses—longer than any other Speaker in the nineteenth century. Because of the respect other representatives had for his abilities and fairness, Clay usually won election as Speaker on the first ballot.

His tenure was interrupted in 1814 when he accepted appointment by President James Madison to serve as one of the ministers assigned to draw up the Treaty of Ghent that concluded the war with Great Britain. Returning to the House after the war, Clay became an ardent nationalist, believing the government should act to strengthen the nation both at home and abroad as it moved into an increasingly industrial age. He called his program the American System. It consisted of government-sponsored public works (the building of canals, bridges, highways, and other transportation facilities); a protective tariff to encourage domestic manufacturing; and a strong central bank to provide and control the nation's currency and credit. He supported the chartering of the second Bank of the United States in 1816, the protective tariffs of 1816 and 1824, the extensions of the National Road, and a number of other bills that implemented his American System.

Clay also became the leading spokesman for independence for Latin America, so much so that his speeches were translated into Spanish and read to the armies rebelling against Spain; statues of him were later erected in his memory in former Spanish colonies; and he remains one of the very few highly respected North American statesmen among Latin Americans. Clay also spoke eloquently for the independence of Greece. Abraham Lincoln contended that Clay's "predominant sentiment, from first to last, was a deep devotion to the cause of human liberty."

The introduction of a bill to admit Missouri as a slave state triggered the first of a series of crises that nearly shattered the Union. Its resolution achieved for Clay lasting recognition as the "Great Compromiser." Only he commanded the respect from southern proslavery advocates and northern antislavery restrictionists necessary to produce a compromise. He once said that he had never worked so hard, wheedling, pleading, and beseeching the other representatives to set aside their differences to reach an amicable solution. The Missouri Compromise "saved" the Union in 1820 and 1821. The Great Compromiser became one of the most popular statesmen in the country, but his ambitious craving for higher office turned many would-be admirers away.

Clay retired from Congress to recoup financial losses he had suffered following the panic of 1819. He spent two years rebuilding his law practice and repaying loans to John Jacob Astor and was then returned to the House of Representatives and again chosen Speaker. Kentucky nominated Clay for the presidency, and he ran against Gen. Andrew Jackson, hero of the Battle of New Orleans; Secretary of State John Quincy Adams; and Secretary of the Treasury William H. Crawford. There was no clear winner in the election and, following the Twelfth Amendment to the Constitution, the choice of president went to the House from among the three leading candidates. Clay was low man in electoral votes and was therefore excluded from consideration by the House, but his influence and power there would otherwise probably have seen him elected. Instead, he became the king maker, and he decided to throw his support to Adams. It was understood, but unspoken, that he would be appointed secretary of State, a position he desperately sought because presumably it positioned him for the presidency when Adams stepped down. Jackson condemned what he called their "corrupt bargain," and the charge resurfaced each time Clay ran for the presidency.

As secretary of State, Clay tried to promote a "good neighborhood" policy, as he termed it, with the liberated South American republics, but the Jacksonians defeated his efforts to participate in a congress in Panama called to discuss problems of mutual concern to nations of the Western Hemisphere.

When Jackson defeated Adams for the presidency in 1828, Clay retired to Ashland, his home in Lexington, and resumed his law practice. On 9 November 1831 the Kentucky legislature elected him to the U.S. Senate, where, except for the period from 1842 to 1849, he served until his death in 1852. Clay assumed control of the National Republican party, which opposed Jackson's Democratic party. On 13 December 1831, the National Republicans nominated him for the presidency, to run against Jackson.

Clay cajoled Nicholas Biddle, president of the United States Bank, into applying for an extension of the bank's charter, even though it had four years to go. Clay was convinced that he could defeat Jackson in the election on the bank issue. Jackson vetoed the recharter bill after it passed Congress and went on to defeat Clay in the election. Subsequently, the president removed the government's deposits from the bank and placed them in selected state "pet" banks. Condemning Jackson's actions as violations of the Constitution and the rights of the Congress, Clay introduced, and won passage in the Senate for, two resolutions censuring the president and the secretary of the Treasury—an unprecedented action that has never been repeated. Jackson replied in a protest message, declaring the censure

unconstitutional because it infringed on the power of the House to initiate impeachment proceedings against the president.

Clay also guided the Tariff Act of 1832 through Congress. South Carolina declared the tariff null and void and threatened secession if the government forced it to comply. Again, Clay provided the leadership and ideas that resulted in the Compromise Tariff of 1833. South Carolina repealed its ordinance of nullification and spared the nation possible secession and civil war.

Clay, Daniel Webster, and John C. Calhoun—known as the Great Triumvirate—led congressional opposition to Jackson's policies and appointments in the Senate. In 1834, on the Senate floor, Clay dubbed the opposition the "Whig party." He exercised such control of this party and the Congress during the presidency of John Tyler that his enemies called him "The Dictator." Clay's efforts to legislate Whig policies into law, especially the push for a new national bank, provoked a series of presidential vetoes, and he resigned from the Senate on 16 February 1842.

In 1844, the Whigs nominated Clay for the presidency, to run against Democratic nominee James

CAMPAIGN BANNER. With Henry Clay's likeness, for the 1844 presidential race of Clay and his vice presidential running mate, former senator Theodore Frelinghuysen of New Jersey.

COLLECTION OF DAVID J. AND JANICE L. FRENT

K. Polk. Openly hostile to the annexation of Texas, which he believed would precipitate a war with Mexico, Clay lost the election in a very close contest. His opposition to the Mexican War that followed further alienated many of his constituents and kept Clay from receiving the presidential nomination in 1848. In February of that year, the Kentucky legislature again elected him to the U.S. Senate, where he formulated his final compromise, a plan to resolve a quarrel over the spoils of the war.

The treaty concluding the Mexican War provided the United States with extensive territory in the Southwest, including California and New Mexico. Northern abolitionists opposed the extension of slavery into these territories, while southern radicals demanded access to them for their "peculiar institution." A convention in Nashville to demand southern rights took on the appearance of a move toward disunion. Clay had opposed slavery all of his life, even though he owned slaves; he sought to bring about gradual emancipation through compensation, with blacks to be returned to Africa upon gaining their freedom.

In 1850, with the threat of secession and civil war ever more real, Clay brought to the Senate a series of eight resolutions dealing with California, New Mexico, Utah, the Texas boundary and debt, slavery in the District of Columbia, and fugitive slaves. The compromise scheme attempted a balancing act that would placate both sides in a fair and equitable arrangement. Later, the most critical resolutions were packaged into a single "omnibus" bill, but the entire bill went down to defeat in a flurry of amendments in July 1850. The resolutions were reintroduced as single bills and in late summer were shepherded safely through Congress by Sen. Stephen A. Douglas. The compromise undoubtedly prevented secession.

BIBLIOGRAPHY

Eaton, Clement. *Henry Clay and the Art of American Politics.* 1957.
Howe, Daniel Walker. *The Political Culture of the American Whigs.* 1979.
Remini, Robert V. *Henry Clay: Statesman for the Union.* 1991.
Van Deusen, Glyndon G. *The Life of Henry Clay.* 1937.

ROBERT V. REMINI

CLAYTON ANTITRUST ACT

CLAYTON ANTITRUST ACT (1914; 38 Stat. 730–740). When the Democrats won control of both Congress and the presidency in 1912, theirs was a long agenda. Occupying a prominent place was the desire to strengthen antitrust law. The Supreme Court's "rule of reason" approach in its *Standard Oil v. United States* and *United States v. American Tobacco Co.* decisions of 1911 distressed those who saw in it a significant modification of the declaration of the Sherman Antitrust Act (1890) that all restraint of trade was illegal.

A number of proposals to remedy this were combined into the Clayton Antitrust Act. The bill was identified especially with House Judiciary Committee chairman Henry D. Clayton of Alabama and Nevada senator Francis G. Newlands. It specified unfair trade practices such as price discrimination and exclusive dealer contracts and prohibited intercompany stockholding and interlocking directorates. Such provisions, said a contemporary, represented Congress's recognition "that the trust problem was not a single problem but a large number of problems."

Big business interests objected. But so too did small business advocate Louis D. Brandeis, who wanted protective fair trade legislation of the sort that the Clayton Act appeared to prohibit. And Samuel Gompers of the American Federation of Labor wanted—and got—unions specifically exempted from the antitrust law, since the courts were beginning to strike at picketing and boycotts as illegal conspiracies in restraint of trade.

So amended, the Clayton Antitrust Act swept through Congress and became law on 16 October 1914. Gompers welcomed it as an "industrial Magna Carta" for American workers, but, in fact, the courts continued to wield the Sherman Act against the unions' strike weapon. Nor can it be said that the Clayton Act transformed antitrust law, which remained a judicial more than a legislative instrument of public policy.

[*See also* Sherman Antitrust Act.]

BIBLIOGRAPHY

Link, Arthur. *Wilson: The New Freedom.* 1956. Pp. 423–444.
Kolko, Gabriel. *The Triumph of Conservatism.* 1963. Pp. 257–267.

MORTON KELLER

CLEAN AIR ACT. The Clean Air Act established one of the country's most ambitious, extensive, and expensive regulatory programs. Air pollution legislation passed in the 1960s was designed to help the states improve air quality. The Clean Air Act of

1970 (P.L. 91-604), in contrast, established a variety of nationally uniform, legally binding pollution control standards. The law's most controversial section required automakers to cut new cars' pollutant emissions by 90 percent within five years. It also authorized the Environmental Protection Agency (EPA) to establish new source performance standards for all major categories of stationary sources of air pollution. These standards had to "reflect the degree of emission limitation achievable through the application of the best system of emission reduction which . . . has been adequately demonstrated." Most important, the law directed the EPA to establish national ambient air quality standards for all pollutants that "endanger the public health." States were given responsibility for writing implementation plans that would ensure that ambient standards were achieved by 1975. Under the act both the EPA and the states had authority to enforce the standards contained in these plans.

The 1970 legislation was the product of both the enthusiasm for environmental protection that followed the first Earth Day on 22 April 1970 and the presidential ambitions of Sen. Edmund S. Muskie (D-Maine). Muskie, at that time favored to win the 1972 Democratic presidential nomination, chaired the Public Works Committee's Subcommittee on Environmental Pollution. For over a decade he was the Senate's leading authority on air and water pollution. Muskie was intent on demonstrating his commitment to the environment; President Richard M. Nixon was equally determined to deprive Muskie of credit for the legislation. The result of this political one-upmanship was a law that included many unrealistically ambitious goals.

The EPA quickly established a regulatory program to reduce levels of sulfur dioxide, particulate matter, ozone (smog), and carbon monoxide. Although most areas met sulfur dioxide standards by the 1975 deadline, violations of other standards remained. In 1977 Congress completed a massive revision of the act. These amendments (P.L. 95-95) extended the deadlines for meeting emission standards for new automobiles and for attaining some ambient air quality standards. At the same time they imposed stringent restrictions on new coal-burning power plants, added more controls on polluters in nonattainment areas (areas that fail to meet ambient standards), established a program to prevent the "significant deterioration" of air quality in areas currently meeting ambient standards, and gave the EPA significant new enforcement powers.

Congress expected to make additional "mid-course corrections" in 1982. But heated disputes within Congress and between Congress and President Ronald Reagan produced a stalemate that lasted until 1990. The logjam finally broke when President George Bush endorsed legislation that significantly expanded the reach of the regulatory program.

The Clean Air Act of 1990 (P.L. 101-549) was one of the most important pieces of legislation passed during the 101st Congress. Among its many provisions were an acid rain program requiring utilities to reduce sulfur dioxide emissions by ten million tons per year; stringent new limitations on tailpipe emissions; a wide variety of new federal controls on sources contributing to smog; and an ambitious program to reduce toxic pollutants, especially carcinogens. The act also allowed private firms to buy and sell the right to emit certain pollutants. The law was notable for both its length and its level of detail.

The new law placed billions of dollars of additional control costs on industry and imposed new administrative demands on the EPA and the states. As a consequence, it was highly likely that Congress would make further changes in the law before the end of the decade. It was also likely that clean air politics would remain contentious.

BIBLIOGRAPHY

Bryner, Gary C. *Blue Skies, Green Politics: The Clean Air Act of 1990.* 1993.
Melnick, R. Shep. *Regulation and the Courts: The Case of the Clean Air Act.* 1983.

R. SHEP MELNICK

CLERK OF THE HOUSE. When the House of Representatives reached its initial quorum on 1 April 1789, the second order of business after the election of a Speaker was the appointment of a clerk. In naming John Beckley of Virginia as the first clerk, the representatives were fulfilling their constitutional authority "to chuse their Speaker and other Officers." The clerk was to serve the House as the chief administrator of the legislative process, much as the secretary of Congress had acted in the Continental Congress and clerks had assisted the colonial assemblies before independence.

The First Congress assigned the clerk duties that still define the office. His first action was to receive and certify the credentials of newly elected members, a responsibility the clerk has had ever since. From the First Congress, the clerk also has kept the Journal of House Proceedings, as required by the Constitution. In a resolution that gave the clerk's

Clerks of the House of Representatives

CONGRESS	NAME	STATE
1st–4th (1789–1797)	John Beckley	Virginia
5th (1797–1799)	Jonathan W. Condy	Pennsylvania
6th (1799–1801)	John H. Oswald	Pennsylvania
7th–9th (1801–1807)	John Beckley	Virginia
10th–13th (1807–1815)	Patrick Magruder	Maryland
13th–17th (1815–1822)	Thomas Dougherty	Kentucky
17th–22d (1822–1833)	Matthew St. Clair Clarke	Pennsylvania
23d–25th (1833–1838)	Walter S. Franklin	Pennsylvania
25th–26th (1838–1841)	Hugh A. Garland	Virginia
27th (1841–1843)	Matthew St. Clair Clarke	Pennsylvania
28th (1843–1845)	Caleb J. McNulty	Ohio
28th–29th (1845–1847)	Benjamin B. French	New Hampshire
30th–31st (1847–1850)	Thomas J. Campbell	Tennessee
31st (1850–1851)	Richard M. Young	Illinois
32d–34th (1851–1856)	John W. Forney	Pennsylvania
34th (1856–1857)	William Cullom	Tennessee
35th–36th (1857–1860)	James C. Allen	Illinois
36th (1860–1861)	John W. Forney	Pennsylvania
37th (1861–1863)	Emerson Etheridge	Tennessee
38th–43d (1863–1875)	Edward McPherson	Pennsylvania
44th–46th (1875–1881)	George M. Adams	Kentucky
47th (1881–1883)	Edward McPherson	Pennsylvania
48th–50th (1883–1889)	John B. Clark, Jr.	Missouri
51st (1889–1891)	Edward McPherson	Pennsylvania
52d–53d (1891–1895)	James Kerr	Pennsylvania
54th–61st (1895–1911)	Alexander McDowell	Pennsylvania
62d–65th (1911–1919)	South Trimble	Kentucky
66th–71st (1919–1931)	William Tyler Page	Maryland
72d–79th (1931–1947)	South Trimble	Kentucky
80th (1947–1949)	John Andrews	Massachusetts
81st–82d (1949–1953)	Ralph R. Roberts	Indiana
83d (1953–1955)	Lyle O. Snader	Illinois
84th–89th (1955–1967)	Ralph R. Roberts	Indiana
90th–94th (1967–1977)	W. Pat Jennings	Virginia
94th–97th (1977–1983)	Edmund L. Henshaw, Jr.	Virginia
98th–99th (1983–1986)	Benjamin J. Guthrie	Maryland
100th– (1987–)	Donnald K. Anderson	California

office a unique procedural importance in the House, the First Congress declared that the clerk should remain in office until a successor was appointed. The clerk thus has served as the formal means of maintaining continuity between Congresses. The resolution, similar to those passed at the closing of each succeeding Congress, also gave the clerk authority to preside over the opening of the next Congress before the election of a Speaker. Normally, the clerk plays a largely ceremonial role at the opening of a new Congress, but on several occasions in the decades preceding the Civil War, such as the opening of sessions in 1839, 1849, 1855, and 1859, he served as presiding officer for weeks as a factionalized House attempted to elect a Speaker. On each such occasion, however, the sitting clerk declined to rule on points of order and refused to settle contested elections.

The House elects the clerk at the opening of the first session of each Congress, generally as the first order of business following election of the Speaker. The vote is usually by resolution, and election requires approval by a majority of representatives assembled. Although the clerk bears no official party designation, the holder of the office is the candidate of the majority party. The clerk serves until the election of a successor, unless the House votes by resolution to remove the clerk from office for misconduct.

As the complexity of the work before the House increased, so too did the legislative responsibilities of the clerk. The officer is today responsible for furnishing the Daily Digest, recording and printing all bills and reports, certifying engrossed bills, affixing the seal of the House to all formal documents issued by the body, certifying bills and resolutions approved by the House, and sending and receiving messages from the president and the Senate. This legislative work is carried out through a staff of bill clerks, journal clerks, tally clerks, enrolling clerks, reading clerks, and recorders of debates. The clerk operates the House Library, which holds official records issued by the House since 1789.

In the twentieth century, with an increased membership and staff in the House, the clerk became responsible not only for the processing of legislation but also for providing the principle administrative support for the institution. Chief among these duties has been the operation of the Office of Finance, which prepares budgets for legislative operations and disburses House funds for all expenses except members' salaries. The clerk also manages the distribution of office supplies and furnishings, the printing services of the House, and various personnel services. In April 1992, the House approved a resolution transferring most financial and administrative duties from the clerk's office to a newly created position of director for nonlegislative and financial affairs.

Since 1789, thirty individuals have served as clerk of the House. Thirteen clerks have been former members of the House.

[*See also* Parliamentarian, *article on* House Parliamentarian; Secretary of the Senate.]

BIBLIOGRAPHY

DePauw, Linda Grant, ed. *Documentary History of the First Federal Congress of the United States of America.* Vol. 3: *House of Representatives Journal.* 1977.

U.S. House of Representatives. Office of the Clerk. *Office of the Clerk, U.S. House of Representatives.* Prepared under the direction of Donnald K. Anderson. 1991.

BRUCE A. RAGSDALE

CLERKS. Both houses employ specialists, called clerks, to handle the extensive paperwork generated by the legislative process. These positions within the offices of the Secretary of the Senate and Clerk of the House have developed and become increasingly specialized largely over the course of the twentieth century. Many of the clerks work from posts at the rostrum.

In each chamber, *journal clerks* are responsible for maintaining the official record of the proceedings. *Bill clerks* assign numbers to introduced bills and resolutions, prepare them for printing, and keep records of papers received (e.g., committee reports, messages from the other chamber and the president, reports from executive agencies, petitions). In the Senate, bill clerks also record chamber action on each measure, but in the House the journal clerks do this.

The House employs *tally clerks* to administer votes and quorum calls and to prepare legislative information for the (printed) House Calendar, as well as *reading clerks* to read bills, amendments, motions, and other official papers to the chamber. In the Senate, *legislative clerks* perform all these functions.

In both chambers, *enrolling clerks* prepare messages passed by the chamber to be printed as engrossed or enrolled bills. In the Senate, these clerks also handle the transmission of such measures to the other chamber and to the president; in the House, the reading clerks and the House Administration Committee, respectively, have these functions.

The Senate also has *executive clerks*, who record action on executive business (nominations and treaties), track its receipt from and transmission to the president, and maintain the Executive Journal.

The offices of the Clerk of the House and Secretary of the Senate also include such related positions as the reporters of debate and the parliamentarians.

BIBLIOGRAPHY

U.S. House of Representatives. Office of the Clerk. *Office of the Clerk, U.S. House of Representatives.* 1991.
U.S. Senate. Office of the Secretary. *The Office of the Secretary of the Senate.* 1991.

RICHARD S. BETH

CLEVELAND, GROVER

CLEVELAND, GROVER (1837–1908), twenty-second and twenty-fourth president of the United States, sought to redress Congress's supremacy over the executive in the post-Reconstruction decades. Born in New Jersey, Cleveland moved as a child to western New York, where his father was a Presbyterian minister. He read law and was admitted to the bar at Buffalo in 1859.

Cleveland never served in Congress or any other legislature and so had little appreciation of the give-and-take of the legislative process. In 1881 Cleveland was elected mayor of Buffalo, the next year he won the governorship of New York, and in 1884 he was elected president. As mayor and governor he showed a propensity for liberal use of the veto power, an inclination that he carried with him to Washington. Moreover, his meteoric rise in politics contributed to his sense that elected executives owed their positions directly to the people and hence had little obligation to compromise with the legislative branch. His conception of the presidency was essentially Jacksonian. Following the prevalent Democratic party belief that government should remain relatively small and frugal, Cleveland saw the president's principal task as defending the public interest against perceived legislative excesses of Congress.

When Cleveland entered the White House in 1885, Congress was divided, with a Republican Senate and a Democratic House, and he fought his first important battle with the Senate over the president's appointments prerogative. When Cleveland began removing Republican officeholders to make way for Democrats, Republican senators invoked the Reconstruction-era Tenure of Office Act to demand that the executive submit all documents relating to the removals. Cleveland refused. Public opinion sided with the president, and the Republicans eventually backed down. Congress repealed the Tenure of Office Act in early 1887.

Cleveland's negative conception of government showed most clearly in his readiness to veto congressional legislation. In his first term (1885–1889), he turned back 414 bills, more than twice the number vetoed by all his predecessors combined. His second term (1893–1897) witnessed another 170 vetoes. Congress sustained all but seven of them. In the vast majority of cases, Cleveland used the veto to block individual veteran pension bills, but in others he demonstrated his general commitment to limited government. In his Texas seed bill veto in 1887, for instance, he argued that "the lesson should be constantly enforced that though the peo-

PROTECTING THE PUBLIC TRUST. Political cartoon depicting President Grover Cleveland guarding the national Treasury. Vetoed private pension bills litter the floor.
NEW YORK STATE HISTORICAL ASSOCIATION, COOPERSTOWN

ple support the Government[,] the Government should not support the people."

For Cleveland, as for his predecessors, the principal vehicle for communicating with Congress was the president's annual message presented at the opening of each session in December. Traditionally, presidents had used the annual message to offer summaries of executive department reports, to report on foreign affairs, and to make policy suggestions. In 1887 Cleveland broke with precedent and devoted his entire message to a single subject, his call for a reduced tariff to alleviate the growing surplus in the Treasury. As much a political move as a legislative maneuver, Cleveland's message inspired the Democratic House to pass a low tariff bill (killed by the Republican Senate) and made the tariff question the central issue in his 1888 reelection bid, which he lost to Benjamin Harrison.

Four years later, when Cleveland defeated Harrison and returned to the presidency, his party controlled both houses of the 53d Congress (1893–1895). Ironically, Cleveland's shortcomings as a legislative leader became most apparent in his second term. Not long after he took office, the Panic of 1893 threw the economy into an abrupt downward spiral, and the Treasury witnessed a rapid depletion of its gold reserves. To stanch the hemorrhage, Cleveland called Congress into special session to repeal the Sherman Silver Purchase Act. Repeal would end the exchange of silver certificates for gold at the Treasury and thus help restore business confidence. To the chagrin of many civil service reformers, Cleveland used patronage unabashedly to garner support in Congress for repeal. A repeal bill passed easily in the House but encountered strong opposition, including a filibuster, in the Senate. Cleveland refused to compromise, however. Although the bill eventually passed, it cost him many allies in Congress and hopelessly divided the Democrats into gold and silver wings.

Having expended all his leverage on the repeal fight, Cleveland failed to win a substantial reduction in the tariff. Again the Senate posed powerful opposition; again Cleveland would not compromise. The resulting Wilson-Gorman Tariff Act became law without his signature. He further alienated opponents by disregarding senatorial courtesy in two Supreme Court nominations. Although Cleveland was assertive in his relations with Congress, he lacked the finesse necessary to secure his legislative goals.

BIBLIOGRAPHY

Nevins, Allan. *Grover Cleveland: A Study in Courage.* 1932.

Welch, Richard E., Jr. *The Presidencies of Grover Cleveland.* 1988.

CHARLES W. CALHOUN

CLINTON, WILLIAM JEFFERSON (BILL)

(1946–), governor of Arkansas and forty-second president of the United States (1993–). Bill Clinton gained the White House as "a different kind of Democrat" with a shaky coalition of traditional Democrats and independents who were impatient with President George Bush's economic policies. Once elected, he struggled to reconcile the divergent elements of his constituency and broaden his fragile base of support.

Born in Hope, Arkansas, on 19 August 1946, Clinton pursued his education at Georgetown University, Oxford University (as a Rhodes scholar), and Yale Law School. Returning to Arkansas, he served as attorney general (1977–1979) and governor

(1979–1981, 1983–1992). Building on his reputation as an innovative but moderate governor, Clinton battled for and won the Democratic presidential nomination, overcoming speculation about his qualifications and his personal life. (Several leading Democrats, noting President Bush's strength after the popular Persian Gulf War, opted to sit out the 1992 race.) Seizing on voter unrest and Bush's inaction during the 1991 and 1992 recession, Clinton captured 43 percent of the vote (against Bush's 38 percent and independent H. Ross Perot's 19 percent) and 370 electoral votes.

Clinton's victory reflected voters' eagerness for change and impatience with partisan "gridlock" in Washington. Yet his victory was narrow, with little public consensus on what changes were needed. "The simple reality is that a 43 percent plurality victory constitutes a fragile base for governing," observed *Washington Post* political commentator David S. Broder. "It falls far short of the public support Clinton will need to achieve the ambitious policy changes he outlined in the campaign." Clinton was the first Democrat since John F. Kennedy to enter the White House as his party lost strength in Congress (a loss of 10 House seats and eventually one Senate seat).

To seize the initiative and push his legislative agenda, Clinton's advisers urged him to "hit the ground running" with a short list of high-priority initiatives. Advisers were aware that the last Democratic president, Jimmy Carter, had squandered his influence by failing to focus his message or limit his legislative agenda. Clinton did not heed this advice. His early months were marked by delays in fashioning proposals, glaring policy reversals (abandoning several key campaign promises), and embarrassing lapses in White House staff work. Old charges of improprieties during his governorship (the so-called Whitewater affair) resurfaced to cast a continuing shadow over Clinton's presidency, and aides complained that Clinton's presidential honeymoon was the briefest on record.

Tardiness in nominating people to fill executive and judicial posts marked the start of the administration. On top of an already burdensome nomination and confirmation process Clinton added his goal of creating a cabinet "that looked like America." Although his appointments met his diversity pledge (his original cabinet included four blacks, four women, and two Hispanics), critics noted that the administration drew heavily on people recommended by traditional liberal Democratic groups. Two nominees for attorney general were dropped because of minor but highly publicized ethical questions; other would-be nominees fell victim to congressional objections. Increasingly, the White House looked for safe appointees assured of quick confirmation. For the Supreme Court, for example, Clinton chose two moderate federal judges, Ruth Bader Ginsburg and Stephen G. Breyer.

Clinton's core economic agenda was soon upstaged by a clutter of other issues, large and small. An effort to redeem a campaign pledge to normalize the treatment of gays and lesbians in military service was met with outcries from high-level military officers, the Senate and House armed services panels, and large segments of the general public. Relatively little change was achieved, at the cost of diverting attention from the president's core agenda. Another early proposal—to hike fees for use of western public lands—was dropped after western lawmakers protested. Like the abandoned nominations, these incidents signaled that the president would cave in under pressure.

Although during his campaign he had kept Democratic congressional leaders at arm's length, as president Clinton quickly moved to cooperate with them, declaring that "Pennsylvania Avenue will run both ways again." He pursued an essentially partisan Capitol Hill strategy, deferring to Democratic congressional leaders' advice on substantive and tactical questions, relying on the party's increased cohesion for votes, and shunning alliances with moderate Republicans. In return he forsook his campaign rhetoric criticizing Congress and advocating such controversial reforms as the line-item veto. A common stake in the administration's success would, it was reasoned, bind the president and his partisans on Capitol Hill.

That strategy paid off in Clinton's first year, when he prevailed on 86.4 percent of the 191 roll calls on which he declared a position (as recorded by *Congressional Quarterly Weekly Report*). That was the highest success rate since 1965, the height of Lyndon Johnson's "Great Society" juggernaut. Most House and Senate Democrats gave Clinton strong support. Many of the early victories involved legislation that had been stalled after twelve years of Republican administrations—for example, providing parental leave, "motor voter" registration, and Hatch Act revisions. Democrats also rallied to support the budget reconciliation bill, which raised taxes on fuels and for upper-income individuals, cut the defense budget, and hiked funds for some social and antipoverty programs. Campaigning intensely and in person, Clinton and his allies managed to overcome defections from conservative Democrats. The plan barely passed the House, 218 to 216, and the Senate, 51 to 50, with Vice President Albert A. Gore, Jr., casting the tie-breaking vote.

Embracing his party leaders on Capitol Hill, though perhaps inevitable, was not without its costs. Many items on Clinton's agenda cried out for bipartisan coalition building: attracting moderate Republican support in order to counter defections from his own party and to gain the sixty votes required to break Senate filibusters. Clinton's worst 1993 defeat was the Senate's rejection of his $16.3 billion economic stimulus package. Unswayed by grumbling from conservative Democrats, House leaders pushed through the bill on a virtual party-line vote. But Senate Republicans united against the measure, which died after four failed attempts to end the Republican filibuster. The next year an omnibus crime bill was stalled in the House by a coalition of anti–gun control forces and Republicans eager to embarrass the president. After frantic lobbying and grassroots efforts, the president wooed enough votes to pass the measure (the Violent Crime Control and Law Enforcement Act of 1994).

The most spectacular legislative victory of Clinton's first two years—congressional approval of the North American Free Trade Agreement (NAFTA) in late 1993—was the fruit of a bipartisan effort. Many Democrats opposed the treaty, among them leaders of organized labor and such House figures as Majority Leader Richard A. Gephardt (Mo.) and Majority Whip David E. Bonior (Mich.). Clinton launched a high-profile public relations campaign, trumpeted the treaty's job-creation benefits, welcomed support from Republican leaders, and cut deals to meet individual legislators' objections. In the end, only 40 percent of House Democrats supported the president, but their 102 votes along with those of 132 Republicans were enough to gain House approval. NAFTA then easily passed the Senate.

The NAFTA victory raised speculation that Clinton might develop a bipartisan strategy to broaden his constituency and gain passage of even more complex goals, especially reform of the health care system and welfare policy. But such a course proved difficult to implement: Democratic leaders were bound by their caucuses' wishes and reluctant to seek bipartisan compromises, at least on key ideological issues. The Republicans, for their part, displayed uncommon unity in the hopes of weakening the administration and laying the groundwork for victories in 1994 and 1996.

Clinton, like Carter before him, teetered between his electoral and governing coalitions. Electorally, he needed to broaden his support among disaffected and increasingly independent voters, many of whom had supported Perot in 1992 and were apt to turn against incumbents in 1994 and 1996. But governing coalitions were paradoxically more partisan than ever: congressional Democrats (and Republicans) were far more consistent and cohesive partisans than the electorates they represented. Their partisanship was reinforced by the parties' core factions—in the Democrats' case, a markedly liberal collection of groups representing women, minorities, environmentalists, and public employees' unions. At the midpoint of his term, Clinton wavered between these electoral and governing coalitions, unable to raise his popularity and facing intensified resistance from Republicans.

BIBLIOGRAPHY

Campbell, Colin, and Bert A. Rockman, eds. *The Clinton Presidency: First Appraisals.* 1995.

Duncan, Phil, and Steve Langdon. "When Congress Had to Choose, It Voted to Back Clinton." *Congressional Quarterly Weekly Report* 51 (December 18, 1993): 3427–3431.

Woodward, Robert. *The Agenda: Inside the Clinton White House.* 1994.

ROGER H. DAVIDSON

CLOAKROOMS. L-shaped rooms located adjacent to the House and Senate chambers and beneath the visitors' galleries, the Capitol cloakrooms were originally used for storing members' personal belongings while they were on the floor. With the opening of the House and Senate office buildings in 1908 and 1909, respectively, every member was supplied with an office for that purpose, and the cloakrooms were modified to become private, partisan lounges. Both the House and Senate have Democratic and Republican cloakrooms, modestly furnished with chairs, sofas, and telephones. Members use the cloakrooms to conduct conversations without disrupting the business on the floor. They may discuss strategy on legislation, conduct business by telephone, purchase a light meal, read newspapers, watch television, or rest.

Cloakrooms are among the few areas of the Capitol restricted to members only. No personal staff members are allowed in the cloakrooms; selected committee staff may be allowed access when they have legislation pending on the floor. Over time, communications equipment has been added, and the cloakrooms have become clearinghouses for information relating to the status of business on the floor and centers for disseminating information from the leadership to the members. Staff persons and pages are assigned to the cloakrooms to relay messages to members, to inform them regarding the scheduling of legislation, and to notify members when their presence is required on the floor.

BIBLIOGRAPHY

U.S. House of Representatives. *Constitution, Jefferson's Manual, and Rules of the House of Representatives, 102d Congress.* 101st Cong., 2d sess., 1990. H. Doc. 101-256.

U.S. Senate. *Senate Manual.* 101st Cong., 1st sess., 1989. S. Doc. 101-1.

JIM OLIVER

CLOTURE. The U.S. Senate has two means for ending debate available to it. One is a unanimous consent agreement, and the other is a petition for cloture. Because its smaller size allows for less restrictive procedural rules than those placed on the House of Representatives and because of the value placed on free debate and deliberation, the Senate has been reluctant to limit the opportunities of members to speak on the floor. Until 1917, debate could be ended only if the Senate adopted a unanimous consent request to close debate. A single senator or a group of senators could prevent a bill from coming to a vote by objecting to unanimous consent requests and extending the debate. This tactic is known as a filibuster.

Although filibusters were relatively rare and successful only under certain conditions, some senators sought to reform the rules to provide another means for bringing debate to a close. During the 64th Congress (1915–1917), twelve progressives engaged in a filibuster against President Woodrow Wilson's bill to arm merchant ships; they succeeded in preventing a vote on it. When the new Senate convened it adopted a substitute amendment to Rule XXII that established cloture.

Under the cloture procedure, any senator may circulate a petition calling for an end to debate on a particular bill, resolution, or motion. After sixteen senators have signed the petition, it may be filed with the presiding officer of the Senate. On the second calendar day after such a petition is filed, the Senate votes on whether to end debate by invoking cloture. As originally established, at least two-thirds of those senators "present and voting" had to vote in favor of cloture for it to be successful. If the cloture motion was defeated, debate would continue.

Rule XXII changed very little between 1917 and 1975. In 1949, the requirements for invoking cloture changed to two-thirds of the Senate membership instead of two-thirds of those present and voting. In 1959, the Senate changed the provision back to two-thirds of those present and voting and allowed motions to change the Senate rules also to be subject to cloture.

Between 1917 and 1937 the cloture procedure was used rarely, on a diffuse group of issues, and with limited success; its use was uncontroversial. From 1937 until the early 1960s, cloture votes, though still infrequent, were primarily taken when southern Democratic senators engaged in filibusters of civil rights bills. In every instance cloture was defeated. Senate liberals and reformers sought to reduce the cloture vote requirement to three-fifths or to a simple majority of senators. Efforts to reduce the cloture requirements in 1957, 1963, 1965, and again in 1967 were defeated.

One interesting aspect of the issue involved limitations on debate on motions to change Senate rules. Reformers argued that because the Senate started anew with each Congress, preexisting Senate rules were not in effect and a simple majority vote could end debate on a motion to adopt a set of rules. The other side contended that the Senate was a continuing body because two-thirds of its membership automatically carried over from one Congress to the next. Prior to 1959 such an interpretation meant that debates on changing Senate rules could only end by unanimous consent, and even after 1959 ending such debates was subject to the two-thirds provision of Rule XXII.

By 1975, changes in the Senate had made possible an alteration of the cloture requirements. The filibuster was a growing problem. With the growing legislative workload, Senate sessions were running nearly year round; no longer could the Senate afford the luxury of unlimited debate. And because of the increased time pressures, the filibuster became a more effective tactic, more easily forcing legislative concessions. Thus there were both more filibusters and more cloture votes. In the forty-four years from 1917 to 1960, there were twenty-one cloture votes. In the following ten years, from 1961 to 1970, there were twenty-six cloture votes. And in the less than five years from 1971 until Rule XXII was altered in 1975, there were fifty-four cloture votes. Filibusters were no longer limited to southern Democrats trying to prevent action on civil rights bills. They were used by diverse senators and against diverse kinds of legislation.

The Senate voted in 1975 to change the cloture requirement from two-thirds of those present and voting to three-fifths of the Senate membership. (Only motions to change the Senate rules remained under the two-thirds cloture requirement.) Efforts to invoke cloture in the Senate were more successful after this change. But another effect was the development of the so-called post-cloture filibuster. Once cloture was invoked Senate rules allowed each member to speak for one hour on the bill or any amendments to it, up to a total of one hundred hours. In addition, procedural motions and votes could be used to extend the process well beyond that period. In reaction to post-cloture filibusters, the Senate in 1979 placed all activity following cloture under the one-hundred-hour limit. In 1986, as part of the legislation allowing television coverage of the Senate floor, the Senate restricted all post-cloture activity to thirty hours.

[*See also* Filibuster; Unanimous Consent Agreements.]

CLEANING HOUSE. Cartoon depicting the successful and easy adoption of Senate Rule XXII, which established the cloture procedure. Clifford K. Berryman, *Washington Evening Star*, 9 March 1917.

U.S. SENATE COLLECTION, CENTER FOR LEGISLATIVE ARCHIVES

BIBLIOGRAPHY

Oleszek, Walter J. *Congressional Procedures and the Policy Process*. 3d ed. 1989.
Smith, Steven S. *Call to Order*. 1989.

BRUCE I. OPPENHEIMER

CLUBS. Since the beginning of the nineteenth century, both houses of Congress have seen small and typically informal groups of legislators meet either regularly or on an ad hoc basis to socialize and discuss business. Because the gatherings unite, in some combination, serious political discussions with sociability, they have sometimes been styled "sociolegislative groups."

The earliest of these groups were the "boarding-house fraternities" that thrived during the first thirty years of the nineteenth century. Members from the same states or regions lived and ate together in boardinghouses on Capitol Hill. Their living arrangements promoted strong regional attachments and retarded the growth of nationalism.

In the late nineteenth century, the Philosophers Club met at the Washington home of Sen. James McMillan (R-Mich.). The members of the group—all Republican senators—were McMillan, Nelson W. Aldrich of Rhode Island, Orville H. Platt of Connecticut, William B. Allison of Iowa, and John C. Spooner of Wisconsin. The group was united by their partisanship, their personal wealth, and their membership on such critical committees as Finance and Rules. Allison was the chairman of the Republican caucus. From about 1880 until the death of Allison in 1908, the Philosophers Club served as the informal directorate of the Senate Republicans.

In the House of Representatives early in the twentieth century, the Tantalus Club was founded for the purpose of coordinating legislative activity among House Republicans. Of an avowedly nonpolitical purpose was the Statesmen's Sunday Morning Marching Club organized by Nicholas Longworth, Speaker from 1925 to 1931. The club gathered in Washington's Rock Creek Park for strenuous two-hour walks. While charter members of the club were under an informal injunction not to discuss politics, it was a regulation honored in the breach. Longworth was a cofounder of a bipartisan group of House members in the 1920s along with John Nance "Cactus Jack" Garner, a Texas Democrat. Calling itself the Bureau of Education, this club had its name appropriated by House Speaker Sam Rayburn's famous Board of Education.

In the late 1920s and early 1930s, New York representatives Fiorello H. LaGuardia (later mayor of New York) and John J. Boylan organized a bipartisan club calling itself the LaGuardia-Boylan Spaghetti Association. But by reason of its duration and the influence its members wielded in Congress, Sam Rayburn's Board of Education was the most

prominent gathering since the days of the Philosophers Club. According to his biographers, D. B. Hardeman and Donald C. Bacon, Rayburn himself never used the title "Board of Education" but would merely invite some friends "downstairs" to his private hideaway office on the ground floor of the Capitol. Invitees were asked "to strike a blow for liberty"—a euphemism for having a drink.

Among the small group of regulars were some of the most powerful committee chairmen and members. One of them, Clinton P. Anderson of New Mexico, described meetings of the board as occasions where business was rarely discussed but where bridge and poker were played, bourbon and branch water was the beverage of choice, and Speaker Rayburn could then adjourn to his favorite Chinese restaurant for dinner.

While formal discussions of pending matters might have been considered a breach of the board's informal protocol, the club served as a clearinghouse for intelligence and sometimes simple gossip. It enabled the Speaker to take the pulse of the House in a relaxed and unofficial way. Vice President Harry S. Truman, a board regular, learned about the death of President Franklin D. Roosevelt on 12 April 1945 while in the Rayburn hideaway.

Such clubs have arisen more frequently in the House than in the Senate, both because the House's larger size prompts representatives to seek intimacy in smaller groups and because senators are typically more individualistic than House members. An organization of Republican members who were World War II veterans joined forces to defeat a veterans' benefits bill that they considered extravagant. They called their group the Chowder and Marching Society. In the post–World War II period, liberal Republicans in the House established the Wednesday Club, and there were other clubs called the Acorns and SOS. The Republican equivalent of Rayburn's Board of Education was Minority Leader Charles A. Halleck's Clinic, where Republicans wounded in battle against the numerically superior Democrats could come for care and sympathy. The Clinic was more informal and more purely social than Chowder and Marching, Acorns, or SOS.

More akin to Halleck's Clinic and Rayburn's board were the two Senate watering holes of Majority Leader Lyndon B. Johnson and Minority Leader Everett M. Dirksen that thrived in the 1950s. Johnson's group had no name but met habitually at the office of Secretary of the Senate Felton M. "Skeeter" Johnston.

Distinct from the earthy tone of the sociolegislative clubs are the prayer breakfasts in the House and Senate. These groups grew out of the National Prayer Breakfast movement of the 1950s with which President Dwight D. Eisenhower was associated. While these meetings are officially nonsectarian, the membership consists largely of southern and midwestern members affiliated with Protestant denominations. The prayer breakfasts, which were active during the 1960s and 1970s, were to some degree supplanted in the 1980s by ad hoc groups of "born-again" senators and representatives who met in members' personal offices for worship.

In general, the sociolegislative club has gone into decline in Congress for a number of reasons. The need to attend to reelection concerns such as fundraising has cut increasingly into legislators' discretionary time. By the 1990s colleagues no longer viewed as lazy or uncollegial those members who preferred spending leisure time with their families. There has also been a proliferation of specialized caucuses that bring together members sharing common concerns. Modern transportation, moreover, makes it easier for members to return to their constituencies and reduces the amount of time they spend in Washington with colleagues.

Changes in the values of American society have also taken their toll. Drinking liquor and playing cards—activities that were central to most of the clubs—have, at least temporarily, fallen into disfavor. Furthermore, the symbolism of such groups—small cliques of influential men—seems at variance with the image of democratic government.

[See also Alcoholic Beverages in Congress; Boardinghouses; Caucus, article on Special Interest Caucus.]

BIBLIOGRAPHY

Baker, Ross K. *Friend and Foe in the U.S. Senate.* 1980.
MacNeil, Neil. *Forge of Democracy: The House of Representatives.* 1963.

ROSS K. BAKER

COALITIONS. *See* Blocs and Coalitions.

COAST GUARD. The United States Coast Guard has undergone substantial evolution in both name and functions since it began in 1790 as the Revenue Cutter Service (also known as the Revenue Marine Service) within the Department of the Treasury. Initially, its only responsibility was to collect revenues for the Customs Service. However, since its founding, the Coast Guard and its missions have been gradually broadened through many statutes that reflect Congress's and the country's strong commitment to this agency.

In 1790, the Department of the Treasury was authorized by the First Congress to acquire not more than ten cutters, which were to be used for the collection of "the duties imposed by law on goods, wares and merchandise imported into the United States, and on the tonnage of ships or vessels." In 1797, with a war against France threatening, Congress expanded the Revenue Cutter Service's responsibilities to include authority, at the direction of the president, "to defend the sea coast and to repel any hostility to their vessels." Thereafter, until an enlarged Coast Guard was formed in 1915, the missions assigned to the Revenue Cutter Service grew to include many of the traditional missions that the Coast Guard currently exercises, including interdiction of illegal immigrants, rescue at sea, fisheries enforcement, enforcement of navigation regulations, and service as part of the military force protecting the U.S. coastline.

Several proposals were put forward in the 1790s to transfer the Revenue Cutter Service to the navy. Although none were adopted, Congress in 1799 enacted legislation that placed the Coast Guard under the navy's control during a declaration of war. In both world wars, the Coast Guard was transferred to the navy by executive order of the president. In addition, although not officially transferred to the navy, the Coast Guard played an important role in the Korean, Vietnam, and Persian Gulf wars.

Apart from the Revenue Cutter Service, a separate lifesaving service existed from 1837 until its merger into the Coast Guard in 1915. It began as a series of lighthouses, with later appropriations for rescue boats. In 1878 an act was passed providing for the appointment of a general superintendent of the Life-Saving Service, a separate appointment of a gulf coast superintendent, rates of compensation and duties, the schedule of times when lifesaving stations would be open, and support for the service.

In 1915 Congress officially established the Coast Guard under its current designation. The Revenue Cutter Service was merged with the Life-Saving Service in the new Coast Guard, which was in the Department of the Treasury. The president retained the authority to transfer the Coast Guard to the navy in time of war. When the Department of Transportation was established in 1967, the Coast Guard was transferred to that agency because of the Coast Guard's important role in maritime transportation.

In recent years, the Coast Guard's duties have been expanded to encompass a broad array of domestic law-enforcement missions, search-and-rescue functions, military readiness operations, marine environmental protection responsibilities, the maintenance of aids for safe navigation, and many more.

Congress exercises legislative and oversight control of the Coast Guard through several standing committees. Authorization bills are the jurisdiction of the House Merchant Marine and Fisheries Committee, through its Subcommittee on Coast Guard and Navigation, and of the Senate Committee on Commerce, Science, and Transportation, through its National Ocean Policy Study Subcommittee. Funding proposals for the Coast Guard must go through the House Appropriations Subcommittee on Transportation and the Senate Appropriations Subcommittee on Transportation and Related Agencies.

Major acts giving additional responsibilities to the Coast Guard under the Department of Transportation include:

Natural Gas Pipeline Safety Act of 1968
Recreational Boating Fund Act, as amended by the Federal Boat Safety Act of 1971
Ocean Dumping Act of 1972
Ports and Waterways Safety Act of 1972
Trans-Alaska Pipeline Authorization Act of 1973
Deepwater Port Act of 1974
Intervention on the High Seas Act of 1974
Hazardous Materials Transportation Act of 1975
Fishery Conservation and Management Act of 1976 (Magnuson Fishery Conservation and Management Act)
Federal Water Pollution Control Act Amendments of 1977
Outer Continental Shelf Lands Act Amendments of 1978
Port Tanker Safety Act of 1978
Hazardous Liquid Pipeline Safety Act of 1979
An Act to Prevent Pollution from Ships of 1980
Maritime Drug Law Enforcement Act of 1980
Omnibus Diplomatic Security and Antiterrorism Act of 1986
Anti–Drug Abuse Act of 1986
Marine Plastic Pollution Research and Control Act of 1987
Anti–Drug Abuse Amendments Act of 1988
Oil Pollution Act of 1990
Abandoned Barge Act of 1992
Passenger Vessel Safety Act of 1993

[*See also* Commerce, Science, and Transportation Committee, Senate; Merchant Marine and Fisheries Committee, House.]

BIBLIOGRAPHY

U.S. House of Representatives. *Report on the Activities of the Merchant Marine and Fisheries Committee.* 102d Cong., 1992. H. Rep. 102-1092.
U.S. Senate. Committee on Commerce, Science, and Transportation. *The U.S. Coast Guard.* 97th Cong., 2d sess., 1982.

ELIZABETH R. MEGGINSON

COBB, HOWELL (1815–1868), representative from Georgia, prominent Democratic party leader, Speaker of the House, secretary of the Treasury. Cobb epitomized the power of the South in national politics before the Civil War. A large, affable man who enjoyed the perquisites of office, Cobb was a consummate politician. He was born to the plantation aristocracy of his state, a position he secured by his 1835 marriage to Mary Ann Lamar, who belonged to an even more prominent southern family. Cobb regarded power as his birthright. Following his education and admission to the bar, he moved quickly into Georgia Democratic politics. After serving as a circuit solicitor (1837–1841), he was elected to the U.S. House of Representatives while still in his twenties. A representative for ten years (1843–1851, 1855–1857), he was a skilled manager and the most partisan of the powerful antebellum Georgia triumvirate that included Robert Toombs and Alexander H. Stephens. Unlike the latter two, who began their national careers as Whigs, Cobb was a lifelong Democrat.

Cobb used his power within the Democratic party and Congress to protect the South and to advance his intense ambition. In 1849, he was chosen Speaker of the House by a plurality vote after a long balloting that foreshadowed the deeper conflicts over slavery during the fractious 31st Congress (1849–1851). Because of his support for the Compromise of 1850, which temporarily diminished sectional antagonisms, Cobb gained a reputation as a Unionist. From that time on, he was never fully trusted by the southern radicals.

After interrupting his congressional service for a term as governor of Georgia (1851–1853) and then returning to the House, Cobb became secretary of the Treasury in the fateful administration of James Buchanan. One of the president's closest political friends, he helped shape the southern policy of the

HOWELL COBB. As Speaker of the House, Cobb helped pass the Compromise of 1850.   LIBRARY OF CONGRESS

administration. His position at the Treasury placed a large share of the federal patronage at his disposal, and he unhesitatingly employed it in pursuit of the administration's goals. In this way he was able to exercise behind-the-scenes influence in Congress, particularly at critical moments such as the 1857 drive to secure passage of the proslavery Lecompton constitution for Kansas. From within the cabinet, Cobb competed with Illinois senator Stephen A. Douglas for the Democratic presidential nomination in 1860. Having failed to stop Douglas, however, the longtime partisan supported the separate southern Democratic ticket headed by Vice President John C. Breckinridge.

Following the election of Abraham Lincoln, the former Unionist resigned his cabinet position and returned to Georgia, where he actively campaigned for the state's secession. Cobb hoped to play a major role in the Confederacy. Because of his legislative reputation, he was elected by acclamation to preside over the Confederacy's provisional congress, but he failed to win higher office in the permanent government. Although Cobb served as a Confederate general, he was more involved in political than in military action. His running criticisms of Vice President Alexander Stephens and other opponents of President Jefferson Davis reflected his prewar loyalties within the Democratic party. After the Confederate defeat, he did not return to office.

BIBLIOGRAPHY

Nichols, Roy F. *The Disruption of American Democracy.* 1948.
Phillips, Ulrich B., ed., *The Correspondence of Robert Toombs, Alexander H. Stephens, and Howell Cobb.* 1913.
Simpson, John Eddins. *Howell Cobb: The Politics of Ambition.* 1973.

JOHANNA NICOL SHIELDS

COLD WAR. Toward the end of World War II, the uneasy alliance between the United States and the Soviet Union deteriorated as both countries positioned themselves to compete for influence in the postwar world. By 1947, the former allies had become bitter adversaries in a global geopolitical and ideological struggle that would last half a century. "Let us not be deceived," Bernard M. Baruch said at the outset of this struggle, "We are today in the midst of a cold war." His phrase neatly captured the ambiguity of international relations in a bipolar system dominated by two hostile superpowers: the world was neither at war nor at peace, but living in the twilight somewhere in between.

The Cold War had a profound effect on how the American political system dealt with foreign policy issues. The Constitution divides authority for foreign policy between Congress and the presidency so that the effective conduct of international affairs requires a partnership of the two branches. In E. S. Corwin's famous phrase, the division of power is also "an invitation to struggle." Since the founding of the Republic, there have been struggles aplenty, and the dominant role in foreign policy has swung between the branches.

The Cold War ushered in a period of executive dominance that went unchallenged for a generation. Not until the war in Vietnam did Congress endeavor to reassert an active role in formulating the nation's foreign policy—an activism that was fiercely resisted by the executive until the Cold War ended abruptly in the late 1980s.

The decades between the two world wars marked a period of congressional assertiveness. Spurred by the public's strong isolationist sentiment, Congress rejected American participation in the League of Nations in 1919 despite the best efforts of Woodrow Wilson. Even Franklin D. Roosevelt, who opened new vistas of presidential power in domestic affairs, was constrained by Congress in his ability to help the Allies in Europe resist the rise of Nazism.

During World War II, Congress acceded to presidential leadership, but with the return of peace came a reassertion of congressional prerogatives. In 1945 and 1946, Republicans assailed President Harry S. Truman's policy toward the Soviet Union as too soft, while at the same time advocating a domestic agenda of military demobilization and tax cuts that made global leadership impossible. The domestic policies were firmly rooted in public opinion reminiscent of prewar isolationism. People wanted the president to "bring the boys home" as soon as the war ended, and they were reluctant to pay for a large peacetime military establishment or a big foreign aid program to rebuild Europe.

In 1945, it was not certain that Congress would approve U.S. membership in the United Nations if the Republicans opposed it. Truman worked hard to build bipartisan support for his foreign policy, dealing primarily with Arthur H. Vandenberg of Michigan, a senior Republican on the Senate Foreign Relations Committee and later its chairman (1947–1949). Vandenberg was less of an isolationist than many other Republicans, but he was also a staunch defender of Congress's right to participate in foreign-policy–making. For both Truman and Vandenberg, a major impetus for cooperation was the memory of how the peace had been lost after World War I because of partisan bickering.

Prompted by Soviet actions in Eastern Europe and Republican criticism in Congress, Truman's policy toward the Soviet Union was moving to a harder line by late 1946. The event that crystallized that policy and marked the first major Cold War confrontation was the civil war in Greece. When Britain withdrew its backing from the anticommunist side, Washington was forced to decide whether it would take up the mantle of world leadership and use force to contain the expansion of Soviet influence.

At a famous White House meeting called to convince Republican congressional leaders of the necessity of interceding in Greece, Undersecretary of State Dean Acheson painted the struggle between the United States and the Soviet Union as a struggle between democracy and communism, between good and evil—a struggle every bit as urgent and morally compelling as the struggle against nazism and fascism had been. Vandenberg replied that if the president would explain his policy to the American people in exactly those terms, he would have Republican support. Truman agreed.

With Vandenberg's help, Truman won two landmark legislative battles against Republican isolationists. In May 1947, Congress approved aid for Greece and Turkey, thereby endorsing the Truman doctrine, which committed the United States to the global defense of nations threatened by communism. In March 1948, Congress approved the Marshall Plan for European reconstruction, which speeded economic recovery in the West, but reinforced the division of the continent into hostile blocs. With these two victories, Truman forged a bipartisan consensus on the need for the United States to serve as leader of the "free world" and global policeman.

Some foreign policy analysts, George Kennan foremost among them, were uneasy with the sweeping rhetoric of the Truman doctrine and the unlimited commitments it implied. Kennan worried that not even the United States had the capacity to police the globe, and that U.S. commitment in a region ought to be proportionate to the real interests at stake. But the rationale for America's Cold War foreign policy was not cast in terms of interests; it was a moral imperative that admitted of no bounds.

POSTWAR AID. At the beginning of the Cold War, partly as an effort to increase the influence of the United States in areas seen as vulnerable to communist domination, Congress returned for a special session to act on numerous foreign aid bills. Clifford K. Berryman, *Washington Evening Star*, 12 November 1947.

U.S. SENATE COLLECTION, CENTER FOR LEGISLATIVE ARCHIVES

The Manichaean rhetoric in which the Cold War struggle was presented to the American people had the intended effect of scaring them out of any isolationist instinct. It had the unintended effect of unleashing a witch-hunt. Congressional Republicans had used the issue of internal security as a partisan bludgeon to bash New Deal Democrats. The Truman administration, hoping to harness popular fears of domestic communists to rally support for the Marshall Plan, fed the tempest rather than resisting it. While Rep. Richard M. Nixon (R-Calif.) and the House Un-American Activities Committee (HUAC) were investigating Hollywood and Alger Hiss, Truman imposed loyalty tests on federal employees and inaugurated the attorney general's list of subversive organizations.

The growing hysteria over "the enemy within" successfully undercut Republican opposition to Truman's foreign policy, but like the sorcerer's apprentice, Truman could not control the demons he unleashed. The victory of Mao Zedong's Communist guerrillas in 1949 sparked Republican recriminations about who "lost" China, and the outbreak of the Korean War intensified the search for domestic traitors. In 1950, Congress passed the McCarran Act over Truman's veto, and Sen. Joseph R. McCarthy (R-Wis.) rose to prominence by charging that the government was riddled with communists. The resulting "red scare"—the investigation and persecution of suspected communists and communist sympathizers in the United States—constituted one of the worst threats to civil liberties in the history of the Republic, and its legacy poisoned domestic political discourse for the remainder of the Cold War.

Amid the anticommunist fervor of the late 1940s and early 1950s, Congress authorized fundamental and lasting structural changes in the executive branch. For the first time in its history, the United States built a peacetime military establishment that grew so large that even Dwight D. Eisenhower was moved to warn against the influence of the "military-industrial complex." The United States also built an intelligence apparatus with covert capabilities extending to nearly every nation in the world and a propaganda apparatus in the United States Information Agency (USIA) to wage global ideological war.

During the 1950s and 1960s, the intelligence agencies operated with little or no congressional scrutiny. Presidents authorized military interventions and covert operations from Latin America to the Far East without seeking congressional sanc-

tion and without fear of congressional challenge. The bipartisan consensus remained intact. So long as there was no disagreement over the basic aims and methods of foreign policy, Congress felt no compelling need to assert its authority.

Power that is not exercised atrophies. As the Cold War escalated, presidents no longer felt obligated to seek a declaration of war before committing American troops abroad, even to conflicts as vast as Korea and Vietnam. They authorized covert operations, including the subversion of foreign governments, without informing Congress. Only a handful of members even knew what the Central Intelligence Agency's budget was, and most preferred not to know.

The war in Vietnam ended congressional complacency. Domestic opposition to the war grew as U.S. policy faced the dilemma foreseen by Kennan. Vietnam was a country so far away, where tangible American interests were so slight, that the mounting cost of the war seemed patently out of proportion to any conceivable gain. The bipartisan consensus fractured.

To the chagrin of Lyndon B. Johnson, Democrats led the congressional revolt against the "imperial presidency." In 1966, televised hearings on Vietnam before J. William Fulbright's Senate Foreign Relations Committee spotlighted the growing division between "Cold War Democrats" and "antiwar Democrats." It marked the end of congressional acquiescence to presidential unilateralism in foreign policy. The revolt within Johnson's own party, capped by Eugene McCarthy's unexpectedly strong showing in the 1968 New Hampshire primary, prompted Johnson to quit the presidential race. His departure did not heal the rift among Democrats, however, and Richard M. Nixon succeeded to the presidency.

With a Republican in the White House, opposition to the war took on a more partisan flavor. Frustrated congressional Democrats soon discovered that it was not easy to end a war the president wanted to prosecute. In 1971, Congress repealed the Gulf of Tonkin Resolution, which had authorized Johnson's use of force against North Vietnam since 1964. Nixon took no notice. Efforts to halt appropriations for the war were routinely introduced, but during the first Nixon administration Congress could not bring itself to cut off support for American troops in the field.

Growing public frustration with the war, combined with the debilitation of the executive branch caused by the Watergate scandal, finally emboldened Congress to reclaim its foreign policy prerogatives. In 1973 and 1974, Congress passed seven different restrictions limiting the president's ability to spend funds for the war in Southeast Asia, finally prohibiting U.S. involvement in combat activities anywhere in the region.

Not content simply to end one war, Congress in 1973 passed the War Powers Resolution over Nixon's veto. The resolution sought to recapture the war power for Congress by specifying in detail what sorts of U.S. military involvement abroad required explicit congressional approval, by either resolution or declaration of war.

No subsequent president has fully accepted the constitutionality of the War Powers Resolution, and most have honored it just barely. On balance, the resolution did not achieve its authors' aim of returning to Congress the power to send the nation to war. At best, its passage put the executive branch on notice that U.S. involvement in hostilities abroad would be subject to congressional debate and challenge.

The congressional activism sparked by Vietnam was by no means restricted to issues of war and peace. Once Congress's acceptance of presidential leadership on foreign policy broke down, all issues became potential points of contention.

During the height of the Cold War (1947–1973), Congress had accepted the idea that foreign assistance was a necessary, albeit politically unpopular, instrument in the global struggle for influence between East and West. The criteria for providing aid were relatively straightforward: the United States helped countries that were strategically important and friendly to the United States, regardless of their domestic policies. Issues such as human rights were subordinated to the national security interest in building a network of anti-Soviet allies.

In the early 1970s, however, congressional activists began to look at aid programs as leverage to force recipients to modify their behavior, especially in the field of human rights. Moral complaints about how the United States conducted the war in Vietnam threw into disrepute the "realist" balance-of-power politics practiced by Secretary of State Henry Kissinger. Critics argued that American foreign policy should promote the values of American society. Human rights violations by U.S. allies in the less developed countries, heretofore tolerated, came under close congressional scrutiny.

In 1974, Congress cut off military assistance to the dictatorship in Chile and directed the president to reduce aid to any government guilty of a "consistent pattern of gross violations of internationally recognized human rights." The Ford administration ignored the injunction. In 1975, Congress adopted the Harkin amendment, sponsored by Rep. Tom Harkin (D-Iowa), prohibiting economic aid to human rights violators. A year later, the ban was extended to military assistance and sales. Finally, in 1977, Congress mandated that the United States oppose loans from international financial institutions to governments that violated human rights. More than six U.S. military assistance programs around the world were ended as a result of the legislation.

President Jimmy Carter embraced the human rights issue as his own, but Ronald Reagan regarded such limitations on military aid programs as crippling Washington's ability to halt the spread of Soviet influence in less developed countries. For the most part, he ignored existing human rights conditions on aid, simply refusing to characterize any U.S. ally as a gross human rights violator.

El Salvador proved to be the most contentious case. The U.S.-backed government was fighting the largest Marxist guerrilla army in Latin American history when Reagan assumed office. Carter had limited military aid to the Salvadoran regime, because of the military's horrendous human rights record. Reagan poured in more than $1 billion in military assistance, justifying it as essential to block a Soviet and Cuban thrust onto the North American mainland.

To prevent Reagan from ignoring the human rights issue, Congress passed a "certification" law in 1981, making continued military aid to El Salvador contingent upon a semi-annual presidential determination that the Salvadoran human rights situation was improving. Every six months, Reagan certified improvement, despite bitter complaints from congressional Democrats that the evidence proved the contrary. In the course of the decade, the Salvadoran military killed about sixty thousand unarmed combatants in its war against the left, but U.S. military aid continued to flow uninterrupted.

The Reagan administration's refusal to allow human rights legislation to constrain its military assistance programs showed how difficult it is for Congress to control presidential behavior if the president's attitude is one of defiance rather than cooperation. Congress's ultimate weapon—cutting off funding for a program—is a blunt one and its application often has a high cost. In the case of El Salvador, even Reagan's congressional opponents recognized that if military aid were ended, the government was likely to fall to the guerrillas. Many were unwilling to risk opening themselves to the charge that they "lost" El Salvador to communism.

In the wake of Vietnam and Watergate, Congress also sought to assert some measure of control over the conduct of intelligence operations. After its creation by the National Security Act of 1947, the CIA had been largely immune to congressional oversight. Defenders of the agency argued that the Soviet spy agency, the KGB, fought dirty in the covert theater of the Cold War, so the CIA had to be free to respond in kind.

Questionable CIA operations in Southeast Asia—particularly the Phoenix assassination program in Vietnam and the secret war in Laos—led to a full-fledged investigation of the agency in 1975 and 1976. The Senate investigation, headed by Frank Church (D-Idaho), revealed some of the CIA's most closely guarded secrets—what veteran intelligence officers called "the family jewels." During the 1960s, the CIA had plotted to assassinate various foreign leaders, including one scheme to kill Fidel Castro in which the agency teamed up with the Mafia. A CIA destabilization program had set the stage for the 1973 overthrow of the democratically elected Marxist government of Salvador Allende in Chile, ushering in a decade and a half of brutal military dictatorship. The agency had conducted brainwashing experiments in which psychokinetic drugs were tested on unwitting subjects. And during the heyday of the domestic opposition to Vietnam, the CIA had illegally spied on dissident American citizens, including members of Congress, inside the United States, in clear violation of its legal mandate.

Congress reacted to these revelations by establishing a new oversight system designed to keep the legislative branch adequately informed of covert operations and to assure that they had the approval of the president. The Hughes-Ryan Amendment, passed in 1974, required the president to sign a "finding" justifying every new covert operation and to convey that finding to Congress "in a timely fashion." Both the House and Senate created oversight committees with jurisdiction over the intelligence community's budget and operations.

In 1975, Congress for the first time voted to cut off funding for a covert operation when it passed the Clark Amendment (sponsored by Iowa senator Dick Clark) banning covert involvement in the Angolan civil war. Secretary of State Kissinger's argument that Angola was a new Soviet test of U.S. resolve in the wake of Vietnam was not enough to overcome congressional skepticism and fear that Angola could become "another Vietnam."

Ronald Reagan came to office determined to overcome the "Vietnam syndrome," which he believed had paralyzed American foreign policy for nearly a decade. The Cold War, Reagan insisted, had not waned during the 1970s era of détente. Washington's fearfulness had simply prevented the United States from challenging Soviet advances from Angola and Ethiopia to Grenada and Nicaragua. Reagan sought to reestablish executive preeminence in foreign policy, which inevitably meant confronting Congress. In addition to reinvigorating U.S. military relationships with friendly "moderate authoritarian" regimes, Reagan sought to revitalize the CIA's program of covert operations.

Reagan and CIA director William Casey believed that the United States should seize the initiative in the Cold War, seeking not merely to contain Soviet influence but to roll it back by destabilizing Soviet allies in the less developed countries. Under the Reagan doctrine, as this policy came to be known, covert operations were either launched or expanded against governments in Afghanistan, Cambodia, Laos, Grenada, and Nicaragua. Only Nicaragua proved to be controversial.

From the outset, Congress was skeptical of the covert war against the Marxist Sandinista government in Nicaragua. Although Nicaragua's close ties to Cuba and the Soviet Union were undeniable, such a small and poverty-stricken country seemed to pose little threat to the United States. And the rapacious behavior of the U.S.-backed Contra army seemed no better than that of the Sandinistas. In 1983, Congress voted to limit U.S. support for the Contras, and in 1984, it passed the Boland Amendment, sponsored by Rep. Edward P. Boland (D-Mass.), banning Contra aid entirely.

The Reagan administration circumvented the ban. Management of the covert aid program was moved from the CIA to the White House and run by National Security Council staff member Lt. Col. Oliver North. When the secret operation was revealed in late 1986 during the Iran-contra investigation, it touched off the most serious domestic political crisis since Watergate. Ironically, just before North's operation was uncovered, Congress had succumbed to Reagan's intensive lobbying and voted to lift the ban on Contra aid. The Iran-contra scandal, however, doomed any further U.S. military support for the Contras.

Nicaragua proved to be one of the last battlefields of the Cold War. By the time the Iran-contra scandal had subsided, relations between the United States and the Soviet Union were warming rapidly as a result of Mikhail Gorbachev's reforms. In 1990,

Moscow actively cooperated with Washington to assure that the Sandinistas conducted a fair election in Nicaragua and abided by the result.

The depth of the change in Soviet foreign policy became apparent in 1989, when the Red Army did not intervene to prevent the collapse of the communist regimes in Eastern Europe. The failure of the attempted coup against Gorbachev in 1991 marked the beginning of the disintegration of the Soviet state.

The end of the Cold War appeared to have a soothing effect on presidential-congressional relations in the field of foreign policy. With the United States left as the world's only military superpower, congressional fears that using military force abroad could lead to another quagmire seemed to recede. The waning of the Vietnam syndrome revived the idea that the United States should serve as a global policeman—a need that intensified with the ethnic and nationalist conflicts in the former communist states and beyond. In a reversal of recent roles, some congressional critics in 1994 demanded that President Bill Clinton intervene more actively in Bosnia and Haiti.

The disappearance of the Soviet threat also made the executive branch more willing to accept congressional insistence that foreign aid and trade preferences be tied to recipients' behavior on human rights, democracy, and nuclear proliferation. Presidents Bush and Clinton both emphasized that promoting democracy abroad rather than containing communism would be the principle aim of U.S. foreign policy in the post–Cold War era, and both found substantial congressional support.

With the end of the Cold War came a revival of some isolationist sentiment. Having defeated the international menace of communism, many Americans were inclined to look inward to domestic social and economic problems. Although Clinton was no isolationist, he nevertheless campaigned effectively against Bush by arguing that Bush was more interested in foreign policy than in America's domestic problems.

As the domestic economy struggled with huge budget deficits, the foreign aid program became a target for cost cutters. The political constituency for foreign aid had never been large; no longer justifiable as a bulwark against communist expansion, foreign aid to all but a few countries shrank to the vanishing point.

As the United States entered the post–Cold War era, both the president and the Congress seemed to be seeking a more balanced partnership in the field of foreign policy, rejecting the executive unilateral-ism of the early Cold War period and the bitter conflicts of the later period. At issue still was the question of whether the American public and its representatives in Congress would be willing to support a foreign policy of world leadership and engagement, with all its attendant costs, in the absence of the overarching international threat of communism.

BIBLIOGRAPHY

Arnson, Cynthia. *Crossroads: Congress, the Reagan Administration, and Central America.* 1993.

Crabb, Cecil V., Jr., and Pat M. Holt. *Invitation to Struggle: Congress, the President, and Foreign Policy.* 3d ed. 1989.

Destler, I. M., Leslie H. Gelb, and Anthony Lake. *Own Worst Enemy: The Unmaking of American Foreign Policy.* 1984.

Draper, Theodore. *A Very Thin Line: The Iran-Contra Affairs.* 1991.

Franck, Thomas M., and Edward Weisband. *Foreign Policy by Congress.* 1979.

Freeland, Richard M. *The Truman Doctrine and the Origins of McCarthyism.* 1971.

Gaddis, John Lewis. *Strategies of Containment: A Critical Appraisal of Postwar American National Security Policy.* 1982.

Gaddis, John Lewis. *The United States and the Origins of the Cold War, 1941–1947.* 1972.

Gibbons, William Conrad. *The U.S. Government and the Vietnam War: Executive and Legislative Roles and Relationships.* Parts I and II. 1985.

Halberstam, David. *The Best and the Brightest.* 1972.

Johnson, Loch K. *A Season of Inquiry: Congress and Intelligence.* 1988.

Navasky, Victor S. *Naming Names.* 1980.

Schoultz, Lars. *Human Rights and United States Policy toward Latin America.* 1981.

WILLIAM M. LEOGRANDE

COLFAX, SCHUYLER

COLFAX, SCHUYLER (1823–1885), Whig editor and politician, Republican representative from Indiana, Speaker of the House (1863–1869), and vice president (1869–1873). Widely admired for his skills as presiding officer, Colfax ended his political career tarnished by scandal and belittled for his affability.

Colfax was a loyal party man, uncreative and cautious. A Whig delegate to Indiana's 1850 constitutional convention, he showed himself hostile to slavery and friendly to rights for blacks, but careful not to go far beyond what voters in his district would accept. At the height of anti-Catholic hysteria in 1854, he even joined the Know-Nothings, converting to Republicanism only a year later.

SCHUYLER COLFAX. As vice president.

PERLEY'S REMINISCENCES, VOL. 2

Colfax's record in the House, where he served from 1855 to 1869, left no mark in the statute books. His good nature earned him the sobriquet "Smiler," though a *New York World* reporter (21 January 1870) saw his face as that of a hypocrite set in "the shape of a smile without its humor." Still, he proved a capable Speaker during Reconstruction. The *Cincinnati Commercial* (20 December 1866) credited his vigilance alone with keeping the House from dissolving into "a disorganized mob—worse and more chaotic than any town meeting." A soothing demeanor helped mollify both Radical and conservative Republicans, no easy accomplishment. The House sustained his rulings whenever they were challenged, and his successors would build on some of the precedents he set. "High and central over the debates sits a mild-mannered gentleman, after whom three hundred babies (none of his own) have been named by admiring mothers in the South Bend district of Indiana," the *Independent* (12 April 1866) opined. "O, urbanity, thy name is Colfax!"

Still, despite the esteem in which he was held for his capacity, quick wit, and impartiality, his good nature made him easy to dismiss as a "good fellow"

but no "great man" (*Independent*, 19 April 1866). Thrice Speaker, he was still an immensely popular figure when he left the House to serve as Ulysses S. Grant's vice president, only to retire from politics four years later under a barrage of criticism. What damaged him most was his scramble for money. On a cross-country tour, he lectured nightly, delivering well-paid encomiums to the Northern Pacific Railroad. He accepted every gift that came his way, from free railway passes to silver utensils. When Colfax was accused of involvement in the Crédit Mobilier scandal, his sanctimonious attitude and the improbability of his explanations dealt a last, fatal blow to his political future—though he may actually have been telling the truth.

Already having declined a second term as vice president in 1872 (and reconsidering too late), Colfax quickly faded from the public eye. His charm has ultimately worked against him in historical memory. "Colfax's name always suggests the warmth of a summer afternoon," wrote a historian of the speakership early in the twentieth century, and that seems a fair evaluation of so beaming and temperate a partisan.

BIBLIOGRAPHY

Hollister, Ovando J. *The Life of Schuyler Colfax.* 1886.
Smith, Willard H. *Schuyler Colfax: The Changing Fortunes of a Political Idol.* 1952.

MARK WAHLGREN SUMMERS

COLORADO. Congress created the Colorado Territory, with the same boundaries as the present state, in February 1861, soon after voting statehood for Kansas with its present western boundaries. (There had been an earlier indigenous effort to convert the "homemade" Jefferson Territory into a congressionally sanctioned entity.) Colorado remained a territory for fifteen years. Attempts to gain statehood failed in 1864, 1865, 1866, and again in 1868. Bitter factional divisions among the Republicans in the territory and the slow growth of population combined to defeat all these efforts. Finally, in March 1875, after Congress approved enabling legislation, delegates were elected to a constitutional convention and on 1 July 1876 voters overwhelmingly approved the constitution drafted by the convention by a vote of 15,443 to 4,062. President Ulysses S. Grant proclaimed Colorado a state on 1 August 1876.

The "Centennial State" was entitled to two senators and one representative. The first representative, Democrat Thomas M. Patterson, was chosen over the Republican candidate, James B. Belford, by the House of Representatives after the election returns became hopelessly contested and disputed. A second member of the House of Representatives was authorized after the 1890 census, a third district was created ten years later, and a fourth followed the 1910 enumeration. For the next six decades no further change occurred. Then, after both the 1970 and 1980 censuses, an additional seat was allotted, bringing the delegation up to two senators and six representatives.

Generally the delegation has been divided between the two major political parties. Exceptions include the 1890s and early years of the twentieth century, when Populists and Fusionists (often Republicans supporting the "free silver" issue) were elected; 1912, when the Democrats held both Senate seats and all four seats in the House; and the years from 1934 to 1938, when Democrats repeated that success. Only six of Colorado's twenty-nine senators in the years from 1876 to 1990 were members of the House of Representatives before gaining their Senate seats. In the early era, men who had amassed personal fortunes in mining were chosen senators by the state legislature; more recently, most senators have had previous experience in state governance.

Henry M. Teller was one of the first two senators from Colorado. He began his career as a Republican but shifted to the Democratic party on the silver issue, serving as U.S. senator from 1876 to 1882 and again from 1885 to 1909. He sponsored the amendment renouncing U.S. intent to annex Cuba in 1898 at the time of the declaration of war with Spain. He has been termed "the first statesman of national stature to emerge from Colorado politics."

Long-tenured representatives include Edward T. Taylor, a Democrat, elected from the 4th (Western Slope) District for fifteen terms (1909–1941), and Wayne N. Aspinall, also a Democrat from the Western Slope, who served twelve terms (1949–1973). Rep. Patricia Schroeder, another Democrat, became the first woman from Colorado to serve in Congress in 1973.

BIBLIOGRAPHY

Abbott, Carl. *Colorado: A History of the Centennial State.* 1976.
Ubbelohde, Carl, Maxine Benson, and Duane A. Smith. *A Colorado History.* 6th ed. 1988.

CARL UBBELOHDE

COMITY. The norms that sustain cordial relations in decision-making bodies and that facilitate the bargaining essential to policy-making are collectively referred to as comity. At the core of comity are courtesy and reciprocity. The tenets that sustain comity are institutional patriotism, apprenticeship, specialization, and hard work.

Members of Congress are expected to respect one another. This courtesy builds mutual confidence by creating a veneer of friendliness that often translates into good working relationships among legislators of different parties and ideologies. Most party leaders have enjoyed good personal relationships in the twentieth century. Members must not make unflattering comments about each other. They routinely refer to one another as "my good friend" and "the distinguished gentleman (gentlewoman)." Reciprocity makes compromise possible by enabling legislators across the spectrum to negotiate with each other. Members regularly exchange votes for constituency projects in what has become known as "logrolling." Institutional patriotism puts devotion to congressional procedures ahead of individual goals. Apprenticeship depersonalizes conflicts over power by setting up a prescribed order of advancement. Under this norm junior members were expected to keep their counsel and not even to speak on the floor until the leadership gave them their political baptism. Specialization divides the labor of legislation and promotes exchanges (reciprocity) among expert committees. Hard work encourages members to be workhorses rather than show horses.

There is no consensus as to when the norms took hold. Estimates range from the mid-nineteenth century to the early twentieth century. Comity has declined since the late 1960s, as the system of norms has frayed. Specialization and hard work are still valued, but apprenticeship, institutional patriotism, and especially courtesy and reciprocity have waned, leading to stalemate in the Congress since the 1970s.

BIBLIOGRAPHY

Matthews, Donald R. 1960. *U.S. Senators and Their World.* 1960.
Uslaner, Eric M. *The Decline of Comity in Congress.* 1993.

ERIC M. USLANER

COMMEMORATIVE LEGISLATION. For more than two centuries Congress has formally recognized especially noteworthy individuals, causes,

Perpetual Commemoratives

DATE ENACTED	EVENT
8 May 1914	Mother's Day
24 April 1972	Father's Day
6 September 1979	National Grandparents' Day
18 May 1928	Child Health Day
22 September 1959[1]	
20 May 1933	National Maritime Day
30 April 1934	Columbus Day
23 June 1936	Gold Star Mother's Day
16 August 1937	Commemoration of Thomas Jefferson's Birth
28 March 1938	Cancer Control Month
11 May 1939	Aviation Day
10 October 1940	Pan American Aviation Day
29 February 1952	Citizenship Day
11 August 1945[2]	National Disability Employment Awareness Month
8 October 1970[3]	
7 November 1988[4]	
30 June 1948	National Freedom Day
3 August 1949	Flag Day
9 June 1966	National Flag Week
13 June 1975	Honor America Days
27 October 1951	Stephen Foster Memorial Day
2 August 1956	Constitution Week
16 May 1957	National Defense Transportation Day

[1]Day of commemoration for Child Health Day changed from "May 1" to the "first Monday in October."
[2]Initially designated "National Employ the Physically Handicapped Week."
[3]Commemorative broadened to include all handicapped workers.
[4]Commemorative designation changed to "National Disability Employment Awareness Month."

and events. The Continental Congress used the earliest commemoratives, individually struck medals, to express public gratitude for distinguished contributions, to dramatize the virtues of patriotism, and to perpetuate the remembrance of significant events of the American Revolution.

Independence from Great Britain had not yet been proclaimed when, on 25 March 1776, George Washington was tendered the first congressional gold medal for his "wise and spirited conduct" in bringing about the evacuation of the British from Boston. Congress has since (through one of its longest-running customs) periodically commissioned more than one hundred individually struck gold medals bearing the portraits of those honored or images of the events in which they participated. Recipients have included actors, acclaimed lifesavers, aeronautical and space pioneers, antarctic explorers, athletes, authors, entertainers, military leaders, musicians, scientists, and political leaders, as well as

notable Americans and foreigners from other walks of life. The American Red Cross was similarly honored in 1979. Bronze duplicates of each medal are available to the public through the Bureau of Engraving and Printing.

During the nineteenth century Congress gradually broadened the scope of commemorative legislation by creating federal holidays, recommending special days for national observances, funding monuments and memorials, commissioning busts and painted portraits, authorizing the minting of commemorative coins, and establishing commissions to celebrate important anniversaries. These resolutions included everything from a commemorative half dollar for the World's Columbian Exposition of 1892 in Chicago and a commission to celebrate the 1876 centennial of the signing of the Declaration of Independence to a gold chronometer presented to Capt. James G. Smith of the British brig *Victoria* in appreciation of his rescue of the of-

Perpetual Commemoratives (Continued)

DATE ENACTED	EVENT
4 June 1958	National Safe Boating Week
3 October 1980[5]	
18 July 1958	Loyalty Day
13 September 1960	National Forest Products Week
7 April 1961	Law Day USA
26 September 1961	National Poison Prevention Week
14 May 1962	National Transportation Week
1 October 1962	Peace Officers Memorial Day
9 October 1962	National School Lunch Week
17 December 1963	Wright Brothers Day
30 December 1963	Save Your Vision Week
30 December 1963	American Heart Month
2 September 1964	Leif Erikson Day
6 October 1964	White Cane Safety Day
2 November 1966	Steelmark Month
17 September 1968	National Hispanic Heritage Month
17 August 1988[6]	
11 May 1950	Memorial Day as Day of Prayer for Permanent Peace
17 April 1952	National Day of Prayer
8 May 1988[7]	
27 August 1986	Federal Lands Cleanup Day

[5]Week of commemoration changed from "week which includes July 4" to "week commencing on the first Sunday in June."
[6]Commemoration designation changed from "National Hispanic Heritage Week" to "National Hispanic Heritage Month."
[7]Day of Commemoration changed from "a suitable day each year other than Sunday" to "the first Thursday in May each year."
SOURCE: Congressional Research Service (April 1993).

ficers, crew, and passengers of the American brig *E. H. Fitler* in 1867.

In the twentieth century, Congress has increasingly used commemorative legislation to name public buildings, dams, scholarships, fellowships, and historic sites. Since 1981, commemorative observances (special days, weeks, months, and years) have been the most popular commemorative legislation by far. These resolutions authorize the president to issue proclamations "calling upon the people of the United States" to observe the occasion with appropriate programs, ceremonies, and activities.

Presidents can issue commemorative proclamations without congressional request and did so regularly until the administration of Ronald Reagan (1981–1989). During the 1980s, Congress initiated most observances. They included, for example, Anne Frank Day, National Theater Week, National Ice Cream Month, and Oil Heat Centennial Year.

While Congress approves most commemorative observances only for a particular year, since 1914 it has approved nearly forty perpetual observances that call for the president to issue annual proclamations.

Before 1900, commemoratives rarely comprised more than 1 percent of all legislation enacted by a particular Congress and never exceeded 5 percent until the 85th Congress (1957–1959). During the next two decades commemoratives accounted for 5 to nearly 10 percent of all legislation.

Then a dramatic change occurred. In the 96th Congress (1979–1981) commemorative legislation increased by more than 70 percent. In the next Congress commemoratives rose by nearly 50 percent. By the 98th Congress (1983–1985) they constituted more than one-third of all bills signed into law by the president, with special observances (commemorative days, weeks, months, and years) making up nearly 80 percent of that total.

Because commemorative legislation is so diverse, jurisdiction over such bills belongs to several House and Senate committees. Holidays and commemoratives, for example, are generally handled by the Subcommittee on Census and Population of the House Post Office and Civil Service Committee and by the Senate Judiciary Committee. Commemorative coins and medals are the responsibility of the Subcommittee on Consumer Affairs and Coinage of the House Committee on Banking, Finance, and Urban Affairs and of the Senate Committee on Banking, Housing, and Urban Affairs.

While commemorative legislation is usually not complicated—frequently requiring neither hearings nor reports—it has proved costly to Congress's image. As commemorative observances became increasingly popular in the 1980s, the media frequently poked fun at what they perceived to be misplaced priorities. Strict House and Senate procedures for considering commemorative observances, adopted in the mid 1980s, specify that no measure may commemorate: a commercial enterprise, industry, specific product, or fraternal, political, business, labor, or sectarian organization; a particular state or any political subdivision, including city, town, county, school, or institution of higher learning; or a living person. Committee policy also provides that this type of commemorative legislation not be reported in the House or taken up by the Senate unless at least half the members of the originating chamber have agreed to cosponsor it. Still, commemorative observances continue to be approved in large numbers.

Members advocating reform of the commemorative process have argued that commemoratives are too costly and that Congress should devote its efforts to bills addressing substantive issues. Estimates of the total cost of all commemorative observances range from $100,000 to $1 million annually. These concerns prompted several proposals either to prohibit Congress from considering such legislation or to establish an independent advisory commission to determine what will be honored.

During February 1990 congressional hearings on a proposed advisory commission on national commemorative events, reformers argued that a commission would save Congress time and money and might ensure a more coordinated and rational commemorative process. Opponents of reform maintained that commemorative legislation serves an important constituency function and provides an important forum for organizations engaged in a broad range of charitable and public services. Certainly the system needs to be fine-tuned, they argued, but it should not be disregarded.

Several factors have contributed to the spectacular growth of commemorative observances since 1980. These include more organized lobbying efforts; an increased attentiveness to constituents, due in large part to the electronic media's broader coverage of Congress; a renewed empathy for philanthropic institutions; and the attractiveness of commemoratives for satisfying a multitude of constituencies at little cost. Despite the tendency of the media to dismiss such legislation as trivial, the sheer number of commemoratives being introduced and enacted is evidence of the primacy of the constituency role for members of Congress.

BIBLIOGRAPHY

Stathis, Stephen W. *Commemorative Legislation.* Congressional Research Service, Library of Congress. CRS Rept. 93-407 GOV. 1993.

U.S. House of Representatives. *Advisory Commission on Commemorative Events.* 101st Cong., 2d sess., 1990. Serial No. 101-42.

STEPHEN W. STATHIS

COMMERCE, SCIENCE, AND TRANSPORTATION COMMITTEE, SENATE.

The Committee on Commerce, Science, and Transportation has one of the widest-ranging jurisdictions of the seventeen standing committees in the Senate. The present-day committee traces its roots back to the Committee on Commerce and Manufactures, which was created in 1816 when the Senate first established standing committees charged with legislative duties. Tension between manufacturing and trade interests over the tariff issue led to the creation of a separate Manufactures Committee in 1825, and the original committee was renamed the Committee on Commerce. These two committees existed separately until the Legislative Reorganization Act of 1946, when they again were joined, this time as the Committee on Interstate and Foreign Commerce. The reorganization of 1946 also incorporated two other committees under Interstate and Foreign Commerce: the Committee on Interstate Commerce and the Committee on Interoceanic Canals. In 1961, a Senate resolution simplified the name of the committee to the Committee on Commerce; in 1977, it became the Committee on Commerce, Science, and Transportation. In short, the core of the committee's jurisdiction always has included matters related to commerce, but the specific policy issues under its purview have changed considerably over time.

The Committee's Changing Jurisdiction. The committee's jurisdiction has changed significantly several times as a result of entrepreneurial efforts to expand its jurisdiction. Perhaps the best example occurred in the mid 1960s, when Chairman Warren G. Magnuson (D-Wash.) pushed the committee into the area of consumer protection. As David E. Price (1972) documents, committee activity on these issues was driven largely by the political motives of Magnuson and an ambitious staff seeking a new legislative niche for its chairman. While this initial movement into consumer protection encompassed issues such as fair package labeling and traffic safety, the committee eventually came to enjoy a wide claim to consumer affairs issues as a result of Magnuson's agenda entrepreneurship. Indeed, the 1977 jurisdictional reforms in the Senate formally ratified the committee's jurisdiction over the regulation of consumer products and services.

The 1977 committee reforms also granted Commerce, Science, and Transportation jurisdiction over space programs with the abolition of the Aeronautics and Space Sciences Committee. At the same time, the reforms threatened to eliminate the committee's jurisdiction over coastal-zone management and related matters. However, strong objections from several coastal state committee members, especially Magnuson, Ernest F. Hollings (D-S.C.), and Russell B. Long (D-La.), resulted in the preservation of this part of the committee's jurisdiction.

After the 1977 reforms, the committee expanded gradually through bill referral precedents. While the pace of expansion was considerably slower than that of its House counterpart, the Energy and Commerce Committee, the Senate committee did move into some new and important legislative areas. As concerns over the competitiveness of U.S. firms in international markets grew during the 1980s, the committee moved more aggressively into trade issues that had previously rested more squarely within the province of the Senate Finance Committee. Hollings, who became chairman in 1987, found such jurisdictional excursions valuable for protecting the large textile industry in his home state, which had been losing jobs and market share to foreign firms. As chairman, Hollings also engineered the committee's claim to issues related to the development of high-technology industries. And from the early 1980s on, the committee's actions on such issues as product liability and methanol-based fuel represented significant policy initiatives not obvi-

ously reflected in the committee's statutory jurisdiction. The committee's jurisdiction in the 1990s spanned the domains of communications, including telecommunications, cable television, and broadcasting; transportation, including highway safety, inland waterways, common carrier regulation, and the transportation of toxic substances; oceans policies, including marine and ocean navigation, the Merchant Marine, the Coast Guard, marine fisheries, and coastal zone management; consumer protection and product liability; space programs; travel and tourism; private insurance regulation; and even professional sports.

Committee Leadership. The leadership of the Commerce, Science, and Transportation Committee underwent relatively frequent turnover after 1977. After chairing for nearly twenty-five years, Magnuson stepped down in 1977 and was succeeded by Howard W. Cannon (D-Nev.). But Cannon's chairmanship was short-lived and marked the beginning of a period of high turnover. In part, this can be attributed to the changes in party control of the Senate. But even during the six years of a Republican majority (1981–1987), there were two different committee chairmen. Bob Packwood (R-Oreg.) led the committee from 1981 to 1984, and John C. Danforth (R-Mo.) took over the chair in 1985, when Packwood chose to head the Finance Committee. After the Democrats regained control of the Senate in the 1986 elections, Hollings served as chairman, Danforth becoming the ranking minority member.

Despite frequent changes in the committee's leadership, the demands placed on committee leaders and their responses to these demands have remained relatively stable. By dint of its highly diverse jurisdiction, the work load of the committee is one of the largest in the Senate, one that requires a great deal of coordination if it is to be handled effectively. But much of the committee's work is of rather low salience to many committee members, so the leaders often can allow the rank and file substantial independence without fear that it will cause conflict. From Magnuson's tenure on, committee leaders have tended to retain control over the major formal prerogatives while allowing other members substantial independence in practice. All markups continue to be held in full committee, giving the chairman important formal prerogatives that have devolved to subcommittee leaders in some other Senate committees. Similarly, decisions on majority and minority staff hiring and assignment remain largely the responsibility of the respective committee leaders. Control over the committee's agenda certainly helps the chairmen to pursue their own legislative goals and is also an important source of power. For instance, Hollings has used his agenda powers to move cable television regulation quickly through committee.

Of course, leadership is, at least in part, followership, and the Commerce, Science, and Transportation Committee leaders are no exception to this rule. While they have succeeded in retaining control over such formal prerogatives as scheduling markups and hiring staff, committee leaders have clearly been able to do so in part because they have considered the views of the committee rank and file. Price (1972) asserts that Magnuson ran the committee with an eye toward achieving consensus and making sure that members with a particular interest in a piece of legislation had a chance to have those interests incorporated into the bill. Likewise, C. Lawrence Evans (1991) notes that when Danforth became chairman in 1985, he was sensitive to members' objections to the content of proposals. Hollings continued the emphasis on consensus and allowed subcommittees to operate with some independence. While pursuing legislation of concern to him, he allowed other committee members an active role in shaping the bills that interested them. In sum, the relative centralization of the committee persisted not so much because its leaders tightly held onto and exploited their prerogatives but rather because of their responsiveness to the political interests of committee members.

The emphasis that these leaders placed on consensus and coordination also is reflected in the relatively close working relationships between majority and minority leaders. Danforth worked closely with Hollings when Danforth was chairman and Hollings the ranking minority member, and the two men continued to consult with each other frequently after their positions were reversed. In particular, Danforth's restrained leadership style frequently defused emerging conflicts on the committee.

Committee Composition. If the committee's leadership has been consensus oriented, it has been helped in this regard by the panel's composition. Because of the breadth of the committee's jurisdiction, members with a wide range of policy interests are attracted to it. The vast majority of the committee's members sought a seat on it because of its relevance to their constituents' interests. Evans (1991) claims that members come to the committee to help private industries and other economic interests particular to their home states. Lacking clear regional affinities or mutually compatible con-

stituency interests, the committee is fairly heterogeneous in terms of the values, priorities, and preferences of its members.

Unlike other heterogeneous committees (House Energy and Commerce, for example), however, the diversity of interests on Senate Commerce, Science, and Transportation does not often produce significant internal divisions. First, the salience of most committee issues is quite low in the eyes of the membership as a whole. Particular subsets of committee members will be intensely interested in particular bills, but given the diversity of the committee's agenda, these interested subsets tend to be small, with their composition varying across issues. Second, the committee's major issues do not often evoke strong ideological impulses, so there has been some tendency for the committee to attract relatively moderate legislators. This characteristic of the committee's membership seems to be relatively stable. Price's 1972 study of the committee in the mid 1960s and Evans's study twenty years later both emphasized the moderate character of the committee's membership.

This is not to say that the committee is without conflict. While many issues within the committee's jurisdiction evoke the intense preferences of relatively few committee members, other issues have much broader policy implications and, thus, much larger audiences on the committee. In the 1960s, for instance, consumer protection legislation had more far-reaching effects than most committee bills. More recently, the Federal Trade Commission's efforts to regulate the professions in the 1980s, product liability, and tort reform were committee issues involving significantly broader interests, and thus more conflict, than typical committee concerns. Although these sorts of bills are the exception in the committee, it is important to recognize that panel members at times find the committee's jurisdiction relevant to their broader policy concerns. At such times, the committee's usual tendency toward consensus grows weaker.

Committee Decision Making. Because the formal authority to mark up legislation remains with the full panel, decision making in the Commerce, Science, and Transportation Committee is more highly centralized than in many other committees. Still, this formal authority is only one aspect of committee decision making, and it is important to recognize the many ways in which committee deliberations have become more decentralized over the last two decades. As they have throughout Congress, subcommittees have become increasingly important locations for much of the committee's legislative work. Commerce subcommittees typically hold hearings on bills within their jurisdiction, whereas Price (1972) found that a majority of the hearings on bills during the 1960s were conducted at the full committee level. At the information-gathering stage, then, subcommittees have become more important, even if they remain relatively weak in their formal prerogatives. Moreover, committee staff have become increasingly specialized, with some staffers assigned to specific subcommittees. This shift has helped subcommittee leaders to develop the expertise and political intelligence that enhance a panel's power at subsequent stages of the legislative process.

Finally, it should be noted that these sorts of informational advantages become especially important given how selective participation in committee decision making can be. While the typical Commerce, Science, and Transportation subcommittee is composed of from five to fifteen members, even these small numbers typically overstate the number of members who seriously participate in framing a committee bill. As Richard L. Hall (1993) points out, senators' involvement on issues is shaped less by their mere panel membership than by other factors: personal policy or constituency interests; the opportunity costs to them in terms of some other activity that might be displaced; and the time and resources they are able to commit relative to potential committee competitors. In view of the heavy demands on legislative time and staff, many participate actively during pre-floor consideration.

Another important feature of decision making concerns the committee's relationship with external groups and actors. With its broad jurisdiction, the committee deals with a wide range of interest groups. On many issues, such as the cigarette labeling legislation of the 1960s or the changes in policies related to long-distance telephone service in the 1980s, the committee confronts highly organized, politically sophisticated private interest

MEETING OF THE SENATE COMMERCE COMMITTEE. *Left to right*, Clifford P. Hansen (R-Wyo.), James B. Pearson (R-Kans.), Norris Cotton (R-N.H.), and committee chairman Warren G. Magnuson (D-Wash.).

groups such as the tobacco lobby or the telecommunications industry. These relatively narrow groups often have important constituency ties to the committee members who are most active on the particular bill. But some issues affect much broader interests, and in these instances the committee often deals with important public interest groups. For example, Ralph Nader's fledgling movement in the 1960s to improve traffic safety eventually had a significant impact on the committee's actions in that area, and today virtually all of the consumer-related legislation the committee produces involves interactions with similar public interest groups. In short, interactions with interest groups run the gamut, although commercial, resource-rich interests are invariably the most prominent.

The Committee and the Senate. In the Senate, every committee interested in passing legislation must anticipate the more-or-less intense preferences of committee nonmembers. Every senator, regardless of committee assignment, enjoys substantial latitude to amend, delay, or obstruct a bill reported out of the committee with jurisdiction. Indeed, Steven S. Smith (*Call to Order*, 1989) shows that floor amending in the Senate has grown considerably more common over the last three decades and that consistently more than half those amendments have been sponsored by a member not on the committee of origin. However, less than one bill out of four reported by the Committee on Commerce, Science, and Technology has been amended from the floor since the early 1950s. No doubt this pattern is due in part to the fact that most of the committee's bills deal with state-specific concerns and so are low in salience to the wider membership. But there is little reason to expect considerable conflict between the committee and the Senate. Relatively heterogeneous in membership, consensus-oriented in its internal decision-making processes, and moderate in its preferences, the committee tends more than most others to produce legislation that roughly agrees with the preferences of the Senate majority.

[*See also* Energy and Commerce Committee, House; Public Works and Transportation Committee, House.]

BIBLIOGRAPHY

Evans, C. Lawrence. *Leadership in Committees.* 1991.
Hall, Richard L. "Participation, Abdication, and Representation in Congressional Committees." In *Congress Reconsidered.* Edited by Lawrence Dodd and Bruce I. Oppenheimer. 5th ed. 1993.
Price, David E. *Who Makes the Laws?* 1972.
U.S. Senate. Committee on Commerce. *History, Membership, and Jurisdiction of the Senate Committee on Commerce from 1816 to 1966.* 89th Cong., 2d sess., 1966. S. Doc. 100.

GARY McKISSICK and RICHARD L. HALL

COMMERCE POWER. One of the central problems with the Articles of Confederation was the ineffective powers of regulation of commerce bestowed on the Continental Congress. For that reason, as James Madison explained in *Federalist* 42, the Constitution in Article I, section 8 specifically empowers Congress "to regulate Commerce with foreign Nations, and among the several States, and with Indian tribes." Initially, Congress confined itself to regulating foreign commerce and did not assert its power domestically. In the absence of congressional legislation in the early nineteenth century, the Supreme Court nevertheless laid the basis for expanding congressional power under the commerce clause. Ironically, in the late nineteenth and early twentieth century, when Congress asserted its power over interstate commerce, the Court then sought to curb the legislature. But during the 1937 battle over the New Deal, the Court retreated, and since then Congress has regulated an ever-wider range of social and economic activities in the United States. On the basis of the commerce clause, Congress has authorized the regulation of monopolies, labor relations, and telecommunications; has expanded protection of civil rights and civil liberties, along with health, safety, and the environment; and has greatly enlarged the scope of federal criminal law. As a result, the power of Congress and the federal government has grown enormously, preempting state power in many areas.

Congress remained reluctant to assert its authority over interstate commerce until after the Civil War. Yet in *Gibbons v. Ogden* (22 U.S. 1 [1824]), Chief Justice John Marshall set forth enduring constitutional law principles to govern Congress's exercise of power over commerce. Marshall held that congressional power is plenary, and he broadly defined "commerce" as all "intercourse" that "affects more states than one." His standard for determining the scope of congressional power was nationalist, which would prove to be important in securing the freedom of interstate transportation. *Gibbons* and other rulings of the Marshall Court (1801–1835) eliminated tax and tariff barriers erected by the states, laid the basis for a national "common market," and promoted nationwide economic

Federal Statutes Preempting State Authority, 1790–1991

	CIVIL RIGHTS	COMMERCE	HEALTH, SAFETY, AND NATURAL RESOURCES	TAX, FINANCE, AND MISCELLANEOUS	TOTAL
Before 1900	7	15	5	3	30
1900–1909	—	7	7	—	14
1910–1919	—	16	4	2	22
1920–1929	—	12	3	2	17
1930–1939	—	21	2	10	33
1940–1949	—	9	5	2	16
1950–1959	1	10	9	7	27
1960–1969	7	9	26	5	47
1970–1979	10	31	41	26	108
1980–1989	6	35	32	27	100
1990–1991	2	11	6	6	25
Total	33	176	140	90	439

growth. In addition, the Marshall Court's definition of commerce as "intercourse among the states" later served as a basis for upholding federal regulation of activities as wide-ranging as the sale of lottery tickets, prostitution, telecommunications, and the disposal of hazardous wastes.

Gibbons also implied a distinction between Congress's power over interstate commerce and that of the states over intrastate commerce. Although holding that the power of Congress does not "stop at the external boundary line of each State, but may be introduced into the interior," Marshall observed that "the completely internal commerce of a State may be considered as reserved for the State itself." Relying on that dictum the Court under Chief Justice Roger B. Taney (1836–1864) developed the distinction between interstate commerce (which Congress may regulate) and intrastate commerce (which the states may regulate). The constitutional law touchstone for determining the respective powers of Congress and the states became whether or not commerce crossed state lines. But because Congress did not generally assert its power over commerce until after the Civil War, the Court could, and did, uphold state regulations while not directly challenging Congress's power under the commerce clause.

In the late nineteenth century, though, the distinction between interstate and intrastate was used to limit congressional power. This development reflected political changes in both Congress and the Court. A new era in government regulation was inaugurated with congressional passage of the Interstate Commerce Act of 1887 and the Sherman Antitrust Act of 1890. The Interstate Commerce Act created the Interstate Commerce Commission, the first regulatory commission in the United States, and authorized it to regulate the operation of interstate railroads. The Sherman Antitrust Act made it illegal for interstate businesses to form trusts, combinations, or monopolies.

This expansion of congressional power was due to economic and political pressures brought by the Industrial Revolution. It also registered a new conception (that had developed during the Civil War–Reconstruction era) of the federal government's role in promoting national interests. Industries, railroad companies, and corporations opposing federal regulation contended that only states could regulate their own activities, even though states could not regulate businesses operating in more than one commonwealth. Coincidentally, the Court's composition changed with the addition of justices who had been corporate lawyers and sympathized with private business interests. In 1888, Melville Fuller, a successful commercial attorney, was appointed chief justice, and he was followed by several other justices who embraced laissez-faire capitalism and opposed progressive social and economic legislation.

Between 1887 and 1937, more than fifty congressional acts were struck down by the Court on the basis of the line drawn between interstate and intrastate commerce. In challenging congressional power, the Court invented additional rules for further defining the boundaries between the powers of the states and those of Congress. One of the most important was the distinction drawn between the activities of production or manufacturing (over which states enjoyed virtually exclusive authority), and those of distribution or transportation (which Congress might regulate). This production and distribution rule enabled the Court to uphold state regulation or taxation of commercial interests that sought exemption by claiming that their activities were subject only to congressional regulation. And the rule also empowered the Court to strike down federal regulations and thereby limit the reach of congressional power.

United States v. E. C. Knight Company (156 U.S. 1 [1895]) illustrates the Court's use of the production and distribution rule in the late nineteenth century to defeat Congress's power under the commerce clause. A majority ruled that the Sherman Antitrust Act's regulation of monopolies did not apply to the country's largest sugar refining company. In the Court's view, the company's production of sugar was an entirely local activity, even though E.C. Knight controlled the distribution of 99 percent of all sugar in the United States.

The Court later applied the production and distribution rule to limit the scope of congressional power over mining, fishing, farming, oil production, and hydroelectric power. The most extreme use of the Court's rule in thwarting congressional power came in *Hammer v. Dagenhart* (247 U.S. 251 [1918]), which struck down the Keating-Owen Child Labor Act of 1916. A bare majority on the Court ruled that Congress impermissibly barred interstate shipment of goods produced in factories that employed children under fourteen or allowed children between the ages of fourteen and sixteen to work more than eight hours a day or more than six days a week. Justice William Day construed Congress's power over commerce to be limited to regulating the means of transportation. Earlier cases upholding congressional regulation of lottery tickets, prostitution, and impure food were distinguished on the ground that those goods were harmful per se, whereas goods produced by child labor were deemed harmless in themselves.

Even when progressive congressional legislation was upheld in the early twentieth century, the Court relied on other formalistic rules and tests derived from the distinction between interstate and intrastate commerce. For example, the Court deliberated on federal regulation based on whether or not an activity within a state had an obvious effect on interstate commerce sufficient to justify the exercise of Congress's power. But this rule also required the Court to invent various tests for gauging the impact of local activities on interstate commerce. One test was whether or not local activities were in the "stream of commerce"; that is, whether local activities were intimately part of interstate

commerce. This was the basis in *Swift & Company v. United States* (196 U.S. 375 [1905]), in which the Court rejected a claim by a Chicago stockyard firm that the purchase and sale of cattle in Chicago stockyards was not commerce among the states, but instead a completely local activity.

Another test centered on whether or not intrastate commerce was so physically intermingled or intertwined with interstate commerce as to make it impractical to distinguish federal and state powers. In *Southern Railway Co. v. United States* (222 U.S. 20 [1911]), the Court upheld federal regulations applied to a company that carried on its interstate railroad three cars not equipped with safety couplers required under the Federal Safety Appliance Act of 1893, even though these cars were used solely in intrastate transportation.

Finally, the Court employed a distinction between the direct and indirect effects on commerce in order to limit congressional power. In *United States v. E. C. Knight Company*, Chief Justice Fuller had ruled that the government could not forbid the merger of sugar companies under the Sherman Antitrust Act based on the possibility that "trade or commerce might be indirectly affected." Even though the company would control 98 percent of all the sugar produced in the United States, the Court held that it was exempt from the Sherman Antitrust Act because the production of sugar was a local activity that only indirectly affected interstate commerce.

Ultimately, the Court's rigid application of its line-drawing rules to limit executive and congressional power led to a constitutional crisis over the New Deal. During President Franklin D. Roosevelt's first term, the Court overturned major pieces of legislation aimed at achieving economic recovery from the Depression. In *Schechter Poultry Corporation v. United States* (295 U.S. 495 [1935]), Chief Justice Charles Evans Hughes struck down the National Industrial Recovery Act of 1933 after concluding that the Schechter Corporation in Brooklyn, New York, was neither engaged in "interstate commerce" nor part of the "stream of commerce." Nor did Schechter's purchase and transportation of chickens from elsewhere in New York and Pennsylvania to its slaughterhouse, where they were sold to local retailers, have a "direct effect" on interstate commerce. Although Hughes did not try further to define direct and indirect effects, he observed that without some distinction between the two "there would be virtually no limit to the federal power and for all practical purposes we should have a completely centralized government." One year later, in *Carter v. Carter Coal Company* (298 U.S. 238 [1936]) the Court struck down another major piece of New Deal legislation, the Bituminous Coal Conservation Act of 1935, under which codes for employment practices were established for the coal industry.

The invalidation of New Deal legislation resulted in a major confrontation between the Court and the president and Congress. After winning a landslide reelection in 1936, Roosevelt responded by proposing judicial reforms that would expand the size of the Court from nine to fifteen justices. His Court-packing plan called for the appointment of a new member of the Court for every justice over seventy years of age. That would have enabled Roosevelt to secure a majority on the Court sympathetic to his and Congress's New Deal legislative programs.

In February 1937, while the Senate was considering Roosevelt's Court-packing plan, the Court, by a 5 to 4 margin, upheld a vital part of the New Deal program, the Wagner-Connery National Labor Relations Act of 1935, in *National Labor Relations Board v. Jones & Laughlin Steel Corporation* (301 U.S. 1 [1937]). Chief Justice Hughes's opinion in *Jones & Laughlin* affirmed the power of Congress to give the National Labor Relations Board jurisdiction over any person engaging in unfair labor practices "affecting commerce." Hughes also reaffirmed Congress's plenary power under the commerce clause. He at once returned to the principles expounded in *Gibbons V. Ogden* and laid the basis for the contemporary exercise of congressional power over commerce.

The Court's "stitch-in-time-that-saved-nine" in 1937 contributed to the Senate's defeat of Roosevelt's Court-packing plan. Congress in turn responded by passing the Fair Labor Standards Act of 1938, one of the last major pieces of New Deal legislation. That law makes it illegal to ship in interstate commerce goods produced in violation of federal employment standards set by the law for all employees "engaged in commerce or in the production of goods for commerce." The Court unanimously upheld that legislation in *United States v. Darby Lumber Company* (312 U.S. 100 [1941]) and expressly overruled its earlier decision in *Hammer v. Dagenhart*. The following year, in *Wickard v. Filburn* (317 U.S. 111 [1942]), the Court again demonstrated that it would not challenge Congress's power and in the process discarded the direct and indirect effects rule. In that court case, marketing penalties under the Agricultural Adjustment Act of 1938 were upheld against a farmer who grew only

twenty-three acres of wheat for consumption solely on his farm; for that he ran afoul of the act's limitations on the amount of wheat and other crops farmers were permitted to grow.

The rulings in *Darby* and *Filburn* exemplify the modern Court's approach to congressional power under the commerce clause. With few exceptions since the New Deal crisis, the Court has legitimated Congress's steady expansion of its power over interstate commerce. One consequence has been to enlarge congressional power to establish federal criminal law. Under the commerce clause, for instance, Congress passed the Consumer Credit Protection Act of 1968, the Omnibus Crime Control and Safe Streets Act of 1968, and the Federal Travel Act of 1970, all of which imposed criminal penalties for various activities bearing some connection to interstate commerce and transportation. The ruling in *Perez v. United States* (402 U.S. 146 [1971]) underscores the Court's deference to Congress after its 1937 turnaround. In that decision the Court upheld Congress's prohibition of "loan sharking"—that is, organized crime's extraction of payments for loans—under the Consumer Credit Protection Act on the ground that congressional hearings had established a connection between local loan sharks and interstate commerce.

Another significant use of Congress's commerce power has been in the realm of civil rights legislation. On the authority of the commerce clause, Congress enacted the Civil Rights Act of 1964, which bans racial discrimination in public accommodations and employment. So, too, does Title VIII of the Civil Rights Act of 1968 prohibit discrimination on the basis of race, color, religion, or national origin in the sale or rental of housing. When constitutional challenges were raised against the Civil Rights Act of 1964, the Court rebuffed them in *Heart of Atlanta Motel, Inc. v. United States* (379 U.S. 241 [1964]) and *Katzenbach v. McClung* (379 U.S. 294 [1964]), again reaffirming Congress's broad powers under the commerce clause.

Since 1937 the Court has generally deferred to Congress's authority under the commerce clause. Besides abandoning efforts to define certain activities as inherently local and exempt from congressional power, the Court has tended to legitimate Congress's assertion of power by enforcing the doctrine of federal preemption; that is, congressional legislation preempts state and local laws. Even when Congress fails to state expressly that it is preempting the states when enacting a statute, the Court tends to find state regulations preempted.

When determining whether or not the states have been implicitly preempted, the Court examines whether a state law conflicts with Congress's policy goals or whether congressional legislation so occupies an area as to preempt the states.

Even if Congress does not assert its powers under the commerce clause, the Court may strike down state laws under the theory of dormant commerce clause powers. The classic justification for the Court's enforcement of the commerce clause's dormant powers was offered in *Cooley v. Board of Wardens of the Port of Philadelphia* (53 U.S. 299 [1851]): "Whatever subjects of this power are in their nature national, or admit only of one uniform system, or plan of regulation, may justly be said to be of such a nature as to require exclusive legislation by Congress." Thus, even if Congress has not asserted its commerce power, the Court may strike down state laws that discriminate against interstate commerce. In *Fort Gratiot Sanitary Landfill, Inc. v. Michigan Department of Natural Resources* (112 S.Ct. 2019 [1992]), for example, the Court struck down a state law authorizing counties to bar within their jurisdictions the disposal of solid wastes that were generated in another county or state.

Since 1937, and particularly during the 1970s and 1980s, Congress has enacted a broad range of legislation on the basis of its authority in the commerce clause. See the table for an indication of Congress's expanding regulatory powers and preemption of state laws. The expansion of congressional power under the commerce clause has been criticized for intruding upon state powers and the Tenth Amendment. That amendment provides that "The powers not delegated to the United States by the Constitution, nor prohibited by it to the States, are reserved to the States respectively, or to the people." But with only one exception, since 1937 the Court has not enforced the Tenth Amendment as a limitation on Congress.

Congressional power over commerce was held to threaten "the separate and independent existence" of the states in *National League of Cities v. Usery* (426 U.S. 833 [1976]). Justice William H. Rehnquist struck down three 1974 amendments to the Fair Labor Standards Act, which extended minimum-wage and maximum-hours standards to all state, county, and municipal employees. But four dissenters protested that the Constitution neither guarantees state sovereignty nor requires or permits its judicial enforcement. They reiterated that since 1937 the Court had taken the position that "restraints on [Congress's commerce power] must proceed from political rather than judicial processes." Almost a decade later, Justice Harry Blackmun, who cast the crucial fifth vote in *National League of Cities,* changed his mind about the wisdom of the Court's attempt to limit congressional power in defense of states' interests. In *Garcia v. San Antonio Metropolitan Transit Authority* (469 U.S. 528 [1985]), he joined the four justices who had dissented in *National League of Cities* and expressly overturned that earlier ruling.

Whether or not the Tenth Amendment limits Congress's power was reconsidered in *New York v. United States* (112 S.Ct. 2408 [1992]). At issue was Congress's imposition of a deadline, among other regulations, for the states to provide disposal sites for low-level radioactive waste generated within their borders by 1996. New York contended that the Low-Level Radioactive Policy Amendments of 1985 infringed on its powers and asked the Court to overturn *Garcia.* The Court, however, upheld all but one provision of that legislation. It struck down Congress's stipulation that states failing to provide disposal sites by 1996 take title of and assume liability for all undisposed waste. The Court ruled that Congress had gone too far in that regard, though Justice Sandra Day O'Connor's opinion for the Court did not reach that verdict on the basis of the Tenth Amendment and balked at overturning *Garcia.* O'Connor concluded that the commerce clause itself limits Congress and does not empower it to direct the states to enact particular laws. Congress may force the states to participate in or comply with federal programs by preempting their laws and through its spending power. Under the commerce clause, however, Congress may not direct the states to pass specific laws or, in O'Connor's words, "commandeer state governments into the service of federal regulatory purposes."

The power of Congress under the commerce clause is not unlimited. But Congress and the Court have so enlarged the scope of that power that few activities remain solely within the domain of the states or conceivably beyond the reach of Congress. The commerce clause is one of the principal bases for congressional legislation and expanding federal regulatory powers.

[*See also* Regulation and Deregulation.]

BIBLIOGRAPHY

Frankfurter, Felix. *The Commerce Clause under Marshall, Taney, and Waite.* 1971.
McCloskey, Robert G., ed. *Essays in Constitutional Law.* 1957.

O'Brien, David M. *Constitutional Law and Politics: Struggles for Power and Governmental Accountability.* 2d ed., 1994.

U.S. Advisory Commission on Intergovernmental Relations. *Federal Statutory Preemption of State and Local Authority: History, Inventory, and Issues.* 1992.

DAVID M. O'BRIEN

COMMITTEE OF THE WHOLE.

Known as the Committee of the Whole, the Committee of the Whole House on the State of the Union is the House of Representatives meeting as if it were a committee on which each member of the House serves. (The procedural device is employed frequently in the House but has been abandoned by the Senate.) This alternative debate forum is utilized to take advantage of more expeditious rules of procedure. The Committee of the Whole continues to meet in the same chamber, but other changes signal the shift.

When the House transforms itself into the Committee, the mace is moved to a lower position on the rostrum. The Speaker leaves the chair and a majority party member is instead designated to preside over the Committee. Members seeking recognition from the chair change the form of address from "Mister (or Madam) Speaker" to "Mister (or Madam) Chairman."

The most significant changes are procedural. First, the quorum requirement in the Committee is only 100 members, whereas 218 are needed to constitute a quorum in the House. Second, obtaining a recorded vote in the Committee requires a sufficient second of 25 members. In the House, one-fifth of those present must approve taking a vote for the record. If a quorum is present, the sufficient second is 44, rising even higher when more than 218 members are on the floor.

Third, consideration of a measure is more flexible in the Committee of the Whole. The one-hour rule of debate governs in the House, permitting up to one hour per question. In the Committee, however, general debate is provided for by the unanimous consent of the House or pursuant to a special rule from the House Rules Committee. It can range from one hour to several hours in length. Overall, the Committee spends most of its time in the amending process, where the five-minute rule prevails: five minutes for the proponents, five for the opponents. On controversial questions, the period for debate and amending is frequently extended by unanimous consent or by offering of pro forma amendments, which are amendments in form only, that is, their only purpose is to obtain debate time.

The use of the Committee of the Whole has been accepted House practice since 1789. The purpose behind its use has changed considerably over time, however. Its antecedents were found in the English parliamentary practice of concealing proceedings from the Speaker, who was viewed with suspicion as a conduit to the Crown. Many colonial legislatures as well as the Continental Congress utilized a committee of the whole to provide members with a temporary forum in which debate could be exercised in a freer manner. Until the early 1800s, the House of Representatives used the Committee of the Whole to work out the broad outlines of a legislative proposal, which would then be sent to a select committee for further refinement. After the select committee completed its work, the Committee of the Whole would again meet to debate and amend the measure before the House would vote on it. In modern House practice, use of the Committee is limited to this final stage of consideration: debate and amending up to the point of final passage. In the Senate, the use of Committee of the Whole for the consideration of legislative measures was abolished in 1930, and its use for the consideration of treaties ended in 1986.

[*See also* Amending; Five-Minute Rule.]

BIBLIOGRAPHY

Alexander, De Alva Stanwood. *History and Procedure of the House of Representatives.* 1916. Pp. 256–272.

Nickels, Ilona B. *Committee of the Whole: An Introduction.* Congressional Research Service, Library of Congress. CRS Rept. 85-943. 1985.

U.S. House of Representatives. *Deschler's Precedents of the United States House of Representatives*, by Lewis Deschler. 94th Cong., 2d sess., 1977. H. Doc. 94-661. Vol. 5, chap. 19, pp. 39–286.

ILONA B. NICKELS

COMMITTEES.

[*This entry includes nine separate articles on the role, formation, operation, and types of congressional committees:*

An Overview
Assignment of Members
Committee Hearings
Committee Jurisdictions
Markups
Committee Reports
Standing Committees
Select and Special Committees
Joint Committees

See also Conference Committees; Subcommittees. For discussion of particular congressional committees, see under the name of each committee.]

An Overview

Committees and parties are the central organizational features of the U.S. Congress. The entire jurisdiction of each house of Congress is divided among a set of committees. Most legislative details are drafted in committee, and most investigations are conducted by committees. Further, committees provide most members of Congress their most important base of power.

Organization of the Modern Committee Systems. The U.S. Constitution makes no provision for committees, except to allow each house to devise its own rules to govern procedure. House and Senate rules list the standing committees, specify their jurisdictions, and prescribe certain features of committee procedure and organization. The two chambers have adopted rules affecting committees that differ in important ways. Committee activity is also regulated by a variety of statutes, party rules, and informal practices.

Modern committees have two basic functions: (1) collecting information through hearings and investigations and (2) drafting and reporting legislation. Committees are the primary means for formally receiving the testimony of representatives of the executive branch, organized interest groups, and the general public. The vast majority of legislation introduced by members is routinely referred to the committee or committees of appropriate jurisdiction. And most of the details of legislation are scrutinized or written in committee markups. Various types of committees perform these informational and legislative functions.

Standing committees have legislative authority and permanent status. Their jurisdictions are specified in chamber rules and precedents, and they may write and report legislation on any matter within their jurisdictions. In the House, which must approve its rules at the start of each Congress, the jurisdictions of standing committees are routinely reapproved every two years. In the Senate, all rules remain in force until they are changed. Table 1 lists the standing committees in the 103d Congress (1993–1995).

Ad hoc committees may be created and appointed to consider and report legislation, but they are temporary and usually dissolve upon reporting legislation or at a specified date. Since 1975 the Speaker of the House has been permitted to ap-

TABLE 1. *Standing Committees of the House and Senate, 1993–1994*

HOUSE	MEMBERSHIP
Agriculture	45
Appropriations	57
Armed Services	52
Banking, Finance, and Urban Affairs	51
Budget	35
District of Columbia	11
Education and Labor	34
Energy and Commerce	43
Foreign Affairs	43
Government Operations	39
House Administration	21
Judiciary	35
Merchant Marine and Fisheries	43
Natural Resources	37
Post Office and Civil Service	23
Public Works and Transportation	50
Rules	13
Science, Space, and Technology	49
Small Business	44
Standards of Official Conduct	12
Veterans' Affairs	34
Ways and Means	36

SENATE	MEMBERSHIP
Agriculture, Nutrition, and Forestry	19
Appropriations	29
Armed Services	20
Banking, Housing, and Urban Affairs	21
Budget	23
Commerce, Science, and Transportation	20
Energy and Natural Resources	19
Environment and Public Works	16
Finance	20
Foreign Relations	19
Governmental Affairs	14
Judiciary	14
Labor and Human Resources	16
Rules and Administration	16
Small Business	19
Veterans' Affairs	11

point ad hoc committees, with House approval, but this authority has been used on only a few occasions.

Joint committees are permanent but lack legislative authority. Composed of members from both houses, with the chairmanships rotating between

SENATE COMMITTEE ROOM. Photographed in 1902.

members of the two chambers, these committees conduct investigations, issue the results of studies, and recommend legislative action. Bills are not referred to them, and they cannot report legislation directly to the floor. The Joint Economic and Joint Taxation committees house sizable staffs and conduct newsworthy hearings from time to time. The Library and Printing committees, by contrast, perform the more ministerial duties of overseeing the operations of the Library of Congress and the Government Printing Office.

Select or special committees are, in principle, temporary committees without legislative authority. They may be used to study problems falling within the jurisdiction of several standing committees, to symbolize Congress's commitment to key constituencies, or simply to reward particular legis-

lators. Unfortunately, committee nomenclature can be misleading. For example, without eliminating the word *select* from their names, the House and Senate have made their intelligence committees permanent and granted them the power to report legislation. Some select committees are routinely re-created at the beginning of a new Congress.

In addition, the House and Senate jointly create conference committees to resolve the differences between their versions of legislation. The Constitution requires that legislation be approved by both houses in identical form before it is sent to the president. For important, complex legislation, the task of resolving differences often is difficult and time-consuming. While there are other ways to resolve interchamber differences, conference committees are named for most important legislation.

These committees have wide but not unlimited discretion to redesign legislation in their efforts to gain House and Senate approval. When a majority of House conferees and of Senate conferees agree, a conference committee issues a report that must be approved by both houses. Conference committees dissolve as soon as one house takes an action on the conference report.

The committees of greatest interest are the standing committees. In the modern Congress, standing committees originate most legislation and their members manage the legislation on the floor and dominate the conference committee dedicated to it. The organization and role of standing committees in the two chambers is the further subject of this essay.

The Legislative Power of Modern Committees. Committees have no power that is not granted to them by the parent chambers and parties. While the parent chambers approve committee assignments and budgets and must approve committee legislation, it is the parties that construct the committee lists routinely ratified by the chambers. This function gives the parties a source of leverage with committee members and allows the parties to regulate the behavior of committee members through formal and informal rules. In the main, committees must function in a procedural fashion and with a substantive effect that is consistent with the interests of their parent chambers and parties.

Nevertheless, committees exercise real power in the modern Congress. Their power stems in part from the indifference of the two parties and most members as to the details of legislation. Parties and their leaders focus on the few issues each year that are likely to affect party reputations and electoral prospects. The average member does not and could not take an interest in the details of most of the legislation that is considered on the floor. Party and member indifference varies from jurisdiction to jurisdiction, as well as over time, but it is common for the vast majority of measures that Congress processes.

When members are not indifferent, committees still have advantages that give their members disproportionate influence over policy outcomes. If committees abuse their advantages, it is yet often difficult to mount credible challenges to their power. Threats to strip a committee of jurisdiction, funding, or parliamentary privileges, or to retract members' committee assignments, usually are not credible, if for no other reason than that such actions might set precedents that members of other committees would not like to have established. The most practical means for keeping committees in check is to reject their policy recommendations.

Committee power comes in two forms. Negative power is the ability of committees to block legislation favored by others; positive power is the ability of committees to gain approval of legislation opposed by others. On both counts, committees have substantial advantages over rank-and-file members of the parent chambers and parties. Indeed, modern congressional committees have sources of negative and positive power that committees lack in most other national legislatures.

Negative power rests in committees' ability to control newly introduced legislation and obstruct alternative routes to the floor. This is accomplished more effectively under House rules than under Senate rules. In the House, such "gatekeeping" power is supported by rules that give committees near-monopoly control over newly introduced legislation and make it very difficult to circumvent them. Since 1880, all legislation relating to a committee's jurisdiction must be referred to that committee. Prior to 1975, this meant that the committee with the most relevant jurisdiction received the referral. Since then, the Speaker has been able to refer legislation to each committee with relevant jurisdiction. Short-circuiting the bill referral rule and bringing legislation directly to the floor requires either that the rules be suspended by a two-thirds vote or that a resolution from the Rules Committee be approved by majority vote.

House and Senate committees are granted wide latitude on most legislation that is referred to them. They may simply refuse to act, hold hearings but take no legislative action, amend the legislation in any way, or accept it without change. Or they may write their own legislation. They may vote to report legislation with a recommendation that it pass, with no recommendation, or with a recommendation that it be rejected.

Circumventing House committees is difficult but not impossible under current rules. The House operates under a germaneness rule that requires a floor amendment to be relevant to the section of the bill or resolution it seeks to modify. Thus, it is difficult to bring to the floor as an amendment a policy proposal whose subject has not been addressed in legislation reported by a committee. The germaneness rule can be waived, but only if the Rules Committee approves a resolution (a special rule) to this effect and the resolution is approved by a majority on the House floor. House rules provide other means for bringing legislation to the floor—a motion to suspend the rules, a special rule, and a petition to discharge a measure from committee—but these are difficult to employ and are used infrequently.

House committees' blocking power is further enhanced by their members' domination of conference committees. House-Senate differences on complex legislation are usually resolved in conference, and conferees usually are named from the membership of the committees that originated the legislation. The power of these conferees rests in their wide latitude in negotiating with the Senate conferees and in a rule that prohibits amendments to the conference report. The House must usually accept or reject the entire report. This process gives conferees substantial discretion in designing the final form of legislation as long as they can gain the support of the Senate conferees and of the majority in both houses.

The situation in the Senate is very different. Although measures are routinely referred to Senate committees upon introduction, it is easy to object to a referral and keep a measure on the calendar for floor consideration. Furthermore, the Senate lacks a germaneness rule for most measures, allowing senators to circumvent committees by offering whole bills as amendments to unrelated legislation. Senators often hesitate to bypass committees in this way but do so much more frequently than in the House. And most conference reports are subject to filibusters, giving Senate minorities a source of bargaining leverage with conferees that does not exist in the House. In sum, the Senate's rules combine to create only very weak blocking power for its committees.

Committees depend on majority floor support for their policy proposals. Most positive power results from general indifference to the issues and details of specific legislation. Yet committees do have ways to gain the support of interested members who are adverse to committee legislation. By threatening to use their blocking power, for example, committees may gain bargaining leverage with members who want something from them on this or another matter. And committees may force their chambers to enact certain policy positions by giving them ultimatums in the form of conference reports.

Committee proposals benefit from the body's extraprocedural resources. Committees gain a tactical edge over opponents, for example, through their advantages in political and policy information. After sitting through hearings and after their previ-

ous experience with the issues, committee members are usually better informed than other members about the political and policy implications of their recommendations. Committees' large, expert staffs and their extensive networks of allies in the executive branch and in the interest-group community further enhance their informational advantage.

The Investigative Power of Modern Committees. Committees monitor or investigate the activities of the executive and judicial branches, as well as private activity that is or might be the subject of public policy. Congress's power to compel cooperation with its investigations, courts have ruled, is implicit in its constitutional functions of legislating and appropriating funds. Without broad powers to investigate and compel cooperation, Congress and its committees would not be able to act knowledgeably on public policy or authorize the use of public moneys. Beginning with the Legislative Reorganization Act of 1946, committees have been assigned the duty of maintaining "continuous watchfulness" over executive branch activities within their jurisdictions.

Oversight appears to have become an increasingly important part of committee activity in recent decades. According to Joel Aberbach's count in *Keeping a Watchful Eye* (Brookings, 1990), the number of days of oversight hearings conducted by House and Senate committees increased from 159 in 1961, to 290 in 1973, to 587 in 1983. The proportion of committee meetings and hearings devoted to oversight grew from less than 10 percent to more than 25 percent. The surge in the 1970s appears to be the product of several factors: the new independence of subcommittee chairs to pursue oversight at their discretion; a general expansion of committee activity made possible by larger staffs; the frequency of split party control of Congress and the White House; and a generally more assertive Congress.

Committee Assignments. At the start of each Congress, freshman members are named to committees and nonfreshmen may attempt to transfer from one committee to another. Nonfreshmen who do not seek to transfer are routinely reappointed to their committees.

The majority party in each chamber holds a majority of the seats on most committees, roughly in proportion to its size in the chamber as a whole. The exceptions are the House Appropriations, Budget, Rules, and Ways and Means committees, crucial committees on which House Democrats have reserved a disproportionate number of seats for themselves, and the House and Senate ethics committees, on which there are equal numbers of majority and minority party members. The specific size of committees is negotiated by majority and minority party leaders, with the majority leaders having the upper hand because of their ability to win a vote for the resolutions providing for committee sizes. Over the last few decades committee sizes have grown to accommodate members' requests for desirable assignments.

Each congressional party has its own Committee on Committees. Party leaders chair these committees, although the degree to which they dominate the proceedings varies. Assignments are constrained by the availability of vacancies, the number of members competing for assignments, and certain rules on the number and type of assignments each member may hold, to which exemptions are frequently granted. Only for Senate Republicans is seniority a decisive consideration in choosing among competitors for coveted assignments. Democrats and House Republicans consider seniority among many other factors, such as party loyalty, electoral needs, and geographic balance. Since the 1950s both Senate parties have granted every senator who seeks one a seat on one of the top four committees before any senator gets two such seats.

Distinct patterns are observable in committee assignments. A committee's appeal to members and importance to a party varies widely according to its jurisdiction, its active policy agenda, and its general political environment. The money committees (House Appropriations, Budget, and Ways and Means; Senate Appropriations and Finance) and certain other committees with large and important jurisdictions (for example, House Energy and Commerce and Senate Armed Services) have wide appeal and are considered vital to the parties' policy interests. There is intense competition for assignments to these committees, and party leaders exercise care in making appointments to them. Other committees attract only the few members whose constituencies are most affected by policy under their jurisdictions. Party leaders have little interest in these committees and seek to accommodate members requesting seats on them.

Scholars have ranked committees according to their attractiveness, as indicated by the balance of transfers to and from each committee. Table 2 lists House committees according to this measure of attractiveness (recent ratings are not available for the Senate). The table also indicates what research

TABLE 2. *House Committees Ranked by Attractiveness, with Member Goals*

NAME AND RANKING	GOALS
1. Ways and Means	prestige, influence
2. Appropriations	prestige, influence
3. Rules	prestige, influence
4. Energy and Commerce	policy
5. Armed Services	constituency
6. Foreign Affairs	policy
7. Budget	prestige, influence
8. Interior and Insular Affairs	constituency
9. Banking, Finance, and Urban Affairs	policy
10. Agriculture	constituency
11. Education and Labor	policy
12. Government Operations	policy
13. Small Business	constituency
14. Science, Space, and Technology	constituency
15. Merchant Marine and Fisheries	constituency
16. Post Office and Civil Service	constituency
17. Judiciary	policy
18. Veterans' Affairs	constituency
19. Public Works and Transportation	constituency

NOTE: Three committees are not included: the District of Columbia and House Administration committees attract very few members; members generally do not take the initiative to request seats on Standards of Official Conduct but rather are solicited by party leaders.
SOURCE: The attractiveness rating is an updated transfer ratio for the 95th–99th Congresses, as reported in Michael Munger, "Allocation of Desirable Committee Assignments," *American Journal of Political Science* 32 (May 1988), p. 325; member goals are based on freshmen's motives for committee requests in the 100th and 101st Congresses, as reported in Steven S. Smith and Christopher J. Deering, *Committees in Congress* (Washington, D.C.: CQ Press, 1990), Chap. 3.

shows to be the distinctive political motivation for seeking assignment to each committee. Committees noted for their influence within the House are the most attractive. Committees with jurisdictions concerning which members have personal policy interests tend to be more attractive than committees that draw members because of their relevance to particular types of constituencies. A few committees attract the interest of virtually no members because of their limited jurisdiction or focus on housekeeping matters.

Committee Leadership. Both the majority and minority parties designate formal leaders for each committee and subcommittee. The majority party names the chairmen of all committees and subcommittees, and the minority party appoints a ranking minority member for every committee and subcommittee. The seniority norm dictates that the member with the longest continuous service on the committee serve as chairman, although there are limitations on the number and type of chairmanships a member may hold. Subcommittee chairmen and ranking minority members are chosen, in most cases, on the basis of committee seniority as well. Accruing seniority toward leadership posts is one reason members are reluctant to transfer to other committees, where they must start at the bottom of the seniority ladder.

In the last two decades, the seniority norm has been checked in both houses by new party rules that require a secret-ballot election of full committee chairs and ranking minority members. House Democrats led the way by requiring that all committee chairs and the chairmen of the Appropriations Committee subcommittees stand for election in the Democratic caucus at the start of each Congress. Three full committee chairs were deposed in 1975, another was defeated in 1985, two were defeated in 1990, and an Appropriations subcommittee chairman was replaced in 1977.

Subcommittee chairmen traditionally were appointed by the full committee chairman, who could thereby manipulate subcommittee activity. That procedure also was made more egalitarian in the 1970s. House Democratic rules require that committee Democrats bid for subcommittee chairmanships in order of seniority and that their choices be ratified by a majority vote of the committee's party members. While seniority generally is observed, party members on a committee have the right to reject the most senior member and elect someone else, as has happened more than a dozen times since the mid 1970s. House Republicans leave the appointment process to each committee's ranking minority member, but in practice Republicans also select most of their subcommittee ranking members by committee seniority. Both Senate parties also allow committee members to select their subcommittee chairmanships or ranking positions in order of seniority.

Restrictions on chairmanships were developed in the 1970s to spread the chairmanships among more members. The House Democratic caucus rules limit members to one full committee and one subcommittee chairmanship. Full committee chairmen may chair only one subcommittee, and that within the full committee they chair. This rule,

along with the increasing number of subcommittees, greatly increased the number of members holding subcommittee chairmanships—more than half of the House Democrats now hold a subcommittee chairmanship, up from one quarter in 1955.

Senate rules permit a member to hold only one chairmanship—the full committee chairmanship or a subcommittee chairmanship—on each committee on which he or she sits. Because most senators are limited to three standing committee assignments, they can have up to three subcommittee chairmanships, in addition to a full committee chairmanship of one of those standing committees. Nearly all majority party members hold at least one subcommittee chairmanship today, and more than half of the majority party Democrats hold two or three subcommittee chairmanships.

On most full committees, the chairman is the most powerful member. The chairman controls the committee's agenda; schedules meetings and hearings of the full committee and influences the scheduling of subcommittees' meetings and hearings; benefits from years of dealing with the committee's policy problems and constituencies; normally names conferees; controls the committee budget; supervises a sizable full committee staff; and often serves as a spokesperson for the committee and party on issues that fall under the committee's jurisdiction. Consequently, the committee chairman's support is critical to bill sponsors or opponents. That is as true today as it was thirty or forty years ago.

Nevertheless, compared with their predecessors of the 1950s and 1960s, committee chairmen now are more accountable to their party colleagues and face more effective competition for control over policy choices. This is due in part to changes in the formal rules limiting chairmen's discretion on a variety of procedural matters, particularly in the House, and in part to the acquisition of resources by other members who may not share the chairs' policy views.

The House and the House Democratic caucus adopted rules in the 1970s to reduce the influence of full committee chairmen over the decisions of their committees. Chairmen were required to stand for election by the Democratic caucus at the start of each Congress; subcommittees were required on committees with fifteen or more members and were empowered with written jurisdictions and staffs; proxy voting was restricted; the minority party contingents on committees were guaranteed staff; committees were required to open their meetings to the public unless a majority of committee members agreed to close them; a procedure for committee majorities to call meetings was created so the chairs could no longer refuse to hold meetings; and chairmen were required to promptly report legislation to the floor that had been approved by their committees.

The ability of committee chairmen to delay the referral of legislation to subcommittees or to delay the reporting of committee-approved legislation to the floor was curtailed. And House Democrats adopted a self-selection procedure for subcommittee assignments so that full committee chairmen could no longer stack important subcommittees with their supporters.

Like the House, the Senate adopted rules to provide guidelines for the conduct of committee meetings, hearings, and voting and required committees to publish additional rules governing committee procedure. In both houses, committee meetings were required to be held in public session, except by a recorded majority vote of the committee, making all committee members, including chairmen, more accountable to outside colleagues and constituents. And in both houses a majority of committee members may call and set the agenda for committee meetings if chairmen refuse to do so on their own authority.

But, unlike the House, Senate chamber and party rules do not specify internal committee organization in any detail and are silent on the functions of subcommittees. Compared with the rules of House committees, most Senate committees' rules are very brief, usually not even mentioning the structure, jurisdiction, or function of subcommittees. In most cases, committee chairmen are assumed to have great discretion, although even that is left unstated. The referral of legislation to subcommittees, the discharge of legislation from subcommittees, and the distribution of legislation between the full committee and subcommittees remain under the formal control of nearly all Senate committee chairmen. Thus, Senate chairmen are granted more discretion in designing the internal decision-making processes of their committees than House chairs, and Senate subcommittee chairs enjoy less autonomy than their House counterparts.

It is in the House, then, that the full committee chairmen's control of committee decisions by procedural means has declined most in recent decades. Even their ability to keep issues off the agenda was undermined by the empowerment of subcommittees. House chairmen must be responsive to the demands of the Democratic caucus or risk losing

their posts in the future, and they must tolerate independent subcommittees with professional staffs. Senate chairmen enjoy greater freedom in the internal affairs of their committees but must tolerate and anticipate more frequent and successful efforts to circumvent their committees altogether.

Subcommittees. Subcommittees became more important on many committees after the Legislative Reorganization Act of 1946 consolidated committee jurisdictions and reduced the number of standing committees in both chambers. The number of subcommittees grew after World War II and continued to grow into the 1970s as individual committees responded to new policy problems and to demands from members for their own subcommittees. By the early 1990s, there were more than 130 House subcommittees and more than 90 Senate subcommittees. Currently, of the committees with authority to report legislation, only the House Budget and Standards of Official Conduct committees and the Senate Budget, Rules and Administration, Ethics, Indian Affairs, and Veterans' Affairs committees lack standing subcommittees.

In the House, the resistance of some full committee chairmen to efforts to create legislative subcommittees was eventually overcome by a 1974 rule that requires that "each standing committee . . . , except the Committee on the Budget, that has more than twenty members shall establish at least four subcommittees." Later, problems associated with the growth in the number of House subcommittees—jurisdictional squabbles among subcommittees, scheduling difficulties, the burden of subcommittee hearings on executive officials—led the Democratic caucus to limit the number of subcommittees. The 1981 caucus rule limits large committees (at least thirty-five members) to eight subcommittees, with the exception of Appropriations, and small committees to six subcommittees.

Neither the Senate nor its parties have a formal rule on the number of subcommittees any committee may have, although restrictions on the number of subcommittee assignments that individual senators may hold effectively limit the number of subcommittees that can be created. The stricter enforcement of limits on subcommittee assignments in 1985 led five committees to eliminate one or more subcommittees after a few senators were forced to give up one of their subcommittee chairmanships. On other committees, enforcement of the rule meant that not enough members were able and willing to take subcommittee assignments, forcing the abolition of some subcommittees. A total of ten Senate committees were compelled or chose to eliminate at least one subcommittee that year.

Subcommittees have gained great importance in committee decision making in the House. As noted above, the House adopted rules in the early 1970s that substantially weakened the ability of full committee chairs to control subcommittees. The net result is that decision-making processes within House committees are now more decentralized than they were in the 1950s and 1960s. Most legislation originates in subcommittees, the vast majority of hearings are held in subcommittees, about half of all committee staff are allocated to subcommittees, and subcommittee leaders usually serve as the floor managers for legislation originating in their subcommittees. The pattern in the House has led some observers to label House decision making "subcommittee government."

The empowerment of House subcommittees greatly increased the importance of subcommittee chairmen. One indication of the change is increased contention for subcommittee chairmanship: several House members in line for a chairmanship by virtue of their seniority have been rejected by committee colleagues in favor of competitors. The few systematic studies of intracommittee decision making since the reforms of the 1970s indicate that subcommittee chairmen, full committee chairmen, and ranking minority members are the most influential members of their committees. Because of their limited jurisdiction, most subcommittee chairmen are not as powerful as many full chairmen were in the 1950s and 1960s, but their independence of action makes them central players on most legislation.

In the Senate, subcommittee appointment practices are much like those of the House. Committee rules often guarantee members a first (or second) subcommittee choice before any other member receives a second (or third) choice, and all party contingents operate in this way even in the absence of a formal rule. Consequently, committee members are no longer dependent on the full committee chair for desirable subcommittee assignments. But the lack of formal rules empowering subcommittees in the Senate has produced great variation among committees in their reliance on subcommittees. Several Senate committees hold very few hearings in subcommittee, and only a few Senate committees use subcommittees to write legislation. The concept of "subcommittee government" does not fit decision-making processes in most Senate committees.

In addition to standing subcommittees, committees occasionally create other subunits. Most but not all committees allow their chair to create ad hoc subcommittees to handle matters that fall under the jurisdiction of more than one subcommittee. Unfortunately, there is no reliable record of how frequently such ad hoc arrangements are employed, but the relative ease of altering subcommittee jurisdictions keeps the number very small. Committee rules generally imply that the ad hoc subcommittees dissolve upon completing action on the specific matters assigned to them.

Committee Staff. The size of committee staffs increased steadily between 1946 and the early 1980s. The Legislative Reorganization Act of 1946 granted each standing committee authority to hire four professional staff assistants and six clerical aides, and the 1970 act increased to six the number of professional assistants each committee could hire. In 1974 the House increased the number to eighteen professional assistants and twelve clerical aides, where it remains today. The 1970 act guaranteed minority party selection of at least two professional staff assistants on each committee, and both chambers later adopted rules guaranteeing even larger staffs to the minority party. The House now gives the minority party control over one third of professional and clerical staffs, and the Senate requires that staff be allocated to the minority party in proportion to the number of minority party members on each committee. Since the early 1980s, budget constraints have caused many committees to reduce staff sizes somewhat, and there has been little overall growth.

Staffing has buttressed committee power and altered the distribution of power within committees. In rules adopted in the early 1970s, the House allowed both the chair and ranking minority member of each standing subcommittee to appoint at least one staff member. Unless the House authorizes additional staff, subcommittee staff positions come out of the allocation guaranteed to the full committee and so directly reduce the number of staff under the control of the full committee chairman and the ranking minority member. This rule dramatically altered staffing patterns in House committees. Between 1969 and 1985, the proportion of all committee staff assigned to subcommittees grew from about 23 percent to nearly 46 percent. Some House subcommittee staffs have grown far beyond the minimum required by House rules, to levels as high as fifteen to twenty aides in a handful of particular cases.

In the Senate, where no rule guaranteeing sub-committee staff was adopted, subcommittee staff has made up about 40 percent of all committee staff. Indeed, while the total number of House committee staff more than tripled between 1969 and 1979, due primarily to the expansion of subcommittee staffs, Senate committee staff grew by only 80 percent or so.

House committees, operating under requirements that committee staff be shared with subcommittees and the minority party, now have very similar distributions of staff between full committee and subcommittees. In some cases, most notably Ways and Means, the full committee chairman, through the senior full committee staff, exercises substantial control over at least the majority party staff of the committee and subcommittees. Senate committees, because they are not constrained by chamber or party rules requiring separate subcommittee staffs, continue to vary widely in the manner in which they staff subcommittee activities.

Committee Decentralization. The extent of decentralization in the decision-making processes found within House and Senate committees is indicated in an index of "subcommittee orientation." The higher the index score, the more the committee relies on subcommittees. The greater the reliance on subcommittees, the more decentralized the committee's decision-making process is said to be.

Table 3 lists House and Senate committees according to the degree of decentralization found in the 100th Congress (1987–1989). House committees were more decentralized than Senate committees. House committees had an average subcommittee orientation of 47 percent from 1969 to 1971, 62 percent from 1979 to 1981, and 57 percent from 1987 to 1989. In contrast, the respective levels for the Senate were 26 percent, 25 percent, and 20 percent. Compared to the situation in the late 1960s, all but one of the fourteen House committees examined became more subcommittee oriented by the late 1970s. In sharp contrast, eight of the twelve Senate committees for which complete data are available became less subcommittee oriented during the 1970s.

"Subcommittee government" clearly is a more appropriate description of the internal decision-making processes of House committees than of Senate committees. House subcommittees have developed a more thoroughly institutionalized role. This role is established not only in the rules of the House and the Democratic caucus, but also in the interests of individual representatives. Representatives with sufficient seniority to chair a subcommittee

TABLE 3. *House and Senate Committees Ranked by Subcommittee Orientation (Most Decentralized to Least Decentralized), 1987–1988*

1. House Energy and Commerce
2. House Science, Space, and Technology
3. House Judiciary
4. House Banking, Finance, and Urban Affairs
5. House Government Operations
6. House Interior and Insular Affairs
7. House Public Works and Transportation
8. House Education and Labor
9. House Agriculture
10. House Merchant Marine and Fisheries
11. House Foreign Affairs
12. House Armed Services
13. House Veterans' Affairs
14. Senate Judiciary
15. Senate Commerce, Science, and Transportation
16. House Small Business
17. Senate Governmental Affairs
18. Senate Environment and Public Works
19. House Ways and Means
20. Senate Labor and Human Resources
21. Senate Energy and Natural Resources
22. Senate Banking, Housing, and Urban Affairs
23. Senate Armed Services
24. Senate Agriculture, Nutrition, and Forestry
25. Senate Finance
26. Senate Rules and Administration
27. Senate Foreign Relations
28. Senate Small Business
29. Senate Veterans' Affairs
30. House Budget
31. Senate Budget

NOTE: The index is the mean of the following measures: (1) the percentage of measures considered on the floor that are managed by a subcommittee chair, (2) the percentage of measures reported to the floor that were referred to a subcommittee or on which a subcommittee hearing was held, (3) the percentage of meetings (primarily markups) that were subcommittee meetings, and (4) the percentage of staff specifically allocated to subcommittees. Data not available for House Appropriations, House Rules, and Senate Appropriations. Excludes three minor House committees: House Administration, Standards of Official Conduct, and District of Columbia.
SOURCE: Adapted from Steven S. Smith and Christopher J. Deering, *Committees in Congress* (1990), pp. 157–158.

ordinarily chair only one. That chairmanship gives them additional staff, control over hearings on matters under their subcommittee's jurisdiction, and the power to initiate or block legislation in the absence of actions by the full committee.

In contrast, a typical majority party senator chairs two or three subcommittees. A senator is not very dependent on any one subcommittee or subcommittee chairmanship for his or her legislative livelihood. The tremendous demands on senators' time make senators less likely to insist that their subcommittees be active, effective decision-making units. As a result, Senate subcommittees vary more in importance. On several Senate committees, subcommittees play no formal role in writing legislation. And over the last decade or so, reliance on subcommittees has declined on some Senate committees. Rather than developing a central role in Senate policy making, Senate subcommittees have proved to be one component of a very individualistic decision-making process.

Forces Shaping the Power of Committees. The decision-making processes of the House and Senate represent an interaction of committees, parties, and the parent chambers. The relationship among the three varies through time, as does the relative importance of each in shaping public policy. Committees have been used since Congress's first session in 1789, but their functions and influence have changed as the chambers, parties, and their political environment have evolved.

The potential importance of committees can be seen in three contrasting models of committee power. Each model is a highly stylized view of what congressional decision making could be like. The models highlight the advantages and disadvantages of the modern committee systems and provide a basis for specifying the conditions that shape the role of committees.

In the autonomous committee model, members of each committee determine policy within their jurisdiction, irrespective of the policy preferences of the parent chamber and parties. That is, committees have monopoly control over both setting the agenda for their parent chamber and making policy choices.

In the party-dominated committee model, committee members are agents of their parties. The parties have the capacity to shape the composition and policy outlook of their committee contingents because they control appointments to committees. Committee members take direction from their party leaders on what issues to consider and what policy choices to make.

In the chamber-dominated committee model, committee members are agents of their parent chambers. Committees are created to meet the needs of the chamber for a division of labor, the development of expertise, the acquisition of informa-

tion, and the organization of a supporting staff. Committees must obtain majority support on the floor for their legislation and so tailor their proposals to the expectations of floor majorities.

Each of the three models has attractive features. Autonomous committees allow Congress to manage a large work load by providing a division of labor and encourages the development of expertise among committee members, who know that their work will be respected and approved by others. A party-dominated system allows for the emergence of strong party leadership, which can supervise the development of coherent, timely policy and makes it possible to hold a party accountable for congressional decisions. A chamber-dominated system seems quite democratic because it preserves the equality of all members, regardless of their committee assignments or party affiliation, and allows all members to have an active voice in important decisions.

The fit of these models to actual House and Senate practices has varied over time in response to several sets of factors: the character of Congress's policy agenda, the distribution of policy preferences, and the institutional context. The effects of these factors can be summarized in several propositions.

Issue agenda. The larger the agenda, the more separable the issues, the more issues recur frequently, and the less salient the issues, the more Congress relies on committees to make policy choices. Large agendas require a division of labor to handle the work load, and a system of powerful committees provides such a division of labor. If the issues are easily separable into distinct categories, then committees with distinct jurisdictions work well. If issues recur frequently, then committee jurisdictions can be fixed without concern that some committees will become superfluous over time. Moreover, if most issues concern only a few members, committees can make decisions without serious challenge on the floor. Over its two-hundred-year history, Congress's expanding policy agenda has produced a nearly continuous elaboration of its committee systems, which provide the basic means for dividing labor and increasing Congress's capacity to process legislation.

Alignment of policy preferences. The more issues are salient to most members and the more cohesive the majority party, the more Congress relies on the majority party to make policy choices. When more issues are salient to most members and the majority party lacks cohesiveness, however, Congress relies more on the chamber floor to make policy choices. When most members take an active interest in policy decisions, they will not tolerate autonomous committees that do not share their policy views. If members' policy preferences reflect partisan alignments so that the majority party is cohesive, the majority party will have both the incentive and the capacity to control committees. Party leaders will be encouraged to see to it that committees either have little influence over outcomes or are stacked with friendly members. If issues are salient to most members, preferences are not aligned by party, and the majority party lacks sufficient cohesiveness, coalitions cutting across the parties—perhaps different coalitions on different issues—may assert themselves on the floor and determine policy outcomes. Historically, the partisanship of policy alignments has varied greatly.

Institutional context. The more chamber rules and practices preserve the right of individual members to debate and offer amendments at will on the floor, the less autonomy committee members and party leaders will have. The House and Senate are very different institutions. There is greater need for a strong presiding officer and for observance of formal rules in the larger, more unwieldy House. In the Senate, there is greater tolerance of individual initiative and greater resistance to committee- or party-imposed policy choices. That tolerance is represented in Senate rules that protect the individual member's right to offer amendments on any subject and conduct extended debate. Such rules preserve individual senators' bargaining leverage with committee and party leaders.

The critical feature of past procedural and structural choices is that they limit the range of feasible institutional arrangements for the future. Neither house has the time or capacity to completely reconstitute its decision-making processes. Elaboration of existing procedures and structures is the common response to new demands. Different institutional arrangements in the House and Senate are likely to cause different responses to similar changes in issue agendas and policy alignments. In general, the committee autonomy and party-dominated committee models generally fit the Senate less well than the House.

Recent Trends. Committee power has come under attack during the past two decades. While committees continue to draft the details of nearly all legislation and their members remain central players in nearly all congressional policy decisions, they no longer operate as autonomously as they once did. Change has been most dramatic in the House of Representatives, where committees traditionally dominated policy-making more completely than they did in the Senate. But both houses have become less committee centered.

Changes in both the policy agenda and political alignments have led to a decline in committee autonomy in recent decades. In the 1960s and 1970s, many new issues, like energy, the environment, and consumer protection, were interconnected and fell under the jurisdiction of several committees. The agenda became less predictable and recurrent. In the 1980s, concern about the federal budget deficit began to dominate policy-making. Most other domestic policy issues were set aside or reinterpreted in terms of their budgetary consequences. The agenda contracted and the remaining issues, all seen as connected to fiscal policy, concerned nearly all members.

These changes stimulated intercommittee conflict, which has sometimes been fueled by multiple referrals. Noncommittee members have more frequently challenged committee recommendations. Floor amending activity increased in the last two decades, and demands for recorded votes on committee and conference recommendations have increased. And in the area of budgeting, a number of procedures to limit committee discretion and order committee action have been imposed.

While the agenda fluctuated, the political alignments among members shifted. Due to electoral changes and a new agenda, the party coalitions proved far more cohesive in the 1980s. Party leaders and caucuses became more assertive in structuring the agenda and formulating policy on important issues.

The decline of committee autonomy is most apparent in the House, where committees had more to lose than in the Senate. House committees recovered to some extent in the 1980s by the more creative use of special rules to limit amendments, but the fact that restrictive special rules are necessary indicates how much committee autonomy has declined in the House.

Committees are integral to a remarkably complex congressional decision-making process. For most of the past century, the basic structure of the committee systems has remained stable, reflecting fundamental features of Congress itself—a large, diverse agenda, weak parties, and the great variation in the salience of issues among members. Nevertheless, the House and Senate committee systems are not rigid and fixed. They have demonstrated substantial variability in their place in the policy-making process and will continue to do so in the future.

BIBLIOGRAPHY

Davidson, Roger H. "Subcommittee Government: New Channels for Policy Making." In *Congress Reconsidered*, 3d ed. Edited by Lawrence C. Dodd and Bruce I. Oppenheimer. 1985.

Evans, C. Lawrence. *Leadership in Committee*. 1991.

Fenno, Richard F., Jr. *Congressmen in Committees*. 1973.

Fenno, Richard F., Jr. *The Power of the Purse: Appropriations Politics in Congress*. 1966.

Goodwin, George. *The Little Legislatures*. 1970.

Huitt, Ralph K. "The Congressional Committee: A Case Study." *American Political Science Review* 48 (1954): pp. 340–365.

Kiewiet, D. Roderick, and Mathew D. McCubbins. *The Logic of Delegation*. 1991.

Krehbiel, Keith. *Information and Legislative Organization*. 1991.

Manley, John F. *The Politics of Finance*. 1970.

Matthews, Donald R. *U.S. Senators and Their World*. 1960.

Parker, Glenn R., and Suzanne L. Parker. *Factions in House Committees*. 1985.

Price, David E. *Who Makes the Laws?* 1972.

Shepsle, Kenneth A., and Barry Weingast. "The Institutional Foundations of Committee Power." *American Political Science Review* 81 (1987): pp. 85–105.

Smith, Steven S. *Call to Order*. 1989.

Smith, Steven S., and Christopher J. Deering. *Committees in Congress*. 2d ed. 1990.

Strahan, Randall. *New Ways and Means*. 1990.

STEVEN S. SMITH

Assignment of Members

Members of both chambers generally seek assignment to committees with certain jurisdictions: those that relate to their own professional background (e.g., former teachers to the panels that have responsibility for education issues); those that reflect the demographic complexion of their district or state (e.g., members from farm states to the Agriculture committees, the type often referred to as "constituency committees"); or those involved in policy areas of particular personal interest (e.g., tax-policy specialists to the tax writing committees). Some seek influence through assignments to so-called power or prestige committees. Once members are assigned to committees, it is fairly uncommon for them to change assignments, although given the opportunity to serve on a prestige committee, such as Appropriations, very few members elect not to seek the appointment. Therefore, the committee assignment process largely determines committee membership, especially since that membership is usually very stable.

Senate. Many key regulations affecting committee assignments are included in the rules of the Senate. The political parties in the chamber make their initial decisions regarding committee sizes following an election and then include those provisions in the Senate rules changes adopted early in the new Congress. Obviously, changes to those rules require a majority vote in the chamber in addition to agreement within one of the party conferences.

Senate Rule XXV contains the basic elements of the committee assignment process. The assignment portion of the rule, substantially rewritten in 1977 and modified in 1984, is traditionally adjusted at the beginning of each Congress to reflect the party ratios in the chamber and to determine the size and ratio of each committee. If changes in Senate membership occur during the course of a Congress, the ratios also may be altered. Despite the periodic changes, the rule still serves as the preeminent determinant of committee membership.

Rule XXV divides Senate committees into three categories, designated "A," "B," and "C." Included in the "A" category are the standing committees on Agriculture, Nutrition, and Forestry; Appropriations; Armed Services; Banking, Housing, and Urban Affairs; Commerce, Science, and Transportation; Energy and Natural Resources; Environment and Public Works; Finance; Foreign Relations; Governmental Affairs; Judiciary; and Labor and Human Resources. In the "B" category are the remaining standing committees—Budget, Rules and Administration, Small Business, and Veterans' Affairs—the permanent select committees on Aging and Intelligence, and the Joint Economic Committee. In the "C" category are the remaining select and joint committees.

Each member is required to serve on two A committees, may serve on one B committee, and can serve on as many C committees as he or she desires and the parties agree to. Many members serve on more committees than the rules allow. This is done by including a waiver, called a grandfather provision, approved by the party caucus and included in Rule XXV for that Congress. The waiver basically says that the particular senator may serve on a specific committee notwithstanding the rule that would otherwise limit such service. Numerous members have such waivers.

The rule also lists the size of each committee for each Congress. The ratio of majority to minority party members on the committee approximates the ratio of majority to minority party members in the full chamber, within the confines of the committee's size as determined by Rule XXV. In order to accommodate the political orientation of the members and majority party control of committees, the rule provides for a so-called working majority, which in effect allows an additional member to serve on the majority side if there are majority party members who frequently vote with the other party on committee business. Committee sizes usually remain fairly constant from Congress to Congress, and it is the ratios that change as party strength in the chamber varies. For sizes to change, amendment of Rule XXV is required.

Once committee sizes and ratios are determined, usually at organization meetings in early December after the November election, each of the parties begins the assignment process. (If a member is elected to the Senate from a party other than the Democratic or Republican party, that member selects which of the two parties he will associate, or caucus, with for assignment purposes.) Each party maintains a committee that is responsible for committee assignments, called the Committee on Committees. This entity reviews the members' requests for assignments and tries to match those requests with available slots. Also, this panel is responsible for internal party rules relating to committee assignments. For example, both parties try to discourage senators from the same party and the same state from serving on the same committee. This is usually accomplished, although there have been exceptions. Further, each party designates "exclusive" committees within the A category and tries to limit members to service on only one such exclusive panel. Regional and philosophical balance also serve as variables that the parties weigh in making assignments. Finally, although waivers (called grandfathers) are included in Rule XXV, each party caucus determines which senators will receive such waivers.

Senators are limited to one full committee chairmanship, although such a chairman can also chair a joint committee whose jurisdiction is directly related to that of his standing committee; for instance, the Finance Committee chairman can chair the Joint Committee on Taxation. Exceptions to this limitation are rare. Ranking minority slots are usually also limited to one per member, although the application of this restriction depends on the party ratio and the number of minority slots that need to be filled.

Generally, senators are limited to service on three subcommittees on each of their class A committees and two subcommittees on their class B committee. There is no limitation on subcommittee service on class C committees. Senators with full committee assignment waivers are entitled to corresponding additional subcommittee assignments. Regarding subcommittee chairmanships, senators are usually limited to one such chairmanship on each full committee on which they serve, although waivers can be granted to exceed this limit.

House of Representatives. Unlike the Senate, which incorporates some committee assignment procedures in chamber rules, the House of Representatives invests almost all of the assignment process in its party machinery, especially that of the majority party. In addition, the party decisions never appear in House rules and occasionally do not appear in writing at all.

As the Democrats have been the majority party all but four years between 1931 and 1993, most of the committee assignments have rested with that party and are handled by the Democratic caucus and its Steering and Policy Committee. The Democratic caucus manual details the specific rules and regulations guiding committee assignment procedures for the Democrats; it is modified as necessary each Congress, and occasionally during the Congress, to reflect shifts in party strength.

Committees are divided into three basic categories: exclusive, major, and nonmajor (with general agreement that the divisions in the latter two categories do not carry value judgments regarding the importance of the committees, although the former are the most desirable). Exclusive committees are Appropriations, Rules, and Ways and Means. Major committees are Agriculture; Armed Services; Banking, Finance, and Urban Affairs; Education and Labor; Foreign Affairs; Energy and Commerce; Judiciary; and Public Works and Transportation. Nonmajor committees are Budget; District of Columbia; Government Operations; House Administration; Interior and Insular Affairs; Merchant Marine and Fisheries; Post Office and Civil Service; Science, Space, and Technology; Small Business; and Veterans' Affairs.

Select, special, and joint committees are not included in the categorization, and indeed, assignments to these panels are made outside the limitations discussed below. Select and special committee membership procedures are either included in the resolution creating the panel or made by the Speaker of the House. Joint committee membership is generally drawn from the corresponding standing committee.

Sizes of committees are determined by the Democratic caucus, with ratios usually reflecting majority-to-minority party strength in the chamber. In a few cases, ratios do not reflect party strength (e.g., the Rules Committee has a 2-to-1 plus 1 ratio, and the Committee on Standards of Official Conduct has an equal number of Democrats and Republicans). Also, sizes are often altered to reflect interest in a panel; that is, sizes can be raised to accommodate members' requests, or limited to deny assignment. It is rare for sizes to be decreased in order to eliminate members already serving on the panel.

Democratic members are generally limited to service on one exclusive committee, or one major and one nonmajor committee, or two nonmajor committees. However, members often receive waivers to serve on more than the requisite number of major and nonmajor panels. Waivers most often result from assignments to those committees that are perceived to be less desirable and thus are more difficult to fill. In addition, for some committees, such as Budget and Standards of Official Conduct, the Democratic caucus limits the terms a member can serve and these committees therefore have what has been called a rotating membership. They are also outside the assignment limitations. For the Budget Committee, some members are appointed because of their other committee assignments; for instance, some members represent the Appropriations Committee, others the Ways and Means Committee, and so forth. Finally, waivers regarding the exclusive committees are rare.

The Democratic caucus rules state that the chairman of an exclusive or major committee may not serve on any other exclusive, major, or nonmajor committee. Further, a full committee chairman may not serve as a chairman of any other full committee without a waiver from the caucus. Finally, no committee chairman can serve as a member of the Committee on Standards of Official Conduct.

Generally, members are limited to service on a total of five subcommittees among their standing committee assignments. Members usually bid for three subcommittee assignments on their major committee and two on their nonmajor committee, although there is no rule governing this selection. However, because of the numerous waivers discussed above, some members exceed the five subcommittee limit. The caucus rules also limit members to election to one subcommittee chairmanship on their legislative committees. Because of their unique nature, the subcommittees of the Appropriations and Ways and Means Committees have a distinct set of assignment guidelines, which basically provide more authority to the full Democratic caucus, rather than to the Democrats on the committee.

Because the majority party determines committee sizes and ratios, assignment decisions by the Republican party's Committee on Committees must wait until the Democrats have completed their initial assignment processes. Accordingly, the Republican rules and practices are much more flexible, much less formal, and rarely found in writing. However, they do categorize committees as "red," "white," and "blue," a categorization roughly the same as the Democrats', the major difference being that Energy and Commerce is a red committee. Generally, most Republican members serve on only one standing committee, with some limited exceptions. Members are limited to service as a ranking member (often called vice chairman) on only one full committee, and as a ranking member on only two subcommittees.

As in the Senate, members from third parties receive their committee assignments through one of the two party caucuses, although past practice has been inconsistent regarding how these members are counted toward committee size, ratio, and other seniority questions.

[See also Congress, article on Politics and Influence in Congress; Seniority.]

BIBLIOGRAPHY

Schneider, Judy. *Senate Rules and Practices on Committees, Subcommittees, and Chairmanship Assignment Limitations as of October 31, 1992.* Congressional Research Service, Library of Congress. CRS Rept. 92-780. 1992.
Shepsle, Kenneth A. *The Giant Jigsaw Puzzle.* 1978.
Smith, Steven S., and Bruce A. Ray. "The Impact of Congressional Reform: House Democratic Committee Assignments." *Congress and Presidency* 10 (Autumn 1983).
Smith, Steven S. and Christopher J. Deering. *Committees in Congress.* 1990.

JUDY SCHNEIDER

Committee Hearings

Scholars have differed as to the role committees play in the legislative process. The traditional view is found in Joseph Chamberlain's classic *Legislative Processes* (1936) and Arthur Maass's *Congress and the Common Good* (1983). By this view committees are tools used by the larger chamber to arrive at the "common good" of the larger society. The committee acts as the guardian of the general public interest after hearing from special-interest advocates who appear before it. From this perspective, committee hearings take on features of a legislative court where members decide what to do based upon the evidence of law and fact brought before them by the interested parties. These open hearings at the same time act as a public forum where the public interest will emerge from the clamor of competing special interests.

By a second view, first proposed in 1908 by Arthur Bentley in *The Process of Government* but not popularized until the publication of David Truman's *The Governmental Process* in 1951, the legislative process is but a struggle between competing groups, none of whom are concerned with a guiding abstraction like the "common good." Public policy emerges from the push and pull of competing groups, each seeking its own interests. In this process, individual legislators act as advocates of these parochial interests and not as neutral judges seeking the general good. Committee hearings are not neutral legislative fact-finding courts but vehicles to further the interests of members.

Truman argues that committee hearings serve three purposes. First, the hearings allow for the transmission of information from the various interest groups to the committee. Second, because committee members are not acting in the role of neutral judges, the hearings are used as a propaganda platform by the interest groups, with little thought given to a meaningful debate on the subject at hand. Third, the hearings act as a safety valve whereby group conflicts can be adjusted before they become explosive.

The most recent view to emerge takes the group concept one step further by relying upon econometric research to focus upon the economic calculus of individuals and thus to explain committee activity. A laudable attempt to summarize in a nonmathematical manner the two classes of formal theory that make up much of this literature is Keith Krehbiel's *Information and Legislative Organization* (1991).

Authority to Hold Hearings. The authority of committees to hold hearings rests on the constitutionally granted power to legislate, which includes the power to conduct inquiries and investigations (*Kilbourn v. Thompson*, 103 U.S. 168 [1881]; *McGrain v. Daugherty*, 273 U.S. 135 [1927]; *Watkins v.*

United States, 354 U.S. 178 [1957]; *Barenblatt v. United States*, 360 U.S. 109 [1959]). Both chambers of Congress have developed sets of rules to guide their conduct based upon the power to legislate. Rule X of the Rules of the House of Representatives and Rule XXV of the Standing Rules of the Senate provide for the establishment and jurisdiction of standing committees. Rule XI, clause 1 (a) (2) (b) of the House rules stipulates, "Each committee is authorized at any time to conduct such investigations and studies as it may consider necessary or appropriate in the exercise of its responsibilities under Rule X. . . ." Furthermore, clause 2 (m) (1) of Rule XI authorizes committees or their subcommittees to hold hearings and require, by subpoena or otherwise, the attendance and testimony of such witnesses and the production of such records or documents as it deems necessary.

Authority for Senate committees to hold hearings is found in Rule XXVI, clause 1 of the Senate rules. This provision states:

> Each standing committee, including any subcommittee of any such committee, is authorized to hold such hearings, to sit and act at such times and places during the sessions, recesses, and adjourned periods of the Senate, to require by subpoena or otherwise the attendance of such witnesses and the production of such correspondence, books, papers, and documents, to take such testimony . . . as may be authorized by resolutions of the Senate. Each such committee may make investigations into any matter within its jurisdiction. . . .

Besides the Standing Rules, the authority for committee action may also be found in statutes or in chamber rules and resolutions not specifically focusing on developing the committee's basic charter. The Senate has simplified the process of determining the rights of individuals subpoenaed or otherwise called to appear before a committee by publishing a document that identifies the authority and rules of Senate committees (S. Doc. No. 102-6). Here can be found the authority for matters including provisions for the administration of oaths to witnesses; the payment of witnesses' expenses; the criminal and civil enforcement of Senate subpoenas; immunity for witnesses; the preservation and disclosure of Senate records; and authorization of testimony.

Hearing Process. Roger Davidson and Walter Oleszek in *Congress against Itself* (1977) describe most committee hearings as being conducted with little fanfare, with participation usually confined to the persons giving testimony, a rotating cast of committee or subcommittee members, and a sprinkling of observers, generally interest-group representatives. Witnesses usually give testimony from prepared texts while committee members occasionally follow along. More often than not, members will use this time to review their correspondence or consult with staff. When the testimony ends, the questioning begins, with committee members most often proceeding in order of seniority. There is little interchange between members at this point, and, since witnesses usually appear alone, there is no opportunity for them to exchange views on the subject.

It would be a mistake, however, to believe that committee hearings are used solely for the purpose of collecting information. Various interests vie with one another in the legislative arena to decide public policy, and it should come as no surprise to see the committee hearing process used as a tool in that struggle.

Legislation ultimately needs majority support to be successful. Legislators need to know what the various positions are on an issue before proceeding, and the hearing process can serve the purpose of legislative coalition building by providing a forum for the public discussion of issues. The support of the administration on an issue, for example, might be necessary before members sign on to a bill, or, conversely, presidential opposition might be enough to doom any serious consideration of the proposal.

Hearings, in the hands of a skillful full or subcommittee chairman, can also be used to promote or retard the chances of proposed legislation. For example, scheduling friendly or critical witnesses early in the hearing process when outside interest may be high might be critical to the subsequent success or failure of the legislation. Badgering opposition witnesses or setting up and coaching friendly witnesses can also have an impact on the outcome of a proposal.

Before the Legislative Reform Act of 1970 forced Congress to open up its process, over a third of all committee hearings were closed to the public. Today virtually all hearings are open with many now televised, primarily by C-SPAN (Ornstein et al., 1992). The televised proceedings of the nomination hearings of Robert Bork and Clarence Thomas riveted millions of viewers to their television sets and gave many a revealing look at just how the process is used by legislators to further aims other than the elucidation of an issue.

Investigative Hearings. The hearing most familiar to the average person is the investigative hear-

ing. From the very beginning of the Republic, when the House of Representatives in 1792 appointed a select committee to inquire into the St. Clair expedition, to present-day concerns over government malfeasance, congressional investigations have captured the nation's attention in a manner not possible with other forms of legislative activity.

The power to investigate is not one of the powers expressly granted to Congress, but the Supreme Court has ruled that it can be exercised as an implied power (*McGrain v. Daugherty*, 1927). There is little controversy over whether Congress has or needs the power to investigate in order to meet its obligation to enact legislation, to oversee the administration of its enactments, and to inform the public. Criticism has, for the most part, focused on the extent of the legislature's power and the manner in which investigations are carried out. Initially, the courts attempted to limit the scope of congressional investigations by insisting that they be related to some legislative purpose (*Kilbourn v. Thompson*, 1881). The modern Court, however, has come to take a much less restrictive position: "To be a valid legislative inquiry there need be no predictable end result" (*Eastland v. United States Serviceman's Fund*, 421 U.S. 491, 509 [1975]).

Primarily because of the abuses of investigative power by such individuals as Sen. Joseph R. McCarthy and by the House Un-American Activities Committee (later known as the Committee on Internal Security) in the 1950s, Congress has adopted procedures to assure fairness in committee investigations (Fisher, 1990). The courts have also moved to define the scope and proper authorization for congressional hearings (*United States v. Rumely*, 345 U.S. 41 [1953]; *Gojack v. United States*, 384 U.S. 702 [1966]).

Future of Hearings. The extent to which hearings are utilized by committees depends upon the number of committees and the level of their workloads. The trend since the early 1950s (for which the first reliable figures are available) reveals, first, a dramatic increase in overall levels of congressional activity including committee hearings. This activity peaked in the mid 1970s and has been followed by a slow but steady decline in all levels of committee activity, but not to the levels of the 1950s. The total number of committees in the House and Senate peaked at 385 in the 94th Congress (1975–1977) and then began a steady decline of almost one-third, reaching a total of 284 in the 102d Congress (1991–1993). Likewise, the number of Senate committee and subcommittee meetings grew from 2,607 in the 84th Congress (1955–1957) to a high of 4,265 in the 94th Congress (1975–1977) and then declined to 2,340 in the 101st Congress (1989–1991). The House peaked in the 95th Congress (1977–1979) at 7,896 meetings, up from a total of 3,210 meetings in the 84th Congress. The House then declined, but not as precipitously as the Senate, to a total of 5,305 meetings in the 101st Congress (Ornstein et al., 1992).

Hearing Publications. Because one of the primary purposes of hearings is to gather opinions and information regarding proposed legislation, much valuable information is contained in the hearing publications. This information may range from a full transcript of the proceedings, to statistical analyses, texts of related reports, and expert testimony.

The Congressional Information Service's *U.S. Congressional Committee Hearings Index* (1981, pp. vii-ix) explains that committee hearings began to be recorded and printed only when committees became an important part of the legislative process. Well into the late 1800s, committee hearings were published only sporadically, and as late as the 1930s, committees viewed their hearings as internal documents for their own use and not as public documents. As a consequence, many hearings were never printed. Since that time, however, there has been a more systematic effort to preserve these valuable records.

Through the years committee publications have been stored in a number of places, including the U.S. Senate Library, the Library of Congress, congressional committee collections, and the Supreme Court Library, as well as a number of libraries maintained by major federal departments and private organizations. Many of these facilities are not open to the public.

In 1975 a project was completed that included placing on microfiche more than twenty-seven thousand congressional committee hearings publications held by the U.S. Senate Library, as well as an index and checklist of hearings held before 1935 that had been compiled from major sources outside the U.S. Senate collection.

One can refer to congressional committee hearings by consulting the indexes of the Congressional Information Service (CIS), which cover materials from the early 1800s through the first session of the 91st Congress. Subsequent Congresses are covered through CIS five-, four-, and one-year indexes.

The National Archives are another source of committee hearings. Committees have periodically turned over their records to the National Archives for storage and safe keeping. The extent of each committee's records held in the National Archives has been documented in two companion volumes compiled by the Archives staff (S. Doc. No. 100-42; H. Doc. No. 100-245).

[*See also* Investigations; Investigative Power; Subpoena Power; Witnesses, Rights of.]

BIBLIOGRAPHY

Bentley, Arthur F. *The Process of Government.* 1908. Repr. 1967.
Chamberlain, Joseph P. *Legislative Processes: National and State.* 1936. Repr. 1969.
Congressional Information Services, Inc. *U.S. Congressional Committee Hearings Index (1833–1969).* 1981.
Davidson, Roger H., and Walter J. Oleszek. *Congress against Itself.* 1977.
Fisher, Louis. *American Constitutional Law.* 1990.
Krehbiel, Keith. *Information and Legislative Organization.* 1991.
Maass, Arthur. *Congress and the Common Good.* 1967.
Ornstein, Norman J., Thomas E. Mann, and Michael J. Malbin. *Vital Statistics on Congress, 1991–1992.* 1992.
Truman, David B. *The Governmental Process: Political Interests and Public Opinion.* 1951.

JOSEPH K. UNEKIS

Committee Jurisdictions

Committee jurisdiction is a complex matter, determined by a number of factors. Paramount among these are House Rule X and Senate Rule XXV, which designate the subject matter within the purview of each standing committee. The rules list jurisdictions in broad topical terms rather than narrowly drawn language or programmatic references.

Select and special committee jurisdiction is generally included in the resolution authorizing a panel. Select committees usually do not have legislative jurisdiction and therefore cannot have measures referred to them. In the case of select or special committees, therefore, *jurisdiction* usually refers to investigative responsibility.

Within each chamber, some standing committees' jurisdictions overlap those of other committees, and the parallel yet distinctive House and Senate committee systems distribute policy responsibilities in somewhat different ways. Major analogous jurisdictional clusters can be identified, however, many of which correspond with committee names. (Table 1, adapted from Steven S. Smith and Christopher J. Deering [1990], identifies these jurisdictional clusters.)

All the areas over which a standing committee

has jurisdiction cannot necessarily be inferred from the committee's name, however. Because of the complexity of issues, jurisdictional divisions and matchups often seem arbitrary. For example, child nutrition falls within the purview of the Agriculture Committee in the Senate, where it is viewed as a food-related issue, but under the Education and Labor Committee's jurisdiction in the House, where it is viewed as an education-related issue.

Subcommittee jurisdictions further delineate these broad topical areas. Subcommittee jurisdictions are determined not by chamber rules but by the individual full committees and are often defined in committee rules. The level of specificity of subcommittee jurisdiction varies widely from committee to committee. In fact, some Senate subcommittee jurisdictions are designated solely by the name of the subcommittee, while other Senate committees merely number their subcommittees, giving the chairman (often on behalf of the full committee) the authority to determine the panels' responsibilities. House subcommittee jurisdiction is usually more formally defined.

Both House Rule X and Senate Rule XXV are broad and largely the products of an era in which governmental activity was not so extensive and relations between policies not so complex as now. Most of Rule X and Rule XXV was drawn from nineteenth- and early-twentieth-century precedents and codified in the Legislative Reorganization Act of 1946. Although both rules underwent modest revision in the 1970s (the Senate rule once and the House rule three times), there are legislative topics still omitted from the purview of any specified jurisdiction, as well as unclear and overlapping jurisdictions among those specified.

Accordingly, the formal provisions of the rules are supplemented by an intricate series of precedents and informal agreements governing the referral of legislation. In general, once a measure has been referred to a given committee, it remains the responsibility of that committee; if the measure is enacted into law, amendments to the law are presumed to be within the originating committee's responsibility. Relatedly, bills that are more comprehensive than the measure they amend or supersede are presumed to be within the jurisdiction of the committee reporting the more comprehensive measure. Therefore, policy areas considered in a broad manner may enable a committee to attain jurisdiction; if a more narrow approach were taken, this might not occur. The resultant procedural accretions of responsibility greatly expand the range and scope of subjects assigned to each committee.

In considering jurisdictional overlap, a distinction needs to be made between legislative and oversight responsibility. The former entails the authority to report measures to the full chamber; the latter, the authority to review or investigate. Although oversight jurisdiction may be given by a specific legislative enactment, it also accrues when committees accept responsibilities for broad topical areas. Hence, there are more likely to be broader and more frequent overlaps in oversight jurisdiction than in legislative jurisdiction. Legislative jurisdiction, however, is usually the occasion of the majority of overt conflicts between standing committees.

Several other factors are at work in fixing committee jurisdiction, although these are not formal or even acknowledged in rules or precedents. First, when determining the appropriate referral of a bill, the Speaker of the House and the House and Senate parliamentarians may take into account the committee assignments and generally acknowledged policy expertise of a measure's sponsor. This is especially true if the sponsor is a committee or subcommittee chairman or ranking minority member. Similarly, members may draft bills in such a manner as to possibly influence the referral to committee, especially in the Senate, where predominant jurisdiction is the controlling factor in referrals.

Second, the timing of a measure's introduction may also affect which committee receives a bill referral. For example, if a member introduces a bill following hearings on or press coverage of a subject in which that member was involved, there could be an implicit understanding that the sponsor wants the bill referred to his committee.

Third, even if a committee did not originally consider a measure, representation from its membership at the conference on the measure could be used to argue that the committee has an implicit claim on the measure's subject. The committee might thus begin to accrue jurisdictional prerogatives.

Fourth, on some occasions committee jurisdiction over specific authorizing legislation has been influenced or, arguably, specifically determined by which subcommittee of the Appropriations Committee considers appropriations requests for the programs authorized. Too, even though the rules of the House forbid legislating in an appropriations bill (i.e., making policy decisions in a bill limited to making monetary choices), the Appropriations Committee occasionally does make legislative policy in an annual, supplemental, or continuing appropriations bill that has not been considered by

TABLE 1. *Standing Congressional Committees and Their Jurisdictions*

SENATE COMMITTEE	HOUSE COMMITTEE	JURISDICTION
Agriculture, Nutrition, and Forestry	Agriculture	Agriculture and forestry development and conservation; farm credit and farmer assistance programs; nutrition programs, including food stamps; in House, rural electrification
Appropriations	Appropriations	House and Senate appropriations of money for government agencies and federal programs and activities
Armed Services	Armed Services	Military and defense matters, including human resources and weapons research and development
Banking, Housing, and Urban Affairs	Banking, Finance, and Urban Affairs	Regulation of banking industry and other financial institutions; money supply and its control; public and private housing; urban development; aspects of international finance and foreign trade; in Senate, mass transit
Budget	Budget	Setting annual spending targets and priorities for broad categories of governmental functions—health, education, defense, and so on—and reconciling revenues with expenditures
Commerce, Science, and Transportation	Energy and Commerce Merchant Marine and Fisheries Science, Space, and Technology	Coast Guard; Merchant Marine; science and technology; nonmilitary aeronautics and space sciences; communications; coastal zone management; interstate commerce; regulation of interstate transportation, including railroads; in Senate, also ships, pipelines, and civil aviation; in House, national energy policy generally; energy research and development; securities and exchanges; health care; consumer affairs and protection; Panama Canal
Energy and Natural Resources	Interior and Insular Affairs	Mining; national parks; wilderness areas and historic sites; territorial possessions of the United States; public lands; in Senate, regulation, conservation, research and development of all forms of energy (Energy and Commerce in House); in House, regulation of domestic nuclear energy industry

TABLE 1. *Standing Congressional Committees and Their Jurisdictions (Continued)*

Senate Committee	House Committee	Jurisdiction
Environment and Public Works	Public Works and Transportation	Environmental protection; water resources and flood control; watershed development; rivers and harbors; public works and buildings; highways; noise pollution; in House, surface transportation, except railroads, and civil aviation
Finance	Ways and Means	Taxation; Social Security; tariffs; in House, health care programs financed through payroll taxes
Foreign Relations	Foreign Affairs	Foreign relations and foreign policy; United Nations; in Senate, treaties; in House, international trade and economic policy
Governmental Affairs	District of Columbia Government Operations Post Office and Civil Service	Organization and reorganization of executive branch; intergovernmental relations; in Senate, municipal affairs of District of Columbia, civil service, postal service, census, while in individual committees in House; in House, revenue sharing (Government Operations)
Judiciary	Judiciary	Federal courts; appointment of judges (Senate only); constitutional amendments; crime; drug control and policy: immigration and naturalization; antitrust and monopolies; patents, trademarks, and copyrights; impeachment; in House, presidential succession
Labor and Human Resources	Education and Labor	Education; labor, including vocational rehabilitation, minimum wages; in Senate, public welfare and health (Energy and Commerce and Ways and Means in House); in House, school lunch program (Agriculture in Senate)
Rules and Administration	Rules House Administration Standards of Official Conduct	Rules of chamber; administration and management of chamber; federal elections; Smithsonian Institution; Library of Congress; in Senate, presidential succession
Select Indian Affairs (has legislative jurisdiction)	Interior and Insular Affairs Education and Labor	Indians generally, including land management and trust responsibilities, education, health, special services, claims against the United States
Select Intelligence (has legislative jurisdiction)	Select Intelligence (has legislative jurisdiction)	Intelligence activities and programs
Small Business	Small Business	Small business generally and Small Business Administration
Veterans' Affairs	Veterans' Affairs	Veterans' affairs, including pensions, medical care, life insurance, education, and rehabilitation

the appropriate authorizing committee of jurisdiction. Relatedly, since passage of the Budget and Impoundment Control Act of 1974, budget reconciliation measures (which, in mandating budget cuts, may effect program changes) have had potential influence on committee jurisdiction. For example, when the Budget Committee directs a particular committee to respond to reconciliation instructions (especially in an area of overlapping jurisdictions) or when a committee traditionally considers programs under specific budget functions, these circumstances can be used to support a committee's jurisdictional claims. (It should not be assumed, however, that legislative committees deliberately use the Appropriations Committee or Budget Committee, or the appropriations or budget reconciliation process generally, to avoid jurisdictional disputes, although these options are always open.)

In 1974, with the adoption of the Committee Reform Amendments (H. Res. 988, reported by the Select Committee on Committees chaired by Rep. Richard W. Bolling and modified by a Democratic caucus panel chaired by Rep. Julia Butler Hansen), the House authorized the referral of measures to more than one committee. House Rule X, clause 5(c) invested in the Speaker the authority to refer measures in a joint, split, or sequential manner. Multiple referrals have since been used frequently, often to acknowledge overlapping jurisdictions and often to avoid choosing among committees' jurisdictional prerogatives. The effect has been to further broaden committee jurisdictions and further fragment policy and program responsibility.

In the Senate, multiple referrals are possible but rarely used. Unanimous consent is often difficult to obtain, and a motion to make multiple referrals, granted to the leadership in 1977 (pursuant to recommendations reported by the Select Committee on Committees chaired by Sen. Adlai E. Stevenson III), has not yet been invoked.

[*See also* Referral.]

BIBLIOGRAPHY

Smith, Steven S., and Christopher J. Deering. *Committees in Congress.* 2d ed. 1990.

U.S. House of Representatives. Select Committee on Committees. *Monographs on the Committees of the House of Representatives.* 93d Cong., 2d sess., 1974.

U.S. Senate. Temporary Select Committee to Study the Senate Committee System. *The Senate Committee System: Jurisdictions, Referrals, Numbers and Sizes, and Limitations on Membership.* 94th Cong., 2d sess., 1976.

JUDY SCHNEIDER

Markups

Markups are sessions held by a congressional committee during which the text of a bill is discussed and revised. The term *markup* is derived from the practice of literally marking up the original text of the bill to reflect the committee's proposed changes. Bills may be examined and revised by the committee line-by-line, paragraph-by-paragraph, section-by-section, or title-by-title. Alternatively, a complete substitute text for the entire bill may be offered. Committees also may decide not to alter the original bill at all, although this is rare.

The measure used for purposes of discussion and revision in committee is usually a previously introduced bill that had been referred to the committee. However, sometimes an informal draft, which has never been introduced, is used instead. The bill or draft, typically presented by the chairman to the committee for consideration, is known as "the chairman's mark." The decision of which bill or draft to use for the markup session is an important strategic choice because it is generally simpler to defend existing language than it is to form the consensus necessary to alter it.

Markup sessions are held at either the subcommittee or full committee level, or both. The full committee may choose to accept the subcommittee's modifications or may decide to repeat the entire markup process. Markups normally follow the completion of hearings, but committees need not have held hearings prior to holding a markup session on a bill. Conversely, not every bill on which hearings were held is guaranteed a markup. Many measures receive some committee consideration but do not complete the committee process for political or policy reasons.

Markup practices vary among the legislative committees of the House and Senate. Most committees follow formal parliamentary procedure, which requires that proposed changes to the text under review be offered as motions, known as amendments. These amendments modify or strike out existing language or insert new text. They are discussed, then adopted or rejected by a majority vote. Some committees, however, utilize a more informal procedure. Their members discuss and negotiate any changes to the text, reach a consensus, and defer to the committee staff the responsibility for drafting the precise language to reflect their agreements.

Markup sessions may end with a vote on whether or not to report the committee version of the bill to the floor for further consideration. Or a committee may choose to wait for all its members to have an opportunity to examine the marked up version of the bill, taking the vote on reporting the measure to the floor in a subsequent session. In both the House and Senate, the decision to report must be made by majority vote, with a quorum physically present, or the vote may be challenged on the floor.

In 1973, the House changed its rules to encourage committees and subcommittees to open markup sessions to the press and public. The Senate followed suit in 1975. Committees in both chambers retain the right to close any particular session if a majority of its members so vote. While open sessions remain the general practice, markups on appropriations, tax, defense, and national security bills are frequently closed.

BIBLIOGRAPHY

Calmes, Jacqueline. "Fading Sunshine Reforms: Few Complaints Are Voiced As Doors Close on Capitol Hill." *Congressional Quarterly Weekly Report*, 23 May 1987, pp. 1059–1060.
Oleszek, Walter J. *Congressional Procedures and the Policy Process*. 3d ed. 1989. Pp. 101–103.
Tiefer, Charles. *Congressional Practice and Procedure*. 1989. Pp. 167–170.

ILONA B. NICKELS

Committee Reports

Since 1880, the House has required its committees to issue a written report accompanying each bill sent to the floor for consideration. In the Senate, however, committee reports are voluntary. Committee reports explain committee actions on a bill and present the case to the full chamber for passage of the legislation.

Reports must contain a section-by-section analysis of the measure and describe the changes recommended by the committee to the original introduced version of the bill. In addition, reports must contain a side-by-side comparison with existing law to show how the proposed measure would alter it. This requirement for a current law comparison is termed the *Ramseyer Rule* in the House and the *Cordon Rule* in the Senate, after the lawmakers who first proposed it in each house (Rep. C. William Ramseyer [R-Iowa] and Sen. Guy Cordon [R-Oreg.]). Roll-call votes taken in committee also must be listed in committee reports. Other content requirements include cost estimates of implementing the legislation, a regulatory impact statement, and an analysis of the impact on the inflation rate. Executive comments received from federal agencies on the proposed legislation are frequently included in the report as well, although these are not mandatory.

Committee members may also insert in the report their own views on the proposed measure. If they are essentially in agreement with the viewpoint expressed in the committee report, their statements are included as "supplemental" or "additional" views. The statements of individual members in opposition to the committee's perspective are termed "minority" or "dissenting" views. These individual views often forecast possible future floor amendments and dissent.

Committee reports serve as an essential part of a bill's legislative history. Should the measure be enacted into law, federal agencies responsible for its implementation will turn to the committee report for guidance regarding congressional intent when the language is not clear. If the measure is ever challenged legally, courts of law may refer to the committee report as an aid in interpreting the text. It is because of this value to the legislative history of a measure that most Senate committees choose to issue reports, even though they are not required to do so.

At times, however, the press of legislative business makes expediting the normal reporting procedure necessary, especially if time constraints would make preparation of a committee report difficult prior to its scheduled floor consideration. While Senate committees can simply choose to send a measure to the floor without a report, House committees must use special procedures to circumvent the written report requirement. One procedure used in the House for this purpose is "suspension of the rules." Because all rules of the House are waived when a bill is under suspension, no point of order can be lodged against its consideration on the grounds that a committee report is not available. House committees may also arrange for a friendly floor motion or unanimous consent request to discharge themselves from further consideration of a specific measure. The effect of discharging obviates the requirement for a written report.

BIBLIOGRAPHY

Tiefer, Charles. *Congressional Practice and Procedure*. 1989. Pp. 180–186.
U.S. House of Representatives. *Procedure in the U.S. House of Representatives*, by Lewis Deschler and

William Holmes Brown. 4th ed. 97th Cong., 2d sess., 1982. Chap. 17, secs. 39–45.

U.S. Senate. *Riddick's Senate Procedure, Precedents, and Practices*, by Floyd M. Riddick and Alan S. Frumin. 101st Cong., 2d sess., 1992. S. Doc. 101-28. Pp. 1176–1201.

ILONA B. NICKELS

Standing Committees

Standing committees are primarily responsible for crafting the legislative proposals that are subsequently debated on the floor of the U.S. House of Representatives or U.S. Senate. Standing committees are characterized by their permanence and legislative authority: standing committees continue from Congress to Congress, and they have the power to receive and report legislation.

The House and Senate have independently developed parallel standing committee systems; each body has organized its committees to correspond roughly to the responsibilities of executive branch departments. Most standing committees in both bodies have further divided their work into subcommittees. In modern Congresses there have been slightly fewer than twenty standing committees in the Senate and slightly more than twenty in the House.

Standing committees serve as Congress's issue specialists. When members believe a problem requires a legislative remedy, the committee considers policy options and writes a legislative proposal to address the issue. Measures agreed to by a majority of committee members are reported from committee and may then be debated by the entire House and the entire Senate and enacted into law.

In addition to processing legislation, standing committees plan and conduct public hearings and other fact-finding activities. Committees also review, or oversee, the progress of programs administered by federal agencies.

Legislators tend to remain on the same committees throughout their congressional careers. Standing committees are an integral part of the legislative process, and their activities can and often do shape legislative decision making.

BIBLIOGRAPHY

Davidson, Roger H., and Walter J. Oleszek. *Congress and Its Members.* 3d ed. 1990.
Smith, Steven S., and Christopher J. Deering. *Committees in Congress.* 2d ed. 1990.

MARY ETTA BOESL

Select and Special Committees

Select and special committees are temporary, ad hoc study panels that function without legislative authority. Both the U.S. Senate and U.S. House of Representatives usually set specific boundaries within which each select or special committee must operate. House or Senate rules that create the panels specify the length of time a committee will exist and the specific policy issue it will investigate.

Traditionally, select committee members were appointed by the Senate or the House, and special committee members were appointed by the leadership. In modern Congresses, the traditional distinction is no longer valid in either the House or the Senate. Both select and special committees are authorized by a resolution passed by a majority vote and are provided with operating budgets, staff, and office space. Members are assigned to both select and special committees by their respective political party organizations.

Generally select and special committees exist for one or two Congresses and are then disbanded. Only a few have continued over several Congresses. In the 103d Congress (1993–1995) select and special committees came under fire as wasteful expenditures that could no longer be afforded in the era of federal budget cutbacks, and the House of Representatives consequently eliminated all four of its ad hoc committees.

The House and Senate have created select and special committees in response to a variety of situations. Some have been investigative panels. An example is the House Select Committee to Investigate Covert Arms Transactions with Iran (the Iran-contra Committee), organized in 1987. Select or special committees have also been appointed when a necessary study would cross the jurisdictions of several standing committees, as with the Senate Select Committee to Study the Senate Committee System (1984). Other select and special committees have been formed around highly visible public policy issues or particular interest groups, such as the

---

Select and Special Committees of the 103d Congress

Permanent Select Committee on Intelligence (House)

Select Committee on Ethics (Senate)

Select Committee on Intelligence (Senate)

Special Committee on Aging (Senate)

SOURCE: U. S. Congress. Joint Committee on Printing. *Congressional Directory, 1993–1994.* 1993.

Senate Special Committee on Aging, created in 1977, and the House Select Committee on Children, Youth, and Families, first organized in 1983.

The House Permanent Select Committee on Intelligence and the Senate Select Committees on Intelligence, which function as standing committees in spite of their names, represent a special case. Created in the mid 1970s to study federal intelligence issues, these panels were later given legislative and budget authority.

BIBLIOGRAPHY

Congressional Quarterly. "The Committee System." In *Congressional Quarterly's Guide to Congress.* 4th ed. Edited by Mary Cohn. 1991.

Smith, Steven S., and Christopher J. Deering. *Committees in Congress.* 2d ed. 1990.

MARY ETTA BOESL

Joint Committees

Joint committees are permanent legislative panels organized by and responsible to both the U.S. House of Representatives and the U.S. Senate. Joint committee membership is equally divided between senators and representatives. The chairmanship of joint committees is rotated between the Senate and the House in alternating Congresses.

Congress now rarely grants legislative authority to joint committees; the last to have such authority was the Joint Committee on Atomic Energy, which disbanded in 1977. Many scholars attribute this reluctance to permanent standing committees' fears that a joint committee might infringe on their jurisdictions and an unwillingness on the part of the two houses to closely share the development of legislative proposals.

JOINT COMMITTEE ON INAUGURAL ARRANGEMENTS. *Left to right,* Senate minority leader Everett M. Dirksen (R-Ill.), chairman; Speaker of the House John W. McCormack (D-Mass.); Senate majority leader Mike Mansfield (D-Mont.); Sen. Benjamin Everett Jordan (D-N.C.); House majority leader Carl B. Albert (D-Okla.); and House minority leader Gerald R. Ford (R-Mich.), preparing for the inauguration of president-elect Richard M. Nixon, 1968. Photograph by A. E. Scott.

OFFICE OF THE HISTORIAN OF THE U.S. SENATE

However, joint committees do provide important options to Congress, and their value is reflected by the five panels that exist in the 103d Congress (1993–1995). First, joint committees have traditionally been utilized for shared administrative housekeeping tasks. The Joint Committee on the Library oversees the Library of Congress, and the Joint Committee on Printing oversees the Government Printing Office.

Second, panels such as the Joint Economic Committee and the Joint Committee on Taxation provide Congress with an additional layer of staff specialists on the complex issues of the national economy and the federal tax laws. Staffs of both joint committees work closely with individual members and with the House and Senate standing committees that do write legislation. These panels also provide Congress with additional opportunities to focus and mold legislative decision making through the use of studies and public hearings on selected policy issues.

[See also entries on the following joint committees: Atomic Energy Committee; Conduct of the War Committee; Congressional Operations Committee; Economic Committee; Library Committee; Organization of Congress Committee; Printing Committee, Joint; Reconstruction Committee; Taxation Committee.]

BIBLIOGRAPHY

LeLoup, Lance T. "Congress and the Dilemma of Economic Policy." In *Making Economic Policy in Congress*. Edited by Allen Schick. 1983. Pp. 6–37.
Smith, Steven S., and Christopher J. Deering. *Committees in Congress*. 2d ed. 1990.

MARY ETTA BOESL

COMMON CAUSE. A nonpartisan citizens' lobby, Common Cause concerns itself with correcting the abuses of money, secrecy, and power in the political system.

The organization's first newspaper ads in August 1970 successfully solicited members with the slogan, "Everybody Is Organized but the People." It grew to 70,000 members in its first six months. Since 1973, it has maintained a membership of more than 200,000. It grew to 275,000 members in the late 1980s and early 1990s, when its budget grew to more than $11 million.

Since its inception, Common Cause has shown a determination to tangle with political power. Its whistle-blowing, watchdog style creates ongoing

Common Cause Leadership

BOARD CHAIR	DATES OF SERVICE
John Gardner[1]	1970–1977
Nan Waterman	1977–1980
Archibald Cox	1980–1992
Edward Cabot	1992–

PRESIDENT	DATES OF SERVICE
Jack Conway	1971–1975
David Cohen	1975–1981
Fred Wertheimer	1981–

[1]Founder

public conflict with Congress. It has sued, filed complaints against, and publicly attacked Republican presidents and Democratic committee chairmen, and it urged the House Ethics Committee to investigate House Speaker James C. Wright, Jr.'s violation of House rules. The ensuing probe led to his resignation in June 1989. The organization wins no popularity polls on Capitol Hill, even though it is one of the few interest groups that defends salary increases for Congress combined with a ban on outside earned income and honoraria.

As an organization that focuses on accountability, Common Cause has its own strict rules of procedure. Its meetings are open; its finances are public; and board members are limited to two consecutive terms, except for the chairperson and president. Common Cause does not accept funds from corporations, labor unions, foundations, or government. The great bulk of its contributions are in sums of under $100.

From its start, the organization has created a culture of independence. Common Cause was deliberately structured as a lobbying organization with no tax-deductible arm. By raising so-called hard dollars, organizers sought the freedom to oppose any established interest, including the politically powerful in Congress and the executive branch.

Common Cause's organizational structure eschews the traditional chapters. Instead, it has established networks of Common Cause members by congressional districts, thereby allowing people to become active as issues excite and engage them. Common Cause has an organized capacity in all fifty states and nearly all 435 congressional districts.

BIBLIOGRAPHY

McFarland, Andrew S. *Common Cause: Lobbying in the Public Interest*. 1984.
McFarland, Andrew S. *Public Interest Lobbies*. 1976.

Rothenberg, Lawrence S. *Linking Citizens to Government: Interest Group Politics at Common Cause.* 1992.

DAVID COHEN

COMMUNICATIONS. Even before the ratification of the Constitution, communications was one of the services that national governments were expected to shape through legislation, judicial action, and administration. In English common law and in statutes, communication and transportation were included in a group of industries known as public utilities or public services. That classification, which can be traced back to the fourteenth century, imposes certain obligations on the firms in such an industry, such as the duty to serve all who apply for the service at a reasonable charge and in a nondiscriminatory manner. In contrast to other economic activities, then, communications has a long history of regulation (and even public ownership) to guarantee the performance of these obligations. As other new technologies such as electricity and gas were developed during the nineteenth century, they too were classified as public utilities and closely regulated. Thus, even in the period of U.S. history when regulation was largely anathema to the Supreme Court, public-utility industries were regulated and usually could not construct plants or market their services without a government franchise.

It is therefore unsurprising that the Constitution explicitly granted Congress power over the mails. Article I, section 8, clause 7 states that Congress shall have power "to establish Post Offices and post Roads." Congress enacted its first communications statute in 1792, creating the position of postmaster general, authorizing him to appoint an assistant and deputies, to make rules on how often to carry the mail, and to make regulations for the service and contracts of carriage. Scandal and charges of inefficiency have plagued the Post Office (now the Postal Service) from its beginnings up to the present. Nevertheless, from its inception it grew rapidly, and it continues to grow, notwithstanding the development of technologically more advanced forms of communication. These later forms of communications have been regulated nationally not under the Post Office clause but pursuant to the commerce clause, which gives Congress the power "to regulate Commerce with foreign Nations, and among the several States." While considerable controversy has surrounded the commerce clause in U.S. constitutional history, that controversy has not generally affected the communications business because communications industries have traditionally been viewed as public utilities. If information crosses state borders or the national border, the means of its transmission can be regulated by Congress.

The first communications device to which the commerce clause was applied was the telegraph. Less than twenty-five years after Samuel F. B. Morse invented a practical telegraph in 1837, the United States had thirty-two thousand miles of pole line transmitting five million messages per year. In 1861 it became possible to communicate coast to coast by telegraph, and in 1866 the second Atlantic cable was activated, permitting rapid communication between the United States and Europe. It is impossible to overstate the revolutionary impact of this new communication technology on business, the dissemination of information, and personal contact. Early on, Congress responded to the new industry in a number of constructive ways, most importantly by rejecting the postmaster general's request for government ownership. In this way the U.S. telegraph and, later, telephone industries were spared the retarding effects of government ownership and operation that long characterized European telecommunications.

Congress did, however, respond to Morse's request for $30,000 to build a demonstration line between Washington and Baltimore (the line, which opened in 1844, was a commercial failure). Many state legislatures facilitated telegraph development by allowing telegraph companies to incorporate, use public thoroughfares to erect poles and string wires, and condemn private property. In exchange, the states required telegraph companies to fulfill the public utility obligations of dealing with customers in a reasonable and nondiscriminatory manner and serving all who could pay reasonable charges and would agree to the company's reasonable regulations. These state statutes provided the model for federal legislation in telecommunications.

When the federal government provided a right-of-way in 1860, authorizing the submission of bids to construct a telegraph line from Missouri to the Pacific, it introduced an issue that would continue to plague telecommunications policy: Should the industry be subject to the laws of competition, or should it be a regulated monopoly? The legislative debates manifested concern in the U.S. government about the growing dominance of one of the telegraph carriers—Western Union. In that statute and in the Pacific Railroad Act of 1862, which authorized government support for railroad and telegraph construction to the Pacific, Congress groped toward a public utility policy. In the 1862 act, for example, it authorized a rate reduction if realized earnings in these industries were greater than 10 percent of cost. But this act and subsequent telegraph legislation did little more than spell out general public utility principles, providing no means to enforce them at the federal level. Western Union's growing dominance was unchecked during the telegraph era. Only a new technology—the telephone—was able eventually to erode the power of Western Union.

The Telephone and the Development of Commission Regulation. The patent for the telephone is considered the most valuable ever granted. Yet on the same day in 1876 two claims were filed in the Patent Office within hours of one another, one by Alexander Graham Bell and the other by Elisha Gray. Today, Bell is generally credited as the inventor of the telephone, and Gray is known only to historians of technology. Yet until the expiration of the basic patents in 1893 and 1894, contested patent claims continued to plague the telephone, shaping both the industry's structure and congressional responses to it. In brief, because American Telephone and Telegraph (AT&T) and its predecessor companies were monopolies, Congress manifested hostility toward them virtually from the start.

At the outset, telephone service was almost entirely local. Not until 1880 was long-distance calling possible. Accordingly, states and municipalities enacted most of the early regulatory statutes. For example, in 1881 New Hampshire made its telegraph legislation applicable to telephones, and in 1882 Wisconsin enacted legislation directed at telephone rate discrimination. The right of states to engage in such regulation was confirmed by the Supreme Court in the landmark 1877 *Munn v. Illinois* case, which reasserted common law public utility principles, allowing states to undertake comprehensive regulation over utilities. By analogy, Congress could enact similar legislation over public utilities engaged in interstate commerce. The mechanism that state legislatures, and then Congress, chose to carry out such legislation was the independent regulatory commission.

In 1887 Congress enacted the Interstate Commerce Act, establishing the Interstate Commerce Commission (ICC), whose job was to regulate railroad industry practices. That revolutionary statute and its state counterparts were noteworthy in several respects. First, the commissions set up under these statutes were intended to be relatively free from executive branch interference. For example, commissioners were appointed for fixed terms and, unlike other executive branch appointees, could not be removed at the discretion of the president or a governor. In addition, no more than a simple majority of commissioners could be members of a single political party. These and other provisions were designed to promote agency independence. At the same time, the statutes creating the agencies were relatively vague; they abounded, for example, in phrases such as "reasonable rates" and "unjust discrimination." Accordingly, it fell to these agencies, acting in part like courts adjudicating disputes and in part like legislatures making rules, to flesh out Congress's (or state legislatures') general pronouncements. In a word, independent regulatory commissions were given very wide discretion in regulating the businesses under their control.

Though independent regulatory commissions were originally designed to regulate railroads, at the end of the nineteenth century this began to change at the state level as the powers of the railroad commissions were extended over the telegraph and telephone. In 1910 the federal government followed suit as the Mann-Elkins Act, primarily concerned with railroads, empowered the ICC to regulate interstate telephone rates. Telephone regulation under Mann-Elkins came about almost as an afterthought; most of the debate about the act had concerned railroad short-haul–long-haul price discrimination. But on the House floor an amendment was offered requiring telephone companies to make "reasonable" long-distance charges and requiring the ICC to judge the reasonableness of rates. The ICC was empowered to declare unreasonable rates unlawful and to prescribe new ones. The act, however, was notably silent on the subject of telephone industry structure. The necessary implication of this silence was that the Justice Department could bring antitrust charges against telephone companies (more specifically, AT&T) under the Sherman Antitrust Act that congress enacted in 1890, even though they were subject to comprehensive regulation. This dual and conflicting governmental responsibility created considerable tension and uncertainty that persisted even after the AT&T breakup in 1984.

Between 1907 and 1913 AT&T and independent telephone companies made many acquisitions, contributing in part to increasing concentration in the industry at both the local service and long-distance levels. After investigation by—and negotiations with—the Justice Department, AT&T in late 1913 agreed to cease its acquisition policy. But when Congress next acted in the area of telecommunications, it had changed policy direction considerably. The Esch-Cummins Transportation Act of 1920, like other federal statutes covering telecommunications, was primarily concerned with railroad regulation but granted the ICC considerable power over telephone rate discrimination, rebates, and accounting practices, especially those dealing with depreciation charges.

A year later Congress enacted the Willis-Graham Act, extending ICC jurisdiction over telephone company mergers and consolidations. The ICC was given authority to approve such mergers and acquisitions if they "will be of advantage to the persons to whom service is to be rendered and in the public interest." The statute further exempted telephone mergers and acquisitions from the coverage of the antitrust laws—one of the few times Congress gave complete jurisdiction over telephone service to a single governmental authority. The Willis-Graham Act passed by wide margins in both chambers, and during the thirteen years when it was in effect, the ICC approved 271 mergers and acquisitions. Both long-distance and local service expanded rapidly, and long-distance rates tumbled during the 1920s. But the onset of the Great Depression in 1929 considerably changed the political climate, and public hostility toward public utilities reached the boiling point. At the same time, radio, a new technology, was altering the structure of telecommunications. Both of these factors led to the enactment of the Communications Act of 1934, the most important federal statute ever enacted in this area.

The Advent of Radio. In 1896 Guglielmo Marconi saw the commercial possibilities of the new wireless communications technology that had been discovered a few years earlier. At the age of twenty-two he was granted a patent and soon demonstrated that radio had a practical application as a navigational aid for ships. The safety role that could be played by wireless inspired the Wireless Ship bill of 1910, which would have required oceangoing steamers to be equipped with radio apparatus. The bill, however, was not enacted. It took a disaster, the sinking of the *Titanic* in April 1912, to prompt the passage of legislation requiring ships to carry radio equipment. The legislation, authorizing the secretary of Commerce and Labor to issue appropriate safety regulations for seagoing vessels, was enacted in June. It was followed by the Radio Act

of 1912, the first radio regulatory statute. At the time of its enactment, the major users of radio were the U.S. government, ships, and amateur operators; mass broadcasting had not yet been conceived. In consequence, the secretary of Commerce's discretionary authority to allocate frequencies and set standards was insufficient for the broadcasting boom that began in 1920, when the number of radio license applicants vastly proliferated.

Radio broadcasting was one of the new high-technology industries that triggered the prosperity of the 1920s, and as the stakes in radio increased, the rivalries grew increasingly intense. A series of conferences conducted under the auspices of the secretary of Commerce failed to resolve the hot issue of radio stations interfering with each other's signals. The Radio Act of 1927 was designed to resolve interference chaos and other problems. Congress placed the administration of the new law in the hands of a new independent regulatory commission, the Federal Radio Commission (FRC), consisting of five members. The new commission was intended to last for only one year, but Congress extended its authority thereafter. While the FRC's powers were much broader than those of the secretary of Commerce under the 1912 Radio Act, the anticompetitive bias of the older statute was retained. Property rights in the radio spectrum would not be bought and sold in an open market. Rather, the administrative agency would allocate spectrum licenses based on a set of presumed public interest criteria. That fundamental system continued under the Communications Act of 1934.

Communications Act of 1934. When the 1920s boom collapsed into the Great Depression, the U.S. political landscape changed forever. This was as true in communications policy as in other areas. By the time the Communications Act of 1934 was being considered, the industry consisted of a number of interests, each sometimes at odds with the others. These included the telephone giant AT&T, independent telephone companies, radio networks, and independent radio stations. While broadcasting was considered to be a different business from the telephone industry because it lacked the point-to-point communication characteristic of the telephone, there had been turf and interconnection disputes between the two fields, the most important of which was spurred by AT&T's short-lived participation in broadcasting.

In keeping with the New Deal's legislative impulse to draw strict boundaries between industries (as typified by the banking statutes), the Communications Act erected walls between public utility communication (telephone and telegraph) and broadcasting (radio and television). Many advocates of the new statute also made the common-sense argument that it was inefficient and clumsy to divide communications policy responsibility between the ICC and FRC. The communications jurisdiction of each should be combined into a new agency, they argued, the function of which would be to adopt policies that would provide a rapid, efficient, nationwide communications service with adequate facilities at reasonable charges. Thus the 1934 act also embraced the integrated planning theme advocated by many early New Dealers. But at the same time the idea of creating a unified communications agency indicated a dawning awareness of one of the persistent themes in telecommunications technology—market convergence. Technological advances always point to new applications in different markets—meaning that previously discrete markets inevitably converge.

Need for a Federal Communications Commission. Congress's genius in enacting the 1934 act was to create an agency with sufficiently broad powers to deal with all the technological, market, social, and other changes that were to come. Communications satellites, cellular telephones, and computer communications—to name a few technologies—were not even on the horizon in 1934, but neither the agency established then—the Federal Communications Commission (FCC)—nor the way in which it regulates has fundamentally changed in the face of these new advances. Thus, Congress has not been compelled, as in so many other policy areas, continuously to enact new statutes when new policy issues arise. In most instances it has left actual "legislating" to the FCC, and so the agency has accumulated much expertise in the process. The only cloud has been the problem of dual jurisdiction, for while the FCC has regulated interstate common carriers and broadcasting (although in different ways), these industries have still been subject to antitrust laws and judicial appeal.

The impetus to consolidate communications can be seen in legislative and executive pronouncements before the New Deal. President Franklin D. Roosevelt assumed the presidency in 1933 with a mandate to force fundamental changes in the American political economy. He carried a rubber-stamp Congress into office with him, so that during the early New Deal years, Roosevelt got what he wanted. One of the reforms he sought was a major reorganization of federal public utility regulation. Roosevelt envisioned three regulatory agencies devoted, respectively, to transportation, power, and communications. Virtually every actor in the process of preparing a new communications bill vocally supported the notion of unifying the regulation of communications under one agency. Public utility companies, however, were shy of changes to the regulatory structure: public utilities generally were under fire, and some of their detractors attributed much of the economic distress of the Depression to their activities. The electricity and gas utility scandals that erupted after the 1929 stock market crash, congressional investigations, a lengthy Federal Trade Commission inquiry of public utility holding companies, and the focus of public anger on utility magnate Samuel Insull clearly placed big utilities on the defensive. Although the large communications firms might have done nothing wrong, so much anger at big business had erupted in the early 1930s that all utility firms were wary of any new legislation.

There was much to justify their fear. For example, the House report on Roosevelt's communications bill envisioned a future report by the new regulatory agency on whether AT&T ought to be forced to engage in competitive bidding for equipment instead of largely relying on its subsidiary Western Electric. The new agency was expected to conduct a massive investigation into every controversial aspect of the telephone industry—an investigation that would doubtless lead to further legislation. And the House complained that there were significant gaps in ICC telephone regulation. Interestingly, although a massive investigation did take place and reached highly critical conclusions about AT&T, the feared legislation never materialized after the FCC made its final reports to Congress in 1939 and 1940. Instead, center stage in telecommunications policy shifted from Congress to the FCC, the Justice Department, and the courts.

Of course, this outcome could not have been predicted in 1934. AT&T, the largest actor, with the most to fear, opposed the new bill in congressional hearings. AT&T argued that neither it nor any other telephone company was a holding company in the negative sense. Nor had there been any complaints about interstate rates, which, it showed, had been declining since 1926. Nor had there been any significant complaints about the quality of telephone service. Indeed, AT&T proclaimed, the industry's behavior had been exemplary and ICC regulation had been satisfactory. Nevertheless, AT&T was un-

Landmark Communications Legislation

TITLE	YEAR ENACTED	REFERENCE NUMBER	DESCRIPTION
Mann-Elkins Act	1910	36 Stat. 539	Primarily a railroad statute, it added "telegraph, telephone, and cable companies" engaged in interstate commerce to Interstate Commerce Commission (ICC) rate regulation.
Radio Act of 1912	1912	37 Stat. 302	First radio regulatory statute. Its primary purpose was to promote the use of radio for marine safety and navigation. Repealed in 1927 (44 Stat. 1174).
Transportation Act of 1920	1920	41 Stat. 456	Imposed on the ICC an affirmative duty to develop and maintain adequate telephone and telegraph service.
Willis-Graham Act	1921	42 Stat. 27	Removed the telephone and telegraph industries from antitrust restrictions and imposed on the ICC jurisdiction over telephone company mergers and consolidations.
Radio Act of 1927	1927	44 Stat. 1162	Comprehensive regulatory statute for radio that required stations to be licensed and created the Federal Radio Commission to regulate the industry. Repealed in 1934 (48 Stat. 1102).
Communications Act of 1934	1934	47 U.S.C. 151	Created Federal Communications Commission (FCC), which assumed the ICC's telephone and telegraph jurisdiction and the Federal Radio Commission's jurisdiction over broadcast media. The new agency's jurisdiction over both common carriers and broadcasting was greatly expanded.
Communications Act Amendments	1943	57 Stat. 5	Granted the FCC power over telephone and telegraph company mergers, consolidations, discontinuances, and service reductions.
Communications Satellite Act of 1962	1962	76 Stat. 419	Created the Communications Satellite Corporation (COMSAT) as a quasi-public corporation to provide satellite communications services. The FCC regulates the relationships between COMSAT and its customers.
Cable Communications Policy Act of 1984	1984	98 Stat. 2779	Deregulated most cable rates, allowed the FCC to set franchise fee limits, and required utilities to give cable operators access to poles.
Cable Television Consumer Protection and Competition Act of 1992	1992	106 Stat. 1460	Re-regulated cable rates by requiring FCC to reduce rates to a level consistent with those facing effective competition. The act also granted alternative multichannel firms greater access to cable programming.

able to counter either the argument that communications regulation should be consolidated in one agency or the proposal that an investigation into the relationship between a telephone operating company and its supplier was in order when rates were based, in part, on equipment costs and the principal equipment supplier was owned by the operating company. A reasonable and impartial investigation, legislators argued, could determine whether there were arrangements that could guard against the very real incentive to inflate equipment costs.

AT&T also sought to avoid becoming embroiled once again in the broadcasting battles that promised to be ever more intense as the stakes in broadcasting increased. The telephone giant, which had abandoned broadcasting in the 1920s because it felt that such conflicts would make its telecommunications business more vulnerable to governmental critics, felt that it would inevitably be drawn into such controversies if a single agency was charged with jurisdiction over both broadcasting and telephone communication. Within the broadcasting industry the motives were more complex. But one thing is eminently clear. None of the broadcasting interests shared AT&T's perspective, and none were satisfied with the FRC's performance.

The developing structure of the broadcasting industry promised to make future disputes over communications regulation even more antagonistic than they had been in the past. Controversies between independent stations and the National Broadcasting Corporation (NBC), the first "network," continued unabated after the FRC's creation. But networking was so financially successful that the Radio Corporation of America (RCA) established two—the Red and the Blue. Meanwhile, a group of promoters created their own network—the Columbia Broadcasting System (CBS)—after having been rebuffed when they sought to produce shows for NBC. The new network, which needed telephone lines to link stations that would broadcast programs simultaneously and to link studios (often located outside city business districts) with remote broadcasting locations, charged that an NBC–AT&T conspiracy was denying them interconnection. The FRC lacked the power to order interconnection. Given the high transaction costs of lobbying each state public utility commission or legislature to require mandatory interconnection under these circumstances, the independents and CBS had a clear incentive to promote the establishment of a new federal agency with comprehensive jurisdiction over wire and wireless transmission and the boundaries between them. Notably, RCA, which controlled the Red and Blue networks, also supported the creation of a new commission that would have the power to compel interconnection. Although Owen D. Young, RCA's chairman, did not charge that AT&T had impeded interconnection, he wanted the security of a formal rule.

Many independent broadcasters who feared their demise in the face of the growing networks favored the creation of the FCC for different reasons. The FRC was effectively lending the imprimatur of government to the new system of network broadcasting in which the networks controlled program production (even if they did not necessarily produce programs) and transmission. Since RCA controlled patents in every phase of wireless transmission, this corporation seemingly held monopolistic hegemony in the broadcasting industry. Many radio stations, therefore, viewed the FRC with suspicion or hostility for permitting this continued control. For example, in January 1929 the president of the independent New Jersey State Broadcasters Association charged that the FRC was incompetent and had been used to effect a monopoly in the radio business.

The independents, however, did not call for the end of regulation but rather for better regulation. For example, they approved enlarging an aggrieved party's right to appeal an adverse commission decision to the courts. They also favored expanding the right of radio stations to intervene in agency proceedings. Thus, both the independents and the networks supported the creation of an FCC, but for very different reasons. The large number of interests favoring the creation of a new agency, the anti–big business spirit of the times, and the apparent plausibility of the agency-consolidation argument virtually assured that the new statute would be enacted.

The president's bill (known as the Dill bill, after sponsor Sen. Clarence C. Dill, D-Wash.) was debated in the Senate on 15 May 1934. The debate concerned various amendments, not the heart of the bill, and the bill passed without a roll-call vote. In the House, where a related bill was sponsored by Sam Rayburn (D-Tex.), the entire debate took only two hours on 2 June 1934. Once again there was virtually no disagreement on the bill's substance, and once again the bill passed without a roll-call vote. Differences in the House and Senate versions were resolved in conference committee, with Rayburn's version by and large prevailing. President Roosevelt signed the Communications Act into law on 19 June 1934.

Structure of the Communications Act. The 1934 statute purports to provide a comprehensive scheme of telecommunications regulation. It is divided into six titles. Title I covers general matters such as the act's purpose, definitions of legal terms, and the structure of the FCC. Title II deals with telephone companies and other common carriers. Title III concerns radio broadcasting and, after the advent of television, came to encompass television broadcasting. Title IV covers procedural and administrative matters. Title V contains a few criminal provisions, and Title VI details a variety of miscellaneous matters. Titles I through III contain the act's most important provisions for the regulation of communications.

Title I begins with a preamble that states in general terms the purposes of the act and the reasons that a new agency is being created to attain these objectives. Before looking at this language, it is important to deal with a very important misconception. Preambles of necessity speak in very general terms. But that does not mean they must be dismissed as carrying as little weight as political party platforms or Fourth of July speeches. To the contrary, agencies can be compelled to take such language seriously, and courts have taken agencies to task for failing to attempt to fulfill their missions. Only two years before the enactment of the 1934 statute, the Supreme Court criticized the ICC in the famous *New York Central Securities v. United States* (287 U.S. 12, 24 [1932]) case: "It is a mistaken assumption that the [public interest] criterion is a mere general reference to public welfare without any standard to guide determinations. The purpose of the Act, the requirements it imposes and the context of the provision in question show the contrary." In writing the Communications Act, Congress was clearly aware of that decision, in which the Court measured ICC actions against such statutory goals as efficiency, adequacy of service, and the best use of transportation facilities.

It is within this context that we must look at the language of section 1, which charges the FCC with promoting "a rapid, efficient, nation-wide and world-wide wire and radio communication service with adequate facilities at reasonable charges." One might assume that such phrases as "adequate facilities" and "reasonable charges" are so elastic that they can mean anything the agency decides to make them mean. But this is not the case. Those who draft such legislation are aware of the way in which a long history of similar matters at the federal and state levels has sharply narrowed the permissible limits of such phrases. Many court cases, for example, have restricted the zone in which the FCC can determine whether a charge is "reasonable" or not. For these reasons, the FCC must make constant reference to the requirements set forth in the preamble in justifying its pronouncements. At the same time, this dynamic also helps to explain why parties adversely affected frequently challenge agency pronouncements—sometimes successfully.

Title I, section 4 sets up the Federal Communications Commission as an independent regulatory commission in which no more than a simple majority may be members of the same political party. Originally the commission had seven members, but 1982 legislation reduced the number to five. Commissioners, one of whom is the chair, are nominated by the president and confirmed by the Senate. Terms are for seven years and vacancies are staggered. Like the other independent regulatory agencies, commissioners may not be removed by the president before their terms have expired. All these constructs are intended to preserve the independence of commissioners and their staffs, and the evidence indicates that these provisions have worked well. Because the stakes in telecommunications have become so high, the FCC has been subject to considerable congressional scrutiny. Many of its decisions have been bitterly contested, and those who have been ill-served by the FCC's rulings have sought to involve Congress in reversing adverse opinions. Yet the agency has been largely free of scandal. Many of its decisions have favored small, upstart companies such as MCI and Carterfone against the interest of the giants such as AT&T. And while one may disagree with many of its decisions, the commission has always provided reasoned opinions for its actions. For these reasons, the FCC has largely escaped calls (not uncommon in other fields) to abolish or reorganize the agency.

Title II of the statute lists the responsibilities that the FCC inherited from the ICC. The agency requires common carriers to furnish service on reasonable request at reasonable rates. Carriers are required to file accounting data that justify rates and to show that rates, practices, and subscriber rules are reasonable. The FCC examines rates and practices and may suspend rates and disallow practices, and it can order refunds to customers who have been overcharged. Finally, the agency approves or disapproves applications for new services and firms, mergers and acquisitions, the construction of new lines, and the reduction and abandonment of service. Many of the matters that fall under Title II jurisdiction are highly complex and decisions numbering one hundred pages or more are not unusual.

Title III deals with radio and television. This part of the agency's jurisdiction was inherited from the FRC. But as with its authority over common carriers, the FCC's power over broadcasting is more extensive than was the predecessor agency's. The most important set of activities in this area is the licensing and renewal of radio and television stations. These proceedings are often contested, involving several competing applicants for a slot. The agency also engages in the difficult process of spectrum allocation—an activity that overlaps with the common-carrier side of its responsibilities since common carriers require spectrum allocation for long-distance and overseas transmission. This responsibility also includes assigning frequencies for automatic garage-door openers and ham radios.

The overall system worked relatively well even in the post–World War II era, during which there have been massive technological advances in telecommunications. In the face of these changes, beginning with the development of commercial television on the broadcasting side and microwave transmission of long-distance messages on the common-carrier side, Congress legislated very little. It left the basic structure of the Communications Act of 1934 intact, allowing the FCC, the courts, and the Justice Department to make policy. In only a few instances since World War II has Congress enacted new communications legislation. But technological events are rapidly occurring that have crumbled the traditional regulatory divisions erected in the Communications Act of 1934. Lines between computing and communications are now blurred, while the same fiber, wires, or wireless can now carry traditional voice transmission, video and audio programming, streams of data, facsimile, and images. The digital revolution, breaking down traditional barriers, has arrived, and Congress is preparing a response that will dramatically revise the Communications Act of 1934.

Space Communications. The idea of using satellites for communications was publicly advanced by science fiction writer Arthur C. Clarke in 1945. But not until the mid 1950s did technology advance to the point of making the idea technologically feasible and economically practical. During that period rockets became sufficiently powerful and receiving equipment sufficiently low-noise to make communications satellites a real possibility. Russia's launch of *Sputnik I*, the first artificial satellite, in late 1957 spurred U.S. efforts to overtake the Soviets. As space experiments proceeded, the potential of satellites to supplant land lines and microwave for both broadcasting and telephone communication became clear to observers, Congress included. The potential benefits in international communication were especially provocative. When one combines the commercial possibilities with the national defense implications at a time when the Cold War

was most intense, the reason for Congress's near-unanimous support for the rapid development of commercial satellites becomes clear. In other words, the focus of congressional debate concerned not the objective itself but the way that the objective should be attained.

The critical question was what role the private sector would play. Specifically, many feared that AT&T would come to dominate satellite communication as it had long-distance telephone communication. The Kennedy administration concluded in 1961 that it wanted private, not public, ownership and operation of the coming communications satellite system. AT&T and other firms urged Congress to permit existing private carriers to operate the system on a nonprofit basis, while some left-wing Democratic legislators sought government ownership and operation, excluding private interests entirely. In February 1962 President John F. Kennedy proposed a compromise solution to Congress. His plan called for the creation of a for-profit corporation with two classes of stock: voting stock, which could be purchased by the public and by carriers up to certain limits, and nonvoting stock, available only to carriers and on which no dividends would be paid.

The debate in Congress was heated; the Senate tabled 122 amendments before passing the bill, 66 to 11. The House voted 372 to 10 to accept the Senate version, which spelled out how public stock would be sold, how directors would be selected, and other business details. The FCC was given substantial power to regulate the new corporation—called COMSAT—and the other carriers that would be involved in space communications. Notwithstanding the heated legislative debate, it would be hard to find a commercial statute that has worked more effectively than the law establishing COMSAT. COMSAT eventually became only one of several firms participating in the dramatically expanding field of international space communications. During the Nixon administration, communications satellites came to be used for domestic communication. But this was effected entirely by FCC action—once again a testament to Congress's genius in designing the 1934 statute.

Cable and Broadcasting. While the FCC, the courts, and the Justice Department have played the principal roles in postwar common-carrier policy, Congress has been far more active in the broadcasting realm. And in almost every instance Congress has failed to resolve the policy issues. Even legislative support for public television has led to charges that left-wing interests have come to dominate the production of such programs—at public expense. But it was the advent of cable television that led to the most heated controversy.

Cable television originated when local entrepreneurs put up television antennas on mountaintops to pick up over-the-air signals that they then transmitted through coaxial cable to homes out of the broadcast range of television stations. That initial use, known as community antenna television, was modest, merely supplementing over-the-air television in areas that went unserved. But, gradually, other entrepreneurs began to see additional uses, transforming community antenna television into cable television, with cable operators becoming full-fledged competitors of local television stations and networks.

The FCC first showed an interest in cable in 1952. It presented a memorandum stating the two essential questions: "(1) Do such operations constitute broadcasting within the meaning of the Communications Act of 1934, or (2) do such operations constitute interstate common carrier operations within the meaning of the act?" Since under the Communications Act of 1934 the FCC had express jurisdiction only over common carriers or broadcasters, if cable TV did not fall within either category, the commission could take no action to regulate it. At that time, the FCC decided not to assert jurisdiction, claiming that it did not have the authority. It soon reversed itself on the grounds that cable TV was ancillary to over-the-air television as well as being a common-carrier service. The latter claim was especially tenuous since, under traditional concepts, cable-TV companies more closely resembled broadcasters than common carriers. Nevertheless, the FCC in 1966 asserted jurisdiction over all cable systems. It asserted such authority because of the adverse impact that cable was perceived to be inflicting on over-the-air television, especially ultra-high-frequency (UHF) television. In 1968 the Supreme Court upheld the FCC's authority, leading to the promulgation of comprehensive rules beginning in 1969. But in 1979 the Supreme Court rejected those rules, emphatically asserting that the FCC could not regulate cable systems as common carriers and that the agency had gone far beyond what was reasonably ancillary to discharging its broadcasting regulatory obligation. The Court invited Congress to clarify the situation, but not until 1984 did Congress enact legislation regarding cable television.

The heart of the 1984 Cable Communications Policy Act was the decision to deregulate cable, a decision based on three important issues. First, Congress feared that without a check on franchise fees local governments would be tempted to solve their fiscal problems by levying a discriminatory tax on the cable industry. In addition, legislators believed that the cable-TV industry had matured and was capable of competing with over-the-air television. Consequently, rate regulation at the local level was no longer a necessity. Finally, Congress concluded that cable services, unlike electricity or gas, were nonessential and did not possess any of the characteristics of public utilities. In short, Congress backed cable deregulation because legislators felt that the benefits of cable technology were being impeded by local regulation and should be offered in a competitive market environment.

Assurance of enactment was aided by the political climate of the mid 1980s, which favored deregulation of many industries. As enacted by Congress, the legislation largely deregulated the cable communications industry and removed most of the ability of municipal, state, or federal franchising authorities to regulate the rates charged by franchisees for the provision of cable service where there was "effective competition." It also recognized the power of municipalities to grant and renew franchises and outlined standard franchise procedures to protect cable companies from potentially unfair local decision-making processes. But the 1984 act amounted to little more than a deal between municipalities and the cable industry, ratified by Congress. Rates skyrocketed, and critics claimed that cable operated as an unregulated monopoly.

Under the 1984 law cable companies lived in the best possible world—local monopolies largely unregulated by the FCC. Large increases in cable rates after the enactment of the 1984 statute coupled with service deficiencies in many local markets antagonized large segments of the middle class, which pressured Congress to either promote competition or re-regulate cable rates. In the heat of the 1992 election campaign Congress sought to promote both re-regulation and competition in the Cable Television Consumer Protection and Competition Act of 1992, enacted over the veto of President George Bush. The 120-page law and the voluminous FCC regulations that it has generated are models of imprecision and ambiguity. While the ultimate interpretations of the law are impossible to forecast, the primary intentions of the act's sponsors are clear. The FCC was required to implement regulations that would reduce rates to "competitive" levels and permit alternative distribution modes, such as direct broadcast satellites, greater access to cable programming. The act required network-affiliated stations to negotiate retransmission agreements with local cable companies, but required the cable companies to carry many independent commercial and noncommercial TV stations. At the same time, most telephone companies were still barred from entering the cable business. Few communications analysts predicted that the 1992 statute would be the last word in broadcast regulation. Events, especially the market convergence stemming from the rapid technological change alluded to earlier, were undermining the statute in 1994.

No End in Sight. Probably no sector has witnessed such dramatic changes since the founding of the Republic as communications. The pace of change continues to accelerate. The marriage of computing and communicating, and such new technologies as direct broadcast satellites (DBS), high-definition television (HDTV), videotext, compact discs, cellular telephones, personal communications networks, and others now in development will further transform the telecommunications landscape. Through it all the Communications Act of 1934 has endured, providing an expert agency with the tools to make policy. Nevertheless, market convergence will mandate the act's overhaul.

[See also Communications Act of 1934; Communications Satellite Act of 1962; Sherman Antitrust Act; Telegraph.]

BIBLIOGRAPHY

Allard, Nicholas W. "The 1992 Cable Act: Just the Beginning." *Hastings Communications/Entertainment Law Journal* 15 (Winter 1993): 305.
Brock, Gerald W. *The Telecommunications Industry.* 1981.
Coase, Ronald H. "The Federal Communications Commission." *Journal of Law and Economics* 2 (1959): 1–40.
Coll, Steven. *The Deal of the Century.* 1986.
Douglas, Susan J. *Inventing American Broadcasting.* 1987.
Kinsley, Michael. *Outer Space and Inner Sanctums.* 1976.
Le Duc, Don R. *Cable Television and the FCC: A Crisis in Media Control.* 1973.
Loeb, G. Hamilton. *The Communications Act Policy toward Competition: A Failure to Communicate.* 1977.
Rosen, Philip T. *The Modern Senators.* 1980.
Stone, Alan. *Public Service Liberalism.* 1991.
Stone, Alan. *Wrong Number.* 1989.
Thompson, Robert L. *Wiring a Continent.* 1947.

ALAN STONE

COMMUNICATIONS ACT OF 1934 (48 Stat. 1064–1105). The most obvious purpose of the Communications Act of 1934 was to unify communications regulation under one agency. Prior to its enactment, interstate telephone regulation was under the jurisdiction of the Interstate Commerce Commission (ICC), whose primary responsibility was railroad regulation. Indeed, some critics felt the ICC was so occupied by railroad regulation that it devoted very little attention to the increasingly important interstate telephone business. The other important communications regulator was the Federal Radio Commission, which controlled the allocation of radio spectrum frequencies to broadcasters. The agency created by the 1934 act—the Federal Communications Commission (FCC)—inherited jurisdiction over both forms of communication. But the new agency was given far more extensive powers to regulate communications than its predecessor agencies had had.

This expanded authority has much to do with the fact that the statute was enacted during the early New Deal. Many New Dealers held that government planning constituted the wave of the future. The preamble of the statute reflected this viewpoint by outlining a comprehensive national plan for communications. The seven members of the new agency were directed to make decisions that would lead to "a rapid, efficient, nation-wide, and world-wide wire and radio communications service with adequate facilities at reasonable charges." For this reason the new agency was given powers over two very different sets of activities. On the traditional telephone, or common carrier, side it was to be largely concerned with interstate rates and service, while on the broadcast side it was to be principally concerned with spectrum allocation and comparative licensing procedures.

The act was favored by all communications interests except American Telephone and Telegraph (AT&T) and its allies in the independent telephone industry. The act passed Congress overwhelmingly, and until the technological developments of the 1990s, it provided the FCC with sufficient powers to deal with a modern communications world that differed vastly from that of 1934.

[See also Communications.]

BIBLIOGRAPHY

Loeb, G. Hamilton. *The Communications Act Policy toward Competition: A Failure to Communicate.* 1977.
Stone, Alan. *Public Service Liberalism.* 1991.

ALAN STONE

COMMUNICATIONS SATELLITE ACT OF 1962

(76 Stat. 419–427). When confronted in 1962 with the need to establish an organization to promote commercially the emergent space telecommunications technology, Congress passed the Communications Satellite Act (P.L. 87-624), creating a privately owned Communications Satellite Corporation (ComSat). ComSat was the product of compromise in a highly charged legislative struggle between those who wanted space communications development to be a government-dominated activity and those promoting the establishment of a privately owned corporation that would function according to market discipline. The latter group essentially won the debate, and ComSat was established as a private, shareholder-owned corporation under the regulatory supervision of the Federal Communications Commission. ComSat was designed to be a "carriers' carrier" and to represent the United States in the international space communications consortium INTELSAT. As a nod toward those desiring governmental participation in ComSat, it was decided that three of its directors would be appointed by the president. Their role in directing ComSat's corporate affairs is still subject to dispute.

ComSat is not a government corporation. By and large, Congress has been reluctant to use the statutory process for the establishment of private corporations, but, as in the case of ComSat, it has occasionally done so. ComSat is a private, profit-seeking corporation chartered by Congress, and its obligations are not explicitly or implicitly guaranteed by the federal government. Since there is no national law for incorporating corporations (this is a state function), the rights, responsibilities, immunities, and regulatory authorities for this corporation are contained in the enabling act. ComSat is a domestic provider of mobile communications services—maritime, aeronautical, and land based. It is a regulated communications carrier that has the right to merge with other corporations and own noncommunications corporations (e.g., ComSat is the majority stockholder in the Denver Nuggets, a franchise in the National Basketball Association) and presumably has the private right to declare bankruptcy.

BIBLIOGRAPHY

Galloway, Jonathan. *The Politics and Technology of Satellite Communications.* 1976.
Musolf, Lloyd D. *Uncle Sam's Private, Profitseeking Corporations.* 1983.

RONALD C. MOE

COMMUNISM AND ANTICOMMUNISM.

The issue of communism did not become a major preoccupation of Congress until the Cold War magnified the perceived threat of internal subversion and external attack. Nonetheless, individual members of Congress had been inveighing against such "un-American" phenomena as socialism, anarchism, and communism since the late nineteenth century. Between the two world wars congressional committees on occasion investigated communist activities in the United States. Then as later, Congress used its power of investigation more than its power to make laws in its efforts to combat communism. Because the American Communist party (CP) was usually seen as the agent of a hostile Soviet Union, Congress could invoke internal security as justification for "exposing" communists.

Congress first took formal note of the prospect of a communist revolution during the "red scare" of 1919, when the Senate's Overman Subcommittee, examining German propaganda, was empowered to extend its scrutiny to Bolshevik propaganda. Witnesses told lurid tales of the progress of the Russian Revolution, and the subcommittee issued solemn warnings about the Bolshevik menace. The red scare, however, was less the work of Congress than of the Justice Department, and when it began to subside in 1920, Congress failed to provide the sedition law requested by the attorney general. Congressional nerves were jolted again by the stock market crash of October 1929. Because of subsequent American Communist party involvement in the International Unemployment Day demonstrations of 1930 and charges about the subversive activities of the Amtorg Trading Corporation, the House established a committee, chaired by Rep. Hamilton Fish (R-N.Y.), "to investigate Communist propaganda in the United States and particularly in our educational institutions." This committee concluded that the CP should be outlawed, but no legislation resulted. In 1934 the appearance of Nazi groups prompted the House to establish the McCormack-Dickstein Committee to investigate subversive activities, but its hearings were unsensational. In 1935 the committee reported that neither communism nor fascism had made much impact in the United States.

This temperate view did not survive the decade, for New Deal experimentation fostered suspicions that the federal government itself had been penetrated by communism, and conservative Democrats and Republicans exacerbated these fears for ideological and partisan reasons. Henceforth, not only

A GOLD STRIPE ORGANIZATION

EDWIN PARNELL POST NO. 3615
VETERANS OF FOREIGN WARS

HENRY G. RISER, COMMANDER

HOWARD C. DAVIS, SR. VICE COMM.

LESCAR W. HARLAN, JR. VICE COMM.

RALPH J. SMELLEY, POST ADJUDANT

J. T. RHINEHART, QUARTERMASTER

FRED N. GRAY, CHAPLAIN

GEORGE B. HOLSTEAD, JUDGE ADVOCATE

DR. W. H. KIMBELL, M. D., POST SURGEON

P. O. BOX 155

RUSTON, LOUISIANA

Nov.11,1954

TO: President of the Senate, Senate Office Building, Washington, D.C.

Subject: A Petition To The Senate Of The United States.

WHEREAS, the Senate of the United States plans to convene in a special session for the purpose of censuring one of its own members, and,

WHEREAS, this action is strongly advocated and highly approved by the Daily Worker, by Leftists elements, by the Committee for an Effective Congress, as well as by other definite affiliates of the Communist Party or subversive groups, and,

WHEREAS, it has become common knowledge that the primary reason for such approval by these subversive forces is prompted by their desire to have the Senate of the United States lower its dignity and bring discredit upon itself by such action, and,

WHEREAS, such a censuring of one of its ownmembers, a Veteran, a patriot, and a scourge to RED elements in America, will lend aid and comfort to present and potential enemies of the United States, and,

WHEREAS, even contemplating such action has, in fact, reduced the prestige, the reputation of, and the respect due, this most august and pre-eminent law-making body in the World.

NOW, THEREFORE, BE IT RESOLVED, THAT WE, THE UNDERSIGNED AMERICANS, AND VETERANS OF FOREIGN WARS, RESPECTFULLY AND EARNESTLY REQUEST THAT THE MEMBERS OF THE SENATE CONTINUE TO MAINTAIN THE DIGNITY OF THE SENATE OF THE SENATE OF THESE UNITED STATES BY DEFEATING ON THIS OCCASION ANY MOTION TO CENSURE ONE OF THEIR OWN MEMBERS.

Edwin Parnell Post No.3615
Veterans of Foreign Wars
Ruston, Louisiana

Henry G. Riser,
Commander

PETITION TO THE SENATE. From a veterans' organization, urging the defeat of the motion pending before the Senate to censure Sen. Joseph R. McCarthy (R-Wis.). Revered by the petitioners as a genuine patriot and opponent of communist elements in the United States, McCarthy was censured by the Senate in 1954 for bringing that body "into dishonor and disrepute." NATIONAL ARCHIVES

would radical aliens and labor activists be suspect but also well-connected liberals, and both party competition and executive-legislative friction on occasion encouraged the deployment of the communism issue in American politics in the 1940s and 1950s. International tensions and the Cold War sustained and intensified Congress's interest in communism.

In May 1938, conservative Texas Democratic representative Martin Dies, Jr., secured a majority to investigate "subversive and un-American propaganda," launching the House Committee on Un-American Activities (HUAC) on its long career. In the late 1930s it pursued popular-front groups and New Deal agencies but enjoyed little prestige and limited influence. The Hitler-Stalin pact and the outbreak of war in Europe in 1939, when for a time international communism seemed to be abetting Nazi aggression, did more to disrupt the American Communist party, which both liberals and conservatives viewed with heightened distrust.

Fearing fifth-column operations, whether Nazi or communist, Congress in 1940 passed the Alien Registration Act (better known as the Smith Act), which in addition to regulating aliens made it unlawful for any person knowingly to advocate the overthrow of the government by force or even to be a member of any group with that objective. The Smith Act was thus a wide-reaching sedition law that could be used against any group perceived to believe in violent revolution. It was deployed against the Socialist Workers party (as well as "native fascists") during World War II, although the CP itself was for the moment left alone because the Soviet Union had become an ally of the United States. This circumstance also served to marginalize HUAC.

The advent of the Cold War, however, revitalized HUAC, and by the 1950s other congressional committees had joined in the hunt for reds. The highly conservative 80th Congress (1947–1949) indulged the forays of HUAC under the chairmanship of Rep. J. Parnell Thomas (R-N.J.); its 1947 hearings into communist influence in Hollywood in particular earned it much publicity and notoriety. The 80th Congress also sought to curb communism in labor unions with the Taft-Hartley Labor-Management Relations Act of 1947. Critics in Congress accused the Truman administration of negligence in the area of internal security, and these attacks—as well as the executive's anti-Soviet foreign policy objectives—served to harden the administration's stance against domestic radicalism. It invoked the Smith Act against CP leaders in 1948.

The Democratic administration and Republicans in Congress vied to display their anticommunist credentials, and as the Cold War deepened, American communists were cast even more starkly as traitors to their country. Close Democratic-Republican competition encouraged politicians to smear their rivals as "soft on communism." The Republicans resorted to such tactics even more vehemently after unexpectedly losing the presidential election of 1948: foreign policy reverses (such as the "fall" of China in 1949) added some resonance to their charges. When a well-connected former State Department official, Alger Hiss, who had first been accused in a HUAC hearing, was in effect convicted of being a Soviet spy in January 1950, the Republican charge that communists had penetrated the very heart of government seemed proved. In February 1950 Sen. Joseph R. McCarthy (R-Wis.) gave a spurious specificity to the charge with his claim to have documented proof of 205 communists, or, alternatively, "fifty-seven card-carrying members of the Communist party," in the State Department.

The escalation of the Cold War into the Korean War (1950–1953), during which Americans died in the fight against communism, encouraged McCarthyism, which abused civil liberties in the name of internal security. McCarthy was, however, more the product than the cause of this impulse, which was also displayed in the McCarran Internal Security Act of 1950. This act required communist and communist-front organizations to register with the government. The lives of private citizens and government employees were to be subjected to scrutiny and regulation. In the November 1950 election McCarthy's principal critic in the Senate, Democrat Millard E. Tydings of Maryland, lost his seat, seeming evidence of the potency of McCarthyism.

In the early 1950s congressional anticommunism reached its peak, and investigative committees focused on organizations and groups suspected of giving aid and comfort to an alleged communist conspiracy to overthrow the Republic. HUAC summoned entertainers, labor officials, and others to account for themselves. The Senate Internal Security Subcommittee was established with a similar agenda in 1951 and led the assault on the academic community. In 1953, following Republican success in the 1952 elections, Senator McCarthy assumed the chairmanship of another committee (the Government Operations Committee's Permanent Subcommittee on Investigations) with the mission of scrutinizing "government activities at all levels." These committees perfected techniques of exposure. Hostile witnesses could be sent to prison for contempt of Congress, a fate from which they might protect themselves by pleading the Fifth Amendment against self-incrimination. Resorting to the Fifth, however, usually cost them their jobs or put them on a blacklist. The investigating committees thus purged hundreds from the professions, the defense industry, the labor movement, and government service, summoning them in the knowledge that such exposure would deprive them of their livelihoods.

By the mid 1950s civil libertarians were pressing the question of whether such probes had any legitimate congressional purpose. With the end of the Korean War in 1953 quieting fears of a third world war, there seemed less reason to subordinate civil liberties to the demands of internal security. McCarthy's excesses also undermined the credibility of congressional investigators. His probe of Fort Monmouth, the site of army radar laboratories, led to an unseemly quarrel over an army dentist of allegedly "disloyal tendencies," and McCarthy's relations with the army further deteriorated when his chief counsel, Roy Cohn, sought favors for a friend who had been drafted. When McCarthy's bullying methods were exposed to millions during the televised Army-McCarthy hearings in the spring of 1954, his popularity waned. By this time the Republicans occupied the White House, and Republican leaders had been angered by McCarthy's continued indiscriminate attacks on governmental agencies. In December 1954 half the Republicans in the Senate joined with the Democrats to condemn McCarthy formally, after which he became a political leper, shunned by politicians and press alike.

McCarthy's real offense had been to apply the smear of communism to people who were patently not communists, and while his disgrace weakened congressional anticommunism it did not kill it. Soon after the Army-McCarthy hearings Senate liberals introduced the Communist Control bill, imposing criminal penalties for CP membership. In its final form in August 1954 it passed the Senate without opposition and the House with only two negative votes. Wary of the elections coming up in the fall of 1954, these liberals were hoping to protect people like themselves by making membership (not beliefs or associations) the mark of disloyalty. The Internal Security Subcommittee and HUAC also continued to operate for several years, HUAC retaining its distinctive existence until 1968 (although some of its functions were assumed for a time by the Committee on Internal Security). But in the late

1950s the Supreme Court was curbing the federal internal security program and even congressional powers of investigation, as it also largely dismantled the Smith Act. Congressional conservatives were furious at the Court's actions, but their power in Congress was diminishing with the resurgence of liberalism in both the Democratic and Republican parties. Because both major parties had established impeccable anticommunist credentials, there was little further partisan advantage to be gained in deploying the issue of communism.

[*See also* Army-McCarthy Hearings; Civil Liberties; Cold War; Internal Security; McCarran Internal Security Act of 1950; National Security Act; Un-American Activities Committee, House.]

BIBLIOGRAPHY

Griffith, Robert. *The Politics of Fear: Joseph R. McCarthy and the Senate.* 2d ed. 1987.

Heale, M. J. *American Anticommunism: Combating the Enemy Within, 1830–1970.* 1990.

Goldstein, Robert Justin. *Political Repression in Modern America: From 1870 to the Present.* 1978.

M. J. HEALE

COMPREHENSIVE ENVIRONMENTAL RESPONSE, COMPENSATION, AND LIABILITY ACT OF 1980

(94 Stat. 2767–2811). The program popularly known as Superfund was created by the Comprehensive Environmental Response, Compensation, and Liability Act (CERCLA; P.L. 96-510). Passed by Congress and signed by President Jimmy Carter in 1980, the law was Congress's response to the immense publicity surrounding an abandoned toxic waste dump in the Love Canal neighborhood of Niagara Falls, New York, where in 1978 the State of New York reported that buried wastes constituted a serious threat to the health of the residents. The Environmental Protection Agency (EPA) warned that thousands of dangerous dumpsites—frequently referred to as "ticking time bombs"—dotted the nation.

Two basic premises underlay the act: "shovels first" (meaning that top priority should be given to quick removal of hazardous waste) and "polluters pay." The law gave the EPA the task of identifying waste dumps, establishing a list of "priority sites," and cleaning them up, starting with the most dangerous. "Superfund" refers to the $1.6 billion trust fund established to finance the initial cleanup. Nearly 90 percent of this money came from a special tax on chemicals and petroleum. The law also authorized the government to replenish the fund by suing for damages those responsible for the pollution. It imposed "strict, joint and several" liability on all responsible parties: any responsible party—regardless of the extent of its involvement—could be forced to pay the full cost of remedial action.

Superfund soon became the focus of a major confrontation between the Reagan administration and Congress. In 1981 and 1982 several House committees criticized the EPA for failing to meet statutory deadlines and for negotiating "sweetheart" deals with polluters. Two committees—the House Public Works Committee and the House Energy and Commerce Oversight Subcommittee—issued subpoenas for thousands of pages of EPA documents. Following the advice of the Justice Department and citing executive privilege, Anne Gorsuch, administrator of the EPA, refused to comply. The House then voted to hold her in contempt of Congress. Within a few months Gorsuch had resigned. The assistant administrator in charge of Superfund spent time in jail for lying to Congress. Twenty top EPA officials resigned or were fired as a consequence of the scandal. Even after Gorsuch's exit, however, progress on cleaning up hazardous waste sites remained slow. Congressional Democrats continued to blame the Reagan administration and to push for more effective action.

In 1986, Congress reauthorized the program for another five years and made a number of important changes in the law. The Superfund Amendments and Reauthorization Act (SARA) increased the trust fund nearly fivefold, to $8.5 billion. It not only hiked the tax on chemicals and crude oil but added a new $2.5 billion broad-based tax on corporations. It established a detailed schedule for the EPA to begin work on the most dangerous sites, directed the agency to employ a strategy of detoxification rather than containment whenever feasible, required the EPA and the states to provide local communities with extensive information about environmental hazards and the cleanup process, and authorized citizen suits against those who violate any portion of the Superfund law.

Superfund spawned an enormous amount of litigation over who bears financial responsibility for hazardous waste dumps. But very few sites—less than one hundred—had been fully cleaned up by 1993. One reason for this was the inherent difficulty of the task, given the lack of a readily available technology for completely removing waste that has leached into the ground. Moreover, many scientists and EPA officials have come to believe that the

health risks posed by these sites are not nearly as severe as originally feared.

Many members of the public, Congress, and the media nonetheless continue to believe both that the danger posed by toxic waste dumps is very serious and that the federal government's response has been far from adequate. For this reason Superfund is likely to remain a source of legislative-executive conflict and media attention for some time to come.

BIBLIOGRAPHY

Congressional Quarterly Inc. *Congress and the Nation.* Vol. 5 (1981), pp. 583–585; vol. 6 (1985), pp. 449–461.

Landy, Marc, Marc Roberts, and Stephen Thomas. *The Environmental Protection Agency: Asking the Wrong Questions.* 1990. Chap. 5.

R. SHEP MELNICK

COMPROMISE OF 1850. Actually a series of laws, the Compromise of 1850 was the last great sectional adjustment before the Civil War. It grew out of the congressional deadlock over the status of slavery in land ceded by Mexico to the United States in 1848 as a result of the Mexican War. When President Zachary Taylor proposed to organize the entire region into two free states, Sen. Henry Clay of Kentucky, alarmed by southern threats of disunion and eager to reassert his political leadership, stepped forward in January 1850 with a plan to settle all the important differences between the North and the South.

Clay's scheme included the following measures: admission of California as a free state, organization of the territories of Utah and New Mexico without restriction of slavery, adjustment of the Texas–New Mexico boundary at approximately its present placement, assumption of the debt of the Republic of Texas by the federal government, enactment of a more rigorous fugitive slave law, abolition of the slave trade—but not slavery—in the District of Columbia, and approval of a resolution that Congress had no power over the interstate slave trade. The territorial bill was subsequently amended to incorporate the principle of popular sovereignty, which authorized the residents of a territory to decide the status of slavery at some unspecified time.

Clay's proposals offered something to both sections. To reinforce the idea of a genuine compromise, he combined the admission of California, the organization of the Utah and New Mexico territories, and the settlement of the Texas–New Mexico

SEN. DANIEL WEBSTER (W-MASS.). Addressing the Senate on the compromise measures, 7 March 1850. Lithograph by R. Van Dien.   LIBRARY OF CONGRESS

boundary into a single bill known as the Omnibus. Clay gambled that there was a workable majority in favor of compromise in Congress. This strategy was also designed to prevent a presidential veto by forcing Taylor, who favored California's admission, to accept the other parts of the compromise as well.

Congress debated Clay's proposals for six months. But when the Senate finally voted in July, radicals from both sections combined to defeat the Omnibus bill. Clay's strategy had failed: he had given some seventy speeches in the Senate to no avail, and, physically exhausted, he left Washington. At this point, Sen. Stephen A. Douglas of Illinois assumed leadership of the compromise forces. Douglas proceeded to pass Clay's proposals as separate pieces of legislation by uniting the pro-compromise minority with shifting sectional blocs to form a series of majorities. He was aided by Taylor's sudden

death in July, which removed the threat of a veto; the new president, Millard Fillmore, threw his influence behind the compromise movement. Northerners and southerners in general voted for those parts that benefited their sections and only once in either house did a majority from both sections vote in favor of a bill. Nevertheless, by 17 September all of Clay's proposals had passed and been signed into law by Fillmore.

The Compromise of 1850 was merely an armistice in the sectional conflict. Public opinion in both sections rallied behind the compromise measures, but before long the controversy over the expansion of slavery was reignited by the Kansas-Nebraska Act, northern resistance to the Fugitive Slave Act hardened, and each side accused the other of failing to abide by the settlement of 1850. The Compromise of 1850 did not work as its supporters had envisioned, and the hope of permanently defusing the slavery controversy proved futile.

BIBLIOGRAPHY

Hamilton, Holman. *Prologue to Conflict: The Crisis and Compromise of 1850.* 1964.
Potter, David M. *The Impending Crisis, 1848–1861.* 1976.

WILLIAM E. GIENAPP

CONCURRENT POWERS.

Concurrent powers are those exercised simultaneously by both national and state governments. Taxation is an example of a concurrent power, which falls under national as well as state authority.

Concurrent powers were created to promote the independent exercise of national and state governance—what James Madison called a "compound republic" of two sovereignties. Yet concurrent powers have not yielded wholly independent governments. As the "supremacy clause" of Article VI and the "necessary and proper clause" of Article I of the Constitution intended, the doctrine of national preemption has generally governed. When a conflict of authority arises, even in the presence of a concurrent power such as taxation, the federal government is said to prevail over the state. Early disputes over concurrent powers to tax (*McCulloch v. Maryland*, 1819) and to regulate commerce (*Gibbons v. Odgen*, 1824) were resolved decidedly in favor of the national government in decisions by Chief Justice John Marshall. This occurred despite the Tenth Amendment's grant of reserved powers to the states in the face of federal preemptive authority. Significantly, the idea of concurrent powers was cited only once in the Constitution: in the Eighteenth Amendment's enforcement clause (1919), later repealed by the Twenty-first Amendment (1933).

The political significance of concurrent powers and the preemption doctrine have remained a critical part of constitutional law. Congressional authority is said to preempt state action when the legislature intends to "occupy a field" exclusively. The case of *Pennsylvania v. Nelson* (1956) illustrates such a point. Even in the face of the Tenth Amendment's promise of state police power to govern the welfare of its citizens, the Supreme Court stated that Congress intended to occupy the field of sedition with the passage of the 1940 Smith Act. The state's sedition act was declared unconstitutional, thus weakening the concurrent power of the state to regulate so-called repugnant speech. A more recent controversy over environmental regulation of the nuclear industry has dominated the debate over concurrent powers, the preemption doctrine, and the Tenth Amendment.

[*See also* Implied Powers; McCulloch v. Maryland.]

BIBLIOGRAPHY

Ducat, Craig, and Harold Chase. *Constitutional Interpretation: Powers of Government.* 1974.
Fisher, Louis. *American Constitutional Law.* 1990.

JANIS JUDSON

CONDUCT OF THE WAR COMMITTEE, JOINT.

Prompted by popular impatience with Gen. George B. McClellan's apparent inactivity, frustration over the Union rout at Bull Run in July 1861, and outrage over the October 1861 Ball's Bluff disaster, the 37th Congress (1861–1863) created the Joint Committee on the Conduct of the War by an almost unanimous vote on 19 December 1861. The composition of the seven-member select investigating committee reflected both Radical Republicans' dislike of President Abraham Lincoln's wartime policies and a general determination to assert congressional authority over the increasingly strong executive branch of government. Radical Republicans dominated the committee, and no members had military experience. Senators Benjamin F. Wade (chairman, Ohio), Zachariah Chandler (Mich.), and Andrew Johnson (Tenn.), whose place, left empty when he returned home as military governor, was filled by Joseph A. Wright (Ind.), and Representatives Daniel W. Gooch (Mass.), John Covode (Pa.), George W. Julian (Ind.), and Moses F. Odell (N.Y.) sat on the committee in the 37th Congress. When the 38th Congress (1863–1865) reappointed the committee with additional instructions to investigate war contracts, first Benjamin F. Harding (Oreg.) and then Charles R. Buckalew (Pa.) replaced Wright, and Benjamin F. Loan (Mo.) replaced Covode. Investigating military engagements, the committee defended Republican generals while attacking McClellan and other Democratic officers; it exposed waste and fraud in military procurement; and it published testimony alleging abuse of captured Union soldiers and the mutilation of Union dead by Confederates. The committee's investigations stirred popular opposition to McClellan, increased pressure for more open government contracting, and exacerbated Northern anger toward the South.

BIBLIOGRAPHY

Pierson, William W., Jr. "The Committee on the Conduct of the Civil War." *American Historical Review* 23 (April 1918): 550–576.

U.S. Senate. *Report of the Joint Committee on the Conduct of the War.* 37th Cong., 3d sess., 1863. S. Rept. 108.

U.S. Senate. *Report of the Joint Committee on the Conduct of the War at the Second Session Thirty-Eighth Congress.* 38th Cong., 2d sess., 1865. S. Rept. 142.

U.S. Senate. *Supplemental Report of the Joint Committee on the Conduct of the War.* 38th Cong., 2d sess. 1866. Supplemental to S. Rept. 142.

HEATHER COX RICHARDSON

CONFEDERACY. *See* Civil War; Congress of the Confederacy; Secession.

CONFEDERATION CONGRESS. *See* History of Congress, *articles on* The Origins of Congress *and* The Road to Nationhood.

CONFERENCE COMMITTEES. The United States legislative branch is divided into two separate and equal chambers, the House of Representatives and the Senate. Constitutionally, the House and Senate must each pass measures with absolutely identical language before they can be sent to the White House for presidential consideration. The issue, then, is how to unite what the Constitution divides when each chamber passes different versions of the same bill.

Because the Constitution is silent, Congress has devised three techniques for achieving agreement. First, many bills are enacted into law when one chamber simply accepts the other's version. One chamber's deference to the other house's bill has various explanations, ranging from lack of controversy to political necessity because time is running out in a legislative session. Second, the House and Senate can motion—or "ping-pong"—measures back and forth between them until substantive disagreements are ironed out. In this case, each chamber agrees to some of the other's amendments or amends the other's amendments until both agree to identical language for all provisions of the legislation. Members and staff aides from each chamber consult frequently to facilitate the compromise. There is a parliamentary limit, however, to the number of times measures may be sent between the two bodies.

Finally, the House and Senate may agree to estab-lish a conference committee, composed of selected senators and representatives charged with reconciling the items of disagreement. Only a relatively small number of public laws passed by a Congress (15 to 25 percent by one estimate) reach the conference stage, but these measures are often the most controversial and important. Moreover, recent decades have witnessed an even more important role—reconciliation—for these bicameral panels, sometimes dubbed the "third house of Congress."

Several factors account for the heightened significance of these committees. First, institutional rivalry between the House and Senate is long-standing. Then, during the 1980s, another factor increased the competition: split party control. For the first time in twenty-six years the Senate went Republican after the November 1980 elections, staying in Republican hands for the next six years while the House remained Democratic. Conference committees during this period reconciled not only bicameral policy differences but sharp partisan disagreements as well.

Second, a new form of policy-making emerged on Capitol Hill: bills of massive size and scope. These "megabills" (called omnibus bills and sometimes

"AFTER THE BATTLE." Satirical view of the chaotic results of a congressional conference that has been a knock-down-drag-out affair. Clifford K. Berryman.

HOUSE-SENATE CONFERENCE. In the Old Supreme Court Chamber in the Capitol, discussing a minimum wage bill, 30 August 1960.   LIBRARY OF CONGRESS

thousands of pages long) cut across the jurisdictions of many standing committees. As a result, omnibus bills are commonly referred to more than one standing committee for simultaneous or sequential consideration. When conference committees are convened to deal with megabills, they frequently involve hundreds of lawmakers. The biggest conference in history—more than 250 conferees from the House and Senate—met on the Omnibus Reconciliation Act of 1981 to reconcile hundreds of matters in bicameral disagreement. Big conferences regularly shape the final content of these massive and major instruments of national policy-making.

Finally, before the 1970s junior lawmakers rarely served on conference committees. Instead, senior leaders of House and Senate committees dominated the conferences. Today, participatory democracy characterizes lawmaking in both chambers, with entrepreneurial members active in all phases of congressional policy-making. As scores of commit-

tees, subcommittees, task forces, and ad hoc groups strive to shape policies, it is often harder for Congress to act coherently. Thus, conference committees can function as important centralizing forces, capable of producing integrated policies from a more fragmented legislature.

Once the House and Senate agree to establish a conference committee, several major steps ensue: the selection of conferees (or managers, as they are sometimes called), conference negotiations, and House-Senate action on the conference report (the product of the bicameral negotiations). Each merits discussion.

Selection of Conferees. Selection of conferees is regulated by rules and precedents in both chambers. Each time a bill is sent to conference, the House Speaker and the presiding officer of the Senate formally appoint the respective conferees. In fact, both chambers usually rely on selections made by the chairman and ranking minority member of the committee or committees that originally considered and reported the bill. Some committees have their own rules or customs that influence conferee selection, such as naming subcommittee members as conferees. Rules of the House Democratic caucus obligate committee chairmen to ensure that conference delegations reflect the distribution of majority and minority members on the full committee. House and Senate committee leaders also name as conferees lawmakers who have special knowledge of the subject or whose states or districts are affected by the matters at hand.

The House Speaker does not simply rubber-stamp the committee leaders' list. The Speaker may choose conferees in addition to those the committee chairman has proposed or even veto some who offend the Speaker's personal or political sensibilities. In both chambers party support is sometimes especially critical in conferee selection. House and Senate leaders will seek to name conferees whose work is likely to reflect the goals and preferences of the Democratic or Republican leadership and who are skilled and shrewd negotiators.

Rules and precedents in both chambers require that a majority of conferees have "generally supported" the bill under discussion. Adhering to this standard is not always easy. Usually, for purposes of selection to a conference committee, a lawmaker's floor vote on final consideration is taken as evidence of an overall position on the measure.

Both the House and Senate may select as many conferees as they want. Neither chamber gains an edge over the other by naming more conferees because the respective delegations vote as a unit. The two chambers have one vote each, with a majority in each delegation deciding how its vote is to be cast on the various issues in bicameral disagreement. This feature facilitates compromise.

Although the size of conference delegations does not affect the bargaining authority of either chamber, it does have several consequences. The more conferees from each chamber, the more time and effort are invariably required to resolve bicameral differences. Moreover, size affects the mechanics of decision making. Large conferences regularly and of necessity divide into smaller groups, which means that size can affect the pace of decision making. Simply scheduling negotiating sessions for many conferees is sometimes difficult.

Bargaining in Conference. Bargaining strategies and tactics used in the conference committee are shaped to a considerable extent by several pre-conference considerations, such as the unity of each chamber's delegation, the amount of tradable material that each side brings to the negotiating table, and whether a chamber's conferees have been instructed by their parent body to insist on a certain provision, although such instructions are not always followed. Bargaining in conference is a process based on a carefully planned strategy and the skilled use of resources and opportunities during bargaining.

House-Senate conferences typically operate in an informal, agreement-oriented context. As professional politicians, conferees are accustomed to the personal give-and-take, bargains, and trade-offs that foster bicameral accord. Their objectives are to fashion an agreement acceptable to at least a majority of each chamber's conferees and to create an agreement (compromise legislation) that will attract majority support in the House and Senate. As conferees strive to achieve these broad objectives, only a few formal rules guide the bargaining. One rule specifies that conferees are to consider only the items in disagreement; they may not reconsider provisions approved in identical form by both houses. Even these few rules are sometimes waived by the House or Senate when conferees submit their completed product (the conference report) to their respective chambers. House and Senate rules also state that conference committees are to meet in open session, unless specific steps are taken to close them for a reason such as national security. Nonetheless, much conference bargaining occurs in secret as various individual legislators, small groups, or key leaders privately discuss how to iron out differences.

Conference bargaining can best be viewed as multilateral rather than bicameral. Although constituted in terms of House versus Senate negotiating teams, conference bargaining usually involves other participants. Lobbyists, executive branch officials, and White House aides regularly attend conference deliberations and influence the shape of the final compromises.

When at least a majority of the conferees from each chamber has reached agreement, committee staffers prepare the appropriate documents, such as the conference report and the accompanying joint explanatory statement. Preparing these documents might take several weeks, especially when the legislation is controversial and complex or requires intensive, round-the-clock work to meet tight deadlines. House-Senate agreement is reached when at least a majority of each chamber's conferees signs the conference report. When that is done, the conference committee has concluded its work. Its negotiated settlement must now be considered by the House and Senate.

Chamber Consideration of the Conference Report. By custom, the chamber that requested a conference acts second on the conference report, but this is not an inviolable practice. The first chamber to act has three options: to adopt the conference report, reject it, or recommit it—that is, return it to the conferees for further deliberation. When the first chamber adopts the conference report, the conference committee is automatically dissolved and the other chamber is faced with only two options, to accept or reject.

Conference reports are seldom rejected or recommitted to conference by either house, largely because there are procedural and political incentives for their adoption. For one thing, conference reports are "privileged" business in each chamber, which means that they can be brought to the floor at almost any time, sometimes even when key opponents are out of town. They are usually not open to amendment; "take it or leave it" is the rule at this stage of the legislative process. Members understand, too, that the defeat of a conference report is likely to subject the legislation to further arduous and lengthy negotiations.

The conference floor managers in the House and Senate, usually the senior majority conferees, are key actors in developing the strategy for winning enactment of the bicameral accord. Consultations with party leaders, executive branch officials, and affected interest groups, among others, are standard elements of the coalition-building process both before and during floor deliberations. On the floor, the floor managers' primary concerns are to promote and defend their handiwork and to ensure that there are enough votes to adopt the conference report. Once both chambers agree to the conference report, the bill as finally approved by Congress is transmitted to the White House for presidential consideration.

Conference committees make crucial policy decisions. They are often the most important lawmaking forums on Capitol Hill. House and Senate members understand that many bills will end up in conference. Hence, they purposefully plan how they can enhance their leverage with the other body. This feature of congressional policy-making underscores how legislatively locked the House and Senate are, despite their constitutional separation. Conference committees epitomize bicameralism in action and are centrally important in uniting what the Constitution divides.

[*See also* Amending; Bargaining; Bicameralism.]

BIBLIOGRAPHY

Longley, Lawrence D., and Walter J. Oleszek. *Bicameral Politics: Conference Committees in Congress.* 1989.
McCown, Ada C. *The Congressional Conference Committee.* 1927.
Pressman, Jeffrey L. *House vs. Senate: Conflict in the Appropriations Process.* 1966.
Steiner, Gilbert. *The Congressional Conference Committee.* 1951.
Vogler, David J. *The Third House: Conference Committees in the U.S. Congress.* 1971.

WALTER J. OLESZEK

CONFIRMATION. Article II, section 2, clause 2 of the U.S. Constitution gives the Senate the power to confirm or reject presidential nominees to the principal offices in the federal government. Any appointment to those offices must be made by the president "by and with the Advice and Consent of the Senate." This process applies to "Officers of the United States . . . established by Law." Most such officers are in the executive branch, but they also include all federal judges and several officials in agencies in the legislative branch. After Senate confirmation the president commissions the person who has been confirmed.

Political Nature of the Confirmation Process. At the Constitutional Convention in 1787, the Framers debated whether the power to appoint should reside with the president, the Senate, or Congress as a whole. Some delegates argued that the president, as chief executive, should appoint all public officials because it would be easier to hold one person accountable for a bad appointment. Other delegates, concerned about concentrating too much power in the president, argued that the power to appoint should reside with the Senate or Congress, which also were more likely to appoint people from all regions of the country. As with other contentious issues at the Convention, the Framers resolved the dispute with an innovative compromise—the president would select the nominee, but the Senate would have to consent to the choice.

Because the holders of principal appointive offices may have a direct effect on public policy, selection is crucial. Key appointees help the president develop and implement public policy. Justices of the Supreme Court, who hold lifetime appointments, often decide constitutional and legal disputes that set public policy. Sometimes the justices rule on disputes between the legislative and executive branches.

The confirmation process, which is inherently political, may become highly charged when the Senate and the president disagree on the role of government and the direction of public policy. Such disagreement is likely to occur when different political parties control the Senate and the presidency. At such times there may be little or no consultation between the president and Senate leaders about major nominations. As a result, the Senate may refuse to confirm a nominee to the Supreme Court or, more rarely, to head an executive department or agency.

Role of the Evaluating Committee. Nominations received in the Senate are referred to the committee having legislative jurisdiction over the offices involved; the fate of the nomination is determined largely by the committee. The committee may kill a nomination by failing to act on it, or it may report it out to the full Senate favorably, unfavorably, or with no recommendation. Committee hearings provide senators with an opportunity to extract from nominees specific commitments regarding programs they will be administering. Promises to cooperate with committee investigations may also be part of the understanding established.

Some of the most important factors determining confirmation include the character, experience, and competence of the nominee; the policy views of the nominee and how those views may affect public policy; the type and level of the position; and the political environment.

Failed Nominations. Of the tens of thousands of nominations sent to the Senate each year, approximately 99 percent are routine nominations for appointment or promotion in the military and civilian services (the latter including, e.g., the Foreign Service, the National Oceanic and Atmospheric Administration, and the Public Health Service). The remaining 1 percent are nominations to executive departments, independent agencies, regulatory boards and commissions, part-time advisory bodies, and the federal judiciary. While nearly all nominations for these positions also are confirmed, no president can safely assume that all will be approved.

Of the major nominations, the most careful consideration is usually given to Supreme Court nominees. Since the confirmation process began in 1789, approximately 20 percent of the nominations to the Court have not been confirmed. By contrast, fewer than 2 percent of nominees to head executive departments and agencies have failed to win approval. These figures indicate that while the Senate largely defers to the president's wishes, it is less likely to do so for justices of the Supreme Court.

Unsuccessful nominations fall into three categories—those voted on and rejected, those not acted on, and those withdrawn. Most failed nominations fail in committee: a few by committee vote (fewer than fifty since 1945), the majority by not being acted on. Less frequently, nominees are rejected on the Senate floor, which last occurred in 1989 with the defeat of former senator John G. Tower's nomination to be secretary of Defense. Occasionally, as in the 1993 cases of Zoe Baird for attorney general and Lani Guinier to head the Justice Department's civil rights division, the president withdraws a nomination before the Senate has the opportunity to vote.

Since 1960, the number of full-time positions requiring Senate confirmation has increased significantly. While these positions have been increasing, the confirmation process has become more complex, contentious, and time consuming. Nominees are now required to file financial disclosure statements under the Ethics in Government Act of 1978, as well as committee-sponsored financial and personal questionnaires. In addition, most committees require the White House to submit a report on the background investigation conducted by the Federal Bureau of Investigation on each nominee. Consequently, committees now must devote considerable time to reviewing and evaluating the numerous documents associated with each nomination.

Where nominations involve appointment to policy-making positions, the confirmation process enables senators to express their positions on the issues by approving or rejecting the nominees involved. The process may be prolonged and more contentious when ideological differences sharply divide senators and nominees, especially when different political parties control the presidency and the Senate. During the Reagan and Bush administrations, three particularly divisive confirmation hearings were held—the failed nominations of Judge Robert H. Bork to be an associate justice on the Supreme Court (1987) and of Tower to be secretary of Defense (1989), and the successful nomination of Judge Clarence Thomas to be an associate justice of the Supreme Court (1991).

Senatorial Courtesy. Under the unwritten rules of "senatorial courtesy," the Senate usually defers to the desires of a senator from the same political party as the president regarding who should be appointed to positions located within that senator's state. (A senator from the opposition party who holds a key position may also benefit from the practice.) As a result, the president generally nominates the persons recommended by the senator. The custom began during the First Congress, when the Senate rejected the nomination of Benjamin Fishbourn to be naval officer of the port of Savannah because the two senators from Georgia wanted their own nominee. Today, the practice appears to be limited to the appointment of federal district judges, U.S. attorneys, and U.S. marshals.

Holds. Another Senate practice affecting the confirmation process is to put a "hold" on a nomination. A hold may be placed by any senator or group of senators and may remain in place for days or months. No action is taken on the nomination, whether in committee or the full Senate, until the hold is lifted (which generally happens) or the leadership decides to ignore it (which seldom happens). A hold may be placed for almost any reason on almost any nomination. The hold may relate directly to the nomination—that is, it may be placed to express opposition or displeasure or to get additional information about the nominee—or it may have nothing to do with the nomination, being merely a tactic in a dispute with the administration over some other matter. Holds normally are honored, because to ignore them raises the threat of a filibuster and endangers the unanimity that is essential if the Senate is to function effectively.

Historically, the Senate has confirmed the overwhelming majority of nominations submitted to it. Numbers alone, however, fail to indicate those instances in which the president may have refrained from making a nomination for fear either that it would not be confirmed or that it would not be worth the struggle to win.

[*See also* Advice and Consent; Presidential Appointments.]

BIBLIOGRAPHY

Harris, Joseph P. *The Advice and Consent of the Senate: A Study of the Confirmation of Appointments by the United States Senate.* 1968.

Mackenzie, G. Calvin. *The Politics of Presidential Appointments.* 1981.

ROGELIO GARCIA

CONGRESS. [*This entry includes nine separate articles that provide an overview of congressional operations, practices, and traditions as well as introductions to the resources for further study of Congress:*

For a series of articles that surveys Congress's origins and history, see History of Congress. *For general discussion of the relations of Congress with the other branches of the U.S. government, see* Constitution; Executive Branch; Judiciary and Congress; Legislative Branch; President and Congress. *See also* House of Representatives; Senate.]

Powers of Congress

As the first branch of government, Congress has powers that are broader and more profound than is indicated by a mere reading of the constitutional document. In Article I, section 8 and in the enforcement clauses of many of the amendments, there are specific, formal grants of power, but these are enhanced by the fact that the Constitution leaves much to Congress in constituting the other branches of government and in regulating their powers, and Congress has authority both to expand and to contract the scope of state powers.

Congress's Institutional Powers. Each house of Congress has the internal powers of any legislative body: to determine its rules, to determine contests over who has been elected to it, to police its members, and to discipline those who violate its standards of conduct. It determines its internal procedures, largely free of outside forces, although the courts do at times review and sometimes set aside decisions. For example, the decision to exclude a member-elect was voided because the Supreme Court held in *Powell v. McCormack* (1969) that the House of Representatives had added to the constitutional listing of qualifications. Lawmaking procedures have been evaluated to determine, for instance, whether a revenue-raising measure was initiated in the Senate rather than in the House, although the latter has a procedure to police the violation of its privileges. Generally, the political-question doctrine, under which the courts determine that some issues are not suitable for judicial resolution, enables judges to leave many otherwise litigable questions to Congress and the president.

At the conclusion of Article I, section 8, the Constitution in clause 18 authorizes Congress to make all laws that may be "necessary and proper" for executing its granted powers. Chief Justice John Marshall, writing for the Court in *McCulloch v. Maryland* (1819), interpreted this clause as an enlargement of Congress's powers rather than as a constriction. That is, Congress need not show that a law is strictly necessary; rather, Congress may select any means it thinks reasonable to effectuate its granted powers. It is not a judicial function to review whether a particular exercise is "necessary" or "proper," except within the context of the limitations the Constitution imposes, such as in the Bill of Rights. This discretion as to means is critical to the scope of congressional legislation.

The power to investigate to determine whether legislation is needed and how existing laws are being implemented is one of the most important, although unenumerated, powers of Congress. Sometimes abused, it is critical to Congress's role.

Congress also has initiated all twenty-seven amendments to the Constitution, and while Article V authorizes state initiation as well, Congress would play a significant oversight role there.

Congress and the States. The core of the formal grants of power to Congress is in section 8 of Article I, but only some of these are of signal importance. As in so many provisions of the Constitution, these grants serve a dual purpose. Many were intended to demarcate the scope of authority delegated to the national government. Under the supremacy clause (Article VI, clause 2), congressional exercises of these powers are the supreme law of the land, and state law, even state constitutional law, is subordinate to federal law. However, the mere grant of a power does not deny the states the authority to legislate. States may, for instance, enact debtor-creditor legislation despite the grant to Congress in Article I, section 8, clause 4 of the power to enact bankruptcy legislation. Even when Congress acts, the states do not necessarily lose their authority. If Congress expressly provides for federal exclusivity, as for example in copyright law, enacted pursuant to Article I, section 8, clause 4, that concludes the matter. Congress may expressly permit some state role, but if Congress does not specify, then the courts, which have developed an elaborate set of standards to do so, determine

whether state law must yield, because it conflicts with the federal law or interferes with the federal plan or regulates some activity Congress wished to leave free, or whether the state law may coexist in whole or in part with the federal scheme.

Under the Articles of Confederation, Congress lacked the power to impose taxes, and it could not regulate interstate commerce to prevent state discrimination. The grants of these two powers, Article I, section 8, clauses 1 and 3, made national governance possible in the beginning; since then, especially in the twentieth century, they have been the principal engines of federal dominance of the states.

The ability to raise money by direct levy on individuals in the states meant that Congress could obtain the resources necessary for federal functions. Especially with the confirmation of the power to impose income taxes by ratification of the Sixteenth Amendment, Congress also obtained the ability to compete fully with states for all available moneys, to the fiscal detriment of the states, because national legislation was supreme. When combined with the power to spend tax revenues for the general welfare (clause 2), the execution and significance of these two powers cannot be overstated. Beginning in the 1920s but increasingly since, numerous federal programs have been created that offer money to the states if they will administer the programs in accordance with federal standards and subject to federal conditions. Social security programs such as unemployment compensation and assistance to the poor, highway programs, and educational programs are examples. Utilization of state administration is important to the national government, but just as important is Congress's ability to set conditions (often of minimal connection to the purposes of the spending), which gives to the national legislature a regulatory function that it often exercises. For example, the minimum age at which alcoholic beverages can be purchased and the maximum speed limit are two cases in which Congress set national policy through highway expenditures. Conditions of nondiscrimination imposed on the receipt and use of federal moneys are another. (The imposition of mandates on the states to do certain things, but absent federal moneys to cover the costs, is a more recent feature of national legislation; this accompanies the deficit-imposed shortage of federal moneys.)

The growth of an interrelated national economy and judicial latitude in permitting regulation of even *de minimis* activities affecting commerce have transformed Congress's role from overseeing the rules of how interstate business is done to exercising a national police power in the areas of crime, consumer protection, rules of nondiscrimination, protection of the environment, and many others.

Initially, the Supreme Court permitted Congress to regulate only the use of interstate facilities and the crossing of state boundaries. The production of goods for interstate commerce was an intrastate transaction, as was the sale or other disposal at the other end (*Kidd v. Pearson* [1988], *United States v. E. C. Knight Co.* [1895], *Oliver Iron Co. v. Lord* [1923], *Carter v. Carter Coal Co.* [1936]). Now, Congress may regulate the entire stream of commerce from production to disposal (*National Labor Relations Board v. Jones & Laughlin Steel Corp.* [1937], *United States v. Darby* [1941]). It may also reach local activities that involve no state lines but that Congress has determined have an "effect," even a minimal one, on interstate commerce (*Wickard v. Filburn* [1942], *Fry v. United States* [1975], *Hodel v. Indiana* [1981]). It has been permitted to aggregate individual transactions into a class of like transactions that "affect" interstate commerce (*Perez v. United States* [1971], *Russell v. United States* [1985]). Judicial review is negligible; it is limited to ascertaining that Congress is rational.

An exception exists in instances in which Congress seeks to regulate the governmental activities of the states, with the Supreme Court continuing to be inconsistent with respect to limits. Thus in *Maryland v. Wirtz* (1968), the Court held that Congress could impose federal wage and hour laws on state and local employees, but in *National League of Cities v. Usery* (1976), it overruled *Wirtz* and held that such regulation violated the Constitution. Then, in *Garcia v. San Antonio Metropolitan Transit Authority* (1985), the Court overruled *Usery* and held that congressional application of wage and hour laws to state employees violated no provision of the Constitution and that states had to use their political resources in Congress to defend themselves. Most recently, in *New York v. United States* (1992), the justices held that Congress could not compel the states to enforce and implement a program of radioactive waste disposal and that Congress could not "commandeer" state legislative and administrative assistance.

The result is that instead of debates about Congress's ability to prescribe standards of labor-management relations in large or small industries, the constitutional debates at present are whether Congress can declare gun-free zones around local schools and punish possession of firearms in those areas, whether it can set specific punishments for local carjackings, and whether it can bar racial discrimination in a small restaurant that purchases a significant amount of its food from interstate sources.

As has been noted, conferral of a power on Congress does not deny the states the power to act on the same subject. Thus the states have always had the authority to tax and to regulate interstate commerce, subject to congressional dispossession. Although the commerce clause in its terms is only an authorization for congressional action, the Supreme Court has interpreted it as imposing some limits on state authority, even absent congressional action, making it "negative" on some state laws. The result is that states may not discriminate against interstate commerce (on behalf of local businesses, for example), and if they burden interstate commerce too severely by nondiscriminatory taxation or regulation, the courts can set aside such state legislation (*Brown-Forman Distillers Corp. v. New York State Liquor Authority* [1986], *Quill Corp. v. North Dakota* [1992], *Fort Gratiot Sanitary Landfill v. Michigan Natural Resources Department* [1992], *Barclays Bank v. California Franchise Tax Board* [1994]). It is important to note that Congress may authorize the states to enact measures the courts have disapproved or would disapprove because it is congressional power that is overriding; this permits Congress to enlarge as well as contract state power (*Prudential Insurance Co. v. Benjamin* [1946], *South Central Timber Development v. Wunnicke* [1984]).

Another means by which Congress regularly enlarges state power is its approval of interstate compacts, pursuant to Article I, section 10, clause 3. States often come together to work on a common problem (e.g., pollution of a river that passes through more than one state, or cooperation in extraditing criminals), but because these agreements affect important issues of federalism, they are permissible only by congressional consent.

Adoption of the Reconstruction Amendments following the Civil War further strengthened Congress relative to the states. New constraints were imposed—on the power to regulate suffrage and on the power to deny privileges and immunities of citizenship, due process, and equal protection—and with these restraints came authorization to Congress to enforce them. Remedial legislation in the nineteenth century failed, but the civil rights struggle energized Congress beginning in the 1960s, leading to new protections of the franchise. Congress turned from merely banning discrimination in voting, a largely failed initiative, to affirmatively guaranteeing ballot access, fair apportionment and districting, and general effectuation of the right to a valid ballot. In the course of this movement, Congress sought and the Supreme Court approved a power, not yet fully defined, both to enforce discrimination bans and also to define, free of all but the most restrained judicial review, what conduct and acts were in fact discriminatory. Under this exercise, minority voting and districting that enhanced minority power were legislated and enforced. However, the *Shaw v. Reno* (1993) decision and a pending 1994 case suggest that this power may be more limited than was previously thought.

Similarly, Congress has acted under the Fourteenth Amendment, especially the equal protection clause, to bar states and local governments from discriminating in a large number of areas. Congress's ability to interpret the meaning of the amendment contrary to what the judiciary has decided means that it can, for example, engage in more far-reaching affirmative action than the states can, and it may be able to authorize the states to act more broadly to establish affirmative action programs than they could without such authorization.

Inasmuch as it was through the Fourteenth Amendment's due process clause that the Supreme Court applied most of the provisions of the Bill of Rights, which originally limited only the national government, Congress may define and enforce these constraints against the states.

That the Union would be enlarged through the addition of new states was clear to the Framers, who specifically provided in Article IV, section 3 for the admission of new states, subject to limits on breaking up existing states. An unexpressed command of this provision, recognized in the first and subsequent admissions and enforced by the judiciary, is that each new state comes into the Union on an "equal footing," a condition of equality with the states already forming the Union. In framing the provisions for the admission of new states, the Convention looked to the example of the Northwest Territory, which would later be formed into states and for which the Continental Congress was providing a government through the Northwest Ordinance (passed as the Convention was meeting and repassed during the First Congress). Thus, in section 3, the Framers coupled the statehood clause, granting Congress the power to admit new states, with the clause authorizing Congress to provide governments for the territories. Implicit in this section was the power to acquire new territories by conquest, by treaty, or otherwise. This power remained relatively uncontroversial, save for the intrusion of the slavery debate, until overseas colonies (the Philippines, Puerto Rico, and others) were acquired at the end of the nineteenth century.

Separation of powers. The terms *separation of powers* and *checks and balances* do not appear in the Constitution, but they are implicit throughout the document. The first three articles disperse the legislative, executive, and judicial powers. Yet the Framers recognized that paper boundaries would not deter abuse of powers; only individuals and institutions would be able to resist incursions. The experience of the Framers following the Revolution and the creation of state governments had demonstrated that popularly elected legislatures were threats to liberties, and Congress was constructed to reduce that danger. A bicameral body, a popularly elected House, a Senate elected by the state legislatures, combined with the presidential veto and constitutional judicial review (not set out expressly but acknowledged by all Framers who spoke about it) were intended to suppress the opportunities for abuse.

Surprisingly, therefore, it was in Congress that the Framers reposed much of the power to structure, and necessarily to restructure from time to time, the other two branches of the national government. Article II creates the office of the president (and vice president), but the powers set out are general and the system in which he is to operate is sketchy. Congress must, and did from the beginning, legislate to create executive departments and offices, to disperse authority, and to establish qualifications and terms for officeholders. It has lodged authority in executive offices subject to presidential direction, but it also has created numerous independent agencies (independent in the sense of limits on the ability of the president to remove officers and thus to direct them) charged with the execution of national laws. Recently, in upholding the creation of independent counsels in the executive branch, the Court in *Morrison v. Olson* (1988) altered the understanding of the president's removal power to give to Congress some limited discretion in restricting the removal of many of those who hold executive office. The judiciary as envisioned in Article III consists of a Supreme Court of unspecified size (headed by a chief justice) and of inferior courts that Congress may from time to time create, revise, or abolish. The entire appellate jurisdiction of the Supreme Court appears to depend upon congressional sufferance, since Article III, section 2, clause 2 authorizes Congress to make exceptions and regulations to the Court's appellate jurisdiction. Only the Court's original jurisdiction, a tiny part of its entire jurisdiction, is constitutionally immune from congressional defeasance. Even determining when the Supreme Court is to convene requires congressional legislation.

In part, the power proceeds from direct grants—that is, the authority to constitute courts inferior to the Supreme Court (Article I, section 8, clause 9 and Article III, section 1)—but the most important grant flows from the necessary and proper clause (Article I, section 8, clause 18), which empowers Congress not only to legislate to carry out its own powers but also to carry into execution "all other powers vested in this Constitution in the Government of the United States, or in any department or officer thereof." From this language stems the congressional ability to organize and to structure the executive and judicial branches and to structure much of the exercise of power in those branches.

The Constitution also bars the expenditure of any money from the Treasury except pursuant to appropriations (Article I, section 9, clause 7), giving to Congress the power to determine not only whether money may be or may not be spent for something but also the right to impose conditions under which such moneys may be spent. The money power is a potent force in setting policy and structuring execution.

Congressional authority today is much more circumscribed than what is described here; it is limited by political constraints associated primarily with presidential leadership but also by judicial interpretation that, accepting congressional delegations of power to the other two branches, resolutely stands against attempted congressional policing of that delegation and of other activity in those branches. The Court in its opinions continues to refer to the dangers flowing from legislative predominance (*Immigration and Naturalization Service v. Chadha* [1983], *Bowsher v. Synar* [1986], *Metropolitan Airports Authority v. Citizens for the Abatement of Aircraft Noise* [1991]). The result is that the executive and judiciary may legislate through rules and regulation, the former may adjudicate, and the latter may execute, but Congress may act outside its own walls only through the processes of legislation set out in the Constitution.

Other grants in section 8 involve Congress closely in the exercise of powers that are exclusive to the executive in other governmental systems. The texts of Article I, section 8, clauses 11–16 and of Article II, section 2, and the sparse debates in the Convention, disclose a conscious blending across the two branches of the great powers of war and peace. The president is the commander in chief of the armed forces of the United States, but the Framers probably viewed this grant as little more than giving control of the military to the president. In modern practice, begun under Abraham Lincoln and accelerated in the last half of the twentieth century, the power extends beyond simple control to the sole conduct of national and foreign policy in war and peacetime. The Framers intended that the nation ordinarily should go to war only under a declaration of war by Congress and that peace should be restored again through a treaty negotiated by the president and ratified by the Senate.

However, two world wars, regional conflicts, and the long period of the Cold War in effect validated an expansive theory of presidential dominance. Congress reasserted itself in the War Powers Resolution of 1973, defining the terms of presidential use of military forces abroad in the absence of a declaration of war. A combination of presidential assertiveness and congressional acquiescence has minimized the effects of the resolution; although President George Bush sought and obtained congressional approval for the 1991 Persian Gulf War, the president claimed the right to proceed absent any approval. Congress has also, with somewhat more success, sought to rein in the use of executive agreements, in contrast with treaties, and the enhancement of executive powers through declarations of national emergencies.

Here, too, the congressional power of the purse has force. The president needs money to conduct military operations and other activities abroad. Congress successfully required the withdrawal of troops from Indochina through the conditioning of funds; yet the effort to change U.S. policy in Central America by conditions on funds resulted in presidential evasion and led to the Iran-contra controversy.

Finally, the power to impeach and upon conviction to remove from office the president, justices and judges, and high civil officers is one lodged solely in the legislative branch.

Conclusion. Congress is the only entity thoroughly described and empowered in the Constitution. Its internal structure is minutely detailed. Its powers are affirmatively conveyed, and the language defines the relationships between and among the other two branches of the national government and between the federal government and the states. Most important, Congress is given the discretion to determine largely for itself how it should legislate to effectuate its powers, both express and implied.

Congress in the late twentieth century is different from what the Framers envisioned. It is more powerful in that it has more plenary powers vis-à-vis the states than the Framers intended; but it is less powerful in that its role in developing and implementing national policy has increasingly eroded before the power of a chief executive, who, in fact, if not strictly in constitutional terms, is the only nationally elected officeholder and the most visible embodiment of the national government.

[*See also* Concurrent Powers; Emergency Powers; Enumerated Powers; Implied Powers; Investigative Power; Removal Power; Subpoena Power; War Powers.]

BIBLIOGRAPHY

Mikva, Abner J. *The American Congress: The First Branch.* 1983.

Shane, Peter M., and Harold H. Bruff. *The Law of Presidential Power: Cases and Materials.* 1988.

Thompson, Kenneth W., ed. *The Presidency, the Congress, and the Constitution: Deadlock or Balance of Powers?* 1991.

Tribe, Lawrence H. *American Constitutional Law.* 2d ed. 1988. Pp. 297–400. See also chapters 2, 4, and 6.

Van Alstyne, William. "The Role of Congress in Determining Incidental Powers of the President and of the Federal Courts: A Comment on the Horizontal Effect of 'the Sweeping Clause.'" *Ohio State Law Journal* 36 (1975): 788–825.

JOHNNY H. KILLIAN

Congressional Workload

Although the workload of Congress traditionally focuses on Congress's lawmaking function, it embraces such other responsibilities as overseeing the executive branch, providing a forum for constituencies to be heard, and participating in its shared responsibilities with the president. The various components of legislative workload offer some measure of the activities of members of the House and Senate in lawmaking and representation. By considering the different aspects of legislative workload, we can follow their chronology during the life of a bill or resolution, from introduction to final passage.

The Proposal Stage. At the proposal stage, a number of different activities can be used to mea-

sure the productivity of members of Congress. One common gauge is the number of bills or resolutions introduced by members of the House and Senate. Roger H. Davidson (1986) shows that bill introduction in the House rose dramatically from 1947 to the early 1970s, from a low of 7,611 in the 80th Congress (1947–1949) to a high of 22,060 in the 90th Congress (1967–1969). After 1970, the numbers dropped off to a new postwar low of 6,263 in the 100th Congress (1987–1989), as reported by Norman J. Ornstein, Thomas E. Mann, and Michael J. Malbin (1992). By contrast, the numbers in the Senate remained fairly flat, with bill introductions averaging four thousand bills a year during the post–World War II era. During this period, the high point was 4,867 Senate introductions during the 91st Congress (1969–1971). The lowest figure, 3,325, occurred in the 100th Congress (1987–1989). While this provides a rough measure of workload, some problems attend its use. First, it does not address the content of bills. In fact, most measures of workload do not consider the relative importance of legislation. This way of counting workload would give the same weight to a bill making the monarch butterfly the national insect, for example, as to a tax bill.

Second, this measure does not count the changing levels of activity of specific members of the House or Senate. The number of bills or resolutions introduced can easily be affected by the activities of a single member or a small group of members. Also, the seeming hyperactivity of the House compared to the apparently lower activity of the Senate can be corrected by examining the mean number of bills and resolutions sponsored by each member. In the prolific 1960s, House members were sponsoring, on average, forty-two bills or joint resolutions per Congress, a figure comparable to that in the Senate. By the 1980s, House members' activity had substantially lessened to about sixteen bills or resolutions per member. At the same time, the average number of bills introduced by each senator also decreased, to thirty-four. When using such sponsorship data, one must be careful to acknowledge that the rules for sponsorship of legislation have changed over time. For most of the history of the House of Representatives, a piece of legislation could be introduced only by a single member. Beginning in the 1960s, however, a series of rules changes eventually allowed a House bill to have an unlimited number of sponsors. Davidson (1986) links the decline in bill sponsorship in the House partly to this factor, but this still leaves the uniform decline in bill introduction

Figure 1
Number of Bills and Joint Resolutions in the House per Congress
(80th Congress to 102d Congress)

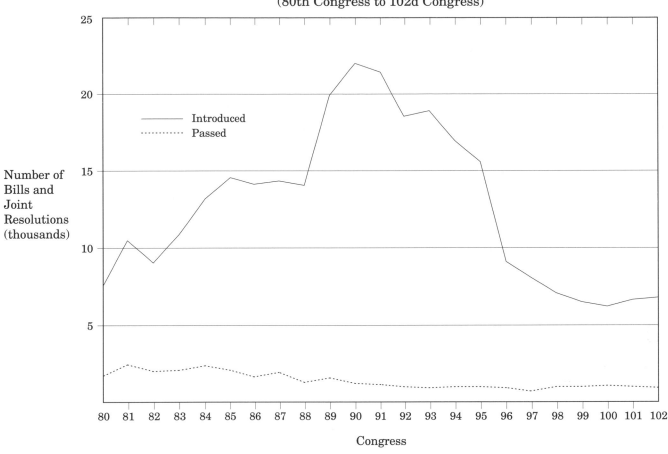

SOURCE: Data for figures 1–4 are from *Congressional Quarterly Weekly Report*, 10 October 1992; *Congressional Record*, 29 October 1992; Roger H. Davidson and Carol Hardy, *Indicators of House Workload and Activity* (Congressional Research Service, 1987); Roger H. Davidson and Carol Hardy, *Indicators of Senate Activity and Workload* (Congressional Research Service, 1987).

by both the House and the Senate in the 1980s unexplained.

Third, measuring workload by the number of bills introduced may not address how the meaning of proposing legislation changes over time. Joseph Cooper and Cheryl Young, in a 1989 article in *Legislative Studies Quarterly*, note that before the 1870s House members were not freely allowed to introduce their own legislation. During the House's early history, most legislation was initially discussed in the Committee of the Whole and was then introduced in the House. Bill introduction by a single member was seen as usurping the judgment of the House. In addition, David Mayhew (1974) and other writers have noted that during the recent history of the House, representatives seem often to in-

troduce legislation solely in order to claim credit for doing so. In other words, legislation is introduced not so that it may be passed but to let constituents or groups know that their representative supports their cause.

In addition to looking at the number of bills and resolutions introduced, scholars who study Congress during its first century examine the number of petitions introduced. In Congress's early years, petitions provided the link between constituent demands and legislative activity; often, petitions would lead to the development of a bill in the Committee of the Whole. Through petitions, constituents would advise members of the House or Senate of their position on an issue; ask that some subject matter be addressed; or ask that some wrong—

Figure 2
Number of Bills and Joint Resolutions in the Senate per Congress
(80th Congress to 102d Congress)

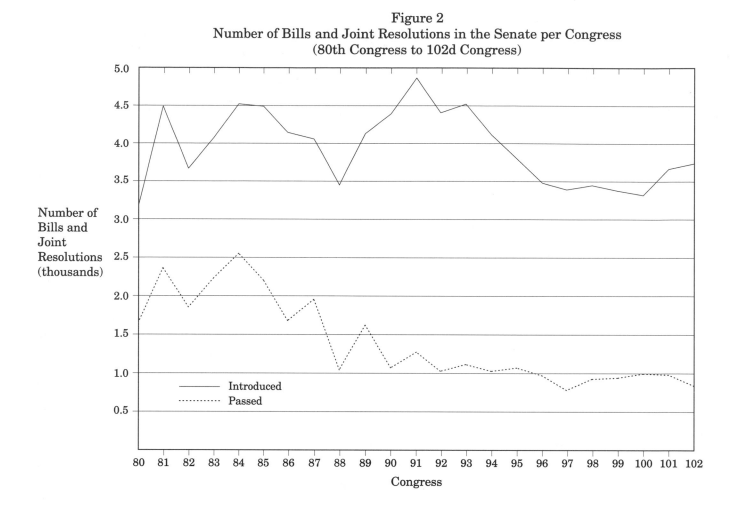

whether caused by nature, other citizens, other nations, or the government—be redressed. Whether or not a petition was ultimately transformed into a piece of legislation, such pleas for action from constituents were ultimately presented to the entire chamber. Finally, measures of nineteenth-century workload not only must include petitions but must accommodate the unusual circumstances that obtained the gag rule that prohibited the introduction of abolitionists' petitions from the 23d through the 28th Congresses (1833–1845).

Committee Workload. As Woodrow Wilson declared in *Congressional Government* (1885), "It is not far from the truth to say that Congress in session is Congress on public exhibition, whilst Congress in its committee-rooms is Congress at work." What Wilson wrote more than a century ago seems still to be true today. After a bill is introduced, it is automatically referred to a standing committee. One way to measure committee workload is to examine the number of bills referred to and reported by committees (Davidson, 1986). Of course, such

counts must, again, be used carefully, because the same problems mentioned in the previous section also apply here. For example, a committee is dependent on the introduction of bills for it to consider. Thus, there is a supply problem. More importantly, the subject matter of bills referred to and reported by committees varies widely.

Other measures can also be used to examine the effort expended in committees. When looking at these other factors, one must recognize that committee output is not limited to producing bills and resolutions. The most important of committees' other tasks is the oversight of executive agencies. The workload involved in this function cannot be monitored by examining the number of bills or resolutions considered or passed. Instead, one must look, for example, at the number and length of committee hearings and reports devoted to the oversight function. These measures might also be used comparatively, to judge the amount of time and effort a committee spends in developing legislation.

Besides oversight, one might also consider the number and length of hearings that the Senate holds in order to give its advice and consent on presidential nominations of judges and other appointees. These hearings may take a great deal of time and require much effort by the senators involved.

Floor Activity. After a bill or resolution has been considered in committee and the committee votes in favor of it, it is sent to the floor of the House or Senate. Here again, one may use the number of bills referred to the floor and the number of bills passed as simple measures of legislative productivity. Both the House and the Senate showed a tremendous decline in the number of bills passed between the 1950s and the 1980s. In the 1950s, the average number of bills and joint resolutions passed per Congress was 2,039 and 2,102 in the House and the Senate, respectively. In the 1980s, the averages had dropped by half, to 937 and 887 (Davidson, 1986; Ornstein et al., 1992). Many cite this decline as evidence of the so-called gridlock of the Reagan-Bush administrations. But interpreting the decline is not that simple since the 1980s also saw an increase in the number of bills consolidated into catchall omnibus bills. Thus the change in how bills were packaged was reflected in the decline in total numbers of bills.

Alternative ways of examining legislative productivity at the floor level are available. Almost all important legislation makes its way to the floor of the House and the Senate through, respectively, a special rule or a unanimous consent agreement. By examining the number of special rules passed in the House and the number of unanimous consent agreements used in the Senate, one can create a rough measure of the amount of important legislation considered.

Alternatively, one might count the length of legislative sessions, either by days or, for a more accurate measure, by the number of hours the House and Senate spend in session considering legislation (Davidson and Hardy, 1987a, 1987b). Other possible measures of floor activity are the number of amendments proposed and the number of roll-call votes taken in each chamber. These methods are time-bound since reforms in the 1970s increased members' access to the floor and relaxed requirements for roll-call votes.

Some measures of legislative activity are applicable only to the Senate. For instance, one might want to consider the number of filibusters pursued in the Senate. As with petitions in the nineteenth-century House, filibusters in the modern Senate represent a different form of legislative "work," in which the interests of a political minority are expressed. As in other cases, counts would have to account for changes over time; regarding filibusters, these changes concern rules of recognition and cloture. Yet rules changes also reflect changing perceptions of what constitutes appropriate use of legislative floor time and thus reflect changes in legislators' "work" roles. Counting the number of cloture votes may also be a method of helping to determine workload, but the same caveats apply.

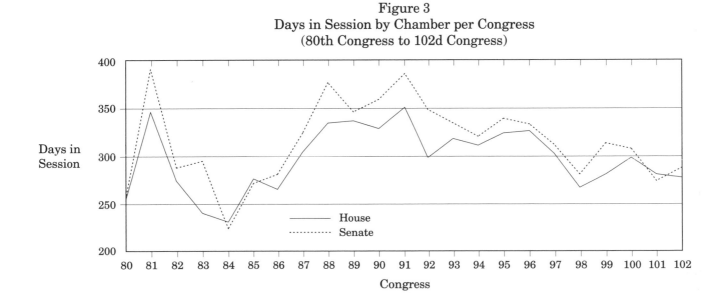

Figure 3
Days in Session by Chamber per Congress
(80th Congress to 102d Congress)

Figure 4
Number of Public Laws Enacted per Congress
(80th Congress to 102d Congress)

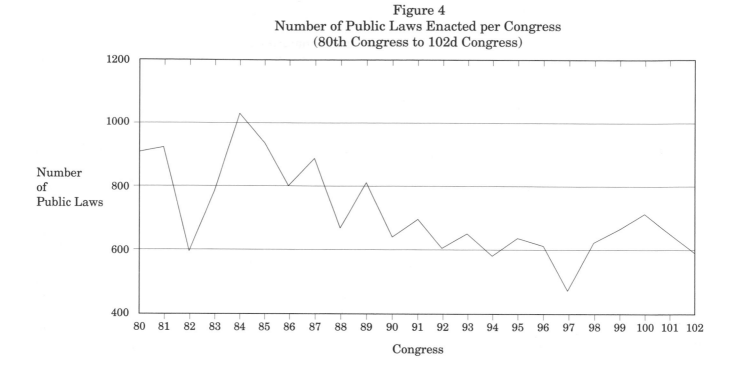

Congress

There are still other measures of floor workload that one may want to consider. If House and Senate disagree on provisions in one another's versions of a bill, they may form a conference committee to resolve their differences. Also, because presidents may veto legislation, it would be helpful to know the proportion of bills vetoed and to measure the effort expended on trying to have those vetoes overriden.

The Final Product. Finally, attention must be given to the amount of legislation passed and then enacted into law. Public laws are the end product of the system. Donald L. Eilenstine, David L. Farnsworth, and James S. Fleming (1978) identified three distinct eras by the number of bills passed by Congress: a limited Congress before 1860; the more active Congress of the industrial era of 1860 to 1921; and the much more active Congress of the era from 1928 through 1957. Since the late 1950s, the steady decline in the number of bills passed by Congress is reflected in the number of public laws. As has been discussed, one problem of measuring workload during the later decades of the twentieth century has to do with bills being packaged into large omnibus bills covering many subjects. Certainly, the number of pages per statute increased more than threefold from the 1950s through the 1990s. Focusing only on this output, however, presents a biased picture of the work of

Congress. Activities such as legislative oversight and the consideration of executive nominations should not be neglected. Likewise, focusing solely on output allows no consideration of time spent developing legislation at the committee and floor stages. Nor does it consider the time spent working on legislation that never becomes law because of disagreements within or between chambers or between Congress and the president.

Numerous activities contribute to legislative workload. To measure Congress's workload accurately, one must cast a wide net, looking at all aspects of the work performed by the House and Senate. One can never disregard, however, the tried and true measures: the number of bills introduced and passed per chamber, the number of public laws enacted, and the number of days in the session. Each of these gauges of legislative activity has stayed relatively constant over the last five to six Congresses.

BIBLIOGRAPHY

Davidson, Roger H. "The Legislative Workload of Congress." Paper presented at the annual meeting of the American Political Science Association, Washington, D.C., 28–31 August 1986.

Davidson, Roger H., and Carol Hardy. *Indicators of House of Representatives Workload and Activity.* Congressional Research Service, Library of Congress. CRS Rept. 87-497 S. 1987.

Davidson, Roger H., and Carol Hardy. *Indicators of Senate Activity and Workload.* Congressional Research Service, Library of Congress. CRS Rept. 87-492 S. 1987.

Eilenstine, Donald L., David L. Farnsworth, and James S. Fleming. "Trends and Cycles in the Legislative Productivity of the United States Congress, 1789–1976." *Quality and Quantity* 12 (1978): 19–44.

Mayhew David. *Congress: The Electoral Connection.* 1974.

Ornstein, Norman J., Thomas E. Mann, and Michael J. Malbin. *Vital Statistics on Congress, 1991–1992.* 1992.

Wilson, Woodrow. *Congressional Government: A Study in American Politics.* 1885. Repr. 1981.

Evelyn C. Fink and Brian D. Humes

Politics and Influence in Congress

Who is influential in the U.S. Congress? Why? To understand influence, one needs to know on what it is based, where it is located, how it is exercised, and how to define and measure it.

Bases of Influence. Influence has three fundamental bases: (1) information and expertise; (2) reciprocity or exchange of favors; and (3) the power to command. In Congress there is a great deal of the first two and very little of the third.

Information. There is much truth in the old saying that "information is power." Some members of Congress are more influential than others simply because they have a greater store of information and a greater expertise. These attributes give them a considerable advantage in persuading their colleagues to cast a favorable vote in committee or on the floor or to take some other form of favorable action.

One incentive for developing such expertise, or for using expertise that predates the member's arrival in Washington, lies in the structure of Congress. Unlike most state legislatures or foreign parliaments, Congress is highly specialized. Its committee system divides the legislative work load, and so command of a subject is prized, while being active in an area without knowing much about it is discouraged. In order to make a mark, a member finds a kind of policy niche—a topic about which he or she becomes expert. Many members develop a genuinely impressive level of knowledge.

However, it is legislative staff who have the most detailed and thorough command of information. Through the 1950s, Congress was not highly staffed, but during the 1960s and 1970s, staffing increased dramatically. Since then, there has been a substantial bureaucracy on the Hill, including the personal staffs of members, committee and subcommittee staffs, and staff agencies like the Congressional Budget Office. Some of this bureaucracy is occupied with clerical duties, constituency service, and reelection efforts. A part of it, though, comprises an impressive source of public policy information internal to Congress and independent of the executive branch or other outside influences.

Because information is power, these centers of staffing figure prominently in drafting bills and amendments, affecting policy outcomes both in committee and on the floor, mounting persuasive efforts internal to the Congress, and mobilizing support outside of the Congress.

Reciprocity. The second of the three fundamental bases of power is exchange. One of the principal norms of Congress is reciprocity: "You do a favor for me, and I'll do a favor for you." Reciprocity, of course, is a norm of social relations in general. Without some expectation that a favor begets a favor in return, most forms of cooperation, including the workings of the legislative process, would collapse.

Some members of Congress are in a better position than others to do favors. A committee or subcommittee chairman, for example, is in a position to see to it that an amendment favored by a noncommittee member is inserted into a bill being marked up by the committee. The chair of a party's campaign committee is able to funnel funds into politicians' campaigns. Those members best situated to do favors can be quite influential in the legislative process, since they can expect favors in return. If a committee chairman helps a member with a provision in one bill, for instance, that member is likely to express appreciation by voting with the chairman on some other bill. If the member does not, he or she will not be able to count on the future cooperation of that particular chairman.

These exchanges occasionally take the form of an explicit quid pro quo. Most of the time, however, the exchanges are implicit and unspoken. Members who do favors for others build up a kind of bank of credit on which they can draw when necessary. But just as with a bank, one can draw down the account, and it needs replenishing from time to time by granting more favors.

The power to command. The third base of influence is the power to command. There are a few cases of that sort of power in the Congress. An elected member, for instance, directs his or her own personal staffers. He or she is in a position to hire and fire them at will, to decide which subjects they will work on, and to direct their activities. Most of the time, of course, that kind of command is not invoked, and the relationships between staffers and their bosses are wholly two-way, compatible, and cooperative. The growth of the Hill bureaucracy, indeed, has led some observers to worry that the elected members are not sufficiently in control. The entire relationship of a member to his or her own personal staff, however, is set in an understanding on both sides that the ultimate power in the situation rests with the elected member.

However, there are hardly any other such examples of command authority on the Hill. Certainly, party leaders are in no position simply to command the troops to follow them. Senators and representatives are elected and returned to office by their own constituents. They do not owe their membership in the body to the sufferance of the party leaders, and everybody understands that fact. Similarly, committee chairs cannot simply command that one type of bill be reported to the floor rather than another version. These leaders are important and influential, to be sure, but their influence does not rest on their power to command committee members. Instead, it is very much linked to expertise and reciprocity. They possess either a fund of information that is hard to match, an ability to do favors for others and profit from the exchange, or both.

Locations of Influence. It is very difficult to identify locations of power and influence in the U.S. Congress. In many ways, it is a remarkably decentralized institution. Its 100 senators and 435 representatives, together with their staffs, make up a body of 535 autonomous enterprises. Far from commanding them, the most that leaders can hope for is some modicum of coordination, and even that is usually quite weak. There is nothing like the hierarchy of superiors and subordinates that one finds in the pyramidal organization charts of business firms or executive branch agencies. Compared to most other legislative bodies, furthermore, the party discipline in Congress is extraordinarily weak.

House-Senate differences. There are some differences between the House and Senate regarding the distribution of influence. First, senators have somewhat more autonomy than House members. When floor business is scheduled, for instance, the Senate majority leader engages in an elaborate process of negotiating among the involved senators regarding when a given bill will be scheduled and how long the debate will take. He then proposes a unanimous consent agreement to schedule the bill,

which can in principle be scuttled by the objection of any single senator. Debate in the Senate is unlimited unless cloture is imposed by a vote of sixty senators or a unanimous consent agreement imposes limits. Nongermane amendments are often introduced, debated, and even passed.

The House, by contrast, schedules its business by a majority vote on a rule for a given bill that is proposed by the Rules Committee. The rule limits debate and often allows only specified amendments to be offered. House members are allowed somewhat less autonomy, in part because the House is bigger and hence potentially more unwieldy. Even House members, however, have greater autonomy than members of parliament in most other democracies.

Another difference between House and Senate involves expertise and hence the distribution of information-based influence. Partly because of the size of the body, senators are spread thinner than House members. The Senate has all of the work of the House, plus the handling of confirmations and treaties, and less than one-fourth the membership. Therefore, more of the detail of legislative business devolves onto staff than in the House. And since information is power, staffers are somewhat more influential on the Senate side of the Capitol.

Formal positions. There are two families of influential formal positions in the Congress: the committee and subcommittee leaders and the party leaders. The committee and subcommittee leaders include the chairmen and the ranking minority members. The party leaders include the majority and minority leaders; the whips on both sides; the chairmen of the party caucuses; the senatorial or congressional campaign chairmen of each party; and, in the House, the Speaker (the top majority party leader, selected by vote of the majority party members).

Committee and subcommittee chairmen derive their influence partly through their expertise and partly through their prerogatives. First, many of them are highly expert in the subject matter of their committees. They have dealt with it for years and know the policy issues, the legislative histories, and the important players in the system surrounding their committees' jurisdictions. Second, their prerogatives are useful in the exchange of favors discussed above. Chairs schedule the meetings and decide what will be taken up and what will be shelved. They direct the majority staff of the committees or subcommittees. So if another member would like a hearing scheduled on a favorite bill, the help of staff members in drafting an amendment, a timely good word from the chairman in favor of a pet proposal, or an endorsement for re-election from a visible colleague, a chairman is in a position to decide whether to help or not.

Party leaders also have a number of resources at their disposal. First, they influence the agenda—which bills will be taken up, when, and under what conditions. Second, the whip system places party leaders at the center of a communications network. That network conducts counts of members for, against, and undecided on a given issue, coordinates campaigns for or against key amendments or bills, and attempts to persuade party members of the virtues of the leadership's position. Third, the party leadership influences the committee assignments of their party's members. Since committee assignments are central to members' careers in the Congress, this prerogative gives leaders an important ability to reward friends and punish enemies and to do favors for new members that build credit. Fourth, the role of party leaders in campaign finance provides another means of building indebtedness that can be used in legislative battles of various kinds. Fifth, party leaders enjoy a publicity advantage over other members, because they are constantly interviewed and featured in the media. Finally, the party leaders of the president's party use the resources of the presidency as well as their own resources.

As noted above, however, the influence of party leadership in Congress is quite limited, especially in comparison with other legislatures. If members cross party leaders, the leaders do not have much redress, especially if the members already hold the committee assignments they want. There is actually a fairly high degree of party cohesion in Congress, but not through the ability of leaders to whip party members into line that one finds in most parliaments. Cohesion, rather, is a result of constituency and coalition differences between the parties, ideological differences between the parties, and the resultant intraparty patterns of communication. Party leaders are overwhelmingly brokers, persuaders, and negotiators. There are very few occasions for command.

Informal influence. An inventory of formal positions of power in Congress does not by any means exhaust the locations of influence. Some senators and representatives are influential beyond their formal positions. They develop reputations among their colleagues for their good judgment, their political savvy, and their expertise. Members have a great many opportunities to observe and to interact

with their colleagues. They see each other daily in committee sessions, in floor debate, in informal conversations, on social occasions, and even in the House gym. Thus, their opinions about their colleagues are based on a rich fund of information.

Also, some members who hold formal positions are not as influential as those positions would suggest. They have not developed reputations for very effective use of their resources. They may not be seen as knowledgeable, tenacious, or skillful. Since members have many opportunities to make judgments about their formal leaders' performance and to differentiate among them, formal position does not necessarily translate directly into influence. Some holders of formal positions are not particularly influential, and some members are influential beyond their positions.

Forms and Exercise of Influence. The forms of influence have two general aspects: individual and institutional.

Individual influence: cue taking. One important way in which members of Congress decide how to vote on the floor, and to some extent even in committee, is by taking cues from each other. Members must cast so many votes that they cannot possibly study each issue with care. They simply do not have sufficient time, and their staffs are occupied with many other matters. So on any particular bill or amendment, they take their cue from a colleague or set of colleagues whose judgment they trust, sometimes following them quite blindly. These cues may take the form of floor speeches, "Dear Colleague" letters, brief conversations with the cue givers, staffs' calls to other staffs, or even the yea or nay lights of cue givers on the electronic display in the chamber. By taking these shorthand cues, members believe they can make the same decisions that they would have made had they studied the issue themselves.

By what criteria do they choose colleagues from whom to take cues? When voting on the floor, they tend to rely heavily on cues from specialists, colleagues with some claim to expertise. These fellow members are overwhelmingly from the committees and subcommittees that considered the legislation. Deciding members also pick cue givers whose judgment they trust and who are likely to come to the same positions they would have had they studied the issue. That criterion for choice implies two things. First, they pick people whose policy positions or philosophies of government are like their own. Second, they pick people whose political judgment is similar to theirs; who are in similar electoral situations; and who share their views about major interest groups, coalition supporters, partisan opponents, and reelection strategies.

These criteria have two major implications. First, most cue taking takes place within parties, not across parties. There may be a regional component to the pattern, with southern Democrats following other southern Democrats or with members following colleagues from within their own state party delegations. One occasionally observes patterns of leading and following across party lines, but it is rare. This intraparty communication pattern is one major reason for the degree of party cohesion that exists in Congress, and it derives from similarities of constituencies, supporting coalitions, and electoral experiences within the parties.

The second and even more important implication of the pattern of cue taking is that, fundamentally, ideology drives voting. Members of Congress choose to follow colleagues whose worldviews, policy attitudes, or ideologies are like theirs. Because they are free to choose whomever they like, this criterion of philosophical agreement with the cue giver means that ideology drives the legislative process to a considerable degree. This implication is quite different from notions about the legislative process that emphasize politicians' efforts to win reelection, buy off pressure groups, or promote their careers through delivering benefits for their districts and angling for favorable media coverage. They do all of those things, to be sure, but the stress on such activities misses the importance of ideas about public policy in the legislative process. It is not that ideas run counter to politics. In fact, because voters tend to elect politicians whose views are not totally unlike their own, elected officials often do both the expedient and principled things at once.

Institutional influence: committee-chamber relations. It follows from the congressional emphasis on expertise that committees and subcommittees are important in the legislative process and in the making of public policy. As discussed above, senators and representatives prize specialization and turn to committee and subcommittee members for cues as they vote on the floor. Thus, the committee system is set up to give an institutional advantage to expertise. Committees also use the influence base of reciprocity to exchange favors with each other. Thus, the pattern, "You help my committee and I'll help yours," also contributes to committee power.

The patterns of cue taking raise a series of critical institutional questions: What is the relationship between committees and the chambers (House or Senate) of which they are a part? Do committees dictate to the floor? What power does the parent chamber have over its committees? Does it make a difference where power rests, or would the outcomes be similar whether committees or parent chambers dominate the legislative process?

Scholars debate whether committees are representative microcosms of their parent chambers or biased subsets of those chambers. Much depends on the answer. If committees are fundamentally representative of their parent chambers, then lodging power in the committees does not produce outcomes very different from those that would be produced if matters resolved in committees were instead decided by votes in the chambers. But if they are unlike their chambers in important ways, then their power raises normative questions concerning whether committee outcomes violate the will of the majority in the parent chamber. Some scholars (e.g., Krehbiel, 1991) assert that committees are not systematically biased, or to the extent that they are, they still must tailor their bills to the wishes of the parent chamber to muster majority votes for passage. Other scholars (e.g., Shepsle, 1978) argue that the committee assignment process, by which members express their preferences for committees and are assigned to one committee rather than another, systematically biases committees away from being representative of the parent chamber.

Probably the best way to reconcile these positions is first to observe that some committees are more representative than others. The Agriculture committees of both houses, for instance, are dominated by farm state members who respond most clearly to farm and agribusiness interests, making them systematically unlike the parent chambers. Second, some types of actions raise concerns about representativeness more than others. For instance, committees are better able to block than to pass legislation without taking much account of chamber majorities, because passage requires floor approval and blocking does not.

One way to think of the committee-parent chamber relationship (Kingdon, 1989) is to picture the parent chamber as setting boundaries for each committee. On matters where most noncommittee members care little about a given provision of a bill, the committee has a great deal of discretion. On matters where most members care a great deal about a provision, committees have less discretion.

These patterns of chamber attention, and hence of the boundaries the chamber sets for the committee, may vary from one committee to another, from one bill to another, and over time.

The importance of selection processes. Many of these observations about flows of influence point to the importance of the selection processes by which officials come to the positions they hold. Members of Congress often make their judgments straightforwardly according to their own attitudes about what constitutes good public policy. That being the case, the processes by which some people rather than others are selected to hold positions critically drive outcomes.

Those selection processes start with nomination and election of members back in individual constituencies and states. More than anything, the larger contours of outcomes in the House and Senate are structured by the distribution of parties and ideologies in the two chambers. Thus, the processes by which these members, rather than their actual or conceivable competitors, are selected to represent their districts and states, go a long way to explaining why the legislative process produces one outcome rather than another.

The ways in which some members rather than others become leaders within the Congress further highlight the importance of these selection processes. To the extent that committees are powerful, for instance, the biases that are built into the committee assignment process fundamentally affect policy outcomes. And to the extent that committee and subcommittee chairs and party leaders affect the workings of Congress, the process for choosing

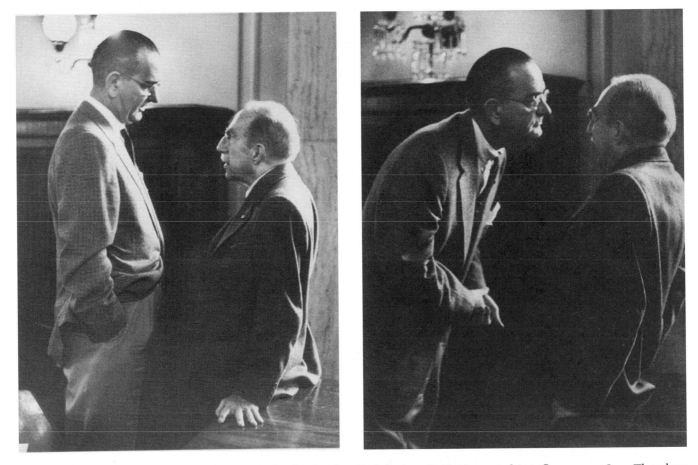

THE JOHNSON TREATMENT. Senate majority leader Lyndon B. Johnson (D-Tex.) exerts his influence on Sen. Theodore F. Green (D-R.I.), 1957. Johnson was the most forceful majority leader to hold that office. Understanding the issues that were important to each senator, Johnson was usually able to persuade his colleagues to vote with him on a given bill. Uncooperative senators faced the so-called Johnson Treatment, in which the majority leader would praise, coax, needle, and threaten his colleagues. In 1955, through his influence, Johnson was able to usher the passage of over thirteen hundred bills, almost two hundred more than in the previous Congress.   GEORGE TAMES, *NEW YORK TIMES*

these leaders affects the orientations and ideologies that drive the institution.

Measurement and Conceptualization. Robert Dahl's (1957) classic definition of power states: "A has power over B to the extent that he can get B to do something that B would not otherwise do." While this is a sensible statement of what we mean when we say that one individual or agent influences or has power over another, it indicates how difficult the measurement of influence is. We need to determine what B would otherwise have done. The problem is that the world often does not hold still long enough for us to do that satisfactorily. At the same time that A is trying to influence B, many other things are happening to B, so it is extremely difficult to isolate the effects of A's activities. It is also extremely difficult to say what B would have done in the absence of A's activities, since determining what might have happened, but did not, must be speculative. Finally, one does not want to commit the fallacy of assuming that just because B acted after A's activities, B's actions were the result of A's activities.

A frequent approach to measurement in legislative studies often is the computation of some sort of agreement score. If legislators vote together, for instance, one might say that they affected each other. But agreement does not tell us the direction of influence; A may have affected B, but B might as easily have affected A. Actually, agreement does not even tell us whether there has been any influence; both A and B might have been affected by some third factor, and the agreement between A and B in that case is unconnected to any relationship between them.

Measurement of influence is also plagued by the problem of anticipated reactions. If one would like to know how much a given president affected Congress, for instance, one might calculate how often Congress passed that president's legislative proposals. But one president might anticipate congressional reaction and scale down his proposals to get them passed, generating a high box score; another president might push for a much more ambitious program and get less of it passed. In that case, one might conclude not that the first president was more successful in getting what he wanted, but only that he tailored his proposals to congressional wishes more skillfully. In fact, one might well argue that he obtained little and that Congress actually ruled the relationship.

The same consideration applies to measures of committee success on the floor. Some committees and committee chairs look tremendously influential because they get their legislation passed intact on the floor. But if they have anticipated floor reaction and tailored their proposals accordingly, then it is the parent chamber that actually controls legislative content, and the committee's surface power is illusory.

The best general solution is not to rely on any one measure. One might want to use agreement scores, combined with interviews, participant observation, analysis of contemporary documents, examination of confidential memoranda and letters, and other indicators. As is often the case, some sort of multimethod design gets better results than any single approach.

[*See also* Bargaining; Committees, *article on* Assignment of Members; Leadership; Logrolling; Seniority.]

BIBLIOGRAPHY

Dahl, Robert. "The Concept of Power." *Behavioral Science* 2 (1957): 201–215.

Fenno, Richard. *Congressmen in Committees.* 1973.

Kingdon, John. *Congressmen's Voting Decisions.* 3d ed. 1989.

Krehbiel, Keith. *Information and Legislative Organization.* 1991.

Matthews, Donald. *U.S. Senators and Their World.* Rev. ed. 1973.

Matthews, Donald, and James Stimson. *Yeas and Nays: Normal Decision-Making in the U.S. House of Representatives.* 1975.

Shepsle, Kenneth. *The Giant Jigsaw Puzzle: Democratic Committee Assignment in the Modern House.* 1978.

JOHN W. KINGDON

Customs and Mores of Congress

The United States Congress comprises some 540 independent actors, counting the one hundred senators, 435 representatives, the four delegates from the District of Columbia and the territories and one resident commissioner from Puerto Rico. Each of these men and women has been elected in his or her own right, and they reach the Congress owing their election to many people: mentors, sponsors, contributors, local political bosses, and the voters of their district or state. They owe very little of their success to each other. Once elected to Congress, of course, members of their party may help them with fund-raising and on rare occasions with campaign appearances, but even this assistance is based largely upon self-interest, such as the desire to further one's advancement within the party hierarchy.

The fact that these men and women are in one sense independent of one another yet depend upon each other to pass legislation means that the way the Congress operates has to do as much with the personal relationships that develop between members and the customs, mores, and rituals of the Congress as with the elaborate written rules and regulations that govern their conduct as individuals and as members of the collective body. Over the two hundred years since the First Congress met in 1789, there have been many changes in the way in which members behave toward each other. Verbal slights and insults, for example, no longer merit challenges to meet on the Bladensburg dueling ground at sunrise. But there has also been continuity in the way members of Congress have treated each other, based largely upon their independence, equality within their respective bodies (with the exception of the nonstate House members, who can vote only in committee), their shared election experience (analogous to the fraternity pledge's "hell week" in terms of building camaraderie, except that it may be a "hell year"—or longer—in the case of a congressional election), and their mutual desire for reelection.

It is difficult to determine which of these factors weighs most heavily in the development of congressional mores and customs. They all have their part in the building of the traditions of Capitol Hill, and together they create a congressional culture that transcends the political and ideological differences that divide the membership.

Some may dispute the notion that there is a culture on Capitol Hill. Actually, there are two cultures: one on the House side of the Hill, and one on the Senate side. They are similar in some ways—being developed and driven by the same forces—but they are different also, just as the House and the Senate are different bodies with different histories and different constitutional responsibilities and expectations. Some of these customs have become clichés, such as Speaker Sam Rayburn's admonition to the members of the House of Representatives: "To get along, go along." But other customs unique to the federal legislative bodies are more subtle and relate to the fact that this is indeed an exclusive club, with two distinct parts.

Joining the Club. Getting elected to Congress is seldom an easy affair. With the exception of those lucky few individuals who are appointed to office to fill an unexpired term, many members run and are defeated several times before finally being granted the grand prize. They are generally successful, well-known men and women, with a drive and desire for public recognition and acclaim that exceeds anything that most people can understand. There is the occasional member who is genuinely self-effacing, but most members necessarily have egos that rival the Washington Monument in size, even if they keep them well hidden most of the time. Given what it takes to put oneself forward to be accepted or rejected publicly by hundreds of thousands—perhaps millions—of one's fellow citizens, it could hardly be otherwise. And once elected they have

"INCIDENTS OF LIFE AT THE NATIONAL CAPITOL DURING A SESSION OF CONGRESS." The captions for the images read: *top, left to right,* "Writing cards for country visitors," "Refreshment room for senators"; *middle, left to right,* "A family lunch at the Capitol," "Female lobbyists"; *bottom,* "Stock speculation in the telegraph station in the corridors of the House." From *Frank Leslie's Illustrated Newspaper,* 9 April 1881.   LIBRARY OF CONGRESS

PHYSICAL CULTURE CLASS FOR SENATORS.   Senators exercising outside the Capitol.   LIBRARY OF CONGRESS

often discovered that reaching Capitol Hill does not immediately make them members of the club.

Twenty years ago curmudgeonly House members like Wayne L. Hays (D-Ohio)—infamous for his dalliance with his secretary, Elizabeth Ray—were reputed to rail at new members with such endearing terms as "potato head," "mush head," and "scum." In the Senate the rites were more sophisticated, such as Henry M. Jackson's mispronunciation of the name of the new senator from Massachusetts: "Tongas," ignoring the "s" that followed the initial "t" in the name. It is barely possible, of course, that the distinguished senator from Washington State might simply have been ignorant of the way Paul E. Tsongas's name was pronounced, but not likely.

As late as the 1940s and 1950s, and perhaps into the 1960s, it could reasonably be said that new members were expected to serve a silent apprenticeship. Donald Matthews reported in his U.S. Sen-

ators and Their World (1960) that even laudatory remarks praising the service of one of the senior colleagues were discouraged when they came from a new member of the Senate. Indeed, the tradition of learning one's specialty before taking an active role in the affairs of the legislative body seems to have been fairly well observed.

Likewise, the tradition that Speaker Sam Rayburn (D-Tex.) observed of inviting new Democratic members of the House to his Capitol "Board of Education" room, where they would sip bourbon and branch water and learn the rituals of the body from their more senior colleagues, died out with the passing of "Mr. Sam." New members of the House are now given an orientation that includes presentations by members of the Harvard University faculty, but it is just not the same.

Observation since the 1980s suggests that there is little if any humiliation involved in the initiation of new members. Indeed, it is unlikely that any member of the Congress would allow himself or herself to be abused by a bully like Hays. Returning members seem to strive to welcome their new colleagues and begin a relationship with them that might prove mutually advantageous. Such a relationship is not enhanced by deliberately insulting someone or implying that they should learn the business of legislation by observing, not by doing.

Courtesies and Conventions. Both the Senate and the House are bodies of elaborate ritual and formality, probably second only to the British Parliament in their historical ceremony. In neither house, for example, do members address each other directly in debate, and neither do they refer to each other by name. In the House all remarks are addressed to the Speaker; in the Senate the president (whoever is presiding at the time) is the addressee. A member wishing to refer to or address a remark to Sen. Ernest F. Hollings, for example, would refer to him as "the senator from South Carolina," leaving it to the listener to determine whether it is to Hollings or to Sen. Strom Thurmond that the remarks are addressed. The *Congressional Record* for that day would make clear who was intended by placing the name of the member in parentheses.

Likewise, in the House the member might refer to "the gentleman from Massachusetts," as if there were only one such in the body. This indirect method of address is customarily observed in both House and Senate, except that in the heat of debate a member will occasionally slip and begin speaking directly to another member. It then falls to the presiding officer to remind the member that all remarks are to be addressed to the chair.

There are also customs as to what can and cannot be uttered on the floor of either body. Members of the House, for example, do not usually refer to the Senate by name, calling it "the other body" or "some other body," when it is found necessary to mention it at all, thereby bringing to mind a homicide detective discussing a multiple killing. Congressional speech when delivered on the floor of the House or Senate is constitutionally protected (Article I, section 6), but this protection does not mean that members can say anything they wish and not be called to account.

The custom of the Congress is that a member is not supposed to attack another member personally. Today's verbal attacks are rather tame affairs when compared with the rough-and-tumble fights—both verbal and physical—that characterized the nine-teenth-century Congress. Still, House Speaker Thomas P. (Tip) O'Neill, Jr. (D-Mass.) discovered in 1984 that there are certain limits beyond which even a Speaker cannot venture with impunity.

Speaker O'Neill was provoked when Rep. Newt Gingrich of Georgia, a conservative Republican, uttered words that O'Neill took as disparaging the patriotism of Democratic members of the House. The imposing Speaker immediately left the presiding position—which a Speaker rarely does—and took Gingrich to task, declaring that the Republican's statement was "the lowest thing I have ever seen in my thirty-two years in Congress." At that point another Republican challenged O'Neill's phrasing, and demanded that the words "be taken down," or stricken from the record. The parliamentarian of the House ruled that O'Neill had indeed violated the prohibition against personal insult, and for the first time since 1797 a Speaker was chastised for his language.

Nineteenth-century members of both bodies would undoubtedly be astonished that language as mild as O'Neill's would bring an official rebuke. An examination of the record of the first hundred years of the Congress reveals that words spoken in the chamber were often the cause of duels, beatings, and fistfights.

In 1838, for example, Rep. Jonathan Cilley of Maine delivered a speech that criticized a New York City newspaper editor. Another member, William J. Graves, attempted to deliver a note to Cilley demanding an explanation. When Cilley refused the note, Graves challenged Cilley to a duel. Though pistols were the usual dueling instrument, these two members chose rifles, and Cilley's death was the result. The House appointed a committee to look into the matter, but decided against expulsion or censure of either Graves or the House members who had served as seconds in the duel.

Neither has the Senate been spared violence arising out of floor debate. In one example, tempers routinely flared during the height of controversy over the great compromise on slavery that had been fashioned by Henry Clay and others in 1850. On 17 April 1850, for instance, Henry S. Foote of Mississippi drew his pistol—there were no rules preventing the well-armed member from entering the Senate chamber—and aimed it at Thomas Hart Benton as the Missouri senator advanced toward him. Benton was unafraid and challenged Foote: "Let him fire! Stand out of the way! Let the assassin fire!" Both men were restrained by others in the chamber, and there was no further breach of proto-

CONGRESSIONAL SOFTBALL. Sen. Mike Mansfield (D-Mont.) as umpire, Sen. John F. Kennedy (D-Mass.) as catcher, and Sen. Henry M. Jackson (D-Wash.) at bat in the 1950s.   OFFICE OF THE HISTORIAN OF THE U.S. SENATE

col that day. But it was abundantly clear, as other members—notably Sen. Charles Sumner of Massachusetts, whose assault on the floor of the Senate by Rep. Preston S. Brooks of South Carolina became a pre–Civil War cause célèbre—discovered throughout the remaining years of the nineteenth century, words could provoke a physical retaliation from another member of Congress.

The standards of today have led to changed mores within the Congress as well, so that it is only on the rarest of occasions when a member physically assaults another. Just such an occasion occurred in the House chamber in March 1985. According to reliable reports, Rep. Thomas J. Downey, a liberal New York Democrat, accosted Rep. Robert

K. Dornan, a conservative California Republican. Downey allegedly grabbed Dornan by the shoulder and spun him around, demanding to know whether Dornan had called him a "draft-dodging wimp" in a recent speech. Dornan took offense at Downey's hands-on approach and grabbed the New York representative by the necktie, hoisting him partway off the floor. As others intervened, Dornan released Downey's tie, explaining that he "only wanted to straighten the knot."

For the most part, senators do not today engage in such unseemly behavior. Indeed, the elaborate rituals and courtesies of the U.S. Senate might make the courtiers of Louis XVI feel quite at home. A member is hardly ever just "the gentleman from

South Dakota." He is "the distinguished gentleman from South Dakota." He or she is "the able Senator from Nebraska" or the "learned Senator from Alabama." All of this is done with the straightest of faces, even if the speaker knows that the member being referred to is in reality dumb as a tree stump. As Sen. Alben W. Barkley of Kentucky was reputed to have said, "If you think your colleague is stupid, refer to him as 'the able, learned, and distinguished Senator.' If you know he is stupid, refer to him as 'the very able, learned and distinguished Senator.'" It is sometimes difficult to maintain the front. As one member said, "I know he is a dumb SOB; everyone else knows he is a dumb SOB. But we must keep up the charade."

Sometimes a member does not display the proper courtesy toward his colleagues, and other than the disdain of his fellows, there is not usually much that can be done about it. Occasionally, though, such a member will leave the Senate and then come back in another capacity, perhaps seeking confirmation for an important post within the executive branch. Consideration of a former member is ordinarily a time for senatorial courtesies to be put on fullest display, and most such nominations sail through without much delay. One such nomination in 1989, however, proved the exception.

John G. Tower, the former senator from Texas, was nominated by President George Bush to be secretary of Defense. Even before credible allegations that touched on Tower's qualifications to be Defense secretary had surfaced, astute observers of the process discerned that there might be some problem with the Tower confirmation. Tower's ego and his prickliness were legendary, even by Senate standards, and during his three-plus terms in the Senate he had apparently aggravated many of his colleagues. Tower's potential difficulty was corroborated when a Republican senator—someone who eventually voted for Tower—was heard to mutter to one of his staff, "I wonder if the little [expletive] expects this to be easy." It was not easy, and Tower was ultimately rejected by the Senate in which he had served for over twenty-three years. It was a rare departure from senatorial norms.

The Tyranny of the Minority. The legislative courtesies of the Senate are much more necessary than are those of the House of Representatives, primarily because of the rules of the two bodies. As more than one observer has noted, the rules of the House are designed to allow the majority to work its will; the rules of the Senate are designed to protect the minority, even if that minority consists of

only one member. The minority in the House of Representatives can often do little more than engage in guerrilla warfare and snipe at the majority, while in the Senate a minority can effectively derail the legislative train by objecting to the usual method by which the Senate does business.

Most of the business of the Senate is conducted by means of what are called "unanimous consent agreements," or "UCs." Unless a member objects, the Senate can violate its own rules with impunity, and the rules are routinely violated every time a bill is called up for floor action. If a member does not want to allow such latitude it is easy enough for him or her to object to the terms of a unanimous consent agreement when it is offered by the majority leader or other sponsor of the bill, and such objections are not uncommon. Through what is called the "hold" system, however, it is possible for a member to indicate his objection even before the UC stage is reached.

To do so, he tells his leader—Republican or Democrat—that he wants to be consulted before a bill is brought up for consideration and that he is placing a "hold" on the bill. This indicates to the leadership that there is no point in seeking a unanimous consent agreement, because the member has a particular problem with that particular piece of legislation. Holds may remain secret for a time, though they are almost inevitably revealed if they are kept in place for longer than a few days. A hold is in many instances an indication that the member wants the sponsor of the bill to accommodate an amendment, but it may signal that a unanimous consent agreement will be objected to no matter what "sweeteners" are offered. As a result, the majority leader or his designee will not generally attempt to bring up for floor action a bill that is the subject of a hold.

Students of the hold system do not know precisely how long it has operated, but it goes back to the 1960s at least. By the 1970s it had developed into the system as it operates now: a powerful brake on the operations of the Senate. The person placing the hold is usually known to the members of his own party, but it can be difficult for a member of the opposite party to discover the identity of the culprit. Both Democrats and Republicans deplore the practice of placing anonymous holds on bills, but members of both parties admit to using holds themselves. It is simply one of the tools of the Senate, and it is one that owes its existence purely to courtesy and tradition.

The unanimous consent agreement also owes its

effectiveness to the courtesies and comity of the Senate. A perfectly naive newcomer, learning about the routine use of such agreements to transact Senate business, might say, "Then that's the answer. If there is anything coming up that I do not like, I will just object to its consideration." That might be within the rules, and if you did not care what your colleagues thought of you, and you never wanted to get anything passed yourself, then this would certainly be a way to delay the passage of objectionable legislation. If one person did it, however, it is a certainty that others would do the same, and the Senate would quickly come to a screeching halt. Senatorial courtesy would have been breached, and the entire nature of the body would change.

The Senate found out in 1957 just what the reaction would be if someone attempted to depart from the norms of the Senate and violate the usual customs and courtesies. According to the *New York Times*, Sen. H. Styles Bridges (R-N.H.) sought the routine permission of the Senate to insert into the *Record* a speech he had delivered some fifteen years earlier. The *Congressional Record* is filled with this sort of drivel, and upon hearing such a request the presiding officer drones almost automatically that "without objection, it is so ordered."

Suddenly, the new (two months in the Senate) member from Ohio, Frank J. Lausche, lodged an objection. Mouths fell open, and there was a dead silence in the chamber. Bridges indicated that if there was to be an objection to his routine request, then he would do the same to others. The Senate leadership could see the cloth unraveling; without such routine comity, the Senate could not function. Majority Leader Lyndon B. Johnson thereupon stepped in; Lausche withdrew his objection; Bridges inserted his speech; and the wheels of the Senate turned freely again.

The same courtesy occurs when a member requests a speaker to yield to him for a question. This is sometimes done for the purpose of helping the speaker make a point, but at other times the purpose is hostile. In both instances the member holding the floor normally yields, but if there is a limitation on his time and he knows the question will be a hostile one, he will sometimes refuse the request to "yield for a question."

It is also part of the courtesy of Senate debate to allow each member to have his say on a bill or amendment before moving to table. "Tabling" a bill or amendment effectively kills the measure, and since the motion to table is nondebatable, offering that motion cuts off debate and causes an immediate vote on the issue at hand. In the normal partisanship of many legislative bodies, such a move would be regarded as a fair and appropriate tactic. In the Senate, though, a member who attempts to shut off debate before each interested senator has had the opportunity (within reason) to have his say will bring down upon him the wrath of his fellows. It has sometimes occurred that someone moves to table an amendment, a member objects that he has not been allowed to be heard on the issue, and the one who moved to table thereupon withdraws his motion.

Seniority. It may come as some surprise to learn that the seniority system, by which the chairmanship and ranking position on a congressional committee or subcommittee are largely determined, is purely a matter of custom and is not a part of the Senate or House rules. Seniority in the Congress is based on (1) length of continuous service within the body (House or Senate), followed by (2) total service in the one body, including noncontinuous service, followed by (3) service in the other body of Congress, followed by (4) service as a state governor. It may also be further determined by alphabetical order.

This system was never as strong in the House as in the Senate, where it still holds sway. A rigid seniority system for committee chairmanships in the House was a fairly recent phenomenon, developing only in the late 1940s and 1950s. Prior to that time the Speaker of the House could influence the committee vote regarding appointments of committee chairmen, and even as recently as 1943 eleven of thirty-four House committees were chaired by other than the most senior member.

Going further back, in the early years of the nineteenth century even presidents got into the act. John Quincy Adams, for example, met with Speaker of the House John W. Taylor in 1825 to discuss the appointment of committee chairmen "so that justice may be done as far as practicable to the Administration." Seniority was not even a consideration in Adams's time.

In the modern House of Representatives Democrats who become chairmen of committees are elected by the Democratic caucus, and a chairman who takes his position for granted may find himself ousted, as occurred in the 1970s with the chairmen of Ways and Means, Agriculture, Armed Services, and Banking and Currency. The days of the all-powerful committee chairman in the House seem gone for good, and it was a sign of the times that the members of the House class of 1992 interviewed the committee chairmen even as they themselves jockeyed for assignments to coveted committees.

In the Senate the seniority system is much more strictly observed. Democratic committee chairmen or ranking members are nominated by the Steering Committee, a part of the Democratic leadership, and these nominations are invariably made by seniority. If 20 percent of the Democratic membership of the Senate wishes to challenge the nominations, the caucus decides the issue by secret ballot. This has not happened, but such a vote theoretically could occur.

On the other side of the aisle, the Republican members of each committee elect the chairman or ranking member, the choice being subject to confirmation by the Republican conference. Seniority has generally been the rule in such selections, and the conference has even overturned the wishes of a committee in order to preserve seniority. Such was the case in 1987, for example, when Jesse Helms (R-N.C.) decided to assert his seniority and bump Richard G. Lugar (R-Ind.) from the ranking position on the Foreign Relations Committee. Republicans on Foreign Relations wanted to keep Lugar, who had chaired the committee during the previous Congress. Helms, however, prevailed in the Republican conference, where even some of those philosophically opposed to the conservative Helms voted with an eye toward the integrity of the seniority system, an example of custom and tradition prevailing over ideological commitment or political compatibility.

Dress. The advent of C-SPAN, the Cable Satellite Public Affairs Network, has allowed the typical voter to see for the first time just how a member of Congress dresses while representing him or her in the halls of Congress. For some voters it is probably quite a shock. For male members, coats and ties are de rigueur for entry onto the House or Senate floor, but beyond that bare code very little else is applicable. Senators generally dress in a conservative fashion, and there is a certain amount of peer pressure to conform to a "Brooks Brothers" look. House members, on the other hand, are all over the place sartorially. Loud plaids and other outrageous patterns are a constant for some members, such that one staffer, in response to a representative's flamboyant attire, was heard to remark that he had "wondered what happened to Pinky Lee's wardrobe," referring to the 1950s children's television star.

There is no actual rule requiring that a male member wear a necktie or even a jacket or suit, but

these are traditions that have been hallowed by the years. Rep. Ben Nighthorse Campbell (D-Colo.), an American Indian, broke one precedent when he wore his bolo tie onto the House floor, but even in the 1970s no member is known to have attempted to pass into the House chamber wearing a polyester double knit leisure suit.

Former Members. Many members who retire or are defeated decide—particularly if they have spent a considerable period of time in the Congress—that they do not really want to go back to Montana or Louisiana or wherever. Instead, they settle into law firms and lobbying operations in the nation's capital and use to great advantage their knowledge of the way legislation is made, the friendships they made while serving in the House or Senate, and the courtesies that are afforded them as former members.

These courtesies are considerable, and they offer the ex-member a distinct advantage as a lobbyist. The former member, for example, has the privileges of the floor, meaning that he can go into the House or Senate chamber while the legislative body is in session and chat with his former colleagues. Both Senate and House tradition prohibits actual lobbying while on the floor, and the House rules even prohibit the presence on the floor of an ex-member who has an interest in pending legislation. But there are few who believe that the presence of a former member who is known to be representing a particular side of an issue goes unnoticed and does not inure to the benefit of his client.

A recent example of the benefits of having an ex-member on a lobbying team comes from the Senate at the close of the second session of the 102d Congress, when Russell B. Long, former chairman of the Finance Committee, ventured into the chamber where he had served for some thirty-seven years. Long was not at that moment lobbying his former colleagues on behalf of the biotech firm that had developed a new and promising possible AIDS vaccine; he had already done his work along those lines. Long was there just to show the flag, so to speak, and his presence was noted by Sen. John W. Warner. Warner affirmed that Long was not there as a lobbyist, but the presence of the former colleague, said Warner, "connoted the importance of the amendment" the Senate was then considering. This amendment proposed $20 million for the Defense Department to conduct clinical trials of the vaccine, and it passed with ease.

Former members are also afforded additional perks that other lobbyists cannot approach, such as the right to enter the "members only" dining rooms in the Capitol, a nice place for schmoozing with one's former colleagues. Former senators qualify for other, lesser privileges, too, ranging from a permanent identification card from the Senate sergeant at arms (which allows unfettered access to the Capitol, including those parts that are off-limits to the general public) to parking in the Senate parking lots (a considerable convenience given the difficulty of parking on Capitol Hill). Some of these privileges, states the *Congressional Handbook*, are derived from statute and Senate rules, "but most are traditional courtesies." There is no publication of the House of Representatives that offers a comparable list of courtesies afforded former members, but knowledgeable insiders suggest ex-representatives are treated about the same as ex-senators.

Equality of Members. All members, with the exception of the nonstate members of the House of Representatives, are equal, whether one is a junior Republican or the Democratic chairman of the Appropriations Committee. This does not mean, of course, that everyone enjoys the same power, prestige, or esteem, but within their own offices they are equally king or queen, or equally despots.

A member can hire and fire staff for no reason at all—even on a momentary whim—and though there are both House and Senate rules that say that a member should not discriminate against his or her staff on the basis of race, color, religion, sex, or national origin, there is little if any enforcement mechanism to ensure that if such discrimination occurs there is real consequence for the member or relief for the victim.

This reluctance among members to involve themselves in one another's domain is perhaps best exemplified in the congressional reaction to allegations of ethics violations by their colleagues, including allegations of sexual misconduct or harassment of staff. Each house of Congress has an ethics committee, and service on it—a duty in which one is compelled to judge one's fellow House or Senate members—is anything but a sought-after assignment. House minority leader Robert H. Michel, for example, described such an assignment as "dirty, dirty duty" and suggested that anyone who served on the ethics committee would fairly much be able to name his or her next committee assignment.

Senators and members of the House have been disciplined for violation of the rules of the body. The extreme reluctance of the membership to recognize and consider accusations against one of

their own, however, only reinforces the notion that there is a "congressional protective society" that turns its collective face away from all but the most egregious violations. It has been suggested that even when the Congress acts against an unethical member, it does so only against conduct that is clearly criminal or in the face of mounting publicity that threatens the body itself. After all, as is a common saying on the Hill, "what goes around comes around," and no member wants to be deprived of the freedom to run his own office and treat his own staff the way he sees fit.

The way in which the Senate and the House conduct their business is the result of some two hundred years of practice, precedent, and tradition. Many of these rules have been codified by the two bodies, beginning with the manual of procedure developed by Thomas Jefferson while he served as vice president of the United States. But many other rules are not written down in any official handbook of the Congress. They are nevertheless just as applicable and operate just as surely as those that have been sanctified by codification. These traditions, mores, folkways, and customs are part and parcel of the Congress, and it is impossible to understand these two legislative bodies without both acknowledging them and accepting their place in the culture of the Hill.

[*See also* Alcoholic Beverages in Congress; Ceremonial Activities; Clubs; Cuisine of Congress; Freshmen; Seniority.]

BIBLIOGRAPHY

Baker, Richard A. *The Senate of the United States: A Bicentennial History.* 1989.

Currie, James T. *The United States House of Representatives.* 1989.

Davidson, Roger, and Walter J. Oleszek. *Congress and Its Members.* 3d ed. 1990.

Jones, Rochelle, and Peter Woll. *The Private World of Congress.* 1979.

MacNeil, Neil. *Forge of Democracy: The House of Representatives.* 1963.

Matthews, Donald R. *U.S. Senators and Their World.* 1960.

Weatherford, J. McIver. *Tribes on the Hill: The U.S. Congress, Rituals and Realities.* 1985.

JAMES T. CURRIE

Public Perceptions of Congress

The public image of the U.S. Congress is paradoxical. Scholars and practitioners who are knowledgeable about the institution admire and respect it as a formidable, influential, and responsive democratic legislature. In contrast to the parliaments in many democratic countries that have only a minor role in making laws, Congress is a powerful lawmaking body. Many ordinary Americans agree, believing that it is Congress that should make the laws of the land and speak for the citizenry in national affairs. At the same time, the drumbeat of public evaluations of Congress, evoked in public opinion polls, is generally negative. To many citizens, Congress is a flawed institution, not to be trusted and requiring reform. And, by criticizing Congress even as they sit as members of the institution, representatives themselves chime in on the chorus of negative voices.

Americans hold ambivalent attitudes toward Congress. On the one hand, they tend to accord quite low performance appraisals to Congress as an institutional entity. On the other, they tend to evaluate their own representative in Congress quite favorably. For instance, at the end of 1991 interviewers conducting a survey for the ABC News–*Washington Post* poll asked a now-standard question: "Do you approve or disapprove of the way the U.S. Congress is doing its job?" Most Americans did not approve—only 35 percent said they approved of Congress's job performance. In the same poll, inter-

viewers asked, "Do you approve or disapprove of the way your own representative to the U.S. House in Congress is handling his or her job?" Most Americans—fully 60 percent—were positive about their own representatives. These results are typical. Americans' consistently more favorable appraisal of their own representatives over the Congress of which their representatives are members has given rise to the aphorism, "We love our congressmen but we do not love our Congress."

Americans' appraisal of congressional performance waxes and wanes over the years, as the two major polling organizations have demonstrated. Figure 1 illustrates the cyclical character of public evaluations from Gallup Poll results, where survey respondents are asked to approve of or disapprove of the way Congress is doing its job. In these Gallup Poll data, the high points of congressional popularity occurred in 1974 (when 47 percent approved of the job Congress was doing) and in response to the activist Congresses of the mid 1980s, prior to the resignation of House Speaker James C. Wright, Jr. (D-Tex.) following charges of improprieties.

The Harris Survey asks its respondents, "How would you rate the job being done by Congress: excellent, pretty good, only fair, or poor?" Typically, "excellent" and "pretty good" are considered posi-

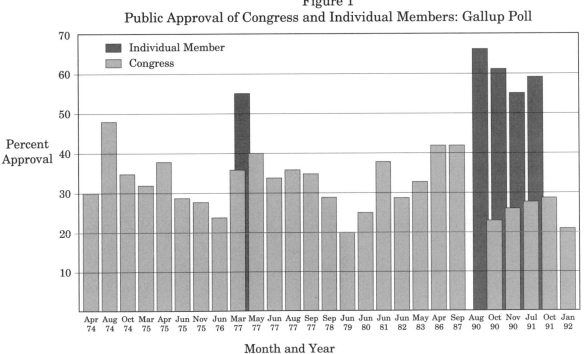

Figure 1
Public Approval of Congress and Individual Members: Gallup Poll

Month and Year

Figure 2
Public Evaluation of Congress and Individual Members: Harris Survey

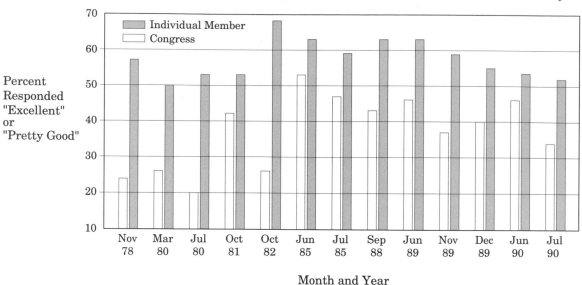

tive evaluations, while "only fair" and "poor" denote negative appraisals. The Harris Survey evaluations are displayed in figure 2. Often, these ratings indicate a more supportive public evaluation of Congress than do the approval-disapproval ratings of the Gallup Poll.

Both the Gallup Poll and the Harris Survey ask their respondents to evaluate their own representative in Congress, as well as Congress itself (shown in figures 1 and 2), although the Harris Survey provides a longer and more complete time over which respondents evaluate their representatives. Although the two evaluations move in tandem over time to some extent (see especially figure 2), Americans always accord their immediate representative much more support than they give to the more remote Congress, and substantially so. This helps to account for the fact that, despite much antipathy toward Congress, Americans regularly reelect their own representatives, making the incumbent return rate very high. By the same token, Americans' strong feelings for their representatives help to explain why they tend to favor term limitations for members of Congress generally while supporting the perpetual reelection of their own representatives.

In addition to these appraisals of Congress and its members, the polls frequently record the extent to which Americans feel a degree of confidence in institutions, including Congress. Gallup pollsters

regularly ask respondents the following: "I am going to read you a list of institutions in American society. Please tell me how much confidence you have in each one—a great deal, quite a lot, some, or very little." Figure 3 shows trends in public confidence in Congress as well as in the military, organized religion, the Supreme Court, big business, and television. Americans' confidence in institutions has generally declined since the 1970s, perhaps with the exception of the military (which was not included in the 1973 poll). The military's Desert Storm operation in the Persian Gulf in 1991 added to the already high confidence Americans seemed to have in the armed forces. As with most institutions in U.S. society, public confidence in Congress declined; only 18 percent expressed "a great deal" or "quite a lot" of confidence in Congress in October 1991. This plunge in confidence was influenced by the variety of scandals and bad publicity surrounding Congress in 1990 and 1991—the savings and loan debacle, the resignations of the House Speaker and the Democratic whip, controversy about the Senate confirmation hearing for Supreme Court justice Clarence Thomas, and misuses of banking, postal, and other privileges by House members.

Whether one considers ratings of Congress's job performance or measures of confidence in the institution and its leaders, three observations may be made about oscillations in congressional popularity. First, these ratings tended to be relatively high as late as the 1960s and then declined, although there have been occasional short bursts of performance approval. Second, more often than not Congress receives lower ratings on performance and confidence than do the president or the Supreme Court. Third, the erosion of public confidence in Congress appears to be part and parcel of a much more general ebbing of faith in major institutions in general.

What factors account for variations in public evaluations of Congress and its members? Major events may boost the congressional approval rate. Recent examples would include the high positive evaluations recorded after the Senate Watergate hearings and the resignation of President Richard M. Nixon or following the joint House-Senate Iran-contra hearings. Generally, Americans evaluate Congress mainly on the basis of their feelings about major policy issues and their appraisal of how the legislative process is working. When the Gallup Poll asked Americans in 1990 why they disapproved of "the way Congress is handling its job," 23 percent

said they disapproved because of the way Congress handled the budget, failing to cut government spending and to solve the deficit problem. Another 31 percent complained that Congress was "not getting anything done" or that the members were "not working together" and "can't agree on anything."

In contrast, Americans evaluate their own members of Congress mainly on the basis of their personal characteristics and constituency-service efforts. On these criteria, representatives tend to be accorded favorable evaluation. Because the basis on which Americans evaluate Congress leads to negative appraisals and the basis for assessment of individual representatives tends to produce positive evaluations, it is easy to see why there is such a disparity between public attitudes toward Congress as a whole and representatives individually.

What factors help to bring about the fluctuation in public evaluations of Congress? Ratings of congressional job performance are quite volatile over the years and are greatly influenced by two factors. First, levels of approval or disapproval of how Con-

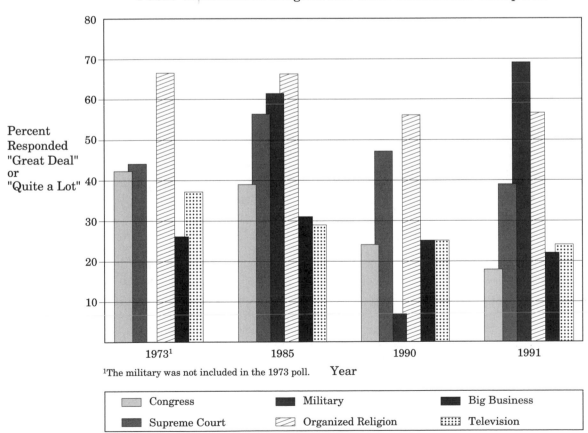

Figure 3
Public Confidence in Congress and Other Institutions: Gallup Poll

¹The military was not included in the 1973 poll.   Year

"THE OPTIMIST." Political cartoon reflecting the public's skepticism over Congress's ability to make good on its campaign promises. The cartoon presents the Republican Congress elected in 1946 as a hen trying to hatch a doorknob labeled "campaign promises." Edwin Marcus, published 9 February 1947.　　LIBRARY OF CONGRESS

gress performs are strongly affected by the popularity of the president. Other things being equal, when the president's popularity is high, there is a strong tendency for Congress to be popular; when the president's popularity falters, public evaluation of congressional performance likewise declines. This effect of presidential popularity on congressional job evaluation occurs whether or not the party affiliation of the president is the same as that of the congressional majority. Moreover, the extent of support for the president in congressional voting does not appear to divert or modify the impact of presidential popularity on congressional performance evaluation.

Second, public approval or disapproval of the job Congress does is very sensitive to the valences of media reporting. Media coverage of Congress is extensive. But at the same time, Congress normally receives less media coverage than the president, and congressional news coverage is often derivative of presidential news. Senators are more visible in

the news than are House members, and leaders of both houses attract the lion's share of news coverage of Congress. Finally, news coverage of Congress is inclined to be very negative. Media reportage of the operations of Congress as a legislative body—lawmaking activity, committee work, party leadership—and coverage of members' ethical behavior, both of which generally accentuate the negative, have powerfully depressing effects on public evaluations of Congress.

Public confidence in Congress runs on a different track than appraisal of job performance. Expressions of public attitudes toward almost all societal institutions have, since the 1960s, shown diminished levels of confidence, and Congress has been no exception. Public confidence in Congress and its leadership is especially attuned to the general condition of the economy. When the unemployment rate goes up, confidence in Congress drops. And confidence in Congress varies over time according to the salience of national versus international problems. When Americans perceive that foreign affairs present the most important national problems, confidence in Congress rises; when Congress is mired in vexing domestic policy problems, confidence abates. Confidence in Congress and appraisal of congressional job performance are distinctive features of public evaluation. Perhaps surprisingly, confidence in Congress's leaders can decline even when evaluation of congressional performance improves.

Americans' evaluations of Congress and its members are complex, reflecting ambivalence and contradiction and involving an intricate intertwining of perceptions of a remote institution, of the behavior of members of Congress in general, and of the performance of the citizen's own representative. Of course, Americans may disapprove of congressional performance and yet strongly approve the work of their own representatives. They may think that most members of Congress should be replaced while favoring the reelection of their own senators and representatives; they may think most members of Congress are dishonest and unethical while rating the ethics and honesty of their own representative very favorably; and they may vote for term limitations for members of Congress and at the same time vote to reelect their incumbents. Americans' own individual evaluations of congressional performance are strongly colored by their sense of the responsiveness of their own representatives, how much they know about their representatives, and how much contact they have had with them. And citizens' attitudes toward Congress, on the one hand, and toward their representatives, on the other, interact so that each can influence the other. While individual members, beloved of their constituents, may have considerable immunity from public hostility toward Congress as an institution, at some threshold of congressional disapproval public attitudes toward Congress may rub off on incumbent representatives accustomed to the immunity of strong local approval and the luxury of "running for Congress by running against Congress."

[*For a variety of related discussions, see* C-SPAN; Constituency Outreach; Literature on Congress; Movies on Congress.]

BIBLIOGRAPHY

Ladd, Everett Carll. "Public Opinion and the 'Congress Problem.'" *The Public Interest* 100 (1990): 57–67.

Parker, Glenn R. *Characteristics of Congress.* 1989. Pp. 45–64.

Parker, Glenn R., and Roger H. Davidson. "Why Do Americans Love Their Congressmen so Much More Than Their Congress?" *Legislative Studies Quarterly* 4 (1979): 53–61.

Patterson, Samuel C., and Gregory A. Caldeira. "Standing Up for Congress: Variations in Public Esteem since the 1960s." *Legislative Studies Quarterly* 15 (1990): 25–47.

Patterson, Samuel C., Randall B. Ripley, and Stephen V. Quinlan. "Citizens' Orientations toward Legislatures: Congress and the State Legislature." *Western Political Quarterly* 45 (1992): 315–338.

SAMUEL C. PATTERSON

Comparative Perspectives

Most countries have legislatures, though the consequences that legislatures have for their respective political systems differ significantly. Legislatures are constitutionally created institutions that have one core defining role: they assent to measures of public policy that by virtue of that assent are to have binding applicability, with that assent given on behalf of a body that extends beyond the elite responsible for formulating those measures. For some legislatures, this core defining task is the only task they undertake. Others are more functionally adaptable, fulfilling a number of tasks.

This variety in legislatures has allowed scholars to devise a number of typologies. One of the most useful is that offered by Michael Mezey in *Comparative Legislatures* (1979). He categorizes legislatures according to two criteria: their policy-making power and the degree of support they enjoy at both the mass and elite levels. Using the first criteri-

on, Mezey distinguishes between legislatures with strong, modest, or little or no policy-making power; using the second, he offers a simple dichotomy of more-supported and less-supported legislatures. The result is a six-box classification, though only five of the six boxes are actually occupied. (There are no less-supported legislatures with little or no policy-making power.) The more-supported legislatures that have strong policy-making power he calls *active legislatures;* the more-supported with modest policy-making powers he terms *reactive legislatures.* Of the remainder, the more-supported with little or no policy-making power are termed *minimal;* the less-supported with strong policy-making powers are termed *vulnerable,* and those with modest policy-making power are termed *marginal.*

The U.S. Congress is distinctive. It is the only major national legislature to be classified as active. The only other significant legislatures to be placed in this category are the U.S. state legislatures. Though Congress shares with most Western legislatures the feature of being more-supported, it stands apart in its policy-making powers. Congress has the power not only to amend or reject measures brought forward by the executive but also to formulate and substitute policy of its own. Reactive legislatures can amend, even reject, measures advanced by the executive but lack the capacity to formulate and substitute policy of their own.

The U.S. Congress's distinctiveness is more marked in the twentieth century than it was in the nineteenth, an age of parliamentarianism. This age of parliamentarianism was, however, short lived. In *Modern Democracies* (1921), the scholar-statesman Lord Bryce asserted that legislatures were in decline. Though he qualified his assertion, the notion of legislative decline is one that has pervaded perceptions of legislatures ever since. Other legislatures have ceased to be "active." Yet Congress has stood apart from this trend.

Three principal explanations—constitutional, procedural, and ideological—account for Congress's continued activeness. The first two explanations are necessary but not sufficient for creating the dichotomy; the third provides the sufficient condition.

Constitutional Explanations. The U.S. Constitution prescribes a separation and an overlap of powers. The executive and legislature are elected separately. Though there is an overlap of powers, there is no overlap of personnel (other than the vice president, who serves as presiding officer of the Senate, but this exception is irrelevant to this discussion). Furthermore, neither relies on the other for contin-

BRITISH HOUSE OF COMMONS. Aquatint from R. Ackermann, *Microcosm of London*, 1808–1811, vol. 1.
THE METROPOLITAN MUSEUM OF ART, ROGERS FUND, 1921. [21.36.164-1 (PLATE 21)]

uation in office. (The president may, in exceptional circumstances, be impeached, but he is not dependent on the political confidence of Congress for his continuation in office.) Each branch serves until the next fixed-term election.

These characteristics distinguish Congress from the parliamentary (or, as in the case of France, hybrid) system employed in most Western countries, in which the executive is normally drawn from the legislature and where each is dependent on the other for its continuance in office. The legislature may withdraw its confidence from the executive; the head of government may seek to dissolve the legislature. There is thus a mutual dependence. As demands on government have grown since industrialization and the spread of the franchise in the nineteenth century, parliaments have increasingly

deferred to the executive. The executive has the advantage of superior resources of information, administrative expertise, and, as we shall see, political muscle.

Procedural Explanations. In terms of formal procedures, the distinction between Congress and other Western legislatures is not as sharp as at the constitutional and ideological levels and so does not go far toward explaining Congress's uniqueness. For example, the examination of bills in committee prior to floor consideration by the full legislature tends to enhance the legislature's capacity to influence the contents of legislative measures. However, this procedure is not peculiar to the U.S. Congress nor, indeed, to a congressional form of government as such.

Congress exhibits additional similarities to other

BRITISH HOUSE OF LORDS. Aquatint from R. Ackermann, *Microcosm of London*, 1808–1811, vol. 2.

THE METROPOLITAN MUSEUM OF ART, HARRIS BRISBANE DICK FUND, 1917. (17.3.1167-128)

legislatures in terms of procedures. The filibuster, for example, is not unique to the U.S. Senate. Also, terminology is often shared. (It does not always impart the same meaning, however. In the British Parliament, for example, "to table" a motion is to start a process; in Congress, it is to end one.) There are also similarities in lengths of sittings. Congress is among the world leaders in the number of days it sits each year (though it is usually surpassed by one or two others, such as the United Kingdom and Canada), but it is not so exceptional in the number of hours per sitting. In common with most other Western legislatures, Congress does not hold plenary sessions in the morning.

What is noteworthy but not, in terms of formal rules, peculiar about Congress is the extent to which the legislative process constitutes a multiple check process. Several hurdles must be overcome in both chambers before a measure can be sent to the president for signing. What distinguishes Congress from other Western legislatures is the extent to which these constitute active hurdles. The explanation for this is to be found in ideology.

Ideological Explanations. Louis Hartz, in his seminal work, *The Liberal Tradition in America* (1955), made a point vital to understanding the contemporary role of Congress. Unlike the countries of Western Europe, the United States lacks a feudal history. It therefore lacks the legacy of social division and political conflict bequeathed by feudal hierarchies. The United States is characterized by ideological consensus. Within that consensus, parties exist but lack the ideological focus and commitment exhibited by political parties in other Western nations.

In the United States, the distinctions between the Republican and Democratic parties are narrow, sometimes to the point of being indiscernible. There is party competition for Senate and House seats and for the presidency, but there is no sharp ideological conflict. By Western standards partisanship is muted, which deflates voter turnout. It also acts as a reinforcement of the separation of powers; with strong partisanship—commitment to party programs uniting the president and members of Congress—an overriding of the barriers erected by the Constitution between the executive and legislature would be more likely. Though party is an important influence in Congress and, according to studies, is growing stronger, it remains but one of several influences.

In most Western legislatures, party is the strongest and sometimes almost the exclusive determinant of voting behavior. The contrast with the U.S. Congress is sharp—and long-standing. A. Lawrence Lowell, in *The Government of England* (vol. 2, 1908), analyzed party votes in Congress and in the British House of Commons during the second half of the nineteenth century. He recorded that party voting in Congress varied from session to session (in some sessions it was nonexistent) and did not "follow any fixed law of evolution." In contrast, party voting in the British House of Commons increased markedly during this period, becoming both extensive and fairly constant by century's end.

Party voting has remained a central feature of parliamentary behavior. In *British Politics in a Collectivist Age* (1965), Samuel Beer noted that party cohesion in the House of Commons had increased "until in recent decades it was so close to 100 percent that there was no longer any point in measuring it." Though there has since been an increase in cross-party voting in the House of Commons, party voting remains overwhelmingly the norm. Such cohesion is the norm in other Western legislatures as well, reinforcing an us-versus-them mentality. Legislators adhere to a particular philosophy; they want to achieve its implementation; party provides the means for its realization. They thus vote with their party to achieve it. Their opponents vote against them in pursuit of another ideology. This ideological imperative in party voting means that to vote against the party is equivalent to betraying the ideology.

There are also political imperatives to party voting. A failure to support his or her own side in parliamentary votes may result in the legislator being denied renomination by the local party or, in systems employing regional or national lists, being relegated to a lowly place on the list. In some parliaments, such as that of India, a single act of defiance can result in immediate sanction. A parliamentary form of government also encourages cohesion through a desire not to jeopardize the continuation of one's own party in government. Provision for formal votes of confidence—with the government resigning or calling an election if the vote is lost—usually exists in parliamentary systems. In some parliaments, important (and some not so important) votes are treated—formally or by popular perception—as tantamount to votes of confidence. Additionally, where ministers are drawn from the legislature, the desire for preferment encourages party loyalty. Unlike Congress, most legislatures offer no significant alternative career path to that of ministerial office. The only path to ministerial office is through the legislature. The relationship of legislators to the head of government, where they are of the same party, is usually one of dependence. In Congress, the relationship is one of independence.

It is thus possible to identify a particularly sharp dichotomy between a system that is parliamentary and partisan and one that is congressional and nonpartisan. The former is marked by a strong whipping system, a high level of cohesion in roll-call votes, executive dominance of the parliamentary timetable, and an emphasis on the chamber as a whole rather than on committees. Examples include the Irish, British, Canadian, and Indian parliaments. The congressional system, by contrast, is marked by a weak or nonexistent whipping system, a relatively low level of cohesion in roll-call votes, control by the chamber of its own timetable, and an emphasis on committees. Indeed, the U.S. Congress is remarkable for the extent to which it uses committees, especially subcommittees.

Congress as an Active Legislature. Congress thus epitomizes an active legislature. Despite the greater emphasis since 1933 on the executive as the initiator of legislative proposals, Congress remains, in Mezey's words, "one of the few legislative institutions in the world able and capable of saying no to a popularly elected president and making it stick."

This has significant consequences for the generation of public policy. Parties compete for power on the basis of party programs. In parliamentary systems, where one party—or a stable coalition with a dominant partner—is returned to power, a party majority is available to implement that program.

(Examples include Germany, the United Kingdom, Canada, Ireland, New Zealand, and Australia.) Parliamentary systems are "responsible"—that is, there is a clearly defined body that the electorate can hold responsible for the public policy enacted during the lifetime of a parliament. Systems in which there is a separation of powers or in which governments are formed on the basis of shifting coalitions or postelection bargaining are essentially "irresponsible"; no single body can be held accountable by the electorate in a subsequent election. Is a large budget deficit the responsibility of Congress or the president? Parliamentary systems tend to ensure coherence of policy over constraints on executive power. Congressional systems tend to emphasize constraints to the detriment of coherence.

Consequences of Legislature Types. Legislatures have consequences for their political systems other than making laws. Robert Packenham, in a 1970 article (in Allan Kornberg and Lloyd D. Musolf, eds., *Legislatures in Developmental Perspective* [1970]), identified eleven consequences and grouped them under three heads: legitimation; recruitment, socialization, and training; and political decision making, or influence. These, he noted, would vary in importance from legislature to legislature. Although legislatures are often associated mainly with value allocation (i.e., lawmaking), Packenham's study of several developing nations supported the hypothesis that a legislature's legitimation of government and of measures of public policy was the consequence with the greatest impact on the political system. His research concentrated on Brazil but was supplemented by impressionistic evidence from other countries. "Specialists in legislative studies," he wrote, "have not studied the functions of legislatures very much, but what knowledge we have suggests that the Brazilian case is much closer to the mode in terms of ranking of consequences than the U.S. Congress."

This conclusion is borne out by Mezey's study. Congress is atypical because of its capacity to allocate values. This capacity has also increased the impact of other functions. Its administrative oversight is conducted through its committees and subcommittees. Cabinet secretaries cannot rely on political loyalty or patronage to ensure a supportive environment. What Packenham calls "errand running" for constituents also constitutes a major activity for legislators. Lacking the protective cloak of partisanship—and of parties that undertake fundraising and campaigning on candidates' behalf—members of the House and Senate are highly responsive to constituent demands. In more partisan systems, legislators can often rely on the party label rather than constituency attentiveness to ensure reelection and, in countries with list systems of election, on party patronage rather than constituents' choice.

Similarly, the lack of a strong protective party cloak also ensures that interest articulation constitutes a significant congressional activity. Members of Congress are able to articulate the demands not just of constituents but of attentive publics. Packenham used the term to refer to the articulation of public interests. In the United States, the interests of special groups compete with those of the public. In strong party systems, opinions of electors are aggregated and channeled through political parties. On the one hand, this ensures that special interests do not monopolize the political system. On the other, it reduces the capacity of legislatures dominated by partisan conflict to act as agents of conflict resolution. The absence of such partisanship in the United States increases the potential for Congress to resolve conflicts and serves to mobilize popular support for measures of public policy. Congress provides an important arena in which interests of competing groups can be brokered.

Also, in the congressional system recruitment is of minor significance in comparison with parliamentary systems. In the latter, the legislature is an important avenue of recruitment and training for executive office. Ministers will normally be drawn from, and usually remain in, the legislature. (This is not, however, the case in all parliamentary systems.) Parliamentary service constitutes a form of apprenticeship. It is a necessary condition for achieving office. In hybrid systems such as that of France and, in practice, Brazil, and in congressional systems such as that of the United States, service in the legislature is but one—and not always the most important—of several possible routes to executive office.

In parliamentary systems where ministers remain in the legislature, the chamber continues to offer a form of political training. Ministers have to respond to debates and to answer questions. The twice-weekly appearance of the British prime minister in the House of Commons to answer questions contrasts sharply with the almost total detachment of U.S. presidents from congressional activity.

Congress resembles other legislatures in its legitimizing function. Like all legislatures, it fulfills the core defining function of "manifest" legitimization—that is, of giving the formal seal of approval to measures of public policy. Like other Western legislatures, it also fulfills the function of "latent" legitimization. That is, by being elected and by meeting regularly and uninterruptedly, it serves to legitimize the political process. In this respect, Congress and the British Parliament are closer to each other than to other Western legislatures that have not enjoyed the same uninterrupted history.

The consequences of Congress for the political system are notably different from those of most other legislatures. By virtue of retaining, and on occasion exercising, strong policy-making powers, Congress has an impact that distinguishes it from most others. It is distinguishable in another respect: it is the most studied of all legislatures. The development of the discipline of political science and of behavioralism in particular in the United States has ensured the subjection of Congress to more intense quantitative as well as qualitative analyses than any other legislature. Not only did advances in the study of legislatures, and especially legislative behavior, in the 1960s and 1970s take place in the United States, but such studies were also largely focused on the U.S. government. There was an existing literature to build on. Hard data in the form of roll-call votes were available. Senators and representatives could be observed and interviewed. Constituents could be surveyed and interviewed. Other legislatures—aside from U.S. state legislatures—were geographically distant from U.S. researchers, and the existing literature was poorer and less accessible. Knowledge of Congress—and of the state legislatures—has consequently outstripped knowledge of other legislatures.

We know from existing literature and observation that Congress is atypical. Study of Congress, therefore, does not allow generalization about legislatures as a species. As the study of other legislatures grows, not only will there be a stronger body of literature from which to generalize, but there will also be an ever-richer body of comparative material that will permit a better understanding of Congress. Most of the existing generalizations and hypotheses about legislatures have been generated by Congress-watchers rather than parliament-watchers. The more that observers look elsewhere, the greater number of tools they will have to understand the atypical, active legislature that is the U.S. Congress.

BIBLIOGRAPHY

Blondel, Jean. *Comparative Legislatures.* 1973.
Mezey, Michael. *Comparative Legislatures.* 1979.
Norton, Philip. *Legislatures.* 1990.
Norton, Philip. *Parliaments in Western Europe.* 1990.
Olson, David. *The Legislative Process: A Comparative Approach.* 1980.
Polsby, Nelson. "Legislatures." In vol. 5 of *Handbook in Political Science.* Edited by Fred I. Greenstein and Nelson W. Polsby. 5 vols. 1975.

PHILIP NORTON

The Study of Congress

The U.S. Congress has long fascinated scholars, students, politicians, and professional observers of politics. This fascination has produced a wealth of books, articles, and stories about the processes, structures, and members of Congress. Studies of Congress have often been characterized by contradictions, controversies, and diverse findings, rather than by agreement. These divergent results stem from the fact that the study of Congress, like the institution itself, is very complex and that writers vary markedly in their focus (what they study), their method (how they study), and their intent (why they study).

Topics of Congressional Research. The earliest scholars of Congress, primarily historians and political scientists, focused on the legislative institution as a whole and its place in the American political system. Alexis de Tocqueville (*American Institutions and their Influence*, 1851), Woodrow Wilson (*Congressional Government*, 1885), and other pioneers of the study of Congress were primarily intent on examining its activities, as well as its place in the American structure of government, and how it compared to the legislative bodies of other nations. Such studies approached Congress as an institution. They focused on interactions within the legislative branch or the interplay between the legislative branch and the executive, the courts, the public, or the international community. While this institutional approach yielded a thorough understanding of the constitutional role and performance of the legislative branch, it failed to address the less formal activities and roles of the institution.

Congressional subunits. Congress is comprised of smaller institutions or subunits. Some scholars and other writers have chosen to focus on these units rather than on the institution as a whole. The standing committees, the primary working units of Congress, have been the focus of much research, with scholars describing the organization, activities, interactions, and decision-making processes of the various committees. Such studies have revealed that members are purposeful in their selection of committee positions and that com-

NATIONAL ARCHIVES RESEARCH ROOM AND LIBRARY. East Search Room, a public room in which researchers may study government records. In the fall of 1994, the room became part of the Center for Legislative Archives and now serves as a research room for viewing records of the legislative branch.   NATIONAL ARCHIVES

mittees function in their own different and very predictable ways.

Congressional parties constitute another set of institutional subunits that have been subjected to a good deal of study. Led by David Truman (*The Congressional Party*, 1959), academics and journalists have dutifully analyzed the organization, purposes, and activities of congressional Democrats and Republicans. These studies have shown that the significance and activities of the congressional parties change markedly over time, adapting to the changing nature of society and the political system.

Additionally, some of the earliest historical studies of Congress focused on the elected leaders. These studies have demonstrated that while leaders generally possess several common traits, such as a propensity for ideological centrism and consensus building, each leadership style is somewhat unique

because of individual experiences and particular political environmental constraints. Finally, since the mid 1970s, Congress has witnessed an increase in the number of caucuses that are not affiliated with either party but are composed of members united by a common characteristic or purpose. Such groups, based on race, gender, region, state, economic interests, or ideology, are becoming increasingly important in the legislative process and as subjects of congressional research.

Individual members. At its most basic level Congress is composed of 535 members, each driven by their own ambitions, motivations, personalities, and constituencies. Historical biographies of prominent members of Congress have been, and remain, a mainstay of the literature. Historical depictions of individual members have helped readers understand the modern institution. Furthermore, many studies since the mid 1960s have focused on the importance of individual members in determining the nature and direction of congressional activity. This attention to individuals enables writers to weave stories from the personal and professional lives of members that catch readers' interest while offering insight into the congressional process. This focus on individual members has also contributed a wealth of information that scholars have used to compare the attitudes, behaviors, and opinions of members, discovering interesting differences. For example, studies of roll-call votes have revealed the correspondence between a member's vote and his or her ideology, electoral situation, party, seniority, constituency, and state or region. Furthermore, the focus on members, combined with the increasing availability of accurate campaign data, has led to the development of intriguing and intricate theories concerning the predictability of electoral success, the sources to which incumbents will go for campaign contributions, and the impact of varying levels of campaign financing. While gathering information about attitudes is a much more difficult task than observing behavior, studies of individual members and groups of members are fruitful for discovering why members act as they do and hence why Congress acts as it does.

Process. Finally, some of the richest studies of Congress have focused on the process rather than the players. Well-written case studies of particular legislative efforts are instructive and can be quite entertaining. Efforts to chronicle the perilous paths of particular pieces of legislation (for example, Eric Redman's *The Dance of Legislation*, 1973) have brought the legislative process to life for millions of students, activists, and scholars. Other legislative events that have been the focus of popular books and articles include judicial and executive confirmations, legislative scandals, leadership elections, and conflicts with the executive.

Methods of Congressional Research. The methods that people have used to study Congress have changed markedly over the years, each offering its own brand of insight into the activities, purposes, and motivations of the institution, its component parts and its individual members. However, the study of Congress, by historians and political scientists, has followed a general path of increased methodological sophistication.

Legalistic approach. Early scholars adopted what has been called a legalistic, or constitutional, approach, analyzing the constitutional place and responsibilities of the legislative branch. This method relied almost exclusively on the analysis of legal documents, including the Constitution, the formally defined rules and responsibilities of each legislative chamber, and the formal avenues of interaction between Congress and other branches. The evaluation of congressional performance in light of constitutional and historical demands was often subjective. While offering a great deal about how Congress was supposed to work, these studies revealed little about the actual day-to-day workings of Congress.

Descriptive approach. The first half of the twentieth century saw a shift to a more descriptive approach, as political philosophers gave way to political practitioners and historians. The 1930s, 1940s, and 1950s were marked by an emphasis on the factual depiction of the activities of Congress and its component parts. The studies offered detailed and often intricate descriptions of Congress, its organization, and its processes, as well as the relationships with external actors. It was the job of the writer to present the facts, but the task of the reader to draw any conclusions or implications.

Several studies in the early 1950s by congressional staffers exemplified this approach to the study of Congress. These studies explained not how Congress was supposed to function but described how it worked in actuality. They relied on a great deal of observational as well as quantitative data, which the authors utilized to write about the stages of the legislative process, the responsibilities and composition of the leadership, the importance of particular informal membership coalitions, the work of standing committees, the number of bills passed, and the number of members defeated for reelection, as well as the constitutional responsibilities

of the legislative branch. While these facts were used to paint a detailed portrait of Congress, they offered little analysis concerning how and why congressional processes or characteristics might change or be altered. These concerns were left to the next generation of congressional scholars.

Behavioralist approach. The late 1950s witnessed the rise of the social-scientific movement known as behavioralism, and the analyses of political practitioners gave way to those of political scientists. Behavioralist scholars made a concerted effort to understand political activities rather than merely observe or describe them. This new generation of scholars shifted the emphasis of congressional research away from the examination of rules, regulations, and the activities of groups of actors to the behaviors and attitudes of individual members. Borrowing heavily from colleagues in sociology, social psychology, and anthropology, behavioralists used various methods to gather and analyze objectively data about the activities and attitudes of members of Congress.

For example, David Truman in his famous 1959 study, *The Congressional Party,* went beyond noting the existence of partisan blocs to dissect them and explain their sources. Congress was an appropriate topic for this more objective approach, since many of the activities could indeed be measured and then analyzed for patterns of variation. For example, individual members can readily be sorted according to their positions on individual issues, cumulative positions on several issues, seniority, partisanship, presidential support, electoral success, campaign finances, and the character of their districts. An analysis of these variations reveals much about the motives and actions of individual members of Congress and contributes to our understanding of the institution as a whole. But, this method is not without faults. It has been argued that the behavioral emphasis on measurement and objectivity has encouraged a discipline that is data rich and theory poor. There exists the very real danger of validating numerous pieces of information with no real understanding of how those pieces fit together.

Postbehavioralist approaches. Efforts to give theoretical underpinnings to data-intensive behavioral studies have led scholars in several directions. Some writers have sought solace in the application of formal models, primarily game theory and social choice theory, to the world of congressional decision making. This approach, borrowed from economics and psychology, assumes that decisions are made based on an established set of rules and constraints. Since the mid 1970s, it has been used primarily to explain the probability that a policy will or will not be adopted by Congress.

Others, often called "neo-institutionalists," have turned to the institutional context to understand individual decisions. These writers assume that individual behaviors are constrained by characteristics of the institutional and environmental context, as well as qualities peculiar to the individual. The institution influences the behavior of its members. Scholars are finding this approach useful in understanding the activities of leaders as well as the behaviors of members.

Finally, others have responded by combining objectivity with more traditional subjective methods of inquiry, such as case studies. They recognize the value of studies of a few cases, or even a single case, as well as the importance of statistical analysis of hundreds of cases. For instance, while studies comparing the election results in 435 congressional races are informative and offer considerable insight into why certain people win, a case study of a single district, like Linda Fowler and Robert McClure's *Political Ambition* (1989), may offer information—about how candidates decide to run for office—that is just as significant. The methods of congressional research reflect the search for a balance between scientific objectivity and practical application.

Purpose of Congressional Research. There are as many reasons for studying Congress as there are people conducting studies. Each writer is motivated by his or her own goals and informed by his or her own perspectives. Some have approached Congress with the intent of explaining and evaluating the place of Congress in the structure of American government. These writers attempt to evaluate the activities and performance of Congress in light of the Framers' expectations or the wishes of the voting public. This intent is often associated with the legalistic method described earlier.

Other writers, particularly politicians and political historians, approach the study of Congress with the intent of describing its structure, responsibilities, and activities. Their goal is to describe what is, rather than to speculate on what should be. This is often the intent of those who adopt the descriptive or behavioral approaches. The objective is to utilize an event, an activity, or a behavior to gain generalized knowledge about Congress and its members.

A third set of studies might be termed *critical.* The purpose of a critical study is to examine the facts to discover Congress's weaknesses and failures. Such normative studies, often engaged in by journalists and public interest groups, evaluate par-

ticular aspects of the congressional process and generally arrive at negative conclusions. Unlike more purely descriptive studies, their primary intent is to compare actual congressional performance with some ideal level of performance.

Finally, academics, politicians, and journalists have also written about Congress to propose changes to correct perceived flaws in process and performance. Such studies offer practical solutions to the structural, procedural, and political problems that plague Congress. Among the aspects of Congress that have been the subject of serious reformminded studies are the committee process, the budget process, and campaign finance.

BIBLIOGRAPHY

Cooper, Joseph, and David W. Brady. "Toward a Diachronic Analysis of Congress." *American Political Science Review* 75 (1981): 988–1006.
Huitt, Ralph K. "Congress: Retrospect and Prospect." *Journal of Politics* 38 (1976): 209–227.
Huitt, Ralph K., and Robert L. Peabody. *Congress: Two Decades of Analysis.* 1969.
Lowenberg, Gerhard, et al., eds. *Handbook of Legislative Research.* 1985.
Rieselbach, Leroy N. "The Forest for the Trees: Blazing Trails for Congressional Research." In *Political Science: The State of the Discipline.* Edited by Ada W. Finifter. 1984.

THOMAS H. LITTLE

Bibliographical Guide

This bibliography serves as an overview of the most important secondary research tools covering Congress.

Research Guides. There are several useful guides to the primary and secondary sources of information about Congress and the legislative process. These guides can be used for finding many additional bibliographic tools not mentioned in this article, as well as for obtaining more details about some of the topics covered in this overview. The following are listed in order of publication date, the most recent first.

Morehead, Joe, and Mary Fetzer. *Introduction to United States Government Information Sources.* 4th ed. Englewood, Colo.: Libraries Unlimited, 1992.
Jacobstein, J. Myron, and Roy M. Mersky. *Fundamentals of Legal Research.* 5th ed. Westbury, N.Y.: Foundation Press, 1990.
Goehlert, Robert U., and Fenton S. Martin. *Congress and Law Making: Researching the Legisla-*

tive Process. 2d ed. Santa Barbara, Calif.: ABC-Clio Press, 1989.

Zwirn, Jerrold. *Congressional Publications and Proceedings: Research on Legislation, Budgets, and Treaties.* 2d ed. Englewood, Colo.: Libraries Unlimited, 1988.

Dictionaries. Dictionaries on Congress can be used for finding the answers to ready reference questions, such as dates, terms, concepts, definitions, procedures, rules, and information about individuals.

Kravitz, Walter. *Congressional Quarterly's American Congressional Dictionary.* Washington, D.C.: Congressional Quarterly, 1993.

Congress A to Z: Congressional Quarterly's Ready Reference Encyclopedia. 2d ed. Washington, D.C.: Congressional Quarterly, 1993.

Dole, Robert J. *Historical Almanac of the United States Senate.* Washington, D.C.: U.S. Government Printing Office, 1989.

Elliot, Jeffrey M., and Sheikh R. Ali. *The Presidential Congressional Political Dictionary.* Santa Barbara, Calif.: ABC-Clio, 1984.

Handbooks. The handbooks cited below contain lengthy essays, written by experts in the field, providing concise overviews on the history, development, and procedures of Congress.

Guide to Congress. 4th ed. Washington, D.C.: Congressional Quarterly, 1991. As a handbook concentrating on Congress, the *Guide* explains how Congress works, beginning with an account of its origins and history. There are chapters on the structure, powers, and procedures of Congress and its relations with the other branches of government. There are new sections on the growth of subcommittees, the budget process, redistricting, pay, and honoraria. The volume is most valuable to the researcher seeking a basic, yet thorough, understanding of how Congress operates. This is the best single-volume reference work on the Congress.

Congressional Quarterly Almanac. Washington, D.C.: Congressional Quarterly, 1945–. This annual work summarizes congressional action for the previous year. Included are accounts of major legislation enacted, presidential programs and initiatives, analyses of Supreme Court decisions, results of all federal elections held in the preceding year, an examination of lobbying activities, and other special reports.

Congress and the Nation. 7 vols. Washington, D.C.: Congressional Quarterly, 1945–1988. This reference set, consisting of one volume for every four years, is a well-organized work providing quick access to descriptions of major legislation and issues in the Congress, White House, and Supreme Court. The set provides an excellent chronological history of major legislative programs and political developments during each Congress and executive administration, including biographical information, major votes, key judicial decisions, and election issues.

Lowenberg, Gerhard, Samuel C. Patterson, and Malcolm E. Jewell, comps. *Handbook of Legislative Research.* Cambridge, Mass.: Harvard University Press, 1985. This excellent volume summarizes the state of research on legislative studies about the Congress and other legislative bodies. It includes chapters on the organization and workings of legislative bodies as well as on elections, campaigning, the media, and relations with other branches of government. It is especially useful for identifying the key writings, both books and articles, on various aspects of Congress.

Biographical Directories. These tools direct a researcher to information about members of the Congress, their staff, committee staff, and other key government officials.

Biographical Directory of the United States Congress, 1774–1989: Bicentennial Edition. Washington, D.C.: U.S. Government Printing Office, 1989. This directory provides short biographies, arranged alphabetically, of senators and representatives who served in Congress from 1774 to 1989. Also included is a chronological list of executive officers of administrations from 1789 to 1989, a listing of delegates to the Continental Congress, and a listing of Congresses by date and session.

U.S. Congress. *Official Congressional Directory.* Washington, D.C.: U.S. Government Printing Office, 1809–. This biennial directory contains biographical and statistical information about members. It also includes information about their state delegations, terms of service, committee memberships, congressional sessions, votes cast for members of Congress, maps of congressional districts, and an index by names of individuals. Brief biographies supplied by members themselves indicate party membership, birth date and place, education, military career, religion, memberships, occupations, political career, and family.

Congressional Staff Directory. Mount Vernon, Va.: Staff Directories, Ltd., 1959–. This directory lists the staffs of all of the members of Congress as well as the committees and subcommittees of both houses and gives short biographical sketches of key staff personnel. Included are committee and subcommittee assignments, key federal officials and their liaison staffs, and an index of personal names. The *Congressional Staff Directory* is published every April and September. A C.S.D. *Advance Locator* is issued in February. The *Congressional Staff Directory* is also available on disk from the publisher and on CD-ROM, which is called *Congress Stack.* This CD-ROM product includes district maps, staff listings, and a biography of each member.

Politics in America: Members of Congress in Washington and at Home. Washington, D.C.: Congressional Quarterly, 1980–. This biennial directory provides a description of each member's performance, including legislative influence, personal style, election data, campaign finances, voting records, and interest group ratings. Each member's birth date, education, military career, election returns, family members, religion, political career, and address are provided. The directory contains profiles and maps of each congressional district. Also included is the membership of Senate and House committees and subcommittees.

Barone, Michael, and Grant Ujifusa. *The Almanac of American Politics.* Washington, D.C.: National Journal, 1972–. This biennial guide is arranged alphabetically by state. An introductory description of the state's political background precedes a section covering that state's members of Congress, which provides a sketch of each one's background, ideology, and record. The section contains a short outline of their career, the committees they serve on, their record on key votes, and their electoral history. Also included are ratings of members by interest groups. Finally, there is a profile of each district within a state that provides the district's political background, including census data, federal outlays, tax burdens, and voter characteristics.

In addition to the above directories, the following works provide the same kinds of information:

Who's Who in Congress. Washington, D.C.: Congressional Quarterly, 1991–.

Buhler, Michaela, and Dorothy Lee Jackson, eds. *Congressional Yellow Book: A Directory of Members of Congress, Including Their Committees,* and Key Staff Aides. Washington, D.C.: Washington Monitor, 1977–.

Francis, Charles C., and Jeffrey B. Trammell. *The Almanac of the Unelected: Staff of the U.S. Congress. . . .* Washington, D.C.: Almanac of the Unelected, Inc., 1988–.

Voting Guides. While there are many sources in which one can find roll-call votes, the following two guides are easy to use and very comprehensive.

Congressional Roll Call. Washington, D.C.: Congressional Quarterly, 1970–. This annual series began with the first session of the 91st Congress. Each volume opens with an analysis and legislative description of key votes on major issues, followed by special voting studies such as freshman voting, bipartisanship, voting participation, and so forth. The remainder of the volume is a member-by-member analysis, in chronological order, of all roll-call votes in the House and Senate. There is also a roll-call subject index. In the compilation of roll-call votes, there is a brief synopsis of each bill, the total vote, and vote by party affiliation.

Busnich, Victor W. K. *Congressional Voting Guide.* 4th ed. New York: H. W. Wilson, 1992. This ten-year compilation is arranged in two main sections, the House Voting Records and Senate Voting Records. A brief biography of members of the 102d Congress, arranged state by state, includes a record of how each voted since 1982. Two additional sections, on House measures and Senate measures, describe each bill and present the date and results of the vote by party. The work also includes a name and subject index.

Committees. While most of the biographical directories mentioned earlier provide current committee information—both committee assignments by member and committee rosters—the following reference tools are invaluable for historical purposes.

Nelson, Garrison, ed. *Committees in the U.S. Congress 1947–1992.* 2 vols. Washington, D.C.: Congressional Quarterly, 1993. This two-volume set is the most comprehensive reference work on congressional committee membership for the period since 1947. It includes each member's length of membership and leadership positions. The first volume is organized by committee, showing all members for each Congress and their seniority. The second volume lists each member's committee assignments throughout his or her career. This volume also includes descriptions of committee jurisdictions and a history of each committee and of the committee system.

Stubbs, Walter, comp. *Congressional Committees, 1789–1982: A Checklist.* Westport, Conn.: Greenwood Press, 1985. This volume is useful for identifying the more than 1,500 committees that have existed since 1789. It identifies standing, select and special, select and joint special, and statutory joint committees.

Staff Directories, Inc., has published two CD-ROM products that include committee information. *Modern Congress Committee Assignments* (1947–1991) contains the membership of all committees for the time period indicated. *Historical Congress Committee Assignments* (1789–1991) contains the information provided on the first disk as well as all committee assignments back to 1789.

Journals. Scholarly articles about Congress can be found in many journals; several contain articles about some aspect of congressional politics on a regular basis. Those journals are *American Political Science Review, American Politics Quarterly, Journal of Politics,* and the *American Journal of Political Science.* In addition, there are four journals that deserve special mention, since they all focus on the Congress.

Congress and the Presidency: A Journal of Capitol Studies. Washington, D.C.: Center for Congressional and Presidential Studies, American University, 1983–. This journal covers both the Congress and the presidency, the interaction between the two, and national policy-making in general. Published twice a year, it contains a mix of articles on both political science and history. In addition to research articles, it includes research notes, review essays, and book reviews.

Congressional Quarterly Weekly Report. Washington, D.C.: Congressional Quarterly, 1946–. This journal recounts important congressional activities of the previous week, including developments in committees as well as on the floor. When covering major pieces of legislation, it often provides voting records and excerpts of testimony in hearings. Lobbying activities are given considerable coverage, with special reports on the relationship between congressional voting and interest groups. Most issues of the publication contain several articles on special issues or major legislation pending in Con-

gress. Congressional Quarterly indexes the *Weekly Report* both quarterly and annually. The *Weekly Report* is also indexed in *Public Affairs Information Service Bulletin* and *Social Sciences Index.*

Legislative Studies Quarterly. Iowa City: Comparative Legislative Research Center, University of Iowa, 1976–. Although this journal is devoted to the publication of research on legislatures and parliaments in all settings and all time periods, the bulk of the articles deal with Congress, especially its processes, history, and behavior. Each issue of the journal also includes a Legislative Research Reports section that provides abstracts of articles on legislative bodies from other scholarly journals. This section also provides abstracts of papers on legislative studies presented at the annual meetings of various associations, such as the American Political Science Association and the Midwest Political Science Association.

National Journal: The Weekly on Politics and Government. Washington, D.C.: National Journal, 1969–. The *National Journal* covers all areas of the federal government. It provides excellent analyses of activities of the Congress. Each issue usually contains two or more feature articles on some aspect of congressional politics. At the end of each issue, there is a detailed index for that issue as well as an index for recent weeks. The *National Journal* is self-indexed by subject semiannually. It is also indexed in *Public Affairs Information Service Bulletin.*

Indexes. Indexes and abstracting services are crucial for finding journal articles on Congress. Many indexes are now available on CD-ROM, which can save time and effort. The following indexes are the most useful for finding journal articles that pertain to Congress.

ABC POL SCI: A Bibliography of Contents: Political Science and Government. Santa Barbara, Calif.: ABC-Clio, 1969–.

America: History and Life. Santa Barbara, Calif.: ABC-Clio, 1964–.

Public Affairs Information Service Bulletin (PAIS). New York: PAIS, 1915–.

Humanities Index. New York: H. W. Wilson, 1974–.

Index to Legal Periodicals. New York: H. W. Wilson, 1908–.

International Political Science Abstracts. Paris:

International Political Science Association, 1951–.

Legal Resources Index. Menlo Park, Calif.: Informational Access Corporation, 1980–.

Social Sciences Citation Index. (SSCI) Philadelphia: Institute for Science Information, 1973–.

Social Sciences Index. New York: H. W. Wilson, 1975–.

Sociological Abstracts. San Diego, Calif.: Sociological Abstracts, 1952–.

United States Political Science Documents. Pittsburgh, Pa.: University Center for International Studies, University of Pittsburgh, 1976–.

Writings on American History: A Subject Bibliography of Articles. Millwood, N.Y.: Kraus, 1903–.

An important new compilation of journal literature on Congress has been published by Carlson Publishing. The twenty-three-volume set is entitled *The Congress of the United States, 1789–1989.* The volumes are published in a series of ten titles. The entire set includes 356 articles that the editors felt should be available to every student and scholar. Each of the ten titles includes a detailed index to the events, individuals, concepts, and topics discussed. The indexes make the set a very comprehensive reference work on Congress.

Compact Disk Products. Many reference sources are now being published in the compact disk (CD-ROM) format. Printed indexes previously cited that are now in compact disk format include: *ABC POL SCI* (the CD-ROM version is called *ABC POL SCI on Disc*); *Humanities Index; Index to Legal Periodicals; Legal Resources Index* (the CD-ROM version is called *LegalTrac*); *Public Affairs Information Service Bulletin* (the CD-ROM version is called *PAIS on CD-ROM*); *Social Sciences Citation Index; Social Sciences Index;* and *Sociological Abstracts* (the CD-ROM version is called *Sociofile*). The following are two additional CD-ROM products that are of special interest to students of Congress.

Facts on File News Digest on CD-ROM. The full texts of articles in *Facts on File News Digest* since 1980 are included in this data base. The primary press sources for the articles are over fifty U.S. and foreign newspapers, including the *Congressional Record, State Department Bulletin,* official government press releases, and the publications of Commerce Clearinghouse and Congressional Quarterly.

InfoTrac: General Periodicals Index/Academic Library Edition. Citations to articles from general interest periodicals are contained in this data base. Coverage includes the current year and the three previous years. It indexes the *Congressional Quarterly Weekly Report* as well.

In addition, there are three CD-ROM products—*Government Publications Index on Infotrac, Government Documents Catalog Subscription Service,* and *GPO on Silver Platter*—that can be used for identifying U.S. government publications, including those useful for the study of Congress.

Data Bases. On-line data bases are extremely useful because they retrieve information quickly. The following on-line services are especially useful for scholars of Congress.

CQ'S WASHINGTON ALERT. Washington, D.C.: Congressional Quarterly. This congressional tracking service provides the full text of bills and resolutions and all committee reports, summaries of bills and resolutions, committee and floor schedules, committee and subcommittee action, votes, rosters, and roll-call votes. Articles from the *Congressional Quarterly Weekly Report* and information from other CQ publications are included in the data base.

LEGI-SLATE. Washington, D.C.: LEGI-SLATE. This data base tracks and updates congressional and regulatory activity and provides the full text of bills, resolutions, and the *Congressional Record.* Also included are updates of committee schedules, congressional votes, and the full daily text of the *Federal Register.* There is also a news service with articles from the *National Journal, Congressional Quarterly Weekly Report,* and the *Washington Post.*

LEXIS/NEXIS. Dayton, Ohio: Mead Data Central. This system can be used for finding information about Congress, including the progress of legislation, floor votes, committee membership, district profiles, member profiles, ratings of members, data from the Federal Election Commission, and analyses from news transcripts of CNN, ABC, NPR, and other media outlets. There are two major services within the system that are especially useful, Legislation and Campaign News. Both provide information from a variety of sources, including the *National Journal* and the *Almanac of American Politics.* One can also access the *Index to Legal Periodicals* on this system.

WESTLAW. St. Paul, Minn.: West Publishing Co. This data base is most useful for finding citations related to the interpretation of public laws. The data base includes not only case law, statutes, and administrative materials but also a periodicals data base and access to other commercial data bases, including the *Index to Legal Periodicals*. West publishes a *Westlaw Database List*, which describes the various data bases that comprise WESTLAW, and a student guide entitled *Discovering WESTLAW*.

Newspapers and Indexes. The two best general circulation newspapers for following Congress are the *New York Times* and the *Washington Post*, although it should be noted that several other major newspapers occasionally have exceptional articles or series, e.g., the *Los Angeles Times, Baltimore Sun, Boston Globe, Chicago Tribune,* and *Wall Street Journal*. UMI (University MicroFilms) has put full-text versions of the *New York Times* and the *Washington Post* on CD-ROM starting with 1990. They call these versions *NYT on Disc* and *Washington Post on Disc*. The *National Newspaper Index* provides indexes for the *New York Times*, the *Washington Post*, and other major newspapers. This microfilm index is cumulative and updated regularly. The *National Newspaper Index* is also available on CD-ROM on *InfoTrac*. Another newspaper that deserves special mention is *Roll Call: The Newspaper of Capitol Hill*. Published twice weekly except for August and two weeks in December, *Roll Call* has become indispensable to observers of Congress not only for its coverage of institutional issues, policy briefings, and reports on candidates and campaigns, but also for its regular guest columns and editorials.

An important on-line data-base service is the *NewsBank Electronic Index*. *NewsBank* indexes selected articles from more than 450 U.S. newspapers, beginning with January 1982. The full text of articles is available on microfiche. The CD-ROM version of this index is called the *Newsbank Electronic Library*. Another on-line data base is DATATIMES, which indexes U.S. and international newspapers, news services, and business journals. Especially useful is its indexing of the *Washington Post* and the *Congressional Quarterly Weekly Report*.

Bibliographies. The following bibliographies cover all kinds of materials, including books, periodical literature, dissertations, and selected government documents.

Goehlert, Robert U., and John R. Sayre. *The United States Congress: A Bibliography.* New York: Free Press, 1982. This is the most complete bibliography on Congress. It includes 5,620 citations to books, dissertations, journal articles, research reports, and selected documents. The citations are classified according to fourteen major topics: History and Development of Congress; Congressional Process; Reform of Congress; Powers of Congress; Congressional Investigations; Foreign Affairs; Committees; Legislative Analysis; Legislative Case Studies; Leadership in Congress; Pressures on Congress; Congress and the Electorate; Members of Congress; and the Support and Housing of Congress. An updated version of this bibliography, by Robert U. Goehlert and Fenton S. Martin, containing citations since 1980, is to be published by Congressional Quarterly in 1995. This volume will be similar in design to the earlier volume, except that all the entries will be annotated.

Kennon, Donald R., ed. *The Speakers of the U.S. House of Representatives: A Bibliography, 1789–1984.* Baltimore, Md.: Johns Hopkins University Press, 1986. This bibliography is arranged in chronological order by Speaker. For each Speaker, there is a brief biographical profile followed by a listing of manuscript collections. Finally, there is a bibliography of books, dissertations, and articles about and by each Speaker. The work includes a subject and author index.

CRS Studies. Publications of the Congressional Research Service are available on microfilm in the series *Major Studies of the Legislative Reference Service/Congressional Research Service: 1916–1974* and in yearly supplements called *Major Studies and Issue Briefs of the Congressional Research Service*. The original collection and each supplement comes with a printed guide providing a title-author guide and subject index. These sets cover such areas as legal and constitutional issues, the Congress, government and political issues, and foreign and defense issues. University Publications of America, which publishes the series, has also published a two-volume cumulative index for the years from 1916 to 1989. The first volume of this index contains a bibliography and supplementary indexes and the second volume contains an index organized by subjects and names.

The Congressional Research Service has published a number of bibliographies on Congress, which are updated irregularly. All of the bibliographies cover the same areas, including history, procedure, reorganization and reform, party leadership, committee system, staff and support agencies, roll-call analysis, and policy studies. These bibliographies are available on microfilm in the *Major Studies and Issue Briefs of the Congressional Research Service*.

Since 1980, CRS has also published a journal, *CRS Review*. Aimed at individuals interested in congressional affairs, it focuses on public-policy issues. Another useful tool is the CRS journal *Major Legislation of the Congress*. It is designed to provide summaries of congressional issues and major legislation. Each issue is cumulative, and the final issue, published at the end of each Congress, is meant to be used as a permanent reference tool.

Statistical Sources. In addition to data about voting and election returns, students and researchers can obtain statistical information about a variety of other congressional activities.

Vital Statistics on Congress. Washington, D.C.: Congressional Quarterly, 1980–. This handbook, issued biennially, contains statistical data on Congress as an institution, including membership, elections, campaign financing, committees, staff, work load, operating expenses, budgeting, and voting alignments. The data are historical, spanning more than two decades.

Ratings. Over one hundred organizations rate members of Congress on key votes. Most publish their ratings in their own newsletters or magazines. The addresses and telephone numbers of the groups that rate members and the title and frequency of publication of the serials in which the rating can be found are listed in a Congressional Research Service report entitled *Organizations That Rate Members of Congress on Their Voting Records*. The most recent edition of this report was published in 1991. It is available on microfilm in *Major Studies and Issue Briefs of the Congressional Research Service*.

Two weekly publications, *Congressional Quarterly Weekly Report* and *National Journal*, publish ratings each year. *CQ Weekly Report* publishes the ratings and the key votes on which four rating groups evaluate members of Congress. *CQ Weekly Report* began publishing their ratings in 1961. Ratings by the same four groups can also be found in Congressional Quarterly's directory, *Politics in America*. Only the ratings are given in this volume, not the key votes on which they are based. The *National Journal* conducts its own rating, published in the *National Journal* each year since 1982. It analyzes votes in the economic, social, and foreign policy areas. The *Almanac of American Politics* provides the ratings, but not the key votes, for ten groups. The addresses and telephone numbers of the groups whose ratings are cited are provided in the front of the *Almanac of American Politics*.

Sharp, J. Michael. *Directory of Congressional Voting Scores and Interest Group Ratings*. 2 vols. New York: Facts on File, 1988. This volume provides a comprehensive voting study and group rating data compilation for every member of Congress since the beginning of the 80th Congress in 1947. Four categories of ratings scores, all generated by Congressional Quarterly, are included: conservative coalition; party unity; presidential support; and voting participation. The volume also presents ratings by eleven groups that represent various areas of concern. The real value of this volume is that it provides ratings back to 1947, when the first ratings were done.

Broadcast Media. The Congressional Satellite Public Affairs Network (C-SPAN), available on cable TV, is one of the most important developments for students of Congress. Its live broadcasts of congressional proceedings, which began in 1979, provide gavel-to-gavel coverage of the House and Senate, plus other public affairs programming such as National Press Club speeches, policy addresses, debates, and public-policy forums and call-in programs. C-SPAN broadcasts on two twenty-four-hour channels, including C-SPAN I, which carries the House of Representatives, and C-SPAN II, which carries the Senate. This coverage of Congress allows one to study it at first hand as well as to gather other background information. For anyone researching Congress or a specific piece of legislation, C-SPAN helps to make the process come alive. C-SPAN also publishes a *U.S. Congress Handbook*, a handy reference tool that contains a special section with information about C-SPAN and many of the organizations whose events the network covers. Two guides for users of C-SPAN are:

Greenberg, Ellen. *The House and Senate Explained: A TV Viewer's Fingertip Guide*. Dobbs Ferry, N.Y.: Streamside, 1986.
Green, Alan. *Gavel to Gavel: A Guide to the Televised Proceedings of Congress*. Washington, D.C.: Benton Foundation, 1986.

The Public Affairs Video Archives, located at Purdue University, records, catalogs, indexes, and distributes all programming on both channels of C-SPAN. The archives has recorded and cataloged all C-SPAN programming since October 1987.

Archives. Archives contain original documents such as letters, memos, reports, and other forms of primary research material. The difficulty in utilizing archival material lies in locating archives and finding out what they contain. Fortunately, there are several guides that can help:

Miller, Cynthia P. *Guide to the Research Collections of Former Members of the U.S. House of Representatives, 1789–1989.* Washington, D.C.: U.S. Government Printing Office, 1988.

Jacob, Kathryn A., ed. *Guide to Research Collections of Former United States Senators, 1789–1982.* Detroit: Gale, 1986.

McDonough, John J., comp. *Members of Congress: A Checklist of Their Papers in the Manuscript Division, Library of Congress.* Washington, D.C.: Library of Congress, 1980.

Campaigns. The Federal Election Commission publishes the *FEC Reports on Financial Activity* and the *FEC Index of Independent Expenditures. Congressional Quarterly Weekly Report* and the *National Journal* also publish articles based on federal campaign data. The most recent research guide to campaign spending was published by Congressional Quarterly and is to be published every two years:

Makinson, Larry. *Open Secrets: The Encyclopedia of Congressional Money and Politics.* 2d ed. Washington, D.C.: Congressional Quarterly, 1992.

The series *Vital Statistics on Congress* (see above) has an excellent section on campaign finance, including information on expenditures and political action committees.

Informal Congressional Groups. In addition to formal groups, there are numerous informal congressional groups. Informal groups are those for which membership is optional or a membership fee is required. These groups normally form around common issues, interests, or geographic concerns. Some of them are bipartisan. They have increased in number since the late 1970s and continue to grow, particularly in the House. More than 170 currently exist. The best access to materials published by congressional groups is the new Congressional Information Service, Inc. (CIS) guide and microfiche collection, *Congressional Member Organizations and Caucuses: Publications and Policy Materials.* The first annual guide and companion microfiche collection of this series was published in 1992 and covers publications issued during 1991. The index provides access by subject, person, institution, bill and act names, and bill numbers.

District Data. To cover the latest district changes, Congressional Quarterly has published a two-volume set, *CQ's Guide to 1990 Congressional Redistricting* (Washington, D.C.: Congressional Quarterly, 1992). This is the most up-to-date guide on new districts, providing demographic, economic, and business data and maps for them. Congressional Quarterly's *Congressional Districts in the 1990s* was published in 1993. There is also a CD-ROM product, the *1990 Census of Population and Housing-Public Law 94-171 Redistricting Data,* that provides the census data gathered for redistricting purposes. Users can search for data on this CD-ROM by state, county, census tract, voting district, block group, and block.

The following three volumes provide population data for both the districts and counties. Along with districts and county maps is included information about the creation of the counties. Also given are the names and party affiliations of representatives for each district by Congress.

Parson, Stanley B., William W. Beach, and Dan Herman. *United States Congressional Districts, 1788–1841.* Westport, Conn.: Greenwood Press, 1978.

Parsons, Stanley B., William W. Beach, and Michael J. Dubin. *United States Congressional Districts, 1843–1883.* New York: Greenwood Press, 1986.

Parsons, Stanley B. *United States Congressional Districts, 1883–1913.* New York: Greenwood Press, 1990.

Finally, if the kind of data or information one is seeking about a district is of a general nature, two of the almanacs cited earlier, *Almanac of American Politics* and *Politics in America: Members of Congress in Washington and at Home,* can be used as ready reference guides.

Atlases. The following three atlases graphically document the history of apportionment, redistricting, and legislative and social trends. They provide a unique way to analyze congressional voting and the growth of party politics.

Martis, Kenneth C. *The Historical Atlas of the Congresses of the Confederate States of America, 1861–1865.* New York: Simon & Schuster, 1994.

Martis, Kenneth C. *Historical Atlas of Political Parties in the United States Congress, 1789–1988.* New York: Macmillan, 1989.

Martis, Kenneth C. *The Historical Atlas of the United States: Congressional Districts, 1789–1983.* New York: Free Press, 1982.

Martis, Kenneth C., and Gregory A. Elmes. *Historical Atlas of State Power in Congress, 1790–*

1990. Washington, D.C.: Congressional Quarterly, 1993.

Election Returns. The following guides are the best sources for election returns.

Congressional Quarterly. *Guide to U.S. Elections.* 2d ed. Washington, D.C.: Congressional Quarterly, 1985. This work is the most definitive source of statistical data on elections. Included are the complete voting records of elections for the presidency, Congress, and governorships. This volume is an excellent reference guide to all aspects of elections, including extensive background material on the history of parties, preference primaries, demographic data, and redistricting. Accompanying each major section of the work is a topical bibliography. The format makes this an especially useful reference work. There are three ways by which to locate information. First, a detailed table of contents provides an overall view of the scope and coverage of the work. Second, candidate indexes for presidential, gubernatorial, Senate, and House candidates are provided. Third, a general index, which covers all subjects discussed in the work, is included. The volume is supplemented by *The People Speak: American Elections in Focus* (Washington, D.C.: Congressional Quarterly, 1990), which includes data for the 1988 presidential, congressional, and gubernatorial elections.

Scammon, Richard M., and Alice V. McGillivray, comps. *America Votes: A Handbook of Contemporary American Election Statistics.* Washington, D.C.: Congressional Quarterly, 1955–. This biennial work includes presidential, congressional, and gubernatorial returns. The total vote (Republican and Democratic), pluralities, and percentages per county and congressional district are reported. Sections on each of the states include the following: a political profile of the state; a map of the state depicting counties and congressional districts; a geographical breakdown by county and districts for presidential, senatorial, and gubernatorial returns; and tables of the congressional returns. The volume includes data since 1928.

The *National Journal* and *CQ Weekly Report* also publish the results of the elections in a special issue a week or two after an election. For a week-by-week analysis of a campaign and election, these two journals are indispensable, as are the *New York Times*

and the *Washington Post.* The series *Vital Statistics on Congress* (see above) also has election statistics and includes tables on shifts in House and Senate seats, incumbents reelected, and ticket splitting.

[*See also* C-SPAN; Congressional Directory; Congressional Quarterly; Congressional Record; Congressional Research Service; Records of Debate; Roll Call.]

ROBERT U. GOEHLERT and FENTON S. MARTIN

Congressional Publications

In the course of its legislative, fiscal, confirmative, inquisitive, and analytical work, Congress produces various kinds of literature. Furthermore, since the earliest days of the Republic, Congress has made a conscientious effort to publish (print and distribute publicly) documentary accounts of its activity.

Publications History. During the Constitutional Convention of 1787, James Wilson of Pennsylvania stressed the importance of official publication by the new government. Addressing a proposal that would allow each house of Congress discretion as to the parts of its journal that would be published, he told the delegates: "The people have the right to know what their Agents are doing or have done, and it should not be in the option of the Legislature to conceal their proceedings." The following year, James Madison and George Mason made a similar point during the Virginia convention on the new Constitution when discussing the importance of having the federal government publish accounts of all receipts and expenditures of public money.

Consistent with these views, the new Congress readily mandated the printing and distribution of all laws and treaties, the preservation of high state papers, and the maintenance of official files in the new departments. In its own domain, Congress provided for the publication of the House and Senate journals in 1813. Arrangements also were made for a contemporary summary of chamber floor proceedings to be produced in the *Registry of Debates* beginning in 1824. In 1833, this publication was superseded by the weekly *Congressional Globe,* which sought to chronicle every step in the legislative process of the two houses. A daily publication schedule for the *Globe* was established in 1865. In early 1873, the *Congressional Record* succeeded the *Globe* as the official congressional gazette.

Other publication developments were also afoot. In 1846, Congress initially provided for the routine printing of the reports, special documents, and bills of the two houses. For many years, these responsibilities were met by contract printers. Such arrangements, however, were subject to considerable political abuse. Consequently, in 1860, Congress established the Government Printing Office (GPO) to produce all of its literature. The GPO prints all congressional documents and operates a sales office to enable the public to purchase many governmental materials.

Contemporary Congressional Literature. Several kinds of congressional publications have been produced in the modern era. The daily chamber activities and events of the House of Representatives and the Senate continue to be recorded and published in the *Congressional Record*. Published each day that a chamber is in session, it contains a transcript and digest of floor proceedings and information concerning committee and subcommittee meetings.

When the committees or subcommittees of either house of Congress hold hearings on legislation to examine some matter, or, in the Senate, to consider a nomination, a transcript of these proceedings is made and usually published. Until supplies are exhausted, copies of these documents are available from the committees at no charge.

Studies and supplemental materials aiding the hearing process are sometimes published as so-called committee prints. These are also available from the issuing committee while the supply lasts.

House and Senate reports, sequentially numbered, usually result when a committee completes action on legislation, concludes an investigation, or, in the Senate, votes on a nomination. They are available from the issuing committee as well. Committee reports indicate the action taken by the panel—findings and recommendations resulting from an investigation, modifications made in a bill and the reasons for such changes, or the reason for approval or rejection of a nomination. Reports on legislation often guide legislators when floor action is taken on a measure, and they may be used by courts to clarify congressional intent concerning pertinent provisions of law. Similarly, reports on nominees guide final floor votes on the individual in question.

Other auxiliary materials of importance to each congressional chamber, such as presidential messages or official submissions by congressional officers, may be published as House or Senate documents, another sequentially numbered series. The rules of each chamber and the annual reports of the clerk of the House and the secretary of the Senate are also produced in this category.

Proposals introduced by representatives and senators are published as bills, simple resolutions, concurrent resolutions, and joint resolutions of each chamber. They are noted in the *Congressional Record* when introduced, and copies often are available from the principal sponsor.

These kinds of congressional literature may be found in most federal depository libraries and law-school libraries, as well as many major public libraries. Subscriptions to the *Congressional Record* and copies of selected congressional hearings, committee prints, reports, and documents may be purchased from the GPO. The *Monthly Catalogue of United States Government Publications* is issued by GPO to assist in this regard. There are also commercial indexes and microform versions of these kinds of congressional literature. Public and law-school librarians may be consulted regarding the availability of these materials.

Support-Agency Materials. During the twentieth century, Congress has been assisted by special agencies of the legislative branch that also produce publications. The oldest of these is the Congressional Research Service (CRS), established in 1914 as the Legislative Reference Service and given a modified mandate and renamed in 1970. Using the collections of its parent organization, the Library of Congress, CRS responds to information requests from congressional legislators and their personal and committee staffs. Memoranda and specially prepared studies often result, not publications. Indeed, with the exception of a few products, such as its *Bill Digest*, an annotated version of the Constitution, and national high-school and college debate manuals, CRS materials are statutorily proscribed from direct dissemination to the public by the agency. Nonetheless, printed copies of *CRS Reports for Congress* and computer-generated CRS issue briefs on current legislative topics are increasingly obtained indirectly by scholars, attorneys, the press, and the general public through requests to congressional personnel. CRS products also appear in House and Senate literature and the *Congressional Record*.

The General Accounting Office (GAO), another support agency, was established in 1921 and is headed by the comptroller general. GAO staff produce reports on a vast array of matters, often through field research using various techniques including audits, investigations, surveys, operations evaluations, and policy analyses. Studies may be initiated by legislators or congressional committee staff, a statutory requirement, or the comptroller general. Resulting reports are usually issued as a general *Report to the Congress by the Comptroller General of the United States* or as a so-called letter report to a particular requester or group of requesters. Each report is given an identification number in addition to its topical title. Most GAO reports are publicly available. As of 1992, the first five copies of a report could be obtained without charge, while supplies last, directly from GAO. Copies also may be purchased from GPO for a small fee. GAO produces the *Monthly List of GAO Reports* to assist in identifying its studies. This list and GAO reports may be found in many major public and federal depository libraries.

Two other relevant congressional support agencies are the Office of Technology Assessment (OTA) and the Congressional Budget Office (CBO). OTA, established in 1972, prepares studies for Congress, through contract research, on the scientific and technical impact of government policies and proposed legislative initiatives. Its reports may be purchased from GPO. Often, summaries of these reports may be obtained, while supplies last, from OTA.

CBO, established in 1974, produces public reports on federal budgeting and the economy, including both routine and special studies. Some reports may be obtained, while supplies last, from CBO; public reports also may be purchased from the GPO. CBO and OTA reports are listed in the GPO *Monthly Catalogue of United States Government Publications*, and many of them may be found in major public and federal depository libraries.

[*See also* C-SPAN; Committees, *article on* Committee Reports; Congressional Record; Congressional Research Service; Debate, Reporters of; Government Printing Office; Records of Debate.]

BIBLIOGRAPHY

Relyea, Harold C. "Historical Development of Federal Information Policy." In *United States Government Information Policies: Views and Perspectives*. Edited by Charles R. McClure, Peter Hernon, and Harold C. Relyea. 1989.
Schmeckebier, Laurence F., and Roy B. Eastin. *Government Publications and Their Use.* 2d rev. ed. 1969.

HAROLD C. RELYEA

CONGRESSIONAL BUDGET AND IMPOUNDMENT CONTROL ACT OF 1974

(88 Stat. 297–339). The Congressional Budget and Impoundment Control Act of 1974 represented an ambitious attempt to increase congressional control of the purse strings and to counter growing presidential power in budgeting. It created a new system for managing budget totals and sharply reduced the president's ability to impound (refuse to spend) moneys appropriated by Congress. Although formally amended and informally modified on numerous occasions, twenty years later the law still formed the statutory basis for congressional budgeting.

Dissatisfaction with the old authorization-appropriations process, which had dominated the congressional budget process for nearly a century, was rampant by the early 1970s. The fragmented process divided the budget into thirteen separate parts that were never considered as a whole. The House and Senate were increasingly unable to pass spending bills by the start of the fiscal year. Federal spending increased rapidly, and Congress seemed incapable of exerting restraint. President Richard M. Nixon lambasted the Congress as irresponsible and began to impound appropriated moneys. Members of Congress were increasingly suspicious of budget information presented by Nixon's Office of Management and Budget (OMB). With bipartisan sentiment for budget reform, Congress created the Joint Committee on Budget Control in 1972.

Many diverse interests were represented on the joint committee. Conservative Republicans wanted to force a recorded vote on the deficit to facilitate balancing the budget. Liberal Democrats wanted a debate on national priorities in which they could question the proportion of spending going to defense compared to that going to social programs. Members of the appropriations committees wanted to protect their power over spending. Balancing these diverse interests resulted in a hybrid system that, rather than replacing the old system, superimposed a new process over the old. The final version of the Budget and Impoundment Control Act passed overwhelmingly, in the House by 401 to 6 and the Senate by 75 to 0; Nixon signed it into law in July 1974. However, sharp partisan cleavages appeared as soon as implementation began.

The act developed a new process to enable Congress to make decisions on the budget as a whole. It created the House Budget Committee and Senate Budget Committee, which were responsible for reporting budget resolutions to their respective houses and following a strict timetable for action. The first concurrent resolution on the budget, to be enacted by 15 May, set targets for budget authority and outlays, for spending by functional category, for revenues, for surplus or deficit, and for public debt. By 15 September, Congress was required to pass the second budget resolution, which set binding totals. Those figures had to be reconciled with the actions of the Appropriations committees in time for the start of the new fiscal year, which was moved from 1 July to 1 October. To provide analysis and information to members and committees, the act created the Congressional Budget Office. Banning impoundment, the act created a process whereby the president could request that Congress temporarily delay spending (deferral) or permanently eliminate spending (rescission). Deferrals automatically went into effect unless either house disapproved. Rescissions were automatically rejected unless both houses approved within forty-five days.

At first, the performance of the new congressional budget process disappointed many. Most scholars agree that the process did little to restrain spending since the budget resolutions Congress approved generally accommodated the totals reached by actions of the spending committees. Because the process became extremely partisan in the House, the process's survival was initially in doubt. The potency of reconciliation and the ability of the process to shape the budget from the top down did not become clear until 1981, when President Ronald Reagan used the process to enact his sweeping economic and budget plan.

[See also Deferral; Impoundment; Rescission.]

BIBLIOGRAPHY

Ippolito, Dennis. *Congressional Spending.* 1981.
LeLoup, Lance T. *The Fiscal Congress: Legislative Control of the Budget.* 1980.
Schick, Allen. *Congress and Money.* 1980.

LANCE T. LELOUP

CONGRESSIONAL BUDGET OFFICE. Created by the Congressional Budget Act of 1974 (Title I–IX, P.L. 93-344; 88 Stat. 297), the Congressional Budget Office (CBO) started operations on 24 February 1975 with the appointment of its first director, Alice M. Rivlin. Compared with the other congressional support agencies—the Congressional Research Service, the General Accounting Office, and the Office of Technology Assessment—CBO has a narrow mission. It provides economic and budgetary information for the congressional budget and legislative processes. CBO's work covers a wide range of activities, however, in keeping with the diversity and scope of the federal budget. Before CBO existed, only the president had a complete source of data on the budget and the economy. With CBO,

Congress has its own source of budgetary information, knowledge that can be used to make policy decisions or to challenge presidential information.

CBO has three primary responsibilities in assisting Congress with the budget process: monitoring the economy and estimating its impact on government actions; improving the flow and quality of budgetary information to members and committees; and analyzing the costs and effects of alternative budgetary choices. The Congressional Budget Act directs CBO to produce an annual report "with respect to fiscal policy taking into account projected economic factors," "national budget priorities," and "alternative allocations of budgetary resources." In carrying out these responsibilities, CBO has been instrumental in preserving a nonpartisan, professional reputation, which has enhanced the credibility of its budget estimates and analysis.

CBO meets these responsibilities by providing analysis and data to the Senate and House Budget committees, analytic assistance to the Appropriations, Ways and Means, and Finance committees; and similar services, to a limited degree, to other committees and members. Prior to CBO's creation, Congress had no unit comparable to the Office of Management and Budget (OMB) of the Executive Office of the President. Through its director, CBO is authorized to obtain data, estimates, statistical analyses, and other information from executive branch agencies, departments, and commissions. It also allows Congress to be more independent of the president and the executive branch in determining final budget figures.

CBO spends a great deal of its time (about 40 percent) on program and budgetary analysis for the two Budget committees and other money committees of Congress. The Budget Act requires CBO to prepare an annual report analyzing the president's budget recommendations, economic conditions, and budget policy. This report, considered essential to the congressional budget process, focuses on fiscal policy, five-year budget projections, and deficit reduction. CBO is also required to prepare five-year cost projections on every piece of legislation reported out of committee. It spends approximately 25 percent of its time providing these five-year projections. Additionally, CBO helps committees determine the cost of programs proposed in pending legislation (20 percent of its time). "Scorekeeping," which takes about 15 percent of CBO's time, consists of periodically informing Congress of the impact of legislation on the spending limits in its most recent budget resolution. This function gives

Organization of the Congressional Budget Office

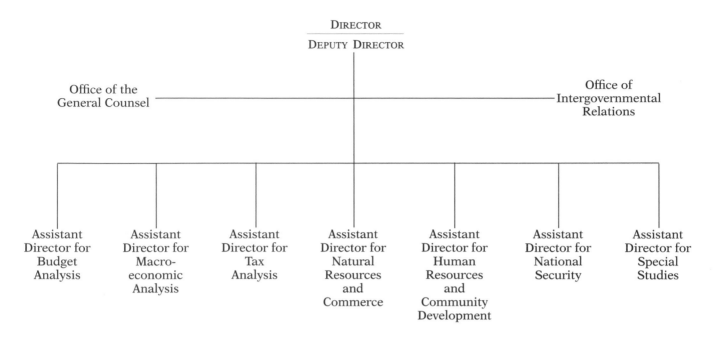

SOURCE: Congressional Budget Office. *Responsibilities and Organization of the Congressional Budget Office.* 1993.

Congress information that can lead to significant budgetary control.

Congress has assigned additional responsibilities to CBO since 1974. CBO was given a major role in the sequestration process established by the Balanced Budget and Emergency Deficit Control Act of 1985, more popularly called the Gramm-Rudman-Hollings Act. Under Gramm-Rudman-Hollings, CBO and OMB initially played equal roles in calculating whether the annual deficit targets specified by the act were met and, if not, in determining the amounts and percentages of budgetary resources that would be cut to meet the deficit target. In *Bowsher v. Synar* (1986), however, the Supreme Court ruled that in allowing the comptroller general to make the final determination on the amount of required spending reductions, the act had delegated the executive's responsibility to carry out the law to a legislative branch official. Consequently, in 1987 the Gramm-Rudman-Hollings Act was amended to give the responsibility for determining whether a sequester should occur to OMB, and CBO's role was reduced to providing advisory reports.

In 1981, CBO's original responsibility was expanded when it was directed to estimate the costs that state and local governments would incur in complying with proposed federal legislation. Con-

gress also may direct CBO to undertake specific studies on various subjects, such as the costs of including coverage of outpatient prescription drugs under Medicare, the outlook for farm-commodity program spending, and the cost of curbing acid rain. These policy-analysis reports are widely used and highly respected. The influence of many CBO reports has extended well beyond Capitol Hill, helping to shape public debate on many issues.

The most widely used CBO publication is its annual report to the budget committees. This report has evolved over time, and in 1993 consists of two volumes. One makes economic and budget projections for the next five years, and the other (first issued in 1982) suggests spending and revenue options for reducing the budget deficit. The economic and budget volume also includes an excellent discussion of fiscal policy and the implications of federal deficits for economic growth. The Budget Act requires that this two-volume annual report be submitted by 15 February; it is customarily updated by mid-August of each year.

Another highly respected and popular CBO report is the annual analysis of the president's budget, prepared at the request of the Senate Appropriations Committee. The executive's budget is recast using CBO's economic assumptions and estimating techniques, thus allowing Congress to see how CBO's baseline estimates would be affected by the president's revenue and spending projections. The CBO analysis has often shown that the president has underestimated the size of the deficit. For example, in nine of the ten years from 1982 to 1992, CBO estimated that adoption of the president's budgetary proposals would result in baseline deficits much higher—averaging $22 billion higher—than those estimated by the administration.

CBO also prepares cost estimates for every public bill reported by congressional committees to show how these legislative proposals will affect spending or revenues over the following five years. The number of cost estimates prepared by CBO each year varies depending on the amount of legislation being considered and reported by committees, but the number has tended to increase: for example, CBO produced 553 such reports in 1980 and 861 in 1989.

One of CBO's most important functions is "scorekeeping," or keeping track of all spending and revenue legislation that is considered each year. Scorekeeping helps Congress know whether or not it is acting within the limits set by the annual budget resolutions, bringing more discipline to the budget process. Scorekeeping can be quite controversial. There are no written rules, and the conventions are frequently challenged by committees that feel pinched by the limits set in the annual budget resolutions. The two budget committees are the ultimate scorekeepers for Congress; they often settle disputes by political compromises rather than using a formal written rule.

CBO is structured along lines of production and responsibility. In 1993 CBO's organizational structure remained almost identical to that established in 1975. The number of employees at CBO, which is limited by its annual appropriations, rose from 193 in fiscal year 1976 to 226 positions in 1993. CBO's director is appointed jointly by the Speaker of the House and the president pro tempore of the Senate after considering recommendations from the two budget committees. The director's term is four years, with no limit on the number of terms he or she may serve. As of late 1993, there had been three directors, each a prominent economist with knowledge of the federal budget process. Rivlin served two terms, from 1975 to 1983; Rudolph G. Penner served one term, from 1983 to 1987; and Robert D. Reischauer became the third director in March 1989. The process of jointly appointing the CBO director has proved

difficult. It took seven months after passage of the 1974 Budget Act for the two budget committees to agree on the Rivlin appointment, eight months for them to agree on the Penner appointment, and more than two years to agree on the Reischauer appointment.

[*See also* Balanced Budget and Emergency Deficit Control Act; Bowsher v. Synar; Congressional Budget and Impoundment Control Act of 1974.]

BIBLIOGRAPHY

Schick, Allen. *Congress and Money: Budgeting, Spending, and Taxing.* 1980.

Thurber, James A. "The Evolving Role and Effectiveness of the Congressional Research Agencies." In *The House at Work.* Edited by Joseph Cooper and Calvin MacKenzie. 1981. Pp. 292–315.

U.S. Congress. Congressional Budget Office. *A Profile of the Congressional Budget Office.* 1990.

U.S. Congress. Congressional Budget Office. *Responsibilities and Organization of the Congressional Budget Office.* 102d Cong., 2d sess., 1993.

JAMES A. THURBER

CONGRESSIONAL CEMETERY. Situated on a thirty-three-acre site overlooking the Anacostia River less than two miles east of the Capitol, Congressional Cemetery was founded in 1807 by a group of citizens who purchased the property and ceded its jurisdiction to Christ Episcopal Church Washington Parish in 1812. (The church itself is located a mile closer to the Capitol, at 620 G Street, SE.) The vestry of Christ Church designated portions of the site, originally named Washington Parish Burying Ground, for the use of the U.S. government for the interment of members of Congress, heads of departments, and their families. Because of the government's use of the cemetery, it became known as Congressional Cemetery. Over time, two vice presidents, eighty-four members of Congress, and several diplomats, including emissaries of Native American tribes, were interred at the cemetery. Some remains were later removed.

In 1835, the government built a receiving vault (the Public Vault) on the grounds for temporary interment of remains until a gravesite could be prepared or transportation arranged to take the body to another city. The state funeral processions of Presidents William Henry Harrison, Zachary Taylor, and John Quincy Adams terminated at the Public Vault.

In 1844, a White House funeral was held for Sec-

Members of the U.S. House of Representatives Interred at Congressional Cemetery

William L. Ball, Virginia (1817–1824)	James Jackson, Georgia (1789–1791)
Phillip P. Barbour, Virginia (1814–1825, 1827–1830)[1]	Charles C. Johnston, Virginia (1831–1832)
James Blair, South Carolina (1821–1822, 1829–1834)	James Jones, Georgia (1799–1801)
Theodorick Bland, Virginia (1789–1790)	David S. Kaufman, Texas (1846–1851)
Thomas Blount, North Carolina (1793–1799, 1805–1809, 1811–1812)	Charles W. Kendall, Nevada (1871–1875)
	Joab Lawler, Alabama (1835–1838)
Thomas T. Bouldin, Virginia (1829–1833, 1833–1834)	Joseph Lawrence, Pennsylvania (1825–1829, 1841–1842)
John E. Bouligny, Louisiana (1859–1861)	Richard Bland Lee, Virginia (1789–1795)
Edward Bradley, Michigan (1847)	James Lent, New York (1829–1833)
Elijah Brigham, Massachusetts (1811–1816)	Rowland B. Mahany, New York (1895–1899)
Jacob Broom, Pennsylvania (1855–1857)	Francis Malbone, Rhode Island (1793–1797)
Daniel A. A. Buck, Vermont (1823–1825, 1827–1829)	Felix G. McConnell, Alabama (1843–1846)
William A. Burwell, Virginia (1806–1821)	Jeremiah McLene, Ohio (1833–1837)
Timothy J. Carter, Maine (1837–1838)	George E. Mitchell, Maryland (1823–1827, 1829–1832)
Charles Case, Indiana (1857–1861)	Frank Morey, Louisiana (1869–1876)
Levi Casey, South Carolina (1803–1807)	William S. Morgan, Virginia (1835–1839)
Thomas H. Crawford, Pennsylvania (1829–1833)	George Mumford, North Carolina (1817–1818)
Ezra Darby, New Jersey (1805–1808)	Tilman B. Parks, Arkansas (1921–1937)
Warren R. Davis, South Carolina (1827–1835)	Isaac S. Pennybacker, Virginia (1827–1839)
John Dawson, Virginia (1797–1814)	William Pinkney, Maryland (1791, 1815–1816)
Littleton P. Dennis, Maryland (1833–1834)	Christopher Rankin, Mississippi (1819–1826)
Philip Doddridge, Virginia (1829–1832)	Thomas D. Singleton, South Carolina (1833)
William P. Duval, Kentucky (1813–1815)	Jesse Slocumb, North Carolina (1817–1820)
Lemuel D. Evans, Texas (1855–1857)	John Smilie, Pennsylvania (1793–1795, 1799–1812)
John Forsyth, Georgia (1813–1818, 1823–1827)	Alexander Smyth, Virginia (1817–1825, 1827–1830)
Philip B. Fouke, Illinois (1859–1863)	Richard Stanford, North Carolina (1797–1816)
Henry Frick, Pennsylvania (1843–1844)	Philip Stuart, Maryland (1811–1819)
Elbridge Gerry, Massachusetts (1789–1793)	Clyde H. Tavenner, Illinois (1913–1917)
James Gillespie, North Carolina (1793–1799, 1803–1805)	William Taylor, Virginia (1843–1846)
Francis J. Harper, Pennsylvania (1837)	Benjamin Thompson, Massachusetts (1845–1847, 1851–1852)
Albert G. Harrison, Missouri (1835–1839)	Uriah Tracy, Connecticut (1793–1796)
Nathaniel Hazard, Rhode Island (1819–1820)	Thomas Tudor Tucker, South Carolina (1789–1793)
William Helmick, Ohio (1859–1861)	Charles H. Upton, Virginia (1861–1862)
George Holcombe, New Jersey (1821–1828)	David Walker, Kentucky (1817–1820)
Jonathan Hunt, Vermont (1827–1832)	Henry G. Worthington, Nevada (1864–1865)
Narsworthy Hunter, Mississippi (1801–1802)	

[1]Speaker of the House (1823–1825)

retary of State Abel P. Upshur, Secretary of the Navy Thomas W. Gilmer, Capt. Beverly Kennon, Ambassador Virgil Maxcy, and Hon. David Gardiner, all killed in the explosion of a gun being demonstrated for a group of officials aboard the USS *Princeton*. The bodies of all but Maxcy were held in the Public Vault and most were interred on the grounds.

Benjamin Latrobe, the second Architect of the Capitol, designed cube-shaped sandstone markers for the government graves. Congress later decided that an identical marker would be erected at Congressional Cemetery as a memorial for each member of Congress who died in office. A total of 118 of these cenotaphs had been erected by 1875, when government interments essentially ceased because of the increasing practicality of transportation to distant cities and the opening of Arlington

CONGRESSIONAL CEMETERY. Sandstone cenotaphs with square bases and conical tops were designed by the second Architect of the Capitol, Benjamin Henry Latrobe, and placed as memorials to members of Congress who died in office from 1807 to 1877.   LIBRARY OF CONGRESS

National Cemetery, which provided a local alternative. The custom of erecting cenotaphs was revived in 1981, when such a marker was dedicated in memory of House majority leader Hale Boggs and Rep. Nicholas J. Begich, who were presumed killed when their plane disappeared on a flight in Alaska in 1972.

Congressional Cemetery is the first "national" cemetery in the sense that it contains the first sites designated for government use. Unlike modern national cemeteries, however, it is not solely military and governmental. Of the sixty thousand burials there, fewer than a thousand are in government gravesites. The rest of the graves belong to citizens of Washington, D.C. While other old cemeteries in Washington have been closed or relocated, Congressional has been in constant use since it was established. In the mid-twentieth century, Christ Church found itself unable to maintain the ceme-

tery, and the grounds fell into disrepair. In 1976 it was leased to a nonprofit group, the Association for the Preservation of Historic Congressional Cemetery, which relies on private contributions to maintain and restore the grounds.

Prominent persons buried at Congressional include Elbridge Gerry, vice president, governor of Massachusetts, and signer of the Declaration of Independence; William Thornton, original architect of the U.S. Capitol; Robert Mills, architect of the Washington Monument; Alexander Macomb, general in chief of the U.S. Army (1827–1841); Joseph Wood, portrait artist; Mathew Brady, Civil War photographer; Belva Lockwood, women's rights pioneer; John Philip Sousa, composer and leader of the Marine Band; and J. Edgar Hoover, director of the Federal Bureau of Investigation.

[See also National Cemeteries, Monuments, and Battlefields.]

U.S. Senators Interred at Congressional Cemetery[1]

Joseph Anderson, Tennessee (1797–1815)

George M. Bibb, Kentucky (1811–1814, 1829–1835)

Lemuel J. Bowden, Virginia (1863–1864)

James Burrill, Jr., Rhode Island (1817–1820)

John Forsyth, Georgia (1818–1819, 1829–1834)

John Gaillard, South Carolina (1804–1826)

J. Pinckney Henderson, Texas (1857–1858)

James Jackson, Georgia (1793–1795, 1801–1806)

Francis Malbone, Rhode Island (1809)

James Noble, Indiana (1816–1831)

William Pinkney, Maryland (1819–1822)

William N. Roach, North Dakota (1893–1899)

Samuel L. Southard, New Jersey (1821–1823, 1833–1842)

Buckner Thruston, Kentucky (1805–1809)

John M. Thurston, Nebraska (1895–1901)

Uriah Tracy, Connecticut (1796–1807)

William A. Trimble, Ohio (1819–1821)

William Upham, Vermont (1843–1853)

Richard M. Young, Illinois (1837–1843)

[1]Sen. Edward Dickinson Baker of Oregon (1849–1851; 1860–1861) was placed in the Public Vault on 21 October 1861 after he was fatally wounded at the Battle of Balls Bluff, Virginia.

BIBLIOGRAPHY

U.S. Senate. *History of Congressional Cemetery*. 59th Cong., 2d sess., 1906. S. Doc. 72.

JIM OLIVER

CONGRESSIONAL DIRECTORY. The *Congressional Directory* is the official almanac of Congress. Early predecessors of the modern *Directory*, compiled and printed in very small numbers by private firms, were little more than lists of members of the House of Representatives and the Senate. Produced as broadsides and pamphlets, they were temporary documents that were readily discarded at the end of each Congress or when a new issue was published.

Over time, new details were added to the directories. When Congresses first began arriving in Washington, D.C., members were listed by boarding-house groups. By 1814, the compilation included the postal address of each legislator, and the next version contained a list of the principal officers of the government and their residences. Issues for the 14th Congress (1815–1817) first specified the American ministers serving abroad and the foreign diplomats stationed in the United States, followed by an enumeration of the standing committees of each house. For the period from 1801 to 1840, directories grew from seven to sixty-nine pages, with an average of forty-five pages.

The *Directory* for the first session of the 30th Congress (1847), compiled and published by the postmaster of the House of Representatives, is generally considered to be the initial official edition because it was the first to be ordered and paid for by Congress. The Joint Committee on Printing began supervising the production of the *Directory* in 1864.

When biographical sketches of legislators were added in 1867, the *Directory* had essentially attained its modern format. Today, the *Directory* is published at the outset of each Congress. Its contents, totaling 1,314 pages in 1992, include lists of all individuals currently serving in Congress (with biographical information supplied by members); the principal officials and entities supporting and assisting Congress; the existing congressional committees, boards, and commissions; the committee assignments of legislators; the primary entities and leaders of the executive branch, the judicial branch, and the government of the District of Columbia; U.S. diplomatic offices; international organizations of which the United States is a member; and journalists accredited to the congressional press galleries. It also includes certain congressional statistical data, historical information on and floor plans of the Capitol, and current congressional district maps. The *Directory* may be purchased from the Government Printing Office and is available in many public libraries.

BIBLIOGRAPHY

Goldman, Perry M., and James S. Young, eds. *The United States Congressional Directories, 1789–1840*. 1973.

HAROLD C. RELYEA

CONGRESSIONAL MEDAL OF HONOR.

Among the most enduringly popular misnomers in American English, the term *Congressional Medal of Honor* reflects a long-standing confusion regarding two entirely separate awards: the special medals presented by Congress from time to time for distinguished achievements (generally known as congressional gold medals or, simply, Congressional Medals); and the highest of all military awards for valor, officially designated as the Medal of Honor.

The Medal of Honor, authorized in 1862, has been awarded to some thirty-four hundred persons, nearly half of them for "gallantry in action" during the

Civil War. More than seven hundred additional awards were made over the following half century, in connection with the Indian campaigns and various U.S. ventures in the Philippines, China, Mexico, and elsewhere. The large number of Medals of Honor given prior to World War I was due to the absence, until the war, of any other medals for valor.

The inception in 1918 of several new awards raised the Medal of Honor to its present exalted and unique stature: it is to be given only for actions involving actual conflict with an enemy, distinguished by "gallantry and intrepidity at the risk of life above and beyond the call of duty." Consequently, awards became far less common following World War I; only about 430 were made for all of World War II, roughly 130 for the Korean War, and about 240 for the Vietnam War. In addition, there have been a handful of "special legislation" awards by Congress, such as that made in 1927 to Charles Lindbergh, to whom Congress also awarded a Congressional Medal the following year.

Under existing law, the Medal of Honor is presented by, or by the direction of, the president, following a set of procedures for nomination, investigation, verification, endorsements, approvals, and so on, all governed by the regulations of the respective armed services. While Congress plays no part in the selection of recipients or other aspects of the process (except in the rare instances of the special legislation awards mentioned above), the medal is presented "in the name of Congress" (10 U.S.C. 3741)—probably the main reason for the widespread use of the term *Congressional* Medal of Honor. Although this remains the award's popular name and occasionally appears even in the text of federal laws and other documents, the correct, official designation has been "Medal of Honor" since 1905, when the matter was the subject of a ruling by the War Department.

[*See also* Awards and Prizes.]

BIBLIOGRAPHY

Editors of Boston Publishing Company. *Above and Beyond: A History of the Medal of Honor from the Civil War to Vietnam.* 1985.

U.S. Senate. Committee on Veterans' Affairs. *Medal of Honor Recipients 1863–1978.* 96th Cong., 1st sess., 1979. Committee Print 3.

E. RAYMOND LEWIS

CONGRESSIONAL OFFICE BUILD-INGS. The Capitol complex includes six major office buildings for the House and Senate: the Can-

non, Longworth, and Rayburn House office buildings and the Russell, Dirksen, and Hart Senate office buildings. Several were named long after their construction and occupancy; their current names are used below for easy reference.

The first congressional office buildings were constructed immediately after the start of the twentieth century to relieve overcrowding in the Capitol. Previously, members who wanted office space had to rent quarters or borrow space in committee rooms. In March 1901 Congress authorized the Architect of the Capitol, Edward Clark, to draw plans for fireproof office buildings adjacent to the Capitol grounds. The acquisition of sites and construction of the buildings were authorized in March 1903. The House Office Building Commission selected a site south of the Capitol bounded by Independence Avenue, First Street, New Jersey Avenue, and C Street SE for the Cannon Building (completed in 1908). The Senate Office Building Commission selected a site north of the Capitol bounded by Constitution Avenue, First Street, Delaware Avenue, and C Street NE for the Russell Building (completed in 1909).

In April 1904 the Architect of the Capitol engaged the prominent New York architectural firm of Carrère and Hastings. Thomas Hastings took charge of the House project, while John Carrère oversaw the construction of an almost identical office building for the Senate. Their Beaux Arts designs were restrained complements to the Capitol. Architecturally, their elevations are divided into a rusticated base and a colonnade with an entablature and balustrade. The colonnades with thirty-four Doric columns that face the Capitol are echoed by pilasters on the sides of the buildings. Both buildings are faced with marble and limestone; the Russell Building's base and terrace are gray granite. Modern for their time, they included such facilities as forced-air ventilation systems, steam heat, individual lavatories with hot and cold running water and ice water, telephones, and electricity; the Russell Building also included physical fitness facilities. Both are connected to the Capitol by underground passages. Originally, there were 397 offices and 14 committee rooms in the Cannon Building. After remodeling in 1932, there were 85 two- or three-room suites, 10 single rooms, and 23 committee rooms. The Russell Building had 98 suites and 8 committee rooms; the First Street Wing, completed in 1933, added 2 committee rooms and 28 suites.

Of special architectural interest in both buildings are the rotundas. In each, eighteen Corinthian columns support an entablature and a coffered dome, the glazed oculus of which floods the rotunda with natural light. Twin marble staircases lead from each rotunda to an imposing Caucus Room, which features Corinthian pilasters, a full entablature, and a richly detailed ceiling; the Russell Caucus Room retains its original 1910 benches and settles with carved eagles. This space has been used for many hearings on subjects of national significance, from the sinking of the *Titanic* (1912) to the Watergate break-in (1974) and the nomination of Justice Clarence Thomas (1991).

The Russell Building was occupied in 1909 by the Senate of the 61st Congress. The growth of staff and committees in the twenty years following its completion necessitated the addition of a fourth side, the First Street Wing, to the originally U-shaped building. Nathan C. Wyeth and Francis P. Sullivan were the consulting architects for the new wing, which was completed in 1933. In 1972 the building was named for former senator Richard B. Russell.

The Cannon Building was occupied by the House of the 60th Congress in December 1907. By 1913, however, the House had outgrown the available office space, and 51 rooms were added by raising the roof and constructing a fifth floor. In 1962 the building was named for former Speaker Joseph G. Cannon.

By 1924 the need for additional space led to the renovation of the Cannon Building and the construction of the Longworth House Office Building, which occupies a site opposite the Capitol on the south side of Independence Avenue. It is the smallest office building, with a floor area of just under 600,000 square feet. Preliminary designs for the building were prepared in 1925 by a local firm known as the Allied Architects of Washington. Principal architects were Frank Upman, Gilbert La-Coste Rodier, Nathan C. Wyeth, and Louis Justemente. They produced two schemes for a simple, dignified building in harmony with the rest of the Capitol complex. In January 1929 Congress authorized $8 million for acquiring and clearing the site and for constructing the new building. The foundations were completed in December 1930, and the building was accepted for occupancy in April 1933.

Because of its position on a sloping site the rusticated base of the Longworth Building varies in height from two to four stories. Above the granite base stand the three principal floors, which are faced with white marble. The Longworth Building is a fine example of the Neoclassical Revival style popular in the second quarter of the twentieth cen-

tury. Ionic columns supporting a well-proportioned entablature are used for the building's five porticoes, the principal one of which is topped by a pediment. Two additional stories are partially hidden by a marble balustrade.

When the Longworth Building was completed, it contained 251 congressional suites, 5 large committee rooms, 7 small committee rooms, and a large assembly room now used by the Ways and Means Committee. It was in this room, which seats 450 people, that the House of Representatives met in 1949 and 1950 while its chamber in the Capitol was being remodeled. The building was named in honor of former Speaker Nicholas Longworth.

The Dirksen Senate Office Building was the next office building constructed. In 1941 the Senate Office Building Commission directed the Architect of the Capitol, David Lynn, to prepare preliminary plans and cost estimates for an additional office building. The sum of $24.2 million was appropriated for the building. The site east of the Russell Building was acquired and cleared in 1948–1949, and New York architects Otto R. Eggers and Daniel Paul Higgins were engaged to prepare the preliminary plans.

Eggers and Higgins submitted a plan for a simple, seven-story building faced in marble. Each committee room was designed with a committee rostrum and space for reporters and witnesses. Features incorporated into the design of the building, which reflected the technological advances of the time, included an auditorium seating approximately five hundred people and equipped with radio, television, motion picture, recording, and broadcasting facilities; a cafeteria seating seven hundred people; a telephone exchange system; a parking garage for two hundred cars; and a fluorescent lighting system. The original subway system, which had been installed in 1909, was expanded to a double-track system in a new tunnel to the Russell and Dirksen buildings.

The final plans and specifications were approved by the Senate Office Building Commission in 1949, but construction was delayed until 1954. As a result of the delay and increasing costs, it became necessary to postpone construction of the entire interior center wing of the building. The latter was finally completed in 1982, as part of an entirely new building that was named the Hart Senate Office Building. The ground-breaking exercises for the Dirksen Building, named in 1972 for former minority leader Everett M. Dirksen, were held in January 1955, and the building was occupied in October 1958.

The principal (First Street) elevation of the Dirksen Building was designed with a pilastered central bay with an entablature and pediment. The bronze doors at the north and south entrances were designed by Eggers and modeled by the Rochette and Parzini Corporation. In the center are the American eagle and symbols representing equality and liberty. Five figures on the spandrels of the doors represent shipping, farming, manufacturing, mining, and lumbering.

In March 1955 Speaker Sam Rayburn decided that more office space was needed and introduced an amendment for a third House office building, although no site had been identified, no architectural study had been done, and no plans prepared. The Architect of the Capitol, J. George Stewart, with the approval of the House Office Building Commission, selected the firm of Harbeson, Hough, Livingston, and Larson of Philadelphia to design a simplified, classical building in architectural harmony with other Capitol Hill structures. An area west of the Longworth Building was chosen, with the main entrance on Independence Avenue and garage and pedestrian entrances on South Capitol Street, C Street, and First Street SW. The cornerstone was laid in May 1962. The building was completed in 1965, at a cost of $87.3 million.

The design of the building is a modified H plan with four stories above ground, two basements, and three levels of underground garage space. A white marble facade above a pink granite base covers a concrete-and-steel frame. One hundred sixty-nine members of Congress were accommodated in three-room suites, with such features as toilets, kitchens, and built-in file cabinets; nine committees also moved to this building. Amenities include a cafeteria, first aid room, Library of Congress book station, telephone and telegraph room, recording studio, post office, gymnasium, and facilities for press and television. A subway tunnel with two cars connects the building to the Capitol, and pedestrian tunnels connect it with the Longworth Building.

On either side of the main entrance to the building stand two ten-foot marble statues by C. Paul Jennewein, *Spirit of Justice* and *Majesty of Law*. On the east and west walls are eight marble rhytons, drinking horns formed of the mythical chimeras. Speaker Rayburn, for whom the building was named in 1962, is represented in the building in an oil portrait by Tom Lea, a marble relief by Paul Manship, and a six-foot bronze statue by Felix de Weldon.

By 1967 the Senate was experiencing strain on its existing office facilities and decided to construct an additional building. In 1972 the Senate Office Building Commission authorized George M. White, Architect of the Capitol, to commission John Carl Warnecke and Associates to prepare studies; a contract for construction was signed in 1973. In addition to satisfying space and design requirements, the architects were required to preserve the neighboring nineteenth-century Belmont House.

In August 1974 the Senate Office Building Commission and the Senate Committee on Public Works approved the design of the proposed Hart Senate Office Building, a nine-story structure that would complete work begun on the Dirksen Building in the 1950s. The building included suites for

HART SENATE OFFICE BUILDING. Interior, photographed February 1983.

fifty senators, with more than one million square feet of interior space, including three floors of garage and service facilities, eight floors of office, and a mechanical equipment floor at the top. A central atrium provides offices and corridors with natural light. To allow flexible use of office space, Warnecke introduced a two-story duplex suite, consisting of a senator's office with traditional sixteen-foot ceilings and two staff levels that can be easily rearranged.

Excavation began in December 1975, and in August 1976 the building was named in honor of former senator Philip A. Hart. The first occupant, Majority Leader Howard H. Baker, Jr., moved into the building in November 1982. The cost of the building was $137.5 million.

Installed in 1986 in the building's atrium was the sculpture *Mountains and Clouds* by Alexander Calder. The matte black aluminum clouds, the largest of which weighs one ton, are suspended from the roof and revolve above the thirty-nine-ton steel mountains.

Two other buildings have been acquired for office space by the House of Representatives: in 1972 the House began large-scale occupancy of the Congressional Hotel on C Street, which the government had owned since 1957; in 1975 a building located at Second and D streets, originally built for the Federal Bureau of Investigation, was acquired. These buildings have been named for late Speaker Thomas P. (Tip) O'Neill, Jr., and former minority leader Gerald R. Ford, respectively.

BIBLIOGRAPHY

U.S. Congress, Architect of the Capitol. *Report of the Architect of the Capitol.* 1909–1947, 1976–.
U.S. House of Representatives. *Report of the Commission to Direct and Supervise the Construction of the House Office Building.* 61st Cong., 3d sess., 1912. H. Rept. 2291.

PAMELA N. VIOLANTE

CONGRESSIONAL OPERATIONS COMMITTEE, JOINT.

The Joint Committee on Congressional Operations was created by the Legislative Reorganization Act of 1970 (P.L. 91-510). This act was a bipartisan effort nearly six years in the making. Its essential provisions grew out of recommendations of a special congressional study group, the Joint Committee on the Organization of the Congress (1965–1966). The panel recommended that Congress create a new joint committee that could serve "as a centrally constituted agency under which certain [congressional] functions can be consolidated, and which can be charged with new and important functions that significantly involve the Congress as an institution, as well as continuing scrutiny of its organization and operations, including implementation of the recommendations [in this final report]." The joint committee was to have ten members, three Democrats and two Republicans from each chamber.

The Joint Committee on Congressional Operations was given jurisdiction in three general areas. The first concerned the organization and operation of Congress. The authors of the act clearly intended that this joint committee be the successor and heir to the joint committee that had recommended its creation. Second, it was to keep track of court proceedings and other actions of interest to Congress. Third, it was given the responsibility to create and to supervise the operation of an Office of Placement and Office Management for Congress.

The joint committee's primary jurisdiction made it responsible for studying and making recommendations in such areas as the scheduling, staffing, and operation of congressional committees; the work load of Congress; communications, travel and other congressional allowances; strengthening the congressional power of the purse; finance and congressional campaigns; and lobbying laws.

Before the Joint Committee on Congressional Operations was established, members of the House and Senate had no obvious way to find out what their congressional allowances were in such important areas as office space, staff support, and salaries. The administration rules existed, but they never had been promulgated. The joint committee lifted the secrecy surrounding the rules by publishing its *Congressional Handbook,* which for the first time collected and identified all relevant rules.

The joint committee was a prime mover behind televising the proceedings on the floor of the House of Representatives. Another of its pioneering studies concerned the telecommunications and computer needs of Congress.

Budgetary reform was a high priority for the joint committee. It outlined a number of possible changes, including a biennial appropriations process and a shift of the fiscal year. The later recommendation eventually was adopted by a special committee that recommended sweeping changes in the congressional budget process, ultimately leading to enactment of the Congressional Budget and Impoundment Control Act of 1974.

Even it is most active period, the House of Representatives had greater interest in the joint committee than did the Senate. This was primarily due to the energetic leadership of Rep. Jack Brooks (D-Tex), the joint committee's first chairman.

In 1977 the joint committee was terminated. The House established a five-member Select Committee on Congressional Operations to carry on the functions that had been performed by the joint committee, and the Senate transferred those functions to the Committee on Rules and Administration. Brooks continued as chairman of the select committee until the House abolished it on 31 December 1978. Its legacy remains in the technological innovations it introduced, the way it modernized and streamlined congressional operations, and the televising of congressional floor proceedings.

[*See also* Legislative Reorganization Acts.]

BIBLIOGRAPHY

"Joint Committee Proposes Congressional Reform." *Congressional Quarterly Weekly Report*, 29 July 1966, pp. 1627–1629.

U.S. Senate. Committee on Government Operations. *Improving Congressional Control over the Budget: A Compendium of Materials.* 93d Cong., 1st sess., 1973.

NICHOLAS A. MASTERS

CONGRESSIONAL PUBLICATIONS. *See* Congress, *article on* Congressional Publications.

CONGRESSIONAL QUARTERLY. Congressional Quarterly Inc., known as CQ, is the preeminent private publisher of readily accessible information on the U.S. Congress. Through a variety of directories and reference works, most notably the *Congressional Quarterly Weekly Report*, the Washington, D.C.–based editorial research and publishing company serves clients in the fields of news, education, business, and government.

Founded by Henrietta and Nelson Poynter in 1945, CQ became a major postwar information source for and about congressional activities. Its success stemmed primarily from CQ editors' ability to condense accounts of legislation into readable form for the *Weekly Report*, placing them in intelligible political and governmental contexts. For much of the print and broadcast media, the *Weekly Report*, together with the companion *CQ Almanac*, published annually, is a preferred alternative to Congress's own official daily, the *Congressional Record*, with its cumbersome format and hard-to-read typography.

Perhaps the most valuable service rendered by Congressional Quarterly in its early days was its new way of presenting roll-call votes in the House and Senate. CQ's format for roll calls differed from the official formats of the *Congressional Record* and the House and Senate journals, which were extremely difficult for news organizations, academic observers, and other serious Congress-watchers to use in examining voting patterns. CQ's roll-call reports listed House members alphabetically by state, identifying each member by district and party affiliation. Senate roll calls were arranged alphabetically by state with majority-party members listed first. This simple innovation permitted roll-call analysis to flourish as a research technique and opened a window on congressional behavior and attitudes.

CQ's editors also used roll-call tallies for a number of computations of their own. Four of these measurements became standard in the field of congressional studies. The first was a simple measure of attendance at roll calls, which also led CQ to poll absent members of Congress on how they would have voted had they been present on the floor. The second was a party-voting index (first used in 1947) that measured the degree of cohesiveness within the congressional parties and the degree of differentiation between them. The presidential support scores (first used in 1953) reflected legislative voting for presidential initiatives in Congress. The conservative coalition index (first used in 1960) measured ideological voting in Congress by weighing the combined votes of Republicans and southern Democrats against those of nonsouthern Democrats. CQ's voting measures have been used in virtually every contemporary study of the U.S. Congress.

During the 1960s CQ became a major reference-book publisher through the regular compilation of its own reports in its Congress and the Nation series, published every four years to coincide with presidential terms. Other Congress-related publications later added to the CQ lineup include *Guide to Congress, CQ Researcher, Congressional Monitor, Congressional Insight, Congress A to Z, Campaign Practices Reports, Guide to U.S. Elections, Politics in America,* and a variety of college political-science textbooks published under the CQ Press imprint.

[*For broad discussion of publications of and about Congress, see* Congress, *articles on* Bibliographical Guide *and* Congressional Publications.]

BIBLIOGRAPHY

Congressional Quarterly Inc. *Congressional Quarterly's Guide to Congress.* 4th ed. Edited by Mary Cohn. 1991.

GARRISON NELSON

CONGRESSIONAL RECORD. The *Congressional Record* is the primary written source for a daily account of the floor proceedings of the House and Senate. The courts and federal agencies rely on it to interpret legislative intent, and scholars use it to compile a bill's legislative history. However, much more than legislative matters such as roll-call votes, texts of bills, amendments, conference reports, and floor debates appear in its pages. A regular reader of the *Congressional Record* might well qualify for a liberal arts degree, for he or she would be exposed to an astounding variety of material: articles reprinted from newspapers and magazines, speeches on a broad variety of topics, copies of correspondence between federal officials, tributes to athletic teams, eulogies to the departed, renditions of local and regional concerns and celebrations, and even occasional attempts at poetry and humor.

The official records of House and Senate proceedings, as mandated by Article I, section 5, clause 3 of the Constitution, are the House and Senate journals. The journals, akin to the minutes of a meeting, describe only briefly the procedural actions and votes that occurred on a given day and do not contain the text of the debates surrounding them or any extraneous material. Therefore, although not the official account, the *Congressional Record* remains the more complete source of legislative activity and debate.

The *Congressional Record* is not, however, a word-for-word account of all that is spoken on the floors of the two chambers. Rather, the *Record* is required to be only a "substantially verbatim" rendition of chamber action. The expectation of a more verbatim account grew simultaneously with technological innovations such as audio amplification and phonetic shorthand, which made more accurate reporting possible. Omissions and errors in the reporting of debates were commonplace in earlier years due to the poor acoustics within the chambers and a necessary reliance on longhand. As a result, members often took the opportunity to revise, expand upon, and edit words they spoke on the floor, a tradition that remains the practice today.

In addition to revising their remarks, many members also "extend" them by inserting supplementary material into the *Congressional Record*. This includes items such as newspaper or magazine articles, scholarly essays, constituents' letters, and research studies. The daily practice of revising and extending remarks means that the *Congressional Record* is not a perfectly verbatim record of the floor proceedings of Congress.

Each daily edition of the *Congressional Record* is divided into four separately numbered sections. The "H" pages signify the House floor proceedings for that day; the "S" pages, the Senate's. The "E" pages denote the "Extensions of Remarks" section, which is used almost exclusively by House members to insert material not spoken on the floor. The "D" pages designate the "Daily Digest," which appears at the back of each issue and serves as a combined index and table of contents. It summarizes legislative action that occurred in each chamber by giving capsule descriptions of bills and amendments considered. It also lists committee meetings held, often including the names of the witnesses who testified. Future floor and committee schedules are also published when announced.

The *Congressional Record* presents other significant legislative information in addition to the daily renditions of congressional proceedings. Periodically, the editors of the *Congressional Record* include a "Résumé of Congressional Activity" that provides useful legislative statistics, such as the numbers of measures introduced, reported, and passed by each chamber, as well as the number of hours and days each chamber has been in session. Lists of registered lobbyists and the policy issues they contact legislators about are also periodically published in the *Congressional Record*. In addition, the text of all conference reports and floor amendments are printed in the *Record* when submitted. Sometimes the text of newly introduced legislation also is provided, but this is not a consistent practice. More often only the fact of introduction, along with the names of the sponsor and any cosponsors, and the committee of referral are noted. The *Congressional Record* does not contain any text of committee proceedings on legislation. Committee information is limited to announcements of scheduled hearings and markups and daily summaries of those committee meetings that were actually held.

After each two-year Congress ends, the Government Printing Office issues a hardbound edition of the *Congressional Record* for that Congress. This becomes the permanent edition maintained by depository libraries across the nation, and most discard the softcover daily edition when the permanent edition is published. There are discrepancies between the two editions, however. In the permanent edition, pages are numbered consecutively within each volume, and the separate "H," "S," "E," and "D" page indicators are removed. In addition, members routinely receive permission from their colleagues to correct, revise, and extend their remarks for the permanent edition, even after the original version of those remarks has already been published in the daily edition.

Highly skilled reporters, known as the "Official Reporters of Debate," most using stenographic machines, but some still using shorthand, take down each word spoken on the House and Senate floor for shifts of approximately ten to fifteen minutes each. A new reporter takes over while the first transcribes the notations just taken. Computer technology is used to hasten the process and to begin the electronic printing of the *Congressional Record* while floor proceedings continue to unfold. The daily edition is kept open until midnight so that all the revisions and extensions from members can be received. Any floor proceedings held after midnight are published separately in the subsequent day's edition. The first printed copies of the *Congressional Record* are ready for distribution by about 6 A.M. the following morning.

The House and Senate differ somewhat in their editorial practices for their respective sections of the *Congressional Record*. For example, the House provides time blocs, while the Senate does not. The House editors insert square indicators approximately every ten to twenty minutes using the military time style (e.g., "1400 hours" for 2 P.M.). Members find this indicator useful for identifying the point at which they might wish to obtain videotape of that portion of the day's session. Researchers have used the indicators to estimate the time spent on specific legislative actions on the floor. The Senate, however, provided time blocs only in the late 1980s and then dropped them. The start-and-stop nature of Senate sessions (due largely to quorum calls and other delays) contributed to this decision.

In another difference between the two chambers, text inserted but not spoken is designated in the House proceedings with a unique type face that visually separates such inserted material from the spoken word. On the Senate side, black dots, referred to as bullets, are used at the beginning and at the end of inserted material. However, the Senate practice is more casual than that of the House. Senators routinely obtain unanimous consent to have their remarks appear "as if spoken." Although this

material is never fully delivered on the floor, no bullets appear when such permission has been granted.

Congress controls the reporting and editing of the content of the *Congressional Record*; the Government Printing Office is responsible for printing and distribution. This division of responsibility goes back to 1873. The House and Senate first began to take direct responsibility for the recording of their debates in 1855 by hiring the reporters of debates as congressional employees. Then in 1872 Congress decided to publish the debates as well as supervise their reporting, first assigning the work to the Congressional Printer and in the following year, to the Government Printing Office.

From 1789 to 1848, the floor proceedings of Congress were recorded by private entrepreneurs, mostly journalists. In addition to leading newspapers, which sometimes carried accounts of congressional floor proceedings, several commercial publications dedicated to floor coverage appeared, although none lasted for any length of time. Among them were *Lloyd's Congressional Register, Carpenter's American Senator, Callender's Political Register,* and *The Congressional Reporter.*

The first issue of the *Congressional Record* appeared on 4 March 1873. Its predecessors were the *Annals of Congress* (1789–1824), the *Register of Debates* (1824–1837), and the *Congressional Globe* (1833–1873). However, many of these earlier volumes had been compiled well after the fact, relying on news accounts, private journals, and the recollections of members of Congress and their employees. Over the course of the history of Congress, the recording of congressional proceedings has progressed from mere notations of floor actions to reconstructed abstracts, to admittedly flawed transcripts, to substantially verbatim accounts.

The *Congressional Record* is still published by the Government Printing Office under the supervision of the Joint Committee on Printing. The "Laws and Rules for Publication of the Congressional Record" appear on an unnumbered page near the back of every daily edition. These guidelines combine the mandates of the Joint Committee on Printing with the applicable provisions of public law (82 Stat. 1255–1256.)

In recent years, the average length of the *Congressional Record* has been about 218 pages per issue; the average printing cost has been about $485 per page. Printing costs are influenced not only by the length of daily floor sessions, but also by fluctuating prices of newsprint, technical equipment, and personnel. Approximately twenty thousand issues are distributed to the offices of members of Congress, congressional committees, and private subscribers per year. The subscription cost in 1994 is $225 annually, although members of Congress receive three free subscriptions for their office use and twenty-five free subscriptions for designated constituents, most of whom are depository libraries.

[*See also* Congress, *article on* Congressional Punlications; Debate, Reporters of; Records of Debate.]

BIBLIOGRAPHY

Amer, Mildred. *The Congressional Record: Content, History, and Issues.* Congressional Research Service, Library of Congress. CRS Rept. 93-60. 1993.
Block, Bernard A. *The Congressional Record.* Serials Review, January–March 1980, pp. 23–28.
McPherson, Elizabeth Gregory. "Reporting the Debates of Congress." *Quarterly Journal of Speech* 28 (April 1942): 141–148. (Reprinted in the *Congressional Record,* 10 June 1942, pp. A2182–2185.)

ILONA B. NICKELS

CONGRESSIONAL RESEARCH SERVICE.

A department of the Library of Congress, the Congressional Research Service (CRS) provides research, analysis, and information services to Congress. CRS was established by the Legislative Reorganization Act of 1970 as the successor to the Legislative Reference Service (LRS). LRS was established by an amendment to the Legislative, Executive, and Judicial Appropriations Act of 1914 "to enable the Librarian of Congress to employ competent persons to prepare such indexes, digests and compilations of law as may be required for Congress and other official use." LRS was the brainchild of Herbert Putnam, who served as the librarian of Congress from 1899 to 1939 and effected major developments in the library's policies and operations.

Putnam's recommendations were influenced by the experience and example of Melvil Dewey, creator of the Dewey Decimal System, who established a Legislative Reference Department in the New York State Library in 1890, and by Charles McCarthy, who established the Legislative Reference Department in the Wisconsin State Library in 1903. McCarthy stressed that representative government requires well-informed legislators with independent access to full and accurate information. As Samuel Rothstein (1989) observes, McCarthy's leadership helped transform library legislative departments from passive repositories of information into active participants in the legislative process. This transformation was marked by professional anticipation of and response to legislative needs for impartial information and analysis.

The original legislative mandate of LRS was expanded in the Legislative Reorganization Act of 1946. The Legislative Reorganization Act of 1970 renamed the agency the Congressional Research Service and further expanded its size and mission to emphasize policy analysis and research, particularly for congressional committees. The mission statement of CRS, based on the 1970 act and related legislation, states:

> The Congressional Research Service works exclusively and directly for all Members and committees of the Congress in support of their legislative, oversight, and representational functions. The department of the Library of Congress provides research, analysis, and information services that are timely, objective, nonpartisan, and confidential. The Service's staff responds to and anticipates congressional needs and addresses policy issues in an interdisciplinary, integrative manner. The Service maintains close ties with the Congress and, consistent with its broad congressional mandate, provides a variety of services with the goal of contributing to an informed national legislature. (Ross, 1992, p. 1)

By law, the director of CRS, though head of a department within the Library of Congress, reports directly each year to Congress's Joint Committee on the Library. That joint committee and the Legislative Appropriations subcommittees of the House and Senate Appropriations committees are the governing bodies of the library and of CRS. These committees provide legislative direction and funding through authorizing legislation and appropriations. The library and CRS also receive limited funds through contracts and agreements with other government entities and grants from other organizations.

In fiscal year 1991, CRS had an authorized staffing level of 864 permanent positions and a budget of $52.7 million. Salaries and benefits accounted for approximately 90 percent of expenditures. In fiscal year 1991, $5 million was transferred to CRS from the Agency for International Development to pay for work by CRS and a bipartisan task force created by the House of Representatives and the Special Task Force on the Development of Parliamentary Institutions in Eastern Europe. A similar program was created by the Senate. With substan-

Organization of the Congressional Research Service

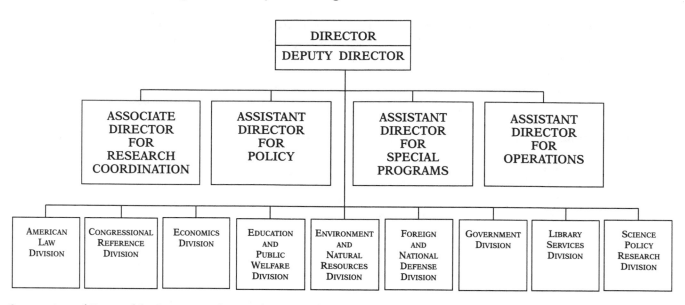

SOURCE: *Annual Report of the Congressional Research Service of the Library of Congress for Fiscal Year 1989 to the Joint Committee on the Library.*

tial CRS assistance, the task force supported the development of new legislatures and legislative information and research systems in Hungary, Poland, the Czech and Slovak Federal Republic, and Bulgaria.

CRS is organized into offices of the director and deputy director, seven research divisions, two reference divisions, and several specialized offices, including the Office of Senior Specialists and the Office of the Associate Director for Special Programs. The organizational form reflects the diversity of products and services provided by CRS.

Products and Services. CRS annually develops and delivers to members and committees of Congress an extensive range of both printed publications and services such as information in electronic form, technical advice, background briefings, and seminars. CRS employs a distinctive form of applied policy analysis and information tailored to the cycles, pressures, and time limitations of the legislative, oversight, and representational functions of Congress. It is the only congressional support agency that provides information, analysis, and technical assistance for all these functions. The crucial factor in the effectiveness of such support is the integration of information and analysis into the daily work of the Congress, which requires an ability to combine understanding of a subject with understanding of the distinctive phase of congression-

al operations in which the information and analysis are to be used.

Legislation. CRS supports the initiation, analysis, debate, and enactment of legislation by providing information, analysis, and consultation throughout the process. The process includes development of agendas and proposals, introduction of bills, analysis of bills and amendments, organization and conduct of hearings, preparation of reports, conduct of conference proceedings, conduct of floor debates, and related activities.

Oversight. CRS supports the congressional oversight of the programs and activities of the executive branch and independent agencies. It organizes and analyzes background data, assists in defining issues, and helps identify specialists and sources of data outside of Congress.

Representation and constituent service. CRS also assists in the representational functions through which members inform constituents about legislative developments and respond to constituents' requests for information and assistance. CRS provides extensive information to members for use in responding to constituent concerns.

In fiscal year 1991, CRS responded to 509,780 requests from Congress for analysis, information, and other forms of assistance. The responses included seven thousand original written analyses designed to meet the individual needs of members and committees; distribution of 334,700 copies of standard reports prepared for the Congress on a range of subjects; distribution of 295,400 copies of issue briefs; and distribution of 153,400 information packs containing factual background on subjects of current interest, often used by members in responding to constituent requests. CRS was also engaged in 1,438 major projects for committees and members, such as an extensive analysis of Japan's science and technology strategies and policies. Additionally, it provided extensive personal briefings, translations, bibliographies, and other reference services and conducted more than one hundred seminars for members and their staffs.

Assessment. In 1989, CRS initiated an extensive strategic management review to assess its success in carrying out the mission established for it by Congress. Interviews with members and congressional staff established that CRS is widely regarded as being very successful in accomplishing its mission of supporting the legislative, oversight, and representational functions of the Congress. Its success is attributed to the professionalism of its staff, its close working relationships with and under-

standing of the Congress, and its continuous adoption of new information technologies and new products and services.

The strategic management review also defined several major challenges. One involves the continuing increase in demand from Congress for CRS products and services, as shown in figure 1. In fiscal year 1985, with a staff of 899 and a budget of $40,433,000, CRS responded to 457,837 requests. In fiscal year 1991, with a staff of 864 and a budget of $52,743,000, CRS responded to 509,780 requests. Members of Congress and their staffs attributed increases in demand to greater use of electronic data bases and other information formats, increases in the technical nature and complexity of public policy problems, and increases in requests for constituent services.

A second challenge is how to plan and direct the CRS research process to meet the legislative priorities of committees. The heavy volume of requests from individual members challenges CRS's ability to maintain and strengthen its contacts with committees so that committee priorities and CRS work plans are coordinated.

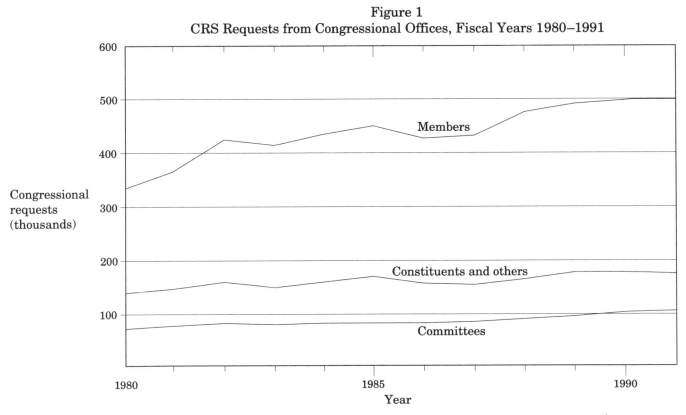

Figure 1
CRS Requests from Congressional Offices, Fiscal Years 1980–1991

SOURCE: Congressional Research Service.

MADISON BUILDING. The Congressional Research Service is located in this building, which is part of the Library of Congress.

The strategic review also defined a number of other issues, including continuing innovations in information technology, particularly with regard to simplifying access to CRS information by congressional offices; measurement of program performance; assessment of the usefulness of products and services; and conducting performance reviews, staff training, staff orientation, and other human-resource-related activities. While CRS's divisional structure is essential to professional specialization by subject area and task, the structure does create continuing challenges in managing major research and analysis projects as well as initiatives and issues involving CRS as a whole.

BIBLIOGRAPHY

Carroll, James D. *New Directions for the Congressional Research Service on Science and Technology Issues.* 1990.

Congressional Research Service. *CRS Strategic Management Review.* 1990.

Englefield, Dermot. *The Parliaments of the British Commonwealth: The Growing Role of Legislative Libraries.* 1989.

Robinson, William H. *The Congressional Research Service: Policy Consultant, Think Tank, and Information Factory.* 1989.

Robinson, William H., ed. "Symposium Policy Analysis for Congress." *Journal of Policy Analysis and Management* 8 (1989).

Ross, Joseph E. *Annual Report of the Congressional Research Service of the Library of Congress for Fiscal Year 1991.* 1992.

Rothstein, Samuel. *The Growth of Reference Services and Special Librarianship and Its Consequences for Legislatures.* 1989.

JAMES D. CARROLL

CONGRESS OF THE CONFEDERACY. From 1861 to 1865 there were three Congresses that convened as the legislative bodies for the Confederacy. The first, known as the Provisional Congress, was a unicameral body consisting of delegates chosen by state legislatures to organize a government for the Confederate States of America. It held five sessions between 4 February 1861 and 17 February 1862 and drafted both the provisional and permanent Confederate constitutions. Elections for the first regular Congress were held in November 1861; the first Congress met for two years beginning in February 1862. The second Congress held two sessions before adjourning on 18 March 1865, just weeks before the collapse of the Confederacy.

Under the permanent constitution, the Confederate Congress was a bicameral body like its Union counterpart. Contrary to the U.S. Congress, however, most sessions were held in secret, and the absence of an organized system of two-party competition deprived the Confederate Congress of an effective institutional framework for either supporting or opposing administration policies. The result was a bitter factionalism that hampered the Confederate war effort.

The Confederate Constitution closely followed the U.S. Constitution in creating a system of limited, separate powers. The Confederate Congress differed, however, in the extent of its subordination to executive authority. The Confederate president had the power of a line-item veto over appropriations bills, and a two-thirds majority in Congress was required for passage of any appropriations measure not submitted by the president.

In response to an invitation issued by Virginia,

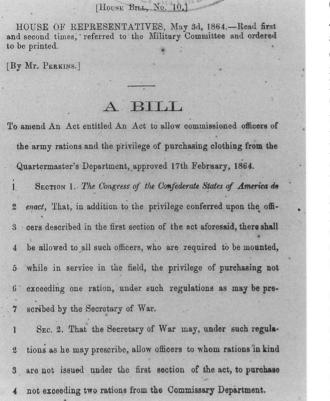

[HOUSE BILL, No. 10.]

HOUSE OF REPRESENTATIVES, May 3d, 1864.—Read first and second times, referred to the Military Committee and ordered to be printed.

[By Mr. PERKINS.]

A BILL

To amend An Act entitled An Act to allow commissioned officers of the army rations and the privilege of purchasing clothing from the Quartermaster's Department, approved 17th February, 1864.

1   SECTION 1. The Congress of the Confederate States of America de
2   enact, That, in addition to the privilege conferred upon the offi-
3   cers described in the first section of the act aforesaid, there shall
4   be allowed to all such officers, who are required to be mounted,
5   while in service in the field, the privilege of purchasing not
6   exceeding one ration, under such regulations as may be pre-
7   scribed by the Secretary of War.

1   SEC. 2. That the Secretary of War may, under such regula-
2   tions as he may prescribe, allow officers to whom rations in kind
3   are not issued under the first section of the act, to purchase
4   not exceeding two rations from the Commissary Department.

CONGRESSIONAL BILL. Approved by the Confederate House of Representatives on 17 February 1864. The bill amends procedures for purchasing rations and clothing from the Quartermaster's Department, the Confederate bureau responsible for providing nonfood and nonordnance items to the Confederate armies. Printed on 3 May 1864.   CIVIL WAR LIBRARY AND MUSEUM, PHILADELPHIA

the Confederate government moved from Montgomery, Alabama, to Richmond in the summer of 1861. There, in quarters shared with the Virginia legislature, the Congress struggled both to build a nation and wage a war. Of the 267 men who sat in Congress, only 27 served continuously. The most effective leaders were Robert M. T. Hunter of Virginia and Benjamin H. Hill of Georgia in the Senate and Thomas S. Bocock of Virginia and William W. Boyce of South Carolina in the House.

BIBLIOGRAPHY

Alexander, Thomas B., and Richard E. Beringer. The Anatomy of the Confederate Congress. 1972.
Martis, Kenneth C. The Historical Atlas of the Congresses of the Confederate States of America, 1861–1865. 1994.
Yearns, W. Buck. The Confederate Congress. 1960.

WILLIAM L. BARNEY

CONGRESS WATCH. Founded in 1973 by Joan Claybrook, Congress Watch is the lobbying arm of Public Citizen, Inc., a public-interest-group conglomerate organized by Ralph Nader, representing in 1994 approximately 100,000 members. Public Citizen also includes the Health Research Group, the Critical Mass Energy Project, the Litigation Group, and Buyers Up, a heating oil cooperative. Of these organizational entities under the Public Citizen umbrella, Congress Watch, the Litigation Group, and the Health Research Group receive the bulk of the Public Citizen program funding. Congress Watch is composed of approximately twenty professional staff members as well as a legislative director and executive director. It has no board of directors; rather, it relies on the larger Public Citizen board for policy direction.

Congress Watch, along with several other watchdog organizations, has raised and maintained the issue of campaign finance reform on the congressional agenda. This effort began in 1989 as its "Clean Up Congress" campaign, continuing into the 103d Congress as Congress Watch lobbyists pressed for severe limits on PACs, the elimination of "soft money" contributions, and overall campaign spending limits.

In addition to the campaign finance issue, Congress Watch has monitored the savings and loan crisis, and it formed a coalition of citizen, environmental, farm, labor, and civil rights groups to publicize the environmental, health, and safety issues raised by the North American Free Trade Agreement (NAFTA). Congress Watch has been active in the health care debate, supporting a single-payer plan modeled after the Canadian system.

BIBLIOGRAPHY

Congress Watch, Inc. Public Citizen. Published bimonthly.
Rosenzweig, Leslie Swift, ed. Public Interest Profiles, 1992–1993. 1992.

RONALD G. SHAIKO

CONKLING, ROSCOE (1829–1888), Republican representative and senator from New York and leader of the Republican party's "stalwart" faction. Born in Auburn, New York, Conkling read law in Utica, where he was elected mayor at age twenty-eight. He was elected to Congress in 1858 and re-elected in 1860. One of the more prominent young Republican members, Conkling was narrowly defeated in 1862 in a voter reaction to the stumbling war effort, but he was sent back to the House in

"BORROWED PLUMES—MR. JACKDAW CONKLING."
Roscoe Conkling, who dominated the New York Republican party, sought the party's presidential nomination in 1876, and, as the cartoon suggests, would seek the nomination again in 1880. A notably vain and pompous man, Conkling was a leader among the machine-oriented Republican members of Congress who during the 1870s superseded the more issue-oriented Radical Republicans of the Civil War–Reconstruction era. In an 1866 clash in the House with his party rival Rep. James G. Blaine (R-Maine), the latter spoke crushingly of Conkling's "majestic, supereminent, overpowering turkey-gobbler strut," a characterization captured in this cartoon. Wood engraving after Thomas Nast, *Harper's Weekly*, 20 December 1879.   LIBRARY OF CONGRESS

1864. Handsome, vain, and arrogant, Conkling served on the Joint Committee on Reconstruction and embarked on a long and bitter feud with James G. Blaine (R-Maine) after Blaine attacked him for his "turkey-gobbler strut."

Easily reelected to the House in 1866, Conkling was chosen by the state legislature for the U.S. Senate in 1867, displacing Ira Harris. Grasping the essentials of patronage politics, he gained control of the Republican party in New York State by placing an ally in the powerful position of collector of the New York Customhouse, and he used patronage to create a powerful political machine in New York. Conkling soon became one of the leaders in the Senate for the administration of Ulysses S. Grant as well as Grant's close personal friend. In 1873, Grant named him to the Supreme Court as chief justice, but Conkling turned the position down. Personally honest, he was a principal defender of the ill-starred Grant administration.

Conkling was a presidential aspirant in 1876, but his imperious nature and dubious connections made his candidacy a short-lived one in the convention that nominated dark horse Rutherford B. Hayes. Conkling refused to campaign for Hayes.

Conkling was one of the principal architects of the Electoral Commission Act of 1877, which resolved the Hayes-Tilden electoral snarl. He was quickly alienated from the new president, Hayes, who attacked him at the source of his strength by ousting Collector Chester A. Arthur from the Customhouse. After four years of Hayes, Conkling looked forward to restoring Grant and the "stalwart" wing of the party to the White House. But after a protracted deadlock in the 1880 Republican convention between Grant and Blaine, the unheralded James A. Garfield won the nomination. Garfield attempted to placate Conkling by choosing Arthur as his running mate. After winning what he thought were appropriate assurances from Garfield on patronage, Conkling stumped the country for the ticket, aiding immensely in a narrow Republican victory.

Garfield fell under the influence of Conkling's enemy Blaine and named an opponent of Conkling to the key post of customs collector. Conkling resigned his Senate seat in protest, and his effort at reelection was doomed when a deranged stalwart shot Garfield. Thus, Conkling's active political career ended in 1881. Conkling spent the remainder of his life practicing law in New York, becoming quite wealthy. Meanwhile, the split in the Republican party caused by his and Blaine's mutual enmity helped to end the party's dominance.

Intelligent, able, and a powerful orator, Conkling chose to devote himself to narrow political issues and left little mark on the substantive questions of his day.

BIBLIOGRAPHY

Chidsey, Donald Barr. *The Gentleman from New York: A Life of Roscoe Conkling.* 1935.

Jordan, David M. *Roscoe Conkling of New York: Voice in the Senate.* 1971.

DAVID M. JORDAN